PUBLIC LAW

LONGMAN LAW

GENERAL EDITORS

PROFESSOR I. H. DENNIS, *University College London*
PROFESSOR R. W. RIDEOUT, *University College London*
PROFESSOR J. A. USHER, *University of Edinburgh*

PUBLISHED TITLES

PETER STONE, *The Conflict of Laws*
CHRISTOPHER HARDING AND ANN SHERLOCK, *European Community Law: Texts and Materials*
R. J. SMITH, *Property Law*
ANDREW LE SUEUR AND MAURICE SUNKIN, *Public Law*

ANDREW LE SUEUR AND
MAURICE SUNKIN

PUBLIC LAW

LONGMAN
LONDON AND NEW YORK

Addison Wesley Longman
Edinburgh Gate
Harlow, Essex CM20 2JE, England
and Associated Companies throughout the world.

*Published in the United States of America
by Addison Wesley Longman Inc., New York.*

First published 1997

ISBN 0 582 08730 9 PPR

British Library Cataloguing-in-Publication Data

A catalogue record of this book is available from the British Library

Library of Congress Cataloging-in-Publication Data

A catalog entry for this title is available from the Library of Congress

Set by 35 in 10/12pt Plantin
Produced by Longman Asia Limited, Hong Kong
NPCC/01

This book is dedicated to the memory of:
Andrew Le Sueur's father, G. A. Le Sueur;
Maurice Sunkin's parents, Solomon and Betty Sunkin;
and of his father-in-law, Maurice Mann.

CONTENTS

PREFACE

Many will ask: 'Why another book about Public Law?' Our answer is straightforward: despite the existence of several excellent texts on the subject (and there are more of these than when we first started to write this book), there is still a need for a book which introduces readers to the ways public law and its processes work, which shows how particular public law issues emerge from broader political disputes, and which reveals the interconnections between the courts and the legislative and other institutions in the constitutional system.

Although often comprehensive in their coverage, traditional textbooks have tended to be too static, giving little sense of the dynamics of the processes which generate the law described and analysed. Cases-and-materials books have done much to help students acquire easier access to extracts from written sources; but again they often provide only tantalising glimpses of the realities of the constitutional system and show little of the ways issues evolve over time. Moreover, there is rarely space for the authors to provide adequate contextualising commentary.

What we have tried to write is a book which reveals something of how things happen in a complex and changing world, seen from the point of view of public lawyers. Throughout we draw upon four carefully selected case studies; at the beginning of Chapter 2 we explain some of the ways in which readers may use these accounts of events.

Part A introduces the public law system from a variety of perspectives: as a set of institutions (Chapter 3); as an element of a *policy* cycle (Chapter 4); as a system through which governmental *power* is exercised (Chapter 5); and as a set of *principled* constraints on power (Chapter 6). The themes of these chapters—policy, power and principles—recur throughout the rest of the book.

In Part B we examine the main sources of legal authority by which government acquires its legal powers: statute (here we draw on the battles over the deregulation of Sunday trading); delegated legislation (a case study on the controversial Board and Lodging Regulations provides the backdrop to this); the prerogative and residual non-statutory powers of central government (such as the ability to regulate employment in the civil service to ban trade union membership at GCHQ); and finally European Community legislation (here we examine how the Working Time Directive was made).

Part C is concerned with the mechanisms which exist for questioning and regulating the exercise of governmental power. As we say: 'The ability of people to challenge government and to seek redress against official action is a hallmark of a mature constitutional system.' The chapters look in turn at the work of MPs, the ombudsmen, tribunals, judicial review and the role and work of the European Court of Justice. The case studies again provide the backdrop. We see how the GCHQ trade unionists sought redress from the House of Commons, by applying for judicial review, petitioning the International Labour Organisation and finally the European Commission of Human Rights. Simon Cotton, a young unemployed man from Birkenhead successfully used judicial review to challenge the Secretary of State's attempt to reduce his benefits by arguing that delegated legislation was invalid. Protagonists in the campaigns for and against Sunday trading also used litigation: in the High Court, magistrates courts and before the European Court of Justice.

During the past five years many busy people spared time to talk to us, to share ideas and information, and to comment on drafts. We thank them. First there are our students both at UCL and at Essex who have used earlier versions of chapters in their public law courses and who have always been willing to offer their constructive criticism and practical guidance: they have helped to remind us that books are things to be used by real people. We also owe a debt of gratitude to many friends and colleagues who read and commented on earlier drafts of various chapters. They include: Rodney Austin; Tony Barker; Nick Bernard; Patrick Birkinshaw; Charles Blake; Lee Bridges; Tom Cornford; Richard Drabble QC; staff in the office of Frank Field MP; Richard Gardiner; Stephen Grosz; Françoise Hampson; Jeffrey Jowell QC; Dawn Oliver; Sebastian Payne; Steve Peers; Genevra Richardson; Richard Rawlings; Nicholas Warren; Bob Watt; Jane White; Barry Winetrobe; and three anonymous readers who offered criticisms of our first draft. Naturally, we alone are responsible for the omissions (whether made deliberately to keep the book reasonably accessible to those for whom it is intended or unconsciously) and for any errors which may remain despite our best efforts.

Two highly effective research assistants helped us while they were undergraduates at UCL: Shaun Mills at the start of the project; Stephen Kempner towards the end. Our publishers, in particular Brian Willan, were patient and encouraging throughout, as were the advisory editors, Ian Dennis and Roger Rideout. Sylvia Lough (at UCL) and Alison Smith (at Essex) skillfully typed, faxed, wordprocessed and juggled e-mails; we could not have managed without them.

The Faculty of Laws at UCL and the Department of Law at Essex have continued to provide intellectually stimulating environments which are perfect for writing, as well as much-needed periods of study leave and funds for research assistance. St Andrew's College and the Faculty of Law, University of Sydney, also gave Andrew Le Sueur an opportunity to work intensively on the book in early 1996.

Finally and most importantly, Maurice Sunkin is more grateful than words can say to his family—Shirley, Sarina, Naomi and baby Michael (who was born three days after the completion of the typescript) for living with this book for what must seem to the children to be a lifetime. Andrew Le Sueur is grateful to his good friends who always knew exactly when to tempt him away from the wordprocessor and when to let him get on with this project.

Public law continues to develop at an astonishing pace and we were fortunately able to incorporate references to Lord Woolf's important report, *Access to Justice*, and to the ECJ's judgment in the Working Time Directive case at proof stage.

Andrew Le Sueur
Faculty of Laws
University College London

Maurice Sunkin
Department of Law
University of Essex

February 1997

TABLE OF CASES

TABLE OF LEGISLATION

EUROPEAN LEGISLATION

TABLE OF ORDERS, RULES AND REGULATIONS

TABLE OF ABBREVIATIONS

BNFL	British Nuclear Fuels
C&AG	Comptroller and Auditor General
CAO	Chief Adjudication Officer
CBI	Confederation of British Industry
CCSU	Council of Civil Service Unions
CCT	compulsory competitive tendering
CICS	Criminal Injuries Compensation Scheme
CND	Campaign for Nuclear Disarmament
col. (*pl* cols.)	column
COREPER	Committee of Permanent Representatives
CPAG	Child Poverty Action Group
DHSS	Department of Health and Social Security
DSS	Department of Social Security
DTI	Department of Trade and Industry
EAT	Employment Appeal Tribunal
EC	European Community
ECHR	European Convention on Human Rights
ECJ	European Court of Justice
ECOSOC	Economic and Social Committee
ECSC	European Coal and Steel Community
EEC	European Economic Community
EU	European Union
EURATOM	European Atomic Energy Community
GCHQ	Government Communications Headquarters
HSC Act 1993	Health Services Commissioners Act 1993
IAT	Immigration Appeal Tribunal
IGC	inter-governmental conference
ILEA	Inner London Education Authority
ILO	International Labour Organization
IPPR	Institute of Public Policy Research
IRC	Inland Revenue Commissioners
JCSI	Joint Committee on Statutory Instruments
KSSC	Keep Sunday Special Campaign
LGA 1974	Local Government Act 1974

MEP	Member of the European Parliament
MP	Member of Parliament
NDPB	non-departmental public body
NEDC	National Economic Development Council
NHS	National Health Service
Ord	Order
p. (*pl* pp.)	page
PCA	Parliamentary Commissioner for Administration
PC Act 1967	Parliamentary Commissioner Act 1967
PQs	Parliamentary Questions
r	rule
RSAR	Retailers for Shops Act Reform
RSC	Rules of the Supreme Court
s (*pl* ss)	section
Sched	Schedule (to Act)
SHRC	Shopping Hours Reform Council
SI	statutory instrument
SSAC	Social Security Advisory Committee
SSAT	social security appeal tribunal
TUC	Trades Union Congress
UKIAS	United Kingdom Immigration Advisory Service
UKREP	United Kingdom's permanent representatives
vol. (*pl* vols.)	volume
WDM	World Development Movement

Part A

PERSPECTIVES ON THE CONSTITUTION

1

WHAT IS PUBLIC LAW?

Public authorities and office-holders in the modern state carry out many functions: they provide education and health care; restrict immigration; build roads; pay welfare benefits and retirement pensions; attempt to control pollution; regulate the transport of animals—a list could go on for many pages.[1] Debates and controversies about these and other responsibilities fill the newspapers every day.

On a level of high politics, people disagree over which functions should be carried out by the state, and which left to the market place.[2] There are also many other, more particular controversies. For instance, which institution or person should be entrusted with each function? What tools will enable these responsibilities to be carried out? To what extent, and how, should citizens (as individuals or groups) be able to participate in decision-making? What is there to prevent powers being exercised corruptly, unwisely or unfairly? What happens when a decision-maker makes a mistake and harms people? Questions like these are of different types. Some enquire into how things *are*; answers to these need to describe and explain what occurs in practice. Other questions, however, are normative ones: they ask what *should* happen, how *ought* the institutions of the state to act in their relationships with each other and with citizens.

NAMING THE SUBJECT

The study of 'public law' is one way of understanding this intricate network of state activity and exploring the many issues which arise. Academics have

[1] A random A to Z of illustrations of the functions carried out by state institutions could read as follows: asylum applications are determined; building construction and use is regulated; care in the community provided; dangerous dogs controlled; employment of tens of thousands of people; fire fighting; grants for students; housing for the homeless; inspection of work places to ensure safety standards; judicial review; licensing of all kinds of activity; monetary policy is made and implemented; national insurance system operated; overseas aid; postal services are run; the Queen reigns; railways are regulated (but not now owned); social work carried out; taxis licensed; unemployment benefits paid; victims of crime compensated; water quality regulated; X-ray use controlled; youth training schemes set up; and zoos licensed. Dozens of equally eclectic lists could be drawn up.

[2] See p. 130.

often sought to sub-divide public law into 'constitutional law' and 'administrative law'.[3] Few of these attempts have proved to be coherent and most commentators concede that the dividing line between these two sub-branches is very unclear.[4] The more general expression 'public law' is therefore better, though the terminology is not without its problems.

The 'law' in public law

It might suggest to newcomers that the scope of the subject is confined to 'law' in some narrow sense. If you were to begin studying the subject by reading *Statutes in Force*, the volumes containing legislation made by the institutions of the European Community and a complete set of the *Law Reports*, you would certainly learn some things about the constitution. For a start, you would see that laws relating to government functions often take the form of highly complex legislation and extremely subtle case law. But your understanding of the constitution would be incomplete and misleading. It makes no sense to look at the 'legal bits' of the system in isolation. It has been said, by way of a backhanded criticism of lawyers, that 'if you can think about something which is attached to something else without thinking about what it is attached to, then you have what is called a legal mind'.[5] 'Law', in the sense of court judgments and the texts of legislation, is only one aspect of the whole constitutional system in the United Kingdom: every legal rule, legal principle and legal process is connected to something larger. What more, then, is needed to complete the picture?

Rules other than those enforced in national courts

Many of the 'rules' which influence how people and groups act within the constitutional system are not set out in legislation or case law enforced by the national courts. Constitutional conventions (or 'understandings') upon which the system operates—for instance that the monarch appoints as Prime Minister the leader of the largest political party in the House of Commons and that ministers are required to explain and justify their actions and omissions to Parliament—have tended to be regarded as distinct from 'law', yet clearly they are of key importance.[6] Two other important types of rules are the United Kingdom's international treaty obligations and the standing orders

[3] For early attempts see John Austin, *Outline of the Course of Lectures on Jurisprudence* (1873), vol. 1, p. 73 and the discussion in F. W. Maitland, *The Constitutional History of England* (1919), pp. 526–36.

[4] Cf. E. C. S. Wade and A. W. Bradley, *Constitutional and Administrative Law* (11th edn., 1993) where the following working definitions are adopted: constitutional law refers to 'those laws which regulate the structure of the principal organs of government and their relationship to each other and to the citizen, and determine their functions' (p. 9). Administrative law 'may be defined as the law which determines the organisations, powers and duties of administrative authorities' (p. 10).

[5] D. Horowitz, 'Decreeing Institutional Change: judicial supervision of public institutions' [1983] *Duke Law Journal* 1265, 1307 (quoting T. R. Powell).

[6] See Chapter 6.

which govern the operation of Parliament. These types of rule certainly qualify to be called 'law', yet neither are enforceable by the national courts. Public law has therefore to concern itself with a broad range of normative influences on how actors within the constitutional system behave.

Process

More than most other law degree core subjects, public law also has to extend beyond looking at rules and their theoretical underpinnings, into *processes*. Court judgments and legislation do not grow like mushrooms in the darkness of law libraries; these texts are the end products of complex human interactions. To understand judgments in the round, it is important to know how and why the disputes which prompted them came to court and also what happens after a judge has delivered his decision. Similarly, with legislation, it is important to appreciate what pressures may lead to a bill being introduced into Parliament, how MPs and peers deal with bills and, once enacted, what effects statutes have on the ways people behave.

The study of the processes in the constitution is not something unique to lawyers. On the contrary, some of the best empirical research and theorizing about processes has been by people working within academic disciplines such as political science and public administration. Public law, like these other fields of study, is often concerned with evaluating how in practice administrative decisions are made, how the whole legislative system operates, how disputes are resolved and so on. This can be a difficult task. The sequence of interactions we call 'processes' is intangible. Often all that is left behind, apart from an end product (such as the text of an Act of Parliament or a court's judgment), is documentary *evidence* of what has happened. Much of this is not in the public domain nor easily accessible to researchers. The core material with which public lawyers work in order to understand and evaluate processes tends therefore to be official publications such as reports of parliamentary debates, minutes of evidence and committee reports.

The 'public' in public law

The 'public' in public law is just as tricky as the 'law'. It might seem to suggest that in the British legal systems it is possible to make a clear demarcation between 'private law' (legal rules, such as contract and tort, applying to individuals and to companies) and 'public law' (legal rules relating only to the relationships between government bodies, and between government bodies and individuals). In practice, no such divide exists. While some important legal rules (notably the grounds of judicial review) do apply only to bodies operating in the public domain,[7] much of the general law (for instance contract and tort liability) applies both to government institutions and office-holders

[7] The courts have spent a great deal of effort attempting to make a workable distinction between 'public' and 'private' in this context: see Chapter 22.

in similar ways as it does to private individuals and companies. Perhaps, then, the term 'public' qualifies 'law' in some broader, less legalistic sense? It could signify that the subject matter affects the public as a whole or a section of it, rather than just the specific parties to a particular transaction (as in a contract) or particular litigation.[8] In other words, we all have an interest in seeing that government bodies carry out their legal responsibilities to regulate and provide.[9]

PERSPECTIVES ON THE CONSTITUTION

It is an elementary observation that different groups of people will look at the constitutional system, and the role law plays in it, in different ways.

A government minister's outlook

Imagine for a moment that you are a government minister. You have been elected as an MP for a constituency somewhere in the United Kingdom and the Prime Minister has chosen you to be the political head of one of the central government departments. You are sitting at your desk in Whitehall,[10] reading a memorandum from the Chief Government Medical Officer. It informs you that tests have proved there to be a link between a disease carried by dogs and a severe type of asthma in children. His advice is that immediate steps ought be taken to ensure that all dogs are vaccinated annually against the canine disease. Assuming you accept this recommendation, civil servants in your department (and other departments) will need to devise a strategy for achieving this goal. Because the policy involves imposing new legal obligations on dog owners, the existing law will have to be changed. You and your officials will need to call on the expertise of the department's lawyers at this stage. Perhaps they will recommend that a bill (a draft statute) has to be introduced into Parliament. The programme for parliamentary scrutiny and approval of bills is notoriously overloaded and it might just not be possible to find time for another bill this year. Backbench MPs of your own party, and MPs in opposition parties, will also be able to scrutinize the proposal in some detail. In theory at least, they also have the power to veto it. Perhaps, though, an existing Act of Parliament already confers rule-making powers on you in your official capacity as a minister. If so, this will enable

[8] For a discussion of this idea, see Abram Chayse, 'The Role of the Judge in Public Law Litigation' (1976) 89 Harv LR 1281.

[9] See e.g. Sir Harry Woolf, *Protection of the Public—a New Challenge* (1989).

[10] Whitehall is the street in London running between Trafalgar Square and the Palace of Westminster (where both Houses of Parliament meet). Many of the main government departments, such as the Department of Health and the Ministry of Agriculture, Fisheries and Food, have their headquarters on this street and for this reason the term 'Whitehall' is often used as a synonym for 'government'. 'Westminster' is a term which can be used to refer to 'Parliament'.

a lawyer in your department to draft rules ('delegated legislation') which will have the force of law but be subject only to minimal parliamentary scrutiny before they come into effect.

Whichever legal basis you are advised to use (a statute or delegated legislation), decisions will have to be made about a range of other matters. For instance, is the department going to consult with interested parties, such as the RSPCA, the Kennel Club and the British Medical Association, before going ahead? If so, what information will be released and how much time will be allowed for representations to be made? Will consultations take place because this is just accepted as normal practice, or because there is some *legal* requirement that this happens? If the latter, what will be the consequence of not complying with it? As a minister under pressure to take action, you may be eager to be seen to be acting firmly and decisively in dealing with a problem of public concern, even if this means that you fail to follow strictly the legal procedural requirements which apply to rule-making.

These are some of the sorts of decisions which ministers, civil servants and their legal advisors often have to make. In the United Kingdom, elected local authorities also have powers (though much more limited ones than ministers) to make and implement public policy decisions. Since 1973, decisions affecting the United Kingdom have also been taken by the institutions of the European Community.[11] From the perspective of people in these three tiers of government—the EC, central government and local authorities—one of the prime roles of the constitutional system is that it *enables* government action to take place.

A citizen's perspective

As well as appreciating how government bodies operate within the UK constitutional system, there is also the perspective of the citizens, groups and business enterprises. On a general level, most people welcome (or at least accept) most of what government does. Indeed, there are more or less constant calls for government action to tackle new or recurring problems. In a democracy, the constitution needs to provide opportunities for citizens to participate in decision-making. Policy-making and implementation is not a one-way process, with government 'deciding' and 'commanding' people to do things. Law facilitates interactions between the government and the governed in various ways. For instance, legislation ensures the right to vote in elections for MPs, local councillors and Members of the European Parliament (MEPs). It may also place duties on ministers and other decision-makers to consult with people before particular policies are formulated or implemented and the common law aims to ensure that decisions affecting people are made fairly.

While legal rights to participate are of great importance to citizens, they

[11] See further Chapters 13 and 14.

also want more from the constitutional system. In any system of government intervention, whether it be the provision of services or regulation of activity, problems inevitably arise from time to time. An individual may be upset because an official treated them rudely or because there was an undue delay in dealing with their request. A person may believe that an official has misinterpreted the law, or misunderstood a factual situation, and therefore wrongly denied some benefit or imposed some obligation. Campaigning groups may want opportunities to challenge the whole legal basis for a government action: perhaps they claim that the minister did not have the power to make delegated legislation, or that an Act of Parliament is incompatible with Community law and therefore ought not be recognized by the UK courts.

In short, citizens—either as individuals or in groups—look to the constitutional system to provide ways of participating in decision-making, redressing their grievances and scrutinizing the ways in which government uses its legal and political powers.

An academic viewpoint

Often during this book you will be invited to stand in the shoes of one of the participants in the constitutional system, such as a government minister having to deal with a problem, or a citizen. A third perspective is also needed: an academic one, which involves standing back and attempting to make sense of the often confused and frenetic activity that seems to take place. In other words, this perspective seeks to explain how the system fits together and what makes it tick.

Mapping out the institutions

A first step along this road can be the naming the parts of the constitutional system; this is the subject of Chapter 3. So far we have used the term 'government' and the even broader expression 'the state'. While both these terms are useful in a general way, neither has any precise legal meaning.[12] In order to map out official bodies in the constitution and describe their legal responsibilities and powers within the system, we will therefore need to use a range of more specific names. To a newcomer, this task may seem daunting, particularly because the United Kingdom has no codified legislation setting out the main office-holders and institutions, their responsibilities and powers, their relationships to one another and to citizens.[13]

[12] See further Geoffrey Marshall, *Constitutional Theory* (1971), Chapter 2. Cf. Community law where the concept of 'emanation of the state' has become important (see p. 687, below). The term 'state' is widely used by other social scientists.

[13] In recent years, several attempts have been made to produce texts of a codified constitution for the United Kingdom, including the Institute of Public Policy Research's *The Constitution of the United Kingdom* (1991) and Tony Benn's Commonwealth of Britain Bill (set out in T. Benn and A. Hood, *Common Sense* (1993)). None of these, however, describes the system as it is; they are all attempts at reform.

The best introductory guides to the system are therefore academic textbooks, but these, especially those written by lawyers, reveal a wide array of approach and emphasis. In particular, public lawyers have often worked on different assumptions about which aspects of the institutional map ought be at the heart of the subject. For some commentators what is truly significant is *what happens in the courts* (i.e. how the judges ensure that government bodies carry out their legal duties and how the common law protects people from abuses of power by government). For other public lawyers, however, the primary objects of study are *government and Parliament* and the ways in which law (particularly legislation) enables the regulation of social and business activities and provision of services in the public interest. We will return to this dichotomy of view later in the book.

A policy cycle

Chapter 3 concludes by saying that while an institutional map is a useful basis for understanding state activities, it is ultimately a limited one. It emphasizes the institutions of the constitution as objects of study in themselves, whereas what is more important is how they *function* in dealing with the real political, economic and social problems of society. In Chapter 4 we therefore move on to consider a model of a 'policy cycle' developed by social scientists which describes how the constitutional system enables public policy to be formulated, put on a legal footing and implemented. This will help to identify when, where and how law and legal processes are particularly significant in the way the modern state takes practical action.

Power and principles

What emerges from the policy cycle model (and this is a point already touched upon in this chapter, because it is a constantly recurring theme) is that law and legal processes are both concerned with enabling government to operate *and* controlling government action in various ways. Chapters 5 and 6 explore this dual aspect in much more detail, both by describing some of the basic characteristics of the constitution (such as parliamentary sovereignty and constitutional conventions) and delving deeper into the theoretical justifications for them. Like most books on public law, this one mentions the name of A. V. Dicey, an academic lawyer most famous as the author of *Introduction to the Study of the Law of the Constitution* (first edition 1885, seventh edition 1908). With phenomenal success, he popularized an explanation of how and why the United Kingdom constitutional system, and in particular its legal aspects, operates as it does.[14] Today, Dicey's idealized nineteenth-century view of law and politics still hangs over us and exerts a real influence on what lawyers in particular say and do. Many academics, and now some judges, strongly reject both Dicey's explanation of the system

[14] See Chapter 5 for an overview of Dicey's model.

and the prescriptive power of his theoretical framework. The search is now on to find a satisfactory framework capable of giving coherence to the modern constitutional system. This is a theme to which the book will return several times.[15]

WHERE TO GO FROM HERE

In order to explore more fully all the perspectives described above, this book provides case studies into four controversial episodes of the last few years. Frequent reference is made to these events and so the next chapter presents an overview of each of them and explains in more detail how the use of case studies can help to understand the UK public law system.

[15] See especially Chapters 5, 6 and 20.

2

THE CASE STUDIES

INTRODUCTION

The use of case studies helps solve several problems faced by anyone trying to understand the constitution of the United Kingdom. One is that public law can seem static, abstract and even dull. Some textbook accounts of the constitution have been guilty of presenting it as a series of more or less unconnected institutions ('Parliament does this'; 'the Cabinet does that'; 'local authorities do the other'). Some have also lapsed into dry expositions of abstract notions such as parliamentary sovereignty and the rule of law. The *real* work of public law is different. It is about how government actions can dramatically affect the lives of ordinary people up and down the country, occasionally propelling them into the news. It can also be about how law prevents businesses from operating and enables pressure groups to 'play the system' to further their goals. In short, public law provides tools which can be used to achieve often controversial ends. Case studies emphasize this well.

A second virtue of case studies is that they enable people to form their own reasoned opinions about the strengths and the weaknesses of the constitutional system. The constitution can only be understood properly if a critical stance is adopted. This does not mean blindly disparaging every institution, process or principle in the constitution, but rather being open-minded and searching in the questions asked. It is easy, however, for people new to the subject either to accept too easily the assertions made by textbook writers or, having read an impartially presented list of the pros and cons of some aspect of the constitution, to shrug their shoulders and wonder how they are meant to decide between them.

Thirdly, for many years progressive law teachers have believed that law is best understood by looking at primary materials. In many branches of law this means judicial decisions and legislation, but in the field of public law a much wider range of sources needs to be drawn upon: parliamentary debates, minutes of evidence of committees, official reports, decisions of international organizations and so on. More than this, though, the day-to-day practices and problems which are mediated through the institutions and processes of the constitution are of central importance. These events are recorded in history books, newspapers and biographies. In short, public law cannot be confined to the analysis of 'legal' literature. As a genre, law textbooks have had a considerable influence on the development of English law; in some ways they are the common law's substitute for a codified system of law. But textbooks have their limitations. While they may be a good medium for presenting knowledge about legal rules and principles, and exploring the conceptual and policy issues underlying the law, textbooks have very serious drawbacks for describing how *processes* work. They tend to draw attention to the static: in the context of public law this has often meant examining, in turn, the work of formal institutions of the constitution such as the House of Commons, local authorities and the ombudsmen and also the principles of judicial review. The printed page, and maybe the common law legal method itself with its emphasis on judicial decisions, has also resulted in the presentation of the constitution as a series of snapshots. Court judgments, for instance, tend to be viewed as isolated events, as if they are in themselves the beginning and end of an episode. Case studies can show how issues develop over time, how events are linked, and how systems overlap.

The case studies

Throughout this book four case studies are used to illustrate and explore different aspects of public law. The studies are interspersed between chapters which, in a more conventional way, seek to describe and analyse general features of the constitution and how they operate. These bite-size portions of case study enable readers to test the generalizations which have been made in the chapters which precede them against real-life events while also pursuing in more detail some interesting and important angles. The studies are as follows:

(1) The 1984 ban on civil servants at GCHQ from belonging to trade unions.
(2) The attempts to deregulate Sunday trading, partially achieved in 1994.
(3) Changes made in 1985 to welfare benefits for people living in board and lodging accommodation.
(4) The EC directive on working time which regulates working conditions such as working hours and entitlement to holidays.

The purpose of this chapter is to provide an overview of the case studies. If, while using the book, readers feel they have lost the thread of events in any of the case studies, they should turn back to this chapter.

THE GCHQ CASE STUDY[1]

In 1984 the Appellate Committee of the House of Lords gave judgment in *Council of Civil Service Unions v Minister for the Civil Service*.[2] Judicial review proceedings had been brought by civil servants working at the Government Communications Headquarters (GCHQ, the government's electronic eavesdropping organization responsible for collecting signals intelligence)[3] whose terms of employment had been changed to forbid them from belonging to any independent trade union. The law lords' speeches contain several important statements about the circumstances in which judicial review may be obtained by a person aggrieved by the action of a public body. It was held that if a public body or official had in the past regularly consulted with a person or organization about a matter, then those people had a legitimate expectation which could be protected by the courts, to be consulted in the future.[4] The case can also be regarded as authority for the proposition that the mere fact that the source of the power exercised was the prerogative (the powers of central government not based on statute)[5] did not of itself prevent the court intervening. Lord Diplock's speech has also become well known for his attempt to restate the general grounds on which judicial review may be sought in English law: 'illegality', 'procedural impropriety' and 'irrationality'. (All these points are examined later in the book.)[6]

If we approach the GCHQ episode solely in terms of the principles of law decided by the House of Lords, we will fail to see how the court's decision fits into the constitutional system as a whole and how the work of the courts is just one part of the public law process. What we need is a virtual reality machine which can transport us backwards and forward in time, allowing us to see the entire episode unfold, which then enables us to zoom in at any point to examine what is happening in detail, or to pan out to take in the whole panorama of events. However, the following outline of details leading up to the case shall have to suffice.

In 1981, a small group of very senior civil servants met, probably in central London. The main item on the agenda of the Permanent Secretaries' Intelligence Steering Committee (PSIS)[7] was a proposal made by Sir Brian Tovey, the Director of GCHQ, that GCHQ be de-unionized. On several occasions

[1] See further Hugh Lanning and Richard Norton-Taylor, *A Conflict of Loyalties: GCHQ 1984–1991* (1992).

[2] [1985] AC 374. Extracts from the judgment are set out in Chapter 28.

[3] On the functions of GCHQ, see p. 64.

[4] On the facts of the GCHQ case, the argument was that officials acting on behalf of the Minister for the Civil Service had, in the past, always consulted the unions at GCHQ about proposed changes to the terms and conditions of employment there.

[5] For an explanation of prerogative powers see Chapter 12. Note that there is considerable dispute as to which non-statutory powers ought to be classified as 'prerogative' (a term of art) and some commentators would argue that the powers exercised by Mrs Thatcher here should not be described in this way.

[6] See Chapters 20–25.

[7] The existence and role of the PSIS was officially acknowledged only in October 1993.

during the previous two years, the work of GCHQ had been disrupted by many of its several thousand employees taking industrial action organized by trade unions as part of an acrimonious pay dispute which affected the whole of the civil service. After a lengthy discussion the PSIS committee decided to advise the Prime Minister (Mrs Thatcher) to reject the proposal, believing that the benefits of de-unionization would not be worth the fuss it would cause.[8]

Two years later, in the winter of 1983, a meeting was held at 10 Downing Street. The meeting was chaired by Margaret Thatcher (the Prime Minister at the time also held the post of Minister for the Civil Service). With her were Sir Geoffrey Howe (the Foreign Secretary), Lord Whitelaw (deputy Prime Minister), Michael Heseltine (Secretary of State for Defence) and Tom King (Secretary of State for Employment). Sir Robert Armstrong, who was then the country's most senior civil servant,[9] was in attendance. Since the PSIS's decision two years earlier, an employee at GCHQ[10] had been convicted as a Soviet spy and, for the first time, the government had publicly acknowledged the existence of GCHQ. One obstacle to de-unionization had thereby been removed. Without taking the matter to Cabinet, the five ministers decided the time was now ripe to ban the unions, even though there had been no industrial action at GCHQ for three years.

A few days before Christmas 1983, Margaret Thatcher telephoned the Director of GCHQ to inform him of the decision. (A judge was later to comment that it seemed odd that such an important decision should be communicated in this way.) A public announcement needed to be made, but had to wait until the House of Commons met again after the Christmas recess.

Giving legal advice to government

Imagine you are a government lawyer; your role is to ensure that the correct legal steps are taken to implement the ministerial decision. What would you need to consider? The oral instruction given over the telephone by Margaret Thatcher (which you decide not to mention in the Commons' statement you are drafting for the Foreign Secretary) was an exercise of prerogative power delegated by an Order in Council (a type of legislation formally made by the Queen on the advice of the Privy Council without any involvement by Parliament).[11] The instruction had legal effect in itself, but further steps were necessary to implement it fully. Government lawyers needed to ensure that the management at GCHQ could lawfully dismiss staff who refused to give up membership of their trade union. Normally such discrimination against an employee on ground of union membership would amount to unfair dismissal

[8] Peter Hennessy, *Whitehall* (1990), p. 684.
[9] Secretary to the Cabinet and Head of the Home Civil Service.
[10] Geoffrey Prime, who was not a member of a union.
[11] The technicalities are examined in Chapter 12.

and there would be a statutory right to apply to an industrial tribunal for compensation or an order that the worker be reinstated. This statutory protection was removed from GCHQ staff by the Foreign Secretary issuing certificates under the Employment Protection legislation (explained in outline in the Foreign Secretary's statement to the House of Commons, below).

But as well as working out what 'tools' to use, as a government lawyer you need to be aware of the legal and political constraints within which you must operate. For instance, a number of international treaty obligations, such as the European Convention on Human Rights (ECHR) and treaties made under the auspices of the International Labour Organization (ILO), contain protections of fundamental rights such as freedom of association and restrict a state's right lawfully to deprive a person of trade union membership. You need to be able to interpret these broadly phrased provisions and understand how they relate to domestic law. If, for example, you conclude that the proposed action by the minister may be contrary to ECHR provisions, does this mean that the union ban must be abandoned, or can you proceed anyway?[12]

Other important constraints within which you must work are the judge-made principles of judicial review. The role of the High Court (and the Court of Appeal and the House of Lords) in judicial review cases is to ensure that there is a proper legal basis for the government decisions challenged and, if there is not, to quash the decision, declare it unlawful or issue an order compelling the public body to carry out its proper legal duties. In carrying out this task, the court's function is not to look at the merits of the particular decision ('is this a good decision: could a better one have been made?'), but the more limited one of determining whether the decision-maker has acted *ultra vires* (outside his or her powers).[13] Sitting at your desk in Whitehall at Christmas time in 1983, you are fairly confident that there is little prospect of any GCHQ employees making a successful judicial review challenge of the decision. This is because until now the courts have been extremely reluctant to review decisions of central government taken under the prerogative as opposed to statutory powers.[14]

The decision was announced

25 January 1984 was the day set by the government to announce the decision, taken a few weeks before, to ban union membership. Obviously the individual employees at GCHQ had to be informed; but so concerned was the management at GCHQ that the decision might leak out before it was announced in Parliament that it had the letters to the staff printed at the

[12] The relationship between international treaty obligations and domestic law is dealt with at p. 112 and pp. 271–3.

[13] As with so many aspects of public law, the courts' role in reviewing government action is controversial: see further Chapter 20.

[14] See Chapter 12.

National Security Agency in Maryland, USA and flown across the Atlantic.[15] They were distributed at the same time as the Foreign Secretary stood at the despatch box (the place where ministers stand to speak) in the House of Commons.[16]

GCHQ (Employment Protection Acts)

3.30 pm

The Secretary of State for Foreign and Commonwealth Affairs (Sir Geoffrey Howe): With permission, Mr Speaker, I shall make a statement on the Government communications headquarters and the Employment Protection Acts.

As the House knows, the Employment Protection Acts contain provisions that enable the Government to except Crown employees from the application of the Acts. These provisions can only be used for the purposes of safeguarding national security, and reflect the acknowledged need for particularly sensitive functions of Government to be protected so far as possible from the risk of exposure or disruption.

Government communications headquarters is responsible for intelligence work of crucial importance to our national security. To be effective, this work must be conducted secretly. Moreover, GCHQ must provide a service that can be relied on with confidence at all times. It is clear, therefore, that the conditions envisaged in the special provisions of the Employment Protection Acts exist in this case.

The House will wish to know that, for these reasons, I have today signed certificates under s 121(4) of the Employment Protection Act 1975 and s 138(4) of the Employment Protection (Consolidation) Act 1978, excepting GCHQ employees from the application of the relevant provisions. The certificates have immediate effect and the new conditions of service are at the same time being introduced at GCHQ. Under these new conditions, staff will be permitted in future to belong only to a departmental staff association approved by their director.

The very special nature of the work will be apparent from what I have said. The action I have taken stems directly from that. The Government fully respect the right of civil servants to be members of a trade union, and it is only the special nature of the work of GCHQ that has led us to take these measures. I can assure the House therefore that it is not our intention to introduce similar measures outside the field of security and intelligence.

GCHQ staff are being informed of these measures this afternoon. Those who decide to remain at GCHQ will each receive a payment of £1,000 in recognition of the fact that certain rights that they have hitherto enjoyed are being withdrawn from them in the interests of national security. Those who do not wish to continue to serve at GCHQ will be offered the opportunity of seeking a transfer to another part of the civil service.

Mr Denis Healey (Leeds, East) [Labour frontbench spokesman on foreign affairs: the 'Shadow Foreign Secretary']: I found the Foreign Secretary's statement at once disturbing and perplexing. Government communications headquarters,

[15] See *The Guardian*, 25 January 1994, p. 5.

[16] What follows is an extract from the Official Journal of the House of Commons (colloquially known as *Hansard*): HC Deb, vol. 52, cols. 917–24. You will need to read *Hansard* in different ways according to *why* you are looking at it. You should be able to read this particular extract quite rapidly as its purpose is to build up a general picture. At other times, you may need to go through *Hansard* with a fine tooth comb. In *Pepper v Hart* [1993] AC 593, the Appellate Committee of the House of Lords held that in litigation about the meaning of legislation, counsel could in certain circumstances refer the court to debates during the passage of a bill where this would assist to make the meaning of the statute clear: see p. 533.

of which I know something from the six years I spent as Secretary of State for Defence, has performed an indispensable service to the nation since the war by providing vital intelligence with an efficiency and dedication that is the envy of the world. It is not, like some other branches of the security services, a small body of professionals. It is a large industrial enterprise employing thousands of skilled technicians. Any of the very few offences against security that have been committed by members of GCHQ have been dealt with under the law, as in the Prime case not long ago. As far as I am aware, there has been no industrial action for the past three years since 1981 by members of GCHQ.

The House must be told by the Foreign Secretary why the Government have decided after all these years to deprive GCHQ employees of the rights that are enjoyed by civil servants in the Ministry of Defence and the Foreign and Commonwealth Office, who are doing work of equal security and operational importance. Why is the Foreign Secretary depriving GCHQ employees of the rights of industrial organisation that are enjoyed by employees of the royal ordnance factories and those in private firms such as Vickers and Plessey, who are doing work that is equally secret and equally central to the nation's security?

I wish to ask the Foreign Secretary two questions about how he took his decision. What consultations did he have, before taking his decision, with the elected representatives of GCHQ employees? Secondly, did he discuss his decision with the Security Commission which, although it was not set up specifically to deal with a broad question of this nature, comprises people with a deep and long standing knowledge of the work of GCHQ and whose impartiality would be accepted on both sides of the House?

I put it to the right hon. and learned gentleman that he has announced a very grave decision. I appeal to him not to implement it before he has consulted the representatives of the employees concerned and put the matter to the Security Commission for an objective judgment.

Sir Geoffrey Howe: Members of the Security Commission were not consulted. It is not a matter for them. They are normally involved only in cases where there has been a breach of security. Nor was there any consultation with the trade unions at GCHQ. [HON. MEMBERS: 'Why not?'] It would not have been appropriate in such a matter to consult in that way. In parallel with my announcement, letters are being sent today to all GCHQ staff, and the non-industrial trade unions are being informed this afternoon.

I appreciate the importance of this matter. That is why there has been long and careful consideration of the issue and, for example, of the need to avoid a repetition of the industrial action that took place in the three years from 1979 to 1981, which faced staff doing this work with a severe conflict of loyalties. Bearing in mind the need for confidence in the stability and reliability of the service, the Government have concluded that it is right to take these measures. It is right to remind the House that the provisions that I am invoking are already applied to other aspects of the security services and are contained in statutes passed by the Labour government of whom the right hon. Member for Leeds, East (Mr Healey) was a member.

Further questions were asked. The Speaker refused a request by Dr David Owen (leader of the now defunct Social Democratic Party) for an urgent debate on the matter.[17] At about 4.15 pm the House moved on to other business.

[17] See p. 371.

Remember that the purpose of following through an episode like the GCHQ union ban is to understand how the public law process operates. So far, we have looked at the events from the perspective of the decision-makers in government and their legal advisors, and considered how the constitution provides tools for the executive to implement policy. The public law process is also about how institutions and procedures can be used to scrutinize and call into account the actions of government. The announcement of the government's decision on GCHQ caused the furore that some senior civil servants predicted it would. Even the *Daily Telegraph*, a newspaper normally supportive of the Conservatives, was critical of the government action, describing it as 'little short of shambolic'. How, then, were this opposition and the grievances about the union ban channelled and mediated by the constitution?

Select committee investigation and adjournment debate

Almost immediately after Sir Geoffrey Howe's statement, the House of Commons' select committee responsible for scrutinizing the work of the Department of Employment decided to carry out an investigation of the matter.[18] A few days later, twelve backbench MPs (six Conservatives and six Labour) sat together around a horse-shoe-shaped table in a committee room and questioned the Foreign Secretary, the Secretary of State for Employment and Sir Brian Tovey (by then retired as Director of GCHQ) about the events leading up to the imposition of the ban on trade union membership.[19] But the government prevented the new GCHQ Director and any of the employees actually affected by the ban from giving evidence to the committee. One (Conservative) member of the committee even alleged that the committee had been 'nobbled' by the government whips.[20] Within three weeks of the Foreign Secretary's announcement of the ban, the committee published its report. It was highly critical of the way in which the ministers had set about handling the situation, especially their failure to consult the unions and refusal to accept the no-strike agreement which had quickly been proffered by the unions. Two weeks later there was a debate on the floor of the Commons and during the whole period Prime Minister's Questions were often occupied by set-piece exchanges about GCHQ.[21]

But what did all this parliamentary activity actually achieve? Are select committees able to scrutinize the executive effectively? A relatively small number of MPs have always been critical of the select committee system, believing it deflects attention from the true task of opposition and government backbench MPs, which should be to further the party political battle on the floor of the House of Commons through debates and questions to ministers. Many claim, however, that select committees have helped restore

[18] On select committees, see Chapters 16 and 17.
[19] See p. 376.
[20] On whips, see p. 181.
[21] See p. 403.

some of the power of Parliament to call the executive into account. In a later chapter we test these rival claims by examining in detail the role of the Employment Select Committee and the subsequent adjournment debate.[22]

Legal challenges

Political accountability through Parliament is only one aspect of the public law process; legal challenges to governmental decisions, on the domestic and international plane, are also important. As soon as the union ban was announced, the Council of Civil Service Unions (CCSU, an umbrella organization for the main trade unions) and a number of individual employees from GCHQ took legal advice and began judicial review applications in the High Court to challenge the legality of the union ban. The main ground was that the government had, contrary to principles of common law developed by the courts, failed to consult the unions before changing the terms of employment for civil servants at GCHQ and that, accordingly, the decision was invalid.

As a second line of attack, in February 1984 (on the same day as the Employment Select Committee published its critical report), Len Murray, the then General Secretary of the Trades Union Congress (TUC), made a formal complaint to the ILO, a body first set up in 1919, to which the United Kingdom is a signatory to treaties made under it. Like the other 172 member states, the United Kingdom has agreed to abide by its conventions and recommendations. It was said that the GCHQ union ban had breached Art 2 of the 1948 ILO Convention on Freedom of Association which provides that 'workers and employers, without distinction whatsoever, shall have the right to establish and subject only to the rules of the organisation concerned, to join organisations of their own choosing without previous authorisation'.[23] This convention is not part of national law in the United Kingdom; the unions were therefore not able to rely on it directly in their application for judicial review.[24] Nor would any findings by the ILO be enforceable against the UK government in the domestic courts.

A committee of the ILO considered the TUC's complaint. With considerable speed, the ILO concluded in May that the government's actions were not in conformity with its ILO treaty obligations. Yet as the treaty was not part of national law, the government felt able to ignore these recommendations with impunity.

Less than two months later in July 1984, to the government's dismay, Glidewell J granted the unions' application for judicial review in the High Court, declaring that the oral instruction given by Margaret Thatcher was invalid as there had not been proper consultation with the trade unions before the decision was made. Three weeks later (with much more speed

[22] See p. Chapter 17.
[23] Freedom of Association and Protection of the Right to Organise Convention, published in the United Kingdom as Cmd 7638.
[24] See p. 534.

than usual) this ruling was reversed by the Court of Appeal. In November 1984, the Appellate Committee of the House of Lords upheld the Court of Appeal's decision. Their Lordships found that although the government's failure to consult was contrary to the principles of natural justice, the court should not interfere because the decision had been taken on grounds of national security, something that the judicial process could not enquire into. The House of Lords' decision came as a great disappointment to the CCSU and many of the employees at GCHQ. There were, however, other avenues still open to them. From the unions' perspective, a battle had been lost but the war was certainly not over.

The European Convention on Human Rights

In the wake of the Second World War, European states had come together to enshrine certain fundamental rights and democratic freedoms in an international treaty: the European Convention on Human Rights (ECHR).[25] The UK government of the time played a leading role in drafting the Convention and in establishing the European Commission of Human Rights and the European Court of Human Rights in Strasbourg to adjudicate on complaints brought under it. Like the ILO treaties, the ECHR being an international treaty is not as such part of national law in the United Kingdom and so cannot be relied upon directly in domestic courts. Since 1966, however, the United Kingdom has permitted 'any person, non-governmental organisation or group of persons' who claim to be victims of violations of the ECHR in the United Kingdom to petition the Commission of Human Rights.[26] The CCSU used this procedure claiming that the ban on union membership was contrary to Art 11 of the Convention which provides, *inter alia*, that:

> Everyone has the right to freedom of peaceful assembly and to freedom of association with others, including the right to join trade unions for the protection of his interests.

The unions received little comfort from the European Commission of Human Rights. In January 1987, three years after the ban on unions was imposed, it found that the unions' application was 'manifestly ill-founded' and rejected it.[27]

International Labour Organization continues to criticize

Almost every year since the union ban, the ILO has called upon the UK government to reverse its policy. In June 1995 the ILO's criticisms of the union ban were repeated at its annual conference in Geneva: a statement

[25] See further p. 78.
[26] ECHR, Art 25.
[27] Appl No. 11603/85. The European Commission of Human Rights' reasoning is set out at p. 675.

'deeply regretting and deploring ministers' failure to solve the problem' was issued.[28] The government's response was to dismiss the statement as the product of 'a politically inspired campaign by the TUC to manipulate the ILO for partisan purposes'. This comment by Michael Portillo MP (Secretary of State for Employment) did little to hide what Labour MPs claimed was 'open warfare' between the Employment Department and the Foreign Office over whether the United Kingdom should quit the ILO in protest at its sustained and embarrassing criticisms. Earlier that week Foreign Office ministers had made commitments in Parliament that the United Kingdom's membership of the organization was not under threat, yet Portillo now seemed to suggest that the United Kingdom might well withdraw.[29] The Speaker, Miss Betty Boothroyd MP, told the Commons that she hoped ministers would 'take an early opportunity of clearing up this matter so we can all understand what the position is'.[30]

The on-going campaign

Pressure to reverse the union ban continued. Some of the 14 civil servants who were sacked for refusing to give up union membership or be transferred to other work continued to campaign for the reinstatement of trade union rights at GCHQ from two rooms above a shop in Cheltenham. The civil service unions paid them on a basis equivalent to their salaries at GCHQ, and funded the campaign, at a cost of over £1 million a year.[31] The Labour Party and the Liberal Democrats remained pledged to restore union rights.

In December 1993 there had appeared to be a glimmer of hope when the Prime Minister, now John Major, agreed to meet union officials in Downing Street to discuss the issue; all that was offered was a right for the GCHQ staff association (the body set up by management in place of independent trade unions) to affiliate to the CCSU. During the passage of the Intelligence Services Bill in 1994, which was to put GCHQ on a statutory basis for the first time and introduce some degree of accountability to Parliament for its work,[32] Labour MPs proposed an amendment to restore union rights, but this was defeated by a government majority of 61.

Meanwhile, life at GCHQ was changing. Many posts were cut as a result of the end of the Cold War and the need for cost savings in government generally; the aim was to reduce staff from 6,500 in 1993 to 4,500 by 1997. In a recent twist in the tale, the government announced in March 1995 that some of the activities carried on at GCHQ (particularly in the engineering and logistics departments) would be contracted out to firms in the private sector.[33] Some of these firms will have unionized workforces.

[28] *The Independent*, 15 June 1995.
[29] *The Independent*, 9 June 1995, p. 10.
[30] *The Independent*, 9 June 1995, p. 10.
[31] *The Independent*, 30 January 1994, p. 6.
[32] See p. 65.
[33] *The Independent*, 23 March 1995.

Interpreting the GCHQ episode

Admittedly this narrative of events is a poor substitute for the virtual reality machine envisaged at the beginning of the chapter. But you can see that by following an episode through, rather than just looking at one particular snapshot of the constitution, we can begin to see different institutions interacting as part of a process which lies at the heart of any proper understanding of the working of the modern British constitution.

Some of the methodological difficulties of public law should also be emerging. First, whereas in other areas of law the focus of study is often on interpreting and evaluating rules or principles of law set out in case law and statute, the raw material of public law is more diverse. Much of the subject matter of public law is not 'law' in a strict sense of rules enforceable in English courts. The ILO treaties and ECHR are part of the body of public *international* law, but are not enforceable in the domestic courts. Nor is there any statute stipulating that there has to be a select committee, or Prime Minister's Questions; rather the standing orders of the House of Commons, a body of rules not justiciable in the courts, provide that there shall be. Further, constitutional *conventions*, rather than legally enforceable rules, dictate procedure, for example that the Foreign Secretary was required to announce the government's decision to the House of Commons. Lawyers need to know how these different categories of norms operate and how they relate to the more familiar territory of common law and statutory rules developed or enforced in the court room.

A second methodological challenge is *how* to evaluate an episode like the GCHQ union ban. As you use this book, you should learn the skill of understanding the mechanics of the constitutional process at work. Another is the ability to critically evaluate and to form opinions about how well or badly the modern British constitution operates. For example, do parliamentary debates and the select committees merely add a gloss of legitimacy to executive action, without altering outcomes in any significant way? What, if anything, does judicial review achieve for applicants?[34]

Exercise

Look back at the sketch of events surrounding the decision to ban unions at GCHQ and draw up a chronology. Do the same as you read the summaries of the other three case studies which follow. (This will be useful for answering the questions at the end of the chapter on the similarities and differences between the episodes.)

The main 'tool' used by the government to ban trade unions at GCHQ was an 'instruction' issued by the Minister for the Civil Service under the

[34] In the GCHQ case, even if the unions had won in the House of Lords (as they did before Glidewell J), the court's power would have been limited to quashing the government's decision. The government would have been able to make the decision again, this time consulting properly, and the substantive outcome could well have been as before: a ban on union membership.

prerogative. A more usual source of power for government, however, is derived from legislation that has passed through Parliament. In theory, this should give MPs an opportunity to participate in law-making and open policy decisions to scrutiny *before* they are put into effect. (In GCHQ, it was only *after* a legally effective decision had been made that Parliament had a chance to question the government.) The next two case studies, on Sunday shopping and welfare benefits, show how Acts of Parliament and statutory instruments can provide legal authority for particular policy choices made by government.

THE SUNDAY TRADING CASE STUDY[35]

While most people deplore law breaking, almost everyone who lived in England and Wales during the 1980s and early 1990s participated in a widespread flouting of the criminal law by shopping on Sundays. Local authorities had statutory responsibility for enforcing the law yet many turned a blind eye; others, however, adopted a policy of prosecuting shop owners, particularly chain stores. It was not an offence to buy prohibited goods, only to sell them.

There is a long history. Since the Sunday Fairs Act 1448, governments in England have attempted to regulate Sunday trading. Originally the motivation was religious: it was seen as right that in a Christian country the sanctity of the Christian sabbath should be protected by law. But from the later part of the nineteenth century, additional reasons became important in the continued prohibitions on Sunday opening of shops, particularly the paternalistic desire to protect shopworkers from extreme forms of exploitation. Today still further concerns, for example to do with environmental and competition policies, form a complex matrix of conflicting arguments for and against some regulation of Sunday trading.

The Shops Act 1950

For most of the period after the Second World War the main legislation was the Shops Act 1950. Section 47 prohibited Sunday opening except for the sale of a rather odd-looking range of goods specified in the fifth schedule to the Act.[36] Many retailers pursued a strategy of unlawful opening while at the same time attempting to bring legal and political pressure on the government to change the law. The campaign over Sunday trading took place in and around two main arenas: Parliament and the courts. In two of the other case studies (GCHQ and the Board and Lodging Regulations) the government appeared to have a firm policy it wished to implement. The position was less clear in relation to Sunday trading. While some in the Conservative Party

[35] To follow this case study in more detail, read Chapters 9 and 30.
[36] For the section, see p. 200.

(the governing party throughout the 1980s and early 1990s) supported complete deregulation in line with its generally free market outlook, others were intent on preserving what was seen as the 'traditional Sunday,' which did not include shopping.

The events surrounding attempts at legislative change often feature powerful and well-organized interest and campaigning groups. As Harlow has put it:

> Behind the monolithic facades of Government and Opposition, Parliament operates as a network of interest groups—official party groupings, back bench committees, All-Party Groups. It acts, too, as a magnet of outside interest groups. Hypnotised by the Burkeian myth, we dismiss these from our minds.[37]

Two broad coalitions of interest groups formed to campaign on the issue of Sunday trading. The Shopping Hours Reform Council (SHRC) had close links with the Conservative Party. Its main supporters were the do-it-yourself retailers (B&Q, Wickes, Texas Homecare) and some supermarkets (Asda and Tesco). On the other side was the Keep Sunday Special Campaign (KSSC) supported by trade unions and churches as well as many small retailers and some larger chains (Iceland Foods and the Co-Op).

Independent inquiry and a government bill

Faced with significant differences of opinion within its own party, in August 1983 the government set up a committee of inquiry under the chairmanship of Robin Auld QC 'to consider what changes are needed in the Shops Act, having regard to the interests of consumers, employers and employees and to the traditional character of Sunday, and to make recommendations as to how these should be achieved'. In November 1984, the committee reported; it came down in favour of complete deregulation.[38]

Although the government had a majority of over one hundred MPs in the Commons, it proceeded cautiously. Instead of introducing a bill (primary legislation was necessary to alter the existing Shops Act) straight away, it held a Commons debate on the Auld Report.[39] The government won the vote and decided to introduce a bill in the House of Lords, where it was passed with only a few amendments.[40] When the bill came to be considered by the Commons, however, an almost unprecedented thing happened: the government lost the second reading vote on the principle of the bill.[41] It was humiliated and legislative action on opening hours had to be shelved for a long while.

37 Carol Harlow, '"A Community of Interests"? Making the Most of European Law' (1992) 55 MLR 331, 335. On Burke's views of the role of MPs, see further p. 122 below.
38 See p. 201.
39 See p. 202.
40 See p. 205.
41 See p. 211.

Litigation strategies

When it became clear to the pressure groups in favour of Sunday opening that no further progress was going to be made through the parliamentary process, their attention turned to the courts. When local authorities, which were responsible for enforcement of the restrictions under s 47 of the Shops Act 1950, brought prosecutions against shops in magistrates' courts, or sought injunctions from the High Court to prohibit unlawful trading, lawyers for the retailers came up with several types of ingenious defence, often relying on Community law.

One 'European defence' was to argue that s 47 of the Shops Act was contrary to Art 30 of the European Community Treaty, which states: 'Quantitative restrictions on imports and all measures having equivalent effect shall . . . be prohibited between Member States.' Unlike the treaty provisions in the GCHQ case study, the EC Treaty *is* part of national law and some provisions in it can be relied upon directly in litigation in the domestic courts. This is because s 2 of the European Communities Act 1972 incorporates it into national law; furthermore, EC law is supreme in its operative areas and so courts in the United Kingdom have to follow it and disregard any incompatible national law.[42] Since about 10 per cent of the goods sold at B&Q plc, one of the retailers most often prosecuted, were manufactured in other EC member states, when local authorities sought to prosecute a retailer it was argued for the defence that s 47 would prevent the sale of goods manufactured in other member states and for this reason the court had to disregard s 47 as it was incompatible with Art 30. As this argument raised questions about the correct interpretation of the EC Treaty, the national courts referred the points to the European Court of Justice (ECJ) based in Luxembourg for preliminary rulings on how Art 30 ought to be interpreted.[43] As we shall see, the answers received from the ECJ were not always clear; in the end the ECJ washed its hands of the matter holding that Art 30 just had no application to national laws restricting Sunday trading.[44]

Undeterred, and having realized the considerable tactical advantage of delay by raising Community law issues, lawyers for B&Q plc and other retailers came up with another so-called European defence: that s 47 of the Shops Act was in contravention of an EC directive on equal treatment of men and women because women were more likely to be employed in retail outlets on Sundays.[45] Like the one before, this defence failed; but, as before, it created uncertainty and so deterred local authorities from enforcing the Shops Act for some time and kept the Sunday trading issue firmly on the political agenda.

[42] The relationship between Community law and national law is an important aspect of modern public law; see p. 115.

[43] On the various functions of the ECJ, see Chapter 29. Be clear that the ECJ is an institution of the European Union, quite separate from the European Commission on Human Rights and the European Court of Human Rights in Strasbourg which have responsibilities for adjudicating on the ECHR (a treaty between member states of the Council of Europe).

[44] See p. 721.

[45] EC directives are secondary legislation made by the Community institutions under the terms of the EC Treaty: see Chapter 13.

The legislative campaign revived

Having failed in the courts, the reform campaign turned its focus once more on to Parliament. In March 1993 a Labour MP's Private Member's Bill on Sunday trading received considerable cross-party support in the Commons, but by May it had suffered the fate of numerous other private members' bills on the subject by running out of parliamentary time before it had completed all the necessary stages.[46]

The government's response was to publish its own bill in July 1993. It was in an unusual format in that it contained three different options:

(1) total deregulation with all shops allowed to open;
(2) larger shops able to open on the four Sundays before Christmas and smaller shops able to open all year round; and
(3) unlimited opening for small shops and large shops able to open for six hours on a Sunday.

The option which received an overall majority would be accepted and the others would fall without a vote.

In the months that followed intensive lobbying took place. A new coalition of retailers (Retailers for Shops Act Reform) sympathetic to some degree of regulation became active, but was criticized by other pressure groups for not working more effectively with another umbrella organization (the KSSC). An important step forward came in November 1993 when USDAW, the shop-workers' union, dramatically withdrew its opposition to general opening on Sundays. In December, MPs voted for the third option. The government made a number of concessions including statutory protection for all shop-workers against being forced to work on Sundays and increasing the fines for breach of the new rules from £5,000 to £50,000. No significant amendments were made in the House of Lords. The Sunday Trading Act 1994 was given Royal Assent in July 1994 and became law on 26 August 1994.[47]

The aftermath

Government success in deregulating Sunday shop opening encouraged it to pursue similar deregulatory policies in other contexts. In May 1995 it became legal for betting and horse racing to take place on Sundays; and in August 1995 restrictions on pub Sunday opening hours were relaxed, allowing them to open from noon to 10.30 pm. So far as shops were concerned, *The Guardian* reported that 'supporters of [the] change must be pleased with the way things turned out, because virtually all opposition to Sunday trading has gone underground or gone bust since the law was changed'.[48] Not everyone was pleased, however. The same report stated that 'as far as the economy

[46] See p. 213.
[47] Extracts from the Act are set out at p. 219.
[48] *The Guardian*, 20 May 1995, p. 20.

is concerned, Sunday trading has been an almighty flop'. Early statistics from the government's Central Statistical Office suggested that the main effect of Sunday trading has been to encourage the existing trend towards people spending less at small independent stores and much more at large out-of-town supermarkets. Marks & Spencer, one of the chain stores which opposed deregulation, remained unconvinced by the new law which allowed larger shops to open for six hours: Sunday trading had produced no improvement in profits for the company, the chairman Sir Richard Greenbury said, the extra revenue being generated at the expense of trading in the rest of the week and the cost of double-time payments to staff.[49]

This was not the end of the dissatisfaction with the new law. Very soon anomalies and loopholes began to be identified. Under the Sunday Trading Act DIY stores and garden centres with indoor premises above 3,000 square feet had to stay closed on Easter Sundays (previously one of the busiest days of the year). Many people had not realized this. Some retailers were prompted to resort to tactics reminiscent of those used to side-step the restrictions imposed by s 47 of the Shops Act. The owner of one garden centre, backed by the Horticultural Trade Association, moved his entire stock of plants and goods into the open air to circumvent the new rule; it took a dozen staff over four hours to achieve this.[50] Another garden centre applied for a liquor licence for Easter Sunday so that it could sell drinks to disappointed customers who turned up not realizing the effect of the new law.

Meanwhile, some employers began searching for loopholes in the provisions of the Sunday Trading Act designed to protect shopworkers. Staff of one supermarket chain were reported to have received letters from management saying that their wages would be cut if they refused to work on Sundays because they would not be offered alternative weekday shifts. The workers concerned were said to be taking legal advice.[51]

THE BOARD AND LODGING CASE STUDY[52]

During the summer of 1984 national attention was caught by a problem. The tabloid press ran stories concerning what was dubbed the 'Costa del Dole' scandal. Considerable numbers of young unemployed people (it was claimed) were moving to live in boarding houses at seaside holiday resorts around England during the summer and claiming welfare benefits there including supplementary benefit for board and lodging accommodation.[53]

[49] *The Times*, 24 May 1995.

[50] *The Guardian*, 17 April 1995, p. 4.

[51] *The Guardian*, 17 April 1995, p. 4.

[52] To follow this case study in more detail, read Chapters 11 and 27.

[53] Supplementary benefit has now been replaced with new forms of welfare payments including income support, family credit and social fund loans. The social security law at the heart of the case study has therefore been superseded. This does not matter as we are not concerned with the minutiae of the substantive law for its own sake, but rather for what it shows us about the public law process.

The Department of Health and Social Security (DHSS)[54] was under pressure to curb this expenditure and to stamp out abuse. We can begin this saga with an announcement made by the Secretary of State to the House of Commons at 4 pm on 29 November 1984.

The Secretary of State for Social Services (Mr Norman Fowler): With permission, Mr Speaker, I should like to make a statement on changes I am proposing in the system for making board and lodging payments under the supplementary benefit scheme. I have referred these proposals to the Social Security Advisory Committee for it to report its views to me after a process of consultation. Copies of the consultative document are available in the Vote Office.

Supplementary benefit expenditure on board and lodging is escalating. During 1983 it rose from £205 million a year to £380 million a year. My latest information suggests that unless action is taken expenditure will grow by a further 50 per cent each year during 1984 and 1985. No responsible Government can allow expenditure to increase in this way unchecked. As an immediate measure of cost control, I laid before the House on 22 November regulations which will empower me to impose a temporary freeze on the existing local limits governing board and lodging payments. These regulations will be debated soon. They will be replaced by new arrangements which will come into operation in early 1985, following the consultative process.

There is particular concern about the growing number of young people receiving board and lodging payments, especially those spending long periods on benefit in seaside resorts. The number of such people aged 25 and under went up by 60 per cent during 1983. The increasing evidence of abuse makes it essential to move quickly to bring ordinary board and lodging expenditure under control . . .

My consultative document proposes several changes. The responsibility for setting the maximum amounts of benefit payable will be transferred to Ministers. For ordinary board and lodging accommodation, the existing locally determined limits will be replaced by two new limits—one for the Greater London area and another for the rest of the country. I am also proposing limiting the eligibility of 16- and 17-year-olds to claim board and lodging payments in their own right. We shall also prevent young people from setting up in long-term board and lodging accommodation, but we shall safeguard the position of the genuine job searcher . . .

Subject to the process of consultation I have mentioned, I propose bringing regulations before the House in February next year with a view to implementing new arrangements in April 1985 . . .

The supplementary benefit scheme is there to help people in need. The Government are committed to that . . . but we are equally determined to make sure that the supplementary benefit scheme is not abused or exploited. I am determined that we should no longer make unjustified board and lodging payments. I therefore give this warning: if claimants do not need board and lodging accommodation, or if the charges are too high the supplementary benefit scheme will no longer pick up the bill.

The Opposition frontbench spokesman asked several, mostly rhetorical, questions (in effect, he made a statement) and several backbench MPs also made points.

[54] In a subsequent reorganization of government departments, the DHSS was split into two: there is now a separate Department of Health and a Department of Social Security. The two departments nevertheless still continue to share the same legal advisors.

Giving the new policy legal effect

Imagine for a moment it is 1984 and you are a lawyer in the DHSS. One of your main tasks is to advise how the new policy can effectively be given legal backing. You sit at your desk and think about the possibilities. One can be ruled out immediately. It is obvious that the government's historic non-statutory prerogative powers (like those used to regulate the civil service and so ban unions at GCHQ) cannot be used because entitlement to welfare benefits has always been governed by legislation and it is a principle of law that no new prerogative powers can now be created.[55] You therefore come up with two options.

First, new primary legislation (a statute) could be enacted. The prospect of spending several months steering a bill through all its legislative stages in both Houses of Parliament before receiving the Royal Assent does not appeal to you.[56] You would need to draft detailed instructions, in conjunction with senior civil servants in your department, for the Parliamentary Counsel, the government's specialist law draftsmen housed in offices at 36 Whitehall. There might be many meetings before the bill could even be published. The minister is putting pressure on you and his civil servants to tackle the problem quickly; an Act will take far too long. But it is not just the laboriousness of getting an Act passed that makes primary legislation an unattractive option. The main problem would be finding room in the legislative timetable for such a bill. The Cabinet's Future Legislation Committee will have planned which bills are to be introduced during the summer recess in time for the Queen to announce the programme at the State Opening of Parliament.[57] Now, in November, there is no realistic prospect of you being able to squeeze another bill into the schedule. You therefore rule out an Act. (The minister will later be criticized for this decision by Frank Field MP, a Labour backbencher.)[58]

The obvious solution seems to be to make the proposed new rules on entitlement to supplementary benefit by using rule-making powers that have been delegated by Parliament to a minister.[59] As the existing rules are already set out in a statutory instrument (SI) called the Board and Lodgings Regulations 1983, a new SI can be used to amend those rules. All delegated legislation requires enabling power from an Act; you decide that s 2(1A) of the Supplementary Benefits Act 1976 provides a legal basis for the proposed new scheme of greater ministerial control.[60] You therefore advise the minister and senior civil servants in the DHSS that this is the best course to follow, and (as we have seen) the minister announces this in his Commons statement.

55 See Chapter 12.
56 On the legislative process for bills, see Chapter 8.
57 See p. 177.
58 See Chapter 27.
59 'Regulations', 'statutory instruments', 'subordinate legislation' and 'secondary legislation' are, for most purposes, synonyms and the terms can be used interchangeably. The use of delegated legislation is discussed in Chapters 10 and 11.
60 The text of that section is set out at p. 244.

As the minister stated, the new scheme is to be in operation by April 1985. This gives you less than five months. First, you will have to draft the new regulations. (Drafting of SIs, unlike bills, is done in-house by each department.) It may be difficult to find adequate time to do this in your hectic and gruelling working day because, of course, you have to continue giving advice on other matters and probably preparing for various pieces of litigation, especially judicial review challenges to departmental decisions taken in the past. But as well as actually drafting the SI you are going to have to steer it through the formal stages it needs to go through on the way to becoming law. Although the procedures are considerably less cumbersome than those for primary legislation, nevertheless your text will be subject to some scrutiny. (Outsiders often suggest that this scrutiny is inadequate.)

The need to consult

First, the Social Security Act 1980 imposes a requirement that draft regulations on welfare benefits are referred to a body known as the Social Security Advisory Committee (SSAC).[61] You will have to ask SSAC to report back quickly if you are to meet the April deadline. But regulations are not yet drafted! What can you do? You decide that the SSAC will have to make do with an outline of the proposals. How much time will you need to give the SSAC to report back to you? (The 1980 Act is silent on the point.) The department decides to ask for the formal SSAC report by the end of January. This does not give SSAC much time, but then you do have to have the new rules up and running by April.

Parliamentary scrutiny of delegated legislation

You can now carry on drafting the new SI.[62] As soon as the text is finished, it can begin its progress through Parliament. There are two main hurdles: gaining approval by the Joint Committee on Statutory Instruments (JCSI)[63] and obtaining an affirmative resolution by the House of Commons. You give a big sigh of relief when the SI passes through these stages without trouble. You are quite unaware of the catastrophe that will occur a few weeks later.

The claimant's perspective

Now switch hats. You are a 21-year-old unemployed person living in board and lodging accommodation. It is a fine May morning in 1985. You see the postman walking up your landlady's path. A letter drops on to the door mat. It is addressed to you, from your local DHSS office:

61 This is not a select committee of MPs (as was the Employment Select Committee which considered the GCHQ union ban) but a committee of experts appointed by the Secretary of State for Social Security.

62 Extracts from the final version are set out at p. 251; notice how complicated it is.

63 This is a select committee of backbench MPs and peers whose task is to scrutinize draft SIs and report to Parliament any technical irregularities: see p. 235.

> We are writing to tell you that you are affected by changes in the rules for paying Supplementary Benefit to unemployed people who are aged 16–25 and who are living as boarders. The new rules say we can only pay them as boarders in any one area for a limited number of weeks in any 26 week period. The length of time we can pay you as a boarder depends on where you are living. The time limit for paying you as a boarder in this area is four weeks. This means that if you remain unemployed and living as a boarder we will pay you as a boarder until week commencing 3 June 1985. After that date we will reduce your money . . .

What impact will this have on your life? What do you think you would do about it? Whom would you turn to for advice? One person who was really in your imaginary position was Simon Cotton. He was 22, unemployed and living in Birkenhead, in northwest England. He received £103 a fortnight in welfare benefit and paid his landlady £30 a week for bed, breakfast and evening meal. He had had no contact with his parents since he was a baby. Worried by the letter from the DHSS, he went to see a nun whom he had known when in a children's home. She referred him to the Birkenhead Resource Unit, a charity giving legal advice, then run by solicitor Nicholas Warren from a spare bedroom in his home. (If this charity had not existed, where, if at all, do you think Simon Cotton would have obtained legal advice?)

A judicial review challenge is launched

Warren looked at the new regulations carefully and came to the conclusion that s 2(1A) of the Supplementary Benefits Act 1976 did *not* give the minister the necessary legal powers to make the new SI. Further research suggested an additional ground, that the mandatory consultation process with the SSAC had been inadequate. (Remember how it was necessary to rush them, and that the text of the SI was not yet drafted?) Cotton's lawyers decided to make an application for judicial review to obtain an order to quash the new SI. Great speed was needed: not only was Simon Cotton to be affected by the new regulations in a couple of weeks, but the rules of court require applications for judicial review to be made 'promptly'.[64]

In the weeks that followed, the implementation of the government's new supplementary benefits policy was stopped in its tracks. Simon Cotton's application for judicial review was successful; having heard submissions from Cotton's barrister and counsel for the Secretary of State Mann J held on 31 July 1985 that the new SI was *ultra vires*.[65] From the government's point of view, the timing of this judgment was truly disastrous. It was on the last day of the legal term (so a speedy appeal to the Court of Appeal was impossible) and Parliament had already risen for its annual summer recess (so new regulations could not be made until it met again in the autumn). The DHSS

64 The documents necessary to begin the legal action are set out in Chapter 27.

65 See p. 643.

agreed to continue paying the full amount of benefit to Simon Cotton and thousands of other claimants in his position during the summer.

The government tries again (and again)

As soon as Parliament resumed in October, a new SI on board and lodging payments was laid before it. But the smooth passage enjoyed by the first regulations in April was not afforded to these regulations. The JCSI of backbench MPs and peers, after subjecting lawyers and officials from the DHSS to gruelling cross-examination,[66] reported to Parliament that the latest regulations suffered from the same legal defect as the April ones and were accordingly *ultra vires* s 2(1A) of the Supplementary Benefits Act.[67] It is difficult to understand what the department was doing. The proposed regulations were withdrawn.

In December, the Court of Appeal upheld Mann J's decision granting Simon Cotton's application for judicial review.[68] By this time, the DHSS had produced yet another set of regulations, which went on to pass the scrutiny of both Parliament and (in a judicial review brought by another applicant) the courts.

WORKING TIME DIRECTIVE CASE STUDY[69]

No exploration of the modern UK constitution can now be complete without an examination of the work of the Community institutions. The ECJ has already been mentioned in the context of the litigation over Sunday trading; the next case study examines the work of several others by tracing the often tortuous steps which preceded the adoption of an EC directive: the Directive on Certain Aspects of Working Time.[70]

Initiation by the European Commission

The starting point in each of the previous case studies has been the initiation of a policy by central government, either in a department or, in the case of GCHQ, a small group of ministers acting collectively. In relation to the directive, national government stood in quite a different position. We therefore begin not in Whitehall, but in the office of the European Commissioner with responsibility for social affairs (at that time, Mrs Vasso Papandreou). It

66 See the Minutes of Evidence at p. 259.
67 See the report at p. 261.
68 See p. 649.
69 To follow this case study in more detail, read Chapter 14.
70 A directive is one of the main types of secondary legislation made by Community institutions acting under the terms of the EC Treaty; the other main type is regulations. See further Chapter 13.

was here that the first draft of the directive was prepared with the assistance of her personal staff of six or so working together with the Community legal service. As is usual, Mrs Papandreou and her staff would have consulted very widely with interest groups and representatives of national governments on the proposed policy implications during the preparation of the first draft of the directive.

Decisions needed also to be made about the legal basis on which the Commission planned to introduce the draft directive. The EC Commission has only those powers granted to it under the EC treaties. Some specific treaty provision therefore had to be found; in the end it was decided that Art 118a of the EC Treaty was to be used. It gave power to the Commission to initiate legislation designed 'to encourage improvements, especially in the working environment, as regards health and safety of workers'.[71] The legislative procedure which applies to Art 118a allows a directive to be adopted by the Council of Ministers[72] on the basis of a majority vote in its favour. (Some other articles in the treaty enabling directives to be made require there to be unanimity; in other words, any member state is able to veto a proposed directive.)

In July 1990 Mrs Papandreou took the draft text to the regular Wednesday-morning meeting of the whole Commission, where decisions are taken behind closed doors, usually on the basis of majority voting. The Commission agreed to propose the draft directive to the Council of Ministers.[73]

The Community legislative process

The task then before Mrs Papandreou was to steer the draft directive though the Community's notoriously complex legislative processes. There are several different procedural routes which directives may follow; the procedure used for the directive on working time was the cooperation procedure. It was necessary first for the Commission to seek the 'opinion' of the Economic and Social Committee (ECOSOC), a purely advisory body established by the treaty now with 222 part-time members (24 from the United Kingdom) representing employers, workers and other interests such as farmers, academics and consumers. In December 1990, ECOSOC published a report rather critical of the draft directive.[74] For example, it 'failed to understand why the Commission has not put forward health provisions in respect of weekend working . . .'.

At the same time, the draft directive had to be considered by the European Parliament, an institution now comprising of 626 directly elected MEPs. In its response in February 1991, the European Parliament approved the draft

[71] Art 118a is set out at p. 323, below.

[72] See p. 297 below.

[73] Extracts from the draft directive are set out at p. 320. The Council of Ministers consists of a ministerial representative from each of the member states.

[74] See p. 324.

directive, but proposed two very significant changes:[75] restrictions on weekend working and a maximum 48-hour working week.

Directive considered in the United Kingdom

Given its general policy of deregulation, the UK government was implacably opposed to the draft directive, believing that it would place undue burdens on businesses. Very soon after the Commission had formally published the draft directive, the Department of Employment[76] issued a formal consultative document, hoping to elicit responses which it could use to put pressure on the Commission to water down its policy proposals, if not abandon them entirely. Comments were received from many workers' and employers' organizations such as the TUC and CBI. This national consultation was not a formal part of the Community legislative process, but it helped inform the British government.

The draft directive was also considered by the UK Parliament (at about the same time as ECOSOC and the European Parliament were doing so). Again, this was not a formal part of the legislative process stipulated by the EC Treaty. A sub-committee of the House of Lords' Select Committee on the European Community took evidence from more than 20 different organizations and issued a report suggesting that further research was needed into the health effects of long working hours.[77] Even though the principles contained in the proposed directive would have had a far-reaching effect on British industry, there was no debate in the chambers of either the Lords or the Commons.

Both the government and the House of Lords' select committee also raised concerns about whether Art 118a of the EC Treaty was a proper legal basis on which the Commission was entitled to proceed: they doubted whether there was sufficient connection between restrictions on working time and the granting of entitlement to holidays and 'health and safety'. The government would have preferred for the directive to have been based on another article of the treaty, to which majority voting in the Council of Ministers did not apply. This would have enabled the United Kingdom to veto the proposed directive.

Commission proposal to Council of Ministers

Having received formal responses from the European Parliament and ECOSOC, and also feedback from national governments and some national parliaments, the Commission was able now, under the cooperation procedure,

[75] See p. 325.
[76] The Department of Employment has since been merged with the Department for Education.
[77] See p. 322.

to make a formal proposal to the Council of Ministers.[78] The text of the Commission's directive was little different from that published at the start of the consultation process; it had rejected, as it was entitled to, the proposed amendments made by the European Parliament and the opinion of ECOSOC.

Common position in the Council of Ministers (eventually)

Under the cooperation procedure, the way was now clear for the Council of Ministers to adopt a 'common position' on the directive; a qualified majority of ministers needed to vote in favour.[79] Sometimes agreement is reached with relatively little difficulty with no real discussion at the Council meeting. The Working Time Directive, however, was one of the most fraught and long-drawn-out episodes of deadlock in recent years. The process lasted over two years.

The employment ministers met in June 1991 to discuss formally the Commission's proposal, but failed to reach any consensus. In a move that must have appalled the UK government, the German government, backed by Luxembourg, then proposed an amendment at this stage: that the mandatory 36-hour rest period in the Commission's text should include Sundays. The French government also proposed a maximum 48-hour working week (averaged out over two months). For the UK government, still intent on deregulating Sunday shop opening, this was anathema. There was much behind-the-scenes lobbying between ministers. By coincidence, Britain had held the presidency of the Community during part of this period; one of the responsibilities of the member state holding the six-month revolving presidency is to convene and chair Council meetings. Gillian Sheppard MP, the UK employment minister, was roundly condemned by the Commission for calling only one meeting of the Council of Ministers on social affairs which, it was said, had been inadequately prepared. The directive on working time was not included on the Council's agenda in December 1992; this was the first time that the Council had not included in its agenda a point the Commission had asked for. At the press conference after that meeting Mrs Papandreou could hardly mask her disappointment and anger, saying that 'the British presidency has been effective to its aim which was to make as few decisions as possible'. Answering a journalist who asked her if one could speak of 'deliberate sabotage', the Commissioner replied pointedly: 'Not very well; as the United Kingdom, they did their job.'[80]

78 Remember that the Council of Ministers consists of a ministerial representative from each of the member states. As the directive concerned employment matters, it was employment (or social affairs) ministers who were involved here.

79 Votes are weighted so that the votes of the larger member states, such as Germany, France and the United Kingdom, are worth more than those of smaller states like Luxembourg and Portugal.

80 'Europe' No. 5872 (new series), 5 December 1992, p. 9.

In June 1993 the Council finally agreed, by the necessary qualified majority, to adopt a common position on the Working Time Directive: the United Kingdom abstained, with all other member states voting in favour.

Back to the European Parliament

The next stage in the cooperation legislative procedure was for the Council's common position, and also the Commission's position, to be communicated to the European Parliament. As before, the Parliament approved the draft directive, subject to some amendments.

Back to the Commission

The Commission accepted only some minor amendments made by the European Parliament.

Final adoption by the Council of Ministers

Finally, on 23 November 1993, the Council of Ministers adopted the final text of the directive.[81] Directives do not automatically take effect in national law. They usually specify a period of 12 or 18 months by the end of which each member state must have amended its legislation, or taken steps to alter administrative practices, so as to bring its domestic law in line with Community law. As part of the many compromises made during its tortuous passage through the Community legislative process, the Working Time Directive contains a more than usually complex formula determining the date by which there must be compliance. Had the UK government accepted that the directive had been validly made, it would have either introduced a bill into Parliament or made an SI to bring the law in the United Kingdom into line with the new directive.

UK government commences legal proceedings in ECJ

The government, however, remained bitterly opposed to the directive. In a relatively unusual move, it sought to challenge the directive's legality before the ECJ under Art 173 of the EC Treaty, which gives the ECJ responsibility for adjudicating on disputes between member states and the institutions of the Community.[82] The ground on which review was sought was that it was unlawful for the directive to be made under Art 118a;[83] the United Kingdom

[81] See p. 337.
[82] Remember that the jurisdiction of the ECJ in the Sunday trading case study was under Art 177 (preliminary ruling to national courts on the interpretation of the treaty).
[83] The text is set out at p. 323.

claimed that if there had to be a directive regulating working time then it should have been introduced under Art 100 (which would have resulted in a requirement that there be unanimity in the Council of Ministers before the directive was adopted).[84]

In March 1996, Advocate General Léger advised the court to dismiss the United Kingdom's application in its entirety. The ECJ delivered its judgment on 12 November: the directive was held to be valid, except for the provision that the weekly rest period 'shall in principle include Sunday'.[85] It was a victory for the Commission. The Conservative government remained implacably opposed to the directive (which under Community law it was now obliged to incorporate into national law by 23 November 1996). *The Times* reported that within hours of the court's decision, the British Ambassador to the European Union had tabled proposals for the inter-governmental conference due to be held the following month in Dublin: the UK was going to demand that the treaty be amended to exempt it from the Working Time Directive and that in the future health and safety legislation be subject to unanimous voting in the Council of Ministers (rather than qualified majority voting).[86] If the other member states did not agree to this, the UK would block agreement on other issues at the IGC.

WHERE TO GO FROM HERE

The summaries above have outlined the events in each of the case studies. We will be returning to these episodes throughout the book, either to use as brief illustrations within the narrative chapters or, in the case study chapters, by setting out and exploring in detail primary materials such as the court judgments, select committee reports and debates in Parliament. The study of public law cannot, though, merely be the analysis of several 'stories'. The next four chapters therefore present a variety of ways of understanding the constitutional law system and what happens in it, beginning with an overview of the institutional structure.

[84] See p. 323.
[85] *United Kingdom v Council of the European Union* (1996). *The Times*, 21 November.
[86] See *The Times*, 12 November 1996, p. 1, and *The Times*, 13 November 1996, p. 10.

3

AN INSTITUTIONAL APPROACH

INTRODUCTION

In order to learn how something complicated works, its various component parts have first to be named. We therefore need to map out and label the main institutions and office-holders in the modern constitutional system, identify some of their interrelationships and highlight what is of particular importance from a legal perspective. Most of the features described in this chapter are examined again later in the book.

A general survey like this inevitably hits snags. For a start, how do we decide what needs to be included? (In the United Kingdom there is, of course, no formal codified constitutional document to use as a starting point.) Then there is the problem that the system appears to be constantly changing: new government departments are set up; local government is reorganized; state-owned enterprises are privatized and so on. The institutional map therefore needs to try to capture this dynamism while also explaining continuities in the constitution. A further set of complications arises when we try to attribute functions to each institution and office-holder. In the United Kingdom there is no strong principle of 'separation of powers'. Nor were many of the institutions expressly *designed* to carry out the roles they now perform; rather they *evolved*. Before plotting out the main constitutional framework, some thought has to be given to these difficulties.

Deciding what should be included

An initial problem with institutional descriptions of the constitution is knowing what to include. A glance at the contents pages of the standard legal textbooks on the UK constitution shows considerable consensus about which institutions are regarded as central to the study of public law: Parliament, the Cabinet, local authorities, the civil service and so on. But should we, for instance, also examine the main political parties, pressure groups, charities, the now privately-owned gas, electricity and water utilities (which until recently were state-owned), the self-regulatory bodies which exist in the financial services and some other industries?

To take just political parties for the moment. We could, for example, look at questions such as internal party democracy and accountability.[1] In some countries, such as Germany, political parties are given formal status under the constitution and they receive funding from the state. In the United Kingdom, parties receive little formal recognition in public law and no direct financial support from taxation. However, many constitutional conventions[2] and almost all modern parliamentary procedure are premised on their existence. Who is to be Prime Minister is effectively determined by the internal elections within the Labour and Conservative parties[3] (though *formally* the Prime Minister is appointed by the monarch) and, in the many 'safe seats', the question of who is to represent a constituency in Parliament is for all intents and purposes determined by local party officials or members. Political parties are therefore important—though they are not, from a strictly legal perspective, necessarily regarded as part of 'the constitution'. In short, the borderlines between public and private institutions, government and non-government, the formal and the informal are often indistinct. This is of practical importance because we need to know which bodies are subject to the special mechanisms of public accountability and public law.[4]

Design or evolution?

Metaphors have often been used by writers in their descriptions of the constitution. Some have used images of architecture or machines; others have used references to living organisms.[5] Implicit in the former, but not the latter, is the idea that constitutional arrangements are, or ought to be, *designed* by someone or a group of people to carry out specific functions. F. A. Hayek has suggested a distinction between two different types of order (he also uses the synonyms 'systems, structures and patterns') which may be of use here.[6] First there is 'made' order (which Hayek terms *taxis*): in the context of the constitution, it means that constitutional institutions and arrangements are invented and designed by a group of people sitting down to plan how the system will work and what it is intended to achieve. Distinct from this, there is 'spontaneous' or self-generating order (*kosmos*) which describes patterns of interaction between people and institutions that is of nobody's deliberate making; prime examples are the free market and the common law.

[1] See e.g. R. K. Alderman 'Electing the Leader of the Conservative Party: revision of the rules' [1992] PL 30 and 'Electing the Leader of the Labour Party: revision of the rules' [1994] PL 17; Rodney Brazier, 'The Next Labour Government' [1990] PL 9.

[2] On conventions, see p. 137.

[3] Margaret Thatcher ceased to be Prime Minister in 1989 when she lost an internal leadership election in the Conservative Party in which only Conservative MPs could vote.

[4] For example which bodies are subject to judicial review (see Chapter 22) and which institutions are 'emanations of the state' for the purposes of being directly subject to European Community directives (see Chapter 29).

[5] For example Sir Ivor Jennings, *The Law and the Constitution* (5th edn., 1959), p. 81: 'The short explanation of constitutional conventions is that they provide the flesh which clothes the dry bones of the law.'

[6] See *Law, Legislation and Liberty: vol. 1* (1973).

Much of the British constitution has not been designed; there is no constitutional document which sets out systematically the purposes of, and relationships between, the institutions of governance. Institutions and constitutional practices have developed piecemeal over time, adaptations being made to suit changing needs. To take one prime example, the UK Parliament was not 'designed' in its current form. Its origins can be traced back to 1265 when Simon de Montfort called a Parliament (from the French *parler*, 'to speak') for the King at Westminster. In its early period, Parliament met only sporadically, often not for several years. It became a democratic institution only late in its history, and the process was gradual. During the nineteenth century the right to vote for MPs to sit in the House of Commons was extended by a series of Acts of Parliament to more and more ordinary people in pragmatic response to pressure; women were finally enfranchised on the same basis as men only in 1928. Even today, the House of Lords is not organized on democratic principles, with the majority of peers being entitled to sit and vote in Parliament because of the hereditary principle. Were a group of people to sit down to design a *legislature* for the United Kingdom today, it is improbable that they would base parts of their design on the use of the hereditary principle.[7] Contrast this with the written constitutions in countries such as France and the USA, which are much more the product of purposive, rational planning.[8] Proposals for constitutional reform in the United Kingdom also assume that rational design and express purpose is better than spontaneous and piecemeal development.

It is not only constitutional institutions which tend in the United Kingdom to emerge piecemeal and slowly over time. For many writers it is the common law, evolved over the centuries by judges deciding particular cases, which contains the important legal constraints on government action and statements of the important civil rights of individuals.[9]

Separation of powers

Any description and analysis of the constitution which focuses on institutions needs also to look at the principles which govern their interrelationships. The doctrine of separation of powers is often presented as being of key importance in Western constitutions.[10] The phrase can be used to refer to several different concepts, as Vile makes clear:[11]

[7] There may be more agreement that hereditary monarchy is suitable for a head of state.

[8] For an introduction to these, see S. E. Finer, Vernon Bogdanor and Bernard Rudden, *Comparing Constitutions* (1995).

[9] See further Chapter 6.

[10] See further Eric Barendt, 'Separation of Powers and Constitutional Government' [1995] PL 599.

[11] M. C. J. Vile, *Constitutionalism and the Separation of Powers* (1967), Chapter 1. For discussion of how the concept applies to the EC see Koen Lenaerts, 'Some reflections on the separation of powers in the European Community' (1991) 28 CMLRev 11.

> The first element of the doctrine is the assertion of a division of the **agencies** of government into three categories: the legislature, the executive, and the judiciary .... The growth of three separate branches of the government system in Britain reflected in part the needs for a division of labour and specialization, and partly the demand for different sets of values to be embodied in the procedures of the different agencies, and in the representation of varying interests in the separate branches. This aspect of the doctrine ... is clearly central to the whole pattern of Western constitutionalism. The diffusion of authority among different centres of decision-making is the antithesis of totalitarianism or absolutism.
>
> The second element in the doctrine is the assertion that there are three specific **'functions'** of government. Unlike the first element, which *recommends* that there should be three branches of government, this second part of the doctrine asserts a sociological truth ... that there are in all government situations three necessary functions to be performed, whether or not they are in fact all performed by one person or group, or whether there is a division of these functions among two or more agencies of government. *All* government acts, it is claimed, can be classified as an exercise of the legislative, executive, or judicial functions....
>
> The third element in this doctrine ... is what, for want of a better phrase, we shall describe as the **'separation of persons'**. This is the recommendation that the three branches of government shall be composed of quite separate and distinct groups of people, with no overlapping membership.

These versions of the separation of powers are premised on the notion that different sorts of governmental powers either must be or ought to be dispersed, not concentrated. However there is no very strong sense in the United Kingdom's constitutional arrangements of either a 'separation of agencies' or a 'separation of persons': judges sit in the Upper House of the legislature (the law lords in the House of Lords); the Lord Chancellor, a judge, exercises executive functions which in many other countries are performed by a minister of justice and he also participates in the legislature by chairing parliamentary sessions of the Lords; members of the executive (ministers) sit in the legislature (Parliament); and so on. In one particular sense, however, elements of the separation of powers are evident in the UK constitution: the independence of the judiciary from executive influence is an important element of the rule of law.[12] On the whole, though, writers have instead stressed the fusion or balance of powers (rather than their separation) as a characteristic of the UK constitution. For Walter Bagehot, the 'efficient secret' of the nineteenth-century constitution was the Cabinet in which there was a 'nearly complete fusion of the executive and legislative powers'.[13] These themes are taken up again in Chapter 5, below.

The dignified and efficient constitution

As a description of constitutional realities, Bagehot's *The English Constitution* (1867) was soon regarded as outdated. One of the reasons for its lasting

[12] See Chapter 6.

[13] *The English Constitution* (1867), p. 65; and see further p. 53 below.

importance, however, is the distinction Bagehot draws between the 'dignified' and the 'efficient' parts of the constitution. He argued that some institutions—the 'dignified' ones such as the monarchy and the House of Lords—were 'very complicated and somewhat imposing, very old and rather venerable . . . august with the Gothic grandeur of a more imposing age'. Bagehot was an elitist who had little but contempt for the extension of the franchise to the male working class. Modern-day commentators stress Bagehot's view that the dignified constitution was 'merely wool to pull over the eyes of the unlettered clods who make up the vast majority of the population'.[14] The ordinary people of the United Kingdom were not aware of the realities of government power which were exercised through what he termed the 'efficient' institutions:

> They defer to what we may call the *theatrical show* of society . . . The apparent rulers of the English nation are like the most imposing personages of a splendid procession; it is by them the mob are influenced; it is they whom the spectators cheer. The real rulers are secreted in second-rate carriages; no one cares for them or asks about them, but they are obeyed implicitly and unconsciously by reason of the splendour of those who eclipsed and proceeded them.

In the 1990s, Bagehot's distinction (if not his strident snobbery) remains a useful one. There is still much 'theatrical show' in the constitution such as the annual State Opening of Parliament. Ceremony is also important away from the public gaze: Cabinet ministers, chosen by the Prime Minister, are still formally appointed by the Queen delivering to each one three sets of seals.[15] Privy Counsellors are appointed to office when they kiss the Queen's hand.[16] This suggests that function of ceremony and symbolism extends beyond just impressing the *general* population.

The concept of 'dignified' aspects in the constitution can also be extended today. It can be argued that much of what now happens in the House of Commons belongs to the dignified part—there to impress rather than to make real decisions or exercise real influence over events. The twice-weekly 15-minute ritual of Prime Minister's Questions, introduced in 1961, is a good example of this.[17] Some commentators have even suggested that the Cabinet is only a decorative vestige in the constitution, hiding the fact that real power is now exercised by the Prime Minister and through Cabinet committees.[18]

Where to begin?

A final difficulty is knowing where to start drawing the map. For convenience, public bodies and officers can be arranged into three broad tiers:

[14] F. Mount, *The British Constitution Now* (1992), p. 42.
[15] See A. J. C. Simcock, 'One and Many—The Office of Secretary of State' (1992) 70 Public Administration 535.
[16] See Chapter 12.
[17] See Chapter 16.
[18] See p. 54 below.

national; sub-national (or 'local') and supra-national ('European' or 'international'). Several different starting points are possible. Some might suggest starting at sub-national level, with those institutions of law and government closest to individuals, such as the several hundred elected local authorities. An alternative starting point could be the European Union, the supra-national organization which has been emerging in Western Europe since the devastation of the Second World War. More and more political and legal action is carried out not by the governments of individual nation states, but though the institutions of the European Community (the most developed of the three 'pillars' of the European Union).[19]

There are, however, good reasons for taking the 'United Kingdom of Great Britain and Northern Ireland' as the point of departure. Writing at the end of the nineteenth century, A. V. Dicey said that one of the features which has 'at all times since the Norman Conquest characterised the political institutions of England [*sic*] is the omnipotence or undisputed supremacy throughout the whole country of the central government'.[20] This is still largely true today. There is no tradition of regional (as opposed to local) government in the United Kingdom, in contrast to countries such as Germany and Spain where many governmental functions are carried out at a level below that of the nation state; the *Länder* and Spanish 'autonomous regions' have a considerable degree of autonomy. Local authorities in the United Kingdom are by comparison small units with very restricted governmental powers granted to them by central government.[21] They have no protected constitutional status and can have functions given and taken away by central government and councils can be abolished or restructured by Act of Parliament like any statutory body. Also, although the European Union operates through supra-national institutions and decision-making processes, it has only those powers which have been conferred on it from time to time by member states through its constituent treaties. The European Union has no general, inherent competence similar to the prerogative powers of central government.

A second reason for taking the United Kingdom as the starting point is that it is intimately connected with ideas about sovereignty, a concept which is at the heart of public law.[22] In an influential school of British jurisprudence known as legal positivism, associated particularly with the work of John Austin, 'law' is conceived as a set of sovereign commands and all law as emanating from a single source of political power. This is not the place to discuss difficult questions of jurisprudence; the point is that the nation state is not merely a territorial entity, but has shaped our whole understanding of the nature of law.[23]

[19] On the terminology 'European Union' and 'European Community', see p. 76 below.

[20] *Introduction to the Law of the Constitution* (10th edn.) p. 183. Dicey (1835–1922) is the most influential writer on the British constitution. His ideas, now often criticized and rejected, are considered in Chapters 5 and 6 below.

[21] See p. 67 below.

[22] See Chapter 5.

[23] See further Neil MacCormick, 'Beyond the Sovereign State' (1993) 56 MLR 1.

NATIONAL INSTITUTIONS

The United Kingdom of Great Britain and Northern Ireland is often described in textbooks as a unitary state, distinguishing it from states which have a federal structure.[24] A thumbnail sketch of the United Kingdom's history and the current arrangements for the government of its constituent parts—England, Wales, Scotland and Northern Ireland—shows, however, that the term 'unitary' disguises as much as it reveals.

An historical sketch[25]

The legal and political integration of England and Wales was firmly established by the sixteenth century. England and Wales then formed a union with Scotland in 1603 when King James IV of Scotland succeeded Queen Elizabeth I of England to the English throne. Such a union, based on little more than a shared monarch, lasted for over a hundred years before being transformed into a more formal, political union in 1707 when both countries abolished their own parliaments, created a single Parliament and established the United Kingdom of Great Britain. Despite several hundred years of union between Scotland, and England and Wales, the legal system of Scotland remains distinct from that in England and Wales, and many statutes enacted by Parliament still apply only to one or other, rather than to both.

From the twelfth century, the English and Scottish colonized the island of Ireland; there followed centuries of conflict and repression of the Irish. British domination culminated in the enlargement of the United Kingdom of Great Britain to include the whole of Ireland in 1800 and Irish MPs and peers came to sit in Parliament in London. The legal historian Maitland comments that the 1800 union between Great Britain and Ireland was 'the union of two independent kingdoms, not the absorption of a dependent kingdom'.[26] From the outset of colonization, Irish nationalists (most by religion Catholics) denied the legitimacy of the union. During the nineteenth century there were ever-stronger demands for Home Rule or independence from the United Kingdom by the majority of the Irish. Continuing political and social turmoil in Ireland led to a succession of Home Rule Bills being introduced by Gladstone's and Asquith's Liberal governments from the 1880s onwards, but none was enacted until 1922, when the UK Parliament passed the Government of Ireland Act, granting independence to what was then called the Irish Free State.

Six counties in the north of Ireland, where the population was made up predominantly of the Protestant descendants of English and Scottish settlers, were retained within the United Kingdom as 'Northern Ireland'. Between

[24] In a federal system there are two main levels of government, each having specified powers and functions. The regional level is not, however, dependent on the federal level for its powers, as each level of government is regarded as autonomous within its own sphere.

[25] See further F. W. Maitland, *The Constitutional History of England* (1908).

[26] *The Constitutional History of England*, p. 335.

1921 and 1972 there was a bi-cameral parliament housed at Stormont Castle on the outskirts of Belfast to which the UK Parliament devolved a great deal of legislative power. Executive power was exercised by a Governor (representing the Crown) and a Prime Minister of Northern Ireland and ministers. In 1972, amid growing civil unrest and terrorist activities, the UK government introduced direct rule of Northern Ireland from London, and the Secretary of State for Northern Ireland (an MP and Cabinet minister in the UK Parliament) became responsible for all major executive decisions in the province. Over 3,000 people were killed in the 'Troubles' between 1972 and 1995. Unsuccessful attempts were made in 1974 and again in 1982 to set up a legislative assembly in Northern Ireland. The Northern Ireland Constitution Act 1973 continues to make it clear that Northern Ireland's status as part of the United Kingdom will not change without the consent of the majority of people who live there.[27]

Devolution and decentralization[28]

Even leaving aside the special situation in Northern Ireland, many people are dissatisfied that so much legislative and executive power lies at national level in the United Kingdom. A handful of MPs in the UK Parliament represent political parties campaigning for Welsh or Scottish independence. In 1978 the Labour government held referenda in Wales and Scotland about devolving more legislative and executive powers to assemblies in those parts of the United Kingdom; in neither did the necessary majority of the electorate approve of the proposals, which were later shelved. The issue has not, however, gone away. Both the Labour and Liberal Democrat parties are committed to establishing Welsh and Scottish assemblies and some sort of regional government in England. The Conservative Party is implacably opposed to this, even making the maintenance of the United Kingdom in its present form an important part of its successful election campaign in 1992.

The Crown

So far our description of the United Kingdom has focused on its territorial boundaries. Another important feature in traditional understandings of the sovereign state of the United Kingdom is the notion of the 'Crown'. Until quite recently official publications still described the United Kingdom as a 'monarchical state' (rather than a parliamentary democracy).[29] The enduring

27 See p. 110.
28 See further Dawn Oliver, *Government in the UK* (1991), Chapter 6.
29 See comments by Tony Benn, *Arguments for Democracy* (1981), pp. 8–9 and Ferdinand Mount, *The British Constitution Now* (1994), Chapter 3. On the legal status of the Crown generally, see further Joseph M. Jacob, *The Republican Crown* (1996) and M. Sunkin and S. Payne (eds.), *The Nature of the Crown* (1997).

importance of the Crown can be seen by glancing at previous editions of volume 8 of *Halsbury's Laws of England*, the leading practitioners' encyclopaedia, where the editors arrange their discussion of English constitutional law under the following very traditional subtitles: the title to the Crown; relations between Crown and subject; the Royal Family; the Royal Prerogative; the Crown and the Executive; the Revenue; and the hereditary revenues of the Crown. (Other volumes deal with Parliament, Local Government and so on.) So despite Bagehot's argument that the function of the monarch was symbolic—part of the dignified, not the efficient, constitution[30]—some analysts still take the Crown as a starting point for descriptions of government. Certainly, the language of monarchy continues to litter constitutional vocabulary: Her Majesty's Government; Her Majesty's Loyal Opposition; ministers of the Crown; the Royal Prerogative; the Royal Assent; Queen's Bench Division of the High Court; the Crown Office; the Crown is the nominal applicant in applications for judicial review and prosecutions are brought in the name of the Crown; senior lawyers are Queen's Counsel (QCs); United *King*dom; the Queen-in-Parliament enacts statutes; children convicted of serious crimes may be detained at Her Majesty's pleasure.

In the early 1600s the Stuart kings claimed to occupy the throne by divine right,[31] but after the Glorious Revolution of 1688 a *constitutional* monarchy developed (in the sense that the Crown's powers became dependent on express parliamentary consent or its tacit acquiescence). Today the Queen reigns not merely because she is her father's daughter, but because Acts of Parliament dictated that it was she who would succeed to the throne.[32] In the years which followed the constitutional settlement in 1688, more and more of the monarch's governmental powers passed to ministers, many later being put into a statutory basis, but some still authorized by the prerogative.[33] The result of this long and complex history is, as the editors of *Halsbury's Laws* put it, that:[34]

> the greater part of the machinery of cental government may be regarded, historically and substantially, as an emanation from the Crown. It is for that reason that, from very early days, the central government has been exercised in the name of the Sovereign.

[30] See p. 41, above.

[31] This was the belief that the monarch's authority to rule stemmed from God and divine authority rather than from any sort of 'contract' between the king and the people. It was associated with a concept known as the Great Chain of Being: 'According to this theory the universe consisted of a series of hierarchies. In heaven there was God and below him a descending series of angelic beings. In the skies there was the sun, and below it a descending series of planets. In the animal kingdom the king of the beasts, the lion, stood atop a descending series of beasts. In the political order the king ruled over a descending series of authorities reaching down to village constables and churchwardens' (David Wootton, *Divine Right and Democracy* (1986), p. 28).

[32] Bill of Rights 1688, Act of Settlement 1700 and His Majesty's Declaration of Abdication Act 1936.

[33] See Chapter 12.

[34] 8 *Halsbury's Laws of England*, para. 807 (4th edn.). Volume 8 was reissued in November 1996 in substantially revised form.

Parliament

It is a popular misconception that 'Parliament' consists of the House of Commons (elected MPs) and the unelected House of Lords. This is to miss out a third vital component: the monarch. Together these three parts, 'the Queen-in-Parliament', form the legislature of the United Kingdom. For a bill (a draft statute) to become law, it needs to be approved by a plurality of members in each House *and* to receive Royal Assent. As we shall see later,[35] statute law (Acts of Parliament) and the processes by which it is made are of great practical and theoretical importance to the whole constitutional system. Most, but not all, of the legal powers of central government and other bodies stem from Acts of Parliament. In other words, a minister or other public authority is generally able to take action only if authorized to do so by a specific statutory provision.[36]

As well as acting jointly to enact statutes, each of the constituent parts of Parliament also has its own particular functions. The monarch has the duty of appointing the Prime Minister. She alone also has the power to summon the Houses of Parliament to meet, power to prorogue Parliament (stop it meeting) and power to dissolve Parliament (effectively, to cause there to be a general election of all MPs). The monarch also has the sole power to appoint people to be members of the House of Lords, either for their own lifetimes only, or by creating a hereditary peerage. Decisions in relation to all these matters are carried out on the basis of advice from ministers or other members of the Privy Council[37] and are constrained by law and constitutional conventions.

The Commons

The House of Commons consists of an elected representative of each of the 651 parliamentary constituencies in the United Kingdom. With a few exceptions, all citizens of the United Kingdom, and also of the Irish Republic, who are resident in a particular constituency are entitled to vote in elections for its MP, though voting is not compulsory. In recent years all MPs have belonged to a political party, though in principle any individual citizen could be elected by a constituency. The Parliament Act 1911 (as amended) stipulates that in normal circumstances MPs are elected for a period not exceeding five calendar years. The minimum term of each Parliament is not fixed, however, and the Prime Minister may request the monarch to dissolve Parliament for a general election to be held before a five-year period is up. Arguably, this gives an unfair advantage to the government, which is able to choose the time most favourable to it.

Elections use the 'first past the post' system under which the candidate who obtains the largest number votes cast in each constituency is elected as

[35] See Chapter 8.
[36] See Chapter 7.
[37] See Chapter 12.

the MP for that constituency. Where more than two candidates stand for election (as is almost always the case), the MP elected may have been supported by only a minority of those who voted—not to mention those who did not vote at all.[38] This system, some argue, should be replaced by one based on some form of proportional representation, which would ensure that there is a closer relationship between the number of votes cast for parties and their representation in the House of Commons.

After a general election, the political party with the largest number of MPs forms the government. The leader of that party is appointed Prime Minister by the Queen, and the Prime Minister then recommends to the monarch other MPs and peers to be appointed to other ministerial posts. The House of Commons Disqualification Act 1975, s 2 limits to 95 the number of ministers who may sit and vote in the Commons at any one time. The second largest party in the Commons becomes the 'Official Opposition'; frontbench spokesmen from that party 'shadow' the work of particular government ministers. MPs who are not government ministers or members of the frontbench team of the Official Opposition are termed 'backbenchers'.

All MPs outside government have a constitutional role in calling ministers to account. When bills are steered through the parliamentary legislative process by ministers, MPs scrutinize both the policy goals of bills and the words used to give legal effect to these aims.[39] When MPs are not debating bills, they may spend their time debating on the floor of the chamber, asking ministers formal written and oral Parliamentary Questions (PQs) and participating in the system of select committees which have powers 'to examine the expenditure, administration and policy of the principal government departments'.[40]

The House of Commons[41] is also responsible for authorizing (through passing bills) and scrutinizing the raising and expenditure of money by government. The Public Accounts Committee, a select committee of backbench MPs first established in 1861, scrutinizes departmental accounts to ensure that money has been spent for the purposes prescribed by Parliament and that these funds have been used economically. A very senior civil servant from each department acts as an accounting officer, and may be questioned by the committee in a formal hearing. This committee is assisted in its work by the Comptroller and Auditor General (C&AG),[42] an independent officer of the House of Commons who heads the National Audit Office (which is responsible for certifying the accounts of central government departments and some other bodies). The C&AG is also responsible for examining the 'economy, efficiency and effectiveness' of the ways in which departments use their resources.

[38] For instance in 1951 the Conservatives won with 26 more seats than Labour, but having gained 230,000 fewer votes.
[39] See Chapters 8 and 9.
[40] See further Chapter 16.
[41] By convention, the unelected House of Lords does not involve itself in detailed discussion or scrutiny of public finance.
[42] Formally, the 'Comptroller and Auditor General of the Receipt and Issue of Her Majesty's Exchequer and Auditor General of Public Accounts'.

MPs also help particular constituents to obtain redress for their grievances against central government, sometimes with the assistance of another independent officer of Parliament, the Parliamentary Commissioner for Administration (the 'Ombudsman').[43]

The Lords

The upper chamber of Parliament is the House of Lords.[44] Like the Commons, it participates in the legislative process and calls ministers to account. Because the House of Lords is unelected, law and constitutional conventions restrict its powers in relation to legislation and scrutiny about taxation and public expenditure. It has over 1,200 members, though many attend only irregularly. The majority of these are aristocrats who inherited their right to sit in Parliament. Other peers are appointed for life from a variety of backgrounds:[45] some on their retirement as MPs, some as senior members of the judiciary (the law lords), others are bishops of the Church of England. Although the current composition based on the hereditary principle and patronage still has some supporters,[46] for most of the twentieth century there has been consensus that the House of Lords needs to be reformed. Indeed, the preamble to the Parliament Act 1911 (which restricts the powers of the Lords to reject or delay bills)[47] states 'whereas it is intended to substitute for the House of Lords as it at present exists a Second Chamber constituted on a popular instead of hereditary basis . . . such substitution cannot immediately be brought into operation'. The Labour and Liberal Democrat parties are committed to reforming the upper chamber. The view of the Conservatives appears to be that the House of Lords as presently constituted in fact carries out a great deal of important work very effectively, and for this reason there is no urgent need for change. This view is also influenced by the support Conservative governments can usually expect to receive from hereditary peers.

Ministers and departments

Ministers and the departments which they head are at the heart of modern central government. Departments vary enormously in size and some are

43 See Chapter 18.

44 See further Chapter 8.

45 The creation of life peerages was first permitted by the Life Peerage Act 1958.

46 For a long time after the passing of the Life Peerages Act 1958 it was thought no longer appropriate for new *hereditary* peerages to be created. However during her premiership, Mrs Thatcher created several: Lord Tonypandy (George Thomas, a former Speaker of the House of Commons who had no heirs) in 1983; Lord Whitelaw (who had only daughters who cannot inherit a Viscountcy) in 1983; and in 1984 the Earl of Stockton (formerly Harold Macmillan, an ex-Conservative Prime Minister whose title is now held by his grandson, the 3rd Earl, a director of a publishing company). In August 1995 a small committee of peers, chaired by the Earl of Carnarvon, published a report which criticized plans by the Labour Party to scrap the rights of hereditary peers to vote in the Upper House as 'irresponsible'.

47 See Chapter 8.

responsible for diverse areas of policy activity.[48] The Home Office, for instance, oversees among other things prisons, immigration and the Metropolitan Police. The three territorial departments (the Scottish Office, the Welsh Office and the Northern Ireland Office) have legal and political responsibilities for most central government activities in those parts of the United Kingdom. Departments are subject to periodic amalgamation, splitting and restructuring to suit the government's changing needs.[49] Although departments play a key role in the policy-making process, little academic research has been carried out into 'the relationships and networks that exist within and between departments and how departments react to events and interests in the outside world'.[50]

The spheres of interest of several departments may overlap on a particular decision and when this happens their roles need to be coordinated by the Cabinet Office. The GCHQ case study shows this well, with the Cabinet Office,[51] the Foreign and Commonwealth Office, the Ministry of Defence and the Department of Employment all participating in the decision to ban unions and its subsequent implementation. Relationships between departments, however, are not always harmonious and co-ordination can break down, as happened during the later stages of the GCHQ saga when it was evident that the Foreign Office and the Department of Employment had different views on whether the United Kingdom should leave the ILO in protest at its criticisms of the union ban.[52]

Most departments have as their political head a minister who bears the title 'Secretary of State' and sits in the Cabinet; he or she will have a team of junior ministers (often known as 'Ministers of State'). By convention all ministers must either be MPs or peers in order that they can be made answerable to one or other of the Houses of Parliament for their departments' actions. Ministers are chosen by the Prime Minister but are still conferred with their general legal authority by being presented with a set of three seals by the monarch, which they must return when they resign from office or are sacked by the Prime Minister. The office of Secretary of State is of great importance, both legally and politically, because statutes frequently confer powers or impose duties on 'the Secretary of State'. For instance, the National Health Service Act 1977, s 1(1) provides:

> It is the Secretary of State's duty to continue the promotion in England and Wales of a comprehensive health service designed to secure improvement—

[48] For an account of the structure of departments see Peter Hennessy, *Whitehall* (1990).

[49] For example, the Department of Health and Social Security (DHSS) was split into two separate departments in 1988. For the legal powers to do this, see the Ministers of the Crown Act 1975.

[50] See M. Smith, D. Marsh and D. Richards, 'Central Government Departments and the Policy Process' (1993) 71 Public Administration 567. When dealing with what happened inside departments, the case studies in this book have therefore had to rely mainly on information in the public domain, such as press reports and answers to PQs.

[51] As well as being responsible for the coordination of government policy, the Cabinet Office is also responsible for civil service security.

[52] See p. 21.

(a) in the physical and mental health of the people of those countries, and
(b) in the prevention, diagnosis and treatment of illness, and for that purpose to secure the effective provision of services in accordance with this Act.

Legislation normally refers simply to 'the Secretary of State' without specifying which particular one will have responsibility for the duty in question. (In the case of the NHS Act, in practice it will be the Secretary of State for Health.) This is because the strict legal position is that there is only one office of Secretary of State which is occupied by several different people at the same time, each in charge of different areas of policy.[53] A major concern of public law is with how ministers exercise their statutory powers, duties and discretions—and how they are made to account for them through legal processes (especially judicial review) and in Parliament. Ministers are frequently conferred with statutory powers to make delegated legislation (often in the form of SIs); these rules are usually subject to only minimal parliamentary scrutiny.[54] Also, in some circumstances, ministers are able to base their actions on the legal authority of the prerogative (the special non-statutory powers of 'the Crown' to take action which do not stem from Acts of Parliament). Here again, Parliament often has relatively little power apart from retrospectively scrutinizing what ministers have already done.[55]

Individual ministerial responsibility and accountability

The constitutional convention of individual ministerial accountability is of central importance to parliamentary scrutiny of executive action.[56] This means that ministers are answerable to Parliament for the policies pursued and implemented by their departments. It involves making statements to Parliament, answering PQs, defending their department's actions or proposed actions in debates on the floor of the Commons or Lords, and appearing before select committees of backbench MPs. Some commentators are sceptical of the efficacy of these mechanisms. Austin writes:[57]

> In practice a minister can decide for himself what information to disclose to Parliament and what to withhold. Accountability to the House is therefore dependent on ministerial goodwill, there being no effective enforcement sanction at the disposal of the House.

Closely intertwined with individual ministerial accountability is the convention of individual ministerial *responsibility*. In essence this means that where error has occurred (either in the formulation of policy or its implementation

[53] See further A. J. C. Simcock, 'One and Many—The Office of the Secretary of State' (1992) 70 Public Administration 535.

[54] See Chapter 10. The Board and Lodging Regulations were an SI.

[55] As in the GCHQ union ban, when ministers were able merely to announce their decision to Parliament as a *fait accompli*: see the case study in Chapter 17.

[56] On constitutional conventions generally, see Chapter 6.

[57] Rodney Austin, 'Freedom of Information: the constitutional impact', Chapter 14 in Jowell and Oliver (eds.), *The Changing Constitution* (3rd edn.).

by civil servants within a minister's department), a minister must make amends. This often means making a statement to Parliament explaining what has happened and what is proposed to be done about it. At its most extreme, the convention of individual ministerial responsibility may require a minister to resign from government office and return to being a backbench MP.[58] Resignations following the acceptance of responsibility for departmental or personal error are, however, relatively rare. Recent instances are the resignation in 1982 of Lord Carrington as Foreign Secretary following the invasion of the Falkland Islands by Argentina and, in 1988, Edwina Curry for remarks made about British eggs being contaminated by salmonella which led to public panic and the collapse of domestic egg production. More often, a minister who has the support of the Prime Minister and Cabinet colleagues can survive even the most ferocious criticism, such as that made of the fiascos concerning the Child Support Agency,[59] the Community Charge (or poll tax, a highly controversial form of local taxation), the Pergau Dam affair,[60] and the Scott Report.[61]

Until recently it was often said that ministers were responsible under the convention for the wrongful acts or omissions of civil servants in their departments, at least where the minister knew, or ought to have known, about the conduct.[62] One reason for this was the principle of civil service anonymity,[63] which meant that individual civil servants were not generally named in Parliament. Today, however, it is very unusual for ministers to resign because of operational blunders by their officials. This is particularly so given changes

[58] Ministers may also resign for other reasons, unconnected with accepting responsibility for departmental errors. As discussed on p. 55 below, ministers who decide that they no longer support the policies of the government, including those pursued by other departments, must resign under the convention of *collective* ministerial responsibility. Also, a number of ministers have been forced to resign following sexual scandal or revelation of other personal misdeeds: see further Geoffrey Marshall, *Constitutional Conventions*, Chapter 6 (The morality of public office).

[59] For the Parliamentary Commissioner for Administration's report on this, see p. 412–13.

[60] On 14 December 1994 Douglas Hurd MP (the Foreign Secretary) made a statement to the Commons stating that the government would not appeal against a finding by the High Court (*R v Secretary of State for Foreign and Commonwealth Affairs, ex p World Development Movement* [1995] 1 WLR 386) that a grant made under the Overseas Development and Co-operation Act 1980 to build the hydro-electricity station in Malaysia was unlawful. George Foulkes MP, Labour frontbench spokesman on overseas aid, called on him 'if not to offer his resignation, at least to offer his apologies'. Mr Hurd refused to do either. Prior to the judicial review challenge to its legality, the £234 million grant had been subject to investigation and critical report by the Comptroller and Auditor General and then by two select committees of backbench MPs: see further F. White, I. Harden and K. Donnelly, 'Audit, accounting officers and accountability: the Pergau Dam Affair' [1994] PL 526.

[61] *Report of the Inquiry into the Export of Defence Equipment and Dual-use Goods to Iraq and Related Prosecutions* (1995–96) HC 115. Much of the criticism in this report was directed at William Waldegrave MP (for misleading Parliament) and at the Attorney General Sir Nicholas Lyell QC MP (for the advice he gave to ministers on public interest immunity certificates, on which see further p. 498). There were no resignations.

[62] For a 'classic' statement of this principle, see the parliamentary discussion of the Crichel Down Affair in 1954 when the Minister of Agriculture (Sir Thomas Dugdale) resigned because of wrongdoing by officials in his department in connection with compulsory purchase of land: HC Deb, vol. 530, col. 1285 (20 July 1954).

[63] On which see p. 58 below.

in the structure of the civil service[64] which have meant that almost all operational matters have been delegated to agencies headed by chief executives who are themselves regarded as answerable to parliamentary select committees and the press. As we shall see at various stages in the book, the line between policy and operational matters can be very blurred. This is dealt with below (see p. 58) when we look at recent reforms to the civil service.

The workload placed on ministers is crushing. They work in Cabinet and Cabinet committees, in their departments, attend meetings of the European Community Council of Ministers, prepare to defend government policy and steer bills through the legislative process in Parliament, deal with constituents' problems, carry out the work of their party and appear on radio and television. This overload is almost certainly a factor contributing to some failures of policy-making and implementation. Signs of panic and chaos are, for instance, evident in the board and lodgings saga.[65]

The Cabinet

Twenty or so of the senior ministers form the Cabinet, which has its weekly meeting chaired by the Prime Minister at 10 Downing Street. Discussion around the Cabinet table is regarded as highly confidential and journalists are only briefed afterwards on those matters authorized by the Prime Minister.[66]

As with so many other institutions of central government, the Cabinet is not a statutory body, but exists as a matter of constitutional convention. Although the Cabinet is 'the ultimate embodiment of the executive government' in the United Kingdom,[67] for practising lawyers its work is of much less direct importance than that of individual ministers. The Cabinet has no statutory decision-making authority. Almost all decisions taken by the Cabinet, or in the system of Cabinet committees which underpin it, have to be implemented by individual Secretaries of State and their departments using the appropriate statutory or prerogative powers. So, for example, although the government's policy on deregulating shop opening hours is likely to have been discussed in Cabinet at some stage (because of its political sensitivity), and almost certainly by a Cabinet committee, it was left to the Home Secretary and Home Office officials to prepare and steer the Shops Bill and the Sunday Trading Bill through Parliament.

The origins of the modern Cabinet system go back to the early nineteenth century,[68] but Bagehot in *The English Constitution* (1867) was the first constitutional analyst to recognize its real importance. As mentioned earlier in

64 Described at p. 58 below.

65 See Chapters 11 and 27.

66 In the 1970s, the Attorney-General unsuccessfully attempted to obtain an injunction to stop publication of the first volume of Richard Crossman's account of Cabinet discussions which had taken place ten years earlier: see *Attorney General v Jonathan Cape Ltd* [1976] QB 752.

67 Douglas Wass, *Government and the Governed* (1984), p. 10.

68 P. Hennessy, *Cabinet* (1986), pp. 1–3.

this chapter, he saw in the Cabinet 'the nearly complete fusion, of the executive and legislative powers'. As he put it, it is:[69]

> a *hyphen* which joins, a *buckle* which fastens, the legislative part of the State to the executive part of the State. In its origin it belongs to the one, in its functions it belongs to the other.

Today one of the most important functions of the Cabinet, at least from a legal perspective, is that it controls the legislative timetable in Parliament: a Cabinet committee determines which government bills are introduced and when.[70]

Like other parts of the constitutional system, the Cabinet is a dynamic institution whose work and approach to decision-making has changed over the years. This has partly been the result of the different leadership styles of the various post-war prime ministers (Margaret Thatcher during her 1979–90 term as premier was, for example, credited with reducing collective decision-making in government). Change has also been due to the sheer growth in size and complexity of the government machine.

Cabinet committees

Commentators have often stressed that the function of the Cabinet is not to make government policy. Policy will usually have been formulated within a department or in one of the 27 or so Cabinet committees which form a central part of the Cabinet system. It is typical of the secrecy surrounding central government that although these committees have been a feature of decision-making since the Second World War their existence was not officially acknowledged until 1992. In practice, at its weekly meeting the full Cabinet is only able to discuss a handful of issues in any detail. Even highly contentious decisions have been made without the Prime Minister allowing the matter to be considered in full Cabinet; this means that not all Cabinet ministers may be directly involved in making controversial government decisions, such as to ban unions at GCHQ. Nevertheless they are required, like all junior ministers, by the convention of collective ministerial responsibility (see below), to support all government decisions in public or, if they cannot do so, to resign.

The Cabinet as a 'court of appeal'

The accepted wisdom has regarded the Cabinet as 'the place where disputes [between departments] are settled, where major policies are endorsed and where the balance of forces emerges if there is a disagreement'.[71] Today the role of the Cabinet as a 'court of appeal' for ministers is said to be diminishing. It has been suggested that since the mid-1980s there has been a 'revival of the discursive Cabinet', allowing ministers to use the weekly meetings to

[69] p. 68.

[70] There are relatively few opportunities for backbench MPs to initiate legislation: see Chapter 8, below.

[71] J. P. Mackintosh, *The British Cabinet* (1962), Chapter 2.

'raise any matter which troubled them or thought that colleagues should know about' so that the Cabinet acts 'as a sounding board for a whole range of government policy'.[72]

Numerous commentators, some of them former Cabinet ministers or senior civil servants, have expressed dissatisfaction with the Cabinet system. For instance, Sir Douglas Wass, a former senior civil servant, has suggested that the Cabinet needs to give more emphasis to considering and planning the *totality* of government policies which cut across departmental responsibilities. At the moment, the 'Cabinet's staple diet consists of a selection of individually important one-off cases or of issues on which the ministers departmentally concerned are unable to agree'.[73] Between 1971 and 1983, the Central Policy Review Staff, a so-called 'think tank' of career civil servants and specially recruited outsiders, did attempt to provide a basis for the Cabinet to engage in strategic planning and coordination of government policy by working for ministers collectively, but its role was not without problems and it was eventually abolished by Mrs Thatcher.

Collective Cabinet responsibility

Although problems with coordination of government policy may exist in practice, the Cabinet has always attempted to work collectively. In its earliest incarnations in the eighteenth century, when the Cabinet met in the presence of the king in his 'closet', ministers met beforehand to agree a common position in order to prevent the king exploiting any differing views there may have been among Cabinet members. Today, the practice of collective ministerial responsibility means that:

(a) discussion in Cabinet, and particularly differences of opinion between ministers, is not made public;
(b) once a common position is agreed (almost always by a consensus emerging and only exceptionally by a vote), all ministers—even if they expressed contrary views during discussion—are bound by the collective decision and must loyally support and defend it in Parliament and to the public; and
(c) a minister who feels unable to do this must resign from office and return to the backbenches.[74]

Sometimes the appearance of ministerial solidarity gives way to reveal obvious disagreements. In 1986 Michael Heseltine MP, then Secretary of State for Defence, strode out of a Cabinet meeting and announced to the press that he had resigned. Although some confusion surrounded the stated reason for the resignation, it was clear that the real reason was his disagreement with

[72] See Simon James, 'The Cabinet System since 1945: fragmentation and integration' (1994) 47 Parliamentary Affairs 613, 627.
[73] *Government and the Governed*, p. 25.
[74] Making collective decisions in secret and then being bound by them is not unique to the Cabinet: a similar approach to decision-taking applies in the European Commission (see Chapter 13) and even to the judges in the ECJ (Chapter 29).

his Cabinet colleagues over government policy towards Westland, a British company in financial difficulties which manufactured helicopters (including military ones used by the armed services). In the past, splits in the Cabinet have been so fundamental as to necessitate 'agreements to differ' permitting members of the Cabinet to dissent publicly from government policy. In 1975, for example, ministers in a Labour Cabinet were able to campaign against continued membership of the European Community in the run-up to a referendum even though official government policy supported membership.

Collective responsibility, however, is the norm and it does perform a number of constitutional functions. Its main justification is said to be to further strong government. It also presents MPs who belong to the governing party with a stark choice: either to support decisions of the Cabinet or not to do so; they cannot pick and choose which ministerial policies to back in votes in the Commons. If the government loses a vote on an important issue in the Commons (where confidence in the government is at stake), convention requires ministers to resign collectively and a general election to be held. Not every vote is one of 'confidence' in the government. The government did not resign, for instance, when it lost the second reading vote on the Shops Bill in 1986.[75] The clearest situations where resignation has to follow are where the government itself declares in advance that a vote is a matter of confidence (as the Conservative government did in one vote relating to the European Communities (Amendment) Bill in 1993)[76] or where the Official Opposition has tabled a vote of censure. For most backbench MPs belonging to the governing party 'bringing the government down' by voting against a particular policy is unthinkable, however much they might disagree with that one particular policy.

The Prime Minister

Like the Cabinet, the office of Prime Minister is a matter of constitutional convention rather than statute law. The Prime Minister, who convention dictates must be an MP, is the leader of the largest political party in the Commons. Unlike the Secretaries of State, the Prime Minister has no specific statutory powers or duties, and so from a narrowly legal point of view is of less importance than these ministers. One consequence is that decisions taken by the Prime Minister are rarely subject to challenge in the courts by judicial review.[77] The fact that the Prime Minister has no political responsibility

[75] See Chapter 9. Finer, Bogdanor and Rudden state that 'defeats on the second reading of a Bill used to be regarded as a matter of confidence entailing the government's resignation': see *Comparing Constitutions* (1995), p. 68.

[76] See Chapter 13.

[77] The instruction issued by Mrs Thatcher to ban staff at GCHQ from belonging to independent trade unions was subject to judicial review, but in that case she was acting in her capacity as Minister for the Civil Service, a ministerial post she occupied at the same time as that of Prime Minister. In 1992 a new ministerial post of Minister for Public Service and Science was created.

for specific policy areas is also used to justify the convention that prime ministers (and former prime ministers) do not appear before parliamentary select committees.[78]

Although the Prime Minister may have few specific legal powers and duties, the holder of that office has many constitutional responsibilities and political powers. These include:

(a) to appoint and dismiss government ministers and deciding on the allocation of functions between departments;
(b) to chair Cabinet meetings and some of the most important Cabinet committees;
(c) to defend government policy in the House of Commons, mainly through the twice-weekly ritual of Prime Minister's Questions;[79]
(d) to inform the Queen, normally in person once a week, about matters of government; and
(e) as Head of Government of the United Kingdom, to represent the country at important inter-governmental conferences.

Above all, the Prime Minister is expected to provide strategic leadership to the government and the country.

Changing constitutional status of the Prime Minister

From the 1960s onwards, commentators began to write of a transformation in the constitutional status of the Prime Minister: the office was said no longer to be merely *primus inter partes* (first among equals) with other Cabinet colleagues, but had taken on a 'presidential' function. Richard Crossman, himself a Cabinet minister, wrote of the Prime Minister having become the focal point of public attention and governmental power.[80] During the height of Mrs Thatcher's premiership, it was perhaps too easy to believe that a Prime Minister, especially one whose party has a large majority in the House of Commons, had great personal power. Subsequent events, however, have shown that a Prime Minister who refuses to work collegiately with Cabinet colleagues risks losing their support, and ultimately the premiership.[81] In the light of this experience constitutional analysts have revised this 'presidential view' of the Prime Minister's role.[82]

[78] For example, Lady Thatcher declined an invitation to answer questions by the foreign affairs select committee when it was investigating the Pergau Dam affair on the grounds (explained in her letter to the committee chairman) that 'in such cases evidence is given by ministers who have departmental responsibility for the subjects under discussion': see further Foreign Affairs Committee, Third Report 1993–94 Session, para. 8.

[79] See Chapter 16.

[80] See *Inside View: three lectures on Prime Ministerial government* (1972).

[81] Mrs Thatcher resigned as Prime Minister in 1990. She was deeply unpopular among the general public, but had also been damaged by resignations of senior Cabinet colleagues Michael Heseltine, Geoffrey Howe and Nigel Lawson.

[82] See Simon James, 'The Cabinet System Since 1945: fragmentation and integration' (1994) 47 Parliamentary Affairs 613. Arguments that there is now a system of 'Prime Ministerial government' may also overlook the fact that the powers of patronage of any future Labour

The civil service

In the earliest days of government, the monarchs' Secretaries of State carried out many executive functions personally. By the nineteenth century, however, the size and diversity of government functions had grown so much that several thousand civil servants were employed. The civil service is not a statutory body; it is still regulated by means of the prerogative.[83] Civil servants are not regarded as constitutionally separate from the departmental minister they serve. This is reflected in the legal rule known as the *Carltona* principle which recognizes that it is often civil servants who make decisions where statute confers legal powers on 'the Secretary of State'.[84] Like ministers, civil servants may be sued in tort for loss or damage caused by them in the course of carrying out their official duties.[85]

The modern civil service was created by reforms in the late nineteenth century based on recommendations made by two senior officials, Sir Stafford Northcote and Charles Trevelyan. Since the late 1980s the civil service has been subject to further radical restructuring. New career patterns have been introduced, with senior posts now being advertised rather than filled by internal selection. Many day-to-day operations have been allocated to agencies or contracted-out to private firms.[86] The apparent motivation for these changes has been to make administration more efficient and effective by separating the 'policy-advice' function of the civil service from practical 'service delivery' (such as issuing passports, calculating and paying welfare benefits, running prisons and so on). In consequence of these changes, the number of civil servants employed directly in the main government departments has been drastically reduced. These 'core' civil servants are now mainly concerned with giving policy advice to ministers. Almost all the service delivery tasks formerly carried out by departments have now been transferred to semi-independent executive agencies. So, for example, the Department of Social Security is no longer directly responsible for collecting national insurance contributions and paying welfare benefits; these functions are now carried out by the Contributions Agency and the Benefits Agency respectively. Likewise in the context of prisons, whereas previously prisons were run under the auspices of the Home Office, now while the Home Office is responsible for issues of general policy, responsibility for the day-to-day running of prisons falls upon the Prison Service Agency and its director general. The relationship between each department and the executive agencies is regulated by 'framework agreements' (which are public documents) setting out in broad terms the main policy objectives, the performance targets and the resources

Prime Minister will now be constrained by the standing orders of the Parliamentary Labour Party which, for instance, require a Labour Prime Minister to appoint to the Cabinet all Labour MPs elected to the Parliamentary Committee of the party: see further R. Brazier, 'The Next Labour Government' [1990] PL 9.

83 See p. 275.

84 *Carltona Ltd v Commissioner of Works* [1943] 2 All ER 560, discussed further at p. 543.

85 See Chapter 26.

86 See Diana Goldsworth, *Setting Up Next Steps* (1991).

available to the agency. Responsibility for achieving these aims is placed on the chief executive of each agency.

The changes have had important repercussions for the convention of individual ministerial responsibility to Parliament.[87] To what extent, for example, are ministers still answerable and responsible for the operational performance and failures of executive agencies?[88] If ministers are accountable does this undermine the agency's relative autonomy from ministerial control? If they are not, what political controls are there over the way these important governmental activities are performed?

One typically pragmatic response to this division of responsibility has been the establishment of a system whereby MPs wishing to raise concerns on behalf of their constituents about operational matters no longer write to the relevant minister, but instead write directly to the relevant chief whose replies are published in *Hansard*.[89] However, recent events involving the Prison Service Agency have revealed deeper tensions in the relationship between ministers and heads of executive agencies. Following serious criticism of the Prison Service in an official report into a break-out from Parkhurst Prison,[90] the Home Secretary first requested the director general of the Prison Service Agency (Derek Lewis) to resign, and then (following his refusal) dismissed him with immediate effect. In the acrimonious events surrounding this saga (which later led to Derek Lewis starting proceedings against the Home Secretary for wrongful dismissal) a number of important general issues emerged concerning the division of responsibility and lines of accountability. Who was responsible for security lapses and escapes? Were these the consequence of general ministerial policy which affected such things as the allocation of resources? If so, surely the minister should have been responsible? Or were the security lapses the agency's responsibility? Lewis argued that although the Home Secretary disclaimed responsibility for operational matters, in fact he interfered with day-to-day decision-making in ways which prevented Lewis from doing his job. On the other hand, the Home Secretary claimed that he was carrying out his responsibility in sacking Lewis because it is managers—not ministers—who are responsible for the human error of their staffs. Opposition MPs and others saw the saga as an example of the way the policy/operational divide may be used by ministers to shield themselves from political responsibility and to further undermine the convention of ministerial accountability.[91]

[87] See p. 51 above.

[88] See G. Drewry [1988] PL 505 and R. Baldwin (1988) 51 MLR 622.

[89] This method of ensuring some degree of public accountability for the first time involves publishing statements of non-Parliamentarians which have been published in *Hansard*. For further analysis of some of the constitutional problems, see P. N. Leopold, 'Letters to and from "Next Steps" Agency Chief Executives' [1994] PL 214.

[90] The Report of General Sir John Learmont, *Review of Prison Service Security in England and Wales and the Escape from Parkhurst Prison on 3 January 1995*, Cm 3020 (1995). See further, Anthony Barker, 'Political Responsibility for UK Prison Security: Ministers Escape Again', *Essex Papers in Politics and Government* (1995).

[91] Ms Ros Hepplewhite resigned as head of the Child Support Agency in September 1994 after considerable criticism of the way the CSA carried out its functions of tracing absent fathers and requiring them to contribute to their children's upkeep.

Servants of whom?

Civil servants working in departments may face conflicts of responsibility. The dilemma confronting Clive Ponting, a senior civil servant in the Ministry of Defence in the mid-1980s, provides an extreme but important example. He believed that he was being instructed by ministers to prepare documents in such a way as to mislead Parliament about the circumstances in which the Argentinean battleship *General Belgrano* had been sunk during the Falklands war. What ought a civil servant to do in such a situation? (What would you do?)

The fundamental duties of civil servants are now set out in the 'Armstrong Memorandum'.[92] This states the principles that:

(a) civil servants are servants of the Crown (meaning the government of the day);
(b) 'the duty of the individual civil servant is first and foremost to the Minister of the Crown who is in charge of the department in which he or she is serving'; and
(c) 'the determination of policy is the responsibility of the Minister [and] in the determination of policy the civil servant has no constitutional responsibility or role, distinct from the Minister'.

The memorandum makes it clear that once a minister has made a decision it is the duty of the individual civil servants 'to carry out that decision with precisely the same energy and good will, whether they agree with it or not'.

Ponting was faced with stark choices. He could handle the information in the way the minister instructed him to and so, in his view, mislead Parliament. He could resign—a course of action that would not only have ended his career but would not alter what he believed was ministerial wrongdoing because civil servants who resign or retire are under civil and criminal legal obligations not to divulge information about their work. Ponting therefore chose another option: anonymously he passed on information about the true position of the *General Belgrano* to a backbench MP who raised the matter in the Commons. An inquiry into the leak tracked it down to Ponting and he was prosecuted for breaching s 2 of the Official Secrets Act 1911.[93] Despite the judge giving directions to the jury which appeared to leave them no real alternative but to find Ponting guilty,[94] the jury acquitted him.

The government responded to the Ponting case by amending s 2 of the

[92] A note by Sir Robert Armstrong (Head of the Civil Service 1983–87 and Secretary to the Cabinet 1979–97) called *Ministers and Civil Servants* published in 1987. A version of the memorandum may also be found in HC Deb, vol. 123, col. 572 (2 December 1987).

[93] The Official Secrets Act 1911 was enacted in great haste in the run-up to the First World War (there was less than an hour's debate on the bill in the Commons) in response to fears that German spies were posing as tourists and photographing fortifications at Dover Harbour. Section 2 was astonishingly broad, making it an offence for any public servant to reveal any information about their jobs, or any information obtained during the course of their work, if the disclosure had not been authorized by a superior.

[94] See *R v Ponting* [1985] Crim LR 318.

1911 Act[95] and putting in place mechanisms which allowed civil servants to discuss matters of conscience with senior officials. The Pergau Dam affair prompted further change: Sir Tim Lankester, the senior civil servant in the Overseas Development Administration, believed (rightly) that making a grant towards the electricity project in Malaysia was 'unequivocally a bad one in economic terms'. His advice to this effect was ignored by the Foreign Secretary. Although Sir Tim's reservations were noted in official files, the Foreign Secretary was under no obligation to inform Parliament of what had happened. Details only emerged after the C&AG's investigation and the inquiries by two select committees of backbench MPs. Now senior civil servants are able to report such matters to the C&AG, who in turn refers the matter to the Public Accounts Committee (a parliamentary select committee).[96]

Who controls policy?

Although the Armstrong Memorandum repeated the orthodox view that it is ministers, not officials, who are accountable for policy, for many years there has been a debate about who really controls policy-making in departments—ministers or senior civil servants?[97] Arguably, ministers are under several considerable handicaps when it comes to controlling policy: they tend to stay in any given ministerial post for a relatively short time between ministerial reshuffles; they have many other duties outside the department (for instance Cabinet work, party matters, their constituencies); and they often lack necessary technical expertise. In many other countries, including Germany and the USA, senior civil servants are political appointees who are replaced when a new government is elected. The concept of political 'neutrality' in the British civil service is in any event a difficult one. It does not mean 'impartiality'; senior civil servants are expected to show commitment to the policies of the government of the day, but, like a chameleon, to be prepared to show the same commitment to a government of different political complexion. Some commentators, and a few ex-ministers, have identified a problem with neutrality: that it may really mean in fact that senior civil servants pursue their own 'civil service policy', rather than that of the elected government in power.[98] Others, however, argue that the current civil service has become politicized—sympathetic to the Conservative Party—because so many officials have spent all their careers since 1979 serving Tory governments.

Policy advice and the relationship between civil servants and their ministers is regarded as highly confidential and so information about what happens

[95] Official Secrets Act 1989. The stated purpose of this Act was to reduce the scope of the criminal law to situations where disclosure of information would be harmful to the public interest. Critics have argued, however, that its primary rationale was to *tighten* the criminal law of secrecy with the aim of making convictions more likely. See further S. Palmer, 'Tightening Secrecy Law: the Official Secrets Act 1989' [1990] PL 243 and G. Robertson, *Freedom, the Individual and the Law* (6th edn., 1989).

[96] See p. 52, n. 60, above.

[97] See G. Drewry and T. Butcher, *The Civil Service Today* (1988), Chapter 8.

[98] See e.g. Tony Benn, *Arguments for Democracy* (1982), Chapter 4.

behind the closed doors of the departments is largely absent from the case studies. One justification for this secrecy is that disclosure would take away the shield of anonymity from senior civil servants and so compromise their political neutrality and dampen their willingness to consider issues thoroughly. Even if this was once a justification for secrecy, it is now fast becoming weakened by the changes we have sketched. As the Ponting,[99] Howard/Lewis,[100] Pergau Dam[101] and Arms to Iraq affairs indicate,[102] officials are now increasingly pushed into the public domain, and senior civil servants now regularly appear before parliamentary select committees to justify their department's actions.[103] In any event, people outside government concerned with a particular policy (for example lobbying for changes to the Sunday trading laws) are usually aware of the identity of the officials involved in it.

Non-departmental bodies

Not all central governmental functions are performed by departments and their executive agencies. Many non-departmental public bodies (NDPBs) carry out regulatory,[104] advisory, policy-making and other activities.[105] They present considerable problems for public law, particularly as to how they ought to be made accountable for their actions and expenditure of public funds.

Privatized industries and statutory regulators

During much of the post-war period, when people were still used to the extensive government direction of industry that had occurred during the war, there existed a fairly broad consensus that certain industries and utilities which were of national strategic importance ought to be owned and controlled by government in the national interest. The gas, water, electricity and telephone utilities, British Airways, British Rail, the coal and steel industries and shipbuilding (to name but a few) were carried out by public corporations. Many required government subsidies to keep operating and there was often great uncertainty (or secrecy) about the extent to which ministers should direct their operations.

In the years since 1979, Conservative governments have privatized most of these public corporations. In part this general policy has been prompted by

[99] See p. 60 above.

[100] See p. 59 above.

[101] See p. 52 above.

[102] Sir Richard Scott, *Report of the Inquiry into the Export of Defence Equipment and Dual Use Goods to Iraq and Related Prosecutions* (1995–96) HC 115.

[103] See further Chapter 16.

[104] Regulation by government is a subject area of study in its own right: see further R. Baldwin and C. McCrudden (eds.), *Regulation and Public Law* (1987) and Anthony Ogus, *Regulation: legal form and economic theory* (1994).

[105] There is dispute as to how many such bodies exist. This is partly because they can be classified in different ways. The government claimed that there were 1,389 in 1993 (down from 2,169 in 1979). An academic study has, however, suggested that there are over 5,500: see Stuart Weir and Wendy Hall (eds.), *Extra-governmental Organisations in the UK* (1994).

a belief that governments ought not to act as entrepreneurs and that these industries would be more innovative, efficient and responsive to consumer needs if they were subject to the rigours of competition in the free market.[106] Selling shares in these industries has also brought considerable funds to government. It was clear, however, that some (sometimes considerable) state regulation remained vital, especially for utilities such as the water companies and the railways which operate in monopoly situations. Even after many years of Conservative government committed to the free market, entry into many major industries, such as broadcasting, civil aviation and telecommunications, is still controlled by a system of state licensing.

A plethora of statutory regulators has therefore been created, often with far-reaching powers to control prices and impose standards of performance. As with the executive agencies,[107] the paths of accountability and responsibility for often controversial decisions taken by the regulatory bodies (such as OFGAS for the gas industry and OFWAT for water) are unclear. Powers to make some kinds of decision were allocated to regulatory bodies precisely to make them seem less 'political' and so protect newly privatized industries from undue ministerial interference; yet in theory ministers remain accountable to Parliament for government policy in relation to particular industries.

Other non-departmental bodies

A great raft of specific governmental functions is carried out by public bodies such as the Equal Opportunities Commission, the British Council and the Countryside Commission (to name just a few). Such bodies normally have a considerable degree of independence, but a government minister is ultimately answerable to Parliament for their actions and often has power to appoint people to work on these bodies. This has often attracted controversy, it being suggested, for example, that there has been over-representation of Conservative Party sympathizers on bodies such as National Health Service Trusts. As with executive agencies and regulators, much confusion and uncertainty remains as to how such unelected bodies can be made answerable for their actions.

Intelligence and security institutions

One of the most basic roles of government is to safeguard national security. During the Cold War, this meant in large part monitoring the USSR and other communist states. It also involved collecting information about the work of terrorists (particularly the IRA) and, much more controversially, the work of trade unionists in the United Kingdom (especially during the 1984–85 miners' strike) and peace campaign organizations such as CND.

[106] On public choice theory, see p. 130.
[107] See above, p. 58.

For public law, the state intelligence-gathering bodies pose a conundrum. Almost everyone agrees that some form of monitoring of subversive and criminal action is necessary to protect society: the problems are concerned

(a) with how and by whom national security ought to be defined;[108] and
(b) how government counter-subversion institutions can be constrained to act within the boundaries proper to a parliamentary democracy and be made accountable for their work.

To open up the necessarily highly secret work of the intelligence-gathering institutions to public scrutiny in Parliament and the courts could well destroy the value of their work and the very reason for their existence.

The work of the intelligence and security institutions has caused controversy—both about their effectiveness and the constitutionality of their activities. Several court cases revealed that they had indulged in activities considered by many to be unacceptable in a constitutional democracy,[109] but the unease was brought spectacularly to global attention when a former secret agent, Peter Wright, wrote his autobiography *Spycatcher*. The UK government tried unsuccessfully to obtain injunctions preventing the book being published. It described how he and other agents 'bugged and burgled [their] way across London'. He claimed that MI6 was riddled with KGB agents and that people in the service had attempted to destabilize Harold Wilson's Labour government during the 1960s and early 1970s. It is difficult to know whether these allegations are true, but the publicity surrounding them was certainly one reason why the government decided to introduce legislation putting the services on a statutory footing for the first time and offering some degree of scrutiny of their work. Three main bodies are involved; until recently, the government avoided publicly acknowledging their existence and their legality depended on the government's non-statutory prerogative powers.[110]

(1) *GCHQ*. The Government Communications Headquarters is an electronic eavesdropping institution based in Cheltenham and with outposts around the world. It collects and interprets signals intelligence—telephone calls, satellite communications and, increasingly, electronic messages sent from computer to computer by foreign diplomats and military organizations.[111] It also has powers to listen in to communications between people within the United Kingdom. In the early 1980s over 10,000 people were employed by GCHQ, but the workforce has since been reduced considerably, partly as a result of the break-up of the USSR.
(2) *Secret Intelligence Service*. Like GCHQ, the Secret Intelligence Service (MI6) works under the auspices of the Foreign Office. It has fewer than 2,000 full-time staff. Its function is to conduct espionage and covert

[108] For detailed discussion, see L. Lustgarten and I. Leigh, *In from the Cold: National Security and Parliamentary Democracy* (1995).

[109] See *R v Secretary of State for the Home Department, ex p Ruddock* [1987] 1 WLR 1482 (telephone tapping of members of CND) and *Malone v United Kingdom* (1985) 7 EHRR 14.

[110] See Chapter 12.

[111] Intelligence Services Act 1994.

activities overseas, with its main priorities being to investigate nuclear proliferation and assisting agencies, such as the Special Branch of the Metropolitan Police, to fight serious crime such as illegal drugs and money laundering. Doubts now surround the future of this agency, some people suggesting that it ought to be merged with the Metropolitan Police.

(3) *The Security Service* (MI5)[112] exists 'to safeguard the economic well-being' against threats from 'outside the British Islands' from espionage, terrorism and also domestic subversion ('actions intended to overthrow or undermine parliamentary democracy by political, industrial or violent means'). MI5 employs about 2,000 people. According to information released in 1993, 44 per cent of the agency's resources were devoted to domestic terrorism and 26 per cent was spent on international terrorism.

In 1994 a special Intelligence and Security Committee was set up to oversee the expenditure, administration and policy of MI5, MI6 and GCHQ.[113] Although the special committee is comprised of MPs and peers, it is not a parliamentary select committee and decisions as to who should sit on it are made by the Prime Minister after consultation with the leader of the Official Opposition. The Prime Minister has power to dismiss committee members and may censor its annual reports if it 'would be prejudicial to the continued discharge of the functions' of the services. Critics have dismissed the committee as toothless. One of its weaknesses is that it can be denied information 'because the Secretary of State has determined that it should not be disclosed'.[114] Perhaps an even more fundamental defect is that the Act places the initiative on the committee to ask for information rather than placing a primary duty of disclosure on the security services to supply it; this means that the committee may remain unaware of problem areas which ought to be subject to scrutiny.

The 1994 Act also established a Commissioner (a post to be occupied by a judge) responsible for reviewing the Secretary of State's powers under the Act to issue warrants 'for the entry on or interference with property or with wireless telegraphy' which would otherwise be burglary and bugging. A tribunal to consider individual complaints about action done by the security services was also set up. Its work cannot be questioned in the courts.

Courts

Courts are a final and important set of institutions organized on the level of the nation state. For many writers on public law, the work of the courts forms the core of the subject. Government and parliamentarians are viewed with suspicion; the adjudicatory process is, in contrast, regarded as the prime

112 Security Service Act 1989; for commentary see I. Leigh and L. Lustgarten (1989) 52 MLR 801.

113 Intelligence Services Act 1994, s 10.

114 Intelligence Services Act 1994, Sched 3, para. 3(1)(b)(ii).

means by which aggrieved citizens may seek protection from abuses of state power. The common law itself is thought to embody important principles including respect for liberty, fairness and equality.[115] A substantial proportion of Part C of this book examines in detail how the courts (and also tribunals) operate, especially in the context of judicial review of governmental action. What follows here is therefore no more than the briefest of outlines of the position in England and Wales.[116]

Most cases raising issues about the legality of actions taken by public authorities come to court by way of applications for judicial review. Judicial reviews are handled by a special part of the Queen's Bench Division of the High Court in London where they are dealt with by High Court judges nominated by the Lord Chief Justice.[117] The modern judicial review procedure was set up in 1978, but the supervisory role of the High Court and its predecessors goes back centuries. Judicial review is not the same as an 'appeal'. So, for instance, if a would-be student refused a discretionary grant by a local authority seeks judicial review, the court will not be interested in the merits of the decision (whether the person really deserves to get a grant), only in whether the decision is a valid one in the sense that there is a proper legal basis for it. The grounds on which judicial review may be granted form an elaborate and subtle web of legal principles and policy considerations.[118]

The status of all judges is a matter of constitutional importance. If judges merely decided particular cases brought against the government in a manner directed by ministers, then plainly the system would be useless. The judiciary has to be independent of government. Judges in England and Wales are either appointed by the Lord Chancellor or 'the Crown' (here meaning in effect the Prime Minister), depending on which court they will be serving in. Statutes lay down basic criteria for appointment to the bench (such as the minimum number of years a person has had to have spent practising as a barrister or a solicitor) and set down mandatory ages for retirement. Parliament plays no part in approving individual judicial appointments. High Court and superior judges may not, however, be removed from office during the term of their appointment, except on an address to the Crown (the monarch) presented by both Houses of Parliament, something which has not been done this century.

In any constitutional system, the interrelationships between the powers of the courts, the government and the legislature are of central importance. The terms 'separation of powers' and 'checks and balances' are often used to

[115] See Chapter 6.

[116] As we have noted, Scotland has a distinct legal system. There civil cases are heard by the Court of Session (divided into the Inner House and the Outer House) and by the Sheriff Court. There is an appeal from the Inner House to the House of Lords. Criminal cases are heard by district courts, the Sheriff Court and, on appeal, to the High Court of Justiciary. In Northern Ireland, magistrates' courts, county courts, the High Court and the Court of Appeal have civil jurisdiction, with a further appeal in some situations to the House of Lords. Criminal cases are heard mainly by magistrates' courts and the Crown Court.

[117] See Chapter 21.

[118] See Chapter 20.

describe these. Issues surrounding these matters are explored in detail throughout the book. However, some of the key questions can be raised here. First, ought the courts to be able to declare legislation passed by Parliament unconstitutional and invalid? The answer given by orthodox constitutional theory and practice in Britain is in the negative: Parliament is said to have legislative supremacy.[119] There is, however, growing scepticism about this basic arrangement, including among some members of the judiciary.[120] Secondly, the relationship between the courts and ministers (and other public bodies) is, we will see, a highly sensitive one. Until fairly recently, many commentators were prepared to accept the orthodox explanation that the courts can interfere with the actions of ministers and public bodies in order to ensure compliance with the law laid down by Parliament. This seemed quite neatly to justify why unelected judges had power to set aside decisions and actions taken by elected bodies such as local authorities and ministers. Here again there is now scepticism about the cogency of this constitutional justification for judicial review.[121]

LOCAL AUTHORITIES AND SUB-NATIONAL GOVERNMENT

A local primary school is in desperate need of repairs. A child is subject to sexual abuse by her stepfather and needs to be removed to a place of safety. A mother and her two young children have their house repossessed by a building society because they cannot afford to pay the mortgage and now have nowhere to live. A market-trader is selling dangerous electrical goods. Your neighbour wants to build a large extension to his house which will plunge your garden into shade. You like to listen to loud music late at night but your neighbours complain. These are a few of the problems about which people may turn to the state for help and protection. In these contexts it is 'local government', rather than central government departments, which is likely to have the necessary legal powers to intervene. In the mapping exercise of this chapter, we therefore need to turn to look at the layer of governmental institutions organized at a local level.[122]

Many of the difficulties identified at the beginning of the chapter apply with just as much force here as they do to the institutions of the nation state: it can be difficult to decide what institutions ought to be included. The institutional arrangements of local government have been in a state of more or less constant flux; and they are more the product of piecemeal evolution than rational design. One characteristic may, however, help. Local authorities are

119 See Chapter 5.

120 See Chapter 6.

121 See Chapter 20.

122 Useful starting points for further reading include J. Stewart and G. Stoker (eds.), *Local Government in the 1990s* (1995) and M. Loughlin, 'The Restructuring of Central–Local Government Relations' in J. Jowell and D. Oliver (eds.), *The Changing Constitution* (3rd edn., 1994).

statutory bodies. So, unlike many of the institutions of central government, it is possible to sit down in a law library and gain some sort of understanding by reading the many Acts of Parliament relating to local government.

Structure

There are over 500 local authorities in the United Kingdom. In some parts of the country there is a two-tier system, with several district councils sharing powers with a county council; in other areas there is a single layer of unitary authorities.[123] Frequent reorganization of the structure of local government has occurred, often (but not always) following recommendations by the Local Government Commission, the statutory body with the responsibility for reviewing the size and structure of local authority units.[124]

Spheres of responsibility

The statute book shows that certain important functions have been allocated to local authorities. They have legal responsibilities and permissive powers within their areas, for:

- town and country planning;[125]
- primary and secondary education;[126]
- the provision of social housing, a duty to secure the provision of accommodation to homeless people and payment of housing benefit;
- the provision of personal social services and 'care in the community';[127]
- the provision of recreational facilities such as playgrounds and sports centres;
- environmental health services;
- trading standards officers who act to protect the interests of consumers;
- providing and maintaining some public highways;[128]
- enforcing Sunday trading legislation.[129]

During the last few years, there have been important changes in the spheres of responsibility of local government. In education, for example, central government now has considerably more influence than it once did. Under the Education Act 1944, national policy on schooling was stated to be secured by local education authorities, under the control and direction of the Secretary

123 The main, and much amended, piece of legislation establishing the structure and general powers of local authorities is the Local Government Act 1972.
124 See Local Government Act 1992.
125 Town and Country Planning Act 1990.
126 Education Act 1944.
127 Children Act 1989; National Health Service and Community Care Act 1990.
128 Highways Act 1980.
129 Sunday Trading Act 1994.

of State for Education; and for over 35 years councils were in the forefront of determining and implementing policy on education. During the 1980s and 1990s, however, these arrangements were considerably altered: a national curriculum was introduced;[130] schools may now opt out of local authority control and receive finance directly from a body set up by central government, the Funding Agency for Schools; decision-making powers have been devolved to boards of governors in each school (elected by parents); and head teachers have more day-to-day managerial powers and responsibilities than before. In 1995 the Prime Minister expressed the view that *all* schools ought to opt out of local authority control and become self-governing, thus effectively ending—or at least fundamentally changing—the role of local councils in the sphere of education. Parents have been given more legal rights, not only to stand and vote at elections for school governors but to express preferences as to which school their children will attend, and have been supplied with more information than before about the performance of schools. In 1992, further education was removed from local authority control.[131]

In housing, which was once the main role for many councils with almost a third of all housing in the United Kingdom owned and managed by local authorities during the 1970s, there has been similar radical change. Most notably, central government introduced legislation giving council tenants 'the right to buy' their flats and houses from local authorities, often at very substantial discounts and with subsidized mortgages.[132] Over 1.5 million tenants did so. The policy has been taken still further, with tenants now having the right to convert their council rents into mortgages,[133] and whole estates have, following votes taken by tenants, been transferred from local authority ownership and management to voluntary housing associations. The discretion of councils to determine what rents to charge for their property has been significantly reduced and is now subject to stringent control by central government,[134] as is the ability of authorities to build new homes for rent.

Commentators have often presented the changes as signifying a rapid trend to centralization, with powers and responsibilities being removed from elected local councils and given to central government departments. Such an analysis is far too crude. First, local government has actually been given important *new* areas of responsibility in recent years, notably in respect of 'care in the community': under the National Health Service and Community Care Act 1990 and other legislation, social services departments in councils have duties to plan, assess, purchase and provide assistance to elderly, ill, disabled and other vulnerable people living in their areas. Secondly, it does not *necessarily* follow that because power and responsibility have been removed from local authorities that they have been transferred to central government; many of the changes were designed to empower individuals directly, for example,

[130] Education Reform Act 1988.
[131] Further and Higher Education Act 1992.
[132] Housing Act 1980.
[133] Leasehold Reform, Housing and Urban Development Act 1993.
[134] Housing Act 1988, Part VI.

parents of school children and tenants of council houses. What is undeniable, however, is that much of the legislation introduced by central government to bring about these and other changes has reduced the discretion of local government to formulate and implement the policies it considers best and has increased the degree of direction and control from central government.

Decision-making in local authorities

Duties, discretions and powers are placed by statutes on local authorities as corporate bodies. Typical statutory formulae include the following.

> It shall be the duty of every local education authority to secure that there shall be available for their area sufficient schools—
>
> (a) for providing primary education . . . ; and
> (b) for providing secondary education . . .

(Education Act 1944, s 8).

> (1) If the local housing authority have reason to believe that an applicant may be homeless and have a priority need, they shall secure that accommodation is made available for his occupation pending a decision as a result of their inquiries under section 62.
> (2) This duty arises irrespective of any local connection which the applicant may have with the district of another local housing authority

(Housing Act 1985, s 63).

Councils only have those powers expressly or impliedly granted to them by statute and are constrained by the principles of judicial review.[135]

Some decision-making in local authorities is done by elected councillors at meetings of the full council, but in practice more decisions are taken by committees and sub-committees of councillors or, in some situations, may be delegated to a local government officer (the politically impartial executive employees of the council). The membership of the committees must reflect the party political composition of the whole council.[136] By law, council and committee meetings must, subject to a few exceptions, be open to members of the public, who also have rights to inspect agendas, minutes of meetings and certain other documents.[137] There is some dissatisfaction with this system for decision-making.[138] Only a few years after a formal inquiry into the subject (chaired by David Widdicombe QC),[139] the Department of the Environment, the central government body with overall responsibility for local government, set up a working party to reconsider the arrangements.

135 See further Chapter 7.
136 Local Government and Housing Act 1989.
137 Local Government (Access to Information) Act 1985.
138 For an overview, see John Stewart, 'The Internal Management of Local Authorities,' Chapter 5 in J. Stewart and G. Stoker (eds.), *Local Government in the 1990s*.
139 See the *Report of the Committee of Inquiry into the Conduct of Local Authority Business*, Cmnd 9797 (discussed by M. Loughlin (1987) 50 MLR 64).

Local authority funding

The work of local authorities is funded in several ways, most importantly by annual grants from central government and by revenue raised by local taxation (now called Council Tax). In some situations, councils have power to levy charges, for example for use of recreational facilities. Funding has been a battleground between the Department of the Environment and local authorities. For central government during the 1980s, control of local government spending was a vital part of its overall aim of reducing public expenditure in order to control inflation; for most local authorities it was a matter of the highest importance for them to secure the maximum grant possible from central government and to have the ability to impose as high a rate of local taxation as possible in order to preserve essential services. Central government attempted various reforms: domestic rates were replaced by Community Charge (the infamous poll tax) and when that caused mounting public dissatisfaction, with a new tax known as Council Tax; the tax-levying powers of local authorities were 'capped'; restrictions were placed on the council's ability to spend capital receipts. In response, local government resorted to ever-more creative ways of raising revenue, some of which were held to be unlawful.

As central government introduced a morass of legislation designed to restrict the discretionary powers of local authorities and, generally, 'to reduce the political capacity of local government as a tier of government',[140] law became the principal mechanism for structuring the relationships between the two tiers of government where in previous decades this had been done more informally through bargaining and administrative practice. There was also frequent resort, by both sides, to judicial review. In this intra-state litigation the courts became central players in the regulation of relationships between the two tiers of government.

Service delivery

Over the last decade or so, dramatic changes have occurred in the ways local authorities implement their duties. Before 1980, it was normal for councils to employ directly a large workforce to carry out their diverse range of responsibilities, such as building and maintaining social housing and highways, providing school meals, refuse collection and road-sweeping. Prompted by considerations such as the need for greater efficiency and the desire to restrict the influence of trade unions in local authorities, and by ideological commitments to the free market, the Conservative central governments in power since 1979 have required councils to put out to 'compulsory competitive tender' (CCT) an increasing range of service delivery functions.[141] What

[140] M. Loughlin in Jowell and Oliver (eds.), *The Changing Constitution* (3rd edn.), p. 273.

[141] See: Local Government and Housing Act 1989; Transport Act 1985 (bus undertakings had to be operated commercially); Local Government Act 1988; Environmental Protection Act 1990 (waste disposal). For analysis, see Kieron Walsh, 'Competition and Public Service Delivery', Chapter 3 in J. Stewart and G. Stoker (eds.), *Local Government in the 1990s*.

this means in practical terms is that a local authority must invite tenders from firms in the private sector to carry out specified tasks; only if, applying set criteria, the council's own workforce is able to do the task more cost-effectively will it be allowed to do so. Otherwise, the council must enter into a contract for the delivery of the particular service (such as refuse collection and supervision of on-street parking) with the private sector business able to offer best value for money. Most recently CCT has been extended further than the practical delivery of services to the public into the council's own internal support services such as surveying, housing management and architectural services, and some legal work now needs to be put out to tender.[142]

As well as contracting-out, local authorities have also set up 'internal markets': different parts of a local authority enter into agreements with other parts (e.g. for the provision of legal services) and have to 'pay' for this in the internal accounting arrangements. Combined with contracting-out, this has altered the ethos within many councils, with much more awareness of the need for value for money and commercial considerations; whether there has actually been any appreciable improvement in the quality of service to local inhabitants is a moot point.

Are councils merely agents of central government?

The description so far of the work of local authorities may suggest that they are little more than agents for central government. After all, it is central government which decides what functions councils are to perform, determines levels of funding for these activities and controls the ability of authorities to raise their own revenue through local taxation, and ultimately can (with parliamentary consent) abolish and reorganize the units of local government. This view of the purpose of local government is implicit in many of the recent reforms, such as CCT, which appear to envisage the prime function of local authorities to be organizers of *services* to the public. For one academic commentator 'it is quite possible to envisage the local authority of the future as a network of internal and external trading'.[143] Some members of the Conservative central government clearly hope that this is the case: speaking at a fringe meeting at the 1986 Conservative Party Conference, the then Secretary of State for the Environment said that in an ideal world councils would 'meet once a year to award contracts, have lunch, and go away again for another year'.[144]

There is, however, an alternative. Local authorities are democratically elected bodies, they have knowledge of local conditions and they are highly politicized.

[142] See Local Government Act (Competition)(Defined Activities) Order 1994 (SI 1994 No 2884) and Local Government Act (Competition)(Construction and Property Services) Order 1994 (SI 1994 No 2888).

[143] K. Walsh in J. Stewart and G. Stoker (eds.), *The Future of Local Government* (1989), p. 30.

[144] Quoted in Mike Radford, 'Competition Rules: the Local Government Act 1988' (1988) 51 MLR 747, 767.

They ought, therefore, to have a role much broader than merely facilitating the delivery of public services. Through elections and lobbying their councillors, citizens ought to be able to participate and influence policy formulation and implementation at local level. Certainly during much of the 1980s Labour-controlled authorities saw themselves as possessing a mandate to pursue policies which often brought them into conflict with Conservative central government. These councils often pursued high-profile policies in areas to do with nuclear disarmament (some authorities proclaiming themselves to be 'nuclear-free zones'), race, sex and sexual orientation anti-discrimination[145]—policy areas far removed from those which politicians on the Right believed to be the appropriate concerns for local government.

Police

Detailed consideration of the police falls outside the scope of this book.[146] A striking constitutional feature needs to be noted, however: police forces in the United Kingdom are part of sub-national, rather than national, government. There are 43 police forces (or 'constabularies') in England and Wales. Their work is in part controlled by regulations set by the Home Office, and in part by police authorities. The membership of each authority is made up of local councillors, magistrates and lay members.[147] Neither the Home Office nor the police authorities have powers to issue orders on operational matters, with the chief constable of each constabulary having very considerable freedom from political control. Police constables take their orders from their chief constable, who is also legally responsible for any wrong-doing by officers under his command.[148] Complaints about police conduct may be made to an independent body, the Police Complaints Authority.[149]

SUPRA-NATIONAL INSTITUTIONS

One of the greatest changes to have occurred to Britain's public law system over the last 50 years has been its 'Europeanization' and 'internationalization'. Back in 1945, major states in Europe were at war with each other. In Germany the government was pursuing policies of international aggression and genocide. Italy was ruled by a dictatorship. Spain continued to be ruled by General Franco's military junta until 1975 (after which there was a peaceful transition to democracy). Yet now, remarkably, governments of nation states in Europe act collectively through international organizations to make public policy. International bodies also subject the actions of national governments

145 See further Davina Cooper, *Sexing the City* (1994).
146 See further Geoffrey Marshall, 'The Police: independence and accountability,' Chapter 11 in Jowell and Oliver (eds.), *The Changing Constitution* (3rd edn.).
147 Police and Magistrates' Courts Act 1994.
148 Police Act 1996.
149 Police and Criminal Evidence Act 1984.

to scrutiny and seek to protect people's fundamental civil and political rights. This all takes place through a variety of international organizations including the European Union (part of which is the European Community), the Council of Europe (responsible for the European Convention on Human Rights) and, on a global level, by bodies such as the United Nations and the International Labour Organization.

The significance of the work of international organizations, so far as it impacts on the public law system in the United Kingdom, is examined later in the book.[150] Here we need only briefly map out the main institutions.

The European Union/European Community

The United Kingdom's decision to join the European Economic Community (EEC or 'common market' as it was colloquially known) in 1973 was one of the most momentous events in Britain's constitutional history. It continues to be deeply controversial. For some, membership has created new rights for ordinary people in the work place and elsewhere (particularly in respect of sex anti-discrimination) and created the single market necessary to promote economic growth. For others, the Community is perceived as imposing bureaucratic regulations on businesses and threatening parliamentary democracy in the United Kingdom. What is beyond doubt, however, is that membership of the Community has brought about huge changes in the legal systems of the United Kingdom and the sources of law which need to be referred to in solving practical legal problems. As we have already seen,[151] Community institutions and law play parts in two of the case studies examined in this book: the Working Time Directive and in the litigation over legal restrictions on Sunday trading.

Origins

The origins of the Community lie in the devastation of Europe at the end of the Second World War. Jean Monnet, a Frenchman and international statesman, was instrumental in bringing about what only a few years previously would have been impossible: an agreement for limited economic co-operation between France and West Germany. Italy and the small Benelux countries (Belgium, the Netherlands and Luxembourg) were also attracted to the scheme and in 1952 the European Coal and Steel Community (ECSC) came into operation with the governments of those countries agreeing to pool decision-making about those key industries under a single multi-national authority. Britain, under Attlee's Labour government and then Churchill's post-war Conservative administration, refused to join this new organization. The ECSC was seen as a great success by its member states and they formed

[150] On the European Community, see Chapters 5 (pp. 115–19), 13, 14, 29 and 30. On the European Convention on Human Rights and the International Labour Organization, see Chapters 6 and 28.

[151] Chapter 2.

two other similar organizations: the European Atomic Energy Community (EURATOM) and the much broader European Economic Community. The three communities, ECSC, EURATOM and the EEC, were for many practical purposes amalgamated in 1967.

The United Kingdom began negotiations to join the Communities in 1961, but these were at first unsuccessful because the French government vetoed the proposal for British membership. Finally in 1973 the United Kingdom, along with Ireland and Denmark, became members and the Six became the Nine. Greece joined in 1981; Portugal and Spain in 1986; and Austria, Finland and Sweden in 1995. There are therefore currently 15 member states.

The treaty framework

A good way to understand the development of the Community from the 1950s is by looking at the main treaties which, in effect, provide it with a written constitution. The treaties set out the institutional arrangements: how, when and by whom decisions are taken.

(1) *The EC Treaty.* The first is the Treaty Establishing the European Community (often referred to as the Treaty of Rome). It is here that the important provisions concerning the 'four freedoms' of persons, goods, services and capital are to be found, along with the basic frameworks for policy areas such as the Common Agricultural Policy and statements on the role of each of the institutions through which collective decisions are made. The EC Treaty was incorporated into United Kingdom law by the European Communities Act 1972.[152]

(2) *Single European Act.* The Single European Act of 1985 (despite its name an international treaty, not a British statute) amended the Treaty of Rome. It was incorporated into national law in the United Kingdom by an Act amending the European Communities Act 1972. Changes were made to some of the institutions in order to encourage further progress towards the creation of the single market. It set a target date of the end of 1992 for the removal of the remaining trade barriers between member states. It also made it more difficult for any one member state to veto some types of decision and it increased the powers of the European Parliament.

(3) *Treaty of European Union.* The Treaty of European Union (known as the Maastricht Treaty after the Dutch city where it was agreed) further amended the Treaty of Rome and created important new areas on which the member states agreed to act collectively. The treaty marked a very significant step forward in the process of 'ever closer union' (an expression used in all the treaties). It increased the powers of the European Parliament still further and set a target date of 1999 for the last

[152] On the relationship between Community law and national law in the United Kingdom, see Chapter 5.

major elements of the single market: a single currency and a central bank to control monetary policy throughout all member states. It also created European Union citizenship.

In addition to this, the treaty added two new facets to the relationships between the 15 member states. The new European Union thus has three pillars:

(a) the European Community which has been developing since 1958;
(b) a framework for inter-governmental cooperation on foreign and security policy; and
(c) inter-governmental cooperation in the fields of justice and home affairs.

There are important differences in the ways in which decisions are taken in the pillars (a)–(c) above. In the Community decisions are taken through a set of institutions (described below) in which a wide range of interests are represented, including representatives of the peoples of the member states in a directly elected parliament. The government of any one member state often has no power to veto decisions taken through these institutions. In other words, the pooling of sovereignty which has occurred through collective decision-making in the Community institutions may result in a national government becoming legally bound by a decision which it strongly opposes (as happened in relation to the Working Time Directive which the UK Conservative government resisted). The style of decision-making in pillars (b) and (c) is quite different, much more along the lines of classic international diplomacy with sovereign states meeting as equals. Unanimity is required and the institutions which play central roles in the Community (such as the Court of Justice, the Commission and European Parliament) have little or no function.

The institutions of the Community

Later chapters describe in some detail the network of Community institutions and how they operate in practice. The treaties agreed by the member states have conferred powers on institutions to make secondary legislation (such as 'directives' and 'regulations') within the ambit of the treaties.[153] The details of the legislative process vary according to the treaty provision on which a particular piece of secondary legislation is based. On a level of generality, however, it is possible to characterize the main features as follows.[154]

Formal initiatives to make legislation are proposed by the European Commission, a body consisting of 20 people nominated by the governments of member states but who, once appointed, act independently in the interests of the Community itself. The Commission's proposals are formally scrutinized by the directly elected European Parliament and, in some situations, also by other specialized bodies representing various interest groups. The final

[153] On the making of the Working Time Directive, see Chapter 14.
[154] For a more detailed account of this highly complex process, see Chapters 13 and 14.

decision on whether or not to adopt proposed legislation usually rests with the Council of Ministers, a body consisting of one ministerial representative from each of the member states. (When legislation relates to agriculture, ministers responsible for agriculture attend; when it relates to employment, employment ministers attend, and so on.) Here voting is normally on a 'qualified majority' basis, with ministers from larger member states (such as the United Kingdom) having their votes weighted more than those from smaller states (such as Belgium). As a result of member states agreeing to modify the treaties, the power of the European Parliament to amend, and now even to veto, legislative proposals has increased considerably over the years. That, in the very barest of outlines, is the legislative process; in reality it is highly complex.

The secondary legislation which is produced interconnects with the UK national legal systems in different ways. 'Regulations' are 'directly applicable', meaning that they are capable of taking effect and being enforced by the national courts without the UK government or Parliament taking any action.[155] The other main sort of secondary legislation, 'directives', are really instructions addressed to the member states themselves to take administrative action, or to pass national legislation, to ensure that national law complies with the directive.[156] In some circumstances, provisions in a directive are said to be 'directly effective' meaning that national courts will regard them as creating rights and obligations which may be relied upon in litigation.[157]

As well as providing methods for making Community legislation, the institutional structure also establishes a system for adjudicating on disputes concerning rights and obligations under Community law. Most 'euro-litigation' (the term often given to disputes involving Community law issues) takes place in national courts. Where, however, a British court is faced with a difficult question of the interpretation of European Community law, it may seek a preliminary ruling on the issue from the European Court of Justice based in Luxembourg.[158] The procedure is known as an 'Article 177 reference'. An illustration of this is when a magistrates' court in Wales adjourned hearing a prosecution of a DIY-goods retailer charged with unlawful Sunday trading, in order to obtain a ruling on how to interpret Arts 30 and 36 of the EC Treaty. The ECJ also determines other types of proceedings, such as challenges by a member state to the validity of secondary legislation made by the Community institutions (as in the case of the United Kingdom's dispute over the Working Time Directive).[159]

The concepts of sovereignty and subsidiarity

A central political concern in recent years has been over the principles that ought to guide the allocation of decision-making powers between the European

155 See p. 685.
156 See p. 686.
157 See p. 686.
158 See p. 696.
159 See Chapter 30.

Union and its member states. Discussions often revolve around two concepts: sovereignty and subsidiarity. As we will see in Chapter 5, 'sovereignty' has a variety of political and legal meanings. Sometimes it is used to refer to the location of ultimate political power (itself a rather dubious concept);[160] at other times (as in the expression 'parliamentary sovereignty') it relates to the rules applied by the national courts to determine the hierarchy of different types of legal rules.[161] In both these senses, the United Kingdom's membership of the European Union has far-reaching impacts.

Subsidiarity, similarly, is a concept that has both political and legal aspects, though these are difficult to disentangle. The principle was part of the compromise reached between member states at the time of the Maastricht Treaty. It was decided that where the Community treaties had not already allocated power to take action exclusively to the Community, the Community would take action

> only if and in so far as the objectives of the proposed action cannot be sufficiently achieved by the member states and can therefore, by reason of the scale or effects of the proposed action, be better achieved by the Community.[162]

The concept is said to stem from principles adopted by the Roman Catholic Church that:[163]

> It is an injustice, a grave evil and disturbance of right order for a large and higher association to arrogate to itself functions which can be performed efficiently by smaller and lower societies.

This general principle of organization is in fact highly complex and subtle.[164] It could well apply not only to the relationship between the European Union and the national governments of member states, but much more widely to include the functions of local authorities. In the United Kingdom this has not happened.

The Council of Europe and European Convention on Human Rights

Separate from the European Union is the international treaty organization known as the Council of Europe, much of whose work is concerned with the European Convention for the Protection of Human Rights and Fundamental Freedoms (ECHR). It comprises 32 states. Like the Community it was founded in the aftermath of the Second World War but its objectives were not primarily economic ones: its aim was furthering the ideals of political democracy, the rule of law and the protection of fundamental human rights.

The status of the ECHR within the legal systems of the United Kingdom

160 See p. 119.
161 See p. 104.
162 Treaty of European Union, Art 3b.
163 Pope Pius XI, Encyclical letter, *Quadragesimo Anno* (1931).
164 See further David O'Keeffe and Patrick Twomey (eds.), *Legal Issues of the Maastricht Treaty* (1994), Chapters 3 (A. G. Toth), 4 (J. Steiner) and 5 (N. Emiliou).

is contentious. Unlike Community law, the ECHR has not yet been incorporated by Act of Parliament into national law. Many people argue that it ought to be in order to provide a modern Bill of Rights guaranteeing basic political and civil rights for people. The arguments are not, however, all one way.[165] Some critics view the ECHR's text, drafted during the late 1940s and 1950s, as outdated; some also believe that its incorporation into national law would give too much power to judges over government and Parliament. As national law now stands, courts in the United Kingdom may hear arguments based on the text of the ECHR, and the case law of the European Human Rights Commission and the Human Rights Court, in only very limited circumstances.[166]

Procedures and remedies

In 1994 signatory states agreed to a radical reform of the procedures for determining whether rights protected by the ECHR and its other Protocols have been infringed.[167] These changes will not, however, become effective until at least 2000 and so it is necessary to outline briefly the current arrangements.

The United Kingdom, like most signatory states, permits individuals and groups to petition the European Commission of Human Rights. This is composed of a person from each signatory state elected for terms of six years by the Committee of Ministers of the Council of Europe. The roles of this institution are to establish the facts of complaints, consider whether they meet the requirements for the admissibility of a complaint[168] and, if possible, to secure a 'friendly settlement' between the complainant and the signatory state. Such a petition is in no sense an 'appeal' from the UK courts; the issues before the Commission may be distinctly different from those canvassed in the national courts. This is well illustrated by the GCHQ case.[169] In the House of Lords the issues were concerned with whether there ought to have been consultation with the unions before the ban had been imposed. When the dispute went to the European Commission of Human Rights, the case turned on whether the government had infringed the right to freedom of association under Art 11 of the ECHR.

If the Commission decides that a friendly settlement cannot be reached between the parties and that the petition is 'admissible', the matter is referred to the European Court of Human Rights. Judges are elected for terms of nine years by the Parliamentary Assembly of the Council of Europe from lists nominated by signatory states. The judges sit in an individual capacity, independent of their own national state. Procedures before the court are

[165] See Chapter 6.

[166] See p. 34.

[167] See Alistair Mowbray, 'Reform of the control system of the European Convention on Human Rights' [1993] PL 419 and 'A new European Court of Human Rights' [1994] PL 540.

[168] Under Arts 25–7 these include: that the petitioner has exhausted all remedies available under national law; that the matters giving rise to the complaint occurred within the past six months; and that substantially the same matter has not already been examined by the Commission.

[169] See Chapter 28.

adversarial in nature. The judgments of the court are declaratory; it has no power to compel a signatory state to amend its national legislation or alter administrative practice to comply with the ECHR. The court may, however, award compensation to a person whose rights have been infringed.

The Committee of Ministers of the Council of Europe, comprising of a foreign minister from each signatory state, is responsible for supervising whether states comply with judgments of the court. 'Compared to most other international human rights treaties, the Convention has very strong enforcement mechanisms.'[170] Ultimately, it has power to suspend or expel a state from membership of the Council of Europe if it persists in refusing to comply with a judgment of the court. These steps, however, have never had to be used.

Other international organizations

Foreign relations law and any detailed examination of the work of the organizations such as the United Nations, NATO, the Western European Union (WEU), the International Monetary Fund (IMF), the General Agreement on Tariffs and Trade (GATT) and the Organization for Economic Co-operation and Development (OECD) fall outside the scope of this book. It is, however, important to appreciate that the work of such institutions may have an important impact on government, businesses and people in the United Kingdom. We do, though, return later in the book to examine the work of one such organization and the UK government's reaction to it: the International Labour Organization (ILO) and its highly critical views of the union ban at GCHQ.[171]

Question

The government is concerned about the general public's lack of knowledge about the constitution. It wishes to place a series of advertisements in British newspapers explaining the current system. What are the main points about 'law' which such a campaign should emphasize?

WHERE TO GO FROM HERE

This chapter has sketched in outline the main institutions and office-holders in the modern constitution. As a way of describing the public law system this institutional analysis is useful: it describes who does what. There are, however, limits to what it can describe and explain. One important aspect which it fails to emphasize is that the constitution exists in order to enable decisions to be made. In the next chapter we therefore turn to consider how public policy is formulated and, in particular, what roles are played by law and lawyers in the process.

170 Harris, O'Boyle and Warbrick, *The Law on the European Convention on Human Rights*, p. 5.
171 See Chapter 28.

4

THE POLICY CYCLE AND PUBLIC LAW

INTRODUCTION

The description of institutions in the previous chapter provides useful information about the constitution. It does not, however, convey any real sense of the constitution as *a dynamic entity in which things happen*. A different sort of route map through the system is needed to do this. This chapter therefore introduces an analytical tool developed by social scientists which can be described as the 'policy cycle'.[1] As its name suggests, the policy cycle is concerned with the way the constitutional system enables public policy to be formulated, put on a legal footing, and implemented. Not only does it help us to see that institutions such as Parliament and the courts do not exist for their own sake or in isolation, it also highlights the different tasks expected of the constitution. While the government looks to the constitution to provide efficient and effective mechanisms to achieve its policy goals,[2] for citizens, businesses and groups the constitutional arrangements afford opportunities to participate in formulating policy, scrutinize proposals, and challenge governmental actions.

The policy cycle model

The word 'policy' is an everyday word which is used in many different senses.[3] It can refer to the aspirations and promises made by political parties and government in manifestos and in statements of intent: 'it is the government's policy to create a society in which all are "stake-holders"' or more specifically to 'improve education' or 'reduce unemployment'. It can also be used in more concrete terms to refer to what government delivers and achieves. The policy to improve education might, for example, be achieved by the

[1] See further Brian W. Hogwood, *From Crisis to Complacency? Shaping Public Policy in Britain* (1987) and Christopher Ham and Michael Hill, *The Policy Process in the Modern Capitalist State* (2nd edn., 1993).

[2] Unless the context requires otherwise, 'government' in this chapter means central government. Rather different considerations apply at other levels of government—local authorities and the European Community institutions.

[3] On the meaning of policy, see further Hogwood, *From Crisis to Complacency?*, Chapter 1.

building of more schools, employing more teachers, etc. In this chapter we are concerned with the *process* by which the system seeks to put aspirations and proposals such as these into practice.

The policy cycle model is particularly helpful in revealing what happens during episodes such as those described in the case studies used in this book. The model breaks down events into a number of stages.[4] This can be shown as a diagram.

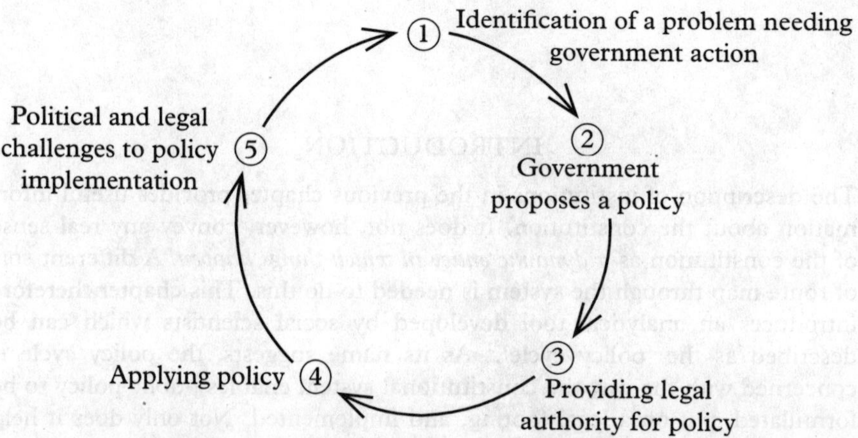

A brief illustration will demonstrate the basic idea. Suppose there is public concern that certain breeds of dog are attacking and seriously harming people (stage 1).[5] The government may decide, perhaps after consultation with animal welfare and other pressure groups, that action needs to be taken, such as requiring dog owners to muzzle dogs in public and to take out liability insurance (stage 2). It may be felt that persuasion and encouragement of dog owners to do these things, for instance by television adverts, would be insufficient and that it is necessary to make muzzling and insurance compulsory; officials such as the police or another agency may therefore need to be given powers to impose sanctions on dog owners who fail to comply with these requirements. Powers to impose fines or, for example, to arrest offending dog owners will require legal backing in the form of an Act of Parliament or delegated legislation (stage 3). Implementation of the new law is stage 4. Here, for instance, police officers may use powers conferred on them to stop and arrest people walking unmuzzled dogs. There may, however, be complaints about the ways in which the law is being enforced and perhaps also criticism of the requirements themselves once people see how they operate

[4] In this chapter we divide the policy cycle into five stages. There is no particular magic in this. In other contexts, writers have chosen to characterize the stages in different ways: see e.g. the three stages ('policy formulation', 'policy application' and 'policy validation') used by Genevra Richardson, 'The Legal Regulation of Process', Chapter 5 in G. Richardson and H. Genn (eds.), *Administrative Law and Government Action* (1994).

[5] For a case study on the Dangerous Dogs Act 1991, see Hansard Society Commission on the Legislative Process, *Making the Law* (1993), pp. 388–98.

in practice (stage 5). The government may then have to deal with these new problems (stage 1) possibly by considering changes to the policy.

Caution in using the model

Because a model such as this is a highly simplified representation of reality, some caution is needed in using it. First, although the model set out above breaks down the policy cycle into distinct stages, bear in mind that this does not mean that these are always easily identifiable as separate phases in the real world. Government, for instance, may not have a clear and certain view about the detail of its policy when it first introduces a bill into Parliament,[6] or the policy may change as Parliament deliberates the matter. When such things happen stages 2 and 3 of the model merge or overlap.

Secondly, the model should not be taken to imply that every policy episode will necessarily complete the chronological sequence. A good illustration of this was the government's attempt to deregulate Sunday trading in the mid-1980s which ended, for several years, midway through stage 3 with the defeat of the Shops Bill in the House of Commons.[7] Nor will a policy necessarily have to pass through every stage of the model. Central government may be able to pursue policy objectives without having specific legal authorization for it if, for instance, the policy does not involve altering people's pre-existing legal rights. Thus if the Department of Health wishes to discourage smoking it may launch an anti-smoking advertising campaign without the need to obtain the specific consent of Parliament.[8] If, however, the goal is to be achieved by taking more coercive steps, such as by making it a criminal offence to smoke in a public place, specific legislation would be needed.

A third reason for caution is that models of the policy cycle tend to emphasize the importance of the *processes* by which policies are made and implemented rather than the content or *substance* of those policies.[9] In some ways this serves our purposes well, because public law is often much more concerned with the processes of decision-making than it is with the content of government action.[10]

Finally, be aware that the policy cycle model tends to be associated with 'top-down' versions of how government operates. To some extent it assumes a hierarchy in which policy is formulated at one level and then subsequently implemented by another, lower level of government. As discussed later, much of our constitutional theory presents the constitutional system in this hierarchical way.[11] Recent reforms in the structures of central and local

6 See further Chapter 8.

7 See further Chapter 9.

8 Provided it has statutory authorization to spend the money to do so, on which see Chapters 16 and 23.

9 For an overview of this and other difficulties, see Hogwood, *From Crisis to Complacency*, pp. 9–14.

10 For instance, judicial review is traditionally said to be confined to matters of procedure rather than substance: see Chapter 20.

11 For example, in Chapter 5 we consider the principle of parliamentary supremacy. See also the 'power-based' approach to judicial review, discussed in Chapter 20.

government have also tended to reinforce the idea that 'policy formulation' and 'practical implementation of policy' are distinct operations.[12] Nevertheless, a rigid top-down analysis can be misleading. Take the Sunday trading case study as an example. The old policy reflected in s 47 of the Shops Act 1950 can be seen as having been decided by central government and implemented by local authorities.[13] Such an analysis of the events would, however, downplay the importance of these authorities. If we look at the actual events we see that their role was far more than simply to implement policy which had been decided by others. Different authorities, for instance, adopted different attitudes towards prosecuting shop owners who breached s 47. The fact that many authorities were loath to enforce what they regarded as outdated restrictions on trading not only highlighted the inadequacies of the existing law, but also became an important impetus for the changes ultimately made by the Sunday Trading Act 1994. Examples such as this show that lines between policy-making and implementation are often very blurred.

How the model helps understanding

The policy cycle model is useful because it raises some fundamental questions about the interconnections between the types of activity called 'politics', 'policy-making', 'administration', and the 'law'. For law students and practitioners it is important to know when and how 'legal' issues arise. Many textbooks and law courses emphasize the constitutional importance of legal issues which arise at stage 3 (Acts of Parliament, delegated legislation, prerogative powers and so on) and stage 5 (parliamentary accountability, ombudsmen, tribunals, and especially judicial review). To a large extent, the main focus of this book fits into that tradition.[14]

However, this book also attempts to show that 'law' and legal values are capable of permeating the political process, including those aspects of the system with which lawyers are not normally concerned. This is not to suggest that politicians and officials necessarily know what the law requires in particular circumstances. Nor indeed does it imply that compliance with the law is necessarily of prime importance to them. As the case studies show, other considerations may be given more weight. It might, for example, be thought politically more important to make speedy decisions than to comply with legal requirements to consult.[15] However, one of the recent lessons of judicial review is that government may come unstuck in the courts when insufficient weight is given to the legal dimension during the policy formation and implementation stages of the policy cycle (stages 2 and 4). It is an aim of this

[12] See below and p. 58.

[13] See further Chapter 30.

[14] Stage 3 (providing legal authority for policy) is considered in some detail in Part B of the book; stage 5 (political and legal challenge to policy implementation) is the subject matter of Part C.

[15] Was this what happened in the Board and Lodgings Regulations saga? See Chapters 11 and 27.

chapter, therefore, to introduce what goes on during these stages in order to show that they too have relevance to public lawyers.

A difficulty with trying to do this is that much of what happens during these stages goes on beyond closed doors within government offices. Consequently, we have much less information about these stages than we have about the more open and visible activities of institutions such as Parliament and the courts. To a large extent it is the very fact that so much of government is not open to public scrutiny that underscores the importance of knowing more about the actual and potential role of law and legal values in government decision-making. If we want to have a system of government in which law and legal values are taken seriously, then it may be exactly this sort of behind-closed-doors activity which is of central importance. When, for example, we discuss the rule of law in Chapter 6 we shall note the argument that it is vital that people working in government internalize legal requirements and follow them, even when they are not told to do so directly by a judge in a particular case. In other words it may be important for law to be an accepted part of the culture within government and not merely something imposed from the outside.

Armed with these words of introduction and caution, we now look at each of the stages in the policy cycle in turn.

STAGE 1: PROBLEMS ARE IDENTIFIED

Different types of problem arise which need the attention of the government. Some problems stem from a particular crisis or scandal or from one-off circumstances. An illustration of this type of problem was the crushing to death of people at a football ground which led to an inquiry, conducted by a judge, into safety at soccer matches and eventually to the government introducing a bill into Parliament which set new safety standards for football grounds.[16]

Other problems needing to be tackled by government are of a recurring or systemic nature. Principal among these is the need to provide basic income and services funded out of taxation, such as health care, education, welfare benefits and social services. Also of great importance is the need for there to be some government regulation of commercial activities. Problems needing attention can also be caused by previous attempts to make and implement policy.

STAGE 2: POLICY PROPOSALS

At the second stage of the model it is for government to consider how to respond to problems. For central government, the main institutions involved

[16] See the Football Spectators Act 1989.

are departments and their ministers. Decisions inevitably have to be taken within the context of the overall political and economic climate. But room for manoeuvre available to policy-makers is also subject to several different forms of restrictions which are of particular importance from a legal perspective. Some constraints relate to *how* they arrive at a policy decision (procedure); others to *what* that policy actually is (its substance). Some constraints are set down in *law* (the common law, legislation and the United Kingdom's international treaty obligations); other constraints result from *political* practices. These legal and political limitations may be direct or indirect. Legal constraints might be direct, for example, when a court has told government that a decision is unlawful and must be changed, but indirect when the government takes account of the *possibility* that a decision *might* be challenged in the courts in the future.

Procedural constraints on policy-making at Stage 2

Non-legal procedural constraints

Many decision-making methods at the policy formulation stage are dictated more by conventions and political practices than by law. It is for instance routine for there to be consultation with interested parties before the government introduces a bill into Parliament; there is however no general legal requirement for this. The manner in which consultation is carried out in any given case is also normally a matter of political practice or convention.

For example, when ministers and their advisors have a firm view of what needs to be done to tackle the problem they may have little interest in undertaking widespread consultation in order to discover what other interested parties think about the various possibilities. They may even decide that it would be counter-productive to consult with those who will be directly adversely affected by the decision. However, as can be seen from the GCHQ case, in this situation there may be duties to consult imposed by the legal principle of legitimate expectation (see below). In other situations the government may not be wedded to any particular course of action and may see it as highly desirable for there to be widespread consultation, particularly with interest groups, as in the Sunday trading case study.[17] Consultation may also be seen as desirable in order to get potential critics 'on board' or to deflect later criticism of the policy which is eventually adopted.

When a major new policy is being considered, a department often publishes a Green Paper, a document formally presented to Parliament inviting a response from the general public and interest groups to initial proposals. Having received representations, the government may publish a White Paper stating what the government's policy decisions are before any bill is introduced. *Ad hoc* committees of inquiry of various types, including Royal Commissions, may also be set up by government, though there is no mandatory

[17] See also the discussion on pluralism at p. 125.

legal requirement to do so. The Auld Committee on Sunday trading, for example, heard evidence from all sides of the debate. Inquiries are often established after a scandal or disaster; here the role of the inquiry may be confined to establishing what happened, though its terms of reference may also include the task of making policy recommendations, which may or may not be accepted by government.

Commentators have identified trends in these practices in recent years. As Harlow and Rawlings put it:[18]

> The Thatcher era inaugurated a retreat from the consultative and participatory towards the directive—what a lawyer might call the 'command theory of government'. Her relations with Parliament have been analysed to show her distaste for parliamentary accountability. The breakdown in central/local relationships to which the new managerial style has contributed is also well documented. A similar shift is noticeable inside government departments where policy-making was increasingly seen as a government responsibility dominated by politicians and sympathetic officials. Goodbye to Royal Commissions, consultative committees, 'Think Tanks' and leisurely Green Papers; enter instant legislation.

Many people view such changes as highly undesirable. Not only do they mean that individuals, groups and businesses are denied opportunities to participate effectively in the process of decision-making at this early stage of the policy process,[19] they may also mean that government acts on the basis of incomplete or wrong facts.[20]

Law as a procedural constraint

In many situations there are few, if any, legal obligations on government to follow particular procedures while formulating its policy. Government, for example, is often not obliged by law to consult or to provide opportunities to individuals or groups to participate; although as indicated above, government may be willing to do so on the grounds that it is useful to get people involved and to benefit from their views. In particular circumstances procedural obligations may, however, be imposed by statute or the common law.

PROCEDURES SET DOWN BY STATUTE

Requirements to consult or to invite objections to proposals may exist in particular contexts, such as in relation to plans to build roads.[21] However, the main general situation in which statute sets down procedures which are relevant at this stage arises when government is proposing to give legal backing to its policy either by amending existing regulations or introducing new

[18] *Pressure Through Law* (1992), p. 297 (footnotes omitted).

[19] Should the GCHQ employees and their union representatives have been given an opportunity to discuss with the government the union ban before it was imposed? See Chapter 16.

[20] Did inadequate consultation lead to 'legislation on the basis of anecdote' rather than proper research in the case of the Board and Lodgings Regulations? See Chapter 11. Could the same be said of the Working Time Directive? See Chapter 14.

[21] See, for example, *Bushell v Secretary of State for the Environment* [1981] AC 75, discussed at p. 590.

delegated legislation.[22] An illustration of this can be seen in the Board and Lodging Regulations case study where the minister was required by s 10 of the Social Security Act 1980 to submit his proposals to an independent committee of experts, the Social Security Advisory Committee, before seeking parliamentary approval for his plans to cut welfare benefits.[23]

PROCEDURES REQUIRED BY THE COMMON LAW

The common law rules on fair procedures potentially provide a set of procedural requirements which are of more general application at the policy formulation stage. However, as we shall see when we discuss these rules in Chapter 25, until recently the judges have been unable or reluctant to impose common law procedural requirements at this point of the policy cycle. There are several practical and constitutional reasons for this.[24] The first practical reason is that until policy decisions are made and implemented in particular situations, people may not be sufficiently interested to take the case to court. If a challenge is made, judges may take the view that it would be constitutionally improper to intervene, particularly where this would involve them in politics. Judges might also prefer to await a challenge to the way the policy actually impacts upon individuals because then they are dealing with concrete situations rather than hypothetical possibilities.

In recent years, however, the courts have developed principles which are relevant to policy-making procedures. The most important is the concept of 'legitimate expectation'. As we have already seen, at its core this provides that if a public body has indicated that it will consult, or has in the past consulted, with a person or an organization before taking action, then those to whom the indication is given or those who have been consulted in the past have a legitimate expectation that they will be consulted in the future. If the body fails to consult it may be held to have acted unfairly, unless there is some good reason to justify its actions. The GCHQ case illustrates this. Had the government been unable to justify its union-ban decision on grounds of national security, the House of Lords would have held the government to have acted unfairly in a legal sense.[25]

Ministers and officials often complain that principles such as legitimate expectation are too general and vague to provide adequate guidance on what steps have to be taken in particular situations: when, for example, do legitimate expectations arise and who has to be consulted? Such issues are discussed later in the chapter. Suffice to say that this is one reason why government lawyers may find themselves involved in decision-making early on in the cycle, trying to predict how the courts might respond should a legal challenge be made.

[22] On SIs and other types of delegated legislation, see further Chapters 10 and 11, below.
[23] See further Chapter 11, below.
[24] For a general discussion, see Genevra Richardson, 'The Legal Regulation of Process' in Chapter 5, G. Richardson and H. Genn (eds.), *Administrative Law and Government Action.*
[25] See further Chapter 28, below.

Constraints on the content of policy

So far, this section of the chapter has been examining the procedural requirements on government policy-makers. We now move on to consider what, if any, constraints exist on the content of the policy choices made by government. We shall consider first the political constraints, and then the legal constraints.

Political constraints

Many of the most important controls on choices about social and economic goals are political ones. In a system of parliamentary democracy, policy decisions by the government normally have to be authorized by a plurality of MPs, most explicitly when the government needs to introduce a bill into Parliament to give ministers or other public bodies new legal powers. Here factors such as the size of a government's majority in the House of Commons are important, though even with a large majority the government may want to test the water in the Commons before introducing a controversial bill by having a debate on a paving motion, as with the debate on the Auld Committee report on Sunday trading.[26]

Policy-makers are also aware that a parliamentary majority is not in itself enough to ensure that policies will be effective. They must also consider how their policies are likely to be received by those directly affected. In Chapter 5 we discuss various theories about the location of political power, including the theory that 'political sovereignty' resides with the electorate, which has been used to provide a democratic justification for the doctrine of parliamentary supremacy. While most discussions of political power nowadays highlight its complexity, there is no doubt that it is ultimately possible for policy to be frustrated when those affected refuse to comply with it. This occurred when the Sunday trading laws were widely flouted by shopkeepers. The organized campaign for non-payment of the Community Charge also played an important part in forcing government to reconsider its policy and its eventual decision to replace this 'poll tax' with a new Council Tax.

Various legal constraints

In addition to the political limits on the content of policies which may be proposed and pursued by government, there are also a range of legal constraints imposed by statute, Community law, common law and international treaties.

STATUTE

When ministers wish to pursue a new policy, they and their advisors consider whether an existing Act of Parliament confers the necessary legal powers to

[26] See Chapter 9. A similar tactic was used for the European Communities (Amendment) Act 1993 when a general debate on the Maastricht Treaty was held before the bill was introduced: see Chapter 13.

take the proposed action. In the Board and Lodgings Regulations saga, for instance, it was decided that the Supplementary Benefit Act 1976 gave the minister power to make the regulations that were considered necessary to reduce the sums spent on board and lodging payments. The court later held that that statute did not confer the necessary legal powers and that the action of the government was therefore unlawful.[27] This illustrates the basic rule of public law that where ministers purport to rely on statutory authority they must ensure that they use the powers granted by the specific Act to further the objects and policy of that Act.[28] Expressed in these terms it might appear that the issues are often clear, but this is not always so (see p. 000). The meaning of legislative provisions is often uncertain and even experienced government lawyers (*if* they are asked by ministers for their advice) may find it difficult to predict how courts will eventually interpret specific provisions. The rider is important because ministers do not always seek legal advice at the policy formulation stage.

Where it has been decided that existing legislation does not confer the necessary powers, thought needs to be given to whether it is necessary to draft a new bill for presentation to Parliament. If this is the case the need to prepare the necessary bill and, most importantly, to find time in the legislative timetable may well force government either to rethink the policy or to shelve the matter until legislation can be enacted.[29]

COMMUNITY LAW

Since the United Kingdom's accession to the European Community in 1973, British governments have had considerable and growing constraints placed on their policy choices by Community law.[30] The case study on the Working Time Directive provides a good illustration of this. Even though the Conservative government was committed to deregulation of commerce and employment, it was outvoted at the Council of Ministers by the other member states and because its legal challenge to the directive was unsuccessful, it had to amend national law to bring it into line with the directive.

COMMON LAW

As already discussed ministers and their advisors may seek to reduce the possibility of policy decisions being later challenged by taking steps to avoid falling foul of the common law principles of judicial review. Reference has already been made to the principles relating to procedures and to the need to comply with statutory provisions. There are also a number of other principles of judicial review which may be relevant to the substance of policies. Two particular issues can be mentioned here. First there are the rules developed by the courts on 'unreasonableness' which seek to ensure that action

[27] See Chapter 27.

[28] See *Padfield v Minister of Agriculture, Fisheries and Food* [1968] AC 997, discussed further in Chapter 23.

[29] See further Chapter 8.

[30] See Chapters 13 and 30, below.

proposed by a minister or other public authority is within the range of *legally acceptable* outcomes.[31] Secondly, judges may force ministers to justify actions which impinge upon the fundamental rights and interests of citizens. As discussed in later chapters, the level of justification may vary depending on the importance of the rights infringed, so that in some circumstances the courts may intervene with the substance of a government's decision where it is considered unreasonable or disproportionate.

It would, however, be misleading to give the impression that the judges are waiting to leap in and to overturn government policy. On the contrary, the courts have tended to give ministers a wide 'margin of appreciation': in most cases only if a decision is 'outrageous in its defiance of logic or accepted moral standards' will a court strike it down on grounds of unreasonableness. And it is very rare indeed for a minister's action to be held invalid for this reason. As a leading textbook puts it, 'judges should not lightly interfere with official decisions on this ground'.[32] The courts continue to show great deference to Parliament and government as the institutions most appropriate to formulate public policy, and they are acutely aware of the practical and constitutional limits of the adjudicative process. This is well illustrated by the recent applications made by homosexual ex-service personnel, challenging the validity of the Ministry of Defence's total ban on gay men and lesbians serving in the armed forces. Simon Brown LJ had this to say at first instance:[33]

> I have to say that the balance of argument . . . appears to me to lie clearly with the applicants. The tide of history is against the ministry. Prejudices are breaking down; old barriers are being removed. It seems to me improbable, whatever this court may say, that the existing policy can survive much longer. I doubt whether most of those present in the court throughout the proceedings now believe otherwise.

In spite of this, he held that the policy could not be characterized, in a legal sense, as 'unreasonable'. His decision was upheld by the Court of Appeal.[34]

INTERNATIONAL TREATY OBLIGATIONS

A further constraint on the content of government policy comes from the international treaty obligations entered into by the United Kingdom, particularly the European Convention on Human Rights (ECHR).[35] Treaties are not, as such, part of domestic law but government may be loath to pursue policies which are contrary to their provisions. The GCHQ case study provides a convenient, though complex, illustration of this. When questioned by the Employment Select Committee, the Secretary of State for Employment (Mr Tom King MP) was keen to stress that, before taking the decision to ban union membership, ministers had 'considered each of the relevant sources

[31] See Chapter 24; note also the discussion of proportionality and the influence of legitimate expectations on the content of policy.
[32] De Smith, Woolf and Jowell, *Judicial Review of Administrative Action* (5th edn., 1995) p. 549.
[33] *R v Ministry of Defence, ex p Smith* [1995] 4 All ER 427, 440.
[34] [1996] 1 All ER 257.
[35] See p. 78.

of international law . . . the ILO Conventions, the European Convention of Human Rights, the European Social Charter and the United Nation Declaration [on Human Rights] and Covenants'.[36] Government advisors had told ministers that the union ban would not be contrary to any of these international treaties. As it happened, the ILO later held that the union ban was contrary to its treaty.

STAGE 3: PROVIDING LEGAL AUTHORITY FOR POLICY

So far we have been considering how policy is made and its content. Normally, though not always, ministers and other public bodies need to have specific legal authorization before they may go ahead and put the policy into practical effect.[37] Statutory authority is required, for example, where the policy involves the levying of taxes[38] or the interference with rights and individual liberties which are already established by legislation or the common law. Legislation may not be required if the government seeks to pursue its policy by persuasion, but it is necessary if the government wants to use coercive powers such as criminal sanctions.

Part B of the book examines in some detail the main types of legal authorization that may be given to government in order to pursue its policies. In outline they are as follows:

(1) Acts of Parliament;
(2) delegated legislation made by ministers;
(3) the prerogative; and
(4) European Community law.

The procedures by which government is given powers under each of these sources of law is described and evaluated. Here one point may be noted: the extent to which people outside government are able to participate at this stage of the policy cycle depends on the form of legal authority chosen by the government. If *new* legislation is to be made, whether primary or subordinate, *some* form of parliamentary approval normally has to be obtained, subjecting the proposal to a degree of scrutiny by MPs before it becomes effective. Rules may, however, sometimes be made by central government without the participation of Parliament, such as primary prerogative legislation like the Civil Service Order in Council (on which see Chapter 10) and informal quasi-legislation (on which see Chapter 7).

Some commentators argue that Parliament is ineffective at subjecting government's legislative proposals to scrutiny and that too often it does little more than act as a rubber stamp.[39] It would be better, some say, for MPs to

[36] See p. 382, below.
[37] For more detailed discussion, see Chapter 7.
[38] Bill of Rights 1688.
[39] On scrutiny of statutes see Chapters 8 and 9; on delegated legislation see Chapters 10 and 11.

be involved earlier in the policy cycle, at stage 2. Special Standing Committees of MPs could, for instance, hear evidence from experts and interest groups about a problem and help to formulate the bill in question, rather than, as often seems to happen, the whole matter being left to ministers and civil servants.[40]

Critics also argue that prerogative powers give too much power to government without there being any prior parliamentary debate or scrutiny.[41] These issues will be returned to in later chapters.

STAGE 4: IMPLEMENTATION OF POLICY

Having obtained legal backing for its policy the focus now shifts to the task of putting the policy into practice. It is at this stage that government and public come into direct contact. Simon Cotton came face to face with the government's public expenditure policy when he received the letter informing him that his benefits were to be withdrawn. The workers at GCHQ experienced government policy when they were forced to relinquish their union membership; individuals will experience immigration policy when they confront immigration officers at airports; and so on. These personal contacts are the end products of complex administrative processes possibly involving many thousands of officials working in government departments and other official bodies. Here we can only sketch the bare outlines of what may be involved.

Even before a new scheme is introduced preparations ought to have started to consider such things as the effects of the new policy on staffing levels and workload in the relevant departments.[42] Once the Act has been passed or regulations made, steps must be taken to deploy and appoint the necessary staff. Staff will also have to be told about the changes and this may require lawyers and managers to draft internal instructions and give guidance on what the legislation means and how it is to be applied in particular cases. Such instructions and guidance become very important to officials who may never look at the original legislation. While sometimes these internal instructions are published, they will often remain secret (for example the internal instructions to immigration officers on how to apply the Immigration Rules). Officials will also need to be told how to respond to questions from the public and how to interview people, and what sort of letters to write to those affected by the policy.[43] Systems may need to be established to monitor how the scheme is working and to pick up problems which might require aspects of the scheme to be reconsidered.

[40] See Chapter 8.

[41] As in the decision to ban unions at GCHQ. The select committee investigation and debate in the Commons took place only after the government's decision had already been carried into effect.

[42] New institutions may also be established: see for example Chapter 3.

[43] Decision letters may be generated by computers. For criticism of computer-generated decisions, see *Annual Report of the Social Fund Commissioner for 1989–90*, Chapter 5.

Sometimes things can go horribly wrong. When we consider the work of the Parliamentary Commissioner for Administration (or 'parliamentary ombudsman') in Chapter 18 we shall see some of the problems which arose when the Department of Social Security miscalculated the expected workload imposed when a new policy on disability allowances was introduced. The result was that the department found itself unable to cope with the flood of claims, with disastrous consequences:

> many letters were not responded to or dealt with; files were 'lost' for long periods; and there were heart-rending delays in the payment of some disabled claimants' benefits.[44]

Within two years an almost identical fiasco occurred, this time involving the new Child Support Agency, for which the Department of Social Security is also responsible.

These examples illustrate that although much of what goes on within official departments is private, administration can have a direct and serious impact on individuals. There are also a number of other important reasons why public lawyers have an interest in this stage of the policy cycle.

In orthodox constitutional theory the implementation stage involves putting policy into effect and the administrative process is simply a conduit by which general policies are delivered and applied to practical situations. Within this theory administration does not change policy, and it would be constitutionally improper for it to do so. The reason for this should be clear: the task of the administration is to apply the policies which have been made by those who are politically accountable and, where these policies are enshrined in legislation, made law by Parliament. Civil servants and other officials are not elected or politically accountable and they have no authority to alter the law. It might appear from this theory that there will be little within the implementation stage to interest public lawyers.

However, the reality is different. Despite the theory, the complex process of administration is likely to influence and change the content of policy. The policy which comes out of the administrative machine is not necessarily identical to the policy that was originally fed into it. The issue might be described as the problem of refraction by analogy to the way a stick placed partly under water looks bent. Why such refraction occurs and how it can be controlled are two key questions of concern to political scientists and lawyers.

Let us briefly consider why refraction might occur. First, of course, is the possibility that officials might make deliberate decisions to change policy. However there are also a number of factors associated with the very nature of implementation, some of which we have already touched upon. For instance, the process by which policy is explained to officials can, like Chinese whispers, lead to misunderstandings and mistakes of interpretation. Internal guidance and instructions, for example, might wrongly interpret legislation

[44] Annual Report of the Parliamentary Commissioner for Administration for 1993 (HC 290 of 1993–94), para. 26. See further p. 412 below.

and in turn be wrongly interpreted by administrators. Problems can also arise when discretion has been given to officials to decide how to handle particular problems, such as when the police are given discretion whether to arrest people in particular situations or whether to charge speeding drivers, or when immigration officers are given discretion to allow people into the country. In such cases there might be a risk of these officials exercising their discretion improperly and in ways which do not further the policy. The police, for instance, might be accused of using their discretion to charge young drivers who are exceeding the speed limit only slightly, but doing nothing to stop middle-aged men who are driving much faster, and who might pose a greater threat to road safety.

As we shall see in later chapters various responses have been made to such problems and much thought given to whether government policy is likely to be more effectively implemented if officials are told in rules what to do or are given discretionary powers.[45] For example, the nineteenth-century constitutional lawyer, A. V. Dicey, argued that officials should not be given discretion because this would undermine the rule of law. More recently, writers have argued that discretion is often necessary and desirable, provided ways can be found to control its exercise by such things as internal checks, the provision of appeals and judicial review. This aspect is discussed below when we consider stage 5 of the policy cycle.

Why does implementation fail?

Legislation sometimes fails to achieve its desired goal of regulating a type of activity or providing certain services. This may be for a variety of reasons, as can be seen in the Sunday trading case study, where there was very widespread non-compliance with the rules contained in s 47 of the Shops Act 1950. One reason was that a large number of shop owners and shoppers did not agree with the restrictions on trading. Also, local authorities in different parts of England and Wales adopted very different attitudes towards the obligation placed on them by s 72 to enforce the restrictions. Some authorities were very loath to inspect and prosecute; others were very eager. Another reason for implementation failure in this context was that the sanctions for non-compliance were ineffective. For many large stores, a fine of £1,000 for contravening s 47 represented only a small fraction of the profit that could be earned by Sunday opening. A further cause of failure may also have been lack of clarity in the rules themselves. Shop owners were able to exploit uncertainty over what was meant by 'motor supplies' which could be sold (claiming, for instance, that this included kitchen sinks because these could be fitted inside caravans) and, more fundamentally, to argue that s 47 was incompatible with provisions in the EC Treaty which prevent restrictions on the import and export of goods between member states.[46]

[45] See p. 145.
[46] See Chapter 30.

As we will see in the next chapter, some influential theorists and politicians believe that most government regulatory schemes and state-provided services are doomed to failure. They argue that decision-making activity of the institutions, elected politicians and state officials described in a policy cycle model (such as the one being described in this chapter) ought instead to be left to the 'public choice' made by individual 'consumers' through the mechanism of markets.[47]

STAGE 5: CHALLENGING POLICY IMPLEMENTATION

The final stage of the policy process model involves the legal, political and administrative mechanisms by which the implementation of policy is challenged and scrutinized. Issues connected to this stage are explored in much more detail in Part C of the book and only a brief discussion is needed here. As we shall see, a range of institutions is involved.

Parliament

As well as being a legislature doing work at stage 3 of the policy cycle, Parliament also has a more general role in scrutinizing government policy and its practical effects, including helping to redress grievances which arise. Members of Parliament help perform this role by maintaining contacts with their constituents, handling complaints made to them by the public, corresponding with ministers and officials, asking PQs and participating in debates, as well as through the work of select committees.[48]

Ombudsmen

The Parliamentary Commissioner for Administration was established to improve Parliament's ability to investigate complaints about the quality of central government administration and to provide more effective redress to victims of maladministration. Similar bodies have since been established to investigate complaints against local government and the health services, and in recent years the ombudsman concept has become increasingly popular in the private sector as well. The work of the main public sector ombudsmen is considered in Chapter 18.

Tribunals

Whenever a government is proposing a new policy initiative, thought ought to be given to ways of dealing with complaints from those who are unhappy

[47] On public choice theory, see p. 130.
[48] See further Chapter 16.

with the way the policy has been applied to them. It might be anticipated, for example, that claimants for a new social welfare benefit will complain that their claims have been rejected, or that they have been offered less than they feel they are entitled to receive. Those responsible for new immigration rules will consider how best to deal with people who might object to being refused permission to enter or to stay in the country. A response to such situations may be to establish special tribunals; another may be to allow appeals to the courts. Whether or not to establish such opportunities to appeal can be very contentious. There are, for example, currently very intense debates about rights of appeal and the quality of appeal procedures in areas such as housing and immigration. Where appellate tribunals are established, they handle many times more cases than are dealt with by the courts and they play a very important part in the public law system, both in providing redress to individuals and in helping to regulate the quality of decision-making. We deal with tribunals in Chapter 19.

Judicial review

In Part C of this book, particular emphasis is given to judicial review. It used to be said that the role of judicial review in the policy-making system was 'inevitably sporadic and peripheral',[49] meaning that there were not many applications for judicial review and that it had little real impact on the way government operated.

More recently the situation appears to be changing. Court decisions, including Simon Cotton's case about board and lodging payments, have highlighted the potential impact of judicial review on government policy. The importance of this has grown as greater use has been made of judicial review.[50] As we have already suggested, a consequence is that ministers and officials are now encouraged to consider the possibility of judicial review challenge from the very outset of the policy cycle. To help them, government lawyers have prepared a booklet entitled *The Judge Over Your Shoulder*, which summarizes the principles of judicial review for the benefit of civil servants. Elsewhere we have argued that:[51]

> the most profound and enduring influences of judicial review are not to be found by examining the statute book, or by seeking formalised and public shifts of policy in response to litigation. Rather they are to be found in the effects of litigation on the less accessible aspects of governments, their management systems and decision-making culture.

Unfortunately, as yet, there has been no comprehensive empirical research into the impact of judicial review on administrative systems and decision-making

[49] See de Smith, Woolf and Jowell, *Judicial Review of Administrative Action* (5th edn., 1995), para. 1–003, quoting earlier editions of that work.

[50] See further L. Bridges, G. Meszaros and M. Sunkin, *Judicial Review in Perspective* (1995). For more discussion of the use of judicial review, see Chapter 20 below.

[51] Maurice Sunkin and A. P. Le Sueur, 'Can Government Control Judicial Review' (1991) 44 CLP 162.

culture within central government, and we are forced to rely on specific studies and anecdotal evidence.[52] Our pilot study into the impact of judicial review on central government found that officials were being encouraged to be more aware that their decisions could be challenged, to make more use of legal advice, to be more careful in drafting, and more thorough in internally reviewing decisions. Although some, particularly government lawyers, emphasized the positive aspects of judicial review in improving the quality of decision-making, the dominant view was that the threat of legal challenge had led to administrators becoming more defensive, to 'emphasise the need to "reduce the risks of challenge," to "take precautions" and to "protect ministers" from "embarrassment in the courts"'.[53] Research into the impact of judicial review on local government found a similar response with local authorities adopting procedures which would enable them to demonstrate to the courts (if they were challenged) that their decisions had been properly taken.[54] This means, in the words of one officer, that:[55]

> we generate a lot more paper . . . there is more writing down of relevant factors and irrelevant factors in decisions. We are now setting down many things that were previously implicitly understood . . . [this] . . . all contrive[s] to lengthen and complicate the decision process.

From this research it seems that judicial review has led to more bureaucracy, a greater attention to formality, and a greater role for lawyers within government. This, of course, assumes that administrators are aware of judicial review and are responding to it. Loveland's research into local housing authorities, however, cautions against this assumption.[56] He found that judicial review had little effect on day-to-day decision-making. Officials were more concerned about issues of resources, inter-agency relations, conceptions of morality and expediency than they were about the law in general, or judicial review in particular. Even where senior officials took account of judicial review their main interest was in avoiding costs and unfavourable publicity, rather than in more positive matters.

The overall impression from the little research which has so far been done on the use and impact of judicial review seems to indicate that while particular decisions can have a profound effect, few areas of a government are regularly called to account by judicial review proceedings; where judicial review does impinge, its effect on governmental policy is usually short-lived; its longer-term effects tend to be on administrative systems and bureaucratic behaviour. Here the research suggests that its effect is to encourage more formal and more cumbersome procedures. Whether this improves the quality of government is an open question which clearly warrants more comprehensive research.

[52] For a general discussion, see further Genevra Richardson and Maurice Sunkin, 'Judicial Review: Questions of Impact' [1996] PL 79.

[53] Sunkin and Le Sueur, at p. 172.

[54] L. Bridges *et al.*, *Legality and Local Politics* (1987).

[55] Quoted by Ross Cranston, 'Reviewing Judicial Review', in G. Richardson and H. Genn (eds.), *Administrative Law and Government Action* (1994) pp. 72–3.

[56] I. Loveland, *Housing Homeless Persons* (1995).

Compensation

For individuals and businesses, one major concern at stage 5 of the policy cycle may be to obtain financial recompense for government action.[57] As a general principle the courts will not award damages for losses and injuries solely on the grounds that the relevant minister or official has acted beyond their powers. Negligence or some other tort must be established. Even then the courts are very reluctant to award damages to those injured by policy decisions.[58]

In general, the only type of situation in which government is likely to have to pay compensation for pursuing unlawful policies (as opposed to specific practical mistakes at stage 4 in the implementation of policies) is where the policy adopted is contrary to Community law.[59] The government has had to pay considerable sums to women forced to resign, contrary to Community law, from the armed forces when they became pregnant and to Spanish trawler owners unlawfully prevented from registering their boats as British vessels.[60]

CONCLUSION: THE ROLES OF LAW IN THE POLICY CYCLE

This chapter has introduced an analytical tool used by social scientists, a model of the policy cycle. Use of this model helps to show the main stages by which government policy is made and to highlight the various roles played by law in this process. The most familiar of these roles are associated with stage 3, where legal authority is given to policy by Parliament, and stage 5, where the courts are used to challenge and scrutinize governmental decisions. However, our discussion shows that legal issues also arise at the other stages and in particular during the implementation process.

The main legal stages (3 and 5) reflect the two fundamental roles performed by law in the constitutional system. In one the law, in the form of legislation, may be seen as a tool which *enables* government to pursue its policies. In the other, law in the form of legal principles enforced by the courts becomes a mechanism for *controlling* government power.[61] The next two chapters explore these two facets of law in more detail. Chapter 5 considers how orthodox theory reinforces the power of government to use law as a tool for achieving its ends principally by means of the doctrine of parliamentary supremacy. Chapter 6 takes the other perspective and examines the principal

[57] See further Chapter 26.

[58] See *Rowling v Takaro Properties Ltd* [1988] AC 473, discussed in Chapter 26.

[59] See especially *Francovich v Republic of Italy* (Joined Cases C-6&9/90) [1991] ECR-I 5357, discussed in Chapter 29.

[60] See the *Factortame* litigation discussed in Chapters 26 and 30.

[61] On this dichotomy, see further Carol Harlow and Richard Rawlings, *Law and Administration* (1984), Chapters 1 and 2: they coin the terms 'red light theories' for the focus on control and 'green light theories' for those which emphasize that law facilitates government action. See also Martin Loughlin, *Public Law and Political Theory* (1992).

limitations on government, including the principles usually associated with the 'rule of law'.

Questions

1. Choose a 'problem' (stage 1 of the policy cycle) facing government which has been in the news recently. How do the events which have happened, or are likely to happen, fit into the policy cycle model? What do you learn about how the constitution operates by analysing an episode in this way?

2. Imagine you are a senior civil servant. Following a general election, the Prime Minister appoints several ministers to your department who have never held ministerial office. The ministers ask you to write a short memorandum outlining the constitutional constraints which exist on the policies which they may pursue, and explaining the relative importance of each of these constraints.

3. To which stages of the policy cycle is judicial review relevant and why?

5

POWER AND PUBLIC LAW

INTRODUCTION

We concluded the previous chapter by identifying two ways of viewing the role of law in the policy-making process: as a means of *enabling* government to pursue its policies and as a mechanism for *controlling* government power. We now move on to look at these two aspects more closely. In this chapter we first consider the way orthodox constitutional theory, particularly the doctrine of the legal supremacy of Parliament, accommodates the government's use of law. The chapter then moves on to question the democratic basis and political justification for this orthodox theory. The next chapter considers law as a mechanism of control.

DICEY'S LEGEND

For over a century one particular story about where power lies in the constitution has been retold to students and is now so well known that it has become an accepted part of our constitutional theory. The story was popularized by A. V. Dicey,[1] in his *Introduction to the Study of the Law of the Constitution*, first published in 1885 and still read and debated today.[2] This book has had an influence far beyond its intended undergraduate audience. Indeed, it has even been claimed recently that 'Dicey's word has in some respects become the only written constitution we have'.[3] The apparent vigour

[1] Albert Venn Dicey (1835–1922) was a well-known public figure during his lifetime as well as a professor of law at Oxford. His political views are often described as 'liberal', meaning he had a commitment to individualism and free trade. Above all he was against 'state collectivism', believing there was a contradiction between such 'socialism' and democracy. He was concerned by the increasing state regulation of economic activity and the growing provision of services by the state. He was a passionate, obsessive, Unionist and opposed all proposals that any part of Ireland should cease to be part of the United Kingdom.

[2] There is a voluminous literature responding to Dicey, including: R. A. Cosgrove, *The Rule of Law: Albert Venn Dicey, Victorian Jurist* (1980); P. McAuslan and J. McEldowney (eds.), *Law, Legitimacy and the Constitution* (1985); P. P. Craig, 'Dicey: Unitary, Self-correcting Democracy and Public Law' (1990) 106 LQR 105; M. Loughlin, *Public Law and Political Theory* (1992); T. R. S. Allan, *Law, Liberty, and Justice* (1993).

[3] J. Jowell and D. Oliver (eds.), *The Changing Constitution* (3rd edn., 1994), p. v.

of Dicey's work, however, is not to be taken as evidence that commentators necessarily agree or approve of what he had to say. On the contrary, one reason why public lawyers still use Dicey is that we love to hate him. His theories continue to be used for illustration and criticism and they continue to provide a foil for explaining the system, its theoretical and cultural heritage and the assumptions which have dominated orthodox viewpoints. In short, if you want to know what principles and attitudes have made judges tick for the past 100 years you can do no better than read Dicey. If you want a critique of these attitudes, start by considering criticism of Dicey. In a way Dicey has become a metaphor for an idealized or mythological constitution which is often used to illustrate the failings of the modern British system and to expose fundamental shortcomings in our constitutional theory.

Dicey's model constitution

Any summary of Dicey's understanding of the constitutional system is inevitably prone to overlook the undercurrents, the gaps, the uncertainties and the contradictions in his influential ideas. Nevertheless, an overview is a good starting point.

Political sovereignty

Dicey believed that ultimate political power in the constitutional system lies with the electorate who every five years or so vote for MPs to sit in the House of Commons. 'The electors can in the long run always enforce their will,' he wrote.[4] As a liberal, he regarded the primary political units to be individual citizens. In later life he came to believe that the use of referenda would be a way of enhancing the electorate's power and preventing Parliament from enacting imprudent legislation, but Parliament and representative democracy were central to his view of the constitution. His view of democracy can therefore be described as Parliament-centred and majoritarian.

Legal sovereignty

Dicey distinguished between political power and legal power. Ultimate law-making power, he argued, lies with Parliament: it has

> under the English constitution, the right to make or unmake any law whatever; and . . . no person or body is recognised by the law of England as having a right to override or set aside the legislation of Parliament.[5]

[4] *Law of the Constitution*, p. 73. During Dicey's lifetime there was a significant increase in the proportion of people entitled to vote in parliamentary elections. The Great Reform Act 1832 enfranchised only 14 per cent of adult males, all property owners. The major change came in 1867 when for the first time working-class men were able to vote and modern mass-membership political parties began to be organized. Women received the vote on the same basis as men only in 1928.

[5] *Law of the Constitution*, p. 40.

This view of Parliament's legal supremacy belongs to a theory known as legal positivism.[6] In essence, this views 'law' as the commands of a legal sovereign (person or body) backed by sanctions. One of the features of legal positivism is that it distinguishes law from morality. Even legislation whose content is morally repugnant is nevertheless to be regarded as valid law and ought to be applied by the courts.[7]

Another feature is that it assumes a hierarchical legal system with the sovereign law-maker at the top and those subject to the sovereign's commands at the bottom. In such a system the courts have no power to set aside or declare invalid any Act of Parliament—even if a provision is immoral or contrary to international law; and Parliament can enact legislation to alter the common law developed by the judges. Ultimately, the constitutional role of the judges is to ensure that ministers, civil servants and other officials comply with the sovereign's will and do not exceed the powers conferred on them by Acts of Parliament. Even today, this *ultra vires* principle is regarded by many as the main justification for judicial review of administrative action.[8]

Legislation reflects public opinion

The main guarantee against abuse and tyranny lies in Dicey's division between legal and political sovereignty. Parliament is legally sovereign but it has to comply with the wishes of the electorate, which is politically sovereign. This relationship in the long run prevents government from abusing its powers because the system is self-correcting. Legislation made by MPs reflects the will of the majority of the electorate; if it does not, then MPs will not be re-elected and the government will fall at the next general election.[9]

Parliamentary control of government

In short, then, Parliament controls the government and the electorate controls Parliament. In Dicey's constitutional model Parliament is able to control government power in two main ways. First, in order to carry out its executive functions, government usually needs specific legal authorization from an Act of Parliament. To maximize Parliament's leverage over executive action, Dicey argued that statutes ought not to confer wide discretionary powers on ministers and other office-holders.[10] If Parliament *does* confer such powers, then

[6] For further reading on the much-criticized theory of legal positivism see M. D. A. Freeman (ed.), *Lloyd's Introduction to Jurisprudence* (6th edn., 1994), Chapter 4 ('Bentham, Austin and Classical English Positivism').

[7] Consider, for instance, the race laws once made by the apartheid governments in South Africa and in Nazi Germany.

[8] See further Chapter 20 below. But cf. Dicey's theory of the rule of law discussed in Chapter 6.

[9] On this subtle idea, see further P. P. Craig (1990) 106 LQR 105.

[10] *The Law of the Constitution*, p. 188. The absence of 'wide, arbitrary or discretionary powers' conferred on government was, for Dicey, a key element in the definition of the rule of law: see p. 145 below.

the courts are there to ensure that those to whom discretionary powers are delegated do not exceed or abuse this power.

Secondly, Dicey recognized that the government had residual non-statutory powers (prerogative powers)[11] which had passed from the monarch to ministers after the Glorious Revolution of 1688. But Parliament is able to control these too, not by law but by means of a body of constitutional 'ethics' and 'understandings' which he described as conventions. These conventions are not, he argued, enforced by the courts and are not therefore in Dicey's scheme constitutional 'law'.[12] Nevertheless they help to make government accountable to Parliament and the electorate for its use of non-statutory powers. The ultimate purpose of conventions is, in Dicey's theory:[13]

> to secure that Parliament, or the cabinet which is indirectly appointed by Parliament, shall in the long run give effect to the will of that power which in modern England is the true political sovereign of the state—the majority of the electors . . .

Let us now turn to consider the idea of the legal supremacy of Parliament, and the implications of this theory within current constitutional practice.

THE LEGAL SUPREMACY OF PARLIAMENT?

Practising lawyers, judges and legal commentators have, perhaps naturally, focused their attention on the 'legal' aspect of Dicey's constitutional model—Parliament's *legal* supremacy rather than his views of political sovereignty. In practical terms the essence of this is that Parliament is not subject to any *legal* constraints as to what it may enact and judges cannot claim any right to declare Acts of Parliament 'unconstitutional'.[14] Strictly speaking, when we refer to Parliament in this context we mean the 'Queen-in-Parliament' because it is necessary for Acts of Parliament to receive the Royal Assent, although by convention the monarch now has no power to withhold assent. Note the words of enactment at the start of statutes:

> Be it enacted by the Queen's Most Excellent Majesty, by and with the advice and consent of the Lords Spiritual and Temporal, and Commons, in this present Parliament assembled, and by the authority of the same, as follows . . .

As stated above, the main modern justification for the rule of parliamentary supremacy is that it embodies democratic principles.[15] The House of Commons

[11] See Chapter 12 below.
[12] See further p. 138.
[13] *Law of the Constitution*, p. 429.
[14] Compare the position in the USA where in *Marbury v Madison* (1803) 5 US (1 Cranch) 137 the US Supreme Court first refused to give effect to provisions in a federal statute which, it held, Congress had enacted contrary to its legislative powers under the constitution. Constitutional review of federal and state legislation is now a principal part of US constitutional arrangements.
[15] There is also an *historical* explanation for the principle: the new constitutional settlement in the wake of the 1688 Glorious Revolution was concerned to give *Parliament* power over the monarch.

comprises of MPs who must put themselves forward for re-election at least once every five years. Between elections, MPs are responsive to public opinion and so it can be expected that the government's legislative programme has majority support. In these circumstances, it can be argued, it would be wrong for unelected judges, especially given that the judiciary in the United Kingdom are overwhelmingly from a small social and cultural elite, to adjudicate on the legality of Acts of Parliament and, in effect, substitute their own views of what is proper and acceptable for those of the nation's elected representatives.[16]

Nevertheless, to many people this appears to be a potentially dangerous constitutional arrangement. In particular, its focus on the link between Parliament and the wishes of the majority of the electorate seems to provide little safeguard for minority interests and particularly individuals and groups who may be unpopular and who may be oppressed by actions of the majority. One riposte to this is that Parliament would never, in fact, use its power to enact oppressive legislation because it is constrained by public opinion from doing so. Indeed, it has been suggested that the practice of not legislating to infringe fundamental rights has actually crystallized into a constitutional *convention* binding on Parliament.[17] This is a dangerously complacent attitude. Public opinion may well be against oppressive legislation, but in a constitutional system where the executive effectively controls Parliament and public opinion is often uncertain or easily influenced, stronger legal protection for individuals and groups, many now argue, is necessary.

Over the last few years there has been a real change of attitude towards parliamentary supremacy. Later in the chapter we consider the impact of Community law on parliamentary supremacy. In addition to Community law, the Labour and Liberal Democrat parties are now committed to constitutional reforms including a new Bill of Rights (a charter of fundamental legal rights) which may empower the courts to review parliamentary legislation. The judges, too, have become more outspoken in advocating a more expansive constitutional role for themselves. We shall return to these issues in the next chapter. For the present our concern is to examine the orthodox view in more detail.

There are two main dimensions. One is the proposition that Parliament can make or unmake any law it wishes. The other is the proposition that in the United Kingdom no person or institution has independent legislative power except Parliament.[18]

16 See further J. A. G. Griffith, 'The Political Constitution' (1979) 42 MLR 1.

17 See G. Marshall, *Constitutional Conventions* (1986), p. 9: 'Though it is rarely formulated as a conventional rule the most obvious and undisputed convention of the British constitutional system is that Parliament does not use its unlimited sovereign power of legislation in an oppressive or tyrannical way.' On conventions as a constraint on governmental power, see Chapter 6, below.

18 Ministers, local authorities and some other statutory bodies have powers to make delegated legislation (SIs, bylaws etc.), but these law-making powers are limited and conferred by Parliament. See further Chapter 10.

Parliament has unlimited legislative power

What is immediately striking about Dicey's writing on this subject is his method: he sets out to 'prove' that Parliament is legally sovereign, drawing on 'evidence'. His conclusion is that 'parliamentary sovereignty is . . . an undoubted legal fact' which is 'shown historically in a large number of instances'.[19] On this approach the enactment of far-reaching or draconian statutory provisions is evidence of Parliament's legal power. Modern examples are not hard to find; three can be given as illustrations.

Retrospective legislation has been passed to overturn a court's decision which was inconvenient to government. In *Burmah Oil Co Ltd v Lord Advocate*,[20] the House of Lords held that the government had a common law duty to pay compensation to an oil company whose installations in Burma had been destroyed by the British army in 1942 to prevent them falling into the hands of the invading Japanese; the government found this ruling unacceptable and immediately enacted the War Damage Act 1965 to reverse the decision.[21]

The second example concerns local democracy. In some countries local and regional government have a protected status under the constitution; in the United Kingdom, however, elected local authorities are merely statutory bodies and may be abolished by Act of Parliament. Section 1 of the Local Government Act 1985, for example, abolished the Greater London Council (GLC) and the county councils in five other metropolitan areas in England.[22] Because of the rule of parliamentary supremacy, the GLC and concerned citizens had no scope for seeking judicial review of the 1985 Act on the ground that it was 'unlawful' or 'unconstitutional' for an institution of democratic government to be abolished.

Section 28 of the Local Government Act 1988 provides a third example of draconian use of parliamentary legislation.[23] This provides that 'a local authority shall not . . . promote the teaching . . . of the acceptability of homosexuality as a pretended family relationship'. Section 28 was 'widely seen as a

[19] *Law of the Constitution*, p. 43.

[20] [1965] AC 75.

[21] For another illustration see the governments retrospective reversal, by means of Sched 1 to the Social Security (Persons From Abroad) Miscellaneous Amendments Regulations 1996, of the Court of Appeal's Decision in *R v Secretary of State for Social Security, ex p Joint Council for the Welfare of Immigrants* [1996] 4 All ER 385.

[22] Section 1:

'(1) On the date on which this subsection comes into force—

(a) the Greater London Council; and

(b) the metropolitan county councils, shall cease to exist.

(2) The date on which subsection (1) above comes into force is in this Act referred to as "the abolition date" and shall be 1st April 1986.'

[23] This inserted a new s 2A into the Local Government Act 1986.

major and shameful attack on civil liberties'[24] that was concerned with pandering to populist prejudice against a minority rather than with addressing any real problem. The provision may well be contrary to the non-discrimination principle contained in Art 14 of the European Convention on Human Rights,[25] but the ECHR cannot be relied upon directly within the domestic legal system to challenge its lawfulness.

It would be possible to continue in a similar vein, giving further examples of harsh enactments. Although this was Dicey's *method* for 'proving' that Parliament was, as a matter of law, legislatively omnipotent, what exactly do such illustrations prove? Arguably all they show is that the courts in the United Kingdom *have not* adjudicated on the constitutional validity of statutes, but not that they *cannot*. The orthodox assertion that Parliament has legally unlimited powers to legislate appears also to mean that the British courts *ought* to refuse to consider the lawfulness of any Act of Parliament, even one which (say) disfranchised Jews from voting in parliamentary elections. This, as we shall see, is becoming an increasingly contentious proposition.

Can Parliament bind itself in the future?

From the time of the creation of a single Parliament for Great Britain in 1706, politicians have occasionally sought to embed statutory provisions into law for all time in order to prevent or reduce the possibility of their future amendment or repeal. This desire to 'entrench' some Acts of Parliament has occurred when politicians regard the content of the legislation as being of fundamental importance. For example, the Act of Union with Scotland 1707 stated that it was 'a fundamental and essential condition . . . in all time coming' that teachers at Scottish universities had to be members of the Presbyterian Church. Yet this restriction was later repealed by the Universities (Scotland) Act 1853. Questions of entrenchment are now being debated in the context of the possible adoption of a modern Bill of Rights. Some argue that if such a bill is introduced it will have to be entrenched in order to prevent a future government using its majority in the Commons to repeal or amend its provisions too easily.

Dicey used the amendment to the Act of Union (see above) as evidence that entrenchment was not possible in this constitution. There could not be, he asserted, any special statutes:

[24] See M. Colvin with J. Hawksley, *Section 28: a practical guide to the law and its implications* (1989), p. 11.

[25] Art 14 of the ECHR provides that the enjoyments, rights and freedoms *set out in the Convention* shall be secured 'without discrimination on any ground such as sex, race, colour . . . or other status'. The other substantive rights under the convention which parents in same-sex relationships and their children might benefit from, and to which Art 14 might apply, include those protected by Art 8 ('Everyone has the right to respect for his private and family life . . .'). On the ECHR generally, see p. 78.

> none of them when passed will be, legally speaking, a whit more sacred or immutable than the others, for they each will be neither more nor less than an Act of Parliament, which can be repealed as it has been passed by Parliament.[26]

For Dicey, the main reason why it was impossible for Parliament to entrench legislation was because attempts at entrenchment in the past had all 'failed', in the sense that they had in fact been repealed or amended by later legislation.

A somewhat different argument against the possibility of entrenchment is to say that part of the very *meaning* of 'parliamentary sovereignty' is that Parliament, being sovereign, can do everything *except* limit its sovereignty for all time. If it could do this, a *future* Parliament would not be sovereign.

The 'doctrine of implied repeal'

The normal rule is that a later Act which is inconsistent with an earlier one implicitly repeals the former, even if it does not do so expressly. This is often referred to as the 'doctrine of implied repeal'. This doctrine may apply even where the earlier Act purports to say that its provisions shall prevail over inconsistent provisions in a later Act. Consider the Court of Appeal's decision in *Ellen Street Estates Ltd v Minister of Health*.[27] The minister made a compulsory purchase order under powers in the Housing Act 1930 so as to clear an area of slum housing for redevelopment. The property owned by the plaintiff company was to be demolished and it applied for compensation. The Housing Act 1930 set out one way of calculating the award. An earlier statute which had not been expressly repealed, the Acquisition of Land (Assessment of Compensation) Act 1919, had set out a different and more generous one. Section 7(1) of the 1919 Act stated:

> The provisions of the Act or order by which the land is authorised to be acquired, or of any Act incorporated therewith, shall, in relation to the matters dealt with in this Act, have effect subject to this Act, and so far as inconsistent with this Act, those provisions shall cease to have or shall not have effect.

In rejecting the plaintiff's case (that because the 1930 Act was inconsistent with the 1919 Act, it had no effect and so the more generous scheme applied), Maugham LJ held:

> The legislature cannot, according to our constitution, bind itself as to the form of subsequent legislation, and it is impossible for Parliament to enact that in a subsequent statute dealing with the same subject-matter there can be no implied repeal. If in a subsequent statute Parliament chooses to make it plain that the earlier statute is being to some extent repealed, effect must be given to that intention just because it is the will of the legislature.

[26] *Law of the Constitution*, p. 89.

[27] [1934] 1 KB 590, 597. See also *Vauxhall Estates v Liverpool Corporation* [1932] 1 KB 733.

Absolute entrenchment

Absolute entrenchment of a statutory provision would occur if Parliament were able to bind all future Parliaments from *ever* repealing or amending the provision in question. As the above discussion indicates absolute entrenchment would conflict with orthodox conceptions of parliamentary supremacy. Even if this were not so, there are good reasons for saying that such entrenchment is undesirable because it is not possible for us to foresee what future generations may hold to be important. For example, it might be argued that Parliament should entrench fundamental legal rights provisions contained in a new Bill of Rights. However, the virtue of doing so depends on how we view fundamental rights. Absolute entrenchment would only make sense if we accept the idea that some rights are absolute and fixed, and that they do not vary over time. However, many rights we currently regard as fundamental and relatively uncontroversial, such as equality between men and women, would have been regarded as absurd only a few generations ago.[28] We look back at the religious discrimination (as we would now view it) of the Act of Union 1707 with disapproval; yet at the time many people thought that the Protestant ascendancy was essential. In short, attitudes and beliefs change and it would surely be wrong for Parliament now to be able to bind its successors for all time.[29]

Procedural entrenchment and the re-definition theory

There may therefore be little to be said in favour of making a statute irrepealable for all time, even if this were possible. But this is not to say that Parliament can do nothing to protect its legislation from future alteration. Changes, for example, have been made to procedures by which legislation is enacted. Jennings referred to such changes as the 're-definition theory':[30]

> Legal sovereignty is merely the name indicating that the legislature has for the time being power to make laws of any kind in the manner required by law. That is, a rule expressed to be made by the Queen 'with the advice and consent of the Lords spiritual and temporal, and the Commons in this present Parliament assembled, and by the authority of the same'. If this is so, the 'legal sovereign' may impose legal limitations upon itself, *because its power to change the law includes the power to change the law affecting itself.*

Parliamentary procedures and the definition of the Queen-in-Parliament have been changed in the past in order to make it *easier* to legislate. The Parliament Acts 1911 and 1949 made it possible for a bill to receive Royal Assent

[28] For example in *Roberts v Hopwood* [1925] AC 578, the House of Lords held that it was unlawful for a local authority to adopt a policy of paying its male and female employees the same basic wage.

[29] On the need to situate what we now regard as 'fundamental' human rights in a particular time and place, see Sir Stephen Sedley, 'Human Rights: a Twenty-First Century Agenda' [1995] PL 386, discussed at p. 154 below.

[30] Sir Ivor Jennings, *The Law and the Constitution* (5th edn., 1959), pp. 152–3.

without the agreement of the House of Lords.[31] If it is possible to change procedures to make it easier to legislate, is it not also possible to change procedures in order to make it more difficult to legislate?[32]

Consider the following example. The Northern Ireland Constitution Act 1973, s 1 provides an illustration of procedural entrenchment currently on the statute book:

> It is hereby declared that Northern Ireland remains part of . . . the United Kingdom, and it is hereby affirmed that in no event will Northern Ireland or any part of it cease to be part of Her Majesty's dominions and of the United Kingdom without the consent of the majority of the people of Northern Ireland voting in a poll held for the purposes of this section in accordance with Schedule 1 to this Act.

Suppose some future UK Parliament wishes Northern Ireland to be part of the Republic of Ireland and, without first having ascertained the wishes of the majority of the Province's population, passes a new Act which provides that: 'It is hereby declared that Northern Ireland shall cease to be part of the United Kingdom.' If in litigation a court is required to consider these two provisions, to which ought it to give effect? Would the courts be bound to accept the later Act as the most recent expression of parliamentary intention, or would they hold that the legislation was invalid because it had been improperly enacted?

Irregular parliamentary procedures

The above example raises a further question, namely: to what extent will the courts be prepared to consider the legality of Acts of Parliament on the grounds that the appropriate procedures have not been followed? The main procedural rules for making primary legislation are set out in standing orders (internal rules of Parliament) rather than in an Act of Parliament or delegated legislation.[33] From the time of the Glorious Revolution in 1688, Parliament has vigilantly asserted an unfettered right to regulate its own proceedings. Thus the Bill of Rights 1688, art 9 provides that 'the freedom of speech and debates or proceedings in Parliament ought not to be impeached or questioned in any court or place out of Parliament'. This legislative provision has sometimes been relied upon by the courts to justify their refusal to adjudicate on the validity of Acts of Parliament, especially where the ground of challenge has been that incorrect parliamentary procedures were followed. In *The Prince's Case*,[34] a court examined the validity of an Act.

[31] See p. 187.

[32] See Heuston's argument on 'manner and form' in R. F. V. Heuston *Essays in Constitutional Law* (2nd edn., 1964), pp. 7–8 and also *Attorney-General for New South Wales v Trethowan* [1932] AC 526; *Bribery Commissioner v Ranasinghe* [1965] AC 172 (both decisions of the Privy Council and so not strictly binding on UK courts).

[33] An exception is the Parliament Act 1911 as amended by the Parliament Act 1949 (on which see further Chapter 8). For Standing Orders and commentary on them see C. J. Boulton (ed.), *Erskine May's Treatise on the Law, Privileges, Proceedings and Usage of Parliament* (21st edn., 1989), hereafter referred to as *Erskine May*.

[34] (1606) 8 Co Rep 1a.

In this pre-Glorious Revolution decision it was held that even if an Act was formally recorded in the official record of proceedings of Parliament, if there was an error on the face of the Act showing that the Lords, Commons and King had not all[35] assented to it, but only for example the King and the Lords, then it would not be regarded as a valid Act. Today, however, the courts in the United Kingdom cannot question the validity of an Act of Parliament on the ground that it did not pass through the proper procedures laid down by parliamentary standing orders. There is no shortage of authority for this. In several cases litigants have attempted to argue that Acts of Parliament have, in some sense, been obtained fraudulently.[36] These were all private Acts of Parliament,[37] but this makes no difference of principle.

In one of the most recent cases, *Pickin v British Railways Board*, it was alleged that contrary to the preamble to the British Railways Act 1968 certain plans and lists of owners of land adjoining a railway line had not been deposited in a local authority's office for inspection. A unanimous Court of Appeal (including Lord Denning MR) held that it was a triable issue whether the Act had been obtained fraudulently.[38] The House of Lords unanimously overturned the Court of Appeal, Lord Reid stating that:[39]

> The function of the court is to construe and apply enactments of Parliament. The court has no concern with the manner in which Parliament or its officers carrying out its Standing Orders perform these functions. Any attempt to prove that they were misled by fraud or otherwise would necessarily involve an inquiry into the manner in which they had performed their functions in dealing with the Bill which became the British Railways Act 1968. . . . For a century or more both Parliament and the courts have been careful not to act so as to cause conflict between them. Any such investigation as the respondent seeks could easily lead to such a conflict, and I would only support it if compelled to do so by clear authority. But it appears to me that the whole trend of authority for over a century is clearly against permitting such an investigation.

Other competing legislative authority

So far we have introduced the proposition that Parliament has unlimited legislative authority. We shall return to this later in this chapter when we consider the impact of Community law. Before doing this, however, we need to examine briefly what Dicey called 'the negative side' of the doctrine of

35 Subject now to the provisions of the Parliament Acts 1911–49.

36 Leading cases include *Lea v Bude and Torrington Junction Railway Co* (1871) LR 6 CP 576 and *Edinburgh and Dalkeith Railway v Wauchope* (1842) 8 ER 279.

37 Defined in *Erskine May* as 'legislation of a special kind for conferring particular powers or benefits on any person or body of persons—including individuals, local authorities, statutory companies, or private corporations—in excess of or in conflict with the general law'. Private Acts should not be confused with 'Private Members' Bills', on which see p. 191.

38 [1973] QB 219.

39 [1974] AC 765, 787–8.

parliamentary sovereignty: that in the United Kingdom no person or institution has independent legislative power except Parliament. Dicey wrote that:[40]

> The Queen, each House of Parliament, . . . and the Law Courts, either have at one time claimed, or might appear to claim, independent legislative power.

None of these institutions, he argued, had won that claim.

The Crown acting alone without Parliament

'The Queen' in this context refers to the monarch's inherent powers which today are *used by government ministers*—in other words, the prerogative and other non-statutory powers of the government.[41] The Queen-in-Council still retains some power to make primary legislation:[42] examples include the Civil Service Order in Council (the legislation which delegated to the Minister for the Civil Service the power to issue instructions used to ban union membership at GCHQ) and the Order in Council which requisitioned merchant ships to aid the United Kingdom's efforts in the war to recapture the Falkland Islands. Although important, the powers of ministers to use the prerogative to make primary legislation without Parliament is now restricted to a handful of situations and in any case these powers may be removed or limited by Parliament.

Of more general importance today is the ability of government to use the prerogative to enter into international treaties. Dicey had relatively little to say about treaties, perhaps because a century ago such agreements between states had little impact on the domestic legal system. Today, however, treaties deal with matters of direct importance to individuals and businesses, such as aviation landing rights, financial transactions, transport, the environment and fundamental human rights. The government still has exclusive authority to negotiate and enter into treaties under the prerogative without any effective parliamentary scrutiny or approval.[43] Ministers are also able to make other types of 'informal' or 'quasi legislation' without the participation of Parliament.[44]

Dicey's analysis may therefore be criticized for downplaying the ability of government to make binding rules of general application *without the participation of Parliament*. Against this it should be recognized that the prerogative and other non-statutory government powers to make rules may be replaced by statute at any time; the executive can only 'legislate' or act without parliamentary approval so long as Parliament acquiesces in this state of affairs;

40 *Law of the Constitution*, p. 50.
41 See Chapter 12.
42 The term 'Queen-in-Council' refers to the fact that the monarch acts on the advice of the Privy Council. Contrast this with the 'Queen-in-Parliament', pp. 277–8.
43 See further Chapter 12. The principle that the Crown cannot make law without Parliament's consent explains why international treaties do not become part of domestic law until their provisions have been incorporated into domestic law by an Act of Parliament.
44 See Chapter 10.

Parliament can, if it wishes, legislate to abolish or limit any prerogative power and in its place confer a statutory power. Thus, whereas GCHQ was once set up under the prerogative, it has now been put on a statutory footing by the Security Services Act 1993.

The House of Commons or Lords acting alone

Much of the time of each House of Parliament is occupied with debates and votes on bills and amendments to bills as part of the legislative process. There are, however, other types of debates which lead to votes on *resolutions* or *motions* which formally express the view of the majority of the particular House.[45] As in Dicey's day, it is clear that they do not, in themselves, have the force of law. For example in 1985, in an attempt to find out how the Commons viewed proposals to deregulate Sunday trading, the government proposed and won a division on a motion welcoming the Auld Committee's recommendations.[46] The vote did nothing to change the existing law: a bill receiving Royal Assent was needed for this.

The 'legislative' power of judges

In relation to the law courts, it is commonplace to speak of judicial decisions (especially those of the House of Lords) which depart from precedent as 'judicial legislation'. Judges, however, show great deference to Parliament and disclaim any right to 'legislate' generally saying that innovations ought to be left to Parliament. This, of course, does not mean that judges never make new law. The whole of the common law is the product of judicial creativity and this creativity has been nowhere more important than in the context of the principles of judicial review. Nor does it mean that judges are limited to the mechanical application of statutory provisions. Statutory interpretation is a vital judicial activity and can sometimes enable judges to explain legislation in ways that may surprise those responsible for its enactment.[47] However, the orthodox theory is that these activities are done with Parliament's implied consent and Parliament is ultimately free to alter the common law and to override judicial interpretations of its statutes. As Dicey put it:

> English judges do not claim or exercise any power to repeal a statute, whilst Acts of Parliament may override and constantly do override the law of the judges.[48]

This deserves further comment.

The courts have no power to pronounce any statute void on substantive grounds

The orthodox view is that courts in the United Kingdom have no jurisdiction to decide that any Act of Parliament is void on the ground its provisions are

[45] See generally Chapter 16.
[46] See Chapter 9.
[47] See Chapter 23.
[48] *Law of the Constitution*, pp. 60–1.

immoral or unjust,[49] or that it breaches the United Kingdom's obligations under international treaties. A good illustration is provided by *Cheney v Conn*[50] in which Ungoed-Thomas J rejected an argument made by a taxpayer that an income tax assessment under the Finance Act 1964 was unlawful because part of the money would be used for nuclear weapons which, it was submitted, was contrary to international law. The judge said:

> What the statute itself enacts cannot be unlawful, because what the statute says and provides is itself the law, and the highest form of law known to this country. It is the law which prevails over every other form of law, and it is not for the court to say that a parliamentary enactment, the highest law in this country, is illegal.

Until recently, this proposition was regarded as so fundamental that it was rarely questioned. However, the effect of Community law and developing ideas about fundamental rights force us to reconsider the legal basis for the theory. Countries which do have judicial review of primary legislation also tend to have written constitutions and/or a charter of fundamental rights against which the actions of the legislature may be judged. Similar provisions do not exist in the United Kingdom and therefore it cannot be said that Parliament's legislative competence is limited by express constitutional provisions. But, by the same token, nor is the jurisdiction of the courts limited by a written constitutional document. If a written constitution does not limit judicial power, what does? One possibility is statute. However, there is no *general* prohibition in any Act of Parliament preventing the courts from reviewing Acts of Parliament on substantive grounds.[51] Indeed, even if there were, it is not self-evident that this would be conclusive of the issue, or provide a satisfactory explanation for why judges cannot review legislation. After all, an attempt by Parliament to protect itself by enacting a general prohibition on judicial review of its actions might be exactly the type of power that the judges ought to be able to question.

The limitation on the courts' ability to review statute has not been imposed upon the judges by Parliament; rather it seems that the courts have restricted themselves as a matter of common law. Professor Wade has argued that this is no ordinary common law rule:

> The rule of judicial obedience [to Parliament] is in one sense a rule of the common law, but in another sense—which applies to no other rule of common law—it is the ultimate political fact upon which the whole system of legislation hangs.[52]

Wade goes on to argue that it follows from this that no Act of Parliament can alter or abolish the rule of parliamentary supremacy. If the rule is 'the ultimate

[49] Remember as a legal positivist Dicey drew a distinction between law and morality.
[50] [1968] 1 WLR 242.
[51] Compare specific provisions in statutes ('ouster clauses') which may seek to prevent judicial review of decisions or actions taken under powers conferred on a minister or other body by Act of Parliament: see further Chapter 22.
[52] H. W. R. Wade, 'The Basis of Legal Sovereignty' [1955] CLJ 172. See also P. J. Fitzgerald (ed.), *Salmond on Jurisprudence* (12th edn., 1966), p. 111.

political fact' does this mean that the rule will change if political facts alter? Are the facts now altering?

Parliament's legislative authority and Community law

A major challenge to the orthodox assertion that there are no legal limits on Parliament's legislative power has been provided by the United Kingdom's membership of the European Community. Judges in the United Kingdom no longer apply provisions of Acts of Parliament where those provisions are inconsistent with Community law. In short, statutes are no longer recognized by the courts as supreme law in the United Kingdom. Surely traditional thinking about parliamentary legislative supremacy cannot survive this revolution in the legal system? Its adherents, however, believe that it has: they argue that when Parliament enacted the European Communities Act 1972 to incorporate Community law into the legal systems of the United Kingdom it was merely *delegating* some of its law-making powers to other bodies (institutions of the European Community)[53] in much the same way as it frequently delegates power to ministers to make SIs. On this view

(a) the effect of Community law on the domestic system derives from Parliament;
(b) Community institutions have only been given power to legislate in strictly limited areas; and
(c) the 1972 Act could be repealed or amended at any time by Parliament if it wished to regain its legislative supremacy.

The European Communities Act 1972

The importance of this dramatic change in the way judges treat Acts of Parliament justifies a close look at the key provisions of the European Communities Act 1972. Sections 2 and 3 are particularly important. The drafting of s 2 is breathtaking in its obscurity.

> 2.—(1) All such rights, powers, liabilities, obligations and restrictions from time to time created and or arising by or under the Treaties, and all such remedies and procedures from time to time provided for by or under the Treaties, as in accordance with the Treaties are without further enactment to be given legal effect or used in the United Kingdom shall be recognised and available in law, and be enforced, allowed and followed accordingly; and the expression 'enforceable Community right' and similar expressions shall be read as referring to one to which this subsection applies.

This subsection achieves several things. First, it makes the various EC treaties a source of law *within* the UK legal systems.[54] As we mentioned earlier, international treaties are not part of domestic law unless and until they are

[53] On which see Chapters 13 and 14.

[54] For a full list of all the treaties, see T. C. Hartley, *The Foundations of European Community Law* (3rd edn., 1994), pp. 257–8. For an overview, see p. 75 above.

incorporated by an Act of Parliament. Section 2(1) goes further, however, and also incorporates without further enactment rights etc made 'under' the treaties prior to the United Kingdom's accession *and in the future*—in other words, rights etc contained in *secondary* EC legislation such as directives and regulations made by the Community institutions. The subsection also expresses the principle of 'direct effect' of Community law in national legal systems.[55] In essence it means that certain provisions in the EC treaties, in regulations and (less commonly) in directives are to be directly applied by UK courts.

Section 2(2) of the 1972 Act gives ministers powers to make SIs in order to bring UK law into line with Community law when they are required to do this by EC legislation.[56] Section 2(4) is so unclear that even distinguished Community lawyers disagree over some aspects of its meaning.[57] The emphasis is added.

> (4) The provision that may be made under subsection (2) above includes, subject to Schedule 2 to this Act, any such provision (of any such extent) as might be made by Act of Parliament, *and any enactment passed or to be passed, other than one contained in this Part of this Act, shall be construed and have effect subject to the foregoing provisions to this section*; but, except as may be provided by an Act of Parliament passed after this Act, Schedule 2 shall have effect in connection with the powers conferred by this and the following sections of this Act to make Orders in Council and regulations.

What does seem reasonably certain is that the overall effect of s 2(4) is to make Community law supreme within the UK legal systems. This is because Acts of Parliament, whether already enacted in 1973 or after this date, are to be interpreted and applied by the UK courts 'subject to the foregoing provisions' which includes, of course, s 2(1). That section had incorporated all Community law into the national legal systems, including the case law of the European Court of Justice. Long before the United Kingdom joined the Community, the ECJ had laid down this fundamental rule of primacy.[58]

> By contrast with ordinary international treaties, the EEC Treaty has created its own legal system which, on the entry into force of the Treaty, became an integral part of the legal systems of the Member States and which their courts are bound to apply. By creating a Community of unlimited duration, having its own institutions, its own personality, its own legal capacity and capacity of representation on the international plane and, more particularly, real powers stemming from a limitation of sovereignty or a transfer of powers from the States to the Community, the Member States have limited their sovereign rights, albeit within limited fields, and have thus created a body of law which binds both their nationals and themselves.

Section 3(1) of the 1972 Act makes it clear that issues of Community law are questions of law (contrary to the usual rule in the United Kingdom that

[55] See Chapter 29.
[56] See further Chapters 10 and 13.
[57] See T. C. Hartley, *Foundations of European Community Law*, p. 261; cf. Lawrence Collins, *European Community Law in the United Kingdom* (4th edn., 1990), pp. 28–9.
[58] *Costa v ENEL, Case 6/64* [1964] ECR 585, 593. See further Chapter 29.

questions of foreign law are treated as questions on which experts may give evidence at a trial). It also provides that the ECJ is the final court on EC matters and recognizes the procedure by which national courts may refer questions on Community law to the ECJ for a preliminary ruling under the provisions of Art 177 of the EC Treaty.[59]

The 1972 Act in practice

The practical legal effect of Community membership can be seen in *R v Secretary of State for Transport, ex p Factortame Ltd (No 2)*[60] where the domestic courts found themselves having to deal for the first time with litigation which sought directly to challenge the applicability of provisions contained in an Act of Parliament on the basis that they were inconsistent with Community law. In order to conserve fish stocks, the Community's common fisheries policy allocated fishing quotas to each of the member states. The UK government wanted to ensure that the trawlers whose catches counted against the UK quota were British-owned; Spanish fishermen were 'quota-hopping' by forming companies in England to buy fishing boats and registering them under the British flag, thus allowing their catches to count against the UK fish quotas rather than Spanish ones. Royal Assent was given to the Merchant Shipping Act in 1988. Section 14 required that three-quarters of the shareholders of any company that owned a British-registered trawler be either British citizens or domiciled in the United Kingdom. Over 90 Spanish-owned (and other) trawlers thus ceased to be entitled to be registered as British and have their catches counted against the British quota. Their owners applied for judicial review in London seeking, among other things, an order that s 14 of the Act was legally ineffective because it was inconsistent with Community law.[61] Following guidance from the ECJ, the House of Lords eventually granted the Spanish owners an interim injunction suspending the operation of the relevant parts of the 1988 Act while the case awaited final resolution.

The British newspapers put the *Factortame* decision on their front pages with headlines saying this was 'rewriting the British constitution'. Most British lawyers were rather less surprised as *Factortame* seemed to be a logical and inevitable consequence of s 2 of the European Communities Act 1972.

In 1994 the House of Lords again considered the lawfulness of provisions in an Act of Parliament: it declared that provisions in the Employment Protection (Consolidation) Act 1978, which gave less generous rights in respect of unfair dismissal to part-time workers (most of whom are female) than to full-timers (most of whom are male) were indirectly discriminatory against women contrary to Art 119 of the EC Treaty.[62] Interestingly, there

[59] As to Art 177 references, see Chapter 29.

[60] (Case C-213/89) [1991] 1 AC 603 (ECJ), 658 (HL). The case is discussed further in Chapter 26 below. See also D. Oliver, 'Fishing on an Incoming Tide' (1991) 54 MLR 442.

[61] Rights under Art 7 (prohibiting discrimination on the ground of nationality) and Art 58 (the right to freedom of establishment) of the EC Treaty.

[62] *R v Secretary of State for Employment, ex p Equal Opportunities Commission* [1995] 1 AC 1.

had been no Art 177 reference to the ECJ in this case (for guidance as to the interpretation of the EC Treaty) because the courts considered the issues of Community law *acte clair*;[63] for the first time, British judges determined without prompting that statutory provisions were not enforceable.

Is there a residual right to legislate contrary to Community law?

One doubt about the priority of Community law over Acts of Parliament remains. The expression 'any enactment passed or to be passed' in s 2(4) seems to be a rather half-hearted attempt at entrenchment. In other words it seeks to ensure that all Acts passed *after* the commencement of the 1972 Act will be interpreted by the UK courts as being intended by Parliament to be subject to the 1972 Act (including the rule that they will be effective only in so far as they comply with Community law). But what would an English court do in a case where a statute *intentionally and expressly* enacts provisions which are inconsistent with Community law? (This was not the situation either in *Factortame*, where the government actually believed that the Merchant Shipping Act 1988 was furthering Community fishing policy, or in the *Equal Opportunities Commission* case.) It is unlikely that the UK government would introduce such legislation into Parliament, but it could perhaps happen through a successful Private Member's Bill.

In these circumstances would a judge apply Community law or follow the statute? In a couple of early cases, Lord Denning MR considered this hypothetical problem. His conclusion (which was *obiter* and so not binding in any subsequent case) was that:[64]

> If the time should come when our Parliament deliberately passes an Act with the intention of repudiating the Treaty or any provision in it or intentionally of acting inconsistently with it and says so in express terms then I should have thought that it would be the duty of our courts to follow the statute of our Parliament.

There seems little real doubt that Lord Denning is correct in respect of a situation where the United Kingdom has expressed its intention to leave the Community entirely: ss 2 and 3 of the European Communities Act 1972 are not firmly entrenched into national law and there is no reason in national law why these sections could not be repealed by Parliament in the future. As we have noted it can be argued that by s 2 of the 1972 Act, Parliament has merely delegated for the time being some of its sovereign law-making powers to the Community institutions and that it is therefore able to reclaim these powers to itself by repealing or modifying s 2.

Moreover, it is possible for the United Kingdom to agree with other member states that it alone will not be bound by certain parts of Community law. This was done by a protocol in the Treaty of European Union under which

[63] In other words, the Community law on this issue is so clear that it does not require 'interpretation' by the ECJ.

[64] *Macarthys Ltd v Smith* [1979] 3 All ER 325, 329 and also [1981] 1 All ER 111, 120 (under Art 119 of the EC Treaty, a woman was entitled to equal pay even though the man had left before she joined a firm and she had taken his job afterwards; employment did not have to be contemporaneous). See also *Blackburn v Attorney General* [1971] 1 WLR 1037, 1040.

the United Kingdom is not bound by the provisions of the Social Chapter in that treaty.[65] It remains to be seen how this complex and politically contentious arrangement will work in practice.

Lord Denning goes further than this, however. He is suggesting that if Parliament expressly legislates contrary to Community law, without the consent of other member states and while the United Kingdom remains a member of the EC, then a court in the United Kingdom ought to apply the Act of Parliament. This is questionable. Much would depend on the exact form of words used by the Act. At first sight, though, Lord Denning appears to overlook the fact that a national court in these circumstances would be obliged under Community law to refer this uncertain issue to the ECJ for a preliminary ruling under Art 177 of the EC Treaty. It is likely that the ECJ would take the view that a UK court, as an institution within the EC legal order, has an obligation to give effective protection to Community law rights and enforce obligations created by Community law. This stems from Art 5 of the EC Treaty which provides that member states (including their courts) are required to

> take all appropriate measures, whether general or particular, to ensure fulfilment of the obligations arising out of this Treaty or resulting from action taken by the institutions of the Community. They shall facilitate the achievement of the Community's tasks. They shall abstain from any measure which would jeopardize the attainment of the objectives of this Treaty.

The national court would be bound by this obligation so long as the United Kingdom remains a member of the EC. Moreover, if a national court failed to do this, the EC Commission would have power to commence enforcement proceedings before the ECJ.[66]

THE SOCIAL REALITIES OF POLITICAL POWER

So far this chapter has outlined the main 'legal' rules of parliamentary supremacy; it is these rules which have traditionally been the focus for judges and practising lawyers and, until quite recently, for academic lawyers too. These legal rules, however, were not created and do not work in a vacuum for they assume a certain structure of political power and authority. In particular, Dicey's model of the constitution asserts that legal and political power are located in particular places within the system and that they flow in certain directions. Political power flows from the electorate and controls Parliament (in this sense it flows upwards) whereas legal power is located in Parliament and flows downwards. In this way political and legal powers are balanced against each other to create a self-correcting system which continues to function in accordance with the general needs and ethos of the society.

Many commentators have challenged Dicey's explanation of how the legal and political system fits reality. In later life even Dicey himself became less

[65] See further Chapter 13.
[66] See Chapter 29 below.

optimistic about the system. Certainly his model of parliamentary democracy begs questions about the nature of political power, how public opinion is formed, how MPs are made aware of it and how they respond. We therefore now need to examine how well the orthodox model of political power stands up.[67] The issues to be considered are important for lawyers, not least because if we reject Dicey's understanding of politics, we might also find ourselves rejecting the justifications for Parliament's legislative supremacy.

What exactly is power? How, and by whom, is it exercised? These questions of social and political science are important ones for students and practitioners of law. For example, we have seen that two ideas are central to Dicey's theory: one is the importance of individuals; the other is the idea that 'law' can be understood as commands of a sovereign. The work of social and political scientists may show that it is misleading to focus on individual electors as the basic unit of political power. It might show, for instance, that political power in the constitution is in fact exercised by various organized *groups*.[68] Social science might also reveal that power is exercised in ways other than by making decisions and issuing authoritative commands backed by sanctions. While central to legal positivism, for many social scientists such an instrumental view of power—that a institution or person intentionally makes a decision, then takes action to implement it in order to effect change—is too limited and simplistic.[69]

An illustration from the case studies may be helpful at this point. Consider the struggles over whether or not Sunday trading ought to be regulated.[70] To understand what happened (and so, perhaps, to go on to generalize about how the constitution works more broadly), social scientists could investigate various aspects of the episode. What roles were played by pressure groups, business corporations, individual voters, consumers, the news media, MPs, government and others in an attempt to influence and win public opinion? What social, political and organizational factors made different local authorities adopt different policies towards the enforcement of the old restrictive trading rules? Why in this episode was 'law' an ineffective tool for controlling social behaviour? What factors determined that the deregulatory Shops Bill failed to become law in 1985 whereas the Sunday Trading Act succeeded nine years later?

Sovereignty, pluralism and public choice

We now introduce three broad approaches to theorizing about where power lies, or ought to lie. Each has practical implications for our constitutional

[67] For more detailed critical appraisal of Dicey's model constitution and its relation to social reality, see A. H. Birch, *Representative and Responsible Government: an essay on the British constitution* (1964), especially Chapter 5, and P. P. Craig, *Public Law and Democracy in the United Kingdom and USA* (1990), especially Chapter 2.

[68] See the discussion of pluralism, p. 125 below.

[69] For one thing power may be exerted by 'non-decision-making', in other words by preventing pressure for change or action from building up in the first place. See Steven Lukes, *Power: A radical view* (1974).

[70] For an overview of the case study, see Chapter 2.

arrangements and the functions which public law serves. First we question Dicey's view that ultimate political power resides with the electorate.[71] We then consider the theory that political power is dispersed between different groups in society which compete with one another, and the state, for control and influence over public policy: this is usually referred to as a *pluralistic* view of power. Finally we look at *public choice* theory. This rejects the democratic political process as the main means of meeting the needs and desires of individuals. It is hostile to the activities of politicians, civil servants and sectional interest groups. Public choice theorists see power as residing in every individual who is best able to exercise it through the mechanisms of the market.

Notions of political sovereignty in the electorate

As we have seen, for Dicey political sovereignty lies with the electorate: 'the electors can *in the long run* always enforce their will'.[72] Note that the electorate is not the same as the general public. Certainly when Dicey was writing many people (including all women) had no right to vote. It is unclear how precisely Dicey envisaged that the electorate would exert its influence and control within the constitutional system. On this he tended to be vague:

> the arrangements of the constitution are now [1885] such as to ensure that the will of the electors shall by regular and constitutional means always assert itself as the predominant influence in the country.[73]

The most important of these 'arrangements' was the regular participation by people in parliamentary elections by voting for MPs, although in later life he also advocated the use of referendums on particular issues. How effective are these arrangements as a way of the electorate exercising political power?

Representative democracy in Parliament

Several factors combine to reduce the importance of the act of voting in parliamentary elections as an effective channel of powers. First, it was commonplace in Dicey's time, and still today, to view MPs not as delegates of their constituents bound by the electorate's views to vote in particular ways, nor as representatives for particular sectional interest groups, but rather as independent actors who once elected speak and vote in Parliament according to their own conscience and their view of the national interest. This idea is associated with Edmund Burke, the eighteenth-century writer and politician. In his famous speech to the electors of Bristol in 1774, Burke asserted that Parliament was:[74]

71 At other times, other 'political sovereigns' have been identified. For instance during the reign of the Stuart kings in the early 1600s, the monarch was accepted by most people as having absolute authority. This stemmed from a theory that the king ruled by divine right: see p. 46, n. 31.

72 *Law of the Constitution*, p. 73 (emphasis added).

73 *Law of the Constitution*, p. 73.

74 Quoted in A. H. Birch, *Representative and Responsible Government*, p. 29.

> not a *congress* of ambassadors from different hostile interests; which interests each must maintain, as an agent and advocate, against the other agents and advocates; but Parliament is a *deliberative* assembly of *one* nation, with *one* interest, that of the whole; where, not local purposes, not local prejudices ought to guide, but the general good, resulting from the general reason of the whole.

In short, once elected, MPs acquire independence from the electorate and interest groups. Some MPs, mostly in the Conservative Party, still claim that this is the position. Certainly this view forms one justification for the rules of parliamentary privilege which seek to protect MPs from illegitimate threats from outsiders attempting to persuade them to vote or act in particular ways.[75] In the past, parliamentary privilege even prevented the publication of reports about debates in Parliament on the ground that this would be seen as an 'admission of accountability to the electors'.[76] If Burke's view is still correct electors have relatively little power over MPs except to *select* them every four years or so.

With the organization of mass-membership political parties from the 1830s onwards, the Burkian ideal of independent MPs, entrusted by the electorate to use their conscience for the national interest, began to appear unconvincing (if ever it was). Throughout the twentieth century, almost all successful candidates have stood for election as a representative of one of the main political parties; and once elected they are expected to support party policy in Parliament. Labour MPs are bound by party rules to accept and conform to the 'programme, principles and policy of the Party'. Although the Conservative Party internal rules speak of the independence of MPs, a Conservative MP who defies party discipline by abstaining or voting against party policy in Parliament may cease to be recognized as a Conservative MP by the party (though remaining the MP for his or her constituency).[77]

It is difficult to see how party discipline and manifesto commitments provide particularly effective ways for the electorate to make known their views to MPs. The manifestos published by each party before a general election refer to specific items of proposed legislation only in the most general terms, if at all. Governments develop many ideas on policy and legislation between elections. In any event, research has shown that voters often disagree with many proposals which are included in the manifesto of the party which they support.

A second reason why voting in elections may not be effective at influencing the content of legislation is that the first-past-the-post electoral system creates a Parliament which is 'unrepresentative' of public opinion, in that the political complexion of the House of Commons tends not to reflect overall national support for each party. In particular, it leads to the third largest party (the

[75] Although the privileges were originally intended to protect Parliament from the monarch rather than the electorate. See Chapter 8 below.

[76] See Birch, *Representative and Responsible Government*, p. 15.

[77] For instance in 1995 nine Conservative MPs, 'Eurosceptics' who failed to support the government in Commons' votes relating to government policy on Europe, had the party whip removed for several months.

Liberal Democrats) having disproportionately few seats and minority parties (such as the Greens) having no representation at all.[78]

Thirdly, in discussions of representative parliamentary democracy it is easy to overlook the fact that only one of the two Houses of Parliament is actually elected: the House of Lords remains selected by the hereditary principle and the appointment of life peers. Amendments to government bills by the upper House can have important impact on legislation,[79] yet the existence of the unelected part of the legislature presents a challenge to the notion that the content of legislation is influenced by public opinion as represented in Parliament through the electoral system.[80]

Referendums

Another way in which the general public might assert its political sovereignty is by the use of referendums in which electors are asked to vote 'yes' or 'no' on a particular proposal. In later life Dicey came to advocate their use. Only four referendums have been held during the 1900s: on whether or not Northern Ireland should remain part of the United Kingdom;[81] on whether the United Kingdom should remain a member of the European Community;[82] and in 1979, over devolution of government and legislative powers to Wales and Scotland.[83] There have been frequent calls for a referendum on the restoration of capital punishment (abolished in 1966 against the wishes of the majority of the population, according to informal opinion polls) and also on steps towards further European integration (such as the adoption of a common currency throughout the Community). More generally, though, referendums are not, and are unlikely to become, a way of the electorate directly controlling

78 See p. 47.

79 See Chapter 8 below.

80 These and other related issues are explored in more detail in a later chapter, in the context of the legislative battles over deregulation of Sunday trading. Here the House of Lords was more than merely a 'revising chamber' for the 1985 bill, as the bill was introduced there; deregulation of Sunday trading had not been part of the Conservative manifesto at the 1983 general election; a Labour MP complained that Conservative MPs had been 'paid' by the pro-deregulation Shopping Hours Reform Council; there was much discussion about the use of 'free votes' (divisions in which MPs are not instructed by their party whips which way to vote); one Conservative MP even complained that he had been subject to a 'threat' by a supermarket chain that if he did not support deregulation they would tell their Sunday workers that the MP was destroying their jobs. Above all, the Sunday trading episode raises important questions about what is meant by *public* opinion: is the opinion of every individual voter to be given weight, or does the constitution regard the informed and organized 'opinions' of pressure and interest groups as more important?

81 Every referendum needs statutory authorization—here the Northern Ireland (Border Poll) Act 1972.

82 Referendum Act 1975. The United Kingdom had joined the EC two years previously and so the referendum was, in effect, asking for retrospective validation or rejection of that decision. Prime Minister Harold Wilson almost certainly supported the idea of the referendum on this issue primarily as a way of resolving the deep divisions within the Labour Party on the question.

83 Scotland Act 1978; Wales Act 1978. Both Acts required there to be a qualified majority of the electorate in favour in both countries, rather than just a bare majority.

legislation. One reason for this is that they may be seen to challenge the very idea of parliamentary representative democracy.

Majoritarian democracy

Whether it is through the election of MPs, or more directly through voting in referendums, many people today would question whether it is right that legislation should always reflect the wishes of the majority of the electorate. This is especially so where popular opinion favours legislation which discriminates against minorities in society (for example, opinion polls suggest that a majority of the population are against homosexuals having equal rights). There is no reason to believe that the majority will always do what is wise. Dicey's analysis of political and legal sovereignty contains no convincing explanation of how the majority could be prevented from oppressing minorities.[84]

An elective dictatorship?

Even leaving aside the many questions about *how* the electorate may make their views known on the content of legislation, the orthodox model is now subject to two further fundamental challenges. The first is concerned with the concentration of power. The orthodox theory assumes that MPs, representing the people, control government. This no longer fits reality, if ever it did. Today the collective power of ministers dominates Parliament. Although the executive is drawn from Parliament,[85] once in office it exercises a whip hand by dictating how its supporting MPs will vote, determining the parliamentary timetable, controlling how long debates will be, what legislation is introduced[86] and in the last resort effectively determining when Parliament will be dissolved (within its maximum five-year lifespan) and a general election called. Government also keeps tight controls over the flow of information available to MPs and the public. It is therefore implausible today to argue that political power moves exclusively in one direction—from the electorate, to MPs and then to government. Parliament has at most power to ratify, veto and legitimate the exercise of executive and legislative power.

Concern about the government's control of Parliament surfaced in popular discussions during the 1970s. In the words of Lord Hailsham, a former Conservative MP and Lord Chancellor:[87]

> the sovereignty of Parliament has increasingly become, in practice, the sovereignty of the Commons, and the sovereignty of the Commons has increasingly become the sovereignty of the government . . . which controls the party whips, the party machine and the civil service.

[84] On this, see Chapter 6.

[85] On the absence of any strong principle of separation of powers in the United Kingdom, see p. 40.

[86] Bills introduced by backbench MPs normally have no chance of actually reaching the statute book: in relation to Sunday trading, see further Chapter 9.

[87] Lord Hailsham, *The Dilemma of Democracy: diagnosis and prescription* (1978).

This Hailsham called the 'elective dictatorship'. That was said during a period of Labour government. Concern about the waning of parliamentary power is not confined to people on the Right in politics. Indeed the period of Conservative government since 1979 has seen a considerable centralization of power within the United Kingdom. The independent political decision-making powers of local authorities have been dramatically reduced.[88] The growth of non-departmental public bodies (so-called quangos), giving ministers powers of appointment rather than selection by elections, is further evidence of the process.[89] Reference is also made to the Thatcher governments' 'distaste for parliamentary accountability'.[90] In the light of these tendencies it is not surprising that it is now people in the Centre and Left of British politics who are most vocal in their concern about the concentration of power.

Sovereignty, the nation state and the internationalization of power

The second fundamental challenge to the notion that ultimate political power resides in the British electorate, and legal sovereignty in Parliament, is posed by the internationalization of political decision-making and law-making. Political and legal sovereignty, it is often said, has been 'lost' to the institutions abroad. Both the executive and legislature in Britain are now constrained in many areas of public policy—mainly regarding the functioning of the internal market and many aspects of European Union social policy—by decisions taken by the Commission and the Council of Ministers. Of course the United Kingdom participates in the latter, through ministers, but as more and more Council decisions are now taken under the qualified majority voting procedure the ability of British ministers to assert 'sovereign' powers by vetoing a proposal has diminished significantly. Issues surrounding sovereignty and Community law are considered in more detail in Chapter 13.

Pluralism: political power shared by groups

So far this chapter has considered the orthodox view, upon which the theory of parliamentary legislative supremacy rests, that ultimate political power resides with one identifiable group within society, the electorate. A number of influential theorists, however, have questioned the very notion that political sovereignty can or should rest in any one person, group or institution. One of them, Harold Laski, saw society:[91]

> not as a pyramid in which the State sits crowned upon the summit, but as a system of cooperating interests through which, and in which, the individual finds his

[88] See p. 67.
[89] See p. 62.
[90] P. Dunleavy *et al.*, 'Prime Ministers and the Commons: patterns of behaviour' (1990) 68 Public Administration 123. See also C. Harlow and R. Rawlings, *Pressure Through Law*, p. 297 (quoted at p. 87 above).
[91] *Grammar of Politics* (1925), pp. 286–7.

scheme of values . . . Law then emerges as the evaluation of the interests by the interweaving of interests. It is a function of the whole social structure and not some given aspect of it . . .

For pluralists, politics is about the competition and interplay between different interest or pressure groups.[92] Trade unions, consumer groups, employer organizations, bodies such as the National Farmers' Union and welfare rights and environmental groups put issues on to the political agenda, develop policies and seek to persuade the public and government. On this view of politics, it is also important for there to be effective local democracy as well as at national level; conflict between local authorities and central government is not a bad thing.

Pluralism has repercussions for the constitution and the public law system. For one thing, it throws doubt on the image of strong government and relatively weak individuals. It also challenges the notion that the electorate can be viewed as a single homogeneous whole; on the contrary, it highlights the degree to which there are differences between sections of society. If the pluralist view is correct, then the function of institutions and processes may be seen as being to facilitate the making of various claims, to structure conflicts and to produce collectively made decisions. Parliament is to be seen as one forum in which these diverse claims can be articulated and collective decisions made; and it does this in a necessarily complex and subtle way. In formal terms, MPs are elected to represent their geographical constituencies, but they are all also members of a political party,[93] and MPs may act as 'advisors' or be 'sponsored' by organizations (such as trade unions, the Police Federation and so on).[94]

Lobbying for legislative change

The pluralist view sees consultation and participation through political organizations as key constitutional activities. These are essential features of the policy-making and legislative processes. As seen in Chapter 9, the Sunday trading saga provides a striking illustration of this. The Auld Committee heard evidence from various groups, including church organizations, bodies representing business interests and trade unions prior to the formulation of government policy in 1984. And throughout the legislative process—in the

[92] How to classify groups is a notoriously vexed question for social scientists. Some groups exist to represent the economic interests of their members, such as trade unions and the Confederation of British Industry. Other groups have been set up to campaign on single or fairly specific issues, such as the Keep Sunday Special Campaign. For present purposes it is not essential for us to differentiate between them. Some are large organizations with paid research and campaigning staff. Other groups, such as local amenity groups, are small, informal and run on shoe-string budgets. What the groups have in common is that they attempt to exert influence in an *organized* way. See further G. Alderman, *Pressure Groups and Government in Great Britain* (1984).

[93] The Labour Party is strongly associated with the representation of trade unions; the Conservatives with business interests. See further Chapter 8.

[94] On representation by MPs, see further Chapters 8 and 9 below.

1984 Shops Bill and the 1994 Sunday Trading Act—the Home Office (the government department responsible for this area of policy) was subject to intense lobbying from well-organized and -resourced interest groups representing different viewpoints.

Litigation as a method of pressure

Citizen participation through interest or pressure groups, and the collective influence of business corporations, is not confined to the processes leading up to legislation: the court room may also provide opportunities. Litigation can be a method of campaigning and influencing policy formulation; it is a way in which *collective* aims are pursued and is not confined to the resolution of disputes between individuals, or between individuals and the state.[95] The litigation in the GCHQ case study clearly had the aim of furthering collective rights; so too did the court cases over Sunday trading, even though the prosecutions and applications for injunctions were brought against particular corporations (especially B&Q plc) rather than the interest group to which they belonged.[96] Even though an interest group may not 'win' a case by obtaining a favourable judgment from the court, litigation may nevertheless be a successful tool to use if it keeps an issue on the political agenda and improves the group's profile.[97]

Pluralists thus see litigation as part of the wider political process and as far more than the impartial application of legal rules to individual problems. Access for groups to the legal system therefore plays an important role in the political life of the system and should be encouraged by liberal rules of standing, appropriate court procedures and by adequate public funding. We look more closely at these issues later in the book.

Direct collective action

Another tactic used by groups is to organize direct action which may or may not involving breaking the law. From pluralist perspectives, such activity is legitimate in a democracy because formal institutions such as Parliament do not have a monopoly—or even, perhaps, any primacy—as fora for debating issues of public importance. There is a long tradition in the United Kingdom of groups using civil disobedience as a technique of pressure. For instance, in the early years of the twentieth century public demonstrations, people chaining themselves to railings of public buildings and hunger strikes were a central part of the eventually successful Suffragette campaign for votes for women in parliamentary elections. More recently, confrontational demonstrations have been associated with pressure groups against nuclear weapons,

[95] See further Carol Harlow and Richard Rawlings, *Pressure Through Law* (1992); Tony Prosser, *Test Cases for the Poor* (1983); and David Feldman, 'Public Interest Litigation and Constitutional Theory in Comparative Perspective' (1992) 55 MLR 44.

[96] On the litigation strategies over Sunday trading, see further Chapter 29. For discussion of the ability of groups to gain access to the courts, see Chapter 21.

[97] For instance the litigation on environmental issues brought by Greenpeace: see p. 492.

blood sports, opposition to the Community Charge, the transportation of live animals, road building and other environmental problems, and claims for rights for disabled people. Picketing of entrances to work places has also long been used by trade unions as a way putting pressure on employers and non-striking workers.

Confrontational demonstrations and picketing can easily be seen in stark terms, either as the practical embodiment of freedom of expression in a tolerant society or as illegitimate intimidation by mob tactics. In the United Kingdom, neither the common law nor legislation grants to individuals or groups any positive right to assemble and protest. There is only the residual freedom to do what is not contrary to the criminal and civil law. The courts have been scathing of public bodies which succumb to direct action. In *R v Coventry Airport, ex p Phoenix Aviation*, Simon Brown LJ warned that:

> tempting though it may sometimes be for public authorities to yield too readily to threats of disruption [here, by animal rights protesters at harbours and airports], they must expect the courts to review any such decision with particular rigour—this is not an area where they can be permitted a wide measure of discretion.[98]

The Public Order Act 1986 created new statutory criminal offences of riot, violent disorder and affray. Under s 51 of the Police Act 1964 it is an offence to assault, or wilfully obstruct, a police officer in the execution of his duty. Other offences which protesters may commit include obstructing the highway and acting in breach of the peace. Organizers of protest marches must give written notice of their intended action to the local police station and restrictions may be imposed on their proposed action, or it may be prohibited altogether for up to three months at a time.[99]

In short, the forms of collective direct action that can be lawfully taken by groups are restricted. People who decide not to comply with a law because they object to it are subject to the same sanctions as those who break the law for less principled motives. There is no doubt, however, that law breaking can be a powerful impetus for change. For example, deregulation of Sunday shopping may have been achieved more slowly (or not at all) had shopkeepers —including major retail chains—not deliberately set out to flout s 47 of the Shops Act 1950. The principled non-payment of the Community Charge was also a factor in the government's decision to abandon that tax in 1992 after only four years.

Problems with pluralism

Critics of pluralism point to problems. One is that the image of groups interacting with one another and government to arrive at collective decisions overlooks the fact that not all interests are represented by groups or have equal opportunities to participate in the political system. In the battles over

[98] [1995] 3 All ER 37, 62.

[99] Public Order Act 1986, ss 11, 12.

deregulation of Sunday trading, for example, while there were highly organized networks of organizations representing the interests of retailers, shop workers and the churches, there was no significant group putting forward the views of the many people all over England and Wales who lived near supermarkets and who were directly affected by the increased disruption of seven-day-a-week trading.

Another potential problem is that pressure and interest groups may be thought to have inadequate internal democratic controls or mechanisms for accountability to their members. In short, it may be argued that some groups are not truly representative.[100] This was a charge often levied against trade unions in the 1960s and 1970s, when it was said that union leaders were out of touch with the real wishes of their members. It prompted the Conservative government during the 1980s to impose requirements of secret ballots in elections for officers, before industrial action is called and decisions taken to give financial support to political parties (in effect, of course, the Labour Party).

Another attack on the idea and practice of pluralism is made on the grounds that the activities of organized groups undermine parliamentary democracy. Sometimes the criticism is that one group manages to exert undue influence and power. Often it is that the very existence of well-organized sectional groups is dangerous. Attacks from the Right focused on the political power which trade unions were said to have to influence governments, particularly during the 1960s and 1970s. One professor of law had this to say:[101]

> In public law unions are not only consulted by governments on every matter, but assert and dictate their views, arrogantly claim to represent the people of the country and make and unmake governments . . . They represent the gravest threat to democracy, liberty and economic progress and prosperity yet known and constantly call for the law to be kept out of industrial relations to enable anarchy to be promoted.

From a different standpoint, Harden and Lewis write that:[102]

> Traditional assumptions concerning cabinet government are no longer sustainable: the major locus of public power in Britain is focused around a federation of the great departments of state and their client groups.

They are describing a phenomenon known as corporatism, 'whereby a centralised state combines with the giant enterprises of modern capitalism to channel power into the hands of a powerful elite'.[103] The term corporatism describes a particular type of pluralism under which tripartite arrangements existed between government, organized groups representing workers (especially the TUC) and business. Specific institutions were set up to facilitate

[100] See p. 486.

[101] David Walker, *The Oxford Companion to Law* (1980), p. 1229. Lord Hailsham makes similar claims in *The Dilemma of Democracy*.

[102] Ian Harden and Norman Lewis, *The Noble Lie: the British constitution and the rule of law* (1986), p. 70.

[103] See further Carol Harlow and Richard Rawlings, *Law and Administration* (1984), p. 49.

this, notably the National Economic Development Council (NEDC) with its network of sub-committees which sought to develop policies in respect of various sectors of the economy. The main strategy for controlling the economy became a prices and incomes policy which was negotiated between the three groups. As Grant says:[104]

> The pressure groups thus became intermediaries of a new kind between their members and the state, not simply articulating their members' views to government, but sharing in the development of policy, and acquiring a responsibility for its implementation which may include the disciplining of members.

Public choice theory: empowerment through markets

Antipathy to academic theories and the practical implementation of pluralism led to the development of a new set of theories about the proper role of government, what power is and how it ought to be exercised. Public choice theories have been put into practice by many of the policies pursued by the Conservatives since 1979.[105]

At the heart of the public choice view of power is a belief that the political process (including the activities of government, civil servants, local government officers and interest and pressure groups) is unresponsive to the needs and desires of individuals. This is because the participants are motivated by their own private interests of ambition, status and pay. In short, they are manipulative and self-serving. Interest groups are blamed for exploiting events for their own ends and undermining the efficiency of markets. The restrictive practices of trade unions, for example, are from this perspective seen as a prime example of interest group activity preventing economic progress. Professional groups, such as the British Medical Association and its opposition to reforms in the National Health Service, provide another illustration of this phenomenon, as does the Law Society's objection to opening up conveyancing to competition from outside the solicitors' profession. Representative democracy is also suspect, with participation through periodic elections for MPs or local councillors seen as giving almost no power at all to individuals since the choice available to voters is limited to the three 'packages' of policies put forward by the main political parties. In any event, how a particular individual votes is unlikely to affect the overall outcome of elections.

Public choice theory therefore favours 'de-politicization' of the supply of public goods and services (such as health care, low-cost housing and education), with individuals empowered as *consumers participating in markets* rather than as voters for politicians.

The participation of individuals in the free market is seen as intrinsically superior to collective decision-making through the political system and public administration. Advocates of public choice theory therefore call for 'less

[104] Wyn Grant, *Pressure Groups, Politics and Democracy in Britain* (1989), p. 32.

[105] For a fuller explanation and trenchant critique, see Peter Self, *Government by the Market? The Politics of Public Choice* (1993).

government'. Where a continuing governmental presence is necessary, they argue that market concepts should replace traditional notions of public administration. Some of the particular proposals by public choice theorists, such as issuing every citizen with an education voucher to be used to purchase schooling either at (former) state schools or in the private sector, have yet to be adopted by the Conservative government at the national level. However, many other proposals have been. These have been described in Chapter 3 and include:

- the privatization of state-owned utilities and public corporations;
- the selling off of publicly-owned low-rent housing;
- the creation of an internal market within the NHS and the introduction of CCT by local authorities;
- giving to head teachers and school governors responsibility for their school's financial management;
- the provision to parents of more information about examination results achieved by pupils;
- more recently giving schools greater freedom to select their pupils.

The Citizen's Charter initiative is also an aspect of this market-oriented approach.[106] Charters are intended to identify the level of performance which citizens can expect from those providing public services. If these levels are not achieved citizens are given opportunities to complain and in some cases to obtain financial compensation. With increased competition between providers of services, consumers are free to take their custom elsewhere—with the result that low standards of service will lead to a loss of business and potentially loss of revenue.

In *Government by the Market?* Peter Self makes fundamental criticisms of public choice theory. He argues that corporatism

> has not (despite much rhetoric) been dismantled but has been turned into a narrow partnership between government and business on appointed boards, with other interests largely excluded . . . Democracy requires a return to a more balanced pattern of pluralist representation, while renewing its capacity to judge claims fairly and to control the more powerful interests.[107]

Self is also critical of 'the thin concept of citizenship' offered by many public choice theorists who assume that everyone is motivated by self-interest and politics is seen as primarily about the satisfaction of personal wants.[108]

A NEW VIEW OF POWER AND PUBLIC LAW?

The orthodox theoretical framework about the location of power owes much to Dicey's argument that political sovereignty resides with the electorate and

[106] *Citizen's Charter* (1991) Cm 1599. See further Chapter 15.
[107] *Government by the Market?*, p. 267 and Chapter 6.
[108] *Government by the Market?*, p. 256.

legal sovereignty with Parliament. However, the foundations of this framework have taken a battering. His view that the electorate exercises ultimate political power has for many years lacked plausibility, yet this view is still assumed to provide the main democratic justification for Parliament's legal supremacy. Given the criticisms of its democratic foundations, can continued faith in the concept of parliamentary supremacy be justified? Should the courts remain subservient to Parliament's will? Is there not a broader notion of democracy that might justify restricting the power of Parliament?

As we have noted in relation to Community law, ideas associated with parliamentary supremacy are changing and a new understanding is emerging. There are indications that the judges are no longer content with a role limited to policing the 'intention of Parliament' as expressed in statutes. The courts are now adopting a far more ambitious role within the system with some judges questioning the traditional legal dominance of Parliament.[109] One High Court judge has described the notion of the sovereignty of Parliament as 'outdated'.[110] Another has said that:[111]

> . . . we have today in this country . . . a new and still emerging constitutional paradigm, no longer Dicey's supreme Parliament to whose will the rule of law must finally bend, but of a bi-polar sovereignty of the Crown in Parliament and the Crown in its courts, to each of which the Crown's ministers are answerable—politically to Parliament, legally to the courts. That the government of the day has no separate sovereignty in this paradigm is both axiomatic and a reminder of the sharpest of all lessons of eastern Europe: that it is when state is collapsed into party that democracy founders.

In the next chapter we turn to consider the idea that the constitution and law has to provide more than merely a set of tools for government to pursue its policies. The constitutional system and public law are not just about enabling power to be exercised: they are also about the need to impose constraints upon the powers of government and possibly also on Parliament itself.

Questions

1. Consider each of the case studies summarized in Chapter 2. How well do the events in each one fit into Dicey's model constitution in which ultimate political power lies with the electorate and Parliament has legislative supremacy?

2. Would you have been in favour of holding a referendum on whether to deregulate Sunday shopping?

3. On 6 September 1994 *The Times* carried the following report:

> Macfarlanes, the city solicitors, are warning clients with large shops that open on Sundays that they could still be fined up to £50,000 if they do not give notice of opening to local authorities under the new Sunday Trading Act. Roy Edey, who once worked for Macfarlanes, says that the shops are 'breaking the Fourth Commandment'.

[109] See further Chapter 20.
[110] Sir John Laws, 'Law and Democracy' [1995] PL 72.
[111] Sir Stephen Sedley, 'Human Rights: a Twenty-First Century Agenda' [1995] PL 386, 389.

> His private prosecutions under the old Shops Act are still being heard. Last Thursday, Kennedy's, a chain of garden centres, was fined £75 and ordered to pay costs of £125 to Mr Edey. But Mr Edey was ordered to pay costs of nearly £2,000 to Sainsbury and Safeway in Folkestone when his case against them was thrown out on a technicality. His reward will, no doubt, be in heaven.

Three days later the editor published a letter from Mr Edey.

> Sir, The reference to my activities over unlawful Sunday trading requires clarification. . . . I am to ask the Court of Appeal to declare the provisions of the Sunday Trading Act 1994 unconstitutional and unlawful. The Home Secretary misinformed the Sovereign and Parliament in alleging that the former law was muddled and unenforceable. My successful private prosecutions have shown that argument to be invalid . . . If my action fails there will be nothing to stop a future government with a majority carrying through Parliament a measure to abolish the monarchy, the Church of England or even the loyal Opposition in Parliament.

(a) Imagine you were a barrister instructed to advise Mr Edey in 1994 in his proposed proceedings. Write a short opinion setting out your reasoned views, supported by authorities, on his prospects for success.
(b) Is Mr Edey right to say that there is *nothing* to stop Parliament abolishing the monarchy and the Official Opposition?

4. A backbench MP believes that 'a married woman's place is in the home'. In order to encourage married women to leave the workforce he introduces a Private Member's Bill permitting employers to pay married women less than men. The bill will amend the Sex Discrimination Act 1975 by including a new section:

> x.—(1) Nothing in this Act shall make it unlawful for a person, in relation to employment by him at an establishment in Great Britain, to discriminate against a married woman—
>
> (a) in the arrangements he makes for the purpose of determining who should be offered that employment, or
> (b) in the terms on which he offers her that employment, or
> (c) by refusing or deliberately omitting to offer her that employment.
>
> (2) Subsection (1) shall be applied in the courts and tribunals of the United Kingdom notwithstanding any inconsistency with the law of the European Community.

Imagine that as soon as the bill receives Royal Assent the Equal Opportunities Commission applies for judicial review seeking a declaration that the new provisions are contrary to Art 119 of the EC Treaty[112] and therefore ineffective. You are a judge in the Court of Appeal. Write a short reasoned judgment.

[112] Art 119 provides: 'Each Member State shall . . . maintain the application of the principle that men and women should receive equal pay for equal work . . .'

6

PRINCIPLES OF LIMITED GOVERNMENT

INTRODUCTION

The previous chapter presents the constitution as a system of power, the dominant theme being that, provided government has the support of Parliament, it can generally use legislation to achieve whatever policy it considers desirable or necessary. We now explore a rather different view of the role of law within the constitution. The theme of this chapter is that the system is not merely a conveyor-belt for government policy; the constitution also reflects certain 'principles' which limit governmental power and which, in particular, help to protect the rights and liberties of citizens.

A government *could*, for instance, rule by fear and force but if it did so it would lack legitimacy. Government *could* perhaps implement its policies more easily by side-stepping or restricting judicial and parliamentary scrutiny of its activities. Elected local authorities *could* be abolished to ensure that there are no other public bodies capable of frustrating the work of central government. People suspected of plotting to undermine the state by violence or subversion *could* be picked up off the streets and detained in prison without charge or trial; they could also be tortured. A minority group *could* be singled out as a scapegoat by government and officially vilified and discriminated against in order to appease popular opinion. Many would say government action such as this is wrong. Surely a constitutional system ought to be able to prevent it happening?

For some commentators, the current constitutional arrangements in the United Kingdom provide insufficient constraints on government power and fail to ensure reciprocity between the interests of individual citizens, groups within society and the goals of government. As seen in previous chapters, parliamentary supremacy puts statutes at the top of the hierarchy of legal rules.[1] If Parliament is now controlled by government (and not, as Dicey assumed, the other way around) this may give too much unrestricted power to the government. But equally if, as Dicey asserted, MPs and government *are* responsive to public opinion, there may be a danger that the views of the majority will trample over the rights and interests of unpopular minorities. For instance, the majority may want to ban an extremist religious or political

[1] See Chapter 5.

group from meeting and publicizing its views, but this may well be contrary to a desirable principle of 'freedom of expression'.

The legal limits on government

There are at least three different senses in which we can talk broadly about 'law' as a controlling and limiting device, each of which is explored in this chapter. First there are *constitutional conventions*.[2] These are habitual practices regarded as binding, such as that ministers make themselves answerable to Parliament for the work of their departments and that Royal Assent is now never withheld from bills which have passed through Parliament. Although most conventions are the result of pragmatic responses to circumstances, it can be argued that important principles do lie at the heart of them. As discussed below, there is much debate over whether such 'conventions' rules are different in nature from 'legal' rules. Secondly there is *the notion of the 'rule of law'*.[3] In its minimal sense this means that government ministers and officials, like everyone else, ought to comply with particular legal rules contained in legislation[4] and the common law. A larger and more complex claim may also be made: that the rule of law means there is, or ought to be, a constitutional ethic regarding legality which pervades the ways in which government acts and which imposes limitations on all the institutions of the constitution, including Parliament. A third, and more specific, sense in which 'law' may be said to constrain government in the interests of liberty is the need for government to respect and comply with the United Kingdom's *international treaty obligations dealing with human rights*.[5]

These three sources of constraint on government are not dependent on legislative enactment. They cannot easily or quickly be changed by a government with a majority in Parliament. They may also operate as a brake on government power because they are underpinned by basic principles of constitutional propriety to a greater extent than is statute law (which is often more concerned with giving legal effect to shorter-term policy considerations). Discovering the 'principles' of any constitution is not, however, easy.

What are principles and how are they to be discovered?

In the United Kingdom the task of identifying principles is made more difficult because there is no single constitutional document to use as a guide.[6]

[2] See p. 137 below.
[3] See p. 141 below.
[4] If the United Kingdom had a written constitution and a modern Bill of Rights, the rule of law would require compliance with these written instruments as well as ordinary legislation.
[5] See p. 158 below.
[6] Even if there were a single document it would almost certainly not contain a complete and uncontroversial statement of constitutional values and principles. The document would not, for example, set out actual practice and conventions. Concentrating on the document would lead to 'flat constitutionalism': see Michael Foley, *The Silence of Constitutions* (1989).

Some analysts deny that there are any such things as 'basic principles' or 'fundamental rights' in the constitution. Even among those who accept that there are or ought to be fundamental rights, there can be disagreements over how to define them. Moreover, attitudes change over time. Fundamental attitudes regarded as good sense a century ago now seem outrageous. Not so long ago the principle of one person–one vote in parliamentary elections was viewed with hostility[7] and the notion that men and women ought to be treated equally was derided.[8]

One of the best-known critics of fundamental rights, J. A. G. Griffith, argues that statements of rights, such as the right to freedom of expression contained in Art 10 of the European Convention on Human Rights,[9] 'sounds like the statement of political conflict pretending to be a resolution of it'.[10] He believes that discussions about rights merely present as questions of law what are really issues of politics and economics: 'Law is not and cannot be a substitute for politics.' There are, he says, no overriding or inherent 'human rights' or 'principles'; rather individuals and groups have political claims against government. Griffith's extremely positivist stance drives him to the conclusion that:[11]

> The constitution of the United Kingdom lives on, changing from day to day for the constitution is no more and no less than what happens. Everything that happens is constitutional. And if nothing happened that would be constitutional also.

If this is correct, then while it is possible to criticize government for acting 'unlawfully' when it breaches a particular rule of the common law or misapplies a statute, the term 'unconstitutional' can have no real force.[12] As Grant puts it, it can only be 'a code-word indicating disquiet'.[13]

In contrast to this approach, the idea of 'principles' and 'rights' lies at the heart of Ronald Dworkin's highly influential writing on legal and political philosophy. He draws a distinction between arguments of principle and arguments of policy:[14]

[7] See for instance the contempt for popular participation in government expressed by Bagehot in *The English Constitution* (1867).

[8] For instance, women were not allowed to vote in parliamentary elections on the same basis as men until 1928. In *Roberts v Hopwood* [1925] AC 578 the House of Lords held that it was unlawful for a local authority to pay women the same basic wage as men.

[9] On the ECHR, see p. 161 below. Art 10 provides:

'1. Everyone has the right to freedom of expression. This right shall include freedom to hold opinions and receive and impart information and ideas without interference by public authority and regardless of frontiers. . . .

2. The exercise of these freedoms, since it carries with it duties and responsibilities, may be subject to such formalities, conditions, restrictions or penalties as are prescribed by law and are necessary in a democratic society . . .'

[10] J. A. G. Griffith, 'The Political Constitution' (1979) 42 MLR 1.

[11] p. 19.

[12] For examples of discussions using these terms, see P. McAuslan and J. McEldowney, *Law, Legitimacy and the Constitution*, p. 13 and Malcolm Grant, 'Central–Local Relations' in J. Jowell and D. Oliver (eds.), *The Changing Constitution* (2nd edn., 1989).

[13] Grant, 'Central–Local Relations' in *The Changing Constitution*, p. 253.

[14] *Taking Rights Seriously* (1977), pp. 82–3.

> Arguments of policy justify a political decision by showing that the decision advances or protects some collective goal of the community as a whole. The argument in favor of a subsidy for aircraft manufacturers, that the subsidy will protect national defense, is an argument of policy. Arguments of principle justify a political decision by showing that the decision respects or secures some individual or group right. The argument in favor of anti-discrimination statutes, that a minority has a right to equal respect and concern, is an argument of principle. . . . The justification of a legislative program of any complexity will ordinarily require both sorts of argument.

Those arguing that the constitution does or should further principles and protect rights use the term 'unconstitutional' as more than merely a vague criticism. Government action may be said to be unconstitutional if it unjustifiably fails to respect a principle or right, even if that action is in accordance with specific laws.

We now turn to look in turn at the three types of constraint on government, all of which have been claimed to embody important constitutional principles: conventions; the rule of law; and international human rights.

CONSTITUTIONAL CONVENTIONS

Brazier has written that 'the whole system of British central government is based on practice, not law'.[15] It is certainly the case that the rules relating to vast tracts of the constitution are not to be found in case law or legislation, but rather in practices that are regarded as binding and which have evolved either by agreement or custom. Such binding practices are usually described as 'conventions'.

The importance of conventions is reflected by the fact that institutions such as the Cabinet and the office of Prime Minister exist by virtue of convention, not law. Jennings tells us that the Cabinet and ministerial system was established out of the need to evolve a working relationship between the King and the new Parliament at the end of the seventeenth and the beginning of the eighteenth centuries.[16] The King needed money which Parliament controlled, and Parliament needed the symbolic authority that the King could provide. As Jennings puts it: 'If Parliament had said, "You get no money," the King might have said, "Then I go back to the Netherlands."' This mutual dependency produced an arrangement whereby the King appointed the members of the Cabinet, but because it was necessary for these members to have the general support of the House of Commons a party system in the House of Commons evolved to support the Cabinet. As real authority shifted from the King most of the Crown's prerogative powers were in practice exercised by ministers, although in theory the King was merely

[15] Rodney Brazier, *Constitutional Practice* (1988), p. 3.
[16] Sir Ivor Jennings, *The Law and the Constitution* (5th edn., 1959), p. 85.

acting on the basis of their advice. The way prerogative discretions were exercised was also determined by convention. Although the monarch remains responsible for appointing the Prime Minister, it is convention that the person appointed will be the leader of the party able to secure the support of the majority of MPs after a general election. Likewise, convention dictates that the monarch always grants Royal Assent (a prerogative power) to bills that have been passed by Parliament.

Are conventions legal rules?

There is an influential line of theory for which Dicey is primarily responsible which argues that 'law' and 'conventions' are distinct types of binding norm.[17] Legal rules, so this argument runs, are to be found either in statutes enacted by Parliament or in the common law enunciated by the judges. Within this positivist approach, since conventions evolve through practice (rather than legislation or judicial decisions) they do not give rise to legal rules and will not be directly enforced by the courts. They exist as part of the political rather than the legal domain, and although failure to follow a convention may ultimately have legal consequences, it is not the law which compels compliance with a convention.

Dicey was not suggesting that conventions are necessarily less important than law. The examples already given clearly show that conventions can affect key areas of the constitution whereas, by contrast, laws often relate to minor matters of detail of little general constitutional significance. His argument was about the nature and limits of law and the competence of judges and lawyers. But Dicey's approach did imply that lawyers and the courts ought *not* to be concerned with those parts of the constitutional system regulated by convention, such as the exercise of prerogative power,[18] for these were better regulated by political, administrative, or even moral considerations. Not only did this narrowly limit the scope of legal regulation of government, it also reinforced the view that law and lawyers are of marginal importance within the British constitutional system and helped to create an intellectual environment in which legal scholarship has tended to be isolated from broader political science concerns.

Thankfully public lawyers are now escaping from these restrictions and Dicey's split between law and convention is now widely disputed, largely due to the criticism of Dicey by Jennings, especially in his book *The Law and the Constitution* first published in 1933.[19] Jennings accepted that there may be formal differences between conventional rules and legal rules, but denied that there was a distinction of substance between them. Both, he argued, were ultimately based on general acceptance and acquiescence. If conventions are not recognized and generally followed, they will not exist. Likewise,

[17] Dicey, *Law of the Constitution*, p. 422.

[18] Dicey, *Law of the Constitution*, p. 426. This is particularly anomalous in the light of his theory of the rule of law and his criticism of discretion, on which see p. 146 below.

[19] Note the subtle difference between the titles of Dicey's book (*The Law of the Constitution*) and Jennings' *The Law and the Constitution.*

he reasoned, anyone can draft a written constitution, but it will not be law unless people generally accept and obey it. He acknowledged that it was true that legal rules are enforced by the courts whereas conventions are not; but he argued that the key to law lay not in enforcement, but in obedience. He illustrated his point by speculating about what might happen if a citizen attempted to use the law to force a minister to act contrary to his wishes:[20]

> . . . it is difficult to believe that a metropolitan policeman under the control of the Home Secretary would arrest the Home Secretary or one of his colleagues in order to put . . . [them] . . . into a prison controlled by the Home Secretary. A legal remedy against the Crown or a minister is useful not because it could be enforced but because it would be obeyed. If the Government decided to break the law, it could not be enforced against them except by revolution.

Jennings goes on to say that:

> In truth, members of the Government do not know and need not bother to know whether a rule is a matter of law or convention. If it is proposed to do something, a technical adviser will tell them that it cannot be done, and unless there is an urgent reason to the contrary it will not be done. Indeed, it is better that the rule should be law and not convention, for a law may be changed by legislation and a convention is rather difficult to change abruptly. The real question which is presented to the Government is not whether a rule is law or convention, but what the House of Commons will think about if a certain action is proposed.

Although Jennings argues that law and conventions are not fundamentally distinct, he accepts that there are three important differences. These are worth noting. First, courts can declare that rules of law are breached and there is then no doubt about it. Secondly, legal rules are either formally expressed or formally illustrated by court decisions, whereas conventions arise out of practice, and it is never quite certain at what point practice becomes or ceases to be convention. The third difference is psychological: 'Formal enunciation through the proper constitutional authorities gives a rule of law a greater sanctity than a convention; an Opposition feels that it has a more effective remedy if it can point out that the Government has acted illegally than it would have if it could say only that it had acted unconstitutionally.'[21]

[20] *Law and the Constitution*, p. 127. The courts have often been very reluctant to make mandatory orders against central government, believing that coercion was unnecessary to ensure compliance with the law. An illustration of this can be seen in *R v Secretary of State for Social Services, ex p Cotton* (1985) *The Times*, 14 December (Chapter 27, below) when Mann J at first instance decided to make no formal order to quash the Board and Lodgings Regulations even though he had held them to be unlawful. A significant departure from this general attitude occurred in *M v Home Office* [1994] 1 AC 377 when the House of Lords held for the first time that a minister could be found in contempt of court for disobeying a court order. In this case the Home Secretary was held to be guilty of contempt for ordering that a man claiming to be a refugee be sent back to the country from which he was fleeing, despite the fact that counsel for the Home Secretary had apparently given an undertaking to the court that the man would not be expelled. But even here, the House of Lords stopped short of imposing a fine on the Home Secretary on the ground that the mere finding of contempt was sufficient to indicate the court's disapproval of what had happened. This case is examined in more detail in Chapter 26.

[21] Jennings, *Law and the Constitution*, p. 133. See also J. D. B. Mitchell, *Constitutional Law* (2nd edn., 1968), p. 18.

Do conventions embody principles of limited government?

It might be said, then, that conventions resemble the common law. Unlike governmental decisions and legislation, which tend to be driven by short- or medium-term policy goals, both conventions and the common law develop over time;[22] and the principles they contain are not determined by the needs of particular governments. For this reason, it is widely argued that conventions and the common law both contribute to the constitutional framework within which government functions.

Allan has recently adopted this approach to argue that constitutional principles developed by the judges through the common law are essentially the same as the political principles reflected in conventions.[23] To support this claim he says that while judges may not directly enforce conventions they are prepared to recognize their existence and support their underlying purpose. The Crossman Diaries case illustrates the point.[24] Here it was argued that publication of the diaries kept by an ex-minister while in office would be contrary to the convention of collective responsibility[25] of the Cabinet because the diaries would reveal differences of opinion between ministers in Cabinet discussions. Although the court decided the case by applying common law principles of confidentiality, it accepted that the convention was in the public interest and necessary for the working of government.

One practical consequence of the argument that legal and conventional principles are essentially the same is that judges ought to be free to review decisions taken in areas of the constitution from which they would be excluded by Dicey's distinction between law and convention. There is evidence that judges are willing to accept this, the best example being the decision of the House of Lords in the *GCHQ* case.[26] Dicey argued that the prerogative powers of the Crown were regulated by convention and not by law and prior to the *GCHQ* decision the judges took the same view. The traditional legal doctrine was that the courts could determine whether a prerogative power existed, but they could not review the manner of its exercise. In the *GCHQ* case the House of Lords altered this view and held that the mere fact that an action was taken under prerogative powers did not mean that the courts were barred from reviewing the action on normal grounds of illegality, irrationality and procedural impropriety. In reaching this decision, Allan says the House vindicated Lord Denning MR's earlier assertion that it is a fundamental principle of the constitution that the law will impose limits on the scope of the prerogative.[27]

Not only did the *GCHQ* decision hold that the courts could review prerogative powers, it also illustrates the way in which a conventional practice

[22] See also Hayek's distinction between *taxis* and *kosmos* noted at p. 39.
[23] T. R. S. Allan, *Law, Liberty, and Justice* (1993).
[24] *Attorney General v Jonathan Cape Ltd* [1976] QB 752.
[25] On which, see p. 55.
[26] *Council of Civil Service Unions v Minister for the Civil Service* [1985] AC 374, extracts from which are set out in Chapter 28.
[27] In *Laker Airways v Department of Trade* [1977] QB 643, 705.

can be used to establish legal principle. The House of Lords accepted that before the Prime Minister had issued her oral instruction to ban unions, it had been normal practice to consult with trade unions about changes in conditions of service. Employees had no legal right to be consulted, but the past practice generated a legitimate expectation that they would be consulted before changes in the conditions of employment were introduced. This the government had failed to respect. In the event the House of Lords accepted that national security justified the decision not to consult, but had there been no such justification the House would have held that the government had acted unlawfully.

As discussed later in this chapter, Allan's treatment of conventions is part of an argument that the rule of law can play a far more active and pervasive role in the constitution than orthodox constitutional theory has permitted.[28] Having challenged the law and convention distinction, Allan goes on to argue (controversially) that there is a principled justification for enabling the courts to review Parliament's legislative powers.[29]

One of the main criticisms levelled at those who argue for principles of limited government is that they choose the principles which they regard as desirable and then find the evidence to support their view. The arguments just considered make a case that conventions and law reflect the principles of limited and accountable government. However, not all commentators would agree that conventions necessarily further clear and consistent principles. Arguably, many conventions operate to protect government and to insulate it from criticism, thereby stifling accountability. Oliver has written that 'the conventions of collective responsibility operate to protect [the government] from public scrutiny and comment rather than to expose it to public or political accountability'.[30] Collective responsibility seems to be more concerned with *effective* and *efficient* government than with accountability. A similar criticism can be made of the convention that ministers are responsible for the work of their departments; this has often been used as a way of protecting civil servants from criticisms and scrutiny. Another illustration is the convention that present and former prime ministers do not give evidence to select committees. Examples such as these suggest that any 'principles' underlying conventions are complex, contradictory or non-existent.

THE RULE OF LAW

The idea of the rule of law is part of the stock in trade of lawyers, politicians and theorists. What does this idea mean? No single answer can be given to this question: the rule of law has been (and is) defined and used in many different ways to serve many different purposes. The only common feature

[28] See p. 153.
[29] See p. 154 below.
[30] Dawn Oliver, *Government in the United Kingdom* (1991), p. 57.

is the notion that governmental powers should, in some broad sense, be exercised in accordance with the law. There is, however, heated debate over the implications of this apparently straightforward proposition. This section examines the main understandings of the rule of law. Our purpose is twofold: to explain understandings of one of the key constitutional ideas, and to use this explanation as a way of illustrating more general lines of theorizing about constitutional principles. The main ideas associated with the rule of law may be summarized as follows.

(1) *Compliance with the law*: like citizens, government and public bodies must act in accordance with the law and must have legal authority for actions which impinge on the rights of others.
(2) *The requirement of rationality*: the rule of law implies rule by reason rather than arbitrary power or whim. In order to comply with the rule of law, decisions must be properly and logically reasoned in accordance with sound argument.
(3) *The rule of law and fundamental rights*: the rule of law requires the protection of the fundamental rights of citizens against government.

Compliance with the law

In its minimal and least contentious sense people use the phrase 'the rule of law' to refer to the obligation upon government and public bodies to comply with the law and to ensure that legal authority exists for actions which infringe the rights of others. The eighteenth-century case of *Entick v Carrington*[31] is a classic illustration of these basic propositions. Two messengers of the King were sued in trespass by Entick after they had broken into his house and seized his papers. For their defence they relied on a warrant issued by the Secretary of State ordering them to find Entick and bring him, and his allegedly seditious books, to the Secretary of State for questioning. The Secretary of State accepted that no specific legal authority, either in the common law or in statute, permitted him to issue the warrants, but argued that the warrants were necessary in order to protect the interests of the state and that similar warrants had been used in the past without question. These arguments were rejected by the court, which emphasized that government needed specific authority to arrest people and claims of state necessity were insufficient. Since the general warrants were illegal and void the King's messengers could be sued for trespassing. Of course, we do not have to go back to the eighteenth century to illustrate the idea that government must have legal justification for its actions:[32] this principle was employed by Simon Cotton when he argued that the Secretary of State lacked legal authority to make the Board and Lodging Regulations.[33]

[31] (1765) 19 St Tr 1030.
[32] See further Chapter 7. The chapters in Part B of this book are concerned with the different forms which such legal justification may take.
[33] See Chapter 27.

Even the basic obligation to 'comply with the law', however, can be problematical. As any practitioner or judge will tell you, it is not always self-evident what the law requires. In the words of H. L. A. Hart:[34]

> in the vast majority of cases . . . neither statutes nor precedents in which the rules are allegedly contained allow of only one result. In most important cases there is always a choice . . . all rules have a penumbra of uncertainty where the judge must choose between alternatives.

Government rarely openly and deliberately flouts the law and in most cases that get to court there is a reasonable argument to be made for both the government and those challenging its decisions.[35] As we see later in the book this uncertainty may arise for a variety of reasons, including the fact that statutory provisions may be very complex and their meaning unclear. Statutes may also confer apparently unlimited discretionary power on ministers or public bodies. A minister may, for example, be permitted to act 'when he thinks fit' or 'when he is satisfied that it is desirable to do so'. In the above situations, implicit in the concept rule of law is the principle that courts are ultimately responsible for determining what the law is and what a statute requires, though the judges are bound to interpret the words actually used in the legislation.[36] This basic principle can produce controversy, particularly when ministers or elected local authorities believe that they have legal power to act in a certain way, but judges say otherwise. The orthodox judicial response is that ministers may be elected, but they only have the legal authority that Parliament has conferred upon them and it is the task of judges to determine what these powers are in cases where the legality of ministerial decisions are challenged.

Substance and procedure

Notice that so far we have been assuming that the rule of law says nothing about the quality of the laws that the judges are enforcing. From this perspective the rule of law would be satisfied whatever the content of the statutory rules enforced by the courts. Suppose, for example, that Parliament gave a minister power to arrest those 'he believed harboured thoughts critical of the government'. Somebody detained might argue that the provision was unfair, but provided the minister had the appropriate belief his actions would comply with the rule of law in the sense so far discussed.[37]

The argument that the rule of law requires compliance with the law is uncontentious. It fits well with the command theory of law[38] and the orthodox view that the task of courts is to ensure that government and other public

[34] *The Concept of Law* (1961), p. 12.

[35] The leave requirement in the judicial review procedure ensures that applicants have an arguable case: see Chapter 21.

[36] On approaches to interpretation, see Chapter 23.

[37] But such a law would be contrary to the United Kingdom's international treaty obligations: see p. 161 below.

[38] See Chapter 5.

bodies act in accordance with laws which are either expressly promulgated by Parliament or which are implicitly acceptable to the sovereign Parliament. What is controversial is the claim that the rule of law *only* requires compliance with the law. Critics of this minimalist view, as we discuss below, argue that the rule of law would be an empty idea if it could be satisfied by a regime that faithfully complied with oppressive and unjust laws. It is inconceivable, they would say, that a government such as that in Nazi Germany could in any sense be said to comply with the rule of law.

Those adopting a strict legal positivist approach respond to this argument by saying that we should not confuse law with justice and morality. The rule of law has nothing to do with these ideas, however important they may be. Raz presents one of the best-known arguments of this type. For him, the rule of law is linked to what he sees as the basic need to ensure that laws can be complied with. Laws which people cannot comply with do not satisfy the requirements of the rule of law.[39] Since people cannot comply with rules that are secret or are constantly changing, the rule of law demands that laws be open, clear, relatively stable and not retrospective. If people are to know what the law requires of them they must also have access to independent courts operating fair procedures and able to resolve disputes over the meaning of the law. He goes on, however, to say that the rule of law:[40]

> is not to be confused with democracy, justice, equality (before the law or otherwise), human rights . . . A non-democratic legal system, based on denial of human rights, on extensive poverty, on racial segregation, sexual inequalities and religious persecution may, in principle, conform to the requirements of the rule of law better than any of the legal systems of the more enlightened western democracies. This does not mean that it will be better than those western democracies. It will be an immeasurably worse legal system, but it will excel in one respect: in its conformity to the rule of law.

Here then the rule of law is concerned with the form in which laws are promulgated, with the existence of independent courts and the procedures that they adopt. According to this view, government can comply with the rule of law but be unjust and undemocratic. The implication, of course, is not that this would be a good state of affairs. Rather it warns us not to expect too much from the rule of law, that if we want just government and fair laws we must look beyond the legal system to such matters as the moral values of the community and the adequacy of the political system.

Rational decision-making

A second idea associated with the rule of law is contained in Aristotle's famous edict that government by laws is superior to government by men. The problem with 'government by men' is that decisions are likely to be taken in

[39] J. Raz, 'The Rule of Law and its Virtue' (1977) 93 LQR 195.
[40] (1977) 93 LQR 195, 195–6.

order to further the interests of those in power—perhaps on the basis of whim, passion or prejudice. By contrast, 'government by laws' implies that decisions are rational, taken in accordance with reason and based on sound argument. The association of the rule of law with rational decision-making and its opposition to arbitrary government still plays a key role in public law. We discuss below that judges expect decisions of public bodies to be rational and properly reasoned.[41] Contrasts between 'the rule of law' (associated with rationality) and 'discretion' (associated with arbitrariness) also inform the way public lawyers have approached the more general relationship between law and governmental power. Two views can be identified. The first, which is associated with Dicey, argues that governmental discretion is incompatible with the rule of law. The second, more modern approach challenges this.

The rule of law against discretion

Dicey drew on Aristotle's distinction between government by law and government by men when he argued that in its first sense the rule of law meant:[42]

> the absolute supremacy or predominance of regular law as opposed to the influence of arbitrary power, [it] excludes the existence of arbitrariness of prerogative, or even of wide discretionary authority on the part of the government.

The proposition that the existence of wide discretionary powers is contrary to the rule of law has been widely criticized, not only by those who disagree with Dicey's political antagonism to government,[43] but also on the grounds that it showed that Dicey had failed to come to terms with the realities of government. The concept of discretion is examined later;[44] for the time being it is sufficient to adopt a definition used by Lord Diplock:[45]

> The very concept of administrative discretion involves the right to choose between more than one possible course of action upon which there is room for reasonable people to hold differing opinions as to which is to be preferred.

Three main specific criticisms have been made of Dicey's aversion to discretionary powers.[46] First, as a matter of reality government has always possessed wide discretionary powers and such powers are necessary and often desirable: without them the system would be inoperable.[47] Secondly, it has

41 See Chapter 24.

42 *Law of the Constitution*, p. 202. This he called his 'first meaning' of the rule of law. For his second and third definitions, see pp. 149–50 below.

43 Jennings once wrote that 'Dicey is reported to have told a Harvard audience . . . that if you scratch an Englishman you will find a socialist. It is doubtful if even a pick-axe would have produced such a discovery in Dicey himself and what he meant by "socialist" is not what we mean by it now' (Preface to the 2nd edn. of *The Law and the Constitution* (1938)).

44 See Chapter 24.

45 *Secretary of State for Education and Science v Tameside Metropolitan Borough Council* [1977] AC 1014, 1064.

46 For example, W. A. Robson, *Justice and Administrative Law* (1928) and Jennings, *The Law and the Constitution*.

47 See R. F. V. Heuston, 'The Rule of Law' in *Essays in Constitutional Law* (2nd edn., 1964) pp. 40–2.

been said that his view that discretion and law are incompatible and contradictory cannot be right. Judges as well as officials have wide discretionary powers which can impinge upon individual liberty. Courts, for example, have power to punish for contempt of court and have discretion over sentencing. Indeed, it may be argued that the common law is itself created by judicial discretion. Thirdly, writers have also criticized Dicey's view that governmental discretion is necessarily and implicitly bad. As well as these specific criticisms there is the more general complaint that Dicey's rule of law fails to come to terms with the realities of modern government. Dicey appeared to believe that his rule of law could keep the tide of government at bay when in fact the power of government was growing and was likely to continue to grow despite the law. The result is that this version of the rule of law is incapable of imposing an effective system of legal controls on governmental power.

The rule of law and discretion

Many today argue that if a theory of the rule of law has a role to play in imposing limitations on governmental discretion that theory must acknowledge that discretion exists and come to terms with the way powers are actually exercised. This requires public lawyers to recognize that law has a role to play *within* government and is not simply a means of imposing external controls on government when (or if) decisions are challenged in the courts. The law must, as it were, roll up its sleeves and participate in government. It must be relevant and useful to those who make decisions so that it can influence what happens on a day-to-day basis inside government departments, local authorities and other public bodies, whether or not legal proceedings are taken.[48] After all, only a tiny proportion of decisions are likely to be challenged in the courts.

To this end writers such as Davis, writing in the USA,[49] have developed the idea of the rule of law by explaining how legal techniques can be used to control discretionary power of officials *at the time they make their decisions*. Put simply, the general concern of these writers is to ensure that officials comply with the rule of law in their routine work so that illegality and unfairness are prevented. In his book *Discretionary Justice*, Davis makes the familiar argument that Dicey was wrong to suggest that discretion was necessarily bad. For Davis the problem was not discretion in itself, but the tendency to allow officials too much discretion. The great virtue of discretion, he argues, is that it allows officials to 'individualise justice' by enabling them to apply general rules to individual circumstances. A general rule might, for example, say that welfare payments should be paid to those 'financially in need' and discretion is then necessary to decide who is in need. To take

[48] See Chapter 4.

[49] K. C. Davis, *Discretionary Justice* (1969). For critiques of Davis on the ground that his approach is too legalistic see Keith Hawkins (ed.), *The Uses of Discretion* (1992), especially pp. 16–18 and Chapter 11 (Nicola Lacey). See also Robert Baldwin, *Rules and Government* (1995), especially pp. 19–41.

another example, a rule might say that it is an offence to travel at more than 40 miles per hour on a particular road. There may, however, be virtue in allowing a police officer discretion not to charge a doctor who was driving at 43 mph on her way to a dangerously ill patient in the early hours of the morning when there was no other traffic on the road.

The difficulty is that if we allow discretion in these circumstances we also need to ensure that the discretion is not abused. It would be wrong, for example, for officials to decide which applicants are in financial need, or which motorists should be charged, on the basis of criteria that had nothing at all to do with need or road safety—say, their religion. If officials had complete freedom to choose their own criteria for reaching decisions, this would enable them to act arbitrarily and to further their own objectives rather than the policy for which the scheme was established. Davis' response is not that discretion ought to be eliminated altogether; instead, he argues, steps must be taken to eliminate *unnecessary* discretion. Three techniques are available to do this: confining, structuring and checking.

(1) *Confining discretion* is where rules limit the scope of discretion. The admissions tutor in a university department has unconfined discretion if he or she is able to admit 'whichever applicants appear to him most suitable'. This broad discretion could be confined by the tutor being told to admit applicants who have obtained 'three A levels at grade B or an equivalent examination result, save in exceptional circumstances when the tutor should consider the age, experience and social background of applicants'. Here the scope of discretion is much more limited.

(2) *Structuring discretion* means that decision-makers should have to follow certain procedures before they make their decisions and in particular that decisions should be made openly. Openness, Davis argued, is the enemy of arbitrariness. A university could choose to structure the admission tutor's discretion by ensuring that it makes its admissions policy public and by requiring the tutor to provide reasons why candidates have been admitted or rejected.

(3) *Checking discretion* can be done internally by ensuring that someone other than the decision-maker, such as a superior or a manager, has a second look at the decision, or it can be done externally by providing rights of appeal against the decision to a tribunal or the courts, establishing complaints procedures, or by relying on judicial review.

In this version of the rule of law the courts play only a small part in the overall scheme. Rather than being something imposed on policy-makers and officials from the outside by judges the rule of law becomes an accepted part of the internal culture of the system, or as Jowell puts it 'a principle of institutional morality'.[50] Whether, and if so to what extent, this institutional

[50] J. Jowell, 'The Rule of Law Today' in Jowell and Oliver (eds.), *The Changing Constitution* (3rd edn., 1994), p. 57.

morality exists in practice is difficult to say. Much of what goes on within government is not available for public scrutiny and little research has yet been done on the relevance of legal techniques within government. The studies that are available warn us that while there are signs that officials are becoming more familiar with the law and more aware of the legal implications of their actions, we cannot yet assume that government has imbibed the rule of law as its institutional morality.

Fundamental rights

So far in our discussion, the rule of law has been principally associated with controlling decision-making procedures, with ensuring that government complies with Parliament's wishes and that these wishes are promulgated in a form that can be obeyed. Used in these senses, the idea of the rule of law is comparatively uncontroversial largely because it has not been claimed that the rule of law imposes limits on the *substance* of policy or the content of governmental decisions. It has been assumed that such matters are for those who are politically accountable: for Parliament and the government that is answerable to Parliament. Most legal positivists would be able to accept the ideas of the rule of law so far enunciated. So too would those who believe that in a democratic system the content of public policy ought ultimately to be driven by the wishes of the majority of the electorate.

There is however a strong and well-established line of thinking which argues that the rule of law is also concerned with matters of substance; that as well as imposing limits on the *way* government reaches its decisions, it also imposes limitations on the content of decisions that can be made. In particular, it has for long been argued that the rule of law reflects fundamental rights and liberties of citizens and therefore constrains action which adversely affects these rights and liberties. This line of argument is put in different ways.

(1) Within the established orthodoxy of parliamentary supremacy,[51] the argument for fundamental rights is expressed inevitably in weak terms. Parliament's legal authority is unlimited and it can therefore abrogate rights and liberties. The thrust of orthodox theory about the rule of law is therefore to say that ministers, officials and public bodies may only infringe existing legal rights and liberties if they have Parliament's authority for doing so. If they act without this authority, the courts can step in and provide remedies to the aggrieved person.[52]

(2) Recently, stronger rights-based arguments have been developed by academics and judges.[53] The argument is that the rule of law can impose

[51] On which see Chapter 5.

[52] See the power-based approach to judicial review, p. 471.

[53] See also the impact-based approach to judicial review, p. 473.

obligations to respect rights and liberties not only on government, but also on Parliament itself. Within this new approach, there are two main strands: one stresses the continued vitality of the common law tradition; the other that the common law needs the support of a Bill of Rights to protect effectively individuals against government. By challenging the orthodox view of parliamentary supremacy, these arguments also challenge the legitimacy of the democratic process upon which it is based. They do so by arguing that majoritarian electoral democracy, though necessary, is insufficient. As well as giving too much power to majorities and too little power to minorities, it provides inadequate controls over government between elections. This being so, the courts must step in to fill gaps left by the electoral process to ensure that the system is democratic in a broader sense of the term.

Having sketched the main lines of thinking about fundamental rights and liberties, let us now look at the arguments more closely, beginning with the orthodox approach.

Parliamentary supremacy, rights and the common law

The established orthodox view is still associated with Dicey's explanation of the rule of law and parliamentary supremacy. His second and, especially, his third meanings of the rule of law are particularly significant.[54] Here his ideas are outlined to show, in particular, the importance he attached to the common law.

In his second meaning of the rule of law, Dicey argued that it required the equal subjection of all classes to the 'ordinary law' of the land administered by the 'ordinary courts'.[55] So even though government possessed legal powers and responsibilities which citizens did not have, it was for Dicey important that the same laws, administered by the same judges, applied to ministers and officials. They did not, and should not, possess special legal privileges or immunities, he claimed. In practice this meant that a citizen could use the common law to sue ministers or civil servants who in the course of carrying out official duties trespassed or acted negligently. By contrast he criticized the French system of administrative law (*droit administratif*) on the grounds that it provided a special form of justice that allowed officials to be judged by specialized courts staffed by officials, rather than by the ordinary courts with independent judges.[56] Such a system, he said, was 'fundamentally inconsistent

[54] For his first meaning, see p. 145 above.

[55] *The Law of the Constitution*, pp. 202–3. A word of caution is needed: although Dicey refers to equality he was only concerned with equality between individuals and officials during the litigation process. He was not concerned with issues such as social, sex or economic equality. In this context the rule of law is not about living or working conditions, access to education or housing, discrimination between sexes, races or social classes.

[56] Administrative law courts are staffed by judges who have administrative experience. See further, L. Neville Brown and John S. Bell, *French Administrative Law* (4th edn., 1993).

with our traditions and customs'. There are several reasons to doubt whether Dicey was correct in his descriptive analysis. When he was writing, and still to some extent today, the Crown (often, in effect, ministers) enjoyed privileges in litigation not shared with ordinary citizens.[57] He also overlooked the existence of a network of specialized courts and tribunals.[58]

In explaining his third meaning of the rule of law Dicey wrote:[59]

> We may say that the constitution is pervaded by the rule of law on the ground that the general principles of the constitution (as for example the right of personal liberty, or the right of public meeting) are . . . the result of judicial decisions . . . thus the constitution is the result of the ordinary law of the land.

Here Dicey argues that the rule of law and the values that it represents pervade the constitution so that the constitution is the result of the common law. He goes on to contrast the rule of law with the situation in countries where rights and liberties are stated in written constitutions and bills of rights. Such statements may reflect aspirations, but they do not necessarily represent the actual working principles and the real culture of the system, as the rule of law does in this constitution.

So we can see that throughout his discussion of the rule of law, Dicey emphasizes the importance of the common law. He was well aware that, by rooting his rule of law in the judge-made common law, he was drawing on a system that was centuries old and which pre-dated the growth in governmental power which he so disliked. However, it was not just its history that appealed to him. He was also attracted by the notion that principles of the common law had evolved from thousands of individual cases in which judges were forced to deal with the practical problem of reconciling the conflicting claims of individual litigants. The common law was therefore moulded out of practical needs to do justice in particular situations. Unlike legislation, it does not serve the short-term policy objectives of whatever government happens to be elected, but rather reflects deeper and more profound constitutional values, chief of which are the values of individual liberty and freedom. In this way, the common law provides a bedrock of stability within the system. While Parliament has legal power to change the common law, Dicey believed that it would be unable to alter fundamental values because the electorate—the political sovereign—would not permit it to do so and would exert 'serious or insuperable resistance' if necessary.[60]

Dicey's views on this had changed by 1914, by which time he seemed to accept that the French system is capable of providing at least as much control over government as the English system. In the United Kingdom today many disputes with government are handled by specialized tribunals: see Chapter 19.

57 See Chapters 12 and 26.

58 See H. W. Arthurs, *Without the Law: administrative justice and legal pluralism in nineteenth century England* (1985).

59 *Law of the Constitution*, p. 193.

60 See Chapter 5.

The enduring common law tradition

Judges and academics continue to assert that the common law reflects and promotes fundamental rights such as free speech,[61] freedom of conscience,[62] to gain access to the courts,[63] freedom from arbitrary detention,[64] equality[65] and freedom of movement.[66] Claims like these can be found in dozens of cases. Lord Browne-Wilkinson has written that:[67]

> It has become so fashionable to urge constitutional reform by means of a Bill of Rights or by incorporating the European Convention on Human Rights in our domestic law that attention has been diverted from the principles of our indigenous domestic law ... Whenever the provisions of the European Convention on Human Rights has been raised before the [English] courts, the judges have asserted that the Convention confers no greater rights than those protected by the common law.

Sir John Laws, a High Court judge, has echoed the same sentiments:[68]

> The contents of the European Convention on Human Rights, *as a series of propositions*, largely represent legal norms and values which are either already inherent in our law, or, so far as they are not, may be integrated into it by the judges.

He went on to argue that the courts have power to override the apparently plain words of a statute where 'there is a naked assertion of a power to interfere with fundamental rights without a demonstrated justification'.[69] This is an interesting statement which throws light on the way orthodox theory has approached fundamental rights issues. Two questions need to be considered:

(a) what are the characteristics of fundamental rights within orthodox constitutional theory; and
(b) how in practice are these rights protected?

[61] In *Derbyshire County Council v Times Newspapers* [1993] AC 534 a local authority was barred from suing a newspaper for libel over allegations that council funds had been improperly invested. Lord Keith said that the Court of Appeal had reached its conclusion 'principally by reference to Art 10 of the European Convention on Human Rights ... I have reached my conclusion upon the common law of England without finding any need to rely upon the European Convention'. Cf. *R v Secretary of State for the Home Department, ex p Brind* [1991] 1 AC 696 (although the House of Lords held it was lawful for the government to ban radio and TV from broadcasting the direct speech of members of the IRA and other terrorist organizations, Lord Ackner stated, at p. 757, that 'in a field which concerns a fundamental human right—namely that of free speech—close scrutiny must be given to the reasons provided as justifications for interference with that right').

[62] See Browne-Wilkinson LJ's dissenting judgment in *Wheeler v Leicester City Council* [1985] 2 All ER 151, 155–9.

[63] *R v Secretary of State for the Home Department, ex p Leech (No 2)* [1993] 4 All ER 539, 548, CA. See also *R and W Paul v The Wheat Commission* [1937] AC 139. See further Chapter 21 below.

[64] See *R v Secretary of State for the Home Department, ex p Khawaja* [1984] AC 74.

[65] See J. Jowell, 'Is Equality a Constitutional Principle?' (1994) 48 CLP vol. II 1.

[66] *R v Secretary of State for the Home Department, ex p McQuillan* [1995] 4 All ER 400, 421 ('Freedom of movement, subject only to the general law, is a fundamental value of the common law').

[67] 'The Infiltration of a Bill of Rights' [1992] PL 397, 404–5.

[68] 'Is the High Court the Guardian of Fundamental Constitutional Rights?' [1993] PL 59, 61 (emphasis in original).

[69] At p. 78. See further Chapter 20.

THE CHARACTERISTICS OF FUNDAMENTAL RIGHTS WITHIN ORTHODOX CONSTITUTIONAL THEORY

The orthodox view of rights is based, as was Dicey's theory, on what can be described as liberal individualism. Within this theory rights and liberties protect the autonomy and freedom of individuals against other individuals and especially against the state. Rights and liberties are therefore essentially negative in character: they protect individuals *from* interference with freedom to speak, *from* deprivation of liberty, *from* trespass and so on. In so far as the state has a role, it is limited to providing the conditions necessary to ensure that these freedoms are protected. For extreme liberals this would limit the state to providing such things as a legal system and a police force that would help prevent people infringing the rights of others.[70] Today few people adopt this view. Most argue that even within liberal theory it is possible, and some would say necessary, to adopt a more positive view of rights which is more appropriate for a system in which the role of the state extends to providing a minimum income in the form of welfare benefits, health care, education, housing and environmental protection. Negative liberties are only useful if they can actually be used.[71] Serious inequalities of wealth or health, or lack of educational facilities, mean that some people simply cannot be as free to enjoy their 'liberty' as others and this in itself undermines the rights of individuals and the principle that individuals are equal. People who cannot afford to travel have no freedom of movement; those who are illiterate or who do not have access to the news media are not free to express themselves. Negative freedoms therefore can only be fully protected if people have *positive* rights which demand the society as a whole to create conditions in which everyone's autonomy may flourish.

Here then is one reason why many liberals would not place their trust in the ability of the common law to fully protect fundamental rights. Common law rights are essentially negative and concerned with a narrow range of traditional freedoms. They do not impose positive obligations on government to provide such things as decent housing, education or health care. Of course there are a number of good reasons for this. Perhaps the most important is that judges do not control resources. This is a matter for politicians who hold the public purse; and judges can only enforce such obligations when they have been imposed by Parliament or some other source such as Community law.

HOW IN PRACTICE ARE RIGHTS PROTECTED BY THE COMMON LAW?

There are two answers to this question. Where the body which adversely affects the rights of an individual does not have any statutory or other legal authority for its actions, the normal method for protecting rights in orthodox theory is to sue in tort. Where statutory or other legal authority does exist for interfering with an individual's rights, private law litigation may not succeed

[70] For more recent advocacy of this approach, see R. Nozick, *Anarchy, State and Utopia*, Chapters 5 and 6; F. Hayek, *The Constitution of Liberty* (1960).

[71] For a fuller discussion, see David Feldman, *Civil Liberties and Human Rights* (1993), Chapter 1.

because the courts may hold that Parliament permitted interference with the right.[72] The important point is that while we may talk about rights being 'fundamental', this term is misleading in the sense that in orthodox theory individual rights can always be overridden by the parliamentary legislation.

The New Orthodoxy: the rule of law to control Parliament?

Allan is one writer who has recently refurbished Dicey's theory of the rule of law with a view to strengthening the ability of the judges to protect rights against government and also against Parliament.[73] Like Dicey, Allan links the rule of law with the common law which 'embodies the traditional bias . . . in favour of individual liberty' and which 'has been generally regarded as providing a bulwark against the erosion of the most important civil liberties'.[74] However, he presents the rule of law as part of a more all-embracing theory which helps to define not only the nature of governmental power but also 'the nature of the constitution' itself.[75] He says that like our commitment to democracy, the rule of law embodies both a formal and a substantive commitment to equality between citizens:[76]

> it is . . . inextricably linked with certain basic institutional arrangements. The fundamental notion of equality, which lies at the heart of our convictions about justice and fairness, demands an equal voice for all adult citizens in the legislative process: universal suffrage may today be taken to be a central strand of the rule of law. There is also a commitment implied to some form of the principle of separation of powers . . . A government which could make laws at its own pleasure, and determine the extent of its own infractions of the laws, would not be a government under the rule of law.

Here Allan stresses the link between the principle of equality, the rule of law and the universal franchise. By so doing he extends the rule of law beyond the traditional province of the courts and into the political domain (which Dicey argued was regulated by convention rather than by law). This enables Allan to challenge Dicey's view of the supremacy of Parliament. The legal doctrine of legislative supremacy, he argues, is based on the 'courts' commitment to British parliamentary democracy . . . [and] must entail a commitment to some irreducible, minimum concept of democratic principle'.[77] In *most* cases that political commitment demands that the judges respect parliamentary legislation, but this does not mean that judges should always respect the will of Parliament. The respect cannot be limitless and would not extend to:[78]

> A parliamentary enactment whose effect would be the destruction of any recognizable form of democracy—for example, a measure purporting to deprive a substantial

[72] See e.g. *Manchester Corporation v Farnworth* [1930] AC 171.
[73] T. R. S. Allan, *Law, Liberty, and Justice* (1993).
[74] p. 40.
[75] p. 21.
[76] p. 22.
[77] p. 282.
[78] p. 282.

> section of the population of the vote on the grounds of their hostility to government policies—could not consistently be applied by the courts as law. Judicial obedience to the statute . . . could not coherently be justified in terms of the doctrine of parliamentary sovereignty, since the statute would violate the political principle which the doctrine itself enshrines.

Allan argues that limitations on Parliament do not imply a conflict between the rule of law and democratic principle. On the contrary, since both ideas flow from a basic moral commitment to democracy they are both necessary and each supports the other. Sir John Laws has recently taken a similar approach, arguing that:[79]

> as a matter of fundamental principle . . . the survival and flourishing of a democracy in which basic rights (of which freedom of expression may be taken as a paradigm) are not only respected but enshrined requires that those who exercise democratic, political power must have limits set to what they may do: limits which they are not allowed to overstep. If this is right, it is a function of democratic power itself that it be not absolute.

The constitution, he goes on to argue, must guarantee such rights as freedom of expression 'since otherwise its credentials as a medium of honest rule are fatally undermined'. This requires a 'higher-order law' which cannot be abrogated by a statute promoted by a government with the necessary majority in Parliament. It is, he argues, the constitution rather than Parliament which is sovereign. By implication it is the judges who are responsible for interpreting the constitution and ensuring its imposition on Parliament.

A fellow judge, Sir Stephen Sedley, also questions the doctrine of parliamentary sovereignty—but he doubts whether there can be a higher-order law of the type envisaged by Laws.[80] Times change and assumptions about the content of fundamental rights also change. One of the examples he cites is that of the American constitution which in 1896 legitimated racial segregation in public services and then in 1954 forbade it.[81] Another example, drawn from closer to home, is the decision of the Court of Appeal in 1925 that it was lawful for an education authority to sack married women teachers on the ground that their duties lay at home with their family.[82] Neither of these decisions, he says, is intelligible today except 'by situating the reasoning of the . . . court in its peculiar time and place'.[83] He goes on to remind us that democracy itself has only recently been accepted as a desirable idea: not so long ago it was used as a term of abuse synonymous with mob rule. Sedley predicts that it is unlikely to remain a valued principle for all time.

Sedley's argument here is part of a broader reflection on the role courts can play in constitutional matters in general and human rights issues in particular.

[79] Sir John Laws, 'Law and Democracy' [1995] PL 72. Cf. Lord Irvine, 'Judges and Decision-makers: the Theory and Practice of Judicial Review' [1996] PL 556.

[80] Sir Stephen Sedley, 'Human Rights: A Twenty-First Century Agenda' [1995] PL 386.

[81] *Brown v Board of Education* 347 US 483 (1954).

[82] *Short v Poole Corporation* [1926] Ch 66.

[83] p. 387.

As well as being sceptical about the notion of a higher-order law, he is also far from sanguine about the ability of judges to decide cases so that their outcomes consistently further human rights. To illustrate his concern he compares two Australian cases decided on the same day in 1992. In the first the courts struck down a statute which made it a criminal offence to criticize members of the Industrial Relations Commission on the grounds that the statute restricted free speech.[84] In the second case, the court struck down a statute which in the run-up to elections provided free airtime for all political parties, but banned other political advertising.[85] The purpose of the statute was to reduce the political advantage that candidates and parties with wealthy supporters would have by expensive advertising and thereby achieve electoral equality. The court decided that the legislation obstructed the fullest flow of opinion and was therefore unconstitutional. For Sedley these cases illustrate both the trend in free market democracies for the courts to keep government within the law and also the fickleness of outcomes. While the first decision removed immunity from criticism and strengthened free speech, the effect of the second was to strengthen the political voice of the wealthy at the expense of others.

There is no need to go to Australia to see that despite the rhetoric of the common law, judges are not always able to ensure that the outcomes of their decisions are to protect liberty. We can point to cases such as *GCHQ* in which the courts have refused to protect individuals in the face of government claims that the interests of the state justify restricting freedom.[86] Lord Lester QC has written of the 'ethical aimlessness in the common law' and cites 'a catalogue of unprincipled decisions' in which the courts have upheld racial discrimination and failed to develop an implied constitutional right to free expression.[87]

A Bill of Rights?

For the reasons set out above, many people believe that the common law is unable to protect fundamental rights and liberties. For them, the solution is the enactment of a new Bill of Rights. Lester has been a leading proponent of this and recently steered such a bill through the legislative process in the House of Lords.[88] Many of the issues associated with debates over a Bill of Rights can be conveniently discussed by considering Lester's bill.

Before doing this, however, let us consider why some people critical of the

84 *Nationwide News Pty Ltd v Wills* (1992) 177 CLR 1.

85 *Australian Capital Television Pty Ltd v Commonwealth of Australia* (1992) 177 CLR 106.

86 See e.g. *Liversidge v Anderson* [1942] AC 206.

87 'English Judges as Law Makers' [1993] PL 267. He is particularly critical of the decision in *R v Secretary of State for the Home Department, ex p Brind* [1991] 1 AC 696 in which the House of Lords held that where Parliament confers broad powers on ministers and public authorities there is no presumption that Parliament intended those powers to be exercised in accordance with the ECHR.

88 A. Lester, 'The Mouse That Roared: The Human Rights Bill 1995' [1995] PL 198.

current constitutional situation are none the less against enacting a Bill of Rights whereas others are strongly in favour of doing so. The views of two well-known commentators capture the key issues: in the anti-Bill of Rights corner is Griffith; in the pro-corner is Dworkin.

Dworkin suggests that as well as providing citizens with rights against government, a Bill of Rights would halt and reverse the 'decline in the *culture* of liberty' in this country.[89] In so doing it would strengthen the concept of 'government under law'. Griffith sees two principal dangers in this. One is that it skews the nature of arguments about important questions of policy. Questions of real substance are put to one side and (in Griffith's words) members of the legal profession 'embark on the happy and fruitful exercise of interpreting woolly principles and even woollier exceptions'.[90] A second danger is that a Bill of Rights is 'undemocratic'. Griffith believes that political decisions should be taken by politicians and not judges:[91]

> the law is not and cannot be a substitute for politics . . . proposals [for a Bill of Rights] are not only mistaken but positively dangerous. They seem to indicate a way by which potential tyranny can be defeated by the intervention of the law and the invention of institutional devices. There is no such way. Only political control, politically exercised, can supply the remedy.

Dworkin denies that there is anything undemocratic about a Bill of Rights; he distinguishes the notion of *statistical* democracy (the need only for there to be a plurality of MPs in favour of a policy or law) and the 'true' idea of *communal* democracy, which forms the foundation of his justification for a Bill of Rights. This conception of democracy means:[92]

> majority decision is legitimate only if it is a majority within a community of equals. That means not only that everyone must be allowed to participate in politics as an equal, through the vote and through freedom of speech and protest, but that political decisions must treat everyone with equal concern and respect, that each individual person must be guaranteed fundamental civil and political rights no combination of other citizens can take away, no matter how numerous they are or how much they despise his or her race or morals or way of life.

Here then we see a fundamental disagreement between writers like Griffith, who adopt an essentially positivist conception of law, and those like Dworkin, who adopt an essentially value-based approach to law. For Griffith, values are controversial and controversies cannot be resolved by statements of legal rights. In this sense Griffith agrees with Dicey's view that written statements of principle are only valuable if the principles they enshrine actually pervade the constitution. Griffith would, however, disagree with Dicey's view that principles can be discerned from the common law. Rather they are things which are fought over in the political arena. If rights require greater protection,

[89] Ronald Dworkin, *A Bill of Rights for Britain* (1990).
[90] 'The Political Constitution' (1979) 42 MLR 1, 14.
[91] p. 16.
[92] *A Bill of Rights for Britain*, pp. 35–6.

what is needed is reform of political systems to ensure more freedom of information, greater participation and greater powers for Parliament. A Bill of Rights would codify a particular set of values based on individual rights which many would find inadequate and unsuited to the broader needs of the community as a whole.[93] Unless it were easily amended it would also crystallize values which, as Sedley shows, are likely to change over time, thereby producing a rift between the written law and the cultural values of society.

Lord Lester's Human Rights Bill

Lester's Human Rights Bill illustrates some of the more specific issues associated with the Bill of Rights debate. This bill was presented as a modest reform designed to attract as much support as possible. Its purpose was to incorporate the rights set out in the ECHR and its first protocol into domestic law.[94] Some, like Sedley, argue that the ECHR

> is a full generation out of date. The Convention, devised in 1950, took a limited view of human rights, based on the nineteenth century paradigm of the individual whose enemy is the State; I don't believe that is a workable premise.[95]

New 'second-generation' substantive rights could be included: the right to health care, education and housing for example. 'Third-generation' environmental rights could also form part of a Bill of Rights. The advantage of the ECHR, however, is that it is widely accepted as providing a minimal statement of rights which are generally accepted by Western nations and many other Commonwealth countries. Some might feel its rights do not go far enough; on the other hand its rights are relatively uncontentious from a political point and likely to attract support across the political spectrum.

As well as its symbolic value, a Bill of Rights would enable British courts to provide remedies for citizens who were victims of breaches of the ECHR by public bodies without having to make an application to the Human Rights Commission and Court in Strasbourg. Lester's proposal did not seek to entrench its provisions in a way that would prevent Parliament enacting future legislation that was inconsistent with it. Entrenchment might be desirable but it was felt that this too would be controversial because it would raise too many questions about parliamentary sovereignty. In its original form the bill would, however, have prevented an Act of Parliament from being relied on in legal proceedings to the extent that it was inconsistent with ECHR rights.[96] In other words it would have given similar effect to the ECHR as s 2(1) and (4) of the European Communities Act 1972 gives to Community

[93] Cf. P. McAuslan's argument that the 'public interest' is a fundamental principle: 'For the Welfare Statists there *is* something we call the "public interest" . . . to "advance the public interest" is to adopt policies and practices which advance the good of all citizens . . .': 'Public Law and Public Choice' (1988) 51 MLR 681, 688.

[94] On the ECHR, see further p. 161 below.

[95] *The Times*, 10 October 1994.

[96] The original bill also contained a right of action for damages for any violation of the ECHR by those performing public functions. This was also dropped. See further Chapter 26.

Law.[97] It would therefore have given power to the courts to set aside legislation inconsistent with the ECHR—but, argued Lester, it would not have undermined Parliament's sovereignty because Parliament would still be free to expressly amend or repeal the Bill of Rights Act. This proposal proved too contentious. Many MPs were already concerned about the effect of Community law on parliamentary sovereignty. Lester decided to amend the bill by substituting for the court's power to override inconsistent legislation a new rule of statutory interpretation requiring that: 'So far as the context permits, enactments (whenever passed or made) shall be construed consistently with' the ECHR rights and freedoms.[98] Lester believed that this rule would make the 'Convention a full part of our system of public law'. Although he believed that this would undo the restrictive effect of the decision in *ex p Brind*,[99] there is enough leeway in the phrase 'So far as the context permits' to enable judges to continue to adopt a pro-government approach in sensitive cases.

Despite Lester's willingness to moderate the effects of the bill ('as a result of . . . changes my Bill became more a mouse than a lion')[100] and the widespread support it received,[101] the government continued to object to the bill. According to Lester the real objection to the bill in Whitehall 'is not that it would diminish parliamentary sovereignty . . . [but] that the Bill would reverse the *Brind* case and so require Ministers to comply with the European Convention'.[102] The bill passed through the Lords but was lost in the Commons due to lack of time, as were three previous bills seeking to introduce a Bill of Rights.

INTERNATIONAL HUMAN RIGHTS OBLIGATIONS

So far, this chapter has examined two broad types of constraint on governmental power: constitutional conventions and the rule of law (which is defined in many different ways). We now move on to consider a third type of constraint: the international treaty obligations of the United Kingdom dealing with human rights.

The United Kingdom has entered into several treaties with other states under which it has agreed to respect certain fundamental rights of its citizens. These treaties include the International Covenant on Civil and Political Rights

97 See Chapter 5.

98 This was modelled on the New Zealand Bill of Rights 1989.

99 [1991] 2 AC 696.

100 A. Lester [1995] PL 198, 201.

101 Lords Ackner, Browne-Wilkinson, Scarman, Lloyd, Simon, Slynn, Taylor (the Lord Chief Justice), Woolf and Sir Thomas Bingham MR spoke or voted in favour. It was also thought to have the support of most other law lords. Lord Donaldson (a former Master of the Rolls), however, spoke against the bill.

102 [1995] PL 198, 201.

1966 (under the auspices of the United Nations);[103] the European Convention on Human Rights (ECHR) (under the auspices of the Council of Europe);[104] and the International Labour Organization (ILO) Convention on Freedom of Association.

International treaties and national legal systems

Treaties emerge from bilateral or multilateral negotiations between independent sovereign states and bind states in international law.[105]

Under the UK constitution, the complex network of international treaties which now exists is generally viewed as a *separate* 'system' of law from internal national law (or domestic law). Under this approach, commonly known as 'dualism', treaties by themselves cannot alter national law nor do they confer rights recognized by national law on individuals—even where the treaty itself (as does the ECHR) expressly sets out individual rights. Lord Oliver has put the general position succinctly:[106]

> Treaties . . . are not self-executing. Quite simply, a treaty is not part of English law unless and until it has been incorporated into the law by legislation. So far as individuals are concerned, it is *res inter alios acta*[107] from which they cannot derive rights and by which they cannot be deprived of rights or subjected to obligations and it is outside the purview of the court not only because it is made in the conduct of foreign relations, which are prerogatives of the Crown, but also because, as a source of rights and obligations, it is irrelevant.

In other words, the rights and obligations of the United Kingdom under international law are regarded as separate and distinct from the rights and obligations of citizens of the United Kingdom under domestic law. Although the ECHR has yet to be directly incorporated,[108] it and other human rights treaties do have an internal influence. They may for example help to elucidate principles of the common law, and they also help judges interpret ambiguous statutes.[109] Such treaties may also provide a method of redress against the UK government on the international plane.

103 Published in the United Kingdom as Cmnd 6702.

104 Published in the United Kingdom as Cmnd 2643. For discussion and analysis of its provisions see D. J. Harris, M. O'Boyle and C. Warbrick, *Law of the European Convention on Human Rights* (1995).

105 On the formal process of treaty-making see Chapter 12.

106 *Maclaine Watson & Co Ltd v Department of Trade and Industry* [1990] 2 AC 418, 500 (the International Tin Council case).

107 This Latin phrase means 'a transaction between others'. In this context it refers to treaties as being agreements between states and not involving individuals.

108 Art 1 of the ECHR requires signatory states to 'secure' its rights and freedoms to people within the state's jurisdiction, but this stops short of compelling the states to incorporate the Convention into their national law.

109 See Chapter 23.

European Convention on Human Rights[110]

In the wake of the Second World War, an international organization called the Council of Europe was established in 1949. Its member states (today totalling 36) 'accept the principles of the rule of law and the enjoyment by all persons within [their] jurisdiction of human rights and fundamental freedoms'.[111] Under the auspices of the Council of Europe, the ECHR came into force in 1953 and today all members of the Council of Europe are obliged to ratify it.

The ECHR has had a significant impact in the United Kingdom. First, it gave to individuals the opportunity[112] to bring legal proceedings against the United Kingdom before the European Commission of Human Rights and the European Court of Human Rights (both based in Strasbourg). This does not form a further 'appeal' from the House of Lords; neither the European Commission nor the Court of Human Rights will consider an application which merely alleges that a national court has erred in misinterpreting or wrongly applying domestic law. Rather, the applicant has to show that the United Kingdom has breached one of the rights set out in the Convention.[113] This is well illustrated by the GCHQ case study. In the national courts the issues concerned whether there ought to have been consultation before the union ban had been imposed.[114] When the dispute went to the European Commission of Human Rights, the case turned on whether the government had infringed the right to freedom of association under Art 11 of the Convention.[115]

In comparison to applications for judicial review in England and Wales, the number of individual applications made by UK citizens to Strasbourg is not great: in 1994, 236 applications were registered with the European Commission of Human Rights; 141 were held inadmissible or struck off and 16 were held admissible. However, the importance of the ECHR extends well beyond the numbers of individual applications. As Harris, O'Boyle and Warbrick put it:[116]

> The real achievement of the Convention system can be said to go beyond the statistical tally of cases and the provision of remedies for individuals. It resides in the deterrent effect of an operational system. States, confronted with a system that works, must keep their law and administrative practices under review. As happens in Whitehall, new legislation must, as far as possible, be 'Strasbourg proofed'. In this way the Convention radiates a constant pressure for the maintenance of human rights standards and for change throughout the new Europe.

110 In the context of the GCHQ case study, see Chapter 28.
111 Art 3, Statute of the Council of Europe 1949 (published in the Unitd Kingdom as Cmnd 7778).
112 Subject to the United Kingdom accepting the right of individual petition, which it does on a periodical basis, see below.
113 Individuals must exhaust domestic remedies, see below.
114 See Chapter 28.
115 See p. 675.
116 *Law of the European Convention on Human Rights*, p. 31.

Rights protected under the Convention

The ECHR is concerned primarily with civil and political rights, rather than economic and social rights (such as rights to housing and health care). Most rights require governments of the signatory states to *refrain* from infringing the right in question, though the state may in some instances have a positive obligation to take steps to ensure that the right is protected.

The main rights are as follows:

- that the right to life shall be protected by law (Art 2);
- freedom from torture or inhuman or degrading treatment or punishment (Art 3);
- freedom from slavery, servitude or forced or compulsory labour (Art 4);
- the right to liberty and security of the person (Art 5);
- the right to a fair trial (Art 6);
- freedom from retroactive criminal offences and punishment (Art 7);
- the right to respect for private and family life, home and correspondence (Art 8);
- freedom of religion (Art 9);
- freedom of expression (Art 10);
- freedom of assembly and association (Art 11);
- the right to marry and to found a family (Art 12);
- the right to an effective national remedy (Art 13);
- freedom from discrimination in respect of the rights protected by the Convention (Art 14);
- the right to property (Art 1 of the First Protocol);
- the right to education (Art 2 of the First Protocol); and
- the right to free elections (Art 3 of the First Protocol).

Other protocols set out the following:

- freedom from imprisonment for non-fulfilment of a contractual obligation;
- freedom of movement within a state and freedom to leave its territory;
- the right of a national not to be expelled from and to enter a state's territory;
- freedom of aliens from collective and individual expulsion;
- freedom from the death penalty;
- the right to review in criminal cases;
- the right to compensation for miscarriages of justice.

Not absolute rights

Most of the rights set out in the ECHR are expressed in qualified terms; they are often qualified by expressions allowing interference with the right 'in accordance with the law [of the state]' or in circumstances where interference with the right is 'necessary in a democratic society'. Article 15 also states that:

> In times of war or other public emergency threatening the life of the nation any High Contracting Party may take measures derogating from its obligations under this Convention to the extent strictly required by the exigencies of the situation . . .

The European Commission and Court of Human Rights have both, at various times, accepted that terrorist action in Northern Ireland during the 1970s and 1980s justified the United Kingdom making declarations of derogation. The United Kingdom made its last declaration of derogation on 23 October 1988 to enable it to operate the Prevention of Terrorism Act, which permitted police to detain suspects for lengthy periods after their arrest. But for the derogation, this would almost certainly have been contrary to Art 5.

SUMMARY

The previous chapter examines the role of law as a tool to be used by government. This chapter explores the part law plays in the notion of 'limited government'. We have seen how constitutional conventions, the rule of law (including common law principles) and international treaty obligations can work to constrain and limit the freedom of government. Running through this chapter is the assumption that to be legitimate, governmental actions need to be supported by more than a majority, either in the House of Commons or of the electorate. This assumption implies that democracy is about more than elections and that judges also have a part to play in developing and applying principles to limit governmental actions. How far they should go is, however, an increasingly controversial issue. Should they, for example, be able to question the actions not only of government and the administration, but also the legality of legislation enacted by Parliament?

The book now moves in Part B to look more closely at the way the constitution facilitates government's use of law and in Part C to look at methods of redress and scrutiny which impose limitations on governmental actions.

Questions

1. Should government be able to legislate and implement its policies as it pleases, provided that it has the consent of Parliament and the support of the majority of the electorate?

2. Is Parliament subject to the rule of law? If so, what does this mean in practice?

3. During the early 1980s some criticized government policy towards local government on the grounds that the centralization of control over local government, including the abolition of the GLC by the Local Government Act 1986, was 'unconstitutional'.[117] In what senses might it be said to be unconstitutional to abolish local authorities? Can an action be unconstitutional if it is authorized by an Act of Parliament?

4. In 1971 police in Northern Ireland interrogated 14 people to find out information about the IRA. Five techniques were used.[118]

(a) Wall standing: forcing the detainees to remain for periods of some hours in a 'stress position' . . . spreadeagled against the wall with their fingers put high above

[117] See p. 136.

[118] These facts are taken from the report of the decision of the European Court of Human Rights in *Ireland v United Kingdom* (1980) 2 EHRR 25.

their head, the legs spread apart and the feet back, causing them to stand on their toes with the weight of the body mainly on the fingers.

(b) Hooding: putting a black bag over the detainees' heads and keeping it there at all times except during interrogation.

(c) Subjection to noise: pending their interrogations, holding the detainees in a room where there was a continuous loud and hissing noise.

(d) Deprivation of sleep: pending their interrogations, depriving the detainees of sleep.

(e) Deprivation of food and drink.

When these matters became public, the British government set up a committee of inquiry chaired by the judge, Lord Parker. The Parker Report contained a majority and a minority opinion. It was revealed that the use of the five techniques was authorized at 'high level', though never put into writing. All three members of the Parker Committee agreed that the methods used, or at least some of them, were illegal under English law. Two members, however, concluded that the use of such techniques 'need not be ruled out on moral grounds'. In a statement to the House of Commons in 1972, the Prime Minister said the five techniques would not be used in future, but if the government decided additional techniques were required 'then I think that they would probably have to come to the House and ask for powers to do it'.

The detainees brought civil actions against the government and received between £25,000 and £10,000 each in out-of-court settlements. In 1978, the European Commission and Court of Human Rights found that the United Kingdom had contravened Art 3 of the ECHR ('No one shall be subjected to torture or to inhuman or degrading treatment').

Do you think the use of the five techniques should be described as 'morally wrong', 'unlawful' or 'unconstitutional'?

Does your classification change according to *who* made the decision to treat the detainees in this way: (i) a police officer without approval of his senior officers; (ii) the Prime Minister; (iii) under authority of an Act of Parliament; (iv) with the approval of the vast majority of the electorate?

Part B

THE LEGAL BASIS OF GOVERNMENT ACTION

7

INTRODUCTION TO PART B

THE LEGAL BASIS OF GOVERNMENT ACTION

Almost everything we do in our daily lives is at some level controlled or facilitated by government. Consider just the first half an hour in a typical person's day: they get up in the morning, turn on the radio, have a bath and make breakfast. Even though these activities take place in the privacy of one's home, they are underpinned by a complex network of government regulation.

The bed and mattress slept on, if they were bought relatively recently, have to conform to safety standards set by delegated legislation.[1] Law determines the time to which we set our clocks and watches.[2] A pressure group called Daylight Extra Now is currently campaigning for the United Kingdom to adopt European Summer Time; an Act of Parliament will be needed to achieve this.[3] So far as the radio is concerned, all radio stations have to be licensed by government; the Broadcasting Act 1990 and delegated legislation[4] prohibits any one company owning more than six licences to provide independent radio services.

The person's radio may well be powered by mains electricity. The Electricity Act 1989 prohibits the unlicensed supply, transmission or generation of electricity. The Secretary of State is given power to grant licences and the Act sets up a regulatory system for the industry. The quality of water for the bath and the kettle are also regulated. European Community Directive 80/778 imposed obligations on the United Kingdom to ensure that domestic water meets certain standards.[5] The Water Industry Act 1991 and delegated

[1] See e.g. the Furniture and Furnishings (Fire) (Safety) Regulations 1988 (SI 1988 No 1324), made by a minister under s 11 of the Consumer Protection Act 1987, and the Bunk Beds (Entrapment Hazards) (Safety) Regulations 1987 (SI 1987 No 1337).

[2] See Summer Time Act 1972 and delegated legislation made under it such as the Summer Time Order 1994 (SI 1994 No 2798).

[3] A Private Member's Bill designed to adopt European Summer Time was put to Parliament on 19 January 1996.

[4] Broadcasting (Restrictions on the Holdings of Licences) Order 1991 (SI 1991 No 1176).

[5] In 1989 the EC Commission brought proceedings in the ECJ under Art 169 of the EC Treaty (on which see Chapter 29) against the United Kingdom seeking a declaration that the United Kingdom was failing to fulfil its obligations under Directive 80/778 because of high levels of nitrates in domestic water: see *EC Commission v UK* [1992] ECR I-6103. In the United Kingdom, a pressure group later used judicial review proceedings (unsuccessfully) to challenge the steps being taken by the UK government to comply with the ECJ's judgment: see *R v Secretary of State for the Environment, ex p Friends of the Earth* (1995) 7 Admin LR 26.

legislation[6] impose obligations on the water companies (formerly publicly-owned corporations) to meet these standards. The breakfast milk arrives on the doorstep, its production, sale and quality having been controlled by government. Farmers are permitted to produce only the amount of milk allocated to them by a quota determined by the Ministry of Agriculture, Fisheries and Food in accordance with Community legislation.[7] Under the Agriculture Act 1993, the Secretary of State approves schemes for the marketing of milk.[8] The hygiene standards of cornflakes, like other foods, are controlled by the Food Safety Act 1990;[9] this statute confers power on the Secretary of State to make detailed rules by delegated legislation.[10] Legislation also creates rules about the packaging, provision of nutrition information, labelling and weights in which foodstuffs may be sold.

Whether we realize it or not, we all live very highly regulated lives: public law is at the heart of social and business activity. The constitution provides a framework within which regulatory schemes and standards are set and disputes mediated. As previously noted, the extent to which government has legal capacity to intervene in social and economic activity is politically contentious.[11] Many people on the political Right believe that government intervenes too much; they call for the 'rolling back of the frontiers of the state' and view deregulation as a necessary precondition to economic growth. They see markets as a better way of satisfying needs than collective political decision-making. For others, however, government action to regulate the operation of the free market and fill its gaps is one of the great achievements of the twentieth century; intervention in the form of provision of welfare benefits, old-age pensions, personal social services, the enforcement of trading standards and the NHS are essential for a just and fair society.

Law as an instrument of government

Whichever view is taken, some degree of government intervention is inevitable. Part B of this book is about how legal authority is conferred on ministers, local authorities and other public bodies to do this. The general position is stated by Laws J in *R v Somerset County Council, ex p Fewings* (a case in

[6] See e.g. Water Supply (Water Quality) Regulations 1991.

[7] See EC Regulation 89/764/EEC and Dairy Produce Quota Regulations 1993. A farmer aggrieved by the quota allocated to him may appeal to the Dairy Produce Quota Tribunal (on tribunals generally, see Chapter 19 below). Determinations by the tribunal may be subject to judicial review: see e.g. *R v Dairy Produce Quota Tribunal for England and Wales, ex p Caswell* [1990] 2 AC 738.

[8] An interest group unsuccessfully applied for judicial review of the Secretary of State's decision to approve the new Milk Marque scheme in 1994: see *R v Ministry of Agriculture, Fisheries and Food, ex p Dairy Trade Federation Ltd* [1995] COD 3.

[9] This was enacted to give effect to obligations imposed on the United Kingdom by EC Directive 93/43/EC.

[10] See e.g. the Food Safety (General Food Hygiene) Regulations 1995 (SI 1995 No 1763).

[11] See Chapter 5.

which a local authority was held to have acted unlawfully in passing a resolution to ban deer hunting on its land):[12]

> Public bodies and private persons are both subject to the rule of law; nothing could be more elementary. But the principles which govern their relationships with the law are wholly different. For private persons, the rule is that you may do anything you choose which the law does not prohibit. It means that the freedoms of the private citizen are not conditional upon some distinct and affirmative justification for which he must burrow in the law books. Such a notion would be anathema to our English legal traditions. But for public bodies the rule is opposite, and of another character altogether. It is that any action to be taken must be justified by positive law. A public body has no heritage of legal rights which it enjoys for its own sake; at every turn, all of its dealings constitute the fulfilment of duties which it owes to others; indeed, it exists for no other purpose. . . . Under our law, this is true of every public body. The rule is necessary in order to protect people from arbitrary interference by those set in power over them.

Without proper legal underpinning for their actions, government officials are powerless to regulate, inspect, raise money by taxation, license, impose new criminal sanctions and so on. If they attempt to do so without legal authority, their action may be invalid; they may even commit a tort or criminal offence. The corollary of this is that if public authorities have been given legal authority to act, they may do things which no individual would be able to do. To give an example, if a neighbour enters your home and snatches your young child without your consent, believing you are neglecting the child, the neighbour may well commit a crime (child abduction) and a tort (trespass). If, however, similar action is taken by a social worker empowered by the Children Act 1989 and an order of a court to intervene to protect children from harm, the child's removal is lawful.

Is government sometimes free to act without legal authority?

In *ex p Fewings*, Laws J stated the uncontroversial proposition that for 'private persons, the rule is that you may do anything you choose which the law does not prohibit'. In the past it has been suggested that this principle also applies to government. In other words, that it is not always necessary for a public body to have positive legal authority for its actions. Consider the following case.

In 1978 James Malone, an antiques dealer, was prosecuted for handling stolen goods. During his trial, it emerged that the Metropolitan Police had, without entering on to his land, collected evidence by secretly monitoring his telephone conversations. This they had done by seeking a warrant from the Home Secretary which authorized the Post Office to make the recordings. In a subsequent civil action against the police, Malone unsuccessfully sought a declaration that this covert tapping was unlawful.[13] At the time no statute

[12] [1995] 1 All ER 513 at 524; affirmed by the Court of Appeal at [1995] 1 WLR 1037. This case is discussed further in Chapter 24.

[13] *Malone v Metropolitan Police* [1979] Ch 344. See further John Lambert, 'Executive Authority to Tap Telephones' (1980) 43 MLR 59.

expressly authorized telephone tapping; nor, in this case, did the police or Home Secretary claim to have any specific legal power under the prerogative to authorize the interception.[14] Giving judgment in the High Court, Sir Robert Megarry V-C said:[15]

> . . . there is the contention [by counsel for Malone] that as no power to tap telephones has been given either by statute or common law, the tapping is necessarily unlawful. The underlying assumption of this contention, of course, is that nothing is lawful that it is not positively authorised by law. . . . England is not a country where everything is forbidden except what is expressly permitted. One possible illustration is smoking. I enquired what positive authority was given by the law to permit people to smoke. Counsel for the plaintiff accepted that there was none; but tapping, he said, was different. It was in general disfavour, and it offended against usual and proper standards of behaviour, in that it was an invasion of privacy and an interference with the liberty of the individual and his right to be let alone when lawfully engaged on his own affairs.
>
> I did not find this argument convincing. . . . The notion that some express authorisation of law is required for acts which meet with 'general disfavour' and 'offend the proper standards of behaviour', and so on, would make the state of the law dependent on subjective views on indefinite concepts, and would be likely to produce some remarkable and contentious results. Neither in principle nor in authority can I see any justification for this view, and I reject it. If the tapping of telephones by the Post Office at the request of the police can be carried out without any breach of the law, it does not require any statutory or common law power to justify it: it can lawfully be done simply because there is nothing to make it unlawful.

Megarry V-C held that secret interception of telephone conversations in the circumstances of this particular case had not been unlawful: the law of tort did not protect any general right to privacy; and in carrying out the tapping, the police had not unlawfully infringed any of Malone's property rights. Megarry V-C's approach has been criticized.[16] The law on telephone tapping has since been altered by the Interception of Communications Act 1985 which now gives the Home Secretary specific statutory powers to authorize tapping in defined circumstances and so *Malone* no longer regulates what is lawful in this particular context. The more general question remains, however, whether the government does indeed have freedom to act in some situations without specific legal authority.

Taken as assertions of general principle, the statements in *Malone* and *Fewings* cannot both be correct. Our view is that the approach taken by Laws J in *Fewings* is the proper one. The rule in *Malone* is capable of applying in only a very limited range of situations.

The 'freedom to act' has no application to public bodies created by an Act

[14] Many complex issues arose in the case. Having lost in the High Court, Malone successfully made an application to the European Court of Human Rights, where he argued that his rights under Art 8 of the Convention had been infringed: see *Malone v United Kingdom* (1987) 7 EHRR 14.

[15] At p. 638.

[16] See e.g. Carol Harlow [1980] PL 1 and Graham Zellick, 'Government beyond Law' [1985] PL 283.

of Parliament: in these circumstances statute law provides a comprehensive catalogue of all the legal powers possessed by such a body. Thus (as Laws J explains in *ex p Fewings*) a local authority has only those powers which are specifically conferred upon it by statute.[17] Every action by such a body has to have definite legal authority, even if there is nothing in the general law to make the proposed action unlawful. In the absence of such specific legal authorization, the action may be struck down as *ultra vires* (outside the powers) by the court if a citizen applies for judicial review.

The principle set out in *Malone* can therefore apply only to non-statutory public bodies. As seen in Chapter 3, some important institutions and office-holders in the United Kingdom were not set up by Act of Parliament, but exist by reason of constitutional conventions or were originally emanations of the Crown. A prime illustration of this is the office of Secretary of State. Although Secretaries of State are now conferred with many powers by various Acts of Parliament, the office of Secretary of State owes its existence to the prerogative: a Secretary of State is formally created when the monarch presents the person with three seals.[18] Because the office of Secretary of State was not created by statute, statutes do not provide a comprehensive definition of all the legal powers and duties of the Secretaries of State. In addition, a Secretary of State may have specific legal powers and duties recognized by the courts as part of the prerogative (the unique and residual legal powers of the Crown).[19]

Malone's case suggests that in addition to these statutory and prerogative powers and duties, a minister carrying out official functions may also have a 'freedom to act' similar to that of private citizens. In practice, however, this is possible only in respect of a very narrow range of activities. The implementation of government policy normally requires either the alteration of people's existing legal rights or the spending of public money, or both. But as with private citizens, a minister is 'free to act' only in so far as this does not infringe any other person's existing legal rights. Moreover, if the action involves spending a significant amount of public money, especially if it is to recur annually, then the minister is required to seek parliamentary approval for this expenditure (if not the actual action itself).[20] For these reasons the proposition in *Malone* ought not to be treated as a statement of broad principle.

Four sources of legal authority

It can therefore be said that public officials and bodies do indeed require 'distinct and affirmative justification' from a specific law for almost all their actions. The chapters which follow in this part of the book examine four main sources of legal authority for government action:

[17] See further Chapter 23.

[18] See p. 50 and A. J. C. Simcock, 'One and Many—The office of Secretary of State' (1992) 70 Public Administration 535.

[19] See Chapter 12.

[20] See p. 181, n. 31.

(a) Acts of Parliament;[21]
(b) delegated legislation made by ministers;[22]
(c) the prerogative;[23] and
(d) the European Community treaties agreed by member states and secondary legislation (especially regulations and directives) made by institutions of the Community under powers delegated to them by the treaties.[24]

When government wishes to act to achieve its policy or fulfil its obligations under Community law, it may depend on one or more of these sources as the basis for its action. From a legal point of view, the result is often a complex web of overlapping and interconnecting types of legal authorization: statute law, delegated legislation, prerogative power and Community legislation may all confer powers and impose duties on government to regulate or enable a particular sphere of activity. Consider just one transaction which at first glance may seem only to be a matter of contract law: flying abroad on holiday. Underlying this contractual exchange is a whole raft of public law. To enable air transport between the United Kingdom and the destination (if it is outside the European Community), there is likely to be a bilateral treaty detailing the routes which airlines may operate and imposing conditions and restrictions. Although there is some academic debate about what authorizes the government to enter into international treaty obligations, from the point of view of the national legal system, many people regard this as an exercise of prerogative power.[25] Within the EC there is now a single market in air travel, regulated by EC regulations[26] and directives.[27] The package holiday directive was turned into national law in the United Kingdom by delegated legislation.[28] An Act of Parliament, the Civil Aviation Act 1982, creates a regulatory framework for aviation in the United Kingdom; the Secretary of State for Transport and a special statutory body, the Civil Aviation Authority, have responsibility for formulating and applying policies about matters such as the licensing of air transport and air travel organizers.

Why legal authority is important

In the chapters which follow, we examine both the processes by which government is conferred with each sort of legal power and the end result (the nature of the power put into the hands of government). We have already said that 'a government *could* rule by fear and force but if it did so it would lack

[21] See Chapters 8 and 9.
[22] See Chapters 10 and 11.
[23] See Chapter 12.
[24] See Chapters 13 and 14.
[25] See further Chapter 12.
[26] For example, Council Regulation 91/3922/EEC on aviation technical requirements. As to the constitutional status of EC regulations, see Chapter 13.
[27] For example, the directive on package holidays 90/314.
[28] Package Travel, Package Holidays and Package Tours Regulations 1992 (SI 1992 No 3288).

legitimacy'.[29] The existence of legal authority for government action is one reason for saying that that action is acceptable. For this to be so, however, the constitutional system must do more that simply allow government itself to determine what the law is by unilateral decree. The sources of law examined in the following chapters may be justified as 'being legitimate' in several different ways.[30]

Acts of Parliament are the paradigm form of legal authority for government action in orthodox constitutional theory. As we have seen,[31] the democratic justification for parliamentary legislation is that it is 'made' by MPs who are elected at least once every five years in elections in which almost all adults are entitled to vote. In Dicey's idealized model, Parliament is therefore at the centre of the constitution; MPs are responsive to the wishes of the electorate; and MPs effectively scrutinize and, if necessary reject, government bills. The reality of enacting statute law may be far from this ideal. The problems are arguably even worse in relation to the other sources of legal authorization for government action—delegated legislation made by ministers, the prerogative and Community legislation. Often Parliament plays no real part in deciding what powers and obligations ought to be conferred on government by these means. Some critics go so far as to suggest that Parliament has now become part of the 'dignified' constitution:[32] while the Commons and the Lords provide a public spectacle, the real work of deciding what legal powers government ought to have takes place behind the scenes, away from the public gaze. Government dominates the House of Commons and dictates to MPs in its party how to vote. On top of all of this, much law is now made through the institutions of the Community. People in the United Kingdom are able to vote for MEPs, but even though the European Parliament now has more power to participate in the Community legislative process than it once did, critics argue that national parliaments ought to have a larger role.[33] In short, while orthodox constitutional theory places trust in the public's elected representatives, the reality is that MPs are often marginal to the processes of deciding what legal powers government ought to have.

The participation in the law-making process by elected representatives is not, however, the only reason for saying that government action authorized by law is legitimate. Two others are worth noting at this point. First, the ability of interested individuals and groups to take part in the process may be said to make outcomes acceptable. Pressure and interest groups are often actively involved in seeking to persuade government to take or refrain from action. In the battles of Sunday trading they were even involved in framing the wording of the Sunday Trading bill.[34] In the legislative process for making

[29] See p. 134.
[30] For a useful discussion, see Robert Baldwin, *Rules and Government* (1995), pp. 41–7.
[31] See Chapter 5.
[32] See p. 41.
[33] See p. 313.
[34] See p. 216.

the Working Time Directive, some interest groups were formally represented through the Economic and Social Council.[35]

A different type of claim for the legitimacy of government's legal authority is to say that it is the product of technical expertise. Whether or not MPs or pressure groups have participated in shaping the legal power, it may be justified on the basis of objective scientific or other expertise. Thus rules on the safety of beds, food and so on may be said to be legitimate on this basis. As Baldwin points out, there are difficulties with using expertise as a reason for claiming legal authority is legitimate,[36] not least because it may often be difficult to know how competent and impartial the professional experts are.

The worry about all of this is that if government controls the processes by which it obtains legal power, and if it is able to evade proper scrutiny, the outcome may be that ministers and other public bodies hold too much power which is liable to be used oppressively or abused.

Questions

1. Think of an activity you do in a typical day. Research the ways in which it is regulated and facilitated by public law. What are the implications of your findings?

2. Does central government need direct legal authority to take the following actions: (a) to run a poster campaign warning the public of the dangers of smoking; (b) to ban smoking in all government buildings; (c) to ban smoking in all public places?

3. Imagine you are a lawyer advising a local authority. Elected councillors decide that the council should print and distribute leaflets in its area encouraging local businesses to plant hanging baskets of flowers outside shops and offices in order to beautify the neighbourhood. A prize of £1,000 will be offered for the best show. Will you need to 'burrow in the law books' for direct legal authority to carry out this proposal, or is the local authority free to act without such authority?

[35] See p. 324.
[36] *Rules and Government*, p. 45.

8

ACTS OF PARLIAMENT

The failure of Parliament to produce effective and sensible legislation may seem a dry, 'dull government' thing but it affects the lives of millions, year after year.

Andrew Marr, Ruling Britannia (1995), p. 141

INTRODUCTION

Statutes are the principal legal tools available to government. Their use enables government to change existing law, create new criminal offences, impose taxes, abrogate rights and limit freedoms. Using this tool, the constitution could be 'rewritten' and government given absolute power. Parliament's control over legislative proposals is therefore of vital importance and its procedures for law-making are fundamental to the system. Yet for many years there has been dissatisfaction with aspects of statute law;[1] several factors may be to blame. Parliamentary Counsel, the specialist draftsmen employed to write bills, are said sometimes to use inappropriate techniques for giving verbal effect to government policy. Ministers and civil servants may fail to consult with expert opinion and interest groups. Connected to this is the unnecessary haste with which government attempts to turn its ideas into law, with the result that there is a 'legislate as you go' approach, with many bills being half-baked first or second drafts when they are introduced into Parliament. For other critics, it is Parliament itself and the anachronistic procedures it uses which are the reasons for many of the difficulties. As Marr puts it:[2]

> Let us be conservative and acknowledge entirely the right of the government to propose and push through the legislation it wants, irrespective of whether the ministerial

[1] There have been two major reviews. The Renton Committee on the preparation of legislation reported to the government in 1975 (Cmnd 6053), but many of its recommendations remain unimplemented. In 1991 the Hansard Society for Parliamentary Government, an independent pressure group, appointed a commission to examine how government and Parliament produce legislation and to assess whether the system is in need of overhaul and change. Its report, *Making the Law*, was published in 1992 (and debated by the House of Lords on 14 December 1994: see HL Deb, vol. 559, col. 1291). Both Houses of Parliament have also carried out their own reviews of the legislative process: for the most recent, see *Select Committee on sittings of the House* (HC 20 of 1991–92, the Jopling report) and *Sitting Hours Reform*, 8th report of the Procedure Select Committee (HC 491 of 1994–95).

[2] *Ruling Britannia* (1995), p. 141.

> wheezes are brilliant or batty. Accept that and you are still left with the duty of Parliament to ensure that the laws MPs pore over and vote on are legally and practically effective. What else is a legislature for? If it cannot or will not achieve that minimal requirement, we would be as well building a replica of Westminster in balsa-wood, ceremonially stuffing legislation through a slot in the roof, pulling it out through another in the bottom, and declaring it passed.

Some caution is needed, however, before dismissing entirely what currently happens in Parliament as merely rubber-stamping decisions made elsewhere:

> the facility Parliament provides for public ventilation of policy issues cannot be brushed aside as worthless merely because it falls short—even a long way—of a Utopian view of what representation and democracy in a complex pluralist society should really be about.[3]

But there *is* something of a crisis in the way we legislate in the United Kingdom, though many (including in government) choose to ignore this.

The problems stretch beyond the alleged practical difficulties of haste, inadequate consultation, weaknesses in drafting and the failing of MPs to assert their powers of scrutiny over government; the problems go to the core of constitutional theory. The orthodoxy reassures us that MPs are responsive to public opinion and so will not, in the long run, pass legislation which does not have the support of the majority of the electorate.[4] A culture of liberty is also said to 'pervade' the system. But Dicey's idealized constitutional model—in which Parliament controlled government, not vice versa—lacks credibility today. The governing party now effectively controls what bills are introduced into Parliament and when and how they are scrutinized. This is particularly worrying given the responsibility which the orthodox constitutional model places upon Parliament (rather than the courts or some other institution) to ensure that statute law is constitutionally acceptable.

This chapter considers the criticisms made of the process of enacting statutes, highlighting issues of broad constitutional importance. Chapter 9 goes on to survey the legislative process at work in one context—attempts to deregulate Sunday trading. Issues regarding the use of statutes to give effect to Community law are considered in Chapter 13.

DRAFTING AND INITIATING LEGISLATION

Almost all parliamentary legislation is initiated by government.[5] As we have seen, policy may emerge from protracted negotiation within government and between government and interest groups.[6] Much of the 'legislative process'

[3] Gavin Drewry in Michael Ryle and Peter Richards (eds.), *The Commons Under Scrutiny* (1988), p. 127.

[4] See Chapter 5.

[5] On Private Members' Bills, see p. 191 below. Like government bills, Private Members' Bills deal with matters of public concern. Parliament can also legislate in private matters: see Chapter 5, note 41.

[6] See Chapter 4.

can therefore be regarded as happening before any bill is actually introduced into Parliament. Indeed, Drewry comments that 'most bills are the products of hard bargaining in Whitehall, with Parliament being presented, in effect, with a *fait accompli*, too late to exert any real influence'.[7]

How does government decide which bills to introduce?

A legislative programme for the forthcoming parliamentary session (which normally runs from November to November) is drawn up by a Cabinet committee (the Future Legislation Committee). Parliamentary time is very limited[8] and departments always make 'bids' for more bills than can be accommodated. Difficult decisions therefore need to be made about priorities.[9] This may mean that worthwhile but politically unexciting bills are continually postponed, a fate often suffered by law reform bills recommended to the government by the Law Commission.[10] Bills are required to complete their legislative passage through both Houses of Parliament and to receive Royal Assent within a single parliamentary session (which is normally no more than 12 months long), so careful planning and management of the timetable is essential.

By convention, the government's legislative programme for a forthcoming parliamentary session is announced in the Queen's Speech at the State Opening of Parliament each autumn. At this event, proposed legislation is announced in only the most general terms. For instance, the Queen's Speech in November 1994 referred to plans to legislate on Sunday trading using these words: 'My Government will bring forward a bill to reform the law on Sunday trading in England and Wales.'

Who drafts bills?

Once a department knows that time will be found for one of its bills in the legislative programme for the forthcoming session, senior civil servants and departmental lawyers draw up detailed instructions for Parliamentary Counsel, the 30 or so specialist lawyers at 36 Whitehall who draft all government bills. What happens at this stage takes place behind closed doors and so, as the Hansard Society Commission found out, 'it is difficult for anyone outside the system to understand properly how it works'.[11] We therefore have to speculate. Often civil servants and ministers still seem to be formulating policy at this stage, and so initial instructions to Parliamentary Counsel may

[7] Drewry in Ryle and Richards (eds.), *The Commons Under Scrutiny*, p. 126.

[8] The House of Commons sits on average for about 175 days each session; the Lords for 150 days. During this time, MPs and peers also have to carry out work not directly connected to the legislative process: see Chapter 16.

[9] On the general role of the Cabinet in coordinating the work of government departments and, where necessary, resolving conflicts between them, see p. 54.

[10] See further p. 197 below.

[11] *Making the Law*, para. 164.

be sketchy. Drafting work is rarely completed by the time a bill is published and introduced to begin its passage through Parliament, resulting in many amendments being made by the government to its own bills as they are considered by Parliament;[12] Parliamentary Counsel are responsible for drafting and advising upon these amendments. The Hansard Society Commission heard evidence critical of a 'legislate-as-you-go' approach when bills are introduced into Parliament with many particulars still to be worked out.[13] The example of the Companies Bill in 1989 is not unusual: 'the government's own amendments had reached the thousand mark and included no fewer than fifteen new clauses which were introduced on the last day of the committee's sitting'.[14]

Are bills poorly drafted?

Over the years, a drafting style has emerged in the United Kingdom which is markedly different from the 'continental' approach used in EC directives and in legislation of most other member states. Generally legislation in civil law jurisdictions tends to be simple, short and concerned with setting down broad statements of principles and rules, whereas Acts of Parliament are inclined to be much more detailed and precise.[15]

The criticism most often made of Acts of Parliament is that they are usually incomprehensible to non-lawyers, and sometimes even to lawyers, because of the complexity of their language, grammar and structure.[16] There may be several reasons for this. First, the statute may seek to give legal effect to a policy which itself is inherently highly complex. Secondly, in some contexts it may be important for people's rights and obligations to be spelt out with great precision so that they may plan their affairs accordingly. An aspect of the rule of law is that law needs to be certain,[17] and sometimes certainty may go hand in hand with complexity. This is particularly so where a statute imposes a tax (the right of government to require a transfer of wealth from a citizen or business) or penal sanctions. A third reason for complexity is incremental change to policy, which is often given legal effect by several Acts amending earlier ones over a period of time. Until such time

[12] See p. 182 below.
[13] *Making the Law*, para. 173.
[14] Andrew Marr, *Ruling Britannia*, p. 142 (quoting John Garrett MP).
[15] For an illustration of this compare the Sunday Trading Act 1994 (Chapter 9) with the Working Time Directive (Chapter 14). Is the difference that great? Bear in mind that directives are often intended to set out a broad framework for a policy which member states then adapt to their own particular circumstances.
[16] For an illustration of this, look back at the European Communities Act 1972, ss 2, 3 (set out in Chapter 5). Should such a major piece of legislation affecting people's rights and obligations and the UK constitution really have been expressed in such opaque terms? Is this possibly a situation in which obscure drafting was politically desirable because it helped to hide the enormity of what was being enacted?
[17] See Chapter 6.

as these Acts are consolidated, people and their legal advisors may have to look at several different statutes to understand what the law requires.

Fourthly, complexity may arise from a desire to control and restrict discretion in the implementation of policy. A government department may fear that unless contingencies are anticipated and details spelt out, other people may misunderstand exactly what the Act is intended to achieve: there may be 'misinterpretation' by the agency responsible for giving practical effect to a policy (such as a local authority) or, if litigation should arise, the courts. According to the Hansard Society Commission, the pressure for detail comes from 'middle-ranking civil servants'.[18] An illustration of this sort of drafting can be seen in the Local Government (Miscellaneous Provisions) Act 1982. When the Home Office set up a system for the licensing of sex shops[19] by local authorities, it was thought necessary to specify that, for the purpose of the Act, 'premises' include 'vessels' which means 'any ship, boat, raft or other apparatus constructed or adapted for floating on water'.[20] A plethora of detail such as this can stand in the way of easy comprehension.

Obscurely drafted legislation is obviously a matter of concern to the businesses and citizens affected by it. For instance, a woman who believes that she has been discriminated against by her employer because of her sex has to look in several places to find her rights and remedies, and in doing so she will find them set out in unfamiliar language, prompting the Equal Opportunities Commission to comment that:[21]

> If the final form of the legislation is such that individuals cannot even form a basic understanding of the scope of the legislation which affects their fundamental rights and which they are expected to utilise unaided, then the whole legislative process has been in vain.

Complexity and parliamentary scrutiny

Legislation which is difficult to understand may create problems not only for the people whose rights and interests are affected by it, but also for Parliament. If MPs during the legislative process cannot understand what a bill really means, they will not be able to probe and scrutinize the government's policy proposals effectively. On the one hand there are calls for detailed legislation. As we have seen, Dicey argued that statutes ought to confer as little discretion as possible on ministers and other public bodies and one way of restricting discretion is to spell out in statutes with considerable particularity what powers ministers and others have and how they ought to set about making their decisions. Today some commentators continue to argue that the traditional British drafting style has the virtue of both prompting certainty and enabling democratic control.[22]

18 *Making the Law*, para. 168.
19 Establishments where pornography and other sexually explicit material are sold.
20 Sched 3, para. 5.
21 *Making the Law*, p. 263.
22 See e.g. Francis Bennion, *Statute Law* (2nd edn., 1983), p. 25.

On the other hand, there are also calls for shorter, less detailed legislation.[23] An editorial in *The Times* claimed:[24]

> Because British laws are five times longer than comparable continental measures, Parliament faces a legislative workload that has become intolerable. There may be a case, therefore, for adopting some of the practices used in continental lawmaking to improve efficiency.

More and more, statutes do set out only the broad framework for the government's policy, leaving the detail to be filled in later by delegated legislation drafted in government departments. There are several problems with the use of such 'skeleton' Acts. One is that in the absence of detail, Parliament may be unable to see clearly how a bill will work in practice. The controversial Child Support Act 1991, for instance, creates over 100 regulation-making powers for ministers. While there was widespread agreement about the general purpose of the Act (that absent parents be compelled to give financial support to their children), there was equally widespread disagreement about the detailed working out of the rules. As we will see later,[25] delegated legislation is subject to significantly less parliamentary scrutiny than bills and it cannot be amended, only approved or rejected by Parliament as drafted by a government department. So while skeleton-style bills may give ministers maximum flexibility to alter and amend policy to suit changing circumstances,[26] and while such bills may appear to be clearer, there are fears that they confer too much unsupervised discretion on government.

There is a risk that we are ending up with the worst of all worlds: Acts which are in part over-elaborate and so detailed as to prevent MPs and the public understanding them, and which also confer too much regulation-making power on ministers. There is probably, however, no *general* cure-all for the ills which are diagnosed. The search for clearer, more easily scrutinized legislation needs to have regard to particular circumstances. Legislation likely to be read only by specialist practitioners (for example, accountants and lawyers advising companies) may well need to be phrased and structured differently to a statute dealing with basic rights and entitlements of ordinary citizens.

THE PASSAGE THROUGH THE COMMONS

Once the text of a bill is in existence, the next task for government is to steer it through the parliamentary legislative process.[27] As the Hansard Society

[23] For criticisms of the English style of drafting see Sir William Dale, *Legislative Drafting: a new approach* (1977) and the Hansard Society Commission, *Making the Law*, Chapter 4.

[24] Editorial in *The Times*, 15 November 1993. Cf. T. St J. N. Bates, 'The Drafting of European Community Legislation' (1983) 5 Statute Law Review 24, where EC drafting is criticized for its lack of precision and drafting errors.

[25] Chapter 10.

[26] Even to the extent of permitting ministers to amend the Act of Parliament itself: on Henry VIII clauses, see Chapter 10.

[27] The definitive guide to parliamentary procedure is known as 'Erskine May': see C. J. Boulton (ed.), *Erskine May's Treatise on the Law, Privileges, Proceedings and Usage of Parliament* (21st edn., 1989).

Commission puts it, 'statute law must be rooted in the authority of Parliament and thoroughly exposed to open democratic scrutiny by the representatives of the people in Parliament'.[28] The constitutional function of Parliament in giving its consent to bills is, first, to make the executive account publicly for its proposals, and secondly to participate in validating the words of enactment, so giving them legal effect. There is widespread concern that parliamentary scrutiny is inadequate. In most instances, Parliament 'improves' bills only marginally—on points of detail rather than forcing government to rethink a bad policy behind a bill. Very few government bills are defeated outright and few amendments suggested by MPs outside government are incorporated into the bills.

The term 'whips' is used frequently in this description of the legislative process.[29] They are small teams of MPs appointed by each party leader to ensure that other MPs in the party attend Parliament and vote as instructed to do so. The whips indicate to MPs how important their attendance for a particular vote is by sending them a notice of the Commons' business for the forthcoming week. If an item is underlined three times ('a three-line whip'), this means that attendance is absolutely essential. MPs who fail to vote as instructed in such a situation are likely to be disciplined, perhaps even ceasing to be recognized as a member of the party.

Deciding where to start

Government 'business managers' (whips and ministers) have to decide whether to introduce a bill into the House of Commons first, or into the Lords. In exceptional situations bills may also be introduced in each of the Houses concurrently, usually when speed is seen as vital.[30]

The House of Commons has exclusive initiative in relation to taxation and expenditure, and bills with financial implications are therefore introduced there.[31] Non-contentious bills, including consolidation bills which tidy up the statute book and law reform bills sponsored by the Law Commission,[32] are

28 *Making the Law*, para. 22.

29 The term derives from whippers-in, men who keep hunting hounds in order.

30 This occurred in the cases of the Commonwealth Immigrants Act 1968, the Northern Ireland (Temporary Provisions) Act 1972 and the Community Land Act 1975.

31 In bare outline the process is as follows. Each year the government presents 'supply estimates' to the House of Commons on Budget Day. In essence this large, several-volume document sets out requests by central government for permission to spend money under various categories. Eight days are spent by the Commons voting on these estimates, though the debates normally deal with very broad topics rather than the details of particular categories of expenditure. The Commons has no power to increase any of the categories, though MPs can propose a motion to reduce expenditure. Shortly after these debates, the government introduces a Consolidated Fund Bill (which itself is not usually debated) to give statutory authorization to the Bank of England to pay the sums in question. Because of highly complex accounting arrangements, normally three Consolidated Fund Bills are passed during an annual parliamentary session. One of these becomes known as the Appropriation Act: it appropriates sums to the individual purposes set out in the supply estimates, in effect making it unlawful for government to use funds set aside for one purpose for another.

32 See p. 197 below.

almost always introduced in the Lords first. Other practical and political factors may also be relevant, for example the need to balance the flow of legislation between the two Houses during the annual parliamentary session and the desire to spread the legislative load for a particular government department. As discussed later in relation to the Shops Bill in 1985, the decision in which House to begin may be of great tactical importance.[33]

The procedural steps in outline

Wherever the bill is first introduced, it must go through five stages in one House, then the other, before it can receive Royal Assent: First and Second Readings, the committee stage, report stage and Third Reading. The procedure must be completed within an annual parliamentary session; bills cannot be held over from one year to another.[34] It is possible, though highly unusual, for a bill to be introduced into Parliament and to complete all its stages in both Houses and receive Royal Assent in a single day;[35] normally the process takes several months. In sketching out the legislative process, we assume that a bill is introduced into the Commons.

First Reading

The First Reading is purely formal (there is no debate or vote). Its purpose is to give notice that the bill is being introduced. The short title of the bill, 'the Sunday Trading Bill' for example, is read out by a clerk and a day is named for its Second Reading. The bill is then officially ordered to be printed. Often at this stage the bill's text is still being drafted by Parliamentary Counsel and, although the Commons has ordered it to be printed, there is in fact nothing yet fit to print. This creates delay before a printed version of a bill is made available to MPs and to interested individuals, groups and businesses outside Parliament and may prevent full and effective consultation taking place. Even then, what is published may be no more than a first or second draft.[36]

Second Reading

At the Second Reading debate of a bill held in the Chamber of the House, often several months after the First Reading, the House is asked to accept the general principles of the bill; it is not concerned with the detailed provisions. The Second Reading debate on a bill may occasionally take place not in the Chamber of the House, but in a committee room with only some MPs present. This may happen in the case of a consolidation bill (a bill intended merely to tidy up the statute book, not to make new law) and any bill

[33] See Chapter 9.

[34] For criticisms of this, see p. 197 below.

[35] The most notorious example is the Official Secrets Act 1911. Until its repeal in 1989, s 2 imposed draconian restrictions on the release of government information.

[36] *Making the Law*, para. 178.

primarily intended to implement proposals contained in a report of the Law Commission. Such bills are politically uncontroversial and by having their Second Readings in committee, time is freed up on the floor of the House for other matters.

The Second Reading has been said to be the 'most important stage through which the bill is required to pass; for its whole principle is then at issue'.[37] While this may well be true of the theory, in practice the Second Reading is usually a rather predictable debate in which the minister responsible for directing the bill through Parliament sets out the reasons, aims and broad principles of the proposed legislation and opposition MPs oppose knowing that their criticisms are unlikely to be accepted. The vast majority of bills receive an unopposed Second Reading (in other words, there is no vote). When there is a vote, it is extremely rare for a bill to be defeated on the Second Reading: what happened to the Shops Bill in 1986 was therefore exceptional.[38]

Ministerial statements made during Second Reading debates have assumed a new legal significance since in *Pepper (Inspector of Taxes) v Hart* the House of Lords overturned long-standing court practices. It was held that parties to litigation which turns on the interpretation of an Act may, in limited circumstances, refer in court to these statements as an interpretive aid.[39]

Committee stage

Once the general principles of the proposal have been accepted at the Second Reading, the bill is referred to a 'committee' for examination in detail. It is here that MPs subject the bill to detailed scrutiny.

STANDING COMMITTEES

Most bills are considered by Standing Committees. The term Standing Committee is apt to confuse: the committee does not stand during its deliberations nor is it in continuous existence throughout the parliamentary session. They are convened for the purpose of considering one bill and are disbanded once this has been completed. Standing Committees consist of between 16 and 50 MPs in proportion to party strength in the House of Commons as a whole, so the government will always have a majority of MPs from its party on each committee. The actual number of members depends on the bill's importance and the extent of interest in it. Standing Committee members are appointed by the Committee of Selection, which in practice works very closely with the whips of each party.

These committees resemble a mini-House of Commons chamber, with members representing the government on one side of the room and the Opposition on the other. Whips from each party try to ensure that their MPs attend and vote as instructed.[40] Typically, a Standing Committee meets for

[37] *Erskine May*, p. 52.
[38] See Chapter 9.
[39] [1993] AC 593. See further Chapter 23.
[40] Compare this with select committees, where activities of whips are regarded as highly improper: see Chapter 16.

two mornings each week to consider a particular bill. It will go through the bill clause by clause,[41] debating and voting by show of hands on amendments as it does so. These committees are essentially debating chambers and in this respect they differ from the inquisitorial and investigative select committees scrutinizing the work of government departments.[42] Standing Committees do not take evidence or question witnesses.[43] In this sense they do not have a character of their own. The committee cannot identify issues that it would like to explore or collect evidence that it feels desirable in considering whether a particular legislative proposal should be adopted. For its information about the likely impact of the government's proposed policy, the committee is heavily dependent on what it is told by the minister steering the bill through the Commons: one of the problems with the committee system is that there is an inequality of informed advice as between the government side and the Opposition. While the minister has the support of his departmental officials, opposition MPs have to rely either on their own resources or on the work done by interest and pressure groups who prepare briefing papers for MPs on particular topics. Opposition and backbench MPs also do not have access to the skills of the Parliamentary Counsel, and so must draft amendments (often very complex) themselves or rely on legal advice from groups outside Parliament.

COMMITTEE OF THE WHOLE HOUSE

In the Commons, the committee stage of bills is almost always taken in a Standing Committee away from the floor of the Chamber. It is possible, however, for bills requiring rapid passage and bills of real constitutional importance or political sensitivity to be dealt with on the floor of the House by a 'Committee of the Whole House' so that all MPs have a chance to participate in debates on particular clauses.[44] Unfortunately the result is that such bills may actually receive rather inadequate detailed scrutiny.

CONSIDERATION OF OPPOSITION'S PROPOSED AMENDMENTS

The direct impact of the committee stage on the contents of bills is small if measured by the number of amendments made to a bill against the wishes of the government. In his study of government bills in three sessions (1967–68, 1968–69 and 1970–71) Griffith found that while all amendments proposed by government ministers were adopted, of the 3,074 amendments moved by the Opposition only 4 per cent (131) were successful.[45] The indirect impact of committee scrutiny is greater. Ministers do agree to reconsider proposals made by the opposition and backbencher MPs, often in order to make

[41] A 'clause' becomes a 'section' after a bill receives Royal Assent and becomes an Act.

[42] See Chapters 16 and 17.

[43] But see p. 196 below on 'Special Standing Committees'.

[44] In 1994 the Sunday Trading Bill was considered by a Committee of the Whole House in the Commons, as was the European Communities (Amendment) Bill which incorporated the Maastricht Treaty into UK law.

[45] J. A. G. Griffith, *Parliamentary Scrutiny of Government Bills* (1974).

progress, and this may result in the government itself making amendments at a later stage, though few of these are likely to have a significant effect on the main policy of the bill.

Report stage

After completion of the committee stage, the bill returns to the floor of the House. This provides an opportunity for the House as a whole to consider the bill in its revised form. There is a report stage even if a bill has been considered by a Committee of the Whole House; this is needed because committee and report stages may be several weeks apart, and not all MPs will have attended the committee discussions. Amendments made in committee may be altered and further amendments may be made. Government amendments are often made either in response to undertakings given in committee or to reverse changes that a committee made. During the sessions studied by Griffith, of the 26 defeats suffered by government in committee, 14 were reversed on report, three were modified and only nine accepted.[46]

Third Reading

The Third Reading normally follows immediately after the report stage. This is usually a formality, although minor amendments are very occasionally allowed and a few bills have been defeated on a Third Reading. At this stage, the Commons approves or rejects the bill as a whole.

Government control of the Commons' timetable and its MPs

In relation to the process just described, it is vital for government to control both the legislative timetable and the way in which MPs in its party vote. Whips are used throughout the process, though occasionally MPs are allowed a free vote when a bill deals with an issue on which there are strong differences of opinion within parties,[47] or on matters of conscience.

So far as keeping to the timetable is concerned, there is no doubt that government dominates Parliament. It would, however, be misleading to overlook the fact that government must work with the cooperation of the Opposition, particularly in the timetabling of day-to-day parliamentary business. These agreements are secured by a process referred to as 'the Usual Channels'.[48] This includes, for example, agreements on the numbers of sittings required for the committee stage of a bill. When real agreement cannot be reached, government resorts to a range of powerful procedural devices to prevent the Official Opposition and backbench MPs delaying a bill in the Commons. (The government has much less power to curtail debate in the

[46] *Parliamentary Scrutiny of Government Bills*, p. 206.
[47] For further discussion of free votes, see Chapter 9.
[48] See further J. A. G. Griffith and M. Ryle, *Parliament: functions, practice and procedure* (1989), p. 298.

Lords.) These include closure motions and guillotines. Today, closure motions are usually used to end debate at a time agreed by all parties, and they are rarely voted upon. This does not necessarily mean, of course, that the opposition parties are necessarily happy to accept a closure: they may simply realize that they would lose a vote if one was put. Once imposed, a 'guillotine' sets a strict limit on the amount of time that will be devoted to discussing clauses of a bill at committee stage. Once the time is up, the Standing Committee chairman stops debate. This is recognized as an extreme measure and is only adopted where passage of bills within a single session appears to be impossible.[49] According to Griffith and Ryle, since 1974, governments have been reluctant to move for a guillotine until a Standing Committee has sat for 70–80 hours.[50]

THE PASSAGE THROUGH THE HOUSE OF LORDS

The United Kingdom, like many countries, has a bi-cameral legislature. So, assuming that a minister has managed to steer a government bill through the Commons, it must then be referred to the upper chamber, the House of Lords. Essentially, the bill follows the same sequence of scrutiny as in the Commons: First and Second Reading; committee stage; report and Third Reading. The main difference is that the committee stage is normally taken in the Chamber of the Lords rather than in a Standing Committee.

The House of Lords has over 1,000 members, though average daily attendance is in the region of 360–70. The large majority are hereditary peers, only a little over 400 being life peers, including the Lords of Appeal in Ordinary (the law lords). In addition, 26 bishops of the Church of England are entitled to speak and vote.[51] Because so many of the hereditary peers support the Conservative Party, there is in general a majority—though not necessarily an absolute one—of peers willing to support bills introduced by a Conservative government.[52] Conservative governments, when they need to, have been able to call in 'backwoodsmen' (hereditary peers who rarely attend) to support them in vital votes which otherwise they might lose. This was the case, for instance, in relation to the bill introducing the highly controversial Community Charge (or poll tax) in 1988 where the government feared it might lose a vote on an opposition amendment to relate this tax to people's ability to pay: 'Of 317 peers who decided that poor people should

[49] The controversial Police and Criminal Evidence Bill 1983–4, which took 59 sittings in Standing Committee, was not guillotined. During the same session the passage of the Telecommunications Bill was considered impossible without a guillotine.

[50] Griffith and Ryle, *Parliament*, pp. 302–7.

[51] On which, see Francis Brown, 'Influencing the House of Lords: the role of the Lords Spiritual 1979–1987' (1994) XLVII Political Studies 105. His main conclusion is that 'in terms of voting, the Lords Spiritual achieved virtually nothing in the period under review, affecting the outcome of only one division in eight years. Their attendance was patchy.'

[52] The party allegiances were as follows at the end of the 1994–95 session: Conservative 476; Labour 109; Liberal Democrat 52; Crossbenchers (i.e. peers not taking the whip of any party) 289; Other 52. See The Constitution Unit, *Reform of the House of Lords* (1996), p. 14.

pay the same as the rich, 233 were there because an ancestor of theirs had done some service to the Crown.'[53] Generally, however, party discipline is much less strong in the Lords than in the Commons, and Conservative governments since 1979 have lost a number of important votes. While for many years there is widespread agreement that the composition of the Lords lacks legitimacy, attempts at radical reform of the second chamber have not so far succeeded.[54]

The main constitutional role of the House of Lords in the legislative process[55] is said to be the 'revision' and very occasionally the delay of bills approved by the Commons, allowing time for the government and MPs to think again.[56] It is popularly believed that peers have more specialist expertise than MPs and are therefore able to take a more informed view of bills. They are also more likely to take an independent stance from their party whips (if they belong to a party). What really lies behind most justifications for a second chamber is little more than an appreciation that the House of Commons cannot cope adequately with the number of bills it has to scrutinize; bills often receive woefully inadequate scrutiny in the Commons and so passage through similar procedures in the House of Lords is a palliative. This is particularly helpful to a government with a legislate-as-you-go approach: 'the government now uses the House of Lords to amend legislation more than ever before'.[57] As Walter Bagehot put it in 1867:[58]

> With a perfect Lower House it is certain that an Upper House would be of scarcely any value. If we had an ideal House of Commons . . . it is certain we should not need a higher chamber.

Limitations on the powers of the House of Lords

Because it is unelected, there is broad consensus that the Lords ought normally to give way to the wishes of the elected House of Commons: the power of the Lords to delay or reject a bill approved by the Commons is therefore limited both by constitutional convention and by legislation.

In the post-Second World War period, a convention emerged that the Lords does not reject bills at Second Reading which were mentioned in a governing party's general election manifesto. This is known as the 'Salisbury

[53] Charter 88, *A Democratic Upper House* (1990).

[54] For instance, following a White Paper in 1968 (Cmnd 3799), the Labour government introduced the Parliament (No 2) Bill 1969 to remove the right of hereditary peers to vote. It failed to reach the statute book. See further the proposals of the Institute for Public Policy Research: Jeremy Mitchell and Anne Davies, *Reforming the Lords* and The Constitution Unit (Nicole Smith), *Reform of the House of Lords* (1996). See also Chapter 3 above for attempts to justify the hereditary principle.

[55] This chapter is concerned with bills. For discussion of the role of the Lords in relation to delegated legislation see Chapter 10; on its work scrutinizing proposals for Community legislation, see Chapter 13.

[56] For analysis of the impact of the Lords on one piece of legislation, see D. N. Clarke and Donald Shell, 'Revision and Amendment of Legislation by the House of Lords—a case study' [1994] PL 409.

[57] Mitchell and Davies, *Reforming the Lords*, p. 9.

[58] *The English Constitution* (1867), pp. 133–4.

convention' after Lord Salisbury, the leader of the Conservative peers during 1945–51 when, for the first time, the Conservative-dominated House of Lords was faced with having to consider bills approved by a House of Commons with a radical Labour government in power. This convention does not prevent the Lords in such circumstances attempting to 'improve' bills during committee stage. More generally, convention and practice also dictate that the role of the House of Lords in relation to bills dealing with central government taxation and expenditure is very limited.

The Parliament Acts 1911 and 1949

The main legal constraints on the Lords' powers in the legislative processes are set out in the Parliament Act 1911, as amended by the Parliament Act 1949.

The 1911 Act was enacted following a constitutional crisis in which the Lords refused assent to a finance bill (which raised taxation) introduced by a Liberal government.[59] The 1911 Act removed the Lords' power of veto in most situations. It enabled bills which had been passed by the Commons, but rejected by the Lords, to receive Royal Assent two years later. The period of delay for 'money bills' was even shorter, limited to one month.

In 1947 Attlee's Labour government feared that the Conservative-dominated Lords would, despite the Salisbury doctrine, use its remaining powers of delay to wreck the government's nationalization programme. Enacted under the terms of the 1911 Act, the Parliament Act 1949 further reduced the Lords' general delay powers for non-money bills in effect to one year. The combined provisions of these Acts are as follows:

> **Powers of the House of Lords as to Money Bills**
>
> **1.**—(1) If a Money Bill, having been passed by the House of Commons, and sent up to the House of Lords at least one month before the end of the session, is not passed by the House of Lords without amendment within one month after it is sent up to that House, the Bill shall, unless the House of Commons direct to the contrary, be presented to His Majesty and become an Act of Parliament on the Royal Assent being signified, notwithstanding that the House of Lords have not consented to the Bill.
>
> (2) A Money Bill means a Public Bill which in the opinion of the Speaker of the House of Commons contains only provisions dealing with all or any of the following subjects, namely, the imposition, repeal, remission, alteration, or regulation of taxation . . .[60]
>
> **Restriction of the powers of the House of Lords as to Bills other than Money Bills**
>
> **2.**—(1) If any Public Bill (other than a Money Bill or a Bill containing any provision to extend the maximum duration of Parliament beyond five years) is passed

[59] For an account, see Roy Jenkins, *Mr Balfour's Poodle: an account of the struggle between the House of Lords and Mr Asquith* (1954).

[60] Although the original purpose of this provision was to ensure that the Lords could not prevent the government securing passage of its budgetary proposals, not all finance bills are money bills for they often contain non-taxing provisions.

by the House of Commons in two successive sessions (whether of the same Parliament or not), and, having been sent up to the House of Lords at least one month before the end of the session, is rejected by the House of Lords in each of these sessions, that Bill shall, on its rejection for the second time by the House of Lords, unless the House of Commons direct to the contrary, be presented to His Majesty and become an Act of Parliament on the Royal Assent being signified thereto, notwithstanding that the House of Lords have not consented to the Bill:

Provided that this provision shall not take effect unless one year has elapsed between the date of the Second Reading in the first of those sessions of the Bill in the House of Commons and the date on which it passes the House of Commons in the second of those sessions . . .

The Parliament Act does not apply to all bills. In particular it does not apply to bills originating in the House of Lords, nor to bills which seek to extend the life of Parliament beyond five years. In other words the Lords could veto a bill postponing a general election. Perhaps surprisingly, a bill amending the Parliament Act itself is not exempt; the 1949 Act was enacted under the terms of the 1911 Act without the Lords' agreement. In theory therefore a government intent on postponing a general election could amend the Parliament Acts by removing the Lords' power to block bills seeking to achieve this result and then having done so, introduce such a bill.

There has been academic debate about the constitutional status of the Parliament Acts. Zellick[61] and Hood Phillips[62] argue that the 1949 Act is invalid on the ground that the 1911 Act in effect delegated legislative powers to the Commons and the Crown; these two institutions were therefore not then legally entitled to use their new powers to enlarge their powers still further in 1949 because of the basic legal rule that a delegate cannot enlarge his own power (*delegatus non potest delegare*).[63]

The Parliament Acts have been used only five times to enact statutes which otherwise would not have reached the statute book.[64] Most recently it was used to enact the War Crimes Act 1991, an Act giving courts in the United Kingdom jurisdiction to try offences of murder and manslaughter committed by persons in Germany or German-occupied territory between 1939 and 1949.[65] MPs in the Commons, on a free vote, approved the bill; however, in two successive parliamentary sessions, the Lords rejected the bill. Many peers believed that, given the length of time which had elapsed, defendants would not receive a fair trial; many also objected on the principle that the bill imposed retrospective criminal liability.

[61] 'Is the Parliament Act Ultra Vires?' (1969) 119 NLJ 716; see also Trevor Tayleur, 'A Valid Act?' (1995) 145 NLJ 1328.

[62] O. Hood Phillips and P. Jackson, *Constitutional and Administrative Law* (7th edn., 1988), pp. 90–1.

[63] On which see further Chapter 23.

[64] Welsh Church Act 1914; Government of Ireland Act 1914; Parliament Act 1949; Aircraft and Shipbuilding Industries Act 1977; War Crimes Act 1991.

[65] See further A. T. Richardson, 'War Crimes Act 1991' (1992) 55 MLR 73 and Gabrielle Ganz, 'The War Crimes Act 1991—why no constitutional crisis?' (1992) 55 MLR 87.

AGREEMENT BETWEEN BOTH HOUSES AND ROYAL ASSENT

If the Commons does not accept the Lords' amendments, the Lords must decide what to do. Eventually there must either be agreement between the two Houses or a decision to disagree, in which case the bill will be lost at the end of the annual parliamentary session or, in rare cases, there may be an application of the Parliament Acts. Usually, after a shuttling process between the two Houses, agreement is reached. If Lords' amendments are accepted by the Commons, the bill is ready for Royal Assent.

Royal Assent is given by the monarch on the advice of her ministers. Although the possibility of refusal was raised between 1912 and 1914 over the Home Rule Bill for Ireland, it has not been refused since 1707 and is now regarded to be a pure formality. The monarch no longer gives assent in person. Instead, there is a quaint ceremony in Parliament in which the Gentleman Usher of the Black Rod is sent by three peers (who act under commission from the Queen) to the chamber of the House of Commons. The door is shut in his face. The Sergeant-at-Arms reluctantly allows Black Rod into the Commons chamber where he invites the MPs to attend the Lords Commissioners at the Bar of the House of Commons. The Speaker and any MPs with nothing better to do follow. The long title of the bill is read and the Clerk declares '*la Reine le veult*'. The Act is then enrolled (formally put on the record).

COMMENCEMENT DATES

The Act may come into effect immediately on Royal Assent. This has sometimes created practical problems because printed copies of the Act may not be available to the general public for several weeks. It may take even longer for lawyers and interest groups to appreciate the practical effect of new legislation and advise their clients and members accordingly.

Even more problematic can be the common situation in which an Act provides that it shall come into force on such dates as may be decided by a minister. To bring sections of an Act into force, a minister lays before Parliament an SI[66] known an a 'commencement order' specifying the date which he has decided upon. Such an SI is almost always approved without any debate or vote.

It may take several years for a complex piece of legislation to be brought into force—over ten years in the case of the Consumer Credit Act 1974, for instance. Legal practitioners and the public therefore often have to do tricky legal research to find out whether a section is actually effective. The Lord Chancellor's department has estimated, but did not know for certain, that about 1 per cent of provisions in Acts passed between 1989 and 1992 had

[66] On SIs generally, see Chapter 10.

not been brought into force. Lord Nathan, during a debate in the Lords on the Hansard Commission report, complained that legislation is 'now not mandatory on government but permissive'.[67] Various safeguards have been suggested. One proposal is that provisions of an Act could lapse if not brought into force within a specified time; alternatively, provisions could come into force a specified time after an Act receives the Royal Assent unless previously brought into force by a commencement order.[68]

Delayed commencement dates may produced constitutional as well as practical problems. In 1993 the Home Secretary announced that he would not be bringing into force sections in the Criminal Justice Act 1988 which set out in statutory form the methods by which the Criminal Injuries Compensation Board calculates its payments to victims of crime. (The board had, in fact, been operating on a non-statutory basis since 1964.) Instead, he said, the government would instruct the board to make future payments according to a tariff system set by the Home Office (which was to reduce the amounts of compensation payable in many cases). The Appellate Committee of the House of Lords, by a majority, held that the Home Secretary's decision was unlawful:[69] although he was entitled to decide when to bring a section into force, he was not able to declare he would never do this and make rules contrary to the will of Parliament expressed in the Act.[70] The government subsequently introduced its tariff scheme in a new Act.[71]

PRIVATE MEMBERS' BILLS

So far this chapter has considered government bills, by far the most common type. Backbench MPs may also introduce bills into Parliament.[72] Because the parliamentary timetable is so strongly controlled by government, bills from backbenchers do not usually complete their passage through Parliament unless they have government support; as a way of initiating legislation they are therefore of relatively little importance. Nevertheless, there are a few notable examples of Acts that originally started life as Private Members' Bills, including the Chronically Sick and Disabled Persons Act 1970, the Housing (Homeless Persons) Act 1977 and the Abortion Act 1967. Peers in the House of Lords may also introduce Private Members' Bills.[73]

The real role of backbench bills is often to attract or maintain publicity for a particular issue or to put pressure on government to introduce a bill of its

[67] See HL Deb, vol. 559, col. 1291 (14 December 1994).

[68] See further Peter Riddell, 'Quality control deficiency that lets down the law', *The Times*, 16 December 1994.

[69] *R v Secretary of State for the Home Department, ex p Fire Brigades Union* [1995] 2 AC 513. See further E. Barendt, 'Constitutional Law and the Criminal Injuries Compensation Scheme' [1995] PL 357.

[70] For further discussion, see p. 283.

[71] Criminal Injuries Compensation Act 1995.

[72] See further David Marsh and Melvyn Read, *Private Members' Bills* (1988).

[73] For example, Lord Lester's unsuccessful Human Rights Bill 1995, considered in Chapter 6 above.

own on the subject. For example, in 1988 Richard Sheppard MP, a Conservative backbencher, introduced a bill to repeal the infamous s 2 of the Official Secrets Act 1911 which made it a criminal offence for any government information to be disclosed without authorization. The government had to use its whips to secure defeat for the bill, but as a *quid pro quo* undertook to introduce its own reforms (which it did in the Official Secrets Act 1989). In the context of Sunday trading very many Private Members' Bills—for and against—were introduced before the government finally succeeded in steering the controversial Sunday Trading Act 1994 to the statute book. All were unsuccessful in the sense that they failed to reach the statute book, but they kept the issue alive in Parliament.

The best chances for backbench MPs to promote legislation is offered by a ballot procedure which enables approximately 20 MPs a year to present their bills on one of the 12 or so Fridays in each annual session allocated to private members' business. Members who succeed in the ballot find themselves subject to intensive lobbying from pressure groups seeking to persuade them to adopt their bill (which often has been drafted by lawyers in private practice or by academics).

Another method of presenting bills is under the so-called Ten Minute Rule. Each Tuesday and Wednesday a backbencher may move that leave be given to bring in a bill for a stated purpose. When introducing the bill the MP is not allowed to make a full speech but can only give a 'brief explanatory statement' lasting about ten minutes. The main point of using the Ten Minute Rule procedure is to obtain publicity and very few bills introduced in this way eventually reach the statute book.[74]

MEMBERS' LINKS WITH OUTSIDE GROUPS

In Chapter 5 we saw that some MPs still argue that their role, once elected, is to exercise their own conscience in the interests of the whole nation. MPs are not, on this view, delegates of their constituents nor representatives of particular sectional interest groups. This was the view famously put forward by Edmund Burke in his 1774 speech to the electors of Bristol. Times have changed. All MPs now belong to one of the major political parties and the way they act in scrutinizing government bills is to a very large extent determined by instructions from their party's whips. Indeed, most parliamentary practice is now premised on the existence of a government party and opposition parties. This seems uncontroversial today.

More problematical are the links between MPs and outside interests, in the form of businesses, interest and pressure groups. The case study on Sunday trading legislation reveals just how important this is in practice.[75]

[74] In 1984–85 there were two, but none in 1983–84, 1985–86, or 1986–87: see Griffith and Ryle, *Parliament*, p. 391.

[75] See Chapter 9.

There are two aspects here: first, the extent to which it is permissible for an MP to act as an advocate in Parliament for a sectional interest group or cause; secondly, the extent to which it is permissible for outside interest groups to apply pressure on MPs to support a cause.

MPs as advocates for interest groups

MPs may want to advocate or oppose proposals in a bill for a variety of reasons apart from being instructed to do so by their party's whips. An MP may have a personal interest in the matter because (say) they own a business that is affected by a bill. Such pecuniary interests are no bar on their participating in debates and voting. However, since 1974 there has been a rule that in debates every MP has to declare 'any relevant pecuniary interest or benefit of whatever nature, whether direct or indirect, that he may have had, may have or may be expecting to have'.[76] Thus, during the Sunday trading legislation debates several MPs began their speeches by saying that they owned businesses which would be affected by deregulation of opening hours. MPs are also expected to place on a Register of Members' Interests, which is open to public inspection, details of pecuniary interests or benefits 'which might be thought to affect his conduct as an MP or influence his actions, speeches or votes in Parliament'.[77] Such interests include, for example, directorships of companies and 'financial sponsorships'.

During 1995 there was a thorough reappraisal of the rules regarding outside interests. The Nolan Committee on Standards in Public Life recommended that the existing rules were insufficient to safeguard the reputation of Parliament.[78] An official of the House, the Parliamentary Commissioner for Standards, was appointed to oversee the new requirements.[79] One of the most important changes made by the Commons is that it is now forbidden for MPs to receive money from any business, interest or pressure group to advocate any proposal during debates or in PQs to ministers. One type of arrangement which this has affected is the 'sponsorship' of Labour MPs by trades unions.[80] Until recently, many Labour members received several hundred pounds a year from a union; the money was normally used to employ research assistants or to pay for office expenses. In return the MP was expected to represent the union's interests in Parliament. In November 1995 the Labour Party announced that such arrangements would come to an end.[81]

[76] See *Erskine May*, p. 385.
[77] See *Erskine May*, p. 386.
[78] See further Dawn Oliver, 'Standards of conduct in public life—what standards?' [1995] PL 497.
[79] Sir Gordon Downey. A new select committee on standards and privileges has also been established.
[80] During debates on the Sunday trading legislation, several MPs began their speeches by declaring that they were sponsored by USDAW, the shopworkers' union.
[81] See *The Times*, 4 November 1995.

MPs as targets for outside interests

For pressure or interest groups campaigning for changes in the law, it is essential that MPs are won over to their cause. There are limits on what types of influence are permissible. The House of Commons has traditionally been quick to investigate and punish those who threaten or intimidate MPs; to do so is a contempt of Parliament which may be punished by fine or even imprisonment. *Erskine May* lists actions which have been regarded as improper.[82] These include threats by a company to cease investing in an MP's constituency if the member persisted in making speeches in favour of a particular proposal and summoning an MP to a disciplinary hearing of his trades union because of the way he voted.

LEGISLATING FOR SCOTLAND AND NORTHERN IRELAND

Many Acts of Parliament, such as the Sunday Trading Act 1994, apply only to England and Wales. Scotland and Northern Ireland each have legal systems separate from that of England and Wales. Detailed consideration of how the UK Parliament legislates for these parts of the United Kingdom alone falls outside the scope of this book; suffice to say that continuing demands are made for devolution of legislative powers to regional assemblies. Scottish and Northern Irish MPs complain, with justification, that present arrangements lead to insufficient parliamentary time being spent on their legislation. In bare outline, the position is as follows.

Scotland

The Conservative governments of the United Kingdom since 1979 have found legislating uniquely for Scotland politically difficult due to the fact that the vast majority of MPs from Scottish constituencies are not Conservatives. If the Speaker certifies that a bill relates only to Scotland, it may be referred for what is in effect a Second Reading debate to the Scottish Grand Committee, comprising all 72 MPs representing constituencies in Scotland. The committee stage clause-by-clause scrutiny of Scottish bills is then taken in a Scottish Standing Committee, which unlike the Grand Committee includes (Conservative) MPs from other parts of the United Kingdom to enable the committee's party political composition to reflect that of the House of Commons as a whole. As part of a series of reforms to the Scottish legislative process, the government announced in 1994 that greater use would be made of Special Standing Committees.[83]

[82] See *Erskine May*, p. 128.

[83] For an overview see B. Winetrobe, 'Governing Scotland' (1994) 39 Jnl of the Law Soc of Scotland 459. On Special Standing Committees generally, see p. 196 below.

Northern Ireland

The Parliament of Northern Ireland was suspended in 1972 because of mounting civil unrest in the Province. Since then there has been 'direct rule' of Northern Ireland.[84] Most executive functions and legal powers in relation to the Province are now in the hands of the Secretary of State for Northern Ireland. Legislation on areas of responsibility which before 1972 remained within the powers of the UK Parliament (essentially security and constitutional matters) continue to be subject to the general procedures described in this chapter. The bulk of legislation affecting Northern Ireland, however, is now carried out by means of SIs (Orders in Council) made by the Secretary of State for Northern Ireland under powers conferred on him by the Northern Ireland Act 1974 or other enabling statutes. In practice bills applying to England and Wales normally include a clause enabling the Secretary of State to make an Order in Council in terms similar to that of the bill itself; the Order in Council then becomes the equivalent legislation in Northern Ireland.

REFORM PROPOSALS

The current arrangements for making statutes cry out for improvement. It is important to recognize that legislative drafting and parliamentary procedures operate within a wider context.

Drafting

Criticisms of statutory drafting styles have already been considered.[85] They are inescapably linked to the policies which government pursues and the attitude government has to formulating its policies. It is, perhaps, too easy to look for technical solutions to the current problems. If policy formulation has been rushed and ill-thought out, no amount of clear drafting will make the policy intelligible to MPs or effective in practice. The Hansard Society Commission concluded that 'the whole process at present is cramped and hurried, with the result that bills are often introduced into Parliament "half-baked" or not fully drafted'.[86]

Should there be pre-legislation committees?

A recurring theme is that government ought to consult earlier and more fully about its policy proposals. Once policy is set out in a bill, there is a reluctance on the part of government to allow changes suggested by outsiders.

[84] For an overview, see Derek Birrell, 'The Westminster Parliament and Northern Ireland Business' (1990) 43 Parliamentary Affairs 435.
[85] See p. 178 above.
[86] *Making the Law*, para. 484.

More effective scrutiny may therefore be secured by consultation outside Parliament before a bill is introduced, rather than making government defeats on bills more frequent. MPs could, however, be involved in earlier scrutiny if government proposals were referred to 'pre-legislation' committees with powers to call expert witnesses and interested groups in order to consider the likely impact of what the government is proposing before the First Reading of a bill. But there is an argument against setting up such committees. If a committee of all-party MPs approves of a government policy from the outset, this would reduce the degree to which government could be held responsible for the failings of the statute which emerges from the process. Public anger and concern about the Child Support Act 1991, for instance, has been directed at the ministers responsible for the policy and the bill, and those ministers have had to answer to Parliament for the Act's faults. If a parliamentary committee had been involved from the outset, it would have been more difficult for Parliament to hold ministers responsible.

Should MPs have better access to information and expertise?

A second related problem with the present arrangements is that there is an imbalance in information and expertise between government and other MPs. Ministers are advised by civil servants and use the skills of Parliamentary Counsel. MPs, on the other hand, have inadequate opportunities to question people with know-how in the area covered by a bill or to consider the practical implications of legislation. If the committee stage were to be less of a party political debating chamber and instead provided more scope for MPs of all parties to take evidence from experts, this might improve the situation. Interest groups might also value the opportunity to present their arguments for or against proposed legislation to MPs.

There is in fact already provision in Parliament's standing orders for this to happen in the form of Special Standing Committees.[87] Since 1986 such committees have been empowered to take written evidence and hear oral evidence before adopting the debating and scrutiny function of ordinary Standing Committees. So far the use of these committees has been limited to a few non-contentious bills. In 1995 the government rejected calls from opposition parties for a Special Standing Committee to be set up to consider the controversial Asylum Bill, on the ground that this 'would lead to serious practical problems, including a queue of special interest groups lining up to put their case'.[88]

Special Standing Committees might be particularly suitable for uncontentious law reform bills. The Law Commission, the official law reform agency, regularly recommends legal reforms to government which require a statute to give effect to them. For several years there has been concern that Law Commission bills are given insufficient priority by government—even when

[87] See *Erskine May*, pp. 479, 549.
[88] *The Times*, 18 November 1995, p. 2.

the government accepts the need for change. Law Commission bills may not be included in the legislative programme. As a result opportunities are lost to make important, normally politically uncontentious, improvements in the law. The Law Commission has called for special parliamentary procedures for its bills.[89]

A need for less hasty scrutiny of bills by Parliament?

As we have seen, the planning and content of the legislative timetable is of obvious constitutional importance. Critics of current arrangements present a picture of rushed policy-making, an overloaded programme and inadequate drafting which Parliament is then ill-equipped to scrutinize effectively. Reforms could therefore be aimed at slowing down the legislative process. The Hansard Society Commission recommended that government adopt two-year legislative programmes, that there be set intervals between each stage of a bill's consideration by Parliament[90] and that if a bill has failed to complete its passage by the end of one parliamentary annual session it should be allowed to be carried over into the next one. The argument against the last proposal is that to allow bills to roll over into the next session might actually make it more difficult for opposition parties to prevent an unsatisfactory bill reaching the statute book.

Better protection for fundamental rights

Parliamentary supremacy places considerable responsibility on Parliament (rather than the courts) to ensure that statute law is constitutionally acceptable. The present arrangements do not, however, provide any systematic scrutiny of bills to see how they will affect important civil and political rights and liberties.[91] Legislation must now comply with Community law on matters such as sex equality, but its effect on other rights and liberties is less easily constrained. It is to be hoped that government departments always carry out an 'audit' of a bill to ensure what discriminatory effect it may have, and to detect provisions which might infringe the United Kingdom's international treaty obligations (such as the ECHR). There should, however, also be routine external scrutiny to draw MPs' attention to legislative proposals which will adversely affect human rights. One reform which could go some way to dealing with these concerns would be to set up a committee of MPs and/or peers to consider all bills and report to Parliament if a bill, expressly or otherwise, trespasses unduly on rights and liberties.[92] More radical proposals

[89] See further Sir Henry Brooke, 'Special Public Bill Committees' [1995] PL 351.
[90] *Making the Law*, para. 362.
[91] See Chapter 6.
[92] See further F. Klug and J. Wadham, 'The "Democratic" Entrenchment of a Bill of Rights: LIBERTY's proposals' [1993] PL 579. Cf. the House of Lords' Select Committee on the Scrutiny of Delegated Powers (discussed at p. 232, below) and the Joint Committee on Statutory Instruments (p. 235, below).

include entrenching a Bill of Rights limiting the legal power of Parliament to enact such legislation.[93]

Exercise

Select from the shelves of a law library a statute enacted in the past ten years.

(a) Outline its legislative history, stating why the bill was introduced, what was intended to be achieved, and how it was scrutinized in Parliament.
(b) Are all its sections currently in force? Was it difficult to find this out?
(c) To what extent is the Act a 'skeleton'? What 'flesh' has since been added in the form of SIs?
(d) Who are likely to be the main readers of the Act? Do you think that the langauge and structure is such that these readers are likely to be able to understand it? Does the Act include any statement of principle of what it seeks to do?
(e) Have there been any significant judicial decisions interpreting provisions of the Act?

WHERE TO GO FROM HERE

To explore the statute-making process in more detail, in the context of deregulation of Sunday trading, turn to Chapter 9. For general accounts of other types of legislation, turn to Chapter 10 (delegated legislation), Chapter 12 (which includes discussion of prerogative legislation), and Chapter 13 (Community legislation, including discussion of its incorporation in the UK legal systems by Acts of Parliament and delegated legislation).

[93] See p. 155.

9

CASE STUDY: SUNDAY TRADING ACT

This chapter examines the parliamentary legislative process in the context of the long-drawn-out campaigns to deregulate Sunday trading. One government bill which attempted to do this, the Shops Bill 1985, never reached the statute book because MPs voted it down at its Second Reading in the Commons—a highly unusual event. A second bill some years later did become law: the Sunday Trading Act 1994.

The aim of the chapter is to explore in more detail some of the characteristics of the legislative process. The events described should help you form your own opinions about the problems others identify with the system. For an overview of the episode, turn back to Chapter 2.

SHOPS ACT 1950

The legislation on closing hours had its origin in the late nineteenth century and aimed to protect shopworkers from exploitation and to protect small shopkeepers from excessive competition. Restrictions on Sunday trading had their origin in much earlier legislation to protect Sunday as a day of observance of the Christian sabbath.[1] By the 1940s, there was growing pressure for the law to be changed and the Home Office set up a committee of inquiry under the chairmanship of Sir Ernest Gowers to consider the existing law.[2] The committee reported in 1947. In para. 2 it said:

> Existing shops legislation exemplifies the maxim that hard cases make bad laws. There are too many exemptions; the law tries over much to combine the incompatible goals of compelling shops to shut and allowing people to buy. This has had disastrous consequences, especially in mixed shops; in certain respects the law is neither observed nor enforceable, and has been brought into contempt.

The Gowers Committee concentrated on ways to simplify the law on general closing hours but did not suggest any change of substance in the law on Sunday trading. The government of the day responded to this report by

[1] The main piece of early legislation being the Sunday Observance Act 1677.

[2] Gowers was a retired distinguished civil servant, best known today as the original author of *The Complete Plain Words*, a guide to writing clearly.

introducing a stop-gap and simply consolidated existing law into the Shops Act 1950.[3] While this Act presented the law in a more convenient form, it did nothing to cure the obscurity, the anomalies, and the problems of enforcement identified by Gowers. Section 47 dealt with Sunday trading:

> Every shop shall, save as otherwise provided by this Part of this Act, be closed for the serving of customers on Sunday:
>
> Provided that a shop may open for the serving of customers on Sunday for the purposes of any transaction mentioned in the Fifth Schedule to this Act.

The Fifth Schedule is at the end of the Act and is entitled:

TRANSACTIONS FOR THE PURPOSES OF WHICH A SHOP MAY BE OPEN IN ENGLAND AND WALES FOR THE SERVING OF CUSTOMERS ON SUNDAY

1. The sale of—
   (a) intoxicating liquors;
   (b) meals or refreshments whether or not for consumption at the shop at which they are sold, but not including the sale of fried fish and chips at a fried fish and chip shop;
   (c) newly cooked provisions and cooked or partly cooked tripe;
   (d) table waters, sweets, chocolates, sugar confectionery and ice-cream (including wafers and edible containers);
   (e) flowers, fruit and vegetables (including mushrooms) other than tinned or bottled fruit or vegetables;
   (f) milk and cream, not including tinned or dried milk or cream, but including clotted cream whether sold in tins or otherwise;
   (g) medicines and medical or surgical appliances . . .
   (h) aircraft, motor or cycle supplies or accessories;
   (i) tobacco and smokers' requisites;
   (j) newspapers, periodicals and magazines . . .

Questions

1. Which, if any, of the following items could lawfully be sold on a Sunday under Sched 5: (a) a bible (b) a fish and chips take-away meal? (c) a packet of razor blades?

2. Can you see any rational basis for the exemptions to s 47? Would there have been in 1936? What criteria make the sale of some goods acceptable on Sundays and others not?

3. Apart from listing items that cannot be sold, what alternative ways can you think of for regulating Sunday trading? (You may find it helpful to think about the purpose(s) of regulating shop opening.) Try to identify the relative merits of the different schemes you have devised.

REFORM PROPOSALS

Dissatisfaction with the law did not go away, but it was not until 1961 that the government took any action. In that year the Home Secretary appointed

[3] The Shops (Hours of Closing) Act 1928; Shops (Sunday Trading Restriction) Act 1936; and the Retail Meat Dealers Shops (Sunday Closing) Act 1936.

another committee, this time under the chairmanship of Lord Crathorne, to review the law.[4] This recommended extending the exemptions in Sched 5 of the 1950 Act. Following consultation, however, it became clear to the Conservative government that there would be considerable opposition to these proposals and no legislation was introduced. In the years which followed there were many attempts by Private Members' Bills to amend the Shops Act. All failed to reach the statute book.

In 1983 the Home Secretary appointed yet another committee of inquiry, this time under the chairmanship of Robin Auld QC.[5] The 'Report of the committee of inquiry into proposals to amend the Shops Act' (Cmnd 9376) was published in 1984. Chapter 8 included the following summary of its conclusions and recommendations.

> 289. We are convinced that the removal of restrictions on trading hours offers the best—and indeed the only—way forward. A great deal of our Inquiry has been devoted to considering the adverse effects that such a move might have on some. At the end of the day we are satisfied that any such effects would be far outweighed by the substantial benefits that deregulation would bring. It would give retailers freedom and flexibility to meet and make the most of trading opportunities as they arise. It would be a convenience to shoppers, in keeping with the demands and varied pattern of modern living. These benefits would not be so prejudicial to the interests of shopworkers or to the quality of Sunday in its various guises as to justify retention of any form of control of trading hours.
>
> 290. We began this Inquiry from the premise that the law should not interfere in the conduct of human affairs unless it serves a justifiable purpose or purposes in doing so. We have considered all the interests with a claim to protection in the form of legal regulation of shopping hours [consumers, employers and employees and to the traditional character of Sunday; also self-employed shopkeepers, residents in or near shopping areas and on busy shopping routes, rate and tax payers who finance public services and religious bodies]. . . . we are firmly of the view that there is no interest, or combination of interests, that justifies the retention of such regulation.
>
> 291. We have considered as an independent issue whether, in any event, a form of control can be devised that would be fair, simply and readily enforceable. The present legislation does not satisfy any of these tests. As a result it does not command general acceptance, and has brought the law into disrepute. We examined in great detail a wide range of suggested different forms of legal control . . . none would provide a fair or readily enforceable system.
>
> **For these reasons, we recommend the abolition . . . of all legal restrictions on the hours for which shops may be open to serve customers.**
>
> 292. We have reached our conclusion on the need for abolition of legal controls independently of the predictions as to what decontrol would bring. [From research

[4] Lord Crathorne was a former Conservative MP. As Sir William Dugdale he resigned as Minister of Agriculture following revelations that civil servants in his department had behaved improperly in relation to the sale of land. The 'Crichel Down' affair prompted the setting up of the Parliamentary Commissioner for Administration: see Chapter 18.

[5] Sir Robin Auld is now a judge in the Court of Appeal.

and evidence], we are satisfied that in the long run the impact of deregulating trading hours on our economic and social life would not be so great as to be readily indistinguishable from changes already taking place. . . .

294. We consider that a statutory provision specifically protecting shopworkers from being required to work against their will on Sundays . . . would be impracticable . . . [but] we strongly urge the retention for retail workers of the machinery of the Wages Council for the fixing and proper enforcement of satisfactory wages and premium rates.[6]

Questions

Why do you think governments set up 'independent' committees of inquiry on the Shops Act? Could not civil servants in the Home Office have investigated the problems and advised the minister of the most appropriate policy to rectify them?

A paving motion

Rather than moving directly to introduce a bill embodying the Auld Committee recommendations (which the Home Office accepted), the government found space in the Commons' timetable to hold a debate on the report on 20 May 1985. (Can you think of any reasons for having such a 'paving motion'? As you read these extracts from the six-hour debate, remember what the purpose of a *Second Reading* debate on a bill is: how, if at all, does this debate differ in its purpose?) The following extracts highlight the constitutional and procedural issues raised during the debate; many other issues on the policy of deregulating Sunday trading were also discussed by MPs.

The Secretary of State for the Home Department (Mr Leon Brittan): I beg to move.

> That this House takes note of the Report of the Committee of Inquiry into Proposals to Amend the Shops Acts (Cmnd 9376): accepts the case for the removal of legislative limitations on shop hours, and looks forward to the Government bringing forward legislation to remove such limitations.

Shop opening hours were last considered in depth by this House during the debate on the Bill introduced in 1983 by my hon. Friend the Member for Wycombe (Mr Whitney). By then it was clear that there was hardly anyone who considered the present state of the law satisfactory. The argument for change was put forward on a number of different bases. In the first place, it was almost universally felt that the present distinctions between what could be sold on Sunday and what could not be sold were so arbitrary and outdated as to be indefensible. It was not just a question of a few items that were on the wrong side of the dividing line. There no longer appeared to be a rational dividing line at all. Secondly, there was deep anxiety about the continued existence on the statute book of a law that was being increasingly flouted, and which many if not most local authorities were either simply not prepared to enforce effectively or were unable

[6] Wages Councils were statutory bodies responsible for setting legal minimum wages for workers in certain industries. They have since been abolished by the Conservative government.

to do so. These objections to the present law were not seriously challenged . . . It was because of the combination of almost universal dissatisfaction with the present state of the law, and a widespread feeling of uncertainty about the effects of change and the possible forms that it might take that I decided to accept the suggestions made from all parts of the House, that an inquiry should be appointed to look into the whole question. I accordingly appointed an independent committee of inquiry in July 1983 under the chairmanship of Mr Robin Auld, QC. The following were the terms of reference:

> 'To consider what changes are needed in the Shops Acts, having regard to the interests of consumers, employers and employees and to the traditional character of Sunday, and to make recommendations as to how these should be achieved.'

The House will note that the committee of inquiry was specifically required to have regard, among other factors, to the fundamental character of Sunday.

The membership of the committee was deliberately small, but in order to ensure that the main groups interested could satisfy themselves that the evidence submitted to the committee was comprehensive and rigorously scrutinised, I appointed six assessors. They represented the employers—both large and small—employees, consumers, the churches and the local authorities. Their main task was to ensure that the committee obtained evidence from across the spectrum of their interests and to offer comment on that evidence. My aim was to ensure that every possible solution to the problem was put to the committee and thoroughly examined by those likely to object to it, as well as by the members of the committee themselves. I know that the committee much appreciated the specialist advice it received from its assessors, and I am grateful to them for their work.

In addition, I commissioned the Institute for Fiscal Studies to carry out an economic review, which has been published as appendix 6 of the Auld report. This was designed to meet the concern that had been expressed that there was much speculation but little hard evidence on the economic effects that increased trading hours would have. . . .

Mr Eric S. Heffer (Liverpool, Walton) [a Labour backbencher]: Will the right hon. and learned Gentleman say how, exactly, he decided upon the membership of the committee? Frances Cairncross has written an interesting article in today's edition of *The Times* which tries to persuade hon. Members to go further, in one sense, than the Auld report by agreeing completely that the traditional character of Sunday should be abolished. How was Frances Cairncross chosen? Was she an independent character? Where does she stand and where does the right hon. and learned Gentleman stand in relation to what she said?

Mr Brittan: At the time of the appointments there was no criticism whatsoever that any of those who were appointed to the committee were other than independent. I can assure the hon. Gentleman that I did not have the faintest idea about the views of any of the committee members . . .

Mr Foulkes [a Labour backbencher]: The Home Secretary has detailed all the further consideration that has taken place by the Institute for Fiscal Studies, and the Auld committee and its assessors and he invites hon. Members who voted one way on a previous occasion to reconsider their point of view. How can his hon. Friends reconsider their views if, because of the Whip, they are not allowed to exercise their own judgment and their own consciences?

Mr Brittan: I am sure that my hon. Friends will be greatly assisted by the hon. Gentleman's intervention. The

Government are fully entitled to express their views and to seek to persuade my hon. Friends of the merits of those views. As the hon. Gentleman knows, it has been made clear to my hon. Friends who have deeply held conscientious views, that their views are fully respected. . . .

Mr Cormack [a Conservative backbencher]: The Government are on a dangerous course which carries the serious threat that part of our national life will be seriously undermined. On whatever terms we were debating the motion, I should find myself in the opposite Lobby to my right hon. and learned Friend the Home Secretary and his ministerial colleagues.

I have been here long enough for three-line Whips not to mean a great deal to me. If I believe that the merits of an issue are not particularly great, I shall vote against the party. I have done so on a number of occasions, though not with any relish or enjoyment. I greatly resent the fact that this issue has been made the subject for a three-line Whip. That flies in the face of one of our better and more honourable parliamentary traditions, which is that an issue that is, broadly speaking, one of conscience and not of party politics should be left to the discretion and conscience of hon. Members who should vote accordingly.

I have been given a little licence. I received a pleasant letter from my right hon. Friend the Patronage Secretary [the government chief whip] in which he acknowledges my misgivings and says that my conscientious scruples are fully respected. I appreciate that and I understand that my hon. Friends who have made similar representations have received a similar licence. However, that is not an answer, because I know that other colleagues are disturbed about the Government's policy, but because a three-line Whip has been put on, they feel obliged to support the Government. That applies particularly to Parliamentary Private Secretaries, the great extra army of unpaid members of the payroll vote.

If the Government wish to test the opinion of the House, which should be the object of the debate, there should be no Whip on. The matter should be treated as any other major issue of conscience would be treated, and hon. Members should be allowed to vote without fearing that they are being disloyal. . . .

Mr Prescott [Labour frontbench spokesman]: The Opposition are prepared to operate a free vote on the main question, as we consider it to be a matter of conscience. I favour the traditional Sunday and would not want to see more shops open. However, there is a middle way. The committee funked the issue and did not take the opportunities presented to it. Amendments on the Order Paper take a middle course and people should reach their own decisions. We have, for example, debated abortion and left voting to the conscience of hon. Members, although Front Bench spokesmen have put their point of view. It is an honourable tradition of the House. . . .

The government won the vote.

Questions

1. Eric Heffer MP questioned the membership of the Auld Committee. What does 'independence' mean in this context? Would a committee member have to be independent in the same sense that judges are?

2. If government has won the debate on this 'paving motion', has the House of Commons now accepted the principle that Sunday trading should be deregulated?

3. Mr Cormack MP suggests that there should have been a free vote on this 'matter of conscience'. What exactly does this mean? Are free votes a good thing? If so, why are there not more of them? In exercising a free vote, whom does the MP represent?

THE SHOPS BILL 1985

The government success in the debate on the Auld Report encouraged it to introduce a bill implementing the committee's recommendations. It chose to start the bill in the House of Lords. On 2 December 1985, Lord Glenarthur (Parliamentary Under-Secretary of State for the Home Office, in other words a junior minister) moved that the bill be read a second time. The Bishop of Birmingham moved as an amendment to the motion to insert at the end of the motion 'but that this House considers that the law should be amended so as to rationalise restrictions on trading hours without such extensive de-regulation as the Bill proposes'. In his speech, Lord Simon of Glaisdale (a former Conservative MP, Attorney-General and retired law lord) said of this amendment:

> The last matter that I venture to mention is a purely parliamentary one. When your Lordships give the Second Reading to a Bill, it is, I have always understood, an approval of the principles of the Bill. That does not prevent amendment in Committee. On the contrary, it lays the way open to it. But what is impossible is to have an amendment to a Second Reading which says in effect, 'We approve the principle of the Bill but we think it ought to be some quite different Bill'; and that is what the amendment does.
>
> In the end, those who hold the view that the task of your Lordships' Chamber is only as a revising Chamber—a view which I myself do not share—cannot possibly vote for this amendment; on the contrary, anybody who votes for this amendment is declaring at once that the task of your Lordships' Chamber goes far beyond revision and goes to declaration of principle, if indeed this is not intended as a vote of censure. So, my Lords, even if I myself presumed to think that your Lordships are limited to a revising function I could not possibly vote for this amendment, lying, as it does, in complete contradiction and incompatibility with the vote at Second Reading.

At 11 pm, the Lord Chancellor closed the debate, saying:

> The original Question was that the Bill be now read a second time, since when an amendment has been proposed in the name of the right reverend Prelate the Bishop of Birmingham. The Question, therefore, that I have to put is that the said amendment be agreed to? As many as are of that opinion will say, 'Content': to the contrary, 'Not-Content'.

The government won the division on the motion by 141 votes to 85. The Lords had therefore rejected the amendment and it went on to accept the principle of the bill. The committee stage (as usual, on the floor of the chamber of the House of Lords) was held on 16 and 17 December 1985, 21 January and 11 February 1986. The bill survived more or less intact, except for the clauses which sought to remove employment protection from adult shopworkers.

Following an amendment moved by Lord Denning (the former Master of the Rolls) the employment provisions of the 1950 Act were included in the new bill. The bill, as amended, received a Third Reading on 25 February and was then introduced into the House of Commons.

Questions

1. Lord Simon mentions the 'revising' function of the House of Lords. What is this revising function? How can the Lords 'revise' a bill when it is introduced into the Lords rather than the Commons? What other (more expansive?) functions can the House of Lords perform in the legislative process?
2. To what extent should the fact that the House of Lords is unelected limit its function during the passage of legislation? Why?

The bill goes to the Commons

In the seven weeks between finishing its stages in the Lords and coming to the Commons, the bill's opponents carried out a particularly effective lobbying campaign.[7] MPs received an unprecedented number of letters on this issue. The government had to handle the situation carefully if it was to get the bill through. It was all too aware that large numbers of its own backbenchers might not support the bill and that, despite its success in the Lords, it was in danger of losing the bill. A top priority was to ensure that the basic principles of the bill—to achieve greater deregulation of Sunday trading—were accepted so that the details could, if necessary, be worked out later in committee. To this end, the government was prepared to offer compromises on certain procedural matters.

Moving that the bill 'be now read for a second time' on 14 April 1986, Mr Douglas Hurd (the Home Secretary) proposed a somewhat unusual course:

> We would propose that the Bill be referred to a Special Standing Committee. That will give the bodies and interests involved a clear opportunity to put forward their proposals for building, if they so wish, on the ground that the repeal of the 1950 Act would leave clear. I certainly hope that the critics of the Bill will welcome this opportunity to move from criticism to construction.

Later in his speech, in response to a question from a Labour backbencher, Mr Hurd guaranteed that at no stage would he seek to move a guillotine on the bill. This came as a surprise to his Cabinet colleagues. *The Times* reported that 'looks of surprise and pain passed across the faces of . . . the Chief Whip and . . . the Leader of the House'. The Official Opposition was unimpressed.

Mr Gerald Kaufman (Manchester, Gorton) [Shadow Home Secretary]: This debate has been heralded by an unprecedented outbreak of largesse on the part of the Government. There has been an outpouring of goodies, which when carefully examined appropriately fit in nicely with the nostalgic old slogan of one of

[7] See Paul Regan, 'The 1986 Shops Bill' (1988) 41 Parliamentary Affairs 218, 221.

the Bill's commercial supporters, F. W. Woolworth—'Nothing worth more than sixpence.'

We have the generous extension of the debate until midnight. Is it unworthy of me to wonder whether it has crossed the mind of the Patronage Secretary [the Government Chief Whip] that as midnight approaches some of his frailer Back Benchers may find the lure of a mug of Horlicks and bed more enticing than the attraction of the 'No' Lobby?

There is a motion to commit the Bill to a Special Standing Committee—a procedure rarely granted despite the most earnest pleas on even uncontroversial Bills, but now supplied on this Bill for nothing. I ask myself whether the Government are worried about something. I ask that question even more on hearing the Home Secretary solemnly offering his Back Benchers a free vote on some of the remaining stages of the Bill if only they will vote for the Second Reading tonight. Any fly accepting the spider's invitation will have complete freedom of the web.

The Home Secretary's offer of a free vote is only worth while and meaningful if his hon. Friends vote against the Second Reading in numbers ample enough to gain substantial representation on the Standing Committee. That way, with a committee not packed with Lobby fodder, the free vote will mean something, especially in the light of the promise by the Home Secretary that the guillotine will not apply at any stage of the Bill. No doubt sufficient hon. Members on the Government side will take the hint when the Division bells ring at midnight, and they can have complete confidence that voting against the Bill is in no way a violation of the three-line Whip that was issued to them. . . .

Mr Francis Pym (Cambridgeshire, South-East) [Conservative backbencher, formerly Foreign Secretary]: The Bill did not make any contribution to the large majority that my party achieved at the last general election. Indeed, no mention of it was made during the campaign and, so far as I know, little or no thought was given to the topic. The irony is that it is now evident that the Government need their large majority to get the Bill through.

Tonight's motion should have been on a free vote. I asked my right hon. Friend the Patronage Secretary as long ago as last autumn to allow a free vote. The Government are not prepared to allow a free vote and have chosen instead a three-line Whip on Second Reading, accompanied by the undertaking of free votes thereafter in Committee and on Report. That is an unusual device, to say the least, and might serve the needs of some of my right hon. and hon. Friends, but I think that it is a contradiction. . . .

Mr Thomas Torney (Bradford South) [a Labour backbencher]: I declare an interest as a Member sponsored by the Union of Shop, Distributive and Allied Workers. For many years before I became a Member, I worked as a full-time officer with that union.

The Home Secretary was magnanimous in promising a free vote in Committee if the Bill is passed tonight, which I hope will not happen. A free vote would not be worth anything if the Government Whips insisted on including on the Committee Conservative Members who were yes-men on Government policy. May we have an assurance that the many Conservative Members who oppose the Bill will be fairly represented on the Committee? I hope that the answer is yes, even though I hope that the Bill is defeated.

Sir Bernard Braine [a Conservative backbencher]: . . . Perhaps I might summarise the reasons for rejecting the Bill. The Government have no mandate whatever—[HON. MEMBERS: 'Hear, hear.'] —to change the character of the traditional Sunday. The Bill is not before us to fulfil a solemn pledge to the nation. It did not figure in any election manifesto.

It was not an issue that was placed squarely before the electorate at the last general election. The Bill is not brought before us, like others, as a welcome measure for strengthening the economy and increasing the number of real jobs. On the contrary, it can have only a marginal effect on trade, it may well increase prices, and, while offering some extra part-time employment, it will reduce the number of ordinary weekday jobs.

Mr Ray Powell (Ogmore) [Labour backbencher, sponsored by USDAW, the shopworkers' union]: Why is there a need to introduce the Shops Bill? Was there a manifesto commitment by the Tory party in the 1979 or 1983 elections? Has the electorate given the Government a mandate? If not, what moral or Government emergency compels the Government to introduce the Bill without the country's consent? . . .

The Prime Minister's dream about the Shops Bill resulted in her including one sentence as an afterthought at the end of the Queen's Speech. It read:

> 'A Bill will be introduced to remove statutory restrictions on shop opening hours'.—[*Official Report*, 6 November 1985; vol. 86, c. 5.]

That sentence, produced without a mandate or full discussions with Tory colleagues in either House, resulted in the Bill. [*Interruption.*] I am being told that I have had my 10 minutes. . . .

11.2 pm
Mr Alfred Dubs (Battersea) [Labour]: I beg to move, to leave out from 'That' to the end of the Question and to add instead thereof:

> 'this House declines to give a Second Reading to a Bill which fails to have regard to the principles and conscience of those who wish to preserve the special character of Sunday, and which fails to protect adequately the interests of those workers who will be detrimentally affected by it'.

It has been a good debate, with differences of opinion on both sides of the House. Before I turn to the main issues to which the Bill gives rise I should like to speak about the Government's approach to the Bill.

The way in which the Government have handled the matter is, at the very least, novel, and, at the most, in one or two respects, breaking parliamentary precedents. The Home Secretary developed a new doctrine of what the Second Reading of a Bill is about. He said that the purpose of Second Reading is just to clear away the old legislation, that in effect we are not really voting on anything at all except to clear the ground, and then the Committee can get down to the work.

I know that the Home Secretary has been here much longer than I have, but I question whether he has the doctrine right. 'Erskine May' says on page 528:

> 'The second reading is the most important stage through which the Bill is required to pass; for its whole principle is then at issue.'

The 'whole principle' of total deregulation is before us today. I do not think that any fudge by the Home Secretary as to what Second Reading has traditionally been about will convince many hon. Members—in fact, I doubt whether it will convince any—that we should somehow ignore the fact that we are debating and voting on the key point of principle.

The second rather original approach is that there is to be a three-line Whip for Conservative Members, followed by a free vote on the later stages, up to, but probably not including, the Third Reading debate. As far as I can discover, there are no precedents for that approach. Of course, a great deal depends upon the composition of the Committee. We all know that if the Committee is to reflect fairly the speeches that have been made tonight it will be balanced evenly, or perhaps slightly against the Bill. Therefore, it depends very much on how Conservative Members decide to vote. If tonight's votes are a reflection of the speeches, we shall genuinely have a committee that will be able to act independently of the Government. . . .

Mr Kenneth Clarke [Minister of Employment]: . . . This is not an unusual situation. I have had three jobs in the present Government and it has been my fate that during that time I have had to handle legislation on the compulsory wearing of seat belts and on the addition of fluoride to the drinking water supply in Britain. Now I find myself with the privilege of dealing with the reform of Sunday trading. I am not regretting my fate, because they are all particularly interesting Bills, especially in the way in which the House of Commons approaches them. . . .

The Government set up the Auld committee, which made recommendations to deal with deregulation. We have taken the Bill through another place, which amended it somewhat. The Bill went through the House of Lords where the Government do not have an automatic majority—certainly not against the combined forces of the Opposition and the Cross Benches.

After years of preparation and consideration we believe that we are entitled to ask the House to give the Bill a Second Reading to enable it to proceed. All kinds of compromises can be considered. Some of those compromises are pressed upon us by my right hon. and hon. Friends, as well as by Opposition Members. We have examined them, but we cannot see a compromise which is workable, or which we are sure will command a majority in any sector, including the House. For that reason we ask the House, with the usual Whip that Governments apply to such a measure, to give the Bill a Second Reading, to go into the unique Special Standing Committee procedure and to follow that by free votes on the principle of the amendments. . . .

. . . If this Second Reading is rejected we shall be stuck with the unenforceable 1950 Act, with a steady increase in Sunday trading throughout the country. It will be many a long year before we have this chance again.

How are we to handle the timetabling of the Bill? Unless we have some structure and order in our debates it is possible for a handful of hon. Members to protract any legislation—[*Interruption*]. A Bill in favour of muddle could be talked out by an hon. Member who was determined enough if there were no rules of procedure or conduct. The Government's undertaking is that they will allow a free vote for their supporters—members of Government and Back Benchers. Of course the Opposition will also allow a free vote. However, that freedom has never extended to procedural motions—[HON. MEMBERS: 'Oh.'] It has never extended to procedural motions such as closures.—[*Interruption*]. I apologise to the Opposition for the fact that they have been labouring under a misapprehension. I could tell when the hon. Member for Ogmore (Mr Powell) was speaking that he expected an extremely protracted Committee stage. I am not saying anything now that all hon. Members do not already know. . . . There will be whipping from the Government on procedural motions, and I do not believe that any Labour hon. Member could seriously expect anything else. . . .

It is no good hon. Members getting up because they do not like the answer. As my right hon. Friend the Home Secretary said earlier today, the Government have no plan to introduce a guillotine motion. The right hon. Member for Gorton knows the procedures of this House as well as most hon. Members. He knows what a guillotine means. A guillotine means a timetable motion, laying down a timetable at which each stage is taken. It is a well-honoured procedure which was introduced to beat Irish obstruction, and it has been used by successive Governments since. We have no plans to do that. We are proposing to follow the course that has been described —to invite the House to give the Bill a Second Reading and to submit it to the Special Standing Committee procedure, allowing a free vote on amendments of principle and on Report. If the House responds to the evident public need to resolve the problems of the inherent ridiculousness of our Sunday trading laws, we should be able to have a reasoned and measured debate which reaches a conclusion.

Of course the Government must reserve the right, if individual hon. Members do not like the way in which the Bill is going at any stage—they might be absolute deregulators who do not like the compromises or absolute Sabbatarians who will not accept any change—and try to hold it up, to have closures to enable the House to reach a proper conclusion. . . .

Mr Kaufman: There are two things about which we must be clear. The right hon. and learned Gentleman says that a timetable lays down stages by which a Bill should proceed. A timetable, a guillotine—

Mr Clarke: A timetable motion.

Mr Kaufman: A timetable motion. The right hon. and learned Gentleman should study Standing Orders. A guillotine is a timetable. A timetable motion—a guillotine—also sets a terminal date. Is the right hon. and learned Gentleman giving the House a categorical assurance that no guillotine motion setting a terminal date for completion of the Bill will be moved?

Mr Clarke: The Government have no plans to introduce such a guillotine motion. If the right hon. Gentleman was as familiar with Standing Orders as he claims, he would know the difference between a guillotine and a closure, and we would not have spent so much time on this filibustering nonsense.

Mr James Callaghan [the former Labour Prime Minister]: I am obliged to the right hon. and learned Gentleman for giving way. I do not think that any of us have to be here very long before we know the difference between a closure and a guillotine. I speak for myself, but I cannot conceive of a Government proceeding without moving a closure at certain intervals. That is not the point that I put to the right hon. and learned Gentleman at the beginning. He could have disposed of the matter straight away and saved himself a lot of trouble and publicity.

I understand that I speak with the agreement of the hon. Member for Orpington (Mr Stanbrook). The Government will not move a guillotine, but they will not perhaps resist a movement by hon. Members from any part of the House to put down a motion calling on the Government to introduce a guillotine. Will the right hon. and learned Gentleman give me a clear undertaking? It would be twisting the House, in view of what the Home Secretary said—and I do not believe that the Leader of the House would do it—if, having given the House a pledge, the Government failed to resist any attempt to move a motion that called on them to introduce a guillotine.

Mr Clarke: I have already given the undertaking that the Government have no plans to introduce the guillotine. That is the position from which we started. We obviously trust that the guillotine will not be required. [HON. MEMBERS: 'Oh.'] No one except a Minister of the Crown can move a guillotine motion, and no Minister of the Crown intends to introduce such a motion.

As the right hon. Member for Cardiff, South and Penarth, who is slightly nearer to the real point than to the synthetic ones, will appreciate, the House may reach the stage where it wishes to come to a conclusion. The right hon. Gentleman wants me to say that the Government will guarantee that, even if the House as a whole wishes to bring proceedings to a conclusion, we will not agree. He is giving any individual hon. Member the right, in effect, to obstruct the Bill.

We are glad that the Ulster Unionist Members are back in their place. Let me postulate one theory. The House could be agreed that a measure that had passed through Committee and Report stages was a desirable improvement on the present law in England and Wales. If I gave the right hon. Member for Cardiff, South and Penarth the guarantee he seeks, it would be open to the Ulster Unionist Members to talk out the legislation— although I am sure that they would not— relying on the Government's guarantee that we would never, in response to any pressure, introduce a timetable motion. Speeches about the General Belgrano, let alone other matters, could keep us here until Christmas, if I gave such a guarantee. . . .

Question put, That the amendment be made:—

The House divided: Ayes 227, Noes 279

Division No. 140]   [12 midnight

Despite a three-line whip, many Conservatives voted against the bill and several others abstained with the result that, for the first time this century, the government lost a Second Reading vote. The bill was dropped from the legislative programme. One thing seems clear: that lobbying by interest groups played a key role. Regan writes:[8]

> There is general agreement that . . . the campaign in favour of the Bill was too little and too late. Its supporters assumed that a government Bill would naturally succeed. No real efforts were made to appeal to the public and encourage it to join the campaign, and the effort was only directed at MPs when it was too late to be effective. It was weakened because it came from large organisations rather than ordinary citizens. The 'Anti' campaign, by contrast, was extremely effective, particularly in the writing of letters to MPs. A survey by the Letter Writing Bureau discovered that more than three-quarters of MPs surveyed said Sunday trading was the biggest topical issue in their postbags in the previous year. The same survey showed a similar proportion influenced by the letters they received. In addition, wavering Conservative backbenchers had to face constant personal lobbying from those of their colleagues opposed to the Bill.

Questions

1. How did the purpose of the Second Reading debate differ, if at all, from the debate on the Auld Report held eleven months before?

2. What is a guillotine? Did Mr Hurd and Mr Clarke say different things about the use of the guillotine in the committee stage?

3. How does a Special Standing Committee differ from a Standing Committee? What advantages would the Special Standing Committee procedure have offered (a) for the government (b) for the various opposing interests? Why was there so much scepticism over the proposal to use this procedure?

[8] Paul Regan, 'The 1986 Shops Bill' (1988) 41 Parliamentary Affairs 218, p. 231.

SUNDAY TRADING ACT 1994

After the defeat of the Shops Bill in April 1986 the retailers intent on liberalizing the Sunday trading laws focused their attention on litigation rather than legislation as a way of campaigning for change. Several large retail chains, including B&Q plc (which owned a chain of DIY stores) raised what came to be known as 'the European defence' when they were prosecuted by local authorities for unlawful Sunday trading. The gist of the argument was that s 47 of the Shops Act 1950 was incompatible with Community law and so was legally ineffective. This battle in the courts is examined in detail later.[9] The legal proceedings had an important impact on the government's aim of repealing the 1950 Act and replacing it with a more workable regime. As a minister's statement to the House of Commons in November 1991 shows, the Home Office continued with its behind-the-scenes discussions with the various pressure groups, but felt unable to proceed until the validity of the 1950 Act was clarified by the courts.[10]

Minister of State for the Home Office (Mrs Angela Rumbold): . . . As the House knows, I have held an intensive programme of discussions with a wide range of major and conflicting interest groups on the possible ways of reforming the law on Sunday trading. Those discussions are continuing, although I must report that at this stage the common ground is limited. . . . The current uncertainty in relation to Community law . . . is also a factor [in why proposals have not been brought to the House]. It would not be sensible to settle policy on the merits of proposals for continuing to restrict trading in types of classes of goods until the compatibility of such measures with Community law has been determined. It is our intention, therefore, to bring forward proposals for reform once the legal position is clear.

Mr Stuart Randall (Kingston upon Hull, West) [Labour Party]: . . . Is not the right hon. Lady aware that, particularly after her statement, the Government will be seen not to be in control of Sunday trading, and that their policy will be viewed as dictated by certain large businesses? Is she also aware that there is concern in the country that some of those companies—which are determining Government policy when the Government should be doing so—are substantial donors to the Conservative party?

Is the right hon. Lady aware that many people, both in the House and throughout the country, will be exceedingly disappointed that the consultations with various interest groups about changing the 1950 Act . . . should be taking so long? Why has she been consulting for nearly a year with no results? Why does she not have a joint conference on the matter along the lines proposed by the Labour party?

Lobbying was, indeed, intense. Parliamentary questions by backbenchers extracted the following information from ministers: in the two-month period December 1990 to January 1991 the Attorney-General[11] received over 2,000

[9] See Chapter 30.

[10] HC Deb, vol. 199, col. 919 (27 November 1991).

[11] The Attorney-General is an MP and member of the Cabinet. He has constitutional responsibilities for ensuring that the criminal law is enforced.

letters critical of his decisions not to intervene against retailers who continued to break the 1950 Act where local authorities declined to prosecute; and between June and December 1991 the Home Secretary and his officials had 18 meetings with pressure groups on the subject of Sunday trading.

A Private Member's Bill

While the outcome of the ECJ litigation was still awaited, the backbench Labour MP Mr Ray Powell introduced a Private Member's Bill to amend the Shops Act 1950. The bill originally prevented shops of more than 1,500 square feet trading on Sundays but it was later modified to allow limited opening for DIY stores and garden centres. It received considerable cross-party support. The day for its Second Reading was 21 February 1992, a Friday afternoon when the Commons deals with private members' business. The Deputy Speaker announced the bill, but several MPs shouted 'Object'. Mr Powell was furious and stood up to make a point of order. *Hansard* records the exchange, but customarily not the name(s) of the MP(s) who objected to the bill.

Mr Powell: ... only yesterday, the Minister of State, Home Office [Angela Rumbold], replied to me in a letter regarding my request for Government cooperation to ensure that the Shops (Amendment) Bill went further than Second Reading. ... she said that any Bill, unless it had the approval of the Government, would not proceed further. We have ten-minute rule Bills ... and a ballot for Private Members' Bills. ... I stayed up all night to get a spot for my ten-minute Bill ... if it means that we must have Government approval before a Bill may be read a Second time, why do we go to all the trouble of trying to obtain a spot, either in private Members' time or to introduce a ten-minute Bill?

Mr Deputy Speaker: The hon. Gentleman is an experienced and respected Member of the House, and he knows the procedure very well. It does not operate only at 2.30 pm on Fridays; it operates at other times, too. If an hon. Member shouts, 'Object', the Bill can go no further on that occasion, That is exactly what happened this afternoon. Second Reading what day?

Mr Powell: Next Friday.

Second Reading deferred till Friday 28 February [1992].

The vote at the end of the (deferred) Second Reading debate was in favour of the bill and it was sent to a Standing Committee. In March 1992 it passed its committee stage in the Commons and on 14 May it went back to the floor of the House for its report stage. Its fate there is best described in Mr Powell's own words:[12]

> On 14 May [1992] my Bill hit the rocks. There were a number of reasons for that. The right hon. Member for Mitcham and Morden (Dame A. Rumbold) ... tabled 122 amendments, most of which were called. On Friday 14 May she tabled 99 amendments and 30 new clauses.

[12] See HC Deb, vol. 233, cols. 831–2 (29 November 1993) when Mr Powell was speaking in the Second Reading debate of the government's Sunday Trading Bill.

The bill ran out of the time allotted for its consideration.

Question

Should backbenchers have greater opportunities to promote legislation—or is this a function best left to government?

Lobbying continues

In the months which followed the pressure groups on both sides of the debate continued to lobby ministers and backbench MPs. We know something of the letter-writing campaign because further written and oral PQs were asked of ministers. In reply to an oral question the Home Secretary said that between June and October 1992 the Home Office had received some 4,433 further representations broadly in favour of greater Sunday trading and 190 against.[13] Mr Powell was clearly suspicious of these statistics and two weeks later asked the Home Secretary in a written question 'how many of the stated representations in favour of Sunday trading have come from pre-printed colour postcards supplied by the Shopping Hours Reform Council?' The answer was 'of the 4,433 written representations, 4,086 were postcards'.[14]

In mid-July 1993 the Home Secretary took the unusual step of publishing the government's draft bill far in advance of its introduction in Parliament. Lobbying intensified. Campaigners for Sunday opening declared a Sunday in October 1993 'National Sunday Shopping Day'. A spokesman for the KSSC was unimpressed and made sure *The Times* knew about it: 'We would urge people to just look behind this campaign that is being applied by the retail industry and say they will not be manipulated by money' he was reported as saying.[15]

A few weeks later in October 1993 there was an important development which was probably decisive of the final outcome. USDAW, the shopworkers' union, had been a principal backer and source of financial support for the KSSC which favoured continued regulation. In a surprising turnaround USDAW, following pressure from its members, decided to switch its backing to the proposals for partial deregulation, provided that employee rights were protected.

A new government initiative

Meanwhile, on 26 November 1992 the Home Secretary made a statement in the House of Commons.[16] He said that the government had been told that the ECJ ruling was now not expected before January 1993. He outlined the

[13] HC Deb, vol. 212, col. 556 (22 October 1992).
[14] HC Deb, vol. 213, col. 516 (6 November 1992).
[15] *The Times*, 20 September 1993.
[16] HC Deb, vol. 214, col. 998 (26 November 1992).

government's intention to introduce a bill with three options for reform on which Conservative MPs would be allowed a free vote. He said that work had already begun on drafting the bill with the assistance of the various pressure groups:

> The reason for asking outside groups to be involved at this stage in drafting the legislation is so that the skills of the parliamentary draftsmen can be brought to bear to ensure that what is drafted is in order and we do not become bogged down in technicalities. . . . We shall involve the Keep Sunday Special Campaign in the drafting. I appreciate that those involved with that movement have helped the hon. Member for Ogmore [Mr Powell] to draft his Bill. I hope that they will now discuss the matter with parliamentary counsel and their draftsmen about the technicalities of the measure. We may by that means ensure that the measure is in the best possible shape, thereby avoiding the need for drafting amendments later. It may be complicated, because other amendments will no doubt be tabled to each of the options.

In December 1992, a little earlier than expected, the Court of Justice gave judgment and on 31 March 1993 the House of Lords applied this ruling to hold that s 47 of the Shops Act 1950 was not incompatible with free trade provisions of Art 30 of the EC Treaty.[17] The government felt the way was now clear to introduce the bill.

Queen's Speech and First Reading

It was announced in the Queen's Speech in November 1993, as everyone had expected, that the government was to 'bring forward a Bill to reform the law on Sunday trading in England and Wales'. This time, the government decided to introduce its bill first into the Commons. On 19 November the Sunday Trading Bill received its First Reading (a formality) and was ordered to be printed. In the weeks in the run-up to the Second Reading, the government made an important concession in an attempt to win over wavering Conservative and Labour MPs: on 19 November the government announced that future as well as present shopworkers would have a statutory right to refuse to work on Sundays.

Also of significance was the fact that the anti-Sunday trading lobby was plunged into turmoil. The newspapers reported 'rifts' and 'bitter in-fighting' between the KSSC and a newer lobby group called Retailers for Shops Act Reform (RSAR) (led by Marks & Spencer). The main division was over whether there should be a statutory right to double pay for Sunday working in the bill. By 9 December however, *The Times* was able to report that 'with each [anti-Sunday trading] campaign group facing defeat by fighting independently, the rival camps settled their differences and merged under a single campaign'. Valuable time had been lost though.

[17] See further Chapter 27.

Second Reading debate

The debate was opened at 5.35 pm by the Home Secretary (Mr Michael Howard).[18]

The Bill is, in many respects, unique. It contains three options for reform—regulation,[19] deregulation[20] and partial deregulation,[21] as proposed by the Shopping Hours Reform Council. It is the essence of the Government's position in presenting this Bill that we shall argue neither for nor against any of the options for reform, although I make no secret of the fact that, as an individual Member of Parliament, I favour deregulation.

. . . Each option has been drafted by parliamentary counsel. Each reflects the policy aims of the campaigning group that supports it. Parliament can compare and contrast the options and, on a free vote, choose between them. . . . The question for the House today is whether it agrees in principle that any one of the three options in the Bill should replace the existing provision on Sunday trading in the 1950 Act. It is not being asked to choose today between the three options for reform.

The Home Secretary then explained the rather complex procedure that would be used.[22]

If the Bill secures a Second Reading, the House will be invited immediately to agree the motion on the Order Paper . . . committing clauses 1 and 2 and schedule 4 to a Committee of the whole House. If agreed, that will have the effect, among other things, that clause 1 will be considered on the Floor of the House, ensuring that all hon. Members will be involved in the choice between the options.

So how is that choice to be made? . . . Clearly, there will be a full debate in Committee of the whole House on the options' merits. To choose among the options, the Committee will vote on a series of amendments to clause 1, which will remove from clause 1 references to two of the three options for reform. So if any group of amendments secures a majority, clause 1 will be amended to refer to one option only. That option will then be the choice of the House. . . .

It is not a question of which option gets the biggest vote. It is conceivable that only one option will be voted on if that were to secure a majority. Voting against earlier options is the only way in which hon. Members can seek to ensure that they can vote on their favourite option if it comes later in the order. Hon. Members cannot fudge the issues by abstaining in a vote without risking that their preferred option may fail by default.

When the Committee of the whole House has completed consideration of clause 1, the Standing Committee will consider in detail the chosen option and other provisions of the Bill in the normal way.

Mr Howard explained that a free vote would be allowed on 'the issue of which shops can open on Sundays, which cuts across party lines'. But he made it

[18] HC Deb, vol. 233, col. 815 (29 November 1993).

[19] Proposed jointly by the KSSC and the RSARC. This would require most shops to close other than on the four Sundays before Christmas, with exceptions for some types of retail outlet such as garden centres.

[20] This option would allow any shop to trade on Sundays.

[21] This option would allow all small shops to trade at any hour on Sundays but restrict larger shops to six hours' trading.

[22] HC Deb, vol. 233, col. 816 (29 November 1993).

clear that when at committee stage there was discussion about employees' rights (for example the right of new workers not to be discriminated against on the ground that they objected to working on Sundays, or to premium payments for Sunday working) the government would use its whips: 'the Government have a clear employment policy and we shall defend that policy vigorously'.

During the debate several members referred to letters from constituents and also the work of lobby groups. Mr Hugh Bayley, MP for York, had this to say:[23]

> I have felt under some pressure from managers of the companies in the SHRC group. I recently had a meeting, which it kindly organised, with the York managers of all the stores in the group. Perhaps the final factor that tilted me in favour of the RSAR proposal was that one of the managers of a large food superstore in my constituency, from within the SHRC group, said that if I did not support its proposal he would tell all his Sunday workers that I was putting them out of a job. I regret that threat.

The bill was given a Second Reading by 311 votes to 26, left-wing Labour MPs having forced a division.

Question

A Second Reading debate is when the 'whole principle' of the bill is at issue. What was the 'principle' of the bill here? It contained three mutually exclusive options for change.

Committee of the Whole House

When the House sat as a committee on 8 December 1993 as is customary, rather than the Speaker being in the chair, the Chairman of Ways and Means[24] presided, sitting at a table rather than in the Speaker's raised chair. It was at this stage that MPs had to choose between the various reform options. Once one of the options had been chosen by MPs the plan was for the rest of the committee stage to be 'upstairs' in Standing Committee rather than on the floor of the House.

The meeting began with discussion of various important but tricky procedural questions. In particular, several MPs were very concerned about the order in which amendments to the bill were to be discussed: clause 1 of the bill set out 'alternative schemes for reform of law relating to Sunday trading' and parliamentary procedure dictated that the first amendment to receive a majority would win the day and all other amendments (saying in effect that the bill should comprise one of the other reform options) would fall and not be discussed or voted upon.

Tempers often ran high during the debate and several MPs made reference to the work of the lobbyists.

[23] HC Deb, vol. 233, col. 862 (29 November 1993).
[24] A formal title for the Deputy Speaker of the Commons.

Mr Pike [Labour Party backbencher] . . . Conservatives often accuse the Labour party of jumping when the trade unions so demand and suggest that we are under their tight control. On a free vote, however, the Labour party is completely at liberty to advocate a particular case, unlike some Conservative Members who have been paid by the Shopping Hours Reform Council—which has spent substantial amounts of money—to try to persuade hon. Members how to vote on the issue.

Mr Fabricant [Conservative backbencher]: On a point of order . . . I support the Shopping Hours Reform Council. Is it not an absolute slur on certain Conservative Members to say that those who support the SHRC have been paid by that organisation, when we have not been? Moreover, if we had been, and we have not, we would have made a statement in the Register of Members' Interests.

Mr Pike: I was not casting any slur but was simply referring to the vast amount that has been spent by that organisation to persuade people which option they should support in the debate . . .

At the conclusion of the committee stage debate, MPs voted by a majority of 75 for the SHRC partial deregulation option which permitted small shops to open all day on Sundays but limited larger stores to open for only six hours. The rest of the committee stage was taken in a Standing Committee. Amendments made included a raising of the fine for contravention of the new rules from £5,000 to £50,000. At Third Reading a last-minute effort to overturn the bill failed and in the early hours of 24 February 1994 MPs voted 311 to 218 for the bill.

The House of Lords and Royal Assent

No substantial amendments were made to the bill during its passage through the House of Lords. The Sunday Trading Act 1994 received Royal Assent on 5 July 1994 and came into force on 26 August 1994 when the minister made a commencement order by statutory instrument (SI 1994 No 1841).

Questions

1. It might be objected that this case study is atypical of the normal legislative process and it is therefore dangerous to draw any general conclusions from it. Can you think of any ways in which the Sunday trading legislation was different from the norm?

2. Why did the 1985 bill fail, but the 1994 one succeed?

3. What evidence does the case study provide for and against the views:
   (a) that the legislative process is too dominated by the executive?
   (b) that involvement of interest and pressure groups is undesirable?

4. As we have seen, for Dicey and orthodox constitutional theorists in the United Kingdom, the function of MPs is central. It is said that MPs reflect the will of the majority of the politically sovereign electorate and this provides the democratic justification for parliamentary supremacy.[25] This begs many questions, notably whom exactly do MPs

[25] See Chapter 5.

represent—is it their constituents, pressure groups, their party? How do those represented make their views known?

5. If you were a leader of a pressure group opposed to Sunday trading what would you do now?

6. Whom, if anyone, do members of the House of Lords 'represent'?

7. Imagine you are a lawyer working for a retailers' group. They ask you to summarize the main provisions of the Sunday Trading Act for their members in plain language and not more than 150 words.

8. Look back at the discussion of statutory drafting techniques in Chapter 8.[26] Could the Sunday Trading Act 1994 have been expressed in a more appropriate way? (In answering this question, bear in mind the audience to which the Act is directed.)

THE END PRODUCT

What follows is the product of the many years of lobbying and the parliamentary process.

Sunday Trading Act 1994

An Act to reform the law of England and Wales relating to Sunday trading; to make provision as to the rights of shop workers under the law of England and Wales in relation to Sunday working; and for connected purposes

Reform of law relating to Sunday trading

1.—(1) Schedules 1 and 2 to this Act shall come into force on such day as the Secretary of State may by order made by statutory instrument appoint (in this section referred to as 'the appointed day').

(2) [repeals the Shops Act 1950, ss 47–66, Schs 5–7.]

Loading and unloading at large shops on Sunday morning

2.—(1) A local authority may by resolution designate their area as a loading control area for the purposes of this section with effect from a date specified in the resolution, which must be a date at least one month after the date on which the resolution is passed.

[. . .]

(3) It shall be the duty of a local authority, before making or revoking any designation under subsection (1) above, to consult persons appearing to the local authority to be likely to be affected by the proposed designation or revocation (whether as the occupiers of shops or as local residents) or persons appearing to the local authority to represent such persons.

(4) Where a local authority make or revoke a designation under this section, they shall publish notice of the designation or revocation in such manner as they consider appropriate.

(5) Schedule 3 to this Act (which imposes restrictions on loading and unloading on Sunday before 9 am at large shops in loading control areas) shall have effect.

[26] See p. 176.

Construction of certain leases and agreements
3. [. . .]

Rights of shop workers as respects Sunday working
4. Schedule 4 to this Act shall have effect. [. . .]

Consequential repeal or amendment of local Acts
6.—(1) The Secretary of State may by order made by statutory instrument—

(a) repeal any provision of a local Act passed before or in the same Session as this Act if it appears to him that the provision is inconsistent with or has become unnecessary in consequence of any provision of this Act, and

(b) amend any provision of such a local Act if it appears to him that the provision requires amendment in consequence of any provision of this Act or any repeal made by virtue of paragraph (a) above.

(2) It shall be the duty of the Secretary of State, before he makes an order under subsection (1) above repealing or amending any provision of a local Act, to consult each local authority which he considers would be affected by the repeal or amendment of that provision.

(3) A statutory instrument containing an order under subsection (1) above shall be subject to annulment in pursuance of a resolution of either House of Parliament.

[. . .]

Schedule 1 Restrictions on Sunday opening of large shops (s 1(1))

Interpretation
1. In this Schedule—[. . .]

'large shop' means a shop which has a relevant floor area exceeding 280 square metres,

'relevant floor area', in relation to a shop, means the internal floor area of so much of the shop as consists of or is comprised in a building, but excluding any part of the shop which, throughout the week ending with the Sunday in question, is used neither for the serving of customers in connection with the sale of goods nor for the display of goods. . . .

Large shops not to open on Sunday except in accordance with notice to local authority
2. (1) Subject to sub-paragraphs (2) and (3) below, a large shop shall not be open on Sunday for the serving of retail customers.

(2) Sub-paragraph (1) above does not apply in relation to—

(a) any of the shops mentioned in paragraph 3(1) below, or

(b) any shop in respect of which a notice under paragraph 8(1) of Schedule 2 to this Act (shops occupied by persons observing the Jewish Sabbath) has effect.

(3) Where a notice under paragraph 4 below has effect in relation to a shop, sub-paragraph (1) above does not apply in relation to the shop during the permitted Sunday opening hours specified in the notice, but this sub-paragraph has effect subject to sub-paragraph (4) below.

(4) The exemption conferred by sub-paragraph (3) above does not apply where the Sunday is Easter Day or Christmas Day.

Exemptions
3. (1) The shops referred to in paragraph 2(2)(a) above are—

(a) any shop which is at a farm and where the trade or business carried on consists wholly or mainly of the sale of produce from that farm,

(b) any shop where the trade or business carried on consists wholly or mainly of the sale of intoxicating liquor,

(c) any shop where the trade or business carried on consists wholly or mainly of the sale of any one or more of the following—

(i) motor supplies and accessories, and

(ii) cycle supplies and accessories,

(d) any shop which—

(i) is a registered pharmacy, and

(ii) is not open for the retail sale of any goods other than medicinal products and medical and surgical appliances,

(e) any shop at a designated airport which is situated in a part of the airport to which sub-paragraph (3) below applies,

(f) any shop in a railway station,

(g) any shop at a service area within the meaning of the Highways Act 1980,

(h) any petrol filling station,

(j) any shop which is not open for the retail sale of any goods other than food, stores or other necessaries required by any person for a vessel or aircraft on its arrival at, or immediately before its departure from, a port, harbour or airport, and

(k) any stand used for the retail sale of goods during the course of an exhibition. [. . .]

Notice of proposed Sunday opening

4. (1) A person who is, or proposes to become, the occupier of a large shop may give notice to the local authority for the area in which the shop is situated—

(a) stating that he proposes to open the shop on Sunday for the serving of retail customers, and

(b) specifying a continuous period of six hours, beginning no earlier than 10am and ending no later than 6pm, as the permitted Sunday opening hours in relation to the shop.

(2) The occupier of a shop in respect of which notice has been given under sub-paragraph (1) above may, by a subsequent notice—

(a) specify permitted Sunday opening hours that could be specified under sub-paragraph (1)(b) above but are different from those specified in the earlier notice, or

(b) cancel the earlier notice.

(3) A notice under this paragraph shall not take effect until the end of the period of 14 days beginning with the day on which it is given, unless the local authority agree that it is to take effect at the end of a shorter period.

(4) A notice under this paragraph shall cease to have effect when superseded by a subsequent notice or cancelled as mentioned in sub-paragraph (2)(b) above.

Register of shops

5. (1) Every local authority shall keep a register of shops in respect of which a notice under paragraph 4 above has effect.

[. . .]

Duty to display notice

6. At any time when—

(a) a large shop is open on Sunday for the serving of retail customers, and

(b) the prohibition in sub-paragraph (1) of paragraph 2 above is excluded only by sub-paragraph (3) of that paragraph, a notice specifying the permitted

Sunday opening hours specified in the notice under paragraph 4 above shall be displayed in a conspicuous position inside and outside the shop.

Offences

7. (1) If paragraph 2(1) above is contravened in relation to a shop, the occupier of the shop shall be liable on summary conviction to a fine not exceeding £50,000. [. . .]

Schedule 2, Part I General enforcement provisions

Duty to enforce Act

1. It shall be the duty of every local authority to enforce within their area the provisions of Schedules 1 and 3 to this Act and Part II of this Schedule.

Inspectors

2. For the purposes of their duties under paragraph 1 above it shall be the duty of every local authority to appoint inspectors. [. . .]

[*Part II of this schedule deals with the position of shops owned by persons of the Jewish faith*]

Schedule 3 Loading and unloading at large shops on Sunday morning

[*States large shops must obtain the consent of a local authority*]

Schedule 4 Rights of shop workers as respects Sunday working

Interpretation

1. (1) In this Schedule, except where a contrary intention appears—
'the 1978 Act' means the Employment Protection (Consolidation) Act 1978 [. . .]

Meaning of 'protected shop worker'

2. (1) Subject to paragraph 3 below, a shop worker is to be regarded for the purposes of this Schedule as 'protected' if, and only if, sub-paragraph (2) or (3) below applies to him.

(2) This sub-paragraph applies to a shop worker if—

(a) on the day before the commencement date, he was employed as a shop worker,

(b) on that day, he was not employed to work only on Sunday,

(c) he has been continuously employed during the period beginning with that day and ending with the appropriate date, and

(d) throughout that period, or throughout every part of it during which his relations with his employer were governed by a contract of employment, he was a shop worker.

(3) This sub-paragraph applies to any shop worker whose contract of employment is such that under it he—

(a) is not, and may not be, required to work on Sunday, and

(b) could not be so required even if the provisions of this Schedule were disregarded.

(4) In sub-paragraph (2)(c) above 'the appropriate date' means—

(a) in relation to paragraphs 7 and 8 below, the effective date of termination,

(b) in relation to paragraph 10 below, the date of the act or failure to act,

(c) in relation to sub-paragraph (2) or (3) of paragraph 12 below, the day on which the agreement is entered into,

(d) in relation to sub-paragraph (4) of that paragraph, the day on which the employee returns to work,

[. . .]

3. (1) A shop worker is not a protected shop worker if—

(a) on or after the commencement date, he has given his employer an opting-in notice, and

(b) after giving that notice, he has expressly agreed with his employer to do shop work on Sunday or on a particular Sunday.

(2) In this Schedule 'opting-in notice' means a written notice, signed and dated by the shop worker, in which the shop worker expressly states that he wishes to work on Sunday or that he does not object to Sunday working.

Notice of objection to Sunday working

4. (1) This paragraph applies to any shop worker who, under his contract of employment—

(a) is or may be required to work on Sunday (whether or not as a result of previously giving an opting-in notice), but

(b) is not employed to work only on Sunday.

(2) A shop worker to whom this paragraph applies may at any time give his employer written notice, signed and dated by the shop worker, to the effect that the shop worker objects to Sunday working.

(3) In this Schedule 'opting-out notice' means a notice given under sub-paragraph (2) above by a shop worker to whom this paragraph applies.

Meaning of 'opted-out shop worker'

5. (1) Subject to sub-paragraph (5) below, a shop worker is to be regarded for the purposes of this Schedule as 'opted-out' if, and only if—

(a) he has given his employer an opting-out notice,

(b) he has been continuously employed during the period beginning with the day on which the notice was given and ending with the appropriate date, and

(c) throughout that period, or throughout every part of it during which his relations with his employer were governed by a contract of employment, he was a shop worker.

(2) In sub-paragraph (1) above 'the appropriate date' means—

(a) in relation to paragraphs 7 and 8 below, the effective date of termination

(b) in relation to paragraph 10 below, the date of the act or failure to act,

(c) in relation to sub-paragraph (2) or (3) of paragraph 13 below, the day on which the agreement is entered into, and

(d) in relation to sub-paragraph (4) of that paragraph, the day on which the employee returns to work.

(3) For the purposes of sub-paragraph (2)(a) above, 'the effective date of termination', in any case falling within paragraph 1(6) above, means the day with effect from which the employee is treated by section 56 of the 1978 Act as being dismissed.

(4) For the purposes of sub-paragraph (2)(b) above—

(a) where an act extends over a period, the 'date of the act' means the first day of the period, and

(b) a deliberate failure to act shall be treated as done when it was decided on, and in the absence of evidence establishing the contrary, an employer shall be taken to decide on a failure to act when he does an act inconsistent with doing the failed act or, if he has done no such inconsistent act, when the period expires within which he might reasonably have been expected to do the failed act if it was to be done.

(5) A shop worker is not an opted-out shop worker if—

(a) after giving the opting-out notice concerned, he has given his employer an opting-in notice, and

(b) after giving that opting-in notice, he has expressly agreed with his employer to do shop work on Sunday or on a particular Sunday.

Meaning of 'notice period'

6. In this Schedule 'notice period', in relation to an opted-out shop worker, means, subject to paragraph 11(2) below, the period of three months beginning with the day on which the opting-out notice concerned was given.

Right not to be dismissed for refusing Sunday work

7. (1) Subject to sub-paragraph (2) below, the dismissal of a protected or opted-out shop worker by his employer shall be regarded for the purposes of Part V of the 1978 Act as unfair if the reason for it (or, if more than one, the principal reason) was that the shop worker refused, or proposed to refuse, to do shop work on Sunday or on a particular Sunday.

[. . .]

(3) The dismissal of a shop worker by his employer shall be regarded for the purposes of Part V of the 1978 Act as unfair if the reason for it (or, if more than one, the principal reason) was that the shop worker gave, or proposed to give, an opting-out notice to the employer.

[. . .]

Right not to suffer detriment for refusing Sunday work

10. (1) Subject to sub-paragraphs (2) and (4) below, a protected or opted-out shop worker has the right not to be subjected to any detriment by any act, or any deliberate failure to act, by his employer done on the ground that the shop worker refused, or proposed to refuse, to do shop work on Sunday or on a particular Sunday.

[. . .]

Employer's duty to give explanatory statement

11. (1) Where a person becomes a shop worker to whom paragraph 4 above applies, his employer shall, before the end of the period of two months beginning with the day on which that person becomes such a shop worker, give him a written statement in the prescribed form.

[. . .]

(4) Subject to sub-paragraph (5) below, the prescribed form is as follows

'STATUTORY RIGHTS IN RELATION TO SUNDAY SHOP WORK
You have become employed as a shop worker and are or can be required under your contract of employment to do the Sunday work your contract provides for. However, if you wish, you can give a notice, as described in the next paragraph, to your employer and you will then have the right not to work in or about a shop on any Sunday on which the shop is open once three months have passed from the date on which you gave the notice. Your notice must—

be in writing;

be signed and dated by you;

say that you object to Sunday working.

For three months after you give the notice, your employer can still require you to do all the Sunday work your contract provides for. After the three-month period has ended, you have the right to complain to an industrial tribunal if, because of your refusal to work on Sundays on which the shop is open, your employer—

dismisses you, or

does something else detrimental to you, for example, failing to promote you.

Once you have the rights described, you can surrender them only by giving your employer a further notice, signed and dated by you, saying that you wish to work on Sunday or that you do not object to Sunday working and then agreeing with your employer to work on Sundays or on a particular Sunday.'

(5) The Secretary of State may by order amend the prescribed form set out in sub-paragraph (4) above.

(6) An order under sub-paragraph (5) above shall be made by statutory instrument which shall be subject to annulment in pursuance of a resolution of either House of Parliament. [. . .]

POSTSCRIPT

Government success in deregulating Sunday shop opening encouraged it to pursue further similar deregulatory policies. In May 1995 it became legal for betting and horse racing to take place on Sunday; and in August 1995 restrictions on pub opening hours were relaxed, allowing them to open from noon to 10.30 pm on Sundays. So far as shops were concerned, *The Guardian* reported that 'supporters of [the] change must be pleased with the way things turned out, because virtually all opposition to Sunday trading has gone underground or gone bust since the law was changed'.[27] Not everyone was pleased, however. The same report stated that 'as far as the economy is concerned, Sunday trading has been an almighty flop'. Early statistics from the government's Central Statistical Office suggested that the main effect of Sunday trading has been to encourage the existing trend towards people spending less at small independent stores and much more at large out-of-town supermarkets. Marks & Spencer, one of the chain stores which opposed deregulation, remained unconvinced by the new law which allowed larger

[27] *The Guardian*, 20 May 1995, p. 20.

shops to open for six hours: Sunday trading had produced no improvement in profits for the company, Sir Richard Greenbury, the chairman, said, the extra revenue being generated at the expense of trading in the rest of the week and the cost of double-time payments to staff.[28]

This was not the end of the dissatisfaction with the new law. Very soon anomalies and loopholes began to be identified. Under the Sunday Trading Act DIY stores and garden centres with indoor premises larger than 3,000 square feet had to stay closed on Easter Sundays. Many people had not realized this. Some retailers were prompted to resort to tactics reminiscent of those used to side-step the restrictions imposed by s 47 of the Shops Act 1950. The owner of one garden centre, backed by the Horticultural Trade Association, moved his entire stock of plants and goods into the open air to circumvent the new rule; it took a dozen staff over four hours to achieve this.[29] Another garden centre applied for a liquor licence for Easter Sunday so that it could sell drinks to disappointed customers who turned up not realizing the effect of the new law.

Meanwhile, some employers began searching for loopholes in the provisions of the Sunday Trading Act designed to protect shopworkers. Staff of one supermarket chain were reported to have received letters from management saying that their wages would be cut if they refused to work on Sundays because they would not be offered alternative weekday shifts. The workers concerned were said to be taking legal advice.[30]

WHERE TO GO NOW

Chapter 10 examines another type of legislation—delegated (or subordinate) legislation. If, however, you want to continue exploring the Sunday trading case study you can turn now to Chapter 30, which considers the challenges to the validity of 47 of the Shops Act 1950.

[28] See *The Times*, 24 May 1995.
[29] *The Guardian*, 17 April 1995, p. 4.
[30] *The Guardian*, 17 April 1995, p. 4.

10

DELEGATED LEGISLATION: MAKING STATUTORY INSTRUMENTS

It is the natural object of every government having despotic ends, and seeking to narrow the liberties of the people, to encourage the disposition to delegate legislative authority. By this means the ends of centralisation are more effectively accomplished than by any other that ingenuity can devise. While the outward show of representative institutions is preserved, an arbitrary and wholly irresponsible power is, in reality, lodged in the hands of the few.

Joshua Toulmin Smith, Local Self-Government and Centralisation (1851)

. . . the general balance between primary legislation, on the one hand, and conventional secondary legislation, on the other, is an important issue on which it is possible for sensible and well-informed people to hold divergent views . . . my suspicion is that there may be room overall for somewhat greater use of delegated powers, provided that this can be done without loss of quality and with the necessary degree of parliamentary oversight.

Viscount Cranborne, a minister in the Conservative government, HL Deb, vol. 550, col. 1324 (14 December 1994)

INTRODUCTION

Numerous Acts of Parliament grant powers to ministers, the Crown, local authorities or other public bodies to make rules which are binding on the public. In 1993 over 3,000 pieces of delegated legislation were made (52 Acts of Parliament were passed in the same period). The number of items and length of delegated legislation[1] is likely to increase if the trend towards enacting 'skeleton' or 'framework' Acts continues.[2] Delegated legislation is used across a wide spectrum of government, across issues as important and diverse as immigration control;[3] animal welfare;[4] entitlement to welfare benefits;[5]

[1] 'Subordinate legislation' and 'secondary legislation' are synonyms.

[2] On skeleton Acts, see Chapter 8.

[3] For example the Immigration Rules (1994 HC 395) made under the Immigration Act 1971; Asylum Appeals (Procedure) Rules (SI 1993 No 1661).

[4] For example the Welfare of Animals during Transport Order 1994 (SI 1994 No 3249) made under the Animal Health Act 1981.

[5] For example Housing Benefit (General) Regulations (SI 1987 No 1971).

regulation of prisons;[6] health and safety; town and country planning;[7] censorship of television programmes;[8] and environmental control.[9] Delegated legislation, in the form of 'commencement orders', is also the mechanism used by ministers to bring Acts of Parliament into force when this does not happen immediately a bill receives Royal Assent.[10] Significantly, delegated legislation may also be used to alter national law to conform with Community directives.[11] Both in terms of quantity and subject matter, delegated legislation is therefore an important source of law, defining the rights and obligations of individuals and businesses in the United Kingdom.

Types of delegated legislation

Statutory instruments (SIs) are by far the most common form in which delegated legislation may be made by a minister, and it is on SIs that this chapter mainly focuses. A typical enabling provision in an Act of Parliament will state that 'The Secretary of State may by order made by statutory instrument make regulations' about a particular subject.[12] The general procedures for making SIs are governed by the Statutory Instruments Act 1946. SIs may also be referred to as 'regulations', 'orders' and 'Orders in Council'.[13]

Some Acts confer powers on ministers to make legally binding rules other than by SI. Examples include the Immigration Rules and the codes of practice on questioning suspects and carrying out searches made under the Police and Criminal Evidence Act 1984.[14] More generally, local authorities may make bylaws. An example of a very wide enabling provision is s 235 of the Local Government Act 1972 which empowers district councils and London boroughs to make bylaws 'for the good rule and government of the whole or any part of the district or borough . . . and for the prevention and suppression of nuisances therein'. Delegated legislation authorized by an Act will not necessarily be subject to any parliamentary control and scrutiny if it is not in the form of an SI.[15]

[6] Prison Rules 1964 (SI 1964 No 388).
[7] For example Town and Country Planning (Control of Advertisements) Regulations 1989 (SI 1989 No 670).
[8] Foreign Satellite Proscription Order (SI 1993 No 1024).
[9] Under the Environmental Protection Act 1990.
[10] See p. 190.
[11] See Chapter 13.
[12] See e.g. Sunday Trading Act 1994, s 6.
[13] The term Order in Council can be confusing because it may *also* be used to describe *primary* legislation which the Crown may still make under the royal prerogative in limited situations: see Chapter 12.
[14] For discussion of why the codes of practice are not in the form of SIs, see Michael Zander, *The Police and Criminal Evidence Act 1984* (1985), Part VI.
[15] See further p. 237 below.

CONSTITUTIONAL DANGER OR BENEFIT?

As the opening quotations in the chapter suggest, the use of delegated legislation is, and has long been, controversial.

Delegated legislation is necessary and desirable

On the face of it, there is no conflict between the notion that Parliament has ultimate legislative power and the fact that ministers, local authorities and other bodies also have rule-making powers. As it has legislative supremacy, Parliament is free to delegate even legislative powers to other bodies.[16] Moreover, whenever a minister actually wants to use delegated legislative powers in the form of SIs, his proposed rules will be subject to some, though admittedly limited, scrutiny by Parliament. The validity of delegated legislation may also be questioned in the courts. A person may argue that a minister, in making the delegated legislation in question, has exceeded the powers conferred on him by the particular enabling (or 'parent') Act. Judges therefore also police the use of delegated legislation to ensure that ministers and others do not exceed the powers given to them by Act of Parliament.

There is broad consensus that delegated legislation is both necessary and desirable—provided that it is subject to adequate parliamentary and judicial control. Certainly given the intense pressure already on Parliament, it is unrealistic to argue that there ought to be less delegated legislation and more primary legislation. In addition to being a palliative to parliamentary overload, there are many benefits in having delegated legislation. It enables Parliament to focus on issues of general public interest when considering bills, rather than forcing MPs and peers to concentrate on the minor details at that stage. It allows speedy response to a crisis, in part because SIs are drafted 'in-house' by departmental lawyers, not by Parliamentary Counsel who are responsible for drafting bills. It may also permit experts to be more closely involved in making regulations in highly technical subjects such as pollution control and vehicle safety. It allows departments to deal with unforeseen circumstances which may arise during the introduction of large and complex areas of reform. It is rarely possible to anticipate every eventuality and delegated legislation allows details to be changed without subjecting the whole scheme to fresh parliamentary examination.

These, then, are the justifications for the use of delegated legislation. There are, however, also considerable drawbacks.

Constitutional dangers with delegated legislation

Several influential writers have argued that there are dangers associated with increased use of delegated legislation. In 1929 Lord Hewart CJ articulated

[16] See Chapter 5.

his concerns in a controversial book entitled *The New Despotism*. The main thrust of his argument was that the powers of the executive were expanding at a rate, and in a way, that undermined Parliament and evaded the courts. His ultimate fear was that the UK system could come to resemble that of the Soviet Union. The government responded to fears such as these by establishing an *ad hoc* Committee on Ministers' Powers (the Donoughmore Committee). Its terms of reference were:

> to consider the powers exercised by . . . Ministers of the Crown by way of . . . delegated legislation . . . and to report what safeguards are desirable or necessary to secure the constitutional principles of the sovereignty of Parliament and the supremacy of the Law.

When the Donoughmore Committee reported in 1932,[17] it took the view that delegated legislation was inevitable and desirable. Accepting, however, that there were risks in delegation it argued that in normal circumstances delegation should be limited to matters of detail rather than principle. The Committee, nevertheless, was prepared to accept that circumstances could justify the delegation of very wide powers. To reduce the risks of abuse it recommended the introduction of a systematic scrutiny of delegated legislation laid before Parliament. These recommendations were not acted upon until after the Second World War when backbench reaction to the wide delegation of powers to the executive under the Emergency Powers Defence Acts increased pressure on government and eventually led to the introduction of the Statutory Instruments Act 1946, which forms the basis of the current system of parliamentary control.[18]

Concern is thus not just a question of the *scale* of delegation, but also about the *nature* of the powers being delegated. As we have seen, nowadays Acts of Parliament are often limited to establishing a framework which will be developed by regulations made by ministers.[19] In practice, however, the distinction between matters of detail and the broad policy objectives is often hazy. This may result in important *policy* issues being left to be decided by the minister and his or her department with little or no parliamentary scrutiny. In 1993 several pressure groups, including the Child Poverty Action Group (CPAG) and the Confederation of British Industry (CBI) gave evidence to the Hansard Society Commission on the legislative process which was highly critical of extensive delegation of legislative powers to ministers. CPAG said that it had:

> . . . become increasingly concerned about the trend towards 'skeleton bills' containing only a bare outline, with all the detail necessary to implement the legislative intent contained in statutory instruments. The most recent example was the Child Support Act 1991, which contained over 100 regulation-making powers. Serious

[17] Cmnd 4060.

[18] Concern about delegated legislation continued to be expressed even after the 1946 reforms. See for example G. W. Keeton in *The Passing of Parliament* (1952) and Cecil Carr in Lord Campion (ed.), *Parliament: a survey* (1952), Chapter 11.

[19] See p. 180.

> concern was expressed, in particular by peers during debate in the House of Lords, about this. Although statutory instruments are subject to parliamentary scrutiny, this is of a very limited nature. In particular, given our long experience of unsatisfactory drafting of regulations and the problems this can cause to benefit claimants, CPAG is concerned at the lack of opportunity for amendment in the parliamentary scrutiny of regulations.[20]

Apart from problems associated with framework Acts of Parliament, delegated legislation may be criticized on the grounds that it gives ministers excessive power in two specific contexts: the use of SIs to transpose Community directives into English law;[21] and so-called Henry VIII clauses.

Henry VIII clauses

A number of Acts of Parliament grant to ministers powers 'which enable primary legislation to be amended or repealed by subordinate legislation with or without further parliamentary scrutiny'.[22] The Donoughmore Committee explained in its report in 1932 that this type of provision had acquired its nickname 'because that King was regarded popularly as the impersonation of executive autocracy'.[23] Such powers may be used by a minister to make very minor amendments to an Act, for example to increase sums of money specified in the Act in line with inflation or as a kind of 'insurance policy' by Parliamentary Counsel in case some minor matter has been overlooked. Such a clause may also be used to make consequential amendments or repeals of a subsidiary character. Here there is little to object to. The Donoughmore Committee recommended that Henry VIII clauses should be limited to such minor matters and in any event should be included in an Act of Parliament only in the most exceptional cases.

The powers conferred on a minister by a Henry VIII clause may, however, be used for purposes other than minor amendments, including to change the policy which the statute enacted. Here there is good cause for concern. The Hansard Society Commission recommended that future Acts of Parliament should not normally include Henry VIII clauses and welcomed the decision of the government to set up, initially as a one-year experiment, a House of Lords committee to scrutinize bills as to delegated powers.[24] 'Henry VIII clauses are, of their nature, undesirable,' the commission stated. 'Unless absolutely necessary, a single Minister should not be given power to change the law made by Parliament as a whole.'[25] These clauses continue to be used,

[20] *Making the Law* (1993), pp. 185–6.

[21] See p. 315.

[22] House of Lords Select Committee on the Scrutiny of Delegated Powers, 1st Report, HL 57, 1992–93, para. 10.

[23] Cmd 4069, p. 36.

[24] *Making the Law*. This Select Committee on the Scrutiny of Delegated Powers was established in 1992 and re-established in the following parliamentary session.

[25] *Making the Law*, para. 270.

as can be seen in the Sunday Trading Act 1994 set out in Chapter 9. Can you spot the Henry VIII clause in it?

STATUTORY INSTRUMENT PROCEDURE

So far, this chapter has surveyed the benefits and disadvantages of having delegated legislation. There is broad consensus today that delegated legislation is constitutionally acceptable, *provided* that there are adequate mechanisms to ensure that ministers and others do not abuse the rule-making powers conferred upon them. We therefore need to examine when and how scrutiny of delegated legislative powers takes place. In essence there are four main opportunities for scrutiny:

(1) when a bill conferring delegated legislative powers is being considered in Parliament;
(2) when a government department consults interested parties over proposals to make specific regulations;
(3) when the proposed regulations are brought before Parliament for scrutiny and approval; and
(4) in rare cases, when there is judicial review of delegated legislation.[26]

Scrutiny of bills which delegate legislative powers

The first opportunity Parliament has to control delegated legislative power is when scrutinizing a bill conferring rule-making capacity on a minister or public body. Until very recently, there was no systematic way for Parliament to do this. In 1992, however, following pressure from several members of the House of Lords, that House set up a Select Committee on the Scrutiny of Delegated Powers. This committee's terms of reference are 'to report whether the provisions of any bill inappropriately delegate legislative power; or whether they subject the exercise of legislative power to an inappropriate degree of parliamentary scrutiny'. Reports by the committee have led to several delegated powers clauses in bills being defeated or reconsidered by the government.

Consultation over proposed regulations

When a government department intends to use its minister's delegated powers it will almost always engage in *some* form of consultation over the contents of the proposed legislation with individuals, business and interest groups whose members are likely to be affected. There is, however, no *general* statutory obligation imposed upon ministers or departments to consult about delegated legislation. Individual statutes may impose obligations to consult,

[26] See Chapter 27.

but in Britain there is nothing resembling the situation in the USA where interested parties have rights to be heard as part of the process of administrative rule-making.[27] Government departments, nevertheless, regularly consult with interested parties:[28]

> The almost complete absence of parliamentary scrutiny and debate contrasts with the high degree of consultation, mostly non-statutory, which departments engage in with affected interests in the making of delegated legislation.

They do this because it is felt to be good practice to take account of the interests and experience of those affected by the legislation, particularly where technical or specialized issues are involved. The voluntary and informal procedures may work in practice but there are important questions that need to be asked. Is it right, for example, that departments should be left to decide whom will be consulted, what the nature of that consultation will be, and what weight will be placed on views expressed during the consultation? What checks are there to ensure that the consultation procedures are working properly, and what would happen if departments decide to change their practices and choose not to consult? What, if anything, can be done by those who would like to be consulted but have not been?

Hundreds of advisory bodies, some set up by statute, others not, play a key role in the consultation stage. Examples include the Advisory Committee on Pesticides, the Social Security Advisory Committee[29] and the Commission on the Safety of Medicines. Weir and Hall have expressed concerns about these bodies, in particular that ministers have considerable power to appoint whomever they think fit to these organizations,[30] that there is no legal obligation that members of the bodies reflect an appropriate range of interests and that work of the bodies often takes place in secret.[31] They argue that:

> The aim must be to re-define them in law as agents of the public interest, not the creatures of ministers and government departments. They must work as openly as possible in the sight of the public and media, with clear rules to establish an appropriate balance in their composition, to give the public access to their meetings, documents and data, and to provide for public participation in their work.

27 (USA) Administrative Procedure Act 1946. For a recommendation that a similar procedure be adopted in the United Kingdom, see the JUSTICE/All Souls Report, *Administrative Justice: Some Necessary Reforms* (1988), para. 10.118.

28 Ian Harden and Norman Lewis, *The Noble Lie: The British Constitution and the Rule of Law* (1986) p. 112.

29 See p. 245.

30 Labour MPs expressed surprise in August 1995 when Sir Thomas Boyd-Carpenter was appointed to chair the Social Security Advisory Committee. He is a former army officer with no experience of the benefit system. He is also the son of a former Tory minister and the brother of Sarah Hogg (who headed the Prime Minister's policy unit until 1994). On 31 August 1995, *The Times* reported that: 'Donald Dewar, Shadow Social Security Secretary, accused the Government of "keeping the appointment in the family" and said the committee was at risk of losing its independence . . . Social security officials insisted, however, that the recruitment process had been fair, with Sir Thomas having been selected from a shortlist drawn up by civil servants from 50 applicants.'

31 Stuart Weir and Wendy Hall, *Behind Closed Doors: advisory quangos in the corridors of power* (1995).

Unless there is reform, there is a real danger that the sort of unhealthy 'corporatist' arrangements that many people, including the Conservative government, criticize will develop[32] with representatives of sectional interest groups able strike bargains with government behind closed doors with no proper opportunity for public participation in the decision-making.

Perhaps to meet some of these general concerns, Acts of Parliament do sometimes make consultation a mandatory obligation.[33] But obligations in statutes differ. For example, the organizations or groups to be consulted may be specifically named or it may be left to the minister or department to decide whom to consult. A typical provision to this effect might provide, for instance, that there shall be consultation with 'such organisations as appear [to the minister] to be representative of interests likely to be affected' by the regulations.

Parliamentary procedures

Many of the advantages of using delegated legislation would be lost if it were subject to the same level of parliamentary scrutiny as bills. The inevitable question is whether the right balance is being struck between the desirability for speed and flexibility on the one hand, and the interests of maintaining proper controls over law-making on the other.[34] The procedure described below concentrates on the making of delegated legislation in the form of SIs. As you will see parliamentary scrutiny of draft SIs differs from that of bills in that it is normally extremely perfunctory and draft SIs cannot be amended by MPs; they either stand or fall in the form they were introduced.

Negative resolution procedure

The vast majority of SIs are laid before Parliament and come into operation unless within 40 days either House passes a motion (a 'prayer') to annul the instrument.[35] Such challenges are extremely rare and most SIs therefore usually come into effect without any discussion in either House.

Affirmative resolution procedure

Every year about 200 or so SIs are required (by the enabling Act under which they are made) to be subject to somewhat fuller scrutiny by Parliament. These regulations do not come into effect unless positively affirmed by

32 On corporatism, see p. 129.

33 The Board and Lodgings Regulations (considered in Chapter 11) were subject to mandatory consultation. For another example see *Agricultural, Horticultural and Forestry Industry Training Board v Aylesbury Mushrooms Ltd* [1972] 1 WLR 190. See further A. Jergeson, 'The Legal Requirements of Consultation' [1978] PL 290, and see Chapter 27.

34 See further J. D. Hayhurst and Peter Wallington, 'The Parliamentary Scrutiny of Delegated Legislation' [1988] PL 547 and G. Alderman [1989] PL 38.

35 Statutory Instruments Act 1946, s 5.

one or both of the Houses.[36] This affirmative resolution procedure obviously guarantees a higher degree of parliamentary involvement than does the negative resolution procedure. Although the vote has to be taken on the floor of the House, often any detailed consideration of the SI occurs in an *ad hoc* Standing Committee which will meet only once and have a maximum of one and a half hours to debate the regulations.[37] The style of debate resembles that of a second reading of a bill, with MPs discussing in general terms the policy of the draft SI. The Hansard Society Commission on the Legislative Process has called for the 'artificial' time limit for debate to be lifted.

The Joint Committee on Statutory Instruments

At the same time as an instrument is laid it is referred to the Joint Committee on Statutory Instruments which consists of seven MPs and seven peers and by convention is chaired by an opposition backbench MP. It considers every SI which is required to be laid before both Houses. (SIs laid only before the House of Commons are considered by the MPs alone, sitting as a Select Committee of the House of Commons.) The joint committee meets weekly in private and publishes a report after each meeting. It may require a government department to explain an SI and to send witnesses for examination.[38] Indeed, if it is proposing to report adversely on a particular SI it must give the department concerned an opportunity to explain itself. Where there are problems, the committee may negotiate directly with the department rather than making a formal report.

The committee's task is to draw the attention of Parliament to any SI which falls foul of any of the following grounds:[39]

(1) that it imposes a charge on the public revenues or contains provisions requiring payments to be made to the Exchequer or any government department or any local or public authority in consideration of any licence or consent, or of any services to be rendered, or prescribes the amount of any such charge or payment;
(2) that it is made in pursuance of any enactment containing specific provisions excluding it from challenge in the courts, either at all times or after the expiration of a specific period;
(3) that it purports to have retrospective effect where the parent statute confers no express authority so to provide;
(4) that there appears to have been unjustifiable delay in the publication or in the laying of it before Parliament;
(5) that there appears to have been unjustifiable delay in sending a notification under the proviso to s 4(1) of the Statutory Instruments Act 1946

[36] The House of Lords has not actually debated or voted on any motion approving an affirmative SI or on a prayer annulling a negative SI since 1982. On 20 October 1994 the House of Lords did, however, pass a motion confirming that it does indeed still have unfettered freedom to vote on any SI submitted for its consideration: see HL Deb, vol. 559, col. 356.

[37] The Board and Lodging Regulations (see Chapter 11) were subject to this procedure.

[38] This happened in respect of the Board and Lodging Regulations (see Chapter 11).

[39] House of Commons Standing Orders, Order 124.

where an instrument has come into operation before it has been laid before Parliament;[40]

(6) that there appears to be doubt whether it is *intra vires* or that it appears to make some unusual or unexpected use of the powers conferred by the statute under which it was made;
(7) that for any special reason its form or purport calls for elucidation;
(8) that its drafting appears to be defective; or
(9) on any other ground that does not impinge on its merits or the policy behind it.

This last limitation on the committee's powers is important. The committee is not concerned with the merits of instruments or with policy issues. Its functions are limited to technical, drafting and procedural matters and to ensuring that the Houses are aware of SIs that may be making an unusual and unlawful use of ministerial power. The committee considers over 1,000 instruments a year and draws less than 1 per cent of these to the attention of either House. This may suggest that it has relatively little direct impact. It is not, however, known how many SIs are withdrawn or modified prior to a reference being made, nor is it possible to know what types of SI would have been enacted had the committee not existed. The indirect impact of the committee may therefore be considerable.[41] Matthew Parris, a former Conservative backbench MP and now a journalist, gave an insider's eye view of the work of the committee in *The Times*.[42] While he was an MP he sat on the committee for several years.

> It is 14in long, 8in wide and 5in high. It weighs about 20lb. It arrived in two jumbo manilla envelopes, tied together with eight rubber bands. It comprises, I reckon, 2,000 to 3,000 pages of mostly closely printed typescript. 'What is all this about parcels?' you ask. . . . 'was your sketch writer not in the Chamber?'
>
> I was not. Nor, unless they plan to lock themselves away from their constituents for the next four days, were the MPs who serve on the joint committee on statutory instruments. We were all reading. For all of them will have received, like me, an identical parcel. It is a little light reading for their meeting in committee room seven at 4.30 pm next Tuesday.
>
> How can they even read, let alone understand all this? How can this meeting, a regular occurrence, the first and last look Parliament gets at the great bulk of red tape and regulation that its own legislation is spewing out, semi-digested, every week, be anything other than a sham? Acts of Parliament, these days, tell you nothing. But the powers they give to ministers to make orders is immense. It is these—the [SIs] that Parliament can really do little more than nod at glumly as they pass—that are the nub of modern policy-making. . . .

40 The proviso to s 4(1) allows SIs to come into operation before copies have been officially presented to Parliament if this is essential and provided copies have been sent to the Lord Chancellor and the Speaker of the House of Commons drawing their attention to the fact that the SI has not yet been laid and explaining why it came into operation before this.
41 D. Miers and A. Page, *Legislation* (2nd edn.) p. 123.
42 20 November 1993.

> It is not working. The scandal is one of the great, unremarked disgraces of our modern constitution. . . . One little committee cannot possibly attend to it all. Not to half of it; not to a tenth of it; not to a hundredth. I know. I sat on the joint committee for years as an MP. The whips asked me to do it, no doubt to make me feel useful. I was useless. So were most of the others.

As we shall see in the next chapter, the committee was not altogether 'useless' in its scrutiny of the Board and Lodgings Regulations—though it was only alerted to the fact that they were *ultra vires* by a decision of the High Court.

Publication

SIs have to be printed and formally published by the Queen's Printers (Her Majesty's Stationery Office).[43] Each SI is given a reference number (for example SI 1995 No 999).

Exceptions to the obligation to publish exist: where SIs are of limited application because they only apply to particular localities or because they are private in nature; where publication is certified as being contrary to the public interest; and where the SIs are temporary or bulky.[44] The requirement to publish is not regarded as being a mandatory requirement and failure to publish appears not to invalidate the SI. One reason for saying this is that s 3(2) of the 1946 Act provides a qualified defence to a person charged with an offence against an SI that has not been published. There would be no need for such a defence if the SI were invalid.[45]

DELEGATED LEGISLATION OTHER THAN BY SI

It is possible for an Act of Parliament to confer rule-making powers on a minister to be exercised in ways other than by SI. Such rules may sometimes have the status of binding law capable of altering people's legal rights and obligations;[46] sometimes they have no direct legal force in themselves but are merely advisory or exhortatory in nature.[47] Some of these rules are subject to parliamentary scrutiny before they take effect, some are not.

Ministers may also make rules, often in the form of 'circulars' issued by departments, without specific authorization by an Act; this is part of central government's freedom to do everything that is not prohibited.[48] The word 'quasi-legislation' is sometimes used to refer to rules of all these sorts, but

[43] Statutory Instruments Act 1946, s 2(1). See now the Statutory Instruments (Production and Sale) Act 1996 which permits printing of official copies to be done by firms in the private sector, something that has in fact been done for many years.

[44] Statutory Instruments Regulations 1947 (SI 1948 No 1).

[45] *R v Sheer Metalcraft Ltd* [1954] 1 QB 586.

[46] For example, the Immigration Rules (HC 395). These are published as a House of Commons paper.

[47] For example the Highway Code.

[48] See Chapter 7.

this is not a technical term.[49] Informal instructions and rules such as these have sometimes been used by government to implement important policies. For instance, in the mid-1960s the Labour government issued circulars to local education authorities exhorting them to create comprehensive schools.[50] Only later did the government resort to legislation when persuasion failed.[51]

In short, the picture is very complex. One practical problem is that (unlike SIs) there are no uniform arrangements for the publication of the various different types of rules made by government and so it may sometimes be difficult for people to know what exactly they are being told or asked to do.

Homer nods

For our purposes it is sufficient to look at just one example of delegated legislation made other than by SI to highlight the constitutional difficulties. The Social Security Act 1986 replaced supplementary benefit with a range of new welfare payments. Part III of the Act created the 'Social Fund'. Claimants apply for various types of financial help from the Social Fund, including one-off payments to cover exceptional costs such as the need for furniture after a house fire or funeral expenses.[52] Officials have broad discretion, but must keep within a set budget. The discretion must also be exercised in accordance with general 'directions' issued by the Secretary of State, taking into account 'guidance' that may also be issued by the minister. Section 33 of the Act provides that:

> (9) In determining whether to make an award to the applicant or the amount of value to be awarded an officer shall have regard, subject to subsection (10) below, to all the circumstances of the case and, in particular—
>
> (a) the nature, extent and urgency of the need;
>
> (b) the existence of resources from which the need may be met;
>
> (c) the possibility that some other person or body may wholly or partly meet it;
>
> (d) where the payment is repayable, the likelihood of repayment and the time within which repayment is likely;
>
> (e) any relevant allocation under section 32[(8A) to (8D)] above.
>
> (10) An officer shall determine any question under this section *in accordance with any general directions* issued by the Secretary of State and in determining any such question shall take account of any general guidance issued by him.

These binding 'directions' are not in the form of an SI subject to parliamentary oversight. (In this respect, they are therefore different to the Board and Lodgings Regulations.) In judicial review proceedings brought by a person who was refused a Social Fund payment the question arose whether the

[49] See further Gabrielle Ganz, *Quasi-legislation* (1987) and Robert Baldwin, *Rules and Government* (1995). Baldwin uses the term 'tertiary rules'.

[50] Department of Education Circulars 10/65 and 10/66, discussed by Ganz, *Quasi-legislation*, p. 18.

[51] Education Act 1976, ss 1–3.

[52] See Tom Mullen, 'The Social Fund: cash-limiting social security' (1989) 52 MLR 64.

minister could issue 'directions' designed to limit the scope of the Social Fund itself by excluding help for 'domestic assistance and respite care' from the scheme. The Court of Appeal expressed its surprise that under the 1986 Act 'such wholesale unregulated and unsupervised powers effectively to pass subordinate legislation had been granted to a Minister of State'.[53] Purchas LJ went on to say:

> It may be that in this case in the execution of the legislative process that 'Homer nodded' with the result that wholly exceptional and, it might be thought by some objectionable, powers without any parliamentary fetter or supervision other than the annual report (s 32(7B)) was achieved by the Secretary of State. On the other hand it may be an unwelcome feature of a dominating executive in a basically two-party democracy. That having been said . . . it is no part of the function of this court to import into the exercise of construing the intention of Parliament from the words of the statute any such sentiments however genuinely and justifiably held. The limit to which the construction exercise can be so affected is that where an ambiguity is detected the court will lean against an interpretation which would have the effect of granting to the executive unbridled powers to pass subordinate legislation of this kind.

With some reluctance, the court concluded that the Secretary of State was indeed entitled to issue 'directions' excluding all claims relating to expenses incurred for 'domestic assistance and respite care'.

Questions and exercises

Exercise 1

The Deregulation and Contracting Out Act 1994 aims to reduce the bureaucratic burdens on businesses and individuals. It has been criticized by Lord Rippon, the chair of the Lords' Select Committee on Delegated Powers, as 'one big Henry VIII clause'.[54] Others have praised its special consultation procedures as 'more systematic and formal than the consultation normally undertaken in the preparation of delegated legislation'.[55] In the light of the discussion above, carefully consider the following sections of the Deregulation and Contracting Out Act 1994 and explain fully whether you are concerned about its constitutional propriety. Consider in particular the power given to a minister to change the law and the obligation to consult.

Power to remove or reduce certain statutory burdens on businesses, individuals etc

1.—(1) If, with respect to any provision made by an enactment, a Minister of the Crown is of the opinion—

(a) that the effect of the provision is such as to impose, or authorise or require the imposition of, a burden affecting any person in the carrying on of any trade, business or profession or otherwise, and

(b) that, by amending or repealing the enactment concerned and, where appropriate, by making such other provision as is referred to in subsection (4)(a) below, it would be possible, without removing any necessary protection, to remove or

[53] *R v Secretary of State for Social Services, ex p Stitt* (1990) *The Times*, 5 July.
[54] *The Times*, 20 January 1994.
[55] Michael Ryle, 'The Deregulation and Contracting Out Bill 1994—a blueprint for reform of the legislative process?' (1994) 15 Statute Law Review 170.

reduce the burden or, as the case may be, the authorisation or requirement by virtue of which the burden may be imposed, he may, subject to the following provisions of this section and sections 2 to 4 below, by order amend or repeal that enactment.

(2) . . .

(3) In this section and sections 2 to 4 below, in relation to an order under this section,—

(a) 'the existing provision' means the provision by which the burden concerned is imposed or, as the case may be, is authorised or required to be imposed; and

(b) 'the relevant enactment' means the enactment containing the existing provision.

(4) An order under this section shall be made by statutory instrument and may do all or any of the following—

(a) make provision (whether by amending any enactment or otherwise) creating a burden which relates to the subject matter of, but is less onerous than that imposed by, the existing provision;

(b) make such modifications of enactments as, in the opinion of the Minister concerned, are consequential upon, or incidental to, the amendment or repeal of the relevant enactment;

(c) contain such transitional provisions and savings as appear to the Minister to be appropriate;

(d) make different provision for different cases or different areas;

but no order shall be made under this section unless a draft of the order has been laid before and approved by a resolution of each House of Parliament.

[. . .]

(7) Where a restriction, requirement or condition is subject to a criminal sanction (as mentioned in subsection (5)(b)(i) above), nothing in this section shall authorise the making of an amendment which would have the effect of leaving the restriction, requirement or condition in place but producing a different criminal sanction or altering any procedural provisions relevant to the criminal sanction.

Limitations on the power under section 1

2.—(1) If an order under section 1 above creates a new criminal offence, then, subject to subsections (2) and (3) below, that offence shall not be punishable—

(a) on indictment with imprisonment for a term of more than two years; or

(b) on summary conviction with imprisonment for a term exceeding six months or a fine exceeding level 5 on the standard scale or both.

[. . .]

(4) An order under section 1 above shall not contain any provision—

(a) providing for any forcible entry, search or seizure, or

(b) compelling the giving of evidence,

unless, and then only to the extent that, a provision to that effect is contained in the relevant enactment and is abolished by the order.

Preliminary consultation

3.—(1) Before a Minister makes an order under section 1 above, he shall—

(a) consult such organisations as appear to him to be representative of interests substantially affected by his proposals; and

(b) consult such other persons as he considers appropriate.

(2) If it appears to the Minister, as a result of the consultation required by subsection (1) above, that it is appropriate to vary the whole or any part of his proposals, he shall undertake such further consultation with respect to the variations as appears to him to be appropriate.

(3) If, after the conclusion of—

(a) the consultation required by subsection (1) above, and

(b) any further consultation undertaken as mentioned in subsection (2) above, the Minister considers it appropriate to proceed with the making of an order under section 1 above, he shall lay before Parliament a document containing his proposals in the form of a draft of the order, together with details of the matters specified in subsection (4) below.

(4) The matters referred to in subsection (3) above are—

(a) the burden, authorisation or requirement which it is proposed to remove or reduce;

(b) whether the existing provision affords any necessary protection and, if so, how that protection is to be continued if the burden, authorisation or requirement is removed or reduced;

(c) whether any savings in cost are estimated to result from the proposals and, if so, either the estimated amount or the reasons why savings should be expected;

(d) any other benefits which are expected to flow from the removal or reduction of the burden, authorisation or requirement;

(e) any consultation undertaken as required by subsection (1) or subsection (2) above;

(f) any representations received as a result of that consultation; and

(g) the changes (if any) which the Minister has made to his original proposals in the light of those representations.

(5) In giving details of the representations referred to in subsection (4)(f) above, the Minister shall not disclose any information relating to a particular person or business except—

(a) with the consent of that person or of the person carrying on that business; or

(b) in such a manner as not to identify that person or business.

(6) If, before the day on which this section comes into force, any consultation was undertaken which, had it been undertaken after that day, would to any extent have satisfied the requirements of subsection (1) above, those requirements shall to that extent be taken to have been satisfied.

Parliamentary consideration of proposals

4.—(1) Where a document has been laid before Parliament under section 3(3) above, no draft of an order under section 1 above to give effect (with or without variations) to proposals in that document shall be laid before Parliament until after the expiry of the period for Parliamentary consideration, as defined in subsection (2) below.

(2) In this section 'the period for Parliamentary consideration', in relation to a document, means the period of sixty days beginning on the day on which it was laid before Parliament.

(3) In reckoning the period of sixty days referred to in subsection (2) above, no account shall be taken of any time during which Parliament is dissolved or prorogued or during which either House is adjourned for more than four days.

(4) In preparing a draft of an order under section 1 above to give effect, with or without variations, to proposals in a document laid before Parliament under section 3(3) above, the Minister concerned shall have regard to any representations made during the period for Parliamentary consideration and, in particular, to any resolution or report of, or of any committee of, either House of Parliament with regard to the document.

(5) Together with a draft of an order laid before Parliament under section 1(4) above, the Minister concerned shall lay a statement giving details of—

(a) any representations, resolution or report falling within subsection (4) above; and

(b) the changes (if any) which, in the light of any such representations, resolution or report, the Minister has made to his proposals as contained in the document previously laid before Parliament under section 3(3) above.

(6) Subsection (5) of section 3 above shall apply in relation to the representations referred to in subsection (5)(a) above as it applies in relation to the representations referred to in subsection (4)(f) of that section.

Exercise 2

Choose two SIs at random from the shelves of a law library and answer the following questions about them:

(a) Which minister or public body made them?
(b) What was the enabling Act under which they were made? Are they 'framework' Acts?
(c) Was there any statutory obligation for the minister or public body making each SI to consult?
(d) Were the SIs subject to negative or affirmative resolution procedure in Parliament?
(e) What was the purpose of each SI?
(f) Are the SIs still in force? How do you find this out?

WHERE TO GO FROM HERE

If you wish to continue examining delegated legislation, turn to Chapter 11 for a case study on the making of an SI (the Board and Lodgings Regulations). If, however, you want to move on to consider other legal bases for government action, turn to Chapter 12 (Prerogative Powers) and Chapter 13 (Euro-legislation, including the use of delegated legislation to incorporate Community directives into national law).

11

CASE STUDY: MAKING BOARD AND LODGING REGULATIONS

The regulations should be set in concrete and thrown into the Thames so that they are never seen again.

Margaret Beckett MP

This chapter looks at how one piece of delegated legislation was made: the less-than-snappily-titled Supplementary Benefit (Requirements and Resources) Miscellaneous Provisions Regulations 1985 (SI 1985 No 613).[1] A later chapter examines how this SI was held unlawful in judicial review proceedings.[2]

In many ways these regulations enjoyed a far greater degree of scrutiny than is normal: there was a mandatory statutory consultation procedure; an affirmative resolution was needed from the Commons to give the SI validity; and there was a judicial review challenge. Most SIs are subject to much less examination. Here there was a high degree of political controversy and scrutiny. Most SIs become law more with a whimper than a bang.

The main aim of this case study is to provide material from which you can learn more about the general characteristics of the delegated legislative process (described in Chapter 10) and to provide a basis for you to form your own opinions of the essential benefits and dangers of the current arrangements for making SIs.

Some of the legislative drafting and legal arguments are complex and subtle; do not be too daunted by this. In public law, people's legal rights and obligations are as much determined by detailed legislation as by broad constitutional principles of the type considered in Chapter 6. It is therefore important to develop lawyerly skills of statutory interpretation; some of the questions asked are intended to encourage this. Also bear in mind that much of the legislation dealt with in the case study has now been repealed and replaced by legislation establishing a new range of welfare benefits. The aim of this chapter is not to learn about the substantive law; rather it is to learn skills and understand the process of making delegated legislation. Before going further, you may want to look at Chapter 2 for an overview of the events.

[1] See further Neville Harris, 'Board and Lodging Payments for Young People' [1987] Journal of Social Welfare Law 150 and Gill Stewart, Robert Lee and John Stewart, 'The Right Approach to Social Security: The Case of the Board and Lodging Regulations' (1986) 13 Journal of Law and Society 271.

[2] See Chapter 27.

FINDING AN ENABLING PROVISION IN AN ACT

Imagine you are lawyer in the DHSS (as it was then). Your minister has decided on the policy and announced it, in general terms, in a statement to the House of Commons.[3] It has been decided that the time constraints within which he wants to change the law dictate that an SI, rather than a bill, be used to give the policy legal effect. To do this, you will need to find somewhere in a statute a provision conferring power on the minister to make regulations implementing the policy.

Lawyers in the DHSS decided that s 2(1A) of the Supplementary Benefits Act 1976 provided a proper legal basis for making the new regulations. Section 1(1) established that a person of or over the age of 16 whose resources were insufficient to meet his requirements should be entitled to supplementary benefit. Section 2 provided (the emphasis is added):

> (1) Subject to sections 15 and 15A of this Act (appeals), the *question* whether any person is entitled to supplementary benefit and the amount of any such benefit and any *other question* relating to supplementary benefit which arises under this Act . . . shall be determined by an adjudication officer appointed under section 97 of the Social Security Act 1975, a social security appeal tribunal constituted under that Act or a Social Security Commissioner in accordance with regulations made for the purposes of this section . . .
>
> (1A) *Regulations may provide for prescribed questions to be determined otherwise than by adjudication officers, social security appeal tribunals or Social Security Commissioners* . . .
>
> (2) Entitlement to, and the amount of, any supplementary benefit shall be determined in accordance with the provisions of this Part of this Act and Schedule 1 to this Act.

Schedule 1 gave the provisions for determining rights to benefit and the amounts of benefit that could be awarded:

> 1. (1) The amount of any supplementary benefit to which a person is entitled shall . . . be the amount by which his resources fall short of his requirements.
>
> (2) For the purpose of ascertaining that amount—
>
> (a) a person's requirements shall be determined in accordance with paragraph 2 of this Schedule; and
>
> (b) a person's resources shall be calculated in the prescribed manner . . .
>
> 2. (1) For the purposes of this Schedule requirements shall be . . . normal requirements . . . and . . . the weekly amounts for [that category] shall be such as may be prescribed.

Section 34(1) provided: 'In this Act . . . "prescribed" means specified in or determined in accordance with regulations . . .'.

Questions

1. The Act was passed in 1976 when a Labour government was in power. Is there any constitutional problem with a Conservative government furthering its policies by using legislation enacted by an earlier Labour government, or vice versa? Would the new

[3] See p. 28.

Board and Lodging policy have been within the intention of Parliament when it enacted the 1976 Act? Does this matter?

2. Explain in your own words what s 2 means. These pointers may help:

(a) The word 'questions' crops up a several points. What, in the context of this legislation, are 'questions'?
(b) How were 'questions' relating to supplementary benefit *normally* determined? (The answer is in s 2(1).)
(c) What does 2(1A) mean?

3. At what stage of the policy cycle described in Chapter 4 are the adjudication officers and tribunals mentioned in s 2(1A) normally going to carry out their tasks? Is it at stage 3 (giving a legal basis for a general policy or scheme) or at stage 5 (redressing individual grievances arising from the application of rules to particular cases)?

MANDATORY CONSULTATION

The role of the Social Security Advisory Committee

The department was required by statute to consult with an official body called the Social Security Advisory Committee (SSAC) established by the Social Security Act 1980. SSAC members work part-time and are appointed by the Secretary of State. Its main statutory functions are to advise the Secretary of State for Social Services on any social security matter within the SSAC's remit on which he seeks advice; to offer advice on social security matters at the SSAC's own initiative; and to consider proposals for social security regulations referred to it by the Secretary of State and to report on them. Section 10(1) of the Act requires proposals for changes in regulations to be submitted to the SSAC 'whether in the form of draft regulations or otherwise'. In most cases the SSAC receives draft regulations together with an explanatory paper setting out the effect of the proposed changes and the reasons for them. The 1980 Act does not enable the Secretary of State to impose any limitation of time upon the SSAC and neither is the SSAC required by statute to present its report within any prescribed time. Except where regulations are made as a matter of urgency without prior reference to the SSAC, under s 10(2)(a) of the Act, the SSAC's report must be laid by the Secretary of State before each House of Parliament together with his response, at the time when the regulations or draft regulations are themselves laid.

The department's consultative document

The Secretary of State referred a consultative document *outlining* his proposals to the SSAC on 29 November 1984. Departmental lawyers had not yet produced a text of the regulations and the SSAC was therefore unable to comment on *specific* proposals or the ways in which government policy was to be given legal effect. In the consultation paper the government outlined its policy of centralizing control over expenditure by removing the power of local adjudication officers (civil servants) to set limits on the maximum rents which would be paid under the scheme and instead give this power to the Secretary of State. It envisaged two maximum amounts: one that applied in the Greater London Area (where claims could be made for £60–70 per week) and the other outside the Greater London area (where claims could be for £50–60 per week). Because government wanted to move quickly the Secretary of State asked the SSAC to respond by the end of January 1985. The SSAC was 'anxious that this was rather a short period in which to seek public views about such far reaching proposals, especially since it included the main Christmas holidays'.[4]

Although under no statutory duty to do so, the SSAC immediately issued notices seeking comments. Despite the short time scale, 504 organizations and individuals made representations about the proposals. This far outweighed any previous response made to the SSAC and clearly indicated the level of concern about and interest in the proposed changes. During its deliberations the SSAC wrote back to the department seeking clarification or more detailed information on a number of issues contained in the consultative document. For example, on the issue of abuse it asked:[5]

> The proposals have been presented to a large extent as an attempt to crack down on unjustified profiteering by landlords . . . and on holidays by unemployed people, especially young people, who are not genuinely seeking work. As they stand, the proposals will affect many people against whom there is no suspicion of abuse. What financial estimate has the department made of the extent of abuse by claimants in board and lodging accommodation, and of 'excess' charges by landlords . . .? . . . where abuse exists or is suspected, what consideration has been given to the use of existing remedies against claimants whose availability for work is in doubt . . .?

The department receives the SSAC report

The lawyers in the department were still busy drafting the new regulations as the SSAC was completing consideration of the government's proposals and publishing its report (Cmnd 9466):

REPORT OF THE SOCIAL SECURITY ADVISORY COMMITTEE MADE UNDER S 10(3) OF THE SOCIAL SECURITY ACT 1980 ON PROPOSALS FOR THE SUPPLEMENTARY BENEFIT (REQUIREMENTS AND RESOURCES) MISCELLANEOUS PROVISIONS REGULATIONS 1985

Scope and purpose of the proposals

4. The consultative document describing the proposals is reproduced at Appendix 2 to this report. This explanatory material is couched in much more general

[4] Report of the Social Security Advisory Committee (Cmnd 9466), para. 1.

[5] By letter dated 7 January 1985. The department replied a week later.

terms than is usual when proposals for regulations are referred to us, and does not include explicit information on how existing legislation is to be amended. We recognise that this absence of detail is part of the price for receiving an outline of the proposals at an early stage of policy formulation, and we welcome the Government's readiness to seek advice from us and from other interested bodies at this point.

5. We are however concerned that the tight timetable which we understand the Government desires to keep will mean that neither we, nor other interested organisations, will have an opportunity to see draft regulations, or a detailed description of the proposed method of achieving amendments, in advance of the laying of drafts before Parliament. This is a matter of particular anxiety because, as we note later on, we understand that substantial changes are contemplated in part of the proposals as a result of the comments made by our Committee and by the representations to us. The proposals have serious implications for large numbers of claimants, many of whom are very vulnerable, and it is unfortunate that the regulations themselves will not be available for scrutiny in the normal way. Our past experience suggests that even where draft regulations are subject to affirmative resolution and thus to debate in Parliament, a prior examination is nevertheless helpful in identifying possible *lacunae* and in avoiding unintended consequences of complicated provisions. Such defects are slower to be corrected when regulations have actually come into force. We hope therefore that Ministers will be prepared to give a commitment to bring forward early amendments if the regulations when implemented should prove to need correction. We should also be grateful ourselves for an opportunity to consider the proposals again, when a full draft of the changes is available.

[. . .]

General comments

8. We can well understand the Government's wish to revise the present arrangements for supplementary benefit board and lodging payments, which we agree have a number of defects. We also appreciate Ministers' concern for value for money, and we share their anxiety at the steep increase since 1982 in the number of supplementary benefit claimants living in board and lodging accommodation. However, as the extraordinary range of representations to us makes clear, the 64% increase since 1982 in claimants in ordinary board and lodging accommodation . . . [has] worrying implications not only for supplementary benefit expenditure, but also for the effectiveness of many current policies in housing . . . The representations are almost united in their concern at many aspects of the proposed changes; but they are also worried that the proposals make an attempt only to tackle the immediate benefit problem, and do nothing to resolve the underlying difficulties. The wider social issues which have contributed to the growth in supplementary benefit board and lodging claims are complex, and to a considerable extent well outside the remit of DHSS. We doubt, however, whether any satisfactory control can be imposed on the use of supplementary benefit board and lodging accepted that the current proposals may not offer a final solution to the problems they see. In our view, it is because they tackle the symptoms rather than the causes of growth in costs and numbers, that they are unlikely to provide a long-term solution.

9. Some aspects of the proposals have much to commend them, and we welcome these sensible developments, for example in the establishment of a separate hostel category . . . However, we have serious reservations about the proposed switch to uniform national limits in each category, and about the fairness and feasibility of the restrictions imposed on unemployed people in ordinary board and lodging accommodation, and especially on 16–17 year olds. We are deeply concerned that in attempting to limit spending and control abuse where it exists, the proposals are likely to affect large numbers of unemployed claimants who have no real option but to stay in board and lodging accommodation, and whose ability to search for jobs will be much impeded by the restrictions on place and length of stay as a boarder. No-one can condone abuse of the system by claimants, or manipulation by proprietors: we of course support measures to prevent them where possible. However, we are not convinced that the proposals as they stand are focused sufficiently on the problem area.

[. . .]

14. Before considering the present proposals in detail, we want to emphasise that the problem of increased expenditure about which the Government is naturally concerned seems to us to be primarily the result of this increase in the *numbers* claiming rather than in the average cost per claimant. Without an adequate explanation for the reasons for the surge in numbers, we suspect it will be difficult to introduce effective measures for containment. We therefore *recommend* that, as an essential part of preparing a long-term solution, the Department undertakes research into the reasons why claimants entered board and lodging accommodation over recent months . . . Without research of this kind supplementary benefit will continue to try to control the predicted growth of claims without knowing the cause—which may well be more effectively tackled by other Government Departments, for example housing.

[. . .]

17. The public presentation of the proposals has concentrated very much on improving value for money and on curbing abuse. In connection with them a number of claims have been made about abuses of the system, for example by young people taking up board and lodging accommodation in resort towns without a genuine intention of seeking work there, and about collusion between claimants and proprietors of boarding establishments to make fraudulent claims. Anecdote is not a safe basis for legislation, and we therefore sought fuller information from DHSS on the extent of suspected abuse, both by claimants and by proprietors. We were disappointed that no estimates of the size of the problem could be produced, although we recognised that it would be a difficult task. However we were provided with a number of examples of fraudulent or abusive behaviour, and some worrying information about dubious claims in several areas . . . We readily recognise that the existing system may provide room for abuse, and for undesirable developments which are nevertheless well within the rules; but in the absence of good evidence on the cost and extent of abuse, it seems unfortunate that the proposals have been depicted so widely as an attempt to clamp down on unjustified benefit claims. In considering the proposals, we think it is important to remember that the vast majority of claimants are honest, and should not be subject to punitive restrictions.

Many also are forced by circumstances beyond their control to live in thoroughly unsatisfactory accommodation.

[. . .]

National versus local limits

19. The most significant general feature of the proposed changes for all types of board and lodging accommodation is the replacement of a system of local limits with a centrally-fixed limit appropriate to the particular category of accommodation. This proposal attracted a great deal of criticism from those who wrote to us on two main grounds:—

(i) board and lodging provision incorporates an element for rent and in many cases for a certain amount of care. There are inevitable geographical variations in the cost of property and labour, which need to be recognised in the supplementary benefit provision;

(ii) a national limit can take no account of the real variations in the level of care provided in different establishments and thus of the costs incurred. It may well be excessive in some areas, but far too low in others where there is a concentration of special provision.

20. We have serious doubts about the realism of a single national limit, with or without a London weighting, in coping with the wide variety of circumstances and costs applicable in board and lodging.

[. . .]

23. If it is not possible to devise a satisfactory scheme based on local decision-making, a second option which would in our view offer a satisfactory compromise between the need for more secure financial control and the need also to take account of local variations would be the construction of a new scheme of *regional* limits. In some regions these might appropriately be lower than the national limits suggested in the consultative document, providing the level set could be supported by reference to actual charges. Under this scheme, the limits would necessarily be a matter for a Secretary of State's decision rather than that of adjudication offices locally.

[. . .]

87. . . . Our doubts about the consequences of the suggested changes are so great that we cannot readily contemplate them as a permanent modification to the supplementary benefit system, especially since—as we have remarked—we do not believe the root of the problem to be a benefit issue at all. However we acknowledge Ministers' desire to make expenditure savings urgently, and their recognition also that the proposals may not be a permanent solution to the phenomenon of rapid growth in this area of the system. In view of these points we *recommend* that whatever system is finally introduced as a result of our suggestions and of the consultation process, should be introduced overtly as a temporary change and that the regulations giving effect to the proposals should lapse after a limited period during which it should be possible to examine their workings, identify new solutions to the problem areas that emerge in practice, take account of the outcome of

the social security reviews if they impinge on this aspect of the system, and liaise with other Government Departments as necessary to devise a more satisfactory long-term solution to a difficult and complex problem. A sensible time to introduce long-term changes would be when any changes stemming from the social security reviews are implemented.

THE PARLIAMENTARY PROCESS

Ministerial statement

By 21 March 1985, some four months after the new policy was first announced to the Commons, departmental lawyers had completed drafting the text of the new regulations and the SI was ready to begin its progress through Parliament. Remember that the purpose of the regulations was to enable the Secretary of State to fix the periods for which claims could be made and the maximum amounts which could be claimed. The Social Security Act 1976 required regulations to be subject to the affirmative resolution procedure, which is more rigorous than the more common negative resolution procedure. A draft of the new regulations, the SSAC report and the government's response to it were all laid before the Commons. The Minister for Social Security made a statement and several questions were asked:

Mr Michael Meacher (Oldham, West) [Labour]: Is the Minister aware that his statement makes a farce of the consultation process since it almost completely dismisses the overwhelming evidence put before him, severely criticising his proposals, in more than 500 submissions, four times more than the DHSS has ever received on any other issue? [. . .]

Mr Newton: On the so-called 'farce of consultation', the hon. Gentleman has only to read the Government's response to recognise that we have responded in many ways to the suggestions of the Social Security Advisory Committee. If the hon. Gentlemen wishes me to do so, I shall list eight ways in which we have significantly responded to the committee's suggestions . . .

The text of the new regulations

Bear in mind that this SI was seeking to amend an existing one. The method of amendment used was textual: the new regulations were to insert new articles (the SI equivalent of sections in an Act) into the existing SI 1983 No 1399 and add new schedules to it. The new regulations are therefore incomprehensible without having the existing SI open next to it; to make sense of it all one then needs to do some mental or physical cutting and pasting of passages. To see this, look at this very brief extract from the new regulations. No attempt was made produce a single consolidated text for debate in Parliament.

1985 No. 613

SOCIAL SECURITY

The Supplementary Benefit (Requirements and Resources) Miscellaneous Provisions Regulations 1985

Laid before Parliament in draft
Made -------- 15th April 1985
Coming into Operation 29th April 1985

The Secretary of State for Social Services, with the consent of the Treasury, in pursuance of paragraph 2 of Schedule 1 to the Supplementary Benefits Act 1976 and in exercise of powers conferred by sections 1(3), 2(1A) and (2) . . . and of all other powers enabling him in that behalf after reference to the Social Security Advisory Committee of the proposals . . ., hereby makes the following regulations of which a draft has, in accordance with section 33(3) of that Act been laid before Parliament and approved by resolution of each House of Parliament:—

[. . .]

New arrangements as to boarders

4.—(1) For paragraph (6) of regulation 9 of the Requirements Regulations (maximum amounts) there shall be substituted the following paragraph—

'(6) Subject to paragraphs (7) and (17), the maximum amount in respect of the assessment unit as a whole referred to in paragraph (1)(a) shall be the aggregate of the following amounts—

(a) in respect of each member of the assessment unit who is a dependant aged less than 11, $1^1/_2$ times the amount referred to in paragraph (5)(c); and

(b) in respect of each other member of the assessment unit, the appropriate amount specified in or as the case may be determined in accordance with Schedule 1A.'

Remember that the main feature of the policy was to enable the Secretary of State to set limits on the amount that could be claimed and periods for which claims could be made. These were to vary between areas (though the government was minded to have only two). The key provisions were set out in Schedules 1A and 2A. Schedule 2A, paragraph 5 deals with the new policy on *time limits* (or 'initial periods') for claiming board and lodging payments, after which claimants would have their benefit cut or would have to move to another area where the initial period would start to run again. Schedule 1A paragraph 6 deals with board and lodging *areas*.

Questions

1. What is so special about regulations on welfare benefits that they are subject to affirmative, rather than negative, resolution procedure in Parliament?

2. Imagine you are a law student working as a research assistant to an MP. She asks you to write a short note explaining in plain English the meaning of each of the sub-paragraphs of the following schedules to the new regulations. The first deals with time limits:

SCHEDULE 2A

PERSONS WHO ARE NOT BOARDERS FOR THE PURPOSES OF REGULATION 9

[. . .]

5.—(1) Subject to sub-paragraphs (2) to (5) below, a person who—

(a) is aged under 26 but not less than 16 and, if a relevant person, whose partner is also under 26 but not less than 16 and

(b) is required to be available for employment.

(2) Sub-paragraph (1) above shall not have effect in respect of such a person during the initial period (including the initial period extended under sub-paragraph (5) below) determined under sub-paragraph (3) below as appropriate in respect of the board and lodging area determined under paragraph 6(2) of Schedule 1A, in which that person's accommodation is situated.

(3) Any question as to the number of weeks in the initial period for the purposes of sub-paragraph (2) above, in relation to each board and lodging area determined under paragraph 6(2) of Schedule 1A, shall be determined by the Secretary of State in his discretion; and his decision of such question—

(a) shall be given generally and not in relation to a particular case;

(b) may be revised from time to time as he considers desirable;

(c) may make different provisions for different classes of case or otherwise for different circumstances;

(d) shall be published in such form as he considers suitable; and

(e) shall be conclusive for the purposes of this Schedule.

(4) Sub-paragraph (1) above shall not have effect also where such a person—

(a) has a dependant; or

(b) is in a hostel; or

(c) is, or has a partner who is, pregnant; or

(d) is, or has a partner who is, chronically sick, mentally handicapped, physically disabled or suffering from a mental disorder [*etc.*].

SCHEDULE 1A

MAXIMUM AMOUNTS FOR BOARDERS

[. . .]

Ordinary board and lodging accommodation

6.—(1) Subject to sub-paragraphs (2) and (3) below, where the accommodation provided for the claimant is not a residential care home, a nursing home or a hostel, the appropriate amount shall be the amount specified as appropriate under sub-paragraph (2) below for the board and lodging area in which that accommodation is situated.

(2) Any question as to the location of board and lodging areas and as to the amount appropriate for each board and lodging area for the purposes of sub-paragraph (1) above shall be determined by the Secretary of State in his discretion; and his decision of such questions—

(a) shall be given generally and not in relation to a particular case;

(b) may be revised from time to time as he considers desirable;

(c) may make different provisions for different classes of case or otherwise for different circumstances;

(d) shall be published in such form as he considers suitable and

(e) shall be conclusive for the purposes of this Schedule.

Questions

1. How wide are the powers which the minister sought to give himself in the regulations? How important are they in terms of their effect on individuals?

2. If you were an MP, what questions would you be able ask about the regulations? What opportunities would you have to do so?

3. Is complexity inevitable in SIs dealing with welfare payments? Could you have made the rules more straightforward?

4. How will people claiming benefit (or their advisors) know what the 'initial period' and 'appropriate amount' are? Will the rules about these important matters be in the form of another SI laid before Parliament?

Your first impression, almost certainly, is that the regulations are complicated, unclear and extremely difficult to understand. Do not worry: these regulations, like most in this and other areas, *are* very complex. This creates problems. First, it makes the law difficult for members of the public and their advisors to understand. Secondly, complexity increases the risk that policies may not be implemented properly by administrators. Thirdly, it reduces the effectiveness of parliamentary scrutiny. Given these points, why do you suppose it is that these rules are so complex? Might one reason for the complexity have been the government's desire to *clarify* precisely who was entitled to benefit? The rules were drafted in order to remove discretion from local adjudication officers. The earlier rules may well have been clearer on their face, but the exercise of discretion by local officials no doubt created its own problems and may not have produced a system that was any clearer.

There can be little doubt that these regulations did require the Secretary of State to 'legislate' further, to make further rules setting out the actual length of the initial periods and the maximum amounts payable. These additional rules would effect people's eligibility for benefit but there appears to be no formal procedure for making them or for publishing them and they would not be subject to any direct parliamentary scrutiny. Nor would the minister be required to consult with the SSAC about them. They would in effect be equivalent to internal or administrative rules sometimes referred to as 'quasi' or 'tertiary' legislation.[6] As you will see, one of the central issues in the litigation that followed the enactment of these regulations centred on the important constitutional question: did the Social Security Act 1976 give power to make a statutory instrument which, in turn, gave power to the Secretary of State to make further 'informal' rules?

'Technical' scrutiny of the regulations by the JCSI

The new regulations had to be referred to the Joint Committee on Statutory Instruments. The committee meets in private and we therefore do not know

[6] See p. 237.

what, if any, discussion took place. In its normal weekly report, the committee however 'determined that the special attention of both Houses does not require to be drawn to them'. This proved to be a mistaken decision.

Question

Look back at the list of grounds on which the JCSI may draw the attention of the House in relation to an SI.[7] Had you been a member of the JCSI would you have spotted any problems with the SI? If so, why do you think the JCSI failed to draw attention to them?

'Merits' scrutiny by Parliament

The motion for the affirmative resolution was moved by Mr Tony Newton MP at 10.30 pm on 2 April. The debate was held on the floor of the Commons and was limited to 90 minutes. Here MPs were concerned with the general merits of the government's proposals.

The Minister for Social Security (Mr Tony Newton): I beg to move:

That the Supplementary Benefit (Requirements and Resources) Miscellaneous Provisions Regulations 1985, which were laid before this House on 26th March, be approved.

The total of expenditure on supplementary benefit on board and lodging has risen from around £60 million in 1979 to something approaching £600 million in 1984, both in the residential care sector and in the sector of ordinary board and lodging. The number of people in receipt of these payments has risen in a somewhat comparable, though not precisely comparable, fashion.

The effects of this situation have been disturbing hon. Members on both sides and many people outside the House. There is clear evidence of a considerable degree of abuse and exploitation of the rules . . . But just as bad as the abuse and exploitation that have been going on is the fact that we have ended up with many tens of thousand of young people trapped in accommodation which they could not possibly afford if they were in work, and they are thus in a peculiar version of the unemployment trap. That, as I have said on many occasions, is doing no service to them or to the rest of the community . . . It was in response to the growing evidence of this increasingly unsatisfactory situation that the Government acted last year to freeze the limits then in operation subsequently to put to the Social Security Advisory Committee the proposals which, substantially modified in the light of the advice of that committee, have led to the regulations that the House is debating tonight. . . .

Mr Donald Anderson (Swansea, East) [Labour]: The Minister says that the proposals have been substantially modified as a result of the SSAC response, but will he nevertheless confirm that that committee has said that the current proposals are unacceptable?

Mr Newton: That is an exaggeration by a long chalk of what the SSAC has said. It has made a number of important points which we shall continue to take into account in monitoring the progress of changes under the regulations. The SSAC clearly acknowledged the need for something to be done about the problems that I have described. It made a number of suggestions and welcomed many of the

[7] See p. 235.

changes that the Government have made in response to those suggestions and, as I said, we shall continue to take account of the committee's comments in monitoring progress. The main element in what we are proposing is to lay down firm limits, set by Ministers, for particular kinds of accommodation, in some cases varied according to different parts of the country, and to substitute those firm limits for the existing thoroughly unsatisfactory position in which the local limits for board and lodging vary from £40 a week in some places to £110 in others . . . [The minister went on to describe the new scheme].

Mr Roland Boyes (Houghton and Washington) [Labour]: . . . The average number of people giving evidence to the Social Security Advisory Committee has been exceeded six or seven times. Indeed, the number of people giving evidence on this matter is four times more than the previous highest total. How much more evidence does the Minister want? He has all the evidence in a booklet produced by the Social Security Advisory Committee, but he has ignored almost every one of its recommendations.

Mr Newton: I accept that we are not short of evidence in the sense of claims about the consequences of certain sets of proposals and about the desirability of higher limits—mostly from those who have an interest in the matter. However, we are short of sufficient objective data to go beyond the best assessment that we have been able to make in the figures that we have set out in the regulations. I really cannot go further tonight than to re-emphasise that these regulations and figures are not set in concrete. The Government are approaching this matter in the spirit of being willing to listen to further representations and, above all, to consider further detailed information that would enable us to refine the proposals. That is the sensible way in which to proceed.

Sir Kenneth Lewis (Stamford and Spalding) [Conservative]: I am sure that what my hon. Friend has said about keeping the matter under review is a fair offer. He also said that these figures were not set in concrete. What would he have to do if he decided, after four or five months, that there was need for adjustment? Would we need another set of regulations or does he have the power to raise the figure slightly if that is required?

Mr Newton: The Secretary of State simply has to set different figures. One of the advantages of the way in which we are proceeding is that we have the flexibility to respond to the concerns that hon. Members are expressing tonight. That is sensible . . .

Mrs Margaret Beckett (Derby, South) [Labour]: . . . The regulations should be set in concrete and thrown into the Thames so that they are never seen again. . . . Even before the resolution is carried, the Minister says that the regulations are faulty and unsatisfactory, that there is not enough evidence or data, and that they will be reviewed. . . . The Minister had said that the Government intended to review the figures in November 1985. Now they intend to review them in April 1986, despite the fact that the Social Security Advisory Committee said that the denial of an uplift and review in November 1985 seemed 'punitive', so unsatisfactory did the committee consider the figures in the document to be. Now the Government plan to delay the review by six months, unless Government Members influence Ministers. . . . The Government ask why so many young people are going into board and lodging. It is because the vast number of young people—almost 50,000—who go into this board and lodging accommodation which is often expensive and even more often squalid, have no real choice . . . The Government have presided over a catastrophic slump in housing. It is complacent twaddle for the

Secretary of State to refer in his report to the ready availability of housing. He said:

'there continue to be large numbers of unoccupied local authority dwellings'.

That was the right hon. Gentleman's reply to the Social Security Advisory Committee. . . . The committee pointed out that the regulations 'do nothing to resolve the underlying difficulties'.

Referring to the proposals, the committee stated:

'We doubt, however, whether any satisfactory control can be imposed on the use of supplementary benefit board and lodging accommodation until these issues are faced and dealt with . . . In our view, it is because they tackle the symptoms rather than the causes of growth in costs and numbers, that they are unlikely to provide a long-term solution.'

Even during the past couple of days hon. Members have received telephone calls and letters from the many agencies and groups involved in dealing with those who will be affected by the regulations. Those groups would normally, if not always, be wholly sympathetic to the Government. They certainly seek to be non-partisan and non-party political [*Laughter*]. An hon. Member laughs. Does he call the Royal National Institute for the Blind partisan and party political? Perhaps he does if they do not agree with his Government. . . . [Mrs Beckett refers to the role of other interests groups, including the British Refugee Council and the Church of Scotland] . . . I come to board and lodging. The SSAC mentions the strong possibility—this is perhaps the most dangerous part of the Government's proposals—that the Government are on the verge of creating

'a class of homeless and rootless young person who is unable to return to the parental home, for whatever reason, and who cannot remain long enough in any one location to find permanent accommodation or a job'.

The Government suggest—

'other acceptable accommodation is available to these young people if they choose to seek it—a proposition which we doubt'.

Ironically, the current proposals may actually hamper young people from moving into more settled housing by preventing them 'from establishing the continuous residence qualification required both for local authority accommodation and for housing associations property'. . . .

One reads the Government's proposals first with incredulity and then with mounting anger as one realises the effects on, as is usually the case, some of the most vulnerable sections of the population. Realistically, four weeks is just not enough time to find a job for anybody who has the slightest difficulty. I notice that in his statement the Secretary of State says that 25 per cent of young people find a job in under four weeks. That means that 75 per cent of young people do not. In many parts of the country, after four weeks they will have to move on.

My hon. Friend the Member for Swansea, East (Mr Anderson) drew the Minister's attention to criticisms of the proposals. The Minster said that he thought that my hon. Friend was harsh about what the SSAC said, so let me remind the Minister of what it said:

'the proposed changes seem to us to have serious defects'.

They are so serious that:

'we recommend that the changes are seen overtly as temporary changes . . . We think this is particularly the case with the proposals for ordinary board and lodging.'

One of the worst aspects—although it appears to be the most minor—of the board and lodging proposals is the proposal that a couple with a child under 11 will be allowed only the rate for one and three quarter people rather than for two people, irrespective of the fact that the rate for two people is probably charged where they live. Despite the scathing comments of the SSAC about anecdotal evidence not being a sufficient basis for legislation, it did not seem to be able to discourage the Government from legislating on that basis. . . .

I shall finish with just one other quote from the SSAC about all the people who want, the Government appear to think, to go and live in this board and lodging:

> 'In some cases . . . claimants were enduring substantial domestic and other stress before moving into accommodation. The conditions . . . are often of an extremely low standard, and may involve sharing rooms with strangers, having to vacate rooms during the day, dirty and unsafe accommodation, and inadequate meals of poor quality. This is far from the luxurious lifestyle which it is sometimes implied that board and lodging claimants follow.'

That option cannot be the foundation of a workable benefits policy. The regulations are possibly the biggest shambles that the Government have put before the House so far on supplementary benefit. . . . They are more than a shambles; they are a disgrace. I say to the Minister and his colleagues that not only his Government and his party but the whole country will ultimately suffer from the systematic, step-by-step removal of dignity and hope from thousands of the most vulnerable young people in the country.

Several other MPs spoke and the minister made a concluding statement. The House divided and the SI was affirmed by 227 votes to 168, a government majority of 59.

Questions

1. What part did the SSAC report play in the debate?

2. What, if anything, did the consultation process achieve? Was it helpful for:

(a) the government;
(b) the Opposition in Parliament;
(c) interest groups?

Did it alter any outcomes?

3. The Hansard Society Commission called for an end to the 'artificial' time limit of one and a half hours for debating affirmative resolutions. Would further debate of this sort have achieved anything in this case? Surely the government would still have won the vote even if MPs had debated the regulations for several hours? (At the time, it had a majority of over 100.)

4. Would scrutiny of regulations be improved if MPs were permitted to make amendments, rather than having to accept or reject them as they stand? If the answer is 'yes', surely one of the main benefits of having delegated legislation—it saves Parliamentary time—would disappear?

The regulations come into force

Having been affirmed by the House of Commons on 2 April 1985, the new regulations (SI 1985 No 613) came into effect. Lawyers in the DHSS may have sighed with relief; but, as we shall see when we examine the role of the courts in scrutinizing subordinate legislation, this was premature. Trouble was in store for the department.

JUDICIAL REVIEW CHALLENGE

Simon Cotton, an unemployed person living in board and lodging accommodation in Birkenhead, applied for judicial review.[8] His lawyers argued that the regulations were *Wednesbury* unreasonable, that the mandatory consultation requirements had not been complied with, and that s 2 of the Supplementary Benefit Act 1976 did not authorize the regulations. On 31 July 1985, Mann J held that the new SI was indeed *ultra vires* on the last of these grounds. He stated (emphasis added):

> . . . but what of section 2(1A)? In my judgment, the subsection must be read in conjunction with section 2(1). If it is so read, I do not doubt that the *questions* which may be prescribed for determination by other than adjudication officers, appeal tribunals, or commissioners are those *questions* which are referred to in subsection (1). Those questions are *questions in regard to individual cases and are not questions as to the entitlement to benefit of a class of claimants which are answerable in terms of rules of general application*. Adjudication officers and the appellate bodies are not concerned to formulate rules. Their duty is to apply them to the individual cases before them . . . Of course, decisions may have a precedent value but that is not a consequence of the performance of a legislative function. In my judgment paragraphs 6(2) of Schedule 1A and 5(3) of Schedule 2A as inserted into the 1983 Regulations by regulation 4(8) and (10) of the 1985 Regulations are not within the powers conferred and are accordingly void. The decision manifested in regard to the Applicant in the letter dated 11th May 1985 must consequentially fall but I do not regard specific relief as being necessary as against the Secretary of State.

In other words, the enabling provisions relied upon by the department were intended to deal with disputes about particular individuals' entitlement to benefit; they were not intended to permit rule-making about entitlement generally.

From the government's point of view, the timing of this judgment was truly disastrous. It was on the day before the courts stopped sitting for the summer vacation (so a speedy appeal to the Court of Appeal was impossible) and Parliament had already risen for its annual summer recess (so new regulations could not be made until it met again in the autumn). The DHSS agreed to continue paying the full amount of benefit to Simon Cotton and thousands of other claimants in his position during the summer until any appeal. On this basis the judge agreed not to make a formal declaration that the regulations were invalid.

THE GOVERNMENT TRIES AGAIN (AND AGAIN)

When Parliament resumed in October, the Secretary of State made a statement to the House of Commons reporting on the High Court's decision and announcing that he would now be seeking the approval of the House of Commons for a set of *temporary* Board and Lodging Regulations. Extracts

[8] For detailed consideration of this part of the board and lodgings saga, see Chapter 27.

from this statement are set out in Chapter 27.[9] In response to what the minister said the Labour frontbench spokesman Mr Meacher asked (HC Deb, 21 October, col 48):

> . . . is the Secretary of State aware that my initial legal advice is that there may be grounds for holding that the new draft regulations are illegal, because, contrary to the Minister's statement, they still do not address the main reason why Mr Justice Mann ruled in the High Court on 4 August that the original regulations were illegal?

This 'advice', together with the publicity surrounding *R v Secretary of State for Social Services ex p Cotton*, alerted the JCSI to problems with the new regulations. The smooth passage enjoyed in April was not to be afforded to these new regulations.

Technical scrutiny (again) by the JCSI

The day after the minister's statement to the Commons, the JCSI received a memorandum from the DHSS and met to cross-examine lawyers and officials from the department.[10] The chairman of the committee was Andrew Bennett, a Labour MP.

Examination of witnesses

Mr P. K. THOMPSON, Principal Assistant Solicitor; Mrs S. TAYLOR, Assistant Solicitor, and Mrs E. WOODS, Assistant Secretary, Administration, Department of Health and Social Security, called in and examined.

Chairman

1. Could I welcome you all to the Committee? I would like to start by asking you to explain to the Committee why it was felt necessary to bring this forward so quickly?

(Mrs Woods.) As the Secretary of State explained in his statement yesterday, ministers felt it was very important, to bring clarity on an issue which had already caused doubt and confusion, and where there was not only the case of Mr Cotton which gave rise to the need for the regulations but also issues before the Social Security Appeal Tribunals. Of course, it was not possible before Parliament returned to bring regulations, and it was felt necessary to do so at the earliest moment, so when the outcome of the appeal was known, there would be no problems for claimants or local office staff in ensuring that people got the benefit to which they were entitled. At the moment, nobody knows what the outcome of the appeal is going to be, and it would be very difficult indeed for everybody if local offices had not known what claimants were entitled to and if the claimants had not known.

2. Would it not have been possible to print orders last week, so they were available for people to see, rather earlier than yesterday?

(Mrs Woods.) They were printed as soon as it was possible for us to do so. There has been a whole series of events, and as soon as ministers reached their decisions, effect was given to them.

[9] See p. 647.
[10] Minutes of Evidence (HL 247, HC 25-xli).

3. So how long did it take to draft the regulations?

(Mr Thompson.) We have gone through several drafts, Chairman. I am not sure when a first draft was put forward.

(Mr Taylor.) Drafting was not able to be completed until political decisions were taken as to the way the policy was going to be and therefore, as you can see from the regulations, they are not simple, they are complex. This did present a big task to the draftsman, and that could not be completed until policy views were clear.

4. It does seem to present Parliament with some problems of scrutiny. Could I go on to ask you particularly about paragraph 5? As we understand it, it relies on the same powers as were used in the original regulations for the sections which the judgment has called into question. I think this is paragraph 5, Schedule 1A to the requirements regulations, as added to the 1985 regulations which were in issue before Mr Justice Mann, and I think his point is this: by repromulgating the whole of the regulations, you are repromulgating, *inter alia*, that paragraph, and that paragraph would also fall to the ground as *ultra vires* on the reasoning of Mr Justice Mann in the Cotton case, although I think it would be fair to say you are illustrating the fact that you are not at the moment operating power there, by reason of the fact that you have included in Regulation 3 of the new regulations, specific upratings of the figures, which you could otherwise have changed to paragraph 5.

(Mr Taylor.) That is absolutely right. We are not, at this stage, proposing to revoke that provision for several reasons. First of all, this provision was not directly challenged in the Cotton appeal, although I do agree that it was drafted on the same principles as the two provisions that were directly challenged in the Cotton case, but it is a provision that is generally of a beneficial nature. Secondly, as indicated, while the appeal is pending, we do not propose to invoke that power, as is illustrated by the fact that we have put into effect the increases by means of direct amendments by the provisions in the proposed Regulation 3.

5. Surely it raises a question, whether it is beneficial, or to someone's disadvantage, it is still *ultra vires*; you cannot claim that because it is for somebody's benefit rather than their disadvantage it is all right—it is either within the powers or not. Surely the question is not whether someone challenges the powers, but the question is still whether you have the powers to make those regulations or not?

(Mrs Woods.) As I understand it, our position is we are challenging the ruling in the High Court. The Secretary of State has appealed against it, and this particular provision is not, as I understand it, at issue in this case; nobody has said it is *ultra vires*. [. . .]

[The chairman asked several other questions; then handed over to Alex Carlile MP, a Liberal Democrat who is also a QC.]

Mr Carlile

15. Are you saying that it has been difficult to translate into legislative form, *intra vires*, the political will which does intend to translate into legislative form?

(Mr Taylor.) I do not quite understand the question, but I myself have no difficulty in that at all. There was difficulty in drafting, in the sense that one had to await the final definitive policy on this matter, but once that was known, there was no drafting difficulty within the powers available under the Act.

16. But at the time of the drafting of the latest regulations [. . .], is it not correct that you were aware there was a doubt as to whether Regulation 5, as amended was in fact *intra vires*? You were aware of a doubt as to the *vires*?

(Mr Taylor.) Yes, certainly. [. . .]

19. No doubt you are aware that one of the terms of reference in this Committee is that the Committee should make a report to the House, if there is a doubt as to whether the regulations are wholly *intra vires*?

(Mr Taylor.) Yes, I am aware of that function.

20. So it can be no surprise to you that we are investigating this very subject this afternoon?

(Mr Taylor.) No, it is of no surprise.

21. We have great sympathy with you in the DHSS with the number and complexity of the regulations which you have to draft. However can you point to any precedent in any previous regulations, when in the face of a clearly expressed judicial opinion, albeit *obiter*, that there were *ultra vires* aspects to regulations, notwithstanding that the Department has taken the view that the *ultra vires* part should be retained, albeit with an undertaking to postpone the effect; has it ever happened before?

(Mr Taylor.) I cannot recall any such precedent.

(Mr Thompson.) My experience does not go back that far, but what is unusual here is that we are appealing. If we were not appealing, it would be a different situation. [. . .]

[16 other questions were asked.]

Questions

1. What is your impression of the quality of the questions asked and the answers given during the JCSI hearing?

2. Why did the JCSI spot the *ultra vires* problem this time when it had not seen it first time around?

3. How does the type of scrutiny by the JCSI differ from:

(a) that on the floor of the Commons in the 90-minute debates on affirmative resolutions; and
(b) a court hearing an application for judicial review of the validity of an SI?

The JCSI reports

The JCSI and its advisors wrote and published the following report:

THIRTY-FIRST REPORT
FROM THE JOINT COMMITTEE OF BOTH HOUSES APPOINTED TO SCRUTINISE DELEGATED LEGISLATION

Ordered to report—

. . .

SUPPLEMENTARY BENEFIT (REQUIREMENTS AND RESOURCES) MISCELLANEOUS AND TEMPORARY PROVISIONS REGULATIONS 1985

2. That the Committee draw the attention of both Houses to the above draft instrument on the ground that there appears to be doubt whether it is *intra vires*, and on the further ground that the Department making the instrument are aware of the doubt . . . [A]lthough the Department have taken the matter to appeal, and secured dates in November for an expedited hearing, they have also chosen to make new regulations before the hearing of the appeal. [. . .]

The Committee accept that these amendments are intended to take proper account of the judgment in the Cotton case and of the resulting undertaking given by the Department to the court in that case. Nevertheless, the amendments (apart from Regulation 3) have only temporary effect and subject to that temporary effect the 1985 Regulations are re-promulgated. The effect of the new Regulations is thus to re-promulgate *inter alia* the very provisions held in the Cotton case to be *ultra vires*. Furthermore, there are other provisions in the re-promulgated Regulations, notably paragraph 5 of the new Schedule 1A, which would also be *ultra vires* on the basis of the judgment in the Cotton case, even though they were not in issue there. Similar considerations apply to certain amendments made by the 1985 amending Regulations also re-promulgated by the new Regulations, since (although they are of an entirely ameliorative character from the point of view of claimants) these also fall foul of the reasoning in the Cotton judgment.

In evidence to the Committee the Department acknowledged that there must be a doubt concerning the *vires* of the new Regulations having regard to the Cotton judgment. Their position was, however, that a holding operation was very desirable pending the appeal. The new Regulations deferred the operation of the actual provisions held *ultra vires* in the Cotton judgment and so far as concerned other provisions that fell foul of the reasoning in that judgment they were not operating them pending the outcome of the appeal. . . . They pointed to the fact that Mann J. had deliberately refrained from making a formal declaration of *ultra vires* so that from their point of view it did not appear improper to re-promulgate the contentious material pending the decision of the Court of Appeal. The position was further complicated by the fact that the plaintiff in the Cotton case had also sought to strike down the whole of the new Regulations, on the ground that the required consultation procedure had not been followed, and although the Department had won on that point before Mann J. there was a cross-appeal on it by the plaintiff.

The Committee sympathise with the Department's difficulties but it seems to the Committee that to make regulations knowing that there is a doubt about their *vires* is a very questionable procedure. The Department were unable to point to any precedent for proceeding in that way, and the Committee do not know of any. Furthermore, the Committee are not persuaded that the making of these regulations in advance of a decision of the Court of Appeal is necessary, given that Mann J. left the way open for the Department to maintain the status quo *either* pending an appeal *or* pending the making of new regulations. The matter has proceeded without new regulations since the hearing of the Cotton case at the end of July and it is now only about a month until the hearing before the Court of Appeal is due to take place.

Government retreat

Following publication of the JCSI report, the government withdrew the proposed temporary regulations. On 11 November, a further set of regulations (SI 1985 No 1385), drafted in a different way, were laid before the House and were passed by an affirmative resolution on 20 November.

THE COURT OF APPEAL DECISION

Three weeks later, on 13 December, the Court of Appeal gave judgment in the *Cotton* case. It upheld Mann J's decision granting Simon Cotton's application for judicial review: see p. 649 below. Four days after the Court of Appeal judgment, the Minister for Social Security made a short statement in the Commons.

17 December 1985

Supplementary Benefit (Board and Lodging Payments)

The Minister for Social Security (Mr Tony Newton): With permission, Mr Speaker, I should like to make a statement about the position concerning supplementary benefit board and lodging payments following the Court of Appeal decision last Friday.

As the House will be aware, the Court upheld Mr Justice Mann's decision in the Divisional Court on 31 July that there was no power to make two paragraphs of the regulations passed by the House in April. The Court rejected a cross appeal that the Social Security Advisory Committee had not been properly consulted before the regulations were made.

The House will wish to know that the Government do not intend to appeal further. We shall take steps to identify from our records those cases in which arrears may be due because we did not meet the full charge, and to pay these arrears as soon as possible. To this end, we have sought and received from the court today further guidance on how such areas should be assessed.

I should make it clear that the Court of Appeal's judgment does not affect the current benefit position of those in board and lodging. Those payments are covered by the fresh regulations agreed by the House last month which came into effect of 25 November.

Mrs Margaret Beckett (Derby, South) [Labour]: Is the Minister of Social Security aware that this statement, both in its nature and in its perfunctory length, is an insult to the House and, much more than that, is an insult to the thousands of . . . vulnerable people who have been illegally cheated and short changed by the Government since the regulations came into effect. How dare the Minister come to the Dispatch Box to make that statement and utter not one word of apology or explanation for all the suffering that has been caused. It is not even as if the Government can complain that they have not been warned. Initially when the regulations were introduced the Social Security Advisory Committee heard from over 500 organisations that wrote to condemn the proposed regulations. It was the largest number ever to condemn such proposals, apart from those who wrote to condemn the Fowler reviews. [. . .]

Mr Frank Field (Birkenhead) [Labour]: On behalf of Simon Cotton, my constituent who took the Government to court over this matter, I thank the Minister for his statement this afternoon.

The Minister must be aware that his policy has been illegal and unlawful, twice by the courts and that that policy has resulted in some young people being made homeless, many being underpaid and others moving around the country in an attempt to claim benefit. Will the hon. Gentleman explain what measures he will take to trace the claimants? . . .

I would like the Minister to look to the future. He confidently asserts that the Government's current regulations are lawful but he must be aware that the Cotton success paves the way for the present legislation to be challenged in the courts. He must also be aware, and should have told the House, that when the Government's lawyers said they might appeal to the House of Lords, the Lord Chief

Justice said that if they had the nerve to return he would reject the application out of hand.

Is the hon. Gentleman aware that on Friday 13 December Camden Council obtained leave for a judicial review against the current regulations? There is a large question mark over the Government's current proposals. Surely it would be advisable for the Minister to follow the advice that is currently offered by the Opposition. In our opinion, the Minister cannot gain the powers by regulation; he needs to seek primary legislation and he will gain the Opposition's support if he deals with the abuse that undoubtedly exists, particularly if he concentrates on the landlords.

Mr Newton: I thank the hon. Gentleman for the characteristic generosity of his opening remark. However, I did acknowledge, although I did not refer directly to Camden, that there were further court cases in process. That is why I did not feel that it was correct to comment, as they are manifestly sub judice. [. . .]

Mr Tam Dalyell (Linlithgow) [Labour]: With my experience of being Parliamentary Private Secretary to the late Dick Crossman 17 or 18 years ago, I have the feeling that Alan Marre or the late Dame Muriel Riddesdell and their lawyers would have warned the Secretary of State. At any time, did any of the hon. Gentleman's lawyers or senior civil servants give him some kind of premonition of the Cotton judgment and that what he was doing might be *ultra vires*? My experience of the Department was that those lawyers, who were jolly clever and competent, would have warned the Minister. Did not they do so in this case, and did not the Minster have an inkling that this would happen?

Mr Newton: The convention is that Ministers do not normally refer in detail to the advice they receive, but I hope that the hon. Gentleman will recognise that Ministers—

Mr Dalyell: Were you warned?

Mr Newton: In view of the imputation that the hon. Gentleman is seeking to make, I would be grateful if he would listen to the end of my sentence. I hope that he will accept from me that it is inconceivable—if he does not, I can only assure him with all the emphasis at my command—that neither I, the Secretary of State nor anyone else would deliberately have proceeded to maintain regulations that we were advised were unlawful.

Mr Tony Baldry (Banbury) [Conservative]: Is it not somewhat bizarre that, whenever the High Court rules against a government department, the Opposition shout that the Minister concerned has broken the law as if that Minister had deliberately offended against the criminal code? Surely the reality is that English law is now so complex that there will inevitably be occasions when the High Court will be asked to interpret legislation and the actions of Government Departments. On occasions it will rule against the Government Departments and on others it will rule in favour. The protection for us all is that there is a High Court that seeks to protect the interests of all citizens by interpreting the laws and ensuring that nothing unlawful is carried out.

Mr Newton: I am grateful to my hon. Friend and I agree with what he says. A number of people both inside and outside the House may have overlooked the fact that these regulations were submitted to the Joint Committee on Statutory Instruments in the normal way. Their vires were not questioned by the Joint Committee and they were passed by Parliament in an affirmative vote.

Questions

1. Were the various new sets of Board and Lodging Regulations being used to give effect to an important change in government *policy*? Or were they dealing with issues of *detail* and *practical implementation*? In the light of your answer, consider whether you agree with Frank Field MP who said that the new board and lodging regime should have been introduced into Parliament in the form of a bill.

2. *Why* did government make regulations that were held to be *ultra vires* by the courts and the JCSI?

3. Do you agree with Tony Baldry MP's comment?

4. Should the minister have apologized, as Margaret Beckett suggested? Is apologizing for errors part of the conventions of ministerial accountability and responsibility?

The aftermath

In February 1986 the High Court refused the application for judicial review brought by the London Borough of Camden challenging the legality of the last set of regulations which had come into force in November 1985 (SI 1985 No 1835). These regulations had been made 'without having referred any proposals on the matter to the SSAC since it appeared to the Secretary of State that by reason of urgency it was inexpedient to do so' (see s 10(2) of the Social Security Act 1980). Subsequently the whole system of welfare benefits was restructured by the government; supplementary benefit was abolished and replaced by other forms of payment.

General Questions

1. In situations (as in this case study) where a department appears to have a choice either to use delegated legislation or to introduce a bill to give legal backing to a policy, what advice would you give to the government?

2. What is your overall assessment of the effectiveness of consultation on and parliamentary scrutiny of delegated legislation in this episode? How do you measure effectiveness?

WHERE TO GO FROM HERE

So far this part of the book has examined two of the main legal bases for government action: Acts of Parliament and delegated legislation. The chapters which follow move on to look at other sources of legal authorization: the prerogative (Chapter 12) and Community legislation (Chapters 13 and 14). If, however, you want to consider Simon Cotton's judicial review of the Board and Lodging Regulations referred to in this chapter, turn to Chapter 27.

12

PREROGATIVE AND NON-STATUTORY POWER

The constitutional history of this country is the history of the prerogative powers of the Crown being made subject to the overriding powers of the democratically elected legislature as the sovereign body. The prerogative powers of the Crown remain in existence to the extent that Parliament has not expressly or by implication extinguished them.

Lord Browne-Wilkinson, R v Secretary of State for the Home Department, ex p Fire Brigades Union [1995] 2 WLR 464, 474

A development of potentially extraordinary significance has breathed new life into the authority of the royal prerogative, adding greatly to its strength and to the government's freedom to [act] against the wishes of Parliament. This change came with British membership of the European Community. Membership of the Community has increased the power of *Government* and reduced the law-making role of *Parliament*, transferring law-making to the executive in a manner which uses the prerogatives on a scale not seen since 1649.

Tony Benn and Andrew Hood, Common Sense (1993), p. 64

INTRODUCTION

Imagine you are the Foreign Secretary. You open your red ministerial box to find a memorandum from a civil servant about Mrs X, a British citizen staying in Morocco. She has approached the British Embassy there requesting a new British passport to replace one that has been stolen. The Metropolitan Police in London want to question her about an incident in London in which animal rights demonstrators caused criminal damage to the gates of 10 Downing Street. Mrs X implacably denies that she is guilty of any crime but refuses to return to the United Kingdom fearing she will not get a fair trial. She says she needs to visit her daughter who is seriously ill in the USA. The civil servant sets out the options available to you. These include granting a passport (which Mrs X may be able to use to travel around the world in order to avoid arrest) and granting a travel document permitting Mrs X to make only a one-way journey back to the United Kingdom (and so preventing her seeing her daughter). You must decide what to do.

Suppose now you are the Secretary of State for Defence. Your red box contains a briefing document setting out the latest developments in a war.

There will be a meeting of the Cabinet later this morning in which British involvement will be discussed. If Britain is to become involved you will have formal responsibility for any decisions taken about the deployment of British troops.

At first glance, these may appear to be decisions quite different in nature but they share a common feature: both may be described as action taken under prerogative powers. The decision-making powers being exercised by the ministers do not stem from an Act of Parliament. No statute regulates the issue of passports or confers discretion upon a minister to withhold them. Nor is there a statute which empowers the government to deploy British troops in war or in support of international peacekeeping or humanitarian action.

WHY DOES THE GOVERNMENT HAVE NON-STATUTORY POWERS?

There are two main ways of explaining why central government, in a parliamentary democracy, has a source of legal authority for its actions other than parliamentary legislation.

An historical perspective

The historical explanation for the prerogative is rooted in the complex constitutional crises of the seventeenth century. At the beginning of the 1600s the monarch asserted rights to exercise judicial, executive and legislative functions personally. During the course of the century, the courts claimed the right to hear cases without interference from 'the Crown' and denied the monarch had any personal right to *adjudicate*. Under the constitutional settlement following the Glorious Revolution of 1688, it was no longer possible for the monarch personally to *legislate* by proclamation; the legislative function was transferred from the monarch to the King-in-Parliament, which was now sovereign. The monarch's role had become a formal one, confined to granting the Royal Assent to bills (which by convention is never refused). Under the new constitutional monarchy, the monarch's governmental powers passed to ministers—who continued to exercise them 'in the name of the Crown'. Blackstone, an eighteenth-century scholar and author of an early encyclopaedia on English law, stressed that the prerogative referred to:[1]

> those rights and capacities which the King enjoys alone, in contradistinction to others, and not to those which he enjoys in common with any of his subjects; for if once any one prerogative of the Crown could be held in common with the subject, it would cease to be prerogative any longer.

On this basis, prerogative powers can be defined as the *special* powers which originally belonged to the monarch personally, and which after the

[1] William Blackstone, *Commentaries on the Laws of England*, vol. 1 (1765), p. 85.

establishment of a constitutional monarchy were effectively transferred to *ministers of the Crown*. As Lord Browne-Wilkinson points out,[2] many of these powers have been replaced by statutory powers. Indeed, it would be possible for *all* prerogative powers to be supplanted by Acts of Parliament conferring powers on ministers or the monarch herself; for this reason, prerogative powers may be described as 'residual'.

Wade approves of Blackstone's formula and argues that it is wrong to fall into the habit of describing as 'prerogative' any and every sort of government action which is not statutory.[3] For him, essential characteristics of the prerogative (properly so-called) are that

(a) it is a legal power to alter people's rights, duties or status which is
(b) unique to the Crown.

Thus, setting up the Criminal Injuries Compensation Scheme in 1964 on an informal, non-statutory basis was not really done under the prerogative (Wade argues) because

(a) a private individual could have dispensed his wealth in a similar fashion;[4] and
(b) the scheme did not create or alter any private law rights, it merely regulated how *ex gratia* payments were to be made.[5]

It was, for Wade, merely an exercise of the freedom which individuals have.[6] Nor, for Wade, is the issue of passports a matter of the prerogative as a passport has no status or legal effect at common law whatever.[7] He also regards the union ban at GCHQ as merely an employment dispute, not different in nature from any dispute between any employer and its workforce. Treaty-making on the international plane is not, for Wade, the exercise of prerogative power by government because treaties in themselves do not either create or alter rights in national law.[8] According to Wade, genuine prerogative powers include matters such as the power to grant pardons where there has been a miscarriage of justice, the dissolution of Parliament, and the granting of Royal Assent to bills because these powers are unique to the Crown and they affect the content of domestic law.

As we can see, Wade draws a distinction between prerogative powers (in the sense of special powers unique to the Crown to alter legal rights) and the

[2] See the quotation at the beginning of this chapter.

[3] H. W. R. Wade, *Constitutional Fundamentals* (1980), p. 46.

[4] The courts, however, have regarded it as prerogative: see *R v Criminal Injuries Compensation Board, ex p Lain* [1967] 2 QB 864 and *R v Secretary of State for the Home Department ex p P* [1995] 1 WLR 845 and the discussion at p. 283 below.

[5] An argument put forward by the Home Secretary in *ex p Fire Brigades Union* [1995] 2 WLR 464, 474.

[6] See Chapter 7, above.

[7] Wade, *Constitutional Fundamentals*, p. 51. Cf. *R v Secretary of State for Foreign and Commonwealth Affairs, ex p Everett* [1989] QB 811, per O'Connor LJ: 'there is no doubt that passports are issued under the royal prerogative in the discretion of the Secretary of State'.

[8] On treaties, see p. 272.

freedom of central government to do everything that is not prohibited by law.[9] The freedom to act in ways which are not otherwise unlawful is a freedom that is not unique to the Crown, because even individuals are said to possess this freedom. Moreover, since the exercise of this freedom must comply with the law, it cannot alter existing legal rights and obligations, and for this reason too it will include powers which Wade would not describe as prerogative powers. Harris calls this freedom the 'third source of authority' for central government (the other two being prerogative as defined by Blackstone/Wade and statute).[10] Included under this third source are such things as powers to issue circulars and guidance designed to encourage compliance with policy, as well as the power to use the government's control over the country's wealth to further policy objectives—as when, for example, it is decided to relocate government offices to a depressed part of the United Kingdom in order to encourage employment, or when the government decides to purchase goods, such as military equipment, from particular companies. As we saw in Chapter 7, this third source of power can sometimes be used in controversial ways: in 1979 Megarry V-C held that it was lawful for the police to tap telephones because this could 'be carried out without any breach of the law, it does not require any statutory or common law power to justify it: it can lawfully be done simply because there is nothing to make it unlawful'.[11]

A functional perspective

A different type of explanation for the existence of non-statutory powers of central government focuses on the functions they perform. From this perspective, the powers considered in this chapter are not merely historical hang-overs from when the monarch ruled. It can be argued that the government needs to have discretion to act in some situations without prior parliamentary authorization or debate. Similarly, in some circumstances it may be necessary for the courts to adopt a limited scrutiny of government action. There are two main practical reasons why central government may claim to need non-statutory powers even where this restricts political or legal accountability. Whether this is actually so is, of course, politically contentious.

First, the government may say that to govern effectively it often has to take sensitive or urgent action; to require the assent of the House of Commons might impede effective government. Thus, the government might be hampered in its treaty negotiations with other states if it had to obtain parliamentary approval before it signed and ratified treaties; national security and lives

[9] See Chapter 7.

[10] See B. V. Harris, 'The "Third Source" of Authority for Government Action' (1992) 109 LQR 626.

[11] *Malone v Metropolitan Police Commissioner* [1979] Ch 344, 367, discussed in Chapter 7. The law on telephone tapping has since been changed: see Interception of Communications Act 1985.

might be endangered by delay and publicity if there was a requirement that the government gain prior authorization from Parliament for the deployment of the British armed forces. The nation's position might be weakened in the eyes of enemies if action proposed by government were criticized in Parliament before it took place.

A second possible argument in favour of central government retaining non-statutory powers is that it would be almost impossible to 'replace' all existing prerogative powers with *specific* legislative schemes covering every eventuality which might arise. Statutes cannot anticipate, and thus authorize, every type of executive action which may need to be taken by government. Government ministers therefore need to have power to do anything that is not prohibited by law. Dicey's definition of the prerogative, which is much broader than Blackstone's, captures something of this. Rather than stressing that an essential characteristic of prerogative power is that the power in question is unique to the Crown, for Dicey the prerogative is 'every act which executive government can lawfully do without the authority of an Act of Parliament'.[12] This broader approach is now more widely adopted than Blackstone's (or Wade's).

The advantages for government of using prerogative power

The ability of 'the Crown',[13] in certain situations, to derive legal authority for its actions from the prerogative provides advantages for government which are not provided by statute. In particular, use of the prerogative *limits parliamentary scrutiny of government action*. Suppose the government wishes to set up a scheme such as the Criminal Injuries Compensation Scheme (CICS). If it does so by means of a statute, a bill will have to be introduced into Parliament and be subject to line-by-line scrutiny in both Houses. If, however, the scheme is set up by the Home Secretary exercising prerogative powers (as the CICS was in 1964), then the most that the constitution probably demands is for the minister responsible to make a statement in the Commons or to announce the scheme in a written answer to a PQ asked by a government backbench MP.[14] Similarly, where executive action (like the deployment of British troops in war zones overseas) is given legal backing by the prerogative, Parliament is unlikely to have any opportunity to debate the government's decision *before* it is implemented. The reality is that Parliament has almost no effective power to veto government action done under the authorization of prerogative powers.

Until relatively recently there was also a second major benefit for government in using the prerogative (in the circumstances where it was free to do so) in comparison to using powers conferred by statute. Traditionally the courts

[12] A. V. Dicey, *The Law of the Constitution*, p. 425.

[13] The meaning of 'the Crown' in this context and who exactly is entitled to use prerogative powers is considered at p. 278, below.

[14] On the methods used by Parliament to scrutinize executive action, see Chapters 16 and 17.

were very reluctant to judicially review action taken under prerogative powers. Government was therefore able to use prerogative power in the relatively safe knowledge that it would be subject only to minimum levels of judicial scrutiny, if any at all. The House of Lords' decision in the *GCHQ* case in 1984 marked an important change in judicial attitudes in this respect.[15]

ILLUSTRATIONS OF PREROGATIVE AND ANALOGOUS POWERS

A difficulty with discussing prerogative powers is that there is no comprehensive list of them. In part this is because there is, as we have seen, considerable dispute over how the prerogative ought to be defined. However even where there is agreement that an area of governmental activity is authorized by the prerogative, there may be substantial uncertainty about the scope of particular prerogative powers. Where there is doubt, it is ultimately for the courts to determine the existence and extent of any prerogative claimed by government.[16] For convenience it is possible to group the main areas of prerogative power into several broad categories.[17] Very often an area of activity is regulated by statute as well as the prerogative; the two may be intertwined in complex ways.

Prerogative powers over international diplomacy and law

The government may sign and ratify international treaties, and break them, on behalf of the United Kingdom under prerogative power.[18] In bare outline, the process of treaty-making is as follows. Treaties emerge from bilateral or multilateral negotiations between independent sovereign states. The formal process of treaty-making normally follows the practices now set out in the Vienna Convention on the Law of Treaties.[19] Once agreement on the text of the treaty has been reached, a representative of each sovereign state (in the case of the United Kingdom, normally a minister or a senior diplomat) signifies this agreement by signing or initialling the text. For the treaty to bind the United Kingdom in international law, such signature often requires ratification, at least in the case of more important treaties.[20] Under the Ponsonby Rule,[21] the text of any treaty which the government intends to

[15] On judicial review of prerogative powers, see further p. 282, below.
[16] See p. 282 below.
[17] The most detailed account of the range of prerogative powers is in 8 *Halsbury's Laws* (4th edn., 1974), para. 889 *et seq.*
[18] See H. W. R. Wade's argument that this is not 'prerogative' (p. 268 above).
[19] See further Ian Sinclair, *The Vienna Convention on the Law of Treaties* (2nd edn., 1984).
[20] Treaties provide for ratification to take place in several different ways. Commonly it involves a signatory state depositing a formal document with the United Nations or a designated state.
[21] Arthur Ponsonby was a diplomat and subsequently an MP during the 1920s and 1930s. He set this practice down in a departmental minute when he was a junior minister in the Foreign and Commonwealth Office.

ratify is laid before Parliament for its information, at least 21 days before ratification—though this need not happen in cases of urgency.

The orthodox British view is that national and international law are separate legal systems.[22] Treaties are not part of national law and so cannot directly create rights and obligations enforceable in national courts unless the treaty has been incorporated into domestic law.[23] The main rationale for this is that it would be wrong for the government to be able to 'impose laws on the people by entering into international agreements' because this would lack democratic legitimacy.[24] The flip side of the coin is that treaties do not impose obligations upon government which are enforceable by individuals in national courts. Thus, a person cannot challenge the validity of government action, nor legislation, in the UK courts on the basis that it is contrary to a treaty which has not been incorporated (such as the ECHR).[25]

Generally,[26] Parliament is actively involved with treaties only in those situations where government chooses to incorporate a treaty into national law by statute.[27] Many treaties entered into by the United Kingdom are never incorporated in this way because the terms of the treaty do not require any change to be made to the signatories' domestic law. Where incorporation does need to take place, by convention this is done *before* the UK government proceeds to use its prerogative powers to ratify the treaty; otherwise, there would be a danger that Parliament would not pass the required statute and the United Kingdom would, in international law, be in breach of its obligations under the treaty.

Normally, then, it is only where there is incorporation of treaty provisions into the UK legal system by statute that Parliament has an opportunity to debate a treaty signed by the United Kingdom; otherwise Parliament has little more than a right to be informed. Like many commentators, Rawlings is critical of this limited role for Parliament, saying there is 'no better illustration of the antiquated and deficiently democratic character of the British constitution . . . than in the field of external relations in general, and the treaty-making power in particular'.[28] Nowadays, treaties affect the rights of individuals and business, yet treaty-making is still a matter solely for government (the Crown) with Parliament playing no significant role in the process.

[22] On 'dualism', see p. 112.

[23] For a critique of this view, see Deryck Beyleveld, 'The Concept of a Human Right and Incorporation of the European Convention on Human Rights' [1995] PL 577.

[24] Sir John Laws, 'Is the High Court the Guardian of Fundamental Constitutional Rights?' [1993] PL 59, 61–2.

[25] *R v Secretary of State for the Home Department, ex p Brind* [1991] 1 AC 696. See further Chapter 6.

[26] See the special position in relation to treaties enlarging the powers of the European Parliament, discussed at p. 294.

[27] See also the discussion in Chapter 5 on the EC Treaty and the European Communities Act 1972. Another example of a treaty which has been incorporated into English law is the Hague-Visby Rules (a treaty made in Brussels in 1924 and amended in 1968) incorporated by the Carriage of Goods by Sea Act 1971.

[28] Richard Rawlings, 'Legal Politics: The UK and Ratification of the Treaty on European Union (Part One)' [1994] PL 254, 257.

In February 1995 Lord Lester of Herne Hill QC introduced a Private Members' Bill into the House of Lords to create a statutory requirement that all treaties concluded by the United Kingdom which are subject to ratification be approved by Parliament before ratification. The system would have been similar to the affirmative and negative resolution procedures for SIs. Where the entry into force and implementation of a treaty would

(a) affect the existing laws of the United Kingdom or the private rights of individuals or corporations in the United Kingdom, or
(b) lay a pecuniary burden upon the inhabitants of the United Kingdom, or
(c) cede any part of the territory of the United Kingdom,

the treaty in question would have to be approved by resolution of each House of Parliament.

Where a treaty did not have these effects, then the government would have power to go ahead and ratify it unless a negative resolution were passed by either House of Parliament within 21 sitting days from the date on which the text of the treaty was laid before Parliament. The Treaties (Parliamentary Approval) Bill was opposed by the government and failed to reach the statute book.

The United Kingdom also has powers to recognize foreign governments and vote at the United Nations and other international organizations without first having obtained approval from Parliament. The issue of passports can also be regarded as being carried out under this aspect of the prerogative.[29]

Prerogatives over defence of the realm

The Bill of Rights 1689 states that 'the raising or keeping of a standing army within the kingdom in time of peace unless it be with consent of Parliament is against the law'.[30] In both the First and Second World Wars, Parliament passed emergency legislation conferring *statutory* powers on government in relation to the war; most of these Acts have now been repealed. Many other government defence functions are, however, authorized only under the prerogative. The prerogative is used to declare war, order British forces into armed combat[31] and enter into peace treaties. There was, for instance, no prior parliamentary approval before the task force was sent to recapture the Falkland Islands or British troops sent by the government, following United Nations resolutions, to Kuwait and Bosnia.[32] Enemy aliens may be lawfully interned in the United Kingdom without statutory authorization.[33] The prerogative may also be used to requisition ships needed by the government in

[29] *R v Secretary of State for Foreign and Commonwealth Affairs, ex p Everett* [1989] QB 811.
[30] The authorization is in the form of the Army Act 1955, which is renewed annually.
[31] See *Nissan v Attorney General* [1962] 1 QB 286.
[32] However, the United Nations Act 1946 gives the government *statutory* powers to take action requested by the UN Security Council under Art 41 of the UN Charter, such as the imposition of sanctions on states.
[33] See Blackstone, *Commentaries* (14th edn.), vol. 1 p. 259.

times of war[34] and property may be destroyed to prevent it falling into enemy hands.[35] It is the prerogative which gives legal authorization to the Ministry of Defence's total ban on homosexual men and women serving in the armed forces.[36]

Associated with the war prerogative is the prerogative power to take action necessary to keep the peace within the realm.[37] Commentators have suggested that, in relation to civil emergency situations within the United Kingdom, 'it would be constitutionally unacceptable today that extraordinary powers of the military should arise by process of common law'[38] (that is, the prerogative) and that the government ought instead to rely on 'statutory provisions conferring on the executive enhanced powers, broad discretion to act and respond to the changing exigencies of the situation and ability to legislate further'.[39]

Aspects of the administration of justice

As *Halsbury's Laws* rather grandly puts it, 'by virtue of the prerogative the monarch is the source and fountain of justice, and all jurisdiction is derived from her'.[40] On a symbolic level, this is represented by the fact that criminal prosecutions and applications for judicial review are nominally brought in the monarch's name—hence the titles to cases: *R v Smith* and *R v Secretary of State for the Environment, ex p Smith.*[41] The practical implication, however, is that today the executive (particularly through the offices of Home Secretary and the Lord Chancellor) retains considerable non-statutory powers in relation to the legal system. For instance, it is under the prerogative that the Home Secretary makes decisions advising the monarch to grant or refuse pardons to people wrongly convicted of crimes, though in some situations the power to grant compensation to victims of miscarriages of justice is now regulated by statute.[42]

The appointment of the judiciary to their posts is done by the Crown exercising prerogative powers on the advice of the Lord Chancellor or the Prime Minister, though again statute now regulates some aspects of the

[34] For instance the Order in Council made at Windsor Castle in 1982 to requisition any British merchant ship needed to assist in the Falklands War (set out in Colin Turpin, *British Government and the Constitution: text, cases and materials* (2nd edn., 1990), p. 383). For a case where the courts have accepted that this prerogative exists, see *The Broadmayne* [1916] P 64.

[35] See D. Bonner, *Emergency Powers in Peacetime* (1985), pp. 8–10.

[36] See *R v Ministry of Defence, ex p Smith* [1996] 1 All ER 257; the Court of Appeal held that the ban was not, in a legal sense, unreasonable.

[37] See further *R v Secretary of State for the Home Department, ex p Northumbria Police Authority* [1989] 1 QB 26, especially at 58.

[38] M. Supperstone (ed.), *Brownlie's Law of Public Order and National Security* (2nd edn., 1981), p. 214.

[39] Bonner, *Emergency Powers in Peacetime*, p. 10. See generally the Civil Defence Act 1948, Public Order Act and Prevention of Terrorism (Temporary Provisions) Act.

[40] 8 *Halsbury's Laws* (4th edn. reissue), para. 305.

[41] In this context, *ex parte* means 'on behalf of'.

[42] Criminal Justice Act 1988, s 133(1).

process (for instance the number of judges and payments of pensions). What concerns some critics of the present system is the total absence of public scrutiny of nominees to judicial posts before they are appointed. In some other countries, such as the USA, there are often rigorous inquiries into the background and views of nominees for senior judicial posts; and if approval from elected legislators is not forthcoming, a nominee cannot be appointed to the bench. In the United Kingdom, there is no open debate about judicial appointments.

In theory Parliament has more control over the dismissal of judges: since the Act of Settlement 1700 judges of the High Court and Court of Appeal hold office 'during good behaviour' rather than merely 'at the pleasure of the Crown'. This protects judges from being dismissed at the whim of the executive.[43] Parliament does however have the right to present an address to the Crown requesting the removal of a person from judicial office; this has happened on only a handful of occasions in several centuries.

Crown immunities

The prerogative also confers immunities on the Crown. Acts of Parliament do not bind the Crown unless they do so expressly.[44] The courts will not issue certain types of coercive orders, such as injunctions, directly against the Crown.[45] In the Citizen's Charter,[46] published in 1991, the government signalled its view that many immunities traditionally enjoyed by central government institutions are anachronistic:

> Public bodies must not be shielded from obligations to their customers and clients by special privileges and immunities. Government activities should not, for example, be immune from inspection and enforcement on matters such as health and safety regulations. Crown Immunities have been removed progressively from the NHS, and Crown bodies have increasingly been exposed to exactly the same regulatory standards as others. As a result of recent food safety and environmental legislation, if a Crown body is found to be falling below standards, enforcement authorities can go to the courts for a declaration of non-compliance, which would be followed by immediate corrective action. The Government will follow this approach in all similar legislation in future. Only if there are special reasons, for example connected with national security, will immunity be maintained.

The civil service

In the distant past, the monarch governed with the assistance of a small number of trusted courtiers. As the size of government increased, so did the

[43] Before the Bill of Rights 1688, judges were sometimes removed from office by monarchs who disagreed with their judgments.

[44] *Lord Advocate v Dumberton District Council* [1990] 2 AC 580. See also public interest immunity, p. 498.

[45] Crown Proceedings Act 1947 and *M v Home Office* [1994] 1 AC 377; this topic is considered in Chapter 26.

[46] Cm 1599, p. 46; see also National Health Service and Community Care Act 1990, s 60; Food Safety Act 1990, s 54; and Environmental Protection Act 1990, s 159.

numbers of officers of the Crown. In time a distinction emerged between political advisors to the Crown (today, ministers who sit in Parliament) and politically neutral salaried civil servants.[47] The courts have recently settled a long-standing uncertainty by holding that civil servants do have contracts of employment,[48] but many key features of the civil service remain controlled by prerogative powers. Many of the basic terms and conditions of civil servants' employment continue to be set out in the Civil Service Order in Council 1982, which is primary legislation made under prerogative powers. Unlike Acts of Parliament and SIs, Parliament played no role in the order becoming part of the law of the land.[49] Using a technique common in statutes, the Civil Service Order in Council delegates powers to a minister to make 'regulations' and issue 'instructions'. It was by issuing such an instruction that Mrs Thatcher gave legal effect to the decision to ban union membership at GCHQ. She derived her power from art 4:

> As regards Her Majesty's Home Civil Service—
>
> (a) the Minister for the Civil Service may from time to time make regulations or give instructions—
>
> . . .
>
> (ii) for controlling the conduct of the Service, and providing for the classification of all persons employed therein and, so far as they relate to matters other than remuneration, expenses and allowances, the conditions of service of all such persons . . .

As in so many areas regulated by the prerogative, statutory powers were also involved in giving effect to this decision: it was also necessary for the Foreign Secretary to issue certain certificates under Employment Protection Acts to take away a civil servant's right to complain to an industrial tribunal if they were dismissed for refusing to give up membership of their union.[50] Curiously, the Foreign Secretary made no reference to prerogative powers when he made his statement to the House of Commons.[51]

The Labour Party has called for an end to the civil service run under the royal prerogative, advocating instead a Civil Service Act which would 'establish a more open and constitutional relationship between ministers and civil servants, and of both to Parliament'.[52]

Government and Parliament

Finally, there is the group of important prerogative powers regulating matters at the heart of the constitution. They include the appointment of the Prime Minister and other ministers and the summons and dissolution of Parliament

[47] See p. 58.
[48] See *R v Lord Chancellor's Department, ex p Nangle* [1992] 1 All ER 897.
[49] On use of the prerogative to legislate, see p. 277.
[50] See Chapters 2 and 17.
[51] See the text set out in Chapter 2.
[52] Michael Meacher MP, *The Times*, 6 October 1994.

within its statutory five-year life, leading to a general election. As *Erskine May* puts it: 'Parliament can only commence its deliberations at the time appointed by the Queen; neither can it continue them any longer than she pleases'.[53] What differentiates this group of prerogatives is that the monarch herself may have a personal, rather than merely formal, input in deciding what ought to be done.[54] The giving of Royal Assent to bills is also performed under the prerogative, but by convention the power can only be exercised in one way. Many commentators regard it as anachronistic for a hereditary monarch to be so directly involved in making important constitutional decisions. For many years, the Queen has been able to avoid controversy about the use of these powers because convention has dictated clearly what ought to be done. This will not, however, always be the case in the future. We return, below, to the position of the monarch personally.[55]

Prerogative legislation

The above illustrations of prerogative powers show how the prerogative authorizes the Crown to take executive action, such as the decision to send troops to war or issue the instruction to ban union membership at GCHQ. In a few limited situations, ministers (or strictly speaking 'the Crown-in-Council') have retained the right to make legislation under the prerogative. Examples include the Civil Service Order in Council 1982 (see above) and the Order in Council made at Windsor Castle in 1982 to requisition any British merchant ship needed to assist in the Falklands war.[56] Both are pieces of *primary* legislation, made without participation of Parliament. In other words, no Act of Parliament *delegated* legislative power to the Crown.[57] Instead of being subject to parliamentary procedures, like bills and SIs, prerogative Orders in Council are conferred with validity at a private meeting of the Privy Council.[58] There is no discussion; the Queen merely signifies her consent to the text which has been agreed in advance within the relevant government departments. The words of enactment of prerogative legislation show clearly how these Orders are legislation made by the Crown, rather than (as in the case of Acts of Parliament) made by the Crown-in-Parliament:

> Now, therefore, Her Majesty is pleased, by and with the advice of her Privy Council, to order, and it is ordered, as follows:—

Compare this with the comparable words in a statute:

[53] See C. J. Boulton (ed.), *Erskine May's Treatise on the Law, Privileges, Proceedings and Usage of Parliament* (1989), p. 60.
[54] See further p. 278 below.
[55] See p. 278.
[56] See p. 273 above.
[57] Confusingly, the term Order in Council is used in a different sense to describe delegated legislation made by the Crown under *statutory* powers conferred by Act of Parliament.
[58] On which, see p. 280 below.

> Be it enacted, by the Queen's most Excellent Majesty, and by and with the advice and consent of the Lords Spiritual and Temporal, and Commons, in this present Parliament assembled, and by the authority of the same, as follows:—

Prerogative legislation is permitted to be made in only a very few situations such as those already mentioned. In 1611 in the *Case of Proclamations*,[59] a conference of judges held that the monarch had no general right under the prerogative to issue proclamations to prohibit new buildings in London or prevent the making of starch from wheat. After the Glorious Revolution of 1688 it became clear that the Crown generally can legislate only as the Crown-in-Parliament, that is through parliamentary legislation. The modern justification for this prohibition is that parliamentary processes facilitate democracy; when a bill passes through Parliament MPs, responsive to their constituents and to pressure groups, are able to discuss legislative proposals and suggest amendments.

The general prohibition on government legislating without parliamentary approval does not prevent ministers making *informal administrative* rules and 'quasi legislation' which do not purport to alter the general law or people's rights, such as those that originally governed the allocation of *ex gratia* payments by the Criminal Injury Compensation Board or in government circulars.

WHO EXERCISES PREROGATIVE POWERS?

Prerogative powers can only be exercised by or on behalf of 'the Crown'. The Crown is in a quite different position to public bodies, such as local authorities, which are created by statute and have only those powers specifically conferred on them, expressly or impliedly, by Acts of Parliament. Such public bodies have no 'prerogative power', at least in the strict sense of the term. In this context, what is the Crown? There are three possible answers:

(1) the monarch personally;
(2) the monarch acting on the advice of the Privy Council; and
(3) a government minister acting in the name of the Crown.

The monarch's personal role

There are some situations where the monarch herself remains constitutionally responsible for the exercise of prerogative power, such as the grant of Royal Assent to bills having completed their passage through Parliament. Other prerogative powers give the monarch more discretion, such as in relation to the appointment of the Prime Minister following a general election. In recent years one or other of the main political parties has always had an absolute majority of MPs in the Commons; in these circumstances convention has clearly dictated who should be summoned by the Queen to form the next

[59] (1611) 12 Co Rep 74; 77 ER 1352.

government (the elected leader of the majority party). But what happens in the case of a hung Parliament, where no party has an overall majority of MPs? One commentator has suggested that it is, or ought to be, a convention that the Queen appoints as Prime Minister the person who before the election was leader of the Official Opposition,[60] but the position is far from clear. In such an instance the Queen would probably be advised by her private secretary, the Secretary to the Cabinet (a civil servant) and perhaps members of the Privy Council not personally involved in the controversy.

In exercising her prerogative powers, the Queen may even in some circumstances act against the advice of her ministers. She might, for instance, quite properly refuse to dissolve Parliament within its five-year life, even though requested to do so by the Prime Minister, if she considers that to do so would be detrimental to the national economy or if some other MP seems able to form a government with the support of the existing Parliament.[61]

Many view these constitutional arrangements as unsatisfactory, both because there is uncertainty over which rules or principles ought to apply and because the monarch's party political neutrality might be compromised. One way forward would be for an inter-party conference or Royal Commission to consider the matter and draw up rules in advance of such a constitutional crisis. Fixed-term Parliaments would also avoid some potential difficulties over the exercise of the prerogative powers over dissolution of Parliament.

The prerogative and the Privy Council

In some circumstances, constitutional convention dictates that the Crown exercises prerogative power through the Privy Council. This is a body of about 300 people (there is no limit on the number) who, as *Halsbury's Laws* puts it, 'are invariably chosen by the Crown from amongst noblemen of high rank, persons who have held or hold high political, judicial or ecclesiastical office, persons eminent in science or letters or very senior civil servants'.[62] In practice, the most active members are current Cabinet ministers and law lords (who form the Judicial Board of the Privy Council to hear appeals from some Commonwealth jurisdictions as well as from the Channel Islands and the Isle of Man).

Today, the Privy Council performs a variety of judicial and legislative functions, in practice through several committees. Some functions are conferred upon it by statute;[63] some are performed under prerogative powers. In

[60] See Geoffrey Marshall, *Constitutional Conventions* (1986), p. 34.

[61] See Marshall, *Constitutional Conventions,* p. 35 and G. Wilson, *Cases and Materials on Constitutional and Administrative Law* (2nd edn., 1977) pp. 17–22 (setting out correspondence from *The Times* on the issue).

[62] 8 (2) *Halsbury's Laws* (4th edn., reissue), para. 522. Privy Counsellors are entitled to use the title 'Right Honourable' before their name.

[63] Statutory functions include the Judicial Board of the Privy Council acting as an appeal court from decisions of disciplinary committees of some august professional bodies (such as the General Medical Council).

the distant past, the Privy Council was the main advisory body for the Crown, but its status and importance came to be eclipsed by the rise of the Cabinet.[64] Convention dictates which Privy Counsellors advise the Queen in any given situation. In relation to domestic political and administrative matters, that role is for Cabinet ministers. In his diary entry for 22 October 1964, Richard Crossman MP describes rather irritably what happened after his appointment as Minister for Housing and Local Government:[65]

> . . . last Monday we new ministers were summoned to the Privy Council offices to rehearse the ceremony of becoming a Privy Counsellor. I don't suppose anything more dull, pretentious, or plain silly has ever been invented. There we were, sixteen grown men. For over an hour we were taught how to stand up, how to kneel on one knee on a cushion, how to raise the right hand with the Bible in it, how to advance three paces towards the Queen, how to take the hand and kiss it, how to move back ten paces without falling over the stools—which had been carefully arranged so that you did fall over them. Oh dear! We did this from 11.10 to 12.15. At 12.15 all of us went out, each to his own car, and we drove to the Palace and there stood about until we entered a great drawing-room. At the other end was this little woman with a beautiful waist, and she had to stand with her hand on the table for forty minutes while we went through this rigmarole. We were uneasy, she was uneasy. Then at the end informality broke out and she said, 'You all moved backwards very nicely,' and we all laughed. And then she pressed a bell and we all left her. We were Privy Counsellors: we had kissed hands.

In its political role, the Privy Council no longer has any deliberative or consultative function. Its regular formal meetings are mainly to confer formal validity on documents which have already been agreed upon in Cabinet or by a government department.[66] Again Crossman is critical. Here he describes the formal procedure for making an Order in Council.

> Last night I caught the ten o'clock sleeper to Aberdeen because I was due to have a Privy Council with the Queen at Balmoral this morning. . . . When we got to Aberdeen at breakfast time I found no rooms had been booked for us to bath and change in and the hotel was full. . . . We started off from Aberdeen at 10.30 this morning to motor to Balmoral—an absolutely perfect windless autumn day, as we went up the Dee Valley climbing slowly into the mountains. As Lord President I had to go and see the Queen first with the papers for the meeting. We chatted for a few moments, then the others came in and lined up beside me and I read aloud the fifty or sixty Titles to the Orders in Council, pausing after every half a dozen or so for the Queen to say 'Agreed'. When I'd finished, in just two and a half minutes, I concluded with the words, 'So the business of the Privy Council is concluded.' The Privy Council is the best example of pure mumbo-jumbo you can find. It's interesting to reflect that four Ministers, busy men, all had to take a night

[64] The Cabinet can, in theory, still be regarded as a committee of the Privy Council. By convention, all Cabinet ministers have to be appointed to the Privy Council.

[65] Anthony Howard (ed.), *The Crossman Diaries*, p. 31.

[66] There is less pomp and circumstance associated with these regular Councils. Crossman describes one in Buckingham Palace, held 'upstairs in a dim, horrible little room with a picture of her corgi over her writing table. She and I had a little chat about stomach upsets' (p. 318).

and a day off and go up there . . . to stand for two and a half minutes while the list of Titles was read out. It would be far simpler for the Queen to come down to Buckingham Palace but it's *lèse-majesté* to suggest it.

The prerogative and ministers

More important today than the Privy Council is the exercise of prerogative power by ministers (who, in theory, act in the name of 'the Crown'). It is this which is at the heart of debate about reform or abolition of the prerogative. By now it should be clear that ministers possess many non-statutory powers of great importance. Before considering whether, and if so how, prerogative powers could be replaced, we need to examine the extent to which they can be controlled. If there is no accountability, prerogatives must be replaced by a system which is more in tune with current democratic needs.

ACCOUNTABILITY FOR THE USE OF PREROGATIVE POWER BY MINISTERS

One major constitutional concern about the prerogative is that its use is subject to inadequate scrutiny and accountability.

The Parliamentary Commissioner and the prerogative

The Parliamentary Ombudsman[67] is expressly prohibited, under the terms of the Parliamentary Commissioner Act 1967, from investigating 'maladministration' in the course of taking or implementing some of the decisions which are authorized by the prerogative. Schedule 3 (Matters not subject to investigation) excludes the following from the Ombudsman's jurisdiction:

1. Action taken in matters certified by a Secretary of State or other Minister of the Crown to affect relations or dealings between the Government of the United Kingdom and any other Government or any international organisation of States or Governments.

2. Action taken, in any country or territory outside the United Kingdom, by or on behalf of any officer representing or acting under the authority of Her Majesty in respect of the United Kingdom, or any other officer of the Government of the United Kingdom other than action which is taken by an officer (not being an honorary consular officer) in the exercise of a consular function on behalf of the Government of the United Kingdom

[. . .]

5. Action taken by or with the authority of the Secretary of State for the purposes of investigating crime or of protecting the security of the State, including action so taken with respect to passports.

[67] See Chapter 18.

[. . .]

7. Any exercise of the prerogative of mercy.

[. . .]

11. The grant of honours, awards or privileges within the gift of the Crown, including the grant of Royal Charters.

Judicial control of prerogative powers

Until quite recently, the courts did not regard themselves as having jurisdiction to judicially review action taken by ministers under the prerogative. The courts limited their role to determining whether or not a prerogative claimed by the government existed; if it did, the courts would not go on to consider whether it had been exercised unreasonably or in breach of common law rules of procedural fairness.[68] It was thought that the only appropriate form of accountability for the exercise of prerogative powers was political, in Parliament. The position was changed radically in the landmark decision of the *GCHQ* case in 1983,[69] where their Lordships held that prerogative powers were not immune from judicial review. The House of Lords did, however, accept that some prerogative powers, such as treaty-making, are not justiciable—as indeed are some statutory powers.[70] In short, the use of prerogative powers are now subject to judicial review in the same way as the exercise of statutory powers.

Parliamentary control of prerogative powers

Parliament is able to control the exercise of prerogative in two main ways: first, by legislating to abolish or restrict prerogative power; and secondly, by scrutinizing action after it has been taken, by means of Parliamentary Questions and debates, select committee inquiries and so on.

Legislation

When a bill regulating a subject area previously occupied by prerogative powers is introduced into Parliament, it may include an express statement preserving the government's rights to use the prerogative. For instance, s 33(5) of the Immigration Act 1971 provides that 'this Act shall not be taken to supersede or impair any power exercisable by Her Majesty in relation to aliens by virtue of Her Prerogative'.

In general, however, the effect of legislation is to restrict the government's ability to use the prerogative. The government for instance cannot use a prerogative power which is inconsistent with a statute conferring power to carry

[68] See Chapter 24.
[69] *Council of Civil Service Unions v Minister for the Civil Service* [1985] AC 374; see Chapter 28.
[70] See p. 513.

out similar action. In *Attorney General v De Keyser's Royal Hotel*[71] the Crown argued that it need not pay compensation to the owner of a building requisitioned during the First World War as it had occupied the hotel under prerogative powers and there was no rule of common law requiring recompense to be made in such circumstances. The House of Lords held that the Crown had in fact occupied the hotel under powers conferred by the Defence Act 1842 which did impose a duty to pay compensation. Lord Dunedin stated:

> Where . . . Parliament has intervened and has provided by statute for powers, previously within the prerogative, being exercised in a particular manner and subject to the limitations and provisions contained in the statute, they can only be so exercised. Otherwise, what use would there be in imposing limitations, if the Crown could at its pleasure disregard them and fall back on prerogative?

In the more recent case of *R v Secretary of State for the Home Department, ex p Fire Brigades Union*,[72] the House of Lords was faced with a somewhat different problem. As we have already noted, the CICS had been set up under prerogative powers in 1964.[73] In 1988 the scheme was to be placed on a statutory footing by the Criminal Justice Act. As quite often happens, however, the parts of the Act dealing with the scheme did not come into force immediately on the bill receiving Royal Assent. Instead, s 171(1) provided:

> Subject to the following provisions of this section, this Act shall come into force on such day as the Secretary of State may by order made by statutory instrument appoint and different days may be appointed in pursuance of this subsection for different provisions . . .

The Home Secretary never made the necessary commencement orders to bring the sections dealing with the CICS into force. Then, under pressure to reduce expenditure, he announced in Parliament in March 1994 that the existing non-statutory scheme would be modified and that in due course the provisions of the Criminal Justice Act 1988 dealing with compensation (which he had not yet brought into force) would be repealed. He also indicated that compensation would no longer be paid according to the principles of common law tort damages and that instead there would be a less generous tariff system set by the Home Office.

The Home Secretary's decision was challenged on an application for judicial review by several trade unions whose members would have been disadvantaged by the change. The situation was different from that in *De Keyser's Royal Hotel* because here statutory provisions allegedly inconsistent with the prerogative had not yet been brought into force. The majority of the House of Lords, nevertheless, held that it was an abuse of power for the Home Secretary to exercise his purported prerogative powers to introduce a tariff

[71] [1920] AC 508.

[72] [1995] 2 AC 513, noted by E. Barendt [1995] PL 357.

[73] Cf. Wade's argument that its establishment ought not to be classed as an exercise of prerogative power, p. 268 above.

system, as this would conflict with his continuing duty to consider whether to make a commencement order to bring the statutory scheme into force. It is a principle of administrative law that where statute confers a discretion on a person, that person cannot 'fetter' himself by deciding in advance that he will use his discretionary power in only one way (here, never to bring the sections into force).[74] Lord Browne-Wilkinson stated:[75]

> In public law the fact that a scheme approved by Parliament was on the statute book and would come into force as law if and when the Secretary of State so determined is in my judgment directly relevant to the question whether the Secretary of State could in the lawful exercise of prerogative powers both decide to bring in the tariff scheme and refuse properly to exercise his discretion under s 171(1) to bring the statutory provisions into force. . . . The Secretary of State could only validly exercise the prerogative power to abandon the old scheme and introduce the tariff scheme if, at the same time, he could validly resolve never to bring the . . . inconsistent statutory scheme into effect.

The Home Secretary was in effect purporting to repeal parliamentary legislation by the exercise of prerogative power when, under the British constitution, 'it is for Parliament, not the executive, to repeal legislation'.[76]

Another situation is where a statute deals with the same general subject matter as a prerogative power but (unlike *De Keyser's Royal Hotel* and *ex p Fire Brigades Union*) it is not clear that use of the prerogative would be incompatible with parliamentary legislation. In 1986 the Home Secretary sent a circular to all Chief Constables in England. In it he explained that a central store for plastic 'bullets' and CS gas would be set up; that Chief Constables would be able to buy this crowd control equipment if they obtained financial approval from their police authority (statutory bodies established to impose local accountability upon each police force); but, if this approval was not forthcoming, Chief Constables could still purchase the equipment directly from the central store. Many police authorities were dismayed by this, believing it was undesirable and unlawful for Chief Constables to be able to purchase this controversial equipment without their approval. In *R v Secretary of State for the Home Department, ex p Northumbria Police Authority*[77] the Court of Appeal held that the Home Secretary did indeed have the statutory power to set up a central store and supply this apparatus directly to the police. Although the case was decided on the interpretation of the Police Act 1964, the court went on to consider whether the Home Secretary also had prerogative power to do what he did. It held that he did. All three judges stated that the Home Secretary could exercise a prerogative 'to maintain peace in the realm', which included taking precautionary steps such as ensuring a supply of weapons; no statute had ever derogated from this. They reached

[74] On fettering of discretion, see p. 554.
[75] [1995] 2 WLR 464, 475–6.
[76] At 474. See also the Bill of Rights 1688, Art 1 ('that the pretended power of suspending the laws or the execution of laws by regal authority without consent of Parliament is illegal').
[77] [1989] 1 QB 26.

this decision even though it meant that Chief Constables could in effect bypass their police authorities. The case is a good illustration of how important prerogative powers can be.

IS THE PREROGATIVE DIMINISHING OR GROWING?

At first sight, it may appear to follow from the fact that the prerogative is residual, and that particular prerogatives can and have been replaced by statutory powers, that the prerogative ought to be seen as a source of legal power which is diminishing in scope and importance.

The general position

Certainly, the orthodox view expressed by the courts is that the government cannot assert new prerogatives. In *BBC v Johns (Inspector of Taxes)*, where the BBC unsuccessfully claimed it was an emanation of the Crown and so entitled to immunity from paying income tax, Diplock LJ stated the position with his customary flair:[78]

> [Counsel for the BBC] has submitted that because wireless telegraphy and telephony were new inventions the Crown had a prerogative right to a monopoly of their use and has chosen to exercise this monopoly as respects broadcasting . . . through the instrumentality of the BBC. This contention involves adopting what he describes as a modern, and I as a 17th century, view of the scope of the prerogative. But it is 350 years and a civil war too late for the Queen's courts to broaden the prerogative. The limits within which the executive government may impose obligations or restraints upon citizens of the United Kingdom without any statutory authority are now well settled and incapable of extension.

European Community legislation

While it may be settled that wholly new prerogatives cannot be created by government, nevertheless the executive may use existing prerogative powers to novel effect. The United Kingdom's membership of the European Community has granted ministers in the United Kingdom wide powers to participate in the work of the Council of Ministers which has power to legislate over UK subjects without the participation of Parliament. Of course, the Council of Ministers itself is not exercising prerogative powers; its authority derives from the treaties establishing the European Community. These treaties have been incorporated into the British legal systems by the European Communities Act 1972,[79] and so when British ministers attend a Council of Ministers' meeting arguably they do so pursuant to a statutory power.

[78] [1965] Ch 32, 79.
[79] See Chapter 5.

When, however, a minister attends a meeting of the Council of Ministers and gives agreement to a directive or a regulation, or is outvoted under qualified majority voting procedure, the minister participates on behalf of the government, and not on behalf of Parliament.[80] Although Parliament may sometimes consider proposed Community legislation in committee or debate it on the floor of the Lords or Commons, this is not a formal part of the legislative process.[81] In any event, views expressed by peers or MPs, or votes taken, do not bind the minister who is not Parliament's delegate. *In effect*, this is like a prerogative power. As the quotation at the beginning of this chapter indicates, Benn and Hood describe this as a 'development of potentially extraordinary significance [which] has breathed new life into the authority of the royal prerogative, adding greatly to their strength and to the government's freedom to implement them against the wishes of Parliament'.[82] They point out that a minister of the Crown (acting collectively with ministers from the other 14 member states) now has power to participate in making Community law which overrides any conflicting law passed by Parliament either before or after the directive. 'The constitutional irony of this position,' argue Benn and Hood[83]

> is that whereas before entry to the EC, Crown powers could only be exercised in the legislative space left by Parliament, the position has to some degree been reversed: Parliament now has law-making power in the space left for it by Crown prerogatives exercised by British ministers in Brussels. The Crown now sets the boundaries within which the House of Commons has legislative freedom.

While the EC now clearly has important law-making powers, Benn and Hood overstate the position. First, they fail to differentiate between different types of Community legislation. So far as EC *treaties* are concerned, the UK Parliament is in fact in a stronger position to scrutinize these than it is with regard to almost all other international treaties. Generally decisions as to the ratification of treaties are entirely a matter of the prerogative and Parliament has little or no role. The situation is different in relation to EC treaties. Where a treaty makes fundamental changes to the Community's constitution, such as the Treaty of European Union made at Maastricht, in practice these changes have to be incorporated into national law by a bill amending the European Communities Act 1972 and the government cannot realistically go ahead and ratify it until such incorporation has taken place. The passage of such a bill, such as the highly controversial one incorporating the Maastricht Treaty into national law in 1993, provides MPs with opportunities to debate and vote and, if so minded, they could prevent the changes proposed by government.[84] Moreover, s 6(1) of the European Parliamentary Elections Act 1978 states that no treaty which provides for an increase in the powers of

[80] See Chapter 13.
[81] See Chapter 13.
[82] *Common Sense*, p. 64.
[83] *Common Sense*, p. 66.
[84] On the 'Maastricht Bill', see p. 295.

European Parliament shall be *ratified* unless it has been approved by the UK Parliament. Furthermore, s 1(3) of the European Communities Act 1972 requires that EC treaties entered into by the United Kingdom have to be approved by affirmative resolution of each House of Parliament before they are regarded as a 'Community Treaty' within the meaning of the 1972 Act.

In relation to *EC secondary legislation* (regulations and directives), while it is true that EC regulations are capable of being automatically effective in the UK legal systems without any prior parliamentary scrutiny or approval, EC directives usually *do* need to be incorporated into domestic law and this is often done by Act of Parliament or SI and here, albeit sometimes to a limited extent, Parliament is able to participate. Each of the above matters is discussed in Chapter 13.

A broader response to the criticisms of Benn and Hood is to say that they view the scrutiny powers of Parliament in relation to national legislation through rose-tinted spectacles. The reality is that the UK Parliament and its legislative process are almost always tightly controlled by government and government bills are rarely defeated and are only occasionally amended in any significant respect. The opportunities for MPs to participate in any worthwhile way in the making of delegated legislation is even more limited.[85] Arguably, Community institutions and the Community legislative process are much more permeable and responsive to public opinion than is the UK Parliament. It might even be argued that the European Parliament, elected by proportional representation and with growing powers, provides democratic legitimacy to laws made in the Community. Moreover, it is also arguable that the EC Commission carries out more effective consultation on proposed Community legislation than do government departments in the United Kingdom intending to introduce national legislation.[86]

REFORM OF PREROGATIVE POWERS

There are two main reasons why the prerogative as a source of legal authority may be regarded as unsatisfactory. For some critics, including Benn and Hood, it is the association of the prerogative with 'the Crown' and 'monarchy' which is a factor in prompting demands for sweeping changes. That a hereditary monarch should have political power is increasingly viewed as anachronistic.

Desire for reform of the prerogative is, however, prompted by more than republican sentiments. The heart of the problem is that the prerogative is capable of giving legal validity to important policy initiatives with Parliament having little or no opportunity to debate, and if necessary amend them, before they are taken; its role, as illustrated by the GCHQ case study,[87] is confined

[85] See Chapter 10.
[86] See Chapter 13.
[87] See Chapter 17.

to scrutinizing events after they have happened. The main issue of reform is not simply the 'abolition' of the prerogative as a source of legal authority; careful thought clearly needs to be given to the type and design of the legislation which will replace it. If prerogative powers which confer very broad discretion on ministers are merely replaced by very broad discretionary powers contained in an Act of Parliament, little if anything will have been achieved. Nevertheless if the employment of civil servants had been regulated by an Act of Parliament, giving the Minister for the Civil Service power to make SIs, MPs may have had a greater chance to influence both the outcome and the way in which the union ban was unilaterally imposed.

Benn's reforms

Benn, in his Commonwealth of Britain Bill, includes the following arrangements.[88] First he would end the constitutional status of the Crown and the Privy Council.

> 37. The legal status of the Crown is hereby ended and the Monarch for the time being, and his or her heirs and successors, shall cease to enjoy, or exercise as Monarch, any political or personal power of any kind, either directly through the person of the Monarch, or by prerogative, or through Ministers.
>
> [. . .]
>
> 43. The Privy Council, and the style and precedence of Privy Counsellor, are hereby abolished.

Benn advocates the establishment of a president who would be elected by MPs from among their number for a period of three years. Clause 14 of his bill provides:

> 14.—(1)(a) The powers now exercised under the Crown prerogative shall be exercised by the President, who shall act solely upon the advice of the Prime Minister, or of a resolution of the House of Commons (which shall prevail if such resolution is in conflict with the advice of the Prime Minister).
>
> (b) the exercise of such powers shall require the assent of the House of Commons before having effect; and
>
> (c) the powers of the President shall include power—
>
> —to give assent to the passage of legislation;
> —to dissolve Parliament;
> —to make orders for any purpose for which Orders in Council were required before the coming into force of this Act;
> —to declare war;
> —to order British forces into armed conflict;
> [. . .]
> —to sign or ratify treaties;
> [. . .] and
> —to exercise other executive powers not conferred by statute.

[88] Benn and Hood, *Common Sense*, Appendix 1.

(2) Instruments previously made by Order in Council and which are legislative in character, after being made by the President, shall be brought in as Bills.

Benn's bill also includes other more specific provisions requiring what are now prerogative powers to be subject to prior debate and agreement in the Commons, for instance:

22.—(1) No vote may be given by a British Minister at the Council of Ministers of the European Communities unless and until the House of Commons has given its approval by resolution to that vote.[89]

The IPPR proposals

Other reformers are less radical. In its proposed written constitution for the United Kingdom,[90] the Institute of Public Policy Research retains the monarch as head of state (art 34) and also preserves in a modified form the Privy Council (art 39). Its composition would be the same as at present. The IPPR argues that:

the essential purpose is to provide the equivalent of a Council of State for situations involving war or other emergencies . . . The primary function of [the Privy Council], and the reason for maintaining [it] under the Constitution is that it remains an important method of giving the force of law to acts of government through Order in Council.[91]

But the IPPR's constitution would abolish the prerogative:[92]

The Constitution is the sole source of authority for all public action, executive, legislative or judicial. Henceforth authority must be sought not in common law principles such as parliamentary sovereignty or prerogative power . . . but in the written provisions of this Constitution.

As in Benn's bill, the IPPR would require prior parliamentary approval for many actions currently taken under the prerogative, for example:

122. Declaration of war

122.1. Declarations of a State of War and declarations of a State of Peace shall be made by the Head of State by Order in Council.

122.2. No such Order in Council shall be made unless a draft of the Order has been approved, by resolution, by a two-thirds majority of those voting in each House of Parliament.

For the reformers then, the real issue is not so much removing discretion from government as ensuring that they are properly accountable for it and that Parliament has adequate opportunities to participate in decisions, many of which affect the nation's destiny.[93]

[89] See further Chapter 13, below.
[90] *The Constitution of the United Kingdom* (1991).
[91] *The Constitution of the United Kingdom*, Commentary, p. 28.
[92] *The Constitution of the United Kingdom*, Introduction, p. 3.
[93] See further Rodney Bragier, 'Constitutional Reform and the Crown' in M. Sunkin and S. Payne (eds.), *The Nature of the Crown* (1997).

Questions

1. How would you define the prerogative?

2. What *exactly* is seen as objectionable about prerogative powers?

3. How would the proposed reforms, designed to put government activities on a statutory basis, improve the situation?

4. Crossman is very dismissive of the ceremony involved in the work of the Privy Council. Is it really, as he suggests, just mumbo-jumbo?

5. Would reform of the prerogative necessarily affect the monarch's status?

WHERE TO GO FROM HERE

For an example of parliamentary scrutiny of prerogative powers in the GCHQ case study, turn to Chapter 17; for legal scrutiny, see Chapter 28. Having considered the main legal bases for governmental action *within* the United Kingdom, we now turn to consider the ever-more important European Community legislation.

13

EURO-LEGISLATION

Our Westminster Parliament is in dire danger of being denuded of its responsibilities, and of being supplanted by a European assembly controlled by a hotch potch of European politicians and bureaucrats who have no love for this country. Our national destiny will be subject to foreign control.

Viscount Tonypandy, Speaker of the House of Commons 1976–83, letter to The Times, 26 April 1995

Jacques Santer, President of the European Commission, last night challenged its British critics, and their stories about the lunacies of Brussels, to go and see how it worked. . . . 'You will find us to be receptive and friendly Europeans, not megalomaniac bureaucrats with a secret agenda.' He compared the 'Brussels scare stories' about bureaucrats trying to change the British way of life to McCarthyism.

Michael Binyon, diplomatic editor of The Times, reporting on a speech at London's Guildhall, 5 May 1995

INTRODUCTION

Previous chapters have examined how Acts of Parliament, delegated legislation and the prerogative may provide a legal basis for government action. We now turn to consider the role of European Community legislation. Until 1973, the only 'law' made by the United Kingdom acting in agreement with other states was in the form of international treaties. As we have seen, treaties are regarded as distinct from national law, incapable of creating rights or obligations enforceable in UK courts.[1] Since joining the European Community there have been new forms of legislation. First, the treaties establishing the Community were incorporated into national law by the European Communities Act 1972.[2] As well as setting out the institutional framework for the Community, these treaties also impose obligations and confer rights on government, individuals and businesses in the United Kingdom. From time to time, the member states have amended and added to these treaties, and these changes too have been incorporated into national law by Act of Parliament.[3]

[1] See p. 272.

[2] See p. 115.

[3] Most significantly the Single European Act (in force in 1987) and the Treaty of European Union, often called the Maastricht Treaty (1993). See further p. 75.

As discussed below,[4] these treaties are negotiated and concluded in broadly similar ways to other international treaties, with states meeting as independent sovereign nations.

Secondly, the treaties empower Community institutions to enact legislation within the scope of the treaties.[5] The method for making this secondary legislation is very different from treaty-making. In particular, an elaborate institutional framework and legislative procedures allow participation of a wide range of different interests (including governments of member states, directly elected representatives of the peoples of the Community, the Community itself through the Commission and interest groups). Whereas treaties require the consent of member states, secondary legislation in the form of 'directives' and 'regulations'[6] may bind a member state even if its government opposes it.[7] This is what happened in respect of the Working Time Directive, which was opposed by the UK's Conservative government.[8]

This chapter is about the Community treaties and secondary legislation—and the rather marginal role of the UK Parliament in the legislative process. The mechanics of the legislative process—who does what and when—should become clearer once you read the case study on the Working Time Directive in the next chapter. Detailed examination of Community institutions and law as a legal system *in its own right* falls outside the scope of this book;[9] the main focus is instead on the *interactions* between the Community and the UK constitution (particularly the UK Parliament, government departments and the courts).[10] The Community is viewed *from the perspective of the United Kingdom*.

MAKING THE TREATIES

Treaties establish the institutional framework and powers of the Community and some provisions also create rights and obligations which are enforceable

[4] See p. 293.

[5] The term 'Community' is used here deliberately. As explained in Chapter 3, the European Union consists of three 'pillars': (a) the European Community; (b) common foreign and security policy; and (c) cooperation in the fields of justice and home affairs. So far, it is only in relation to (a) that there is a developed legislative procedure. Decision-making in the second and third pillars proceeds by more traditional inter-governmental methods.

[6] Confusingly, UK SIs are often also called 'regulations', as in the Supplementary Benefit (Requirement and Resources) Miscellaneous Provisions *Regulations* 1985. Also, EC regulations and directives, together with other sorts of instruments such as decisions and recommendations (not considered in this book) may be described as 'acts'.

[7] Additionally, there is the 'tertiary' legislation made by the Commission, on which see P. Raworth, *The Legislative Process in the EC* (1993), pp. 112–14.

[8] See Chapter 14.

[9] See further: T. C. Hartley, *The Foundations of European Community Law* (3rd edn., 1994); Francis Snyder, *New Directions in European Community Law* (1990); D. O'Keeffe and P. Twomey, *Legal Issues of the Maastricht Treaty* (1994). A detailed description of the Community legislative process can be found in P. Raworth, *The Legislative Process in the European Community* (1993).

[10] On the ECJ and Community law in the national legal systems, see Chapters 29 and 30.

in UK courts and tribunals.[11] The powers of the Community institutions (including the Council of Ministers, the Commission, the European Parliament and the ECJ) arise from several treaties,[12] principally the Treaty Establishing the European Community (colloquially known as the Treaty of Rome), originally signed by six states in 1958. The United Kingdom joined the Community in January 1973. The Treaty of Rome has since been amended quite radically: first, in 1987 when the Single European Act (despite its name, an international treaty, not a piece of domestic legislation) changed decision-making procedures in the Community institutions to speed up the completion of the single market; then, in 1993, the Treaty of European Union (or 'Maastricht Treaty') made further significant changes to the Treaty of Rome.

The treaty-making process

Like most international treaties, the EC treaties emerged from protracted negotiations between states. Periodic inter-governmental conferences (IGCs) are held to review the treaty framework of the European Union (as it now is). These may go on for lengthy periods. There is no regular schedule for IGCs. There was none between 1975 and 1985, when negotiations for the Single European Act began. Negotiations leading to the signing of the Maastricht Treaty in 1992 took over two years. A further IGC began in 1996. As a matter of law, there is no question of any member state being compelled to agree to any provisions in a proposed new treaty. States meet as they do in any international treaty-making conference, as independent sovereign nations.

Prerogative powers and the ratification of EC treaties

In Chapter 12 we saw that the ratification of treaties by government, in the name of the United Kingdom, is done under the prerogative and there is normally no need for there to be any prior parliamentary approval, or even debate, before this happens. The position in relation to the EC treaties may be somewhat different. Ratification is still a matter for the government under the prerogative, but Parliament may play a larger role than normal. First, because of the dualist nature of UK domestic law, each of the EC treaties has had to be specifically incorporated into domestic law by Act of Parliament. The Treaty of Rome became a source of law in the United Kingdom by virtue of the enactment of the European Communities Act 1972.[13] This

[11] The use to which the EC treaties are put in adjudication, including the concepts of direct effect of some of their provisions in the national legal systems, is considered in Chapter 29.

[12] See p. 75.

[13] For discussion of this Act, see p. 115.

Act was amended in 1986[14] and 1993[15] to incorporate the Single European Act and the Maastricht Treaty into the UK national legal systems. Secondly, if the treaty in question alters the powers of the European Parliament, the government has to obtain the approval of the UK Parliament before ratifying the treaty. This is because s 6(1) of the European Parliamentary Elections Act 1978 states:

> No treaty which provides for an increase in the powers of the European Parliament shall be ratified by the United Kingdom unless it has been approved by an Act of Parliament.

Thus in relation to the Maastricht Treaty signed in 1992 there was a statutory requirement for there to be a debate and vote in Parliament before the government was able to use the prerogative to ratify it.[16]

Incorporation of EC treaties into the national legal systems

Parliament had no power to amend the treaties, which had already been agreed by the governments of the member states. In spite, or perhaps because of this, debates on the European Communities (Amendment) Bill in 1993 were contentious and protracted. It brought to the surface fundamental disagreements within the Conservative Party over Europe, and the government had to resort to a 'confidence motion' to ensure the support of potential rebel backbench MPs in its own party. One MP, Rupert Allason, failed to attend Parliament on the day of a crucial vote and 'lost the Conservative whip', meaning that he was no longer recognized as a member of the party in Parliament.[17] The Labour Party, too, was in a somewhat difficult position: although the Official Opposition was in favour of the Maastricht Treaty as a whole, it opposed the United Kingdom's opt out from the Protocol on Social Policy (or 'Social Chapter').[18]

Legal challenges to EC treaties

Decisions to sign or ratify the EC treaties have been subject to legal challenges in the United Kingdom. In 1971 Raymond Blackburn, a litigant in person well known for bringing legal actions about constitutional matters, sought a declaration that the government would be acting unlawfully if it

14 European Communities (Amendment) Act 1986.

15 European Communities (Amendment) Act 1993. For a discussion of the passage of the bill through Parliament, see Richard Rawlings, 'Legal Politics: The United Kingdom and Ratification of the Treaty on European Union (Part One)' [1994] PL 254.

16 See the European Communities (Amendment) Act 1993, s 1(2): 'For the purpose of section 6 of the European Parliamentary Elections Act 1978 . . . the Treaty on European Union signed at Maastricht on 7th February 1992 is approved.'

17 Late in 1994 several other backbench Conservative MPs lost the whip when they failed to support the government in votes on other aspects of government policy towards Europe.

18 See p. 331.

signed the Treaty of Accession to the EC. In essence, his argument was that by signing the treaty the government would be surrendering 'the sovereignty of the Crown in Parliament'. The Court of Appeal struck out his action: 'since the court could not impugn the treaty-making power of the Crown and would only interpret laws when they had been enacted by Parliament, the statements of claim disclosed no causes of action'.[19]

A more recent litigant was Lord Rees-Mogg, a former editor of *The Times*. The day before the bill incorporating the Maastricht Treaty was to receive Royal Assent in July 1993, he applied for judicial review against the Foreign Secretary in an attempt to prevent the government ratifying the treaty.[20] Some MPs, concerned that this litigation was a threat to parliamentary privileges, complained to the Speaker of the House of Commons that the Rees-Mogg application was contrary to Art 9 of the Bill of Rights 1688 which declares that 'the freedom of speech and debates or proceedings in Parliament ought not to be impeached or questioned in any court or place out of Parliament'. In a statement (described by Rawlings as 'carefully crafted'), the Speaker reminded those involved in the litigation of the need to respect the constitutional position of Parliament as set out in the Bill of Rights. In the event, the court dismissed Rees-Mogg's application, so leaving the way clear for the Crown to proceed with ratification.

The arguments put to the court on behalf of Rees-Mogg concerned the Protocol on Social Policy annexed to the Maastricht Treaty, under which the other eleven member states apart from the United Kingdom would use the Community institutions to make legislation on matters such as workers' rights. One of the main arguments was that although the Protocol was distinct from the main treaty, it increased the powers of the European Parliament; however clause 1(2) of the 1993 bill (by which Parliament was being asked to approve the Maastricht Treaty for the purposes of s 6 of the European Parliamentary Elections Act 1978) did not expressly refer to the Social Policy Protocol and therefore the government could not lawfully use prerogative powers to ratify the treaty. The court held that, as a matter of interpretation, the Social Policy Protocol *was* part of the treaty and therefore covered by clause 1(2) of the bill.

Overview of the constitutional problems with the EC treaties

The ratification and incorporation of the European treaties into the UK legal systems has had a profound impact on the constitution. Three broad areas of concern can be highlighted. First, many people argue that the *consequences* of the treaties are unacceptable: that they have led to a flow of political and

[19] *Blackburn v Attorney General* [1971] 1 WLR 1037. See also *R v HM Treasury, ex p Smedley* [1985] QB 657.

[20] *R v Secretary of State for Foreign and Commonwealth Affairs, ex p Rees-Mogg* [1994] QB 552. See further R. Rawlings [1994] PL 245 and [1994] PL 367 and G. Marshall, 'The Maastricht Proceedings' [1993] PL 402. Rawlings explains that the litigation was funded by Sir James Goldsmith, the entrepreneur, French MEP and founder of the Referendum Party.

legislative power away from the UK Parliament towards the UK government and the Community institutions. (The case study on the Working Time Directive should help you form your own opinions on whether this is so.)[21] Secondly some argue that when, as in the case of the Maastricht Treaty, agreeing to a treaty entails fundamental constitutional change, it is appropriate first to hold a referendum of all voters in the United Kingdom.[22] Thirdly, as we have just seen, it can also be argued that the *legal process* of treaty-making is unacceptable; that there ought to be a greater role for Parliament to influence or mandate government action in this context.

THE INSTITUTIONAL FRAMEWORK FOR MAKING SECONDARY LEGISLATION

So far we have been considering in outline how the EC treaties are concluded and the limited role which the UK Parliament plays in the process. We now turn to examine in outline how Community secondary legislation (regulations and directives) are made.

Like UK legislation, the function of Community legislation is to give legal backing to policy choices.[23] In several fundamental respects, however, the EC legislative process is quite different from Parliament's. Many of these differences stem from the fact that the Community is not itself a state, but a relatively new supra-national organization in which the member states have agreed to pool their administrative, judicial and legislative decision-making powers in respect of certain areas of governmental activity. This collective decision-making has been a recipe for controversy—not only about the substantive content of particular pieces of legislation such as the Working Time Directive, but also, more fundamentally, about who ought to exercise legislative power and how they should be made accountable for it. Many tensions exist within the EC legislative processes and also between what happens there and in national parliaments and governments.

Representation of interests and dialogue

The legislative process in the Community, as in the United Kingdom, can be seen as a network of communication channels, some of which are given formal constitutional status, others of which are quite informal (for instance the lobbying of the Commission by pressure groups). To formulate and agree on policy, and to give policy formal legal validity, dialogue is needed between people representing different interests. Each of the Community

[21] See Chapter 14.
[22] See p. 123.
[23] On the general relationships between law and policy, see Chapter 4. On the more specific question of the effectiveness of law as a tool to implement policy in the context of the Community, see further F. Snyder, 'The Effectiveness of EC Law: Institutions, Processes, Tools and Techniques' (1993) 56 MLR 19.

institutions involved in the legislative process has been designed to reflect different types of interests. These are examined in more detail later in the chapter; in summary they are as follows.

The Commission

This institution safeguards and promotes the common interest of the Community itself. It is the executive branch of the Community, responsible for initiating and drafting legislation as well as implementing the decisions taken by the Council of Ministers and ensuring that member states comply with the law. There are 20 commissioners, one of whom is styled the president (Jacques Santer, formerly prime minister of Luxembourg, holds the post at the time of writing). They are nominated by the governments of the member states, but once appointed are expected to act independently from their national interests. The United Kingdom's current nominees are Sir Leon Brittan (a former Conservative minister) and Neil Kinnock (former leader of the Labour Party).

The European Parliament

Six hundred and twenty-six directly elected Members of the European Parliament (MEPs) represent the peoples of the Community. MEPs often work and vote according to their political rather than national affiliations. The powers of the European Parliament in the Community legislative process have increased significantly as a result of amendments to the treaty framework by the Single European Act and the Maastricht Treaty.

The Council of Ministers

This institution comprises of a representative at ministerial level from each of the 15 member states and so reflects the national interests of each country. There is no set membership of the Council; its composition is determined by the particular issues under consideration. Thus agriculture ministers from the member states meet to discuss and make decisions about farming, transport ministers about transport and so on. The Council is assisted by COREPER (the Permanent Representatives Committee or 'ambassadors' to the EC from member states); the United Kingdom's official delegation is known as UKREP.

The European Council

Heads of state/government meet twice a year as the European Council. The Maastricht Treaty, Art D provides that the European Council 'shall provide the Union with the necessary impetus for its development and shall define the general political guidelines thereof'. Unlike the Council of Ministers, the European Council does not have any legislative powers in its own right; its domain is purely political.

The Economic and Social Committee
ECOSOC is an advisory body which must be consulted in respect of proposed legislation on some subjects, such as workers' rights. Its 222 part-time members are representative of employers, employees and 'other groups' such as farmers and consumers.

The Committee of the Regions
This institution represents local and regional authorities in member states and, like ECOSOC, must be consulted about proposed legislation dealing with certain subjects.

In comparison to the UK parliamentary process, the institutional framework of the Community attempts, in a more elaborate and formal way, to ensure participation in the legislative process of those likely to be affected by legislation. Of course, informal lobbying—of the Commission, MEPs and ministers of national governments who sit in the Council of Ministers—is also frequent and important: certainly to understand the legislative process, at least an awareness of what goes on outside the formal procedures and institutions is needed. As Harlow puts it, 'EC institutions are highly permeable to public opinion and . . . interest-representation in the Community is beginning to be both well-understood and well-organised'.[24] Some argue that the Community has eclipsed the UK Parliament as a focus for lobbying on many issues. Giving evidence to a committee set up to consider how to improve the legislative process in the United Kingdom, the Institute of Directors said:[25]

> the Institute sees the legislative process as much wider than Parliament. It is a long drawn out process involving interactions at many levels and today, particularly with the growing scope of the competence of the EC, the Westminster Parliament (Ministers apart) is a residual, last-stage focus of pressure. This conclusion must have very serious implications for our traditional views of Parliament as a legislator.

As in the United Kingdom, questions arise as to which groups have the best access to the legislators: some have the resources to be able to lobby well, whereas others do not. For example, some commentators suggest that while business and trade union interests are well represented, consumer groups are far less effective at influencing decision-makers in the Community.

Limited legislative competence

As explained in Chapter 5, in the absence of a written constitution or Bill of Rights the UK Parliament possesses general legislative omnipotence. The position of the Community institutions is different; they have competence to

[24] Carol Harlow, 'A Community of Interests? Making the Most of European Law' (1992) 55 MLR 331, 332. See also Snyder, *New Directions in European Community Law*, Chapter 2.
[25] Report of the Hansard Society Commission on the Legislative Process, *Making the Law* (1993), p. 125.

legislate only within the boundaries set by the treaties.[26] In terms of subject matter, the Community continues to be concerned mainly with the 'four freedoms' of movement of persons, goods, services and capital which underpin the single market and also, to an increasing extent, social policy (especially workers' rights and the prohibition of sex discrimination). Regulation of markets in agriculture, fisheries and food, competition and employment policies are also all of great importance.

From a legal perspective, limited competence means that legislative power in any given situation has to be derived from a specific provision in the treaties[27] and disputes can arise as to which treaty provision is the correct basis for a piece of proposed legislation.[28] A second legal and political aspect of limited legislative competence is the developing principle of subsidiarity.[29] During the 1980s the Community appeared to be extending its competence into new areas, some suggested illegitimately. Critics argued that treaty provisions were being used to make directives and regulations which did not properly fall within the scope of the treaties (as the United Kingdom claimed had happened with the Working Time Directive). At first sight the catch-all provisions of Art 235 might also seem to provide opportunities for expansion:

> If action by the Community should prove necessary to attain, in the course of the operation of the Common Market, one of the objectives of the Community and this Treaty has not provided the necessary powers, the Council shall, acting unanimously on a proposal from the Commission, and after consulting the European Parliament, take appropriate measures.

In practice however this article was of relatively little importance because it could only be invoked where member states were prepared to act unanimously. To a considerable extent, the critics won concessions during the negotiations for the Maastricht Treaty and afterwards. The Commission curbed its legislative programme during the 1990s and the EC Treaty was amended to include, in Art 3b, the following:

> The Community shall act within the limits of the powers conferred upon it by this Treaty and the objectives assigned to it therein. In areas which do not fall within its exclusive competence, the Community shall take action, in accordance with the principle of subsidiarity, only if in so far as the objectives of the proposed action

[26] Compare this statement with the views of T. C. Hartley, *The Foundations of European Community Law*, p. 110 and P. Raworth, *The Legislative Process in the European Community*, p. 14. Raworth writes: '. . . the Council, acting alone . . . or jointly with the European Parliament, wields what has become in effect primary legislative power. Theoretically this power still belongs to the Member States, who are solely responsible for enacting the Treaties pursuant to which the Council legislates. However, although the Council must remain within the parameters of these Treaties, when enacting its secondary legislation, the scope of the Community's legislative competence has been so widened that it now resembles a federal area of jurisdiction . . .'

[27] See *French Republic, Italian Republic and United Kingdom of Great Britain and Northern Ireland v EC Commission of the European Community* (Joined Cases 188–190/80) [1982] ECR 2545.

[28] See e.g. *United Kingdom v Council of the European Union* (Case C-84/94) discussed in Chapter 14.

[29] On subsidiarity generally, see pp. 77 and 333.

> cannot be sufficiently achieved by the member states and can therefore, by reason of the scale or effects of the proposed action, be better achieved by the Community.
>
> Any action taken by the Community shall not go beyond what is necessary to achieve the objectives of this Treaty.

The principle of subsidiarity clearly cannot prevent Art 235 being used in appropriate circumstances; it has however resulted in a political climate in which the Commission is now very cautious about being seen to assert its powers to initiate legislation too broadly. Raworth goes so far as to comment that Art 3b 'should ensure that, contrary to popular supposition, the [Maastricht Treaty] will actually reduce the legislative role of Brussels'.[30]

No single legislative procedure for EC secondary legislation

Legislative procedures in the Community are notoriously complicated. Depending upon which EC Treaty provision proposed secondary legislation (regulations and directives) is based, the European Parliament performs different functions: sometimes it merely has a consultative role; at other times it has the power to veto legislation even though the Commission and Council of Ministers are in favour of it. In the Council of Ministers, too, different procedures (unanimous voting and qualified majority voting)[31] apply depending upon the EC Treaty provision under which a regulation or directive is made. According to Dashwood,[32]

> all this unavoidably reflects the complexity of the political bargain that was struck at Maastricht; but it must surely be one of the objectives of the review of institutional arrangements in 1996 [at the inter-governmental conference] to simplify and rationalise the Community legislative procedures, so as to make them intelligible to the citizens of the European Union.

In short, generalizations about the Community legislative process may be misleading. Simplification of the process is likely to be a priority when governments meet at the 1996 IGC to consider again amending the treaty framework of the European Union.

THE LEGISLATIVE PROCESS

Policy proposals

Under the EC Treaty, *formal* responsibility for making proposals for directives and regulations lies with the Commission.[33] The treaty states that the

[30] Raworth, *The Legislative Process in the EC*, p. 4.
[31] See p. 305 below.
[32] A. Dashwood, 'Community Legislative Procedures in the Era of European Union' (1994) 19 ELRev 345, 365–7.
[33] See Arts 189a, 189b and 189c.

Council of Ministers[34] and the European Parliament[35] may request the Commission to formulate and introduce any appropriate proposal, though it is unclear whether the Commission is bound to follow such requests.[36] In practice, the Commission may be influenced by a range of interests. National governments may lobby and negotiate with individual Commissioners or the Commission as a whole; this is done at the official level (that is, through diplomats/civil servants and officials at the Commission) through COREPER.[37] Such negotiations are often difficult. Lobbyists on behalf of businesses, trade unions and pressure groups also have regular meetings with the Commission, which publishes a register of groups with which it has contact.[38]

One or more of the 23 directorates-general, the 'departments' of the Commission, is/are closely associated with the formulation of the policy for proposed legislation.[39] Working groups, including relevant experts co-opted from outside the Commission and representatives of national governments, are normally also set up; much decision-making is, effectively, done in these committees. But final decisions as to proposed legislation are taken by the 20 Commissioners. Such meetings take place in private. As with the Cabinet in the United Kingdom, a convention of collective responsibility applies and, after a vote in favour of recommending a piece of proposed legislation, all Commissioners are expected to show support for it publicly.

Preparation of a draft text

During the later stages of the policy formulation, lawyers in the Commission produce a draft text for a regulation or directive. The text has to serve two purposes: not only must it be drafted effectively to achieve the desired policy goals but it must also be politically acceptable and the Commission will not put forward a text unless it knows that it has broad support for a measure. Throughout the legislative process, the Commission remains 'master' of the text of any proposal for legislation: although, as we will see shortly, the European Parliament and ECOSOC may propose amendments, it is up to the Commission to decide which, if any, of these amendments are ultimately put forward to the Council of Ministers for its final decision to adopt or

[34] See Art 152.

[35] Art 138b.

[36] See K. St C. Bradley, Chapter 13 in O'Keeffe and Twomey (eds.), *Legal Issues of the Maastricht Treaty*, p. 198.

[37] Art 157(2) of the Treaty provides: 'The members of the Commission shall, in the general interest of the Community, be completely independent in the performance of their duties. In the performance of these duties, they shall neither seek nor take instructions from any government or from any other body . . . Each Member State undertakes to respect this principle and not seek to influence the members of the Commission in the performance of their tasks.' The reality, however, is that without the cooperation and broad consent of national governments, the Commission could not perform its functions.

[38] On lobbying in the EC, see further C. Harlow, note 24 above.

[39] Thus, DG V (employment, social affairs and education) was responsible for the Working Time Directive examined in the next chapter.

reject proposed legislation. The Council of Ministers can make amendments to a text recommended by the Commission only if it (the Council) acts unanimously. The proposed text has to be translated into the Community's official languages; it is also published in the 'C-series' of the *Official Journal.*

Determining the procedure: consultation, cooperation and codecision

At an early stage the Commission also has to decide under which EC Treaty provision the proposed directive or regulation ought to be made; as noted above, this may be controversial.[40] The EC Treaty provision chosen determines the procedures and institutions through which the Commission has to steer the proposed text through the legislative institutions of the Community. In particular it determines:

(a) the level of involvement by the European Parliament; and
(b) the voting process in the Council of Ministers when it meets to consider the Commission's proposed legislation.

In practice, the Commission consults informally with representatives of the European Parliament and officials connected to the Council of Ministers before taking any final decision on the precise legal basis for proposed legislation.[41]

What happens after the Commission has published the text of its proposed legislation depends on the level of the European Parliament's involvement —whether the procedural route (determined by the EC Treaty provision on which the legislation is based) is that of 'consultation', 'cooperation' or 'codecision'.

Consultation

The most limited form of parliamentary involvement in the legislative process is under the consultation procedure. Here the Commission sends its proposed legislation to the Council of Ministers which in turn refers the proposal to the European Parliament for its opinion, which may be either favourable or negative. Neither the Commission nor the Council of Ministers is under any legal obligation to follow the Parliament's opinion. The Council has the final say, deciding whether to adopt the proposed legislation, including any amendments which may have been suggested by the Commission, the European Parliament or (sometimes) ECOSOC.

Use of the consultation procedure, once the norm, is declining. Today the consultation procedure applies to directives and regulations made under only

[40] See p. 299 above.
[41] See generally Juliet Lodge, Chapter 3, 'The European Parliament—from "assembly" to "co-legislator": changing dynamics' in J. Lodge, *The European Community and the Challenge of the Future* (1989).

a handful of EC Treaty provisions.[42] It has been largely replaced by the cooperation and codecision procedures, discussed below. A procedure which allowed for no more than 'consultation' was part and parcel of the very limited role of the European Parliament during the early years of the Community; originally it was called the Assembly and comprised of members nominated by national parliaments rather than the directly elected MEPs of today.

Cooperation

Many people came to view the consultation procedure as giving inadequate power to the European Parliament to participate effectively in the legislative process. In 1986, the Single European Act gave the European Parliament a greater role in the form of the cooperation procedure (Art 189c). This is used if the proposed legislation is based on one of ten of the EC Treaty articles.[43] As under the consultation procedure, the Commission passes its legislative proposal to the Council of Ministers and seeks the opinion of the European Parliament (often called the 'first reading'). Then the Council, instead of making a final decision to adopt or reject the text of the proposed legislation, adopts a 'common position' and sends this, together with a reasoned statement, to the European Parliament again for a 'second reading'. As discussed in more detail in the next chapter, the cooperation procedure thus gives the European Parliament two opportunities to consider draft legislation. The European Parliament has three months to decide whether to approve or reject the Council's common position. If the Parliament rejects it, the Council may nevertheless adopt the proposed legislation, though only if all ministers are unanimous in agreeing to do so.

Some commentators have been cautious in their assessment of the cooperation procedure. Writing in 1989, Lodge argued that:[44]

> From the outset, the EP [the European Parliament] was convinced that the cooperation procedure was but a first step in a process of increasing its legislative inputs. Not surprisingly, the fruits of the cooperation procedure have been quantified, assessed and found to be wanting by the EP. While the Commission on the first reading has taken up just over 78 per cent of the EP amendments, the Council has accepted just under half. In second reading, the EP approved in the first year of the cooperation procedure just over 50 per cent of the common positions and tried to amend the rest (sometimes reinserting amendments that had fallen at the first reading, or amendments arising out of the Council's amendment of the Commission's first-reading drafts approved by the EP). The EP's second-reading amendments stand a far slimmer chance of survival. Indeed, on a few occasions the Commission reject all the EP amendments; and the Council deleted over 50 per cent of those agreed by the Commission. The EP has clearly been successful in securing some amendment to legislative items.

42 Including Art 100 on the approximation of laws in member states directly affecting the functioning of the single market.

43 For example, Art 7 (prohibitions of discrimination on the ground of nationality).

44 J. Lodge, *The European Community and the Challenge of the Future*, p. 75.

Codecision

Even after the creation of the cooperation procedure, many people thought that the role of the European Parliament in the legislative process needed to be enlarged further. The codecision procedure,[45] introduced by the Maastricht Treaty in 1993, is broadly similar to the cooperation procedure, except that Parliament is given the power of final veto if a majority of MEPs vote to reject the Council's common position. Another feature of the codecision procedure is the existence of a conciliation committee of MEPs and a representative from the Council of Ministers whose function it is to try to iron out disagreements between both institutions.

European Parliament's 'opinion'

In each of the procedures, the next step in the legislative process is for the European Parliament to consider the Commission's proposal. The European Parliament may participate in the legislative process either once (when the basic consultation procedure is being used) or twice (in the case of the cooperation and codecision procedures).

The proposal is considered first by one of 19 or so committees of 20–60 MEPs. Committees are set up with responsibility for different subject areas. Scrutiny includes an examination of the legal basis of the proposed legislation and this may entail consideration by the Legal Affairs and Citizen's Rights Committee. Committees also discuss the substantive policy of the proposed directive or regulation. The committee then makes a report to the European Parliament sitting in plenary session. This in turn passes a formal resolution which often includes suggested amendments to the text of the proposed legislation. During this whole period there may be much lobbying of MEPs by interest groups. In all, this first-reading stage typically takes about six months.

The Economic and Social Committee

Depending on which Article a proposed directive or regulation is made, it may also be necessary for there to be consultation with ECOSOC, as well as the European Parliament. ECOSOC, established by Arts 193–8 of the EC Treaty, consists of 'representatives of the various categories of economic and social activity, in particular, representatives of producers, farmers, carriers, workers, dealers, craftsmen, professional occupations and representatives of the general public'. Its 222 members (24 from the United Kingdom) meet in sub-committees and in plenary session. ECOSOC has an advisory role in the legislative process in relation to some regulations and directives.[46] In

[45] Art 189b of the EC Treaty.

[46] In addition to ECOSOC, the treaties provide for consultation with some other bodies in some circumstances, including the Committee of the Regions, the Court of Auditors and the European Monetary Institute.

1992 over 2,000 opinions were given to the Commission and Council of Ministers by the committee, but its influence on the outcome of proposals is not great.

Unlike the European Parliament, ECOSOC has no power to delay or veto proposed legislation; its role is merely advisory. Raworth states that the 'Commission rarely amends its proposals purely on the basis of ECOSOC's opinions, although it does often include its suggestions where a proposal is amended for other reasons'.[47] Nevertheless, he argues, 'despite its low profile, ECOSOC should not be dismissed as irrelevant, as its views are a valuable indicator of the potential reactions of the various social groups throughout the Community to a particular piece of legislation'.[48]

Consideration of proposed legislation by the Council of Ministers

Next in the process, the ministerial representatives of the member states, normally accompanied by officials, meet as the Council of Ministers to consider the Commission's draft regulation or directive.

If the consultation procedure is being used, the Council of Ministers at this stage has to decide whether to adopt the measure. Depending on the EC Treaty provision on which the legislation is based, this is either on the basis of unanimity, simple majority or qualified majority. If either the cooperation or codecision procedures are being used, then at this stage the task for the Council of Ministers is to adopt a 'common position'. The Commissioner responsible for the proposal is also normally present. Sometimes there needs to be a vote, but much 'horse-trading' will often have taken place before the meeting so that the ministers have effectively agreed on matters (or agreed to disagree).

If the common position corresponds with the Commission's proposal, then the adoption may be by qualified majority (that is, the larger member states having more votes than the smaller). If, however, the Council wishes to adopt a position which differs from the Commission's, then it may only do so by a unanimous vote. The effect of qualified majority voting is, of course, that the United Kingdom like any member state may be outvoted and a common position adopted with which it disagrees. This is what happened in relation to the Working Time Directive (see Chapter 14).

Secrecy

Meetings of the Council of Ministers normally take place in private, even when the Council is acting as a 'legislature' and deciding on proposed directives and regulations.[49] Commentators have argued that this is inappropriate and at the 1992 IGC in Edinburgh, the European Council suggested that

47 Raworth, *The Legislative Process in the EC*, p. 58.

48 Raworth, above n. 47.

49 The Council of Ministers also discusses and makes decisions on political action unconnected to legislation.

there should in future be open debates in the Council of Ministers on significant legislative proposals and that the voting record should also be published. In 1993 the Council and the Commission approved a code of conduct on public access to documents.[50] Procedural rules laid down the general approach:[51]

> Art 1. The public shall have access to Council documents under the conditions laid down in this decision.
>
> Art 4.—(1) Access to Council documents shall not be granted where its disclosure could undermine [certain specified interests].
>
> (2) Access to Council documents may be refused in order to protect the confidentiality of the Council's proceedings.

Operation of the new regime got off to a very shaky start. A journalist from *The Guardian* wrote to the Council asking for access to documents relating to certain Council meetings, including the attendance and voting records. Some documents were refused on the ground that they 'refer directly to the deliberations of the Council and its preparatory instances'. The journalist challenged this decision in the Court of First Instance of the European Communities[52] which held that the refusal was unlawful because the Council, in reaching its decision, had failed properly to balance its own interest with that of citizens having access.[53] Whether the new procedures for obtaining access to documents will actually lead to more openness is debatable. Raworth, for instance, suggests that deliberations will merely take place in private beforehand.[54] It is certainly true that, even now, decisions at ministerial level in the Council of Ministers are more or less a formality, the horse-trading having taken place between national governments in the run-up to the meeting. On less politically contentious issues, officials from the member states, through COREPER and networks of working groups, will also normally have settled areas of disagreement.

'Second-reading' by the European Parliament

If the cooperation or codecision procedure is being used, the European Parliament has a further opportunity to consider the proposed legislation. The text before the Parliament is the common position agreed upon by the Council of Ministers. Scrutiny, as before, is through committees followed by debate by the full Parliament. Further amendments may be suggested by the European Parliament to the Commission. In this context, all resolutions

[50] Council Decision 93/731/EC (OJ 1993 L340, p. 43).
[51] Council Decision 93/662/EC (OJ 1993 L304, p. 1).
[52] On this court generally, see Chapter 29.
[53] *Carvel v Council of the European Union* (Case T-194/94) [1996] All ER (EC) 53.
[54] Raworth, *The Legislative Process of the EC*, p. 121.

made by the Parliament have to be 'by an absolute majority of its component members'.[55] In relatively rare cases, the European Parliament may decide at this second-reading stage to reject the whole proposed directive or regulation.

Final adoption by the Council of Ministers and the conciliation procedure

The Commission decides which, if any, of the European Parliament's amendments to include in a revised text of the proposed directive or regulation. This is then sent to the Council of Ministers, which must decide whether to adopt the text. According to the EC Treaty provision under which the legislation is made, this may either be by qualified majority voting or by unanimity.

In (rare) cases where the European Parliament has decided at second reading to reject the legislation completely (rather than suggest amendments), the powers of the Council of Ministers depend on whether the cooperation or codecision procedure is being used. Under cooperation, the Council of Ministers may, acting unanimously, overturn Parliament's decision to reject the legislation. In practice, unanimity may well be difficult to achieve and so Raworth suggests that this 'almost amounts to a power of veto' in the hands of Parliament.[56] In the codecision procedure, the European Parliament has a real veto; the Council of Ministers cannot resurrect proposed legislation, even if ministers unanimously favour this, and it will fall. At this stage the matter may be referred to the Conciliation Committee which has an equal number of representatives of the Council and the European Parliament, with a representative of the Commission trying to reconcile the position of the Parliament and Council. The procedures adopted by the Conciliation Committee are very complex and fall outside the scope of this book.[57]

SCRUTINY OF PROPOSED EC DIRECTIVES AND REGULATIONS BY THE UK PARLIAMENT

In the above sketch of the Community legislative process, nothing was said about the role of *national* parliaments. The reason for this is that the parliaments of the member states are given no formal functions under the EC treaties. In practice, however, almost all do in fact make some attempt to scrutinize proposed directives and regulations. Some argue that national parliaments ought to have a much greater role than at present and that there is an imbalance in the scrutiny powers of the European Parliament and those of the 15 national parliaments.

Very soon after the United Kingdom's accession to the Community in 1973, both the House of Lords and the Commons set up committees to

[55] Art 189c.

[56] Raworth, *The Legislative Process of the EC*, p. 39.

[57] See further T. C. Hartley, *Foundations of European Community Law*, pp. 44–8.

scrutinize proposed EC directives and regulations.[58] The most important scrutiny work still takes place in these committees, but before looking at them in detail other ways in which MPs and peers at Westminster are involved in EC legislation should be noted. First, it is practice for ministers to make oral statements to Parliament about the agendas of forthcoming Council of Ministers' meetings which will, of course, often include discussion and agreement of proposed Community secondary legislation. Such statements inform MPs and peers about the government's stance on the proposed legislation, and there is often a short time after the minister's statement for opposition frontbench spokesmen and backbench MPs to comment, criticize and question the minister. A second mechanism for UK parliamentary participation in EC legislation is through Parliamentary Questions (PQs):[59] Community-related matters are regularly the subject of written and oral questions to ministers. In the case study in the next chapter we see how, in relation to the long-drawn-out negotiations about the Working Time Directive, ministerial statements and PQs kept Parliament informed about the UK government's negotiating position and allowed MPs and peers to air their views on the proposed directive and whether it should be adopted. Finally, there are periodic debates on Community-related issues on the floor of both Houses of Parliament. The government used to make a formal written report[60] to Parliament every six months on developments in the Community, including progress of proposed legislation. These reports were debated by MPs. Following a recommendation by the Commons' Procedure Select Committee in 1989, these debates were replaced by general debates *before* the twice-yearly meetings of the European Council. United Kingdom ministers are, in these ways, subject to some degree of political accountability for the decisions they take while sitting as members of the Council of Ministers.

The main work of detailed scrutiny of proposed Community legislation, however, takes place in the committees set up by the Lords and the Commons. Over the years since 1973, the committee structures have changed somewhat; the Lords and the Commons have set up rather different systems.

House of Lords' scrutiny

From the outset, the House of Lords has examined proposed directives and Community regulations in much more detail than the Commons' committee (discussed below). The House of Lords' Select Committee on the European Community carries out its work through six sub-committees specializing in

[58] See generally Eileen Denza, 'Parliamentary Scrutiny of Community Legislation' [1993] Stat LR 56 and Vernon Bogdanor, 'Britain and the European Community', Chapter 2 in J. Jowell and D. Oliver (eds.), *The Changing Constitution* (3rd edn., 1994).

[59] On PQs generally, see Chapter 16.

[60] Published as a command paper.

particular subject areas.[61] Thus, the proposed Working Time Directive was considered by sub-committee C on social and consumer affairs in 1990–91. In the next chapter we see how it took oral and written evidence from a range of businesses and interest groups before publishing a report.[62] Over 90 peers are involved in the work of the select committee as a whole, making it one of the most important of all the Lords' committees. In 1986, the select committee considered its future following the Single European Act, the treaty which enlarged the role of the *European* Parliament[63] in scrutinizing proposed Community secondary legislation. Its report made sober reading:[64]

> 12. How will the Single European Act affect the powers of the United Kingdom Parliament? Nothing in the Act is likely to have an immediate impact but in the long term the position of the United Kingdom Parliament will become weaker.
>
> 13. It is already apparent from the preamble that the Act's intention is to make the Community's legislative process more effective. This streamlining, if successful, will increase the extent of Community law and thus Community competence—that is, the areas subject to Community law rather than national law—at the expense of member states. Any enhancement of the importance of the European Parliament will tend to shift the balance of parliamentary responsibility from the member states to Strasbourg. But the main impact of the Act will lie in its effect on the voting strength of individual Ministers. Since the United Kingdom Parliament exercises no control over Community legislation other than through the voice and vote of United Kingdom Ministers in the Council of Ministers, any weakening of the power of United Kingdom Ministers is felt equally by the United Kingdom Parliament.
>
> [. . .]
>
> 17. . . . The power of United Kingdom Ministers will . . . be circumscribed in five ways. They may be outvoted more often. The intervention of the European Parliament is outside their control. They will have less opportunity than at present to influence the Commission through negotiation at the second stage consideration of proposals. Some legislative powers will be delegated to the Commission. Lastly there will be less opportunity for packaged compromises in the Council: some of Council's decisions (the common position) will, for the first time, be subject to scrutiny and amendment by the European Parliament and thereafter by the Commission.

The select committee report went on to consider how the UK Parliament, particularly the House of Lords, could respond to these changes. Some of its recommendations to the government were relatively minor; others more significant. First, the committee noted that its existing terms of reference were

[61] The sub-committees are identified as A–E, but have been given corresponding nicknames by the peers. Thus, sub-committee D (on agriculture) is called the Digging Committee and E (Law and Institutions) is known as the Legal Eagles Committee: see Denzer (1993) Statute Law Review 56, 59.

[62] See p. 14.

[63] Principally through the cooperation procedure, described above.

[64] 'Single European Act and Parliamentary Scrutiny', 12th Report of the Select Committee on the European Communities, 1985–86 Session, HL 149.

sufficient.[65] Secondly, the select committee requested that the government, in its explanatory memoranda to the committee accompanying proposals for directives and regulations, should identify:

(a) the treaty power relied on;
(b) the procedure applicable, i.e. whether consultation or cooperation; and
(c) the voting procedure applicable in the Council of Ministers, i.e. unanimity or qualified majority voting.[66]

Thirdly, the select committee requested that it be given information about significant amendments proposed by the *European* Parliament.

Fourthly, the select committee considered the question of the timing of its scrutiny:

> 24. The House of Lords scrutiny process will continue to apply without alteration to the cooperation procedure up to the point where the Council adopts its common position. For the Committee's report to have maximum effect it must be made before the Council adopts its common position; and the earlier it is produced, the more useful it will be.
>
> 25. Thereafter strict timetables apply and the Committee may have to consider a re-examined proposal, a supplementary memorandum or amendments proposed by the European Parliament at short notice. Generally speaking, the Committee will have to be prepared to move faster than usual, when required to do so, and the number of fast-moving proposals will probably grow.

One of the select committee's greatest concerns was over the so-called 'parliamentary reserve'. In October 1980 a resolution had been passed in Parliament under which the government undertook that no minister would vote in favour of a proposed directive or regulation in a Council of Ministers' meeting in cases where the select committee had not completed its scrutiny or had recommended that the proposed legislation be debated on the floor of the House, but this had not yet occurred.[67] The government's undertaking was subject to the proviso that a minister could vote in favour of proposed legislation if there were 'special reasons' but he or she would explain what these were to the UK Parliament at the first opportunity after the Council of Ministers' vote. The select committee suggested that where the cooperation procedure was used (rather than the original consultation procedure), so

[65] 'To consider Community proposals, whether in draft or otherwise, to obtain all necessary information about them, and to make reports on those which, in the opinion of the Committee, raise important questions of policy or principle, and on other questions which the Committee consider that the special attention of the House should be drawn': see the opening paragraph of the committee's 12th report, above.

[66] 12th report, para. 19.

[67] The text of the resolution of the House of Commons, passed on 30 October 1980, is as follows: 'In the opinion of this House, no Minister of the Crown should give agreement in the Council of Ministers to any proposal for European legislation which has been recommended by the Select Committee on European Legislation, etc for consideration by the House before the House has given that consideration unless—(a) the Committee has indicated that agreement need not be withheld, or (b) the Minister concerned decided that for special reasons agreement should not be withheld; and in the latter case the Minister should, at the first opportunity thereafter, explain the reasons for his decision to the House.'

giving the Council of Ministers two opportunities to make decisions about proposed legislation,[68] there should be a second parliamentary reserve. In other words, the select committee, and if appropriate the House of Lords as a whole, should be given time to reconsider proposed legislation after adoption of a common position by the Council, for example when the Commission makes amendments to its proposed text in the light of amendments suggested by the European Parliament on its second reading.

Finally, the select committee stated 'that their opinions on proposals for European legislation should be made known not only in the House and to Her Majesty's Government but also to the European Parliament and the Commission'.[69] The report noted that 'both these bodies can now influence the legislative outcome in a way that was not available before [the Single European Act] and the United Kingdom scrutiny ought to take account of this fact'.[70]

Commentators are divided over the real efficacy of the work of the House of Lords' select committee. Some have praised the quality of its detailed reports and minutes of evidence on particular pieces of proposed legislation which are said to be regarded as generally influential by the Commission. Little academic study has, however, been carried out into the degree of influence the select committee's reports have on the UK government itself. As we have noted, the select committee may recommend that a particular draft directive or regulation be debated in the floor of the Lords itself. But many important items of legislation (such as the proposed Working Time Directive) are not debated in this way. In any event, it has been said that 'such debates are usually held outside prime parliamentary time, and arouse only limited interest, since ministers rarely commit themselves before Council meetings, and will therefore promise only to take parliamentary views into account'.[71]

House of Commons' scrutiny of proposed EC secondary legislation

From the outset, the mechanisms for scrutiny of proposed Community legislation in the House of Commons were much less elaborate than those in the House of Lords. A Select Committee on European Legislation was set up in 1974 consisting of 16 MPs from all the main political parties (in proportion to their representation in the Commons as a whole). The select committee's task was to report to the House of Commons on the 'legal and political significance' of directives and regulations proposed by the Commission. The view was taken that the House itself should retain control of scrutiny and not

[68] That is, when the Council of Ministers adopts a common position, and later when it finally adopts (or rejects) the final text of the legislation proposed by the Commission.
[69] 12th report, para. 27.
[70] 12th report, para. 27.
[71] Shirley Williams, 'Sovereignty and Accountability in the European Community' (1990) 61 Political Quarterly 299, 303.

devolve too much responsibility to committees. For many years, the select committee has interpreted the scope of its powers restrictively and takes 'the view that it is not its task to express an opinion on the merits of an instrument . . . it sees its role as being able to identify, for example, the controversial aspects of a proposal and to point out the United Kingdom interest or the pressure groups which are opposed to it'.[72]

The select committee in the Commons continues to do essentially the same task today of receiving information about proposed EC legislation (passed to it by the Cabinet Office) and making recommendations to MPs on which ought to receive further attention in the form of debate. Aided by a staff of clerks and a specialist legal advisor, the select committee has power to recommend that proposed Community legislation be debated either on the floor of the House or, alternatively, in standing committees set up for the purpose.[73] A Deputy Principal Clerk to the House of Commons has described the method of work of the select committee:[74]

> Members usually meet weekly to consider an agenda of perhaps 20 to 40 documents and to select those which are legally or politically important and, of these, those which merit debate by the House in a Standing Committee on European Community Documents. They report their findings in a weekly report, and write brief paragraphs of perhaps one to five pages on each of the documents selected as of being of importance. The documents for debate then await that debate, but they may wait for weeks, months or even years because it is for the Government to select the date, and they will not normally arrange a debate on a document which, for example, is nowhere near final consideration, or is still likely to be altered substantially in the Council [of Ministers] working groups.

There is a trend towards increased use of standing committees, rather than the floor of the House, to discuss proposed legislation (and also other Community documents) drawn to MPs' attention by the select committee. If, however, 20 or more MPs rise in their seats in the Chamber to object to a reference to a standing committee, the proposed legislation is referred to the whole House for its consideration. In the 1989–90 session, there were 33 one-and-a-half-hour debates on the floor of the Commons and a further 22 debates in the Special Standing Committee on European Community Documents.

In the late 1980s, both the Commons' Select Committee on Procedure[75] and the Select Committee on European Legislation[76] considered how arrangements for scrutinizing proposed European legislation by the Commons could be improved. The latter report welcomed:[77]

[72] Robert Wilson, 'Westminster and Brussels: The Relationship of Parliament to the EEC' (1985) 63 Public Administration 235, 237.

[73] Bear in mind the fundamental differences between select committees and standing committees, considered in Chapter 16.

[74] Robert Wilson, above n. 72.

[75] See Fourth Report from the Select Committee on Procedure, Session 1988–89, HC 622-I.

[76] First Special Report of the Select Committee on European Legislation, 1989–90 Session, HC 512.

[77] First Special Report, para. 7.

> the acceptance by the Government of the principle that, where Ministers invoke special reasons under the October 1980 Resolution[[78]] and agree a proposal before a debate can be held, the debate should be held within a sitting month of the agreement being given or the Committee's recommendation being made (whichever is later). Whilst debate after agreement is inevitably a poor second best for debate prior to agreement, this undertaking should ensure that debates at least take place while the issues are still reasonably fresh in Members' minds.

An enduring problem with attempts to make the UK Parliament's scrutiny of proposed directives and regulations more effective is the lack of parliamentary time and the fact that the parliamentary timetable is controlled by government.

Assessing the role of national parliaments

For some commentators, one of the most worrying aspects of the United Kingdom's membership of the Community is that the UK Parliament has lost, in relation to matters within the Community's competence, its historical power to reject legislation proposed by the executive. Benn and Hood make the point powerfully that before entry into the Community, Crown powers could only be exercised 'in the legislative space left by Parliament' but now the position has been reversed to a considerable extent.[79]

While the power of the *European* Parliament has grown under the Single European Act and most recently under the Maastricht Treaty, national parliaments remain on the margins of the legislative process, playing (so far as the Community institutions are concerned) no formal role. Shirley Williams, a Cabinet minister in the years immediately after the United Kingdom's accession to the Community, paints what for many must be a dismal picture of the current arrangements:[80]

> [National parliaments] have little or no input into Commission proposals, certainly none formally. Their scrutiny of the process of framing and agreeing on a directive is often limited to hearing a report of what the Council has decided, which can be criticised but cannot be undone. Occasionally, popular discontent with Commission proposals (as on the harmonisation of standards for beer or milk a decade ago) erupts into Parliamentary pressure on ministers in Council which can make them think again. But it is rare.

Her conclusion is that national parliamentary scrutiny, given the weakness of links to the European Parliament, has been largely ineffective.[81] Williams'

[78] That is, the so-called Parliamentary Reserve, discussed above.

[79] Tony Benn and Andrew Hood, *Common Sense*, p. 66. See also the discussion at p. 285 above.

[80] Shirley Williams, 'Sovereignty and Accountability in the EC' (1990) 61 Political Quarterly 299, 302–3.

[81] With the exception of Denmark where, Williams says, a parliamentary committee on EC legislation 'is in near permanent session. The committee extracts statements on the government's position prior to Council meetings, insists on being consulted as negotiations proceed, and holds its minister accountable for what happened. In practice, this strengthens the negotiating hand of the Danes, but makes them rather uncomfortable partners. It also, on occasion, slows down proceedings. Danish insistence on accountability to the national Parliament works for the Danes, but if extended to the other [member states], would make the Community unworkable': see above article (n. 80), at p. 303.

prescription for the future is to improve the institutional links between the European Parliament and the national parliaments. She suggests that each national parliament should have 'a European committee, chaired by a Cabinet minister for Europe, to scrutinise and debate all substantial Community proposals, on which the countries' MEPs would serve alongside national MPs'.[82] She also suggests that when the Council of Ministers is in 'legislative mode', discussing and voting on proposed directives and regulations, it must cease to meet in private and instead 'should act in the open, as any democratic legislative body does'.

Another former Cabinet minister, Norman Lamont MP,[83] is also highly critical of the balance of power between the European Parliament and national parliaments. He questions the need for a directly elected European Parliament at all, describing it as a 'vastly expensive, pretentious assembly'.[84] 'The continued existence of a directly elected European Parliament makes sense only if it is expected to evolve over the years and eventually acquire more powers. The present half-way house has no logic,' he argues. His prescription is as follows:

> There is one simple way of increasing democracy in Europe, and that is to ensure that no decision is taken in Brussels unless it has been debated and approved by national parliaments. British members of the European Parliament are in a permanent minority, and therefore they cannot protect Britain's national interests. For this reason they ought to be restricted to consultative work, and its members ought to be either nominated or elected from national parliaments. A directly elected [European] Parliament is an expensive nonsense, utterly inconsistent with the idea of a Europe of nation-states.

In March 1995 a confidential briefing paper prepared for UK ministers by senior civil servants was leaked to the press. According to *The Times*,[85] ministers were

> warned that any attempt to strengthen the powers of national parliaments over Brussels through amendments to the Treaty of Rome would be 'fraught' with difficulty. Mr Major and his colleagues are advised to 'tread carefully in this area, avoiding treaty amendments whenever possible in favour of practical steps designed to enable the United Kingdom Parliament to enhance its role in European affairs'.

INCORPORATING EC SECONDARY LEGISLATION INTO NATIONAL LAW

Once the text of a regulation or directive has been finally adopted by the Council of Ministers, the next question is how this secondary legislation

[82] Williams, 'Sovereignty and Accountability in the EC', p. 315.
[83] Chancellor of the Exchequer 1990–93.
[84] *The Times*, 13 April 1995.
[85] 9 March 1995.

relates to the domestic legal system.[86] The status of regulations and of directives is quite different.

Regulations

Regulations automatically become legally effective in domestic law once they have been approved by the Community institutions in accordance with the EC Treaty and so the UK Parliament plays no role in their implementation; they are 'directly applicable'.[87] Indeed, it may be contrary to Community law for the UK government to use domestic legislation to implement a regulation, even if it thought that it might be desirable to do so.[88]

Directives

Directives are 'directed' at member states, not citizens or businesses.[89] A directive requires the United Kingdom and other member states to amend their laws, within a set time limit,[90] so as to reach the result specified in the directive. The process by which this happens is known as 'implementing' or 'transposing' the directive. In the United Kingdom when there is a need to change the law, this can be done by Act of Parliament. The Consumer Protection Act 1987, for example, brought Directive 85/374/EEC into domestic law. More commonly, however, the government may choose to transpose a directive into English law by making an SI: for example the Directive on Unfair Terms in Consumer Contracts 93/13/EEC was translated into UK domestic law by an SI. Section 2(2) of the European Communities Act 1972 gives ministers a general power to use SIs to implement directives, though the government may not use SIs to impose taxation, retrospective legislation, sub-delegated legislation or the creation of new criminal offences.[91] Other statutes also confer more specific powers on ministers to use SIs to transpose directives, for example s 17 of the Food Safety Act 1990 and s 156 of the Environmental Protection Act 1990.

Using SIs has obvious advantages for the government;[92] given the already overcrowded legislative timetable for bills in Parliament, it would be impossible to use primary legislation to transpose all directives. The down side is that SIs receive little parliamentary scrutiny in comparison to bills. In particular, there is little opportunity to debate a draft SI and MPs have no

[86] See p. 272 above for discussion of treaties.
[87] See Art 189 of the EC Treaty: 'A regulation shall have general application. It shall be binding in its entirety and directly applicable in all Member States.'
[88] See *EC Commission v Republic of Italy* (Case 396/72) [1973] ECR 101.
[89] Art 189 provides: 'A directive shall be binding, as to the result to be achieved, upon each Member State to which it is addressed, but shall leave to the national authorities the choice of form and methods.'
[90] Usually 18–24 months.
[91] European Communities Act 1972, Sched 2.
[92] See Chapters 9 and 10.

opportunity to make amendments, only to approve or reject it as it stands. Critics, including some MPs, argue that in this respect the UK Parliament is hardly more than a conveyor belt: it has little choice but to incorporate the contents of directives precisely. Although the UK government has the right to choose the 'forms and methods' of achieving the objectives of a directive, in practice this may leave little room for manoeuvre.

One problem for government ministers and their legal advisors is the style of drafting to use. There is no obligation for the Act of Parliament or SI to use precisely the same wording as the directive. In the past there was a tendency for British legislative draftsmen to use traditional English styles which meant spelling out the policy in great detail and trying to anticipate as many contingencies as possible. The danger with this is that discrepancies may arise between the Act or SI and the original directive on which it was based. An alternative, which is being used more and more, is known as the 'copy out' technique; here the text of the directive is just set out almost word for word. A potential problem with this approach is that directives normally only set out broad principles and there is a fear that this will give domestic judges too much discretion to fill in detail when they are called on to interpret the legislation.[93]

In some situations, it may be possible for the United Kingdom to implement a directive without enacting a statute or making an SI merely by changing administrative practices.

National governments and EC legislation

Just as the role of the UK Parliament in the Community legislative process is contentious, so too is the role of the UK *government*. There has been an enormous transfer of power from the UK Parliament to the government.[94] Since accession to the Community, the executive has power to act, in conjunction with the governments of other member states (through the Council of Ministers), to make legislation (regulations) which are automatically legally binding in the United Kingdom without any real input or formal approval from the UK Parliament. Even directives leave the United Kingdom almost no scope for influence: once the UK government acting with governments of other member states has agreed to a directive, the UK Parliament has little choice but to incorporate it into English law either by passing an Act or

93 On interpretation generally, see Chapter 23.

94 See p. 124. Whether there has actually been much of a shift in power in the United Kingdom between Parliament and the executive *as a result of membership of the EC* is a moot point. As Harlow points out, even in relation to purely domestic issues 'the political reality in the United Kingdom is a Parliament and lawmaking process dominated by Downing Street and Whitehall in which it is exceptional for any but a Government Bill to reach the statute books, non-government amendments are rarely accepted and in which full-scale backbench revolts are rare': see C. Harlow, '"A Community of Interests"? Making the Most of European Law' (1992) 55 MLR 331, 333.

approving an SI. The principle of 'direct effect' of Community law further reduces the involvement of Parliament.[95]

Questions

1. The basic law of the Community is contained in the treaties which are amended periodically following inter-governmental conferences of member states. In the United Kingdom, what legal and political constraints exist to make the UK government accountable for the ratification of such treaties and their incorporation into national law?

2. Why is the legislative process for making Community regulations and directives so complex?

3. How effective is the UK Parliament in:

(a) scrutinizing proposed Community regulations and directives? and
(b) scrutinizing the incorporation of directives into national law?

What reforms can you suggest?

4. Assess the relative importance of the following in the euro-legislation process:

(a) the Commission;
(b) the Council of Ministers;
(c) the European Parliament;
(d) the UK government; and
(e) the UK Parliament.

Do your conclusions cause you concern?

WHERE TO GO FROM HERE

This chapter has examined the processes by which European Community legislation is made. Treaties are the product of inter-governmental negotiation, with member states meeting as independent sovereign states. Directives and regulations are made by the Community institutions. The next chapter looks in more detail at the making of one particular directive: the Working Time Directive.

Later in the book, Chapter 29 on 'Euro-litigation' explains how courts in the United Kingdom and the ECJ deal with the various types of Community legislation. There we see that the concept of 'direct effect' is of great importance: provisions in the EC treaties, in directives and in regulations may *in certain circumstances* create rights and obligations which national courts enforce directly, without there being any national legislation to incorporate those rights and obligations into the UK national legal systems.

[95] On direct effect, see p. 684.

14

CASE STUDY: MAKING THE WORKING TIME DIRECTIVE

INTRODUCTION

The previous chapter considered aspects of the Euro-legislation process; this one moves on to examine one specific law-and-policy episode, the making of the highly controversial Directive 93/104/EC on Certain Aspects of the Organization of Working Time. This directive attempts to impose standards for limiting working hours and entitlements to rest periods and paid holidays in all member states. For the UK Conservative government, intent on *deregulating* economic activity including the removal of restrictions on Sunday trading,[1] the policies contained in the directive were anathema. Speaking in January 1993, some ten months before the directive was finally adopted by the Council of Ministers, Mr Michael Forsyth, the then Minister of State in the Department of Employment, said in the UK Parliament that:[2]

> I find it amazing that anyone could believe that it is a proper role for the government to say how long people should work in their work place. That is for agreement between employees and employers. Only very foolish politicians on the Opposition Benches would go along with the proposition that someone should be prevented from working overtime by decisions taken in the House [of Commons], the European Commission or the Council of Ministers.

This chapter traces how the directive was made, looking at aspects of the formal legislative process as well as the more informal pressures and constraints which shaped it. As with the other case studies used in this part of the book, the main purposes of the exercise are:

(1) to examine in more detail some aspects of the legislative process;
(2) to draw out issues of general constitutional significance; and
(3) to provide materials upon which readers may form their own opinions on the problems with this form of legislation.

Because the focus is on the interface between *the United Kingdom* and the EC, and also on legal issues, some events receive less attention than otherwise they would have done.[3]

[1] See Chapter 9.
[2] HC Deb, vol. 217 col. 245 (19 January 1993).
[3] For instance, political pressure placed on the Commission and other member states by France and Germany played a key role in determining the content of the Working Time Directive towards the end of the legislative process.

Again, the case study is not designed to deal with the substantive law for its own sake, but for what it reveals about the public law *process*. The directive, in its final form,[4] regulates several different aspects of employment including:

- minimum daily rest periods;
- weekly rest periods (which 'shall in principle include Sunday');
- annual leave;
- night work; and
- free health assessments for employees.

One of the purposes of the case study is to see who influenced the content of the directive, when and how. To do this in relation to all the matters covered in the directive is too unwieldy; the focus is therefore on just three aspects: the maximum 48-hour working week; Sunday working; and whether junior hospital doctors should benefit from restriction on working hours contained in the directive.

SOCIAL POLICY IN THE EC

From its inception, the EC has had a 'social dimension' including workers' rights and employment conditions. Art 117 of the EC Treaty provides that:

> Member States agree upon the need to promote improved working conditions and an improved standard of living for workers, so as to make possible their harmonization while the improvement is being maintained.
>
> They believe that such a development will ensue not only from the functioning of the common market, which will favour the harmonization of social systems, but also from the procedures provided for in this Treaty and from the approximation of provisions laid down by law, regulation or administrative action.

During the early 1990s real impetus was given to legal regulation of working conditions by the Commission, headed at the time by Jacques Delors. The policy initiative behind the Working Time Directive can be traced back to December 1989 when eleven of the (then) twelve member states made a non-binding declaration called the EC Charter of Fundamental Social Rights of Workers ('Social Charter' for short) in which commitments were made to protect the health, safety and rights of employees within the single market. Article 8 stated that 'Every worker of the European Community shall have the right to a weekly rest period . . .'. This was backed up by an 'action programme' under which the Commission was to initiate concrete proposals, and some 47 separate pieces of legislation and non-binding recommendations and resolutions, to further the general aims of the Social Charter. The UK government, under Margaret Thatcher, vehemently opposed most of these initiatives, seeing them as quite antithetical to Conservative Party deregulation policies.

[4] See text set out at end of chapter.

One piece of legislation contained in the action programme was the directive concerning certain aspects of working time. The text of the draft directive emerged from the 'cabinet' (staff of civil servants) of Mrs Vasso Papandreou, the Commissioner with responsibility for steering it through the legislative process. They had worked in close consultation with civil servants in each of the member states, as well as independent experts and representatives of interest groups: 'It is the Commission's duty to consider as many points of view as it can reasonably assimilate.'[5] On the other hand, it has been suggested that national civil servants frequently complain that although they are often consulted at an early stage by the Commission, they are then left in the dark about the development of the Commission's thinking until it is almost ready to publish the draft directive.[6]

A draft was formally adopted by the Commission at one of its (private) weekly meetings on 25 July 1990. The following day the UK press carried the story prominently. The then Secretary of State for Employment, Michael Howard MP, was hostile:[7]

> These proposals would mean arbitrary restrictions on the organisation of work which would be an artificial obstacle to new working patterns and would damage job prospects not only here but throughout the Community.

Mrs Papandreou appeared conciliatory, saying that the Commission was still open to argument that the policy contained in the directive could be achieved through informal negotiations between the two sides of industry without the need for prescriptive legislation.

The English-language version of the text of the proposed directive was received by the United Kingdom's permanent representatives (UKREP) on 28 September 1990 and was published in the *Official Journal of the European Communities* on 9 October 1990. What follows is an edited version (see OJ C 254, 9 October 1990).

No C 254/4 Official Journal of the European Communities 9.10.90

II

(Preparatory Acts)

COMMISSION

Proposal for a Council Directive concerning certain aspects of the organisation of working time

COM(90) 317 final—SYN 295

(Submitted by the Commission of 3 August 1990)

(90/C 254/05)

[5] S. A. Budd and A. Jones, *The European Community—A Guide to the Maze* (1991), p. 57.

[6] T. St J. N. Bates, 'The Drafting of European Community Legislation' [1983] Statute Law Review 24, 32.

[7] *Financial Times*, 26 July 1990, p. 2.

THE COUNCIL OF THE EUROPEAN COMMUNITIES,

Having regard to the Treaty establishing the European Economic Community, and in particular Article 118a thereof,

Having regard to the proposal from the Commission,

In cooperation with the European Parliament,

Having regard to the opinion of the Economic and Social Committee

Whereas Article 118a of the EEC Treaty provides that the Council shall adopt, by means of Directives, minimum requirements for encouraging improvements, especially in the working environment, to guarantee a better level of protection of the health and safety of workers;

Whereas, pursuant to that Article, such Directives must avoid imposing administrative, financial and legal constraints which would hold back the creation and development of small and medium-sized undertakings;

. . .

Whereas laying down minimum requirements with regard to individual periods of rest and of work improves the working conditions referred to in Article 118a

. . .

HAS ADOPTED THIS DIRECTIVE:

SECTION I

Scope and definitions

Article 1

1. This Directive applies to minimum daily, weekly and yearly rest periods and to certain aspects of night and shift work

. . .

SECTION II

Daily, weekly and yearly rest

Article 3

Member states shall adopt the necessary measures to ensure compliance with a minimum daily rest period of 11 consecutive hours per period of 24 hours.

Article 4

Member states shall adopt the necessary measures to ensure compliance, in every seven day period, with the minimum period of one rest day on average following without interruption the daily rest period as defined in Article 3 calculated over a reference period of not more than 14 days. [. . .]

Article 6

The performance of overtime must not interfere with the minimum rest periods laid down in Articles 3 and 4. [. . .]

SECTION IV

Final provisions

Article 12

Derogations from the provisions set out in Articles 3, 4 and 7 are permitted:

1. in cases of *force majeure*, or of an actual or imminent accident, provided that equivalent compensatory rest periods are granted to the employees concerned;
2. where the seasonal nature of the work performed or the features peculiar to certain activities or exceptional situations limited in time objectively conflict with the said provisions, provided that equivalent compensatory rest periods are granted within a reference period which must not exceed six months;
3. in the case of collective agreements made between employers and representatives of the workers at the appropriate levels, aiming at setting up a comprehensive set of provisions regarding the adjustment of working time corresponding to the specific conditions of the enterprise, including daily and weekly rest periods as well as night and shift work, subject to

the condition that on these specific points equivalent periods of compensatory rest are granted to the workers within a reference period that must not exceed six months. [. . .]

Article 14

Member states shall comply with this Directive by 31 December 1992 at the latest, by bringing into force the laws, regulations or administrative provisions necessary or by ensuring that the two sides of industry establish the necessary provisions through agreement, without projudice to the obligation on the member states to achieve the results obtained by this Directive.

The provisions adopted by the member states pursuant to the first paragraph shall make express reference to this Directive.

Member states shall forthwith inform the Commission of the measures taken thereunder.

Article 15

This Directive is addressed to the member states.

As you can see, this first proposal for the directive contained no express statement that the weekly day of rest was to be on a Sunday. Nor did it set any legal maximum for the total number of hours that could be worked each week. For the UK Conservative government the directive could therefore have been worse. There was, however, also no special exemption for junior hospital doctors; in 1990 their very long working weeks, often up to 100 hours, were beginning to become a political issue in the UK. Note also that the proposal envisaged that the directive would be implemented in member states by the end of 1992.

In the United Kingdom, the government quickly sprang into action to mobilize opposition to the proposed directive. At the beginning of August 1990 it announced that it would be canvassing the opinions of over 200 organizations in the United Kingdom. According to the *Financial Times*:

> the object of the exercise [was] to build up evidence on the alleged damage that the EC reforms could do to industry. This evidence [would] then be used in detailed negotiations with the Commission before the draft directive is presented to the Council of Ministers, probably in November [1990].[8]

The bodies, which included the CBI, the Association of British Chambers of Commerce, small companies and retailers, were given until September to send their evidence to the Department of Trade and Industry. As the government had imagined, the response from these consultees was overwhelmingly hostile to the Commission's proposed directive. The TUC also sent in evidence saying it enthusiastically supported the proposal. During the consultation process other issues emerged. From the outset, in addition to its rejection of the whole policy of regulation of the labour market, the UK government also pointed to an alleged defect with the procedure used. The Commission introduced its proposed directive under powers conferred by Art 118a of the EC Treaty (look back at the preamble to the draft directive, above):[9]

[8] *Financial Times*, 6 August 1990, p. 5.

[9] Note that the wording of Arts 118a and 100 was subsequently changed slightly by the Maastricht Treaty, but not so as to alter their substance.

118a (1) Member States shall pay particular attention to encouraging improvements, especially in the working environment, as regards the health and safety of workers, and shall set as their objective the harmonization of conditions in this area, while maintaining the improvements made.

(2) In order to help achieve the objective laid down in the first paragraph, the Council, acting by a qualified majority on the proposal by the Commission, in cooperation with the European Parliament and after consulting the Economic and Social Committee, shall adopt by means of directives, minimum requirements for gradual implementation, having regard to the conditions and technical rules obtaining in each of the Member States.

Such directives shall avoid imposing administrative, financial and legal constraints in a way which would hold back the creation and development of small and medium-sized undertakings.

The UK government argued very forcefully that it was illegitimate to use Art 118a as a basis for legislation of this kind as the regulation of working hours and annual leave was not really a matter to do with 'health and safety'. It claimed that, if there had to be legislation, it ought to have been introduced under Art 100:

100. The Council shall, acting unanimously on a proposal from the Commission, issue directives for the approximation of such provisions laid down by law, regulation of administrative action in Member States as directly affect the establishment or functioning of the common market.

The European Parliament and the Economic and Social Committee shall be consulted in the case of directives whose implementation would, in one or more member states, involve the amendment of legislation.

Questions

1. What were the tactical reasons for the Commission wanting the directive made under Art 118a rather than Art 100?
2. Imagine you are a journalist; write a paragraph explaining the practical differences in the legislative procedures which have to be used depending on whether a directive is based on Art 100 and, alternatively, Art 118a.
3. If there is a dispute between a member state and the Commission over the proper legal basis for proposed legislation, how is this resolved?

THE COOPERATION PROCEDURE: ART 189C

Because the proposed directive was based on Art 118a, it was to be made using the cooperation procedure (which is now set out in Art 189c of the EC Treaty).[10] After its publication, the draft directive was accordingly sent to ECOSOC and the European Parliament. The Commission requested that they deliver their opinions by December 1990.

[10] See p. 303.

Opinion from ECOSOC

No C 60/26 Official Journal of the European Communities 8.3.91

Opinion on the proposal for a Council Directive concerning certain aspects of the organization of working time

(91/C60/09)

On 5 October 1990 the Council of the European Communities, acting in pursuance of Article 118A of the EEC Treaty, asked the Economic and Social Committee for an Opinion on the above mentioned proposal.

The Committee's work on the matter was prepared by its Section for Social, Family, Educational and Cultural Affairs, which adopted its Opinion on 13 December 1990. The Rapporteur was Mrs Engelen-Kefer.

The Committee adopted the following opinion by 91 votes to 42, with 20 abstentions, at its 282nd plenary session (meeting 18 December 1990).

1. General comments

1.1. The Committee welcomes the proposal, subject to the following comments.

1.2. The draft Directive does not restrict flexibility in working time and operating hours. Nor does it address the question of reducing overall working time. It does not seek to harmonize shift and night work throughout the Community . . .

1.3. In the Committee's view there is a need in the organization of working time to strike a balance between the interests and requirements of the enterprise and those of the employees. In addition to the need for profitability, enterprises must therefore also enable their employees to organize their working time in accordance with their personal, social and cultural needs.

1.4. In view of the fact that the draft Directive covers only some aspects of the organization of working time, the Committee would draw attention to the measures announced by the Commission in their action programme for the implementation of the EC Charter including the restriction of night working especially for women (with regard to the relevant ILO standards). The Committee notes sympathetically the Commission's concern for the EC-level minimum provisions on other aspects of the organization of working time.

1.7. An extension of operating hours can undoubtedly bring cost benefits. There may, however, be considerable variations in the impact of new operating hours on costs and employment at plant level and the level of the national economy. The effects of differing social costs at national economic level ought to be taken into account.

[. . .]

1.9. The duration of the working week is also inextricably bound up with the protection of workers' health. We fail to understand why the Commission has not put forward health provisions in respect of weekend working, contrary to announcements contained in the action programme. The weekly rest period is an important component of workers' health protection. In most member states Sunday is a rest day as a matter of principle although exemptions are permitted for specific reasons in all states. In the light of developments in collective agreements, the weekly rest period should be longer than 24 hours. The Committee draws attention to ILO recommendation No 103 calling for a weekly rest period of 36 hours.

1.10. Fundamental international standards with regard to organization of working time have recently been repealed or called into question even in EC member states. There has also been a clear tendency to re-authorize night working for women and to grant general authorization for Sunday working on purely economic grounds.

1.11. Regrettably, the Commission has not taken sufficient account either of the Council of Europe's Social Charter or the ILO standards in drafting the draft Directive. ILO Conventions 14 and 106, for example, stipulate that the period of rest shall, wherever possible, be granted simultaneously to the entire staff of each undertaking. It shall, wherever possible, 'be fixed so as to coincide with the days already established by the traditions or customs of the country or district' (Convention No 14) or 'wherever possible, coincide with the day of rest by the traditions or customs of the country or district' (Convention No 106). This broadly coincides with the European Social Charter. In countries with Christian traditions the day of rest has to be Sunday.

. . .

[*The Opinion then makes specific comments on the draft Directive.*]

Done at Brussels, 18 December 1990.

The Chairman of the Economic and Social Committee
François STAEDELIN

Questions

1. What were ECOSOC's main criticisms of the draft directive?
2. In the legislative process, what function(s) does consultation with ECOSOC serve?
3. Does ECOSOC represent 'interests' not represented by MEPs sitting in the European Parliament? ECOSOC is an unelected body, its members being appointed by the Council of Ministers on the nomination of the governments of the member states. What is the significance of this?

First reading by the European Parliament

At the same time as the proposed directive was referred to ECOSOC it was also sent to the European Parliament. As a result of consideration by a committee of MEPs, and then a debate on the floor of the European Parliament, a considerable number of amendments were made to the Commission's proposed text. Verbatim reports of debates are not published in the *Official Journal*. What follows is a short extract, dealing with just a couple of amendments, from the text of the European Parliament's formal 'legislative resolution' passed in February 1991.

No C 72/86 Official Journal of the European Communities 18.3.91

Wednesday, 20 February 1991

7. Organization of working time **I
—Proposal for a directive COM(90)0317 final—SYN 295
Proposal for a Council directive concerning certain aspects of the organization of working time
Approved with the following amendments:

TEXT PROPOSED BY THE COMMISSION OF THE EUROPEAN COMMUNITIES	TEXT PROPOSED BY THE EUROPEAN PARLIAMENT
	(Amendment No 14) *Article 6*
Member States shall adopt all the necessary measures *to ensure compliance, in every seven-day period, with the minimum period of one rest day on average following without interruption the daily rest period as defined in Article 3 calculated over a reference period of not more than 14 days.*	Member States shall adopt the necessary measures to ensure **that each worker is in principle entitled to a free weekend and public holidays, except in sectors where cultural, emergency, security or technical constraints exist and where weekly leave days must be subject to negotiated agreements. In this case equivalent rest periods must be agreed on.**
	(Amendment No 16) *Article 6*
The performance of overtime must not interfere with the minimum rest periods laid down in Articles 3 and 4.	The performance of overtime must not interfere with the minimum rest periods laid down in Articles 3, **4 and 5 and must not lead to working time exceeding the average 48 hours each week calculated over a reference period of not more than 14 days.**

[. . .]

LEGISLATIVE RESOLUTION
(Cooperation procedure: first reading)
embodying the opinion of the European Parliament on the Commission proposal for a Council directive concerning certain aspects of the organization of working time

The European Parliament

—having regard to the Commission proposal to the Council COM(90) 0317 final—SYN 295,

—having been consulted by the Council pursuant to Article 118a of the EEC Treaty,

—having regard to the report of the Committee on Social Affairs, Employment and the Working Environment and the opinion of the Committee on Women's Rights,

1. Approves the Commission proposal subject to Parliament's amendments and in accordance with the vote thereon;
2. Calls on the Commission to amend its proposals accordingly, pursuant to Article 149(3) of the EEC Treaty;
3. Reserves the right to open the conciliation procedure should the Council intend to depart from the text approved by Parliament;
4. Asks to be consulted again should the Council intend to make substantial modifications to the Commission proposal;
5. Calls on the Council to incorporate Parliament's amendments in the common position that it adopts in accordance with Article 149(2)(a) of the EEC Treaty;

6. Instructs its President to forward this opinion to the Council and the Commission.

Overall, the European Parliament made over 30 amendments to the Commission's proposed directive. Many of these were substantial, including (as you can see) a work-free weekend and a maximum 48-hour working week. The European Parliament agreed on these by 156 votes to 129, with four abstentions. Some MEPs who voted against, it was reported in the press, felt that there was little point in voting for changes which were ultimately likely to be rejected by the Council.

Questions

1. In voting on the amendments, and considering proposed legislation generally, who do MEPs represent?

2. Do MEPs represent any of the same interests as ECOSOC?

SCRUTINY OF THE DRAFT DIRECTIVE IN THE UNITED KINGDOM: A SIDE SHOW?

As noted above,[11] the national parliaments of the member states have no *formal* part to play in the legislative process of a directive; but during the period when the Commission was seeking the views of ECOSOC and the European Parliament, the UK government had already initiated a process of extensive consultation. Parliament also considers some, though not all, draft legislation proposed by the Commission.[12]

House of Lords' committee

At the beginning of December 1990 the draft directive on working time was considered by sub-committee C (Social and Consumer Affairs) of the House of Lords' Select Committee on the European Communities. Unlike the House of Commons' Select Committee on European Legislation, the Lords' committee has terms of reference which enable it to consider the merits of proposed Community legislation. More than 20 different organizations submitted written evidence to the committee, including the British Medical Association, the CBI (an employers' group), the Equal Opportunities Commission, the Low Pay Unit, the KSSC and some companies including the TSB Group plc. Many of the memoranda responded to the specific questions that had been posed by the Department of Employment in its consultative paper. In addition the TUC, the Amalgamated Engineering Union and the Engineering

[11] See p. 307.

[12] Remember that the UK Parliament does have a role in validating any *domestic* legislation needed to incorporate a directive into English law once it has been adopted by the Council of Ministers.

Employers' Federation gave oral evidence to the committee on 5 December. The committee reported on 14 February 1991.[13] It stated:

> 47. The committee considers that it is open to question how far there should be a rigid approach to the question of working time. . . . It is clearly essential that the health and safety of the workforce should be protected. It may be the case that this aim may be best achieved by allowing the maximum degree of flexibility to suit local conditions and circumstances, to the benefit of employees and employers alike.

The report said that the evidence received by the committee expressed conflicting views over whether the proposals contained in the draft directive could be justified on health and safety grounds and so based, accordingly, on Art 118A of the treaty. Some suggested, for example, that working long hours with inadequate rest makes workers more accident-prone. But the committee expressed no view as to which was the proper interpretation. It also suggested that the EC should coordinate research on the long- and short-term effects of shift work and excessive hours. It found, however, that junior hospital doctors, and employees in other sectors such as catering and agriculture, appeared to be working excessive hours. The report called in particular for restrictions on hours for workers, such as air traffic controllers and train and bus drivers, whose performance could affect the safety of others. The report was not debated in the chamber of the House of Lords.

House of Commons' committee

The House of Commons' Select Committee on European Legislation has a less expansive role than the Lords' committee.[14] It cannot consider the merits of proposed Community legislation, but identifies issues of legal or political importance and recommends that some of them be debated on the floor of the House or in one of the two Standing Committees on EC matters. On 20 March 1991 European Standing Committee B considered the proposed Working Time Directive, along with other measures.

Questions

1. How does the scrutiny of Community legislation by the Lords and Commons differ from the scrutiny of

(i) domestic bills and
(ii) SIs?

2. Was the degree of scrutiny by the Lords—oral evidence taken on a single day and a 14-page report—adequate? What more could have been done?

3. Whom was the Lords' committee seeking to influence or inform? Was it the British government, or the Commission?

[13] House of Lords' Select Committee on the European Communities, Fourth Report of 1990–91.

[14] See p. 307 above.

4. When is the most effective time in the EC legislative process for the scrutiny of draft directives by the UK Parliament? Did it happen too soon in this case?

5. Given that at the end of the day the directive was going to be adopted or rejected by qualified majority voting in the Council of Ministers, does scrutiny by the UK Parliament really matter?

BACK TO THE COMMISSION

Armed with the opinion from ECOSOC and the legislative resolution of the European Parliament, and also representations from the national governments of the member states and pressure groups, the next step in the cooperation procedure was for the Commission to consider these and how, if at all, the proposed directive should be revised. Generally, over 78 per cent of amendments proposed by the European Parliament at the first reading stage are accepted by the Commission. Such decisions will be made inside the Directorate-General responsible for the draft directive, after consultations with the permanent representatives of the member states and relevant interest groups.

The Commission published its response to ECOSOC's opinion and the amendments contained in the European Parliament's resolution towards the end of April 1991.[15] The Commission did not accept ECOSOC's suggestion that Sunday should be the day of rest, nor the European Parliament's proposal that 'each worker is in principle entitled to a free weekend'. Article 4 of the Commission's original proposal therefore remained unchanged. Nor was the European Parliament's amendment to include a maximum 48-hour week accepted by the Commission. But the Commission did amend its original proposal by specifying a minimum four-week paid holiday period and it increased the minimum daily rest period from 11 to 12 hours.

This process of deciding which amendments to accept and which to reject is not a public one, though the Commission is in close contact with civil servants in the member states.

TOWARDS A COMMON POSITION OF THE COUNCIL OF MINISTERS

The way was now clear, under the cooperation procedure, for the Council of Ministers to move towards adopting a 'common position' on the proposed directive. In relation to the Working Time Directive, this proved to be a very protracted process lasting over two years. When the Council of Ministers (here, the employment ministers) met in June 1991 Michael Howard MP, for the UK government, found himself alone out of the 12 ministers in

[15] COM(91) 130 final, OJ C 124 (15 May 1991).

indicating strong opposition to the Working Time Directive; but no decisions were taken at that meeting.

In the months following the publication of the Commission's revised proposal, two further important amendments were suggested by national governments. In October 1991 the German government, backed by Luxembourg, proposed that the mandatory 36-hour rest period should, indeed, include Sundays.[16] At a UK Cabinet meeting at about this time, the Secretary of State for Employment is reported to have urged his colleagues to use every opportunity to lobby their opposite numbers in other member states against this proposal.[17] To the UK government's further dismay, the French government suggested that the directive should place an overall restriction on the length of the working week—48 hours averaged out over two months.

Employment ministers from all the member states met again as the Council of Ministers in October and December 1991. At the latter meeting, the German and French amendments were tabled. This was apparently the first time that the proposed directive had been discussed at any length at a Council meeting, though officials from member states and the Commission had been in regular, and often intense, contact for many months. As normal, the relevant Commissioner attended the Council of Ministers' meeting. United Kingdom newspapers the following day carried stories of a 'clash' between Mrs Papandreou and Mr Howard; she had, apparently, castigated him for 'ignoring the views of trade unions and revising a debate on working hours last heard at the beginning of the century'.[18] We do not, however, know for sure what actually happened as the meeting was held in private, though as was often the case, there was no shortage of official and unofficial 'leaking' of information. Other reports spoke of Mr Howard appearing more conciliatory on the principle of the directive than previously, indicating that the United Kingdom appeared to be ready to accept the directive albeit in a different form.

The proposed directive made little progress, however. This was partly because Portugal (which was lukewarm about the directive) and the United Kingdom in turn held the revolving six-month presidency of the EC. The United Kingdom especially used its position to delay any further discussion of the matter.

The Maastricht agreement

For the United Kingdom, the continued negotiations about the proposed Working Time Directive occurred at an extremely sensitive time. Throughout 1991 the governments of the member states were hammering out their views as to the future direction of the EC, culminating in a ceremony to sign

[16] *The Times*, 4 October 1991.
[17] *The Times*, 25 October 1991.
[18] *Financial Times*, 4 December 1991, p. 2.

the Treaty of European Union in the Dutch city of Maastricht in February 1992. In the United Kingdom the Conservative government had to tread cautiously for risk of disaffecting its supporters by either being seen to be 'too pro-' or 'too anti-Europe'. Prime Minister John Major, to the regret of the other member states, refused to agree to proposed provisions in the treaty which were to provide specific clauses enabling directives to be made giving effect to parts of the Social Charter that had been agreed by the other eleven member states in 1989. The compromise was for a 'Social Chapter' to be included as a Protocol at the end of the main treaty provisions. The eleven other member states signed it, so extending the qualified majority voting procedure in the Council of Ministers (which then currently only applied to health and safety matters) to areas such as general working conditions. The United Kingdom opted out from the Social Protocol, flatly refusing to lose its power of veto in the Council of Ministers over legislation on working conditions and sex equality at work. It was envisaged that this would mean that the eleven other member states would proceed, using the normal Community legislative process and institutions, to agree on policy and laws relating to minimum employment conditions. The United Kingdom would neither take part in the decision-making process[19] nor be bound by directives and regulations which emerged. This opt-out could not, however, halt the Working Time Directive, which was already well on its way through the EC legislative process. Even if the Social Chapter had then been in place, presumably the Commission would still have chosen to base the Working Time Directive on the health and safety provisions of Art 118a, which already specified the co-operation procedure and qualified majority voting in the Council of Ministers.

Continuing negotiations

Throughout the discussions about the Maastricht agreement, the draft Working Time Directive continued to be considered under the auspices of the Council of Ministers by working groups of civil servants from member states and the Commission, coordinated by COREPER. In cases where the officials from each of the national governments agree on the draft legislation, the adoption of a common position by the Council is normally a formality. Where they do not, considerable discussion and disagreement may occur at ministerial level, as occurred here.

By April 1992 there were signs that some progress on the Working Time Directive might be made in the Council of Ministers. As before, we have to rely on leaks to know what happened at the meeting. Spokespeople for other member states claimed that the United Kingdom had accepted the 48-hour maximum working week in principle, but this was denied by Gillian Shephard

[19] As a Commissioner is reported to have put it acidly, the UK minister will be asked to leave the room while the other members of the Council of Ministers discussed proposed legislation relating to the Social Chapter.

MP (who had by then replaced Mr Howard as Secretary of State for Employment). She claimed that it was other governments which had made concessions, conceding that the weekly day of rest stipulated in the directive did not have to be on a Sunday.[20] In the months which followed Mrs Shephard spent considerable time and effort lobbying employment ministers in the other member states. In particular she made several trips to Paris to meet with her French counterpart, Mme Martine Aubry, for bilateral talks on the directive.

In London on 22 June 1992 a Cabinet committee of senior ministers met to finalize the United Kingdom's negotiating stance at the Council of Ministers' meeting two days later.[21] When the Council met on 24 June 1992, however, no concrete progress was made 'despite a significant amount of negotiated compromise reported as having been achieved'.[22] Portugal, which held the presidency of the EC, tried to broker compromise with a suggestion that the United Kingdom (and also Ireland) could opt for a ten-year exemption from implementing the directive, during which time workers could volunteer to work more than a 48-hour week. Other member states would introduce the directive within three years. According to the *Financial Times* the directive 'limped its way towards the EC statute book':[23]

> The UK government has succeeded in stripping out what it found most objectionable, and the United Kingdom and European employers' bodies have generally welcomed the outcome for a directive that most of them opposed in principle. Equally, the trade union vision of a net of basic Europe-wide minimum standards at work has edged forward enough for Mr Norman Willis, president of the European Trades Union Congress, to hail the agreement as a 'major step'.

Negotiations at ministerial level appeared to be reaching areas of compromise. The next meeting of the Council was in December 1992, when, coincidentally, the United Kingdom held the revolving six-monthly presidency of the Community. This meant that the United Kingdom controlled both the timing of Council of Ministers' meetings and, to a large extent, the agenda at those meetings. Mrs Shephard failed to include discussion of the directive on the agenda. This was highly unusual; normally a Council includes in its agenda all points the Commission asks it to. At the press conference after that meeting Mrs Papandreou, the Commissioner responsible for the directive, could hardly mask her disappointment and anger, saying that 'the British presidency has been effective to its aim which was to make as few decisions as possible'. Answering a journalist who asked her if one could speak of 'deliberate sabotage', the Commissioner replied pointedly: 'Not very well; as the United Kingdom, they did their job.'[24]

[20] *Financial Times*, 1 May 1992, p. 1. See also Mrs Shephard's letter to *The Independent* on 13 May 1992 denying any concessions on the 48-hour week had been made.
[21] *Financial Times*, 23 June 1992, p. 11.
[22] *New Law Journal*, 7 August 1992, p. 1132.
[23] 26 June 1992, p. 2.
[24] 'Europe' No. 5872 (new series), 5 December 1992, p. 9.

The UK presidency of the EC and subsidiarity

Just as a year previously discussions on the proposed Working Time Directive had become wrapped up with the broader debates about what should be included in the Maastricht agreement, so in late 1992 the proposed directive became linked to the general agenda the UK government wished to pursue during its six-month presidency of the EC. In the autumn of 1992 Douglas Hurd MP, the UK Foreign Secretary, announced 'a far reaching initiative to push back the limits of European Community influence by asking Whitehall departments to list powers that they want returned from Brussels to national governments'.[25] *The Independent* reported that 'the Department of Employment has made it clear that it is strongly opposed to the Working Time Directive . . . Ministers at the DoE want the EC's competence in employment policy limited to issues of health and safety and freedom of movement.'[26] By November 1992, the *Financial Times* was able to write that the 'Community's social action plans succumb to sabotage and recession':[27]

> The 'social dimension' of the EC relaunched by Mr Jacques Delors in 1989 is proving a disappointment to many of its supporters, especially Europe's trade unions. Slower [economic] growth in Europe and successful sabotage by Britain has ensured that only a small number of key measures contained in the 1989 social action programme have been adopted. . . . Some of the leading strategists inside the European Commission's Directorate-General 5—the social affairs directorate—privately speculate about a less ambitious approach to legislation. Social affairs officials appear to have taken some of the British criticisms about over-centralised, over-prescriptive, legislation to heart. They are thus concentrating their attention on the idea—included in the social chapter [of the Maastricht agreement]—that the European Trades Union Congress (ETUC) and Unice, the European employers' body, should agree the details of the European social employment law between themselves.
>
> This idea, with the Commission itself merely laying down general objectives, is likely to appeal to whoever takes over from Ms Vasso Papandreou, the current social affairs commissioner from Greece.
>
> . . . Even the Working Time Directive, which is unlikely to be passed this year [1992] under the British presidency but will probably be passed early next year [1993], has some useful protection for workers forced to work dangerously long hours, and might encourage more job creation and less overtime when the upturn comes.

David Goodhart concluded his report by writing that:

> like so much else in the EC, enthusiasm for the social dimension waxes and wanes. After the spurt of the late 1980s the outlook for the social dimension is currently bleak, but it would be foolish to write its obituary.

By December 1992 (ten months after the Maastricht agreement) an intergovernmental summit was being held in Edinburgh, under the UK presidency. The *Financial Times* headlined with 'Burning the House that Jacques

[25] *The Independent*, 2 August 1992, p. 2.
[26] 2 August 1992, p. 2.
[27] 19 November 1992, p. 2.

built: United Kingdom plans to torch 71 pieces of EC law at the altar of subsidiarity'.[28]

> The British government wants to throw 71 pieces of EC legislation on the bonfire at the Edinburgh summit this week, to put national governments firmly in control of Europe. As details leaked out of the scale of United Kingdom plans to roll back Community power, the European Commission was preparing a pre-emptive strike with its own more modest list of 24 EC proposals to be burnt at the altar of 'subsidiarity'. ... At the Edinburgh summit [EC leaders] hope to agree on a division of EC power in line with subsidiarity—the notion that decisions should be taken at European level only when national or local action would be ineffectual. ... Draft directives on part-time work, the employment of young people, and working time would all be scrapped ... Mr Delors' riposte, which the Commission will discuss tomorrow, is a careful mix of bread and circus. Trivia, such as the harmonisation of shoe-labelling and changeovers to summer time ... would be torched. But in the 'green' or social policy Brussels plans to offer up only the zoos directive and subcontracting rules.

Continuing negotiations on the Working Time Directive

In January 1993, when Denmark took over the presidency of the EC from the UK government, there was something of a shift in priorities—with social policy much more to the fore.[29] Mrs Papandreou, who had stepped down from the Commission, was replaced by a new Commissioner for Social Affairs, Mr Padraig Flynn (from Ireland). It was reported that he was determined to get progress on the proposed Working Time Directive.

> According to senior European Commission officials, Mr Flynn has been considering whether to redraft the legislation. But following a meeting of social affairs ministers in Copenhagen [on 28 January 1993], he said he would await the report of the working group set up [in June 1992] to resolve outstanding 'technical' differences between France and Germany.[30]

Common position finally agreed

Finally, a date was set for discussion by the Council of Ministers in June 1993. The United Kingdom still had points of strong opposition to the proposed directive and was reported to be making 'last ditch' attempts to secure changes. In particular it was still fighting for total exclusion from the rules for all work at sea and for doctors in training.[31] There were 'high level negotiations between the Commission and the UK government'.[32] On 1 June

[28] 8 December 1992, p. 2.
[29] *Financial Times*, 29 January 1993, p. 2.
[30] *Financial Times*, 29 January 1993, p. 2. The disagreement between France and Germany was over the period in which working hours should be calculated so that *on average* the maximum legal working week would be 48 hours.
[31] *Financial Times*, 29 May 1993, p. 2. The UK government had already decided to cut maximum hours for junior doctors to 56 by 1996.
[32] Loc. cit.

1993 the Council of Ministers formally agreed, without any further debate, on its common position in favour of the Working Time Directive. David Hunt MP (who had taken over from Mrs Shephard as Secretary of State for Employment) abstained in the vote; ministers from the other eleven member states voted in favour. Some 'Euro-sceptics' in the UK Conservative Party would have preferred Mr Hunt to vote against the directive.

It was a defeat for the Conservative government, though it put on a brave face, arguing that 'the Working Time Directive has been so watered down that it will have virtually no effect in Britain'.[33] There was an express exemption for 'the activities of doctors in training' (Art 1.3); and employees are allowed to volunteer to work longer than 48 hours a week, at least until 2003 (Art 18). But the weekly period of rest was 'in principle to include Sunday' (Art 5).

After the vote (which as normal was taken behind closed doors), the Council issued a terse 300-word press release merely listing the matters discussed at the meeting and the agreements which had been reached, including the common position on the Working Time Directive. Commissioner Flynn was rather more expansive at a press conference, welcoming the Council's adoption of a common position.[34] When asked by a journalist how the Commission could possibly justify four and a half pages of derogation, he explained that:

> the Commission has always recognised the need for flexibility in applying the general principles laid down in the directive to specific circumstances and proposed derogations . . . The Council has chosen to go into considerable detail in defining the areas where derogations are possible and I do not think that was necessarily a good idea. However, the scope for those derogations is not significantly wider than was contained in the original proposal and while lacking the conciseness of the Commission's proposal it does have greater clarity. And you must remember that in nearly all cases where derogations are allowed, they are conditional on the worker being given equivalent compensatory rest.
>
> There are of course those who say that the Commission's original proposal was weak and that the text agreed today was weaker still. With regard to both those points I would point out that politics is the art of the possible. . . . while the Commission is not happy with some of the changes made, in particular the exclusion of a number of sectors from the scope of the directive, the introduction of a maximum working week of 48 hours is a considerable strengthening of the directive. So taken as a whole I believe that it is a good package and I will be recommending it to the European Parliament, when it goes there for a second reading.[35]

In a statement released after the Council meeting, the UK government confirmed what it had threatened for most of the three-year-long legislative process: that it would challenge the legality of the directive before the ECJ. Had the directive been introduced under Art 100 of the Treaty, as the UK government claimed it should have been, the United Kingdom would have

[33] *Glasgow Herald*, 1 June 1993, p. 9.
[34] Reuter's, 2 June 1993.
[35] RAPID, 2 June 1993.

been able to use its veto to reject the proposed directive. But because it was based on the health and safety provisions of Art 118a, to which the qualified majority voting procedure applied, Britain had no power to stop the directive which was supported by all other member states. The use of Art 100 and the consultation procedure would also have meant that the Council of Ministers would have had the last word on the content of the directive (assuming it had adopted it). But under Art 118a and the cooperation procedure, the Council was obliged to report its 'common position' on the directive to the European Parliament for further scrutiny.

COMMUNICATION TO THE EUROPEAN PARLIAMENT

The cooperation procedure, Art 189a, provides that:

> If, within three months of such communication, the European Parliament approves this common position or has not taken a decision within that period, the Council shall definitively adopt the act in question in accordance with the common position.

At this stage the European Parliament had three options.

(1) It could approve the common position without suggesting any amendments. Given the highly controversial nature of the Working Time Directive, this was unlikely.

(2) The European Parliament had power to reject the Council's common position outright; if this happened, the Council of Ministers would only be able to adopt the proposed directive if the ministers were unanimous in supporting it, which of course they were not. A significant number of MEPs believed that the proposal for the Working Time Directive had become too watered down and were prepared to follow this option.

(3) The European Parliament could make further amendments to the proposed directive. It would then be up to the Commission to decide which, if any, of these amendments to accept and put the revised text to the Council of Ministers where there would be a vote to adopt it by the qualified majority procedure.

It was this last option which the European Parliament favoured. The Council's common position was considered first by the Parliamentary Committee on Social Affairs in late October 1993. The Social Affairs Commissioner Mr Flynn spoke to the committee; he is reported to have 'underscored the usefulness of this Directive, recalling that it had been very difficult to achieve a compromise within the Council'.[36] He warned that if at this second-reading stage the European Parliament contested any significant aspects of the compromise, there was a risk that the whole package would come undone. Mr Flynn gave several assurances to MEPs, including that the directive would contain a 'non-regressive clause' (which would ensure that current

[36] Agency Europe, 27 October 1993.

protections enjoyed by workers in any member state would not be reduced once the directive was implemented). The committee of MEPs recommended that, subject to this and other amendments, the European Parliament should not reject the Council's common position.

The Parliament, in plenary session, voted on the Council's common position two days later. Socialist MEPs made a proposal that the Council's common position be rejected. But the Parliament approved almost all the recommendations of the committee, including that junior hospital doctors be included within the scope of the directive. In all 19 amendments were made.

RE-EXAMINATION BY COMMISSION

Under the cooperation procedure, it was for the Commission to decide which, if any, of the European Parliament's amendments should be incorporated into the text to be put before the Council of Ministers. The Commission accepted some of the more minor amendments made by the European Parliament, but rejected all the major ones. Thus, the European Parliament's suggested non-regressive clause was included in the revised text, but not its amendment to include hospital doctors. The Commission made it clear, however, that it would bring forward another directive to deal specifically with hospital staff.[37] The Commission then sent its reconsidered proposed directive, together with a statement of its reasons, to the Council of Ministers for final adoption.[38]

DEFINITIVE ADOPTION BY THE COUNCIL OF MINISTERS

The way was now clear for the Council of Ministers to adopt the directive. This it did on 23 November 1993 without discussion. The final text of the directive was published in the *Official Journal* on 13 December 1993.[39]

COUNCIL DIRECTIVE 93/104/EC
of 23 November 1993
concerning certain aspects of the organization of working time

THE COUNCIL OF THE EUROPEAN UNION,

Having regard to the Treaty establishing the European Community, and in particular Article 118a thereof,

Having regard to the proposal from the Commission,

In cooperation with the European Parliament,

[37] *Glasgow Herald*, 28 October 1993, p. 4.
[38] COM(93) 578 final.
[39] Directive 93/104/EC, 1993 OJ L 307.

Having regard to the opinion of the Economic and Social Committee,

Whereas Article 118a of the Treaty provides that the Council shall adopt, by means of directives, minimum requirements for encouraging improvements, especially in the working environment, to ensure a better level of protection of the safety and health of workers;

Whereas, under the terms of that Article, those directives are to avoid imposing administrative, financial and legal constraints in a way which would hold back the creation and development of small and medium-sized undertakings;

Whereas the provisions of Council Directive 89/391/EEC of 12 June 1989 on the introduction of measures to encourage improvements in the safety and health of workers at work are fully applicable to the areas covered by this Directive without prejudice to more stringent and/or specific provisions contained therein;

Whereas the Community Charter of the Fundamental Social Rights of Workers, adopted at the meeting of the European Council held at Strasbourg on 9 December 1989 by the Heads of State or of Government of 11 Member States, and in particular points 7, first subparagraph, 8 and 19, first subparagraph, thereof, declared that:

> '7. The completion of the internal market must lead to an improvement in the living and working conditions of workers in the European Community. This process must result from an approximation of these conditions while the improvement is being maintained, as regards in particular the duration and organization of working time and forms of employment other than open-ended contracts, such as fixed-term contracts, part-time working, temporary work and seasonal work.
>
> 8. Every worker in the European Community shall have a right to a weekly rest period and to annual paid leave, the duration of which must be progressively harmonized in accordance with national practices.
>
> 19. Every worker must enjoy satisfactory health and safety conditions in his working environment. Appropriate measures must be taken in order to achieve further harmonization of conditions in this area while maintaining the improvements made.';

Whereas the improvement of workers' safety, hygiene and health at work is an objective which should not be subordinated to purely economic considerations;

Whereas this Directive is a practical contribution towards creating the social dimension of the internal market;

Whereas laying down minimum requirements with regard to the organization of working time is likely to improve the working conditions of workers in the Community;

Whereas, in order to ensure the safety and health of Community workers, the latter must be granted minimum daily, weekly and annual periods of rest and adequate breaks;

Whereas it is also necessary in this context to place a maximum limit on weekly working hours;

Whereas account should be taken of the principles of the International Labour Organization with regard to the organization of working time, including those relating to night work;

Whereas, with respect to the weekly rest period, due account should be taken of the diversity of cultural, ethnic, religious and other factors in the Member States;

Whereas, in particular, it is ultimately for each Member State to decide whether Sunday should be included in the weekly rest period, and if so to what extent;

Whereas research has shown that the human body is more sensitive at night to environmental disturbances and also to certain burdensome forms of work organization and that long periods of night work can be detrimental to the health of workers and can endanger safety at the workplace;

Whereas there is a need to limit the duration of periods of night work, including overtime, and to provide for employers who regularly use night workers to bring this information to the attention of the competent authorities if they so request;

Whereas it is important that night workers should be entitled to a free health assessment prior to their assignment and thereafter at regular intervals and that whenever possible they should be transferred to day work for which they are suited if they suffer from health problems;

Whereas the situation of night and shift workers requires that the level of safety and health protection should be adapted to the nature of their work and that the organization and functioning of protection and prevention services and resources should be efficient;

Whereas specific working conditions may have detrimental effects on the safety and health of workers;

Whereas the organization of work according to a certain pattern must take account of the general principle of adapting work to the worker;

Whereas, given the specific nature of the work concerned, it may be necessary to adopt separate measures with regard to the organization of working time in certain sectors or activities which are excluded from the scope of this Directive;

Whereas, in view of the question likely to be raised by the organization of working time within an undertaking, it appears desirable to provide for flexibility in the application of certain provisions of this Directive, whilst ensuring compliance with the principles of protecting the safety and health of workers;

Whereas it is necessary to provide that certain provisions may be subject to derogations implemented, according to the case, by the Member States or the two sides of industry;

Whereas, as a general rule, in the event of a derogation, the workers concerned must be given equivalent compensatory rest periods,

HAS ADOPTED THIS DIRECTIVE:

SECTION I SCOPE AND DEFINITIONS

Article 1

1. This Directive lays down minimum safety and health requirements for the organization of working time.
2. This Directive applies to: (a) minimum periods of daily rest, weekly rest and annual leave, to breaks and maximum weekly working time; and (b) certain aspects of night work, shift work and patterns of work.
3. This Directive shall apply to all sectors of activity, both public and private, within the meaning of Article 2 of Directive 89/391/EEC, without prejudice to Article 17 of this Directive, with the exception of air, rail, road, sea, inland waterway and lake transport, sea fishing, other work at sea and the activities of doctors in training; . . .

Article 2

For the purposes of this Directive, the following definitions shall apply:

1. working time shall mean any period during which the worker is working, at the employer's disposal and carrying out

his activity or duties, in accordance with national laws and/or practice;

2. rest period shall mean any period which is not working time;

3. night time shall mean any period of not less than seven hours, as defined by national law, and which must include in any case the period between midnight and 5 am;

. . .

5. shift work shall mean any method of organizing work in shifts whereby workers succeed each other at the same work stations according to a certain pattern, including a rotating pattern, and which may be continuous or discontinuous, entailing the need for workers to work at different times over a given period of days or weeks;

6. shift worker shall mean any worker whose work schedule is part of shift work.

SECTION II MINIMUM REST PERIODS—OTHER ASPECTS OF THE ORGANIZATION OF WORKING TIME

Article 3

Member States shall take the measures necessary to ensure that every worker is entitled to a minimum daily rest period of 11 consecutive hours per 24-hour period.

Article 4

Member States shall take the measures necessary to ensure that, where the working day is longer than six hours, every worker is entitled to a rest break, the details of which, including duration and the terms on which it is granted, shall be laid down in collective agreements or agreements between the two sides of industry or, failing that, by national legislation.

Article 5

Member States shall take the measures necessary to ensure that, per each seven-day period, every worker is entitled to a minimum uninterrupted rest period of 24 hours plus the 11 hours' daily rest referred to in Article 3. The minimum rest period referred to in the first subparagraph shall in principle include Sunday. If objective, technical or work organization conditions so justify, a minimum rest period of 24 hours may be applied.

Article 6

Member States shall take the measures necessary to ensure that, in keeping with the need to protect the safety and health of workers:

1. the period of weekly working time is limited by means of laws, regulations or administrative provisions or by collective agreements or agreements between the two sides of industry;

2. the average working time for each seven-day period, including overtime, does not exceed 48 hours.

Article 7

[*Deals with annual leave*]

SECTION III NIGHT WORK—SHIFT WORK—PATTERNS OF WORK

[*Articles 8–13 deal with night time and shift work*]

SECTION IV MISCELLANEOUS PROVISIONS

Article 14

The provisions of this Directive shall not apply where other Community instruments contain more specific requirements concerning certain occupations or occupational activities.

Article 15

This Directive shall not affect Member States' right to apply or introduce laws, regulations or administrative provisions more favourable to the protection of the safety and health of workers or to facilitate or permit the application of collective agreements or agreements concluded between the two sides of industry which are more favourable to the protection of the safety and health of workers.

Article 16

Member States may lay down:
1. for the application of Article 5 (weekly rest period), a reference period not exceeding 14 days;
2. for the application of Article 6 (maximum weekly working time), a reference period not exceeding four months. The periods of paid annual leave, granted in accordance with Article 7, and the periods of sick leave shall not be included or shall be neutral in the calculation of the average;
3. for the application of Article 8 (length of night work), a reference period defined after consultation of the two sides of industry or by collective agreements or agreements concluded between the two sides of industry at national or regional level. If the minimum weekly rest period of 24 hours required by Article 5 falls within that reference period, it shall not be included in the calculation of the average.

Article 17

1. With due regard for the general principles of the protection of the safety and health of workers, Member States may derogate from Article 3, 4, 5, 6, 8 or 16 when, on account of the specific characteristics of the activity concerned, the duration of the working time is not measured and/or predetermined or can be determined by the workers themselves, and particularly in the case of:

(a) managing executives or other persons with autonomous decision-taking powers;

(b) family workers; or

(c) workers officiating at religious ceremonies in churches and religious communities.

2. Derogations may be adopted by means of laws, regulations or administrative provisions or by means of collective agreements or agreements between the two sides of industry provided that the workers concerned are afforded equivalent periods of compensatory rest or that, in exceptional cases in which it is not possible, for objective reasons, to grant such equivalent periods of compensatory rest, the workers concerned are afforded appropriate protection:

2.1. from Articles 3, 4, 5, 8 and 16:

(a) in the case of activities where the worker's place of work and his place of residence are distant from one another or where the worker's different places of work are distant from one another;

(b) in the case of security and surveillance activities requiring a permanent presence in order to protect property and persons, particularly security guards and caretakers or security firms;

(c) in the case of activities involving the need for continuity of service or production, particularly: (i) services relating to the reception, treatment and/or care provided by hospitals or similar establishments, residential institutions and prisons; (ii) dock or airport workers; (iii) press, radio, television, cinematographic production, postal and telecommunications services, ambulance, fire and civil protection services; (iv) gas, water and electricity production, transmission and distribution, household refuse collection and incineration plants; (v) industries in which work cannot be interrupted on technical grounds; (vi) research and development activities; (vii) agriculture;

(d) where there is a foreseeable surge of activity, particularly in: (i) agriculture; (ii) tourism; (iii) postal services;

2.2. from Articles 3, 4, 5, 8 and 16:

(a) in the circumstances described in Article 5(4) of Directive 89/391/EEC;

(b) in cases of accident or imminent risk of accident;

2.3. from Articles 3 and 5:

(a) in the case of shift work activities, each time the worker changes shift and cannot take daily and/or weekly rest periods between the end of one shift and the start of the next one;

(b) in the case of activities involving periods of work split up over the day, particularly those of cleaning staff.

3. Derogations may be made from Articles 3, 4, 5, 8 and 16 by means of collective agreements or agreements concluded between the two sides of industry at national or regional level or, in conformity with the rules laid down by them, by means of collective agreements or agreements concluded between the two sides of industry at a lower level. . . .

4. The option to derogate from point 2 of Article 16, provided in paragraph 2, points 2.1. and 2.2. and in paragraph 3 of this Article, may not result in the establishment of a reference period exceeding six months. However, Member States shall have the option, subject to compliance with the general principles relating to the protection of the safety and health of workers, of allowing, for objective or technical reasons or reasons concerning the organization of work, collective agreements or agreements concluded between the two sides of industry to set reference periods in no event exceeding 12 months. Before the expiry of a period of seven years from the date referred to in Article 18(1)(a), the Council shall, on the basis of a Commission proposal accompanied by an appraisal report, re-examine the provisions of this paragraph and decide what action to take.

Article 18

1. (a) Member States shall adopt the laws, regulations and administrative provisions necessary to comply with this Directive by 23 November 1996, or shall ensure by that date that the two sides of industry establish the necessary measures by agreement, with Member States being obliged to take any necessary steps to enable them to guarantee at all times that the provisions laid down by this Directive are fulfilled.

(b) (i) However, a Member State shall have the option not to apply Article 6, while respecting the general principles of the protection of the safety and health of workers, and provided it takes the necessary measures to ensure that:

—no employer requires a worker to work more than 48 hours over a seven-day period, calculated as an average for the reference period referred to in point 2 of Article 16, unless he has first obtained the worker's agreement to perform such work,

—no worker is subjected to any detriment by his employer because he is not willing to give his agreement to perform such work,

—the employer keeps up-to-date records of all workers who carry out such work,

—the records are placed at the disposal of the competent authorities, which may, for reasons connected with the safety and/or health of workers, prohibit or restrict the possibility of exceeding the maximum weekly working hours,

—the employer provides the competent authorities at their request with information on cases in which agreement has been given by workers to perform work exceeding 48 hours over a period of seven days, calculated as an average for the reference period referred to in point 2 of Article 16.

Before the expiry of a period of seven years from the date referred to in (a), the Council shall, on the basis of a Commission proposal accompanied by an appraisal report, re-examine the provisions of this point (i) and decide on what action to take.

(ii) Similarly, Member States shall have the option, as regards the application of Article 7, of making use of a transitional period of not more than three years from the date referred to in (a), provided that during that transitional period:—every worker receives three weeks' paid annual leave in accordance with the conditions for the entitlement to, and granting of, such leave laid down by national legislation and/or practice, and—the three-week period of paid annual leave may not be replaced by an allowance in lieu, except where the employment relationship is terminated.

(c) Member States shall forthwith inform the Commission thereof.

2. When Member States adopt the measures referred to in paragraph 1, they shall contain a reference to this Directive or shall be accompanied by such reference on the occasion of their official publication. The methods of making such a reference shall be laid down by the Member States.

3. Without prejudice to the right of Member States to develop, in the light of changing circumstances, different legislative, regulatory or contractual provisions in the field of working time, as long as the minimum requirements provided for in this Directive are complied with, implementation of this Directive shall not constitute valid grounds for reducing the general level of protection afforded to workers.

4. Member States shall communicate to the Commission the texts of the provisions of national law already adopted or being adopted in the field governed by this Directive.

5. Member States shall report to the Commission every five years on the practical implementation of the provisions of this Directive, indicating the viewpoints of the two sides of industry. The Commission shall inform the European Parliament, the Council, the Economic and Social Committee and the Advisory Committee on Safety, Hygiene and Health Protection at Work thereof.

6. Every five years the Commission shall submit to the European Parliament, the Council and the Economic and Social Committee a report on the application of this Directive taking into account paragraphs 1, 2, 3, 4 and 5.

Article 19

This Directive is addressed to the Member States.

Done at Brussels, 23 November 1993.
For the Council
The President
M. SMET

IMPLEMENTATION OF THE DIRECTIVE IN MEMBER STATES

The next stage of the legislative process of a directive moves from the Community institutions to the member states. The directive, addressed to the United Kingdom and other member states (see Art 19 of the directive, above), requires that appropriate action be taken to ensure that national law and practice is brought into conformity with the policy set down in the directive within a set time. The formula commonly used in directives is that 'Member States shall adopt the laws, regulations and administrative provisions necessary to comply with the directive'. Article 18 of the Working Time Directive, the result of several hard-fought compromises, is altogether more complicated. It allows for the policies of the directive to be met by voluntary collective agreements between employers and employees; state action is not required, though the UK government, like the governments of other member states, retains responsibility for ensuring that such agreements work in practice. A second important qualification is that individual employees may, until 2003, volunteer to work over 48 hours a week. It is unclear what will happen after this date.

UNITED KINGDOM CHALLENGE TO DIRECTIVE'S LEGALITY IN ECJ

In the normal course of events, the Community legislative process would have ended here. The UK government, however, remained bitterly opposed to the directive. In an unusual move, it challenged the legal validity of the directive before the ECJ under Art 173 of the Treaty on the grounds that the directive was made on a defective legal basis, that it breached the principle of proportionality and there was infringement of an essential procedural requirement. Views were mixed about the motives and strength of the United Kingdom's legal challenge. *The Times* reported that 'one Community minister said that Britain's legal attack on the 48-hour law "stood no chance" of succeeding. But an EC law expert said that Britain had a 50–50 chance of overturning the decision.'[40] The *Financial Times* said that 'both British and Brussels officials privately concur that the United Kingdom's legal challenge is unlikely to succeed'.[41] The UK government made it clear that it would take no steps to incorporate any part of the directive into English law until the ECJ made its final ruling. The Commission was publicly dismissive of the UK government's legal challenge, saying it was 'nothing more than a ruse'. Mr Flynn, the social affairs commissioner, was 'adamant that the threat from Britain was just an attempt to divert attention from the UK government's failure to derail his Working Time Directive'.[42]

Belgium and Spain joined the Commission in opposing the UK's application for the annulment of the directive (Case C-84/94). The ECJ heard oral argument on 16 January 1996 and on 12 March Advocate General Léger delivered his opinion to the court. He advised that there were no grounds for accepting any of the UK's legal submissions. On 12 November 1996 the ECJ delivered its judgment:

> APPLICATION for the annulment of Council Directive 93/104/EC of 23 November 1993 concerning certain aspects of the organization of working time (OJ 1993 L 307, p. 18) and, in the alternative, of Article 4, the first and second sentences of Article 5, Article 6(2) and Article 7 of that directive,
>
> THE COURT,
>
> composed of: G. C. Rodríguez Iglesias, President, G. F. Mancini, J. C. Moitinho de Almeida (Rapporteur), J. L. Murray and L. Sevón (Presidents of Chambers), C. N. Kakouris, P. J. G. Kapteyn, C. Gulmann, D. A. O. Edward, J.-P. Puissochet, G. Hirsch, P. Jann and H. Ragnemalm, Judges,

[40] 2 June 1993.
[41] 2 June 1993, p. 1.
[42] *Financial Times*, 3 June 1993, p. 2.

Advocate General: P. Léger,
Registrar: L. Hewlett, Administrator,
having regard to the Report for the Hearing,
after hearing oral argument from the parties at the hearing on 16 January 1996,
after hearing the Opinion of the Advocate General at the sitting on 12 March 1996,
gives the following

Judgment

1. By application lodged at the Court Registry on 8 March 1994, the United Kingdom of Great Britain and Northern Ireland brought an action under Article 173 of the EC Treaty for the annulment of Council Directive 93/104/EC of 23 November 1993 concerning certain aspects of the organization of working time (OJ 1993 L 307, p. 18, hereinafter 'the directive') and, in the alternative, of Article 4, the first and second sentences of Article 5, Article 6(2) and Article 7 of the directive.

2. The directive was adopted on the basis of Article 118a of the Treaty, which provides as follows: [see p. 323, above]

[. . .]

9. In support of its action, the applicant relies on four pleas, alleging, respectively, that the legal base of the directive is defective, breach of the principle of proportionality, misuse of powers, and infringement of essential procedural requirements.

The plea that the legal base of the directive is defective

10. The applicant contends that the directive should have been adopted on the basis of Article 100 of the EC Treaty, or Article 235 of the Treaty, which require unanimity within the Council.

The scope of Article 118a

11. The applicant observes in the first place that, because Article 118a of the Treaty must be regarded as an exception to Article 100—which, pursuant to Article 100a(2), is the article that covers provisions 'relating to the rights and interests of employed persons'—it must be strictly interpreted.

12. As the Court pointed out in Opinion 2/91 of 19 March 1993 ([1993] ECR I-1061, paragraph 17), Article 118a confers upon the Community internal legislative competence in the area of social policy. The existence of other provisions in the Treaty does not have the effect of restricting the scope of Article 118a. Appearing as it does in the chapter of the Treaty which deals with 'Social Provisions', Article 118a relates only to measures concerning the protection of the health and safety of workers. It therefore constitutes a more specific rule than Articles 100 and 100a. That interpretation is confirmed by the actual wording of Article 100a(1) itself, which states that its provisions are to apply 'save where otherwise provided in this Treaty'. The applicant's argument cannot therefore be accepted.

13. Second, referring to the actual wording of Article 118a, the applicant argues first that that provision permits the adoption only of directives which have a genuine and objective link to the 'health and safety' of workers. That does not apply to measures concerning, in particular, weekly working time, paid annual leave and rest periods, whose connection with the health and safety of workers is too tenuous. That interpretation is borne out by the expression 'working environment' used in Article 118a, which implies that directive based on that provision must be concerned only with physical conditions and risks at the workplace.

14. In that respect, it should be noted that Article 118a(2), read in conjunction with Article 118a(1), empowers the Council to adopt, by means of directives,

minimum requirements for gradual implementation, having regard to the conditions and technical rules obtaining in each of the Member States, with a view to 'encouraging improvements, especially in the working environment, as regards the health and safety of workers' by harmonizing conditions in this area, while maintaining the improvements made.

15. There is nothing in the wording of Article 118a to indicate that the concepts of 'working environment', 'safety' and 'health' as used in that provision should, in the absence of other indications, be interpreted restrictively, and not as embracing all factors, physical or otherwise, capable of affecting the health and safety of the worker in his working environment, including in particular certain aspects of the organization of working time. On the contrary, the words 'especially in the working environment' militate in favour of a broad interpretation of the powers which Article 118a confers upon the Council for the protection of the health and safety of workers. Moreover, such an interpretation of the words 'safety' and 'health' derives support in particular from the preamble to the Constitution of the World Health Organization to which all the Member States belong. Health is there defined as a state of complete physical, mental and social well-being that does not consist only in the absence of illness or infirmity.

16. The applicant further argues that under Article 118a(2) the Council may adopt only 'minimum requirements' for gradual implementation, having regard to the conditions and technical rules obtaining in the Member States. That provision therefore empowers the Council to adopt harmonization measures only at a level acceptable to all Member States and constituting a minimum benchmark.

17. In conferring on the Council power to lay down minimum requirements, Article 118a does not prejudge the extent of the action which that institution may consider necessary in order to carry out the task which the provision in question expressly assigns to it—namely, to work in favour of improved conditions, as regards the health and safety of workers, while maintaining the improvements made. The significance of the expression 'minimum requirements' in Article 118a is simply, as indeed Article 118a(3) confirms, that the provision authorizes Member States to adopt more stringent measures than those which form the subject-matter of Community action (see, in particular, Opinion 2/91, cited above, paragraph 18).

18. Third, the applicant argues that, in the light of previous directives based on Article 118a, that provision does not authorize the Council to adopt directives, such as that in dispute here, which deal with the question of health and safety in a generalized, unspecific and unscientific manner. Thus, Directive 89/391 established a risk assessment procedure designed to pinpoint specific areas in which action was required to safeguard the health and safety of workers. Similarly, the other directives based on Article 118a fall into two categories, namely 'individual' directives within the meaning of Article 16 of Directive 89/391 (concerning, in particular, the provision of safety and health signs at work or the regulation of risks connected with exposure to carcinogens), and directives which, whilst not based on Directive 89/391, clearly focus upon a specific health or safety problem in a specific situation.

19. It is settled case-law that what is merely Council practice cannot derogate from the rules laid down in the Treaty, and cannot therefore create a precedent binding on the Community institutions with regard to the correct legal basis (see, in particular, Case 68/86 *United Kingdom* v *Council* [1988] ECR 855, paragraph 24, and Case C-271/94 *Parliament* v *Council* [1996] ECR I-1705, paragraph 24). Moreover, measures having a general scope have been adopted on the basis of Article 118a of the Treaty, as is demonstrated in particular by Council Directive

89/654/EEC of 30 November 1989 concerning the minimum safety and health requirements for the workplace (first individual directive within the meaning of Article 16(1) of Directive 89/391/EEC) (OJ 1989 L 393, p. 1).

20. Furthermore, there is no support in the wording of Article 118a for the argument that Community action should be restricted to specific measures applicable to given groups of workers in particular situations, whilst measures for wider purposes should be adopted on the basis of Article 100 of the Treaty. Article 118a refers to 'workers' generally and states that the objective which it pursues is to be achieved by the harmonization of 'conditions' in general existing in the area of the health and safety of those workers.

21. In addition, the delimitation of the respective fields of application of Articles 100 and 100a, on the one hand, and Article 118a, on the other, rests not upon a distinction between the possibility of adopting general measures in the former case and particular measures in the latter, but upon the principal aim of the measure envisaged.

22. It follows that, where the principal aim of the measure in question is the protection of the health and safety of workers, Article 118a must be used, albeit such a measure may have ancillary effects on the establishment and functioning of the internal market (see, in particular, *Parliament* v *Council*, cited above, paragraph 32).

23. Finally, it is to be remembered that it is not the function of the Court to review the expediency of measures adopted by the legislature. The review exercised under Article 173 must be limited to the legality of the disputed measure.

24. It is in the light of those considerations that the Court must examine whether the directive was properly adopted on the basis of Article 118a of the Treaty.

The choice of legal basis for the directive

25. As part of the system of Community competence, the choice of the legal basis for a measure must be based on objective factors which are amenable to judicial review (see, in particular, Case 45/86 *Commission* v *Council* [1987] ECR 1493, paragraph 11). Those factors include, in particular, the aim and content of the measure (see, in particular, Case C-300/89 *Commission* v *Council* [1991] ECR I-2867, paragraph 10).

26. As regards the aim of the directive, the applicant argues that it represents a continuation of the Community's earlier thinking and of a series of earlier initiatives at Community level concerned with the organization of working time in the interests of job creation and reduced unemployment. It is in reality a measure concerned with the overall improvement of the living and working conditions of employees and with their general protection, and is so broad in its scope and coverage as to be capable of classification as a social policy measure, for the adoption of which other legal bases exist.

27. It is to be noted in that respect that, according to the sixth recital in its preamble, the directive constitutes a practical contribution towards creating the social dimension of the internal market. However, it does not follow from the fact that the directive falls within the scope of Community social policy that it cannot properly be based on Article 118a, so long as it contributes to encouraging improvements as regards the health and safety of workers. Indeed, Article 118a forms part of Chapter 1, headed 'Social Provisions', of Title VIII of the Treaty, which deals in particular with 'Social Policy'. This led the Court to conclude that that provision conferred on the Community internal legislative competence in the area of social policy (Opinion 2/91, cited above, paragraph 17).

28. Furthermore, as the Advocate General has demonstrated in points 85 to 90

of his Opinion, the organization of working time is not necessarily conceived as an instrument of employment policy. In this case, the fifth recital in the preamble to the directive states that the improvement of workers' safety, hygiene and health at work is an objective which should not be subordinated to 'purely economic considerations'. Were the organization of working time to be viewed as a means of combating unemployment, a number of economic factors would have to be taken into account, such as, for example, its impact on the productivity of undertakings and on workers' salaries.

29. The approach taken by the directive, viewing the organization of working time essentially in terms of the favourable impact it may have on the health and safety of workers, is apparent from several recitals in its preamble. Thus, for example, the eighth recital states that, in order to ensure the safety and health of Community workers, they must be granted minimum rest periods and adequate breaks and that it is also necessary in that context to place a maximum limit on weekly working hours. In addition, the eleventh recital states that 'research has shown that . . . long periods of night work can be detrimental to the health of workers and can endanger safety at the workplace', while the fifteenth recited states that specific working conditions may have detrimental effects on the safety and health of workers and that the organization of work according to a certain pattern must take account of the general principle of adapting work to the worker.

30. While, in the light of those considerations, it cannot be excluded that the directive may affect employment, that is clearly not its essential objective.

31. As regards the content of the directive, the applicant argues that the connection between the measures it lays down, on the one hand, and health and safety, on the other, is too tenuous for the directive to be based on Article 118a of the Treaty.

32. In that respect, it argues that no adequate scientific evidence exists to justify the imposition of a general requirement to provide for breaks where the working day is longer than six hours (Article 4), a general requirement to provide for a minimum uninterrupted weekly rest period of twenty-four hours in addition to the usual eleven hours' daily rest (Article 5, first sentence), a requirement that the minimum rest period must, in principle, include Sunday (Article 5, second sentence), a general requirement to ensure that the average working time for each seven-day period, including overtime, does not exceed forty-eight hours (Article 6(2)), and a general requirement that every worker is to have a minimum of four weeks' paid annual leave (Article 7).

33. The applicant points out in that connection that Directive 89/391 provides for employers to carry out assessments to evaluate specific risks to the health and safety of workers, taking into account the nature of the activities of the undertaking. The risk assessment procedure laid down by Directive 89/391 could not apply to the restrictions on working time contained in Section II of the contested directive (and is applicable only to a very limited extent in Section III), the provisions in question being quite simply mandatory and leaving no scope for such an assessment in order to determine whether they are to apply.

34. The applicant maintains, moreover, that unlike other provisions based on Article 118a of the Treaty, the contested measures were not referred to the Advisory Committee on Safety, Hygiene and Health Protection at Work for an opinion (on the role of such committees, it cites Case C-212/91 *Angelopharm* [1994] ECR I-171, paragraphs 31 and 32). Although consultation of that committee is not expressly provided for in cases such as this, the fact that the Council did not call on the Commission to undertake such consultation casts further doubt on the link between the directive and the health and safety of workers.

35. Finally, in the applicant's view, contrary to the requirements of Article 118a(2), the provisions of the directive do not constitute 'minimum requirements for gradual implementation, having regard to the conditiions and technical rules obtaining in each of the Member States' and do not take account of their effects on 'the creation and development of small and medium-sized undertakings'.

36. In order to deal with those arguments, a distinction must be drawn between the second sentence of Article 5 of the directive and its other provisions.

37. As to the second sentence of Article 5, whilst the question whether to include Sunday in the weekly rest period is ultimately left to the assessment of Member States, having regard, in particular, to the diversity of cultural, ethnic and religious factors in those States (second sentence of Article 5, read in conjunction with the tenth recital), the fact remains that the Council has failed to explain why Sunday, as a weekly rest day, is more closely connected with the health and safety of workers than any other day of the week. In those circumstances, the applicant's alternative claim must be upheld and the second sentence of Article 5, which is severable from the other provisions of the directive, must be annulled.

38. The other measures laid down by the directive, which refer to minimum rest periods, length of work, night work, shift work and the pattern of work, relate to the 'working environment' and reflect concern for the protection of 'the health and safety of workers'. The scope of those terms has been explained in paragraph 15 of this judgment. Moreover, as the Belgian Government has pointed out, the evolution of social legislation at both national and international level confirms the existence of a link between measures relating to working time and the health and safety of workers.

39. Legislative action by the Community, particularly in the field of social policy, cannot be limited exclusively to circumstances where the justification for such action is scientifically demonstrated (see points 165 to 167 of the Advocate General's Opinion).

40. Similarly, the applicant's argument that the directive precludes any assessment of the risks involved for certain workers or for those working in a particular sector cannot be regarded as well founded. The Community legislature did take certain special situations into account, as is demonstrated by Article 1 of the directive, which excludes certain sectors or activities from its scope; by Article 14, which excludes occupations and occupational activities where more specific Community provisions apply; and by Article 17(1) and (2) which allow derogations from Articles 3, 4, 5, 6 and 8 in respect of certain groups of workers or certain sectors of activity (see points 114 to 117 of the Advocate General's Opinion).

41. It is true that the Council did not consult the Advisory Committee on Safety, Hygiene and Health Protection at Work established by Council Decision 74/325/EEC of 27 June 1974 (OJ 1974 L 185, p. 15) with regard to the measures envisaged by the directive. However, under Article 2(1) of that decision, such consultation is intended only '[to assist] the Commission in the preparation and implementation of activities in the fields of safety, hygiene and health protection at work', and does not therefore constitute a condition precedent for action by the Council. In those circumstances, failure to consult that committee cannot be relied on to cast doubt on the link between the measures laid down by the directive and the protection of the health and safety of workers.

42. Furthermore, the provisions of the directive are 'minimum requirements' within the meaning of Article 118a of the Treaty. Whilst ensuring a certain level of protection for workers, the directive authorizes Member States in Article 15 to apply, or facilitate the application of, measures which are more favourable to the

protection of the health and safety of workers, thereby guaranteeing them a more stringent level of protection, in accordance with Article 118a(3). Similarly, Article 18(3) of the directive states that, whilst Member States may provide for different measures in the field of working time, subject to compliance with the minimum requirements it lays down, implementation of the directive does not constitute valid grounds for reducing the general level of protection afforded to workers.

43. The measures laid down by the directive are also, in accordance with Article 118a, 'for gradual implementation, having regard to the conditions and technical rules obtaining in each of the Member States'. In the first place, it is not in dispute that legislation in all the Member States includes measures on the organization of working time. Furthermore, Article 18 of the directive authorizes Member States, subject to certain conditions, not to apply, after the expiry of the time-limit for implementing the directive (23 November 1996), the provisions of Article 6 on weekly working time or, for a three-year transitional period, the provisions of Article 7 on paid annual leave, which may during that period be limited to three weeks.

44. Finally, the directive has taken account of the effects which the organization of working time for which it provides may have on small and medium-sized undertakings. Thus, the second recital in the preamble to the directive refers to the overriding requirement not to hold back the development of such undertakings. Moreover, as the Court held in its judgment in Case C-189/91 *Kirsammer-Hack* v *Sidal* [1993] ECR I-6185, paragraph 34, by providing that directives adopted in the field of health and safety of workers are to avoid imposing administrative, financial and legal constraints such as to hold back the creation and development of small and medium-sized undertakings, the second sentence of Article 118a(2) indicates that such undertakings may be the subject of special economic measures. Contrary to the view taken by the applicant, however, that provision does not prevent those undertakings from being subject to binding measures.

45. Since it is clear from the above considerations that, in terms of its aim and content, the directive has as its principal objective the protection of the health and safety of workers by the imposition of minimum requirements for gradual implementation, neither Article 100 nor Article 100a could have constituted the appropriate legal basis for its adoption.

46. The applicant further maintains that the Community legislature neither fully considered nor adequately demonstrated whether there were transnational aspects which could not be satisfactorily regulated by national measures, whether such measures would conflict with the requirements of the EC Treaty or significantly damage the interests of Member States or, finally, whether action at Community level would provide clear benefits compared with action at national level. In its submission, Article 118a should be interpreted in the light of the principle of subsidiarity, which does not allow adoption of a directive in such wide and prescriptive terms as the contested directive, given that the extent and the nature of legislative regulation of working time vary very widely between Member States. The applicant explains in this context, however, that it does not rely upon infringement of the principle of subsidiarity as a separate plea.

47. In that respect, it should be noted that it is the responsibility of the Council, under Article 118a, to adopt minimum requirements so as to contribute, through harmonization, to achieving the objective of raising the level of health and safety protection of workers which, in terms of Article 118a(1), is primarily the responsibility of the Member States. Once the Council has found that it is necessary to improve the existing level of protection as regards the health and safety of workers

and to harmonize the conditions in this area while maintaining the improvements made, achievement of that objective through the imposition of minimum requirements necessarily presupposes Community-wide action, which otherwise, as in this case, leaves the enactment of the detailed implementing provisions required largely to the Member States. The argument that the Council could not properly adopt measures as general and mandatory as those forming the subject-matter of the directive will be examined below in the context of the plea alleging infringement of the principle of proportionality.

48. Finally, as regards Article 235 of the Treaty [see p. 299, above], it is sufficient to point to the Court's case-law, which holds that that article may be used as the legal basis for a measure only where no other Treaty provision confers on the Community institutions the necessary power to adopt it (see, in particular, *Parliament* v *Council*, cited above, paragraph 13).

49. It must therefore be held that the directive was properly adopted on the basis of Article 118a, save for the second sentence of Article 5, which must accordingly be annulled.

The plea of breach of the principle of proportionality

50. The applicant points out that the Council may adopt on the basis of Article 118a of the Treaty only 'minimum requirements for gradual implementation, having regard to the conditions and technical rules obtaining in each of the Member States', and that those requirements must avoid 'imposing administrative, financial and legal constraints in a way which would hold back the creation and development of small and medium-sized undertakings'. In its submission, four broad principles are relevant in assessing whether or not the requirements imposed by the contested directive are minimum requirements within the meaning of Article 118a.

51. First, it argues, not all measures which may 'improve' the level of health and safety protection of workers constitute minimum requirements. In particular, those consisting in global reductions in working time or global increases in rest periods, whilst having a certain beneficial effect on the health or safety of workers, do not constitute 'minimum requirements' within the meaning of Article 118a.

52. Second, a provision cannot be regarded as a 'minimum requirement' if the level of health and safety protection of workers which it establishes can be attained by measures that are less restrictive and involve fewer obstacles to the competitiveness of industry and the earning capacity of individuals. In the applicant's submission, neither the Commission's proposals nor the directive provide any explanation as to why the desired level of protection could not have been achieved by less restrictive measures, such as, for example, the use of risk assessments if working hours exceeded particular norms.

53. Third, the conclusion that the measures envisaged will in fact improve the level of health or safety protection of workers must be based on reasonable grounds. In its view, the present state of scientfic research in the area concerned falls far short of justifying the contested measures.

54. Fourth, a measure will be proportionate only if it is consistent with the principle of subsidiarity. The applicant argues that it is for the Community institutions to demonstrate that the aims of the directive could better be achieved at Community level than by action on the part of the Member States. There has been no such demonstration in this case.

55. The argument of non-compliance with the principle of subsidiarity can be rejected at the outset. It is said that the Community legislature has not established that

the aims of the directive would be better served at Community level than at national level. But that argument, as so formulated, really concerns the need for Community action, which has already been examined in paragraph 47 of this judgment.

56. Furthermore, as is clear from paragraph 17 of this judgment, the applicant bases its argument on a conception of 'minimum requirements' which differs from that in Article 118a. That provision does not limit Community action to the lowest common denominator, or even to the lowest level of protection established by the various Member States, but means that Member States are free to provide a level of protection more stringent than that resulting from Community law, high as it may be.

57. As regards the principle of proportionality, the Court has held that, in order to establish whether a provision of Community law complies with that principle, it must be ascertained whether the means which it employs are suitable for the purpose of achieving the desired objective and whether they do not go beyond what is necessary to achieve it (see, in particular, Case C-426/93 *Germany* v *Council* [1995] ECR I-3723, paragraph 42).

58. As to judicial review of those conditions, however, the Council must be allowed a wide discretion in an area which, as here, involves the legislature in making social policy choices and requires it to carry out complex assessments. Judicial review of the exercise of that discretion must therefore be limited to examining whether it has been vitiated by manifest error or misuse of powers, or whether the institution concerned has manifestly exceeded the limits of its discretion.

59. So far as concerns the first condition, it is sufficient that, as follows from paragraphs 36 to 39 of this judgment, the measures on the organization of working time which form the subject-matter of the directive, save for that contained in the second sentence of Article 5, contribute directly to the improvement of health and safety protection for workers within the meaning of Article 118a, and cannot therefore be regarded as unsuited to the purpose of achieving the objective pursued.

60. The second condition is also fulfilled. Contrary to the view taken by the applicant, the Council did not commit any manifest error in concluding that the contested measures were necessary to achieve the objective of protecting the health and safety of workers.

61. In the first place, Article 4, which concerns the mandatory rest break, applies only if the working day is longer than six hours. Moreover, the relevant details, particularly the duration of the break and the terms on which it is granted, are to be laid down in collective agreements or agreements between the two sides of industry or, failing that, by national legislation. Finally, that provision may be the subject of several derogations, relating either to the status of the worker (Article 17(1)) or to the nature or characteristics of the activity pursued (Article 17(2), points 2.1 and 2.2), to be implemented by means of collective agreements or agreements concluded between the two sides of industry at national or regional level (Article 17(3)).

62. Second, the minimum uninterrupted weekly rest period of twenty-four hours provided for by the first sentence of Article 5, plus the eleven hours' daily rest referred to in Article 3, may be the subject of the same derogations as those authorized in relation to Article 4, referred to above. Further derogations relate to shift work activities and activities involving periods of work split up over the day (Article 17(2), point 2.3). In addition, the reference period of seven days may be extended to fourteen days (Article 16(1)).

63. Third, as regards Article 6(2), which provides that the average working time

for each seven-day period is not to exceed forty-eight hours, Member States may lay down a reference period not exceeding four months (Article 16(2)), which may in certain cases be extended to six months for the application of Article 17(2), points 2.1 and 2.2, and 17(3) (Article 17(4), first sentence), or even to twelve months (Article 17(4), second sentence). Article 18(1)(b)(i) even authorizes Member States, under certain conditions, not to apply Article 6.

[. . .]

66. It follows that, in taking the view that the objective of harmonizing national legislation on the health and safety of workers, while maintaining the improvements made, could not be achieved by measures less restrictive than those that are the subject-matter of the directive, the Council did not commit any manifest error.

67. In the light of all the foregoing considerations, the plea of breach of the principle of proportionality must also be rejected.

The plea of misuse of powers

68. According to the applicant, the directive encompasses a number of measures that have no objective connnection with its purported aims, and must therefore be annulled in its entirety. Those measures overshadow the very small elements—minimum daily rest periods, restrictions on maximum duration of night work—where scientific evidence indicates that there may be some causal connection with health and safety. Those two elements, in respect of which limited and specific action might have been justifiable, have instead been addressed in an unspecific, generalized, and thus unlawful manner.

69. The Court's case-law (see, in particular, Case C-156/93 *Parliament* v *Commission* [1995] ECR I-2019, paragraph 31) defines misuse of powers as the adoption by a Community institution of a measure with the exclusive or main purpose of achieving an end other than that stated or evading a procedure specifically prescribed by the Treaty for dealing with the circumstances of the case.

70. As is apparent from the Court's examination of the plea of defective legal base, the Council could properly found the directive on Article 118a of the Treaty. The applicant has failed to establish that the directive was adopted with the exclusive or main purpose of achieving an end other than the protection of the health and safety of workers.

71. In those circumstances, the plea of misuse of powers must be rejected.

The plea of infringement of essential procedural requirements

72. The applicant's primary submission is that the directive is inadequately reasoned. It does not clearly and unequivocally disclose the reasoning of the Community authority which adopted it, because it fails to demonostrate the causal connection relied on by the Community legislature between health and safety, on the one hand, and most of the measures it contains concerning working time (Articles 3, 4, 5, 6(2), 7 and 8), on the other. Nor moreover, does the preamble to the directive explain why Community action was necessary.

73. In the alternative, the applicant submits that the directive is defectively reasoned, in that the legislature should have explained that many of its elements were concerned with the improvement of the living and working conditions of employees or with the social dimension of the internal market, rather than referring, as it did, to the health and safety of workers.

74. As to those arguments, whilst the reasoning required by Article 190 of the EC Treaty must show clearly and unequivocally the reasoning of the Community author-

ity which adopted the contested measure so as to enable the persons concerned to ascertain the reasons for it and to enable the Court to exercise judicial review, the authority is not required to go into every relevant point of fact and law (see Case C-122/94 *Commission* v *Council* [1996] ECR I-881, paragraph 29).

75. In the case of the directive, the preamble clearly shows that the measures introduced are intended to harmonize the protection of the health and safety of workers.

76. Thus, the first, third, fourth and ninth recitals in the preamble refer respectively to Article 118a of the Treaty, to Directive 89/391 on the introduction of measures to encourage improvements in the safety and health of workers at work, to the Community Charter of the Fundamental Social Rights of Workers, and to the principles of the International Labour Organization with regard to the organization of working time.

77. So, too the fifth, seventh, eighth and eleventh to fifteenth recitals point to a direct link between the various measures on the organization of work laid down by the directive and the protection of the health and safety of workers.

78. The argument that the Council should have included in the preamble to the directive specific references to scientific material justifying the adoption of the various measures which it contains must be rejected.

79. As stated in paragraph 39 of this judgment, Article 118a does not require scientific proof to be produced for every measure adopted on the basis of that provision. Moreover, the Court has held that, where a contested measure clearly discloses the essential objective pursued by the institution, it would be pointless to require a specific statement of reasons for each of the technical choices made by it (see Case C-122/94 *Commission* v *Council*, cited above, paragraph 29).

80. Nor can the argument to the effect that the preamble to the directive fails to explain the need for Community action be accepted as well founded.

81. As has been pointed out in paragraphs 75 to 77 of this judgment, the preamble to the directive shows that the Council considered it necessary, in order to ensure an improved level of health and safety protection of workers, to take action to harmonize the national legislation of the Member States on the organization of working time. As stated in paragraph 47, the pursuit of such an objective, laid down in Article 118a itself, through harmonization by means of minimum requirements, necessarily presupposes Community-wide action.

82. Finally, as regards the arguments concerning alleged errors of assessment in the preamble to the directive, it is sufficient to refer to the Court's case-law to the effect that such questions relate not to the issue of infringement of essential procedural requirements but to the substance of the case (see, in particular, Joined Cases C-296/93 and C-307/93 *France and Ireland* v *Commission* [1996] ECR I-795, paragraph 76), and to recall that those questions have been examined in the context of the plea of defective legal base.

83. It follows that the plea of infringement of essential procedural requirements must also be rejected.

84. The application must accordingly be dismissed, save as regards the second sentence of Article 5 of the directive, which is to be annulled.

The UK government reacts

This account of the Working Time Directive must conclude here. At the time of writing (November 1996), its application to the UK remains uncertain.

Under Community law, the UK was required to incorporate the directive into national law by 23 November 1996. This it did not do. The Conservative government announced that, at the forthcoming IGC, it will demand that member states agree to amend the EC Treaty. The UK wants exemption from the Working Time Directive and agreement that in the future health and safety legislation be subject to unanimous voting in the Council of Ministers (rather than qualified majority voting). If the other member states did not agree to this, the UK says it will block agreement on other issues at the IGC.

Will this be a short-lived crisis? A general election must be held in the UK before May 1997; the Labour Party, which opinion polls suggest is likely to win, does not oppose the directive. Indeed some suggest that the Conservative government's stance may have more to do with domestic politics—being seen to be 'strong against European interference in British affairs'—than with the Working Time Directive itself.

Question

Writing in *The Economist* (23 November 1996, p. 49) soon after the ECJ's judgment, Sir Nicholas Henderson, an eminent retired British diplomat, said:

> Not content with the summer drama of the beef crisis, the government now seems bent on defying its European partners, the European Commission, and the European Court over a directive on working hours. Why did the government go to the court in the first place if it had no intention of abiding by the court's judgment? The current policy is strange for a government that is committed to law and order . . .

Do you agree?

WHERE TO GO FROM HERE

This chapter concludes Part B of the book. To consider in more detail the role of the ECJ in the public law system, you should now turn to Chapters 29 and 30.

Part C

CHALLENGING AND SCRUTINIZING PUBLIC POWER

15

CHALLENGING AND SCRUTINIZING PUBLIC POWER: AN OVERVIEW

The ability to challenge government and to seek redress against official action or inaction is a hallmark of a mature constitutional system. Indeed, the very idea of limited and accountable government implies that citizens have opportunities to criticize public bodies and to seek redress for the consequences of decisions which adversely affect them. It implies also that public bodies are forced to respond to challenge and criticism by justifying their actions and correcting errors that they are found to have made. Redress and accountability therefore go hand in hand. Systems of redress are central to achieving accountability and accountability is a crucial element in obtaining redress. This is made clear by Oliver's explanation that accountability is the obligation to 'give an account or explanation of actions and, where appropriate' to suffer the consequences, take the blame or undertake to put matters right if it should appear that errors have been made'.[1] The obligation to give an account, to answer questions, to explain and to justify actions or plans ('explanatory accountability')[2] arises or ought to arise throughout the policy cycle.[3] The obligation to take blame and put matters right ('amendatory accountability')[4] arises if after decisions are made or actions are taken they are criticized and challenged.[5] This aspect of accountability assumes that public bodies can be questioned, that methods exist for identifying error, forcing explanation, recognizing what needs to be done, and providing redress for those who have suffered. It is with these matters that this part of the book is concerned.

There is no single system of redress

By now it should be evident that there is no single system of redress within the United Kingdom's constitution. The constitution has not been designed

[1] D. Oliver, *Government in the United Kingdom* (1991), p. 22.
[2] Geoffrey Marshall in David Butler and A. H. Halsey (eds.), *Policy and Politics* (1978), pp. 61–2.
[3] On which see generally Chapter 4.
[4] Colin Turpin, *British Government and the Constitution* (1995, 3rd edn.), p. 360.
[5] Because it assumes the need to account for action already taken, Turpin says that 'amendatory accountability' is 'evidently retrospective': Turpin, note 4 above.

and carefully planned but has evolved incrementally over the centuries. As it has done so various forms of redress have been developed. Some (such as statutory tribunals set up to deal with certain complaints from particular administrative schemes) have been specifically crafted to deal with particular types of problems; others (such as judicial review) have been adapted as circumstances have changed. Some mechanisms operate in the political context (MPs, parliamentary debates), others are purely legal; some are concerned solely with the quality of administrative procedures (the local and parliamentary ombudsmen), others with the merits of particular decisions affecting individuals (should X obtain income support, should Y be allowed into the country?); some procedures allow complaint to the body which caused the grievance, whereas others pride themselves on being independent. The picture is one of diversity rather than uniformity. It is a patchwork in which forms of redress may overlap, offering several opportunities of challenge in some contexts, but little or none, and correspondingly little or no, accountability in others.[6]

Overlap between systems can have positive effects as when Simon Cotton's successful judicial review enabled the JCSI to spot that the Board and Lodging Regulations were *ultra vires*, something the committee had overlooked when it had first scrutinized them.[7] Also, in the Pergau Dam case[8] the World Development Movement's legal challenge became possible when in select committee hearings Sir Tim Lankester (the senior civil servant in the Office of Overseas Development) revealed that he had advised against the decision to authorize expenditure on the Pergau Dam project. This advice was later vindicated when the court held the Foreign Secretary's decision to do so was *ultra vires*.

More negative effects of overlap occur when citizens try to use one set of procedures (say resort to ombudsmen) only to be told that another process (such as use of judicial review) is more appropriate. It is not only laypeople who find themselves being caught out in this way. Lawyers can also fall foul of procedural complexities, as when litigants are told that their case will be thrown out of court because the wrong court procedure has been used.[9] In such cases layers of redress can easily appear to operate as barriers designed more to stifle and frustrate than to remedy and cure.

Although the systems of redress and accountability are diverse and complex, as we examine the institutions we will notice that several themes recur in our discussion. It is useful to identify the most important of these at the outset.

Identifying the purpose and role of systems of redress

First there is the question of purpose and role: what is the function of the various systems and what role do they perform within the constitution? Do

[6] Consider e.g. the position of bodies which are not amenable to judicial review or political control, on which see further Chapter 22.

[7] See Chapters 11 and 27.

[8] *R v Secretary of State for Foreign and Commonwealth Affairs ex p World Development Movement* [1995] 1 WLR 386; see further at p. 52, n. 60.

[9] On procedural exclusivity, see p. 514.

they work primarily to redress particular grievances or is their role a more general one of working to improve the 'quality' of government decision-making? Or do they try to do both? It is now widely recognized that effective complaints procedures improve the overall quality of government decision-making.[10] Judicial review provides both an avenue of challenge and is at the same time a resource for public authorities, enabling them to identify their legal obligations. This in turn ought also to reduce the risk of legal challenge and thereby help to improve the efficiency of administration. In this sense accountability and efficiency are compatible and public bodies should adopt a positive attitude to scrutiny and not regard it as a threat.

However the extent to which institutions such as tribunals, the parliamentary and local ombudsmen and the courts can contribute to the quality of government is limited. In particular these bodies only operate if and when they are used. The ombudsmen only examine administrative procedures if people take complaints to them (and there is some concern that too few complaints are being referred to the parliamentary ombudsmen). Likewise, the courts can only review government's actions if challenges are made. Had Simon Cotton not challenged the Board and Lodging Regulations they would probably have been brought into effect without their legality ever being questioned. Had the World Development Movement not sought judicial review the government's decision to spend millions of pounds of taxpayers' money to fund the Pergau Dam project would not have been declared unlawful.[11] This is one reason why such procedures can only impose a partial and sporadic form of accountability.

By contrast, some institutions focus on general practice and policy rather than on the impact of particular decisions on individuals. Select committees can take the initiative and investigate policy without having to wait for a grievance to be referred to them and PQs can always be asked. There are some who argue that ombudsmen and courts should also be able to take a more positive and proactive stance, perhaps being able to investigate or audit governmental actions even though particular complaints have not been made. Others argue that this would fundamentally alter the role of these bodies and they should concentrate on dealing with actual grievances. How, for example, could judges become involved with checking that procedures are lawful? What would happen if having certified that a government department is working well they are faced with an individual challenge alleging that its procedures are unfair? As we shall see such debates force us to consider what institutions are intended to do. This is a matter which is often the subject of intense disagreement.

[10] *Citizen's Charter* (1991), Cm 1599. The Charter sets out standards of service expected from public bodies and emphasizes the importance of complaints procedures. See further A. Barron and C. Scott, 'The Citizen's Charter Programme' (1992) 55 MLR 526.

[11] On the Pergau Dam case, see n. 8 above.

Access

A second recurring theme is access. If forms of redress are not accessible they will not be used, grievances will be unresolved and the quality of government will suffer. However, access is often a serious problem. For example, it may be difficult to find an MP who will refer a complaint to the Parliamentary Ombudsman;[12] rights to appeal to tribunals might not be used because appeals are considered to be (often wrongly) a waste of time and energy, and tribunals thought to be too formal and off-putting;[13] resort to the courts may be out of the question because of the costs involved or because suitable legal advice is not available. As noted earlier, multiple layers of redress may also create barriers frustrating even the most determined complainant or litigant. Each of these problems presents obstacles to people who want to seek redress from government. For this reason alone, they are important. They also undermine levels of accountability and threaten the overall quality of government.

Obtaining information

A third recurring issue concerns obtaining evidence against government. Davis wrote that 'openness is the enemy of arbitrariness'.[14] One reason is that openness permits scrutiny of decisions, which in turn enables criticism and forces decision-takers to justify their actions. Unfortunately the culture of government in the United Kingdom does not encourage openness. Despite incremental improvements,[15] secrecy and confidentiality are still regarded as necessary for effective government. One consequence is that select committees may find themselves unable to secure the attendance of witnesses or obtain information. Another is that citizens are often prevented from mounting effective legal challenges because they lack the evidence needed to support their case.[16] For this reason, institutions such as the ombudsmen may be more user-friendly than the courts because once a complaint is accepted the ombudsmen will carry out the investigations into the facts and free the individual of this burden. This brings us to the question of procedures.

What procedures are appropriate

In the chapters which follow we examine institutions which adopt various forms of procedure:[17] some work in public, some in private; some adopt investigative techniques, others are adversarial; some involve oral evidence and cross-examination of witnesses, others do not. We have just noted that ombudsmen operate by investigation. They go into the relevant offices and will question the decision-takers and read the files. But this process does not

[12] There is no direct access to the Parliamentary Ombudsman; complaints must be referred by MPs: see p. 423.

[13] See p. 451.

[14] K. C. Davis, *Discretionary Justice* (1969), discussed at p. 147 above.

[15] See p. 495.

[16] See p. 494.

[17] See Gabrielle Ganz, *Administrative Procedures* (1974).

take place in public and it is also very time-consuming. There is little publicity and certainly nothing resembling the drama of a direct and public confrontation between a select committee and a minister or official. As well as being public and often dramatic, select committees are able to call upon a wide variety of witnesses. By contrast with both ombudsmen and select committees, the courts are adversarial rather than investigative bodies. Two parties appear before the judge who has the task of deciding which of the two sides is to win. The parties define the issues to be considered and are responsible for presenting the evidence which they regard as being relevant to the court. In judicial review the procedure is based on written submissions and the legal arguments of counsel. Witnesses rarely appear to be cross-examined and there is very little of the drama that people might associate with a criminal trial. The process does, however, allow careful scrutiny of the legal justifications for governmental action.

The point is that different procedures achieve different results. A public cross-examination of ministers, as happens at Question Time in the Commons and in select committee hearings, might be dramatic, but it may not be as revealing as a thorough and low-profile ombudsman investigation. Judicial review may not lead to new factual revelations, but it can provide an extremely rigorous scrutiny leading ultimately to a definitive finding that government has acted unlawfully, a funding to which the government is forced to respond. As we shall see, matters of procedure can themselves attract considerable debate; although often regarded as too technical for students, public lawyers must always be aware of their importance. In particular they must ask: do procedures achieve what they set out to achieve? Are the procedures fair?

Participation

Consideration of these questions in turn raises a further dimension regarding citizens' ability to participate in government. Redress and accountability are central to current conceptions of democracy. They imply that people and groups are able to participate in the process of government, not only by voting for representatives at periodical elections, but also by taking a more active part in the life of the nation, by bringing matters to MPs' attention; by using institutions such as the ombudsmen; by presenting arguments about the legality of governmental actions to the courts. By doing such things citizens contribute to, and participate in, the constitutional life of the state. The extent to which procedures of redress encourage or hinder this participation is indeed a measure of the system's democratic vitality. It should not be assumed, for instance, that because there are relatively small numbers using a process such as the ombudsmen or the courts, all is well.

Questions of impact

One of the key questions asked throughout this part of the book is: what can redress achieve? What will citizens achieve by complaining, by appealing, or by seeking judicial review? At one level the answer to this is straightforward. It involves examining the formal remedies, if any, which the various forms of redress provide. An appeal to a tribunal against a refusal of benefit may lead to that decision being reversed and the money paid; a justified complaint to the ombudsmen may lead to compensation, but will more usually only produce an apology and some publicity; judicial review proceedings might produce a declaration that a public body has acted unlawfully or an order quashing a decision or forcing a fresh decision to be taken. However, it rarely leads to financial recompense and may not even produce a favourable outcome at the end of the day. If the ground of challenge is procedural impropriety, for instance, the decision-taker may have to retake the decision using proper procedures but may still be able to reach the same conclusion, say to refuse a licence or refuse permission to enter the country.

Results can also be considered in a broader context. How, if at all, is the quality of government affected? Does policy change? Are procedures improved? Do redress and scrutiny lead to a new culture within government which is more amenable to criticism and more open? Or do they lead to a more defensive approach—where information is withheld in order to reduce the chance of challenge, with more caution and a greater emphasis on matters of form rather than real improvements? These questions must be asked and should be borne in mind as the chapters are read. However, they cannot yet be answered with any certainty because these issues are only just being explored by political scientists and public lawyers in this country.

WHERE TO GO FROM HERE

Chapters 16 and 17 consider the role of Parliament in providing political redress and accountability. Chapter 18 examines the ombudsmen and redress against errors of administration. Chapter 19 deals with the role tribunals play in providing an independent avenue of resolving disputes between individuals and administration. Tribunals have long been regarded as sitting on the frontier between the system of administration and the judicial system. Chapters 20 to 28 move on to look specifically at redress provided by the courts, and are concerned with judicial review. Chapters 29 and 30 focus on the impact of Community law on public law litigation.

16

PARLIAMENTARY SCRUTINY OF GOVERNMENT ACTION

INTRODUCTION

The role of MPs and peers in the legislative process is considered in earlier chapters.[1] Parliament is, however, much more than merely a law-making institution and we now therefore need to examine another aspect of its work, namely the scrutiny of executive action. Outside the legislative process, MPs and peers call the government to account for its actions and inactions through a variety of formal parliamentary procedures, including:

(1) inquiries and reports by all-party select committees of backbench MPs or peers;
(2) debates in the chambers of the Houses of Parliament;[2]
(3) oral and written questions to ministers; and
(4) ministerial statements to Parliament announcing and explaining decisions, to which opposition spokesmen are able to respond briefly.

The constitutional importance of parliamentary scrutiny

Such scrutiny procedures have an obvious importance to the general conduct of government in a parliamentary democracy. They are mechanisms for giving practical effect to the constitutional conventions of individual and collective ministerial responsibility: the procedures require ministers to explain and justify their actions to the nation's elected representatives.[3] This is of particular significance where government has acted without express parliamentary approval as when ministers take action in one of the areas, such as foreign policy and the regulation of the civil service, which are largely carried out under prerogative powers.[4] While ministerial action will not have been subject to prior parliamentary scrutiny, *retrospective* scrutiny is nevertheless still

[1] See Chapters 5 (the Diceyean model and parliamentary supremacy); 8 and 9 (statutes); 10 and 11 (parliamentary supervision of delegated legislation); and 13 and 14 (the limited role of Parliament on the margins of the Community legislative process).

[2] We do not refer here to those debates, such as on the Second Reading of bills, which are part of the legislative process.

[3] See p. 47.

[4] See Chapter 12.

possible. A similar situation occurs where ministers use statutory powers conferred by an Act enacted perhaps many years previously. Here again it is through the procedures listed above, rather than the legislative process, that MPs and peers can call on a minister to explain and justify action.

The GCHQ case study illustrates these points well. The decision to ban union membership was given legal effect by an oral instruction issued by Mrs Thatcher under prerogative powers[5] and by the Foreign Secretary issuing certificates under powers conferred by a statute enacted several years before. The government did not need to obtain the prior approval of Parliament for the ban—it was just announced to MPs as a *fait accompli*.[6] The most Parliament could do was retrospectively to conduct an inquiry into the matter through a select committee of backbench MPs, to ask formal questions of ministers and to hold a debate in the chamber of the House of Commons.

Parliamentary scrutiny and public law

The general constitutional importance of all this parliamentary activity is plain to see. After all, it provides the basic machinary of accountability which is said to underpin the theory of parliamentary supremacy. What is not perhaps so clear is why, precisely, it should be of any special interest to lawyers? When MPs and peers participate in the *legislative* process, the end product is law capable of enabling or constraining government action. In respect of the procedures being discussed here, though, the end product appears to be no more than political criticism. However much a select committee report criticizes a minister, even if the whole House of Commons were to debate and pass a resolution condemning a minister's actions, this would have no direct affect on the *legality* of what the minister had done. As Dicey made clear, 'the resolution of neither House is a law'.[7] There are, nevertheless, several good reasons why these parliamentary procedures are relevant to public lawyers.

Political and legal responsibility overlap

First, ministers are normally both politically accountable to Parliament and legally accountable to the courts for decisions made within their departments. So, for example, when the Home Office makes a controversial decision to deport a person, a campaigning group may well want to put pressure on a minister to reverse a decision by getting a sympathetic MP to ask a PQ about the matter or to initiate a short debate on the floor of the Commons. (We will see below what exactly this entails.) The group may also try to assist the deportee to make an application for judicial review of the minister's decision. This dual-pronged approach is a common one for pressure groups,

[5] See p. 276.
[6] See p. 15.
[7] See A. V. Dicey, *Introduction to the Study of the Law of the Constitution* (10th edn.), p. 55; and see the discussion in Chapter 5 above.

such as Friends of the Earth, which seek to influence broad policy issues by giving evidence to select committees of backbench MPs and to use litigation to challenge specific decisions. In order to operate effectively within the system, public lawyers therefore need an appreciation of both the parliamentary and the legal process, the different scope of each and what each is capable of achieving.

Political accountability for litigation

A second specific reason why lawyers need to know about parliamentary scrutiny is that ministers are politically accountable to Parliament for the ways in which government conducts and responds to litigation. In practical terms, this means that ministers are required by the convention of ministerial responsibility to make statements to the House of Commons whenever a significant government decision has been overturned by a court, and explain how they propose to deal with the situation.[8] An opposition frontbench spokesman will normally be given an opportunity to make a brief response. In other words, public law litigation is a political activity.

Interaction between parliamentary and court scrutiny

Thirdly, parliamentary scrutiny procedures and litigation may occasionally feed into each other. For instance, a select committee inquiry may bring facts and issues into the public domain which reveal dubious action by ministers; this information may in turn be used by an aggrieved person in preparing for an application for judicial review. This happened in the Pergau Dam affair.[9] The process may also work in the opposite direction: an application for judicial review may highlight legal errors by ministers which then prompts a select committee to enquire into the matter. This happened in relation to the Board and Lodgings Regulations when it was only after the judgment in *R v Secretary of State for Social Services, ex p Cotton* that the JCSI scrutinized regulations on the subject carefully and called civil servants from the department to explain official policy.[10] Specific linkages between parliamentary scrutiny and court processes do not arise every day, but they do occur in some constitutionally significant cases and for this reason lawyers need to be aware of the possibility.

Parliamentary scrutiny as a stop-gap in the absence of judicial review

As discussed in later chapters, there are circumstances in which ministers may not be subject to judicial review. For instance: an Act of Parliament may

[8] For examples of this see Chapter 28 (ministerial statement on *R v Secretary of State for Social Services, ex p Cotton*) and Chapter 9 (minister explains that government waiting for the outcome of litigation in the ECJ before introducing new Sunday Trading Bill). Only a small number of the 3,000 or so applications for judicial review made each year will prompt a ministerial statement.

[9] See p. 52, n. 60.

[10] *The Times*, 14 December 1985. See Chapter 11.

expressly exclude judicial review of a particular type of decision;[11] some ministerial decisions are said by the courts to be 'non-justiciable';[12] some statutory duties are expressed in such broad terms that they are said to be 'duties of imperfect obligation' which the courts will not enforce;[13] there may be no person sufficiently affected by a decision to have standing to challenge it in court;[14] or, more generally, no individual or group may be willing or able to risk the costs and anxieties of seeking judicial review. In these situations procedures such as PQs may be the only formal mechanism for making a minister answerable, albeit politically rather than legally, for what has been done.

Parliament scrutinizes the legality of government action

Finally, parliamentary scrutiny is of interest to lawyers because MPs and peers may use it to question the legality of government action (rather than just its political merits). This is seen clearly in the next chapter, when MPs were keen to inquire into whether the GCHQ union ban decision was contrary to the United Kingdom's international treaty obligations. More generally, the Public Accounts Committee (an all-party select committee of backbench MPs) has power to inquire into the 'regularity and propriety' of government expenditure.

Parliament's ability to tackle issues of legality is almost certainly helped by the fact that solicitors and barristers are significantly 'over-represented' in Parliament (in comparison to their numbers in the population as a whole). These MPs are able to deploy their legal expertise in calling ministers to account for their actions.[15] As the case studies used in the book demonstrate, the legal power of government often turns on the interpretation of highly complex legislation, international treaties and very subtle case law. The government is able to call on the considerable specialist expertise of its own lawyers and also has funds to instruct outside counsel to advise it when necessary. The ability of Parliament to obtain outside legal advice is extremely limited: occasionally select committees appoint legal experts to assist their work, and from time to time campaigning groups may also brief MPs on legal issues to do with government policy—but that is about all. In this respect there is therefore a considerable mismatch between the knowledge of government and that of Parliament. The presence of lawyer MPs helps redress the balance a little. To this limited extent it does perhaps make some sense to talk of the 'rule of law', or legal values, 'pervading' Parliament.[16]

[11] See p. 505.
[12] See p. 513.
[13] See p. 539.
[14] See p. 486.
[15] For example, three of the eleven-member select committee of backbench MPs which inquired into the GCHQ affair were lawyers—one of them (Greville Janner QC) an expert on employment law. Sir Geoffrey Howe, now Lord Howe, the then Foreign Secretary questioned by the committee, is also a QC.
[16] See A. V. Dicey, *The Law of the Constitution* and his third definition of the rule of law, discussed in Chapter 6 above.

Erskine May contains rules dealing with the relationship between Parliament and the court system.[17] Within Parliament, the *sub judice* rule prevents MPs discussing matters, especially criminal cases, which are pending hearing. PQs ought not to criticize the judiciary[18] nor ask a minister 'to interpret the law or comment on the legality of action, even of one of the minister's civil servants'.[19] The courts are constrained by rules of Parliamentary Privilege, especially Art 9 of the Bill of Rights 1688 which states that 'the freedom of speech and debates or proceedings in Parliament ought not to be impeached or questioned in any court or place out of Parliament'.[20] In effect, these rules attempt to limit the degree of overlap between the respective functions of Parliament and the courts.

Parliamentary procedures

The remainder of the chapter briefly describes and explains the main parliamentary processes through which ministers are made answerable for their actions. The aim is to provide an overview of the system rather than a highly technical account of these often arcane procedures. In Chapter 17 many of these mechanisms are examined in more detail in the particular context of the House of Commons' response to the GCHQ union ban.

SELECT COMMITTEES

Erskine May defines a parliamentary select committee as one 'composed of a number of Members specially named';[21] this tells us nothing about the functions they actually perform.

The House of Commons

Select committees have been used for many years by MPs for a variety of purposes,[22] but their use was given a thorough overhaul during the 1979–83 Parliament when for the first time a system of committees was set up to 'examine the expenditure, administration and policy of the principal

[17] The rules governing parliamentary procedures are set out in standing orders, published with a commentary in C. J. Boulton (ed.), *Erskine May's Treatise on the Law, Privileges, Proceedings and Usage of Parliament* (21st edn., 1989)—hereafter referred to as *Erskine May*.

[18] But see p. 469.

[19] Paul Silk, *How Parliament Works* (2nd edn., 1989), p. 184.

[20] See p. 110.

[21] See further *Erskine May*, p. 611.

[22] See e.g. the Select Committee on the Parliamentary Commissioner for Administration (Chapter 18), the Public Accounts Committee (p. 48) and the House of Lords' Select Committee on the European Community and the Commons' Select Committee on European Community Legislation (Chapter 13). The Joint Committee on Statutory Instruments (Chapters 10 and 11) is also a select committee.

government departments'.[23] Each of the committees normally comprises of eleven backbench MPs and has a party political composition broadly reflecting that of the whole of the Commons. Each committee elects its own chairman, who takes a full and often robust part in proceedings, but does not vote unless the committee is evenly split on an issue.

How do departmental select committees work?

At the beginning of each Parliament, each committee decides what topics relating to its department's policy responsibilities it wants to look at, though sometimes plans are set aside so that a committee can carry out a speedy inquiry into events which have just arisen.[24] Unlike the standing committees which 'debate' bills during the legislative process, select committees carry out 'inquiries'.[25] In practical terms this means that they receive written evidence and call witnesses to give oral evidence. At hearings, the MPs on the committee sit around a horse-shoe-shaped table and the person giving evidence and being questioned—frequently a minister or civil servant—sits facing them. Representatives of pressure and interest groups are a very important source of information for committees; many such groups have felt in recent years that their views have not been listened to directly by government and so select committee hearings and briefings have provided an important way in which they have been able to influence public debate on issues. Select committee hearings are normally open to the public and their hearings are often reported in the news media and may be televised. Select committees sometimes travel around the United Kingdom and overseas on fact-finding missions, though they rarely hold formal hearings outside the committee rooms of the Palace of Westminster. Committees may appoint expert advisors to help them and they are all assisted by clerks (officials of the House of Commons).

What powers do select committees have?

The departmental select committees have been conferred with powers by the Commons 'to send for persons, papers and records'. Usually committees are able to rely on the cooperation of ministers. Even a very reluctant minister or former minister may give evidence, if only to save the government from embarrassment or out of personal courtesy to the chairman of the committee—though in such circumstances a committee may well get little useful information. Select committees have no coercive powers to compel any MP, including a minister, to give evidence unless the House of Commons as a whole passes a resolution forcing them to do so. By convention, prime ministers and former prime ministers do not give evidence to select committees, leaving matters instead to be dealt with by ministers with direct departmental

[23] Standing Order 130. For a general description of the work of government departments, see Chapter 3.

[24] This happened when the Employment Select Committee investigated the GCHQ union ban.

[25] See Chapter 8. It is possible for 'special standing committees', which have inquisitorial powers, to scrutinize a bill but in practice these are hardly ever used.

responsibility for the issue in question. Ministers may decline to answer questions on public interest grounds. Committees also have no formal powers to require ministers to produce documents needed for an inquiry, though again committees can normally depend on a fair degree of cooperation from government.[26]

Civil servants are frequently invited by select committees to give evidence. They do so on behalf of ministers, not in their own right. Guidance issued by the Cabinet Office[27] lays down instructions as to what they can and cannot say. Generally, they should 'be as helpful as possible to committees'. This said, they should decline to answer a question where this is necessary in the interests of 'good government'; they should not disclose 'advice given to ministers'; 'interdepartmental exchanges on policy issues'; the 'level at which decisions were taken or the manner in which a minister has consulted his colleagues'; 'Cabinet committees or their decisions'; 'questions in the field of political controversy'; and sensitive information of a commercial or economic nature. The guidance reminds officials of the need to protect the convention of ministerial responsibility and not to express their own views on policy. On occasion, the government has refused to allow officials to attend select committee hearings. This happened when the Employment Select Committee investigated the GCHQ union ban and wished to question the director of GCHQ.[28] The chief executives of Executive Agencies,[29] responsible for the day-to-day 'operational' implementation of government policy, give evidence (like other civil servants) to select committees on behalf of the minister whose department remains responsible for the 'policy' in question. There is widespread dissatisfaction with this arrangement, and the Treasury and Civil Service Select Committee has recommended that chief executives become directly answerable, in their own right, to select committees.

So far as members of the public are concerned, as a last resort, a committee may recommend to the House of Commons that contempt proceedings be instituted if a person refuses to attend a hearing or answer questions properly put to them. Ian and Kevin Maxwell were so threatened when they refused to answer questions put to them by the Social Services Select Committee concerning the Mirror Group's pensions funds.[30]

Select committee reports and government's response

Once evidence has been gathered and discussed by a select committee, it is normal practice for the chairman (often assisted by the committee's clerk) to

[26] While investigating the Pergau Dam affair, the Public Accounts Committee could not obtain minutes of the advice given by senior civil servants to ministers, but following repeated requests another select committee (the Foreign Affairs Committee) also investigating the affair was supplied with a summary of these documents.

[27] See *Memorandum of Guidance for Officials Appearing Before Select Committees* (published in Select Committee on Procedure, *The Working of the Select Committee System*, 1989–90 session, HC 19, pp. 206–31). This document updated what used to be called the 'Osmotherly rules'.

[28] See Chapter 17.

[29] See p. 59.

[30] See *The Times*, 14 January 1992. See further Patricia M. Leopold, 'The Power of the House of Commons to Question Private Individuals' [1992] PL 541.

draft a report which is circulated to other members. The report contains observations and recommendations. In a large proportion of cases, the whole committee agrees to sign the report, though it is open to any member to submit a minority report. Reports are presented to the House of Commons and published. In practice the government now almost always makes a formal response to select committee reports (usually in the form of a command paper) within two months.

When the new system of departmental select committees was established in 1979, the government blocked proposals that would have set aside eight days in each parliamentary session specifically for debating select committee reports. As a result, it is very rare for time to be found in the parliamentary schedule for special debates on particular reports. Many reports are nevertheless referred to by MPs during more general debates, as happened when the Commons debated the GCHQ union ban.[31]

Assessing the impact of select committees

Views about the role of select committees are still divided,[32] not least because it is debatable how the 'success' of the committees ought to be measured. To do so merely in terms of how often select committee reports prompt speedy and specific change in government policy is too crude; nor were the committees set up to achieve this.

A number of benefits clearly flow from the work of the select committees. First, committee investigations enable information and opinions to be brought into the public domain and this improves the knowledge of all MPs. To date, over 1,000 reports have been published together with minutes of evidence. The MPs who serve on committees have over the years built up a degree of expertise in areas of policy which would otherwise have been hard to achieve. As government functions become increasingly specialized, it is important that the expertise of MPs also develops if parliamentary accountability is to be effective. Debates on the floor of the chamber are said to have become more effective at scrutinizing ministers and less prone to mere ritualic exchanges.

Select committees are also said to provide backbench MPs of all parties with a fulfilling role in Parliament. They provide an alternative 'career path' from just aspiring to be a minister or opposition frontbench spokesman; the backbench MPs who are involved in select committee work feel able to contribute something to the policy process.

For some commentators, the fact that select committees encourage cooperation between MPs of opposing political parties is itself a mark of success. The committees have established a sphere of parliamentary activity where party whips have much less influence and control than in the legislative process: it is regarded as improper for government to attempt to use its whips

[31] See p. 389.

[32] For a review of the arguments, see Priscilla Baines, Chapter 1 in Gavin Drewry (ed.), *The New Select Committees* (2nd edn., 1989).

to control the activities of the committees.[33] In their methods of work and function, select committees are therefore very different from the standing committees which debate bills during the legislative process.[34] Select committees often produce reports which are unanimously critical of a department, despite the fact that each committee draws a majority of its members from the governing party. To this extent the committees may have helped to redress the executive domination of the Commons.

Critics of the select committee system are less impressed. It is said that investigations have done little to alter the imbalance of information between government and backbench MPs: the committees merely provide another mechanism for ministers and civil servants to disseminate and control the release of information. Also, the information contained in select committee reports is largely irrelevant to the ability of backbenchers to call government into account in debates. For some parliamentarians, the work of the committees—particularly now that hearings are televised—has also wrongly detracted attention away from the floor of the House of Commons, which they regard to be the proper forum for calling ministers to account. This view is often linked to the belief that the temporary 'coalitions' made between government and opposition MPs, which select committee work encourages, is unhealthy. It hides the fact that the Commons is and ought to be an arena in which conflicting interests, represented by opposing political parties, meet and clash. Critics also suggest that sometimes the search for consensus may become an end in itself for a committee, causing it to shy away from investigating party politically contentious issues.

Select committees in the House of Lords

The House of Lords does not duplicate the departmentally related select committee structure of the Commons;[35] instead select committee work is concentrated in two spheres. First, there is the Select Committee on the European Communities, which operates through many sub-committees.[36] Secondly, there is a Select Committee on Science and Technology which monitors the organization of government for dealing with science and technology, the

[33] As discussed in Chapter 17, allegations were made that the government whips applied improper 'influence' on some members of the Employment Select Committee during its investigation of the GCHQ union ban. Similar concerns were voiced in November 1996: the Commons' Standards and Privileges Committee questioned David Willetts MP over allegations that in October 1994, when he was a government whip, he had sought to influence how the chairman of another select committee conducted an inquiry into MPs accepting cash for asking parliamentary questions. The government also has an influence over the Committee of Selection, the committee responsible for nominating MPs to each select committee: in 1992 Nicholas Winterton was controversially not re-nominated to the Health Select Committee, which he had chaired for the two previous parliamentary sessions, after the committee had issued several reports highly critical of government health policies.

[34] See Chapter 8.

[35] See further the House of Lords' Select Committee on the Committee Work of the House, 1991–92 Session, HL 35 (the Jellicoe Committee) and discussion of it at HL Deb, cols 899–937 (3 June 1992).

[36] See p. 308.

contribution of research and development to the renewal of British industry and also the continuation of basic scientific research. The reports produced by both these committees are regarded as influential. The Lords have also from time to time set up *ad hoc* select committees to inquire into specific issues.

DEBATES

Many of the debates in the chambers of each House of Parliament are concerned with legislation,[37] but much time is also spent seeking to call government to account for actions already done, or to prompt government to take action. The general problem faced by Parliament is how to allocate the very limited time it has for debate. The government demands time for its motions to be discussed (both the GCHQ debate and that on the Auld Committee on Sunday trading were debates initiated by government); the Official Opposition wants the chance to put political pressure on the government by initiating debates of its own choosing;[38] and backbench MPs of all parties require opportunities to raise issues affecting their constituencies or other particular concerns they may have (perhaps encouraged by a campaigning group). Whoever initiates a debate, there are two main types of motions that may be debated: adjournment motions and substantive motions.

Adjournment debates

Often MPs debate the formal motion 'that this House do now adjourn', though these debates are not, in fact, about whether or not the Commons stops sitting; they are merely a vehicle for discussion. A half-hour debate (the daily adjournment) is normally held at the close of parliamentary business on most days. The subject matter for debates is chosen by backbench MPs who compete in a ballot for the opportunity. The debate cannot be used to call for the government to initiate legislation. The chamber is often empty except for the backbencher, the minister who is to respond and a handful of other MPs. As part of a recent package of reforms to the arrangements for sittings of the Commons, backbench MPs are also able to initiate debates on certain Wednesdays.[39]

The government may initiate adjournment debates on issues of major controversy, such as the GCHQ union ban.[40] The advantage for ministers of using such a motion is that parliamentary procedure does not permit any amendments to be tabled to it and so the Opposition is unable to seek to

[37] See Chapters 8 and 9.

[38] Each session there are 20 'Opposition Days' in which debates on subjects chosen by the opposition parties take precedence over government business in the Commons. Seventeen of these go to the Official Opposition (i.e. the second largest party in Parliament).

[39] The so-called 'Jopling reforms' in the 1994–95 session, another important feature of which was to reduce late-night sittings: see further *Select Committee on Sittings of the House*, 1991–92 Session, HC 20 (the Jopling Report) and *Sitting House Reform*, 8th report of the Procedure Committee, 1994–95 Session, HC 491.

[40] See Chapter 17.

tempt 'rebel' governing party MPs to vote on an alternative motion. Very often there is no vote at the conclusion of an adjournment debate.

Under Standing Order No. 20, an MP may request the Speaker that there be an adjournment debate on 'a specific and important matter that should have urgent consideration'. Very few such emergency debates are held. After the Foreign Secretary had made his statement about the GCHQ union ban on 25 January 1994, Dr David Owen (then the leader of the now defunct Social Democratic Party) stood up and said:[41]

> I beg leave to move the Adjournment of the House, under Standing Order No. 20, for the purpose of discussing a specific and important matter that should have urgent consideration namely, 'the decision to deprive members of GCHQ of membership of a trade union'. The matter is specific, because it affects the fundamental liberties of well over 5,000 of our citizens. The matter is important because I believe that there are other ways of achieving the desirable objectives—a negotiated non-strike agreement, the exemption from the industrial tribunal provisions of the Employment Protection Act—while still abandoning any attempt to prevent public servants from being members of trade unions. The matter is urgent because, as I understand it, the action has already been taken without any consultation with trade unions or the Security Commission—the body which all sides of the House have trusted on matters dealing with the GCHQ and many other areas of national security. I believe that this matter will cause a great deal of public controversy throughout the country. . . .

The Speaker refused the request for this debate, saying that there had just been a long question-and-answer period on the Foreign Secretary's statement.

Substantive motions

Substantive motions, in 250 words or less, call for a decision of the House. These debates may be initiated by government or, on a set number of days, by the opposition parties. Unlike adjournment debates, amendments may be tabled to the motion which is being discussed. An example of a substantive motion initiated by the government was the discussion of the Auld Committee report on deregulation of Sunday trading.[42]

Every parliamentary session, backbench MPs also table many hundreds of motions 'for which no date has been fixed'; these are known as Early Day Motions and are not intended ever actually to be formally debated in Parliament. They do, however, enable backbench MPs to make their views known to the government. MPs show their support for a motion by adding their names to it, and the motion is printed in the daily order paper (in effect, the agenda) circulated to all MPs every day that a new name is added. Silk comments that Early Day Motions[43]

[41] See HC Deb, vol. 52.
[42] See Chapter 9.
[43] Paul Silk, *How Parliament Works*, p. 209.

can be a useful source of intelligence for the whips. For example in the 1985–86 session, a large number of Conservative MPs signed an early day motion critical of the bill to de-restrict Sunday trading—the Shops Bill. This was one of several indications which government business managers received that the Bill would have a rough ride.

Conduct of debates

Similar rules as to the conduct of MPs apply to the types of debate mentioned above as apply to debates during the legislative process.[44] The Speaker has considerable discretion in deciding which MPs to call to speak and she may limit the length of speeches.

PARLIAMENTARY QUESTIONS

MPs of all parties are able to ask ministers formal questions. Some are answered orally on the floor of the House of Commons, according to a rota in which each principal government department has a question time approximately every four weeks. Other questions are answered in writing. All answers are published in *Hansard*. 'The purpose of a question,' according to *Erskine May*, 'is to obtain information or to press for action.' A complex and often subtle body of rules govern what questions may be asked of which ministers. Ministers may only be asked a question about matters for which their particular department has responsibility and may refuse to give any meaningful answer. Where a question is designed to elicit information, a minister not infrequently states that the information could not be gathered except at disproportionate cost. Generally, if a minister refuses to answer a question, it cannot be asked again until the next parliamentary session.

When a question relates to day-to-day operational matters, it is now answered directly in writing by the chief executive of the relevant executive agency, rather than by the minister. These answers are also printed in *Hansard*.

Prime Minister's Questions

Since 1961, it has been parliamentary practice for the Prime Minister to answer oral questions from opposition MPs and backbenchers from his own party on Tuesdays and Thursdays between 3.15 and 3.30 pm. Although enjoyed by many television viewers, Prime Minister's Questions is 'a raucous shambles' (according to a recent report by a select committee on parliamentary procedures).[45] For one commentator 'Question Time has become a symbol of much that is wrong with Parliament: its introspection and its

[44] See Chapter 8.
[45] *Prime Minister's Questions*, Select Committee on Procedure, Seventh Report, 1994–95 Session, HC 555.

strident partisanship'.[46] It is quite clear that Prime Minister's Questions fails to produce effective scrutiny of government policy. One reason is that it has no theme. MPs dart around from issue to issue, often asking questions of the most general sort which unsurprisingly elicit only short 'sound bite' responses from the Prime Minister. MPs are able to do this because most questions are 'open': in a bizarre ritual MPs ask the Prime Minister about his engagements that day and then ask a supplementary question, usually on an issue of current controversy.[47] The Select Committee on Procedure has recommended that each Question Time should be on a specific issue, notified a day in advance. Arguably, however, this reform would merely allow the government time to prepare answers better for the news programmes and would remove the power of the Opposition to raise very topical questions and spring surprises.

Another problem is that backbench MPs from the governing party use Prime Minister's Questions to attack the opposition parties, for example by asking the Prime Minister to comment on statements made by the leader of the Opposition. As the Select Committee on Procedure has put it: 'It could be said that Prime Minister's Questions have developed from being a procedure for the legislature to hold the executive to account into a partisan joust between the noisier supporters of the main political parties.'

MINISTERIAL STATEMENTS

After the regular time set aside each day for oral questions to ministers, a minister will sometimes make a statement to the Commons. He or she will typically speak for five or ten minutes and this will be followed by a short response from an opposition frontbench spokesman and a handful of questions from backbench MPs. The Speaker determines how long the exchanges last. Ministerial statements may be used to give information to MPs about a wide range of matters, including announcing government decisions[48] and explaining the government's attitude to court judgments affecting government policy.[49] On the whole, statements and the short exchanges which follow them are useful for both government (which is able to disseminate information) and opposition MPs (whose critical responses will often be reported in the news media).

WHERE TO GO FROM HERE

This chapter has outlined the general constitutional significance of parliamentary scrutiny, explained its particular relevance to public law and briefly described the main procedures. Turn to the next chapter to continue exploring

[46] Peter Riddell, 'Questions without Answers', *The Times*, 17 July 1995.
[47] See p. 403.
[48] See e.g. p. 16 (the statement of the Foreign Secretary announcing the GCHQ union ban).
[49] See e.g. p. 28 (the statement made about the Board and Lodgings Regulations).

these procedures in more detail in the context of parliamentary reaction to the GCHQ decision. Chapter 18 examines a further role of MPs: how they and the Parliamentary Commissioner for Administration seek to redress individual grievances.

17

CASE STUDY: GCHQ UNION BAN SCRUTINIZED IN PARLIAMENT

INTRODUCTION

This chapter examines how, in a particular context, the House of Commons scrutinized government action—the ban on union membership at GCHQ. As with the other case studies, some caution is needed before making too many generalizations from one episode. This is especially so in relation to the Employment Select Committee which carried out an investigation in the GCHQ affair, as there is considerable diversity in the work and 'success' (however that is defined) of the various select committees overseeing the work of government departments. Within the scope allowed by the House of Commons' standing orders, the committees formed at the beginning of each parliamentary session will determine their own style. Nevertheless, the material and questions which follow provide useful material for testing some of the general justifications and criticisms made in the previous chapter about Parliament's work.

MINISTERIAL STATEMENT

Several weeks after a group of ministers decided to ban unions at GCHQ, the Foreign Secretary (Sir Geoffrey Howe) announced the decision to the House of Commons on 25 January 1984. See Chapter 2 for his statement.[1] Consider whether the Foreign Secretary's statement is misleading, in that he made no mention of the fact that the union ban was being imposed by use of prerogative power. (Remember that the Prime Minister had issued an oral instruction on 22 December 1983 to the director of GCHQ under power delegated to her by the Civil Service Order in Council, a very unusual piece of primary legislation made under the prerogative.)[2] Could the omission have been because the government felt that the use of prerogative power in this context was itself politically contentious? It was perhaps easier to give the impression that the government was using *only* statutory powers. Confusion surrounded the precise legal basis for the government's decision for some time; the

[1] See p. 16.

[2] See p. 276. Note that some commentators argue that, strictly speaking, this was not an exercise of 'prerogative' power.

Department of Employment eventually submitted a note to the Employment Select Committee clarifying the position.[3]

SELECT COMMITTEE INVESTIGATION

The Employment Select Committee (composed of backbench MPs drawn from the two major political parties) decided to carry out an immediate investigation of the government's decision. It took oral evidence from the Foreign Secretary, the Secretary of State for Employment (Tom King MP), the recently retired director of GCHQ (Sir Brian Tovey) and representatives from the TUC and the CCSU (the national umbrella organization for civil service unions). The committee also wanted to hear from a representative of the *local* trade union (who was an employee at GCHQ) and the *current* director of GCHQ, but the government refused to permit these people (who were its employees) to attend. A Conservative member of the committee made allegations that the committee had in some way been 'nobbled' by government whips. What follows are extracts from the Employment Select Committee's first Report of the 1983–84 parliamentary session. Before you begin reading this, you may want to look at the questions posed at p. 383 below.

Minutes of Evidence
taken before the
Employment Committee

8 February 1984

Examination of Witnesses

Rt. Hon. Sir GEOFFREY HOWE, QC, a Member of the House, Secretary of State for Foreign and Commonwealth Affairs, and Rt. Hon. TOM KING, a Member of the House, Secretary of State for Employment, examined.

(Chairman.) [Mr Ron Leighton, a Labour backbencher] May I first of all welcome you, Foreign Secretary and Secretary of State, to this meeting this morning to help us. We are very appreciative, and I think what I should do is explain the ground that we wish to cover.

(Mr Gorst.) [a Conservative backbencher] On a point of order, I wonder whether before you get launched into the inquiry I might raise two matters? The first is that I would like to raise a matter which is of immediate importance to our deliberations in this Committee, because it has come to my notice that pressure is being applied to some members of this Committee and it is being done not only by senior Government Whips but also by a Minister who I believe is actually affected by our current inquiry. It involves, as I understand it, interference in both how we conduct our inquiry, that is to say, our procedure, but also who should or should not be examined by this Committee. It is the general belief that Select Committees are and should be entirely self-regulating subject to the Standing Orders laid down by the House, and that they should not be subject to interference from party managers and especially those

[3] See Employment Committee, First Report 1983–84 Session, p. 55.

whose responsibilities cover the matters that are being put under investigation. I believe that the action of Government Whips in offering what I would call euphemistically 'guidance' as to who should not be called before this Committee and how Members might even exercise their votes is more than merely against the spirit of Select Committee procedure. I suspect that it may also be against the Standing Orders under which we operate, since it involves discovery of intentions and proceedings that may only be known to those who are Members of this Committee. More important, however, to the Select Committee is the fact that interference could undermine the impartiality and objectivity and standing of the Select Committee system itself. I wonder who will respect our reports if they are thought to be merely exercises either in rubber stamping the errors of the executive or rubber stamping their policies. Select Committees are not like the floor of the House, forums for debate, they are set up to examine facts and collect information. The second one is this: I know it is your intention to give the Foreign Secretary the opportunity to address this Committee right at the beginning of our proceedings, and before any questions are put to him. However, may I request you, Mr Chairman, to seek clarification from him at the very outset as to why one suggested witness has been banned on his authority from appearing before this Committee even though that person would not have been giving evidence in public, and would only have been dealing with topics related to industrial relations practice in GCHQ, and furthermore, he would have been giving this evidence in his capacity as a trade union representative.

Chairman

63. Can I say, Mr Gorst, I was relieved that you did not ask me to respond immediately to your first point, and I think I could ask the Clerk to look into this, and I would hope we need not proceed with it any further at this stage, but perhaps the Committee could discuss it afterwards. Your second point was would I ask the Foreign Secretary to make a comment on the stop put on one suggested witness. Without taking up a lot of time, if he wishes to could he do that?

(Sir Geoffrey Howe) Well, perhaps it would be helpful if I did so quite shortly, Chairman. The Government made clear its position on this matter in its reply to the Report of the Liaison Committee on the Select Committee system. The reference is Hansard 12 May 1983, column 446 of written answers. The position is that there is a long standing convention under which the Government does not provide information or answers to questions in Parliament on matters of security and intelligence, and the Government —this is, of course, a matter for Government decision—would regard itself as bound by that convention in relation to Departmental Select Committees no less than in relation to Parliament itself. In accordance with that convention the Government considers it would be inappropriate for members to give evidence to Select Committees or for other officials to give evidence on matters of security and intelligence. That is the basis of the decision. There has been a suggestion—I am not quite sure, having listened to the present discussion, whether right or wrong—that the Select Committee had requested certain serving members of GCHQ to give evidence for the purpose of this inquiry. For the reasons I have given the Government does not propose to allow those serving members of GCHQ to give evidence to the Select Committee. I am here with my right honourable friend to give evidence and the questions which your Committee wish to address to officials can be addressed to me or my right honourable friend. We will endeavour to answer them so far as we can do so consistent with the requirements of national security.

Mr Gorst

64. I do not understand how he equates discussions and information about purely terms and conditions of employment which is what this Committee would wish to ask the individual concerned and his attitude towards staff associations—how he can equate that with matters of security?

(Sir Geoffrey Howe) It is not a question of equating it, Mr Gorst, it is a question of applying the rule which has been regarded as sensible and justifiable as I have described.

Chairman

69. If we could move on. We feel that the subject we wish to discuss really falls under four headings, four broad headings. First, why was action taken against trade unions at GCHQ and why were they banned altogether, and under that, what is the legal basis upon which the Government's abrogation of GCHQ's contract of employment of terms and conditions of employment is based? Secondly, what alternatives to banning unions were considered and why was there no consultation or negotiation? Thirdly, are the present proposals open to modification through negotiation or are they irrevocable? Fourthly, how would the proposed arrangements operate? That is the broad area we wish to discuss and later we would want to take them in turn. Could I just ask you one question, Foreign Secretary, is there anything you would wish to say to us privately, in camera?

(Sir Geoffrey Howe) I think not, Chairman, at this stage. I am dealing with the questions that have been already widely canvassed. If that point arises at any stage in the questioning, I shall so indicate to you. I am grateful for the opportunity.

70. Could I invite you to make a statement, please?

(Sir Geoffrey Howe) [. . .] The decision which I announced to the House on 25 January was taken by the Ministers after very careful consideration in the light of these new circumstances [the public disclosure of the existence of GCHQ during the Geoffrey Prime trial]. The overall objective is of course to ensure that staff at GCHQ are not in future subject to the kind of pressures put on them in the past. This implies four detailed objectives: first, that staff at GCHQ must be deprived of the right to access to industrial tribunals, for security reasons; secondly, that it needs to be part of the conditions of service of GCHQ staff that there will be no interference in GCHQ's activities and operations by industrial disruption, whether in pursuit of national or of local disputes; thirdly, that negotiations on departmental issues, including questions of structure must, for security reasons, be carried out by departmental staff representatives answerable to the staff of GCHQ and to no-one else; fourth, that the maintenance of GCHQ's service must not be put at risk by any conflict of loyalty to the staff. These remain our objectives.

[. . .] The issue of certificates [under the Employment Protection Act] does not of itself remove the right to be a member of a trade union. That right is removed as a result of the changes in conditions of service now being introduced at GCHQ. These changes will ensure, first, that discussion of local and departmental issues at GCHQ is dealt with not by officials of national trade unions, but by departmental staff representatives, answerable only to GCHQ staff through the departmental staff association: and, second, that GCHQ staff cannot be instructed by, or in the name of, national unions to interfere in or interrupt GCHQ's operations and activities in pursuit of an industrial dispute. The proposed Staff Association will be able to represent all members of GCHQ . . . Staff experienced in Whitley and Industrial trade union affairs, have already been invited to help in forming the Association, but all members of GCHQ will be eligible. [. . .] Staff have thus been given the choice between continuing to be employed at GCHQ under the new conditions and requesting a transfer to suitable alternative employment elsewhere in the Civil Service. If it proves impossible to arrange such a transfer, they will be eligible for premature retirement on redundancy terms. In accordance with rules which apply generally throughout the Civil Service, anyone who refused the offer of a suitable alternative post would not be eligible for redundancy terms. [. . .] It has been suggested that the Government could have achieved the objectives I have stated by other means. The Government did not take their decision lightly, and the offer of an *ex gratia* payment in recognition of loss of statutory rights to staff choosing to remain at GCHQ is only one indication of the importance we attach to the principles at stake. We concluded, however, that the way to ensure freedom from disruption at GCHQ, and that staff would not be subject to the kind of problems which had been apparent in the past, was to treat them in the same way as other intelligence agencies, by excluding national trade unions. We remain ready to listen to any proposals the unions may have, but we continue to believe that the measures I announced on 25 January are the surest and safest way of ensuring our national security. Chairman, I think that my right hon. friend wanted to say something. If it is convenient to do that now perhaps he could. We are in your hands.

[*The Secretary of State for Employment made a statement at this point. The chairman of the select committee then asked the Foreign Secretary the following questions.*]

72. As you say the purpose of GCHQ was avowed at the time of the Geoffrey Prime case. It has been referred to in the ABC Secrets Case. Could I ask you why, if you were concerned with the industrial action of 1979 and 1981, why you had taken so long to take action? If trade unionism constituted a problem then why have you waited between three and five years? Was it not something of a dereliction of duty to have left it this time? Why did you not take it up with trade unions at any time or even with the Security Commission?

(Sir Geoffrey Howe) No dereliction of duty whatsoever, Chairman. We did attach a very great deal of importance to the question of avowal or non-avowal. You have mentioned that reference had been made to GCHQ in earlier cases. The fact remains that the intelligence function of GCHQ had not been avowed until the Prime Minister made her statement after the Prime case on 12 May last year. Obviously the question of taking action along these lines had been considered before. That was considered in the light of disruption to which I have referred, culminating in 1981. The non-avowal of the agency was a critical factor in leading us to come to no conclusion in favour of action along these lines until then. Once avowal took place in May of last year, the matter was reconsidered and brought forward for decision. It was announced in the way I announced in the House. [. . .]

[*The chairman of the committee asked further questions, then handed over to Mr Gorst.*]

Mr Gorst

76. Sir Geoffrey, do you not see an inconsistency in appearing in front of the Foreign Affairs Committee last week and saying the fault of the Americans in going to war in Grenada was they failed to consult in advance, presumably for security reasons, and now coming to this Committee and saying that you have gone to war with the unions without consulting and that you did not believe that for security reasons it was desirable to do so? Is there one law for international relations and another for labour relations?

(Sir Geoffrey Howe) No, both the

parallels are inapposite and far fetched. There is no question of going to war with the unions whatsoever. As Mr King [the Secretary of State for Employment] made clear this is not a question of general campaign or general change of position either. It is a decision taken for a specific area of Crown employment for a specific reason within a framework of statute designed for that purpose. It is designed to enhance the national security in order to enable ourselves to defend ourselves. To suggest this is a matter of going to war with the unions is fanciful and far fetched. The consultation between the United States and the United Kingdom was consultation between Governments at highest level in conditions of intense security which would have been conducted on that basis. The consultation under discussion in this case as suggested by yourself, I gather, would have been consultations with all those employed at GCHQ and would by definition have been public and massively manifest so neither parallel is appropriate.

79. The Chairman raised what I considered to be a very important point as to why it has taken so long for this decision to be made and you gave your answer to that. Would it be true to say that the implications of such matters as the Falklands Campaign or any other international incident between 1981 and now made it less easy at certain times to make this decision, and therefore there is some good reason for choosing around now for doing it?

(Sir Geoffrey Howe) . . . I am sure you are right in saying that, during the Falklands Campaign, at least, ministers very closely concerned would have been very pre-occupied with other matters. But I think the trigger that brought it back again on to the top of the pile for consideration was avowal in May 1983. That had certainly been a significant factor in our early deliberations.

[*Other questions were asked.*]

Chairman

101. I am anxious to move on to look briefly at the legal basis of this. I have got a quick question and then I would like to call Mr Janner [a Labour member of the select committee who is also a QC specializing in employment law]. Do any employees of GCHQ have legally binding contracts of employment and are there any precedents for unilaterally changing civil servants' terms of employment?

(Sir Geoffrey Howe) Shall I go first? I hesitate to cross swords with Mr Janner on this, he has written books on the subject.

102. This is my question not his.

(Sir Geoffrey Howe) In fact, as I understand it, and Mr King can say if I have got it wrong, all employment under the Crown is on the same terms—in the sense that it is subject to the Royal Prerogative and other determinations. That is to make it very simple indeed. I think the appointments of Crown employees are different from the appointments of other employees. So far as precedent is concerned, I do not think I can refer you to any precedent of this kind, simply because the very nature of the operation at GCHQ has been unique.

(Chairman) I appreciate that. So it is unprecedented?

(Sir Geoffrey Howe) Yes.

Mr Janner

103. Sir Geoffrey, as perhaps members of the same trade union [they are both barristers], may I ask you a few legal questions? First, can you help me, you have given a certificate, the purpose of the certificate as, I understand it is to remove the right of employees at GCHQ to take complaints about unfair dismissal and so on to tribunals, that is the fact of it, is it not?

(Sir Geoffrey Howe) Yes and the effect of the certificate is precisely as set out in the statute. It has the effect of disapplying the relevant provisions of the Employment Protection Acts and the most important

of those is for the individual's access to trade unions. It also embraces right of recognition to trade unions, the protection of individuals against discrimination on grounds of trade union membership.

104. It takes away their rights of complaints to tribunals and courts if they are prevented from belonging to trade unions but does not ban trade union members?

(Sir Geoffrey Howe) That is right.

105. There is no proscription in the certificate to the person's right to join the trade union?

(Sir Geoffrey Howe) That is right.

106. There is no intention on the part of the Government to introduce such proscription?

(Sir Geoffrey Howe) Yes, there is an intention. The terms and conditions of service set out in the notice issued by GCHQ management do provide, as you there see, for non-union membership and they do provide for disciplinary action in the case of industrial action.

107. I do understand that. There is no intention to introduce into this House any law, any statute, which would of itself proscribe trade union membership for these people or anyone else?

(Sir Geoffrey Howe) Absolutely right. The changes being made of that kind are being made in the conditions of service which are offered to the GCHQ staff.

108. So the exercise of the right to belong to a trade union is not proscribed by law?

(Sir Geoffrey Howe) No, it is the right—or, the change in that respect is made by the change in the terms and conditions of service.

109. I take it it is the Government's intention to apply . . . international law and its obligations under terms we have ratified?

(Mr King) Yes.

110. May I draw your attention to the International Covenant on Civil and Political Rights, Article 22: 'Everyone shall have the right to freedom of association with others, including the right to form and join trade unions for the protection of his interest. 2. No restrictions may be placed on the exercise of this right other than those which are prescribed by law . . .'. There is no such prescription in our law. It then continues: '. . . which are necessary in a democratic society in the interests of national security or public safety, public order (ordre public), the protection of public health or morals or the protection of the rights and freedoms of others. This article shall not prevent the imposition of lawful restrictions on members of the armed forces and of the police . . .' which does not apply. May I suggest the Government is in breach of Article 22 of the International Covenant on Civil and Political Rights in introducing the measures which it is proposing?

(Mr King) If I may make the point, first of all, the Government does not accept it is in breach of international law in this respect. I think Mr Janner knows the subject well enough to know that it is capable of considerable examination. He knows that the basis of the change in the conditions of service is the Civil Service Order in Council 1982 that provides for ministers of civil servants making regulations or giving instructions and goes on to refer to conditions of service of all such persons. That is the basis of the change. He has quite rightly said the question of prohibition on union membership does not flow from the certificate but from the Order in Council.

111. It does not flow from proscription in law because both you Minister and the Secretary of State for Foreign Affairs have agreed there is no proscription by law?

(Mr King) On that point, my understanding is that it is the Order in Council which covers it. The actual wording of the Covenant is here—you have read out the two alternative sections to it and the Committee have been informed about it. My understanding is on the basis of the legal advice available to Government this

action is in accordance with our international legal obligation.

112. Has the Government's mind been applied specifically to Article 22 or not?

(Mr King) We have considered each of the relevant pieces of international law which Mr Janner will know if he goes through the whole lot—the ILO Conventions, the European Convention of Human Rights, the European Social Charter and the United Nations Declarations and Covenants.

113. Can I then draw your attention to Article 11 of the European Convention of Human Rights which, without repeating what was in Article 22, says much the same and says 'No restriction shall be placed on the exercise of these rights other than such as are prescribed by law'. I draw your attention once again to the agreement of both ministers—one is a very learned counsel—to the fact you agreed there was no such prescription by law, and at the very least will you agree with your own words that this situation is 'capable of considerable examination', in other words, there is room for massive disagreement over the meaning of these clauses in international law.

(Sir Geoffrey Howe) Can I intervene for a second, because I think it is not customary to try to distil answers to questions of law by cross-examination, and it is necessary to examine these things properly and carefully. [. . .] Can I offer one footnote to the discussion: in introducing the new conditions of service at GCHQ, it is the Prime Minister who is acting by virtue of the Civil Service Order in Council 1982, and it is that Order, part of the law of England, which gives her authority from time to time to make regulations or give instructions for controlling the conduct of the service and for the conditions of service of those employed in it. It is as a result of her power to act under the 1982 Order in Council that the changes in the terms and conditions of service are being introduced as set out in the notice. That is the important feature which I just lay on the table for consideration by my learned friend!

Chairman

117. Can we move on to our second major area which is what alternatives to banning unions were considered, and why was there no consultation or negotiation. Could I start by asking you this question: our four major concerns, no disruption, no disclosure, no intrusion and no conflict of loyalty; we put all these points very firmly to the trade unions last week. They accepted all of these points and objectives and expressed their willingness to make concessions to GCHQ's special status and to guarantee no disruption agreements, secret instead of open hearings before industrial tribunals, restrictions on outside union officials, and said that they thought that dealt adequately without any possible conflict of loyalties. I have always thought in the negotiating world you could always reach agreement with the other fellow if you gave him everything he wanted. My question really is why won't you take 'Yes' for an answer? Is it not possible on this basis to secure national security without doing violence to basic human and civil rights of free association?

(Sir Geoffrey Howe) We have obviously considered what is the right way and the effective way. We have considered all these matters before taking our decision and before we met the unions last week, and I think that in negotiations, on topics as complicated as this, the word 'Yes' is too simple a word, as you would appreciate.

[*Several other questions were asked and answered; the chairman of the committee then continued.*]

132. Could we just clear this point and press it just a little more: we put considerable store by the further meeting [of the unions] with the Prime Minister.

Now, is your mind completely shut on this matter? If it is, then there is not really much point in having a further meeting but your first thoughts were to act in the way you did, but sometimes, having heard other views, one can have a second opinion. Everybody makes mistakes, even, if I may be allowed to say so, Foreign Secretaries, sometimes. Is there any give in the situation? Is there anything to be hoped for from this further meeting, or is your mind irrevocably made up?

(Sir Geoffrey Howe) I think you will understand how very important it is not to give false impression of what the position is in a situation of this kind. Plainly there would be no purpose in having a further meeting if our mind was totally and irrevocably closed. The offer of a further meeting was made and accepted last week and a further meeting is to take place. That speaks for itself as far as it goes, but our judgment does remain as the Prime Minister said yesterday that the approach we have adopted is the only way of meeting our full objectives, and as I have said today, it is the safest and the surest way of doing so. That is a position from which it would obviously be very difficult to dislodge us, because we have given it a great deal of thought, and that is our considered view now, but a meeting takes place on the understanding that the footing and the lines are not completely foreclosed.

[*Several other questions were asked and answered.*]

Questions

1. One virtue of select committees is said to be that they encourage MPs of different parties to work collaboratively and to be less partisan. Is there any evidence of this happening here? Is this a good thing?

2. Why was it thought to be improper for government to apply 'pressure' through its whips on members of a select committee? This is routine and accepted in respect of debates on the floor of the Commons and in standing committees (the legislative debating committees considered in Chapter 8, above).

3. How probing were the questions? Had you been a member of the select committee, are there any further questions you would have wished to ask?

4. Were you convinced by the reasons given by the government for not allowing the GCHQ director or local union representative to give evidence to the select committee?

5. Why, according to the Foreign Secretary, did the government not consult with the unions prior to imposing the ban?

6. Was the union ban 'prescribed by law'? If so, what law?

THE SELECT COMMITTEE REPORT

Within 20 days of the first announcement of the government's decision to ban trade unions, the select committee published a unanimous report critical of the government's union ban decision: see Employment Committee, First Report 1983–84 session. Here are some extracts.

First Report from the

EMPLOYMENT COMMITTEE

Session 1983–84

TRADE UNION LEGISLATION—UNIONS IN THE GOVERNMENT COMMUNICATIONS HEADQUARTERS

Together with the Proceedings of the Committee, Minutes of Evidence taken before the Committee on 1 and 8 February 1984 and Appendices

---

Ordered by the House of Commons to be printed
14 February 1984

The Employment Committee is appointed under S.O. No. 99 to examine the expenditure, administration and policy of the Department of Employment and associated public bodies, and similar matters within the responsibilities of the Secretary of State for Northern Ireland.

The Committee consists of a maximum of eleven Members, of whom the quorum is three. Unless the House otherwise orders, all Members nominated to the Committee continue to be members of it for the remainder of the Parliament.

The Committee has power:

(a) to send for persons, papers and records, to sit notwithstanding any adjournment of the House, to adjourn from place to place, and to report from time to time;

(b) to appoint persons with technical knowledge either to supply information which is not readily available or to elucidate matters of complexity within the Committee's order of reference;

(c) to communicate evidence and other documents of common interest to other departmentally-related Committees, and to meet concurrently with any such Committee to deliberate, take evidence, or consider draft Reports.

The following were nominated as Members of the Committee on 14 December 1983:

Mr Tony Baldry
Mr Gordon Brown
Mr Don Dixon
Mr Ken Eastham
Mr John Gorst
Mr Greville Janner
Mr Ron Leighton
Mr Gerry Neale
Mrs Elizabeth Peacock
Mr Andrew Rowe
Mr Peter Thurnham

Mr Ron Leighton was elected Chairman on 20 December 1983.

FIRST REPORT

The Employment Committee have agreed to the following Report:

TRADE UNION LEGISLATION—UNIONS IN THE GOVERNMENT COMMUNICATIONS HEADQUARTERS

[. . .]

2. The Employment Committee were concerned about the implications for Government policy on industrial relations of this announcement removing from the

staff of GCHQ the right to belong to a trade union, and decided to inquire immediately into the matter.

3. We invited the TUC and the Council of Civil Service Unions (CCSU) to give evidence and they appeared before us on 1 February. The CCSU provided a written Statement of Case at the meeting, and followed this on 7 February with a further note in which they set out their proposals to ensure continuing trade union representation at GCHQ while still meeting the requirements which the Government said lay behind their decision.

4. We also invited the Secretaries of State for Foreign and Commonwealth Affairs and for Employment, and they gave oral evidence on 8 February. A written memorandum by the Foreign and Commonwealth Office and the Department of Employment was provided beforehand, and two further notes were provided subsequently on 8 February and 13 February.

5. We took oral evidence in private on 8 February from Sir Brian Tovey, who was Director, GCHQ until his retirement in September 1983. This evidence, apart from one or two small omissions for security reasons, is being published.

6. An exploratory approach was made to the Foreign and Commonwealth Office about taking oral evidence in private also from the present Director, GCHQ and from the Chairman of the union side of the Whitley Council there. The response was that on Ministerial instructions they had been advised not to accede to any invitation, even though in one case the witness would have been invited to speak in his capacity as a representative of the unions and not as a civil servant. The desirability of making a Report quickly before the Government ban on trade unions at GCHQ is due to take effect on 1 March has prevented us from pursuing the matter before making our Report to the House.

7. The effect of the Ministerial decision has thus been that we have heard only the evidence of local management at GCHQ (as expounded by Sir Brian Tovey) and not that of local unions, which has disturbed the balance of evidence that we sought. Sir Geoffrey Howe argued that it would be inappropriate for officials to give evidence on matters of security and intelligence. But this was never in question: our interest would be with the industrial relations implications of the Government's action, terms and conditions of employment, union views on staff associations, and matters of that nature. The union representative would have been seen in private, and in giving evidence would have been subject to the constraints of the Official Secrets Acts and the Code of Guidance for civil servants appearing before Select Committees. It is most regrettable that the Ministerial instruction has prevented us from questioning the union representative on matters not affected by those constraints on which we would wish to have examined him.

8. In approaching our inquiry we began by agreeing on four fundamental points: Governments *have* a responsibility to ensure that national security is protected; questions of national security *do* arise at GCHQ; industrial action at GCHQ *could* affect national security in certain circumstances; and the Government *have* a duty to ensure that the exercise of trade union rights does not adversely affect national security.

9. In trying to reach a view about the Government's action, we have sought answers to a number of questions:—

(i) was it necessary to ban unions at GCHQ?
(ii) what other options did the Government consider and
(iii) why were they rejected? and
(iv) were there any other options that could have been considered?

[. . .]

13. The legality of the Government action in depriving GCHQ staff of union rights has been questioned in some quarters. The certificates issued under the Employment Protection Acts do not in themselves remove the right of staff at GCHQ to belong to a trade union. The Government propose to remove that right by introducing new conditions of service, under the Civil Service Order in Council 1982. This point was not brought out clearly in the Secretary of State's original statement of 25 January [see p. 16, above], but was referred to later, by the Prime Minister in answer to a Question on 1 February, by the Secretary of State for Foreign and Commonwealth Affairs in his opening statement on 8 February [see p. 377, above] and finally in a note from the Department of Employment following up that statement.

14. In their evidence on 1 February the TUC quoted advice from the International Confederation of Free Trade Unions that the Government are in breach of ILO Convention 87 for denying GCHQ staff the right to belong to a trade union. The Secretary of State said in his oral evidence that the Government were satisfied that their action was not in breach of international conventions to which the UK were a party. This difference of view raises issues of international law which we have not attempted to pursue. We concentrated on the reasonableness of the Government's action rather than its legality.

15. One point which has concerned us is the timing of the action. In their evidence the Government have indicated that they were seriously disturbed by the effects on operations at GCHQ of the industrial action there between February 1979 and April 1981. Yet the Government made no announcement of action to deal with the matter until January 1984. We do not consider that the explanation given by the Government justifies the delay. This was that the action they have now taken could not have been decided upon at a time when the intelligence role of GCHQ had not been publicly acknowledged or avowed, and that avowal was not made until May 1983. Does this mean that but for the exposure of a spy, which led to the avowal, the Government would have continued indefinitely to be seriously disturbed about possible threats to national security at GCHQ, and yet be prepared to take no action? They could surely have approached the unions to impress upon them the seriousness of the position, and to discuss other ways of avoiding disruption. But there was no such approach at Government level to the CCSU, though Sir Geoffrey Howe said that there had been informed consultations with the unions at GCHQ by local management on the possibility of a no-strike agreement.

16. When after the avowal in 1983, the Government reviewed the position and eventually took the decision, apparently without full Cabinet consideration, which was announced without prior warning in January 1984, they held no consultations with the staff affected or their unions. The announcement was followed by strong protests from the unions and much criticism in Parliament and outside, both about the decision itself and the way it was introduced.

17. Information was released in instalments. . . . One example was the fact that GCHQ staff who refused to move to an alternative suitable post would have their employment terminated without any compensation. This was not disclosed to the House in the Secretary of State's opening statement [see p. 16, above], but in a subsequent answer by another Minister to a Parliamentary Question. This led to a private notice question seeking clarification of the terms offered to the staff at GCHQ, and a further statement by the Secretary of State.

18. The unilateral alteration of the terms and conditions of employment of the staff at GCHQ was admitted by Sir Geoffrey Howe to be an unprecedented act. (The Secretary of State for Employment assured us that it did not set a precedent

for action outside the security and intelligence field.) The CCSU said that they were outraged at the announcement of the deprivation of trade union rights, and their members, particularly those at GCHQ, shared that sense of outrage. They also considered that the unprecedented offer of *ex gratia* payments of £1000 (subject to tax) to members of staff who would accept the proposed revised conditions of employment had provoked the indignation of the staff.

19. Thus, according to the unions, the Government's actions appear to have soured relations with the staff affected and to have lowered morale, as well as resulting in damaging public controversy and widespread and unwelcome publicity for GCHQ. We do not wish to add further to the criticisms that have been made by others: we would simply observe that the handling of the issue could not be described as a model of its kind.

20. We turn now to the substance of the action taken by the Government, as distinct from its presentation. In giving reasons for the Government's decision the Prime Minister stressed the need to treat GCHQ like other security services. But there are important differences. The staff of services like MI5 have never enjoyed trade union rights, whereas GCHQ employees always have. To remove those rights, which are also enjoyed by many other civil servants in highly secret posts, from GCHQ is a most serious step, which has provoked strong opposition from the staff and the trade union movement, and caused major political controversy. It is necessary to consider whether the Government could achieve their objectives in some other way.

[. . .]

24. The key passages in Sir Brian Tovey's evidence, however, which seem to point the way to a solution that could be acceptable to the trade unions as well as to the Government are in his answers to Questions 160, 161, 162, 179, 193 and 222. In these answers Sir Brian makes it clear that, had the concession now offered by the unions been available at the time he was drawing up plans to ban them, the concessions would have met all the requirements that were necessary. However, he emphasised that the concessions would have needed to be accompanied by foolproof guarantees backed up by the force of law. Sir Brian explained to the Committee that in his opinion the concessions now offered by the unions seemed inconceivable at that earlier time and that, that being the case, there was no alternative but to proceed along the lines now proposed by the Government, and that there was no other way it could have been announced.

25. We have asked ourselves why the Government did not, nevertheless, engage in consultations before making their announcement. It might be argued in the Government's defence that to have done so might have jeopardised the possibility of obtaining concessions from the unions that only the threat of banning them outright could obtain, and that this extreme line has played a part in producing a satisfactory response from the unions. We are not in a position to judge whether this was, in fact, the Government's intention, but given the willingness of the unions to accept the Government's essential objectives and to find a way of meeting them without a complete ban on union activities, we make the recommendations which follow.

26. *Recommendations*

The Select Committee recommend:—

(1) That the concessions offered by the unions as set out in their note to the Committee submitted after the meeting of 1 February be thoroughly examined by the Government to satisfy themselves that they meet every requirement of national security:

(2) That the unions offer whatever legally binding assurances the Government require in order to make these arrangements totally effective:

(3) That if arrangements which involve setting precedents that would in other circumstances be unacceptable to trade unions have to be demanded, these arrangements will be applied solely in matters relating to national security at GCHQ:

(4) That representatives of the TUC and the CCSU should immediately accept the Prime Minister's open invitation for talks in order to reach agreements along the lines recommended above:

(5) That, in the event of a satisfactory agreement being reached which will maintain both the essential continuity of operations at GCHQ and also freedom of association and the right to membership of a trade union, the Government should withdraw the proposal to prohibit employees at GCHQ from belonging to a trade union: and

(6) That in the meantime all action consequent upon the certificates issued by the Secretary of State for Foreign and Commonwealth Affairs should be suspended, together with the requirement to sign the option forms relating to new conditions of employment and the offer of £1000 ex-gratia payments.

Questions

1. Mr Gorst said that select committees are 'set up to examine facts and collect information'. Make a summary of the information collected and facts examined by the committee during their questioning of these ministers.

2. What does it mean to say that a select committee may 'send for persons, papers and records'? (See the terms of reference which the select committee sets out at the beginning of its report and the discussion in the previous chapter.)

3. To what extent do you think the select committee was hindered in its investigation by the government's refusal to allow some witnesses (its own employees) to give evidence?

4. What legal issues did the select committee consider? The report says 'we concentrated on the reasonableness of the Government's action rather than its legality'. Did they?

5. What reason does the select committee give for there being no consultation prior to the union ban?

AN ADJOURNMENT DEBATE

A major debate on the floor of the House of Commons about the union ban took place on 27 February 1984, a little over a month after the government's decision had been announced. It lasted for six and a half hours. As you read the following extracts from *Hansard* (for the full report, see HC Deb, vol. 58, cols 25–111) consider what contribution the select committee's investigation and report had on the quality of scrutiny by MPs of the government's decision. Remember that one of the strengths of the select committee system is said to be that it improves debate.[4]

[4] See p. 368.

GCHQ Cheltenham

Motion made, and Question proposed, That this House do now adjourn—[Mr David Hunt]. [He was a parliamentary private secretary to the Secretary of State for Defence.]

Mr Speaker: Before we start this very important debate, I draw to the attention of the House the fact that I have a very long list of right hon. and hon. Members who wish to take part. This is a day on which I ask for short contributions, please.

3.38 pm

The Secretary of State for Foreign and Commonwealth Affairs (Sir Geoffrey Howe): Just over a month has passed since I announced to the House the Government's decision to bring the conditions of employment at GCHQ into line with those which apply in the other intelligence agencies. The subject has hardly been out of the news since and there should be no surprise at that. The issues involved are of great importance and it is right that they should be debated.

There are points on which we need to be emphatically clear from the outset. First and foremost, GCHQ is one of the security and intelligence agencies on which our national security, and to some degree also the security of our allies, depends. [. . .]

The next point which I hope will now be accepted on all sides is that the decision which we are debating today is not part, and should not be seen as part, of any wider campaign. There is not one word of truth in the wild and extravagant claims which have been made on that point. [. . .] Let me emphasise, too, that the decision we have taken is in no way a departure from established principle. On the contrary.

Successive Employment Protection Acts, repeating the provisions of the Industrial Relations Act 1971, have provided for the need to except certain categories of employment on grounds of national security. Certificates precisely similar to the ones which I have signed have been in force since 1971 for the other intelligence and security agencies. They have been signed by the responsible Ministers of previous Governments of both parties. The only anomaly is that a different situation had been allowed to grow up and exist in GCHQ. I emphasise that it was an anomaly.

It was only once we had specifically and publicly acknowledged that GCHQ was also an agency whose operations and activities are concerned with security and intelligence—as my right hon. Friend the Prime Minister did in the House on 12 May last year—that the way was open to correct that anomaly.

Mr John Smith (Monklands, East): [a Labour frontbench spokesman; also a QC] The Foreign Secretary has once again suggested that previous Governments acted in the same way as this Government in signing certificates under the Employment Protection Acts. Will he confirm that those certificates do not affect the right of anyone to be a trade union member and that the deprivation of trade union membership flows from instructions given by the Government under the Order in Council of 1982, which relates entirely to the Government and their activities?

Sir Geoffrey Howe: That is right. There has been no mystery about that. The terms and conditions of service have to be altered as well as the certificates being enforced. The terms and conditions of service will have the same effect in all intelligence agencies as a result of the instructions given by my right hon. Friend the Prime Minister.

Mr John Morris (Aberavon) [Labour frontbench spokesman on legal affairs and a QC] *rose—*

Mr Speaker: Order. The Foreign Secretary is not giving way.

Sir Geoffrey Howe: I have a number of points to deal with and I am at the outset of my speech. I know that the point about the avowal of GCHQ, to which I have just referred, is one which some, including the Select Committee on Employment, have been inclined to dismiss, but I can assure the House—

Mr Morris *rose—*

Mr Speaker: Order. The right hon. and learned Gentleman knows better than that.

Sir Geoffrey Howe: that is an argument which was given considerable weight by Ministers both when they discussed the matter in 1982 and again more recently.

As I have already reminded the House, the issues before us have been considered in detail by the Select Committee on Employment. The Committee's report, published on 14 February, makes recommendations to which I shall return. I shall also address myself to the points raised by the Civil Service unions in their evidence to the Select Committee, as well as in course of their discussions with the Government.

First, let me underline one point which has become increasingly widely accepted as the debate has proceeded in public, before the Select Committee and in discussions with the unions; it is the absolute necessity for arrangements which, to quote the recommendations of the Select Committee 'meet every requirement of national security'. I very much doubt whether that would have been so widely recognised and endorsed if the Government had not taken the decision which I announced on 25 January. The extent of the support for our objectives is, none the less, welcome. The differences that remain can be seen as differences about means rather than ends.

Some have argued that no great harm was done [during the industrial action in 1979 and 1981], but to call for quantified evidence of damage is to miss the point. We can never know what intelligence has been, or might be, lost. Fortunately, no serious threats to the nation's security materialised during those particular periods of disruption, but that is not an argument for accepting the possibility of disruption as a fact of life. The function of GCHQ is to be continuously, permanently on the alert. Nothing less will do.

Mr John Gorst (Hendon, North) [backbench Conservative and member of the Employment Select Committee]: My right hon. and learned Friend has just pointed out that up to 25 per cent of the work force were engaged in the disruptions between 1979 and 1981. Have 25 per cent or 75 per cent, now accepted the terms which the Government have offered? Surely, if he maintains that we are discussing the means rather than the end, that is crucial as well?

Sir Geoffrey Howe: My hon. Friend is aware, of course, that the offer expires not today but on 1 March. He is also aware that the numbers accepting—I shall return to this later—are growing steadily. The figures that have been given by the Government are based on the counted forms accepted and delivered to GCHQ.

Mr John Morris *rose—*

Sir Geoffrey Howe: The right hon. and learned Gentleman must acknowledge that I have just given way to him. The decision that we took, notwithstanding what I have just said, was not taken lightly.

From 1979 onwards, management was in touch with the unions to seek ways of avoiding disruption, but union officials were thinking along very different lines. A national officer of the Civil and Public Services Association, for example, was quoted as saying in February 1979, when the Labour party was in power, that

> 'the strike would completely paralyse Government communications, both internally and externally'.

A local official is quoted as saying a few days later that

> 'our action will seriously affect operations by at least 80 per cent., as our members are specialists'.

In the following year, 1980, informal soundings about a no-strike or no-disruption agreement were taken locally by GCHQ management. The reaction of local union representatives was not encouraging. Later still, during the period of selective action that followed the one-day strike on 9 March 1981, GCHQ's senior management and a very senior official in the Civil Service Department appealed to officials of the Civil Service Union not to take disruptive action in certain key areas. The only result was deliberately perverse: pressure to continue strike action was brought to bear on GCHQ staff in precisely those areas.

That same month, and after these clear warnings, the unions announced:

> 'There will be a range of selective and disruptive action which will affect Britain's secret communications surveillance network. There will be both national and international repercussions.'

On 3 April 1981 a senior union official said on the eve of a strike at a GCHQ outstation:

> 'This is the most crucial station we have hit so far. We are going to hit this Department "as hard as we can".'

There can be no doubt that the union leaders concerned knew what they were doing. As I said in my evidence to the Select Committee, they deliberately chose to direct action against what they correctly saw as a very sensitive and vital agency of the Government, with the avowed intent of causing both national and international repercussions. [. . .] To put it more bluntly, in the period that I have described, the unions were quite prepared, in pursuance of a dispute about pay, to cause or threaten damage to national security. The attitude of some at the time was well summarised in the CCSU campaign report No. 1 issued in 1981, where it was said that

> 'our ultimate success depends upon the extent to which . . . defence readiness is hampered . . . by this and further action'.

It is against that background that the Government have formulated the objectives that I described to the Select Committee on Employment, and it is in that light that we have considered the report of the Select Committee and the points put to us by the unions.

Let me first remind the House of the objectives, as I put them to the Select Committee. [. . .]

Let me refer now to the recommendations of the Select Committee on Employment. The first recommendation is that we should thoroughly examine the concessions offered by the unions to satisfy ourselves that they meet every requirement of national security. We have done so very carefully, taking into account not only the union proposals submitted to the Committee, but further developments to the proposals which arose in subsequent discussions.

There is no doubt that the unions have made very real attempts to meet our points, but we have reached the conclusion at the end of the day that the unions' proposals unfortunately do not remove the risk of conflicting pressures from outside GCHQ on the undoubted loyalty of those who work there. They do not satisfy the Government's ultimate responsibility for safeguarding national security.

The Committee's second recommendation is addressed to the unions. The Committee's conclusion that the arrangements to be made should be totally effective endorses an important element in the Government's thinking. Its recommendation that the unions should be prepared to offer whatever legally binding assurances the Government require to ensure that is also very relevant. But making assurances legally binding—difficult enough in itself—can only be part of the answer. What is crucial is that those assurances should go far enough to meet the Government's fundamental objectives. And, as I have explained, they do not go far enough to eliminate the risk of conflicting pressures on those who work at GCHQ.

The third recommendation is that any new arrangements involving precedents which would in other circumstances be unacceptable to trade unions should be applied solely in matters relating to national security at GCHQ. As I have already made clear, the Government have no intention of introducing similar measures outside the field of security and intelligence. And it is our firm position that the measures must apply to all GCHQ staff.

Mr John Morris: Given the precedents which the Foreign Secretary has cited on the issue of certificates under the Employment Protection Act and its predecessor the Industrial Relations Act, and as the right to belong to a union of one's choice is made under the Order in Council, which was not referred to in terms in the Foreign Secretary's original statement, can the right hon. and learned Gentleman give even one precedent for withdrawing the right to belong to a trade union under an instruction given under the Order in Council?

Sir Geoffrey Howe: The statutory right to protection of the right to trade union membership first found its way on to the statute books in the Industrial Relations Act 1971, so there has not been a very long time in which to test the proposition, but, beyond that, the provisions under which we are operating apply to security and intelligence. The other agencies which are primarily concerned with security and intelligence are already covered by the certificate. This agency was outstanding as an anomaly and it was therefore appropriate and right for an order of that kind to be made and for the Order in Council to be varied.

Dr David Owen (Plymouth, Devonport) [Leader of the Social Democratic Party, which later merged with the Liberal Party. Owen had been Foreign Secretary in a previous Labour government.]: Did the Government of the day issue an Order in Council following the certification procedure applied in 1976 to MI5 and MI6?

Sir Geoffrey Howe: So far as I know they did not, because the conditions required in that respect already applied there. That is my point. In the other intelligence and security agencies these conditions already applied. In those circumstances, all that was necessary was the making of a certificate. It is because this one agency was an anomaly that it was necessary to act in this way.

In response to the Select Committee's fourth recommendation, exploratory talks between the Government and the Civil Service unions have indeed taken place on several occasions in an attempt to find the necessary amount of common ground. It is no reflection on the seriousness with which the Government and the unions conducted those talks that they were unable to reach agreement.

The Committee's fifth recommendation is conditional on agreement having been reached. As I have just explained, that has unfortunately not proved possible. I come, therefore, to the final recommendation—that the Government should suspend their action while talks with the unions continue. The Government do not believe that it would have been right to act as recommended by the Committee.

As it was, the Government and the unions moved as quickly as possible to explore the scope for an agreement. If one had been possible, I have no doubt that there would have been no difficulty then in drawing the appropriate conclusions for all the staff at GCHQ.

[*The Foreign Secretary went on to deal in more detail with the points which had been put by the government to the unions. Several other MPs interrupted his speech to ask questions.*]

4.17 pm

Mr Denis Healey (Leeds, East) [Labour frontbench spokesman on foreign affairs]: Let me begin by agreeing on one thing with the Foreign Secretary. No one with any knowledge of the matter can underestimate the importance of this issue. GCHQ has been by far the most valuable source of intelligence for the British Government ever since it began operating at Bletchley during the last war. British skills in interception and code-breaking are unique and highly valued by all of our allies. GCHQ has been a key element in our relationship with the United States for more than 40 years. [. . .]

It is just over four weeks since the Foreign Secretary told the House that he had decided to rob those loyal and dedicated men and women of their right to trade union membership—a right that they have enjoyed throughout their employment there and which has been enjoyed by all employees ever since GCHQ was first set up. It is a right that is enjoyed by tens of thousands of other men and women who do work of equal secrecy and of equal national importance in other Government Departments and in private industry. It is a right that is enjoyed by more tens of thousands of men and women in the Post Office, the Health Service and in many other parts of the Government service on whose continuity of work lives might well depend.

The decision that the Foreign Secretary announced to the House just over one month ago was taken without consulting the representatives of the workers concerned and without consulting even his colleagues in the Cabinet. Since then, I must tell the Foreign Secretary, his daily contradictory statements have made him the laughing stock of the world. When reading through them this weekend I was reminded of nothing so much as the five press conferences given by President Reagan on the Lebanon. The Foreign Secretary has been attacked anonymously by fellow Ministers as basing his decision on emotional and not on intellectual judgment. He has been attacked publicly by Conservative Back Benchers, notably the hon. Member for Cheltenham (Mr Irving), in whose constituency most GCHQ workers reside, and by the hon. Member for Hendon North (Mr Gorst)—Gorst of Grunwick as some of us have learnt to call him—who, on radio recently, described the Foreign Secretary's action as

> 'the nasty thin wedge of Fascism'.

The Conservative newspapers have been even more outspoken. The *Daily Telegraph* described the behaviour of the Foreign Secretary and the Government as 'little short of shambolic'. The *Daily Express* described their decision as 'highly illiberal and authoritarian'. Moreover, they were condemned unanimously by the Select Committee of the House which has a majority of Conservative Members.

More important still, the Government's decision has already done immense damage to the morale, not only at GCHQ but of the Civil Service as a whole. It was condemned by Lord Bancroft in a letter to *The Times* as:

> 'breathtakingly inept: a further exploration of the bloody fool branch of management science'.

Lord Bancroft wrote as a former head of the Civil Service. The entire First Division Association, which represents the top rank of the Civil Service, is up in arms. The Cabinet Office members of the First Division Association have already formally complained to the Minister for the Civil Service, and middle and junior staff have walked out both at the Cabinet Office and the Treasury. The whole machinery of Government is now seething with discontent, partly because the Government's decision is seen as a precedent for attacks on union membership in other secret work—public and private—and in other areas where continuity of operation is regarded by the Government as important.

The Foreign Secretary told the House that he had no intention of using this precedent elsewhere. I remember him and the Prime Minister telling us at election after election that they had 'no intention' of cutting Health Service provisions. The fact is, however, that that phrase is used by members of the Government to disguise a decision to do something by not actually denying that they will do it. For the Government, the way to hell is paved with 'no intentions'.

[. . .] In the past month everyone has been asking why on earth the Foreign Secretary took the decision. It was not because he believed that trade unions were likely to be spies, because he knows, as we do, that most spies since the war have been public schoolboys, masons, scientists or service men. I have no doubt that the Government have in hand measures for dealing with that particular threat to our security. The Foreign Secretary told the House this afternoon that he took the decision because the disruption at GCHQ on certain occasions between 1979 and 1981 broke the continuity of work there and might have endangered lives. He concluded—he told us again this afternoon—that membership of the trade union produces an unacceptable conflict of loyalties.

Some hon. Members may have been impressed by some of the quotations that the Foreign Secretary read out in his speech from trade union leaders during those periods of industrial action. However, the trade unions have shown that there was no prejudice to the essential operations of GCHQ at the time, and the Foreign Secretary told the Select Committee that there was no evidence that any damage was done. [. . .]

[The Foreign Secretary] told the Select Committee that Lord Carrington had discussed the matter with a small group of Ministers, including himself, who was then the Chancellor of the Exchequer. The proposal for a ban on union membership, which was discussed by Ministers in 1982, was brushed aside so contemptuously by Lord Carrington that he could not even remember that it had been put to him when he was questioned by his friends, as reported in *The Times* a fortnight ago.

Two years after Ministers rejected a ban on union membership at GCHQ, the Foreign Secretary and the Prime Minister took a decision to ban the unions right out of the blue. Their only excuse was that the Government had not avowed the existence of GCHQ as an intelligence centre until they published the report of the Security Commission on the Prime affair. I have been in the House for more than 30 years and that is the daftest excuse I have ever heard a Government give for an act of policy. [. . .]

The existence and function of GCHQ have been known to any interested person anywhere in the world since the end of the second world war. In 1960 two American defectors from the National Security Agency in Washington held a 90-minute press conference in Moscow describing the work of NSA and its foreign links. Mr Khrushchev joked about it in public when he visited the United States 25 years ago. Mr Prime was recruited in 1968. [. . .]

As an ex-Secretary of State for Defence, may I say that Ministers and officials sometimes have the most peculiar ideas about what are official secrets. [. . .]

It is difficult to find any convincing reason for this sudden decision by the Government—eight months after the publication of the Security Commission report on Prime—except that their fear of staff reaction to the introduction of the polygraph, or lie detector, which is due to begin on an experimental basis in a few weeks' time. [. . .]

There is no doubt but that the Government were terrified of how staff might react if the use of the lie detector was made a ground for dismissal. Perhaps there was also American pressure—we were told that by the previous director of GCHQ, Sir Brian Tovey, who said in an interview with *The Sunday Times* in recent weeks that discreet pressure had been applied. He was so proud of his interview in *The Sunday Times* that in *The Times* the next morning he wrote a letter urging everyone to read it. Someone must have had a word with him within the next 24 hours, because he told a different story to the Select Committee. He said that what *The Sunday Times* had printed was not quite right, but he did not tell us what he said, and I understand from the journalists who conducted the interview that those were his precise words. General Keegan, a retired American general from the intelligence community, said in an interview just after the Government's announcement that subtle pressure would have been applied. I do not know whether there was such pressure. My experience is that the Government are quite capable of making their own mistakes without pressure from other sources. The Government undoubtedly feared that staff at GCHQ might have recourse to industrial tribunals to protect themselves. However, it is interesting to note that the staff have never been interested in using industrial tribunals. In all but three cases during the past 40 years, when there has been a dispute they have taken it to the Civil Service appeals tribunal, and they are prepared to do so now. The only case which required any publicity of an industrial tribunal affecting GCHQ was one brought by Colonel Thwaite recently, because he was not a member of a trade union and was complaining about the effect of union activities on his personal prospects. However, I am glad to see that since the Government's announcement Colonel Thwaite said that if he was still a member he would join a trade union now like a shot. [. . .]

The unions will also be going to the International Labour Organisation because they believe—and I share their belief, although I am not a lawyer—that the Government's decision is in flat violation of an ILO convention that the Government have signed.

I ask the Government to recognise that they have now embarked on a long-drawn-out campaign that they are bound to lose. The campaign will continue until the Government change their mind, or until the Government are changed by the British people, because there is deep feeling on this matter throughout the trade union movement.

The £1,000 bribe was deeply offensive to trade unionists throughout the country. The Permanent Secretary at the Foreign Office told the Select Committee on Foreign Affairs that the cost of the bribe, if successful, could amount to £10 million. [. . .] I have not wasted time on the Foreign Secretary this afternoon [. . . he] is not the real villain in this case; he is the fall guy. Those of us with long memories will feel that he is rather like poor van der Lubbe in the Reichstag fire trial. We are asking ourselves the question that was asked at the trial: who is the Mephistopheles behind this shabby Faust? The answer to that is clear. The handling of this decision by—I quote her own Back Benchers—the great she-elephant, she who must be obeyed, the Catherine the Great of Finchley, the Prime Minister herself, has drawn sympathetic trade unionists, such as Len Murray, into open revolt. Her pig-headed bigotry has prevented her closest colleagues and Sir Robert Armstrong from offering and accepting a compromise.

The right hon. Lady, for whom I have

a great personal affection, has formidable qualities, a powerful intelligence and immense courage, but those qualities can turn into horrendous vices, unless they are moderated by colleagues who have more experience, understanding and sensitivity. As she has got rid of all those colleagues, no one is left in the Cabinet with both the courage and the ability to argue with her. [. . .]

Sir Anthony Kershaw [a Conservative backbencher, chairman of the Select Committee on Foreign Affairs]: [. . .] I understand that it is being proposed to go to international law. I am not an international lawyer, but that step seems unlikely to be successful. The International Labour Organisation convention exempts the police and armed forces from the right to belong to trade unions. The convention was drawn up a long time ago when the police and the armed forces were the only forces that concerned themselves with intelligence. In a nuclear age, however, early intelligence and surveillance are equally important as, if not more important than, the police.

Mr John Morris (Aberavon) *rose—*

Sir Anthony Kershaw: We have an international lawyer with us.

Mr John Morris: I am not pretending to be an international lawyer, but I should have thought that the hon. Gentleman is aware that the convention that the TUC has called in aid is dated no earlier than 1948 and that the exclusion for the armed forces and the police would not apply to his point.

Sir Anthony Kershaw: We shall see who is right. I do not believe that the convention will be found to be applicable in this case. The human rights convention, which specifically mentions security forces, will cover the point if application is made to that court in Europe.

The protestations that we have heard from the Opposition would come better from people who are prepared to make an equal amount of noise about the right not to join a trade union. Closed minds on the closed shop are not the best advocates of freedom. The people at GCHQ still have many rights. They have the ordinary rights of civil servants, including those relating to conditions of transfer and work and protection under various Acts of Parliament to do with health and so on. They still have the same rights as the armed forces and the police, the functions of which, in relation to the state, are similar. The Labour Government enforced that policy in regard to the armed forces and the police. I note that they have fared a great deal better under the present Government than under Labour. The only right that people at GCHQ have lost is that, for negotiating reasons, to endanger the safety of the state. That is a right that no one should have.

6.39 pm

Mr John Morris (Aberavon): I am glad to follow the hon. Member for Stroud (Sir A. Kershaw) because in the last few minutes of his speech he raised matters of law. In my short speech I hope to raise questions about law and shall be grateful if the Minister will answer them when he replies.

It became abundantly clear during the reluctant exchanges between the Foreign Secretary, my right hon. and learned Friend the Member for Monklands, East (Mr Smith) and myself that the withdrawal of the right to join a trade union does not come under the certificate of the Employment Protection Act. It comes from instructions made under the Order in Council—the royal prerogative. It became abundantly clear that while the Government prayed in aid, in the original statement of the Foreign Secretary and his statement today, precedents for signing certificates under the Employment Protection Act, there was no precedent, under this or any other Order in Council, to withdraw the right to join a trade union. That fact must be clearly established in our exchanges with the Foreign Secretary today.

As the Government from time to time make great play of the point that they receive their support partly because of the importance they place on law and order, it is important to examine closely whether they come to the House with clean hands regarding the law in relation to GCHQ. Never mind that they are behaving like an old-fashioned Victorian employer. This is one of the earliest fruits of returning to the Victorian values that the Prime Minister prays so much in aid. However, whether they can use the royal prerogative to vary unilaterally the conditions of service of their employees is open to argument. Under the royal prerogative it is certainly provided that the Government can dismiss and re-engage their employees, but unilaterally to vary the contract without dismissal and re-engagement cannot be done unless the courts can infer that the variations are effectively dismissal and re-employment.

An equally, if not more, important issue is the possible—indeed, probable—breach of Britain's international obligations. I do not recall—I may have missed it and do not wish to be unfair—a reference to that by the Foreign Secretary in his speech. In his statement to the Select Committee, he said:

> 'On the basis of the legal advice available to the Government this action is in accordance with our international legal obligations.'

I shall examine the main obligations that could be affected. The first is International Labour Organisation convention 87. It is dated 1948 and is ratified by the British Government; therefore, we cannot lightly ignore it without being seen to be in breach of international obligations. Article 2 states:

> 'Workers and employers, without distinction whatsoever, shall have the right to establish and, subject only to the rules of the organisation concerned, to join organisations of their own choosing without previous authorisation.'

GCHQ is a case in point. Article 3 states:

> 'Workers and employers shall have the right to draw up their constitutions and rules.'

It continues:

> 'The public authorities shall refrain from any interference which would restrict this right or impede the lawful exercise thereof.'

Article 8 states:

> 'In exercising the rights provided for in this Convention workers and employers and their respective organisations, like other persons or organised collectivities, shall respect the law of the land.
>
> 2. The law of the land shall not be such as to impair, nor shall it be so applied as to impair, the guarantees provided for in this Convention.'

Article 9 states:

> 'The extent to which the guarantees provided for in this Convention shall apply to the armed forces and the police shall be determined by national laws or regulations.'

There is no reference to civil servants. The exclusion is confined specifically to the armed forces and the police.

Mr Nicholls: [Conservative backbencher and a solicitor] Is my recollection correct that article 1.2 of convention 151, which was signed in 1978, is to the effect that public servants who are dealing with information of a peculiarly sensitive nature are also deprived of the right of trade union membership?

Mr Morris: Article 151 is wholly different, stands on its own and in no way seeks to limit the general provision. I agree and accept that there is an exclusion in 151, which is why I do not propose to bring it to the attention of the Minister.

I mention the articles because I seek clarification.

Will the Minister explain the position where there is more than one convention each of which has different exclusions? Some exclude the whole body of public administration, some exclude national security interests and this one excludes the armed forces and the police. The Foreign Secretary has not said a word about that today, and in Select Committee we heard only the confident tone that the Government were satisfied that they had carried out their obligations. Where there are two conventions, both of which are equally binding on the Government, and one provides for a particular exclusion and the other does not, what is the position? We have not had clarification either in Select Committee or from the Foreign Secretary, and so I ask for it this afternoon. I cannot be denied that request.

Contrary to views expressed in the past few weeks, I find difficulty in applying the 1950 European convention on human rights because it excludes persons engaged in the administration of the state. It also provides for restrictions where they are necessary in a democratic society for the protection of national security. This is a parallel point. Whether the Government—I assume that the convention applies—could satisfy the European Court on the second point, that they have made a bona fide determination, allowing them every reasonable margin of appreciation, might be questioned. 'Necessary' is a word with a mandatory nuance about it. How far, given the offer of the unions to provide guarantees for the changes in their conditions of work, the exclusion of the basic rights that they have enjoyed so far is necessary, it might not be easy for the Government to argue. As confirmation, I have the evidence of Sir Brian Tovey that, had the particular proposal of the trade unions been available to the Government at that stage, they would not have needed to carry out the administrative acts that they have done. That would count against the Government if they tried to pray in aid the need to act in this way because it was necessary in a democratic society for the protection of national security.

My hon. and learned Friend the Member for Leicester West (Mr Janner) mentioned in Committee the international covenant on civil and political rights of 1966. That is a United Nations convention and the only restriction it provides is a personal one regarding the police and the armed forces, not unlike the restriction in the ILO convention. It has a restriction similar to that contained in the European convention on human rights, and refers to exclusions

> 'necessary in a democratic society for the protection [. . .] of national security'.

A similar argument applies to the unions' offer. If the offer is excluded, was the Government's action necessary to protect national security? I doubt, given the terms of the offer, whether the Government could make a case on that.

Article 22(2) of the covenant states:

> 'No restrictions may be placed on the exercise of this right other than those which are proscribed [*sic*] by law, which are necessary in a democratic society in the interests of national security or public safety.'

In the Select Committee my hon. and learned Friend the Member for Leicester, West asked the Foreign Secretary whether the right to belong to a trade union was proscribed by law. The Foreign Secretary replied:

> 'No, it is the right—or the change in that respect is made by the change in the terms and conditions of service.'

As reported on page 41 of the report, the Foreign Secretary continued to justify this:

> 'It is the Prime Minister who is acting by virtue of the Civil Service Order in Council 1982, and it is that Order, part of the law of England, which gives her authority from time to time to make regulations or give instructions for

> controlling the conduct of the service and for the conditions of service of those employed in it. It is as a result of our power to act under the 1982 Order in Council that the changes in the terms and conditions of service are being introduced as set out in the notice.'

The Government are obviously relying upon the Order in Council coupled with the Prime Minister's instructions made under it. I note that there is a gap in time between the certificate signed by the Foreign Secretary on 25 January and the confirmation of instruction on 7 February. That became apparent in an answer given last Thursday, and was mentioned by my right hon. Friend the Member for Cardiff, South and Penarth (Mr Callaghan). However, there may be no significance in the gap.

The position is not as clear-cut as the Foreign Secretary would have us believe. The order does not proscribe; it merely empowers the Minister to give instructions

> 'for controlling the conduct of the service, and providing for the classification of all persons employed herein and, so far as they relate to matters other than remuneration, expenses and allowances, the conditions of service of all persons'.

We need a great deal of imagination to understand this, but it would appear that the words, 'the conditions of service', give the Government the power to deny people the right to belong to a trade union.

I return to my original anxiety: whether the Government are satisfied that the royal prerogative allows them unilaterally to vary conditions of employment as opposed to sacking and reinstatement. The House has traditionally been against the royal prerogative since the Magna Carta. In 1611 the courts said:

> 'The Sovereign can claim no prerogative except such as the law allows, nor such as are contrary to Magna Carta or any other statutes, or to the liberties of the subject.'

It would be strange if the House could easily endorse the interpretation that a prime ministerial instruction can automatically be proscriptive in law and a denial of the hallowed liberties of the subject.

The house cannot make law. It is strange that, on this interpretation, the Prime Minister can make law by edict. The Government may be right in this connection, but, if they are, the sooner that the House examines the extent of the royal prerogative, the better. Whatever doubts and difficulties there may be about other conventions—I should be glad to know the Minister's view on this—there is serious anxiety about ILO convention 87. I put forward that convention, having considered all the others in turn, as the greatest hurdle facing the Government. If we cannot have a clear answer tonight, I hope that a paper will be placed in the Library to justify the Government's case that they have adhered to their international obligations. In that way, we can understand how they put their case.

6.55 pm

Mr John Gorst (Hendon North) [Conservative backbencher and member of the Employment Select Committee]: As some of my hon. Friends know, some years ago I was involved in and gave my support in a well-publicised industrial dispute at Grunwick. They may be puzzled by my apparent volte face in now taking the side of the trade union movement at GCHQ, Cheltenham. May I tell those of my hon. Friends who may believe this to be inconsistent that there is no such inconsistency. At Grunwick I argued for the right not to belong to a trade union, and with GCHQ I argue for the right to belong to a trade union; if one makes one such argument, one must be consistent with the other.

As a member of the Select Committee when it embarked upon its examination of the Government's intention to ban membership of a trade union, I began with the assumption that banning union membership could be justified on the very special grounds of national security. However, I wondered even then whether the Government had addressed themselves to their announcement in the best possible way. As the Committee's inquiry progressed, I gradually came to the conclusion that the Government were not necessarily correct in banning unions at GCHQ. Much of the credit for my change of mind—my conversion, if that is what it was—is due to the evidence given by Sir Brian Tovey.

I conceded at the outset of the inquiry—I still do—that drastic action is justifiable to protect national security. I am convinced that dangerous disruption due to industrial action took place in 1979 and 1981. That is common ground among all sides in this argument, but our response to those facts differs. I do not accept that the Government have adequately examined the options that are now open. I admit that those options may not have been available when the decisions were being discussed, but times have changed and options now exist. Nor do I believe that the Government have given convincing reasons for rejecting what the unions have conceded. The unions have offered unprecedented concessions and have said that they are willing to agree to equally unprecedented and legally binding assurances. Why have not the Government pursued those options?

Before dealing with that matter, I should mention the Select Committee. It would be wrong to overlook two aspects of the Committee's deliberations. Important morals for all Select Committees can and should be drawn from the points that I shall make. It is a compliment to the integrity of those on the Committee that it published a unanimous report. It was founded on facts and I believe that we propounded those facts with objectivity. However, while we were examining our subject I had reason to complain of interference by both Whips and Ministers as to how we were conducting our proceedings. That complaint still stands; indeed, I have further noticed, since our report was published, that there are further signs of Whips or Government interests in how we are conducting our affairs in the Select Committee on Employment. Perhaps that is a compliment to our potency and the value of the Select Committee system, but it also has its dangers.

The purpose of Select Committees is to examine facts and to examine how the Executive conducts itself, and for that purpose a Committee must choose its own subjects of inquiry. It must select for itself which witnesses it believes are relevant. There has been interference—subtly applied, of course—in both those areas, and such interference endangers the work of Select Committees. It inhibits one of the most valuable instances of progress made in recent years to provide an extra balance against the overwhelming power of the Executive.

Select Committees must not be undermined. The independence of Select Committees needs to be reinforced. They must not only be independent, they must be seen and known to be so.

The Government refused to allow witnesses to give evidence in private to the Select Committee on Employment. The two witnesses whom the Government disallowed were a leading trade union representative within GCHQ and the present director. I make no complaint about the latter; I do make complaint about the former.

The reasons given for denying the opportunity to give evidence are both specious and anomalous. They are specious because they hide behind a ruling made on the very day that Geoffrey Prime's role at GCHQ was first avowed. That ruling, quoted by the Foreign Secretary, was that

> 'Government does not provide information . . . on matters of security and intelligence'.

But the ban by the Foreign Secretary was upheld, despite his being told that the Committee's purpose was merely to question the witnesses on the terms and conditions of employment and despite his having said in a written answer on the same day that we were questioning him:

> 'elected trade union representatives are allowed to publicise their unions' views on matters which directly affect the conditions of service of members of their union'—[*Official Report*, 6 February 1984; Vol. 53, *c. 490*].

The Foreign Secretary's reasons are, I believe, anomalous because, throughout the subsequent days, trade unionists from GCHQ have had access to the media and access to their Members of Parliament, and they came in droves to lobby Members of Parliament last Thursday. What, I wonder, had been done, is being done, or will be done about that?

Thus we have a ridiculous situation in which a GCHQ trade unionist can talk with other trade unionists outside GCHQ, and talk to Members of Parliament, but a Select Committee wishing to sit in secret, can talk to none of them. I hope that this House will look with disfavour on that undesirable intrusion by the Government into how Select Committees conduct their business.

The Foreign Secretary told the Select Committee, when he was asked how he could equate discussions and information purely about terms and conditions of employment with matters of security:

> 'It is not a question of equating it; it is a question of applying the rule.'

Hon. Members may well regard that reply as being rather short on reasonableness and rather long on pedantry. Suffice it to say, however, that it had the momentary effect of hiding the deep mortification felt by those who work at GCHQ.

One of the reasons given by the Government for not accepting the Civil Service unions' far-reaching concessions is that the fact of union membership creates of itself a condition in which individuals are torn between a loyalty to their union and a loyalty to their employer, GCHQ. I regard that as a dangerous fallacy.

Mr Tam Dalyell (Linlithgow): [a Labour backbencher] Many hon. Members have listened to the hon. Gentleman putting an honourable point of view on radio and in the House. Why does he think that his Government did what it did? What led them to take that action?

Mr Gorst: I should like to be able to answer the hon. Gentleman's question, but nothing I heard in the Select Committee or this afternoon in the House has given me any inkling about the Government's true motives. I can assume only that they are basing their actions on inadequate reasons.

[. . .] The questions are legion and the Government's answers are lame. It is not for me to argue the merits of union membership. This is a democracy, and many millions have a deep attachment to their right to belong to a union. Hon. Members have a duty to remove that right only if there is no other way. The Government have not proven the case that there is no other way. I urge the Prime Minister, even at this late hour, to re-examine the possibilities. In the final analysis, the Government seem to be resting their case on the proposition that they have no other choice and that this is an unpleasant necessity. Regrettably, we do not seem to have learnt as much from our history as we should have done. About 200 years ago the then Foreign Secretary came to the House of Commons to argue for another measure—not on grounds of choice but on grounds of necessity. Charles James Fox, talking of the East India Company Bill, said:

> 'This business forces itself upon me and upon the nation.'

He was answered by a Back Bencher, the 24 year old Mr William Pitt, who said:

> 'This measure is an abrogation of all the ancient charters and privileges by which the company was first established.'

He added:

> 'Necessity is the plea for every infringement of human freedom.'

I will forbear to complete that famous quotation. Surely the Government should ponder carefully the 'necessity' for their chosen course of action [. . .].

Mr Baldry: [a Conservative backbencher, also a member of the Employment Select Committee] I forbore to interrupt my hon. Friend the Member for Hendon, North (Mr Gorst) on this matter because we have tussled before, but lest this idea that the Government Whips nobbled any Members of the Select Committee should grow roots and flourish. I should make it clear that at no time—I think that I speak for my colleagues—were we nobbled or interfered with by any Government Whips. Would that we had been so lucky. [. . .]

Mr Gorst: I was asked whether I could cast some light on the local difficulty by explaining that there is more than one way of nobbling. One does not need to take a man by the arm; one can sometimes wink or nod at him.

Mr Eastham: [a Labour backbencher, another member of the Employment Select Committee] I appreciate the odd nod and wink. This has been the style of management over the centuries. It is still a form of nobbling, and it was for those reasons that the hon. Gentleman, I feel sure, felt that he was compelled to report this to the Select Committee. However, in spite of the problems, when the report was considered, to the credit of the Select Committee members, they were unanimous in their view. Throughout the evidence, nothing was presented that seemed to justify the action taken by the Prime Minister and the Foreign Secretary.

Day by day it became more obvious in Committee that this was an ill-thought-out action and that even the Cabinet had been treated with contempt and not consulted as to its importance. . . . When Sir Brian Tovey came to give evidence to the Select Committee, I felt that Downing Street had sent him along as a pet poodle, but nothing that he said convinced any members of the Committee that there was a case to justify the Government's action. As has been said, Tovey admitted to the Committee that if a deal such as that later presented by the trade unions had been forthcoming he would have snatched agreement with both hands. Regardless of that, the Government went ahead and decided to continue the confrontation.

The trade unions have been more than accommodating. They have offered a no-strike agreement. As has often been said by Ministers and hon. Members on both sides of the House, the loyalty of the workers was beyond doubt. They were already bound by the Official Secrets Act. What more could any Government expect from a loyal band of workers?

This deplorable episode is typical of the Prime Minister's arrogance, and there have been no negotiations. The Prime Minister agreed to meet the trade unions on a second occasion but it was obvious that such a meeting would be a dialogue with the deaf. She had made up her mind and there will be no trade unions. This is an example of the cheating of the workers of their democratic rights. . . .

[*Several other Members spoke during the debate.*]

Mr John Cartwright (Woolwich) [a member of the Social Democratic Party]: *rose in his place and claimed to move*, That the Question be now put.

Question, That the Question be now put, *put and agreed to.*

Main Question put accordingly:—

The House divided: Ayes 25, Noes 201.

[*Hansard goes on to list the MPs who voted for (ayes) and against (noes) the formal motion.*]

The government won the vote by a very large majority because the Labour Party leadership decided not to vote in the division and that party's whips instructed Labour MPs accordingly. A few backbench Labour MPs defied the whip and voted with the Liberals and Social Democratic Party MPs. A handful of Conservative backbenchers failed to vote in support of the government—including three Conservative members of the Employment Select Committee.

Questions

1. What did the prior work of the select committee contribute to this debate? Several MPs, notably Denis Healey, quoted from newspaper reports during the debate; would it be fair to say that investigative journalists were as influential as the select committee report?
2. What was the motion being debated? What was the debate really about?
3. How were legal arguments used?
4. Why do you think the Labour Party leadership instructed Labour MPs to abstain?
5. In constitutional terms, what exactly was achieved by the debate?

PRIME MINISTER'S QUESTIONS

Throughout the GCHQ episode, the union ban has been a topic regularly raised at the twice-weekly Prime Minister's Question Time. On 28 February 1984, the day after the adjournment debate, questions were asked on a variety of topics: strikes on London Transport; redundancies of university lecturers; the sale of Hamilton College and the role of the Public Accounts Committee; Liverpool City Council; Angola; local radio in London; Hamilton College (again). Interspersed with these issues were several questions about GCHQ; other trade unions were taking strike action to show support for the GCHQ union members. (See HC Deb, cols 134–8.)

PRIME MINISTER
Engagements

Q1. Mr Peter Bruinvels [a Conservative backbencher] asked the Prime Minister if she will list her official engagements for 28 February.

The Prime Minister (Mrs Margaret Thatcher): This morning I had meetings with ministerial colleagues and others, including one with the Premier of Bermuda. In addition to my duties in the House I shall be having further meetings later today, including one with Chancellor Kohl. This evening I hope to have an audience of Her Majesty the Queen.

Mr Bruinvels: Will my right hon. Friend find time today to comment on the secondary action being taken by trade union members all over the country—action that is illegal and totally irresponsible? Is it not true that from 1979 to 1981 there was disruption at Cheltenham, with national union leaders interfering with the workers there because of disputes elsewhere?

The Prime Minister: Yes. The action that has been taken by the trade unions today to encourage breaches of contract is further justification for the action that the Government took to protect national security at GCHQ.

Mr Steel: [Leader of the Liberal Party] As the Leader of the Opposition has taken action against two members of his party for voting against the Government last night [the Labour Party abstained at the end of the adjournment debate], what action does the right hon. Lady propose to take against members of her party who refused to support her? Does she accept that yesterday's debate revealed widespread unease in all parts of the House about her continued intransigence on the issue of GCHQ, and has she anything fresh to say to the House?

The Prime Minister: No. A majority of 176 is good enough for me, and I am grateful to the right hon. Gentleman for providing the opportunity.

[*Questions on other subjects were asked.*]

Mr Kinnock: [Leader of the Labour Party] To come back to self-inflicted injuries, and to return to the subject of GCHQ, does not the Prime Minister agree that the refusal to accept money in exchange for the loss of personal liberties is to be applauded?

The Prime Minister: It is a matter of personal choice. [*Interruption.*] Had we not been prepared to give compensation for rights that were lost, I believe that we would have laid ourselves open to criticism.

Mr Kinnock: Will the Prime Minister tell us whether it was necessary to take such powers and offer such freedom of choice during wartime, when this country was fighting for its freedom? If it was not necessary to do so then, what can justify it now? Is it not a fact that the Prime Minister's selfish pride has reached such depths as to require her to threaten the careers of loyal civil servants in order to impose her selfish will?

The Prime Minister: The right hon. Gentleman tries to forget, as do many other trade unionists, the events of 1979 and 1981. Indeed, I thought the right hon. and hon. Members on both sides of the House made the charge against me yesterday that I did not take action sooner, as many people thought we should have done after 1981.

[*Questions on other subjects were asked.*]

Mr Nicholas Winterton: Is my right hon. Friend aware that she has great support in this country and on the Conservative Benches for the concern and commitment that she has shown towards the national security of this country in her decision over GCHQ? Does she agree that all Members of the House should show the same interest and commitment towards the position of Mr Speaker in the way that they behave in the House?

The Prime Minister: I believe that the decision we took on GCHQ was the right one in the interests of national security. I agree that I am stubborn about pursuing matters of national security, but the British people would expect no less.

[*Questions on other subjects were asked.*]

General Questions

1. What criteria should be used for measuring the 'effectiveness' of parliamentary scrutiny? If the main criterion is whether the government is persuaded to change its mind, then parliamentary scrutiny is mostly worthless, is it not?
2. Compare and contrast the scrutiny techniques used

(a) by the Employment Select Committee,
(b) in the adjournment debate on the floor of the Commons and
(c) at Prime Minister's Questions.

3. What, if any, reforms to parliamentary scrutiny procedures would you advocate?

4. MPs spent considerable time discussing international treaty obligations.[5] What does this reveal about the importance of these as a constraint on government?

5. No MP appears to have asked whether the government's ban was contrary to *national* law and there was no discussion of judicial review. Can you speculate why this was so? Might it be because MPs knew less about judicial review than international law? Or did they assume (wrongly) that the domestic courts would not entertain a judicial review challenge to a decision taken under prerogative powers?[6] Or was it because the principle of 'legitimate expectation', which the law lords accepted had been breached by the government in this case, had not yet been established? Or was it that the *sub judice* rule prevented parliamentary discussion of judicial review proceedings?

6. What does this episode reveal about the difficulties of obtaining open government?

WHERE TO GO FROM HERE

This and the previous chapter examine how Parliament calls government to account for the actions it has taken. Historically, MPs have also had a more particular role in helping constituents obtain redress for their individual grievances against government. During the 1960s, there was a growing awareness that MPs and Parliament were failing adequately to fulfil this important constitutional role. The result was the creation in 1967 of the office of Parliamentary Commissioner for Administration (PCA). It is to the work of the PCA and other 'ombudsmen' to which we turn in the next chapter.

[5] See generally pp. 381–2 and 397–9.
[6] See Chapter 28.

18

OMBUDSMEN

. . . [I]n his Second Reading speech, Crossman described the Commissioner as, 'a new and powerful weapon with a sharp cutting edge to be added to the existing antiquated armoury of parliamentary questions and adjournment debates'. . . . Quintin Hogg, the main Opposition spokesman, described the proposals as a 'threat' to a parliamentary democracy in which the constituency MP already provided 'an efficient and relatively sophisticated grievance machinery . . . developed by trial and error in this House'.[1]

I see my task as primarily to investigate an individual complaint; secondly to provide a recommended redress where the redress is justified; thirdly, to recommend improvements in the systems, or where there are no systems, to recommend that there should be in order to minimise the risk of the same mistake being repeated.[2]

INTRODUCTION AND HISTORICAL BACKGROUND

The previous two chapters examine how MPs use formal parliamentary procedures—select committee investigations, debates on the floor of the Commons and PQs—to call the government to account for its executive actions. In scrutinizing government in these ways MPs are often concerned with broad issues of general policy. MPs also have another important constitutional role: to be concerned with the individual grievances of constituents and others who claim to have been badly treated by public bodies. During the 1960s criticism mounted that MPs were failing to deal with such individual grievances effectively. It was said that the convention of ministerial responsibility often prevented complaints being properly resolved.[3] While ministers are answerable for errors made by their departments, in practice when ministers receive complaints about their departments they ask

[1] Gavin Drewry and Carol Harlow, 'A Cutting Edge? The Parliamentary Commissioner and MPs' (1990) 53 MLR 745, 746–7.

[2] Sir William Reid, Parliamentary Commissioner for Administration until 2 January 1997, giving evidence to the Select Committee on the PCA: Annual Report for 1992, HC 751, Minutes of Evidence, para. 24. An extended statement of aims can be found in the Annual Report of the PCA for 1994, HC 307, para. 14 (hereafter 'Annual Report 1994'). The current PCA is Mr Michael Buckley, who took office in January 1997.

[3] See p. 51.

departmental officials to investigate and report back to them. Ministers then tell MPs what they think it is necessary for them to know. The MP and the original complainant are forced to trust that the matter has been properly investigated, even when they remain dissatisfied with the outcome.

It was in order to improve upon this process that the Parliamentary Commissioner for Administration (PCA) was created in 1967 as the first ombudsman-type body established within the British system.[4] It has since led the way for the widespread use of ombudsmen of various types in both the public and private sectors in this country.

The term ombudsman means 'grievance-handler' and owes its origin to the Swedish ombudsman established in 1809 to investigate allegations that the government had been improperly seeking to influence civil servants. The idea of importing the ombudsman concept into Britain took hold during the 1950s and early 1960s in response to mounting public concern about the inadequacy of machinery for redress against government.[5] The most influential advocacy for a British ombudsman came in a 1961 JUSTICE report, *The Citizen and the Administration*. Aware both that MPs might view the ombudsman as a threat to their work as complaints-handlers and also that ministers might see it as a threat to the doctrine of ministerial responsibility, JUSTICE designed their proposal as a way of strengthening the House of Commons *vis-à-vis* the administration and supporting the work of MPs. It recommended that for an initial period of five years, while the new institution was finding its feet, citizens would have to route their complaints through an MP, who could then refer the matter on to the PCA. Only after this initial period would the public have direct access.

While widely supported, like many proposals for reform the JUSTICE recommendations were criticized both by those who thought they did not go far enough and by those who considered them too radical. Professor Mitchell fell into the former group. He argued that a thorough-going reform of administrative law was needed and that the proposals would be an 'administrative palliative'.[6] In his view the PCA was a half-hearted measure that would be more dangerous than doing nothing. It would, he argued, create a sense of self-satisfaction and provide a perfect excuse for continuing inertia.

Objections of a very different type came from the then Conservative government. Incredibly, it viewed the proposals as a threat to the parliamentary system which would so interfere with the process of administration that they would undermine the government's ability to govern efficiently.[7] The proposals were consequently put on ice until Wilson's Labour introduced the

[4] For a detailed history, see Frank Stacey, *The British Ombudsman* (1971).

[5] This concern led to the establishment of the Franks Committee which, as discussed in Chapter 19, did much to modernize the workings of tribunals.

[6] J. D. Mitchell, 'The Causes and Effects of the Absence of a System of Public Law in the United Kingdom' [1965] PL 95, 109; 'The Ombudsman Fallacy' [1962] PL 24; and 'The Irrelevance of the Ombudsman Proposals' in D. C. Rowat (ed.), *The Ombudsman: Citizen Defender* (1965).

[7] Lord Dilhorne LC, HL Deb, vol. 244, cols 384–5 and the quote from Quintin Hogg MP (later known as Lord Hailsham, a Conservative Lord Chancellor) at the beginning of the chapter.

Parliamentary Commissioner Act 1967.[8] This established the PCA (also referred to as the 'Parliamentary Ombudsman') as well as the Select Committee on the Parliamentary Commissioner.

The creation of the PCA was followed by the establishment of a similar body for Northern Ireland in 1969, and the Health Service Commissioner (or 'Health Services Ombudsman') in 1973.[9] Local Commissioners ('Local Ombudsmen') were created in 1974 to investigate complaints against local authorities in England and Wales.[10] The Parliamentary Ombudsman, the Health Services Ombudsman and the Local Ombudsmen are the main public sector ombudsmen operating within Britain and it is with these bodies that this chapter is concerned.

Ombudsmen, however, are now widely used in both the public and private sectors. Several government departments and local authorities, for instance, have recently appointed their own 'ombudsman' to handle complaints against themselves. During 1994 the Inland Revenue established its own complaints adjudicator and a similar appointment was made by Companies House in 1995.[11] A Prisons 'Ombudsman' for England and Wales has also been created, as has a Scottish Prisons Complaints Commissioner. Also in 1995, following a report of the Nolan Committee on Standards in Public Life, a Parliamentary Commissioner for Standards has been set up to investigate complaints that MPs have breached a code of conduct.[12]

The Maastricht Treaty established an Ombudsman for the European Community to deal with complaints 'concerning instances of maladministration in the activities of the Community institutions or bodies, with the exception of the Court of Justice and the Court of First Instance acting in their judicial role'.[13]

In the private sector ombudsman-type bodies have been created to deal, among other things, with complaints against the legal profession, banks, insurance companies, the provision of financial services (including accountants), building societies, the media, and telephone services. Some of these bodies are statutory (such as the Legal Services Ombudsman and the Building Societies Ombudsman) while others are non-statutory, such as the Insurance Ombudsman.[14]

[8] Hereafter the 'PC Act 1967'.

[9] National Health Service Reorganization Act 1973. See now the Health Service Commissioners Act 1993 (hereafter the 'HSC Act 1993'). To date the same person has been both the Parliamentary Ombudsman and the Health Services Ombudsman. The government has recently accepted that it may be impossible for the same person to be both the PCA and the Health Service Commissioner if the range of functions and workload of these bodies increase.

[10] Local Government Act 1974, Part III (hereafter the 'LGA 1974'). The Act established three commissioners in England and one in Wales. The responsibility of the three commissioners dealing with England is divided geographically. Local authorities in Scotland were brought into the scheme in 1975.

[11] P. E. Morris, 'The Revenue Adjudicator—The First Two Years' [1996] PL 309.

[12] *Standards in Public Life*, First Report of the Committee on Standards in Public Life (1995).

[13] EC Treaty, Art 138e.

[14] Birkinshaw has described the 'explosion of the ombudsman concept in the private sector' as '[o]ne of the most dramatic developments in (recent) public law': P. Birkinshaw, *Grievances, Remedies and the State* (2nd edn., 1994), p. 187. Whether these bodies are established by

Why should this proliferation have occurred and what are its implications to public lawyers? The use of ombudsmen reflects the growing recognition in both public and private sectors of the need to provide effective, credible and independent avenues of complaint which can be used without needing the services of lawyers or other costly professional advisors. Access to effective complaints procedures is important both to individual complainants and to the overall quality of decision-making. As the Citizen's Charter emphasizes, complaints and their investigation help to provide feedback on the quality of services being provided and are a valuable source of information for service providers.[15] In the context of the Parliamentary and Health Services Ombudsmen, this feedback can also improve the quality of parliamentary scrutiny.

However, the growth of ombudsman-type bodies has resulted in a plethora of complaints mechanisms. As well as creating confusion among the public,[16] this may detract from the work of the main public sector ombudsmen and make it more difficult for them to project a clear image of their role. It was with these fears in mind that the main ombudsmen in 1993 established the British and Irish Ombudsman Association.[17] The purpose of this association, which Birkinshaw calls 'an ombudsman approval society',[18] is to encourage, develop and safeguard the role of ombudsmen in the public and private sectors and to ensure that 'true' ombudsmen possess certain qualities, such as independence from the bodies about which people are complaining. An 'ombudsman' employed by a government department or local authority, or controlled by an industry, would not satisfy this requirement and would be unable to join.

OMBUDSMAN INVESTIGATIONS

Before going further it is useful to look briefly at the types of problems which have been handled by the three main public sector ombudsmen. As with the case studies, this helps to put the discussion into context, to identify some of the key issues, and better enable us to assess the debates considered later in the chapter.

---

statute or by voluntary agreement may affect the willingness of the courts to review their decisions: see *R v Insurance Ombudsman Bureau and the Insurance Ombudsman, ex p Aegon Life Assurance Ltd* [1994] COD 426.

15 See *If Things Go Wrong*, Citizen's Charter Complaints Task Force Discussion Paper No. 4 on Attitude and Motivation (1994).

16 Aware of this, the select committee has recently recommended (and the government has agreed) that the term 'ombudsman' should not be used to refer to bodies falling within the jurisdiction of the public sector ombudsmen: *The Powers, Work and Jurisdiction of the Ombudsman*, Fifth Report of the Select Committee on the PCA, Session 1993–94, HC 619, para. 10.

17 Originally called the UK Ombudsman Association.

18 P. Birkinshaw, *Grievances, Remedies and the State*, p. 187.

The Parliamentary Ombudsman

In 1995 the PCA received a record 1,706 complaints.[19] The four most highly complained about departments were: the DSS and its agencies (834); the Inland Revenue (160); the Department of the Environment (67); and the Department of Transport (64). During that year 245 complaints were fully investigated. Of these 236 were found to be wholly or partially justified and only nine were found to be wholly unjustified. The PCA obtained a remedy extending beyond an apology in 154 cases and in 108 of these this involved a financial remedy of some sort. In 30 cases the investigation led to a change in departmental practice. The average time taken to complete a full investigation and to report on it was 74 weeks.

Most complaints handled by the Parliamentary Ombudsman involve fairly mundane matters, no doubt of great importance to those concerned but hardly likely to make news headlines. The following are examples of investigations which led to the payments of compensation:

- When the Inland Revenue failed to amend erroneous records affecting the complainant's PAYE code, the complainant received repayment of £1,798.50 tax and £1,008 costs.
- When the Inland Revenue lost documents, having told the complainant to send them to the wrong office, the department repaid tax plus a supplement amounting to £2,105.04.
- When the DSS was found to have delayed and mishandled claims for benefits an *ex gratia* payment was made of £625.62 as compensation for late payment of benefit.

Not all investigations are so mundane and several have recently involved major public scandals concerning important areas of governmental policy affecting large numbers of people. The investigations into the Barlow Clowes affair and the DSS's handling of new schemes involving Disability Allowance and the Child Support Agency are particularly noteworthy.

Barlow Clowes

The PCA described his investigation into the Barlow Clowes affair as 'the most complex, wide-ranging and onerous investigation which the [PCA] has ever undertaken'.[20] It attracted 'public attention on a scale unprecedented in the history of the Parliamentary Commissioner . . . By the end of 1988 . . . complaints relating to the case had been taken up . . . by no fewer than 159 MPs.'[21]

[19] In 1994 there were 1,332 complaints received. The statistics in this paragraph are from the PCA's Annual Report for 1995, Chapter IV.

[20] Sir Anthony Barrowclough (the PCA at the time), Second Report 1989–89, HC 301, para. 62. See further R. Gregory and G. Drewry, 'Barlow Clowes and the Ombudsman' [1991] PL 192 and 408; and Special Report, Session 1989–90 HC 76, and Annual Report for 1989, Session 1989–90, HC 353.

[21] Gregory and Drewry, above.

The story is a complex one but its essence may be summarized as follows. Eighteen thousand investors lost substantial sums of money when parts of the Barlow Clowes investment business went into liquidation in 1988, leaving losses of over £100 million. Many of these investors complained to the PCA that the Department of Trade and Industry (DTI)—the government department responsible for regulating investment companies—had failed to properly investigate the group when granting licences to the investment companies and that these failures led to their losses.

Barlow Clowes had encouraged investors to believe that their money was being put into secure investments such as British Government Stocks when in fact the money was being invested in far more dubious and risky schemes. There were two sets of partnerships operating under the Barlow Clowes umbrella, each with identical names; one was operating in the United Kingdom and the other in Jersey. While the DTI investigated the UK operation it failed to realize that the separate Jersey partnership existed. In fact, investments received by the UK partnership were intermingled (unbeknown to the investors) with the Jersey investments. Had the DTI investigated the Jersey partnership it is almost certain that this part of the operation would have been brought to an end in early 1985. As it happened, the Jersey partnership was able to operate until part of the business went into liquidation owing in excess of £100 million. The PCA found that there had been significant maladministration by the DTI.

Normally government departments accept the conclusions of the Parliamentary Ombudsman, even if they disagree with them—preferring to suffer in silence than to enter into a conflict. In this case the government refused to accept the findings and at first refused to pay compensation to those who had suffered. Eventually, however, after mounting pressure and criticism in the press the government agreed 'in the very exceptional circumstances of the case and out of respect for the office of Parliamentary Commissioner' to make substantial *ex gratia* payments totalling £150 million to the victims. The *Financial Times* reflected the general attitude of the media when it said that the government's concessions had been made in a 'singularly graceless' manner, compounding the sequence of 'incompetence, evasion and rejection of responsibility' which had characterized the DTI's performance throughout the affair.[22]

The eventual outcome was a success for both the complainants and the Ombudsman. While the Ombudsman did not achieve compensation single-handedly—considerable pressure was also imposed on government by the Barlow Clowes Investors Group (a pressure group representing investors) and by the media publicity—it is unlikely that this level of compensation would have been levered out of government had it not been for the Ombudsman's thorough investigation and his detailed report. Overall the PCA had operated, as Gregory and Drewry put it: 'very much as its architects originally envisaged, providing MPs with a "new and powerful weapon"

[22] Quoted by Gregory and Drewry, note 20 above.

when taking up the cudgels against government on behalf of aggrieved constituents'.[23]

Applause, however, must be somewhat muted by the fact that the PCA could not question the merits of any decisions taken by the department and was able only to investigate the actions of bodies within his jurisdiction. He could not, for example, investigate the involvement of the Bank of England, the Stock Exchange, FIMBRA, accountants, solicitors and other advisors, who were involved in the affair and who may also have been at fault.

Disability Allowance

The second example of a recent major investigation concerns financial problems of a rather different nature. In 1993, nearly a third of the new complaints received by the PCA related to social security matters (299 out of 986). One of the most significant investigations concerned the introduction in April 1992 of a new benefit called the Disability Allowance.

Prior to its introduction there had been a campaign to inform people and to encourage those eligible to apply for the new benefit. The DSS had prepared itself to handle the new claims by calculating expected take-up rates and assessing the expected flow of work. Unfortunately, the planners got it wrong. Their calculations assumed that claims would be steady. In fact, they came in a flood and the system was engulfed and brought to breaking point. In the words of the PCA:[24]

> Large backlogs of unprocessed claims, requests for reviews and appeals built up; enquiries and complaints by letter and by telephone from claimants, their representatives and their Members of Parliament rose sharply; many were not responded to or dealt with; files were 'lost' for long periods; and there were heart-rending delays in the payment of some disabled claimants' benefits.

At one stage there were 120,000 claims requiring action. The PCA's investigation revealed a fundamental breakdown in the system stemming from a failure to anticipate the scale and nature of demand, the provision of inadequate training and an absence of administrative flexibility.

Following the PCA's investigation the department agreed to establish a special compensation scheme out of which the department paid more than half a million pounds to 30,000 claimants. The Select Committee on the PCA responded to this report by saying that in 'future we expect there to be much greater preparedness, training and contingency planning before embarking on major projects'.[25]

Some departments never learn . . .

Within two years, however, an almost identical fiasco occurred, this time involving the new Child Support Agency for which the DSS was also responsible.

[23] Gregory and Drewry, note 20 above, p. 442.
[24] Annual Report of the PCA for 1993, HC 290, para. 26.
[25] Second Report from the Select Committee on the PCA, Session 1993–94, HC 6, para. 16.

By the end of 1994, 95 MPs had referred complaints to the Parliamentary Ombudsman about the work of the Child Support Agency and after another detailed investigation the PCA found that many of the earlier errors had been repeated.[26] Following the PCA's report the select committee commented caustically:[27]

> Two such events within Whitehall would be worrying. For them to emanate from the same Department within two years raises the most fundamental questions as to the competence of that Department and its ability to plan administration efficiently.

The Health Service Ombudsman

The Health Service Ombudsman in 1993–94 received a record number of 1,384 complaints. The following extracts from a recent report of the Select Committee on the PCA, which considers reports from both the PCA and the Health Services Ombudsman, illustrate the types of problems handled by this ombudsman.[28]

> **ACCIDENT AND EMERGENCY WARDS AND PSYCHIATRIC CARE—University College Hospital**
>
> 11. A case reported on by the Ombudsman brings tragically to light the failings and difficulties in one not untypical unit in caring for [patients in need of psychiatric care]. The events took place at the A&E ward in University College Hospital London . . .
>
> 12. A GP referred a woman to hospital as a serious suicide risk. The registrar at the hospital did not form the view that she was actively suicidal but accepted that she would benefit from in-patient treatment. The registrar attempted to find a bed but did not follow the recently introduced procedures. As a result she failed to find a bed for the woman, although perhaps as many as six were available. The woman was sent home, no provision being made for the transport of herself and her husband. Nor was there an attempt to contact the GP before she left. On her return she fell to her death from the balcony of her tenth-floor flat.
>
> . . .
>
> 15. The investigation of the Ombudsman and the further questioning of this Committee made clear . . . that there were . . . deep-seated concerns arising from this case. Mr Reid [the Ombudsman] 'was most concerned' that staff in the A&E Department seem to be unaware of the revised procedure for finding beds. He also found disquieting evidence of poor relations between the staff in the A&E Department and the department of psychiatry which must have had an effect on patient care.
>
> 16. The two trusts have attempted to improve the service offered to the mentally ill in the A&E ward . . .

[26] Third Report of the PCA, Session 1994–95, HC 135.

[27] Third Report from the Select Committee on the PCA on the Child Support Agency, Session 1994–95, HC 199, para. 1.

[28] Second Report from the Select Committee on the Report of the Health Service Ombudsman for 1993–94, Session 1994–95, HC 32.

Complaint Procedures

20. In 1992–93 67 per cent of complaints to the Health Service Ombudsman about complaint handling were upheld. We commented at the time that the Citizen's Charter had yet to have an impact 'on the ability of hospitals to deal with complaints speedily and effectively'. It was therefore with concern that we heard that in 1993–94 the proportion of complaints about complaint handling upheld increased to 85 per cent, a trend, to quote Mr Reid, 'wholly in the wrong direction'. . . .

Walsall Hospitals NHS Trust

23. The case involving Walsall Hospitals NHS Trust demonstrated how badly things can go wrong when no one accepts responsibility for the consideration of a complaint. A man underwent a prostate operation but progress after the operation was slow. The consultant suspected cancer but did not communicate this suspicion to the man's son, indeed he was unaware of the son's existence during the time of treatment. He thought his medical team might have spoken to the family, but the junior doctors in his team had not . . . he did not hold case conferences but exchanged views with staff informally on ward rounds and during breaks. He asserted that two unspecific entries in the clinical records were sufficient evidence for one of his team, or the nurses, to have diagnosed possible cancer and for them to have discussed that with the patient and his family, but the nurses did not see that as their responsibility.

24. Dealing with patients suffering from terminal illness, and with their relatives, demands the utmost care and sensitivity. We are appalled to come across arrangements as haphazard as those brought to light in Walsall. It was the consultant's responsibility to ensure that effective communication of suspected diagnosis took place, something he singly failed to do on this occasion, not, it appears, for the first time . . .

The Local Ombudsmen

During 1995–96 the Local Ombudsmen received 15,266 complaints.[29] The main areas of complaint were housing (37.5 per cent); planning (22.1 per cent); local taxes (7.5 per cent); education (7.3 per cent); highways (6.9 per cent); and social services (6.1 per cent). The average time taken to complete a full investigation during 1995–96 was 71.6 weeks.

The following is a selection of cases taken from a recent annual report of the Local Ombudsmen. (Note that the reports are normally anonymized.)

Social services

A council was found to have unreasonably delayed in providing a disabled man with aids which would have improved his quality of life. The council then failed to deal properly with the man's complaint about this. The complainant felt the council had victimized him as a disabled person and ignored

[29] All figures cited are from the Annual Report of the Local Ombudsmen for 1995/96, Chapter 7 and appendices. The years run from 1 April to 31 March.

his complaints. The Ombudsman recommended that the complainant should be paid £500 compensation and that the council should review its procedures for dealing with complaints.

Planning

A council wrongly advised a man that planning permission was not required for his proposed extension. When, however, the extension was almost complete the man was told that permission was required after all. This was applied for and refused and enforcement action was taken by the council to force the man to remove the extension. The Ombudsman recommended that the council should pay for the removal of the extension and compensate the complainant for the costs incurred, loss of amenity of his home, plus £250 for his time and trouble.

Housing

A council unreasonably delayed in transferring a woman and her family to accommodation suited to her needs. The woman was at risk of violence from her ex-husband, but when the council was told of this it failed to take action to rehouse her for six months. The Ombudsman recommended that the council should pay her £500 compensation.

In another case, a council failed over several years to take action to deal with problems of noise transmission between a man's flat and the flat above. There was a delay in establishing the true cause of the problems, after which nothing practical was done to reduce the noise. The Ombudsman recommended that the council should pay the complainant £1,500 compensation.

Conclusion

These examples indicate the range of issues handled by the main ombudsmen, and their potential importance both to those directly affected and to the wider public. In this context you will have noticed that the investigations were principally concerned with errors of procedure (what is called maladministration): delays in the handling of benefits, lost files, the steps taken to find beds, communication between doctors and patients' families, etc. In many cases the investigations led to the payment of *ex gratia* compensation. This meant that the departments concerned agreed to pay compensation but did not accept a legal obligation to do so. As discussed later these ombudsmen do not have power to award compensation, nor to order its payment. Rather than legal coercion ombudsmen rely on cooperation (which, as the Barlow Clowes affair shows, may be rather grudgingly given). Be aware, however, that these examples illustrate ombudsmen successes. In each of them people have managed to get their grievances to the ombudsmen, have them investigated and upheld; and in most, they have obtained some sort of remedy. However, as will be seen, many complainants are far less successful. We turn now to look at the legal status and formal legal powers of the main ombudsmen.

THE STATUS AND POWERS OF THE OMBUDSMEN

Independence

The independence of the ombudsmen from the central government departments and local authorities against which complaints are made distinguishes ombudsmen from internal complaints procedures established by government.[30] To achieve independence the PCA and the Health Services Ombudsman possess broadly the same level of formal independence as High Court judges. They are formally appointed by the Queen and hold office during good behaviour (retiring at 65), and can only be removed by the Queen following 'addresses from both Houses of Parliament'.[31] Like judges, their salary and pension are paid out of the Consolidated Fund (payments from the Consolidated Fund can only be made with Parliament's authority).

These formal requirements, however, do not tell the whole story and in practice appointments are made by the Prime Minister,[32] probably from candidates suggested by civil servants or ministers. Nor do these formalities say anything about day-to-day matters such as the provision of funding for the ombudsmen and their staff. The PCA is not free to appoint as many investigators or advisors as he thinks necessary to work effectively and thoroughly, but is obliged to work within the resource constraints set by the Treasury. In recent years there has been mounting concern that the government's refusal to increase resources in line with the expanding responsibilities of the office may be reducing the effectiveness of the PCA.[33]

The relationship between the PCA and the complainant also poses issues of independence and neutrality. The PCA should be independent from government, but should the PCA also be independent from complainants? Some argue that, like MPs, ombudsmen are defenders of the citizen against government and as such that they should represent complainants and fight their cause. This view has been roundly rejected by PCAs. They have consistently argued that their role is to be neutral and to carry out investigations dispassionately. If their investigations vindicate departments they must be able to say so because it is only by being seen to be neutral that they will gain the confidence of the administration. This, they have argued, is crucial if their work is to be effectively performed. Building up confidence is obviously important for a body which ultimately relies on administrators to cooperate with investigations. However, there has been criticism that ombudsmen are

30 A recent report on the local ombudsmen by Sir Geoffrey Chipperfield recommended that they should no longer handle individual complaints and this role be replaced by a new complaints regime whereby local authorities would have a statutory obligation to establish internal complaints procedures. This recommendation has not been accepted, partly because of the importance of maintaining the ombudsmen as an independent investigative body: see HC Deb, vol. 271, col. 402 (12 February 1996).

31 PC Act, s 1; HSC Act 1993, Sched 1. Local ombudsmen are appointed by the Queen 'on the recommendation of the Secretary of State after consultation with such persons as appear to the Secretary of State to represent authorities in England or . . . Wales': see LGA 1974, s 23.

32 JUSTICE, *Our Fettered Ombudsman* (1977), p. 9.

33 *The Powers, Work and Jurisdiction of the Ombudsman*, Fifth Report of the Select Committee on the PCA (note 16 above), Appendix, para. 4.

too closely associated with the administration and overly influenced by its culture, and that their work could be more effective (and achieve a higher public profile) if they adopted a more vigorous stance.

The current PCA, Mr Michael Buckley, like most of his predecessors, spent most of his career as a civil servant prior to becoming the Parliamentary Ombudsman[34] and his staff are civil servants on secondment from government departments (to which they may return). This experience undoubtedly provides an understanding of administrative systems and culture, but it is unlikely to create an institution which will capture the imagination of the public; and one of the main criticisms of the PCA in particular is that its profile is so low that most people simply do not know it exists, what it does, or how to use it. It may be that this is one reason why more complaints are not being made to the PCA.[35]

What complaints can be taken to the ombudsmen?

Complaints may be taken to the ombudsmen if:

(a) the body concerned falls within the jurisdiction of the ombudsman, and
(b) the complainant alleges that 'injustice has been sustained in consequence of maladministration,'[36] or in the case of the Health Service Ombudsman that 'hardship' has been caused by maladministration or failures to 'provide health services'.[37]

Which bodies fall within the jurisdiction of the ombudsmen?

Broadly speaking the local ombudsmen may investigate the actions of all local authorities, including local police authorities.[38] The Health Services Ombudsman can investigate Regional and District Health Authorities, National Health Service Trusts which are responsible for managing hospitals, and since 1996, family health practitioners under the Health Service Commissioners (Amendment) Act 1996.[39]

The PCA has jurisdiction over the departments and bodies listed in Sched 2 to the 1967 Act (the current list is set out in an appendix to this chapter). This list includes all the main departments of central government and many agencies. However, the PCA has no jurisdiction over the judiciary, the police, nationalized industries or the broadcasting authorities. The list is updated as new agencies are created, old ones abolished or when decisions are made to extend the PCA's jurisdiction.

One of the main reasons why complaints are not investigated is that they concern bodies that are not within the PCA's jurisdiction (in 1994, 14 per

[34] His immediate predecessor, Sir William Reid, was also a civil servant. Sir Cecil Clothier and Sir Anthony Barrowclough were lawyers.
[35] See figures quoted above p. 000.
[36] PC Act 1967, s 5(1) and LGA 1974, s 26(1).
[37] HSC Act 1993, s 3(1). Since 1996, the Health Service Ombudsman can also investigate complaints arising from the exercise of clinical judgment: Health Service Commissioners (Amendment) Act 1996.
[38] LGA 1974, s 25.
[39] HSC Act 1993, s 2.

cent of complaints were rejected on this ground).[40] Both the PCA and the select committee have argued that the present system is an obstacle to access and ought to be reformed. They say that rather than listing bodies that can be investigated it would be easier and clearer to list only those which are specifically excluded. As well as adding clarity this would create a presumption in favour of the PCA having jurisdiction and force the government to justify decisions to exclude newly-created bodies, whereas at present a case has to be made for inclusion.[41] The government has said that it is prepared to consider this reform although it sees the problem as being primarily concerned with providing proper publicity of the PCA's powers.

Complainants must sustain 'injustice in consequence of maladministration'

The terms 'injustice' and 'maladministration' are not defined in the legislation as it was feared that statutory definitions would limit the PCA's ability to develop their meanings with experience. It is now accepted that 'injustice' covers a spectrum of harm, ranging from being a victim of rudeness and not receiving replies to letters, through to the types of injustice that lawyers would normally associate with the term, such as losing legal rights because officials have given incorrect advice.

'Maladministration' refers to administrative errors that affect the *manner* in which decisions are reached and the *manner* of their implementation, rather than the nature, quality or reasonableness of the decisions themselves.[42] Richard Crossman MP, who as Leader of the House steered the Parliamentary Commissioner Bill through the House of Commons, explained maladministration by listing the type of wrong-doing that might be covered. His list, now known as 'the Crossman catalogue', mentioned bias, neglect, inattention, delay, incompetence, ineptitude, perversity, turpitude, and arbitrariness.

The PCA has recently extended and updated these examples of maladministration using language believed to be more appropriate to the 1990s to include:[43] rudeness; unwillingness to treat the citizens as people with rights; refusal to answer reasonable questions; neglecting to inform people of their rights or entitlements; knowingly giving advice which is misleading or inadequate; offering no redress or manifestly disproportionate redress; showing bias whether because of colour, sex, or any other grounds; refusal to inform people of rights of appeal; adopting faulty procedures; failure by management to monitor whether procedures are being followed; and failure to mitigate the

[40] The largest group of these (29 per cent) concerned complaints against local government which should have been referred to the local ombudsmen.

[41] *The Powers, Work and Jurisdiction of the Ombudsman*, Fifth Report of the Select Committee, Session 1993–94, HC 619, para. 20.

[42] See Lord Donaldson MR in *R v Local Commissioner, ex p Eastleigh Borough Council* [1988] 1 QB 855 at 863E and *R v Local Commissioner, ex p Bradford MCC* [1979] QB 287.

[43] Annual Report 1993, para. 7.

effects of rigid adherence to the letter of the law where that produces treatment that is clearly unfair.

Thus maladministration covers a variety of administrative sins which occur when standards of good practice are not met. Often maladministration is about poor, rather than unlawful, administration. However, maladministration may also indicate that bodies have failed to comply with appropriate legal requirements, and in particular the obligations of procedural propriety and fairness. In these circumstances overlap may occur between the jurisdiction of the ombudsmen and that of the courts. As discussed below, people may find themselves caught between these two procedures: told by the ombudsmen to use the courts and by the courts to use the ombudsmen.[44]

The ombudsmen cannot examine the merits of governmental action or policy

This brief discussion of the meaning of maladministration indicates that, like judicial review, ombudsmen do not exist to complain about the merits of decisions or the content of policy.[45] But distinctions between the *merits* of decisions or policies on the one hand and the *process* or *manner* of decision-making on the other are not always easily made. The quality of decisions reached is often affected by the manner in which decisions are taken. Where files have been lost, or correspondence has not been received, or those affected have not been consulted, this may well adversely affect the quality of decisions which are taken by officials. Likewise where decisions seem unreasonable or unfair this may well indicate that maladministration has occurred even though the individual affected has no direct evidence of it. It was for this reason that the select committee recommended that if a decision is found to be 'thoroughly bad in quality' the PCA should infer that there was maladministration in the way the decision had been taken.[46] While the PCA accepted this advice, it does not appear to have had a great impact on the PCA's practice, possibly because the 'thoroughly bad' decisions are rare.[47] Certainly, PCAs have tended to be cautious and have regularly emphasized the limits of their power. One PCA, for example, refused to support the proposal

[44] For a recent situation where this very nearly arose, see *R v Lambeth London Borough Council, ex p Crookes* [1996] COD 398. An applicant for judicial review complained about delay in the payment of housing benefit. He had previously tried unsuccessfully to complain to the Local Ombudsman and then sought judicial review only to be met by the possibility that the judge (Sir Louis Blom Cooper QC, sitting as a Deputy Judge in the High Court) would refuse him a remedy because he thought the complaint more appropriate for the Ombudsman than it was for judicial review. In the event the remedy was not refused.

[45] For example PC Act 1967, s 12(3) provides 'that nothing in this Act authorises or requires the Commissioner to question the merits of a decision taken without maladministration by a government department or other authority in the exercise of a discretion vested in that department or authority'. See also LGA 1974, s 34(3) and HSC Act 1993, s 19(4).

[46] Second Report for the Session 1967–68, HC 350, para. 14. Cf. the grounds of judicial review which allow the courts to review decisions which are unreasonable on the basis that there must have been error made during the making of the decision: see Chapter 24.

[47] R. Gregory, 'The Select Committee on the PCA 1967–80' [1982] PL 49–88.

made by JUSTICE in their report *Our Fettered Ombudsman* that his jurisdiction should be extended along the lines of the New Zealand Ombudsman to include 'unreasonable unjust or oppressive action'. In his view such a change would not materially add to his powers, but it could create confusion and increase the risk of hostility between the PCA and government departments.

This caution has not, however, protected ombudsmen from being accused of overstepping their powers. A recent example occurred following the PCA's criticisms of the way the Department of Transport had handled compensation claims by those whose property had been blighted (declined in value) by uncertainty surrounding the route to be followed by the high-speed rail link between London and the Channel Tunnel. As in the Barlow Clowes case the department took the unusual step of publicly disagreeing with the PCA's findings and issued a separate statement by the Permanent Secretary, Sir Patrick Brown. In this the department denied maladministration and claimed that the PCA had exceeded his authority by criticizing ministerial policy. The PCA responded by saying that his concerns were with the effects of policy rather than with the policy itself.[48] In the context of local government such disputes have even led councils to bring judicial review proceedings against local ombudsmen on grounds that criticism of policy is an excess or abuse of power.[49]

There must be a causal link between the injustice and the maladministration

Before leaving the terms 'injustice' and 'maladministration' note that there must be a causal link between the 'injustice' and the 'maladministration'.[50] People cannot use the ombudsmen to complain about injustices caused by things other than maladministration, such as legislation or administrative actions which have been properly taken. Nor can people use the ombudsmen to complain about alleged maladministration which has not caused them any injustice at all.

Other restrictions and exclusions

This list is so long that it has been said to cover most of the matters about which citizens complain.[51]

[48] Parliamentary Commissioner, Fifth Report, Session 1994–95, HC 193, para. 48. See further Rhoda James and Diane Longley, 'The Channel tunnel rail link, the Ombudsman and the Select Committee' [1996] PL 38.

[49] See e.g. *R v Local Commissioner, ex p Eastleigh Borough Council* [1988] 1 QB 855 and *R v Commissioner for Local Administration, ex p Croydon London Borough Council* [1989] 1 All ER 1033. On the former case, see M. Jones, 'The Local Ombudsman and Judicial Review' [1988] PL 608.

[50] This was one of the issues in *R v Local Commissioner, ex p Eastleigh Borough Council* [1988] 1 QB 855.

[51] H. Street, *Justice in the Welfare State* (2nd edn., 1975), p. 116.

Matters which cannot be investigated

Even if the body concerned falls within the jurisdiction of the ombudsmen and the complaint involves injustice caused by maladministration, the ombudsmen may be unable to get involved. This is because the legislation contains a long list of matters which cannot be investigated.[52] The Act has a long list of exceptions which the Commissioners cannot investigate. The PCA, for example, cannot deal with:

(1) action taken which is certified by a minister to affect relations between the UK government and any other government or international organization;
(2) action taken outside the territory of the United Kingdom under the authority of the Crown;
(3) action taken in connection with the administration of dependent territories outside the United Kingdom;
(4) action taken by the Secretary of State under the Extradition of Fugitive Offenders Acts;
(5) action taken by or with the authority of the Secretary of State for the purposes of investigating crime or of protecting the security of the state, including action taken with respect to passports;
(6) the commencement or conduct of any civil or criminal proceedings;
(7) action taken by administrative staff of courts and tribunals under the direction or authority of someone acting in a judicial capacity or in his capacity as a member of a tribunal;[53]
(8) any exercise of the prerogative of mercy;
(9) action taken on behalf of central government by listed health authorities;
(10) action taken in matters relating to contractual or other commercial transactions by central government, not being transactions relating to the compulsory acquisition of land or its disposal;
(11) action taken in respect of personnel matters relating to the civil service and armed forces, and other branches of the public service; and
(12) the grant of honours, awards or privileges within the gift of the Crown.

The exclusion of commercial transactions and personnel matters

Of this list, exclusion of the government's commercial transactions and personnel matters from the PCA's remit have been the most criticized of these exclusions, and both the PCA and the select committee have pressed for their removal, so far without success.[54]

Why are these matters excluded? The government's view is that ombudsmen should be concerned with purely governmental actions, by which it

[52] PC Act, s 5(3) and Sched 3. For the equivalent list of exclusions relating to local ombudsmen see LGA 1974, s 26(8) and Sched 5. For those relating to the Health Services Ombudsman, see HSC Act 1993, ss 4–7, as amended by the Health Service Commissioners (Amendment) Act 1996.

[53] This exclusion was added by the Parliamentary Commissioner Act 1994.

[54] See further P. Birkinshaw, *Grievances, Remedies and the State*, pp. 198–201.

appears to mean actions which the government carries out in its capacity as a government, rather than with actions which any large organization has to take. All large concerns have to enter into commercial transactions for things like furnishings for offices, or supplies for canteens; and all large employers need systems for handling personnel matters and complaints that arise. In other words, there is nothing specifically governmental about these activities. Another way of putting this is to say that ombudsmen should be concerned with complaints brought by individuals in their capacity as citizens and not in their capacity as employees, or as suppliers of goods and services to a department or public body.

Neither the PCA nor the select committee has been impressed by these arguments. As far as commercial matters are concerned the select committee has said that the government's argument is beside the point. In its view:[55]

> the Government has a duty to administer its purchasing policies fairly and equitably, and if those policies are the subject of complaint then the complaints should be investigated; this is particularly important if any future Government were again to use the award of contracts as a political weapon.

The PCA has also pointed out that since the relationship between citizens and government departments and other non-departmental public bodies is increasingly contractual and commercial in nature it is now becoming increasingly unrealistic to distinguish between governmental and commercial activities.[56] Indeed, bearing in mind that commercial activities are likely to attract little political or judicial scrutiny there is, if anything, a stronger case for allowing these to fall within the PCA's purview.

Ombudsmen cannot investigate if there is a remedy before a tribunal or the courts

Ombudsmen cannot investigate complaints if the complainant can appeal to a tribunal or has a remedy in the courts, unless it is not reasonable to expect the appeal to be used or the legal proceedings to be instituted.[57] As mentioned above, there may be overlap between judicial review and the jurisdiction of ombudsmen and people may find it difficult to know which to use and may be caught between the two.[58] Fortunately the PCA adopts a flexible approach, only refusing to consider complaints 'where there appears . . . to have been a substantial legal wrong for which, if proved, there is a substantial legal remedy'. Where 'there is doubt about the availability of a legal remedy

[55] Select Committee on the Parliamentary Commissioner for Administration, Fourth Report, Session 1979–80, HC 593, para. 8; Sir Cecil Clothier 'The Value of an Ombudsman' [1986] PL 204, at 110–211. (The reference to 'again to use the award of contracts as a political weapon' appears to refer to the previous Labour government's policy not to contract with companies which flouted its pricing policy: see G. Ganz, 'Government and Industry: The provision of financial assistance to industry and its control' [1977] PL 439.)

[56] Annual Report of the PCA for 1988, p. 1.

[57] PC Act 1967, s 5(2); LGA 1974, s 26(6); and HSC Act 1993, s 4(1).

[58] See *ex p Crookes* (above note 44). Lord Woolf has recommended that people should be encouraged to use ombudsmen before seeking judicial review: Lord Woolf, *Access to Justice* (1996).

or where the process of law seems too cumbersome, slow and expensive' the PCA exercises his discretion to investigate the complaint.[59]

The experience of the local ombudsmen, however, provides a warning that the ombudsmen may be challenged by way of judicial review if they fail to consider whether complaints are more suitable for judicial resolution. In *R v Commissioner for Local Administration, ex p Croydon London Borough Council*[60] an education appeal committee rejected an appeal by parents against a local authority's refusal to allow them to send their child to their preferred school. The parents complained to the Local Ombudsman. He investigated and decided that the appeal committee had acted with maladministration. The local authority sought and obtained judicial review of the Ombudsman's decision on the ground that there was no evidence of maladministration. In its judgment the court criticized the Ombudsman for not considering whether judicial review was a more appropriate remedy for the parents.

Note that there have been several notable examples of judicial review being sought following investigations by ombudsmen, of which one of the best-known is *Congreve v Home Office*.[61] Anticipating an increase in the TV licence fee Congreve (and 20,000 others) bought a new licence before the increase was due to take effect and before his old licence expired. The Home Office, hoping to prevent a loss of revenue, at first demanded an extra £6 from each of these 'overlappers' and later amended this demand saying that it would revoke the new licences early. Some of those affected complained to the PCA which, after an investigation, concluded that people had been caused needless distress and confusion through the maladministration of the Home Office.[62] Armed with the PCA's report Congreve went on to successfully challenge the action of the Home Office in the courts.

ACCESS TO THE OMBUDSMEN

Having looked at whom and what can be complained about we now turn to the important issue of access. In theory ombudsmen should be more accessible than the courts. They do not involve the same costs and ought not to require specialist help (although as we have seen there are many technical issues concerning their jurisdiction). Nevertheless access raises a number of fundamental questions about the constitutional role of these institutions.

Most striking is the fact that there is no direct access to the Parliamentary Ombudsman. People who want to use the PCA must within twelve months from the day on which the complainant first had notice of the matters alleged

59 Annual report of the PCA for 1980, 1980–81 Session, HC 148, para. 2. The Barlow Clowes affair shows how flexible the PCA is prepared to be: here the PCA investigated the complaints even though he was well aware that the complainants could have taken the matter to the courts and obtained 'substantial' legal remedies: see R. Gregory and G. Drewry [1991] PL 408 at 422.

60 [1989] 1 All ER 1033.

61 [1976] QB 629.

62 Seventh Report of the PCA for Session 1974–75, HC 680, para. 38.

in the complaint submit a written complaint to an MP (not necessarily their constituency MP) who may formally request the PCA to conduct an investigation into the matter.[63]

This restriction does not apply to the Health Services Ombudsman.[64] As far as the local ombudsmen are concerned, complaints must also be made within twelve months and be in writing; this may be waived if the Local Ombudsman considers it reasonable to do so. However, while the LGA 1974 originally required complaints to be made through elected councillors, since 1988 people have been able to complain directly to the local ombudsmen.[65] Today the vast majority of complaints are made directly.

The PCA and the MP filter

The inability of the public to complain directly has always been one of the most controversial aspects of the PCA.[66] At root the arguments for and against direct access rest on two fundamentally different conceptions of the PCA's role. On the one hand is the view that the PCA's primary role is to provide redress to citizens and that citizens should therefore have direct access. On the other hand is the view that the PCA is an adjunct to the parliamentary process to be used for and by MPs. On this view the involvement of MPs is crucial and direct access would undermine the true purpose of the PCA.

The case for direct access

As noted earlier, JUSTICE originally recommended the use of an MP filter for a temporary period. However, it strongly opposed the decision to make the filter a permanent feature and has continued to campaign for direct access.[67] The current PCA has added his voice to this campaign arguing that the 'MP filter' discourages complaints and reduces the visibility of the PCA in the eyes of the public.[68] The National Consumer Council put these concerns forcefully when it told the select committee that:[69]

63 PC Act, ss 5 and 6. Section 6(3) allows the PCA discretion to consider complaints made after twelve months if he considers there to be special circumstances for doing so. If a complaint is made directly to the PCA he may refer it to an MP who may then refer it back to the PCA.

64 HSC Act 1993, s 9. Complainants must, however, bring their complaints to the notice of the body being complained against and give them a reasonable chance to investigate: s 9(5)(a). This requirement may be waived by the Health Services Ombudsman: s 9(6).

65 Local Government Act 1988.

66 See further Gavin Drewry and Carol Harlow, 'A Cutting Edge? The Parliamentary Commissioner and MPs' (1990) MLR 745, 758–61. Only in Sri Lanka and France is there a similar restriction on access to an ombudsman.

67 JUSTICE, *Our Fettered Ombudsman* (1977) Chapter V, para. 44. See also JUSTICE/All Souls, *Administrative Justice: Some Necessary Reforms* (1988), para. 5.9.

68 Annual Report for 1993, para. 2.

69 Select Committee on the Parliamentary Commissioner for Administration, First Report Session 1993–94, HC 33, para. 62.

> It is extremely difficult for consumers to gain access to the Parliamentary Ombudsman. Complainants must know of the existence of the Office. Secondly, they must know the process for persuading an MP to refer the complaint . . . Thirdly, they must persuade the MP that the complaint should be investigated by the Parliamentary Ombudsman. The limited information which is available indicates that, from the consumer's perspective, the MP filter operates inequitably. A complainant's chance of having a grievance dealt with by the Parliamentary Ombudsman seems to depend on the approach of individual MPs.

This view is supported by figures which show that many MPs rarely if ever use the PCA and that people's chances of getting complaints to the Parliamentary Ombudsman may depend on the attitude of the MP they contact.[70] Having heard these and other arguments the select committee summarized the case in favour of allowing direct access as follows:[71]

(1) there should be direct access as a matter of right;
(2) the filter is an anomaly, almost unknown in other ombudsman systems;
(3) individuals with complaints may be unwilling to approach MPs;
(4) the filter means that the likelihood of the individual's complaint being referred to the Commissioner depends on the views and practice of the particular MP. Some look more favourably on the office of the Parliamentary Ombudsman than others;
(5) the filter acts as an obstacle to the Parliamentary Ombudsman effectively promoting his services;
(6) the filter creates an unnecessary bureaucratic barrier between the complainant and the Ombudsman, involving considerable paper work for the MPs and their offices.

The claim that the MP filter discourages complainants may also be supported by statistical evidence relating to the use of local ombudsmen. Prior to May 1988 complaints to this ombudsman had to be referred through local councillors. Since then people have been able to complain directly. Between 1974 and 1988–89 the number of complaints considered by the local ombudsmen increased on average by 9 per cent every year. In the year after direct access was permitted the caseload increased by 44 per cent. It is often argued that this increase was at least partly attributable to the introduction of direct access.[72]

[70] Gregory and Pearson have observed that 'in 1986 the constituencies represented by some 463 MPs generated altogether only 200 complaints for the Commissioner's attention. The millions of constituents represented by 263 Members evidently produced *no complaints at all*': 'The Parliamentary Ombudsman after twenty-five years: Problems and Solutions' in Neil Hawke (ed.), *The Ombudsman—Twenty Five Years On* (1993), p. 7.

[71] Select Committee on the Parliamentary Commissioner for Administration, First Report Session 1993–94, HC 33, para. 58.

[72] Annual Report of the Commission for Local Administration for 1988–89, p. 4.

The case against direct access

Although the select committee has recognized the arguments in favour of direct access it has steadfastly rejected them. Its views are summarized in the following paragraph:[73]

> We continue to believe that the MP has an irreplaceable role in pursuing complaints of the public against the Executive, notwithstanding the development within public bodies of an array of direct access complaint and redress mechanisms for the citizen . . . The work of the Parliamentary Ombudsman . . . has a vital role in equipping the Member for the tasks of Parliament . . . The knowledge of the details of problems in administration has an important part in any effective scrutiny of the Executive . . . Direct access will result in the denial to Members of expertise in the problems facing their constituents . . . This is to impoverish parliamentary, and thus political, life.

The select committee has also predicted that direct access will lead to large numbers of inappropriate complaints which will overburden the office and threaten the standards of investigations. So firm has the select committee been in its opposition to direct access that it has even rejected a compromise proposal suggested in 1984 by Sir Cecil Clothier, a former PCA, that individuals should have direct access if an MP has refused to refer the matter to the PCA. This important debate highlights:

(1) that even after nearly thirty years the role of the PCA remains contentious; and
(2) that while the select committee is normally an ally of the PCA against the Executive, it will differ on issues, particularly when these impinge upon the work of MPs and the House of Commons.

Should the PCA be able to embark upon investigations even if complaints are not made?

Like the courts, the PCA and the other public sector ombudsmen are passive bodies which can only carry out investigations when complaints are referred to them. Several ombudsmen in different parts of the world, however, can take the initiative and decide to investigate issues even when complaints have not been made. Other officers and committees of the House of Commons, including select committees and the Comptroller and Auditor General, have this power. This being so, should the PCA's powers be extended to allow him to investigate when he wants to, and not just when he is asked to? The debates on this issue draw a distinction between the power to investigate specific decisions or actions and the power to undertake a more general audit of administrative systems without getting involved in specific cases.

[73] Select Committee on the Parliamentary Commissioner for Administration, First Report Session 1993–94, HC 33, paras 75–6.

Should there be power to undertake audits?

The select committee has recommended that while investigation of individual complaints should remain the main work of the PCA, the Ombudsman should also be able to audit the administrative systems of bodies within his jurisdiction. The power might be used, for example, where a number of complaints involving a single department raise concerns about the general administrative standards of that department and indicate that a general examination of its administrative systems would be desirable. Giving the PCA this power would, argue the select committee, complement the work of the National Audit Office and the Audit Commission.[74]

The PCA has expressed some reservations about the power to audit: among these is concern that the independence of his investigations may be prejudiced if a complaint is brought against an organization whose procedures have been previously 'approved' by an audit. The government has also argued that there are other ways of ensuring that administrative systems achieve proper standards by, for instance, granting or withdrawing Charter Marks under the Citizen's Charter.[75]

Should there be power to investigate without a complaint having been made?

The power to investigate individual decisions or actions even where complaints have not been made would, some argue, greatly strengthen the PAC's usefulness to the House of Commons by providing a more comprehensive check on the incidence of maladministration than is allowed by a complaint-dependent system. If the PCA no longer had to wait for complaints he could investigate departments which are rarely complained against and be freer to deal with problems identified by MPs and others. The PCA could also investigate problems that he comes across during an investigation which have nothing directly to do with the complaint being investigated.

On the other hand, the PCA has acknowledged that such a power would represent a fundamental shift away from the concept of the PCA as a body concerned with investigating complaints of individual injustice caused by administration. The select committee, predictably, is less concerned with this aspect and has said that both the PCA and the Health Services Ombudsman should have power to initiate complaints provided this does not reduce their links with MPs and Parliament. It has therefore recommended a compromise situation whereby the ombudsmen should be able to initiate complaints if recommended to do so by the select committee.[76]

The government has rejected this on the rather dubious grounds that the

[74] Select Committee on the Parliamentary Commissioner for Administration, First Report Session 1993–94, HC 33, para. 39.

[75] It has said that the work of the National Audit Office and the Audit Commission would be duplicated if the PCA was given power to audit: see Fifth Report of the Select Committee on the PCA, Session 1993–94, HC 619, Appendix 1, para. 16.

[76] Select Committee on the Parliamentary Commissioner for Administration, First Report, Session 1993–94, HC 33, para. 44.

present system works satisfactorily and that citizens 'will normally complain where alleged maladministration occurs . . . [and since] . . . complaints may be referred by any MP, the PCA can, if necessary, with a member of his Select Committee, take up a deserving case'.[77]

OMBUDSMEN INVESTIGATIONS, REPORTS AND REDRESS

Speaking of the PCA's investigation into the Barlow Clowes affair, Gregory and Drewry have commented that:[78]

> [B]ecause the [PCA] has time and resources, and the right of unrestricted access to persons and papers [he] was able to mount a fact-finding exercise far more formidable than MPs or the media could have possibly undertaken. Rarely, if ever, can any record of administration have been so closely scrutinised, and reconstructed in such detail, as in the Commissioner's report on the Barlow Clowes affair; some of the officials subjected to interrogation certainly felt not a little bruised by the experience . . . the thoroughness of the Commissioner's inquiry turned out to be of crucial importance.

As this quotation suggests the core powers of the ombudsmen lie in their ability to carry out thorough investigations, to examine documents and to question officials, and then to report their findings. We now move on to consider these powers.

Preliminary screening

When a complaint is received by the ombudsmen it will be screened to see whether it falls within their jurisdiction and, if so, whether it warrants an investigation.[79] The vast majority of complaints received by the Parliamentary Ombudsman are rejected at this preliminary stage (71 per cent in 1993 and 77 per cent in 1994).[80] The main reasons were that the complaints did not concern administrative actions (40 per cent in 1994); there was a right of appeal to tribunals (21 per cent); and that the authorities complained about were beyond the Ombudsman's jurisdiction (14 per cent).

[77] Fifth Report of the Select Committee (note 75 above), Appendix, para. 18.
[78] Gregory and Drewry (note 59 above), p. 439.
[79] If the PCA decides not to investigate the complaint he must send a report explaining his reasons for refusing to do so to the MP who referred the matter to him (but not to the individual concerned): PC Act 1967, s 10(1); but cf. LGA 1974, s 30(1) and HSC Act, s 14(2). The local ombudsmen and the Health Services Ombudsman do report back to the complainant if they decide not to investigate a complaint. The government has agreed with the select committee's recommendation that the Health Services Ombudsman should not be required to provide the body complained about with his reasons for not proceeding with an investigation on the grounds that this may prejudice or embarrass the complainant: Fifth Report of the Select Committee (note 75 above), Appendix, para. 22.
[80] PCA's Annual Report for 1994, p. 43.

If the ombudsmen decide to investigate . . .

If the ombudsmen decide to investigate they must conduct their investigations in private and give the department and those named in the complaint a chance to comment on any allegations made about their conduct.[81] Subject to these obligations they are free to choose how to conduct investigations and 'may obtain information from such persons and in such manner, and make such inquiries' as they think fit.[82] They may examine departmental files and compel ministers (in the case of the PCA) and officials to furnish information and produce documents.[83] Like courts they can force witnesses to attend and can examine them under oath.[84] In some respects the PCA's powers actually exceed those of the courts. Documents cannot be withheld from the PCA on grounds of public interest immunity[85] and Cabinet documents can only be withheld if there is a certificate issued by the Secretary of the Cabinet and if the Prime Minister agrees that they should be withheld.[86] Moreover, prohibitions on disclosure imposed by the Official Secrets Acts do not apply to information sought by the ombudsmen for their inquiries.[87] It would, of course, be an offence for the ombudsmen or their staff to make unauthorized disclosures of this information to the public.[88] Finally, unlawful obstruction of the ombudsmen may be treated as if it were a contempt of court.[89]

The reports

The ultimate power of the ombudsmen lies in their ability to report their findings and thereby to attract publicity to their investigations and findings. After an investigation the Ombudsman prepares reports which are sent, in the case of the PCA, to the MP, the principal officer of the department or authority concerned, and to any other person who was alleged to have acted wrongly, but not to the original complainant.[90] If it appears that 'injustice has been caused to the person aggrieved in consequence of maladministration and that the injustice has not been, or will not be, remedied' the PCA may also lay before each House of Parliament a special report upon the case.[91] The PCA also reports annually to Parliament and regularly issues reports on selected cases.[92]

81 LGA 1972, s 26(5).
82 PC Act 1967, s 7(2); LGA 1974, s 28(2); and HSC Act 1993, s 11(3)(a).
83 PC Act 1967, s 8(1); LGA 1974, s 29; and HSC Act 1993, s 12.
84 PC Act 1967, s 8(2); LGA 1974, s 29(2); and HSC Act 1993, s 12(2).
85 PC Act 1967, s 8(3); LGA 1974, s 29(4); HSC Act 1993, s 12(4). Ministers may, however, prevent the PCA from communicating, e.g. in reports, documents or information which would be prejudicial to the state or against the public interest or which belong to a class of documents or information which would be prejudicial to the state: PC Act 1967, s 11(3). On public interest immunity, see p. 498.
86 PC Act 1967, s 8(4). Query whether such a certificate could be challenged by judicial review?
87 PC Act 1967, s 8(3); LGA 1974, s 29(4).
88 PC Act 1967, s 11(2); LGA 1974, s 29(5); and HSC Act 1993, s 15.
89 PC Act 1967, s 9(1); LGA 1974, s 29(8); and HSC Act 1993, s 13.
90 PC Act 1967, s 10(1), (2).
91 PC Act 1967, s 10(3).
92 PC Act 1967, s 10(4). The PCA's reports are privileged from the law of defamation: s 10(5).

Similar provisions apply to the Health Services Ombudsman except that his special and annual reports go to the Secretary of State for Social Services who is required to lay copies of the reports before each of the Houses of Parliament.[93]

Reports by the local ombudsmen

The local ombudsmen do not report to Parliament; instead they publish an annual report which is available to the public free of charge. There is also a rather complex system of reports on particular investigations that is designed to force recalcitrant councils to comply with the Ombudsman's recommendations by attracting embarrassing local publicity to the council's failings.

Basically, if a local government Ombudsman issues an adverse report councils are given three months to say what action they have taken, or propose to take, in response to the report.[94] If the council's response is unsatisfactory the Ombudsman may issue a further report (between 1 April 1974 and 31 March 1996 the ombudsmen had to issue further reports in 357 cases). Decisions to persist in refusing to comply must be taken by the whole council and, if deadlock remains, the council must at its own expense publish a statement in the local press detailing the Ombudsman's findings and its reasons for non-compliance. These statements may well cost more than the cost of compensating the complainant and experience shows that such statements are unlikely to be of any practical benefit to the complainant. Indeed, a satisfactory outcome following a statement is very rare.

The power to bark but not to bite

None of these public sector ombudsmen has power to enforce his decisions. Unlike the Netherlands Ombudsman they cannot award financial redress (as opposed to recommend the payment of compensation), nor can their findings be enforced by county court proceedings for damages, as can the findings of the Northern Ireland Commissioner.[95]

The PCA has consistently taken the view, and independent committees have agreed,[96] that in order to be able to investigate effectively the PCA must develop a culture of cooperation and trust between his office and government departments. They believe that the acquisition of coercive legal powers would not help to secure this and could lead to a more confrontational approach in which departments become more defensive and more difficult to probe.

[93] HSC Act 1993, s 14(3), (4).

[94] LGA 1974, ss 30 and 31, as amended by the Local Government and Housing Act 1989. This report is normally anonymized and councillors and others are only named if they have been found to have acted contrary to the National Code of Local Authority Conduct.

[95] Commissioner for Complaints Act (Northern Ireland) 1969, s 7(2).

[96] For instance JUSTICE/All Souls, *Administrative Justice: Some Necessary Reforms*, paras 5.36–9.

The dominant view is that publicity, coupled with the knowledge that officials may be called for questioning by the Select Committee on the PCA, are sufficient sanctions and that it is unnecessary to add additional powers of enforcement.

There is, however, a stronger case for giving the local ombudsmen legal sanctions to be used against authorities which insist on refusing to provide redress. Indeed, the government, which has less of a vested interest in local government administration than it has in central government administration, has indicated that it is prepared to introduce legislation to make the local ombudsmen's decisions legally enforceable.

The principles of redress

The absence of enforcement powers does not mean that government departments and agencies can regard themselves as free to accept or reject the recommendations of the ombudsmen as a matter of discretion. Nor ought it to mean that there is no compulsion upon them to provide redress for individuals. These points have recently been forcefully made by the select committee in an important report on 'Maladministration and Redress'.[97] This criticized government attitudes to the provision of redress following findings of maladministration and particularly departmental reluctance to compensate victims of their wrong-doing. Drawing on the spirit of the Citizen's Charter, the committee said that:[98]

> current [governmental] guidance on redress in cases of maladministration is outdated, directed more towards the protection of the public purse than to the rights of the complainant . . . Departments and agencies have a duty to grant redress when their maladministration has resulted in injustice to the citizen.

The select committee went on to condemn the defensive attitudes of departments, which should:[99]

> emphasise the value placed on the admission of mistakes and the attempt to make right any harm done . . . It should also be made clear that the attempt to hide maladministration or its consequences will be considered a serious offence.

THE PCA AND 'OPEN GOVERNMENT'

British government is notoriously secret and there have been many calls for greater openness and much argument in favour of enacting statutory rights of access to official information. The government has responded to these by introducing, in April 1994, the Code of Practice on Access to Government

[97] Select Committee on the PCA, First Report for Session 1994–95 on Maladministration and Redress, HC 112.

[98] Report on Maladministration and Redress, paras 5–9.

[99] Report on Maladministration and Redress, para. 13.

Information.[100] This non-statutory code espouses principles of open government but does not provide for any legally enforceable rights.

The aim is to ensure that certain information (rather than documents) is volunteered by government, including facts and analysis of facts relevant to framing policy decisions, explanatory material such as departmental internal guidance, information explaining reasons for administrative decisions, and information relating to standards of service. The Code provides for a wide range of exclusions. It does not cover, for example, information which would harm national security or defence, the frankness and candour of internal discussion; or information whose disclosure would harm public safety or the administration of justice.[101] Moreover, the Code does not apply to bodies outside the PCA's jurisdiction, nor to the PCA itself.

The Code is not enforceable in law. Instead, responsibility for seeing that government acts in accordance with it is placed on the PCA. A person who is denied information can complain to the PCA (not obtaining the information will be regarded as an injustice) and the PCA may investigate the circumstances and the onus is on the governmental body to show why the information was not disclosed. After the investigation the PCA makes a recommendation. If this calls for revelation and is not complied with the department may be called before the select committee for questioning.

In his 1995 report the PCA said that 'by far the most surprising feature is that even now, nearly two years after the Code came into force, the public's use of it remains minimal'. He added, with certain irony, '[t]hat might change if more publicity were given to the existence of the Code'.[102] The previous year he had noted that far fewer complaints had been made under the Code than he had anticipated in the light of experience overseas and in particular in Canada, Australia, and New Zealand.[103] During 1995, 50 complaints were considered, 27 were rejected (19 because they lacked evidence that there was a matter worth investigating).[104] Eight complaints were found to be wholly or partially justified. Two of these were against the DSS and the others involved the Ministry of Agriculture, the Charity Commission, the Department of the Environment, the Department of Transport, and the Treasury. The PCA noted that the Treasury has approached open government in a positive way, as is evidenced by their releasing of the minutes of the monthly meetings between the Governor of the Bank of England and the Chancellor of the Exchequer. However, until he intervened they had refused to publish reports on frauds in Whitehall.

At this early stage the PCA has said that he believes that the Code offers

100 *Open Government* (1993), Cmnd 2290. See further P. Birkinshaw, *Freedom of Information*, Chapter 6. A Code of Practice on Openness in the NHS was introduced in 1995.
101 *Open Government*, pp. 75–9.
102 PCA's Annual Report for 1995, Chapter 11, para. 11.
103 Special Report, HC 14, para. 111.
104 All figures from the PCA's Annual Report for 1995, Chapter 11.

the public genuine benefits, although it is essential for the government to do more to publicize the Code and to ensure that the PCA's interpretations of its provisions are disseminated to departments and those who deal with requests for information under the Code. He has found that his intervention frequently prompts departments to release information previously withheld, although he has expressed disappointment at the level of ignorance regarding the Code's obligation within departments. 'Knowledge of the Code's obligations can fall off quite rapidly as one moves away from those officials who have specific responsibilities in connection with information release.'[105] He has also expressed criticism of the tendency of some departments to use every argument ('whether legally based, Code-based or at times simply obstructive') to try to justify past decisions not to release information instead of being prepared to reappraise the situation with an open mind.[106] On the other hand these are early days and he detected signs that some departments (the DSS and the Treasury in particular) are beginning to adopt a more positive attitude to open government.

ASSESSING THE OMBUDSMEN SYSTEMS

The growth and popularity of the ombudsman concept is some testimony to its value. The work of the established ombudsmen, and the recent growth of new ombudsmen, have shown a need for accessible independent bodies which can investigate complaints, provide redress, and help to educate and inform governmental decision-makers.

The PCA (which has been the model for the public sector ombudsmen) has been said to be 'capable of better things'.[107] As we have seen in this chapter, the PCA is an ambiguous institution. It has never been clear whether it should be a true ombudsman established to serve the needs of the citizen, or an additional agent of the House of Commons established to augment the powers of the House and MPs.

The ombudsmen provide citizens with potentially valuable avenues of complaint against bureaucracy and their reports record examples of cases in which they have secured redress in circumstances where, had they not existed, redress almost certainly would not have been obtained. But those who believe that the PCA should be an effective champion of the citizen against government have always been disappointed. From the outset they have argued that the PCA is more of an 'ombudsmouse' than an 'ombudsman'.[108] They continue to lament the relatively low numbers of complaints made to these bodies; the inability of citizens to complain directly to the PCA; its low

[105] PCA's Annual Report for 1995, Chapter 11, para. 12.
[106] Ibid.
[107] Drewry and Harlow, n. 1 above, at p. 764.
[108] See Mitchell, n. 6 above.

public visibility; the time it takes for investigations to be carried out;[109] the restrictions on jurisdiction; and the absence of power to compel government to provide remedies where it has been found to have acted improperly.

Are those who view the PCA as an additional tool for the House of Commons and MPs any better satisfied? Seen from this perspective it is clear that there have been notable successes for the PCA. We have seen, for example, that its recent investigations into the Barlow Clowes saga not only greatly added to Parliament's knowledge of the affair, but also fed directly into the broader political pressures imposed on government to provide redress. This and other cases illustrate that the PCA has made a very positive contribution to Parliament's armoury. However, from this perspective too, much more can still be done to improve the use made of the PCA by MPs and its usefulness to them. In a recent survey conducted by the select committee, over 50 per cent of MP respondents said that they 'hardly ever' or 'never' read PCA reports[110] and in another study 19 per cent of MPs said that they found the PCA 'very useful', 67 per cent 'slightly useful' and 11 per cent 'not at all' useful.[111] According to Drewry and Harlow one reason why so many MPs make so little use of the PCA is that the PCA and his staff 'seem unaware of the way in which MPs work . . . They function as, and relate more closely to, the civil servants whose work they are called upon to investigate than to the MPs whose servants they are supposed to be'.[112] To remedy this they call upon the select committee to carry out a thorough empirical study of the work of the PCA and its relationship with MPs and the House. They also call for a determined publicity campaign aimed at MPs and their staff; the introduction of new and less formal investigative procedures, such as a telephone advice service; more imaginative recruitment policies so that in addition to lawyers and civil servants, the PCA could be staffed by investigative journalists, academics, people seconded from foreign ombudsmen's offices or industry. An Opposition Chairman to the Select Committee, they say, would also help. Finally, they raise the possibility that the PCA could be a political appointment.[113]

The PCA is, and always has been, an ambiguous institution: a product of compromise between the desires to provide redress for individual citizens and to strengthen the ability of the House of Commons to hold government to account. It is now, however, only one ombudsman among many. Ultimately their success will depend on the level of respect earned from the public and this in turn depends on their perceived independence and integrity, their ability to provide effective remedies; the publicity that is attracted to their

[109] Following rejection of the recommendations of the Chipperfield Report (see note 1 above), the Department of the Environment has commissioned a second-stage review of the local ombudsman which is concentrating on the efficiency and effectiveness of procedures. The report is due to be published in autumn 1996.

[110] Select Committee on the Parliamentary Commissioner for Administration, First Report Session 1993–94, HC 33, para. 25.

[111] Drewry and Harlow, n. 1 above, p. 761.

[112] p. 767.

[113] pp. 768–9.

work, and their accessibility. On each of these matters, much still needs to be done.

Questions

1. Harlow writes of the PCA that 'his *primary* role should be that of an independent and unattached investigator, with a mandate to identify maladministration, recommend improved procedures and negotiate their implementation. Changes in his jurisdiction and procedures should be made only if they facilitate the execution of this task.'[114] Do you agree with this view of the PCA? In particular, does it sufficiently reflect the idea that the PCA should be the citizen's defender?

2. You are asked by the Select Committee on the PCA to identify three reforms that you would like to see introduced to improve the PCA and to write a short briefing paper explaining why they are important. What reforms would you like to see and how would you justify them?

3. Why has the ombudsman concept become so popular in recent years?

4. It may be argued that the term 'maladministration' should now be defined more specifically so that the public know what they may complain about and officials have a better idea of what is expected of them. The PCA disagrees with this. In his view any definition of maladministration would impose limits which would ultimately be prejudicial to potential complainants.[115] Do you think the term 'maladministration' should be defined more specifically, or be left undefined? Can you think of a better term?

5. Do you favour direct access to the PCA or would you retain the 'MP filter', perhaps with modifications?

6. Should the ombudsmen have power to compel recalcitrant authorities to comply with their recommendations?

APPENDIX

Bodies subject to the PCA's jurisdiction[116]

Advisory, Conciliation and Arbitration Service
Agricultural wages committees
Ministry of Agriculture, Fisheries and Food
Arts Council of England
Arts Council of Great Britain
Arts Council of Wales (Syngor Celfyddydau Cymru)
Scottish Arts Council
British Council
British Library Board
Building Societies Commission
Bwrdd yr Iaith Gymraeg (the Welsh Language Board)
Central Statistical Office of the Chancellor of the Exchequer
Certification Officer
Charity Commission
Civil Service Commission
Coal Authority
Co-operative Development Agency
Countryside Commission
Countryside Council for Wales

[114] C. Harlow, 'Ombudsman in Search of a Role' (1978) 41 MLR 446.
[115] Annual Report of the PCA for 1992, Minutes of Evidence, HC 751, para. 36.
[116] Bodies may be added to or taken away from this list by SI: see e.g. Parliamentary Commissioner Order 1996 (SI 1996 No. 1914).

Crafts Council
Crofters Commission
Crown Estate Office
Customs and Excise
Data Protection Registrar
Ministry of Defence
Development Commission
Department for Education
Education Assets Board
Central Bureau for Educational Visits and Exchanges
Office of the Director General of Electricity Supply
Department of Employment
Department of the Environment
Economic and Social Research Council
Equal Opportunities Commission
Export Credits Guarantee Department
Office of the Director General of Fair Trading
British Film Institute
Foreign and Commonwealth Office
Forestry Commission
Friendly Societies Commission
Registry of Friendly Societies
Office of the Director General of Gas Supply
Health and Safety Commission
Health and Safety Executive
Department of Health
Historic Buildings and Monuments Commission for England
Home Office
Horserace Betting Levy Board
Housing Corporation
Housing for Wales
Human Fertilization and Embryology Authority
Central Office of Information
Inland Revenue
Intervention Board for Agricultural Produce
Land Registry
Legal Aid Board
The following general lighthouse authorities:
(a) the Corporation of the Trinity House of Deptford Strond;
(b) the Commissioners of Northern Lighthouses
Local Government Commission for England
The Lord Chancellor's Department
Lord President of the Council's Office
Office of the Director General of the National Lottery
Medical Practices Committee
Scottish Medical Practices Committee
Museums and Galleries Commission
National Debt Office
Department of National Heritage
Trustees of the National Heritage Memorial Fund
Department for National Savings
Natural Environment Research Council
Nature Conservancy Council for England
Commission for the New Towns
Development corporations for new towns
Northern Ireland Court Service
Northern Ireland Office
Occupational Pensions Board
Ordnance Survey
Particle Physics and Astronomy Research Council
The Director of Passenger Rail Franchising
Office of Population Censuses and Surveys
Office of the Commissioner for Protection Against Unlawful Industrial Action
Registrar of Public Lending Right
Public Record Office

Office of Public Service and Science
Commission for Racial Equality
The Rail Regulator
The International Rail Regulator
Red Deer Commission
Department of the Registers of Scotland
General Register Office, Scotland
National Rivers Authority
Royal Mint
Biotechnology and Biological Sciences Research Council
Engineering and Physical Sciences Research Council
Office of the Commissioner for the Rights of Trade Union Members
Office of Her Majesty's Chief Inspector of Schools in England
Office of Her Majesty's Chief Inspector of Schools in Wales
Scottish Courts Administration
Scottish Homes
Scottish Legal Aid Board
Scottish Natural Heritage
Scottish Office
Scottish Record Office
Council for Small Industries in Rural Areas
Department of Social Security
Central Council for Education and Training in Social Work
Sports Council
Scottish Sports Council
Sports Council for Wales
The Staff Commission for Wales (Comisiwn Staff Cymru)
Stationery Office
Office of the Director General of Telecommunication
English Tourist Board
Scottish Tourist Board
Wales Tourist Board
Board of Trade
Department of Trade and Industry
Traffic Director for London
Office of the Commissioner for the Rights of Trade Union Members
Agricultural Training Board
Clothing and Allied Products Industry Training Board
Construction Industry Training Board
Engineering Industry Training Board
Hotel and Catering Industry Training Board
Plastics Processing Industry Training Board
Road Transport Industry Training Board
Department of Transport
Treasury
Treasury Solicitor
United Kingdom Ecolabelling Board
Urban development corporations
Urban Regeneration Agency
Development Board for Rural Wales
Office of the Director General of Water Services
Welsh Office

19

TRIBUNALS

Tribunals are among the main mechanisms provided by Parliament beyond the parliamentary system for resolving grievances between individuals and public bodies and for providing a quality check on administrative decision-making.

There are currently about 2,000 specific tribunals,[1] annually handling over a quarter of a million cases. This is approximately six times the number of cases disposed of at trial by the civil courts and many more times greater than the 3,000 or so applications made annually for leave to seek judicial review. Tribunals are used to dealing with problems across a vast array of subject areas including: educational issues, such as disputes between parents and local education authorities over choice of schools and the provision of special educational support; immigration issues, including appeals against refusals to allow entry into the United Kingdom for various reasons; disputes over the value of property for the purposes of assessing liability to local taxes; appeals by claimants who have been refused social security payments; and adjudications into whether those alleged to be mentally ill should be detained in hospital. As well as disputes involving public bodies, tribunals also deal with landlord and tenant issues (rent tribunals), and conflicts between employees and employers involving unfair dismissal and unlawful discrimination in employment (industrial tribunals).

The examples could be continued. It is clear, however, even from this short list, that the problems handled by tribunals can be of considerable importance, involving matters such as rights to work, basic financial security, personal liberty, and rights not to be discriminated against on grounds of race or sex. Certainly, it would be wrong to assume that the issues handled by tribunals are necessarily less important, or less complex, than those handled by the courts.

For public lawyers, tribunals raise three broad and overlapping sets of concerns, and it is upon these that this chapter is primarily focused. First there are concerns about tribunals as providers of redress. How accessible are they for individuals and how effective are their procedures and powers? How

[1] Hazel Genn, 'Tribunal Review of Decision-Making' in G. Richardson and H. Genn (eds.), *Administrative Law and Government Action* (1994), p. 250 (hereafter referred to as 'Genn').

independent are they? The second range of concerns are in a sense the flip side of the first. They are to do with the role tribunals play in supervising the quality of public decision-making. Are tribunals able to set standards of good practice? Do they have the appropriate powers and, again, are they sufficiently independent to provide an impartial check on administration? Such questions raise a third set of concerns: how are tribunals controlled? What, for example, can people do if they are adversely affected by delayed hearings or an absence of facilities such as interpreters or help with presenting a case? If people are dissatisfied with decisions taken by tribunals, what can be done? Later in the chapter we examine a range of mechanisms which exist to ensure that tribunals operate appropriately. These include:

(a) judicial review of tribunal decisions;
(b) statutory appeals from some tribunals to the courts; and
(c) the supervision provided by the Council on Tribunals.

Table 19.1

Examples of tribunal case loads[2]

	1993	*1994*
Educational appeal committees	25,887	26,658
Industrial tribunals	21,440	21,003
Immigration appeals adjudicators	27,576	26,774
Immigration Appeal Tribunal	6,564	7,148
Valuation tribunals (concerned with valuing property for local taxes)	72,000	101,000
Mental health review tribunals	5,831	6,479
Service committees of family health service authorities	2,520	2,490
Pensions appeal tribunals	2,348	2,863
Rent assessment committees	16,482	14,463
General commissioners of income tax	322,279	215,000
Social security appeal tribunals	77,895	[n/a]
Disability appeal tribunals	15,300	27,512
Medical appeal tribunals	16,513	15,516

WHAT ARE TRIBUNALS?

While some bodies are called tribunals (such as the Immigration Appeal Tribunal or the industrial tribunals), not all bodies which might claim to be tribunals are called tribunals by name. Given this variation and the fact that

[2] The figures are cases decided. This is a selection of tribunals which are under the supervision of the Council on Tribunals. The 1993 figures are from the *Annual Report of the Council on Tribunals 1993/94*, HC 22, Appendix F. The 1994 figures are from the *Annual Report of the Council on Tribunals 1994/95*, HC 64, Appendix E.

names are not always very informative, is it possible to identify characteristics of tribunals so that we know tribunals when we see them, whatever the context and whatever their title?

'Policy-oriented' tribunals and 'court substitutes'

One attempt at classification has drawn the functional distinction between tribunals which are 'policy-oriented' and those which are 'court substitutes'.[3] Policy-oriented tribunals include a wide range of agencies which have regulatory and licensing powers designed to further, develop or apply policy in areas such as monopolies and mergers, commerce and transport, and more general economic contexts. Their work tends to focus on collective issues rather than on the rights and interests of specific individuals. The Monopolies and Mergers Commission, for example, is concerned with issues of market competitiveness, maintaining consumer choice and protecting the public interest from mergers between companies that would produce monopoly situations. Such bodies are not primarily concerned with adjudicating upon conflicts between individuals and the administration or between individuals and, say, employers.

By contrast, court substitute tribunals are adjudicative institutions responsible for resolving disputes between individuals and public or private bodies. They may be described as 'court substitutes' because courts could have been used to handle the disputes if Parliament had wanted them to. It is with this type of tribunal that this chapter is primarily concerned.

Like courts themselves, not all court substitute tribunals are identical. In some cases the body comprises three people (hence *tri*bunal); in other cases decisions are taken by individuals (for example, immigration adjudicators). Some tribunals have original jurisdiction (in other words, they are the first tribunals to which the conflict is taken and reach a decision on the facts and the law), whereas other tribunals are purely appellate bodies (such as the social security appeal tribunals and the Immigration Appeal Tribunal) and only deal with appeals against decisions originally taken by other bodies. Some adopt very formal procedures akin to the civil courts (for example, immigration adjudicators and industrial tribunals); others operate far more informally, bearing a closer resemblance to a meeting around a table than to a court hearing (for example, social security appeal tribunals).

Given these and other variations it has been said that the main common characteristics shared by court substitute tribunals are those that distinguish them from courts. Genn, for instance, has said that 'it might be argued that the *only* common, unifying aspects of adjudicative institutions that bear the label "tribunal" concern their superficially distinctive procedures and personnel'.[4] They tend not to possess complex pre-hearing procedures such as

[3] See B. Abel-Smith and R. Stevens, *Lawyers and the Courts* (1968); J. A. Farmer, *Tribunals and Government* (1974); P. Birkinshaw, *Grievances, Remedies and the State* (2nd edn., 1994), p. 46.

[4] Genn, p. 251.

discovery of documents, or procedures for interim remedies; nor do they follow strict rules of evidence. Their members do not wear court robes, and those appearing before them are often unrepresented. Notice that Genn refers to the 'superficially distinctive' procedures of tribunals. As discussed later, her argument is that informality is more apparent than real: even though they may lack formal procedures many tribunals are more like courts than people tend to assume.

One important reason for trying to draw up a definition of a tribunal has been highlighted in a recent report of the Council on Tribunals, the body charged by Parliament with the task of supervising many tribunals.[5] The legislation under which the Council acts, the Tribunals and Inquiries Act 1992, contains no definition of a 'tribunal' nor any statement of which bodies should be placed under the Council's stewardship. To fill the gap and to help to provide criteria for deciding which bodies should fall within its jurisdiction, the Council has identified five characteristics. Tribunals should be supervised if they:[6]

(a) are established by or under statute;
(b) have adjudicative functions—not merely administrative or advisory functions;
(c) are decision-making bodies rather than bodies that merely make recommendations to a higher authority;
(d) are not one of the 'ordinary courts of law';
(e) are not primarily concerned with complaints-handling or with non-statutory arbitration.

EXAMPLES OF TRIBUNAL SYSTEMS

The provision of a detailed understanding of the way tribunals work would be impossible in a chapter such as this. The best that we can achieve in the space available is to introduce some illustrative examples of tribunal systems in order to provide a basis for discussing the main controversies and policy issues of concern to public lawyers.

Immigration tribunals

When people first arrive in the United Kingdom immigration officers demand to know whether they hold a British or EU passport and whether they have the necessary documentation permitting them entry into the country, such as a visa. If the documentation does not exist, perhaps because the person is a refugee who has been forced to leave their country fearing persecution or because they hoped to obtain the necessary permissions once they arrived at the airport, immigration officers (administrators appointed by the Secretary of State for Home Affairs and responsible for making decisions

[5] See further below p. 457.
[6] *Council on Tribunals Annual Report 1993–4.*

on his behalf)[7] have to decide whether to allow the person in, or turn them away. In making this decision immigration officers have to apply the immigration law as contained in legislation, principally the Immigration Act 1971 and the Immigration Rules made under that Act.

Before the Immigration Appeals Act 1969 it was not possible to appeal against decisions of immigration officers to an independent body. The absence of a right of appeal was criticized by an official committee on the grounds that it was 'fundamentally wrong and inconsistent with the rule of law' not to allow appeals against decisions taken by administrators which could affect 'a man's whole future'.[8] This criticism led to the creation of the current system of appeals.

Today if an immigration officer decides to refuse entry the individual affected *may*[9] be able to appeal to an immigration adjudicator who has power to overturn the original decision if that decision was not in accordance with the law or the relevant immigration rules, or if the adjudicator feels that a different discretionary decision should have been made.[10]

Adjudicators sit alone and are legally qualified. Prior to 1987 they were appointed by the Home Secretary, but following criticism that this undermined their independence from the Home Office, they are now appointed by the Lord Chancellor. Although legal aid is not available to help those using immigration adjudicators, there is a publicly-funded specialist advisory service, the United Kingdom Immigration Advisory Service (UKIAS), which provides free representation to any appellant who requests assistance, and most of those appearing before immigration adjudicators are represented. In 1994 immigration adjudicators decided 26,774 cases.[11]

Hearings conducted by immigration adjudicators tend to be formal. The adjudicator sits some distance from the appellant, sometimes on a raised platform. While the adjudicator asks questions, the overall character of the procedure is adversarial and the case for the Home Office is put by a presenting officer who may cross-examine any witnesses called by the appellant. In contrast, appellants rarely have a chance to cross-examine witnesses for the Home Office because the one person whose actions are in question, the immigration officer who made the original decision, is hardly ever present at the appeal.

From adjudicators there is a further appeal (with leave or 'permission') to the three-member Immigration Appeal Tribunal (IAT). The members of the

[7] See *R v Secretary of State for the Home Department, ex p Oladehinde* [1991] 2 AC 254.

[8] The Wilson Committee on Immigration Appeals, Cmnd 3387 (1967). For a discussion, see C. Harlow and R. Rawlings, *Law and Administration* (1984), pp. 74–8.

[9] Immigration Act 1971, ss 13 and 14 and Asylum and Immigration Appeals Act 1993. Whether a right of appeal exists depends on the grounds for refusing entry. There is e.g. no right of appeal if entry is refused by the Home Secretary on grounds of public good: Immigration Act 1971, s 13(5). In this situation there may be recourse to a specially constituted panel of three 'wise men' who may hear the complaint, but its decision is purely advisory. Following the decision of the European Court of Human Rights in *Chahal v UK*, *The Times* 28 November 1996, this procedure may be contrary to the European Convention on Human Rights.

[10] Immigration Act 1971, s 19.

[11] *Council on Tribunals Annual Report 1994–95.*

IAT are appointed by the Lord Chancellor and the President is a lawyer of at least seven years' standing. Selected decisions of the IAT are published and are binding on adjudicators. In 1993 the IAT decided 7,148 appeals.[12]

Until the Asylum and Immigration Appeals Act 1993 there was no right of appeal from the IAT to the courts. This was criticized for many years because it meant that, apart from making an application for judicial review, there was no way of ensuring that immigration tribunals were dealing with individual cases in accordance with the general law.[13] The Asylum and Immigration Appeals Act 1993 for the first time provides an opportunity to appeal from the IAT, on a point of law, to the Court of Appeal.[14] However, s 10 of the Act also abolished certain rights of appeal to adjudicators. These include decisions affecting visitors and prospective students and their dependants who do not possess a current entry clearance. Some sense of the importance of this can be gained by noting that in 1992, 3,845 decisions refusing a visitor's visa were reversed on appeal.[15] These people can no longer appeal and their only formal legal recourse is by way of judicial review.

Social security tribunals

The social security system deals with millions of decisions annually across a range of welfare benefits.[16] It is a complex system and it is only necessary to outline its bare bones here. The current structure of social security is based on the Beveridge Report of 1942 which itself built on the national insurance scheme established by the Liberal government in 1911. The scheme was intended to ensure that individuals contributed to a fund out of which they would obtain a subsistence level of income if they lost their own income through unemployment, illness or retirement. This scheme was to be supported by a safety net of means-tested discretionary benefits that would help those who were covered by the contributory scheme or who faced particular difficulties. It was originally envisaged that this safety net would decline in importance as the national insurance scheme was extended. In fact the reverse has happened. Government policy since the 1980s has been to erode entitlement to the national insurance benefits with the result that for millions of families means-tested discretionary benefits have become the main source of income.[17] The system for challenging decisions broadly reflects the difference between the national insurance benefits and the discretionary benefits now handled by the Social Fund Scheme.

[12] Ibid.

[13] See e.g. C. Blake 'Immigration Appeals: The Need for Reform' in A. Dummett (ed.), *Towards a Just Immigration Policy* (1986) at p. 180; *Council on Tribunals Annual Report 1987/88*, para. 3.20.

[14] See Z. Chowdhury 'From Tribunal to Court' (1994) 144 NLJ 207–8 and 240–1.

[15] HC Debs, col. 62 (7 June 1993).

[16] See Baldwin, Wikely and Young, *Judging Social Security* (1992) (hereafter 'Baldwin *et al.*').

[17] Baldwin *et al.*, pp. 2–3.

National insurance benefits

The basic system for challenging decisions involving the national insurance benefits may be summarized as follows. Initial decisions on whether people are entitled to unemployment benefit, retirement pensions or income support are taken by officials in local benefit offices named adjudication officers.[18] These officials are appointed by the Secretary of State, although they are formally independent and their decisions are not taken on behalf of the DSS. In practice securing independence is made difficult because adjudication officers are ordinary administrators who spend part of their time working as departmental officials and part of their time as adjudication officers. In other words, they have continuously to switch hats, sometimes working for the Secretary of State and sometimes reaching independent decisions.[19]

If a claimant complains about a determination reached by an adjudication officer, the original determination is always reviewed as a matter of departmental practice, either by the original officer or another officer. Many complaints are resolved in the claimant's favour at this internal stage.[20]

Claimants who remain dissatisfied have a right to appeal to a social security appeal tribunal (SSAT).[21] These tribunals were established in 1983 and are now governed by the Social Security Administration Act 1992. SSATs sit locally. They are chaired by a lawyer of at least five years' standing who is appointed by the Lord Chancellor, and have two lay members appointed by the President of the Independent Tribunal Service (on which see below). The lay members are supposed to have knowledge of conditions in the area and be representative (though not in the sense of being an elected representative) of persons living and working there.[22] Legal aid is not available to help appellants obtain legal representation before the SSAT, although both lay and legal representation is permitted. In 1993 the SSATs decided 77,895 cases.[23]

The SSATs are organized under the general oversight of the President of the Independent Tribunal Service. This position was established to enhance the visible independence of these tribunals from the DSS.[24] The President, who like the SSAT chairpersons is appointed by the Lord Chancellor, is responsible for the appointment of the lay members of the tribunals. The Independent Tribunal Service provides, among other things, training and advice for members of the tribunals.

SSATs are among the least court-like of tribunals and are, for example, far

[18] In 1989, on the income support side alone, adjudication officers dealt with over four million claims for benefit and over ten million reviews of benefit following changes in claimant's circumstances: see Baldwin *et al.*, p. 16.

[19] Baldwin *et al.*, Chapter 2.

[20] Ibid.

[21] In 1989 about 160,000 appeals were lodged, of which approximately a half proceeded to a hearing. For a discussion of the implications of this see Baldwin *et al.*, p. 16.

[22] Social Security Act 1975, s 97(2A) and Sched 10, para. 1(2).

[23] *Council on Tribunals Annual Report 1993–94*. This is the latest figure available at the time of writing.

[24] Also under the umbrella of the Independent Tribunal Service are the medical appeal tribunals, disability appeal tribunals, child support appeal tribunals and vaccine damage tribunals.

less formal than hearings before immigration adjudicators. Hearings are usually conducted across a table with the members sitting on one side and the claimant and the presenting officer from the DSS sitting next to each other on the other, unless the claimant is represented in which case the representative sits between them.

From a decision of an SSAT there is a further appeal, with leave, on a point of law to the Social Security Commissioners. The Commissioners are lawyers of at least ten years' standing. They are appointed by the Crown and sit in London, Cardiff and Edinburgh. Since 1980 there has been a further appeal on a point of law from a Social Security Commissioner to the Court of Appeal in England and Wales.[25]

Discretionary means-tested benefits: the Social Fund

The above system for handling appeals contrasts in a number of important respects with that which exists for discretionary means-tested benefits under the Social Fund. In particular, instead of a system of appeals, claimants from the Social Fund have access to a series of internal reviews coupled with a further right to ask more independent Social Fund Inspectors to review decisions. When the idea of the Social Fund was proposed the government did not provide for any independent appeal on the ground that this would conflict with policy that Social Fund decisions should be taken within a fixed budget. If an independent tribunal could overturn discretionary decisions this would make it difficult to ensure that the budget was maintained. Following widespread criticisms the government finally agreed to establish Social Fund Inspectors as a compromise.[26]

THE GROWTH OF TRIBUNALS

Bodies resembling modern tribunals have existed since the end of the eighteenth century when the General and Special Commissioners of Income Taxes were established to deal with conflicts generated by the imposition of income tax. However, their current importance can be traced to the major social reforms introduced by the Liberal government in the early years of this century, particularly the introduction of pensions for the elderly[27] and national insurance.[28] These schemes inevitably generated disputes between citizens and public administration on a scale that had never before been witnessed. In theory the courts could have been used for dealing with these issues. Indeed many (and particularly many lawyers) thought that they should be, and that the establishment of specialized administrative tribunals to handle

[25] To the Inner House of Court of Session in Scotland.

[26] R. Drabble and T. Lynes, 'Decision-making in Social Security: The Social Fund—Discretion or Control?' [1989] PL 297; B. Hadfield, 'Judge-proofing Reviewable Decisions' in B. Hadfield (ed.), *Judicial Review: A Thematic Approach* (1995).

[27] Old Age Pensions Act 1908.

[28] National Insurance Act 1911.

disputes between individuals and the state would undermine the rule of law. From this perspective, like delegated legislation, tribunals were at best a necessary evil and at worst a sign of a new despotism.[29] In the face of this scepticism, various reasons are given to explain why tribunals have become so common.

Reasons given for the use of tribunals

Judges were thought to be too conservative to deal with social welfare issues sympathetically

Early ideological opposition among Liberals and socialists to using judges to resolve disputes arising from social welfare legislation, based on fear that judges would sabotage the schemes, is given as one reason why alternatives to the courts were sought. Judges were believed to be so innately conservative and out of touch with the needs of ordinary people that they would be unable to approach social welfare issues sensitive to the social goals of the new policies.[30]

It would be constitutionally improper to use courts to further social welfare policy

It has also been argued that it would be constitutionally inappropriate for the courts to be used as part of a scheme established by Parliament for furthering social policy. Genn has put the argument in the following way:[31]

> the idea that judges might be required to substitute their own decision for an administrative decision-maker is contrary to fundamental constitutional principles which require a separation of power between the executive and judiciary.

Those putting this argument reason that the role of judges is to impose an independent check on public administration in order to ensure that it complies with the law. If judges were used to resolve disputes as part of a legislative scheme for furthering social welfare or other policies, this would draw them into the process of administration and they would consequently lose their independence. This would be particularly true, so the argument goes, if judges were required to apply the rules of the scheme and prevented from using general principles drawn from the common law.

This is a difficult argument to accept. Areas of administration such as social welfare and immigration may be rooted in policy, but the task of

[29] Lord Hewart, *The New Despotism* (1929), p. 35; Report on Minister's Powers (1932), Cmnd 4060.

[30] H. Street, *Justice in the Welfare State* (2nd edn., 1975), p. 9; Abel-Smith and Stevens, *In Search of Justice*, p. 111. Fears of this type are still expressed: see J. A. G. Griffith, *The Politics of the Judiciary* (4th edn., 1991).

[31] Genn, p. 253.

tribunals is to determine whether individuals have been properly treated in accordance with legislation. In this respect their role is the same as that of the courts in any dispute governed by statute or regulations. The only difference perhaps is that courts may have more leeway than tribunals because they can apply principles of the common law whereas tribunals can only apply the rules of the scheme itself. This, however, is not a significant distinction because like all other public bodies, tribunals also have to comply with the general principles of the common law and failure to do so can lead to their decisions being judicially reviewed.

A 'Rolls Royce' system was thought unnecessary

There are also more pragmatic concerns that the court system simply could not cope with the scale of disputes likely to be generated by new legislation. It is argued that if the courts are to be used many new judges will have to be appointed and, as well as being costly, this may dilute the quality of the judiciary. It has also been argued that expensive court procedures are unwarranted because many issues handled by tribunals are trifling and relatively unimportant.[32]

Many would reject the suggestion that tribunals handle matters that are insufficiently serious to warrant the use of judges and a 'Rolls Royce' system of justice, as one eminent academic once put it.[33] As we have already seen, issues dealt with by tribunals may be of considerable and even fundamental importance. Whether a person is to be compulsorily detained in hospital, allowed into the country or dismissed from their job are clearly as important as many of the issues which are regularly handled by senior judges in the courts. Moreover, often the significance of an issue is difficult to determine objectively: a claim for a welfare benefit may involve comparatively small sums of money for those who are in paid employment, but the sums may be vital for claimants who are unemployed. Nor can it be assumed that tribunals deal with issues which are less complex and easier to resolve than disputes which are typically dealt with by the courts. On the contrary, tribunals handle some of the most complex, voluminous and rapidly changing fields of law. The law in areas such as immigration, housing, and social security would test even the most experienced and expert of lawyers.

The political advantages of using tribunals

So far we have emphasized the ideological, constitutional and practical reasons which have been given for the use of tribunals. Several commentators,

[32] Evidence of Sir George Coldstream to the Franks Committee (note 38 below) quoted by Genn, p. 255. The desire to save judicial resources by allocating issues such as homelessness disputes to bodies other than the courts and by decriminalizing certain offences—such as parking offences—is of growing importance: see e.g. Sir Harry Woolf, 'Judicial Review: A Possible Programme for Reform' [1992] PL 221.

[33] H. Street, *Justice in the Welfare State*, p. 3.

however, have questioned the significance of these explanations arguing that the real reasons for the popularity of tribunals have been political and managerial. It has been said, for instance, that tribunals enable ministers to shed responsibility for individual decisions while knowing that since tribunals are created by statute ministers can ultimately control their responsibilities and powers. Beveridge adopted this line of argument when he described the establishment of independent insurance officers to determine claims under the unemployment insurance scheme as an ingenious side-tracking of responsibility.[34]

Prosser developed and broadened this form of argument when he contended that statutory tribunals have been established to deal with disputes arising out of the administration of social welfare schemes because they provide a veneer of procedural fairness and 'a symbolic appearance of legality'.[35] The claim is that tribunals help to legitimate controversial policies by presenting an image of procedural fairness. In so doing they deflect criticism from the general policy of the scheme and focus it upon individual disputes within the tribunal system. Referring to the creation, in 1969, of rights of appeal in immigration cases, Blake and Gillespie argued that:[36]

> The prime aim of those who designed and set up the immigration appeals system was to provide a means of demonstrating the assumed and unquestioned fairness and impartiality of decision-making in immigration control. This was necessary in order to make the growing strictness of immigration policy more acceptable both to those directly affected and to the resident immigrant community.

Tribunals can be more accessible and expert than courts

More positive reasons have also been given for the use of tribunals. The most common is that ordinary people will find them cheaper to use, less formal and more accessible than courts.[37] As for SSATs, tribunals can also be staffed by people who have specific expertise and relevant experience. Judges may be highly expert lawyers, but few possess expertise in specific fields of administration, such as social security, immigration and housing, or have practical experience of the way law in these areas impinges upon day-to-day life.

Whether tribunals are in fact easy to use, informal and accessible is still somewhat controversial. As discussed below, although they are expected to work in accordance with principles of openness, fairness and impartiality much of their work is highly technical and they often appear no less formal or distant than courts.

[34] W. Beveridge, *Unemployment—A Problem of Industry* (1930), p. 283 quoted by Nick Wikeley and Richard Young, 'The Administration of Benefits in Britain: Adjudication Officers and the Influence of Social Security Appeal Tribunals' [1992] PL 238, 239.

[35] T. Prosser, 'Poverty Ideology and Legality: Supplementary Benefit Appeal Tribunals and their Predecessors' (1977) 4 British Journal of Law and Society 39, 44. See further C. Harlow and R. Rawlings, *Law and Administration*, pp. 74–8.

[36] C. Blake and J. Gillespie, 'The Immigration Appeal Process—A Study in Legal Ritual' (unpublished) quoted in C. Harlow and R. Rawlings, *Law and Administration*, p. 75.

[37] JUSTICE/All Souls, *Administrative Justice: Some Necessary Reforms*, (1988), para. 9.3.

THE CHARACTERISTICS OF TRIBUNALS

The Franks Committee report

This committee was established in the late 1950s in the wake of the so-called Crichel Down affair.[38] This concerned land (Crichel Down) that had been compulsorily purchased by a government department and then let to a tenant in breach of a promise to invite public tenders.[39] Although the affair had nothing specifically to do with tribunals, allegations of corruption and departmental wrong-doing were widespread and fanned growing public concern about the behaviour of government and particularly its treatment of individuals. One aspect of this focused on the adequacy of machinery for redress and the work of tribunals and inquiries. The Franks Committee was established 'as a governmental response to a crisis of public confidence' to look into these issues.[40]

The terms of reference of the Franks Committee were to examine statutory tribunals and also administrative processes involving inquiry procedures. According to Griffith, this meant that the committee was 'directed in exactly the wrong direction'. Rather than being asked to examine the broad area of internal departmental decision-making, the committee

> was told, in short, to look at procedures which were predominantly open, fair and impartial and . . . to see if they could be made any more so . . . But into the closed, dark and windowless procedures [of government departments] the Committee was not asked to let air and light.[41]

This did not mean that the committee's report was without value. On the contrary, it has been recognized as 'an important landmark in our constitutional history . . .'.[42]

One of the major questions of principle considered was whether tribunals should be viewed as part of the internal administrative system of government (and therefore under the control of departments) or as independent adjudicative bodies operating as part of the legal system. The Franks Committee concluded that tribunals should be viewed as independent adjudicative bodies and a 'valuable and permanent part of the machinery of justice'.[43] It emphasized that they should operate on the basis of three key principles: 'openness, fairness and impartiality'.

To achieve these principles, Franks said that tribunal procedures should, as far as possible, resemble those of the courts. To this end it recommended that:

[38] Report of the Committee on Administrative Tribunals and Enquiries, Cmnd 218.

[39] Report of Sir Andrew Clark into the Disposal of Land at Crichel Down (1954), Cmnd 9176.

[40] Harlow and Rawlings, note 35 above, p. 95.

[41] J. A. G. Griffith, 'Tribunals and Inquiries' (1959) 22 MLR 125. For further criticism of Franks, see P. Birkinshaw, *Grievances, Remedies and the State*, pp. 50–6.

[42] W. A. Robson, 'Administrative Justice and Injustice: A Commentary on the Franks Report' [1958] PL 12, 17; and see M. Loughlin, *Public Law and Political Theory* (1992), p. 179.

[43] W. A. Robson, note above.

- the chairman should be legally qualified;
- members should not be chosen by the department whose decisions they were being asked to consider;
- hearings should normally be in public;
- individuals should generally have the right to legal representation;
- legal aid should be available to help finance this representation;
- tribunals should give reasons for their decisions; and
- there should be a right of appeal on 'fact, law and merits' from tribunals to courts.

The committee also recommended that tribunals should be supervised by an independent body to be known as the Council on Tribunals.

Tribunals and Inquiries Acts 1958–92

The basic principles underlying these recommendations were accepted by the government and most of the detailed recommendations have since been introduced either by administrative reform or by legislation. The key provision was the Tribunals and Inquiries Act 1958 (now the Tribunals and Inquiries Act 1992). This Act applies also to inquiries; however the main provisions relating to tribunals may be summarized as follows.

(1) The 1958 Act established the Council of Tribunals with responsibility for keeping under review the constitution and working of certain tribunals, but with more limited powers than Franks recommended (ss 1–3).[44]

(2) Chairpersons of specified tribunals are to be selected by the relevant minister from panels appointed by the Lord Chancellor (s 6).

(3) Ministers are prevented from dismissing members of specified tribunals without the agreement of the Lord Chancellor (s 7).

(4) Ministers are required to consult with the Council on Tribunals before making procedural rules for tribunals which are under the Council's supervision (s 8).

(5) Tribunals have a general duty to give reasons, provided these are requested on or before the giving or notification of the decision (s 10).[45]

(6) There is a right of appeal on a point of law from specified tribunals to the High Court or Court of Appeal (s 11).

Governments, however, have repeatedly failed to implement all the recommendations of the Franks Committee. The most significant omission has been the refusal to extend legal aid to more than a handful of tribunals. Also notable has been the failure to extend a right of appeal to the courts on matters of fact and on the merits. There has been additional criticism of the limited role

[44] See further p. 457.

[45] There is no obligation to provide reasons if the provision of reasons would conflict with the interests of national security (s 10(2)). We consider the common law obligations regarding reasons in Chapter 25.

given to the Council on Tribunals as well as concern that large numbers of tribunals continue to fall beyond its jurisdiction. These issues are discussed later in this chapter.

'Openness, fairness and impartiality' in practice

Running throughout our discussion has been the assumption that while tribunals may be similar to the courts in some ways, they are none the less distinctive in that they are more accessible and much more 'user-friendly' than courts. These characteristics are said

(a) to make them better suited than courts for handling the type of problems brought before them and
(b) to mean that tribunals provide a more efficient and effective way of supervising the quality of administrative decision-making than can be provided by the courts.

As the Franks Committee confidently asserted:[46]

> [T]ribunals have certain characteristics which often give them advantages over the courts. These are cheapness, accessibility, freedom from technicality, expedition, and expert knowledge of their particular subject.

How accessible and informal are tribunals?

Compare the above quotation with the following view expressed by Genn:[47]

> This description of tribunals has been happily accepted in the literature on tribunals ever since publication of the Report by the Franks Committee . . . despite the fact that the claims have been put to the empirical test on relatively few occasions. Although some of the most up-to-date analyses of tribunals by public lawyers continue to repeat the Franks [sic] description, published research on tribunals suggests that in practice tribunals often fail to display the characteristics of which commentators appear so fond.

As this suggests, recent research and writing has questioned the assumption that tribunals are accessible and informal. We have already pointed out that in reality tribunals are often required to apply legal regimes and resolve factual issues which are at least as complex as those handled by the civil courts. This creates the danger that individuals may suffer the worst of both worlds: they go to tribunals expecting informality and without the benefit of proper representation and preparation, only to be confronted by hearings that are concerned with complex and legalistic issues with which they are ill prepared to cope. The result, says Genn, is that '. . . citizens with genuine and justified complaints against faulty administrative decision-making cannot obtain redress. Wrong decisions therefore go uncorrected.'[48]

46 Franks Report, para. 38, p. 9.
47 Genn, p. 257 (footnotes omitted).
48 Genn, p. 263.

The following quotations taken from the research carried out by H. Genn and Y. Genn into representation at tribunals provide a flavour of the issues facing individuals in social security tribunals and hearings before immigration adjudicators.[49]

> You are dealing with rules and regulations, and a person who is a lawyer or is somebody who deals in that field will be able to know what . . . evidence is required before the tribunal and will be able to present the facts and the evidence that is essential . . . Consider a person who doesn't know anything about statute law—and we are dealing with statute law. It takes a long time for someone who is not associated with the tribunals or who isn't a lawyer to understand what the regulations mean, what the words mean, and what are the conditions under one regulation or another. (SSAT chair)[50]

> The process is very complex. I have problems understanding it all, so I don't know how the appellants manage, and I am legally trained. (SSAT chair)[51]

> I don't think that you can have informal tribunals. They are courts. They are perceived as courts by everybody else, apart from some lawyers who distinguish between the court system and the administrative tribunal system. It isn't informal. How could it ever be like that? You have got to make decisions based on a set of rules. Then you are going to have the interpretation of the rules. Then the rules are always going to be subject to getting it wrong in law and judicial review. How can you have an informal tribunal system? (SSAT solicitor)[52]

> I didn't know what to say about the case. I didn't understand the situation. It's very complicated. I didn't have a clue about what was happening. No one explained who was who and what role they played. I didn't understand what was being said. (unrepresented tribunal applicant)[53]

The Genn research looked in particular at issues of accessibility and representation before certain tribunals. The findings throw valuable light on these issues and are worth careful consideration by public lawyers.

Accessibility

Tribunals handle vast numbers of cases, but they still only deal with a tiny fraction of the disputes that could be referred to them. Why then are they not used more than they are? Consider the situation in the context of social security decisions.

Millions of social security decisions are taken annually. Research carried out by the Department of Health and others has shown, moreover, that there is a very high level of error in social security decision-making and that a high proportion of these errors go uncorrected (and undetected) unless the individual affected decides to challenge the decisions by resorting to tribunals

[49] H. Genn and Y. Genn, *Representation at Tribunals* (1989); the quotations are given in Genn.
[50] Genn, p. 274.
[51] Genn, p. 274.
[52] Genn, pp. 278–9.
[53] Genn, p. 283.

where available.[54] Claimants who are dissatisfied with decisions have an automatic and free right of appeal to the SSAT and they are told about this right when they are notified about any adverse decision. Nevertheless, it has been estimated that despite the ease with which an appeal can be made, less than 1 per cent of those claimants who are refused any benefit exercise their right of appeal.[55]

It is often argued that people are deterred from using the courts because courts are expensive, slow and extremely formal. In theory these deterrents ought not to apply to tribunals. Why then are these tribunals used in such a tiny percentage of cases?

When H. Genn and Y. Genn explored this question they found that the most frequently cited reason people gave for not appealing was the belief that 'appealing would be too time consuming, involve too much red tape, or be too distressing'. Many claimants felt that decisions must be correct and, even if decisions were wrong, people believed that they were powerless to do anything about it and felt that resort to tribunals would be useless. In fact, these beliefs appear to be largely mistaken. Whenever an appeal is lodged the questioned decision is automatically reviewed within the department and in up to one-third of the cases the decision is changed in the individual's favour, without the matter even going to the tribunal. As well as highlighting the poor quality of initial decisions this clearly shows the value of appealing. There is a broader issue as well. Looked at from the perspective of the effectiveness of systems for controlling the general quality of decision-making, the figures suggest that quality control systems which operate only if they are triggered by individuals are likely to leave many errors undetected.

Outcome of tribunal hearings: the importance of representation

The Genn research also studied the outcome of cases that were taken to SSATs and immigration tribunals. They found that of the 1,115 social security appeals examined, 30 per cent had been allowed or allowed in part at the hearing, and 70 per cent had been dismissed at the hearing. Of the 1,050 immigration cases studied, 22 per cent had been allowed or allowed in part and 77 per cent dismissed. Their data showed that applicants had a substantially greater chance of success when they appeared at a hearing than when they either failed to appear or chose to have the matter dealt with on the papers without an oral hearing. This was understandable, thought the researchers, because if the appellant is not present they cannot provide new information, and paperwork submitted by the department is not thoroughly reviewed.

The researchers analysed the factors influencing the chances of success

[54] The Chief Adjudication Officer (CAO) monitors standards of decision-making by adjudication officers in the DSS and the Department of Employment. Three recent reports of the CAO have shown that procedural errors have been made in 46 per cent, 52 per cent and 32 per cent of cases in which decisions have been reviewed and revised by the department. See Roy Sainsbury, 'Internal Reviews and the Weakening of Social Security Claimants' Rights of Appeal' in G. Richardson and H. Genn (eds.), *Administrative Law and Government Action*, p. 304.

[55] DSS, *Social Security Statistics 1990*, discussed in Genn, p. 266.

and their most interesting findings concern the impact that skilled representation can have. It was found that in the SSATs skilled representation increased the likelihood of success from the average of 30 per cent to about 48 per cent. There is much evidence that those represented by expert and experienced non-lawyers, such as welfare rights workers or trade unionists, have more success in some tribunals than those represented by non-specialist lawyers. In immigration cases skilled representation increased the chance of success from 20 per cent to 38 per cent. The reasons why skilled representation makes so much difference almost certainly lie in the fact that, despite claims to informality, these tribunals are in reality extremely formal institutions that are difficult for those who lack technical knowledge and experience to use: '. . . the veneer of informality presents a trap for those who attempt to proceed with their cases without advice or representation'.[56] Unrepresented claimants are:[57]

> likely to face grave difficulties because of the legal complexity of the subject matter . . . their imperfect understanding of the role and powers of the tribunal, their lack of advocacy skills, and their general discomfort at the manner in which tribunals conduct themselves.

Legal aid

Governments have repeatedly failed to implement the Franks Committee recommendation that legal aid should be extended to all tribunals to enable people to apply for publicly-funded help towards the cost of legal representation. The desire to maintain informality is one reason, but the sheer cost that such an extension would entail is undoubtedly the single most important factor. At present legal aid is only available for proceedings before the Lands Tribunal, the Commons Commissioners, the Employment Appeal Tribunal and the Mental Health Review Tribunal. Individuals can, however, apply for assistance to help pay for legal advice and assistance in preparing a case, but this will not extend to representation itself. As discussed above in the context of immigration, individuals may also have access to publicly-funded specialist representation by a body such as UKIAS. It has been argued that a similar body should be established to help people appearing before other tribunals as well.[58]

Independence of tribunals

It has been said that the 'visible independence of the tribunals is the cornerstone of the system'.[59] Certainly it is the independence of most tribunals from

[56] Genn, p. 279.

[57] H. Genn and Y. Genn, Chapter 7. For a summary and discussion, see T. Mullen, 'Representation at Tribunals' (1990) 53 MLR 230. The researchers rejected the suggestion that these disadvantages can be overcome by the tribunal adopting a more inquisitorial approach.

[58] H. Genn and Y. Genn. Cf. the views of the Council on Tribunals, *Annual Report 1989/90*, paras 1.35–50.

[59] JUSTICE/All Souls, *Administrative Justice: Some Necessary Reforms* (1988), para. 9.13.

departmental, agency and local authority control that distinguishes them from internal complaints procedures, and systems of review such as that provided for dealing with complaints about housing benefit decisions.[60] As the quotations from the Genn research show, independence is an important element in providing tribunals with credibility among potential users. Independence from executive control may also be a legal requirement imposed by the ECHR. The government, for instance, was obliged to increase the powers of mental health review tribunals to ensure that they satisfy the level of independence required by Art 5(4) of the ECHR following the decision in *X v United Kingdom*.[61] Independence, however, is not always a clear-cut issue; and formal independence is not necessarily the same as either actual or perceived independence. This is particularly so in circumstances where departments or ministers can exercise informal influence over such things as appointments, day-to-day working practice, and attitudes to law and policy.

Appointment

As with legal aid, successive governments have also refused to implement the Franks Committee's recommendation that members of tribunals be appointed by the Council on Tribunals, rather than by ministers. The result is that ministers who head the department with which the individual is in dispute are often involved in the appointment of tribunal members. This practice is regularly criticized by the Council on Tribunals.[62] Sometimes the criticism produces a positive response. It was, for example, only as a result of repeated criticisms by the Council on Tribunals and others that immigration adjudicators have since 1987 been appointed by the Lord Chancellor rather than by the Home Secretary.[63]

Independence, working practice and legal advice

Perhaps the most notorious example of the tenuous nature of tribunal independence is provided by the social security adjudicators who provide the first level of review for many social security disputes.[64] Their ambiguous status is summed up by the following quotation from an adjudication officer:[65]

[60] The perception that Housing Benefit Review Boards are insufficiently independent of local authorities has been one of the principal criticisms of that system: Roy Sainsbury and Tony Eardley, 'Housing Benefit Review Boards: A Case for Slum Clearance' [1992] PL 551.

[61] (1981) 4 EHRR 181. See further Genevra Richardson, *Law, Process and Custody: Prisoners and Patients* (1993), p. 280.

[62] See e.g. criticism of appeal committees run by local authorities under the Education Act 1980: Council on Tribunals, *Annual Report 1992/93*, para. 2.13.

[63] Moreover, their duties are now allocated to them by the chief adjudicator rather than by the department: Council on Tribunals, *Annual Report 1981–82*, para. 3.24 and *Annual Report 1985–86*, para. 4.40.

[64] See Baldwin *et al.*, p. 56; Nick Wikeley and Richard Young, 'The Administration of Benefits in Britain: Adjudication Officers and the Influence of Social Security Appeal Tribunals' [1992] PL 238, 240.

[65] Baldwin *et al.*, p. 57.

> I think it's possible to be independent to a degree, but basically I think it's a bit of a joke . . . I am paid by the Department, work for the Department, my supervisor works for the Department. I am, to all intents and purposes, a DSS employee.

Recent situations have shown that even tribunals operating at the highest levels, such as the Employment Appeal Tribunal (EAT) and the IAT, may find their independence undermined. One example occurred when the Lord Chancellor applied pressure on the then President of the EAT, Wood J (a High Court Judge), to alter tribunal procedures which the Lord Chancellor thought were contributing to the mounting backlog of cases. The Lord Chancellor wrote to the President seeking an assurance that the procedures would be changed saying that: 'if you do not feel that you can give me this assurance, I must ask you to consider your position'. Although the Lord Chancellor later denied that he had meant to interfere with the principle of judicial independence, the form of words chosen was widely interpreted as a threat to Wood J specifically and to the independence of EATs more generally. This prompted Oliver to ask 'what has happened to the constitutional sense and antennae in the Lord Chancellor's Department [where it] looks very much as if managerialism is . . . taking over from constitutionalism . . . [?]'.[66]

The need to obtain expert legal advice can also affect the independence of tribunals. At one end of the spectrum, lay members of social security tribunals may find it difficult to exercise independent judgment when confronted with complex regulations which they may have to rely on the clerk to the tribunal, who is a DSS employee, to explain.[67] Even expert tribunals may run into difficulties. Until recently, for example, immigration adjudicators and the IAT were provided with legal advice by the lawyers in the Treasury Solicitor's Department, which also advises and represents government departments including the Home Office, from which these tribunals are supposed to be independent. The potential threat that this posed came to light when it was disclosed that the Treasury Solicitor's Department had written to the IAT criticizing decisions of the High Court and the Court of Appeal and accusing the courts of 'undermining' the immigration rules. The letter was widely regarded as an attempt to influence the IAT to interpret case law in a way that was favourable to the government.[68]

One final matter which may be noted in the context of a discussion of independence is the perception that tribunals are unable to be truly independent because they are obliged to apply the same rules and regulations that the administrators use. While this may be true,[69] it misses the main point

[66] D. Oliver, 'The Lord Chancellor's Department and the Judges' [1994] PL 157. See also Sir Francis Purchas, 'Lord Mackay and the Judiciary' (1994) 144 NLJ 527.

[67] S. Legomsky, *Specialised Justice* (1990).

[68] *The Independent*, 10 June 1989 ('Treasury Solicitor barred from giving immigration advice'). See also *The Independent*, 7 June 1989 ('Immigration advice aims to subvert law, Hattersley claims') and *The Independent*, 6 June 1989 ('The primary purpose of the courts').

[69] Note that tribunals may have to apply Community law even when it is inconsistent with domestic legislation.

of most tribunals. Their role is not to rewrite the law, but rather to ensure that departments and officials have properly interpreted the law and correctly applied it to the facts of particular cases. Discussion of independence leads us to a consideration of the controls which exist over tribunals.

CONTROLS OVER TRIBUNALS

Tribunals are subject to two main forms of supervision: that provided by the Council on Tribunals and that provided by the courts.[70]

Council on Tribunals

As noted earlier, the Council on Tribunals was established by the Tribunals and Inquiries Act 1958 following the Franks Committee Report and now operates under the Tribunals and Inquiries Act 1992.[71] It is an advisory body charged with keeping under review the constitution and working of certain (but not all) tribunals and with considering matters which may be referred to it by the Lord Chancellor. The Council lacks many of the powers that Franks thought it ought to possess, including the power to appoint tribunal members and to formulate procedural rules. However, the Council must be consulted before any procedural rules are made for any tribunal under its jurisdiction and before any tribunal is excluded from the obligation to give reasons for its decisions.

The Council is composed of up to 15 people appointed by the Lord Chancellor. In practice its members offer a mix of legal (academic and practising) and non-legal expertise from industry, commerce, the civil service and from trade union and other backgrounds. The PCA is a member by virtue of his office.

The main influence of the Council on Tribunals is exercised through its special and annual reports which are laid before Parliament and which often receive publicity in the quality press. As well as being purely informative, these reports are often highly critical of aspects of the tribunal system and of government policy in relation to tribunals.

A long-term concern of the Council has been the trend towards using internal reviews within administrative systems instead of establishing rights of appeals to independent tribunals. The Council, for example, has repeatedly criticized government's refusal to reform Housing Benefits Review Boards so as to enable people dissatisfied with housing benefit decisions taken by local authorities to appeal to a tribunal.[72] It has said that the present system is

[70] They are also subject to indirect political supervision by the relevant minister, who is accountable to Parliament, and limited supervision by the Parliamentary Ombudsman. Since September 1994 its jurisdiction has been expanded to include the administrative actions of staff of certain tribunals: Parliamentary Commissioner Act 1994.

[71] See *The Functions of the Council on Tribunals: Special Report by the Council* (1980).

[72] Council on Tribunals *Annual Report 1993–94*, paras 2.77–80.

'unfair—not just for dissatisfied claimants but for members of the Review Boards' as well, because these members have to operate without the support and training which is given to people who sit on social security tribunals.[73] The Council also campaigned vigorously against the original proposal to introduce the Social Fund scheme without an independent right of appeal.[74] In 1994 it renewed its criticism of complaints procedures in the NHS which are insufficiently independent of NHS management.[75] More generally, the Council has been critical of the reluctance of government to place tribunals under its jurisdiction.[76] It has recently highlighted the 'alarming' delays in the processing of appeals from the Child Support Agency to the Child Support Appeal Tribunal[77] and deplored the refusal by some tribunals to allow it to view their deliberations. This, the Council has said, is 'quite baffling in the light of the supervisory functions given to us by Parliament'.[78]

The Council on Tribunals has been urging tribunals to establish and publish their own Charter Statements showing the standards of service which their users can expect.[79] Such statements would include target periods for responding to enquiries and correspondence, providing hearings, and written decisions; standards of accommodation, waiting area and facilities for disabled people; the wearing of name badges by tribunal staff; and the creation of complaints procedures for those who may be dissatisfied by the service provided by the tribunal and its staff. As the Council has said 'none of these matters go beyond the basic standard of service and performance to which tribunal users should feel entitled'. It went on to say, however, that 'our visits to tribunals throughout Britain show us how often these basic standards are not met'.[80]

The Council on Tribunals attempts to be an active defender of tribunals and of the principles of openness, fairness and impartiality. However, it lacks power and the resources that are necessary to carry out thorough research and to provide a greater input into policy-making; and there is 'much evidence to suggest that its proposals on more contentious matters are not taken seriously by government'.[81] Another problem is that the scope of the Council's jurisdiction is very limited and Birkinshaw, and others, have argued that the Council should be replaced by a body which is able to provide systematic oversight over administrative justice as a whole modelled on the Administrative Review Council in Australia or the Administrative Conference in the USA.[82]

73 Para. 2.80.
74 See n. 26 above.
75 Council on Tribunals, *Annual Report 1993–94*, para. 1.12.
76 Paras 1.23–36. Among the tribunals which are outside its jurisdiction are the Foreign Compensation Commission, the Gaming Board, Legal Aid Committees and the Parole Board.
77 Paras 1.1–1.5.
78 Para. 1.40.
79 Paras 2.13–16.
80 Para. 2.16.
81 P. Birkinshaw, *Grievances, Remedies and the State*, p. 52.
82 P. Birkinshaw, note above, pp. 291–2; N. Lewis and P. Birkinshaw, *When Citizens Complain: Reforming Justice and Administration* (1993); JUSTICE/All Souls, *Administrative Justice: Some Necessary Reforms*, Chapter 4; A. W. Bradley, 'The Council on Tribunals: Time for a Broader Role?' [1991] PL 6. The US Administrative Conference was abolished in 1995.

The courts

The work of tribunals comes to the attention of the courts either by way of an appeal from a decision of the tribunal to the court where statute permits an appeal, or by virtue of an application for judicial review of a tribunal's decision.

Appeals from tribunals to the courts

There is only an appeal from tribunals to the courts if one is specifically established by statute.[83] Where an appeal is established, the grounds on which appeals may be made depends on the statute. Sometimes an appeal may involve a complete rehearing of the case. More often, an appeal to the courts is only permitted on the grounds that the tribunal has made an error of law. As discussed earlier in the chapter in the context of immigration and the Social Fund, the establishment of rights of appeal can be controversial and government has for a variety of reasons often been very reluctant to allow appeals to the courts. The reluctance may be due to the fear that appeals to the courts slow down decision-making, are too costly, too legalistic, reduce the freedom of public bodies, or conflict with policy or financial constraints.

Judicial review

Decisions of tribunals may be challenged by proceedings for judicial review. The supervision provided by judicial review is not concerned with whether individual tribunal decisions are right or wrong and on a judicial review judges cannot simply overturn tribunal decisions because they would have decided the issue differently. To succeed in a judicial review it must be shown that the tribunal has either exceeded or abused its legal powers or failed to follow the appropriate procedures. The theory is that had Parliament intended judges to be concerned with the merits of decisions it would either have given the courts the task to make the decision in the first place, rather than allocate the decision to a tribunal; or it would have established a right of appeal on the merits from the tribunal to the courts and obviated the need for judicial review. As discussed in later chapters, although the courts have in recent years given themselves greater opportunity to review tribunal decisions, the courts may be cautious about interfering. Often the caution is justified on the grounds that tribunals are expert and that tribunals ought not to become 'the happy hunting grounds of lawyers'.[84] Even if a

[83] The Tribunals and Inquiries Act 1992 provides for a right of appeal on a point of law from certain tribunals to the High Court or the Court of Appeal—but not, as Franks recommended, on facts and merits. See further Lord Woolf, 'A Hotch Potch of Appeals, a Need of a Blender' [1988] CJQ 44 and 'Judicial Review: A Possible Programme for Reform' [1992] PL 221; see also the recommendations of the Law Commission in its 1995 report *Administrative Law: Judicial Review and Statutory Appeals* (Law Com No 226).

[84] *R v Secretary of State for Social Services, ex p Moore* [1975] 1 WLR 624, per Lord Denning MR.

person has been successful on an application for judicial review, the result may be that the matter is referred back to the tribunal for it to make a fresh decision in the light of the court's judgment. That fresh decision may be the same as that originally made, only this time it ought to be made in accordance with the law.

One final point is to be noted: in some circumstances individuals who are aggrieved by decisions of public bodies may have a choice of process—either to use the statutory appeal procedures and go to a tribunal, or seek judicial review. Simon Cotton was in this situation, and as we see in Chapter 27 he used judicial review. In part he chose to do so because he thought that this would be quicker. In that case the court allowed Cotton to proceed, probably because the judge accepted the need for speed. Often, however, judges insist that people exhaust their statutory rights of appeal before seeking judicial review.[85]

SUMMARY

This chapter has examined the role tribunals play in redressing grievances and supervising the quality of public administration. It has considered the definition of tribunals, the reasons for their growth, their working characteristics and the main controls over them. We have seen that while tribunals are supposed to be informal and accessible there is considerable doubt over whether they actually achieve these aims. Although tribunals hear a great many cases, there is good evidence that tribunals, particularly those working in the social security context, only deal with a small minority of administrative errors, the vast majority of which go unchallenged and unchecked. One implication is that like ombudsmen, the network of tribunals, even where it is available to individuals, cannot provide a comprehensive system of redress against administrative action. In the chapters which follow we turn to consider the work of the courts in providing redress against, and supervision of, government.

Questions

1. 'A Rolls Royce system of justice is not required to deal with the types of issues that come before tribunals and this is one of the main reasons why tribunals are used in preference to the courts.' On what grounds might this statement be criticized?

2. Should legal aid be extended to all tribunals so that all individuals can have legal representation if they want it?

3. Why is it important for tribunals to be seen to be independent from government?

4. 'The use of relatively informal systems for handling conflicts between individuals and the state . . . [may be] . . . understood as a "calculated political action" which is intended

[85] For example *R v Secretary of State for the Home Department, ex p Swati* [1986] 1 WLR 477. Lord Woolf has supported this approach in his report: *Access to Justice* (1996).

to deflect attention from oppressive state policies, to protect such policies with a cloak of legitimacy, and to give the impression of the existence of the right to appeal while ensuring that such rights cannot be vindicated.'[86]

(i) How might tribunals achieve these purposes?
(ii) How would you critically assess this view?

[86] Genn, p. 260.

20

INTRODUCING JUDICIAL REVIEW

WHAT IS JUDICIAL REVIEW?

In 1987, concerned by the growing number of successful judicial review challenges against central government, government lawyers produced a short booklet called *The Judge Over Your Shoulder* for civil servants which explained what judicial review was and how it might be avoided. According to this booklet:[1]

> Judicial review is, as the name implies, how the Courts of England and Wales supervise the way in which Ministers, Government departments, agencies, local authorities or other public bodies exercise their powers or carry out their duties. It is therefore merely a means (although a very powerful one) by which improper exercise of power can be remedied . . . it is a part of the whole process of good administration.

The incidence of judicial review

Applications for judicial review are made to the High Court.[2] Over recent years their number has increased considerably: 544 applications were commenced during 1981; by 1995 the annual number had risen to 3,604. Caution is, however, needed in reading too much into these statistics. For a start, compared to other mechanisms for redressing grievances, the incidence of judicial review seems unexceptional. While the PCA only handled 1,332 complaints in 1994, the local ombudsmen handled over 14,000 complaints during the same period and some tribunals handle hundreds of thousands of cases a year. The judicial review caseload also seems small when compared to the number of potentially reviewable decisions taken every year by public bodies.[3]

[1] *The Judge Over Your Shoulder* (2nd edn., 1994), p. 4. For comments, see A. W. Bradley [1987] PL 487 and D. Oliver [1994] PL 514.

[2] As discussed in Chapter 22, 'judicial review' in a broader sense may also occur in other types of litigation, for instance when a person defends a prosecution by alleging that the delegated legislation which creates an offence has been unlawfully made, or defends a tort or contract action on the grounds that a public body has acted outside its powers.

[3] Recent research has shown that even in areas of administration where judicial review is used relatively often, the 'volume of judicial review litigation is tiny by contrast to the scale of

Delving deeper into the statistics, it emerges that most judicial review applications arise from only a handful of administrative activities. By far the largest sources are decisions involving homelessness taken by local authorities (23.8 per cent of all judicial review applications in 1991) and determinations about immigration taken under the auspices of the Home Office (22.7 per cent). The third largest area is challenges to decisions made by magistrates' courts and the police in relation to criminal matters (15.6 per cent).[4] Much of the recent growth in the caseload is attributable to the increasing numbers of challenges to local authority housing decisions. For most central government departments judicial review challenges are still a very infrequent occurrence, happening perhaps only once or twice a year. Commenting on this, Bridges, Meszaros and Sunkin say:

> There are lessons to be drawn here about the constitutional significance of judicial review. Judicial review is often depicted as a weapon in the hands of the citizen to be used against the over-mighty powers of central government, and it has certainly performed this role in a number of recent, high profile cases. Our data suggests, however, that over the past decade it has been used more often as a weapon to further limit the autonomy of local government rather than as a constraint on the power of the central state.[5]

This is not to suggest that the general growth in the judicial review caseload is unimportant. One consequence is that the High Court has at times found it impossible to process applications with acceptable speed and until quite recently applicants were often faced with delays of over twelve months in obtaining a final determination of their cases. Partly in order to control access to the court, the judges have, through case law, devoted a great deal of attention to the important questions of who may commence judicial review challenges,[6] against which bodies,[7] when[8] and how.[9]

Hand-in-hand with the increasing quantity of litigation there has been an extension of the common law 'grounds' of judicial review—the legal arguments for holding that a public body's action is invalid.[10] The judges have set out with growing sophistication the legal requirements for lawful government action. This development has been reflected in, and sometimes prompted

---

administrative decision making': see further L. Bridges, G. Meszaros and M. Sunkin, *Judicial Review in Perspective* (1995), p. 11. In 1994 for example there were 447 applications for judicial review involving homelessness. According to the housing charity SHELTER, in that year 299,053 households applied for assistance from local housing authorities claiming to be homeless or threatened with homelessness, and just over 127,000 were accepted as being entitled to some help. Bearing in mind that the Housing Act 1985 does not provide an opportunity to appeal against these decisions, this left approximately 170,000 people whose applications were rejected and who constituted a potential pool of judicial review applicants.

[4] For more detailed analysis of the caseload, see Bridges, Meszaros and Sunkin, especially Chapter 1.

[5] Bridges, Meszaros and Sunkin, above, p. 194 (footnotes omitted).

[6] On standing, see p. 486.

[7] On amenability, see p. 508.

[8] On delay, see p. 485.

[9] On 'procedural exclusivity', see p. 514.

[10] See further Chapters 23–5.

by, the growing specialist literature in the field.[11] It is to the grounds that we now turn.

AN OVERVIEW OF THE GROUNDS OF JUDICIAL REVIEW

Lawyers advising a potential applicant or respondent must have a thorough knowledge of the grounds of review in order to decide whether or not a client has a case worth fighting and, if so, on what basis the case should be argued. These grounds are examined in much more detail in Chapters 23–5. One difficulty is that the 'principles' of judicial review are very fluid and have been developing rapidly. There has rarely been a time in recent years when some innovative ground of review is not on the boil: during the 1980s it was the doctrine of legitimate expectation;[12] during the early 1990s it was the common law duty placed on public bodies to give reasons for their decisions.[13] The result is that even experienced lawyers may find it difficult to predict the likely success or failure of particular arguments.

As well as providing a set of legal arguments to be deployed against public bodies, the grounds of review may also work to guide public authorities so that they can anticipate and avoid the possibility of challenge by ensuring that decisions are properly made in the normal course of day-to-day administration. One purpose of *The Judge Over Your Shoulder*, for example, was to alert administrators in central government, thereby enabling 'warning bells to ring'.[14]

Categorizing the grounds

Some countries have codified the grounds of review in statute law.[15] No such codification has yet been officially attempted in Britain.[16] We therefore need to start by considering the leading judicial statements of the common law. The function of judicial review is not to overturn decisions which judges disagree with, rather it is to enable judges to supervise governmental actions

[11] See e.g. Richard Gordon QC, *Crown Office Proceedings* (loose leaf) and *Judicial Review: Law and Procedure* (2nd edn., 1996); Public Law Project, *An Applicants' Guide to Judicial Review* (1995); Michael Fordham, *The Judicial Review Handbook* (1994); de Smith, Woolf and Jowell, *Judicial Review of Administrative Action* (5th edn., 1995). A journal, aimed mainly at practitioners, called *Judicial Review* was set up in 1996. There are also now the specialist law reports *Administrative Law Reports* and *Crown Office Digest*.

[12] See Chapter 25.

[13] See Chapter 25. As we shall see, there are also ongoing debates over whether proportionality is a ground of challenge: see Chapter 24.

[14] *The Judge Over Your Shoulder*, p. 4.

[15] For example in Australia: Administrative Decisions (Judicial Review) Act 1977. See also Art 173 of the Treaty of Rome which sets out the grounds on which the ECJ may annul actions (or inactions) of Community institutions: see Chapter 30 and P. Mathijsen, *A Guide to European Union Law*, (6th edn., 1995), pp. 89–97; L. Neville Brown and Tom Kennedy, *The Court of Justice of the European Communities*, (4th edn., 1994), Chapter 7.

[16] Cf. M. Fordham's classification of the principles of judicial review in his *Judicial Review Handbook* (1994).

to ensure that they have been validly taken in accordance with the law. Judicial review is therefore often said to be concerned with the process of decision-making and not with the substance or merits of decisions; this distinction is discussed later.

In the *GCHQ* case Lord Diplock identified three broad categories of challenge: 'illegality', 'irrationality' and 'procedural impropriety'.[17] This classification, although not intended to be written in stone, has been widely accepted and it is often used by judges and commentators.[18] Broadly speaking these three heads emphasize that judicial review is usually concerned with whether authorities have:

(a) complied with their statutory and common law powers and duties ('illegality');[19]
(b) reached decisions which are rational and which have been taken following a proper process of reasoning (the principles of 'reasonableness');[20] and
(c) complied with the common law principles of fairness.[21]

In the chapters which follow we do not use Lord Diplock's phrase 'procedural impropriety' as a heading. This is because the term 'procedural impropriety' covers two quite different types of argument—one alleging failure to comply with procedures imposed by legislation, and the other alleging failure to comply with common law principles of fairness which have been developed by the courts. These two grounds of challenge are very different in nature. The former is essentially concerned with statutory interpretation and here the courts' task is to ensure that authorities act in accordance with Parliament's wishes. While the fairness of the procedures to those affected may influence the way judges interpret the statutory provisions, here fairness is not the primary issue. We deal with compliance with statutory procedures in Chapter 23 on 'illegality'.

A warning is needed at this point: the various grounds of challenge are not water-tight categories. As Lord Donaldson MR has stated: 'judicial review is a jurisdiction which has been developed and is still being developed by the judges. It has many strands and more will be added, but they are and will always be closely interwoven.'[22] Arguments often overlap and different heads of challenge may be used either in support of each other, or as alternatives. For instance, it may be claimed that a body failed to act fairly because it refused to hear a particular argument (breach of the common law duty of fairness) with the result that its eventual decision was improperly reasoned

[17] *Council of Civil Service Unions v Minister for the Civil Service* [1985] 1 AC 374, especially 407–13. Extracts from this judgment are set out at p. 662 below.
[18] Cf. R. Cranston's comment that it constitutes an 'idiosyncratic catalogue' that is 'best ignored': 'Reviewing Judicial Review' in G. Richardson and H. Genn (eds.), *Administrative Law and Government Action* (1994), p. 54, note 44.
[19] See Chapter 23.
[20] See Chapter 24.
[21] See Chapter 25.
[22] *R v Secretary of State for the Home Department, ex p Brind* [1991] 1 AC 696, 722.

because the body had failed to consider a relevant factor (failure to comply with the principles of reasonableness). The court might ultimately reach the view that the body had acted fairly, but had based its decision on inadequate information; or, conversely, the court might decide that the decision had been based on adequate information, but that the body has adopted a procedure which was unfair to the specific applicant. Different judges in the same case often emphasize different grounds of challenge, reach the same conclusion by different routes, or simply disagree with each other about the meaning and relevance of particular principles. Of course, none of this is unique to judicial review. However, it does carry particular significance in this area of law because judicial review is the principal vehicle for defining the legal obligations of public authorities. In such a context uncertainty can be of vital constitutional importance.[23]

THE IMPACT OF JUDICIAL REVIEW

Administrative culture and legality

It often appears that judges and administrators have quite divergent views of the relevance and importance of law. These differences are rooted in their distinctive cultures, outlooks and methods of operation. While lawyers naturally think in terms of legal powers and readily assume the relevance of law and principles of legality, such things may be perceived to be largely irrelevant to administrators who are driven by the desire to implement governmental policy as efficiently as possible. Even officials working in areas of administration which are heavily regulated by statute rarely look at the Act of Parliament establishing the scheme they are administering and they will rarely be aware of case law. Instead, their main interest is with ministerial circulars, internal departmental guidance and managerial instructions issued by their superiors. It has been shown that even when administrators take account of judicial review, their concerns appear to be directed at saving costs and avoiding the bad publicity that may be associated with legal challenges, rather than more positive factors such as the desire to comply with principles of legality and standards of fairness.[24]

[23] By contrast with the Court of Appeal and the House of Lords, the ECJ gives a single judgment; the judges are bound to keep their own personal views on a case secret and may not formally dissent: see Chapter 29. This is the case with supreme courts in civilian jurisdictions generally.

[24] See, in particular, research carried out by Ian Loveland on the administration of the homelessness legislation: 'Legal Rights and Political Realities: Governmental Responses to Homelessness in Britain' (1991) 16 Law and Social Inquiry 249; 'Administrative Law, Administrative Processes, and the Housing of Homeless Persons: A View from the Sharp End' (1991) Jnl of Social Welfare and Family Law 4; 'Irrelevant Considerations? The Connection of Homeless Persons' in G. Richardson and H. Genn (eds.), *Administrative Law & Government Action* (1994); also I. Loveland, *Housing the Homeless: Administrative Law and Process* (1995). And see also Davina Cooper, 'Institutional Illegality and Disobedience: Local Government Narratives' (1996) 16 OJLS 255.

It is not surprising that judges and administrators have different attitudes to judicial review. After all they are involved in very different tasks. Whereas judges are principally driven by a concern to resolve particular legal problems and to clarify the law, administrators are concerned with applying policy and with allocating scarce resources in accordance, we may assume, with the wishes of their political masters and in the interests of the general public. One consequence is that factors which appear highly relevant to an administrator (do we have the money to pay the benefit? do we really have the time to consult?) may appear irrelevant to a judge scrutinizing the administrator's action in the cold light of a court room months, or years, after the action was taken. These differences can lead to misunderstanding and even tension between officials and the courts.[25] They might also generate a feeling within government that judges do not understand the ways of government and that judicial review is an unwelcome intrusion to be avoided, and even to be evaded.

The best-known technique for excluding judicial review is the use of 'ouster' clauses in legislation which are designed to oust the jurisdiction of the courts.[26] Other techniques include the granting of sweeping discretionary powers to ministers and other bodies on terms which are virtually impossible for judges to review. As well as these legislative devices, a bureaucracy that fears judicial review also has a range of less formal ways of limiting the impact of judicial intervention. These might include, for example, refusing to provide information or reasons for decisions, unless forced to do so; avoiding judicial decisions by amending internal administrative rules which receive little publicity, rather than by more open statutory change; and limiting the amount of public money available to subsidize judicial review challenges.[27] Ultimately, of course, a government with a majority in Parliament may overturn or limit the effect of a judicial decision by legislation.

The risk of such developments has made judges and others increasingly aware that it is essential for the courts to bridge the cultural divide. A former Master of the Rolls has even argued that there is now:[28]

> a new relationship between the courts and [the administration,] one of partnership based on a common aim, namely the maintenance of the highest standards of public administration . . . In proceedings for judicial review, the applicant no doubt has an axe to grind. This should not be true of the authority. Provided that the judges observe the proper boundaries of their office, administrative law and administrative power should be friends and not enemies. The contribution that the law can make is creative rather than destructive.

Whether such a partnership is possible or desirable is itself an issue for debate, for it raises questions which are central to the relationship between

[25] See Sir Michael Kerry, 'Administrative Law and Judicial Review: The Practical Effects of Developments over the Last 25 Years on Administration in Central Government' (1986) 64 Public Administration 163.

[26] See *Anisminic v Foreign Compensation Commission* [1969] 2 AC 147, discussed below p. 506.

[27] On legal aid, see Chapter 21.

[28] Sir John Donaldson MR, *R v Lancashire County Council, ex p Huddleston* [1986] 2 All ER 941, 945.

citizens, courts and government. Some may welcome the idea of judges and administrators gaining a better understanding of each other's work. Others, however, will fear that this will undermine judicial independence and discourage judges from rigorously imposing principles of legality upon government.

Political culture and legality

Many judicial review judgments have little long-term impact on government: no novel principle of law is developed by the judge; no minister is required to explain the government's defeat in a statement to Parliament; and there is little interest by the news media or MPs. Some judgments, however, are surrounded by political controversy—notably when a reviewed decision is made or approved at the highest level by a minister, or the whole legal basis of an important government policy has been criticized in court.

When such judgments are handed down, ministers and their advisors have to decide how to respond. If they decide not to appeal or if they cannot appeal, careful thought has to be given as to how to explain the 'defeat' to Parliament.[29] Ministers often attempt to minimize the significance of a judgment by emphasizing that it 'merely' sets aside a governmental decision because of some procedural error in the way it was made (as if this is unimportant), or that the minister's mistake was in some other way only a technical one.[30]

Ministers will not, however, always 'accept' a judgment and its repercussions. A minister may decide that by introducing new legislation into Parliament it is nevertheless possible to continue with the policy which has been derailed by the court. This happened following the High Court's decision in *R v Secretary of State for Social Security, ex p Cotton* when a new SI was laid before Parliament which was designed to avoid the errors in the earlier regulations challenged by Cotton and so enable government to continue with its desired policy of reducing expenditure on welfare benefits by centralizing control in the hands of the Secretary of State.[31]

Whether reluctantly accepting a judgment or seeking to reverse its effects by legislation, by convention ministers and other MPs have always in the past been careful to use respectful and deferential language about judges and judgments. During 1995 this public decorum broke down: ministers and

[29] The convention of ministerial accountability (on which see generally Chapters 3 and 6) includes an expectation that a minister will make a statement to Parliament in these circumstances.

[30] See for instance the minister's statement to the House of Commons after the Court of Appeal's judgment in *ex p Cotton*, set out in Chapter 27.

[31] See Chapter 11. See also *R v Secretary of State for Social Security, ex p Joint Council for the Welfare of Immigrants* [1996] 4 All ER 385 and *Burmah Oil Co Ltd v Lord Advocate* [1965] AC 75, discussed at p. 106 above. Note that where a ministerial decision or piece of legislation is held to be contrary to Community law, this option will not be available as Community law prevails over national law: see further Chapter 5.

their supporters began to be robustly critical about what was seen as increasingly inappropriate judicial activism.[32] This change was largely prompted by a series of high-profile judicial review applications against the Home Secretary, Michael Howard, including the House of Lords' decision that the use of prerogative powers to alter the Criminal Injuries Compensation Scheme was unlawful; Sedley J's judgment criticizing the Home Office's exclusion from the United Kingdom of Rev. Moon without first giving the cult leader an opportunity to make representations;[33] and the decision of Dyson J to quash the Home Secretary's delay in referring the cases of IRA prisoners to the parole board.[34] If ever a relationship based on 'partnership' had existed between ministers and the courts, by the end of 1995 it seemed to have collapsed. *The Times* commented that 'it is tempting to observe a pattern emerging, a potentially alarming hostility between an over-mighty executive and an ambitious judiciary'.[35] The tabloid press sympathetic to the Conservative Party was more outspoken. The *Daily Express* denounced what it saw as 'the sickness sweeping through the senior judiciary—galloping arrogance'[36] and a headline in the *Daily Mail* asked rhetorically of Sedley J's judgment in *ex p Moon*, 'does this judge think he's above democracy?'. The 'hate campaign' against the judiciary[37] was even conducted within Parliament when a backbench Conservative MP asked the Prime Minister the following question:[38]

Mr Faber: Will my right hon. Friend pass on the grateful thanks of those of my constituents who have written to me in recent days to describe the misery and torment that they and their families have suffered because of the activities of the Rev. Moon? Does my right hon. Friend agree that yesterday's extraordinary court decision is yet another, further example of the contempt with which some members of the judiciary seem to treat the views of both this House and the general public?

The Prime Minister: I believe that my right hon. and learned Friend the Home Secretary was right to refuse the Rev. Moon entry into the country. I do not believe that his presence here would be conducive to the public good. If the Rev. Moon decides to make representations, of course they will be considered.

[32] See further A. P. Le Sueur, 'The Judicial Review Debate: from partnership to friction' (1996) 31 Government and Opposition 8.
[33] *R v Secretary of State for the Home Department, ex p Moon* [1996] COD 52.
[34] *R v Secretary of State for the Home Department, ex p Norney* [1996] COD 79.
[35] 3 November 1995.
[36] 4 November 1995.
[37] The term was used by a High Court judge, quoted anonymously in *The Times*, 3 November 1995.
[38] HC Deb, vol. 265, col. 390 (2 November 1995). On Prime Minister's Questions generally, see p. 372. *Erskine May*, the authoritative guide to parliamentary procedure, states that it is out of order for an MP to ask a question which includes 'reflections on a judge's character or motives' or to use 'language disrespectful to persons administering justice' (p. 380).

Interviewed on Radio 4, the Home Secretary himself made an unprecedented *ad hominem* attack on Dyson J following his judgment in *ex p Norney*: 'The last time this particular judge found against me, which was in a case which would had led to the release of a large number of immigrants, the Court of Appeal decided unanimously that he was wrong,' Michael Howard said.[39]

What is the significance of these events? One thing which they emphasize is the political importance of judicial review; it has a real potency to act as an irritant to government. Another is that there is a great deal of public interest in the constitutional limits of what judges can legitimately do—some of their recent judgments have been regarded as 'undemocratic', contrary to public opinion and disrespectful of Parliament and ministers. What then are the constitutional justifications for judicial review in the United Kingdom?

THE CONSTITUTIONAL JUSTIFICATIONS FOR JUDICIAL REVIEW

The current judicial review system has roots going back centuries; like those of Parliament itself, these predate modern conceptions of democracy. Unlike Parliament, however, the courts have no visible democratic credentials in the sense that judges are not elected and are not accountable to the people for their decisions.[40] They cannot be removed if their decisions are unpopular and there is no obvious way of ensuring that they act in accordance with the wishes of the community. Upon what basis, then, can the courts claim authority to review and invalidate decisions taken by elected and politically accountable ministers, elected local authorities and other official bodies? Is it sufficient in a modern constitutional democracy to assert, as the Law Commission recently did, that the 'public interest in the vindication of the rule of law underpins the very existence' of judicial review?[41] In short, how can judicial power to challenge elected authorities and invalidate their decisions be justified? This question is posed wherever courts have power to review actions of elected bodies and it lies at the core of most discussions of the relationship between the courts and government.[42] While many have attempted to reconcile the conflict, tension between judicial review and democratic theory has been said to 'pose a theoretically insoluble contradiction'.[43]

How is this apparent contradiction approached within the British scheme? Two main lines of thinking are used to justify and explain the constitutional justification for our system of judicial review. For convenience these may be described as the 'power-based' approach and the 'impact-based' approach.

[39] 'Today Programme', BBC Radio 4, 29 September 1995. By the time this remark was made, the Home Office had already indicated in open court that it would not be appealing against Dyson J's judgment.

[40] The term democracy is capable of different meanings: see further Anthony H. Birch, *The Concepts and Theories of Modern Democracy* (1993) and Chapters 5 and 6 above.

[41] *Administrative Law: Judicial Review and Statutory Appeals* (Law Com No 226) 1994, para. 2.5.

[42] See generally M. Cappelletti, *The Judicial Process in Comparative Perspective* (1989).

[43] M. Cappelletti, above, p. xvii.

We shall also consider a newer line of thinking associated with process-based approaches to judicial review. Each of these seeks to justify judicial review by reference to the rule of law and democracy, yet each assumes a different understanding of these terms.[44]

The power-based approach

The power-based approach assumes that the principal task for the courts when asked to review the actions of public bodies is to ensure that these bodies have acted in accordance with the powers granted to them by Parliament. The main conceptual tool used by the judges in performing this task is the *ultra vires* doctrine (*ultra vires* is Latin for 'beyond the powers'). This doctrine has underpinned judicial review for much of the past two centuries and, although no longer adequate, it continues to provide the dominant justification for judicial review. It does so because it is said to reflect and re-enforce three key constitutional principles: the supremacy of Parliament, the separation of powers and the rule of law.

In essence the *ultra vires* doctrine rests on the theory that official bodies only have those legal powers which have been conferred on them by, or with the implied consent of, Parliament. If they act beyond these powers their actions lack a legal basis and can be struck down by the courts as invalid and of no legal effect. The corollary to this is that if bodies act within their powers, judges have no right to interfere with the substance of the decisions that have been taken (unless Parliament expressly permits them to do so by establishing rights of appeal to the courts). If the courts did interfere with *intra vires* decisions they would be meddling with functions which Parliament has specifically allocated to other bodies (local authorities, ministers, etc) and thereby breaching the theory of parliamentary supremacy and the separation of powers.[45]

This view of the judicial role is rooted in what has been described as the *imperium* model of legal theory.[46] This model can be traced back through Dicey's account of parliamentary supremacy to Austin's theory that law is the command of the sovereign.[47] It assumes that the constitutional system can be understood as a hierarchy. At the top stands the sovereign law-maker and below are the subordinate authorities of the state to whom legal duties and powers are delegated by the sovereign. Within this structure the judicial role is to ensure that these subordinate authorities do not exceed the powers which have been conferred upon them. In this way the courts play a policing role on behalf of the sovereign power (the Queen in Parliament) and are an integral part of the system concerned with controlling and regulating the

[44] See generally Chapters 5 and 6.

[45] On separation of powers, see Chapter 3. On parliamentary supremacy, see Chapter 5.

[46] R. Cotterrell, 'Judicial Review and Legal Theory' in Richardson and Genn (eds.), *Administrative Law and Government Action* (1994).

[47] See Chapter 5.

agencies of government. Within this tradition the judicial role may therefore be portrayed as being primarily an internal one in the sense that it is concerned with applying the state's law to the state itself.[48]

As Cotterrell points out, this 'top down' conception of a legal system is not inherently democratic and may indeed provide the basic centralized structure for authoritarian and even fascist regimes. In the British system however, law-making power ultimately resides in a Parliament that is politically accountable to the electorate.[49] Today, therefore, this dominant approach to judicial review is based on the idea that judicial review derives its formal constitutional authority from this democratic base.

The main practical implications of this line of theory may be summarized as follows. First, it follows from the theory that judges have no power to question the validity of parliamentary legislation, unless Parliament has authorized them to do so.[50] Secondly, the theory implies that judicial review is essentially a technical process by which the judges are required to apply Parliament's intention *as it is expressed or implied in the words of statutes.*[51] Thirdly, since the main task of the judges is to ensure that ministers and others act in accordance with the will of Parliament, judges are unable to impose upon official bodies obligations derived from principles or values which are not contained in legislation. Finally, this image of the system as a hierarchy within which the courts are primarily concerned with discerning how much power Parliament intended to give public authorities contrasts with the approach that dominates in systems which have constitutional guarantees of individual rights and liberties. In these systems, although issues of power necessarily arise, judicial attention primarily focuses on the impact that official action has on rights and liberties of citizens.

Criticisms of the power-based approach

In recent years writers have questioned the adequacy of both the power-based image of judicial review and of the *ultra vires* doctrine. Oliver, for example, argues that although the *ultra vires* doctrine is still 'very relevant' to judicial review, it is no longer (if it ever was) an adequate basis for the courts' jurisdiction.[52] She says that much judicial practice simply cannot be explained by the *ultra vires* doctrine. For example, judges often adopt a much more liberal approach to the interpretation of statutes than would be permitted by a strict adherence to the doctrine; it is now well established that courts

48 R. Cotterrell, above, p. 26.

49 See generally P. P. Craig, *Public Law and Democracy in the United Kingdom and the United States of America* (1990), especially Chapter 2. For a discussion of judicial attitudes to democracy see D. Feldman, 'Public Law Values in the House of Lords' (1990) 106 LQR 246, and Sir John Laws, 'Law and Democracy' [1995] PL 72.

50 See Chapter 5. Note that the courts may be asked to review primary legislation of Parliament on the grounds that it conflicts with Community law: *R v Secretary of State for Employment, ex p Equal Opportunities Commission* [1995] 1 AC 1.

51 See further on statutory interpretation, Chapter 23.

52 Dawn Oliver, 'Is the *Ultra Vires* the Basis of Judicial Review?' [1987] PL 543, 567. Compare also Christopher Forsyth, 'Of Fig Leaves and Fairy Tales: the *ultra vires* doctrine, the sovereignty of Parliament and Judicial Review' [1996] CLJ 122.

will intervene to invalidate *abuse*, as well as an *excess* of power and that they can do so if official bodies have failed to adopt a proper process of reasoning or acted unreasonably, or followed unfair procedures. These principles are judge-made and are rarely specifically referred to by statute. Moreover, while some may seek to justify their use by reference to the *ultra vires* doctrine, it is difficult to do so unless we are prepared to adopt the fiction that Parliament has implicitly accepted judicial power to develop principles of review. Even if this were accepted, it is difficult to see how the *ultra vires* doctrine would justify judicial review of powers which do not derive, expressly or implicitly, from Parliament (such as the exercise of prerogative powers as in the *GCHQ* case) or the review of decisions of non-statutory self-regulatory bodies (such as the Panel on Take-Overs and Mergers) which have become an important part of modern commercial activity.[53]

More fundamental criticisms may be levelled at the democratic credentials of the *ultra vires* doctrine itself. These credentials rest on a theory of parliamentary democracy which, as discussed in Chapters 5 and 6, is now widely criticized for failing to provide an effective system of accountability (elections are too sporadic and the executive is usually able to control the House of Commons) and for failing to provide adequate protection for minority interests. Effective democracy, it may be argued, requires more than is provided by the parliamentary system.

Impact-based approaches[54]

Unlike the power-based approach which concentrates on the legal powers possessed by public bodies, impact-based approaches to judicial review focus on the impact which governmental decisions have on the rights and interests of citizens. Here the courts may be presented as being guardians of such rights and interests rather than of Parliament's will.

Impact-based approaches have a tradition that can be traced back to such cases as *Entick v Carrington*[55] in the mid-eighteenth century, and beyond. However, as the concept of parliamentary supremacy took hold and the *ultra vires* doctrine grew to dominate judicial thinking, impact-based approaches declined in relative importance. Their recent revival owes much to the renewed interest in human rights and principles of equality.[56]

We have deliberately referred to impact-based approach*es* because there are several strands of thinking which may be considered under this broad

[53] *R v Panel on Take-overs and Mergers, ex p Datafin plc* [1987] QB 815, discussed further in Chapter 22.

[54] We are using this term to include what are sometimes referred to as 'rights-based approaches' and 'principle-based approaches'. See generally R. Dworkin, *Taking Rights Seriously* (1977); T. R. S. Allan, 'Pragmatism and Theory in Public Law' (1988) 104 LQR 422, 438. See also discussion of the new orthodoxy in Chapter 6, p. 153.

[55] (1756) 19 St Tr 1030.

[56] See Lord Lester, 'European Human Rights and the British Constitution' in Jowell and Oliver (eds.), *The Changing Constitution* (3rd edn., 1994).

umbrella, some of which are more likely to receive the approval of the judges than others. It is now increasingly common to find judges arguing not only that official bodies must have technical authority for their actions (as required by the *ultra vires* doctrine) but also that bodies must be able to justify any interference with the interests of citizens by showing that they have acted in accordance with principles of reasonableness, rationality, and fairness. One of the clearest statements of this approach has recently been provided by Laws J. Writing extra-judicially, he advocated that:

> The greater the intrusion proposed by the body possessing public power over the citizen into an area where his fundamental rights are at stake, the greater must be the justification which the public authority must demonstrate . . . The Secretary of State will be largely left to his own devices in promulgating national economic policy . . . [but] the court will scrutinise the *merits* of his decisions much more closely when they concern refugees or free speech.[57]

Laws' argument is that if rights are to be interfered with authorities must be prepared to justify themselves. The level of justification (and the intensity of the judicial scrutiny) varies depending on the importance of the issues at stake; and in some circumstances the courts should even be prepared to scrutinize the merits of governmental decisions. This approach could not be adequately accommodated within the *ultra vires* doctrine and if it has a constitutional justification, this is not to be found in the theory that the courts are simply ensuring that official bodies act within their powers.

Laws clearly anticipates a more interventionist judicial stance than can be accommodated by the *ultra vires* doctrine, but some will argue that he does not go far enough in providing protection for citizens. They will point out that implicit in this view is the acceptance that public bodies can interfere with rights provided they can justify doing so. This, it can be argued, provides inadequate protection for what might be called fundamental rights, namely rights which should be protected at all costs and possibly even from encroachment by parliamentary legislation. This, however, has yet to be accepted within mainstream judicial thinking in this country.

Laws' approach may be justified in two main ways. One is to argue that protection of individual rights and interests is justified because it is fundamental to the dignity of individuals that their interests be protected.[58] No other justification is needed because judges are simply furthering fundamental core values upon which the very notion of the democratic system is based.

The other justification looks beyond the individual to the nature of society and the need to fill gaps which are left by the parliamentary system. The position may be summarized in the following way. By protecting individual rights and interests and forcing official bodies to justify their actions by showing that they have acted rationally and fairly the courts are applying principles

[57] Sir John Laws, 'Is the High Court the Guardian of Fundamental Constitutional Rights?' [1993] PL 58, 69 (emphasis added).

[58] T. R. S. Allan, 'Pragmatism and Theory in Public Law' (1988) 104 LQR 422, 438.

and values which are central to society, but which are not necessarily embodied in specific legislative enactments or indeed in the parliamentary system. In this way, judicial review ensures that government acts in accordance with principles which are stable and which cannot be manipulated by the 'whims of passing majorities'.[59] Moreover, by developing these principles the courts are able to play a more proactive role in society than is possible under the *ultra vires* doctrine. As a result, the courts 'positively help to secure values that make democracy a worthwhile system for all citizens, and not only for those whose interests are directly promoted by those in power'.[60]

Criticisms of impact-based approaches

Impact-based approaches to judicial review may be criticized at various levels. The first practical problem is one of uncertainty. This affects both the nature of impacts and the level of scrutiny which judges will exercise. What types of impact, for example, will the courts regard as worthy of protection? And, if levels of scrutiny vary depending on the nature of the rights and interests involved, will individuals and officials be able to predict the level of scrutiny they can expect? Laws refers to action impinging upon fundamental rights such as free speech and liberty: but in what sense are these rights fundamental and what other rights and interests could individuals and groups claim to be fundamental? Would rights to privacy, to family life, or to a clean and healthy environment qualify? What about rights to housing or education? Moreover, will the courts accept that the same decisions may impact upon people in varying ways depending on their situation: a decision to close a school or a post office, or to build a road will affect some people more fundamentally than others.

There are also constitutional problems.[61] A concern for impact may be said to be justified because it strengthens democracy by filling gaps left by the parliamentary system. However, as with the power-based approach, the democratic credentials of impact-based approaches are also seriously flawed. If, as Laws suggests, the judges are able to scrutinize the merits of ministerial decisions using common law principles, it is not self-evident that these principles are themselves democratically grounded. Why, for example, should the judicial decision on what is appropriate in the circumstances be constitutionally sounder than the ministerial decision? To put this in a practical context, even if we accept that principles such as reasonableness and procedural fairness do exist and would receive general approval, how can we or the judges be sure that judicial understandings of what is appropriate in fact accord with the views of society? After all, there are no formal mechanisms enabling judges to discover what these views are.

[59] M. Cappelletti, *The Judicial Process in Comparative Perspective* (1989).
[60] R. Cotterrell, above, p. 18.
[61] See also Chapter 6.

In practice judges decide for themselves what principles such as reasonableness and fairness mean and require in specific cases. This being so, what is there to stop judges using these principles to strike down decisions of public bodies essentially because they disagree with what the minister or local authority has decided? Cotterrell has said that the 'invocation of values in judicial review appears [to be] a cloak for the exercise of judicial discretion, the activity of judges as essentially political actors'. He goes on to argue that when they interfere with the decisions of ministers and other official agencies by employing principles and values 'they appear, more often than not, to be putting forward their own discretions alongside or in competition'[62] with those of governmental decision-makers. Even if these appearances are misleading they are sufficient to cast serious doubts about the democratic legitimacy of judicial review.[63]

Impact-based approaches which claim to be justified by reference to community or society values can therefore be criticized on the grounds that it is impossible to know for sure what these values are and it is unclear upon what authority judges can decide what they are. This is particularly problematic if judges use their view of society's values to challenge the substance and merits of governmental action in the way that Laws J suggests they should in some circumstances be able to do.

Process-based approaches

Some attempt to avoid these problems may be made by adopting what may be termed a process-based approach to judicial review.[64] Again there are several lines of thinking, ranging from the narrow argument that even if it may be undemocratic for courts to interfere with the substance of governmental action it is not contrary to democratic principles for the courts to ensure that government adopts a certain process of decision-making, to much broader claims for a strong democracy involving full and direct citizen participation in government.[65]

There is more to distinguish these arguments than to link them. However, in the context of a general discussion of the role of the courts, a common thread may be identified which links the various strands of thinking. This is the general idea that democracy requires citizens to be able to participate in government and that courts have a legitimate role in ensuring that they are able to do so as fully and as effectively as possible. At its narrowest, this

62 R. Cotterrell, above, p. 28.

63 Cf. D. Feldman, 'Public Law Values in the House of Lords' (1990) 106 LQR 246.

64 See further Genevra Richardson, *Law, Process and Custody: Prisoners and Patients* (1993), Chapter 2; T. Prosser, 'Towards a Critical Public Law' (1982) 9 Journal of Law and Society 1; M. Partington, 'The Reform of Public Law in Britain: Theoretical Problems and Practical Considerations' in P. MacAuslan and J. McEldowney (eds.), *Law, Legitimacy and the Constitution* (1985).

65 B. Barber, *Strong Democracy: Participatory Politics for a New Age* (1984).

means that administrative procedures should be fair and designed to allow individuals to make representations and to present arguments where decisions affect them directly.[66] Process-based approaches, however, have implications extending beyond the procedures that must be followed by ministers and official bodies in specific situations. If citizens are to participate effectively in government then they must have access to information and official bodies must be prepared to explain and justify their decisions. Participation, in this sense, therefore implies not just procedural rights but effective systems of accountability, a culture of openness, and real opportunities to influence governmental decision-making. This form of participation is not satisfied by the ability to vote at periodical elections for it demands a more continuous involvement in governmental decision-making. Arguably, the courts have a key role in ensuring that this involvement is possible. Not only can judicial review be used to ensure that official bodies adopt procedures which reflect principles of openness and accountability, but judicial review is itself a vehicle for participation to be used by those wanting to challenge official actions and improve the quality of decision-taking (even in situations where there is no political platform for the grievance).

Seen from this perspective, it may be argued that judges are justified in using common law principles in order to further accountability and participation even, some argue, where this requires them to challenge and impose 'quality controls' on primary legislation to ensure that Parliament itself fully complies with democracy and the rule of law.[67]

Criticisms of process-based approaches

Process-based theories of judicial review have many attractions. Ultimately, however, they depend on an acceptance of the underlying theory that democracy justifies the use of judicially created principle to further participation in government. Some will doubt whether the judges are willing or able to develop principles which further such participation. In addition there are problems associated with issues such as access to the courts. Only certain groups and individuals have the resources or the expertise necessary to use the judicial review procedure and these can exercise a disproportionate influence on judicial attitudes and ultimately the attitude of governments. In practice the courts are likely to be more useful to the type of organization or group that can in any event exert pressure through the parliamentary system than they are to individuals or minorities who lack the legal and financial resources necessary to litigate. We turn to the issue of access in the next chapter.

[66] See further Chapter 25.

[67] I. Harden and N. Lewis, *The Noble Lie: The British Constitution and the Rule of Law* (1986); Genevra Richardson, *Law, Process and Custody: Prisoners and Patients* (1993), p. 25.

Question

'Judicial review is inherently undemocratic.' 'Judicial review is central to the British system of parliamentary democracy.'

Which of these two views is the more accurate and why?

21

ACCESS TO JUDICIAL REVIEW

> It is a principle of our law that every citizen has a right of unimpeded access to a court. In *Raymond v Honey* [1983] 1 AC 1 Lord Wilberforce described it as a 'basic right'. Even in our unwritten constitution it must rank as a constitutional right.[1]

Providing access to the courts to challenge the public bodies on the grounds that they have abused their powers is important not only for those directly adversely affected but also for the maintenance of the rule of law and the general quality of public administration. However, if access to the courts is a constitutional right (as Steyn LJ's statement above asserts), then it is clearly a right which is subject to many practical limitations and obstacles.[2] In this chapter we examine some of the more important obstacles facing those seeking to use the judicial review procedure.[3]

ACCESS AND THE JUDICIAL REVIEW PROCEDURE

Reconciling competing interests

Applicants rightly expect the judicial review procedure to be accessible, cheap and not overly technical. They want to be able to make their arguments effectively relying on adequate evidence to support their claims and dispute those made by the respondent public body. The interests of particular litigants, however, constitute only one aspect. Public bodies, by contrast, want to ensure that their work is not interrupted and their resources expended reacting to unwarranted legal challenge and they look to the courts to provide protection. The courts too are concerned to prevent their lists from becoming clogged with weak or frivolous applications thereby delaying more meritorious applications. The judicial review procedure has been designed to allow judges to reconcile these various competing interests. It is in the process of their reconciliation that the practical nature of the right of access is determined.

[1] Per Steyn LJ *R v Secretary of State for the Home Department, ex p Leech* (*No 2*) [1994] QB 198, 210.

[2] Note that the right of access to the courts is implicitly protected by Art 6 of the ECHR: *Golder v UK* (1975) 1 EHRR 524.

[3] See further, M. Sunkin, 'The Problematical State of Access to Judicial Review' in B. Hadfield (ed.), *Judicial Review: A Thematic Approach* (1995).

The judicial review procedure in outline

Judicial review is centralized in London

Applications for judicial review must be made to the High Court in London.[4] Here they will be handled by one of the judges nominated by the Lord Chief Justice to deal with judicial reviews.[5] Judicial review cannot be sought from county courts or from High Court judges when sitting on circuit throughout the country. The reason for this centralization is partly historical: the modern judicial review procedure is based on the older procedures for seeking the prerogative orders (certiorari, prohibition and mandamus) which were only available from the King's Bench Division of the High Court.[6] There are also policy reasons: it is thought desirable for judicial review applications to be determined by a relatively small and expert group of senior judges in order to achieve consistency. While recognizing that centralization does hinder access,[7] and has not eliminated inconsistency, in its recent review of the procedure the Law Commission rejected proposals that would produce a more localized system.[8]

Leave must be obtained to seek judicial review

An applicant must obtain the 'leave' (or permission) of a High Court judge before seeking judicial review. In practical terms, this requires applicants, or their lawyers if applicants are represented, to complete a form (Form 86A) setting out in some detail both the facts of the case and the applicant's legal submissions. The form has to be lodged at the High Court together with an affidavit sworn by the applicant verifying that the facts are true.[9] The application for leave may, at the choice of the applicant, either be determined by a judge reading only these documents or following additional oral submissions at a short hearing in open court.

In order to obtain leave the applicant has to show that:

(a) the application has been brought promptly and in any event within three months of the date on which the decision or action being challenged was taken;

[4] The procedural rules are governed by the Supreme Court Act 1981, s 31 and the Rules of the Supreme Court (RSC), Ord 53.

[5] There are currently 22 nominated judges. There are also 22 deputy High Court judges who are QCs who sit on a part-time basis to deal with judicial review applications, especially those brought by homeless people.

[6] See Chapter 26.

[7] Research has shown that 55 per cent of all applicants during a sample period came from the London area: see L. Bridges, G. Meszaros and M. Sunkin, *Judicial Review in Perspective* (1995), pp. 38–40.

[8] Various proposals were suggested: giving county courts a judicial review jurisdiction; enabling High Court judges to undertake judicial reviews while out on circuit; and establishing a procedure modelled on Art 177 of the EC Treaty (on which see Chapter 30) whereby local courts could refer judicial review issues to the High Court in London. See *Administrative Law: Judicial Review and Statutory Appeals*, Law Com No 226, para. 3.22. Lord Woolf has recommended that judicial reviews should be heard by High Court or deputy High Court judges: Lord Woolf, *Access to Justice* (1996), Chapter 18, para. 6.

[9] For an example of a Form 86A and supporting affidavit in *R v Secretary of State for Social Services, ex p Cotton*, see p. 636.

(b) the applicant has a sufficient interest in the matter;
(c) the application discloses an arguable case; and
(d) the applicant may also have to show that other remedies have been exhausted and that the application is not premature.

Each of these criteria is discussed later. If leave is granted, the Form 86A is served on the respondent public body, which then has 52 days to file a formal written response with the court. The application is then set down for a full hearing, although in practice many applications are withdrawn before then, often as a result of a settlement.

The leave requirement is both an important and controversial aspect of the process.[10] Its practical significance is reflected by statistics which show that approximately half of all applications for leave are refused, so preventing the applicant taking the matter further.[11]

Two types of criticism are levelled at the leave stage. The most basic is that the leave requirement is wrong in principle.[12] It contradicts the view that access to the courts is a right (if access is a right why must permission be obtained to exercise it?). Moreover, since leave is not required in private law proceedings it is harder to challenge public bodies in judicial review than it is to sue them in private law and this, it may be argued, is inconsistent and contrary to the rule of law.

Criticisms are also made of the way leave operates in practice. Two main principal criticisms may be made. One is that the leave criteria are too vague and uncertain with the result that getting leave has become something of a lottery. The other is that leave forces judges to become managers of the system and this undermines their perceived independence and neutrality.

OBTAINING LEAVE IS A LOTTERY: THE LEAVE CRITERIA ARE TOO VAGUE AND UNCERTAIN

The Supreme Court Act 1981, s 31 and the Rules of Court give applicants very little guidance as to the criteria for obtaining leave. The rules refer only to the need for applicants to apply promptly and to establish a sufficient interest in the matter to which the application relates. Both of these requirements, and as we shall see later particularly the latter, give rise to uncertainties. But these express criteria are not the only ones used by the courts. In fact, the most important test confronting applicants is the need to establish an arguable case, and this is not referred to at all. Moreover, judges have been less than clear as to what this requires. Some judges, for example, have said that applicants must show that their application *may* be arguable, while others

[10] See further A. P. Le Sueur and M. Sunkin 'Applications for Judicial Review: The Requirement for Leave' [1992] PL 102. For a more detailed discussion of the operation of the leave requirement, see Bridges, Meszaros and Sunkin (above), Chapters 7 and 8.

[11] The failure rate has increased as the number of applications for judicial review has grown since the early 1980s. At that time the failure rate was approximately 33 per cent: see Bridges, Meszaros and Sunkin (above).

[12] JUSTICE/All Souls, *Administrative Justice: Some Necessary Reforms* (1988), para. 6.23.

now insist that actual, rather than potential, arguability must be established.[13] On occasions, judges have gone further, insisting that the applicant establish not only an arguable case, but also that the application is exceptional in some way, or that it raises a point of general principle.[14]

Given these different views it is perhaps not surprising that empirical research has revealed an alarming degree of judicial inconsistency at the leave stage.[15] After analysing a random distribution of cases, researchers discovered that during 1987 some judges granted up to 82 per cent of the applications for leave that they dealt with while other judges only granted leave in 21 per cent of their cases. Similar differences were revealed both during 1988 and during the first three months of 1991. This evidence suggests that different judges were indeed applying different tests to the applications which came before them, thereby confirming a widely held perception among practising lawyers that obtaining leave is a lottery depending largely on which judge is considering the application.[16]

MANAGERIALISM

Another difficulty with the leave requirement is that it forces judges into a managerial function which may be incompatible with their role as judges of the legal merits of the individual case. It has been said that the leave stage is an important managerial tool which furthers the 'efficient management of the caseload'.[17] But does this mean that judges should take account of factors such as the general pressure of the caseload and the number of cases waiting to be tried when deciding whether to grant leave, or should they be concerned exclusively with the legal merits of applications? Judicial opinion varies. The tendency in recent years has been to favour a more managerial view. As Lord Donaldson MR put it:[18]

> The public interest normally dictates that if the judicial review jurisdiction is to be exercised, it should be exercised very speedily and, given the constraints imposed by limited judicial resources, this necessarily involves limiting the number of cases in which leave to apply should be given.

Against this approach there is a powerful argument that judges should only be concerned with legal merits of cases and not with extraneous managerial considerations. It would surely be contrary to the rule of law for judicial

[13] Cf. Lord Diplock's statement that leave should be granted 'If, on a quick perusal of the material then available, the court thinks that it discloses what might on further investigation turn out to be an arguable case' in *IRC v National Federation of Self Employed and Small Businesses Ltd* [1982] AC 617, 644 and Lord Donaldson MR's insistence that actual arguability is now required in *Winch v Jones* [1986] QB 296, 304–5 and *R v Legal Aid Board, ex p Hughes* (1992) 24 HLR 698.

[14] Butler-Sloss LJ in *R v Harrow Council, ex p D* [1990] Fam 133 at 138; see also *R v Hillingdon London Borough Council ex p Puhlhoffer* [1986] AC 484; *R v Secretary of State for the Home Department, ex p Swati* [1986] 1 WLR 477.

[15] Bridges, Meszaros and Sunkin, note 7 above, Chapter 8.

[16] Bridges, Meszaros and Sunkin, note 7 above, p. 190.

[17] Law Com No 226, para. 5.6.

[18] *R v Panel on Take-overs and Mergers, ex p Guinness plc* [1990] 1 QB 146, 177–8.

control of governmental illegality to depend on the number of cases in the waiting lists or the shortage of judicial resources.

Despite criticisms the leave requirement continues to be justified on the grounds that it enables the court to filter out unarguable and hopeless applications, thereby protecting public administration from unwarranted interference and ensuring that worthy cases are not delayed by the system becoming overloaded. This being so it is now widely accepted that some form of preliminary filter is necessary and desirable. In its 1994 report, however, the Law Commission said that the term 'leave' creates the perception that citizens relying on public law rights are at a disadvantage compared to those relying on private law. It therefore recommended that the term 'leave' should be dropped and the procedure instead be described as the 'preliminary consideration stage'.[19]

The Law Commission also recommended that the grounds for refusing leave should be explicitly set out in the rules, that applicants should have to show that their claim discloses a 'serious issue to be tried' as opposed to an arguable case, and that judges be required to give brief reasons for refusing leave.[20]

No automatic discovery of documents or cross-examination of witnesses

Two further characteristics of the judicial review procedure may be noted at this stage, although both are discussed in greater detail later in the chapter. The first is that in judicial review, applicants will only obtain documentary evidence if the respondent volunteers to reveal the documents or if the court orders their disclosure. Similarly applicants are rarely able to cross-examine witnesses. Both these procedures are normal and automatic in most private law litigation.

Having sketched the procedure we now consider the main obstacles to access. We deal with these under three broad headings: getting to court; standing; and obtaining evidence.

GETTING TO COURT

Access to legal advice

Unlike complaints to the ombudsmen, or seeking the help of an MP or councillor to redress a grievance against a public body, it is very difficult

[19] Law Com No 226, para. 5.7. Lord Woolf has agreed with this: *Access to Justice* (1996), Chapter 18, para. 12.

[20] For criticism of these and other recommendations see Carol Harlow, 'Public Interest Challenges: New Directions?' *Legal Action*, February 1995, p. 6; Richard Gordon QC, 'The Law Commission and Judicial Review: Managing the tensions between case management and public interest challenges' [1995] PL 11; M. Sunkin, 'The Problematical State of Access to Judicial Review' in B. Hadfield (ed.), *Judicial Review: A Thematic Approach* (1995); Bridges, Meszaros and Sunkin, note 7 above, Chapter 9.

indeed for a person without legal expertise to use the judicial review process.[21] For many would-be applicants an initial hurdle on the way to court is therefore finding and paying for appropriate legal advice. This can be a hit or miss affair. Not only is there evidence that advice agencies such as the Citizens' Advice Bureaux regularly fail to identify potential judicial review challenges,[22] but few firms of solicitors have expertise in judicial review litigation. The problem of finding lawyers with specialist knowledge of judicial review is greatest outside London and the South East, particularly if the problem involves areas of law other than homeless persons and immigration (the two areas in which judicial review has been most frequently used).[23]

Legal aid

Even if appropriate advice can be obtained, using judicial review can be expensive. It has been estimated that it costs between £1,500 and £2,500 to commence an application for judicial review and between £7,500 and £15,000 to take a case all the way through to a full hearing. The great majority of potential applicants for judicial review would find it impossible to pay for such costs themselves. The cost is even more daunting because, as in other types of litigation, an applicant who loses is normally ordered to pay the bulk of the legal costs incurred by the other side.[24] The legal aid scheme provides financial assistance out of public funds to those seeking legal advice and representation.[25] When it was established in the 1940s, challenges to the legal validity of decisions taken by government bodies were much less common than they are today; the civil legal system was primarily designed to cater for private law litigation.

Eligibility for legal aid help depends on satisfying two general tests: one is a means test (how poor the applicant is) and the other a merits test (whether the proposed litigation is worth pursuing). The latter has caused problems in relation to judicial review applications. One criterion which the legal aid authorities apply is referred to as the 'general reasonableness' test and involves asking the question: would a solicitor advise an applicant who was paying for the litigation themselves to take or defend the proceedings. Official guidance advises that legal aid is likely to be refused as 'unreasonable' where 'the applicant would get no personal benefit out of the proceedings'.[26]

[21] See further on the number and success rates of litigants in person, see Bridges, Meszaros and Sunkin, note 7 above, pp. 61–2 and 148–9.

[22] D. Forbes and S. Wright, *Housing Cases in Nine CABx* (unpublished 1990).

[23] Bridges, Meszaros and Sunkin, note 7 above, Chapter 4.

[24] In 1994 the Law Commission recommended that where an application for judicial review raises an issue of public importance, the court should have power to order that the respondent public body's costs be paid out of central funds rather than by the unsuccessful applicant: see Law Com No 226, para. 10.6. See also *Access to Justice* (1996), Chapter 18, para. 22.

[25] See Public Law Project, *The Applicant's Guide to Judicial Review* (1995), Chapter 7; Bridges, Meszaros and Sunkin, note 7 above, Chapter 5, especially pp. 89–101; Stephen Grosz, 'Access to Environmental Justice in Public Law' in Robinson and Dunkley (eds.), *Public Interest Perspectives in Environmental Law* (1995).

[26] Legal Aid Notes for Guidance 1994, para. 6-08(i).

This test may be adequate in the context of private law proceedings involving claims for compensation, but since the regulations do not enable the legal aid authorities to take adequate account of the broader public interest,[27] this test may cause problems for potential judicial review applicants, particularly where the individual is unlikely to obtain great financial advantage from the challenge even where issues of government illegality are raised. An applicant who, for example, seeks to challenge a decision about entitlement to a welfare benefit may only stand to gain a few pounds a week—a sum which a solicitor advising a privately-funded person might say is unreasonable to seek to recover even where the challenge may affect many other claimants who would also benefit by any precedent set. Similarly, legal aid may be refused if the proposed judicial review relates to an alleged procedural irregularity in a pubic body's decision-making process and there is no clear monetary or material benefit to be gained by the applicant.

Two other matters are relevant to the obtaining of legal aid for judicial review. First, legal aid is not available for organizations, such as pressure or interest groups. For this reason groups often decide not to litigate in their own name. Secondly, legal aid may be refused to an individual where others have the same interest in the proceedings as that individual and would not be eligible for legal aid because they earn too much or have too much capital.[28] Suppose, for example, a group of parents decide to challenge a decision to close a school. Here each of the parents will have the same interest in the outcome of the case. If one parent seeks legal aid they may be refused help if a richer parent would benefit from the litigation. Legal aid would not be refused on this ground if the other potential litigants would also be entitled to support from the legal aid fund. In a case like Simon Cotton's challenge to the Board and Lodging Regulations others who would benefit from the challenge would also be dependent on social security payments and would also therefore be eligible for legal aid.

The problems of funding judicial review litigation are likely to grow if the government's recent proposals for reform of the legal aid scheme are introduced.[29]

The need for prompt action

Time can also be a problem. The rules allow only a very short time for applicants and their legal advisors to begin judicial review proceedings. An application must be made 'promptly' and in any event within three months of the date on which the offending action was taken, or the decision made.[30] Contrast

[27] In 1994 the Law Commission recommended amendment of the rules to enable the wider public interest to be taken into account: see *Administrative Law: Judicial Review and Statutory Appeals* (Law Com No 226), para. 10.9.

[28] Civil Legal Aid (General) Regulations 1989 (S1 1989 No 339), reg 32; see Public Law Project, *The Applicant's Guide to Judicial Review*, pp. 66–9.

[29] *Striking the Balance: the Future of Legal Aid in England and Wales*, Cmnd 3305.

[30] See Supreme Court Act 1981, s 31(6), (7) and RSC, Ord 53, r 4.

this with the twelve-month period allowed for complaints to the ombudsmen and the six-year limitation period for general tort and contract claims.

Two possible consequences flow from a failure to commence an application promptly. First, the court may refuse to grant leave, even if the application is made within the three-month period.[31] Conversely, the court has *discretion* to allow an application to proceed even if it is made outside the time period, provided that there is some good reason to do so. A second consequence of lack of promptness may arise at the very end of an application for judicial review when the court is considering what, if any, formal remedies to order.[32]

The justification for the requirement of promptness is said to lie in the need to protect public administration (and the public interest in ensuring efficient administration) from the risk of challenge long after decisions have been taken. Imagine, for example, the practical problems that would have been generated had Cotton's successful challenge been brought two years after the regulations had been introduced. How would the system cope with the need to provide remedies to those who had been refused benefits during the intervening period on the basis of regulations which were later held to be invalid? Here too the issue is one of balancing the needs of applicants and the interests of speed and administrative certainty. At present although those who represent the interests of applicants have argued that the time limit is too short, and that it may force litigants to start proceedings prematurely, the Law Commission's view is that the 'principle of certainty' justifies the current rules.[33]

STANDING

Only those who have standing (or *locus standi*) can claim to have a constitutional right to seek judicial review.[34] Applicants only have standing if they have a 'sufficient interest in the matter to which the application relates'. If they do not have a sufficient interest leave 'shall' not be granted.[35]

These propositions are easily stated. However standing has proved to be one of the most difficult issues in public law. First there is the basic question: what constitutes a 'sufficient interest'? As with other aspects of the leave requirement it is 'uncertain what precisely is required'.[36] Before considering the issues in greater detail four broad types of situation may be distinguished.

[31] See e.g. *R v Swale Borough Council, ex p RSPB* (1990) 2 Admin LR 790.

[32] *R v Dairy Produce Quota Tribunal* [1990] 2 AC 738. See further Chapter 26.

[33] Law Com No 226, paras 5.23–30.

[34] See further: Sir Konrad Schiemann, 'Locus Standi' [1990] PL 342; David Feldman, 'Public Interest Litigation and Constitutional Theory in Comparative Perspective' (1992) 55 MLR 44; Peter Cane, 'Standing, Representation and the Environment' in Ian Loveland (ed.), *A Special Relationship? American Influences on Public Law in the UK* (1995) and 'Standing Up for the Public' [1995] PL 276; Robinson and Dunkley (eds.), *Public Interest Perspectives in Environmental Law* (1995), Chapters 3, 10, and 11.

[35] Section 31(3) of the Supreme Court Act 1981 and RSC, Ord 53, r 3(7).

[36] Law Commission, *Administrative Law: Judicial Review and Statutory Appeals*, Consultation Paper No 126 (1993), para. 9.2.

Where the applicant is directly affected

The most straightforward is where applicants can show that they have been personally adversely affected by the action being challenged. Examples include applications by homeless families challenging decisions of local housing authorities refusing them accommodation; applications by would-be entrants to the country challenging refusals to permit entry; and applications against a licensing authority by someone refused a licence. In such cases standing is not a problem.

Likewise, problems ought not to arise where the applicant is a group or an organization which can show that it has been directly adversely affected by official action.[37] It was, for example, accepted that the Child Poverty Action Group (CPAG) had standing to challenge the manner in which the Secretary of State for Social Services administered social security payments partly because delayed payments to claimants meant that the CPAG was having to expend its resources advising greater numbers of claimants.[38] Here the effect of the government's action was quite easy to quantify in the sense that the CPAG could show how it had impacted upon its resources. Adverse effects are not always this tangible, however. Consider the case brought by the British Herpetological Society and the Worldwide Fund for Nature challenging a grant of planning permission to allow development on an area of importance to various breeds of reptile.[39] Here the court held that the British Herpetological Society had standing because it had been closely associated with the particular site, but denied standing to the Worldwide Fund for Nature because it had failed to show a close connection and its interest was too general. The lesson seems to be that applicants have to establish some real connection with the decision in order to be sure of having a sufficient interest. One established exception to this may be noted in passing, namely that people who pay Council Tax have standing to challenge any decision of *their* local authority, whether or not they are specifically affected by it.[40]

Representative applications

In the situations just discussed, the applicants were seeking to establish their standing by relying on their own interests. Applicants, whether individual or more usually organizations, may also seek judicial review on behalf of others, a section of the community or the public in general. Generally speaking the courts allow a representative application if those being represented would have standing if they applied and the actual applicant is a competent representative. The most difficult cases (to which we return) are those in which the applicant seeks to represent, not individuals or the interests of identifiable groups, but wider public interests.

[37] Cf. *R v Darlington Borough Council, ex p Association of Darlington Taxi Owners* [1994] COD 424 where it was held that an unincorporated association does not have legal personality and so cannot bring judicial review proceedings.

[38] *R v Secretary of State for Social Services, ex p Child Poverty Action Group* [1990] 2 QB 540.

[39] *R v Poole Borough Council, ex p Beebee* [1991] 2 PLR 27; [1991] COD 264.

[40] See *Arsenal Football Club Ltd v Ende* [1979] AC 1.

The applicant is an organization with statutory power to litigate

A third situation is where public bodies are given authority to bring proceedings by statute. Local authorities have powers under s 222 of the LGA 1972 to bring legal proceedings (including judicial review applications) where they consider it expedient for the promotion of the protection of the inhabitants of the area.[41] Similarly, it was held that statute gave the Equal Opportunities Commission standing to bring judicial review proceedings against the Secretary of State claiming that he had unlawfully failed to amend legislation that discriminated on grounds of sex.[42]

The Attorney-General

Finally, the Attorney-General has standing to bring legal proceedings in the public interest. The Attorney-General may also give permission for others to sue in his name. This is known as 'relator' proceedings.[43] These are now rare and of limited value both because the rules of standing have been liberalized (see below) and because the Attorney-General in practice does not give consent to relator proceedings against central government.[44]

At what stage in the process is standing relevant?

It seems evident from the rules that standing is a matter to be considered at the leave stage and that applicants who have a sufficient interest should be allowed to proceed and to present their arguments on the substance of their claim. The courts have, however, created confusion by allowing respondents (and third parties) to question the applicant's standing both to argue that the decision to grant leave was wrong and should be set aside or that even if leave was correctly granted the applicant lacks a sufficient interest to obtain the remedies sought.

Because the courts have been prepared to consider such arguments standing issues may arise both at the leave stage (where they are obviously appropriate) and at the full hearing.

The leading example is the House of Lords' decision in *IRC v National Federation of the Self Employed and Small Businesses Ltd* (the *IRC* case).[45] Here the Federation, an interest group representing the self-employed and small businesses, applied for judicial review to challenge the decision by the Inland Revenue Commissioners (IRC) to grant a tax 'amnesty' to print workers employed on a casual basis in the newspaper industry. The Federation was

[41] See further B. Hough 'Local Authorities as Guardians of the Public Interest' [1992] PL 130. See in relation to Sunday trading, Chapter 30.

[42] *R v Secretary of State for Employment, ex p Equal Opportunities Commission* [1995] 1 AC 1. The Sex Discrimination Act, s 53(1) provides that the Commission's duties are '(a) to work towards the elimination of discrimination; (b) to promote equality of opportunity between men and women generally'.

[43] See *Gouriet v Union of Post Office Workers* [1978] AC 435.

[44] Sir Harry Woolf, *Protection of the Public—A New Challenge* (1990), p. 107.

[45] [1982] AC 617.

incensed that the amnesty had been granted when the IRC went to great lengths to collect taxes from its members. The House of Lords accepted that the Federation should have been granted leave, but the majority said that it was only by considering the 'matter' in more detail that the courts could decide whether the Federation had standing. Lord Wilberforce said that:[46]

> There may be simple cases in which it can be seen at the earliest stage that the person has no interest at all, or no sufficient interest to support the application: then it would be quite correct at the threshold to refuse him leave to apply. . . . But in other cases this will not be so. In these it will be necessary to consider the powers or the duties in law of those against whom relief is asked, the position of the applicant in relation to those powers or duties, and to the breach of those said to have been committed. In other words, the question of sufficient interest can not, in such cases, be considered in the abstract or as an isolated point. It must be taken together with the legal and factual context. The rule requires sufficient interest *in the matter to which the applicant relates.*

Having considered the legal and factual context, and in particular the legislative framework within which the IRC operates, the majority held that the Federation did not have a sufficient interest in the IRC's decision such as would entitle it to obtain a remedy. While it was clear that the IRC is subject to judicial supervision, as 'a matter of general principle . . . one taxpayer has no sufficient interest in asking the court to investigate the tax affairs of another taxpayer or to complain that the latter has been under-assessed' and 'an aggregate of individuals [such as the Federation] each of whom has no interest cannot of itself have an interest'.[47]

Lord Diplock disagreed, taking a far more logical approach. His view was that standing should only be a preliminary (or threshold) issue used to reject the 'simple' cases. Once leave has been granted courts should concern themselves with the substance of the arguments. He said there would be

> a grave lacuna in our system of public law if a pressure group, like the Federation, or even a single public-spirited taxpayer were prevented by outdated technical rules of *locus standi* from bringing the matter to the attention of the court and getting the unlawful conduct stopped.[48]

On the facts, however, he too found against the Federation, not on the ground of lack of standing, but because it had failed to show that the IRC had exceeded or abused its powers.

The current position is that standing issues may be raised at both the leave stage and at the substantive hearing stage. As Lord Donaldson MR has explained:

> The first stage test, which is applied on the application for leave, will lead to a refusal if the applicant has no interest whatsoever and is, in truth, no more than a meddlesome busybody. If, however, the application appears to be otherwise arguable and there is no other discretionary bar, such as dilatoriness on the part of

[46] [1982] AC 617, 630.
[47] Per Lord Wilberforce at p. 633.
[48] [1982] AC 617, 644.

the applicant, the applicant may expect to get leave to apply, leaving the test of interest or standing to be re-applied as a matter of discretion on the hearing of the substantive application. At this second stage, the strength of the applicant's interest is one of the factors to be weighed in the balance.[49]

The purposes of the standing requirement

It is evident even from this brief discussion that very different views exist as to the purpose of standing and the nature of the test to be satisfied. The most pragmatic justifications for imposing a standing requirement are essentially the same as those used to justify the leave stage itself, namely that it helps the court to filter out applications which lack merit, so protecting public bodies from undeserved legal challenge and the courts from being overloaded. These justifications are unconvincing. In practice, as research has shown, leave is very rarely refused solely on grounds of standing.[50] As we have seen, standing issues are often raised at the second stage of the process, by which time the respondent has already become involved and court time already been taken with the case. If at the second stage standing is not a filter, what is its purpose?

At least two possible answers may be given. One is that standing helps to define the scope of the court's jurisdiction. When judges decide whether they are prepared to consider arguments presented by applicants with particular interests, such as interests in tax allocation or in the protection of the environment, they are in effect considering whether courts should be concerned to protect such interests. The second answer is that standing is one element relevant to the court's discretion to grant or refuse a remedy. The way judges respond to these matters depends on their perception of the function of the courts in judicial review cases.

Standing and the role of judicial review

The different views of, and approaches to, standing are not simply about technicalities; the differences are rooted in different, and sometimes fundamentally different, views about the constitutional role of judicial review itself. At one extreme is the view that the primary task of the court is to determine the rights and interests of particular litigants and not to adjudicate upon the legality of governmental actions. This being so, applicants will only have a sufficient interest if they can establish that their personal rights and interests are directly adversely affected by the action being challenged. If they cannot show this they may fail, even though the court agrees with them that the public body has abused or exceeded its powers. A case decided in the 1960s

[49] *R v Monopolies and Mergers Commission, ex p Argyll Group plc* [1986] 1 WLR 763 at 773.
[50] See A. Le Sueur and M. Sunkin, 'Applications for Judicial Review: the Requirement for Leave' [1992] PL 102.

illustrates this approach.[51] A landowner sought to challenge a decision of a local planning authority to grant permission for a school to be built near, but not on, his land. The court accepted that the decision was unlawful but refused to intervene because the plaintiff's private law rights were not directly affected.

It is very unlikely that this case would be decided this way today. However, there are recent examples of judges indicating that they would be prepared to allow governmental illegality to go unchecked because the applicant lacked a sufficient interest. The best-known example is Schiemann J's judgment in *R v Secretary of State for the Environment, ex p Rose Theatre Trust Co Ltd.*[52] During construction work in London remains of the Elizabethan Rose Theatre were discovered. A number of people interested in protecting these remains and in securing public access to them put pressure on the Secretary of State to list the remains under the Ancient Monuments and Archaeological Areas Act 1979. The Secretary of State accepted that the remains were of national importance but refused to list them. They then formed a company which applied for judicial review challenging this refusal. Schiemann J decided that the Secretary of State had acted within his powers but that, in any case, the company lacked standing. He accepted that this could mean that unlawful decisions made by the Secretary of State might be unchallengeable. But, in his view:

> the law does not see it as the function of the courts to be there for every individual who is interested in having the legality of an administrative action litigated. Parliament could have given such a wide right of access to the court but it has not done so. . . . We all expect our decision makers to act lawfully. We are not all given by Parliament the right to apply for judicial review.

Notice that Schiemann bases his view on the intention of Parliament. Both the Supreme Court Act 1981 and Ancient Monuments and Archaeological Areas Act 1979 indicated to him that the applicant should be denied standing. He did not seem troubled by the possibility that Parliament might also have assumed that unlawful ministerial decisions would be reviewed by the courts. As we noted in our discussion of the impact-based approach to judicial review,[53] it may be argued that the courts have a general responsibility to control the abuse of legal power which extends beyond serving a fictional intention of Parliament (the power-based approach). In this context this responsibility requires judges to base standing requirements not in legislation, but in broader principles of the common law. Lord Diplock's statement in the *IRC* case[54] summarizes the essence of this approach and reflects the now dominant attitude that standing requirements should not prevent

[51] *Gregory v Camden London Borough Council* [1966] 1 WLR 899. Note that the plaintiff asked for a declaration before this remedy was available in judicial review proceedings and that the case was treated as a private law matter.

[52] [1990] 1 QB 504.

[53] See p. 473.

[54] See p. 489.

the courts from ensuring that public bodies comply with the law. Two decisions epitomize this attitude.

The Greenpeace case

The first is the decision of Otton J in the *Greenpeace* case.[55] Greenpeace challenged the decision of Her Majesty's Inspector of Pollution (HMIP) and the Minister of Agriculture Fisheries and Food (MAFF) to allow British Nuclear Fuels (BNFL) to test its new thermal oxide reprocessing plant (THORP) at Cumbria. In making the application Greenpeace claimed to represent 2,500 of its members who live in the Cumbria region where THORP was situated and who are concerned about the health risks associated with radioactive pollution. They also sought to represent the wider public interest in preventing such pollution. Greenpeace were granted leave. However, BNFL (who were to operate the plant but were not respondents in the case) were permitted to join the litigation and argue that leave should be set aside because Greenpeace had failed to establish a sufficient interest.

Otton J rejected this argument. Following the approach set out in Lord Donaldson MR's judgment in *ex p Argyll Group*[56] he said that the standing of Greenpeace was one of the factors to be considered in exercising his discretion. After applauding the integrity of Greenpeace and its genuine concern for the environment he went on to say that he would be ignoring the blindingly obvious if he were to disregard the genuine concern for their health of the group's 2,500 members who lived near the site. He had no doubt that the issues raised by the application were serious and worthy of determination by the court.

Otton J said that if he were to deny standing to Greenpeace 'those they represent might not have an effective way to bring the issues before the court'. He was, moreover, particularly impressed by the competence and expertise of Greenpeace, saying that if Greenpeace were unable to make the application:[57]

> a less well informed challenge might be mounted which could stretch unnecessarily the court's resources and which would not afford the court the assistance it requires in order to do justice between the parties . . . because of its access to experts in the relevant realms of science and technology (not to mention the law) it is able to mount a carefully selected, focused, relevant and well argued challenge.

The Pergau Dam case

The World Development Movement (WDM), a pressure group which campaigns to improve the quality of British aid to the Third World, challenged the Foreign Secretary's decision to help fund the Pergau Dam project in Malaysia.[58]

[55] *R v HM Inspectorate of Pollution, ex p Greenpeace Ltd (No 2)* [1994] 1 WLR 570.
[56] See above p. 490.
[57] At p. 350.
[58] *R v Secretary of State for Foreign and Commonwealth Affairs, ex p World Development Movement* [1995] 1 WLR 386.

Unlike Greenpeace the WDM did not claim to represent members who were directly adversely affected by the decision but based its application on wider public interests and in particular in ensuring that ministers comply with the law. The court held both that the WDM had standing and that the Foreign Secretary had exceeded his powers. As in the *Greenpeace* case, Rose LJ acknowledged the reputation, status and expertise of the applicants. He also emphasized the importance of vindicating the rule of law; the importance of the issue raised; the likely absence of any other responsible challenger; the nature of the breach of duty against which relief is sought; and the prominent role of the WDM in giving advice, guidance and assistance with regard to aid. All of these, he said, pointed to the conclusion that the WDM had a sufficient interest in the matter.

In both these decisions the judges declined to follow Schiemann J's approach in the *Rose Theatre* case. In both the judges stressed the importance of vindicating the rule of law and the risk that if standing were refused challenges might not be brought. Both also emphasized the integrity and expertise of these particular groups. Whether this liberal approach will be maintained and if so, whether it will be extended to applicants who are less expert, well-resourced or established remains to be seen. If the approach is to be continued, and possibly extended to other applicants, standing will no longer be an issue of importance once leave has been granted. Another possibility is that certain expert groups will be given special status in gaining access while ordinary individuals or inexpert or newly-formed groups may find themselves confronted by a higher hurdle to jump.[59] This would be wrong in principle. The courts can clearly benefit from the expertise of groups like Greenpeace and WDM; however, it is not self-evident that such organizations are necessarily better placed to represent wider public interests than less well-qualified applicants. Moreover, while a general liberalizing of standing is to be applauded the courts need to be vigilant to ensure that their procedures are not abused by applicants who may have far weaker claims to represent genuine public interests than organizations like Greenpeace or the WDM. We might, for example, be sympathetic to the idea of granting leave to pressure groups representing views with which we broadly agree, but do we remain sympathetic when we disagree or abhor the views being advocated?

Bearing in mind that the concept of the public interest is notoriously vague and that pressure groups inevitably adopt a partial view, might it not be better to place responsibility for litigating on behalf of the public on an independent and impartial body? One suggested approach is to appoint a public official who, unlike the Attorney-General, is independent of government and who will be charged with taking public interest applications to the courts, either when asked to do so by others, or at his or her own initiative.[60]

[59] Cf. Standing to use Art 173 of the EC Treaty, p. 699.

[60] The idea has been suggested by J. A. G. Griffith, 'Judicial Decision-Making in Public Law' [1985] PL 564, 595 and by Woolf, *Protection of the Public—A New Challenge* (1990).

The Law Commission's recommendations on standing

In its 1994 report the Law Commission recommended that there should be a 'two-track' approach to standing. Those who are personally adversely affected should normally be given standing as a matter of course. Other applicants should only be granted standing as a matter of discretion. The Law Commission considered the suggestion that judges should exercise their discretion in these cases by having regard to explicit criteria, such as:

(a) the importance of the legal point;
(b) the chances of the issues being raised in any other proceedings;
(c) the allocation of scarce judicial resources; and
(d) the concern that in the determination of issues the courts should have the benefit of the conflicting points of view of those most directly affected by them.

However, having 'carefully considered' whether to enunciate criteria such as these in statute or the Rules of Court, the Law Commission decided that it is preferable not to limit judicial discretion in this way.[61] Instead, it recommended the introduction of the following rule:

> an application should not be allowed to proceed to a substantive hearing unless the court is satisfied that the applicant has been or would be adversely affected, or the High Court considers that it is in the public interest for an applicant to make the application.

No action has yet been taken to introduce this rule. However, it appears to reflect the substance of current judicial practice.

OBTAINING EVIDENCE

As in any other type of litigation those bringing judicial review proceedings must establish the factual and legal basis of their case.[62] In judicial review proceedings this means first presenting sufficient evidence at the leave stage to persuade the court that the allegations are arguable; and, if leave is granted, then being equipped to overcome the respondent's counter-arguments. Here too applicants face a number of obstacles.

No legal duty to give reasons

First, while the courts have increasingly insisted on public bodies providing reasoned decisions, as yet there is no general legal duty on public bodies to give reasons for their actions.[63] People may therefore just not be told why

[61] Law Com No 226, para. 5.22. Lord Woolf agreed with this approach, though he added that the relevant criteria should be set out in a practice guide: Lord Woolf *Access to Justice* (1996) Chapter 18, para. 20.

[62] Contrast this with the investigatory process used by the ombudsmen (see Chapter 18) and the inquisitorial style of parliamentary select committees (see Chapter 17).

[63] See p. 537 (statutory requirements to give reasons) and p. 592 (common law requirements to give reasons).

(for instance) a licence has been refused. A court might ultimately agree that this failure is unfair, but it will not be easy to get the case off the ground initially if the applicant is unable to tell whether, for example, the authority has taken into account legally irrelevant factors.[64]

No freedom of information legislation

This problem is compounded by the long tradition of non-disclosure by all levels of government in the United Kingdom.[65] Despite recent movement towards greater openness,[66] obtaining information from public bodies is often still very difficult. In particular, there is no generalized freedom of information legislation as in other countries.[67] Nor is there a general legal duty to publish administrative rules, guidelines or policies. On the contrary, the emphasis has tended to be on ensuring the confidentiality of information by means of both the criminal[68] and civil law.[69] The civil service codes of discipline also prohibit unauthorized disclosures of information.

However, there has been an incremental growth in the availability of information and a professed change of attitude within government. In 1993 the government issued a White Paper on Open Government which as well as promising a more open approach to policy formation led to the introduction of the code of practice on open government which is now administered by the Parliamentary Ombudsman.[70]

In the context of local government the Local Government (Access to Information) Act 1985 allows members of the public to attend meetings of the 'principal councils', with a right of access to officers' reports and 'background papers' which have been relied on (subject to exceptions designed to protect confidential matters and certain other exempt information).

There have also been extensions in the right of individuals to obtain details of information kept about themselves. Under the Data Protection Act 1984 there is a register of those authorized to hold electronically retrievable personal information which individuals may inspect. Legislation also provides for rights of access to personal information which is kept in paper form, including access to housing and social services files[71] and access to medical

[64] See p. 496.

[65] See generally Patrick Birkinshaw, *Freedom of Information* (1996).

[66] Recent reforms include the Official Secrets Act 1989 and the Citizen's Charter.

[67] The USA Freedom of Information Act 1966 entitles anyone to have access to identifiable documents of the federal government, subject to specific exceptions relating to national defence, foreign policy, and commercial secrets. Similar provisions exist in Canada, Australia and New Zealand.

[68] The Official Secrets Act 1989 creates an offence to make 'damaging' disclosures affecting security and intelligence; defence; international relations; crime, special investigation powers; and confidential information received from other states. There are also over 200 statutes and regulations making it a criminal offence to reveal specific forms of information.

[69] By means of injunctions to prevent publication of information the release of which would be contrary to the public interest, e.g.: *Attorney-General v Jonathan Cape Ltd* [1976] QB 752 (the *Crossman Diaries* case); *Attorney-General v Guardian Newspapers* [1987] 1 WLR 1248 and *Attorney-General v Guardian Newspapers (No 2)* [1990] 1 AC 109 (the 'Spycatcher' litigation).

[70] See p. 431.

files.[72] Despite these improvements, individuals remain largely dependent on the willingness of public bodies to tell them what their policies are and why decisions have been taken; obtaining information is still a major obstacle to preparing a well-supported and well-argued legal challenge.

Discovery of documents

Even when an application for judicial review has been mounted, it may be difficult to obtain relevant information from the respondent authority. In other types of legal proceedings there is normally an automatic obligation upon both parties to disclose and exchange documentary evidence relevant to the case. This is not so in judicial review proceedings. Applicants who want to see documents which the respondent has not willingly revealed must ask the court to order discovery (to compel the respondent to disclose the documents). Such orders are very rarely made.[73] *R v Secretary of State for the Environment, ex p Islington London Borough Council and the London Lesbian and Gay Centre*[74] illustrates the problems applicants may face. Here the Secretary of State refused permission for the London Residuary Body to transfer the freehold of a building to the London Lesbian and Gay Centre (LLGC) in the wake of the abolition of the Greater London Council. The LLGC believed that the minister refused consent because he disapproved of homosexuals. If this were true, it would have been an irrelevant consideration rendering the decision invalid. The LLGC applied for judicial review and sought an order compelling the minister to disclose the relevant departmental documents. The Court of Appeal held that the applicants had to assume that the minister's written evidence—his affidavit evidence said that his decision was not tainted by bias against homosexuals—was true, unless the applicants had some material available which indicated otherwise. The court said that in view of the history of attitudes to homosexuality in this country, it was perhaps understandable that there was a suspicion that the real reason for the decision lay in disapproval of homosexual activities. This suspicion was not, however, enough to go beyond what the minister said in his affidavit and did not justify ordering discovery of documents. In the event therefore they could not obtain the evidence that was necessary to turn their suspicion into a ground of challenge and their challenge consequently failed.

The result is that applicants may be prevented from challenging what government says in its affidavit evidence unless they have access to information from independent sources, such as a prior select committee investigation. In the Pergau Dam case,[75] for instance, the WDM sought disclosure of two minutes of advice given by a senior official to his minister which would

[71] Access to Personal Files Act 1987.

[72] Access to Medical Reports Act 1988 and Access to Health Records Act 1990.

[73] Although the Law Commission has criticized the reluctance of the judges to order discovery in its 1995 report, it declined to recommend a change in the relevant rules: see Law Com No 226, para. 7.

[74] [1992] COD 67.

[75] *R v Secretary of State for Foreign and Commonwealth Affairs, ex p World Development Movement* [1995] 1 WLR 386. See also Stephen Grosz, 'Pergau be Dammed' (1994) 144 NLJ 1708.

show why he had advised against support of the Pergau Dam project. Although the judge accepted that the government's affidavit gave 'manifestly incomplete summaries' of the minutes he refused to grant discovery of the minutes themselves. Fortunately for the WDM, it was able to refer to evidence given by the official to the Public Accounts Committee and Foreign Affairs Select Committee which clearly showed, contrary to the impression given by the Foreign Secretary's affidavit, that the minister had been strongly advised that the proposed aid would not contribute to the development of Malaysia as required by s 1 of the Overseas and Co-operation and Development Act 1980. This evidence was ultimately central to the court's decision that the Foreign Secretary's decision was unlawful. Had the select committees not secured the information from the officials, the legal challenge would probably not have been brought.[76] Documentary evidence may also be withheld on the grounds that its production would be contrary to the public interest. Public interest immunity, as it is now called, is sufficiently important to warrant separate consideration and this topic is discussed later in the chapter.

The absence of cross-examination

The opportunity to cross-examine witnesses is a normal, and indeed a vital, part of criminal and most civil proceedings. Cross-examination provides an opportunity to challenge the veracity and reliability of oral evidence and enables judges and juries to test the credibility of witnesses. In judicial review applications evidence is very rarely given in the form of oral testimony by witnesses. Instead, the alleged facts are set out in sworn affidavits.[77] The deponents (as those who give evidence by affidavit are known) are rarely called to give oral evidence or to be cross-examined.

The reason for this important procedural difference between judicial review and other types of litigation lies in the theory that judicial review litigation is primarily concerned with conflicts of law rather than conflicts of fact. Factual disputes do, however, arise in judicial review cases. Suppose, for example, a prisoner claims that a prison disciplinary hearing was unfairly conducted because he had been prevented from calling witnesses who would have been able to give material evidence supporting his case. The respondents might deny that the proceedings were unfair because all relevant witnesses were called and that no one else could have given helpful information. Clearly, this challenge involves an issue of fact: were there, or were there not, other witnesses who could have given relevant information? In private law proceedings it is normally possible to call the further witnesses and to have

[76] The Foreign Affairs Select Committee obtained summaries of the minutes, but was unable to compel production of the minutes themselves.

[77] See e.g. the extracts from the affidavits in *R v Secretary of State for Social Services, ex p Cotton* (1985) *The Times*, 14 December, p. 640.

them cross-examined in order to find out whether they have anything relevant to say. This is unlikely to be permitted in judicial review.[78]

The *GCHQ* case is an example of a situation in which the absence of cross-examination has been criticized.[79] The justification ultimately given by the government for not consulting with the unions prior to imposing the ban on trade union membership was that consultation would have threatened national security. This claim was made by Sir Robert Armstrong in his affidavit evidence, but it was disputed by the unions. Although the judges said that the government '. . . is under an obligation to produce evidence that the decision was *in fact* based on grounds of national security' and that 'mere assertion' was not enough,[80] Sir Robert Armstrong was not called to give evidence and the unions were unable to cross-examine him on his statement. Griffith observed that:

> In the *GCHQ* case two people knew the real reason why the Government did not consult with the unions: the Prime Minister and the Foreign Secretary. Neither could be required to give evidence.[81]

This case illustrates the way that the absence of cross-examination limits both the parties' ability to challenge the evidence adduced by the other side and the effectiveness of judicial review as a mechanism for scrutinizing government. The absence of cross-examination also protects ministers and officials from the sort of direct questioning that they can expect from select committees and other investigative inquiries.[82]

Public interest immunity

As noted above, in Order 53 applications for judicial review there is no automatic discovery of documents and the courts rarely order public bodies to disclose evidence to applicants.

Documents may also be withheld in court proceedings if their disclosure would be contrary to the public interest. Until 1973 this was described as Crown Privilege, but this term is no longer used because

(a) the rules are designed to protect wider public interests rather than the interests of the Crown, and
(b) bodies other than the Crown can claim immunity from disclosure.[83]

[78] This is one of the reasons why the prisoners in *O'Reilly v Mackman* [1983] 2 AC 237 tried to use private law proceedings to challenge decisions of the Hull Prison Board of Visitors.
[79] See J. A. G. Griffith, 'Judicial Decision-Making in Public Law' [1985] PL 564, 595.
[80] See Lord Fraser [1985] AC 374, 402 and at 420 Lord Roskill (emphasis added).
[81] J. A. G. Griffith, *The Politics of the Judiciary* (4th edn., 1991), p. 315 and 'Judicial Decision-making in Public Law' [1985] PL 564.
[82] See e.g. the questioning of the Foreign Secretary by the Employment Select Committee when it investigated the GCHQ union ban: Chapter 17.
[83] *R v Lewes Justices, ex p Secretary of State for the Home Department* [1973] AC 388.

In *D v National Society for the Prevention of Cruelty to Children*,[84] for example, the House of Lords upheld the refusal of the NSPCC (a charity with some statutory functions) to reveal the identity of an informant who had reported his suspicions that a child was being abused. It was held that it is in the public interest for informants to be assured that their identities would remain secret as otherwise the NSPCC could be deprived of valuable information.

The Cammell Laird decision

The modern law can be traced back to the decision of the House of Lords in *Duncan v Cammell Laird & Co.*[85] In 1939, a submarine called *The Thetis* sank during trials and 99 men were killed. A number of their dependants sued Cammell Laird, the builders of the submarine. The First Lord of the Admiralty, although not a party to the litigation, intervened to object to the disclosure of documents relating to the construction and salvage of *The Thetis* on grounds of national security. The House of Lords held that the courts could not question this claim and therefore the documents should not be revealed even though they might have helped the plaintiffs. Bearing in mind that this was wartime and that *The Thetis* had been fitted with a new and secret type of torpedo, this was a correct decision on the facts. Unfortunately, in their enthusiasm not to obstruct the war effort, the judges laid down principles which gave the executive sweeping and unreviewable powers to withhold all manner of documents. Disclosure could be withheld not only on the ground that revelation of the *contents of particular documents* would be contrary to the public interest, but also on the ground that documents belong to a *class* of document which ought to be withheld in the interests of 'the proper functioning of the public service', irrespective of the sensitivity or otherwise of the particular documents. Moreover, once a claim for immunity had been made it could not be questioned by the courts.

Conway v Rimmer

Although widely criticized, this remained the law until 1967 when the House of Lords decided *Conway v Rimmer.*[86] A probationary police constable sued his former superintendent for malicious prosecution after he had been prosecuted for theft and acquitted. He sought discovery of five confidential reports on his progress during his probationary period. Both parties wanted the documents produced because they both thought them relevant to the issue of malice. The Home Secretary, however, objected. The Court of Appeal (Lord Denning MR dissenting) following *Duncan v Cammell Laird* felt itself compelled to accept this objection. The House of Lords refused to be so. Unanimously reversing its own previous decision, it held that it is for the courts and not for the executive to decide whether it was in the public interest to prevent the disclosure of documents. In reaching this decision judges would have to:

[84] [1978] AC 171.
[85] [1942] AC 624.
[86] [1968] AC 910.

weigh the competing public interests involved—the public interest in concealing the documents in order to prevent harm to the nation or the public service, and the public interest in having the documents available for the proper administration of justice.[87]

Inspection

In order to decide where this balance lies, courts have to inspect the documents. This first step, however, is taken only if it can be shown that the documents are likely to be relevant to the case. This is a burden that applicants for judicial review or plaintiffs in ordinary proceedings may find difficult to surmount. In *Air Canada v Secretary of State for Trade (No 2)*[88] a number of airlines sought disclosure of various high-level policy documents (including Cabinet papers) in an attempt to establish that the government had unlawfully forced the British Airports Authority to increase landing charges at Heathrow Airport. The House of Lords held that it was inappropriate even to inspect the documents because the plaintiffs had failed to show that they were likely to help their case. While it is understandable that the courts are reluctant to become involved in difficult and time-consuming inspections of documents, this test is far too strict. It is often very difficult for a party to establish the likely import of documents which have not been seen.

Class claims

On what basis can public interest immunity be claimed to prevent the release of a whole class of documents, which may include innocuous but potentially helpful documents? The original basis for class claims was that immunity furthered the 'need to secure freedom and candour of communication with and within the public service, so that government decisions can be taken on the best advice and with the fullest information'.[89] The concern was the familiar one that if policy-makers and their advisors feared that their internal papers could later become public this would discourage free discussion and be detrimental to the quality of governmental decision-making. Few would now regard this 'candour argument' as an acceptable justification for granting public interest immunity. In one of the most important decisions on the point, *Burmah Oil v Bank of England*,[90] only Lord Wilberforce was prepared to accept that the need for candour can justify a class claim for immunity from disclosure. As part of a deal in which the Bank of England rescued Burmah Oil, the bank had purchased a large amount of Burmah Oil stock very cheaply. Following the purchase the value of the stock rose sharply. Burmah Oil sued the bank, claiming that it had acted improperly and that the deal imposed upon the company was unconscionable. It sought discovery of documents relating to the bank's discussions with the government. The

[87] Sir Simon Brown, 'Public Interest Immunity' [1994] PL 579, 581.
[88] [1983] 2 AC 394.
[89] Lord Kilmuir, HL Deb, cols 741–8 (6 June 1956).
[90] [1980] AC 1090.

Chief Secretary to the Treasury objected to disclosure on the ground that the documents concerned government policy. The House of Lords agreed to inspect the documents but, after inspection, decided that they did not contain material which it was necessary to reveal for the purposes of the case. However, referring to the candour argument, Lord Keith said that:[91]

> The notion that any competent and conscientious public servant would be inhibited at all in the candour of his writing by consideration of the off-chance that they might have to be produced in a litigation is in my opinion grotesque. To represent that the possibility of it might significantly impair the public service is even more so ... the candour argument is an utterly insubstantial ground for denying ... access to relevant documents.

He went on to acknowledge the 'trend to more open governmental methods' which, he said:[92]

> ... may demand, though no doubt only in a very limited number of cases, that the inner workings of government should be exposed to public gaze, and there may be some who would regard this as likely to lead, not to captious or ill-informed criticism, but to criticism calculated to improve the nature of that working as affecting the individual citizen.

The liberalization of approach means that class claims now need to be rooted in 'specific' aspects of the public interest, such as the need to protect international relations, police operations or national security. The main class claims concerning the business of government relate

(a) to advice to ministers of the formulation of high-level government-policy, and
(b) to Cabinet discussions.[93]

But following *Attorney-General v Jonathan Cape Ltd*,[94] even these claims may not succeed. Sir Simon Brown has indicated that:[95]

> For the future ... those responsible for asserting immunity claims will need to scrutinise those put forward on a class basis with very particular care indeed. They are likely now to face increasing scepticism ... Only if it really can be said that however innocuous the contents, the intrinsic character of the communications themselves requires secrecy can it ever be proper to advance a class claim properly so called. And even then there should be rigorous examination of the class. Is concealment of the whole class really necessary in the public interest? Can the class not be narrowed or refined in some way? Cannot part of the individual documents be revealed?

91 p. 1133.
92 p. 1134.
93 Simon Brown, note 87 above, p. 588.
94 [1976] QB 752.
95 See note 87 above. Simon Brown also called upon the courts to be 'less awe-struck by the mantra of national security and readier to scrutinise the legitimacy' of claims to immunity based on national security (p. 590).

The House of Lords recently reinforced this message when it unanimously overruled a line of authority which had held that documents relating to investigations of the Police Complaints Authority were, as a class, immune from disclosure.[96] If a class-based public interest immunity is claimed, Lord Woolf said 'it requires clear and compelling evidence that it is necessary'.[97]

Criminal trials and public interest immunity

The above discussion is concerned with the principles governing public interest immunity in the context of judicial review litigation and other types of civil litigation. Public interest immunity has also been claimed to prevent disclosure of documents to defendants seeking to establish their innocence in a criminal trial. As Sir Peter Scott points out in his report into the arms to Iraq affair,[98] in civil cases the public interest may justify refusing a claim of immunity even though this means that a sound civil action might fail. But, for the purposes of criminal trials, the balance must always come down in favour of disclosure if there is any real possibility that the withholding of the document may cause or contribute to a miscarriage of justice. The public interest factors underlying the public interest immunity claim cannot ever have a weight sufficient to outweigh that possibility. In forming this view Scott was highly critical of the circumstances surrounding claims for immunity made during the trial of former directors of Matrix Churchill.[99]

The Matrix Churchill trial

Three former directors of a manufacturing company, Matrix Churchill, were prosecuted for exporting machine tools which could be used for military purposes in Iraq, contrary to rules prohibiting the export of military equipment to that country.[100] The defendants claimed that the exports had been made with ministerial knowledge and express or implicit approval. To establish this they sought disclosure of confidential documents relating to the government's policy on arms sales to Iraq. On legal advice, including that given by the Attorney-General, a number of ministers signed certificates claiming public interest immunity for a large number of documents. After inspecting

[96] *R v Chief Constable of the West Midlands Police, ex p Wiley* [1995] AC 274. A civil action for damages had been commenced against the police. The claim for immunity concerned documents acquired by the police in the course of their inquiry into the complaints. The Court of Appeal, following earlier cases, had held that these documents could only be used for the purposes of investigating the complaints or for the prosecution of a crime and not for the purposes of civil proceedings.

[97] *Ex p Wiley* at p. 446.

[98] *The Report on the Export of Defence Equipment and Dual-use Goods to Iraq and Related Prosecutions* (1996), (1995–96) HC 115, Vol. IV, K6.12.

[99] See further David Leigh, *Betrayed: The Real Story of the Matrix Churchill Trial* (1993); Sir Richard Scott, VC 'The Acceptable and Unacceptable Use of Public Interest Immunity' [1996] PL 427; Adam Tomkins, 'Public Interest Immunity after Matrix Churchill' [1993] PL 650.

[100] The Import, Export and Customs Powers (Defence) Act 1939 and delegated legislation made under it.

them the judge ordered disclosure of most of the documents, albeit with some of their contents being blacked out. In essence he considered that interests of justice (affecting as it did the liberty of the defendants) outweighed the public interest in withholding the documents. As a result the prosecution was dropped because the government was not prepared to make the documents public.

The events surrounding this case led to a furore in Parliament and the news media. There was widespread concern that individuals stood to lose their liberty because government ministers were not prepared to release documentary evidence. In addition there was much speculation that ministers had claimed immunity in order to prevent the defendants establishing that they had acted with ministerial support and from showing that ministers had misled Parliament and the public about government policy. It was against this background that the government commissioned Sir Peter Scott to undertake an inquiry. His report was eventually published in February 1996. Great care is taken in the report to set out the circumstances leading to the making of the claims for public interest immunity.[101] The report was ultimately extremely critical of governmental practice, particularly in respect of class claims. These he said are rarely necessary. National security, for example, can be protected by claiming immunity for particular documents on a contents basis. But even so, such claims should not be made unless in the opinion of the minister, or person making the claim, 'disclosure will cause substantial harm'.[102]

Is there a duty or a discretion to claim immunity?

One of the questions to emerge from the *Matrix Churchill* case was whether ministers have a duty or a discretion to claim public interest immunity. In response to criticism that they had been involved in a cover-up ministers argued that they had been advised by government legal advisors and by the Attorney-General that they had a duty to claim immunity for documents falling within a class which had previously been held by the courts to attract immunity. In this situation they believed that they had no choice but to make the claim. The Attorney-General also expressed this view to the Scott inquiry, relying on the authority of the Court of Appeal in *Makanjoula v Commissioner of Police of the Metropolis*.[103] That case was one of the decisions overturned by the House of Lords in *ex p Wiley*.[104] The view that it supported the proposition that ministers have a duty to claim public interest immunity was also severely criticized in the Scott Report.[105] Scott LJ explained that ministers only have a duty to claim immunity once they have decided that the public interest requires the immunity. This decision is for the minister to take. Scott pointed out that ministers:

[101] See Vol. III, Chapters G13 and G14.
[102] This wording comes from Lord Templeman in *ex parte Wiley* (note 96 above).
[103] [1992] 3 All ER 617. See also Tomkins [1993] PL 650.
[104] Note 96 above.
[105] See particularly Vol. III, G18.52–106.

> are well able to decide whether Government documents of a confidential or secret nature should be disclosed . . . Ministers from time to time place such documents . . . before Select Committees . . . Ministers sometimes . . . allow the contents of such documents to be revealed to journalists or political commentators . . . In each case the Minister . . . concerned [should] take a view as to whether . . . the wider public interest requires them to be produced or disclosed . . .[106]

Later Scott adds:[107]

> It is fair to all the Ministers who signed the Certificates to note that their respective departmental lawyers, the lawyers from the Treasury Solicitor's Department and in the case of Mr Haseltine, the Attorney-General, all advised that it was not permissible for Ministers to take into account any administration of justice factors [such as the interests of defendants] in favour of disclosure of the documents.
>
> I do not regard this advice as having any sound legal foundation.

Although there may be some doubt, the better view is that when public interest immunity issues arise, ministers must exercise their own judgement on whether immunity should be claimed. If they decide not to make a claim it is very unlikely that the courts will disagree.[108] If the minister forms the view that the public interest does require withholding documents then there is a duty to claim the immunity. Ultimately the courts decide whether the claim is justified.

Questions

1. Why is access to judicial review so important? Why does it raise so many issues of difficulty?

2. Can it be said that there is a right of access to the courts to seek judicial review?

3. On what grounds can it be argued that the leave requirement is wrong in principle? Do you agree with these arguments?

4. What purposes are served by the rules on standing? Is a standing requirement necessary?

5. Why is there no automatic right to obtain discovery of documents or to cross-examine witnesses in judicial review proceedings? What issues of principle are raised by these limitations?

6. Is a claim of public interest immunity ever justified to prevent disclosure of relevant material to a defendant facing a serious criminal prosecution?

[106] Vol. III, G18.60.
[107] Vol. III, G18.64–5.
[108] Lord Woolf in *ex p Wiley* said that it is conceivable that they might if the documents do not relate to an area for which the minister is responsible. At the time of writing new guidelines on claiming public interest immunity are being prepared by the Attorney-General.

22

IS JUDICIAL REVIEW APPROPRIATE?

In some situations, even though there is an applicant able and willing to use judicial review, the process may be unavailable because either Parliament or the courts regard judicial review as being inappropriate in the circumstances. If Parliament regards judicial review as inappropriate it may seek to restrict or exclude it altogether by an Act of Parliament, although the courts do not look kindly on being prevented from reviewing the legality of governmental actions. Nevertheless the judges have imposed their own limitations on the scope of judicial review, selecting which types of decisions may be challenged, and which bodies are amenable to judicial review. Judicial review does not lie against private individuals or bodies which do not operate in the public domain. Courts have also held that disputes over the legal validity of some types of decisions are inherently 'non-justiciable'.

If a decision may be judicially reviewed the common law rule of 'procedural exclusivity' normally dictates that this may *only* be done by litigants using the Order 53 application for judicial review procedure, and not by using other court procedures, such as an action in the county court.[1]

STATUTORY EXCLUSION OF JUDICIAL REVIEW

According to the orthodox constitutional theory of parliamentary sovereignty, it is possible for Parliament by statute to limit or totally exclude judicial review. When it attempts to do so two constitutional principles clash. The courts are obliged to respect the intentions of Parliament, but must they do so at the expense of the rule of law and with the risk that an abuse of power might go unchecked? If courts were to adopt the power-based approach rigidly the answer would be clear: their sole task is to do what Parliament asks.[2] If Parliament tells judges to 'keep out', judges should keep clear even if this means that there are no legal controls on ministers and others. If, however, the courts were to adopt the impact-based approach their primary concern is not to faithfully follow Parliament whatever it says (bearing in

[1] See p. 514 below.
[2] See p. 471.

mind that in practice it is the government which often controls parliamentary legislation); rather it is to protect citizens by ensuring that government is accountable to the common law.[3] In practice the courts have tended to adopt a middle way. Attempts to exclude judicial review are regarded with great suspicion by judges and will be approached with the following words in mind:[4]

> It is a principle not by any means to be whittled down that the subject's recourse to Her Majesty's courts for the determination of his rights is not to be excluded except by clear words.

The question inevitably to be asked is: what words will be treated as being 'clear'? The prevailing attitude of the courts may be illustrated by the decision of the House of Lords in *Anisminic v Foreign Compensation Commission*, which is the best-known example of judicial reaction to a legislative attempt to oust the courts.[5] The Foreign Compensation Act 1950, s 4(4) provided that a determination of the Foreign Compensation Commission 'shall not be called into question in any court of law'. Despite appearances, their Lordships said that the words in this provision were ambiguous and not clear. They could mean that literally every determination was protected from challenge however the determination had been made. Taken to its extreme this would prevent challenge to even the most blatantly unlawful of purported determinations, such as those induced by corruption or those reached following blatantly improper procedures or on the basis of obviously irrelevant grounds. Alternatively the words could mean that determinations lawfully made could not be questioned. The problem here is that the lawfulness of a determination could only be established once the courts had had a chance to look at the matter, which is precisely what Parliament might have intended to prevent. Ultimately, a three-to-two majority in the House of Lords overturned a unanimous Court of Appeal and held that had Parliament intended the ouster clause to cover unlawful determinations (or 'purported' determinations) as well as lawful determinations, much clearer wording would have been used. There was therefore nothing in the legislation to prevent the courts from examining the determination to see whether it was a valid determination or a 'purported' determination.

Soon after this decision Parliament introduced new legislation allowing an appeal from the Commission on a point of law to the Court of Appeal. It also strengthened the ouster clause by providing that 'determinations' include 'provisional determinations' and 'anything which purports to be a determination'.[6]

Since *Anisminic* parliamentary counsel have attempted to find forms of words that are judge-proof. One example is the Interception of Communications Act 1985, s 7(8). This provides that decisions of the tribunal established to investigate complaints about the interception of mail or telephone

[3] See p. 473.

[4] Per Viscount Simonds, *Pyx Granite Co Ltd v Ministry of Housing and Local Government* [1960] AC 260.

[5] [1969] 2 AC 147. For a contrasting decision see *South East Asia Fire Bricks v Non Metallic Mineral Products Manufacturing Employees Union* [1981] AC 363.

[6] Foreign Compensation Act 1969, s 3.

tapping, '*including any decisions as to the jurisdiction of the tribunal*, shall not be subject to appeal or liable to be questioned in any court'. Notice that words given emphasis refer to the jurisdiction of the tribunal. This is to make it clear that challenges cannot be made to decisions on the ground that the tribunal lacked jurisdiction to make them. Another illustration is found in the Local Government Finance Act 1987, which deals with the calculation of grants paid by central government to local authorities. Section 4 provides that (emphasis added):

> Anything done by the Secretary of State before the passing of this Act for the purposes of the relevant provisions in relation to any of the initial years or intermediate years shall be *deemed to have been done in compliance* with those provisions.

Here the words 'deemed to have been done in compliance' are used to indicate that actions are to be treated as if they comply with the legislation, even if they do not.

Attempts to oust the courts altogether may be contrasted with provisions which allow decisions to be challenged provided the challenge is made within, say, six weeks. These time limit clauses are common in the context of land-use planning and are regarded by the courts as imposing a limitation period for challenge in order to provide administrative certainty so that planning schemes and development can go ahead without fear of later challenge.[7]

Adequate alternative remedies

Judicial review is said to provide a remedy of last resort. Where Parliament has created an adequate alternative remedy, such as a right of appeal to a tribunal, the courts normally require applicants to exhaust these remedies before seeking judicial review.[8] Thus where students or lecturers want to challenge the decision of a university authority, they normally have first to take their complaint to the university visitor (if there is one).[9] Similarly claimants of welfare benefits who allege that an error has occurred in their payments may be required to appeal to a statutory tribunal rather than seek judicial review. Judges, however, have discretion to allow judicial review to be used prior to appealing where they are satisfied that an appeal would not remedy the grievance or is otherwise inappropriate because, for example, it would be too slow.[10] So, for example, Simon Cotton was not prevented from seeking judicial review of the Board and Lodging Regulations because in the circumstances

[7] *Smith v East Elloe Rural District Council* [1956] AC 736; *R v Secretary of State for the Environment, ex p Ostler* [1977] QB 122; *R v Cornwall County Council, ex p Huntingdon* [1994] 1 All ER 694.

[8] See *R v IRC, ex p Preston* [1985] AC 835; *R v Secretary of State for the Home Department, ex p Swati* [1986] 1 WLR 477; cf. *R v Chief Constable of Merseyside Police, ex p Calveley* [1986] QB 424. Lord Woolf has emphasized the importance of using other remedies prior to seeking judicial review: *Access to Justice* (1996), Chapter 18, para. 7.

[9] See e.g. *R v Hull University Visitor, ex p Page* [1993] AC 682.

[10] *R v Hillingdon London Borough Council, ex p Royco Homes* [1974] QB 720.

(the challenge was to the legal validity of the whole basis upon which benefit was to be paid) this procedure was more appropriate than appealing to the social security tribunal (which is primarily equipped to deal with the more specific question of whether the individual is entitled to the benefit).[11]

There are several possible justifications for requiring exhaustion of alternative remedies. One is a concern to ensure that legal disputes are adjudicated upon by the most appropriate body using the most suitable procedures. Statutory tribunals often have particular expertise which is not enjoyed by judicial review judges. This theme recurs as an explanation for many of the rules examined in this chapter. A second justification is deference to the will of Parliament: if an Act has created a special complaints or appeals mechanism, judges ought to respect this before asserting the supervisory jurisdiction of judicial review.[12] Thirdly, there is the concern—already highlighted in the previous chapter—to control the number of applications for judicial review given the limited judicial resources which are available to deal with them.[13] Judges should also bear in mind that the obligation to exhaust appeals can itself create obstacles which may deter those with genuine grievances from pursuing claims.

WHO AND WHAT IS SUBJECT TO JUDICIAL REVIEW?

Over recent years, as the use of judicial review has grown, the courts have been forced to reconsider the question: what decisions of which bodies are subject to the judicial supervision? In the past the courts attempted to answer this question by using highly legalistic criteria such as whether the body in question was making an 'administrative', 'judicial' or 'quasi-judicial' decision.[14] Today such approaches have largely been rejected, although marking out the boundary of judicial review is still a difficult and controversial exercise. This is an important matter not only for would-be applicants (who need to know whether judicial review is available), but also for decision-making organizations (who need to know whether they are subject to judicial review and whether they have to comply with the obligations imposed by judicial review, such as procedural fairness and the principles of rationality). In *R v Jockey Club, ex p Massingberd-Mundy* Neill LJ stated:[15]

> In order to succeed . . . it is necessary for an applicant to show not only that the body concerned is one whose decisions are susceptible to judicial review but also that the relevant decision was one which infringed or affected some public law right of the applicant.

[11] See further Chapters 11 and 27.
[12] This is associated with the power-based approach to judicial review: see p. 471.
[13] See p. 482.
[14] See further de Smith, Woolf and Jowell, *Judicial Review of Administrative Action* (5th edn., 1995), Appendix.
[15] [1993] 2 All ER 207, 220.

As this indicates, potential applicants for judicial review must ensure that the body they propose to challenge is susceptible to judicial review; and if it is, that the specific decision or action which has caused the grievance is reviewable. These two issues are considered in turn.

The source of the body's power

The standard test for determining whether a body is amenable to judicial review is to consider the legal basis on which it functions. If it derives power from legislation or the Crown's prerogative, then its actions are *prima facie* reviewable.[16] If, on the other hand, a body derives decision-making power from a contract or agreement with the aggrieved person, then this is regarded as a strong indication that it is not susceptible to judicial review. One reason for this lies in the obligation to exhaust alternative remedies. If there is a contractual relationship between the body in question and the aggrieved person, then the aggrieved person should sue for breach of contract (for instance, for breach of an express or implied term that the aggrieved person will have an opportunity to present his case to the body before being disciplined or expelled, or before having a licence revoked). This approach can be used to explain why it has been held that judicial review could not be used to challenge a disciplinary committee of the Jockey Club disqualifying a racehorse owner and fining a trainer,[17] against the National Greyhound Racing Club Ltd by one of its members suspended following a dope test on a dog,[18] and against the Football Association Ltd by the Football League Ltd.[19]

Where a contract does indeed provide an aggrieved person with a basis for a claim, there may be no objection to the court barring a judicial review challenge. Contractual remedies, however, may not be available or adequate. For one thing it may be unrealistic to assume that contractual terms have been freely entered into and people may be forced to accept terms which give organizations great freedom and provide few opportunities for redress. Bodies like the Jockey Club, for example, carry out far-reaching regulatory functions and exercise monopoly power in their field of operation: jockeys and trainers have no choice but to accept the authority of the Jockey Club if they want to participate in horse racing. Moreover, the person aggrieved by a decision of such a non-statutory regulatory body may not have any contract

[16] See *R v Criminal Injuries Compensation Board, ex p Lain* [1967] 2 QB 864; *O'Reilly v Mackman* [1983] 2 AC 237, 277E.

[17] See *R v Jockey Club, ex p Massingberd-Mundy* [1993] 2 All ER 207; *R v Jockey Club, ex p The Aga Khan* [1993] 1 WLR 909.

[18] *Law v National Greyhound Racing Club Ltd* [1983] 1 WLR 1302. Law's lawyers used private law procedure (an originating summons) to seek a declaration; it was the club which, unsuccessfully, argued that the 'exclusivity principle' discussed at p. 514 below required such a challenge to the validity of one of its decisions to be made by an Order 53 application for judicial review.

[19] *R v Football Association Ltd, ex p Football League Ltd* [1983] 2 All ER 833. The Football League, which was in a contractual relationship with the FA, argued that the FA had acted unlawfully in setting up the Premier League. Judicial review was not appropriate.

with it. This is the position of people whose grievance relates to the refusal of an organization to allow them to join. Here if judicial review is not available, there may be no other legal remedy. In the *Aga Khan* case, the Court of Appeal expressly left open the question whether in such circumstances the aggrieved person would be able to apply for judicial review.

The nature and impact of the body's powers

In several cases, the courts have recognized that a strict application of a 'source of power' test may be undesirable and result in a powerful body being effectively free from effective legal supervision. In these the courts have been forced to articulate ways of approaching the question of amenability which do not focus exclusively on the source of a body's powers. One situation is where a regulatory body derives its power from neither statute, prerogative, nor contract. Here the courts have accepted that in order to determine whether such a body is amenable to judicial review it is necessary to consider the nature and impact of its actions.

In *R v Panel on Take-overs and Mergers, ex p Datafin plc* the Court of Appeal had to decide whether the Panel on Take-Overs and Mergers was judicially reviewable.[20] The Panel was established by the City of London as part of a voluntary system of self-regulation to oversee the City's Code on Take-Overs and Mergers, which was designed to ensure that shareholders are treated fairly during the course of take-overs. The Panel is an unincorporated association and its powers do not derive from statute, prerogative, or contract: companies are subject to its authority even though they have not agreed to be. In the words of Sir John Donaldson MR, it seems to be 'without visible means of legal support'.

When challenged by a company aggrieved by one of its decisions, the Panel argued that it was not susceptible to judicial review and could only be controlled by Parliament or the financial market place. The Court of Appeal disagreed. Despite the absence of a public source of power there was a sufficient 'public element' to the Panel's work. Not only does the Panel have wide-ranging and influential powers,[21] it has also been incorporated into the statutory network of financial regulation built up under legislation such as the Banking Act 1979. Moreover, it was clear that the government had agreed to limit legislative regulation of take-overs because of the Panel's existence and that had the Panel not existed some other body would have been established by legislation to perform its functions.

This decision was hailed as a major advance which marked a significant

[20] [1987] QB 815. See further J. Jowell, 'The Take-Over Panel: Autonomy, Flexibility and Legality' [1991] PL 149; Lord Alexander of Weedon, 'Judicial Review and City Regulators' (1989) 52 MLR 640; C. F. Forsyth, 'The Scope of Judicial Review "Public Duty" not "Source of Power"' [1987] PL 356.

[21] It is 'Part legislator, part court of interpretation, part consultant, part referee, part disciplinary tribunal—a truly remarkable body', per Sir John Donaldson MR in *R v Panel on Take-overs and Mergers, ex p Guinness plc* [1990] QB 146.

shift in judicial approaches: a 'triumph of substance over form'.[22] One eminent academic went so far as to predict that after *Datafin* 'there may be virtually no limit' to the scope of review.[23] These views were based on the expectation (or hope) that the courts would now be prepared to review any agency which made decisions that could be shown to impact on the public domain, whatever the source of its power. Since *Datafin* there has indeed been a considerable expansion in the range of bodies which are subject to judicial review. It has been held, for example, that the Advertising Standards Authority, a non-statutory, self-regulatory authority for the advertising industry, is reviewable because if it did not exist its functions 'would no doubt be exercised by the Director General of Fair Trading'.[24] Similarly, the Code of Practice Committee of the British Pharmaceutical Association, a voluntary self-regulatory body which applies a code of practice drawn up after consultation with the Department of Health, has also been held to be reviewable.[25]

Recent decisions, however, show that the courts are still capable of adopting a cautious approach. Judges have, for instance, refused to review decisions of religious bodies,[26] and they may still refuse to review bodies originally established by contract even where they have regulatory functions.[27]

Current position on amenability to review summarized

The current position may be summarized as follows.[28] Bodies deriving their powers from statute or prerogative are potentially reviewable. The courts presume that bodies established by contract or agreement are not reviewable unless they exercise statutory powers[29] or a very strong case can be made that

[22] Michael Beloff QC, 'The Boundaries of Judicial Review' in J. Jowell and D. Oliver (eds.), *New Directions of Judicial Review* (1988), p. 7.

[23] H. W. R. Wade, *Administrative Law*, (6th edn., 1988) at p. 640; cf. the 7th edn. by H. W. R. Wade and C. F. Forsyth (1994) at p. 663.

[24] *R v Advertising Standards Authority, ex p The Insurance Services plc* (1990) 2 Admin LR 77.

[25] This decision was made with 'great reluctance' by Popplewell J: *R v The Code of Practice Committee of the British Pharmaceutical Industry, ex p Professional Counselling Aids Ltd* (1991) 3 Admin LR 697.

[26] In *R v The Chief Rabbi, ex p Wachman* [1992] 1 WLR 1036, 1041 Simon Brown J said that the Chief Rabbi's 'functions are essentially intimate, spiritual and religious, functions which the Government could not and would not seek to discharge in his place were he to abdicate his regulatory responsibility'. See also *R v Imam of Bury Park, ex p Sulaiman* [1992] COD 132. But decisions of the Rabbinical Commission chaired by the Chief Rabbi may be reviewable where the Commission exercises statutory functions: *R v Rabbinical Committee, ex p Cohen* (1987) *The Times*, 22 December.

[27] In *R v Insurance Ombudsman Bureau and the Insurance Ombudsman, ex p Aegon Life Assurance Ltd* [1994] COD 426 the Divisional Court held that the Insurance Ombudsman, a body originally established by the insurance industry by contract, was not subject to judicial review. For a critique of the decision, see Richard Gordon and Sam Grodzinski, 'Insuring against judicial review' (1994) 144 NLJ 98. This means that non-parties to the contract cannot take proceedings against such bodies.

[28] For a more detailed discussion, see de Smith, Woolf and Jowell, *Judicial Review of Administrative Action* (5th edn., 1995), pp. 167–77.

[29] A 'private' non-governmental body, such as charity, may be conferred with statutory powers by an Act of Parliament: see e.g. *Re W (A Minor) (Adoption Agency: Wardship)* [1990] Fam 156 (a voluntary adoption society was subject to judicial review when it served a notice on

they carry out public functions; for example, where it can be shown that they have been recognized and used by government as a necessary part of a regulatory system and that they exercise powers of public importance.

It might be added, taking an impact-based approach to judicial review,[30] that judicial review should be primarily concerned with protecting citizens from bodies which have power over them, and that it ought not to matter whether these bodies have been formally established by statute, prerogative, contract or none of these. This argument may lead to the conclusion that judicial review should be available against all powerful concerns, including business enterprises.[31] It might additionally be pointed out that governmental functions (in their broadest sense) are today carried out by a tremendous variety of agencies, some deriving their powers from public sources, some from private contractual sources, and that the courts should be more concerned with *what* bodies do and how much influence they possess than with more technical questions about the source from which their powers derive.[32] It is certainly true that if the courts do focus exclusively on the source of power judicial review is unable to provide redress against, and legal supervision of, many powerful institutions. Many of these are subject to no democratic political controls either.

What actions/decisions are reviewable?

It is a 'well-settled principle that . . . merely because some public body is amenable to judicial review it by no means follows that it is reviewable in all its functions'.[33] In order to use judicial review against a body which is potentially reviewable it must be established:

(a) that there is a 'decision' or action to challenge;
(b) that the decision or action is justiciable; and
(c) that the decision or action gives rise to a claim in public law.

We deal with (c) above later in the chapter.

The need for a decision or action to challenge

Before a challenge can be mounted there must be a 'decision' or an action to challenge. In *GCHQ*, Lord Diplock stated:[34]

prospective adopters under the Adoption Act 1976, s 30 requiring them to return the child within seven days).

[30] See p. 473.

[31] Cf. the Privy Council decisions in *Minister of Justice for Canada v City of Levis* [1919] AC 505 and *Mercury Energy Ltd v Electricity Corp of New Zealand* [1994] 1 WLR 521.

[32] For an analogous argument, see the *GCHQ* case, Chapter 28 below, where Lord Diplock emphasizes that the function being performed is more important than the source of a body's power when deciding whether judicial review is possible.

[33] Simon Brown J in *R v Jockey Club, ex p RAM Racecourses* [1993] 2 All ER 225, 246.

[34] *Council of Civil Service Unions v Minister for the Civil Service* [1985] AC 374; extracts are set out at p. 668 below.

> To qualify as the subject matter for judicial review the decision must have consequences which affect some person (or body of persons) other than the decision-maker, although it may affect him too. It must affect such other person either: (a) by altering rights or obligations of that person which are enforceable by or against him in private law; or (b) by depriving him of some benefit or advantage which either (i) he has in the past been permitted by the decision-maker to enjoy and which he can legitimately expect to be permitted to continue to do until there has been communicated to him some rational ground for withdrawing it on which he has been given an opportunity to comment or (ii) he has received assurance from the decision-maker will not be withdrawn without giving him first an opportunity of advancing reasons for contending that they should not be withdrawn.

Such decisions or actions may be communicated or evidenced in a wide range of forms, including oral instructions;[35] oral decisions;[36] decisions communicated in letters;[37] conduct by officials;[38] policy announcements;[39] as well as other activities such as the issuing of circulars and the making of regulations.[40] Even primary legislation may be reviewed on the grounds that it conflicts with Community law.[41]

Non-justiciability

There are now very few areas of governmental activity which are beyond the reach of the supervisory powers of the courts. Those areas which remain outside the scope of judicial review are said to be 'non-justiciable' either

(1) because they involve the evaluation of information that the courts do not have available to them; or
(2) because the issues involved are too complex or otherwise inappropriate for resolution in a judicial forum; or
(3) because the issues, for historical or political reasons, are said to lie within the exclusive constitutional preserve of the Government.[42]

35 As in the GCHQ union ban.

36 *R v Chief Constable of the North Wales Police ex p Evans* [1982] 1 WLR 1155 (oral decision of the chief constable that an officer could resign or be dismissed).

37 *Padfield v Minister of Agriculture* [1968] AC 997; cf. *R v Secretary of State for Employment, ex p Equal Opportunities Commission* [1995] 1 AC 1 where it was held that a letter written by a minister to the Commission (stating that it was the government's view that a statute was not contrary to Community law) did not amount to a 'decision' capable of being reviewed because it did not itself alter any person's existing legal rights. The House of Lords held, however, that in these circumstances it was possible for the provisions of the statute themselves to be the direct subject of the challenge.

38 *R v IRC, ex p Rossminster* [1980] AC 952 (unlawful seizure of documents by officers of the Inland Revenue).

39 *Re Findlay* [1985] AC 318 (announcement of a change of policy at a Tory party conference later confirmed by a statement to Parliament challenged by judicial review).

40 See the Board and Lodging Regulations case study.

41 See e.g. *R v Secretary of State for Employment, ex p Equal Opportunities Commission* [1995] 1 AC 1.

42 See further A. Le Sueur, 'Justifying Judicial Caution: Jurisdiction, Justiciability and Policy', Chapter 8 in B. Hadfield (ed.), *Judicial Review: a thematic approach* (1995). See also discussion of polycentric issues at p. 549 below.

Under (3) above, these include certain exercises of prerogative powers relating, for example, to the making of treaties, defence of the realm, the grant of honours, the dissolution of Parliament and the appointment of ministers.[43] Decisions taken by ministers in the interest of national security have also been treated by the courts as non-justiciable.[44] Although potentially justiciable, the courts are also extremely reluctant to interfere in matters of high-level policy impinging, for example, upon public expenditure policy; nor will they readily review actions which have been approved by either or both Houses of Parliament.[45]

However, as discussed in the following chapters, even if the courts refuse to interfere with the actual decisions themselves they may be prepared to review the procedures that have been taken to ensure that government has acted fairly. The dynamic nature of the law, moreover, indicates that it cannot be assumed that activities which are unreviewable today will still be un-reviewable tomorrow.

PROCEDURAL EXCLUSIVITY

So far this chapter has examined situations in which, even though there is a person who wants to commence an application for judicial review, the courts may prevent this. In this last part of the chapter we move on to consider the common law rule of 'procedural exclusivity'. If a particular governmental action *is* capable of being subject to review, the applicant is normally required to use the Order 53 application for judicial review procedure, and not another procedure (such as bringing an action in the county court).[46]

Those planning to start litigation are faced with an array of possible routes. In the previous chapter we saw that, from the applicant's perspective, several features of the Order 53 judicial review procedure compare unfavourably with those of standard private law procedures: private law procedures are available locally, there is no leave stage, they have longer time limits, allow automatic cross-examination and discovery of documents.[47] This being so, potential litigants may want to avoid applying for judicial review and prefer one of the private law procedures.

[43] *Council of Civil Service Unions v Minister for the Civil Service* [1985] AC 374, per Lord Roskill (extracts at p. 672 below). Roskill's list of non-justiciable decisions has been dented because in *R v Secretary of State for the Home Department, ex p Bentley* [1994] QB 349 it was held that a minister's refusal to recommend a royal pardon was reviewable. This shows that courts are open to argument as to what is and is not justiciable; it is not a concept set in stone. It has recently been reaffirmed that courts will not review the exercise of discretion of the Attorney-General in relation to decisions taken in the execution of his public office: see *R v Solicitor General, ex p Taylor* (1996) 8 Admin LR 206. This is because of his 'unique constitutional position'.

[44] *Council of Civil Service Unions v Minister for the Civil Service*, especially Lord Diplock (extracts at p. 671 below); and *R v Secretary of State for the Home Department, ex p Cheblak* [1991] 1 WLR 890, especially Lord Donaldson MR at 904. Cf. Chahal v UK, *The Times*, 28 November 1996, in which the European Court of Human Rights indicated a willingness to review decisions taken by the UK government in the interests of national security.

[45] *Nottinghamshire County Council v Secretary of State for the Environment* [1986] AC 240; cf. *R v HM Treasury, ex p Smedley* [1985] QB 657.

[46] See *O'Reilly v Mackman* [1983] 2 AC 237.

[47] See p. 496.

The background

When the Law Commission originally considered reform of judicial review in the mid-1970s, its main objectives were to remove the technicality which had dogged the system for so long and to improve its flexibility. At the time litigants had to use special High Court procedures if they wanted to obtain one of the prerogative orders of certiorari, prohibition and mandamus.[48] If they wanted one of these forms of relief they could not at the same time ask for a declaration, injunctions or damages. Although the prerogative orders were widely considered to be the most appropriate to use in public law situations many of the leading cases, including *Ridge v Baldwin*[49] and *Anisminic v Foreign Compensation Commission*,[50] were proceedings for declarations rather than for prerogative orders.

The Law Commission recommended that people should be able to obtain all or any of these remedies using a single procedure—the application for judicial review. These recommendations were implemented in January 1978 by RSC, Order 53. Since a main concern of the Law Commission had been to improve access and flexibility, it was widely assumed that this reform increased the range of options available to litigants. In particular, it was assumed that litigants now had a choice whether to apply for judicial review under Order 53 or, if it appeared more appropriate, to use ordinary procedures (such as a writ or originating summons) to seek a declaration that a public body had abused or exceeded its powers. Certainly, the Law Commission had taken the view that its reform should not mean that the new judicial review procedure would be the only, the exclusive, way in which public law issues could be litigated.[51] There was also substantial judicial support for the view that litigants now had a choice of procedures.[52] This seemed to be reinforced by decisions such as that in *Royal College of Nursing of the United Kingdom v Department of Health and Social Security* where it was accepted that the RCN was able to commence private law proceedings (rather than make an application for judicial review) claiming a declaration that a circular issued by the DHSS was unlawful.[53]

This flexible approach was by no means universally adopted, however. Even as early as the late 1970s there were signs that some judges were taking the view that if the purpose of the litigation was to question whether a public body had exceeded or abused its powers, litigants had to use judicial review

[48] On these remedies, see Chapter 26.

[49] [1964] AC 40.

[50] [1969] 2 AC 147.

[51] See Law Com No 73 (1976), para. 4.

[52] See especially Lord Denning MR in *De Falco v Crawley Borough Council* [1980] QB 460.

[53] [1981] AC 800. Also *Gillick v West Norfolk Health Authority and DHSS* [1986] AC 112 where the plaintiff used a writ to seek a declaration that a DHSS circular advising doctors that they could give contraceptive advice to girls under the age of 16 without informing their parents was unlawful. She succeeded in the Court of Appeal but lost, again on the merits, when the department appealed to the House of Lords. In both courts it was accepted that jurisdiction existed to grant the declarations even though the remedy being sought was tantamount to a judicial review application.

and could not use private law procedures even though these might be more convenient or suitable to them.[54]

O'Reilly v Mackman

Several prisoners were found guilty by the Hull Prison Board of Visitors of having committed breaches of the Prison Rules during a riot. Their punishment included loss of remission which meant that they would have to serve the whole of their sentences, rather than be released early as good prisoners are normally. After some delay, they applied for declarations that the tribunal had acted in breach of the common law rules of procedural fairness and that its decisions were therefore invalid.[55] Either because they were out of time for judicial review or because they wanted to cross-examine witnesses in order to establish that the tribunal had acted unfairly and knew that this would be unlikely using judicial review, they used writs (and in one case an originating summons) to commence their legal challenges.

The Board applied to have the actions struck out on the ground that it was 'an abuse of the court's procedure' not to use judicial review in this situation.[56] At first instance, Pain J refused to accept this argument and said that the plaintiffs were free to choose whatever procedure they thought was in their best interests. Both the Court of Appeal and the House of Lords, however, disagreed with him and decided that because the plaintiffs had used the wrong procedure their actions should be dismissed, even before they were able to argue their case in full. Since the plaintiffs were out of time for judicial review they were effectively left without legal redress.

Lord Diplock gave the only speech on behalf of a unanimous House of Lords. He said that these prisoners could not use private law procedures because they did not have any private law rights to enforce. They may have lost remission, but remission was not a right, it was a privilege which would be granted to those prisoners who behaved themselves and who were not found guilty of breaches of prison discipline. While there was no right to remission, judicial review could be used to ensure that decisions depriving prisoners of remission were fairly and properly taken. Their claims against the Board were therefore claims in public law and for this reason judicial review had to be used. He said that:[57]

> . . . it would in my view as a general rule be contrary to public policy and, as such, an abuse of the process of the court, to permit a person seeking to establish that a decision of a public authority infringed rights to which he was entitled to protection under public law to proceed by way of an ordinary action and by this means to evade the provisions of Order 53 for the protection of such authorities.

[54] See e.g. *Heywood v Board of Visitors of Hull Prison* [1980] 1 WLR 1386.
[55] On common law procedural fairness, see Chapter 25 below.
[56] Under RSC, Ord 18, r 19. See further J. A. Jolowicz, 'Abuse of the Process of the Court: Handle with Care' (1990) 43 CLP 77, especially pp. 90–3.
[57] [1983] 2 AC 237 at 285D.

Notice that Lord Diplock bases his 'general rule' on public policy, saying that it is contrary to public policy to enable litigants to 'evade the provisions of Order 53' which protect public authorities and which promote the interests of 'good administration' by ensuring that decisions on the validity of official action are speedily taken. The main provisions to which he was referring are the leave requirement, the short limitation period, the absence of both automatic cross-examination and discovery of documents. Clearly, for Lord Diplock the public interest in protecting public administration and obtaining speedy decisions on the validity of official action was more important than the public interest in providing flexible access to those with legal grievances against officialdom.

The *O'Reilly* decision was immediately applied by the House of Lords to prevent a homeless person using the county court to question a decision of a local housing authority, despite the fact that the county court is clearly a more convenient, accessible and cheaper forum for adjudicating upon homeless persons' cases than judicial review.[58]

The problems following *O'Reilly v Mackman*

Although welcomed by public bodies, the decision was heavily criticized by many academics on grounds of principle and practice.[59] There were two main criticisms based on principle. First, it was argued that *O'Reilly* gave too little weight to the public interest in free access to the courts[60] and too much weight to the desire to protect public administration. Secondly, it was argued that the decision introduced a jurisdictional distinction between 'public law' and 'private law' which had never been known to English law and which was both contrary to traditional conceptions of the law[61] and out of step with general developments in government which were leading to a greater mix between the public and private sectors.[62]

Serious practical difficulties were also predicted. There was now a new question to be asked by litigants and their advisors: was their claim in public or private law? Unfortunately there was little guidance from the courts as to how this should be answered and there was every prospect that *O'Reilly* would lead to a new generation of procedural and technical distinctions of the very type that the Law Commission's inspired reform were intended to

58 *Cocks v Thanet District Council* [1983] 2 AC 286.

59 See e.g. M. Sunkin, 'Judicial Review Rights and Discretion in Public Law' (1983) 46 MLR 645; H. W. R. Wade, 'Public Law, Private Law and Judicial Review' (1983) 99 LQR 166; P. Cane, 'Public Law and Private Law: Some thoughts prompted by *Page Motors Ltd v Epsom and Ewell Borough Council*' [1983] PL 202; J. Beatson, '"Public" and "Private" in English Administrative Law' (1987) 103 LQR 34; A. Tanney, 'Procedural Exclusivity in Administrative Law' [1994] PL 51.

60 On the constitutional importance of access, see Chapter 21.

61 See the discussion of Dicey's theory of the rule of law and his argument that there should be no separation between 'ordinary' law and administrative law, Chapter 5 above. And see now John Allison, *A Continental Distinction in the Common Law* (1996).

62 Cf. C. Harlow, '"Public" and "Private" Law: Definition without Distinction' (1980) 43 MLR 241.

eradicate. These fears were reinforced by the uncertain breadth of Lord Diplock's general rule. While Lord Diplock recognized that his rule would not apply in every case, he gave little guidance as to when it would not apply. Two exceptions were specifically mentioned:

(a) 'where the invalidity of a decision arises as a collateral issue in a claim' made by a private law court procedure; and
(b) where 'none of the parties objects to the adoption of the procedure by writ or originating summons'.

Beyond these, all he said was that the existence of other exceptions should 'be left to be decided on a case by case basis'.[63] This was cold comfort for those applicants who ran the risk of finding themselves thrown out of court because judges had yet to establish clear principles.

The fears of the critics have proved to be well-founded. Since the decision in *O'Reilly* there has been considerable litigation, including a number of decisions of the House of Lords,[64] on whether particular claims can or cannot be raised in one type of proceeding rather than another. Among the most difficult questions considered have been the following.

(1) Can public law arguments be used to defend private law proceedings or criminal law prosecutions without resort to judicial review? The answer, in most cases, is that they can.[65]
(2) Are plaintiffs able to use private law proceedings when their claim involves both public law and private law issues? While at first the courts attempted to separate public law issues from private law issues, allowing some to proceed and others to fall,[66] they are no longer ready to do this.[67]
(3) Are plaintiffs able to use private law proceedings if public law and private law issues are so closely entwined with each other that they are difficult to separate? The answer today is that they normally can.[68]

Some judges have remained firm supporters of *O'Reilly* and have steadfastly resisted attempts to limit its application.[69] The general trend, however,

[63] [1983] 2 AC 237, 285.

[64] *Cocks v Thanet* [1983] AC 237: *Davy v Spelthorne* [1984] AC 262; *Wandsworth London Borough Council v Winder* [1985] AC 461; *Gillick v West Norfolk Area Health Authority* [1986] AC 112; *DPP v Hutchinson* [1990] 2 AC 783; *Roy v Kensington and Chelsea and Westminster Family Practitioner Committee* [1992] 1 AC 624; *R v Secretary of State for Employment, ex p Equal Opportunities Commission* [1995] 1 AC 1; *Mercury Communications Ltd v Director General of Telecommunications* [1996] 1 WLR 48.

[65] See *Wandsworth London Borough Council v Winder* AC 461; *DPP v Hutchinson* [1990] 2 AC 783; cf. *Bugg v DPP* [1993] QB 473, in which Woolf LJ held that a defendant could defend a prosecution by arguing that bylaws were 'bad on their face' but not by arguing that they were invalid by virtue of procedural impropriety. The latter argument could only be made by way of judicial review. See also, *Boddington v British Transport Police (1996) The Independent*, 12 July.

[66] *Davy v Spelthorne Borough Council* [1984] AC 262.

[67] *Roy v Kensington and Chelsea and Westminster Family Practitioner Committee* [1992] 1 AC 624.

[68] *Roy*, above.

[69] See Lord Woolf 'Public Law—Private Law: Why the Divide? A Personal View' [1986] PL 220 (but he has sometimes appeared somewhat less enthusiastic: see Zamir and Woolf, *The Declaratory Judgment* (2nd edn., 1993), para. 9.05). Cf. also Lord Woolf's recommendations designed to bridge the divide between public law and private law claims contained in *Access to Justice* (1996), Chapter 18.

has been to soften the harshness of the rule and to limit its application to situations where the issues are concerned solely with public law and in which private law rights do not exist at all.

Is Lord Diplock consistent?

It is worth considering at this stage whether Lord Diplock's 'open' approach to standing in *IRC v National Federation of Self-Employed and Small Businesses Ltd*[70] (where he dissented in stating that an interest group should be able to use judicial review to vindicate the rule of law) is compatible with his 'narrow' approach to procedural exclusivity in *O'Reilly*. At first sight the two judgments seem inconsistent. In *National Federation* he argues that the courts should not be prevented from adjudicating upon the legality of official action by outdated technical rules which restrict access. Yet in *O'Reilly* he prevents a plaintiff from getting into court because he has chosen the wrong procedure without even considering the merits of the claim being made. One way of reconciling these two decisions is to say that in *O'Reilly* Lord Diplock was concerned with forcing litigants to use the specially designed judicial review procedure in public law cases, in much the same way drivers might be forced away from country lanes and on to the motorway system. In *National Federation* Lord Diplock is located at the motorway's entrance, waving motorists along and encouraging them to use it. Whether the system is as effective or as efficient as he seems to believe it to be is another matter. However, it is almost certainly the case that Lord Diplock believed that both these decisions were ultimately concerned with maximizing access to judicial procedures which were best suited for applying the rule of law to government.

Recent case law

In *Roy v Kensington and Chelsea and Westminster Family Practitioner Committee* a general practitioner sued his General Practitioner Committee after it had used its powers under regulations to reduce his practice allowance by 20 per cent on the ground that he had not devoted a 'substantial amount of his time to the General Practice'. The Committee, relying on *O'Reilly*, applied to have the action struck out arguing that the decision to reduce the allowance could only be challenged by an application for judicial review because Dr Roy did not have a private law right to receive any particular allowance. In a mirror image of the *O'Reilly* litigation, the first instance judge accepted this argument and struck out Dr Roy's action. Roy appealed successfully to the Court of Appeal and the Court of Appeal's decision was upheld by the House of Lords.

The House of Lords said that two approaches could be taken to the *O'Reilly* procedural exclusivity rule: these were labelled the 'broad' and the

[70] [1982] AC 617, discussed in Chapter 21.

'narrow' approach. If a 'broad' approach were taken, use of judicial review would only be insisted upon if private law rights were not in issue at all. Presumably, this is a 'broad' approach because it allows litigants a broad choice of procedure, except where private law rights are not involved at all. The 'narrow' approach requires judicial review to be used in all proceedings challenging decisions of public bodies (even where there may be private law rights mixed with the public law issues), subject to some exceptions. This may be described as being narrow because the presumption is that the litigant's freedom is restricted unless the case falls within an exceptional category. Unfortunately the House did not say which of the two approaches is the correct one, although several judges clearly preferred the 'broad' approach. We therefore cannot be sure whether Dr Roy's case was allowed to proceed because it did not fall within the *O'Reilly* rule at all (on the grounds that Dr Roy did have private law rights) or because it fell within an exception to the rule. Lord Lowry, however, did conclude his judgment by saying that:[71]

> . . . unless the procedure adopted . . . is ill suited to dispose of the question at issue, there is much to be said in favour of the proposition that a court having jurisdiction ought to let a case be heard rather than entertain a debate concerning the form of proceedings.

In *Mercury Communications Ltd v Director General of Telecommunications*[72] there was a dispute between the two main telecommunications companies in the United Kingdom. Under the licensing scheme set up by the Telecommunications Act 1984, British Telecom (BT) had to enter into an agreement to let Mercury use its (BT's) telephone lines. Such an agreement ran for five years, after which either party had the right to require a renegotiation. As the parties were unable to agree in their renegotiations, they requested a determination by the statutory regulator. When this had been made, Mercury considered that the Director General had misinterpreted provisions in the licensing scheme and it therefore used the originating summons procedure to seek a declaration from the High Court on the true construction. The Director General and BT applied to strike out these proceedings, contending that the issues raised by Mercury were governed solely by public law and that it therefore ought to have used the Order 53 procedure.

The House of Lords refused to strike out Mercury's originating summons. Their Lordships echoed the approach taken in *Roy*: the overriding question was whether Mercury was abusing the process of the court and it was of particular importance to retain flexibility as to the procedures by which litigants could choose to initiate their claims. Here the dispute was essentially over the effect of the terms of a contract between two parties and Order 53 was not so peculiarly well suited for dealing with the case that it would be a misuse of the court to allow the matter to be dealt with by private law procedures.

[71] [1992] 1 AC 624, 655. In *R v Secretary of State for Employment, ex p Equal Opportunities Commission* [1995] 1 AC 1 Lord Lowry called for further consideration by the House of the *O'Reilly* rule.

[72] [1996] 1 WLR 48.

If practitioners and commentators thought in the wake of *Roy* and *Mercury* questions on procedural exclusivity were of diminishing importance, they were wrong. In *British Steel plc v Customs and Excise Commissioners*[73] Laws J distinguished *Roy* and struck out a writ by which British Steel claimed restitution and repayment of excise duty levied on oil used as part of the steel-making process inside blast furnaces. The Hydrocarbon Oil Duties Act 1979 gave the Commissioners power to exempt oil from excise duty where it was not used as a fuel. In its writ British Steel claimed that it had been entitled to such relief from excise duty and that the Commissioners had acted unlawfully in demanding payment. Laws J held that the 'whole question' of the case was whether the payments made by British Steel were pursuant to unlawful demands. Accordingly, British Steel should first have made an application for judicial review to determine this issue of public law (which it had not done); only if successful on that application could it go on to make a private law claim for restitution. British Steel's restitutionary claim was entirely contingent on a public law decision in its favour. It was therefore unlike the claim for money in *Roy*, where the doctor had a 'settled and existing private law right', albeit one the value of which depended upon a public authority's opinion as to certain factors given to it by legislation to decide.

The Law Commission's 1994 report

The Law Commission has now added its weight to those who advocate the 'broad' approach and it is worth quoting its justification for doing so at length. We have added the emphasis.[74]

> 3.13 We consider that the primary rationale for requiring the use of Order 53 is the need to take account of public interest factors in *purely public law* cases. First, there is the constitutional function of judicial review and the public interest to ensure that public authorities observe the law and are prevented from relying on invalid decisions. Secondly, there is the interest in enabling individuals to obtain a remedy for grievances which are substantiated. Thirdly, there is the need for speed and certainty in administrative decision-making, particularly in cases where a large section of the community will be affected by the decision. *In a case involving only public law issues the public policy interest in ensuring speed and certainty in administrative decision-making may be more important than the private interest of the individual litigant in obtaining a substantive hearing and, if appropriate, a substantive public law remedy*, and is thought to justify, in particular, a very much shorter time limit.
> 3.14. *On the other hand, where a case involves a properly constituted private law cause of action* or where it is necessary to decide whether a person should be prevented from raising a defence in such an action, on the ground that it involves an issue of public law, *a more flexible procedural approach is needed to ensure that private law rights are not 'trumped' by public law justifications*. Where a case involves disputed issues of fact use of a writ procedure may also be appropriate . . .

[73] [1996] 1 All ER 1002.
[74] *Administrative Law: Judicial Review and Statutory Appeals* (Law Com No 226).

The current situation summarized

The current situation appears to be as follows:

(1) A version of the *O'Reilly* rule still remains and it is still necessary to distinguish between public and private law claims.
(2) Although uncertain, it appears that the courts in general will prefer the 'broad' approach and will only insist on the use of judicial review if the matter is purely a public law matter.
(3) A case will involve purely public law issues if:

   (i) the litigant cannot rely on contractual, tortious, or other propriety rights, or establish that a statutory duty is owed to him personally; and
   (ii) the claim is against a body which is in principle amenable to judicial review.

The flip side of the coin

At this point we return to the proposition that judicial review cannot be used to question decisions of public bodies which solely affect private law rights and which do not raise public law issues.[75] In *R v East Berkshire Health Authority, ex p Walsh*,[76] for example, the applicant began an Order 53 application seeking to quash a health authority's decision to dismiss him from his job. His arguments included the allegation that there had been an improper delegation of authority and the officer who purported to dismiss him lacked the power to do so. The Court of Appeal held that his claim was essentially a private law matter and was therefore inappropriate for judicial review. Although the Rules of Court allow judges to deal with cases which are brought by way of judicial review as if they had been started by writ (that is as private law actions)[77] in this case the Court of Appeal refused to allow this to be done.[78]

Discussion of *Walsh* illustrates the difficulty of separating private law and public law issues. While judicial review cannot be used to question decisions which solely affect private law rights the process may be used in cases where private law rights or interests are involved, provided there is a sufficient public law element. In one case, for example, the courts reviewed a local authority's decision not to enter into commercial contracts with Shell because of Shell's contacts with South Africa.[79] By contrast, when a firm which had unsuccessfully tendered for a contract with the Lord Chancellor's Department to report court cases tried to challenge the department using

[75] See 'Who and what is subject to Judicial Review', p. 508 above.
[76] [1985] QB 152. See also *R v Secretary of State for the Home Department, ex p Benwell* [1985] QB 554 and *R v BBC, ex p Lavelle* [1983] 1 WLR 23.
[77] RSC, Ord 53, r 9(5).
[78] On the technical ground that the only remedy Walsh had applied for was certiorari, a remedy which cannot be obtained in a private law action.
[79] *R v Lewisham London Borough Council, ex p Shell UK Ltd* [1988] 1 All ER 938.

judicial review, it was held that judicial review was unavailable because the decision taken was essentially a commercial one which did not have a sufficient 'public law element'.[80] The case might have been decided differently had the department been required by legislation to follow a particular procedure, or to take a particular range of factors into account in its contracting decisions because here the legislative requirement would have added a greater 'public law element'.[81]

As the Law Commission has pointed out, the problem highlighted by cases such as *Walsh* and *O'Reilly* is that litigants may find themselves caught in a 'Catch-22' situation in the sense that they may find themselves defeated by the procedures whichever way they choose to proceed. Had Walsh started his case as a private law claim the authority may well have argued that his action was an abuse of process under the *O'Reilly* rule on the grounds, for instance, that the thrust of his argument was that the public body had improperly delegated its powers and he had no private law rights in respect to that delegation.[82]

WHERE TO GO FROM HERE

Having in the previous chapter considered issues relating to gaining access to judicial review and the appropriateness and scope of judicial review in this chapter, we now move on in the following three chapters to consider the grounds of review.

Questions

1. On what grounds might it be argued that attempts by Parliament to exclude the jurisdiction of the courts are 'unconstitutional'?

2. If bodies are not subject to judicial review how is the exercise of their legal powers to be controlled?

3. Why do the courts appear reluctant to review the decisions of bodies established by agreement?

4. When will the courts be prepared to review contractual decisions of public bodies?

5. What justifications are there for the principle of procedural exclusivity?

[80] *R v Lord Chancellor's Department, ex p Hibbit and Saunders* [1993] COD 326.

[81] See further P. P. Craig, *Administrative Law* (3rd edn., 1994). Cf. S. Arrowsmith, 'Judicial Review and the Contractual Powers of Public Authorities' (1990) 106 LQR 277. Craig disagrees with Arrowsmith's argument that virtually all contractual relations entered into by public bodies should be subject to public law principles. He does so on the ground that a distinction should be drawn between ordinary commercial contracts, say for furnishings, and contracts which are entered into as part of a regulatory scheme or as an aspect of government. Judicial review, he argues, should not be available in relation to the former but should be in relation to the latter.

[82] This type of problem should be alleviated if the Law Commission's recommendations on transfer between private law and judicial review are implemented.

23

ILLEGALITY

. . . the first principle of good administration is to ensure that you understand the legal basis for the action that you wish to take, and are satisfied that the statue or statutory instrument under which you intend to act in fact gives you the power to do what you want.

The Judge Over Your Shoulder (1994), p. 7

The above advice to civil servants encapsulates the basic principle that ministers and official bodies must have legal authority for their actions.[1] This principle, traditionally associated with the *ultra vires* doctrine,[2] is now usually described as the principle of 'legality'. This term is more flexible and less technical than *ultra vires* because it emphasizes that official bodies can be challenged not only if they have exceeded their power but also if they have abused or misused their power, or otherwise failed to act in conformity with their legal obligations. Although legal authority may be conferred by sources other than statute, such as by the prerogative, in most situations public bodies derive their powers from statute. The Benefits Agency cannot, for example, simply *choose* to pay a person a particular sum as Income Support; powers to pay welfare benefits must be granted by statute or delegated legislation. Likewise, as the *Cotton* case illustrates, ministers can only introduce new regulations if they have been given specific powers to do so, and in so doing they must ensure that they follow the required procedures.[3] Nor can a local authority just *choose* (as can a citizen) to make speculative transactions on the money market[4] or ban hunting on its land.[5]

The message for ministers and officials is that they must pay very careful attention to the meaning of statutory provisions. This message is also relevant to students and practising lawyers. When confronted with a potential judicial review issue it is always necessary to consider whether the authority has complied with relevant legislation or acted within the ambit of prerogative

[1] See further Chapter 7 above.
[2] On *ultra vires*, see p. 471.
[3] *R v Secretary of State for Social Services, ex p Cotton* (1985) *The Times*, 14 December. See Chapter 27.
[4] *Hazell v Hammersmith and Fulham London Borough Council* [1992] 2 AC 1.
[5] *R v Somerset County Council, ex p Fewings* [1995] 1 All ER 513 (Laws J) and [1995] 1 WLR 1037, CA, discussed in Chapter 7. (A resolution by a council to ban hunting on its own land for moral reasons was quashed.)

powers.[6] One consequence is that judicial review litigation often involves a rather specific enquiry into the meaning of statutes with judges having to decide between the public body's interpretation of its powers and the applicant's argument that it has in some way exceeded or abused these powers.

The *Smith* case

Consider the following case. Smith challenged the decision of the Registrar General of Births, Deaths and Marriages to refuse to provide him with a copy of his birth certificate.[7] The relevant law was contained in the Adoption Act 1976, s 51:

> . . . the Registrar General . . . shall on an application made . . . by an adopted person a record of whose birth is kept by the Registrar General and who has attained the age of 18 years supply to that person . . . such information as is necessary to enable that person to obtain a certified copy of the record of his birth.

One of the general policies to be furthered by this Act was to enable adopted children to trace their birth parents. To this end, the section appeared to give an absolute entitlement to obtain copies of birth certificates. The courts held, however, that despite the words used it was not Parliament's intention to give such an absolute right in all cases.

The facts of the case were 'stark and disturbing'.[8] Several years ago Smith, for no apparent reason, murdered a man in a park and was sentenced to life imprisonment. One night in prison he killed his cell mate, apparently believing him to be his adoptive mother. Smith had been adopted when a very small child and he blamed his misfortunes on his adoptive parents. He was detained in Broadmoor Special Hospital. There he decided he wanted to find out who his natural parents were. His solicitor applied to the Registrar General on his behalf for his birth certificate. The Registrar General refused to provide it. Smith challenged that decision in judicial review proceedings. In the judgment given by the High Court, Watkins LJ said:[9]

> In our very firm view, having regard to the potential menace to the safety in the future of the natural mother of the applicant and possibly others related to him by blood or otherwise, a public policy consideration positively demands that we refuse to grant the relief sought by the applicant. *It is, we think, beyond belief that Parliament contemplated that an adopted child's right to obtain a birth certificate should be absolute come what may.* The public at large, knowing the essentials of the facts, we consider would, we have no doubt, be outraged if that were so . . . We appreciate, of course, that a public policy consideration cannot be recognised . . . unless there is . . . a compelling reason for it to exist . . . But where, as here, the need for that

6 But note the anomalous powers of self-regulatory bodies such as the Panel on Take-Overs and Mergers, discussed at p. 510.

7 *R v Registrar-General, ex p Smith* [1991] 2 QB 393. See further A. P. Le Sueur, 'Public Policies and the Adoption Act' [1991] PL 326. For an interesting case in which *Smith* was distinguished, see *X (a Minor) (Adoption Details: Disclosure)* [1994] Fam 174.

8 *Per* Sir Stephen Brown P at 397.

9 [1990] 2 QB 253, 269 (emphasis added).

to be done is glaringly clear, the public policy consideration must be regarded as paramount.

So, while recognizing that the words of the statute gave persons an absolute entitlement to a copy of their birth certificate, the court found this unpalatable on the facts of the case and therefore made a fresh 'policy' decision that Smith had no right to see his certificate. Rather than ask 'what do the words of the statute show Parliament's intention to have been?' the judges asked (and answered) the rather different question: 'what would Parliament have intended had it considered these facts when passing the statute?'. The Court of Appeal affirmed the High Court's decision.[10]

The uncertainty of legislation

This case shows that compliance with legislation is not necessarily a straightforward matter and it is not always easy for a public body to know what is required or for citizens to know what their rights are. Several basic reasons for uncertainty and doubt exist.[11] The legislation may be drafted in a way that appears designed to defeat attempts to understand it. Rules may be very long, be subject to a number of qualifications and contain subclauses. Words and phrases may be archaic, technical, ambiguous or vague.[12] Even if the words appear to be easy to understand they may be uncertain, or unduly harsh or absurd in the context of specific situations. (Did the clear words of the Adoption Act 1976 really mean that a person with Smith's background had an absolute right to their birth certificate?) Doubt might also arise because words have been interpreted in different ways in different contexts, or because the same provisions have been given different meanings by different judges.[13] Given the difficulties presented by complex and developing law, it is perhaps not surprising that even the most conscientious official or government lawyer may get the law wrong. But does this provide an excuse for governmental illegality?[14]

INTERPRETATION OF LEGISLATION

For the reasons just explained, interpretation of legislation is central to judicial review litigation. Often both parties are able to present plausible arguments as to why the legislation should be interpreted in the way that best suits their position, leaving judges with difficult and constitutionally important choices. Once interpreted, statutes mean what judges say they mean and the litigants

[10] [1991] 2 QB 393.

[11] See further William Twining and David Miers, *How to Do Things with Rules* (3rd edn., 1991), Chapter 10.

[12] See below.

[13] In *ex p Cotton*, the three judges in the Court of Appeal gave different meanings to the term 'consultation': see p. 649.

[14] Cf. the comments of Tony Baldry MP following *ex p Cotton*, p. 264 above.

(and the rest of us) are bound by this meaning, at least until the provisions are reconsidered by a higher court or amended by further legislation. Understanding how judges go about the task of interpretation is therefore central both to a lawyer's ability to present arguments which judges will find persuasive and to an appreciation of the role played by judges in the constitutional system.

There is a considerable literature on statutory interpretation which seeks to expose, explain and debate the way judges go about their interpretative task.[15] Over the years much of the debate has focused on the competing merits and constitutional implications of two broad approaches. These have been given various labels by commentators but they may be conveniently referred to as the literal and purposive approaches to interpretation.[16]

Literal approaches

The main characteristic of the literal approach is the desire to give effect to the intention of Parliament as it has been expressed by the *actual words* used in the legislation. Judges using this approach see their task as limited to interpreting the specific words or phrases which have been used by Parliament even where this may produce meanings which appear unjust or even absurd in the circumstances.[17] Underlying this approach is judicial concern not to trespass into Parliament's legislative function by 'adding' language which was not used by Parliament.

Purposive approaches

By contrast, the purposive approach does not limit judges to the actual words which have been used. The purposive approach is based on the view that the 'true' intention or purpose of Parliament is not always adequately expressed in the words themselves, perhaps because the legislature cannot foresee every situation or because it is impossible to draft rules covering every eventuality. Given these difficulties it may be assumed that the legislature expects judges to ensure that legislation works and is applied to specific cases as needs arise. Using this approach judges are prepared to infer words into the legislation if in their view this is necessary in order to further the true purpose of the legislation.[18] We saw an example of this in *ex p Smith* where judges assumed, despite the wording used, that Parliament could not have intended to provide an absolute right to a birth certificate.

In the past these two approaches sometimes appeared to reflect two distinct and warring camps of judicial opinion. One of the most famous skirmishes

[15] See generally John Bell and Sir George Engle, *Cross on Statutory Interpretation* (3rd edn., 1995) and Francis Bennion, *Statutory Interpretation* (2nd edn., 1992 and supplements).

[16] Twining and Miers use the terms 'formalist' and 'instrumentalist': see *How to Do Things with Rules*, pp. 166–9.

[17] Lord Esher, *R v Judge of the City of London Court* [1892] 1 QB 273, 290.

[18] See further D. J. Galligan, *Discretionary Powers* (1986), pp. 292–308.

occurred in *Magor and St Mellons Rural District Council v Newport Corporation*.[19] In the Court of Appeal Denning LJ, a great advocate for the purposive camp, stated in his dissenting judgment that:[20]

> We do not sit here to pull the language of Parliament and of Ministers to pieces and make nonsense of it. That is an easy thing to do, and it is a thing to which lawyers are too often prone. We sit here to find out the intention of Parliament and of Ministers and carry it out, and we do this better by filling in the gaps and making sense of the enactment than by opening it up to destructive analysis.

In the House of Lords, Lord Simonds wryly stated that 'the dissenting opinion of Denning LJ appears to invite some comment':[21]

> This [Denning LJ's] proposition . . . cannot be supported. It appears to me to be a naked usurpation of the legislative function under the thin disguise of interpretation. And it is the less justifiable when it is guesswork with what material the legislature would, if it had discovered the gap, have filled it in. If a gap is disclosed, the remedy lies in amending the Act.

Another famous clash of approaches occurred in *Liversidge v Anderson*[22] over the meaning of the words 'if the Secretary of State has reasonable cause to believe any person to be of hostile origin'. Did these words mean that there *had to be* 'reasonable cause to believe' or did they mean that the Home Secretary could act if *he thought that there was* 'reasonable cause to believe'? The majority in the House of Lords adopted the second interpretation. Lord Atkin disagreed and delivered a scathing attack on his brethren arguing that they had read words into the legislation which gave the executive more freedom than Parliament had intended. This case reminds us that literal approaches are not necessarily less 'liberal' or more pro-executive than 'purposive' approaches.

The general approach today

Open conflict of this sort is rare today and several recent cases have indicated the purposive approach is now the normal and more desirable technique. In the decision of the House of Lords in *Pepper (Inspector of Taxes) v Hart* it was emphasized by Lord Griffith that:[23]

[19] The boundaries of Newport Corporation were expanded into areas previously controlled by two other councils with the result that these two councils lost, and Newport gained, revenue. Statute provided a scheme whereby newly expanded councils would pay compensation. In this case the two affected councils were shortly afterwards merged into one. Newport argued the two councils had been amalgamated to form a completely new authority which had not been adversely affected by Newport's expansion and that it therefore did not have to compensate them. Did the statute require compensation to be paid in these circumstances?

[20] [1950] 2 All ER 1226, 1236.

[21] [1952] AC 189, 191. The House of Lords upheld the majority of the Court of Appeal holding that the two new councils were not entitled to any compensation.

[22] [1942] AC 206. See further J. A. G. Griffith, *Judicial Politics Since 1920* (1993), Chapter 2.

[23] [1993] AC 593, 617.

> The days have long passed when the courts adopted a strict constructionist view of interpretation which required them to adopt the literal meaning of the language. The courts now adopt a purposive approach which seeks to give effect to the true purpose of the legislation.

This is not to say that judges no longer focus on the actual words used or that they will never adopt literalist techniques. On the contrary, judges normally apply the actual words where these are clear and unambiguous and will do so even when one of the parties alleges that this produces an unjust result. In *Griffiths v Secretary of State for the Environment*,[24] for example, legislation said that a person who had been refused planning permission could appeal but could only do so within six weeks of the date on which the decision letter was signed and dated by the Secretary of State. The majority of the House of Lords held that this time limit applied even though the letter was never posted. In *Lees v Secretary of State for Social Services* the House of Lords held that a blind person who could only go out with a human guide did not qualify for mobility allowance because his disability did not mean that he was 'unable to walk or virtually unable to do so'.[25]

Literal approaches also tend to be taken where legislation is extremely complex and technical or where judges are reluctant to intrude either because they lack expertise or they are aware that their decisions may have political or policy implications which are beyond their competence. In situations such as these literalism may provide a safe haven for the judiciary. During the 1980s central government's policy to use the law to control local government expenditure led to disputes between local and central government being taken to the courts over issues of funding. As well as being highly political these cases involved very technical legislation. Two cases illustrate the type of issues raised.

In *R v Secretary of State for the Environment, ex p Merton London Borough Council*[26] the court had to determine the meaning of provisions of the Rate Support Grant Act 1988, which established the mechanisms for determining how much grant each local authority received from the Department of the Environment. In assessing the grant the Secretary of State took into account the total expenditure of local authorities. The total expenditure was based on the figure which each authority specified as the 'amount estimated [to be the] local authority's total expenditure' (para. 1(1) of Sched 1). Unfortunately for the London Borough of Merton, a person in their finance department made a slip when calculating the council's estimated total expenditure with the result that the council stood to be deprived of £8 million worth of grant from central government. The court held that the words used in the Act were clear and unambiguous and it was the duty of the court to give effect to them. The statutory provisions made the figure submitted to the Secretary of State the basis for his calculations. Whether the figure was correct or incorrect was

24 [1983] 2 AC 51.
25 [1985] 1 AC 930.
26 [1990] COD 450.

immaterial. The court 'could not provide a remedy for the obvious injustice'. This is a case where the meaning of the words used in the legislation was clear—even though they operated harshly and produced a result which meant that Merton's grant was not based on a true estimate of its total expenditure, as Parliament seemed to intend it to be.

In the late 1980s the Conservative government decided to limit or 'cap' the power of local authorities to raise money by local taxation (in those days, business rates and Community Charge). Lambeth, a Labour-controlled borough in London, was one of the local authorities affected. In 1990 its budget was capped by the Secretary of State for the Environment because he believed the budget to be excessive and he wanted to reduce the amount of Community Charge that the council was proposing to levy on individuals in its area. After the minister had set a cap on the council's annual expenditure, the council lowered the Community Charge it proposed to levy, but not by the full amount envisaged by the minister. In *R v Lambeth London Borough Council, ex p Secretary of State for the Environment*[27] the minister challenged the council's action. The Court of Appeal held, after considering the relevant provisions of the Local Government Finance Act 1988 in great detail, that the council had not acted unlawfully in setting their new Community Charge and that the Secretary of State had misunderstood his powers. The following extract from the judgment of Mustill LJ gives some indication of the frustration felt by judges who were forced to decipher the legislation:[28]

> I acknowledge at once that this conclusion is based on a reading of the Act *which may not have corresponded with the general intention of those who caused it to be enacted.* The important word here, however, is general. In the lengthy conflict now in progress between central and local government for the control of local taxation, central government has the whip hand, since it has the power to enact legislation which the courts must seek to enforce in the *spirit as well as in the letter*. Nevertheless, the courts must have material upon which to work. Here I find it impossible to discern with any accuracy the spirit of s 35(5) simply because I believe that in all the flurry of legislation, evasive action and counter-legislation the point under review has not been fully thought out. *This being so, we must adhere to the written word.*

Although the government intended the Act to give the Secretary of State powers to cap the actual Community Charge set, and not just the council's total expenditure, the 1988 Act did not achieve this. The government acted quickly to change the law after the Court of Appeal's decision by introducing the Community Charges (Substitute Setting) Act 1991 to achieve what government wanted the earlier legislation to do.

Intention of Parliament or legislative purpose?

It is common to find both literal and purposive approaches being justified by reference to the obligation upon judges to give effect to parliamentary

27 [1991] COD 132.
28 At p. 134 (emphasis added).

intentions. While this appeals to the constitutional principle of Parliament's legislative supremacy and to the separation of powers, the idea that Parliament actually has an intention is purely a fiction.[29] After all, it may be asked, how can an *institution* have an intention? We only have to look at the progress of the Sunday Trading Bill[30] and the debates on the Board and Lodging Regulations[31] to see that the views and intentions of MPs vary. Some of the MPs will have voted against the legislation; do their intentions count? Even those who supported it may have done so for a variety of reasons, including that they were instructed to do so by their party whips; some may have had little idea of its specific details, let alone the reason why particular words were used in specific places.

Added to this is the problem that intentions of those who were originally responsible for legislation may become less helpful as times change. The constitution of the United States may be taken as an example. One way of interpreting this constitution is to ask, what did those who drafted it intend? While this question may be helpful in some contexts, in others it is not at all helpful. For example, today the intentions of the founding fathers on issues of racial equality would be regarded as totally anathema: when the constitution was drafted black slavery was still accepted and slaves were regarded as 'beings of an inferior order; and altogether unfit to associate with the white race, either in social or political relations'.[32] Resort to the intentions of those responsible for legislation runs into similar problems in the United Kingdom. For instance, the Supplementary Benefits Act 1976 that was considered by the courts in the *Cotton* case had originally been introduced into Parliament by a Labour government, yet it was being used by a Conservative Secretary of State to achieve policy that was very different to that for which the legislation was originally drafted.

Partly as a concession to these problems judges now tend to refer to 'the purposes of the legislation' rather than to 'the intention of Parliament'. This emphasizes that judges are more concerned with giving effect to legislation than to fictional parliamentary intentions. Emphasis on legislative purpose also acknowledges that the courts are increasingly required to interpret texts which have not been produced by Parliament. European Community treaties, regulations and directives are the most obvious examples, but judges may also be required to interpret other international treaties such as the ECHR.[33]

Before leaving the question of interpretation there are two further issues which deserve attention. The first is concerned with discerning the legislative purpose. If judges do seek to further the legislative purpose how do they go about discovering what that purpose is? The second concerns what are called

[29] See M. Radin, 'Statutory Interpretation' (1930) Harvard LR 863 and Twining and Miers, *How to Do Things with Rules*, pp. 202–11.

[30] See Chapter 9.

[31] See Chapter 11.

[32] Taney CJ in *Dred Scott v Sanford* (1857) 60 US (19 Howard) 393.

[33] See p. 534 below.

the common law presumptions which Parliament is assumed to have intended to respect. As we will see, use of these principles can lead to rather unexpected results.

Understanding the legislative purpose

In order to help them understand statutory provisions it is accepted that judges should interpret the specific words with which they are concerned in the context of the statute as a whole. It is also now accepted that if the meaning of the words is unclear they can refer to *Hansard* reports of debates in Parliament, government publications relevant to the legislative history of the provisions, and relevant international treaties.

The courts should examine the statute as a whole to determine its policy and objects

It is sometimes difficult to understand what words mean without considering them in the context of the legislation as a whole. This is an important approach for public lawyers, particularly when legislation confers discretionary powers without specifically imposing limits on the scope of those powers. In this situation the courts say that the scope of the discretion is limited in the sense that it must be exercised in accordance with the policy and objects of the Act and that these must be discerned by judicial consideration of the Act in its totality. The approach is often associated with the House of Lords' decision in *Padfield v Minister of Agriculture, Fisheries and Food.*[34]

In this case the House had to decide whether a minister's decision not to establish a committee to look into a particular matter was lawful. The Act said that a committee would be established 'if [the minister] . . . so directs'. It said nothing about when or how he should 'so direct'; nor did it specify the criteria to be employed in deciding whether to 'so direct'. In other words, the language used in the Act seemed to give him an unfettered discretion in the matter. In fact, the House of Lords said that this was not the case. Even if the specific words did not provide limits to his power, his discretion had to be exercised in accordance with the policy and objects of the legislation looked at as a whole. In this particular case the Act was concerned with milk marketing, but the minister's decision had been made in order to save him political embarrassment. Since this had nothing to do with milk marketing his decision was based on irrelevant factors and was therefore an unlawful abuse of his powers.

Parliamentary debates

Until 1992 there was one major practical problem facing judges who wanted to discover the actual intention of Parliament. This was the rule that counsel and judges could not refer to the *Hansard* reports on parliamentary debates of the legislation as an aid to construction.[35] The basic reason for this prohibition

[34] [1968] AC 997.

[35] In a number of cases, e.g. *Pickstone v Freemans plc* [1989] AC 66, the courts had allowed reference to *Hansard* for the more general purpose of finding out government policy.

was practical. It was thought that if lawyers were able to refer to *Hansard* this 'would add greatly to the time and expense involved in preparing cases' without greatly assisting the judges.[36] Although criticized (particularly by Lord Denning MR), it was not until 1992 in the House of Lords' decision in *Pepper (Inspector of Taxes) v Hart*[37] that the rule was partially abandoned. Parliamentary debates are now available to the court as an aid to statutory construction where, subject to any question of parliamentary privilege, three conditions are satisfied:

(a) the legislation is ambiguous or obscure, or the literal meaning leads to an absurdity;
(b) the material relied on consists of statements by a minister or other promoter of the bill together with any other parliamentary material needed to understand the statements; and
(c) the statements relied upon are clear.

The scope and implications of the new approach remain uncertain and they are not altogether uncontroversial.[38] At the practical level use of *Hansard* may increase the cost and difficulty of providing legal advice about the meaning of legislation. Many solicitors and some barristers will not have good access to a library which has *Hansard* and the Official Reports of Standing Committee debates on bills. Even if they are able to refer to *Hansard*, lawyers may find that parliamentary speeches provide little help in explaining how specific statutory provisions are to be understood. As well as these practical problems, it has also been suggested that *Pepper v Hart* might be constitutionally dangerous. Oliver, for example, argues that it may reduce the courts' ability to apply common law presumptions which are designed to protect fundamental principles such as the presumption that access to the courts is only to be restricted by express words in legislation: 'This point, taken with the likelihood that ministers will only make statements that are favourable to government,' she argues, 'may well reinforce the dominance of government in the constitution and reduce the power of the courts to operate as checks against the dominant executive.'[39]

Government publications

Courts can look at reports produced by Royal Commissions, the Law Commission and White Papers in order to discover the background to the

[36] Per Lord Reid in *Beswick v Beswick* [1968] AC 58, 73.

[37] [1993] AC 593.

[38] In *R v Warwickshire County Council, ex p Johnson* [1993] AC 583 for example, the House of Lords referred to *Hansard* even though the language of the statute did not appear ambiguous. In *Three Rivers DC v Bank of England, The Times*, 8 January 1996, Clarke J held that the court can look at *Hansard* to discover the general purpose of an Act where the strict criteria in *Pepper v Hart* (see (a)–(c) above) do not apply.

[39] Dawn Oliver, '*Pepper v Hart*: a suitable case for reference to *Hansard*?' [1993] PL 5, 13. See further Scott C. Styles, 'The Rule of Parliament: statutory interpretation after *Pepper v Hart*' (1994) 14 OJLS 151; F. Bennion, 'Hansard—Help or Hindrance? A draftsman's view of *Pepper v Hart*' (1993) 14 Statute LR 149; T. St J. N. Bates, 'Parliamentary Material and Statutory Construction' (1993) 14 Statute LR 46.

legislation and the 'mischief' that it was intended to remedy. However, there has been a difference of opinion as to whether they can use such reports as an aid to interpreting specific provisions even where a report contains a draft bill which uses wording which exactly corresponds to the words in the later legislation.[40] Since the decision in *Pepper v Hart* this reluctance may well diminish.

R v Broadcasting Complaints Commission, ex p BBC[41] provides a recent example of a case where the court examined *Hansard* and the pre-parliamentary history of legislation to help discern the meaning of provisions of the Broadcasting Act 1990. Here the BBC challenged the decision of the Broadcasting Complaints Commission to look into a complaint made by the National Council for One Parent Families (NCOPF) about a *Panorama* programme, 'Babies on Benefit', which NCOPF claimed presented an inaccurate and unfair image of single parents. The essence of the BBC's argument was that the NCOPF did not have *locus standi* to make a complaint since they were not a person affected by the programme because they did not have a 'direct interest' in it as required by s 144(2) of the 1990 Act. Having explored the legislative history, Brooke J said that he could find no evidence that Parliament intended to allow the Complaints Commission to consider complaints by national bodies about the way a programme treated hundreds and thousands of unidentified people whom they purported to represent.

International treaties

International treaties such as the ECHR are not as such part of UK domestic law unless they have been incorporated into the law by statute.[42] Nevertheless, it is assumed by the courts that Parliament intends to act in conformity with the United Kingdom's international obligations, unless clear words to the contrary are used. For this reason treaty provisions can be used by litigants and by judges to help interpret domestic legislation.[43] In *ex p BBC*, to which we have just referred, the court interpreted the provisions of the Broadcasting Act 1990 in accordance with Art 10 (freedom of expression) of the ECHR: the desire to comply with the principle of freedom of expression led the court to give a restrictive interpretation to provisions in the 1990 Act which sought to define who may bring formal complaints about television programmes to the Commission and therefore to adopt a limited view of NCOPF's standing.

[40] See *Black-Clawson International Ltd v Papierwerke Waldhof-Aschaffenburg AG* [1975] AC 591 where the law lords divided on this.

[41] [1995] COD 284.

[42] See p. 112.

[43] *R v Secretary of State for the Home Department, ex p Phansopkar* [1976] QB 606; *R v Chief Immigration Officer Heathrow Airport, ex p Bibi* [1976] 1 WLR 979. In *Brind v Secretary of State for the Home Department, ex p Brind* [1991] 1 AC 696 the House of Lords held that the statutory power authorizing the Secretary of State to impose limits on broadcasting was not ambiguous and that recourse to provisions of the ECHR (particularly those dealing with freedom of expression) was therefore not justified. On the question whether the common law can be ambiguous, see Sir John Laws, 'Is the High Court the Guardian of Fundamental Constitutional Rights' [1993] PL 58, 67–8.

Common law presumptions

Judges use certain presumptions of the common law to help them interpret legislation.[44] As well as the presumption that Parliament intends to act in conformity with international law other examples include presumptions that Parliament does not intend to permit official bodies to act unreasonably or irrationally; to permit bodies to delegate their powers; or to oust the jurisdiction of the courts. These presumptions are said to reflect certain basic principles of the rule of law. Although often vague and uncertain in their application, they can generate significant arguments in judicial review cases. Indeed, the presumption that Parliament does not intend official bodies to act unreasonably or irrationally is often given as a justification for many of the principles of review which are currently used and which are considered in the following chapters.[45] The presumption against delegation is considered later in this chapter.[46] The best-known example of the use of the presumption against ousting the jurisdiction of the courts was in *Anisminic v Foreign Compensation Commission*[47] where the courts effectively demolished an attempt to exclude judicial review of the Foreign Compensation Commission.

The principle of implied powers

One final common law principle needs to be considered. It goes without saying that bodies may do what they have express statutory power to do. However, the common law also contains the principle of implied powers, which enables public bodies to do whatever is *reasonably incidental* to the exercise of their express powers.[48] For instance, a local authority was able to establish a printing, bookbinding and stationery works because the court regarded this as being incidental to its express functions.[49] On the other hand, a local authority authorized to operate a tram service could not operate a bus service.[50] In the context of the powers of local government, this principle is contained in s 111(1) of LGA 1972.

> subject to the provisions of this Act and any other enactment . . . a local authority shall have power to do any thing . . . which is calculated to facilitate, or is conducive or incidental to, the discharge of any of their functions.

[44] These have been described as 'framework principles': 'principles which are not found in the statute, but which the court presumes to have been in Parliament's mind, and which can therefore be used either as an aid to construction of the statutory language, or as an assumed limitation on the scope of apparently unfettered discretion'. See Sir Robert Carnwath, 'The Reasonable Limits of Local Authority Powers' [1996] PL 244, 259.

[45] In particular the so-called *Wednesbury* principles considered in Chapter 24 and the common law principles of procedural fairness considered in Chapter 25 (exemplified by the 19th-century decision in *Cooper v Wandsworth Board of Works* (1863) 14 CB (NS) 180 where Byles J said that even where 'there are no positive words in a statute requiring that the party shall be heard, yet the justice of the common law will supply the omission of the legislature').

[46] See p. 542.

[47] [1969] 2 AC 147, discussed at p. 506.

[48] *Attorney-General v Great Eastern Railway Co* (1880) 5 App Cas 473, per Lord Selbourne LC.

[49] *Attorney-General v Smethwick Corpn* [1932] 1 Ch 562.

[50] *London County Council v Attorney-General* [1902] AC 165.

The scope of this provision turns on the meaning of the word 'functions'. It seems that in order to justify action under s 111 local authorities have to establish that the action facilitates, or is conducive or incidental to the discharge of 'functions' which are themselves expressly authorized by legislation. It has recently been held, for example, that s 111 does not allow local authorities to charge for giving developers advice before an application for planning permission is made. Although a local authority has power to give advice because this facilitates the consideration of planning permission (a function that is specifically authorized by legislation) the court held that charging for this advice was only incidental to the giving of advice and not the consideration of planning permission. As one judge put it, the charges were 'incidental to the incidental'.[51]

DIFFERENT TYPES OF STATUTORY OBLIGATIONS AND POWERS

The discussion of the need for public bodies to comply with their legal obligations has so far examined the role of the courts in interpreting legislation and noted that public bodies have certain implied powers in addition to those expressly spelt out in statute. We now consider in more detail the different *types* of obligations and powers which may be conferred on public bodies by Parliament. There are many ways in which these may be classified, but for present purposes attention can be drawn to three sets of distinctions:

(a) where legislation lays down a procedure to be followed the obligation may be either essential (mandatory) or non-essential (directory);
(b) statutory obligations may be detailed and precise or broad and general;
(c) legislation may impose a firm duty on a body to do some thing, a qualified duty, or a discretion.

Essential and non-essential procedural requirements

Legislation often requires official bodies to follow certain procedures before or during the course of taking their decisions.[52] Previous chapters have discussed the procedural requirements imposed by the Statutory Instruments Act 1946 on the making of delegated legislation as well as the more specific procedural obligations to consult with the SSAC imposed by s 10 of the Social Security Act 1980.[53] Legislation may also require bodies to notify interested parties of their plans by placing advertisements in a newspaper, to

[51] See *R v Richmond-Upon-Thames London Borough Council, ex p McCarthy & Stone (Development) Ltd* [1992] 2 AC 48. See also *R v North Tyneside Metropolitan Borough Council, ex p Allsop* (1992) 90 LGR 483 (the Court of Appeal held that s 111 did not authorize payments under a voluntary redundancy scheme in excess of levels permitted by regulations). See also *Crédit Suisse v Allerdale BC* [1996] 4 All ER 129 and *Crédit Suisse v Waltham Forest LBC* [1996] 4 All ER 176.

[52] The common law also imposes procedural requirements: see Chapter 25.

[53] See p. 245.

give those affected opportunities to comment or object,[54] to notify those affected by their decisions of rights to appeal or of opportunities to complain,[55] or to give reasons for their decisions. This last requirement is now recognized as being particularly important and is worth considering more closely.

Statutory requirement of reasons

There is no general statutory requirement imposed on ministers and other public bodies to provide reasons for their decisions. However, where a specific obligation is imposed, it is extremely important. First, the requirement to give reasons forces decision-makers to think through why they have reached their decision: it has been said that this is a valuable self-discipline for official bodies.[56] Secondly, it provides those affected with insight into how and why the official body acted as it did, thereby creating confidence that the system is working justly and rationally. Thirdly, reasons may show that the body has acted illegally and provide a basis for a challenge which otherwise could not be mounted; the *Padfield* case[57] is a good example of this, where the reasons given by the minister showed that he had acted for improper purposes. In this context it may be noted that the obligation imposed by s 64 of the Housing Act 1985 upon local housing authorities to give reasons in homeless persons cases has been an important factor in enabling people to use judicial review in this field. Finally, a failure to give reasons when they are required by statute may itself be a ground of challenge.

Where reasons are required they must not be vague or unintelligible and they must deal with the substantial points involved in the decision.[58] Officials cannot, for example, simply repeat standard reasons as if making a 'ritual incantation' or simply say something like 'I have considered all other arguments you have raised but they are not sufficient to affect the decision I have reached'.[59] In one case a decision of a Mental Health Review Tribunal was held to be unlawful because instead of giving reasons that were specific to the particular case, it had merely recited the statutory words which permitted it to refuse to discharge the patient.[60]

The effect of failing to comply with a procedural requirement imposed by statute

The legal importance of procedural requirements is sometimes said to depend on whether the requirement is 'mandatory' or 'directory'. If mandatory, failure to comply invalidates the action taken; if directory, failure to comply does not invalidate the action. Following this approach the basic task is to

[54] *R v Lambeth Council, ex p Sharp* (1986) 55 P & CR 232.

[55] *London & Clydeside Estates Ltd v Aberdeen District Council* [1980] 1 WLR 182.

[56] *Per* Sir Louis Blom-Cooper QC (sitting as a Deputy Judge), *R v Islington London Borough Council, ex p Trail* [1994] 2 FCR 1261.

[57] [1968] AC 997, discussed above.

[58] *Re Poyser and Mills' Arbitration* [1964] 2 QB 467.

[59] *The Judge Over Your Shoulder*, p. 15.

[60] *Bone v Mental Health Review Tribunal* [1985] 3 All ER 330.

determine whether the requirement is intended to be mandatory or directory by looking at the words of the statute. Terms such as 'must' or 'shall' usually suggest that the procedure is mandatory, whereas terms such as 'may', and phrases such as 'if it is reasonably practicable', suggest that the obligations are only directory.

In assessing the importance of a failure to follow a procedural step nowadays the courts, however, rarely base their decision solely on the wording of the statute. They are more concerned about the actual importance of the interests safeguarded by the procedural requirement and the impact of the defect on the litigant and the public.[61] In other words, today judges are more likely to ask the question 'is the requirement essential or non-essential?' than they are to ask: 'do the words used indicate whether Parliament intended the requirement to be mandatory or directory?'[62]

R v Lambeth London Borough Council, ex p Sharp provides an example of this approach.[63] Here the Court of Appeal held that a grant of planning permission was invalid because a notice of the proposed development published in a local newspaper had failed both to specify the period during which objections should be made and failed to say that objections had to be in writing. In considering the legal effect of these failures the court asked:[64]

> What is the particular provision designed to achieve? If, as here, it is designed to give the public an opportunity to make objections to what is proposed, then the court is bound to attach considerable importance to any failure to comply with the requirements.

One of the implications of this more contextual approach is that even where judges acknowledge that there has been a failure to comply with mandatory requirements, they may nevertheless decide that it is not essential to invalidate the resulting action in the circumstances of the case. In *R v Secretary of State for Social Services, ex p Association of Metropolitan Authorities*,[65] for example, Webster J accepted that the Secretary of State had failed to comply with his mandatory obligation to consult with the AMA before making or amending housing benefit regulations. However, by the time the case had come to court the regulations had already been brought into effect and were already being used by officials. In order to avoid administrative inconvenience, the judge decided not to quash the regulations.

The *AMA* decision provides a graphic (and in this case rather unfortunate) example of the way judges can temper the strict requirements of the law in the interests of public administration. It was unfortunate because consultation is often time-consuming and inconvenient to ministers and other government bodies who want to press on with their plans as quickly as possible.

61 See p. 473.
62 In so doing their approach is moving closer to the test in Art 173 of the EC Treaty which empowers the ECJ to annul decisions of Community institutions on the grounds that they have failed to comply with an essential procedural requirement.
63 (1986) 55 P & CR 232.
64 *Per* Woolf LJ at 239–40.
65 [1986] 1 WLR 1.

The case seems to imply that government may be able to escape the consequences of procedural failures by hasty implementation of policy so that if there is a challenge the practical difficulties involved in invalidating the action may persuade the court to withhold any formal remedy from the applicant even if the challenge is successful on the law.[66]

Precise and general duties and powers

Many of the duties and powers discussed earlier in the chapter were quite specific, for example the duty imposed by the Secretary of State for Social Security to consult with the SSAC before making SIs about entitlement to benefits,[67] even though the department had room to decide what information to give to the committee and how long the consultation process should last. Some duties, however, are much broader and more general. For instance, the Secretary of State for Health is under an obligation to:[68]

> continue the promotion in England and Wales of a comprehensive health service designed to secure improvement—
>
> (a) in the physical and mental health of the people of those countries, and
> (b) in the prevention, diagnosis and treatment of illness, and for that purpose to secure the effective provision of services in accordance with this Act.

It would be unlikely that a person (for example, a person seeking treatment) would be able to obtain judicial review of any alleged failure by the Secretary of State under this provision.[69] Duties as broad as this have been called 'duties of imperfect obligation' because the courts are extremely reluctant to make orders forcing compliance with them.[70] In part this is because the reasons for non-compliance are often related to policy associated with the allocation of resources which the courts tend to treat as non-justiciable.

An Act of Parliament setting up an administrative scheme often includes a mixture of general and more precise powers and duties. The Children Act 1989, for example, places upon local authorities a general duty 'to safeguard and promote the welfare of children within their area'.[71] It also imposes more specific duties, including the obligation to 'open and maintain a register of disabled children within their area'.[72] Clearly the duty to open and maintain a register of disabled children is far more specific than the general duty to safeguard the welfare of children; for one thing, it is much easier to tell whether an authority has fulfilled the duty to open a register than to determine whether it is safeguarding children, and for this reason its performance is likely to be easier to enforce by legal challenge.

66 On the court's discretion to withhold remedies, see pp. 614–17.
67 See p. 245.
68 National Health Service Act 1977, s 1(1).
69 See *R v Cambridge District Health Authority, ex p B* [1995] 1 WLR 898.
70 De Smith Woolf and Jowell *Judicial Review of Administrative* (1995), para. 16–010.
71 S 17(1).
72 Sched 2, para. 2(1).

Even in cases where a public body has failed to comply with a fairly specific obligation, however, the courts may be reluctant to intervene. Section 8(1) of the Education Act 1944 provides that it shall be the duty of every local education authority to:

> secure that there shall be available for their area sufficient schools—
>
> (a) providing primary education . . . and
> (b) . . . secondary education . . .
>
> and the schools available for an area shall not be deemed to be sufficient unless they are sufficient in number, character and equipment to afford for all the pupils opportunities for education . . .

During the late 1980s the Inner London Education Authority (ILEA) was failing to provide sufficient school places in Stepney and several hundred children were going without education. Parents began legal proceedings against the authority but were unsuccessful.[73] The court held that where an authority was faced with a situation where, without any fault on its part, it could not comply with the standards set by s 8(1) it was not automatically in breach of that duty. (Here there had been a rapid increase in the school-age population.) The court went on to hold that even if the authority *was* in breach, it would have used its discretion to refuse the mandatory order sought by the parents because the authority was doing all it could to remedy the situation. For good measure, the court also held that the parents had no grounds for a claim for damages for the tort of breach of statutory duty because s 8(1) was intended to benefit the public in general rather than to give any individual enforceable rights.[74] Where a broad and general statutory duty is placed on local authorities, such as that in s 8(1) of the Education Act, the statute often gives a minister a so-called 'default power' to take proceedings to compel authorities to comply with the duty.

The distinction between duties and discretion

As we have seen, statutes often impose firm obligations on public bodies to do some thing, such as to open and maintain a register of disabled children. A council has no choice in the matter: it has to set up the register or face the prospect of legal proceedings. Statutes can also give authorities *discretionary* powers. The Children Act 1989 can again be used to provide two contrasting illustrations.

> Every local authority shall take *reasonable steps* to identify the extent to which there are children in need within their area.[75]

[73] *R v Inner London Education Authority, ex p Ali* [1990] COD 317.
[74] See p. 627.
[75] Sched 2, para. 1(1) (emphasis added).

> Every local authority shall provide such family centres *as they consider appropriate* in relation to children within their area.[76]

In both these examples local authorities appear to have duties, but what is it that they have a duty to do? Suppose you are a legal advisor to the social services committee of a local authority. A council considering its obligations under Sched 2, para. 1(1) will probably want to know what is meant by 'reasonable steps'. Would it be sufficient, for example, to place adverts in prominent places such as libraries or clinics inviting those who are in need, or have knowledge of children in need, to contact the authority? Or must an authority do more? A cautious legal advisor might remind the authority of two things. First, the provision refers to 'reasonable steps'; it does not say that they can take 'such steps as *the authority considers* reasonable'. Had this form of words been used it would be easier to argue that the authority is free to decide what steps are required. Secondly, the advisor would point out that the term 'reasonable' is measured by applying objective standards. In other words, the courts will ask 'what would a reasonable local authority do?'. The cautious lawyer would therefore advise that the authority must act in accordance with general standards, tempered perhaps by local circumstances where these can be shown to be relevant.

In the second example local authorities are to provide such family centres 'as they consider appropriate'. Clearly, here they have much more freedom because the legislation specifically allocates to them the decision to decide what is appropriate. In this situation a lawyer might well be asked whether the authority has any legal duty at all, or only a power to provide these centres. Again the cautious lawyer might say two things. First, they might agree that it is misleading to say that the authority has a duty to provide family centres and that it is more accurate to say that there is a power rather than a duty to do so.[77] But the lawyer might add that this does not mean that authorities have a completely free hand. To take an extreme example, they could not decide not to provide these centres for reasons that had nothing at all to do with the objects and the policy of the Children Act (the *Padfield* rule).[78] In other words, the authority must comply with the principles of public law concerned with the exercise of discretionary powers, which are discussed in the next chapter.

[76] Sched 2, para. 9(1) (emphasis added).

[77] The provision does not say that authorities are to provide such family centres as are 'necessary' or 'reasonably required' or even 'as are appropriate'. Cf. s 18 of the Act. While duties are usually imposed by words such as 'shall' or 'must' and powers by words such as 'may' it has been held that a duty may exist even if legislation uses the word 'may': see *Re Shuter (No. 2)* [1960] 1 QB 142; *Alderman Backwell's Case* (1683) 1 Vern 152; *R v Roberts* [1901] 2 KB 117; *R v Metropolitan Police Commissioner, ex p Holloway* [1911] 2 KB 1131.

[78] See p. 532 above.

UNLAWFUL DELEGATION

As already mentioned it is presumed that bodies are not free to delegate their statutory powers to others unless statute specifically authorizes them to do so. Here we consider the way in which unauthorized delegation may give rise to arguments of 'illegality'.[79]

The non-delegation principle is particularly important in a system that is as centralized as that of the United Kingdom. It reflects the basic idea that legal powers are only possessed by those to whom powers have been conferred by Act of Parliament and it is not for ministers or any other public body to shift their powers and responsibilities on to others or to sub-delegate. In practice, however, delegation is a necessary and important part of practical government and often occurs even though it is not expressly permitted. This being so judges are obliged, in this as in many other areas, to reconcile basic theory with the practical needs of modern government.

Examples of delegation (some of it lawful, other instances unlawful) can be seen at several points in this book. In the *GCHQ* case the instruction directed at ordering civil servants to relinquish their trade union membership was issued by the Prime Minister under powers lawfully delegated to her by Civil Service Order in Council.[80] In *R v Secretary of State for Social Security, ex p Cotton* one of the key arguments was that the regulations were unlawful because they purported to delegate more power to the Secretary of State than was permissible under the Supplementary Benefits Act 1976.[81]

The rule against unlawful delegation has been applied in a wide variety of contexts. It has enabled suspended dock workers to challenge their suspension on the grounds that the local dock labour board[82] had unlawfully delegated power of suspension to the port manager.[83] The Director of Public Prosecutions has been held to be unable to delegate certain decisions to non-lawyers within the Crown Prosecution Service.[84] The chairman of the Monopolies and Mergers Commission has been held to lack authority to seek the Secretary of State's approval for the Commission to abandon consideration of a reference that had previously been made to it by the government.[85]

Bearing in mind that delegation is a necessary aspect of the governmental system, Parliament has made life easier by recognizing the need for delegation within local authorities. Section 111 of LGA 1972 permits authorities to delegate functions to committees, sub-committees, officers of the authority, or other local authorities.[86] No similar provision exists to authorize

[79] This principle is sometimes referred to by the Latin maxim *delegatus non potest delegare* (an agent cannot delegate his authority).

[80] See p. 276.

[81] See Chapter 27.

[82] Part of a statutory scheme, now abolished, for regulating employment at harbours.

[83] *Barnard v National Dock Labour Board* [1952] 2 All ER 424.

[84] *R v DPP, ex p Association of First Division Civil Servants* (1988) *The Times*, 24 May.

[85] *R v Monopolies and Mergers Commission, ex p Argyll Group plc* [1986] 1 WLR 763.

[86] But this would not permit delegation to a single member of a committee: *R v Secretary of State for Education and Science, ex p Birmingham City Council* (1985) 83 LGR 79 where it was held that a proposal to close a school was unlawful when the date fixed for the closure was decided upon by a single committee member.

delegation within central government, however. As far as central government is concerned the applicable principles are judge-made and the leading statement is often referred to as the *Carltona* principle.

The *Carltona* principle

Is it lawful for ministerial powers to be exercised by civil servants? In *Carltona Ltd v Commissioners of Works*[87] Lord Greene MR, acknowledging that ministers can never personally attend to all their functions, said that where functions are exercised under the authority of a minister by a responsible departmental official:

> Constitutionally, the decision of such an official is . . . the decision of the minister. The minister is responsible. It is he who must answer before Parliament for anything that his officials have done under his authority . . .

Although Lord Greene MR refers to the political accountability of ministers it has been assumed that Lord Greene MR also meant to say that ministers should be legally as well as politically responsible for the actions of their officials. We have already seen how in the political context ministerial responsibility has helped to protect the internal machinery of central government from scrutiny.[88] It has had a similar affect in the legal context as well, for one of the results of the *Carltona* principle has been to prevent the courts becoming involved in questions affecting the allocation of powers within departments. Until recently it has been assumed that ministers are free to delegate or to 'devolve' powers, as judges nowadays prefer to put it, without legal interference.[89] In *Re Golden Chemical Products Ltd*,[90] for instance, it was held that although legislation formally gave power to petition for the winding up of a company to the minister, he could require an official to take the necessary decisions on his behalf.

However in *R v Secretary of State for the Home Department, ex p Oladehinde*[91] the House of Lords indicated that not all delegations within departments would be lawful. Here the House considered the lawfulness of 'delegation' by the Home Secretary of powers under the Immigration Act 1971 to immigration officers. These included the power to decide whether steps should be taken to deport people. Although in this instance this delegation was held to be lawful, the House made it clear that it might have been unlawful for the

87 [1943] 2 All ER 560.

88 See p. 141.

89 In *Bushell v Secretary of State for the Environment* [1981] AC 75, a case in which a pressure group challenged the fairness of procedures adopted in deciding whether a motorway should be built, Lord Diplock said that in practice a minister inevitably relies on the 'collective knowledge, experience and expertise of [civil servants] in the department of which, for the time being, he is the political head'.

90 [1976] Ch 300. On the application of the *Carltona* principle to executive agencies, see M. Freedlord, 'The Rule Against Delegation and the *Carltona* Doctrine in an Agency Context' [1996] PL 19.

91 [1991] 1 AC 254.

minister to delegate greater powers to immigration officers, such as power to take decisions automatically affecting the immigration status of the persons concerned. This decision indicates that the courts may now be prepared to investigate the way powers are allocated within government. If so, it will open up an area of government which has been previously closed to legal scrutiny.

Relying on others

Delegation of the type that we have just been considering tends to be deliberate and conscious. However, it is possible for bodies to delegate powers without deliberately doing so. As we have seen, bodies are often under a legal requirement to consult with others about their plans. Even where it is not required by law, consultation often makes good administrative sense and is normally to be encouraged. On occasion consultation appears to be a purely formal exercise with those involved feeling that little notice has been taken of their views. However, suppose a body does take notice of what people say and acts in accordance with their opinions. In this situation public bodies may find themselves accused of deferring to others and thereby abrogating their decision-making responsibility.

H Lavender & Son Ltd v Minister of Housing and Local Government[92] provides one of the best-known illustrations. The company applied for planning permission to extract minerals from high-quality agricultural land. The local planning authority refused planning permission and Lavender appealed to the Minister of Housing and Local Government, whose responsibility it was to consider appeals in such cases. The minister rejected the appeal. His decision letter contained the following two sentences:

> It is the Minister's present policy that land in the reservations should not be released for mineral working unless the Minister of Agriculture, Fisheries and Food is not opposed to the working. In the present case the agricultural objection has not been waived, and the Minister has therefore decided not to grant planning permission . . .

In allowing Lavender's challenge to the minister's decision, Willis J said that:

> It seems to me that by adopting and applying his stated policy he has in effect inhibited himself from exercising a proper discretion . . . in any case where the Minister of Agriculture [objects] to mineral working . . . I think that the minister has fettered himself in such a way that in this case it was not he who made the decision for which Parliament made him responsible.

The judge accepted that the minister could have a policy on how to deal with cases of this type and that it was appropriate for him to consult with the

[92] [1970] 1 WLR 1231.

Minister of Agriculture where agricultural land was involved. Here, however, he had effectively given the Minister of Agriculture a veto and consequently had lost control over the decision.

Notice that the judge refers to the minister as having 'fettered his discretion'. This is a reference to another important principle, namely that those charged with exercising discretion must always ensure that they do in fact exercise their discretion. This is considered in the following chapter.

SUMMARY

In the vast majority of situations public bodies derive their powers and duties from statute. Whether bodies have satisfied the test of legality therefore usually depends on interpretation of the relevant statutory provisions. Here we have considered the techniques used to interpret statutes and the different types of powers and duties commonly conferred by statute. The chapter has also considered the general principle that if powers have been conferred upon particular bodies, those bodies cannot delegate these powers to others, unless permitted to do so by Parliament.

Questions

1. 'The main problem with the literal approach is that it may produce a result which is absurd or patently unjust in the circumstances of the case. The main problem with the purposive approach is that it enables judges to decide upon policy issues when they are not democratically accountable for their decisions.' Do you agree? Which of the two approaches do you favour? Why?

2. Is it desirable or dangerous for the courts to use *Hansard* as an aid to construction?

3. Is there such a thing as the 'intention of Parliament'?

4. Can you think of any justifications for not requiring official bodies to give reasons for their decisions?

5. Imagine you are responsible for drafting the Sports Facilities Bill. The minister wants:

(a) to ensure that local authorities monitor the need for sports facilities in their areas;
(b) to confer upon local authorities freedom to provide swimming pools where these are thought to be needed; and
(c) to consider what cycle tracks are needed and to provide these if they feel they can afford to do so.

Draft the relevant provisions.

6. Is the internal organization of government departments any of the courts' business?

7. What advice would you give a minister in the light of the *Lavender* decision?

24

JUDICIAL REVIEW OF DISCRETIONARY POWER

> The very concept of administrative discretion involves the right to choose between more than one possible course of action upon which there is room for reasonable people to hold differing opinions as to which is to be preferred.
>
> *Per Lord Diplock, Secretary of State for Education and Science v Tameside Metropolitan Borough Council*[1]

> It is no part of [the purpose of review] to substitute the opinion of the judiciary or of individual judges for that of the authority constituted by law to decide the matters in question.
>
> *Per Lord Hailsham LC, R v Chief Constable of the North Wales Police, ex p Evans*[2]

This chapter considers the principles used by the courts to review the way public bodies exercise their discretionary powers.[3] Here we are at the very cutting edge of the rule of law, for it is in this area, probably more than any other, that the authority of the courts is likely to clash with the power of government. We have already seen that discretion implies the freedom to exercise choice and to reach decisions with which others might disagree.[4] If discretion has been conferred on ministers or other authorities, it may be assumed that Parliament believes it to be in the public interest for these authorities to have that freedom. After all, Parliament does not need to confer discretionary power: it can impose duties upon the authorities and require them to apply rules.

The scope of discretionary freedom depends, at least initially, on the terms on which discretionary power has been granted. (We say initially because even where these terms do not impose specific limitations on an authority's freedom, limitations may ultimately be implied by the courts if discretionary decisions are challenged.) Generally speaking, the broader the discretionary freedom the narrower will be the scope for judicial intervention; vice versa,

[1] [1977] AC 1014, 1064.

[2] [1982] 1 WLR 1155, 1160.

[3] For general discussions of discretion see K. C. Davis, *Discretionary Justice: a Preliminary Inquiry* (1971); J. L. Jowell, 'The Legal Control of Discretionary Power' [1973] PL 178; D. J. Galligan, *Discretionary Powers: a Legal Study of Official Discretion* (1986); Keith Hawkins (ed.), *The Uses of Discretion* (1992). For a jurisprudential analysis see Ronald Dworkin, *Taking Rights Seriously* (1977), especially pp. 31–9.

[4] See p. 540.

the narrower the discretion the greater the scope for judicial review.[5] However, before this generalization can be applied there are several other issues to consider.

Objective and subjective discretion

In the previous chapter we saw that the Children Act 1989 imposes various duties and grants various powers to local authorities in respect of children in need. In some situations authorities are told what they have to do and they have little freedom in the matter. The obligation to open and maintain a register of disabled children within their area is such an example.[6] In other situations they are permitted more room for manoeuvre. They are required, for example, to take 'reasonable steps' to identify the extent to which there are children in need in their area. Here their discretion is limited to determining what steps are to be taken and the term 'reasonable' implies that their decision must accord with what others would regard as 'reasonable'. This type of discretion may be described as being an *objective discretion* because it has to be exercised on the basis of objective criteria: criteria which cannot be chosen by the authority itself. If courts are called upon to review this type of discretionary power they feel able to enquire into whether these criteria have been considered without fearing that they are thereby trespassing on to the authority's area of responsibility.

By contrast, a local authority has power to 'provide such family centres as *they consider appropriate*'.[7] This power appears to be limited only by the need for authorities to consider what they regard as being appropriate. Since the statute emphasizes that it is the authority's view that matters, the discretion may be described as being *subjective* in nature. Such powers are less easily challengeable as judges are reticent about interfering in issues which are for authorities to decide. This, however, is not to say that apparently subjective powers are unreviewable. As we have already seen in our earlier discussion of the *Padfield* case, judges will insist that powers be exercised in accordance with the policy and the objects of the legislation.[8] If, to take a hypothetical example, an authority decides that it is not appropriate to establish any family centres because in its view it is morally wrong to spend public money on maintaining the institution of the family, then the decision would almost certainly be reviewed on the grounds that the authority has abused its power and acted on the basis of considerations which are irrelevant to the Children Act 1989.

5 We use the terms 'broad' and 'narrow' discretions; others have used expressions such as 'strong' and 'weak': see Ronald Dworkin, *Taking Rights Seriously*. Goodin refers to 'informal discretion' (where language is vague and options are merely implicit in the statement of the rule) and 'provisional discretion' (where officials are subject to review and their discretion is therefore not final): see R. E. Goodin, 'Welfare, Rights and Discretion' (1986) 6 OJLS 232, 236.

6 See p. 539.

7 See p. 541.

8 *Padfield v Minister of Agriculture, Fisheries and Food* [1968] AC 997. See p. 532.

Process and substance

It is one of the basic tenets of judicial review that the courts will not review the merits of decisions, unless those decisions constitute an abuse of power, have been improperly taken, or are unreasonable in the sense of being absurd or perverse. One judge has summarized this by saying that:[9]

> Judicial review is concerned, not with the decision, but with the decision-making process. Unless that restriction on the power of the court is observed, the court will in my view, under the guise of preventing an abuse of power, be itself guilty of usurping power.

This dictum is often referred to and is useful in so far as it reminds litigants that judicial review cannot be used simply to appeal against a decision which they dislike and reminds judges that they cannot interfere with decisions solely on the grounds that they would have decided the issue differently. However, the dictum must be used with caution. There are two main reasons for this. First, it is often impossible to draw a clear distinction between decision-making processes on the one hand and the quality of actual decisions on the other. While courts and other tribunals may adopt two quite distinct stages—first hearing the evidence and/or the legal arguments and then, having done so, reaching a decision—not all bodies work in this way.[10] Secondly, in practice the courts do not limit themselves to reviewing the process of decision-making. It is now accepted that in addition to issues of process and procedure, the courts can also review the quality of decisions—'substantive review', as it is sometimes called. Indeed, debate about the grounds on which they may do so lies at the centre of current controversy over the role of judicial review in the United Kingdom.

Different types of body possess different types of discretion

Discretion is conferred on a wide variety of public bodies and the courts are readier to interfere with the decisions of some than with others. Generally speaking, the courts are more reluctant to impose restrictions on ministers than they are on local authorities. Two main reasons recur in the judgments. One focuses on the theory of the separation of powers which dictates that

[9] Lord Brightman, *R v Chief Constable of the North Wales Police, ex p Evans* [1982] 1 WLR 1155, 1173–4.

[10] For example the situation in *Franklin v Minister of Town and County Planning* [1948] AC 87 (also considered in the next chapter). Residents of Stevenage opposed to its designation as a 'New Town' challenged this decision on the grounds that the minister had decided his policy and had made up his mind *before* holding a public inquiry at which they were able to present their formal objections. The House of Lords accepted that the minister had been biased, but held that this was inevitable and legitimate in situations where decisions are taken by ministers in order to further their government's policy. Here the policy determined both the decision-making process and his eventual decision. This case also illustrates the way in which decision-making procedures are interrelated. One of the arguments used was that the minister had failed to consider the residents' objections to his plan. They believed that this was not only unfair, but also that it adversely affected the quality of his actual decision.

courts should not intervene in matters for which ministers are politically rather than legally accountable. The other centres on the policy content of many ministerial decisions. The courts generally feel more competent reviewing decisions which affect specific individuals or groups than they are reviewing decisions which have wider and more complex implications. This is because courts, being courts, feel at ease with disputes which have two sides—the public authority versus the individual. Bipolar disputes of this type enable the courts to see what the parties believe the issues to be and then to adjudicate upon the matter knowing how their decision will affect the parties.[11] Many discretionary decisions taken by public bodies, however, do not fall within this bipolar model. Rather than affecting only specific individuals, decisions may affect whole communities and authorities may have to weigh and consider a complex range of factors extending beyond the interests of particular individuals or groups. Consider, for example, a ministerial decision to go ahead with a motorway scheme. In making such a decision a minister will not only take into account the interests of those who live on or near the proposed route, but also the interests of business and other economic factors impinging upon national interests. There will also be environmental implications, agricultural implications and implications for other transport systems. Discretionary powers of this type have been described as 'polycentric' because they are complex and have many ('poly') centres of concern.[12] Court procedures are ill-equipped to handle issues of this sort. Judges lack the necessary expertise and, because of the nature of adversarial adjudicative procedures, they will lack the necessary information and will be unable to assess the wider implications of their actions. Where they are asked to review discretionary decisions involving polycentric and complex issues, they are instinctively cautious and may decide either that the decision is not suitable for judicial resolution (that it is 'non-justiciable')[13] or that in the circumstances of the case they will exercise their discretion not to intervene or not to grant a remedy.[14]

Legal and non-legal constraints on discretion

Although this chapter focuses on the legal constraints on discretion, remember that discretionary freedom is also limited by non-legal factors, such as the need to manage limited financial resources or to act quickly. Indeed, as we pointed out when we discussed administrative culture in Chapter 20, officials may regard non-legal constraints as being of greater relevance than constraints which might be imposed by the courts should a decision be challenged. We have seen that in recent years not only have various steps been taken to alert officials to the principles of review, but the judges have also

[11] Abram Chayes, 'The Role of the Judge in Public Law Litigation' (1972) 89 Harvard LR 1281.

[12] See Lon Fuller, 'The Forms and Limits of Adjudication' (1978) 92 Harvard LR 353.

[13] See also p. 513.

[14] See p. 614.

shown greater sensitivity to the needs of administration.[15] Nevertheless, many of the cases considered below highlight the different priorities and cultural attitudes of government and the courts. It is not unusual to find the courts striking down decisions on the grounds that authorities have abused their powers and acted 'unreasonably' when the authority has taken great care to reach a decision which it genuinely believes to be the best one possible in the circumstances. Part of the problem is that terms like 'abuse', 'irrelevant' and 'unreasonable' convey one set of meanings to non-lawyers and quite different meanings to public lawyers and judges.

THE GENERAL PRINCIPLES USED TO REVIEW DISCRETION

The *Wednesbury* case

We can start by considering the Court of Appeal's decision in *Associated Provincial Picture Houses v Wednesbury Corporation*.[16] Although now widely regarded as a landmark case, *Wednesbury* arose from a rather typical dispute over the exercise of a local authority's licensing powers. Legislation required cinemas to be licensed by local authorities. If authorities decided to grant a licence they could impose 'such conditions as they thought fit'. No specific criteria were referred to in the legislation and on the face of it authorities appeared free to impose whatever conditions they thought desirable in the circumstances.

The plaintiffs were granted a licence to open their cinema on Sundays. However, because the authority was concerned to protect the moral welfare of children in the area, a condition was imposed specifying that no 'children under the age of 15 years shall be admitted . . . whether accompanied by an adult or not'. Since this condition was likely to prevent most families with children from going to the cinema on Sundays, the cinema owners feared that the condition would make it uneconomic to open on that day of the week, thereby undermining the practical value of the licence. They therefore challenged the condition in the courts using two main arguments.

First, they argued that although legislation gave local authorities wide discretionary powers, these powers had to be used to further the purposes contemplated by the legislation. This legislation was concerned with licensing cinemas and said nothing about protecting the moral welfare of children and therefore the condition was imposed for reasons which were irrelevant and improper. Secondly, they said that even if protection of the moral welfare of children was relevant, the condition was none the less unlawful because

[15] See e.g. Sir John Donaldson MR, *R v Lancashire County Council, ex p Huddleston* [1986] 2 All ER 941, 945.

[16] [1948] 1 KB 223. See further J. A. G. Griffith, *Judicial Politics Since 1920* (1993), pp. 48–59; Sir Robert Carnwath, 'The Reasonable Limits of Local Authority Powers' [1996] PL 244; and Lord Irvine QC, 'Judges and Decision-Makers: the Theory and Practice of *Wednesbury* Review' [1996] PL 59.

it was unreasonably wide. They argued that it was unnecessary to exclude children altogether for children could be protected by a narrower condition, such as one that required them to be accompanied by a parent or guardian.[17]

In the event the plaintiffs were unsuccessful. It was held that although no specific reference was made in the statute to the moral welfare of children, it was nevertheless appropriate for the authority to take this factor into account. As for the second argument, it was held that the courts would only upset a condition on grounds of reasonableness if the condition was so unreasonable that no reasonable authority could have imposed it. This condition did not fall within this category.

The decision was a relatively ordinary example of judicial restraint and of itself is of no great importance. Its significance lies not in the specific decision but in Lord Greene MR's summary of the grounds on which the courts can review the exercise of discretionary powers. Lord Greene MR approached the case by emphasizing the breadth of the authority's discretion and the absence of a right of appeal to the courts; both factors indicated that Parliament had not intended the courts to interfere with the merits of decisions taken by local authorities. This, however, did not mean that discretionary decisions could not be controlled at all. In the now famous statement of the principles, he said that:[18]

> The exercise of such a discretion must be a real exercise of the discretion. If, in the statute conferring the discretion, there is to be found expressly or by implication matters which the authority . . . ought to have regard to, then . . . it must have regard to those matters. Conversely, if the nature of the subject-matter and the general interpretation of the Act make it clear that certain matters would not be germane to the matter in question, the authority must disregard those irrelevant . . . matters.

He added that the courts could also intervene where:[19]

> although the local authority have kept within the four corners of the matters which they ought to consider, they have nevertheless come to a conclusion so unreasonable that no reasonable authority could ever have come to it.

The basic idea contained in Lord Greene MR's dicta is that the breadth of discretionary power is limited by the express or implicit provisions of the legislation which grants the power. Those exercising discretion must therefore ensure that they act in accordance with the relevant statutory provisions; that they take account of factors that statute requires them to take account of; that they exclude factors that are irrelevant to the statute; and that they do not reach decisions which are so unreasonable that Parliament could not have intended the authority to reach them.

These principles still inform the way the courts review discretion and form the basis of our discussion. However, there have been developments in

[17] Today we might describe this as a 'proportionality' argument: see p. 572 below.
[18] [1948] 1 KB 223, 228.
[19] [1948] 1 KB 223, 234.

judicial attitudes since the late 1940s which are not adequately reflected in Lord Greene MR's summary. In particular, judges now place much more emphasis on what we have described as the 'impact-based approach'[20] and upon the need for authorities to justify themselves by showing that their decisions have been fairly taken and that they are properly reasoned and based on an adequate foundation of fact and evidence.

The grounds of review of discretion summarized

The main grounds on which the courts review discretion may therefore be summarized as follows:

(1) There must be a real exercise of discretion. If a body has discretion in a matter it must exercise that discretion when it deals with the issues to which the discretion relates; and it must remain free to do so.
(2) Discretionary powers must not be abused. They must not be used to further policies or achieve objects for which the discretionary power was not granted.
(3) Discretionary decisions must be properly reasoned and fairly taken. Authorities must adopt a proper process of reasoning, they must be able to justify their actions by showing that they have acted on the basis of relevant factors and that there is an adequate factual and evidential foundation for their decision or action.
(4) The decision must not be unreasonable, absurd or irrational. If a decision is unreasonable it may be assumed that the authority has either abused its power or failed to adopt a proper process of reasoning, even though no specific errors are alleged.

Overlap of the grounds of review

As we warned in Chapter 20, these grounds overlap and do not constitute water-tight categories. For example, if authorities have taken decisions on the basis of factors which are irrelevant to the legislation, this may constitute an abuse of power. The fact that an authority has taken an irrelevant factor into account might also indicate that it has failed to adopt a proper process of reasoning. It might also be a sign of unfairness; for example, the person affected by the decision may not have realized that a particular factor was being considered and therefore did not address this in any representations made to the authority.[21]

Although the grounds of review may overlap, each does, however, have a distinct emphasis which requires judges to ask different questions about the case. The grounds summarized under points (1) and (2) above are essentially concerned with ensuring that decisions are taken in accordance with the

[20] See p. 473.
[21] See Chapter 25.

legislation and require judges to match the decisions against the legislative provisions. Under (3) judges become more concerned with the quality of decision-making processes. Even where authorities are not being challenged on the grounds that they have abused their power they have to show that they can justify and explain their decisions and that they have adopted a proper process of reasoning.

The grounds cover a spectrum from the 'power-based' to the 'impact-based' approaches

The grounds summarized under (1) and (2) are concerned with the powers of the authority and therefore fit within the traditional 'power-based' model of review which is associated with the *ultra vires* doctrine.[22] Those summarized in (3) are more concerned with the quality of an authority's reasoning and its ability to justify decisions which impinge upon the interests of citizens and the community, rather than the formal powers an authority possesses. They fit less comfortably within the *ultra vires* doctrine than they do within an 'impact-based approach' to judicial review.

The ground summarized in (4) is explicitly concerned with the quality of decisions. It is an exception to the idea that the courts will not interfere with the substance of decisions and is based at least in part on the presumption that Parliament could not have intended to permit official bodies to reach decisions that are unreasonable or perverse.

Finally, note that the grounds on which discretion may be reviewed are not exhaustive, and new grounds are being developed. The best-known example is the emerging principle known as proportionality which many see as much more useful (and intellectually honest) than unreasonableness as a ground for reviewing the quality of decision-making.[23]

DISCRETION MUST BE EXERCISED

There must be a real exercise of discretion. If a body has discretion in a matter it must exercise that discretion when it deals with the issues to which the discretion relates, and it must remain free to do so.

If Parliament has given discretionary power to an authority it is assumed that it is in the public interest for the body to have this discretionary power and that Parliament has deliberately chosen not to impose duties on the authority or to require them to apply rules. This being so, authorities must remain free to exercise their powers and cannot surrender their powers to others or prevent themselves from exercising their discretion.

Issues that arise under this heading fall into three main types. First there are those which concern unlawful delegation.[24] Secondly are those concerned

[22] See p. 471.
[23] See p. 572.
[24] See p. 542.

with the argument that authorities have unlawfully fettered their discretion by applying policies. The third type involves claims that an authority's contractual obligations are incompatible with the requirement that they remain free to exercise their discretionary powers. Here we concentrate on unlawful fettering by policy and the relationship between contractual obligations and discretion.

Fettering discretion by applying rigid policy

It is inevitable that authorities will develop policies to help them handle their work.[25] The university admissions tutor might, for example, develop a policy that they will consult with the languages department regarding applicants who do not have English as their first language, or they might want to interview all applicants who lack formal educational qualifications. Policies will guide and inform decision-making and enable officials to achieve consistency; they will also help ensure that the broad objectives are turned into reality. However, policies must be lawful and they must not prevent authorities from exercising their discretionary powers.

The leading modern authority is *British Oxygen Co Ltd v Minister of Technology*.[26] The Board of Trade had discretionary power to make grants to businesses towards capital expenditure. It adopted a policy not to pay grants towards items costing less than £25 each. The British Oxygen Company (BOC) spent £4 million buying new gas cylinders and applied for a grant. Despite the overall expenditure, their application was refused on the grounds that as each cylinder only cost £20 it would have been contrary to the Board's policy to make a grant. BOC challenged the decision arguing *inter alia* that the Board had applied its policy in a way that prevented it from considering the merits of their particular case. In the House of Lords Lord Reid said:[27]

> that anyone who has to exercise a statutory discretion must not 'shut his ears' to an application . . . a large authority may have had to deal already with a multitude of similar applications and then they will almost certainly have evolved a policy so precise that it could well be called a rule. There can be no objection to this, *provided the authority is always willing to listen to anyone with something new to say.*

Their Lordships accepted that the Board was entitled to adopt the policy and found that there was no evidence that the Board had 'shut its ears' to the application by refusing to consider representations made by BOC.

The message for official bodies is that policies may be adopted and used, but bodies must always be prepared, and show themselves to be prepared, to consider arguments as to why a policy ought not to be applied to a particular case. In addition to the principle now being considered, failure to consider

[25] See D. J. Galligan, 'The Nature and Function of Policies within Discretionary Power' [1976] PL 303.
[26] [1971] AC 610. See also *R v Port of London Authority, ex p Kynoc* [1919] 1 KB 176, 185.
[27] [1971] AC 610, 629 (emphasis added).

specific arguments may also give rise to a challenge on the grounds that the body has failed to consider relevant factors (the arguments that the applicant wanted to make) and also that the body has acted unfairly. The idea of unfairness covers a range of sins which cannot be neatly packaged.[28] It might, for example, be unfair in a particular case to apply a policy or practice without paying attention to the specific arguments made by those affected. In other situations it might be unfair *not* to apply a policy or practice. This might be the case where, for example, an authority has indicated that a policy will be applied.[29]

Fettering discretion by entering into contractual obligations

As just seen, authorities cannot prevent themselves from exercising their discretionary power by adopting and rigidly applying policies. Nor can they do so by entering into contracts or making other commitments with specific parties. The reason is that while official bodies may be free to enter into contractual obligations they cannot prevent themselves from performing their public functions.[30] The basic question asked by the courts is whether the contractual obligations are incompatible with the authority's statutory powers.[31] Notice that in the cases involving fettering by policy the decision being challenged is normally the decision that has been adversely affected by the application of the policy, rather than the legality of the policy itself (although this may be challenged as well). Here, however, the litigation usually focuses on the legality of the contractual or other obligations.

In *Ayr Harbour Trustees v Oswald*,[32] harbour trustees had statutory powers and duties to acquire land to be used for the construction of works on the coast. They compulsorily acquired some land and, in an attempt to reduce the compensation payable to the owner, offered the owner a perpetual covenant not to cut off his access to the harbour. This covenant was held to be *ultra vires* essentially because it would have prevented the trustees ever using this land, even where it was necessary to do so in the public interest.

The *Ayr* case is often compared with *Birkdale District Electricity Supply Co Ltd v Southport Corporation*.[33] Birkdale Electricity agreed with Southport Corporation that it would not charge more for the supply of electricity than did the corporation (which also generated electricity). The House of Lords refused to hold this agreement void at common law or *ultra vires* as it was not incompatible with Birkdale's duties as a statutory electricity undertaker. The House of Lords distinguished the earlier case on the ground that in *Ayr*

[28] See also Chapter 25.

[29] See cases on 'legitimate expectation' discussed in Chapter 25, such as *R v Secretary of State for the Home Department, ex p Khan* [1984] 1 WLR 1337, *Re Findlay* [1985] AC 318 and *R v Secretary of State for Health, ex p United States Tobacco International Inc* [1992] 1 QB 353.

[30] *Birkdale District Electricity Supply Co Ltd v Southport Corpn* [1926] AC 355.

[31] *R v Inhabitants of Leake* (1833) 5 B & Ad 469.

[32] (1883) 8 App Cas 623.

[33] [1926] AC 355.

the trustees had prevented themselves from ever exercising their statutory rights in respect to the relevant land, whereas here the agreement only concerned trading profits and not the basic responsibilities of the company. The decision emphasizes that the courts will look closely at the effect any contract entered into has on the ability of bodies to exercise their relevant statutory powers. It has since been held, for example, that a planning authority cannot bind itself by contract to grant or refuse planning permission because such contracts would clearly conflict with an authority's obligation to exercise its discretion in the public interest.[34]

It follows from these cases that contracts cannot implicitly prevent public authorities carrying out their statutory powers. In *Cory (William) & Sons Ltd v London Corporation*[35] the London Corporation had contracted with Cory (William) & Sons Ltd for the removal of waste by barge. The corporation later introduced new regulations which imposed more stringent requirements on those transporting waste by barge. These made the contract uneconomic. The company claimed that the contract implied an undertaking that the corporation would not amend the bylaws so as to impose more onerous burdens than were already imposed by the contract. The Court of Appeal rejected this argument on the grounds that the corporation had statutory powers to make the bylaws and these powers could not be fettered by contract.

R v Hammersmith and Fulham London Borough Council, ex p Beddowes[36] provides another example of a case in which the issue of contractual fettering arose. The council owned a housing estate consisting of blocks of rented flats. The whole estate was in a bad state of disrepair and needed extensive modernization and improvement. The Conservative-controlled council favoured selling the blocks for development and eventual owner-occupation and it decided to embark on this policy by selling one block to a private developer, Barratts. The council agreed with Barratts that if the company were to buy the block it would enter into certain covenants in respect of the remaining blocks, designed to ensure that the sell-off policy would continue and also to protect Barratts from the risk that it would be left owning one modernized block in an estate of unrenovated properties. The applicant, a resident, challenged the council's actions on the ground that the covenants imposed an unlawful fetter on the authority's statutory duties in respect to its property.

The majority in the Court of Appeal held that the covenants were not unlawful. The council had power to create covenants restricting its use of the land it retained and, provided these covenants can reasonably be regarded as furthering statutory functions, they would not be unlawful. The court said that the purpose of the housing legislation was to enable the council to provide housing accommodation. Since it did not matter whether the accommodation was owned publicly by the council or privately, the purpose would

[34] See *Stringer v Minister of Housing and Local Government* [1970] 1 WLR 1281; *Ransom v Windsor and Maidenhead Royal Borough Council* [1949] Ch 180; and *Triggs v Staines Urban District Council* [1969] 1 Ch 10.

[35] [1951] 2 KB 476.

[36] [1987] QB 1050.

be furthered by the covenants because they would help provide good accommodation for owner-occupation. Kerr LJ dissented on the broader ground that the decision was an 'unreasonable and impermissible' exercise of the powers and functions of the housing authority. It was 'predominantly influenced by the political motive of fettering the political aspects of the future housing policy . . . rather than by any immediately necessary or relevant policy considerations', he held.[37]

DISCRETION MUST NOT BE ABUSED

Discretionary powers must not be abused. They must not be used to further policies or achieve objects for which the discretionary power was not granted. The booklet *The Judge Over Your Shoulder*, advising civil servants about judicial review, states:[38]

> Abuse of power is an emotive phrase and you may feel that it could have no application to your work. But a statutory provision may set out the purposes for which a power may be exercised, or those purposes may be implicit, to be ascertained by considering the statute as a whole. To use the power to achieve some other purpose is an abuse of that power . . .

Purposes specified by legislation

Abuse may arise in several different ways; the most straightforward situation is where the statute sets out the purposes for which discretion has been given and there is clear evidence showing that the authority has exercised its power in order to achieve other purposes. In *Sydney Municipal Council v Campbell*,[39] for instance, a statute allowed the authority to acquire land for the specific purposes of 'carrying out improvements in or remodelling any portion of the city'. It was established that the Council had abused this power by using it to acquire land in order to benefit from an increase in land values. However, cases are not always this straightforward.

Legislation does not expressly identify purpose

A more difficult situation occurs where the provisions conferring the discretionary powers make no specific reference to purposes. Here the purpose for which the powers may be used is determined by the courts construing the statute as a whole. The *Wednesbury* case was an example of this situation, but the leading decision is that of the House of Lords in *Padfield v Minister of Agriculture, Fisheries and Food*.[40]

[37] [1987] 1 QB 1050, 1074.
[38] p. 9.
[39] [1925] AC 338.
[40] [1968] AC 997 (also discussed at p. 532 above).

The case involved complaints arising from the administration of the milk marketing scheme. The legislation provided that a complaints committee would be established to investigate complaints 'if the Minister [of Agriculture] so directs'. Milk producers in the south-east of England complained that the pricing policy operated by the scheme treated them unfairly because it meant that they were being paid less for their milk than were producers in other parts of the country. Accordingly, they asked the minister to establish a committee to examine their complaints. He refused to do so. In his decision letter the minister explained his reasons in terms that indicated that his refusal was at least partly based on his desire to save himself the risk of incurring political embarrassment should the committee uphold the complaint.

When the producers sought an order of mandamus to force the minister to establish a committee he responded by arguing that the legislation gave him complete discretion for which he was politically but not legally accountable.[41] He also argued that since he was under no obligation to give reasons for his decision he could not be found to have acted improperly on the basis of reasons that he had voluntarily given. The majority of the House of Lords rejected the minister's argument that he was the final arbiter of his discretionary powers and that his discretion could not be reviewed by the courts. It held that it was not for the minister to determine how much discretion he possessed. Lord Reid said:[42]

> Parliament must have conferred the discretion with the intention that it should be used to promote the objects of the Act; the policy and objects must be determined by construing the Act as a whole and construction is always a matter of law for the court.

Since the minister had been motivated by factors that had nothing to do with the purpose of the legislation (his desire to save his own political skin had nothing to do with milk marketing) he had acted unlawfully. Following the decision, the minister established a committee. In due course it upheld the complaint, as he had feared it would. The saga ended when the minister told the House of Commons that he had refused to accept the committee's findings and that despite the report he had decided not to change the pricing structure of the milk marketing scheme.[43]

There are many examples of this principle in the law reports. Among the most common are those involving authorities who have used one set of powers to achieve objectives which ought only to be achieved by using other powers. Powers to deport, for example, cannot be used to extradite;[44] and powers contained in planning legislation cannot be used to achieve housing functions.[45]

[41] For a recent example of this argument, see the minority opinions in *R v Secretary of State for the Home Department, ex p Fire Brigades Union* [1995] 2 AC 513.
[42] [1968] AC 997, 1030.
[43] See HC Deb, vol. 780, cols 46–7 (31 March 1969).
[44] *R v Governor of Brixton Prison, ex p Soblen* [1963] 2 QB 243.
[45] *R v Hillingdon London Borough Council, ex p Royco Homes* [1974] QB 720. The legislation allows authorities to take 'material considerations' into account. On the meaning of this see *Tesco Stores Ltd v Secretary of State for the Environment* [1995] 1 WLR 759.

Some of the most difficult and most controversial cases involve situations where local authorities have taken decisions in order to further political objectives which are not specifically authorized by statute. The best-known political case is probably *Roberts v Hopwood*.[46] The Metropolis Management Act 1855 gave local authorities powers to pay 'such salaries and wages as [they] may think fit'. During the 1920s, Poplar Borough Council, a socialist council in the east end of London, used its statutory power to pay its male and female employees the same wage (£4.00 per week). At the time, the idea of paying men and women equal wages was regarded by most as an odd one; now, of course, it is unlawful to do otherwise. When the legality of the council's decision was challenged by the district auditor it was held by the House of Lords that the council had used its powers for reasons which had nothing to do with the statute. In the now infamous words of Lord Atkinson, the council had been motivated by 'eccentric principles of socialist philanthropy, or by a feminist ambition to secure the equality of the sexes in the matter of wages and the world of labour'.

More recently, a local authority which opposed apartheid in South Africa was held to have abused its powers when it withdrew a licence to use a council-owned sports ground from a rugby club because some members of the club had, quite lawfully, participated in a tour of South Africa.[47] Another local authority was held to have abused its statutory duty to 'provide a comprehensive and efficient library service'[48] when it refused to provide newspapers, such as *The Times*, published by News International in order to show support for that company's employees who were involved in a long-running industrial dispute with the publishers.[49] As already noted, an authority was held to have abused its statutory powers to 'manage wildlife' on council-owned land when it passed a resolution banning deer hunting because councillors regarded it to be morally repulsive.[50] Similarly, authorities also run the risk of being held to have abused their powers if they take into account financial matters unless their statutory powers expressly or implicitly allow them to do so. Thus local authorities with power to dismiss school teachers on 'educational grounds' cannot dismiss teachers to save

[46] [1925] AC 578. See further B. Keith-Lucas, 'Poplarism' [1962] PL 52; G. W. Jones, 'Herbert Morrison and Poplarism' [1973] PL 11; and J. A. G. Griffith *Judicial Politics Since 1920* (1993), Chapter 1.

[47] *Wheeler v Leicester City Council* [1985] AC 1054. The council argued that it was legally entitled to revoke the licence under its broad statutory powers to manage its own land and in pursuance of the Race Relations Act 1976, s 61 which places a duty on local authorities to 'promote good relations between persons of different racial or ethnic groups'. See also see *R v Lewisham London Borough Council, ex p Shell UK Ltd* [1988] 1 All ER 938, discussed below.

[48] Public Libraries and Museums Act 1964, s 7(1).

[49] *R v Ealing London Borough Council, ex p Times Newspapers Ltd* (1987) 85 LGR 316.

[50] *R v Somerset County Council, ex p Fewings* [1995] 1 WLR 1037. The Court of Appeal held that 'wildlife benefit' was the statutory purpose arising under LGA 1972, s 120(1)(b), but this did not involve (so far as it related to the deer) anything more than the need to look after the 'proper management' of the herd. The council's decision was not taken on the basis that the ban would be for the herd's better management, but entirely for ethical reasons. This was an irrelevant consideration as well as an improper purpose.

expenditure.[51] Likewise, a local authority was held to have abused its powers when it imposed a ceiling on the number of remunerable hours guardians *ad litem* (people appointed by the court in care proceedings to look after the interests of the child) could spend on their cases. The ceiling helped to save cost, but the decision conflicted with the principle that guardians *ad litem* are independent of authorities.[52]

Multiple motives

It should not be assumed that issues are always as clear as these short summaries of the principles may suggest. Often, as we have seen elsewhere in the book, legislation is complex and its objects and policies may be difficult to discern. On occasion it may be arguable that the legislation is intended to achieve several, possibly incompatible objects. Moreover, authorities may take into account a range of factors or be motivated by more than one purpose. Some of these factors or motivations may be legitimate, while the legitimacy of others may be more questionable.

The classic example of this situation was a case involving a council that had power to build public lavatories but no power to build subways.[53] This being so, did it have power to build a lavatory beneath a street with access from either side so that a subway was created? The House of Lords said that it was necessary to determine the *primary object* of the council. In this case it was held the council's primary object was to build a public convenience with adequate access from both sides of the road. The subway that was formed was therefore a secondary and permissible benefit. Had the court formed the view that the authority did not particularly want a public convenience but decided to build one in order to achieve a subway the result would have been different.

In *R v Inner London Education Authority, ex p Westminster City Council*,[54] the ILEA had power to spend money on publishing information in its area 'on matters relating to local government'.[55] It decided to use this power to mount a media and poster campaign to increase public awareness of the implications on local government of the Conservative government's restrictions on public expenditure. When this decision was challenged by Westminster City Council (a Conservative council) the ILEA accepted that the decision involved both lawful purposes (to inform the public) and unlawful purposes (to

[51] See e.g. *Hanson v Radcliffe Urban District Council* [1922] 2 Ch 490; *Sadler v Sheffield Corporation* [1924] 1 Ch 483.

[52] *R v Cornwall County Council, ex p Cornwall Guardians ad litem and Reporting Officers Panel* [1992] 1 WLR 427. See also *R v Gloucestershire County Council, ex p Barry* (1995) *The Times*, 21 June; *R v Lancashire County Council, ex p RADAR* [1996] 4 All ER 421 where a majority of the Court Appeal held that in assessing an individual's needs under the Chronically Sick and Disabled Persons Act 1970 local authorities could not take account of their resources: see further A. Bradley and S. Cragg (1996) 146 NLJ 1071.

[53] *Westminster Corporation v L & N W Railway* [1905] AC 426.

[54] [1986] 1 WLR 28.

[55] LGA 1972, s 142(2).

persuade the public that the policies were wrong), but denied that its decision was for this reason an abuse of power. Glidewell LJ referred to two possible tests.[56] The first of these required judges to ask: what was the *true purpose* for which the power was exercised? If this can be identified and the authority has shown that it has used its powers to achieve the true purpose then it is immaterial that other subsidiary purposes are achieved. The second test required judges to ask: were any of the purposes unauthorized? If any of the purposes are unauthorized then the judge must go on to consider whether the unauthorized purposes materially influenced the actor's conduct. If he forms the view that they did, the power has been abused. Adopting these tests, Glidewell LJ said that the issue in the case came down to a question of fact: whether the unauthorized purpose—persuasion—had materially influenced the making of the decision. He decided that it had. Deciding upon the 'true purpose' or assessing whether particular factors 'materially affected' decisions cannot be a scientific process. Unless the authority has made it obvious why it has acted and stated its priorities judges are forced, as Glidewell LJ was, to reach a decision on the facts as they appear to them. In the event, his judgment suggests that the existence of any unlawful consideration, amongst a number of lawful considerations, may lead to a decision that the authority has abused its powers.

This approach may be contrasted with the decision in *R v Broadcasting Complaints Commission, ex p Owen*.[57] Here May LJ held that where a statutory body takes a course of action for several reasons which can be 'disentangled' its decision will not be disturbed if one of those reasons is found to be invalid and the court is satisfied that precisely the same decision would have been reached on the basis of the valid reasons alone.

R v Lewisham London Borough Council, ex p Shell UK Ltd[58] was a case where proper and improper purposes were inextricably mixed up and could not be disentangled. During the time of apartheid, Shell had subsidiaries in South Africa. Since a substantial proportion of Lewisham's population is black, the council decided, in the interests of promoting good race relations,[59] to boycott Shell and to persuade other councils to do so as well. When Shell challenged the decision the court held that the council was entitled to decide that the boycott was in the interests of good race relations, but it could not use its power to put political pressure on Shell. For this reason the decision was an abuse of power.

[56] Cf. de Smith, Woolf and Jowell, *Judicial Review of Administrative Action* (5th edn., 1995), para. 6–077 where six different tests used by the courts are set out. The authors comment that none of them is entirely satisfactory and that it is not uncommon to find two or more tests applied in the course of a single judgment.

[57] [1985] QB 1153.

[58] [1988] 1 All ER 938. See further T. R. S. Allan, 'Abuse of Statutory Powers: Apartheid Disinvestment and Coercion' [1988] CLJ 334.

[59] Race Relations Act 1976, s 61 places a duty on local authorities to do this: see n. 47 above.

DISCRETION MUST BE PROPERLY REASONED

> If you are making a decision under statutory powers, those powers may not expressly require you to give reasons . . . Nevertheless, you should always know why you made the decision: A time may come when you have to swear an affidavit explaining your actions! . . . Having identified the factors that inform your decision, are you sure they are relevant? Are you sure that the facts on which you based your decision are accurate? Are you sure that you have not overlooked other relevant factors? (Advice to civil servants in the *The Judge Over Your Shoulder*, p. 11)

So far, we have been considering principles which flow directly from the traditional concern to ensure that ministers and other official bodies do not exceed or abuse their powers. We now move to situations in which the emphasis is rather different. Here the claim is that, even though decisions cannot be categorized as an excess or abuse of power, there are none the less grounds for arguing that authorities have acted improperly or unfairly. The basic thrust of the principles to be considered is that official bodies must be prepared to justify their decisions by showing that they have adopted a proper process of reasoning, that they have considered relevant information, and that their conclusions are supported by facts and evidence.[60] In short, they must be able to show that they have brought 'a rational mind to bear' on the matter.

Although judges in the United Kingdom have yet to adopt a rule as strict as the North American requirement that regulatory agencies justify their actions by showing substantial supporting evidence,[61] there is now a presumption that officials have to explain to the courts how they arrived at decisions which impact upon the lives of citizens and the community. Of course, such an obligation only actually arises in the relatively rare cases where the decision is challenged by judicial review. This presumption is rooted in the 'impact-based' approach to judicial review considered in Chapter 20[62] and the related principles of good administration and administrative fairness.

Decisions must be based on relevant factors

What is meant by relevance? The first thing to note is that when used in the context of judicial review the term 'relevant' has a particular legal meaning that does not necessarily coincide with ministerial or administrative concepts of relevance. In the *Wednesbury* case[63] the authority regarded the moral welfare of children to be a relevant factor for it to consider. However, suppose the authority imposed a condition restricting the opening hours of cinemas because the majority of councillors were keen footballers and wanted to discourage forms of entertainment other than football. Or suppose that the authority,

[60] They may also have to give reasons: see p. 592.
[61] See Ian Harden and Norman Lewis, *The Noble Lie* (1989), Chapter 9 and C. S. Diver, 'Policy Making Paradigms in Administrative Law' (1981) 95 Harvard LR 393.
[62] See p. 473.
[63] See p. 550.

concerned to promote house building, decided to impose a condition requiring cinema owners to pay a levy out of their profits to a house building fund. The councillors might be convinced that such decisions are in the public interest and would be popular with their electorate. From their perspective these conditions would be relevant. The courts, however, might disagree.

When Lord Greene MR referred to 'relevance' in *Wednesbury*, he linked it to situations in which authorities had failed to consider factors which statute expressly or implicitly required them to consider. Used in this sense relevance is an aspect of illegality and abuse of power. One of the reasons why Poplar's decision to pay women and men the same wage was an abuse of their power was that it had been based on irrelevant considerations, namely the council's desire to secure equality of the sexes.[64] The minister's decision in *Padfield* was an abuse because his political reputation was irrelevant to the operation of the milk marketing scheme.[65] Somerset County Council's decision to ban deer hunting on its land was unlawful because the councillor's view that deer hunting was morally repulsive was irrelevant to its statutory powers to conserve its area's wildlife.[66]

Lurking within this understanding of 'relevance' is an additional sense of the term, a sense that is pertinent to the quality of reasoning with which we are now concerned. Relevance can also be used to refer to the relationship between the factors which have or have not been considered and the decision that has been made, irrespective of whether the decision-maker is accused of having abused its power. If, for example, factors X and Y would have a bearing on the decision to be reached, failure to take them into account adversely affects the quality of the decision, whether or not the decision is otherwise unlawful.

Consider *Bugdaycay v Secretary of State for the Home Department.*[67] Bugdaycay applied for refugee status in the United Kingdom, claiming that his life would be threatened if he returned to Uganda. The Home Secretary decided to refuse this application and ordered that Bugdaycay be deported to a third country, Kenya. He did so despite representations from Bugdaycay's lawyers that he would not be permitted to enter Kenya and would be sent by the Kenyan authorities to Uganda. The Home Secretary did not attempt to verify whether this was true or not. The House of Lords held that this information was relevant to his decision and his failure to consider it meant that he could not have properly reached a decision on whether Bugdaycay's life would be threatened. The Home Secretary's decision was accordingly quashed.

In this case the House of Lords felt able to intervene because the omitted factors were obviously of central importance to a decision that might literally have been a matter of life and death for the individual. Where a decision has impacts of this potential magnitude judges expect ministers and officials

64 *Roberts v Hapwood* [1925] AC 578.
65 *Padfield v Ministry of Agriculture, Fisheries and Food* [1968] AC 997.
66 *Fewings v Somerset County Council, ex p Fewings* [1995] 3 All ER 20.
67 [1987] AC 514.

to act with the utmost rigour to ensure that every issue that might have a bearing is considered. Even so, had the minister considered the situation in Kenya, it is unlikely that the court would have interfered with his conclusions, unless these conclusions were unreasonable or absurd. They would see such intervention as an unauthorized interference with the very issue that the minister was charged to decide. Had the information been less central, or the issues less important, the courts may not have interfered either. Certainly, a court will not intervene solely because authorities have failed to consider matters which the judges would have taken into account. Authorities are permitted leeway to select the factors to be considered; how much leeway they are permitted depends on the legislative provisions and the nature of the issues. As one judge has put it:[68]

> What has to be emphasized is that it is only when statute expressly or impliedly identifies considerations required to be taken into account by the authority as a matter of legal obligation that the court holds a decision invalid (on the ground of relevance). It is not enough that a consideration is one that may properly be taken into account, nor even that it is one which many people, including the court itself, would have taken into account if they had to make the decision . . . [T]here will [however] be some matters so obviously material to a decision on a particular project that anything short of direct consideration of them . . . would not be in accordance with the intention of the Act.

Failure to consider relevant factors may be only one of several interlinked errors which when added together show that the decision has been unfairly or improperly reasoned. A recent example occurred when the courts declared unlawful a ministerial decision to set new quotas for night flights from Heathrow and other airports.[69] It was established that the effect of the new quotas would be to increase, rather than decrease noise levels and that this had not been considered by the minister. When added to the fact that the increase breached undertakings that had been given, and appeared also to conflict with his stated policy, the cumulative effect was to create the impression that the minister had failed to make a rational decision or to act fairly.

Decisions must be based on a sound evidential and factual foundation

Traditionally judges have been reluctant to consider factual issues in judicial review applications.[70] They have tended to assume that the body being reviewed will have been in a better position than they are to gather the facts and evaluate their significance. Indeed, the Order 53 judicial review procedure

[68] Cooke J in *Creednz v Gov Gen* [1981] 1 NZLR 172, 183 cited with approval by Lord Scarman in *Re Findlay* [1985] AC 318, 333–4.

[69] *R v Secretary of State for Transport, ex p Richmond upon Thames London Borough Council* [1994] 1 WLR 74.

[70] See further Ian Yeats, 'Findings of Fact: The Role of the Courts' in G. Richardson and H. Genn (eds.), *Administrative Law and Government Action* (1994) and de Smith, Woolf and Jowell, *Judicial Review of Administrative Action* (5th edn., 1995), pp. 277–89.

is ill-suited to dealing with factual disputes.[71] One well-known example of this reluctance was a case in which the Privy Council refused to quash a conviction imposed by a magistrates' court even though it had been alleged that the court had acted without proper evidence. Lord Sumner accepted that the magistrates might have acted wrongly, but lack of evidence, he said, did not affect their jurisdiction.[72] More recently, the House of Lords held that because local housing authorities are in a better position than the courts to investigate whether applicants for housing have a sufficient mental capacity to seek their assistance they would not interfere with an authority's decision.[73] And in *R v South Hams District Council, ex p Gibb* it was held that provided authorities applied the correct legal test to the issue they would not interfere with an authority's decision as to whether particular persons were gipsies.[74]

The two main exceptions to this judicial reluctance to become embroiled in factual issues have been:

(a) where the very power (or jurisdiction) of the body depends on findings of fact, and
(b) where discretionary power has been exercised *without any* supporting evidence.

Jurisdictional fact

Suppose a statutory tribunal with jurisdiction to set rents for unfurnished accommodation is alleged to have wrongly dealt with a case involving furnished accommodation. The issue may involve questions of fact, such as was there any furniture present? If there was then arguably the tribunal exceeded its powers; if there was not then arguably the tribunal acted within its powers.[75] Where a tribunal's jurisdiction depends on questions of fact the relevant facts are described as 'jurisdictional facts'. The power to review jurisdictional facts is based on the principle that bodies with limited jurisdiction cannot have final power to determine jurisdictional facts because if they had, they would effectively be able to determine the scope of their own powers. Review of jurisdictional facts therefore fits four square within the traditional power-based model of judicial review with its emphasis on the *ultra vires* doctrine.[76]

No evidence

It is now accepted that the approach taken in the *Nat Bell Liquors* case is too narrow and, in any case, would be inapplicable in the context of review of

[71] See p. 494.
[72] *R v Nat Bell Liquors* [1922] 2 AC 128.
[73] *R v Oldham Metropolitan Borough Council, ex p Garlick* [1993] AC 509.
[74] [1995] QB 158, 170.
[75] *R v Fulham, Hammersmith and Kensington Rent Tribunal, ex p Zerek* [1951] 2 KB 1. Most statutory controls on rent have now been abolished. For another illustration see *White & Collins v Minister of Health* [1939] 2 KB 838 (a local authority had power to acquire land provided it was not part of a park; the court held it could review the authority's decision that the land was not part of a park).
[76] See p. 471.

official discretion, as opposed to review of decisions taken by inferior courts. If decisions are to be properly reasoned they must be based on facts and evidence and administrative systems must be designed to provide decision-makers with the necessary information. This being so, the courts insist that ministers and officials have evidence to support their views.

Coleen Properties Ltd v Minister of Housing and Local Government provides an example in the context of the housing legislation.[77] A company owned a building which a local authority wanted to compulsorily acquire because it was included in the authority's redevelopment plan. The acquisition was possible if the building was 'reasonably necessary for the satisfactory redevelopment of the area'. The company objected to its inclusion on the grounds that since the building was in first-class condition and was on the edge of the area of proposed development, its acquisition was not reasonably necessary. These objections were accepted by an inspector at a local public inquiry and he reported to the minister accordingly. Without taking any fresh evidence the minister disagreed with the inspector's view and confirmed the local authority's decision. The Court of Appeal quashed this decision on the ground that there was no evidence upon which the minister could properly disagree with the inspector's recommendation. In this case there was a straightforward dispute between the minister and his inspector. The minister was not bound by the inspector's recommendation, but the inspector had seen the site and considered the evidence. The court took the view that if the minister were to disagree with the inspector, at the very least he had to have some evidence to support his view.

Inadequate facts

The courts have since gone further than *Coleen Properties* and have been prepared to intervene even where there is some factual or evidential support for a decision, if that support is thought to be inadequate. *R v Secretary of State for the Home Department, ex p Khawaja*[78] concerned the power of the immigration authorities under the Immigration Act 1971, s 33 to detain and remove 'illegal entrants'. The authorities, relying on an earlier decision of the House of Lords in *Zamir v Secretary of State for the Home Department*,[79] argued that they could detain someone under these powers where they had 'reasonable grounds for believing a person to be an illegal entrant'. The House of Lords rejected this argument and reversed its earlier decision on this point. It held that draconian powers to arrest without trial as a first stage in the expulsion of someone from the country could only be given to the immigration authorities by clear statutory language. The legislation gave power only to detain people who were 'illegal entrants'; it did not give power to detain where the immigration authorities believed (even if they had 'reasonable grounds' for believing) that someone was an illegal entrant. The immigration

[77] [1971] 1 WLR 433.
[78] [1984] AC 74.
[79] [1980] AC 930.

authorities therefore had to establish, as a matter of fact, that the person was an illegal entrant before they took action against them.

This decision may be contrasted with that in *Liversidge v Anderson*.[80] Here the majority of the House of Lords held that power to detain a person 'if the Secretary of State has reasonable cause to believe any person to be of hostile origins or associations' could be used if the Secretary of State *thought* that he had reasonable grounds. The case is generally viewed as an example of the way judges will lean over to protect the executive during periods of 'dire national peril' or in situations where national security interests are at stake. This approach would now be regarded as exceptional.

The need for an adequate factual foundation was also emphasized in *Secretary of State for Education and Science v Tameside Metropolitan Borough Council*.[81] After local elections in May 1976 the control of the Tameside Borough Council passed from the Labour Party to the Conservatives. The Conservatives had campaigned on the basis that they would not proceed with the Labour administration's plans to introduce comprehensive education as from the following September. Once in office they stopped the proposed reorganization and set about re-establishing a system for selecting children to go to the grammar schools. The Secretary of State had power under the Education Act 1944, s 68 to issue directions to local education authorities 'if he is satisfied that they are proposing to act unreasonably'. At the time there was a Labour government and the Secretary of State used his power to direct the council to continue with the existing plans on the grounds that he believed that it was unreasonable at this late stage in the school year to try to decide which children should or should not go to grammar school. The council refused to comply with his direction, arguing that since it was acting in accordance with the electorate's wishes its actions could not be said to be unreasonable. At this point the Secretary of State sought mandamus to compel the authority to comply with his direction. Ultimately, the House of Lords agreed with the council and refused to grant the mandamus. Lord Wilberforce said that the Secretary of State 'had fundamentally misconceived and misdirected himself . . . there was no ground, however much he might disagree with the new policy . . . on which he could find that the authority were acting or proposing to act unreasonably'.[82]

Getting to the merits of decisions: evaluating facts and evidence

In these cases the judges are at pains to distinguish between the nature of the information which the authority has available for its consideration and the conclusions that the authority reaches on the basis of that information. While the courts are willing to interfere on the ground that authorities have considered inadequate information, they regularly deny ability to interfere with

[80] [1942] AC 206.
[81] [1977] AC 1014. See further H. W. R. Wade (1977) 93 LQR 4; D. G. T. Williams [1977] CLJ 1; and D. Bull (1987) 50 MLR 307.
[82] [1977] AC 1014, 1057.

an authority's evaluation of information. Evaluation, they say, is a matter of discretion and judgement. Thus in the *Tameside* case, Lord Wilberforce said:[83]

> If a judgment requires, before it can be made, the existence of some facts, then, although the evaluation of those facts is for the Secretary of State alone, the court must enquire whether those facts exist, and have been taken into account.

To similar effect Forbes J has emphasized that:[84]

> when exercising its supervisory jurisdiction, the court is not concerned with whether due or proper weight is given to a material consideration: the weight to be given to such a matter is for the body exercising the discretion to determine.

An example of this distinction between issues of relevance and weight is provided by *Singh v Immigration Appeal Tribunal*.[85] Here the House of Lords held that in deciding to deport a prominent member of the Sikh community, the immigration rules required the authorities to consider the impact of his deportation on that community. However, Lord Bridge went on to say that although this factor had to be considered, the weight to be attached to it was a matter 'entirely' for the immigration authorities.[86]

Despite these apparently clear statements, it is doubtful that there is a difference in principle between issues of relevance and weight. Allan has argued that it would not be contrary to principle for the courts to invalidate a decision of a minister because he gave insufficient weight to a relevant factor if a statute expressly or implicitly permitted them to do so, or if the issues involved so warranted.[87] His argument is essentially that the scope of judicial intervention varies and that no defining cut-off point can be provided by a line such as that between relevance and weight or, for that matter, the existence of facts and their evaluation. Indeed, we saw earlier that in *R v Inner London Education Authority, ex p Westminster City Council* Glidewell LJ was prepared to assess whether an improper purpose had 'materially' influenced an authority.[88] This was a clear example of the way a judge was prepared to assess an authority's *evaluation* of the issues. Laws J, writing extra-judicially, has even gone so far as to acknowledge that 'the most interesting, and important, types of challenge to discretionary decisions [are] likely to be concerned with the way in which the decision-maker has ordered his priorities'.[89] Ordering priorities is surely simply another way of describing the process of giving more weight to some factors rather than others?

Most judges may not be as ready as Laws to admit that the courts are willing to intrude into the very thought processes lying at the core of discretion. However, their reticence is often about admitting to this possibility

83 [1977] AC 1014.
84 *Pickwell v Camden London Borough Council* [1983] QB 962, 990.
85 [1986] 2 All ER 721.
86 See also *Tesco Stores v Secretary of State for the Environment* [1995] 1 WLR 759.
87 T. R. S. Allan, 'Pragmatism and Theory in Public Law' (1988) 104 LQR 422, 424.
88 See p. 560.
89 Sir John Laws, 'Is the High Court the Guardian of Fundamental Constitutional Rights?' [1993] PL 58, 73.

rather than about the possibility itself. It is not difficult, for instance, to find cases in which the courts have reviewed the way bodies have evaluated or weighed competing factors, but have not explicitly admitted to this in their reasoning. Take the fairly straightforward *Coleen* case as an example.[90] The principle in the case is that a decision is unlawful if it is based on no evidence. Expressed in this way there is obviously no question of the courts reviewing how ministers weighed or evaluated factors, because the whole basis on which intervention is justified is that the minister had no evidence to weigh against the inspector's recommendation. However, the substance of the case may be presented rather differently. One of the minister's arguments was that he had taken account of several factors including the inspector's report and the local authority's opinion of what was in the interests of its area. Having considered these he reached the decision that more weight should be given to the authority's view than to the inspector's report. Looked at with this argument in mind, the Court of Appeal's decision is clearly concerned with assessing the minister's evaluation of these competing factors and thereby with judging the merits of his decision.

We now turn to consider the one situation in which the courts are prepared openly to review the merits of discretionary decisions.

DISCRETIONARY DECISIONS MUST NOT BE UNREASONABLE OR IRRATIONAL

The courts can review a discretionary decision on the grounds that the decision made or conclusion reached is 'unreasonable', 'absurd', 'outrageous', 'perverse' or 'irrational' (these different terms are used interchangeably), and they can do so even where no specific error in the decision-making process has been, or can be, identified.

Terms such as unreasonableness and irrationality are often used loosely to indicate that authorities have erred in some way. It is common, for example, to find judges saying that a decision is unreasonable because a local authority has failed to consider a relevant factor or because a minister has acted for improper reasons. Used in this way unreasonableness is a 'general description of things which ought not to be done'[91] rather than a distinct ground for challenge. In the present context, however, we are using 'unreasonableness' in a more specific and distinctive sense to refer to the court's power to interfere solely on the ground of the quality of the decision taken and irrespective of any errors that may have been made by the authority in reaching that decision. The classic example that would justify intervention on this ground would be a decision of an education authority to dismiss a school teacher because she had red hair.[92] No doubt, if the courts were to examine

[90] See p. 566.
[91] Lord Greene MR, *Associated Provincial Picture Houses v Wednesbury Corporation* [1948] 1 KB 223.
[92] Given by Warrington LJ in *Short v Poole Corporation* [1926] Ch 66, 90–1.

why the authority made this decision errors would be found justifying their intervention. However, the decision itself is so blatantly unreasonable that the courts would feel able to intervene without examining why the decision has been made.

In deference to the principle that judges cannot intervene simply because they dislike decisions they regularly emphasize, in the words of Lord Greene MR, that the question is whether the decision is one 'that no reasonable body *could have come to*. It is not what the court considers unreasonable . . . This . . . is a different thing altogether.'[93] Using similar language in *GCHQ*, Lord Diplock said that the courts can intervene on grounds of irrationality if a decision is so 'outrageous in its defiance of logic or of accepted moral standards that *no* sensible person who had applied his mind to the question to be decided *could* have arrived at it'.[94]

On this formulation decision-makers are left with a margin of discretion into which the courts will not trespass: if a reasonable authority in the same position—with the same powers and considering the same issues—*could* have come to the same decision the courts will not interfere, even where the judge thinks that the decision is unreasonable, or that another decision would have been more reasonable. The scope of this margin of discretion cannot, however, be precisely and objectively determined. Judges have accepted that there is inevitably a subjective element which depends on the reviewing court's perception of the authority's role, its legislative powers, the importance of the interests affected and the policy content of the decision that was taken.

Where, for example, the courts are called upon to review decisions of the Secretary of State on matters of political judgement they will only intervene on grounds of unreasonableness in 'very exceptional circumstances . . . and only if a *prima facie* case were to be shown for holding that the Secretary of State had acted in bad faith . . . or that he must have taken leave of his senses'.[95] This was said in a case involving ministerial decisions on levels of public expenditure by local authorities.[96] The same reticence to intervene on grounds of unreasonableness is not always apparent where the policy content of decisions taken by ministers is of a lower level, particularly where a decision affects important interests of individuals or groups. Nor does the same reticence exist where the courts are reviewing decisions of local authorities rather than central government.[97]

Unreasonableness is therefore an idea which is used with varying degrees

[93] *Associated Provincial Picture Houses v Wednesbury Corporation* [1948] 1 KB 223, 230–1, 233 (emphasis added).

[94] *Council of Civil Service Unions v Minister for the Civil Service* [1985] AC 374, 410 (emphasis added).

[95] Lord Scarman, *Nottinghamshire County Council v Secretary of State for the Environment* [1986] AC 240, 247.

[96] See also *R v Secretary of State for the Environment, ex p Hammersmith and Fulham London Borough Council* [1991] 1 AC 521.

[97] See e.g. *Wheeler v Leicester City Council* [1985] AC 1054, where Lord Roskill said that it was unreasonable for a council to ban a football club from playing on its pitches because some members of the club had participated in a tour of South Africa. See also *Champion v Chief Constable of Gwent* [1990] 1 WLR 1.

of rigour depending on the circumstances. Laws J has said that this means, for example, that 'while the Secretary of State will be largely left to his own devices in promulgating national economic policy . . . the courts will scrutinise the *merits of his decisions* much more closely when they concern refugees or free speech'.[98] He argues that courts should accept that intensity of scrutiny should vary, and that in some circumstances judges are able to review the merits of decisions. In particular, he argued that where 'fundamental rights' are involved the courts ought to impose a 'more exacting' judicial scrutiny upon decision-makers than is possible using the principles of unreasonableness and irrationality, and they ought to be prepared to intervene even where decisions cannot be challenged on established grounds such as relevance and unreasonableness. Responding to the argument that it would be constitutionally inappropriate for the courts to have this much power to interfere, he said:[99]

> Such an approach, is I believe, no more a usurpation of constitutional propriety than is the conventional *Wednesbury* approach itself. No one suggests, nowadays, that the courts behave improperly in requiring a Minister to bring a rational mind to bear on a question he has to decide. In doing so, the court imposes a judge-made standard on the decision maker. To bring forward a more exacting standard . . . is not in principle a different exercise . . . the fact is that just as the judges have evolved the *Wednesbury* doctrine, so they can refine it.

In presenting this argument, Laws is joining others who have been arguing for some time that once it is accepted that the courts do review the substance of decisions the idea of 'unreasonableness' is unsatisfactory. Jowell and Lester, for instance, have said that unreasonableness is unsatisfactory for three reasons.[100] First, they say that it is inadequate: 'The incantation of the word "unreasonable" simply does not provide a sufficient justification for judicial intervention. Intellectual honesty requires a further and better explanation as to *why* the act is unreasonable.' The reluctance to articulate precisely why decisions are unreasonable encourages, they say, suspicion that 'prejudice or policy considerations may be hiding underneath *Wednesbury*'s ample cloak'. Secondly, *Wednesbury* unreasonableness is unrealistic. It is an attempt to avoid judicial intervention in the merits of decisions except in cases where officials have behaved absurdly when in practice 'the courts are willing to impugn decisions which are far from absurd'. Thirdly, they argue that the unreasonableness test is confusing and provides little practical guidance to officials. Officials and ministers already know that they must not act absurdly; what they want to know is what types of thing will the courts regard as unreasonable or irrational.

[98] Sir John Laws, 'Is the High Court the Guardian of Fundamental Constitutional Rights?' [1993] PL 58, 69 (emphasis added).

[99] At p. 69 and p. 71.

[100] J. Jowell and A. Lester, 'Beyond *Wednesbury*: Substantive Principles of Administrative Law' [1987] PL 368, 372. See also de Smith, Woolf and Jowell, *Judicial Review of Administrative Action* (5th edn., 1995), Chapter 13. Cf. Paul Walker, 'What's Wrong with Irrationality?' [1995] PL 556.

Like Jowell and Lester, Laws argues that the courts should embrace a variety of additional principles. The most significant is the principle known as proportionality.

PROPORTIONALITY

Proportionality,[101] a principle derived mainly from German law, is an accepted element within both Community law[102] and the ECHR. It has not yet been explicitly accepted as a separate ground of judicial review in cases involving only issues of national law. The principle requires that the means used to attain a given end should be no more than what is appropriate and necessary to attain that end. As Lord Diplock once put it 'you must not use a steam hammer to crack a nut, if a nutcracker would do'.[103]

Proportionality in cases involving Community law

Proportionality may be illustrated briefly by two cases involving Community law. *EC Commission v United Kingdom*[104] concerned UK legislation prohibiting the import into the United Kingdom of milk that had been sterilized by a technique which subjects the milk to ultra-high temperatures (UHT) and which is common on the continent. In an action brought by the Commission, the UK government responded to the allegation that this prohibition conflicted with the principle of free movement of goods contained in Art 30 of the EC Treaty by arguing that the restrictions were necessary in the interests of health (under Art 36). The ECJ held that the measures were not necessary and therefore were not justified because they were disproportionately restrictive; other less drastic means could have been introduced which would have satisfied the health concerns without imposing the same restrictions on freedom of movement.

Johnston v Chief Constable of the Royal Ulster Constabulary[105] is an example from another context. The Chief Constable of the Royal Ulster Constabulary (RUC) decided that the police should be armed in order better to resist terrorism but that women police officers should not be armed. As women were consequently unable to perform general police duties the Chief Constable refused to issue new contracts to or renew existing contracts with women in the RUC reserve, unless they were prepared to perform duties that were assigned exclusively to women officers. Marguerite Johnston was a part-time

[101] See further J. Jowell and A. Lester, 'Proportionality Neither Novel nor Dangerous' in J. Jowell and D. Oliver (eds.), *New Directions in Judicial Review* (1990); S. Boyron, 'Proportionality in English Law: A Faulty Transition' (1992) 12 OJLS 237; J. Jowell, 'Is Proportionality an Alien Concept?' (1996) 2 EPL 401.

[102] See Chapter 14 (proportionality used in the challenge to the validity of the Working Time Directive) and Chapter 30 (in the Sunday trading litigation).

[103] *R v Goldstein* [1983] 1 WLR 151, 155.

[104] Case 124/81 [1983] ECR 203.

[105] Case 222/84 [1987] QB 129.

member of the RUC reserve affected by these decisions when her contract was not to be renewed. She brought proceedings in the industrial tribunal claiming that the Chief Constable had unlawfully discriminated against her and others in similar positions contrary to Northern Ireland and Community law. Her claim was referred to the ECJ for a preliminary ruling on these issues of law under Art 177.[106] Here one of the Chief Constable's arguments was that even if his decisions did discriminate against women, this was not unlawful because his actions were necessary in the interests of safeguarding national security, protecting public safety, and maintaining public order. In response to this the court said that the discrimination would be disproportionate, and therefore unlawful, if the objectives could be achieved in a less discriminatory way. As is normal on an Art 177 reference, the ECJ left it to the national courts to decide whether the decisions were disproportionate in the specific situation.

UK courts now have to apply the principle of proportionality in cases where Community law issues are raised. Some of the most significant examples have been in the field of equal pay and equal treatment in employment and social security where it has been alleged that legislation offends the Community law prohibition of indirect discrimination on grounds of sex. Direct sex discrimination occurs when a person is treated less favourably than others because of their sex. Indirect sex discrimination occurs where a rule or practice which applies equally to both sexes in a formal sense, in practice is far more onerous to those of one sex rather than the other. A minimum height requirement for employment in the police, although formally applying equally to men and women, would adversely affect more women than men. Exclusion of part-time workers from benefits such as pensions or redundancy payments would adversely affect more women than men because many more women than men work part-time. Under Community law requirements such as these would be unlawful unless they can be shown to be objectively necessary according to the principle of proportionality. This argument was recently used to successfully challenge provisions of the Employment Protection (Consolidation) Act 1978.[107]

Proportionality in domestic law

Where Community law issues are not involved, it is now accepted that proportionality may be considered in judicial review cases *as an aspect* of relevance and reasonableness. You will remember that in *Wednesbury* itself one of the arguments used by the cinema owners was that the authority's aim of protecting the moral welfare of children could have been secured by a less onerous condition, and it was for this reason that the condition was unreasonable. Another way of putting this is to say that the condition was unreasonable because it was disproportionate. In *R v Barnsley Metropolitan Borough*

[106] See generally p. 696.
[107] See p. 117.

Council, ex p Hook,[108] the majority of the Court of Appeal used the principle to justify quashing a council's revocation of a stall-holder's licence after he had been caught urinating in a public place. The punishment, which deprived him of his livelihood, was disproportionate to the relatively minor nature of his offence.

However, judges have yet to accept that proportionality can be used as a *separate* and *distinct* ground of judicial review where Community law is not involved.[109] Their basic concern, as we have seen, is that if action of public bodies cannot be impugned on grounds of illegality, relevance or unreasonableness it is not for the courts to intervene, because to do so would inevitably require them to adjudicate upon the merits of official action; this would be a usurpation of power conferred by Parliament on these bodies.

This concern was most clearly expressed by the House of Lords in *R v Secretary of State for the Home Department, ex p Brind*.[110] Brind, a journalist, challenged the legality of directions given by the Home Secretary to the Independent Broadcasting Authority (IBA) and the BBC prohibiting the broadcasting of statements by representatives of proscribed organizations and members of Sinn Fein, Republican Sinn Fein and the Ulster Defence Association. The ban was imposed because in the government's view it was no longer acceptable in the national interest for spokesmen for terrorist organizations, paramilitary organizations and those who supported them to have direct access to television and radio.[111] The journalist argued that the ban was disproportionate in the sense that it constituted an unnecessarily wide restriction of the principle of freedom of speech.

The challenge failed and the judges were unanimously of the view that proportionality could not be used as a separate ground of challenge in this type of case. Lord Lowry delivered a judgment that appeared to damn the prospect of the proportionality principle being used as a separate ground of challenge. He said that this would be an abuse of the courts' supervisory

108 [1976] 1 WLR 1052.

109 Cf. *R v Brent London Borough Council, ex p Assegai* (1987) 151 LG Rev 891: Woolf LJ referred to the banning of Mr Assegai (a member of the public) from council premises because of his unruly behaviour at previous meetings as having 'constituted a reaction wholly out of proportion to what the applicant had done'. The courts have also been prepared to use the principle of proportionality when considering whether criminal penalties are appropriate in particular cases, e.g. *R v Highbury Corner Justices, ex p Uchendu* (1994) *The Times*, 28 January. See also *R v Secretary of State for Transport, ex p Pegasus Holdings (London) Ltd* [1988] 1 WLR 990, a case concerning the Secretary of State's power to suspend a company's permit to operate charter flights after their pilots had failed a Civil Aviation Authority examination. Schiemann J said (at p. 490): 'It would perhaps be difficult for any one appearing for the Government to take issue on the principle of proportionality being applied by administrative authorities, bearing in mind recommendation R(80)2 of the Committee of Ministers concerning the exercise of discretionary powers by administrative authorities which was adopted by the Committee of Ministers of the Council of Europe on 11 March 1980 and which recommends governments of member states to be guided in their law and administrative practice by the principles . . . (which include the proportionality principle).'

110 [1991] 1 AC 696.

111 The banning directives were issued under powers contained in s 29(3) of the Broadcasting Act 1981 (powers relating to the IBA) and, in the respect of the BBC, clause 13 of the licence and agreement between the Secretary of State and the BBC.

jurisdiction because it would allow the courts to review decisions of those who were elected and accountable to Parliament. Judges, he argued, are not equipped by training or experience, or furnished with the requisite knowledge and advice, to decide the answer to an administrative problem where the scales are evenly balanced. 'They have,' he said, 'a much better chance of reaching the right answer where the question is put in a *Wednesbury* form.' He feared that if proportionality were accepted as an argument it would jeopardize stability and relative certainty, because there is nearly always something to be said against any administrative decision and parties who felt aggrieved would be even more likely than at present to try their luck with a judicial review application. This in turn would lead to an increase in applications for judicial review and a consequential prolongation of court time which could otherwise be devoted to other matters. Ultimately the losers will be members of the public. He concluded by saying that 'there can be very little room for judges to operate an independent judicial review proportionality doctrine in the space which is left between the conventional judicial review doctrine and the admittedly forbidden appellate approach'.[112]

Although the other judges did not disagree with the general tenor of Lord Lowry's comments, several, including Lords Bridge and Roskill, acknowledged that proportionality may become a separate ground of review in the future. Lord Roskill said that he was:[113]

> . . . clearly of the view *that the present is not a case on which the first step can be taken* [towards the adoption of the proportionality principle] for the reason that to apply that principle in the present case would be for the court to substitute its own judgment of what was needed to achieve a particular objective for the judgment of the Secretary of State upon whom that duty has been laid by Parliament.

Lord Templeman went further, saying that if interference with freedom of expression was to be justified it had to be both '*necessary and proportionate* to the damage which the restriction is designed to prevent'.[114]

Brind has not been the last word on proportionality. There is evidence that the courts are prepared to apply the principle in an expanding range of situations and that possibly the only areas in which they will continue to refuse to do so are those involving sensitive issues of political judgement, such as national security or national economic policy. We have seen, for example, that it is now arguable that the courts are ready to accept proportionality-type arguments where human rights and issues of personal freedom are involved.[115]

It has also been accepted that proportionality might be used against local authorities, even if not against ministers. This distinction between local authorities and ministers was referred to in *NALGO v Secretary of State for the Environment*,[116] a case involving an unsuccessful challenge to the legality of

[112] [1991] 1 AC 696, 767.
[113] [1991] 1 AC 696, 750 (emphasis added).
[114] [1991] 1 AC 696, 751.
[115] See p. 571.
[116] (1993) 5 Admin LR 758.

regulations preventing local government officers from participating in politics. Here Neill LJ said that:

> there is much to be said for the view that all the courts in the European Community should apply common standards in the field of administrative law. In time the English courts will become increasingly familiar with the principle of proportionality.

He went on to distinguish between cases 'involving the judicial review of decisions made at a lower level' of government where a 'lack of proportionality may well come to be recognised as a separate ground of intervention' and cases involving 'decisions of government ministers'. As he put it: 'The constitutional balance in this country between the courts and the executive is a delicate one.'

While Neill LJ is correct to acknowledge that there may be qualitative differences between the decisions of ministers and those of local authorities, this distinction provides too crude a basis for distinguishing between situations where proportionality can be used and those in which it cannot. Many decisions of ministers are routine and many are made in relation to specific issues affecting individuals, and from this point of view they are no different to decisions taken by lower-level authorities. Moreover, if the courts do not want to become involved in reviewing high-level policy or delicate issues of political judgement it is not necessary for them to exclude the prospect of using proportionality. The courts have various other techniques for ensuring that they do not upset any constitutional balance.[117] Moreover, once courts accept that proportionality can be used when reviewing decisions of some official bodies there is no justification for them refraining, on a wholesale basis, from using the principle when called upon to review decisions of ministers. After all, why should ministers possess an immunity that others lack?

What difference would adoption of the ECHR make?

One final issue needs to be considered. We have seen that beyond issues of Community law the courts are loath to adopt (some would say to admit to adopting) an explicit proportionality test. Despite general acceptance that the principles enshrined in the ECHR inform Community law and the development of English law, this reluctance extends to cases involving fundamental human rights, such as freedom of expression. If the ECHR were to become part of UK domestic law the courts would have to apply the test of proportionality in such cases. What difference would this make?

Consider the recent unsuccessful challenge to the lawfulness of the policy banning homosexuals from serving in the armed forces, *R v Ministry of Defence, ex p Smith*.[118] Applying domestic law, the Divisional Court stated that it could hold this policy legally invalid only 'if it were plain beyond

[117] For instance the discretion to withhold remedies (see p. 614) and to hold that an issue is non-justiciable (see p. 513).

[118] [1995] 4 All ER 427 QBD; [1996] 1 All ER 257, CA.

sensible argument that no conceivable damage to the armed forces as a fighting unit' would occur if it were reversed. In other words, the court was prepared only to review the justification for the policy on grounds of irrationality, not the policy itself. According to Simon Brown LJ, the court could exercise a 'secondary judgment' but not a 'primary judgment'. Had the ECHR been applicable, the court would have been obliged to ask, under Art 8, whether the policy answered a 'pressing social need' and whether the 'restriction on human rights involved can be shown to be proportionate to its benefits'. This would mean that they would be forced to review the 'primary judgment'.

Questions

1. What do you understand to be the difference between subjective and objective discretion?

2. Local authorities have discretionary power to award grants to students on the Legal Practice Course (LPC) and the Bar Vocational Course (BVC).

(a) The London Borough of Cambington writes to Anna, who has a place on the LPC, saying that: 'due to financial constraints we regret to inform you that we are not considering any applications for discretionary grants this year'. Is this legally objectionable?

(b) The London Borough of Wandsbeth write to Ben, who has a place on the BVC, saying 'it is our policy only to give 15 grants for this course per year. Unfortunately you were the 16th applicant.' Ben's application was delayed because he was involved in a serious road accident and has been unconscious ever since. The authority were told this, but no reference to this information has been made in their letter to him. Does he have any legal cause for complaint? Would it have made any difference if he were the 50th applicant?

3. A government department which deals with many issues involving both UK and Community law asks you to provide a summary of the basic grounds on which discretionary decisions may be reviewed by the British courts. It is concerned because many of its officials know little about judicial review and fewer know anything about Community law. They are particularly troubled by the proportionality principle. They want to know whether this always applies or only sometimes. If only sometimes, when? What would your summary say?

4. Schedule 3 of the Local Government (Miscellaneous Provisions) Act 1982 provides that (emphasis added):

> the appropriate authority *may* grant to any applicant and from time to time renew, a licence under this Schedule for the use of any premises, vehicle, vessel or stall specified in it for a sex establishment *on such terms and conditions* and *subject to such restrictions as may be so specified.*

(a) Antbridge District Council decides that all pornography is immoral and that it will not grant any sex shop licences at all. Should it be able to do this?

(b) Thirty people apply to Batbridge District Council for licences to run sex shops. It decides as a matter of policy that only three sex shops should be allowed to operate in its area and that the three licences should be allocated randomly by drawing names out of a hat. Is there anything objectionable about this?

(c) Catbridge District Council decides to refuse a licence to Dan because he recently wrote to the local newspaper criticizing councillors for wasting money on a new children's playground. Should it be able to refuse a licence for this reason?

(d) Dogridge District Council grant a licence to X subject to two conditions:
   (i) that the shop only opens between 9 am and noon, three days a week;
   (ii) that the owner of the shop contributes at least £100 to the annual Mayor's charity.

   X claims that the first condition will make it uneconomic to operate the shop and that the second condition is objectionable because he does not believe in donating money to charity. Does Dogridge District Council have power to impose these two conditions?

25

COMMON LAW FAIRNESS

The previous chapters have examined the duty of official bodies to comply with express and implied requirements of legislation (including those relating to matters of procedure),[1] and to adopt a proper process of reasoning and to reach decisions which are not unreasonable, absurd or perverse.[2] There is, however, a further set of constraints on public decision-makers. These are the common law requirements relating to fairness, and particularly fair procedures, which may be imposed either where legislation is silent on matters of procedure, or where judges perceive legislative provisions to be inadequate. Many of the principles discussed are associated with matters of procedure. However, judges now use the term fairness in a broader sense to encapsulate principles that extend beyond matters of procedure and which have a direct effect on the substance and merits of official action. The most obvious examples arise in the context of the principles associated with legitimate expectations, which are considered later in this chapter.

THE DEVELOPMENT OF FAIRNESS

'Fairness' and 'natural justice'

Ideas of fairness have a very long tradition in judicial review.[3] They were originally associated with matters of procedure and the so-called principles of natural justice. These required:

(a) judges and other decision-makers to be impartial and unbiased;[4] and
(b) that parties be given opportunities necessary to enable them to present their cases effectively.[5]

[1] See Chapter 23.
[2] See Chapter 24.
[3] For a more detailed account see de Smith, Woolf and Jowell, *Judicial Review of Administrative Action* (5th edn., 1994), Chapters 7–12.
[4] Sometimes referred to by the Latin *nemo judex in re sua* (no man should be a judge in his own cause).
[5] *Audi alterem partem* (hear the other side).

These requirements were initially designed to provide minimum standards of protection to those appearing before courts, tribunals, disciplinary bodies and other agencies carrying out adjudicative functions.

As administrative law developed, the courts were called upon to consider whether, and if so to what extent, the principles of natural justice applied to administrative bodies which did not adjudicate or operate like courts. Were ministers, for example, required to be neutral and unbiased when they made decisions implementing government policy? Did local authorities have to provide hearings to those who were likely to be affected by decisions, say, to increase local tax levels or approve a grant for planning permission or a street trader's licence?

During the 19th century judges had held that administrative bodies had to comply with the principles of natural justice when taking decisions affecting an individual's property rights. This required them to provide a hearing to those affected, even where statute did not expressly oblige them to do so. Perhaps the most famous statement of this position was that of Byles J when he said that 'the justice of the common law would supply the omission of the legislature'.[6] This interventionist approach, however, did not survive. During the first half of the 20th century the prevailing view was that although decision-makers always had to act fairly,[7] the rules of natural justice only applied to administrative agencies that followed procedures akin to those of the courts; in other words to bodies which were 'judicial' in character, rather than 'administrative' or 'quasi judicial'.[8]

Judges had two general concerns. At the time the prevailing theory of judicial review was based on the *ultra vires* doctrine which focused judicial attention on the statutory powers of public bodies.[9] First this left little room for judges to imply common law principles into statutory schemes for fear that to do so would trespass into Parliament's domain. Secondly, the judges were also reluctant to impose rigid court-like procedures on administrative systems. These were no doubt legitimate concerns. The result, however, was to render most areas of administrative activity free from any judicial supervision on procedural grounds, except failure to comply with express statutory provisions.

A basic problem was that judges appeared to regard natural justice as an inflexible set of principles which were moulded on court procedure where decisions are taken by an independent judge following argument by two

[6] *Cooper v Wandsworth Board of Works* (1863) 14 CB NS 180, 194.

[7] Cf. *Board of Education v Rice* [1911] AC 179, 182 where Lord Loreburn LC said that the Board must 'act in good faith and fairly listen to both sides, for that is the duty lying upon everyone who decides anything'.

[8] For a definition of these terms see de Smith, Woolf and Jowell, *Judicial Review of Administrative Action*, Appendix. Much of the blame for this has been placed on the judgment of Lord Hewart CJ in *R v Legislative Committee of the Church Assembly, ex p Haynes-Smith* [1928] 1 KB 411 where he appeared to misunderstand an earlier statement of Atkin LJ in *R v Electricity Commissioners, ex p London Electricity Joint Committee Co* [1924] 1 KB 171, 205 which in any case was concerned with the availability of the prerogative writs (as they were then known) rather than natural justice.

[9] See p. 471.

opposing parties. They could see no way of applying this model to less adversarial administrative procedures. It was as if they were trying to fit a square peg into a round hole: natural justice could be used where agencies adopted judicial procedures but not otherwise. Judges paid lip service to the idea that even though natural justice did not apply administrative bodies nevertheless had to act fairly, but fairness was a poor substitute largely because there was no real attempt to clothe it with specific content.

The first serious attempt to escape this sterile and formalistic approach was made in 1964 by the House of Lords in *Ridge v Baldwin*.[10] It is from this decision that the modern law on fairness can be traced. Here the House held it to be unlawful for a Watch Committee (a committee responsible for overseeing the work of the local police force) to dismiss a chief constable without first giving him the opportunity to make representations. The House emphasized that whether natural justice applied depended not on the label attached to the body or its procedure ('judicial', 'administrative' and so on), but upon the rights and interests affected by its decisions.[11]

This represented a fundamental change of approach, for once judges admitted that their first concern was to ensure that individual rights and interests were properly respected, they were obliged to find ways of imposing standards of fairness on decision-makers whatever their formal designation, and whether or not the old rules of natural justice were appropriate. While the idea of fairness had in the past been a poor relation to natural justice, the flexibility it offered now became a useful vehicle for judges. It has since become an overarching concept potentially applying to all official bodies who make decisions affecting individuals or groups, whether or not they adopt adjudicative procedures.[12]

What is meant by fairness?

The word 'fair' is one of those notoriously vague terms that can mean anything to anybody. Most officials probably realize that they must act fairly (as they realize that they must not act unreasonably). They, and individuals affected by their actions, however, need to know what judges mean by fairness and what procedural standards will be expected in particular situations. Do universities, for example, have to provide students with opportunities to appeal against the grades they have been awarded by examination boards? If so, would it be unfair to require a student to make written representations to an appeal panel composed of the student's lecturers? Or would fairness require an opportunity to make oral representations to a panel composed of people who have had no prior contact with the student? If oral representations are allowed, should the student be able to have a representative? If so,

[10] [1964] AC 40.

[11] On the impact-based approach to review, see p. 473.

[12] See *R v Secretary of State for the Environment, ex p Kirkstall Valley Campaign Ltd* [1996] 3 All ER 304.

should the representative be a lawyer? If this is what fairness requires, does it also require that those lecturers whose grades are being challenged be allowed to participate and should they also have the benefit of legal representation?[13]

Each of these questions, and others which could be asked, raise important issues of fairness. They also raise other practical problems including questions of cost and speed. There is no general code of procedural fairness to which institutions and individuals can turn for a definitive list of requirements applicable in every situation. On the contrary, the judges have repeatedly emphasized that fairness is a flexible concept that has to applied pragmatically on a case-by-case basis. Lord Bridge's guidance in *Lloyd v McMahon* is typically general. He said:[14]

> My Lords . . . what the requirements of fairness demand . . . *depends on the character of the decision-making body, the kind of decision it has to make and the statutory or other framework in which it operates.*

The core presumptions of fairness

For the moment we may note that procedural fairness consists of a series of core presumptions which may be summarized as follows.

(1) Decisions affecting an individual's rights and interests should not be taken by those who may be prejudiced against them, or who are motivated by their own interests.

(2) Those affected by decisions should be able to participate in the decision-making. While the level of participation varies depending on circumstances, sometimes there may be rights to oral hearings, at other times written procedures are adequate. Ability to participate does imply that participants are informed of relevant issues and policies and have access to relevant information.

(3) Participation also implies that decision-makers are required to give reasons for their decisions. Reasons are important because they explain why a decision has been made and help those aggrieved to appeal against or challenge the decision.

Factors influencing how these presumptions are applied

In order to obtain a better feel for what fairness requires in specific types of case it is necessary to study the case law, and later in the chapter we look at some of the most important examples. For now it is sufficient to flag some of the issues to which judges pay particular attention. These are noted in no particular order of importance.

[13] For a case on academic disciplinary procedures, see *R v Manchester Metropolitan University, ex p Nolan* (1993) *The Independent*, 15 July; A. J. Carroll, 'The Abuse of Academic Power' (1994) 144 NLJ 729.

[14] [1987] AC 625, 702 (emphasis added).

- Higher standards are normally expected from bodies making final decisions than from those against which appeals may be made; similarly, higher standards are expected when decisions are firm rather than advisory.
- Standards of fairness depend on 'the gravity of the issue which the decision determines'.[15] Accordingly decisions affecting grave issues such as life and liberty are expected to comply with the highest standards.
- Broadly speaking a higher level of fairness is expected of an authority when depriving a person of a licence or privilege that is already possessed than when considering whether to grant the licence or privilege in the first place.[16]
- What is fair to the individual concerned is determined in the context of what is fair to the general public. The courts may not interfere with unfair treatment if the unfairness is justified by other factors. For example, the normal principle that those affected by decisions should be fully informed of the issues does not apply if the provision of information would be contrary to the interests of national security.[17]
- As in other areas of judicial review, the judges are sensitive to the needs of public administration. Accordingly, they need to be persuaded that procedures that are likely to impose substantial administrative burdens are necessary in the interests of fairness to the individual.

FAIRNESS AND THE POLICY CYCLE

The prime area in which fair procedures are demanded by the common law is at the stage when officials apply administrative rules, law or policies to particular individuals and groups.[18] The courts have traditionally refused to impose fairness either at the policy-making or the legislative stages of the policy cycle.[19]

Policy-making

When, for example, the Home Secretary announced to the Conservative party conference that prisoners serving life sentences for violent crimes would have to wait longer for parole, the courts rejected the argument of two prisoners who challenged the new policy on the grounds that it conflicted

[15] See Lords Bridge and Templeman in *Bugdaycay v Secretary of State for the Home Department* [1987] AC 514.

[16] See Megarry V-C in *McInnes v Onslow-Fane* [1978] 1 WLR 1520, discussed below.

[17] *R v Secretary of State for the Home Department, ex p Hosenball* [1977] 1 WLR 766; *R v Secretary of State for the Home Department, ex p Cheblak* [1991] 1 WLR 890. For an example in a different context see *Bushell v Secretary of State for the Environment* [1981] AC 75, discussed below.

[18] Stage 4 of the policy-process model: see Chapter 4.

[19] Stages 2 and 3.

with their legitimate expectations.[20] Similarly, the courts refused to review the government's decision to change its health policy and ban oral snuff, even though the challenge came from a company which had been encouraged by the government to establish a plant to manufacture the product.[21] In *Bushell v Secretary of State for the Environment*[22] it was said that 'a decision to construct a nationwide network of motorways is clearly one of government policy in the widest sense of the term. Any proposal to alter it is appropriate to be the subject of debate in Parliament' not the subject of hundreds of local inquiries all over the country in which people and pressure groups could make representations, and which could then generate judicial review challenges on grounds of unfairness.

Legislating

As we have seen, when it comes to legislating to give legal basis to policy choices there is often considerable voluntary consultation by government departments with those likely to be affected by the new rules.[23] Sometimes, as in the case of the Board and Lodgings Regulations, there is also a *statutory* requirement for government to consult with specific bodies.[24] Generally, however, the courts have been reluctant to impose any *common law* requirements of fair process at this stage. For example, when the Lord Chancellor was about to exercise rule-making powers under the Solicitors Act 1957 to set fees chargeable by solicitors, he was not required to hear representations from the British Legal Association as his function was plainly 'legislative'.[25]

Several explanations for this caution may be offered. It may be said that it would be inappropriate for the courts to become involved in policy-making at a stage before final decisions are taken as this would both encourage litigation over speculative issues and force judges to become improperly involved in policy-making. Related to this is the argument that courts ought only to impose procedural fairness to protect actual rights and interests and that until decisions are made and implemented, there is no right or interest with which to trigger judicial intervention.[26]

TYPICAL COMMON ALLEGATIONS OF UNFAIRNESS

Having considered the history and nature of fairness and its role in the policy cycle, we now move on to consider some of the more common allegations

[20] *Re Findlay* [1985] AC 318, discussed below.
[21] *R v Secretary of State for Health, ex p United States Tobacco International Inc* [1992] QB 353; see further below.
[22] [1981] AC 75.
[23] See Chapters 8 and 9.
[24] See Chapter 11 and *Agricultural, Horticultural and Forestry Industry Training Board v Aylesbury Mushrooms Ltd* [1972] 1 WLR 190.
[25] *Bates v Lord Hailsham of St Marylebone* [1972] 1 WLR 1373.
[26] See below.

of unfairness. We shall consider bias; failure to allow effective participation; failure to give reasons and failure to respect legitimate expectations.

The rule against bias

It has always been a basic principle that parties to litigation in courts have a right to expect judges to be impartial and unbiased. In one of the leading cases, *Dimes v Grand Junction Canal Proprietors*, a decision of the Lord Chancellor was set aside because he owned shares in one of the parties, a canal company, even though there was no evidence that he was in any way influenced by this.[27] Non-financial connection with one of the parties may also act as a disqualification. In *Metropolitan Properties v Lannon*,[28] for example, decisions of a Rent Assessment Committee (a statutory tribunal responsible for setting fair rents for private accommodation) were quashed because the chairman's father (Mr Lannon) was a tenant of a comparable block of flats and the chairman's firm of solicitors had acted for some tenants in his father's block in a similar dispute with their landlords.

The rule against bias also prevents decision-makers being involved in considering appeals against their own decisions. Thus, in *Hannam v Bradford Corporation*[29] a decision to dismiss a school teacher was held to be unlawful because three councillors were members of the school's governing body (which had initially recommended that the teacher be dismissed) as well as being members of the council committee responsible for considering whether the dismissal should be confirmed (one of the councillors actually chaired this committee).

The key element in these cases is the need to ensure that decision-makers are able, and seen to be able, to exercise a proper discretion, untainted by bias. Actual bias or prejudice need not be established. What matters, to quote the famous words of Lord Hewart CJ, is 'that justice should not only be done, but should manifestly and undoubtedly be seen to be done'.[30]

The test of bias in cases involving non-pecuniary interests

The test for determining bias has been expressed in different ways. One formulation asks whether a reasonable and fair-minded person, seeing the proceedings and knowing the material facts, would have a reasonable suspicion that the decision would be unfair.[31] In considering this question the

[27] (1852) 3 HLC 759. A remote financial interest would not necessarily disqualify a decision-maker. In *R v Mulvihill* [1990] 1 WLR 438 a Crown Court judge was not disqualified from sitting just because he had 1,650 shares in one of the banks and building societies the accused was charged with robbing. Note that local councillors cannot participate in making decisions which affect their pecuniary interests whereas MPs can, provided they declare this.

[28] [1969] 1 QB 577.

[29] [1970] 1 WLR 937.

[30] *R v Sussex Justices* [1924] 1 KB 256, 259.

[31] See *R v Liverpool City Justices, ex p Topping* [1983] 1 WLR 119. For other formulations of the test see *Metropolitan Properties v Lannon* [1969] 1QB 577 and *Hannam v Bradford Corporation*

court is not solely concerned with the way the applicant viewed the proceedings and only intervenes if it decides that there are objective grounds for suspecting bias. In *R v Gough*,[32] a case in which a juror recognized the defendant's brother as her neighbour, the House of Lords has recently spoken of the need to show a 'real danger of bias' which, according to Lord Goff, makes it unnecessary in cases of apparent bias to 'have recourse to a test based on mere suspicion, or even reasonable suspicion'. He went on to say:

> I think it possible, and desirable, that the same test should be applicable in all cases of apparent bias, whether concerned with justices or other members of inferior tribunals, or with jurors, or with arbitrators. . . . I think it unnecessary, in formulating the appropriate test, to require that the court should look at the matter through the eyes of a reasonable man, because the court . . . personifies the reasonable man; and in any event the court has to ascertain the relevant circumstances from the available evidence, knowledge of which would not necessarily be available to an observer in court at the relevant time.

This approach has been held to have general application in public law and not to be limited to judicial or quasi judicial bodies or proceedings.[33] Lord Goff's dictum has also been amplified and explained by Simon Brown LJ.[34] Courts dealing with a challenge on the ground of apparent bias must, he said, ascertain the relevant circumstances and consider all the evidence for themselves so as to reach their own conclusions as to whether there is a real danger of injustice having occurred as a result of bias. A real danger involves more than a minimal risk and less than a probability. Injustice, he said, will have occurred if the decision-maker 'was pre-disposed or prejudiced against one party's case for reasons unconnected with the merits of the issue'.

Bias and policy

These basic principles were often developed in the context of court or court-like procedures where the decision-maker is adjudicating on a dispute between opposing parties. Many public law decisions do not fit into this mould. To take one example, for many years ministers responsible for town and country planning and road building have been given specific statutory duties to make decisions about the siting of new airports, new towns and motorways. Normally planning permission for proposed developments is granted by the local authority in which it is to be situated under powers given to them by the Town and Country Planning Act 1990, but projects such as these are of such strategic national interest that the decision has to be made by a minister. Legislation usually requires the minister to set up a public inquiry chaired by a civil servant known as an inspector. The inspector hears evidence from people affected by the proposed scheme and also pressure groups.

[1970] 1 WLR 937 (which considered the 'real likelihood' test and the 'reasonable suspicion' test).

[32] [1993] AC 646.

[33] *R v Secretary of State for the Environment, ex p Kirkstall Valley Campaign Ltd* [1996] 3 All ER 304.

[34] *R v Inner West London Coroner, ex p Dallaglio* [1994] 4 All ER 139, 151–2.

He then evaluates this and makes a recommendation to the minister as to whether the development should go ahead or not. The minister must consider the inspector's report carefully, but he is free to disagree with it if he decides an alternative decision is preferable. Obviously the minister's role in this context is different from that of a judge: he is not simply arbitrating or adjudicating between two opposing parties. Rather he has to make a decision in what he considers to be the public interest. Should the courts quash a decision in this context if, for example, the minister is swayed by government policy on road building or the like?

Franklin v Minister of Town and Country Planning[35] illustrates some of the problems that can arise. After the Second World War the Labour government adopted a policy of building new towns around London. To the dismay of many of the residents of what was then a small town, Stevenage was identified as one of the sites. Before the final decision was made, indeed before a public inquiry was held, the minister spoke at a very hostile public meeting in Stevenage Town Hall. He made it clear that he wanted a new town to be built at Stevenage and the locals made it equally clear that they did not want the plans to go ahead. Following this acrimonious meeting a public inquiry was held at which objections were again expressed. These were summarized by the inspector in his report to the minister. Despite the objections the minister ordered that Stevenage New Town be built. The objectors then challenged the minister's decision arguing that it was tainted by bias: he had made up his mind before the public inquiry and he was so biased that the whole process was a sham. They won at first instance, but lost in the Court of Appeal and in the House of Lords. Their Lordships accepted that the minister had been biased but refused to quash his decision. Ministers, they intimated, are expected to be biased in favour of their government's policy; this 'official bias' was understandable and legitimate. The only obligation upon the minister was to genuinely consider the inspector's report and the objections that had been made. This, they said, he had done.

From the point of view of the objectors this was no doubt a totally unsatisfactory result. After all, their whole case was based on the argument that the minister could not have genuinely considered their objections when he had already publicly committed himself to his decision. The practical problem facing the judges was that if this argument had been accepted it would have left the minister unable to decide the issue in conformity with his government's policy. It was because the judges were unwilling to tie ministerial hands in this way that they rejected the language of bias in this context.

The courts have also had to make adaptations to the basic principles of bias in the context of local authority decisions where members of a council vote on party political lines. (Councillors are elected on the basis of the party they represent and local authorities may be highly politicized.) In *R v Amber Valley District Council, ex p Jackson*[36] a pressure group (led by Mrs Jackson)

[35] [1948] AC 87.
[36] [1985] 1 WLR 298.

challenged the decision of the council to grant planning permission for a recreation and leisure centre on several grounds, including the fact that the political party having a majority of seats on the local authority had met before the formal vote in the council chamber and had decided to support the development. Woolf J, accepting that the council had an obligation to deal fairly with the application for planning permission, stressed that the rules of natural justice were not rigid and had to alter in accordance with the context. Here political realities had to be faced and so the majority of the council could not be held to be 'biased' when all this meant was that they were 'politically predisposed' to answering the question in one way. The fact that there was a declaration of policy by the majority group did not disqualify the council from adjudicating on the planning applications.

Such an approach is not confined to issues of party political controversy. Similar situations arise when local authorities have to exercise their statutory powers to grant or refuse planning permission for development on land in which they have an interest. In *R v Sevenoaks District Council, ex p Terry*[37] a local authority's decision to grant planning permission to construct a supermarket on land it owned was challenged. Glidewell J said that in such cases the court should not apply the normal test of bias; instead it should ask itself whether the council had before determining the application for planning permission acted in a way that makes it clear that 'when the committee came to consider . . . the application . . . it could not exercise proper discretion'.[38]

Similar issues may also arise when councils decide upon matters on which councillors feel strongly and have publicly expressed their views. In *R v Reading Borough Council, ex p Quietlynn Ltd*[39] the court did not invalidate an authority's decision to refuse a sex shop licence where the panel which considered the licence application included a councillor known to have strong views against sex establishments. Sedley J has recently emphasized that these decisions do not mean that the principles relating to bias as expounded in *R v Gough* do not apply to councils. Rather they rest on a different line of reasoning altogether, namely those concerned with fettering of discretion.[40]

The opportunity to participate and be heard

As with the rule against bias, the principle that those affected by decisions must be given a proper opportunity to participate and be heard (*audi alterum partem*) was largely developed in the context of court decisions.[41] It is assumed that here fairness requires parties to the dispute to be informed about the basic allegations made against them and to be given adequate opportunities

[37] [1985] 3 All ER 226.

[38] [1985] 3 All ER 226, 233.

[39] (1986) 85 LGR 387.

[40] *R v Secretary of State for the Environment, ex p Kirkstall Valley Campaign Ltd* [1996] 3 All ER 304.

[41] Including disciplinary tribunals and cases involving deprivation of office, e.g. *Bagg's Case* (1616) 11 Co Rep 93.

to refute these and to present their own arguments. As with the rule against bias, the task for the judges has been to adapt and apply this court-oriented facet of procedural fairness to the vast range of different types of decision-making functions performed by administrative bodies, ministers and officials. The following propositions show that the courts have been sensitive to the practical problems faced by such bodies.

(1) Fairness does not necessarily require administrative bodies to hold oral hearings as this would often be impracticable and too cumbersome.[42]
(2) Even where oral hearings are held, fairness does not necessarily require parties to be legally represented.[43]
(3) Parties are not necessarily allowed to cross-examine witnesses.[44]
(4) Although fairness normally requires people to be told what factors are being taken into account by the body, particularly when these bear upon the person's reputation or are necessary in order to enable allegations to be refuted, this does not necessarily mean that full details have to be disclosed, particularly where issues of confidentiality or national security arise.[45]

These propositions may be illustrated by considering some particular cases.

In *R v Army Board, ex p Anderson*[46] Anderson, a black former soldier, applied for judicial review to challenge the way in which the Army Board had considered his complaints of racial discrimination within the army. The Army Board tried to justify its refusal to disclose evidence to Anderson, or to grant him an oral hearing at which he could cross-examine witnesses and make his own legal and factual submissions, by arguing that it was performing an administrative rather than a judicial function. In rejecting this argument Taylor LJ said that it did not matter whether the procedure of the Army Board could be categorized as judicial or administrative. He stressed that the Army Board must adopt high standards of fairness because it is a forum of last resort dealing with an individual's fundamental statutory rights under the Race Relations Act 1976 not to be discriminated against. The Board, he held, must hold a proper hearing in the sense that it must meet to consider all the relevant evidence and contentions before reaching its conclusions. But this did not mean that the Board had to act as if it were a court of law. Its proceedings need not in all cases include oral hearings, and procedures such as cross-examination are not always required. Whether these procedures are needed to achieve fairness depends, said Taylor LJ, on the subject matter and the circumstances (for example, whether there are substantial issues of fact which cannot be resolved on the available written evidence alone). He emphasized that the Board cannot adopt an inflexible policy never to hold

[42] For example *R v Army Board, ex p Anderson* discussed below.
[43] For example *R v Maze Prison Visitors, ex p Hone* [1988] AC 379.
[44] For example *Herring v Templeman* [1973] 3 All ER 569.
[45] For example *R v Secretary of State for the Home Department ex p Hosenball* [1977] 1 WLR 766; *R v Secretary of State for the Home Department ex p Cheblak* [1991] 1 WLR 890.
[46] [1992] QB 169.

oral hearings or never to allow cross-examination; and he went on to say that the Board had a duty to show complainants all the material that it has seen, apart from any documents for which public interest immunity may be properly claimed. Since the Army Board had failed to comply with these principles certiorari was granted to quash the Board's decision.

A contrasting example of this pragmatic approach is provided by *Bushell v Secretary of State for the Environment.*[47] Mr Bushell, a member of a pressure group campaigning against the construction of the M42 motorway, sought to challenge the ministerial decision to confirm the construction of a section of the motorway on the grounds that the decision had been unfairly taken. At the public local inquiry into the route of that section of motorway, the pressure group questioned the need for the motorway as a whole, arguing that the government's traffic predictions underestimated the capacity of the existing roads in the area. To make their case they wanted to cross-examine departmental officials. The inquiry inspector refused them permission to do so on the basis that the traffic predictions and the way they were calculated (set out in a Department of Trade publication known as the Red Book) were matters of government policy and therefore beyond the scope of the inquiry. After the inquiry the inspector, relying on the predictions, recommended that the scheme be permitted to go ahead. The predictions were later revised to suggest that the existing roads could in fact carry higher volumes of traffic. Despite this revision, the minister accepted the inspector's recommendations and approved the scheme.

One of Bushell's arguments on judicial review was that the inspector's refusal to allow the cross-examination was unfair and contrary to the rules of natural justice. The challenge failed at first instance, but succeeded in the Court of Appeal (by a majority). The Secretary of State successfully appealed to the House of Lords (although Lord Edmund-Davies delivered a powerful dissenting speech). Lord Diplock's speech is particularly interesting. He started by considering the role of inquiries into motorway schemes. Two possible approaches were possible, he said. One emphasizes the importance of inquiries for objectors and places a high premium on the need to promote and protect rights to participate. The other approach sees inquiries as an information-gathering tool for ministers. This view stresses the discretionary nature of the procedure and the absence of procedural rights for participants. Diplock adopted the second approach. He said that although inspectors have a 'constitutional duty' to act 'fairly and honestly' they are not required to apply procedural 'concepts that are appropriate to the conduct of ordinary civil litigation between private parties'. In his view, 'to "over-judicialize" the inquiry by insisting on observance of the procedures of a court of justice . . . would not be fair'.

At first sight it may seem odd to see a judge argue that it would be unfair to provide rights to cross-examination. But for Lord Diplock fairness had to be considered in the context of motorway planning as a whole, and not just

[47] [1981] AC 75.

in the light of the impact of the decision on specific individuals or groups. In his view it would have been unfair to allow these objectors to cross-examine the officials because this might have led to a change in the route of the motorway that would have adversely (and unfairly) affected the interests of others who were not involved in this inquiry. It might also have caused a delay in the motorway programme and this might have been unfair to the general public.

The implication is that fairness is an issue that can only be considered by asking: fairness to whom? In some cases the only contenders to be treated fairly are the individuals who are immediately affected by the official action, as in *Anderson*. In this type of case the court is essentially concerned with balancing the needs of the official body against the interests of the individual. However, in more complex cases, like *Bushell* and *Franklin*, where official decisions affect a wider section of the public, there is a distinction between what is fair to the litigant and what is fair to the wider community. The prevailing tendency appears to be to assume that this decision should be taken by those who are, at least in theory, politically accountable rather than by judges.

Another decision, illustrating the way the courts have adapted the strict principle of *audi alterum partem* to the context of administrative decision-making, was that in *McInnes v Onslow-Fane*.[48] The British Boxing Board of Control had previously withdrawn various licences from the plaintiff including his licence to train boxers. He subsequently applied five times for a manager's licence but was refused each time. He challenged these refusals arguing that the decisions had been made in breach of the rules of natural justice in that he had not been informed of the case against him or been given an oral hearing.

Megarry V-C distinguished between three types of case. First, there are what he called the 'forfeiture cases' where a decision takes away some existing right or position, as where a person is expelled from an organization or where a licence is revoked. Megarry V-C said that in these cases, those affected are entitled to an unbiased tribunal, to notice of charges, and to the right to be heard in answer to the charges. At the other extreme stand the 'application' cases where the decision-maker merely refuses to grant the applicant the right or position that he seeks. This might include membership of an organization or a licence to do certain acts. Here, according to Megarry V-C, nothing is being taken away and normally there are no charges made against the applicant. There is therefore no need for a hearing, nor any obligation to provide reasons. The only duty upon the decision-maker is to act 'honestly and without bias or caprice'.

[48] [1978] 1 WLR 1520. Would decisions of the British Boxing Board of Control now be subject to judicial review on grounds of procedural fairness? Cf. discussion of amenability to judicial review at p. 509 above. Note that obligations to comply with the rules of fairness might be implied into contracts and therefore binding between bodies and their members, even though their decisions are not judicially reviewable in public law. Such a contract could not, of course, assist a person who was not a member but wanted to join the body.

Between these two types of case stands an intermediate class. This he called the 'expectation' cases (though a better label might perhaps have been 'renewal' cases). This includes situations where the applicant is seeking to have an existing licence renewed. According to Megarry V-C, these may be more akin to forfeiture cases than application cases because the failure to fulfil the legitimate expectation raises the question of 'what it is that has happened to make the applicant unsuitable' when the applicant was previously thought suitable. The use of the term 'legitimate expectation' is rather unfortunate because Megarry V-C apparently did not intend to suggest that the applicant had to establish that a legitimate expectation (in the sense used later in this chapter) had been created by the public body.[49]

According to Megarry V-C, *McInnes* was an application case and as there had been no allegation of dishonesty, bias or caprice the challenge failed. In arriving at his decision Megarry V-C took into account policy considerations that had little or nothing to do with the particular facts. In particular, he said that the courts should be cautious before imposing 'undue burdens' on bodies like the British Boxing Board for this could encourage them to try to avoid the prospect of litigation by being too ready to grant licences. Speculation by judiciary of this type is common and is often used to justify non-intervention. It is invariably based on little or no evidence about the way decisions will be received, and what impact they might have.[50] Certainly, it would be very unfortunate if judges were to refuse to impose fair procedures for fear that bodies would simply reach decisions that would not be challenged when there is no evidence that this would in fact occur. Another problem with the decision is that Megarry V-C's threefold categorization takes no account of the impact which decisions may have on the person concerned. Rejection by the Boxing Board of Control, for example, may well have a serious adverse effect on a person's livelihood and reputation regardless of whether it is the first time they have applied for a licence or whether they are seeking to renew a licence they already possess.

The common law and reasons

The courts expect decisions of official bodies to be reasoned and rationally reached.[51] They also expect bodies to be open and cooperative, or, in the words of Lord Donaldson MR, 'to conduct their affairs with the cards face up on the table'.[52] As one judge has put it, there is a 'perceptible trend

[49] In view of the legitimate expectation cases it might be better to say that people in this position can 'reasonably anticipate' that their licence will be renewed.

[50] Cf. Lord Bridge's opinion in *R v Deputy Governor of Parkhurst Prison, ex p Leech* [1988] AC 533 in which he said that judges should not feel themselves unable to impose principles of law by unsubstantiated fears that this would have an adverse effect on prisons.

[51] For discussion of statutory obligations to give reasons, see Chapter 23. Cf. the obligations imposed by Art 190 of the EC Treaty on Community institutions to give reasons for their decisions.

[52] *R v Lancashire County Council, ex p Huddleston* [1986] 2 All ER 941.

towards an insistence on greater openness, or if one prefers the contemporary jargon "transparency", in the making of administrative decisions'.[53]

Nevertheless, as yet there is no general obligation upon bodies to give reasons for their decisions where this is not required by statute. This is not to say that public bodies never have to explain their actions. We have already seen, for example, that fairness may require a decision-maker to tell a person the case against him *before* a decision is made so that he will be able to participate in the decision-making.[54] Bodies are also obliged to justify their actions to *the court* if they are challenged by judicial review; and their actions may be invalidated if they are unable or unwilling to do so, or if their reasons show that they have abused their powers.[55] Here, however, we are concerned with a third situation, namely where fairness requires public bodies to give *those affected* reasons for actions *after they have been taken*, even when this requirement is not imposed by statute. Where reasons are required in the interests of fairness, failure to provide them is now regarded as an independent, self-standing ground for invalidating action.[56]

The advantages and disadvantages of reasons

Before going further it is useful to consider the advantages and disadvantages of imposing an obligation to provide reasons. These were conveniently summarized by Sedley J in *R v Higher Education Funding Council, ex p Institute of Dental Surgery*:[57]

> The giving of reasons may . . . concentrate the decision-maker's mind on the right questions . . . show that the issues have been conscientiously addressed and how the result has been reached; or alternatively alert the recipient to a justifiable flaw in the process. On the other side of the argument, it may place an undue burden on decision-makers; demand an appearance of unanimity where there is diversity; call for the articulation of sometimes inexpressible value judgments; and offer an invitation to the captious to comb the reasons for previously unsuspected grounds of challenge. It is the relationship of these and other material considerations to the nature of the particular decision that will determine whether or not fairness demands reasons.

Also bear in mind that there is no routine discovery of documents in judicial review,[58] and so without reasons an applicant may have no effective way of finding out the real basis upon which a decision was made.

53 Lord Mustill in *R v Secretary of State for the Home Department, ex p Doody* [1994] 1 AC 531, 561.
54 See p. 582 above.
55 *Padfield v Minister of Agriculture, Fisheries and Food* [1968] AC 997, per Lord Pearce 1053–4, Lord Reid at 1032, Lord Hodson at 1049 and Lord Upjohn at 1061; see also *R v Secretary of State for Trade and Industry, ex p Lonrho plc* [1989] 1 WLR 525.
56 As to what constitutes adequate reasons, see p. 537.
57 [1994] 1 WLR 242.
58 See p. 496.

When are reasons required?

In the *Institute of Dental Surgery* case the Institute unsuccessfully challenged the Higher Education Funding Council's assessment of its research rating on the grounds, *inter alia*, that it had not provided reasons for its decision. In giving judgment Sedley J distinguished between two classes of case. First, he said, there are those in which the *nature and impact* of the decision require reasons as a routine aspect of procedural fairness. Secondly there are those cases in which 'some trigger factor' is required to show that, in the circumstances of the particular decision, fairness requires reasons to be given.

CASES WHERE REASONS WILL ALWAYS BE REQUIRED IN THE INTERESTS OF FAIRNESS

The House of Lords' decision in *R v Secretary of State for the Home Department, ex p Doody*[59] illustrates the first class. Here the question to be decided was whether prisoners who had received a mandatory sentence of life imprisonment were entitled to be told how long they could expect to wait before being considered for release. In the words of Lord Mustill:[60]

> The giving of reasons may be inconvenient, but I can see no ground at all why it should be against the public interest: indeed, rather the reverse. This being so, I would ask simply: is refusal to give reasons fair? I would answer without hesitation that it is not. As soon as the jury returns its verdict the offender knows that he will be locked up for a very long time. For just how long immediately becomes the most important thing in the prisoner's life.

The implication is that where a decision impinges upon a person's liberty, and arguably where other fundamental rights are involved, fairness demands that the person be given reasons for that decision. This is both in the general interests of fairness and also because it is necessary to enable those affected to exercise any rights of appeal they may have or to challenge the decision. Lord Mustill said that without reasons, prisoners have:[61]

> virtually no means of ascertaining whether . . . the decision-making process has gone astray. I think it important that there should be an effective means of detecting the kind of error which would entitle the court to intervene, and in practice I regard it as necessary for this purpose that the reasoning of the Home Secretary should be disclosed.

CASES WHERE SPECIFIC FACTORS 'TRIGGER' THE OBLIGATION TO GIVE REASONS

R v Civil Service Appeal Board, ex p Cunningham[62] illustrates the second class of case, namely where 'some trigger factor' is required to show that fairness requires reasons to be given. Cunningham had been unfairly dismissed from a post in the Prison Department of the Home Office. As a civil servant he could not complain to an industrial tribunal but was entitled to seek

[59] [1994] 1 AC 531.
[60] Lord Mustill at 564–5.
[61] Lord Mustill at 565.
[62] [1991] 4 All ER 310.

compensation from the Civil Service Appeal Board. The Board awarded him compensation of £6,500 in circumstances in which, had he been able to go to the industrial tribunal, the tribunal would have awarded him in the region of £15,000. Despite his requests, the Board gave no reasons for the level of its award and he challenged its refusal to do so. The Court of Appeal held unanimously that he was entitled to reasons. Lord Donaldson MR based his decision on the broad ground that 'fairness requires a tribunal such as the board to give sufficient reasons for its decision to enable the parties to know the issues to which it addressed its mind and that it acted lawfully'.[63]

The other judges also emphasized that while there is no general duty to give reasons, reasons ought to have been given in this case. The judges were influenced by several (trigger) factors. These included that the award affected Cunningham's means of livelihood; there was no appeal from the Board's decision and that the only remedy is judicial review (which is difficult to use without knowledge of the reasons for the decision); that statute did not authorize the non-provision of reasons; and that the giving of reasons would not prejudice the public interest or otherwise conflict with the system under which the Board operates.

Legitimate expectations

We have seen that *Ridge v Baldwin* held that principles of fairness should be triggered by rights.[64] Used in this context the idea of rights was never intended to be interpreted narrowly, and certainly not to be confined to those rights which are enforceable in private law. This broader conception of rights has since been further emphasized by the development, in Britain largely since the 1980s, of principles associated with the protection of legitimate expectations.[65] As we shall see in the discussion that follows legitimate expectations may arise where rights do not, and could not, exist. What then are legitimate expectations, to what can they relate, and how are they protected?

What are legitimate expectations?

In order to be protected by public law, expectations must be legitimate and not all expectations, even if they are reasonable, will necessarily be regarded as legitimate. Determining whether an expectation is legitimate can be a rather circular exercise in the sense that applicants may not know whether the courts will respect their expectations as legitimate until the courts have decided the matter.

Legitimate expectations can arise when public bodies indicate either expressly or by their past practice that they will adopt certain procedures (such

63 [1991] 4 All ER 310, 320.

64 [1964] AC 40.

65 See further P. Craig, 'Legitimate Expectations: A Conceptual Analysis' (1992) 108 LQR 79 and 'Substantive Legitimate Expectations in Domestic and Community Law' [1996] CLJ 289; R. Baldwin and D. Horne, 'Expectations in a Joyless Landscape' (1986) 49 MLR 685. Principles associated with the protection of legitimate expectations were already fundamental to Community law: see J. Schwarze, *European Administrative Law* (1992), pp. 867–8.

as consultation) or apply certain policies in their decision-making. Where they do arise, principles of good administration and basic fairness demand that official bodies act consistently with these expectations, unless they can justify not doing so to the courts. In this situation the courts will be interested in both the legality and reasonableness of the authority's action and in whether the authority has acted fairly to those whose expectations have been thwarted.[66]

It is important to note that principles of consistency and obligations to respect legitimate expectations cannot estop public authorities from exercising their public functions, even where they know, or ought to have known, that individuals have relied on their statements or past practice to their detriment. Sedley J has emphasized that such reliance has no bearing upon the legitimacy of the existence of the expectation: 'it is upon the practices or promises of the public authority that any such expectation will be built: whether it stands up depends not at all on how much the decision-maker knew of the applicant's reliance on the practice or promise'.[67] This is not to say that knowledge of reliance is irrelevant; it cannot prevent public bodies from exercising their powers in the public interest but its existence may be relevant to whether the authority has acted fairly towards the individual in the circumstances and may therefore be one of the factors to be weighed by the courts.

In the past a distinction has often been drawn between *procedural expectations* and *substantive expectations*, and it has commonly been argued that legitimate expectations can only relate to matters of procedure and not substance. This distinction is now of limited practical value. Nevertheless its retention is worthwhile for the purposes of explanation.

PROCEDURAL EXPECTATIONS

The most straightforward cases are those where it is alleged that the body has failed to satisfy an expectation that a particular procedure will be followed. The leading example is the *GCHQ* case.[68] Here the House of Lords accepted that the unions had a legitimate expectation that the government would consult with them prior to changing the terms and conditions of employment of civil servants. This legitimate expectation was not conferred by statute nor by contract or terms of employment. It arose because it had been settled practice in the past to consult in this situation. In the circumstances, however, the expectation was overridden by the interests of national security.

The unions' legitimate expectation may be described as being a procedural expectation rather than a substantive expectation because the unions were not claiming that the government was obliged, after the consultation, to reach a particular decision;[69] and presumably their claim, under this head,

[66] See *R v Ministry of Agriculture, Fisheries and Food, ex p Hamble (Offshore) Fisheries Ltd* [1995] 2 All ER 714, 731.

[67] *Ex p Hamble (Offshore) Fisheries Ltd* at 725.

[68] *Council of Civil Service Unions v Minister for the Civil Service* [1985] AC 374, considered in Chapter 28.

[69] Although implicit in the argument for consultation is the further argument that the views obtained following the consultation have to be considered.

would have been satisfied even had the government, following the consultation, arrived at precisely the same decision. In this situation there might have been a dispute as to whether the consultation had been real and adequate.

A second type of case involves allegations that there is a legitimate expectation, again based on promise or practice, that the body will approach their decision-making in a certain way. Unlike the first type of case nothing might have been said or implied about the specific procedures to be followed. Here the courts have held that those affected have a legitimate expectation, either that the authority will act consistently or, if it proposes to change its approach, that it will first give those affected a chance to make representations.

For example, in *R v Secretary of State for the Home Department, ex p Khan*[70] a Home Office circular letter set out the procedure and criteria that would be applied by the Home Office when considering whether to permit a child who was subject to immigration control to be allowed entry into the United Kingdom for the purposes of adoption. Mr and Mrs Khan wished to adopt a relative's child who was living with its mother in Pakistan. The Home Office refused entry clearance on the basis of criteria that differed from those indicated in the letter. The Court of Appeal held that the Home Office had failed to respect the Khans' legitimate expectation that the policy contained in the letter would be followed and quashed the refusal of entry.[71] Parker LJ said that 'the Secretary of State, if he undertakes to allow in persons if certain conditions are satisfied, should not . . . be entitled to resile from that undertaking without affording interested persons a hearing and then only if the overriding public interest demands it'.

This hearing need not be oral. The essential obligation is to provide those affected with a chance to make representations as to why their case should be dealt with in the way they thought it was going to be, rather than in accordance with the new policy. Subject to what is discussed below, these legitimate expectations may be described as procedural because the courts are only insisting that individuals be allowed to make representations as to why a particular approach ought or ought not to be followed. The expectation is not that a particular substantive decision will be reached.

SUBSTANTIVE EXPECTATIONS

So far we have seen that the courts will infer legitimate expectations to procedural fairness. Some judges have argued that legitimate expectations can only relate to matters of procedure and cannot impose restrictions on the freedom of public bodies to make decisions on matters of substance.[72] They argue that individual expectations, however reasonable, cannot force official bodies to apply particular policies or decide cases in particular ways.

This would conflict with the general principle that public bodies cannot fetter their freedom to change their policies or practices whenever their perception

[70] [1984] 1 WLR 1337.

[71] [1984] 1 WLR 1337, 1344.

[72] For example *R v Secretary of State for Transport, ex p Richmond upon Thames London Borough Council* [1994] 1 WLR 74, *per* Laws J.

of the public interest dictates this to be desirable.[73] It may also be argued that the common law cannot prevent public bodies from making decisions that are otherwise within their statutory powers.

In *Re Findlay*,[74] for example, two prisoners sought judicial review when the Home Secretary changed his policy on the granting of parole in a way that meant that these prisoners were likely to spend longer in prison than they had previously, and reasonably, expected. The House of Lords rejected their argument that they had a legitimate expectation that the old and more beneficial policy would continue to apply. Lord Scarman said that:[75]

> The most that a convicted prisoner can legitimately expect is that his case will be examined individually in the light of whatever policy the Secretary of State sees fit to adopt provided always that the adopted policy is a lawful exercise of the discretion conferred upon him.

Similarly in a case involving a change in departmental policy relating to the compulsory retirement age of civil servants, Lord Diplock said that:[76]

> The liberty to make such changes is something that is inherent in our constitutional form of government. When a change in administrative policy takes place and is communicated in a departmental circular . . . any reasonable expectations that may have been aroused . . . by any previous circular are destroyed.

In another case a tobacco manufacturer challenged the Secretary of State's decision to ban oral snuff (a form of tobacco designed to be chewed).[77] The tobacco company had established a factory to manufacture the product with the help of a government grant and had agreed that it would not market the oral snuff to persons under 18 years old. When the total ban was imposed the company argued that the support given by the government created a legitimate expectation that it would be able to continue to produce the oral snuff, unless stronger evidence emerged that the product was a threat to health. In the Divisional Court Taylor LJ said that:[78]

> The applicants are understandably aggrieved that, after leading them on, the government should then strike them a mortal blow by totally banning their products . . . However, a minister cannot fetter a discretion given him under statute. Provided he acts within his statutory powers, rationally and fairly, he is entitled to change his policy.

Even if the government owed the company a moral obligation, it would, he added, 'be absurd to suggest that some moral commitment to a single company should prevail over the public interest'.

These decisions seem to suggest that legitimate expectations can never limit the freedom of public bodies to change policies, provided they have

[73] See Chapter 23.
[74] [1985] AC 318.
[75] [1985] AC 318, 338.
[76] *Hughes v Department of Health and Social Security* [1985] AC 776, 788.
[77] *R v Secretary of State for Health, ex p United States Tobacco International Inc* [1992] QB 353.
[78] At 368–9.

statutory power to do so. This, however, would be too sweeping. It cannot be assumed that the courts will treat all policy decisions in the same way. There may, for example, be a difference between decisions which affect a narrow range of individuals and those which have wider and more diverse impacts.[79] Where, for example, decisions affect particular individuals but have little or no knock-on effect for others, fairness may prevent official bodies departing from previous statements or past practice (particularly where individuals have acted on the basis of those statements or practices), even where this dictates that a particular decision is almost inevitable.

In *Khan*, Parker LJ said that the Home Office should be unable to resile from its undertaking 'without affording interested persons a hearing *and then only if the overriding public interest demands it*'. In other words, he appears to be saying that the Khans not only had a legitimate expectation of a hearing before the policy was changed, but also a legitimate expectation that the policy would not be altered, unless there was an 'overriding public interest' to justify the change. The first expectation is purely procedural, but the second expectation is more than procedural. It imposes a presumption against altering the policy itself and forces the decision-maker to explain why the public interest justifies depriving the Khans of their expectation.[80]

This line of argument was developed in *R v Secretary of State for the Home Department, ex p Ruddock*.[81] Here there was no question of the courts implying an expectation of a hearing before the decision was taken. In this case Joan Ruddock, a leader of the pressure group CND, challenged the legality of a warrant granted by the Secretary of State permitting the tapping of her telephone. She argued that the stated criteria for granting warrants (including that major subversive activity was being carried out) could not have been applied in respect of the activities of CND, and if they were the Secretary of State's decision must have been unreasonable.

Obviously, the whole purpose of tapping would be defeated if the person were told about it in advance. Nevertheless, the courts accepted that the Secretary of State was obliged to act fairly and consistently in accordance with the criteria which had been published and regularly used in the past. By implication he would also be bound to reach decisions which were not unreasonable on the facts having regard to those criteria. In the event, however, the judge accepted the Secretary of State's contention that he had applied the stated criteria and refused to find his decision irrational.

More recently, in a case in which a trawler owner unsuccessfully challenged a change in government policy relating to the granting of fishing licences, Sedley J adopted Parker LJ's approach in *Khan* and, drawing extensively on Community law, argued that 'the question is always whether the

[79] *R v Secretary of State for Transport, ex p Richmond upon Thames London Borough Council* [1994] 1 WLR 74, 93.

[80] It has been said that 'this is as near as public law is able to approach to estoppel': *per* Sedley J in *R v Ministry of Agriculture, Fisheries and Food, ex p Hamble (Offshore) Fisheries Ltd* [1995] 2 All ER 714, 731. Cf. *R v Secretary of State for the Home Dept, ex p Hargreaves*, *The Times* 3 Dec. 1996.

[81] [1987] 1 WLR 1482.

discipline of fairness, imposed by the common law, ought to prevent the public authority . . . from acting as it proposes' in relation to matters of procedure *or* matters of substance.[82] This being so, the courts have ultimate responsibility for determining whether public bodies have adequately respected both procedural expectations and expectations that particular policies will be adopted or criteria applied:[83]

> While policy is for the policy-maker alone, the fairness of his or her decision not to accommodate reasonable expectations which the policy will thwart remains the court's concern (as of course does the lawfulness of the policy). To postulate this is not to place the judge in the seat of the minister . . . it is the court's task to recognise the constitutional importance of ministerial freedom to formulate and reformulate policy; but it is equally the court's duty to protect the interests of those individuals whose expectation of different treatment has a legitimacy which in fairness outtops the policy choice which threatens to frustrate it.

In practice, it seems that the courts now first enquire into whether the applicant has a reasonable expectation, procedural or substantive. This enquiry considers whether, for example, the public body has stated or implied that it will follow a particular procedure or adopt a particular approach. The court also considers claims that public bodies have made changes to policy contrary to legitimate expectations. If such expectations have been thwarted the courts scrutinize both the reasonableness of the authority's action (applying the *Wednesbury* principles) and its fairness to the applicant. In assessing fairness the courts consider the impact of the decision on the individual weighed against the public interest issues involved.

CONSTITUTIONAL JUSTIFICATIONS FOR IMPOSING COMMON LAW STANDARDS OF FAIRNESS

'Fairness' requirements can have serious implications for public bodies

The imposition of common law requirements of fairness can have serious implications for official bodies. Not only will there be practical consequences flowing from the need to redesign procedural systems (for example, to ensure that in future individuals are kept informed and that they are able to make representations), as in the context of legitimate expectations, there may also be policy implications. In some contexts common law notions of fairness can challenge cultural traditions and affect the whole style of work within an organization. The impact of judicial intervention on prison disciplinary systems during the 1980s provides an example.[84]

[82] *R v Ministry of Agriculture, Fisheries and Food, ex p Hamble (Offshore) Fisheries Ltd* [1995] 2 All ER 714, 723. Cf. Laws J in *R v Secretary of State for Transport, ex p Richmond upon Thames*, n. 79 above.

[83] *Hamble Fisheries* at 731.

[84] See further S. Livingstone and T. Owen, *Prison Law* (1993).

Until the late 1970s it had been assumed that the courts would not intervene to regulate prison disciplinary procedures. At that time the prevailing culture saw prison discipline as an internal matter that ought not to be subject to external control. If the courts intervened this would both encourage prisoners to complain and undermine the authorities in the eyes of prisoners. This in turn would make it more difficult for governors to maintain order.

This internal culture was challenged in a series of judicial decisions during the late and early 1980s which held that in making disciplinary decisions Prison Boards of Visitors were bound by the rules of natural justice and, amongst other things, that these rules could require prisoners to be legally represented.[85] When these decisions were first handed down some in the prison service were aghast. They feared that the service would no longer be able to function as it had and prisoners would be given a licence to complain and disrupt the system. Moreover, it was feared that once lawyers were permitted into the procedure the disciplinary system would slow down and become overly formal. There were also industrial relations and cost implications. Now that prisoners could be legally represented prison officers would also want representation, thereby adding cost to the process.

This is one aspect of a complex and continuing saga which we cannot explore here.[86] The main point here is to emphasize that judicial decisions do have impacts, and that these can be controversial and significant. It may be argued that if controversial change is to be forced on administrative systems it should be introduced by politicians using legislation and political influences, rather than by courts using the common law in specific cases—not least because those who are politically accountable have a far stronger claim to represent the public interest than do non-accountable judges.[87]

How then can judicially imposed fairness be justified?

There is a strong argument that the *ultra vires* doctrine cannot justify judicial imposition of procedural standards where statutes are silent or perceived by judges to be inadequate. Such an argument is particularly powerful when statutes say nothing about procedure, for here it is difficult to claim that the requirements may be inferred from the legislation. Nor, it might be argued, can the *ultra vires* doctrine justify imposing principles of the common law

[85] *R v Board of Visitors of Hull Prison, ex p St Germain* [1979] QB 425; *R v Board of Visitors of Hull Prison, ex p St Germain (No 2)* [1979] 1 WLR 1401; *R v Secretary of State for the Home Department, ex p Tarrant* [1985] QB 251. Note that Boards of Visitors no longer have disciplinary functions.

[86] Judicial review is one of several factors which can influence change in situations such as this. For further discussion see G. Richardson, *Law, Process and Custody* (1993); M. Loughlin '"The Underside of the Law": Judicial Review and the Prison Disciplinary System' (1993) 43 CLP 40; M. Loughlin and P. Quinn, 'Prison Rules and the Courts: A Study of Administrative Law' (1993) 56 MLR; and S. Livingstone 'The Impact of Judicial Review in Prisons' in B. Hadfield (ed.), *Judicial Review: A Thematic Approach* (1995).

[87] See Chapter 20.

which had not been developed when the legislation was originally drafted. How then can judicial intervention to achieve procedural fairness be justified?

Instrumentalism and process values

Genevra Richardson considers this question by analysing judicial attitudes against the background of the literature on procedural fairness.[88] From this literature she identifies two broad approaches which might be used to justify requiring procedural fairness. The first, she calls the *instrumental approach*. This argues that fair procedures are important and justified because they are likely to lead to better-quality and more 'accurate' decisions than unfair procedures. From this perspective, bias and prejudice are to be eliminated because they will lower the quality of decisions. Those affected should be allowed to participate because this will make it easier for decision-makers to get their decisions right. In this sense, procedural fairness is an aspect of the requirement that authorities adopt a proper process of reasoning. The second approach she calls the *process values* approach. Fair procedures, she says, may be justified:[89]

> in so far as they protect values which exist independently of the direct outcome of the decision [my] right to be heard . . . is essential in order to protect my personal dignity and autonomy, and is thus justified irrespective of the impact of my participation on the ultimate decision.

This approach, then, is not concerned with whether decisions are properly made or 'accurate', but with ensuring that procedures (particularly those relating to the ability of people to participate in decisions adversely affecting them) further the 'obligation to respect a person's dignity and autonomy as a human being'.[90]

Having identified these two approaches, Richardson moves on to consider judicial attitudes. She points out that since *Ridge v Baldwin*,[91] obligations to act fairly have been triggered by the existence of rights and interests which the courts deem worthy of protection. For Richardson this is significant because it indicates that the courts are not concerned with issues of individual dignity and autonomy as such, but only with the more specific relationship between the alleged unfairness and the *legally recognized interests of the specific applicant*. In her view, this suggests that the common law is primarily instrumental in approach: it focuses upon the correctness of the decision in the light of the interests involved, rather than upon the value of procedural fairness in its own right.

Richardson acknowledges that there are two lines of judicial thinking which appear to conflict with this conclusion. First, there is authority for the view that

[88] Genevra Richardson, *Law, Process and Custody: Prisoners and Patients* (1993), Chapter 3. See also her essay 'The Legal Regulation of Process' in G. Richardson and H. Genn (eds.), *Administrative Law and Government Action* (1994).

[89] Richardson, n. 88 above, p. 26.

[90] Ibid., p. 29. In this respect the approach is an example of the impact-based approaches to judicial review: see p. 473.

[91] [1964] AC 40.

the courts can intervene whether or not the unfairness has actually affected the decision. In other words, that the courts can intervene where a person has, for example, been deprived of a hearing and it is clear that the same decision would have been reached had he been heard.[92] However, she argues that such cases do not affect her overall conclusion because in these situations the courts are likely to exercise their discretion not to intervene anyway.[93]

The second line of judicial reasoning which appears to be against her relates specifically to allegations of bias. As we have seen the principles relating to bias do not require applicants to show that bias actually influenced the decision. The basic view is that justice must be seen to be done and must be rooted in confidence. Judges emphasize that confidence in the system will be undermined if there is a 'real danger' that officials or judges are biased.[94] In this context Richardson appears to accept that the common law may be more concerned with values than with pure instrumentalism.

Fairness and democracy

These cases, however, raise another issue which is not adequately encompassed by either the 'instrumental' or the 'values'-based approaches so far considered. As mentioned above, the cases on bias are rooted in the need to ensure that decision-making systems possess the confidence of those affected by them and, indeed, of the public in general. Without this confidence people will distrust systems and the systems will consequently lose their authority and legitimacy. From this perspective judicial intervention may be justified, not in order to ensure the accuracy of decisions or to further values such as individual dignity, but in order to help maintain the integrity and legitimacy of the procedures themselves—and ultimately the democratic authority of public bodies and the governmental system itself.

In earlier chapters we have seen that modern theories of judicial review justify judicial intervention on the grounds that the courts have an important role to play in furthering democratic values. Whereas the 'old orthodoxy', as we have called it, emphasized the supremacy of Parliament, the 'new orthodoxy' recognizes that the parliamentary system offers inadequate opportunities for citizens to participate in government and inadequate controls over the executive to fully reflect 'true' democracy.[95] This being so, one of the tasks of the courts is to fill the gaps left by political procedures. We identified earlier two broad lines of thinking which seek to explain and justify judges adopting a more assertive role than orthodox theory permits. The 'impact-based' approaches concentrate on the impact of decisions on those affected and reflect the principle that authorities must have legally acceptable justification for taking action which interferes with the rights and interests of citizens, the level of justification varying depending on the importance of the rights and interests involved. As we saw in Chapter 20, a basic criticism of

[92] See e.g. Lord Wright in *General Medical Council v Spackman* [1943] AC 627, 644–5.
[93] *Glynn v Keele University* [1971] 1 WLR 487.
[94] Lord Hewart CJ in *R v Sussex Justices* [1924] 1 KB 256, 259.
[95] See Chapters 5, 6, and 20.

such approaches is that they tend to assume that judges are able, and should be able, to decide which rights and interests society recognizes as worthy of protection in circumstances where Parliament has been silent or unclear. 'Process-based' approaches to judicial review seek to address this problem by emphasizing the role courts can play in facilitating citizen participation in government and the adoption of fair procedures, rather than the importance of substantive rights and interests themselves.

Common law principles of fairness have a role to play within both these approaches to judicial review. For example, as discussed earlier in this chapter, the requirement to provide reasons, where it is imposed by the common law, is central to the idea that public bodies should act rationally and should be able to justify and explain themselves, even where not expressly required to do so by statute. The provision of reasons also helps citizens and groups to decide whether decisions are challengeable and, if so, on what grounds. The importance of considerations such as these may extend beyond the particular dispute. The giving of reasons may lead to greater openness of government more generally, and so to a better-informed community. If this is so, it should enhance democratic processes and improve the overall quality of systems of accountability.

Seen from this perspective, common law fairness is not to be regarded as a threat to parliamentary democracy, nor is it a sign that judges are usurping constitutional power. Rather, this body of principle may be seen as a desirable, and indeed necessary, contribution to the practical application of democratic values. This is particularly so where principles of fairness encourage participation in decision-making and greater openness in government.

The above view assumes that principles of fairness do operate to further democracy. This, however, may be a controversial assumption. There are at least three reasons for this. First, some will oppose the idea that an unelected and unaccountable judiciary can be trusted to further democratic principles. Secondly, it may be argued that while some principles of common law help to further openness and participation, principles such as fairness are sufficiently pliable to be used by judges to restrict participation and limit accountability, where for example, courts regard countervailing public interests to justify doing so.[96] Thirdly, even if judges and others believe that judicial decisions will lead to greater participation and more open and accountable government, we cannot be sure that they will have this effect in practice.[97]

Questions

1. Why is fairness a more flexible concept than natural justice?
2. What are the arguments for and against limiting judicial intervention on grounds of procedural fairness to situations where the rights and interests of identifiable individuals have been adversely affected by decisions?

[96] See e.g. cases referred to in n. 45 above.

[97] See Sir Stephen Sedley, 'Human Rights: A Twenty-First Century Agenda' [1995] PL 386; Genevra Richardson and Maurice Sunkin, 'Judicial Review: Questions of Impact' [1996] PL 79.

3. You are a lawyer working for a local authority. It urgently needs to reduce expenditure and decides to close an old people's home and move residents to other homes in the borough. No formal procedure is set out in any statute as to how this has to be done. Many, but not all, of the residents are confused and their families live all over the country.

(a) Does the common law require you to consult with individual residents? With their families? With the staff? How long a period of notice do you need to give them of the intended closure? Is five days sufficient? Do the people affected need to be given an opportunity to question the councillors about any alternative money-saving schemes they may have considered? (For a case with similar facts, see *R v Devon County Council, ex p Baker*.[98] Here it was held that there was no duty to consult residents of an old people's home about its closure. That decision may be compared with *R v Secretary of State for Transport, ex p Sherrif & Sons*[99] where the Secretary of State was required, before withdrawing a freight licence, to provide an opportunity to make representations.)

(b) Can you think of any good reasons why a council in this sort of situation may want to keep consultation to a minimum, or avoid it altogether? Do you think that a court should ever accept any of these reasons (or excuses)?

4. Some may see *Bushell v Secretary of State for the Environment*[100] as a sensible application of the principle that the courts should leave policy issues to ministers who are answerable to Parliament. Others may view this approach as an example of judicial abrogation of the court's responsibility to protect the right of citizens to participate in the protection of the environment in situations where political accountability is likely to be little more than a fiction. Which of these views would you be happier to adopt?

5. Sophie is a competent law student who expected to pass the LLB examination at Anytown University. In fact, she failed two of the four subjects and so failed the whole examination. She strongly suspects that the only explanation for her low marks is bias by the some of the examiners (who she believes disagree with her strongly-held political views). Sophie was not permitted to see her marked examination scripts, but she was told the marks she obtained. There is no appeal from the Board of Examiners, but there is an internal review procedure. At the review board (which comprised of all the examiners from the original Board plus the vice-principal) Sophie was refused permission to cross-examine the chairman of the Board as to why the examinations are marked with the candidates' names rather than anonymously. But Sophie was allowed to present her case.

At the conclusion of the review board's hearing, the following written statement was issued: 'The Board of Examiners confirms the decision it took in June that Sophie has failed in two subjects and therefore failed the entire Examination. In accordance with its usual practice, the Board declines to give reasons for its decision.'

Advise Sophie.

6. 'The idea that judges can review policy and procedures on the grounds of so-called "fairness"—which really means what judges say it means—is an affront to democracy.'

Discuss.

[98] [1995] 1 All ER 73.
[99] (1986) *The Times*, 18 December.
[100] [1981] AC 75.

26

JUDICIAL REMEDIES AGAINST PUBLIC AUTHORITIES

INTRODUCTION

The applicant's perspective

Many applicants for judicial review have no more than a passing interest in the details of the legal arguments advanced on their behalf. For them, the grounds of judicial review examined in the preceding chapters are merely a means to a successful end. 'Success' may come in different forms, however. Every year a few high-profile cases receive considerable press coverage and the consequential publicity may itself be important to applicants, even if the court does not accept their legal arguments.[1] The mere fact that an application has been granted leave may prompt a public authority to reconsider its original decision before the full hearing. In many cases, though, success (or failure) is measured by the formal remedial orders which a court grants (or refuses) at the conclusion of the full hearing.

Remedies aim to redress grievances. What exactly litigants want varies depending on the nature of their complaint.[2] A family claiming to be homeless may want to force the local housing authority to provide immediate housing. A pharmaceutical company which alleges that the Department of Health has unlawfully refused to grant it a licence to market a new and potentially profitable drug may want to force the department to change its mind; it might also want financial compensation for the loss of profits caused by the delay necessitated by the litigation. A person disciplined by a tribunal which acted unfairly may want the decision quashed and the matter fairly reconsidered so that his name and reputation are cleared.

[1] See e.g. in *R v Cambridge District Health Authority, ex p B* [1995] 1 WLR 898 (the Court of Appeal refused an application by the father of a child who had been refused medical treatment for leukaemia by a health authority, but an anonymous donor was prompted to pay for the girl to be treated in a private hospital).

[2] For a more detailed examination, see C. Lewis, *Judicial Remedies in Public Law* (1992) and de Smith, Woolf and Jowell, *Judicial Review of Administrative Action* (5th edn., 1995), Part IV.

The constitutional importance of remedies

As well as providing redress for particular applicants, remedies also play a broader role in the system of public law. They are the practical method by which the court gives effect to the rule of law. By issuing formal remedial orders, the judges require public authorities to comply with the legal obligations contained in legislation and the common law. Remedies are therefore central to the relationship between legal and political power in the constitution. Many difficult questions arise. What, for example, can the courts do if government is unable or unwilling to comply with their decisions? How sympathetic should the courts be when government concedes that it has acted unlawfully, but claims that administrative pressures, resource constraints and other practical factors mean that it is now in the public interest to overlook the illegality? Bearing in mind that judicial remedies are essentially directed at past actions, should the courts have greater powers to step in so as to ensure that public bodies introduce new systems and behave differently in the future?[3] Questions such as these raise further issues as to the relationship between the courts and government: ought the remedial system to assume that judges should have the power to force government to act against its wishes, or should the relationship between courts and government be based, not on coercion and force, but on trust and guidance?[4]

The remedies available on a judicial review

The Supreme Court Act 1981, ss 29[5] and 31 give the High Court jurisdiction to make several different kinds of formal orders on applications for judicial review to:

(a) compel authorities to comply with the law: mandamus and (mandatory) injunctions;
(b) prevent public bodies from acting or continuing to act unlawfully: prohibition and (prohibitory) injunctions;
(c) quash an unlawful decision by a public authority and where appropriate to remit the matter back to the original decision-maker to reconsider the matter: certiorari and power to remit;
(d) declare what the law is: declarations;
(e) provide compensation: damages;
(f) preserve the position of the parties between the time of the application for leave and the hearing of the full application for judicial review: interim injunctions and stays of proceedings.

[3] As they can in some situations in the United States, see further D. Horowitz, 'Decreeing Institutional Change: judicial supervision of public institutions' [1983] Duke Law Journal 1265.

[4] See discussion of *M v Home Office* [1994] 1 AC 37 at p. 619 below.

[5] 'The High Court shall have jurisdiction to make orders of mandamus, prohibition and certiorari in those classes of cases in which it had power to do so immediately before the commencement of this Act.'

Section 31 states:

(1) An application to the High Court for one or more of the following forms of relief, namely—

(a) an order of mandamus, prohibition and certiorari;

(b) a declaration or injunction under section (2);

. . .

shall be made in accordance with rules of court by a procedure to be known as an application for judicial review.

(2) A declaration may be made or an injunction granted under this subsection in any case where an application for judicial review, seeking that relief, has been made and the High Court considers that, having regard to—

(a) the nature of the matters in respect of which relief may be granted by orders of mandamus, prohibition or certiorari;

(b) the nature of the persons and bodies against whom relief may be granted by such orders; and

(c) all the circumstances of the case,

it would be just and convenient for the declaration to be made or the injunction to be granted, as the case may be. . . .

(4) On an application for judicial review the High Court may award damages to the applicant if—

(a) he has joined with his application a claim for damages arising from any matter to which the application relates; and

(b) the court is satisfied that, if the claim had been made in an action begun by the applicant at the time of his making his application, he would have been awarded damages. [. . .]

(5) If, on an application for judicial review seeking an order of certiorari, the High Court quashes the decision to which the application relates, the High Court may remit the matter to the court, tribunal or authority concerned, with a direction to reconsider it and reach a decision in accordance with the findings of the High Court.

(6) Where the High Court considers that there has been undue delay in making an application for judicial review, the court may refuse to grant—

(a) leave for the making of the application; or

(b) any relief sought on the application, if it considers that the granting of relief sought would be likely to cause substantial hardship to, or substantially prejudice the rights of, any person or would be detrimental to good administration.

As is often the case, the meaning and effect of these statutory provisions are not immediately clear. The following points may help to make sense of them, before we look at the issues more closely. First, certiorari, prohibition and mandamus (which may be referred to collectively as 'the prerogative orders'), and also injunctions and declarations, are discretionary remedies. In other words, they are not granted automatically and may be refused, even where the court agrees with the applicant that the public body has exceeded or abused its powers.[6] In this context, s 31(2) provides guidance on some of the factors to be considered when judges decide whether these remedies are appropriate in judicial review proceedings.

[6] See p. 614 below.

Secondly, s 31(4) gives the court jurisdiction to grant damages on an application for judicial review, but paragraph (b) limits this to situations where damages would be awarded 'in an action begun by the applicant'. The term 'action' refers to private law proceedings commenced by writ and this therefore means that damages are in general only granted if the applicant has a claim in tort.[7]

Thirdly, s 31(5) means that the court can quash a decision by granting certiorari and at the same time send the matter back for reconsideration. This provision is designed to improve the court's power in certiorari cases. Previously the court's power was limited to quashing the decision, and therefore did nothing to force a fresh decision to be taken.

In its 1994 report, the Law Commission said that there is no longer any justification for retaining the archaic Latin titles of the prerogative orders, arguing that the function performed by the remedies should be as clear as possible. It recommended that instead of mandamus, prohibition and certiorari these remedies should be known as mandatory orders, prohibiting orders and quashing orders.[8]

Having set the general background, we shall now look in more detail at when, how and why courts make particular sorts of remedial orders, beginning with interim relief.

INTERIM RELIEF

Often an applicant will not want to wait the many months it may take to have the judicial review application finally resolved before obtaining some form of remedial order from the courts.[9] The applicant may therefore request an interim remedy (or 'interlocutory relief'), usually at the leave hearing. Because the prerogative orders and declarations[10] cannot be granted on an interim basis, the main interim remedy is the interim injunction.[11] At this stage, the court has a very difficult task in deciding what is best done. It still does not have all the information necessary to tell whether or not the applicant will eventually win the case, yet its decision on interim relief may have enormous repercussions for both parties to the application, and also for the general public.

A person who claims a local authority unlawfully refuses to recognize that he is homeless might have to sleep rough if the court does not step in from

[7] See p. 623 below.

[8] *Administrative Law: Judicial Review and Statutory Appeals* (Law Com No 226), paras 8.1–3; in his report *Access to Justice* (1996), Lord Woolf disagrees: see Chapter 18, para. 25.

[9] Some cases take years, particularly if a question of Community law is referred to the ECJ for a preliminary ruling under Art 177 of the EC Treaty: see Chapter 29.

[10] The Law Commission has recommended that the courts should be able to make interim declarations. See further Zamir and Woolf, *The Declaratory Judgment* (2nd edn., 1993), para. 9.05. Cf. *R v Secretary of State for the Environment, ex p RSPB* (1995) 7 Admin LR 434.

[11] The court may also 'stay proceedings': RSC, Ord 53, r 10(b).

the very outset of the legal challenge and order the authority to provide temporary accommodation until the case can be finally dealt with;[12] on the other hand, if the court does step in the local authority may have to spend very scarce funds housing someone not entitled to be housed. A person challenging the legality of a deportation order may want to prevent the authorities putting him on a plane until the legality of the order can be resolved;[13] but a deportee may just be cynically seeking judicial review in order to be able to spend a few more months in the United Kingdom. A pharmaceutical company challenging the validity of a decision to ban one of its products may lose hundreds of thousands of pounds of profit if it is prevented from marketing its products until the full hearing of its application for judicial review; however the medicine may truly carry a risk of harming people who use it.

In deciding whether or not to grant an interim injunction on an application for judicial review, the court takes into account a range of factors.[14] Obviously, it has to be satisfied that the application is not frivolous and that the applicant has at least a reasonable prospect of success at the full hearing. Where the applicant is arguing that legislation is invalid,[15] the court requires the applicant to demonstrate that this argument is *very likely* to succeed at the full hearing. The justification for this is the need for legal certainty and the fact that many third parties might be affected by a temporary suspension of legislation awaiting the full hearing.[16] If an award of damages at the full hearing adequately compensates the applicant for any loss suffered in the period up to that hearing, then generally the court refuses interim relief. In practice, however, damages are rarely available or appropriate in applications for judicial review.[17]

An applicant seeking interim relief is often required to give a 'cross undertaking in damages', though the court does not insist on this if an applicant is legally aided and has no resources. The effect of such an undertaking is that if the applicant loses at the full hearing, he has to pay the respondent damages to cover any loss caused by the interim order having been made.[18]

[12] An interim injunction is normally prohibitive (i.e. it normally *prevents* the public body doing something), but in appropriate circumstances, such as homelessness cases, it can be mandatory: see e.g. *R v Kensington and Chelsea Royal London Borough Council, ex p Hammell* [1989] QB 518.

[13] For a particularly grave case see *M v Home Office* [1994] 1 AC 37, discussed at p. 619 below.

[14] The general approach is laid down in *American Cyanamid Co v Ethicon Ltd* [1975] AC 396. This was a private law case, and many adaptations to the framework it sets out have to be made in the context of applications for judicial review.

[15] For instance, that an SI is *ultra vires* its enabling Act, or that legislation is contrary to Community law.

[16] See *R v Secretary of State for Transport, ex p Factortame Ltd (No 2)* (Case 213/89) [1991] 1 AC 603 and *R v HM Treasury, ex p British Telecommunications plc* [1995] COD 56.

[17] See p. 622 below.

[18] Many local authorities were deterred from commencing proceedings (not of course judicial review) and seeking interim injunctions to prevent shops trading on Sundays contrary to s 47 of the Shops Act 1950 for fear of the enormous sums in damages they might have to pay if the shops eventually won in their argument that the trading restrictions were contrary to Community law: see Chapter 30.

FINAL REMEDIES

At the conclusion of the full hearing, the court has at its disposal a range of remedial orders.

Prohibitory remedies

The prerogative order of prohibition and (prohibitory) injunctions are used to prevent official bodies acting unlawfully. Orders of prohibition have been used, for example to stop a doctor who was incapable of being impartial from deciding that a chief inspector was permanently disabled,[19] and to prevent a local authority licensing additional taxi-cabs without first granting a hearing to existing taxi drivers.[20]

Remedies to compel action

Here too there are two main remedies: mandamus and mandatory injunctions. As with the other prerogative orders, mandamus has a long history and has been widely used. It has compelled public bodies to disclose information where this is necessary in the interests of fairness[21] and in *Padfield v Minister of Agriculture* it was the remedy which forced the minister to establish the complaints committee, despite his claim that the legislation gave him complete discretion in the matter.[22] Mandamus, it may be noted, can only be used to compel performance of duties which are legally enforceable. In *R v Inner London Education Authority, ex p Ali*,[23] for instance, the courts refused to force a local education authority to open more schools because the statutory duty to provide sufficient primary schools in its area was only a 'target duty' and was not enforceable in the courts.[24] At the other end of the spectrum, because mandamus is a public law remedy, it cannot be used to compel the performance of duties which give rise to private law rights. As with the other prerogative orders, mandamus cannot be obtained as an interim remedy, and in future it is likely that use of prohibition and mandamus will decline as more litigants use the more flexible injunction.

Quashing

Certiorari quashes unlawful decisions of public bodies. Its effect is to eradicate the decision thereby rendering it a nullity having no legal effect. At one

19 *R v Kent Police Authority, ex p Godden* [1971] 2 QB 662.

20 R *v Liverpool Corp, ex p Liverpool Taxi Fleet Operators' Association* [1972] 2 QB 299.

21 *R v Kent Police Authority, ex p Godden*, above.

22 See Chapter 23. Cf. *R v Secretary of State for Trade and Industry, ex p Lonrho* [1989] 1 WLR 525 where the House of Lords emphasized that mandamus can only force official bodies and ministers to exercise their discretionary powers lawfully; it cannot be used to dictate what decision should be reached.

23 [1990] COD 317.

24 On duties of 'imperfect obligation', see p. 539.

time there were a large number of technical restrictions on the availability of this and the other prerogative orders. It was thought, for example, that certiorari and prohibition were only available against 'judicial' and not 'administrative' bodies; that they could only protect rights and not other interests; and that they could not be used against delegated legislation.[25] Fortunately, these restrictions have now been eroded by the courts and it is generally accepted that certiorari is available to quash any unlawful action taken by public authorities.

The usefulness of certiorari is limited by its inability to do more than quash a decision: by itself it cannot stop action being taken or compel a body to act. To save time and trouble statute now permits judges, when issuing certiorari, to remit the matter back to the original decision-maker with a direction to reconsider the matter in accordance with their findings.[26] Suppose, for example, a person successfully challenges a tribunal on the grounds that it reached a decision after unfairly refusing to allow legal representation. Certiorari can be used to quash the decision that has been made. But, in order to obtain a fresh decision, the applicant can ask the court to remit the case back to the tribunal with directions as to how it should proceed. It is important to remember that even if certiorari is granted and the matter is remitted back with directions, the tribunal may still reach the same conclusion as it did originally.

Obtaining a declaration of the legal position

As its name suggests, a declaration is a statement by the court of the legal position.[27] Unlike the other remedies declarations are non-coercive and therefore those to whom they are directed cannot be forced to comply and will not be in contempt of court if they do not do so. This apparent weakness is in fact seen as one of the strengths of this remedy, particularly in public law when the courts emphasize (recognizing the ultimate weakness of their position) that their relationship with government should be based on trust and cooperation rather than on force and coercion. Certainly, the non-coercive nature of the declaration partly explains why there have been few restrictions imposed on the scope of declarations compared with those imposed on the other remedies. Declarations are therefore used in a very wide variety of situations both in private and public law and have often been associated with some of the most significant and interesting developments in the law.[28]

[25] Many of these restrictions stem from misunderstanding of Atkin LJ's statement that these remedies were only available against bodies having legal authority to determine questions affecting the rights of subjects and having the duty to act judicially: see *R v Electricity Commissioners, ex p London Electricity Joint Committee* [1924] 1 KB 171, 205. See also Chapter 25.

[26] RSC, Ord 53, r 9(4); Supreme Court Act 1981, s 31(5).

[27] See generally Zamir and Woolf, *The Declaratory Judgment* (2nd edn., 1993).

[28] The flexibility of declaratory relief may be illustrated by the decision early this century in *Dyson v Attorney General* [1911] 1 KB 410 where a declaration was granted that the Commissioners of the Inland Revenue had unlawfully issued tax forms, even though Dyson had

One area where declaratory relief may be particularly significant is in the context of providing judicial guidance on the legality of future conduct. Official bodies are often forced to guess whether their decisions are challengeable and they run the risk that schemes, possibly involving the investment of massive public resources, may be challenged only after they have been implemented. In this situation advisory declarations and prospective declarations may be of assistance.

Advisory declarations

At one time the courts refused to give advisory declarations. This was because of the way the system was abused by the Stuarts in the early 17th century. At that time the judges could be dismissed at the King's pleasure and there was a real danger that the judiciary would be coerced into giving the executive the advice it wanted, thereby legitimating its action and precluding later challenge.[29] As the judges became more independent of the executive the practice of approaching the judges for their advice declined. Today the use of advisory declarations is somewhat controversial, not because it would necessarily threaten the actual independence of the judiciary (as it did in the early 17th century) but because it 'may give the appearance . . . of bringing the judges too close to the executive, making them too associated with the public bodies which may later appear as defendants before them'.[30] Another danger is that if there is no actual opponent, the advisory opinion may be given on an inadequate, and possibly misleading, presentation of the issues. Advisory opinions may also create embarrassment for the courts in future cases where actual problems raise issues that were not anticipated, as well as uncertainty for parties who may be unsure whether their problem falls within the scope of the advisory opinion or not. Their use may also encourage litigants to try to use the courts to raise hypothetical issues.[31] Despite these dangers the courts have on occasion been prepared to grant advisory declarations where these appear to provide certainty and guidance to public bodies and to aid public administration by reducing the risk that decisions will be declared illegal retrospectively. In *R v HM Treasury, ex p Smedley*,[32] for example, Sir John Donaldson MR accepted that delegated legislation could be challenged before it had obtained the necessary approval of both Houses of Parliament. He said that if the court deferred consideration of the matter until after parliamentary approval had been obtained this would cause unnecessary delay and potentially waste Parliament's time. In another case[33] doubt arose over whether, in the light of an

no cause of action. See also *Guaranty Trust Co of New York v Hannay & Co* [1918] 2 KB 623 and Zamir and Woolf, *The Declaratory Judgment*, p. 21. *Anisminic v Foreign Compensation Commission* [1969] 2 AC 147 was another famous declaration case.

29 See further Zamir and Woolf, *The Declaratory Judgment*, p. 121 where they discuss *Peacham's Case* (1615) and the *Shipmoney case* (1637).

30 Zamir and Woolf, *The Declaratory Judgment*, para. 4.046.

31 Paras 4.046 and 4.051.

32 [1985] QB 657.

33 *R v London Transport Executive, ex p Greater London Council* [1983] QB 484.

earlier decision of the House of Lords,[34] the Greater London Council could lawfully make grants to London Transport. Before implementing its proposals the GLC obtained a declaration that the new proposals were within their powers. The Law Commission has recommended that the Supreme Court Act 1981 be amended to put the court's power to give advisory declarations on a statutory basis.[35]

Prospective declarations

The term 'prospective' refers to declarations that guide decision-makers as to their future actions, but which do not retrospectively upset past actions.[36] These declarations may be made, for example, in cases where the court decides not to declare the challenged administrative action unlawful, but nevertheless takes the opportunity to clarify the law for the future. This occurred in the *AMA* decision,[37] where Webster J granted a declaration that the minister was in breach of the mandatory duty to consult before making Housing Benefit Regulations (thereby indicating what needed to be done in the future) but refused to quash the regulations because of the administrative inconvenience that this would have caused.[38]

JUDICIAL CAUTION IN THE GRANT OF REMEDIES

The courts have shown themselves unwilling to grant relief to applicants in certain circumstances. At a general level, all the public law remedies described above are 'discretionary', meaning that a court may refuse to make a formal order even though an applicant has established that the decision being challenged was indeed unlawful. More specifically, the courts have been loath to issue certain orders against 'the Crown' and reluctant to grant remedies which impinge on Parliament and the legislative process. We examine each of these issues in turn.

Judicial discretion to withhold remedies

Certiorari, prohibition, mandamus, declarations and injunctions are all said to be 'discretionary'.[39] The power to withhold a formal remedial order from

[34] *Bromley London Borough Council v Greater London Council* [1983] 1 AC 768.

[35] *Administrative Law: Judicial Review and Statutory Appeals* (Law Com No 226) 1994, paras 8.9–14; see also Lord Woolf, *Access to Justice* (1996), Chapter 18, para. 10.

[36] See C. Lewis, *Judicial Remedies in Public Law* (1992) p. 196 and C. Lewis, 'Retrospective and Prospective Rulings in Administrative Law' [1988] PL 78.

[37] *R v Secretary of State for Social Services, ex p Association of Metropolitan Authorities* [1986] 1 WLR 1.

[38] See also *R v Dairy Produce Quota Tribunal, ex p Caswell* [1990] 2 AC 738 where the court declared the true meaning of the relevant regulations but refused to upset the particular decision because of the applicant's delay.

[39] See further Sir Thomas Bingham, 'Should Public Law Remedies be Discretionary?' [1991] PL 64 and C. Lewis, *Judicial Remedies in Public Law*, Chapter 11.

an otherwise 'successful' applicant raises a number of issues of principle and practice. What justifications are there, for example, for the court refusing to invalidate governmental action which has been found to be unlawful? Does the possibility that government may be allowed to rely on its unlawful decisions not conflict with the very idea of the rule of law? More specifically, the ability of the courts to refuse remedies even to those who have been 'successful' shows the perilous nature of the judicial review process for applicants who have already had to obtain leave and satisfy the courts about their legal submissions at a full hearing.[40] Certainly the idea that relief may be refused even where unlawfulness has been found reinforces the idea that public law is not about rights of individuals.

Precise classification of the factors which may influence the way judicial discretion is exercised is difficult, but six main factors may be mentioned as particularly important.[41] Running through these is the idea that since judicial review is a public law remedy, the courts must balance the interests of the applicant in obtaining the remedy requested against the impact of granting the remedy on the interests of the public, and particularly the interests of the administration.

Conduct of the applicant

Applicants may be refused a remedy, despite the merits of their legal argument, because of their own conduct. For instance, the court refused a remedy to a local authority which sought to challenge ministerial confirmation of its own proposals for reorganizing schools by relying on its own procedural error.[42] Applicants who claim to have been treated unfairly may be refused a remedy if they did not object at the time[43] or because they have acquiesced in the action taken.[44] An applicant may also be refused a remedy because there was a delay in bringing the application for judicial review. In *R v Dairy Produce Quota Tribunal, ex p Caswell* certiorari was refused because the delay was thought to be detrimental to good administration in that if the application were allowed substantial numbers of other challenges would be expected and this could involve reopening many cases that had already been decided.[45]

[40] Note that in its 1994 Report the Law Commission seemed unconcerned with the existence of remedial discretion.

[41] See C. Lewis, *Judicial Remedies in Public Law*, Chapter 11.

[42] *R v Secretary of State for Education and Science, ex p Birmingham City Council* (1985) 83 LGR 79.

[43] A remedy was refused because an applicant had not objected at the time to certain members voting at a council meeting: *R v Governors of Small Heath School, ex p Birmingham City Council* [1990] COD 23.

[44] A person was taken to have acquiesced when he failed to object to the presence of a member of a tribunal despite believing him to be biased: *R v Nailsworth Licensing Justices, ex p Bird* [1953] 1 WLR 1046.

[45] [1990] 2 AC 738 and Supreme Court Act 1981, s 31(6)(b). Delay may also be a reason for the court refusing leave: see p. 485.

Relief of no practical use

The courts may refuse relief where the issue is no longer contentious. The courts, for example, refused to declare that a special prison was unlawful when the unit had already been closed.[46] Remedies have also been refused when procedural errors have had no practical impact on applicants. For instance, a failure to publicize planning proposals may not justify quashing the grant of planning permission if in fact the public was adequately informed of the proposals and the objectors had ample opportunities to make their objections known.[47] In these cases the courts have not been persuaded by the argument that even though granting a remedy serves little purpose, it serves to enhance and underpin the rule of law.[48]

Impact on third parties

The courts are aware that judicial review decisions may affect those who are not party to the proceedings. So, for example, the interests of dealers in the stock market will be considered by the courts when considering applications involving regulatory bodies such as the Monopolies and Mergers Commission or the Panel on Take-Overs and Mergers.[49] Similarly, when a local authority challenged a minister on the status of a particular school the court considered the interests of other schools,[50] and when delegated legislation is challenged the courts consider the impact of the challenge on others who may be affected by the delegated legislation.[51]

Impact on administration

The courts take the view that it is not always in the public interest to quash decisions if this will impose heavy administrative and other burdens on the respondent public body: in *R v Monopolies and Mergers Commission, ex p Argyll Group*,[52] the Master of Rolls emphasized the need to take into account the principles of good public administration when deciding whether to grant a remedy. Here the decision that a take-over bid had been abandoned was taken by the chairman of the Commission when it should have been taken by the Commission as a whole.[53] Despite the unlawful delegation, the Court of Appeal refused to grant a remedy after weighing the interests of the

46 *Williams v Home Office (No 2)* [1981] 1 All ER 1211.

47 *R v Lambeth London Borough Council, ex p Sharp* (1988) 55 P & CR 232. The court may refuse relief where the applicant was not given all the relevant information initially but had been before the final decision was made: *R v Secretary of State for Foreign and Commonwealth Affairs, ex p Everett* [1989] QB 811.

48 This argument was rejected when used by Gerry Adams to challenge an order excluding him from England after it had been revoked: *R v Secretary of State for the Home Department, ex p Adams* (No. 2) [1995] COD 426.

49 See e.g. *R v Panel on Take-Overs and Mergers, ex p Datafin plc* [1987] QB 815.

50 *R v Secretary of State for Education and Science, ex p Avon County Council* [1990] COD 237.

51 *R v Secretary of State for Social Services, ex p Association of Metropolitan Authorities* [1986] 1 WLR 1.

52 [1986] 1 WLR 763.

53 On delegation, see p. 542.

applicant (a commercial rival seeking to prevent the bidder from making a fresh bid) against the need for speedy decision-making, finality and decisiveness in the context of a decision that would affect the wider financial market. The likely administrative inconvenience was also the reason why Webster J refused to quash regulations in the *AMA* case despite the minister's failure to consult.[54]

Alternative remedies and implied exclusion of judicial review

As we have seen, the courts normally expect litigants to exhaust other remedies before applying for judicial review and may either refuse leave or refuse to grant relief where other more suitable remedies exist.[55]

Standing

It has been stated that, in considering what final remedy to grant an applicant, the court must consider the degree of interest which the applicant has in the matter.[56] For instance, it is often said that the standing requirements for obtaining mandamus (an intrusive remedy because it compels public bodies to act) are more stringent than for the other remedies. In *R v Felixstowe Justices, ex p Leigh*[57] for example, a journalist challenged the refusal of magistrates to reveal their identities. He obtained a declaration that their refusal was unlawful, but the court declined to grant him a mandamus compelling the Bench to disclose their identities to him. Had he been a party to the proceedings before the magistrates he might have been entitled to the remedy.[58] Several commentators have argued persuasively that this link between standing and final remedies is misconceived, and that if an applicant has a sufficient interest to apply for judicial review this should be enough to obtain any of the remedies.[59]

The problem of 'the Crown' and ministers

Apart from claiming a general discretion to withhold any public law remedy for the reasons just set out, courts have in the past shown particular reluctance about granting particular remedial orders against the Crown. The term 'the Crown' is a confusing one. It is commonly used as a synonym for 'central government', but in the context of remedies the expression relates to the more specific use of the term in the Crown Proceedings Act 1947. Although in modern times courts have always been prepared to grant the remedies of mandamus and prohibition against ministers (Secretaries of State),[60] until

54 *R v Secretary of State for Social Services, ex p Association of Metropolitan Authorities* [1986] 1 WLR 1.
55 See p. 507.
56 On standing, see p. 486.
57 [1987] QB 582.
58 Per Watkins LJ at 598.
59 See P. Cane, 'Statutes, Standing and Representation' [1990] PL 307.
60 For general discussion of these terms, see p. 50.

very recently courts believed they had no power to grant *injunctions* against ministers. At the final hearing of a judicial review, this did not really matter as mandamus and prohibition have the same effect as mandatory and prohibitory injunctions. This was, however, a problem when an applicant sought interim relief because there is no such thing as an 'interim mandamus', 'interim prohibition' or 'interim declaration'.[61] The extraordinary result was that a person seeking judicial review against a minister could not get any interim relief.

The background to the courts' reticence are some obscure constitutional fictions. One is that 'being the fountain of justice' the Crown 'can do no wrong' and therefore the courts ought not to be able to make coercive orders such as injunctions against the Crown or (it was believed) ministers of the Crown. Another was to say that it would be illogical for the court, the *Queen's* court, to make an order against the Crown as this would mean, in effect, that the Crown (through its judges) was telling the Crown (in the form of its ministers) what to do.

The more specific reason for not granting injunctions against ministers was the Crown Proceedings Act 1947. Introduced in the wake of the Second World War, this legislation sought to remove many, but by no means all, of the legal immunities and privileges of the Crown in litigation. In other words, it was designed to make it *easier* for aggrieved citizens to obtain justice against central government. However, s 21 provided that (emphasis added):

> (1) In any civil proceedings by or against the Crown the court shall, subject to the provisions of this Act, have power to make all such orders as it has power to make in proceedings between subjects . . . Provided that:
>
> (a) where in any proceedings against the Crown . . . *the court shall not grant an injunction* or make an order of specific performance, but may in lieu thereof make an order declaratory of the rights of the parties . . .
>
> (2) The court shall not in any civil proceedings *grant any injunction or make any order against an officer of the Crown* if the effect of granting the injunction or making the order would be to give any relief against the Crown which could not have been obtained in proceedings against the Crown.

For the purposes of the Act, ministers are 'officers of the Crown'.

The *Factortame* litigation illustrates the potential injustice that this could cause.[62] The Spanish fishermen applied for judicial review of the Secretary of State for Transport's decision not to register their trawlers to fish in UK waters under the Merchant Shipping Act 1988. Their lawyers knew that it would take many months for the courts to hear and reach a decision on their application; in the meantime, they wanted an interim injunction to prevent the minister de-registering their vessels until the final outcome of the case was known. At first the English courts refused to grant an interim injunction, on the ground that they had no power to do so as this would fall foul of

[61] See p. 609.
[62] See p. 117.

s 21(2) of the Crown Proceedings Act (judicial reviews were 'civil proceedings'). Moreover, it was said that s 31 of the Supreme Court Act 1981 (see above) was only intended to alter procedures and was not intended to increase the jurisdiction of the court to grant injunctions against the Crown. It was only when the ECJ insisted that the English courts provide adequate remedies to protect rights claimed under Community law that the House of Lords accepted that it did have power to grant interim injunctions against ministers, but only in situations where Community law rights were involved.[63] In private law proceedings and judicial review cases concerned only with domestic national law, the rule continued to be that interim injunctions could not be granted against ministers.

M v Home Office

In 1993 the House of Lords again considered this unsatisfactory state of affairs: *M v Home Office*[64] is a decision of profound constitutional importance and arose out of events that illustrate some of the worst aspects of modern administration. The consequences for the individual involved, however, were probably more tragic than this. The facts, which make chilling reading, were as follows. M, a teacher and political activist in his native Zaire, feared for his life. He travelled to the United Kingdom where he unsuccessfully applied for political asylum. Following this refusal, officials in the Home Office ordered that he be removed from the United Kingdom to Zaire at 6.30 pm on 1 May 1991. At 5.25 pm M's lawyers made an emergency application for leave to move for judicial review. At about 5.50 pm, the judge decided that there might be an arguable point and indicated that he wished M to remain in the United Kingdom so that the judicial review could be considered the following day. Counsel for the Secretary of State gave what the judge took to be an undertaking that M would not be removed. It appears that counsel did not intend to give such an undertaking and had not been instructed to do so. The judge's wish that M should not be removed was communicated to the Home Office but, nevertheless, M was put on a flight to Zaire via Paris. Although the Home Office knew of the judge's wish it was decided not take M off the flight when it landed in Paris.

Later that evening at 11.20 pm, after the plane had left Paris, the judge issued a mandatory interim injunction directing the Home Office to ensure the return of M to the United Kingdom. The next day, after taking legal advice,[65] the Secretary of State decided to challenge the order and not to take steps to return M in the meantime. After hearing argument, the judge accepted that (as the law then stood) he had no jurisdiction to make the mandatory interim injunction against the Secretary of State and he therefore

63 *R v Secretary of State for Transport, ex p Factortame Ltd (No 2)* [1989] AC 603.

64 [1994] 1 AC 377. The applicant's name was not mentioned in the law reports in order to protect him from any possible further threats.

65 From John Laws, then First Treasury Junior (or 'Treasury Devil'), the barrister in private practice briefed to advise and appear for the government in most judicial review cases. Sir John Laws is now a High Court judge.

discharged it. M 'disappeared' shortly after leaving the plane in Zaire; it is thought that he was abducted and killed by the forces from whom he had fled in his attempt to obtain political asylum in the United Kingdom.

Appalled by these events, M's lawyers began proceedings against the Secretary of State alleging that he was in contempt of court for failing to comply with the undertaking and with the mandatory order while it was in force. This led to the first ever finding that a minister of the Crown, Kenneth Baker MP, the Home Secretary, was in contempt of court. Two issues called to be decided. The first was whether the court had jurisdiction to make an interim injunctive order against a minister. The second was whether a minister of the Crown could be found to be in contempt of court.

COULD INJUNCTIVE ORDERS BE MADE AGAINST A MINISTER IN JUDICIAL REVIEW?

The minister, relying on *Factortame (No 1)*, argued that this question had to be answered in the negative because *M*'s case raised no issues of Community law and the Crown Proceedings Act 1947, s 21 prevented injunctive relief being ordered.

Lord Woolf delivered the leading speech. He distinguished *Factortame* which, he said, was primarily about the discriminatory effect of Part II of the Merchant Shipping Act 1988 rather than injunctive relief against the Crown; consequently the House of Lords had not had the benefit of full argument on this issue. Lord Woolf explained that although the Crown Proceedings Act 1947 prevented injunctions being available against the Crown or ministers of the Crown in 'civil proceedings' (unless Community law rights are involved) judicial review proceedings were not 'civil proceedings' and the prohibition in s 21 did not apply to judicial review. He therefore considered judicial review separately, explaining that the courts distinguished between the Crown as sovereign and ministers of the Crown. Prohibition and mandamus, which have the same practical effect as injunctions, are, he said, regularly granted against ministers of the Crown in respect of duties which are imposed by statute or prerogative, and carried out by them or by officials for whom they are responsible.

When declarations and injunctions were made available in judicial review proceedings by s 31 of the Supreme Court Act 1981, their availability was linked to the prerogative orders and statute did not distinguish between the scope of injunctive relief and the other remedies—although it did distinguish between the scope of damages and the other remedies. Lord Woolf therefore saw no reason why injunctions should not be available against ministers in the same situations as the prerogative orders, particularly when the only practical difference would be to enable the courts to grant interim relief against ministers.

This decision brought domestic judicial review in which injunctive relief was claimed against the Crown into line with the position where Community law rights were involved (as in *Factortame*). The bar on the granting of injunctions against the Crown is therefore now limited to proceedings which are expressly covered by the exclusion in s 21 of the Crown Proceedings Act 1947.

THE CONTEMPT ISSUE

As far as the contempt was concerned, Lord Woolf disagreed with the distinction which had been drawn by the Court of Appeal between ministers acting in their official capacity (who could not be the subject of contempt proceedings) and ministers and officials acting in their personal capacity (who could be subject to contempt proceedings). He said that contempt jurisdiction should be coextensive with the courts' jurisdiction to make orders which need to be protected by contempt proceedings. Accordingly, since the prerogative orders and injunctions can be issued against ministers and officials, they should be subject to contempt proceedings if they fail to comply. The need to impose any punishment would be very rare and usually a finding of contempt will suffice. This power, he said is none the less of great importance:

> It would demonstrate that a government department has interfered with the administration of justice. It will then be for Parliament to determine what should be the consequences of that finding.[66]

In the event, the House of Lords found the Secretary of State to be in contempt in his official capacity rather than, as the Court of Appeal had found, in his personal capacity.

In its 1994 report, the Law Commission recommended that in order to remove any remaining doubts the Supreme Court Act 1981 should be amended expressly to enable interim relief to be granted against ministers and against government departments in judicial review proceedings.[67]

Remedies and the legislative process

As well as their cautious attitude to granting injunctive relief against ministers and the Crown, the courts have also shown restraint about granting remedies to applicants which in some way would impinge on the legislative process. This can be seen most obviously in the principle of parliamentary supremacy by which the judges, as a matter of common law or convention, have decided that the courts will not review the legality of Acts of Parliament (except, now, in so far as they are incompatible with Community law).[68] The rules of parliamentary privilege also prevent the courts from granting injunctions to prevent the enactment of any public bill.[69]

In relation to delegated legislation, however, the courts have long accepted jurisdiction to intervene: *R v Secretary of State for Social Security, ex p Cotton* is a good illustration of this.[70] For many years, the courts confined themselves to making declarations that delegated legislation was unlawful (the

[66] [1994] 1 AC 377, 425.
[67] *Administrative Law: Judicial Review and Statutory Appeals* (Law Com No. 226), para. 6.13.
[68] See Chapter 5.
[69] See further de Smith, Woolf and Jowell, *Judicial Review of Administrative Action*, para. 17-038 and also the comments on *R v Secretary of State for Foreign and Commonwealth Affairs, ex p Rees-Mogg* [1994] QB 552.
[70] (1985) *The Times*, 14 December. See Chapter 27.

least intrusive kind of remedy). In more recent years, however, the courts have been prepared to grant certiorari[71] and the Court of Appeal has even indicated that, in appropriate cases, a mandatory injunction requiring a minister to draft and introduce an SI into Parliament may be granted.[72] It would, nevertheless, remain open for Parliament to refuse to enact a draft SI.

HABEAS CORPUS

All the remedial orders discussed so far in this chapter are obtained in applications for judicial review under RSC, Order 53. The writ of habeas corpus is a public law remedy, regarded by many people as being of great constitutional significance. It has its own procedure separate from Order 53.[73] The function of this remedy is to secure the safety and release of people who are unlawfully detained by a public body; the term habeas corpus means 'bring us the body'. Today, it is used mostly to question the legality of detention of immigrants by the Home Office or police and, less often, compulsory detention of people under the Mental Health Act 1983.

Controversially, the grounds on which habeas corpus may be obtained have been narrowed in recent years by the Court of Appeal.[74] It appears that, as the law now stands, habeas corpus can only be used where the allegation made is that the public authority has made a 'jurisdictional error' or acted completely beyond its powers. An allegation that the detention is 'merely' *Wednesbury* unreasonable or that there has been procedural impropriety is insufficient. In practice, lawyers acting for a detained person often make an Order 53 application for judicial review simultaneously with an application for the writ of habeas corpus. Unlike the other public law remedies, the court does not have a discretion to withhold habeas corpus once an applicant's lawyers have established that the detention is unlawful.

DAMAGES

Unlawful administrative action often results in people suffering pecuniary loss. For instance, a person may have a licence to operate a taxi revoked because the licensing authority acting in breach of common law fairness

[71] See *R v Secretary of State for Social Security, ex p Association of Metropolitan Authorities* [1986] 1 WLR 1 and *R v Secretary of State for Foreign and Commonwealth Affairs, ex p Rees-Mogg*, n. 69 above.

[72] See *R v HM Treasury, ex p British Telecommunications plc* [1995] COD 56. They have also been prepared to declare a draft Order in Council unlawful before presentation to Parliament: *R v HM Treasury, ex p Smedley* [1985] QB 657.

[73] See RSC, Order 54.

[74] See *R v Secretary of State for the Home Department, ex p Cheblak* [1991] 1 WLR 890 and *R v Secretary of State for the Home Department, ex p Muboyayi* [1992] QB 244. For further discussion, see A. P. Le Sueur, 'Should We Abolish the Writ of Habeas Corpus?' [1992] PL 13 and Law Com No 226, Part XI.

failed to hear the taxi driver's own version of an allegation made against him. Even if the decision is eventually quashed by the High Court, the driver may be prevented from carrying on his trade for a year or more if an interim injunction, suspending the revocation, cannot be obtained. In a situation like this, it may seem fair to require the public authority to compensate the victim of its unlawful action. Where an authority is carrying out a governmental function (such as licensing) in the public interest, surely the whole community (through its funding of the authority) ought to shoulder the burden of the authority's errors? The response of English law is ambivalent.

On the one hand there is Dicey's much-vaunted definition of the rule of law—that 'every man, what ever be his rank or condition, is subject to the ordinary law of the realm and amenable to the jurisdiction of the ordinary tribunals'.[75] This is given practical effect by the absence of any general immunity for ministers and officials being sued *personally* for tortious acts done while acting in their official capacity. In the case of officials, some corporate body with substantial assets (such as a central government department or a local authority) will normally also be vicariously liable. Not only may these bodies be sued, but in some limited circumstances the court may award exemplary damages (more than mere compensation) when the actions which constituted the tort were also 'oppressive, arbitrary or unconstitutional'.[76]

Set against this is the fact that there is no right to claim damages simply on the basis that a public authority has breached one of the grounds of judicial review. Even if an applicant for judicial review establishes that a decision causing loss was *Wednesbury* unreasonable, was taken in breach of the common law requirements of fairness or was in some sense 'illegal', this *of itself* gives no basis for claiming damages. What has to be shown is that some recognized tort, such as negligence, breach of statutory duty, misfeasance in public office, trespass or false imprisonment, has occurred.[77] Also, for a variety of reasons the courts are often loath to impose tortious liability on those carrying out governmental functions. In short, it may be difficult or even impossible for victims of unlawful government action to obtain compensation in the courts.[78]

Damages in applications for judicial review

Even though the grounds of judicial review and tort liability are distinct, since the 1978 procedural reforms to Order 53 it has been possible for an applicant for judicial review to include a claim for damages. Section 31(4)

[75] *Introduction to the Law of the Constitution*, p. 196, discussed in Chapter 6 above.

[76] The two leading authorities on exemplary damages generally are *Rookes v Barnard* [1964] AC 1129 and *Cassell & Co v Broome* [1972] AC 1027. The Law Commission is currently considering whether exemplary damages ought to be abolished.

[77] Or that a right conferred by Community law has been infringed: on this important area, see Chapter 29.

[78] Cf. the payment of *ex gratia* compensation following ombudsmen investigations: see Chapter 18.

of the Supreme Court Act 1981[79] gives the court power to award damages to an applicant for judicial review when 'the court is satisfied that, if the claim [for damages] had been made in an action [that is, private law proceedings] begun by the applicant . . . he would have been awarded damages'. In other words, s 31(4) is merely intended to streamline procedures and does not itself create any right to damages.

Where litigants seek only damages, and none of the public law remedies discussed earlier in the chapter, they will not normally apply for judicial review under RSC, Order 53 but will instead simply begin an ordinary action in the High Court or county court.[80] Where a litigant wants both a public law remedy (such as certiorari) and damages, an application for judicial review will have to be made. The court deals first with the public law issues, and then goes on to consider whether the applicant can also establish that a tort was committed by the public authority.

Detailed examination of the tort liabilities of government falls outside the scope of this chapter; the following sections merely highlight some of the issues surrounding three of the torts which are of particular importance to public lawyers: negligence, breach of statutory duty and misfeasance in public office.

Negligence

As where individuals sue other individuals or private organizations in negligence, a person suing a public official or authority in negligence has to establish that:

(a) a duty of care situation exists;
(b) the official or authority has breached that duty; and
(c) that the person has in consequence suffered damage.

In various ways, the courts have adapted this basic framework of liability to suit the special circumstances of public bodies carrying out governmental functions.

In deciding whether or not a duty of care relationship exists between a person and a public body in a particular situation, a distinction has often (but not always) been drawn between the 'policy' or planning roles of a public authority and its 'operational' activities.[81] In general the courts have been

[79] See p. 608 above.

[80] See *Roy v Kensington and Chelsea and Westminster FPC* [1992] 1 AC 624 and the discussion of procedural exclusivity in Chapter 22.

[81] For a fuller critical discussion of this distinction, see S. Bailey and M. Bowan, 'The Policy/Operational Dichotomy—A Cuckoo in the Nest' [1986] CLJ 430 and de Smith, Woolf and Jowell, *Judicial Review of Administrative Action*, para. 19-040. The starting point for the use of this idea in English law is Lord Diplock's speech in *Home Office v Dorset Yacht* [1970] AC 1004. It was taken up by Lord Wilberforce in *Anns v Merton London Borough Council* [1978] AC 728.

very loath to impose a duty of care in respect of policy decisions, which in essence are those which entail determining how scarce resources ought to be allocated. Assume, for instance, that local authorities have a permissive statutory power to set up dog warden schemes. (They may set one up, but are not under a statutory duty to do so.) The decisions about whether or not to set up a scheme, and if so how many wardens to employ, can be characterized as policy decisions. The day-to-day work of wardens, once a scheme is set up, may be described broadly as operational activity. The courts have recognized that there is no hard and fast dividing line between these two categories: for instance, a decision by the authority that dog wardens ought to patrol some parts of the borough more frequently than others might be said to be an operational decision with an element of policy.

To see how this approach may work, consider the following situations. If you are bitten by a stray dog in a park and sue the local authority in tort arguing that it was negligent in not providing sufficient dog wardens to patrol parks, a judge is likely to decide that this argument raises questions concerning how the local authority ought to have allocated its resources. If so, then the policy/operation approach suggests that a duty of care may be imposed only if its decision not to allocate more patrols to parks was *ultra vires* (in a public law sense).[82] Here it has to be established both that the authority has acted beyond its powers and that the authority owes a duty of care to you, which it has breached. If, on the other hand, your case is that a dog bit you because a warden carelessly let go of its collar as he was putting it in a van, then this is an operational error and the existence of a duty of care is much more easily established; there is no need to raise issues to do with *ultra vires*.

There are a number of reasons why the courts have developed this rather complicated approach to deciding whether a duty of care situation exists. One is that it helps the court to explain that some governmental decisions concerned with allocating resources are 'non-justiciable', and that the courts ought not to substitute their own decisions about how public money and resources should be spent for those taken by the public body in question.[83] The complication may be linked to the fact that, unlike the judicial review remedies, damages are available as of right so that the court has no discretion to refuse this remedy once a claim has been substantiated. For this reason, judges might be much more cautious about how the duty of care is defined in the first place. Underlying this approach is also a desire to avoid sending mixed messages to public authorities: how can a public authority be acting within the scope of the power conferred on it by Parliament and yet be required to pay compensation to those adversely affected by its actions?[84] The reasoning process set out above in effect tells authorities that their discretionary decisions will not lead to liability in negligence provided they

[82] Maybe this decision was *Wednesbury* unreasonable? Perhaps the words of the statute require a local authority, if it decides to set up a scheme, to provide a 'comprehensive' one?

[83] See further p. 549.

[84] No such conflict arises when Parliament provides for compensation to be paid to those adversely affected by statutory schemes.

are acting within their powers. It also warns them, however, that they must always exercise reasonable care when performing everyday operational tasks.

The Privy Council has doubted the usefulness of the policy/operation distinction in determining whether a duty of care should be imposed by the courts.[85] There are also many judgments in which the court has avoided referring to the test when it well might have done. A recent House of Lords' decision concerning the liability of social workers and education professionals, *X (Minors) v Bedfordshire County Council*,[86] however, used the distinction. Here Lord Browne-Wilkinson stressed that he did 'not believe that it is either helpful or necessary to introduce public law concepts as to the validity of a decision into the question of liability at common law for negligence'.[87] He preferred instead to talk more broadly (and less technically) about public bodies acting altogether outside the ambit of the discretion conferred on them by statute before a duty of care might be imposed on a policy decision.[88]

Apart from the difficulties of the policy/operation dichotomy, there are also numerous other problems standing in the way of a successful claim in negligence arising out of carelessness by public authorities. Just one can be mentioned here. This is the often expressed assertion that if liability in damages is imposed, a public authority might adopt an inappropriately 'defensive' approach to their duties. This has been one of the principal reasons why the courts have declined to impose a duty of care relationship between a financial regulator and investors,[89] and social workers and their clients,[90] and police and victims of crime, in respect of which Lord Keith said:[91]

> The general sense of public duty which motivates police forces is unlikely to be appreciable reinforced by the imposition of such liability so far as concerns their function in the investigation and suppression of crime . . . In some instances the imposition of liability may lead to the exercise of a function being carried out with a detrimentally defensive frame of mind.

Not all judges, however, have shared such cautious views. In *Home Office v Dorset Yacht Co Ltd*[92] Lord Reid rejected arguments put forward on behalf of the Home Office that imposing liability for the negligent actions of prison officers would be prejudicial to good administration. His experience led him to believe that 'Her Majesty's servants were made of sterner stuff'. The

[85] See *Rowling v Takaro Properties Ltd* [1988] AC 473.
[86] [1995] 2 AC 633.
[87] See p. 736F.
[88] See p. 737E. The term 'beyond the ambit' of power might be less technical than *ultra vires*, but in future cases the courts may be called upon to consider whether it covers all the *Wednesbury* errors, as well as failure to comply with common law fairness: would a policy decision which has been unfairly taken be beyond the ambit of an authority's powers?
[89] *Yuen Ken Yeu v Attorney General of Hong Kong* [1988] AC 175.
[90] *X (Minors) v Bedfordshire County Council* [1995] 2 AC 633, Cf. C. Hamilton and B. Watt, 'Do local authorities owe children a duty to take care?' (1995) *Childright* 118, pp. 8–9 where it is argued that the imposition of a common duty of care might improve the investigative work of councils in child abuse cases.
[91] *Hill v Chief Constable of West Yorkshire* [1989] AC 53, 63.
[92] [1970] AC 1004.

reality is that there is little empirical evidence of how public authorities actually respond to the imposition of tortious obligations and judicial attitudes are largely based on guesswork or personal experience.

Tort of breach of statutory duty

In Chapter 23 we saw that an allegation that a public authority has not complied with a statutory duty imposed on it can be a ground for judicial review ('illegality'). The issue here is whether a person who suffers loss as a result of a failure to perform a statutory duty is entitled to claim damages.[93] The basic proposition is that:

> . . . a breach of statutory duty does not, by itself, give rise to any private law cause of action. However, a private law cause of action will arise if it can be shown, as a matter of construction of the statute, that the statutory duty was imposed for the protection of a limited class of the public and that Parliament intended to confer on members of that class a private right of action for breach of the duty.[94]

Two questions must therefore be asked:

(a) was the duty imposed for the protection of a limited class of the public? If so
(b) did Parliament intend to confer on members of that class a private right of action for breach of the duty?

In order to answer these questions judges must construe the words of the Act. Duties imposed for the benefit of the public in general or which are expressed as 'target duties', or as duties of 'imperfect obligation' are not regarded as intended to benefit a particular class of individuals.[95] This is so even where particular individuals benefit more than others from performance of the duties. The courts, for example, have rejected claims for damages by a parent for a failure of a local authority to provide sufficient primary school places contrary to s 8 of the Education Act 1944 which imposes a duty to provide sufficient schools. Although parents and children would derive particular advantage from performance of the duty in s 8 the duty was intended, said the Court of Appeal, to benefit the public generally and not the individual plaintiffs.[96]

Even where a person can show that they fall within a limited class for whose protection the duty was imposed, they may be unable to establish that Parliament intended to confer private rights upon them. In *R v Deputy Governor of Parkhurst Prison ex p Hague*,[97] for example, the House of Lords held that a prisoner could not sue for damages for breach of statutory duties in relation to his treatment in prison. It accepted that the Prison Act and the

[93] See further K. Stanton, *Breach of Statutory Duty in Tort* (1986).
[94] Per Lord Browne-Wilkinson in *X (Minors) v Bedfordshire County Council* [1995] 2 AC 633, 731.
[95] See Chapter 23.
[96] *R v Inner London Education Authority, ex p Ali* [1990] COD 317, discussed at p. 540.
[97] [1992] 1 AC 58.

rules made under it were intended to benefit prisoners, but rejected Hague's action on the ground that Parliament did not intend to confer upon prisoners a right in private law.[98] More recently the House of Lords has held that victims of child abuse and neglect cannot sue local authorities for breach of statutory duties imposed by child support legislation, even though that legislation was enacted to protect children at risk.[99] One reason was that the duties imposed by the legislation required authorities to exercise their discretion and to make difficult decisions 'reflecting the basic tension which lies at the root of so much child protection work: the decision whether to split the family in order to protect the child'. This being so, Lord Browne-Wilkinson said that he found it impossible to construe the legislation as:

> demonstrating an intention that even where there is no carelessness by the authority it should be liable in damages if a court subsequently decided with hindsight that the removal, or failure to remove, the child from the family either was or was not 'consistent with' the duty to safeguard the child.

Here he is referring to situations where carelessness is not alleged. He went on, however, to hold that individuals cannot seek damages for careless performance of a statutory duty either, unless the body owes a common law duty of care in negligence to the plaintiff.

Misfeasance in public office

This is a relatively new tort which imposes liability only on public bodies and officials. To succeed, a plaintiff has to prove:

(a) that there was an exercise or non-exercise of public power, which
(b) was either
    (i) effected by malice towards the plaintiff or
    (ii) taken despite the decision-maker's knowledge that it was unlawful; and
(c) the plaintiff was in consequence deprived of some benefit or suffered other loss.[100]

Thus, in *Jones v Swansea City Council*,[101] a local authority refused a tenant permission to change the use of premises. The tenant alleged that the authority had refused permission because it was motivated by malice towards her husband. Her allegation failed because she had been unable to prove that the

[98] See also *Calveley v Chief Constable of Merseyside* [1989] AC 1228: a suspended police officer could not sue for a failure by his superiors, investigating a complaint made against him, to follow the Police (Discipline) Regulations.

[99] *X (Minors) v Bedfordshire CC* [1995] 2 AC 633. It also held that children with special educational needs cannot sue education authorities on grounds that they have breached statutory duties under the Education Acts.

[100] See de Smith, Woolf and Jowell *Judicial Review of Administrative Action*, para. 19-048.

[101] [1990] 1 WLR 1453. See also *Three Rivers District Council v Bank of England (No 3)* [1996] 3 All ER 558, where the argument was based not on malice (as in *Jones*), but on knowledge of unlawfulness.

majority of councillors had supported the decision to refuse consent owing to a desire to cause financial harm to her husband.

Reform proposals

Concern about how difficult it is for people to recover damages for losses caused by unlawful governmental action has prompted numerous calls for reform of the current law. In 1988 the JUSTICE/All Souls Review recommended the introduction of a statutory right to damages for 'unlawful administrative action or omission which causes a person loss'.[102] In 1991, the Institute of Public Policy Research's draft constitution for the United Kingdom included a right to 'effective remedies (including payment of compensation) in cases where applications for judicial review are upheld'.[103] It seems clear that reform of the common law principle of no liability without proof of a tort will have to come about by statute. The growing number of rights to damages for breaches of Community law may be one impetus for such a change.[104]

LIABILITY TO MAKE RESTITUTION

One final issue may be briefly mentioned in this chapter. If money is paid to a public body in response to a demand by that body, and it is established that the body did not have legal power to make the demand, the money must be returned. If it is not, the person can seek restitution in the courts to compel repayment.[105]

The modern principles relating to restitution from public bodies were established by the House of Lords in *Woolwich Building Society v Inland Revenue Commissioners*.[106] Here the Society paid tax to the Commissioners, but disputed the legality of the regulations under which it had been demanded. They successfully challenged the legality of these regulations. The Commissioners then agreed to repay the tax plus interest from the date of the High Court's decision. The Society argued, however, that it was entitled to the interest from the date of the original payment, a sum of £6.7 million, and not just from the date of the judgment. Many believed that they were not entitled to restitution of this sum because the existing common law did not allow such claims where monies had been voluntarily paid. However, by a three-to-two majority the House upheld the Society's claim. Lord Goff,

[102] Report of the Committee of the JUSTICE/All Souls Review of Administrative Law in the UK, *Administrative Justice—Some Necessary Reforms* (1988), para. 11.83.

[103] *The Constitution of the United Kingdom* (1991), art 118.1.3. Lord Lester's Human Rights Bill (discussed at p. 157) originally contained a right of damages for breach of the ECHR.

[104] See Chapter 29.

[105] See further A. Burrows, *The Law of Restitution* (1993) and J. Beatson, 'Mistakes of Law and *Ultra Vires* Public Authority Receipts: the Law Commission Report' [1995] RLR 280.

[106] [1993] AC 70.

delivering the leading speech for the majority, emphasized that under the Bill of Rights 1688 public bodies can only levy taxes with the authority of Parliament. He said that 'retention by the state of taxes unlawfully exacted is particularly obnoxious . . . the simple fact that the tax was exacted unlawfully should prima facie be enough to require its repayment'.[107] This decision has been greatly welcomed by public lawyers particularly because it rejects the view that money cannot be recovered once it has been paid, even if the payment was under protest. As Professor Wade has put it:

> There is then a clear benefit in public policy, since the law will no longer set a trap for the citizen if he acts on the principle of 'pay now, sue later', which is plainly a becoming attitude *vis-a-vis* the state.[108]

SUMMARY

Most of the highly technical restrictions which once limited the grant of remedies have been removed, but the courts retain a broad discretion to refuse relief even to an applicant who establishes a public authority has acted unlawfully. The judges often show themselves to be acutely aware of the need to be cautious of the disruption and difficulty that a remedial order may cause to a public authority. Arguably the courts have sometimes failed to attach sufficient weight to using remedies to protect the legal rights of applicants.

Questions

1. Helen runs a market stall. Much to her surprise, her annual trading licence is not renewed by the local authority. In breach of the common law requirements of procedural fairness,[109] the authority failed to give her an opportunity to reply to the untrue allegations of her drunkenness which had been made anonymously to the authority. The untruth of such allegations could easily have been verified by the authority, but it failed to do so because of grossly inefficient management of its officers in the market trading department. Helen continues to lose £500 a week profit while her stall is shut down.

   Helen wishes to apply for judicial review of the decision not to renew her licence. Carefully explain to her what remedies she may obtain.

2. What are the arguments for and against judicial discretion to refuse remedies even where the applicant has established that the public body has abused or exceeded its powers? Which of these arguments have the most force?

WHERE TO GO FROM HERE

The next chapter returns to the Board and Lodgings Regulations saga, this time focusing on the application for judicial review made by Simon Cotton. As well as examining issues regarding the Order 53 procedure and the grounds

[107] [1993] AC 70, 172–3.
[108] H. W. R. Wade and C. Forsyth, *Administrative Law* (7th edn., 1994), p. 807.
[109] See Chapter 25.

of judicial review, it also highlights issues regarding remedies. Even though Cotton's lawyers had successfully demonstrated that the delegated legislation was *ultra vires*, at first instance Mann J exercised his discretion to refuse to make the formal declaration which had been requested. He was clearly very aware of the practical difficulties that doing so would impose on the department.

The case study also shows that the grant of a remedy in an application for judicial review is not the 'end' of any story: the public body has to consider how to respond to the court's order. In this case, while the defeat in the application for judicial review temporarily prevented the department pursuing its policy of cutting social security benefit and centralizing control in the hands of the Secretary of State, in the long run it was able to make a new set of regulations to achieve its goal.

27

CASE STUDY: LEGAL CHALLENGE TO THE BOARD AND LODGING REGULATIONS

INTRODUCTION

This chapter returns to the saga of the Board and Lodging Regulations.[1] The government twice tried to introduce rules dealing with board and lodging payments. Although they were controversial the first set of regulations were affirmed by Parliament and brought into effect. However, they were successfully challenged by Simon Cotton in judicial review proceedings. The government responded by introducing a second set of temporary regulations. But here too the government was prevented from doing what it wanted, this time by the JCSI. Chapter 11 examines the legislative process by which the regulations were made; here we consider the role of litigation and the courts in the events.

The previous chapters on judicial review have provided an introduction to the legal principles relating to judicial review arranged and ordered by academic lawyers for law students. We now take a step into the real world of legal conflict. Those chapters may suggest that the law can be understood as a logical sequence of ordered legal principles. Here we shall see how practical factors such as timing, procedural rules of court, litigation strategies and tactics, the perceived needs of public administration and political pressures influence the way law works in practice.

The main issues explored in this chapter may be summarized as follows. First, there are issues concerned with access to judicial review: how did Cotton's case get to court? Second, there are issues of court procedure. Looking at the documentation that Cotton's lawyers had to prepare for the court will provide you with a better understanding of the way the judicial review process works. Consider, for example, whether RSC, Order 53 allows Cotton to present his case fully, and whether it gives a proper chance for the government to respond. Consider also whether the judicial review procedure provides the judges with all the information that is necessary to decide whether the regulations should be invalidated. Bear in mind that others apart from Cotton and the department, such as other benefit claimants and taxpayers in

[1] For an overview of this case study, see Chapter 2.

general, might also have an interest in whether the regulations are lawful. In this context consider whether judges should be able to investigate matters which the parties do not raise, or call for evidence from people that the parties have not relied on. And compare the way judicial review contrasts with the style of scrutiny adopted by the JCSI dealt with in Chapter 11.

Finally, the chapter also illustrates the grounds of judicial review. You will see that the main grounds of challenge used by Cotton involve:

(1) issues of delegation and excess of power: did Parliament intend to delegate to the Secretary of State power to use regulations to limit board and lodging benefit? (see further Chapter 23);
(2) procedural questions: what is meant by the statutory obligation to consult prior to introducing new regulations or amending existing ones? (see Chapter 23);
(3) questions of reasonableness: can the Secretary of State's decision to introduce regulations be impugned on the ground that it was unreasonable? (see Chapter 24).

SIMON COTTON SEEKS JUDICIAL REVIEW IN THE HIGH COURT

Cotton receives a letter

The story of Simon Cotton's judicial review challenge can be traced back to the day in May 1985 when he received an official letter informing him that, due to changes in the rules, '. . . if you remain unemployed and living as a boarder we will pay you as a boarder until week commencing 3 June 1985. After that date we will reduce your money . . .'.

Having read this Cotton went to seek the advice of a nun he had known since he was a child. She referred him to the Birkenhead Resource Unit, a charity which gave legal and other advice.[2] At the time it was run by Nicholas Warren, one of the country's foremost experts on social security law and a former legal adviser at CPAG. The Chairman of the Unit's Board of Trustees and the local constituency MP was Frank Field, another expert in social security issues. He had been a director of CPAG as well as the Low Pay Unit. He is currently the Chairman of the Parliamentary Select Committee on Social Security, a position he has held since 1987. Simon Cotton may well have obtained access to appropriate legal advice through other routes, perhaps by going to a local Citizens' Advice Bureau or even a solicitor, but it was certainly fortuitous for him that he found himself being advised by a legal expert with the support of one of the most experienced opposition MPs working in this area of law and policy.

[2] Unfortunately it was a victim of the collapse of Barings Bank and had to be wound up in June 1995.

Formulating a litigation strategy

The fact that Cotton found himself being helped by a unique blend of legal and political expertise owed much to chance. The element of serendipity here may be contrasted with cases which are fought as part of a deliberate test case strategy by those who want to use the courts as a vehicle for challenging government in particular areas of policy. Often such proactive strategies involve seeking a suitable individual who is adversely affected by the policy and who is willing to take a test case which might affect many others in a similar position.[3] In fact, at about the same time as Cotton was seeking advice from the Birkenhead Resource Unit, a group of lawyers and welfare rights activists in London were trying to find a suitable person willing to take a test case against the Board and Lodging Regulations, but by the time Cotton's application had been made, they had not yet managed to find such a person.

Nicholas Warren knew that he had to act quickly and that the options were limited. Basically, there seemed to be two alternative legal routes to take. Either Cotton could use the statutory *appeal* system provided by the social security legislation and appeal against the decision taken by the Secretary of State to reduce his benefit,[4] or he could try to use the judicial review procedure to challenge the validity of the regulations themselves. Seeking judicial review would be much quicker, but there were a number of potential problems. In the first place there was the problem of costs. Who would pay for the cost of using the High Court, obtaining the services of a barrister, travelling to London and so on? Secondly, judicial review was quicker than using the statutory appeal system, but might it be too quick? The Rules of Court (RSC, Order 53) require applications for leave to seek judicial review to be submitted promptly and in any event within three months.[5] Did this give sufficient time for the case to be properly prepared, for the law to be researched, counsel to be briefed, the paperwork drafted? Finally and most fundamentally, there was the need to identify the specific grounds on which a judicial review challenge could be mounted. Cotton knew that he disliked the decision to reduce his benefit and there was certainly considerable political opposition to the cuts, but were there arguments of law on which to challenge the legality of the new rules? This was likely to be a real problem bearing in mind that the regulations had been vetted by MPs on the JCSI and then debated and affirmed by Parliament. In this situation, Warren knew that the judges would be very reluctant to invalidate regulations, particularly if this were to imply criticism not just of government but of Parliament as well.

Preparing for the legal challenge

Despite these problems, Cotton was advised to apply for judicial review. Legal aid was sought and obtained. The costs problem was therefore substantially

[3] T. Prosser, *Test Cases for the Poor* (1983).
[4] For a discussion of statutory appeals and tribunals, see Chapter 19.
[5] See p. 485.

eliminated. Warren, although an expert on social welfare law, had to work with a barrister who would ultimately argue the case orally in court. Warren decided to brief Richard Drabble who had considerable experience in judicial review and social security cases.[6] Together they developed the arguments which could be mounted, although at the time they were not terribly confident that the challenge would succeed: in private the chance of success was put at about 30 per cent.

In order to get the case to court they had to draft the Form 86A (the application for leave) and an affidavit of evidence sworn by Cotton. As can be seen from the Form 86A (set out below) three main lines of attack were chosen. These are summarized under the part of the form headed GROUNDS ON WHICH RELIEF IS SOUGHT. To understand these arguments you may want to have another look at the primary legislation and extracts from the regulations set out in Chapter 11.

First,[7] it was argued that the Supplementary Benefits Act 1976[8] did not confer power on the minister to make rules about the entitlement of whole groups of people to benefit by dividing the country into areas, imposing time limits on the period for which benefits could be claimed, and capping the amount which could be claimed. In other words, it was argued that the lawyers in the department had chosen an inappropriate enabling provision for the regulations: s 2(1A) could only be used for making regulations dealing with how 'questions' in *individual* cases were to be determined in situations where claimants were dissatisfied with *particular* decisions and used the statutory appeals system. Another aspect of the argument was that the regulations themselves did not specify what the areas and time limits were going to be; this was to be done by the Secretary of State issuing further informal rules which would not be subject to any parliamentary scrutiny.[9] Note that this argument focused on the legality of particular paragraphs of the regulations[10] rather than the regulations as a whole.

Secondly, it was argued that the proper procedure for making the regulations had not been followed because the Secretary of State had not complied with the statutory duty placed on him to consult with the specialist advisory body, the SSAC.[11] This argument challenged the legality of the regulations as a whole.

The final argument was that the imposition by the Secretary of State of the initial four-week period for which Cotton would receive benefit was, in

[6] Incidentally, he had also been involved in the *GCHQ* case as a junior counsel for the unions. He is now a QC.

[7] See p. 637 (paragraphs 1 and 2 of the Form 86A).

[8] See p. 244.

[9] This issue of sub-delegation was not really dealt with in the judgments of Mann J and the Court of Appeal (set out below) because it was held that, in any event, the regulations were outside the scope of s 2(1A) of the 1976 Act. See p. 237 for discussion of the constitutional problems created when ministers make rules which are not subject to parliamentary supervision.

[10] Those set out at pp. 251–2.

[11] See p. 637 (para. 3 of the Form 86A). As to the role of SSAC generally see p. 245.

a legal sense, 'unreasonable'.[12] This was likely to be the most difficult of the arguments, bearing in mind that the regulations had already been affirmed by Parliament. After all, how could regulations accepted by Parliament be unreasonable? If judges were to hold that they were, would this not amount to a review of Parliament itself?

As well as the grounds, note the remedies which Cotton asked for. What are the practical differences between asking for certiorari and the various declarations? What, for example, would be the effect of a judge's decision to refuse to grant certiorari, but to grant one or more of the declarations which are sought?

IN THE HIGH COURT OF JUSTICE CO/799/85
QUEEN'S BENCH DIVISION
CROWN OFFICE LIST

NOTICE OF APPLICATION FOR LEAVE TO APPLY FOR JUDICIAL REVIEW
O.53, r.3

Applicant's Ref No	Notice of Application of leave to apply for Judicial Review (Ord.53 r.3)	Crown Office Ref No

This form must be read together with Notes for Guidance obtainable from the Crown Office.

To the Master of the Crown Office, Royal Courts of Justice, Strand, London WC2A 2LL

Name, address and description of applicant	Simon Cotton Tranmere Birkenhead Unemployed

Judgment, order or other proceedings in respect of which relief is due and the date thereof

1. A letter dated 11th May 1985 to the applicant from the local office of the Department of Health and Social Security . . . indicating that as from 3rd June 1985 the applicant would be paid as a non-householder and not as a boarder.
2. The decision of the Secretary of State for Social Services purportedly made pursuant to paragraph 5(3) of Schedule 2A of the Supplementary Benefit (Requirements) Regulations 1983 S.I. 1983 No. 1399 as amended by the Supplementary Benefit (Requirements and Resources) Miscellaneous Provisions Regulations 1985 that the number of weeks in the initial period referred to in the said paragraph 5(3) should be 4 in the Applicant's area.

[12] See p. 638 (para. 4 of the Form 86A).

RELIEF SOUGHT

1. An order of certiorari quashing the decision to fix the number of weeks in the said initial period at four.

2. A declaration that

(i) the power purportedly given to the Secretary of State to determine the location of 'board and lodging areas' in paragraph 6(2) of Schedule 1A of the said Requirements Regulations and

(ii) the power purportedly given to the Secretary of State to determine the number of weeks in the initial period by paragraph 5(3) of Schedule 2A of the said Requirements Regulations are ultra vires the provisions of the Supplementary Benefit Act 1976.

3. A declaration that the Supplementary Benefit (Requirements and Resources) Miscellaneous Provisions Regulations 1985 are invalid by reason of a failure to comply properly with the requirements of s 10 of the Social Security Act 1980.

Signed: [Richard Drabble] Dated: 29 May 1985

GROUNDS ON WHICH RELIEF IS SOUGHT

1. The powers conferred upon the Secretary of State by paragraph 6(2) of Schedule 1A and paragraph 5(3) of the Schedule 2(A) of the Requirements Regulations (as amended) are expressed to be exercisable generally and not in relation to a particular case; to be capable of making different provisions for different classes of case or otherwise for different circumstances and must be exercised by a published decision. The purported powers accordingly confer on the Secretary of State a power to prescribe the location of the areas and the number of initial weeks. This power to prescribe is not authorised by any provisions of the Supplementary Benefits Act 1976 and is a purported further delegation to the Secretary of State acting otherwise than by statutory instrument of powers intended by Parliament to be exercised by statutory instrument.

2. Further, the power to prescribe the requirements of a boarder in paragraph 2(1) of Schedule 1 of the 1976 Act which, so far as is material, provides:—'For the purposes of this Schedule requirements shall be of three categories, namely, normal requirements, additional requirements, and housing requirements; and the items to which each category relates and . . . the weekly amounts for those categories shall be such as may be prescribed.' Prescribed means 'specified in or determined in accordance with Regulations' (see Section 34(1) of the 1976 Act). It is respectfully submitted that these provisions do not authorise the amount of a boarder's requirements to be determined in accordance with Regulations read together with published decisions of the Secretary of State of general effect. Had Parliament intended to authorise such a form of delegated legislation, clear language would have been necessary.

3. It is apparent from the published material (in particular Cmnd. 9466 and Cmnd. 9477) that the Secretary of State failed to provide the Social Security Advisory Committee with sufficiently detailed proposals in order to provide Parliament with the assistance envisaged under Section 10 of the Social Security Act 1980 before passing Supplementary Benefit (Requirements and Resources) Miscellaneous Provisions and Regulations 1985. In particular:—

(i) In paragraph 1 of Cmnd. 9466 the Committee complained of the time scale.

(ii) In paragraph 5 the Committee remarked 'we are however concerned that the tight timetable which we understand the Government desires to keep will mean that neither we, nor other interested Organisations, will have an opportunity to see draft Regulations, or a detailed description of the proposed method of achieving amendments, in advance of the laying of drafts before Parliament'. The Applicant will submit that on its true construction Section 10 demands that proposals sufficiently detailed to amount to 'a detailed description of the proposed method of achieving amendments' must be put before the Committee.

(iii) In paragraph 5 the Committee continue 'this is a matter of particular anxiety because, as we note later on, we understand that substantial changes are contemplated in part of the proposals as a result of the comments made by our Committee and by the representations to us'. The original proposals were set out in the Consultative Document 'Proposals for Change' Appendix 2 of Cmnd. 9466 it is quite clear that these proposals ceased to accurately reflect the Department's intentions well before the end of January 1985 (see paragraphs 67 and 68 of Cmnd. 9466). It is respectfully submitted that there was no proper time available for the Committee to form a detailed view of the new proposals.

4. The fixing of the initial period at four weeks in the Applicant's area is unreasonable having regard in particular to the matters canvassed by the Social Security Advisory Committee in paragraph 73 of Cmnd. 9466.

[Counsel's signature]

IN THE HIGH COURT OF JUSTICE
QUEEN'S BENCH DIVISION
DIVISIONAL COURT

IN THE MATTER OF: AN APPLICATION BY SIMON COTTON FOR JUDICIAL REVIEW AND IN THE MATTER OF: THE SUPPLEMENTARY BENEFIT (REQUIREMENTS AND RESOURCES) MISCELLANEOUS PROVISIONS REGULATIONS 1985

AFFIDAVIT IN SUPPPORT OF
APPLICATION FOR LEAVE

I, SIMON COTTON of [address] Birkenhead MAKE OATH AND SAY as follows:—

1. I swear this Affidavit in support of my Application for leave to apply for the relief set out in Form 86A.

2. The address I give above is that of my Landlord and Landlady, where I lodge. I have been paying £30.00 per week for bed, breakfast and evening meal. On the basis that I was classified as a boarder by the Supplementary Benefit Authorities I have been receiving £103.30 per fortnight by way of benefit. However I have recently received a letter from the Department of Health and Social Security, dated 11th May 1985, telling me that if I remain unemployed and living as a boarder I will only be paid as a boarder until 3rd June 1985. After that date my money will be reduced and I will be paid as a non-householder. That letter is now produced and shown to me marked 'SC1'[see p. 31]. As I explain below I have absolutely no idea what I shall do if my money is reduced to that as a non-householder. I would have no chance of staying where I am. I have no family to go to. I do not appear to fit into any of the exempt categories set out in the letter.

3. My personal history is as follows. I am now aged twenty two, having been born on 21st February 1963. I have never known my mother or father . . . I have had nearly twenty changes of address including one foster placement where I was deliberately burned. I have also had two substantial heart operations. I am accordingly left without any 'home' of my own to return to. I am obliged to find my own accommodation as best I can . . . I moved in with Mr and Mrs Westbrook as a lodger, as I had been, at different address, for the whole of the period from 1980 to 1983 . . .

6. I have two 'O' levels but am otherwise unskilled. In Birkenhead at the moment the prospects of employment are bleak. If I leave my present address on 4th June the only course I can think of is to start wandering from one Department of Health and Social Security area to another despite the fact that such roots as I have are in the Wirral.

7. I am advised and verily believe that the changes purportedly made to the Supplementary Benefit (Requirements) Regulations 1983 (S.I. 1983 No. 1399) by the Supplementary Benefit (Requirements and Resources) Regulations 1985 are invalid for the reasons set out in Form 86A and I accordingly respectfully ask the Honourable Court to grant me leave to apply for Judicial Review. The matter is one of extreme urgency for me because I simply cannot stay in my present accommodation unless I am able to pay the proper rate for dinner, bed and breakfast to my Landlord and Landlady. I accordingly have no choice but to make this Application.

SWORN by the said SIMON COTTON [Signature
this 25th day of May 1985 of Simon Cotton]

Simon Cotton obtains leave to seek judicial review

On 4 June 1985 Taylor J granted leave to apply for judicial review and ordered that the case be expedited (dealt with speedily). This was an important stage in the process because it had now been accepted that Cotton had an arguable case that the regulations were unlawful and permission had therefore been given for the case to proceed to a full hearing. Since the case had been expedited it would probably be dealt with before the summer legal vacation.

The ball was now in the government's court. Up to this stage of the process the government had not been formally involved in the litigation, but now that leave had been granted government lawyers had to prepare their case in reply and to submit affidavit evidence. At this stage the challenge probably looked like a typical and rather routine piece of litigation. Certainly there is anecdotal evidence that government lawyers did not seriously contemplate losing the case. Since the government would have to be represented in court, government lawyers turned for advice to the 'Treasury Devil', the barrister in private practice who usually represents the government in judicial review cases. At the time this was John Laws.

Extracts from two of the affidavits filed by the government are set out below. The first is from Mr Williams (a Principal in the Department of

Health and Social Security); the second is sworn by Mr Barclay, the chairman of the SSAC.

IN THE HIGH COURT OF JUSTICE
QUEEN'S BENCH DIVISION
DIVISIONAL COURT

IN THE MATTER OF AN APPLICATION FOR JUDICIAL REVIEW

AND

IN THE MATTER OF THE SUPPLEMENTARY BENEFIT (REQUIREMENTS AND RESOURCES) MISCELLANEOUS PROVISIONS REGULATIONS 1985

AFFIDAVIT

I, STEPHEN EDWARD JAMES WILLIAMS of New Court, Carey Street, London MAKE OATH and say as follows:—

1. I am a Principal in the Social Security (Supplementary Benefit) Division of the Department of Health and Social Security ('the Department'). In my capacity as Principal I am responsible for, inter alia, board and lodging aspects of supplementary benefit that is policy and administration. I am duly authorised to make this affidavit on behalf of the Secretary of State for Social Services ('the Secretary of State') and save as otherwise appears the facts herein deposed to are within my knowledge.

2. I have read a copy of the affidavit of Simon Cotton sworn herein on 29 May 1985 and the exhibits thereto. . . . [The affidavit went on to set out the legislative background to the new regulations and the requirement of consultation . . .]

13. The SSAC were asked to report to the Secretary of State in January of 1985. It was made clear in paragraph 26 of the consultative document that the Department wished to strike a balance between a reasonable period for consultation and the need to act speedily to restrain the growth of supplementary benefit expenditure on board and lodging. I would respectfully point out that although the SSAC were asked to report by the end of January of 1985 Section 10 of the 1980 Act does not enable the Secretary of State to impose any limitation of time upon the SSAC and neither is the SSAC required by statute to present its report within any prescribed time parameters. Although it is accepted that the SSAC did comment on the time available they did not assert or complain that they were in any way prevented from considering the proposals and making their report by reason of insufficient time.

14. The Applicant further contends that the fixing of the initial period at four weeks is unreasonable having regard in particular the matters canvassed by the SSAC in paragraph 73 of their report. For the avoidance of doubt the Secretary of State does not accept that the four week period is in any way unreasonable . . .

15. In the circumstances the Secretary of State will aver that the proposals as referred to the SSAC were sufficiently and adequately detailed for the purposes of Section 10 of the 1980 Act and further that the time of four weeks given referred to in paragraph 14 above involved no breach of any legal obligation lying upon the Secretary of State and was in the circumstances entirely reasonable for the purposes

for which it was needed. I would therefore respectfully request this Honourable Court to decline to grant the relief sought.

SWORN by STEPHEN EDWARD JAMES WILLIAMS [signature]
at 11 Breams Buildings, London on this 9th day of July 1985

IN THE HIGH COURT OF JUSTICE
QUEEN'S BENCH DIVISION
DIVISIONAL COURT

IN THE MATTER OF AN APPLICATION FOR JUDICIAL REVIEW

AND

IN THE MATTER OF THE SUPPLEMENTARY BENEFIT (REQUIREMENTS AND RESOURCES) MISCELLANEOUS PROVISIONS REGULATIONS 1985

AFFIDAVIT

I, PETER MAURICE BARCLAY C.B.E., of New Court, Carey Street, London MAKE OATH and SAY as follows:—

1. I am the Chairman of the Social Security Advisory Committee ('the Committee' hereinafter), [. . .] I have read what purports to be true copies of the Affidavit of Simon Cotton sworn 29 May 1985 herein . . . Except as appears hereafter, I make this Affidavit from my own personal knowledge.

2. The Social Security Advisory Committee was established under Sections . . . 10 of the Social Security Act 1980 ('the Act' hereinafter). [Its main statutory functions are then summarised.][13]

3. Section 10(1) of the Act requires that proposals for changes in regulations should be submitted to the Committee 'whether in the form of draft regulations or otherwise'. In most cases the Committee receives draft regulations together with an explanatory paper setting out the effect of the proposed changes and the reasons for them. I am informed that on a number of occasions the Committee has initially received only a detailed explanation of a proposal upon which the Committee has based its preliminary consideration. Additionally, the Committee has in every case the opportunity to discuss all proposed changes with officials of the Department of Health and Social Security ('DHSS' hereinafter) . . .

4. On 29 November 1984 the Secretary of State referred to the Committee proposals which are now set out in the Supplementary Benefit (Requirements and Resources) Miscellaneous Provisions Regulations 1985 (SI No. 613) ('the Board and Lodgings Regulations' hereinafter) and the consultative document . . . was issued. Prior to this on 21 November 1984 the Committee had a brief informal discussion with officials of DHSS at which an earlier version was produced . . .

5. Although there is no statutory requirement to do so, the Committee, as a matter of policy, undertakes a public consultation on all proposed changes which they intend to report in order to gather the views of those affected [. . .] the consultative document was less specific and detailed than other proposals received by the Committee, but it was explained to the Committee that this reflected the

[13] See p. 245.

readiness of Ministers to seek advice on the general thrust of policy change as well as on the detail of draft regulations. The Committee noted in Cmnd. 9466 that 'this absence of detail is part of the price of receiving an outline of the proposals at an early stage of policy formulation . . . we welcome the Government's readiness to seek advice from us and from other interested bodies at this point'.[14] The consultative document was not, however, the only information available to the Committee in their consideration of the proposals. In addition to discussions with officials, the Committee also received written replies to some 40 specific queries on the implications and expected effect of the proposals.

6. I consider specifically whether the information the Committee had received was, in the absence of draft regulations, sufficient to enable the Committee to report. In my view, the full range of information provided to the Committee officials was adequate to enable it to comment reasonably. The Committee did in fact offer a substantial and comprehensive report (Cmnd. 9466). If draft regulations had been available, the Committee should have been able to comment in more detail on some aspects of the proposals, but it did not feel that the information received was insufficient for a report on the central issues raised by the proposed changes.

7. I note that at paragraph 3(iii) of the grounds of relief herein, it is submitted that the Committee did not have sufficient time to consider changes in the proposals in the consultative document. In this connection it is relevant to note that the possible restructuring of the proposals relating to people in ordinary board and lodging accommodation was a direct consequence of the Committee discussions and comments preparatory to our report. There is no specific time laid down in the Act for our consideration, but the Committee is always aware of the practical constraints which govern proposed legislation. These include hoped-for implementation date of changes, considerations of the Parliamentary table, operational issues, such as the time needed to issue instructions to offices, and other factors such as finance. The timetable under which the committee studied all the proposals was admittedly less generous than we should have liked especially in view of the large public response to the consultative document. Despite, however, the time constraints which undoubtedly presented us with considerable difficulties, I consider that the Committee was able adequately to report on the proposals.

SWORN at 100 Fetter Lane, EC4 [signature]
in the City of London
on the 11th day of July 1985

Questions

1. Having read Mr Barclay's affidavit, do you feel that the SSAC had been adequately consulted?
2. Does Mr Barclay's affidavit throw any light on whether the SSAC is:

(a) a body which represents the public as consumers of welfare benefits;
(b) an independent body of experts which gives disinterested advice to the government on the formation of policy; or
(c) a body which serves the Secretary of State?[15]

[14] Extracts from this report are set out at p. 246.
[15] These questions are posed by A. Ogus and E. Barendt, *The Law of Social Security* (1988, 3rd edn.), pp. 534–7.

3. If you were the judge about to hear this case, are there any questions you would like to ask the parties, and is there any more factual information you would like to obtain at this stage?

THE DECISION OF THE HIGH COURT

At the end of July, a little under two months after leave had been granted, the application for judicial review was heard by Mann J. He considered oral argument from Richard Drabble and John Laws. As usual, the only factual evidence before the court was that contained in the affidavits and no witnesses were called. Had you been Simon Cotton's lawyer would you have liked to ask Mr Williams or Mr Barclay any questions? Had you been representing the Secretary of State would you have liked to ask Simon Cotton any questions? Even at this late stage, Warren and Drabble felt that they still had a mountain to climb: while they had a strong case, they foresaw difficulties in setting a practical remedy for Cotton. The government legal team seemed to assume this as well. Certainly Laws did not consider it necessary for him to be in court to hear the judgment. Instead he sent his pupil to take a note of what the judge said. Mann J's judgment was delivered on 31 July 1985.[16] After summarizing the history, describing the complex regulations and referring to the regulations which are set out in Chapter 11 at pp. 251–2, he continued:

> It is to be observed that no criteria are prescribed in the new schedules for the determination of the 'initial period', the 'location of board and lodging areas' or 'the amount appropriate for each board and lodging area'. Each matter for determination is left to the discretion of the Secretary of State. In the event, the Respondent determined there to be an area in which the Applicant boarded (ie Birkenhead) and fixed the initial period as being one of four weeks. The decision was manifested in his letter dated 11 May 1985 of which complaint is made. There is no suggestion that the decision was peculiar to the Applicant. The Applicant deposed that in the light of the decision he did not know what he could do. After the initial period, his benefit as a 'non-householder' would not meet his boarding housekeeper's charges. I need not explain 'non-householder's' benefit. Suffice it to say, that it can be expected to be less in amount than a boarder's benefit and is the category of benefit to which the Applicant would be entitled at the end of the initial period. The options open to Mr Cotton would seem to be to enter a hostel, to obtain rented accommodation or to obtain boarding accommodation outside Birkenhead where there are such roots as he has. Each course would have different consequences in terms of supplementary benefit. Common to all is a necessity to leave the accommodation in which he has been since January 1985.
>
> Mr Drabble . . . argued that the legislation does not confer a power to make paragraph 6(2) of Schedule 1A or paragraph 5(3) of Schedule 2A[17] which were inserted into the 1983 Regulations in the manner which I have described . . . Mr

[16] (1985) *The Times*, 5 August.

[17] See p. 244.

Laws . . . accepted (and I agree with his acceptance) that the only material enabling power is that conferred by s 2(1A) of the Act of 1976.[18] . . . Mr Laws submitted that the questions posed as to the number of weeks in the initial period for each board and lodging area and as to the location of board and lodging areas are 'prescribed questions' within the meaning of the subsection and may thus be properly the subject of provision for their determination by the Secretary of State. [He] . . . submitted (rightly in my view) that 'prescribed' has two meanings; that is to say, the word means either 'specified in regulations' or 'determined in accordance with regulations'. Here, he says, there are questions specified in regulations, which questions are to be determined by the Secretary of State. Regulations to that effect, he submitted, are within the enabling power. He agrees that the questions are questions of a general character which are answerable by rules drawn in general terms without regard to the circumstances of any particular claimant.

As against Mr Law's submissions, Mr Drabble drew attention to the consideration that a person's 'requirements' are to be such as may be specified in regulations or determined in accordance with regulations . . . He pointed to the need for regulations which concern 'requirements' to be the subject of affirmative resolution procedure and of a Treasury consent . . . To permit benefit to be assessed by reference to determinations of a general nature by the Secretary of State would flout the requirement that a person's 'requirements' are to be such as may be specified in regulations or determined in accordance with regulations without reference to any other source. It would, said Mr Drabble, remove decisions on quantum from either Parliamentary or Treasury control if regulations could provide for what was in effect the enactment of a subordinate body of rules by the Secretary of State which controlled the amount of 'requirements' . . .

. . . In my judgment [s 2(1A)] . . . must be read in conjunction with s 2(1). If it is so read, I do not doubt that the questions which may be prescribed for determination by other than adjudication officers, appeal tribunals, or commissioners are those questions which are referred to in subsection (1). Those questions are questions in regard to individual cases and are not questions as to the entitlement to benefit of a class of claimants which are answerable in terms of rules of general application. Adjudication officers and the appellate bodies are not concerned to formulate rules. Their duty is to apply them to the individual cases before them . . . Of course, decisions may have a precedent value but that is not a consequence of the performance of a legislative function.

In my judgment paragraphs 6(2) of Schedule 1A and 5(3) of Schedule 2A as inserted into the 1983 Regulations by regulation 4(8) and (10) of the 1985 Regulations are not within the powers conferred and are accordingly void. The decision manifested in regard to the Applicant in the letter dated 11 May 1985 must consequentially fall but I do not regard specific relief as being necessary as against the Secretary of State.

What I have said is decisive of this application but I should record that Mr Drabble also argued that the 1985 Regulations as a whole were flawed by reason of a failure to comply with the system of reference established by ss 9 and 10 of the Social Security Act 1980[19] [in other words, by a failure to consult with the SSAC] . . .

Mr Drabble submitted that the only fair reading of the Report [of the SSAC] . . .

[18] See p. 244.
[19] See p. 245.

is that the Committee believed themselves unable to perform their normal role because they lacked sufficient knowledge of what was to be proposed. What was in the event placed before Parliament, says Mr Drabble, was never put to SSAC otherwise than in the bald expression of the new concept on 14th January 1985 . . .

The response to this argument by Mr Laws was that . . . the duty under s 10 is not a duty to refer to the SSAC every item that ultimately is to be found in a regulation. The duty, he said, may be performed and sensibly performed before the Secretary of State has taken a definitive view but so long as a topic is placed before the SSAC and they are able to report upon it then the duty is discharged. In my judgment this argument is correct. In the nature of a proposal is the possibility that it may be amended or may be filled up. I cannot accept that amendments or a filling up require a further reference so long as the changes are not such as to justify an allegation that the SSAC never considered the subject matter of the regulations in fact made . . .

Had the point been necessary for me to decide, I would have rejected the argument that the 1985 Regulations have been flawed by reason of a failure to comply with s 10 of the Social Security Act 1980.

I must last discuss an argument advanced by Mr Drabble . . . that in fixing an initial period of 4 weeks for Mr Cotton for whom boarding in the area in which he has such roots as he has . . . the Secretary of State acted unreasonably. By 'unreasonably' Mr Drabble meant, I apprehend, that the decision is 'so outrageous in its defiance of logic or of accepted moral standards that no sensible person who had applied his mind to the question could have arrived at it'. (Per Lord Diplock, *Council of Civil Service Unions v Minister for the Civil Service*.)[20] At one stage Mr Drabble seemed to assert that the Secretary of State did not have in mind the position of or the impact of change upon people such as Mr Cotton at all. Mr Drabble said that the Secretary of State 'had no thought for such people'. I cannot accept that assertion. The SSAC in paragraph 79 of their Report refer to 'people with established residential links with an area, but who have no possibility of alternative accommodation'. This is adverted to on page 15 of the Secretary of State's statement in accordance with s 10(4) of the Act of 1980 (Cmnd 9467).

. . . In summary . . . [it was the] . . . Government's view that the then extant system discouraged young people from finding employment by enabling them to settle down. That a young person ought to be able to establish quickly whether there was work in an area and that the extant system encouraged the provision of expensive and unnecessary board and lodging accommodation. In my judgment, a decision to the effect that all able-bodied and independent young people who live upon supplementary benefit in lodgings should move from one area to another in search of employment after a stay judged appropriate for the quest in the first area does not come within any distance of being 'outrageous'. Had it arisen for decision I would have rejected Mr Drabble's argument.

For the fundamental reasons which I have given, that is to say, that there is no statutory provision which enables the Secretary of State to make the disputed provisions in the 1985 Regulations, but for no other reason, I propose subject to argument to declare the two disputed sub-paragraphs to be *ultra vires* and therefore void.

I should add this. The Applicant and the Respondent were each anxious and for reasons which are obvious, to secure a quick decision upon the question which I

[20] [1985] AC 374. See p. 669, below.

have decided. They were agreed that such a decision could be obtained by invoking the supervisory jurisdiction of this Court. Mr Laws, however, recorded the Respondent's view, that a decision could have been achieved, albeit not quickly, by use of the appeal procedure in the social security legislation (as to this view, see the decision of a Divisional Court in *R v Chief Adjudication Officer, ex parte Bland* (29 January 1985), *The Times*, 6 February 1985 (CO/1486/84)).

Questions

1. Refer back to the Form 86A. On which grounds did Cotton's application succeed?

2. 'It would, said Mr Drabble, remove decisions on quantum from either Parliamentary or Treasury control if regulations could provide for what was in effect the enactment of a subordinate body of rules by the Secretary of State which controlled the amount of "requirements".' What constitutional issues were at stake here?

3. Can you provide a hypothetical example of a situation in which it might be successfully argued that a Secretary of State has acted unreasonably (in the sense that Mann J uses the term) in making an SI?[21]

THE GOVERNMENT REACTS TO THE HIGH COURT DECISION

The decision appeared to come as a surprise to the government. Having expected to win there had been little thought given to the prospects of losing. Moreover, the timing of Mann J's judgment could not have been more inconvenient. Since it was on the last day before the court's summer vacation closure there could be no speedy hearing of an appeal; and since Parliament had already risen for the summer recess immediate amendment of the regulations was also impossible. As a first step the department tried to limit the damage by persuading Mann J not to make a formal declaration that the regulations were invalid. They said that if he did so this would leave a legal vacuum because it was impossible for the government to replace the invalid rules with new rules until either there was a successful appeal or new regulations were approved by Parliament. Mann J recognized this problem and agreed not to make a formal declaration of invalidity on the understanding that the department would not exclude Cotton, and other claimants in his position, from benefit until the matter had been considered by the Court of Appeal or until new regulations were made. This created a rather unusual situation: it was now acknowledged that the provisions were invalid and could not be used to the disadvantage of claimants, but their formal legal status had not been impugned. As discussed in Chapter 11 this created problems for the JCSI which Mann J may not have anticipated (see pp. 259–61).

[21] See further J. D. Hayhurst and P. Wallington, 'The Parliamentary Scrutiny of Delegated Legislation' [1988] PL 38. They show that in the 72 years up to 1986, only 15 pieces of delegated legislation were successfully challenged on substantive grounds. See also G. Alderman [1989] PL 38.

Government introduces new temporary regulations

After some hesitation, the government decided to appeal against Mann J's decision and as soon as Parliament returned after the summer recess, to introduce new temporary regulations. The government lawyers now had the summer to draft these and to prepare the appeal. Cotton would also appeal against the rejection of the argument that there had been inadequate consultation.

When Parliament met again in the autumn, the Secretary of State announced that as a result of the *Cotton* case he would be seeking the approval of the House of Commons for a set of temporary Board and Lodging Regulations.

21 October 1985
Board and Lodging Payments
5.3 pm

The Secretary of State for Social Services (Mr Norman Fowler): With permission, Mr Speaker. I should like to make a statement about supplementary benefit board and lodging payments . . .

On 31 July, after Parliament had risen, the High Court decided an application for judicial review of the regulations. Mr Justice Mann rejected the argument that we had failed properly to consult the Social Security Advisory Committee, and he also rejected the argument that the time limit of four weeks applied in this case was unreasonable. The judge did, however, find that the powers in the Supplementary Benefits Act 1976 were insufficient to make regulations enabling Ministers to determine board and lodging areas and limits. In other words, the judge's view was that the regulations would have been in order if they had themselves contained the board and lodging areas and limits. Mr Justice Mann declined to make a formal order, on our undertaking not to apply the time limits pending the making of new regulations or the outcome of any appeal. Immediate action was taken to put this undertaking into effect and I should like to pay tribute to the efforts of our local office staff in carrying out this work.

We have lodged an appeal against the judgment and arrangements have been made for an early hearing in the Court of Appeal. This will take place at the end of November. However, as Mr Justice Mann specifically recognised, there is a need for a sensible interim operation. It is in the general interest that there should be stability during which the outcome of the appeal can be given proper consideration and the review, which we are committed to carrying out, completed. I have accordingly laid draft regulations today. They include temporary provisions—which will expire at the end of April 1986. There are two important differences from the regulations passed by the House to meet the judge's points. First, time limits will not apply to existing boarders on benefit. They will apply only to new claimants.

The second important difference is that I am also taking powers, in addition to the exemptions in the previous regulations, to exempt from the time limits claimants who would otherwise suffer exceptional hardship . . .

The House will have the opportunity to discuss the new regulations when they are debated next week.

We hope in this way to restrain spending, tackle abuse, but at the same time protect the interests of genuine claimants.

Mr Michael Meacher (Oldham, West) [Labour frontbench spokesman]: . . . On the issue of obedience to the law, about which the Government talk so much, the right hon. Gentleman has been found to have laid illegal regulations which have led to the deaths of at least three young people and have caused public outrage because of the untold hardship and distress inflicted unnecessarily and wrongly, as it turns out, on thousands of others.

... is the Secretary of State aware that my initial legal advice is that there may be grounds for holding that the new draft regulations are also illegal, because, contrary to the Minister's statement, they still do not address a main reason why Mr Justice Mann ruled in the High Court on 4 August that the original regulations were illegal? ... the judge concluded that the regulations were illegal, not simply because, as the Minister said, they did not contain the board and lodging areas and limits, but because they were applied to classes of individuals, and the Secretary of State had no power to do that. Is the Secretary of State aware that, on that basis, we shall be taking legal advice before next week's debate about whether the new draft regulations may also be ruled to be illegal and invalid? ...

Mr Fowler: ... I am sorry that the long lay-off has not made the hon. Gentleman's judgment any better than it was before. The Cotton case resulted from the regulations which were passed by both Houses of Parliament and were scrutinised by the Joint Committee. Three issues were raised—consultation with the Social Security Advisory Committee, the unreasonable time limit and the fact that my own powers are not of a general nature so that I could lay down time limits and board and lodging areas. It was only in the last case that Mr Justice Mann found for Mr Cotton. That position is covered by the new regulations which specify the areas and the limits.

I hear what the hon. Gentleman says about what he terms his initial legal advice. We will obviously want to study what that initial legal advice amounts to. However, there is absolutely no question of our wanting or seeking to withdraw these regulations for the very good reason that the position before we acted was quite insupportable. Payments had increased out of all proportion. When the hon. Gentleman says that the number of boarders, for example, under 26 had trebled, that is far more than can be explained by housing problems or unemployment. We had a situation where the maximum amounts payable were determined by local offices, charges were being pushed up, and there was fraud and abuse. In other words, there was a case for action, and the Government have taken it. We shall seek to protect the interests of claimants, but the hon. Gentleman's basic case is insupportable.

Questions

1. How does the Secretary of State present the government's defeat in the court to the House of Commons? Do you think the government understood Mann J's judgment properly?

2. If you were a member of the government what steps would you now take? Would you, for example, take legal advice on the legality of the proposed new temporary regulations? What would you do if the advice was that the regulations might be unlawful?

Following the Secretary of State's statement, the JCSI met to consider the temporary regulations and heard evidence from government lawyers and departmental officials. Extracts of the hearings and the Committee's conclusions are set out at pp. 259–62, above. In that chapter you will see that the Committee decided that the interim regulations also appeared to be *ultra vires* and the government was forced, with some considerable embarrassment, to withdraw them. In the meantime the *Cotton* case came before the Court of Appeal.

COTTON IN THE COURT OF APPEAL

In November the Court of Appeal considered the appeal against Mann J's judgment. The following are extracts from the three judgments that were delivered on 13 December 1985.[22]

Glidewell LJ

. . . I propose to consider first the issue on which the learned judge found in favour of the applicants, that . . . parts of the 1985 Regulations . . . were not within the powers of the Secretary of State.

Mr Beloff [the QC who now appeared for the Secretary of State] seeks to persuade us that this reasoning is incorrect. His submissions may be summarised as follows:

(i) Section 2(1A) of the 1976 Act as amended,[23] if read alone, empowers the Secretary of State to make regulations which provide for any question to be determined by somebody other than an adjudication officer, an appeal tribunal or a Social Security Commissioner. This is precisely the effect of the regulations to which the applicants object. They prescribe questions, ie the location of board and lodging areas, the amount appropriate for each such area, and the number of weeks in the initial period, which are to be determined by the Secretary of State himself . . .

(ii) There is no reason why the questions prescribed under s 2(1A) should be questions of the kind dealt with by s 2(1), which was the basis of the learned judge's judgment . . .

(iii) But even if that be wrong, the questions to which s 2(1) relates are not restricted to questions relating to individual cases . . .

Mr Drabble, for Mr Cotton . . . argues to the contrary. He accepts that the Secretary of State is entitled to make regulations prescribing certain questions to be answered by himself, but Mr Drabble submits that such questions must be questions which relate to individual cases. The vice of paragraph 6(2) of Schedule 1A and paragraph 5(3) of Schedule 2A to the 1985 Regulations[24] is that they purport to require the Secretary of State to decide generally, not in relation to particular cases. Section 2 of the 1976 Act, he submits, is concerned as a whole with adjudication, ie the process of deciding, initially or on appeal, an individual claimant's entitlement to supplementary benefit, and the amount of such benefit. No part of the section empowers regulations to be made which give power to decide generally questions which must be answered in relation to an individual claim. In my judgment the learned judge's decision on this issue, and Mr Drabble's submissions in support of it, are correct. It is clear that s 2 of the 1976 Act as originally enacted dealt with questions relating to the entitlement of individual claimants to supplementary benefit . . . If Parliament had intended to give to the Secretary of State the powers he claims to make regulations which would permit him to make decisions of general effect, it could and I believe would have achieved this, not by the amendment of s 2(1A), but by the addition of a separate provision setting out the intended powers in clear words . . . It follows, therefore, in my view that s 2(1A) of the 1976 Act as now amended is concerned with questions arising out of individual claims, and does not give a power to make regulations which

[22] *The Times*, 14 December 1985.

[23] See p. 244.

[24] See p. 252.

would themselves permit the Secretary of State, or any other person, to lay down rules, or to make decisions, of general application.

[Turning to the consultation point, he continued . . .] In view of the decision I have reached in relation to the powers of the Secretary of State, it is not strictly necessary to decide also whether the 1985 Regulations as a whole are invalid [on the grounds that the consultation with the SSAC was inadequate]. Nevertheless, we have heard argument on the point, and I think it right to express my view about it shortly.

The Committee delivered their report to the Secretary of State on the 6 February, 1985. It is clear that the Committee still did not know with any clarity the form which the regulations dealing with this issue were likely to take. Thus paragraph 5 of the report says: 'we understand that substantial changes are contemplated in part of the proposals . . .' and concludes 'We should also be grateful ourselves for an opportunity to consider the proposals again, when a full draft of the changes is available.' This last point is repeated in paragraph 68 and paragraph 102(21), which summarises the Committee's conclusions. Paragraphs 71–74 express considerable concern about what are understood to be the intended revised proposals for young people. . . . The Statement by the Secretary of State to Parliament accompanying the regulations notes the Committee's request to consider the actual regulations at an early stage, and says:

> The Government regret that the need for urgent action precludes any opportunity for a formal reference of the regulations to the Committee for consideration.

Despite this, the Secretary of State did not refer the new regulations to the Committee after they had been made, in accordance with s 10(7) so as to enable the Committee to report further on this issue. Mr Beloff accepts for the purposes of these proceedings that the requirement to consult the Committee is mandatory. Nevertheless, he submits that the material put before the Committee was sufficient to satisfy the requirements of s 10. He points to an affidavit before us from the Chairman of the Committee, who said at paragraph 6: [Glidewell LJ sets this out, see above p. 641] . . . Mr Drabble submits that despite the Chairman's view, the material put before the Committee on this issue did not comply with s 10. Without either the draft regulation or a clear exposition of it, and sufficient time to make a considered response, the Committee could not carry out its proper function . . .

After considerable hesitation, I agree with Mann J that what the Secretary of State did was sufficient to comply with the wording of s 10, though I do not think it complies with the spirit of the provision. The whole purpose of having the Advisory Committee is to give advice to the Secretary of State on, amongst other matters, intended new regulations. It can only fulfil that function properly if it knows clearly what is intended and has sufficient time for its members to consider and discuss it and to express its views fully. I agree with Mr Drabble that in this case the Committee lacked both the necessary clarity in the information it received and the necessary time for consideration and reporting. Nevertheless, in the end I cannot say that what was done did not comply with s 10(1) and (4) of the 1980 Act. Like Mann J, I would not declare the whole of the 1985 regulations invalid on this ground.

Conclusion

. . . For the reasons I have sought to give earlier, I conclude that paragraph 6(1) and (2) of Schedule 1A and Schedule 2A paragraph 5 of the 1985 regulations were not made within the powers conferred on the Secretary of State by s 2(1A) of the Act of 1976 as amended. I would therefore dismiss this appeal.

May LJ

[May LJ concurred with Glidewell LJ that the regulations were *ultra vires* the powers conferred on the Secretary of State by s 2(1A) of the Act of 1976 as amended, and then continued . . .] I agree that this appeal should be dismissed . . . In so far as the challenge to the 1985 regulations as a whole is concerned, based upon the provisions of s 10 of the Social Security Act 1980, I respectfully disagree with the view to be expressed by the Master of the Rolls and I also have less hesitation than Glidewell LJ in thinking that it cannot be maintained in this case. Section 10 provides for consultation between the Secretary of State and the Social Security Advisory Committee. The latter is an adviser which the Secretary of State is bound to consult to the extent that the statute provides. However, it neither has, nor should it be held to have, any power of veto on any legislation or regulations which the Secretary of State may consider it appropriate to ask Parliament to approve in this context. The Committee is there to give the Secretary of State the benefit of independent experience in the social security field, which may not be wholly available within his own department . . . In the light of the evidence from the Chairman of the Committee which was before us and the learned judge below, I do not think it possible to mount even a *prima facie* general attack on the regulations based upon a failure to comply with the provisions of s 10 . . .

Nevertheless, for the earlier reasons I have given, I do not think that the Secretary of State did have the power to make the regulations which have been particularly challenged. I therefore agree that this appeal should be dismissed.

Sir John Donaldson MR

I agree . . . Although I have reached the same conclusion as Mann J, my reasons are slightly different. Thus I do not think that the Secretary of State would have been on firmer ground if, in s 33 [of the Supplementary Benefits Act 1976] which deals with rules and regulations, or elsewhere it had been provided that 'Regulations may provide for prescribed questions to be determined by the Secretary of State'. Nor do I think that subsection (1A) is necessarily to be read in conjunction with subsection (1), although it might well be. Again I am not persuaded that the prescribed questions must necessarily be limited to questions in regard to individual cases, since there is no such express limitation and s 2(1) shows that Parliament contemplated that questions could arise either as to the entitlement of a person to supplementary benefit or otherwise under the Act. . . .

That said, the scope of subsection (1A) is limited to making provision for prescribed questions to be determined by someone other than the specified adjudicative trio and for such decisions, and any other prescribed decisions, to be effective or conclusive for prescribed purposes. 'Prescribed' is defined as meaning 'specified in or determined in accordance with regulations' and the matters which the Secretary of State has referred to himself are clearly 'prescribed'. But are they 'questions' within the meaning of the subsection? Section 25(1) of the 1983 Act provides that 'the law relating to social security adjudications shall have effect subject to the amendments specified in Schedule 8 to this Act'. This implies that the amendments relate to the process of adjudication and that 'prescribed questions' and 'prescribed decisions' in subsection (1A) must be limited to questions and decisions relating to that process.

. . . None of the three matters referred to the Secretary of State under the regulations has anything to do with the process of adjudication. All relate to the creation of a right to supplementary benefit. In argument it was submitted that under the previous regulations the benefit officer, and later the adjudication officer, would be required to fix the maximum weekly charge applicable to his area, yet no one has ever suggested that those regulations were *ultra vires*. This neatly illustrates the dividing line between the adjudicative function and the creation or quasi-legislative function. The adjudication officer was called upon to estimate an amount which represented 'the reasonable weekly charge for the relevant area for full board and lodging (inclusive of all meals) which is available in that area or, if the level of charges there is unusually high, in an adjoining area . . .' It is true that is not a question whether any person is entitled to supplementary benefit, but it is a question relating to a justiciable issue arising under the Act. The officer is being asked to apply criteria contained in the regulations to a factual situation. It is a process of adjudication. This is to be contrasted with instructions to determine a maximum sum without regard to any criteria. That is not a justiciable issue and the process of doing so is not adjudicative. Similarly in relation to area and period. It is a justiciable issue and an adjudicative question whether a particular board and lodging establishment is within area A or area B. So too with the initial period, which may vary from place to place. If it has been fixed by legislative act, the adjudicative process can determine what is the relevant length of time in relation to a particular place, but it cannot determine that without reference to some external criteria.

. . . I too would dismiss the appeal, holding that the regulations were in this respect *ultra vires* . . .

In the light of this conclusion, it is not strictly necessary to consider the effect of s 10 of the Social Security Act 1980, but, the matter being of some general interest, I will, nevertheless, express my view. . . .

It is clear that Parliament was not content merely to rely upon its power to disapprove, or, as the case may be, refuse to approve, regulations, but, in this sensitive area, intended that the Secretary of State should have the benefit of the advice of a specialist Advisory Committee and that Parliament should itself be fully informed of any advice which it tendered. It is against this background that s 10(1) falls to be construed. The relevant words are 'where (a) the Secretary of State proposes to make regulations . . . [he] . . . shall refer the proposals in the form of draft regulations or otherwise to the Committee'. This duty is, of course, subject to subsections (2)(a), (7) and (2)(b). Subsection (2)(b) covers the situation, which did not occur here, in which the Committee itself agrees that the proposals should not be referred to it. Subsections (2)(a) and (7) cover emergency situations and entitle the Secretary of State to legislate first and then refer the regulations to the Committee, whose report is to be laid before Parliament. . . .

The key words are 'in the form of draft regulations *or otherwise*' (my emphasis). There may well be cases in which it is preferable to convey the nature of the proposals to the Committee in the form of an explanatory note, rather than in the form of draft regulations. But in my judgement the parliamentary intention must have been that the explanatory note, or other form of communication, would tell the Committee substantially as much as would the regulations themselves. Put in another way, 'proposals' in this context must mean 'precise proposals' and not 'broad proposals' or 'the Minister's present thoughts'. In the instant case it seems to me that at the time when the Secretary of State last communicated with the Committee, his thinking had not reached this stage. I say this because if he had already decided what should be the maximum payments in respect of particular areas, what those areas should be, what should be the length of the initial period and what categories of persons should be exempt, all of which could be of crucial importance, he does not seem to have informed the Committee. If by then he had come to the conclusion that these would have to be capable of variation, speedily and without the need for further regulations, and, for this purpose, must be determined by him, again he does not seem to have informed the Committee. This view is supported by such phrases as 'we are considering the adoption of a system' and 'in drawing up the exemption categories, we shall aim to take account . . . '

If, as may well have been the case, the urgency of the situation did not permit of more refined proposals being referred to the Committee, in my judgement s 10 required the Secretary of State to operate the emergency procedure under s 10(2)(a) and (7) and to refer the regulations to the Committee as soon as practicable after they had been made. Nothing in the Act prevents the Secretary of State giving the Committee advance information which is incomplete, because the proposals are still in a formative stage, and, if pressure of time does not permit a further delay, referring the regulations to the Committee after they have been made, using the emergency procedure. If, on the other hand, time did permit, the Secretary of State should have given the Committee further, better and more precise information as to the proposals before making the regulations, either by sending them a draft or otherwise. . . .

For the reasons which I have sought to express, I do not consider that there was due compliance with s 10, but in the light of my view that the regulations were *ultra vires* as being outwith the power conferred by s 2(1A) of the 1976 Act, I need not explore this further.

Appeal dismissed with costs. Legal aid taxation of respondent's costs. Declaration in terms sought, but to lie in the office until the end of next week with liberty to the appellant to apply to vary terms.

Questions

1. Summarize the findings of Mann J and the Master of the Rolls on the regulation-making power conferred by Supplementary Benefit Act 1976, s 2(1A). The departmental lawyers made a mistake about the scope of this subsection and the JCSI failed to spot that the regulations challenged by Cotton were *ultra vires* this provision. Why was this? Do you think it was because the statutory language is unclear?

2. Four judges (Mann J and the Court of Appeal) make *obiter* statements about compliance with the statutory consultation requirement. Imagine you are a lawyer in the department. Write a memorandum for civil servants explaining, as clearly as you can, what they ought to do in the future to decrease the risk of further successful judicial review challenges on this ground. Think carefully about what, if anything, you will say about the distinction drawn by Glidewell LJ between complying with the 'wording' but not the 'spirit' of the statutory duty.

3. If you were a lawyer in the department what steps would you advise the Secretary of State to take after this decision? For example, should there be an appeal to the House of Lords? Should new regulations be enacted? Should the law on consultation be clarified and, if so, how?

POSTSCRIPT

Following the Court of Appeal's decision the government decided against appealing to the House of Lords and to start afresh with new regulations. There were further attempts to block these in Parliament and to use judicial review to challenge them, but these were unsuccessful and eventually the government achieved its objectives.

The *Cotton* decision was one of a number of decisions in the 1980s which, in the words of one government lawyer, brought 'the full majesty of the law home to officials'. The saga is still remembered as a very unhappy one of the department. Elsewhere we have argued that the 'saga proved to be pivotal in governmental thinking about its reaction to challenge in the courts'.[25] The single most important lesson for government arising from the litigation was probably the need to take more care to anticipate and prepare for legal challenge. Since the decision the government has taken steps to increase legal awareness amongst officials both by providing training courses in judicial review and by publishing *The Judge Over Your Shoulder*—and also to make better and earlier use of lawyers.

As far as its policy implications were concerned, the saga forced government to delay the implementation of a central plank of its social security policy at a time when 'macho ministerial action' and speed was everything (as one non-government lawyer we interviewed put it). The episode attracted media attention, acted as a catalyst for further challenges both in the courts and by the JCSI, and forced the Secretary of State to acknowledge error and to re-present fresh regulations in a political climate that had become better informed and possibly even more hostile. However, the litigation probably had very little influence on the content of government policy and ultimately the government was able to push on with its reforms.

Concluding Questions

1. Professor Ross Cranston has written that: 'It is sometimes said that *Cotton* is the only instance in the social security area where judicial review has had any profound impact on the practices of the Department of Social Security.'[26] What lessons do you think the department should have learnt from this episode?

2. Looked at as a whole, what does this episode tell us about the importance and limitations of judicial review within the constitutional system?

[25] M. Sunkin and A. P. Le Sueur, 'Can Government Control Judicial Review?' (1991) 44 CLP 161.

[26] Ross Cranston, 'Reviewing Judicial Review' in G. Richardson and H. Genn (eds.), *Administrative Law and Government Action* (1994), p. 71.

28

CASE STUDY: LEGAL CHALLENGES TO THE GCHQ UNION BAN

INTRODUCTION

Very early on in the dispute, the trade unions decided to challenge the legality of the government's prohibition of trade union membership at GCHQ.[1] Three lines of attack were anticipated: the TUC complained to the International Labour Organization (ILO); an application for judicial review was launched in the High Court by the CCSU and six individual employees; and should this fail, the applicants were prepared to go further and to allege that the union ban constituted a breach of the United Kingdom's obligations under the ECHR.

In the previous chapter, dealing with *ex p Cotton*, we saw how the judicial review procedure operates, how arguments are presented and how evidential issues are put to the court in the form of affidavits. We also saw how the courts apply legal principles to ensure that ministers do not exceed or abuse powers conferred on them by Acts of Parliament. This chapter focuses on the GCHQ litigation in the Court of Appeal and the House of Lords and examines one of the most important judicial decisions in the area of public law in recent years. The litigation is significant at a number of different levels and for a variety of reasons. At the political level, here was a direct clash between the unions on the one hand and Mrs Thatcher's Conservative government on the other. For years conflict between the civil service unions and the government had rumbled on. This was brought to a head by the government's decision to ban union membership at GCHQ. It was not surprising therefore that by the time the judicial review litigation was under way the ban had already become a red-hot political issue. There had been heated debate on the floor of the House of Commons, a select committee inquiry in which backbench MPs were critical of the union ban, and even criticism of the government in the pages of the *Daily Telegraph*, in which the government's decision was described as 'little short of shambolic'.[2]

The constitutional law issues, although perhaps less highly charged, were if anything even more weighty. In the past the courts had been unwilling to

[1] For an overview of this case study, see Chapter 2. See further: G. Drewny (1985) 38 *Parliamentary Affairs* 371; K. Ewing [1985] CLJ 1; J. A. G. Griffith [1985] PL 564; H. W. R. Wade (1985) 101 LQR 180.

[2] See generally Chapter 17.

review the way the executive exercised its prerogative, as opposed to its statutory powers.[3] Would the courts now accept this jurisdiction or not? If they did, would this lead to a head-on constitutional conflict between the courts and the executive? If they did not, would this weaken the rule of law? Would it mean that over three hundred years after the fall of monarchical government, the executive could still exercise prerogative powers free from both parliamentary and legal scrutiny? If the courts were to intervene what would be the constitutional basis for their doing so? In orthodox theory the courts' role is usually depicted as being to ensure that public bodies comply with the will of Parliament:[4] how can this justify judicial review where the exercise of prerogative power is involved? The litigation also raised important questions about the availability of judicial review to citizens: can citizens seek the protection of the courts when they have been adversely affected by actions of government which might be unlawful, but which the government seeks to justify as necessary in the interests of national security? If the courts are not available in this situation what is to stop the government abusing its power? If the courts are available, what can the courts do? Do judges have the information and experience to question the government's perceptions of the needs of national security? If they lack the necessary tools to do this, can they nevertheless review the action of government to ensure, at least, that the government is acting in good faith and has grounds to believe that its actions are dictated by national security considerations?[5]

THE UNIONS TAKE THEIR CHALLENGE TO COURT

Getting to court

In order to begin the application for judicial review several decisions had to be made. First the particular litigants had to be identified. Those most immediately affected were of course the individual civil servants, but if they were to take the case they would have to be supported financially and their arguments would have to be coordinated and focused on the most effective points. Six national trade unions had members at the GCHQ and potentially each of these could be involved, but this might prove to be unwieldy. It was therefore decided that the umbrella organization, the CCSU, should take the leading role in the litigation. Since it was also engaged in the political and industrial relations dimensions of the dispute, it would be able to coordinate the legal attack. The applicants hoped that by using both an umbrella organization and named individuals who were personally affected, they would be able to defeat an argument that they lacked standing to bring the case.[6]

[3] See p. 282.

[4] See Chapter 20.

[5] Parliament in scrutinizing the ban was also constrained by national security arguments raised by government and some potential witnesses were not allowed to appear before the Employment Select Committee: see Chapter 17.

[6] On standing, see p. 486.

The greatest obstacle was to identify plausible legal grounds for challenging the ban. Since the 1960s the judiciary had shown itself willing to invalidate actions of the executive, even in areas of sensitive policy, where powers granted by statute had been abused. However, it had not yet been accepted that judges could review the way prerogative powers were exercised. This had to be established if the challenge was to be successful. Various lines of argument were developed. The most general relied on the rule of law itself. This argued that the old idea that Crown prerogative powers were immune from review was out of step with modern notions of political and legal accountability. There should no longer be a difference between judicial review of powers granted to the executive by statute and powers authorised by the prerogative. This broad line of attack was bolstered by the more specific argument that, even if the courts are unable to review the exercise of prerogative powers itself, they could nevertheless review the way power delegated by prerogative is exercised. The thrust of this more technical argument was that Mrs Thatcher, in her capacity as Minister for the Civil Service,[7] had been given power to alter the terms and conditions of employment of civil servants by the Civil Service Order in Council. The Order in Council was the direct product of prerogative legislative power and had been enacted by the Queen and the Privy Council.[8] It had delegated power to Mrs Thatcher. Even if judges could not review the legality of the Order in Council (it was argued), they could review the way Mrs Thatcher exercised powers delegated to her by the Order in Council in the same way as the courts review the exercise of power delegated by statute.

If the courts refused to accept jurisdiction to review prerogative powers the case would fail. However, accepting jurisdiction would only be a step towards success; the specific grounds on which the judges could intervene also had to be identified. The main line of argument here emphasized the importance of union membership and the obligation upon government to adopt fair procedures. The right to form and join a trade union is protected by Art 11 of the ECHR.[9] This provision is not part of domestic law but it reflects a general principle and underscores the status of the interests involved. Government, it was argued, can only interfere with these interests if it has legal power to do so and if it follows procedures which are fair.[10] In the past the government had always consulted with the relevant trade unions before altering terms and conditions of employment. The unions therefore had a 'legitimate expectation' that they would have been consulted in this situation. The failure of the government to consult breached this legitimate expectation and was therefore unfair and unlawful, the unions argued.

[7] A ministerial post she occupied at the same time as being Prime Minister.

[8] See p. 277.

[9] See p. 675.

[10] On common law procedural fairness, see Chapter 25.

Leave is granted and affidavit evidence exchanged

On 8 March 1984 Glidewell J accepted that the applicants had established an arguable case and granted leave to seek judicial review. As part of its response the government filed an affidavit sworn by Sir Robert Armstrong, the Chief Secretary to the Cabinet. Although he had no legal responsibility for the decisions which had been taken by the government, he had been intimately involved in the events leading up to the ban and, indeed, had tried unsuccessfully to broker a no-strike agreement between the unions and the government.[11] His affidavit sought both to place the government's decision to ban union membership at GCHQ in the context of past industrial unrest there and the disruption this had caused to work, and to emphasize the importance of preventing the risk of future industrial unrest at GCHQ. It referred, in particular, to industrial action in 1981 which was aimed, Armstrong said, at doing as much damage as possible to government agencies including GCHQ. To support this his affidavit referred to campaign letters and circulars issued by the CCSU highlighting the importance of interfering with key governmental activities. The following examples were amongst those later quoted by Lord Fraser in the House of Lords:

> Our ultimate success depends upon the extent to which revenue collection is upset, defence readiness hampered, trading relations disrupted by this and future action.
>
> Walkouts in key installations have affected Britain's defence capability in general, and crippled the UK contribution to the NATO exercise 'Wintex' . . .
>
> . . . another vital part of the Government's Composite Signals Organisation . . . is to be hit by a strike from Friday, 3 April.
>
> 48 hour walkouts have severely hit secret monitoring stations belonging to the Composite Signals Organisation. The Government is clearly worried and will be subject to huge pressure from NATO allies.

The affidavit went on to explain why the government had not consulted with the trade unions prior to imposing the ban. Significantly, this did not rely specifically on the fear that consultation would have threatened national security, although it did say that the government feared that consultation would have drawn attention to areas of vulnerability to those who might use the information to cause disruption.

The thrust of the government's argument at the first instance judicial review hearing was, therefore, that previous industrial action at GCHQ had made the ban necessary and that it would have been impossible to consult before imposing the ban without generating the risk of more disruption. At this stage the government did not seek to justify the decision not to consult on the basis of national security interests as such.

[11] See further P. Hennessey, *Whitehall*, pp. 585–684.

First instance judgment

On 16 July 1984 Glidewell J gave judgment.[12] He said that he was entitled to examine the way in which the government had chosen to exercise the prerogative:

> The Royal Prerogative Power in relation, amongst other matters, to the qualifications and terms and conditions of service of civil servants is embodied in the Civil Service Order in Council 1982. It is by virtue of the power given to her by art 4 of that Order in Council that the Minister for the Civil Service made or purported to make, her direction of 22 December 1983. I am thus concerned with the jurisdiction of the courts, not in relation to the whole field of the Royal Prerogative nor to any question of treaty making power, but in its application to powers granted to a Minister by an Order in Council.
>
> I see no reason in logic or principle why an exercise by a Minister of a power confirmed by an Order in Council should not be subject to the same scrutiny and control by the courts as would be appropriate to the exercise of the same power if it had been granted by statute. In my judgment therefore, the exercise by the Minister of her power under art 4 is subject to scrutiny and control by this court on the principles normally applicable to the exercise of statutory powers and the making under those powers of decisions which affect the rights of the subject.

Having established that he could intervene, he went on to emphasize the need for government to follow the correct and fair procedures required by the common law and that in the circumstances the failure to consult was a procedural irregularity. He therefore declared that the instruction issued by the Minister for the Civil Service was invalid and of no effect.

The government appeals

This was a major victory for the unions and the workers and a considerable blow for the government. It was also a stunning example of the willingness of the High Court to stand up to the executive and of the potential potency of judicial review. Winning a battle, however, is not the same as winning the war. The government immediately appealed. It also decided that in the Court of Appeal it needed to strengthen its line of argument. In particular, it resolved now to argue that the decision not to consult had been taken in the interests of national security. The government knew that the courts have always been extremely reluctant to interfere where national security considerations are at stake. Even if the Court of Appeal were to agree with Glidewell J that prerogative powers could be reviewed, surely the judges would not upset a national security decision? The government was right.

[12] See [1984] IRLR 309.

THE COURT OF APPEAL'S DECISION

The judgment of the Court of Appeal was given on 6 August 1984, barely three weeks after Glidewell J's decision. The Lord Chief Justice (Lord Lane), and Watkins and May LJJ sat. The judgment was given by the Lord Chief Justice.[13] His Lordship considered the factual background to the appeal and continued:

> There are two main contentions advanced by the appellant [the Minister for the Civil Service] in support of this appeal. First, it is submitted that there is no jurisdiction in this court to supervise what was an exercise of the royal prerogative power in the present circumstances. Secondly, if it be held that the court is entitled to enquire into that exercise, can it be said that the executive in the present case have used that power improperly or upon a mistaken view as relevant matters to be taken into consideration? There is also a third point. If the first two issues are decided in favour of the respondents [the civil servants and the CCSU], should the court nevertheless exercise its discretion to grant relief? . . .
>
> *Is the court entitled to supervise the exercise of the royal prerogative*? [Having referred to the passage from Glidewell J's judgment set out above, he continued] . . . The appellant contends that the learned judge was wrong in this approach . . . The argument on behalf of the appellant is that the role of the court with regard to the exercise of prerogative powers is limited to determining the existence, scope and form of the power that has been exercised, the prerogative being part of the common law. Counsel submits that it is not within the power of the court to review the adequacy of the grounds on which a prerogative power has been exercised. The manner of exercise of a prerogative power cannot, he says, be impugned in, or enquired into by the courts.
>
> The respondents, however, point to certain dicta which appear to support the contrary view . . . Mr Blom-Cooper [counsel for the CCSU] put forward an added reason in the present case for suggesting that the exercise of the royal prerogative is amenable to supervision by the court. That is because the royal prerogative has here been reduced to what he calls 'legislative form' . . . We do not think that those contentions are effective to override any limits which are imposed by the authorities on the powers of the court to supervise the exercise of the prerogative.
>
> The Prime Minister's instruction of 22 December and the Secretary of State's certificates of 25 January were given because the government, which is the body responsible for national security, thought that national security required them. That was a bona fide belief based upon ample evidence as has already been made clear. [His Lordship quoted from *The Zamora* [1916] 2 AC 77 and *Chandler v DPP* [1964] AC 763 and continued.]
>
> In the present case it seems to us that the actions taken by the government with regard to trade union membership at GCHQ were clearly actions taken on the grounds of national security. . . . the ministers were the sole judges of what the national security required and consequently the instruction and certificates were not susceptible to judicial review . . . there may well be areas where the court may be entitled to inquire into the exercise of the royal prerogative, but there are certainly other areas where such inquiries are not permitted. Such an area is any action taken under the royal prerogative which can truly be said to have been taken

[13] See [1984] IRLR 353.

in the interests of national security to protect this country from its enemies or potential enemies. This is such a case.

Accordingly, we respectfully disagree with the learned judge in the conclusions he reached on this aspect of the case . . . The respondents contend that the Prime Minister's instruction and its consequences constituted a breach by Her Majesty's government of their . . . obligations under [international] Conventions, in particular arts 2 and 4 of ILO Convention No 87. They seek to draw support from the finding to this effect in a report dated 1 June 1984 of the Committee on Freedom of Association of the Governing Body of the ILO upon a complaint made to the latter by Mr Murray[14] . . . In our judgment, the correct meaning of the material articles of the conventions is by no means clear. The nature of the obligations with which they seek to deal is no doubt the explanation of the very general terms in which some of them are drafted . . . [I]f it be necessary for this court to reach a conclusion upon the construction of the Conventions, we are respectfully driven to a conclusion different from that reached by the Committee on Freedom of Association. In our opinion, the view taken by the government's advisers that the actions taken by the Prime Minister and the Secretary of State were in accordance with the government's international obligations was correct, at least, with the learned judge below, we are far from being able to say that the interpretation adopted by HM Government was wrong . . .

Strictly speaking there is no necessity for us to go any further. If, however, we are wrong in our view that this court has no power to review the exercise of the royal prerogative in the context of national security, we would like to add these observations. It may be that government failed to satisfy expectations held by the staff at GCHQ that there would be consultations about important changes such as those with which we are here concerned. There are, however, restrictions on the requirements for consultation contained in the various staff and departmental regulations, and we can understand why the government thought fit to act as they did. We can understand the government's anxiety (which is apparent from the evidence given to the Select Committee by the Foreign Secretary and Sir Brian Tovey[15] and also from the statements made by the Foreign Secretary to the House of Commons,[16] including the history of past disruptive actions) lest by premature disclosure of their plans they might precipitate the very trouble which by their decision they were seeking to avoid.

We also doubt whether had the consultations taken place, anything useful could have been achieved. We respectfully doubt whether the judge was correct in his conclusions on this aspect . . .

Finally . . . the judge dealt with the question of discretion. He made no mention in this context of the considerations of national security. We invited Mr Blom-Cooper to address us on this point. It seems to us that it was necessary for the judge when considering his discretion to strike a balance between the public interest in national security (which is pre-eminently a matter for government) on the one hand and the public interest in the non-interference in the private rights of the individual on the other . . . We doubt whether the judge had his attention drawn to this crucial aspect. Had he considered it, his decision would probably have been different. We therefore allow this appeal, and set aside the declaration made by the learned judge.

[14] The then General Secretary of the TUC. This complaint is discussed below.

[15] See Chapter 17.

[16] See p. 16.

Questions

1. Consider again the statement in the Employment Select Committee's report that they had 'concentrated on the reasonableness of the government's action rather than its legality'.[17] How did the Court of Appeal's approach differ from that of the select committee in terms of the questions it asked and answered?

2. In view of its importance, what explanations might there be for the government's failure to rely explicitly on national security as an argument at the hearing before Glidewell J?

3. The Lord Chief Justice commented that 'We also doubt whether had the consultations taken place, anything useful could have been achieved.' Is this is a sound reason for refusing to interfere where the failure to consult is claimed to be unfair? Does this not require the court to substitute its own decision for that of the decision-maker, something judges repeatedly say it should not do when considering applications for judicial review on the grounds that it blurs

(a) the distinction between appellate and review function, and
(b) the distinction between issues which are for public bodies to decide and issues which are for the courts?

Note below p. 665 Lord Fraser's reference to Lord Brightman in *R v Chief Constable of the North Wales Police, ex p Evans* [1982] 1 WLR 1155 at 1173.

GCHQ IN THE HOUSE OF LORDS

The Court of Appeal gave leave to appeal to the House of Lords. There was a six-day hearing in October 1984 before Lords Fraser of Tullybelton, Scarman, Diplock, Roskill and Brightman. On November 6 the House of Lords gave judgment (the reasoned speeches were delivered on 22 November 1984). The Lords were in unanimous agreement that the decision of the Court of Appeal should be upheld. However, as often happens, the speeches of their Lordships expressed a range of views on several of the key issues. Here are extracts from their Lordships' speeches.[18]

Lord Fraser of Tullybelton set out the facts and continued:

> . . . The principal question raised in this appeal is whether the instruction by which the decision received effect, and which was issued orally on 22 December 1983 by the respondent (who is also the Prime Minister), is valid and effective in accordance with art 4 of the Civil Service Order in Council 1982. The respondent maintains that it is. The appellants [the CCSU] maintain that it is invalid because there was a procedural obligation on the respondent to act fairly by consulting the persons concerned before exercising her power under art 4 of the Order in Council, and she had failed to do so. Underlying that question, and logically preceding it, is the question whether the courts, and your Lordships' House in its judicial capacity, have power to review the instruction on the ground of a procedural irregularity, having regard particularly to the facts (a) that it was made in the exercise of a power conferred under the royal prerogative and not by statute and

[17] See p. 386.
[18] See [1985] AC 374.

(b) that it concerned national security. . . . I shall consider first the question which I regard was the most important and also the most difficult. It concerns the royal prerogative.

The royal prerogative

The mechanism on which the Minister for the Civil Service relied to alter the terms and conditions of service at GCHQ was an 'instruction' issued by her under art 4 of the 1982 Order in Council. That article, so far as relevant, provides as follows:

> 'As regards Her Majesty's Home Civil Service—(a) the Minister for the Civil Service may from time to time make regulations or give instructions . . . (ii) for controlling the conduct of the Service, and providing for the classification of all persons employed therein and . . . the conditions of service of all such persons . . .'

The Order in Council was not issued under powers conferred by any Act of Parliament . . . it was issued by the sovereign by virtue of her prerogative, but of course on the advice of the government of the day. In these circumstances counsel for the respondent submitted that the instruction was not open to review by the courts because it was an emanation of the prerogative. This submission involves two propositions: (1) that prerogative powers are discretionary, that is to say they may be exercised at the discretion of the sovereign (acting on advice in accordance with modern constitutional practice) and the way in which they are exercised is not open to review by the courts; (2) that an instruction given in the exercise of a delegated power conferred by the sovereign under the prerogative enjoys the same immunity from review as if it were itself a direct exercise of prerogative power. Counsel for the appellants contested both of these propositions, but the main weight of his argument was directed against the second.

The first of these propositions is vouched by an impressive array of authority, which I do not propose to cite at all fully. Starting with Blackstone's *Commentaries* (1 Bl Com (15th edn) 251) and Chitty, *A Treatise on the Law of the Prerogatives of the Crown* (1820) pp. 6–7, they are at one in stating that, within the sphere of its prerogative powers, the Crown has an absolute discretion. In more recent times the best known definition of the prerogative is that given in Dicey's *Introduction to the Study of the Law of the Constitution* (8th edn., 1915) p. 421, which is as follows:

> The prerogative is the name for the remaining portion of the Crown's original authority, and is therefore, as already pointed out, the name for the residue of discretionary power left at any moment in the hands of the Crown, whether such power be in fact exercised by the King himself or by his Ministers.

Dicey's definition was quoted with approval in this House in *A–G v De Keyser's Royal Hotel Ltd* [1920] AC 508 at 526 by Lord Dunedin and was impliedly accepted by the other Law Lords in that case. In *Burmah Oil Co (Burma Trading) Ltd v Lord Advocate* [1965] AC 75 at 99 Lord Reid referred to Dicey's definition as being 'always quoted with approval' although he said it did not take him very far in that case. It was also referred to with apparent approval by Roskill LJ in *Laker Airways Ltd v Dept of Trade* [1977] QB 643 at 719. As *De Keyser's* case shows, the courts will inquire into whether a particular prerogative power exists or not and, if it does exist, into its extent. But once the existence and the extent of a power are established to the satisfaction of the court, the court cannot inquire into the propriety of its exercise. That is undoubtedly the position as laid down in the authorities to which I have briefly referred and it is plainly reasonable in relation to many of the most important prerogative powers which are concerned with control of the armed forces and with foreign policy and with other matters which are unsuitable for discussion or review in the law courts. In the present case the prerogative power involved is power to regulate the Home Civil Service, and I recognise there is no obvious reason why the mode of exercise of that power should be immune from review by the courts. Nevertheless, to permit such review would run counter to the great weight of authority to which I have briefly referred. Having regard to the opinion I have reached on the second proposition of counsel for the respondent, it is unnecessary to decide whether his first proposition is sound or not and I prefer to leave that question open until it arises in a case where a decision on it is necessary. I therefore assume, without deciding, that his first proposition is correct and that all powers exercised directly under the prerogative are immune from challenge in the courts. I pass to consider his second proposition.

The second proposition depends for its soundness on whether the power conferred by art 4 of the 1982 Order in Council on the Minister for the Civil Service of 'providing for . . . the conditions of service' of the Civil Service is subject to an implied obligation to act fairly. (Such an obligation is sometimes referred to as an obligation to obey the rules of natural justice, but that is a less appropriate description, at least when applied, as in the present case, to a power which is executive and not judicial.) There is no doubt that, if the 1982 Order in Council had been made under the authority of a statute, the power delegated to the minister by art 4 would have been construed as being subject to an obligation to act fairly. I am unable to see why the words conferring the same powers should be construed differently merely because their source was an Order in Council made under the prerogative . . . The 1982 Order in Council was described by Sir Robert Armstrong in his first affidavit as primary legislation; that is, in my opinion, a correct description, subject to the qualification that the Order in Council, being made under the prerogative, derives its authority from the sovereign alone and not, as is more commonly the case with legislation, from the sovereign in Parliament. Legislation frequently delegates power from the legislating authority, the sovereign in one case, Parliament in the other, to some other person or body and, when that is done, the delegated powers are defined more or less closely by the legislation, in this case by art 4. But, whatever their source [such delegated powers] are in my opinion normally subject to judicial control to ensure that they are not exceeded. By 'normally' I mean provided that considerations of national security do not require otherwise.

The courts have already shown themselves ready to control by way of judicial review the actions of a tribunal set up under the prerogative. *R v Criminal Injuries Compensation Board ex p Lain* [1967] 2 QB 864 was such a case . . . [he quoted from the judgment of Lord Parker CJ [1967] 2 QB 864 at 881 and continued] . . . Accordingly, I agree with the conclusion of Glidewell J that there is no reason for treating the exercise of a power under art 4 any differently from the exercise of a statutory power merely because art 4 itself is found in an order issued under the prerogative . . .

The duty to consult

Counsel for the appellants submitted that the minister had a duty to consult the CCSU, on behalf of employees at GCHQ, before giving the instruction on 22 December 1983 for making an important change in their conditions of service. His main reason for so submitting was that the employees had a legitimate, or reasonable, expectation that there would be such prior consultation before any important change was made in their conditions.

It is clear that the employees did not have a legal right to prior consultation. The Order in Council confers no such right, and art 4 makes no reference at all to consultation. . . . The Civil Service Pay and Conditions of Service Code expressly states:

> The following terms and conditions also apply to your appointment in the Civil Service. It should be understood, however, that in consequence of the constitutional position of the Crown, the Crown has the right to change its employees' conditions of service at any time, and that they hold their appointments at the pleasure of the Crown.

But even where a person claiming some benefit or privilege has no legal right to it, as a matter of private law, he may have a legitimate expectation of receiving the benefit or privilege, and, if so, the courts will protect his expectation by judicial review as a matter of public law. This subject has been fully explained by Lord Diplock in *O'Reilly v Mackman* [1983] 2 AC 237 and I need not repeat what he has so recently said. Legitimate, or reasonable, expectations may arise either from an express promise given on behalf of a public authority or from the existence of a regular practice which the claimant can reasonably expect to continue. Examples of the former type of expectation are *Re Liverpool Taxi Owners' Association* [1972] 2 QB 299 and *A–G of Hong Kong v Ng Yuen Shiu* [1983] 2 AC 629 . . . An example of the latter is *R v Hull Prison Board of Visitors ex p St Germain* [1979] QB 425, approved by this House in *O'Reilly v Mackman* [1983] 2 AC 237 at 274. The submission on behalf of the appellants is that the present case is of the latter type. The test of that is whether the practice of prior consultation of the staff on significant changes in their conditions of service was so well established by 1983 that it would be unfair or inconsistent with good administration for the government to depart from the practice in this case. Legitimate expectations such as are now under consideration will always relate to a benefit or privilege to which the claimant has no right in private law, and it may even be to one which conflicts with his private law rights. In the present case the evidence shows that, ever since GCHQ began in 1947, prior consultation has been the invariable rule when conditions of service were to be significantly altered. Accordingly, in my opinion, if there had been no question of national security involved, the appellants would have had a legitimate expectation that the minister would consult them before issuing the instruction of 22 December 1983. The next question, therefore, is whether it has been shown that consideration of national security supersedes the expectation.

National security

The issue here is not whether the minister's instruction was proper or fair or justifiable on its merits. These matters are not for the courts to determine. The sole issue is whether the decision on which the instruction was based was reached by a process that was fair to the staff at GCHQ. As Lord Brightman said in *Chief Constable of the North Wales Police v Evans* [1982] 1 WLR 1155 at 1173: 'Judicial review is concerned, not with the decision, but with the decision-making process.' I have already explained my reasons for holding that, if no question of national security arose, the decision-making process in this case would have been unfair. The respondent's case is that she deliberately made the decision without prior consultation because prior consultation 'would involve a real risk that it would occasion the very kind of disruption [at GCHQ] which was a threat to national security and which it was intended to avoid' (I have quoted from para. 27(i) of the respondent's printed case). Counsel for the appellants conceded that a reasonable minister could reasonably have taken that view, but he argued strongly that the respondent had failed to show that that was in fact the reason for her decision. He supported his argument by saying, as I think was conceded by counsel for the respondent, that the reason given in para. 27(i) had not been mentioned to Glidewell J and that it had only emerged before the Court of Appeal. He described it as an 'afterthought' and invited the House to hold that it had not been shown to have been the true reason.

The question is one of evidence. The decision on whether the requirements of national security outweigh the duty of fairness in any particular case is for the government and not for the courts; the government alone has access to the necessary information, and in any event the judicial process is unsuitable for reaching decisions on national security. But if the decision is successfully challenged, on the ground that it has been reached by a process which is unfair, then the government is under an obligation to produce evidence that the decision was in fact based on grounds of national security. [Authority for these points, he said, is to be found in *The Zamora* [1916] 2 AC 77, in Lord Parker's opinion at 107 and at 106 and 108.] . . . What was required [in that case] was evidence that a cargo of copper in the custody of the Prize Court was urgently required for national purposes, but no evidence had been directed to that point. The claim on behalf of the Crown that it was entitled to requisition the copper therefore failed; considering that the decision was made in 1916 at a critical stage of the 1914–18 war, it was a strong one. In *Chandler v DPP* [1964] AC 763 at 790, which was an appeal by persons who had been convicted of a breach of the peace under s 1 of the Official Secrets Act 1911 by arranging a demonstration by the Campaign for Nuclear Disarmament on an operational airfield at Wethersfield, Lord Reid said:

> The question more frequently arises as to what is or is not in the public interest. I do not subscribe to the view that the government or a minister must always or even as a general rule have the last word about that. But here we are dealing with a very special matter—interfering with a prohibited place which Wethersfield was.

But the court had before it evidence from an Air Commodore that the airfield was of importance for national security. Both Lord Reid and Viscount Radcliffe referred to the evidence as being relevant to their refusal of the appeal ([1964] AC 763 at 796).

The evidence in support of this part of the respondent's case came from Sir Robert Armstrong in his first affidavit, especially at para. 16. Counsel for the appellants rightly pointed out that the affidavit does not in terms directly support para. 27(i) quoted above. But it does set out the respondent's view that to have entered into prior consultation would have served to bring out the vulnerability of areas of operation to those who had shown themselves ready to organise disruption. That must be read along with the earlier parts of the affidavit in which Sir Robert had dealt in some detail with the attitude of the trade unions which I have referred to earlier in this speech. The affidavit, read as a whole, does in my opinion undoubtedly constitute evidence that the minister did indeed consider that prior consultation would have involved a risk of precipitating disruption at GCHQ. I am accordingly of opinion that the respondent has shown that her decision was one which not only could reasonably have been based, but was in fact based, on considerations of national security, which outweighed what would otherwise have been the reasonable expectation on the part of the appellants for prior consultation. In deciding that matter I must with respect differ from the decision of Glidewell J but, as I have mentioned, I do so on a point that was not argued to him . . .

Minor matters

The judge held that had the prior consultations taken place they would not have been so limited that he could confidently say that they would have been futile. It is not necessary for me to reach a concluded view on this matter, but as at present advised I am inclined to differ from the judge, especially because of the attitude of two of the trade union members of CCSU who declared that they were firmly against any no-strike agreement.

The Court of Appeal considered the proper construction of certain international labour conventions which they cite. I respectfully agree with Lord Lane CJ, who said that 'the correct meaning of the material articles of the conventions is by no means clear', but I do not propose to consider the matter as the conventions are not part of the law in this country.

Counsel for the appellants submitted that the oral direction did not qualify as an 'instruction' within the meaning of art 4 . . . There was no obligation to put the instructions in writing, although that might perhaps have been expected in a matter so important as this. Nor was there any obligation to couch the instructions in any particular form. Accordingly, I reject this submission.

For these reasons I would dismiss the appeal.

Lord Diplock[19]

My Lords, the English law relating to judicial control of administrative action has been developed on a case to case basis which has virtually transformed it over the last three decades. The principles of public law that are applicable to the instant case are in my view well established by authorities that are sufficiently cited in the speech that will be delivered by my noble and learned friend Lord Roskill. This obviates the necessity of my duplicating his citations though I should put on record that after reading and rereading Lord Devlin's speech in *Chandler v DPP* [1964] AC 763 I have gained no help from it, for I find some of his observations that are peripheral to what I understand to be *ratio decidendi* difficult to reconcile with the actual decision that he felt able to reach and also with one another.

The only difficulty which the instant case has presented on the facts . . . has been to identify what is, in my view, the one crucial point of law on which this appeal turns. It never was identified or even adumbrated in the respondent's argument at the hearing before Glidewell J and so, excusably, finds no place in what otherwise I regard as an impeccable judgment. The consequence of this omission was that he found in favour of the applicants. Before the Court of Appeal the crucial point was advanced in argument by the Crown in terms that were unnecessarily and, in my view, unjustifiably wide. This stance was maintained in the appeal to this House, although, under your Lordships' encouragement, the narrower point of law that was really crucial was developed and relied on by the respondent in the alternative. Once that point has been accurately identified the evidence in the case in my view makes it inevitable that this appeal must be dismissed. I will attempt to state in summary form those principles of public law which lead me to this conclusion.

Judicial review, now regulated by RSC Ord 53, provides the means by which judicial control of administrative action is exercised. The subject matter of every judicial review is a decision made by some person (or body of persons) whom I will call the 'decision-maker' or else a refusal by him to make a decision.

[19] Lord Diplock had previously been Chairman of the Security Commission and therefore had experience of national security issues.

To qualify as a subject for judicial review the decision must have consequences which affect some person (or body of persons) other than the decision-maker, although it may affect him too. It must affect such other person either:

(a) by altering rights or obligations of that person which are enforceable by or against him in private law; or

(b) by depriving him of some benefit or advantage which either (i) he has in the past been permitted by the decision-maker to enjoy and which he can legitimately expect to be permitted to continue to do until there has been communicated to him some rational ground for withdrawing it on which he has been given an opportunity to comment or (ii) he has received assurance from the decision-maker will not be withdrawn without giving him first an opportunity of advancing reasons for contending that they should not be withdrawn. (I prefer to continue to call the kind of expectation that qualifies a decision for inclusion in class (b) a 'legitimate expectation' rather than a 'reasonable expectation', in order thereby to indicate that it has consequences to which effect will be given in public law, whereas an expectation or hope that some benefit or advantage would continue to be enjoyed, although it might well be entertained by a 'reasonable' man, would not necessarily have such consequences. . . . 'Reasonable' furthermore bears different meanings according to whether the context in which it is being used is that of private law or of public law. To eliminate confusion it is best avoided in the latter.

For a decision to be susceptible to judicial review the decision-maker must be empowered by public law (and not merely, as in arbitration, by agreement between private parties) to make decisions that, if validly made, will lead to administrative action or abstention from action by an authority endowed by law with executive powers, which have one or other of the consequences mentioned in the preceding paragraph. The ultimate source of the decision-making power is nearly always nowadays a statute or subordinate legislation made under the statute but in the absence of any statute regulating the subject matter of the decision the source of the decision-making power may still be the common law itself, i.e. that part of the common law that is given by lawyers the label of 'the prerogative'. Where this is the source of decision-making power, the power is confined to executive officers of central as distinct from local government and in constitutional practice is generally exercised by those holding ministerial rank.

It was the prerogative that was relied on as the source of the power of the Minister for the Civil Service in reaching her decision of 22 December 1983 that membership of national trade unions should in future be barred to all members of the Home Civil Service employed at [GCHQ].

My Lords, I intend no discourtesy to counsel when I say that, intellectual interest apart, in answering the question of law raised in this appeal, I have derived little practical assistance from learned and esoteric analyses of the precise legal nature, boundaries and historical origin of 'the prerogative', or of what powers exercisable by executive officers acting on behalf of central government that are not shared by private citizens qualify for inclusion under this particular label. It does not, for instance, seem to me to matter whether today the right of the executive government that happens to be in power to dismiss without notice any member of the Home Civil Service on which perforce it must rely for the administration of its policies, and the correlative disability of the executive government that is in power to agree with a civil servant that his service should be on terms that did not make him subject to instant dismissal, should be ascribed to 'the prerogative' or merely to a consequence of the survival, for entirely different reasons, of a rule of constitutional law whose origin is to be found in the theory that those by whom the administration of the realm is carried on do so as personal servants of the monarch, who can dismiss them at will, because the King can do no wrong.

Nevertheless, whatever label may be attached to them there have unquestionably survived into the present day a residue of miscellaneous fields of law in which the executive government retains decision-making powers that are not dependent on any statutory authority but nevertheless have consequences on the private rights or legitimate expectations of other persons which would render the decision subject to judicial review if the power of the decision-maker to make them were statutory in origin. From matters so relatively minor as the grant of pardons to condemned criminals, of honours to the good and great, of corporate personality to deserving bodies of persons, and of bounty from moneys made available to the executive government by Parliament, they extend to matters so vital to the survival and welfare of the nation as the conduct of relations with foreign states and (what lies at the heart of the present case) the defence of the realm against potential enemies. Adopting the phraseology used in the Convention for the Protection of Human Rights and Fundamental Freedoms (Rome, 4th November 1950 TS 71 (1953) Cmd 8969), to which the United Kingdom is a party, it has now become usual in statutes to refer to the latter as 'national security'.

My Lords, I see no reason why simply because a decision-making power is derived from a common law and not a statutory source it should for that reason only be immune from judicial review. Judicial review has I think developed to a stage today when, without reiterating any analysis of the steps by which the development has come about, one can conveniently classify under three heads the grounds on which administrative action is subject to control by judicial review. The first ground I would call 'illegality', the second 'irrationality' and the third 'procedural impropriety'. That is not to say that further development on a case by case basis may not in course of time add further grounds. I have in mind particularly the possible adoption in the future of the principle of 'proportionality' which is recognised in the administrative law of several of our fellow members of the European Economic Community but to dispose of the instant case the three already well-established heads that I have mentioned will suffice.

By 'illegality' as a ground for judicial review I mean that the decision-maker must understand correctly the law that regulates his decision-making power and must give effect to it. Whether he has or not is par excellence a justiciable question to be decided, in the event of dispute, by those persons, the judges, by whom the judicial power of the state is exercisable.

By 'irrationality' I mean what can by now be succinctly referred to as '*Wednesbury* unreasonableness' . . . It applies to a decision which is so outrageous in its defiance of logic or of accepted moral standards that no sensible person who had applied his mind to the question to be decided could have arrived at it. Whether a decision falls within this category is a question that judges by their training and experience should be well equipped to answer, or else there would be something badly wrong with our judicial system . . . 'Irrationality' by now can stand on its own feet as an accepted ground on which a decision may be attacked by judicial review. I have described the third head as 'procedural impropriety' rather than failure to observe basic rules of natural justice or failure to act with procedural fairness towards the person who will be affected by the decision. This is because susceptibility to judicial review under this head covers also failure by an administrative tribunal to observe procedural rules that are expressly laid down in the legislative instrument by which its jurisdiction is conferred, even where such failure does not involve any denial of natural justice. But the instant case is not concerned with the proceedings of an administrative tribunal at all.

My Lords, that a decision of which the ultimate source of power to make it is not a statute but the common law (whether or not the common law is for this purpose given the label of 'the prerogative') may be the subject of judicial review on the ground of illegality is, I think, established by the cases cited by my noble and learned friend Lord Roskill, and this extends to cases where the field of law to which the decision relates is national security, as the decision of this House itself in *Burmah Oil Co (Burma Trading) Ltd v Lord Advocate* [1965] AC 75 shows. While I see no *a priori* reason to rule out 'irrationality' as a ground for judicial review of a ministerial decision taken in the exercise of 'prerogative' powers, I find it difficult to envisage in any of the various fields in which the prerogative remains the only source of the relevant decision-making power a decision of a kind that would be open to attack through the judicial process on this ground. Such decisions will generally involve the application of government policy. The reasons for the decision-maker taking one course rather than another do not normally involve questions to which, if disputed, the judicial process is adapted to provide the right answer, by which I mean that the kind of evidence that is admissible under judicial procedures and the way in which it has to be adduced tend to exclude from the attention of the court competing policy considerations which, if the executive discretion is to be wisely exercised, need to be weighed against one another, a balancing exercise which judges by their upbringing and experience are ill-qualified to perform. So I leave this as an open question to be dealt with on a case to case basis if, indeed, the case should ever arise.

As respects 'procedural propriety', I see no reason why it should not be a ground for judicial review of a decision made under powers of which the ultimate source is the prerogative . . . Indeed, where the decision is one which does not alter rights or obligations enforceable in private law but only deprives a person of legitimate expectations, 'procedural impropriety' will normally provide the only ground on which the decision is open to judicial review. But in any event what procedure will satisfy the public law requirement of procedural propriety depends on the subject matter of the decision, the executive functions of the decision-maker (if the decision is not that of an administrative tribunal) and the particular circumstances in which the decision came to be made.

My Lords, in the instant case the immediate subject matter of the decision was a change in one of the terms of employment of civil servants employed at GCHQ. That the executive functions of the Minister for the Civil Service, in her capacity as such, included making a decision to change any of those terms, except in so far as they related to remuneration, expenses and allowances, is not disputed. It does not seem to me to be of any practical significance whether or not as a matter of strict legal analysis this power is based on the rule of constitutional law to which I have already alluded that the employment of any civil servant may be terminated at any time without notice and that on such termination the same civil servant may be re-engaged on different terms. The rule of terminability of employment in the civil service without notice, of which the existence is beyond doubt, must in any event have the consequence that the continued enjoyment by a civil servant in the future of a right under a particular term of his employment cannot be the subject of any right enforceable by him in private law; at most it can only be a legitimate expectation.

Prima facie, therefore, civil servants employed at GCHQ who were members of national trade unions had, at best, in December 1983, a legitimate expectation that they would continue to enjoy the benefits of such membership and of representation by those trade unions in any consultations and negotiations with representatives of the management of that government department as to changes in any term of their employment. So, but again *prima facie* only, they were entitled, as a matter of public law under the head of 'procedural propriety', before administrative action was taken on a decision to withdraw that benefit, to have communicated to the national trade unions by which they had theretofore been represented the reason for such withdrawal, and for such unions to be given an opportunity to comment on it.

The reason why the Minister for the Civil Service decided on 22 December 1983 to withdraw this benefit was in the interests of national security. National security is the responsibility of the executive government; what action is needed to protect its interests is, as the cases cited by my noble and learned friend Lord Roskill establish and common sense itself dictates, a matter on which those on whom the responsibility rests, and not the courts of justice, must have the last word. It is par excellence a non-justiciable question. The judicial process is totally inept to deal with the sort of problems which it involves.

The executive government likewise decided, and this would appear to be a collective decision of cabinet ministers involved, that the interests of national security required that no notice should be given of the decision before administrative action had been taken to give effect to it. The reason for this was the risk that advance notice to the national unions of the executive government's intention would attract the very disruptive action prejudicial to the national security the recurrence of which the decision barring membership of national trade unions to civil servants employed at GCHQ was designed to prevent.

There was ample evidence to which reference is made by others of your Lordships that this was, indeed, a real risk so the crucial point of law in this case is whether procedural propriety must give way to national security when there is conflict between (1) on the one hand, the *prima facie* rule of 'procedural propriety' in public law, applicable to a case of legitimate expectations that a benefit ought not to be withdrawn until the reason for its proposed withdrawal has been communicated to the person who has theretofore enjoyed that benefit and that person has been given an opportunity to comment on the reason, and (2) on the other hand, action that is needed to be taken in the interests of national security, for which the executive government bears the responsibility and alone has access to sources of information that qualify it to judge what the necessary action is. To that there can, in my opinion, be only one sensible answer. That answer is Yes.

I agree with your Lordships that this appeal must be dismissed.

Lord Roskill

. . . If the executive in pursuance of [a] statutory power does an act affecting the rights of the citizen, it is beyond question that in principle the manner of the exercise of that power may today be challenged [by way of judicial review] . . . If the executive instead of acting under a statutory power acts under a prerogative power and in particular a prerogative power delegated to the respondent under art 4 . . . I am unable to see . . . that there is any logical reason why the fact that the source of power is the prerogative and not statute should today deprive the citizen of that right of challenge . . . In either case the act in question is the act of the executive. To talk of that act as the act of the sovereign savours of the archaism of past centuries. . . .

But I do not think that the right of challenge can be unqualified. It must, I think, depend on the subject matter of the prerogative power which is exercised. Many examples were given during the argument of prerogative powers which as at present advised I do not think could properly be made the subject of judicial review. Prerogative powers such as those relating to the making of treaties, the defence of the realm, the prerogative of mercy, the grant of honours, the dissolution of Parliament and the appointment of ministers as well as others are not, I think, susceptible to judicial review because their nature and subject are such as not to be amenable to the judicial process. The courts are not the place wherein to determine whether a treaty should be concluded or the armed forces disposed in a particular manner or Parliament dissolved on one date rather than another.

In my view the exercise of the prerogative which enabled the oral instruction . . . to be given does not by reason of its subject matter fall within what for want of a better phrase I would call the 'excluded categories' some of which I have just mentioned . . . Historically, at least since 1688, the courts have sought to present a barrier to inordinate claims by the executive. But they have also been obliged to recognise that in some fields that barrier must be lowered and that on occasions, albeit with great reluctance, the courts must accept that the claims of the executive must take precedence over those of the individual. One such field is that of national security. The courts have long shown themselves sensitive to the assertion by the executive that considerations of national security must preclude judicial investigation of a particular individual grievance. But even in that field the courts will not act on a mere assertion that questions of national security are involved. Evidence is required that the decision under challenge was in fact founded on those grounds . . . The question is whether, on the evidence before your Lordships, the respondent is entitled to assert that it was the fear of revealing the vulnerability of GCHQ to industrial action that it was decided that advance consultation could not take place . . . [He refers to Sir Robert Armstrong's affidavit evidence and particularly the extracts referred to above at p. 658 and continues] . . . counsel for the appellants claimed that careful reading of Sir Robert Armstrong's first affidavit . . . did not support the view that [national security] was a consideration which the respondent had ever had in mind. My Lords . . . I read Sir Robert as explaining why the possibility of negotiating a non-disruption agreement was considered and rejected . . . Ministers were also of the view that the importance of the decision was such as to warrant its first being announced in Parliament . . . [the affidavit] seems to me to make abundantly clear why the respondent and other ministers declined to engage in consultations . . .

. . . [T]he respondent has established [first] that the work at GCHQ was a matter of grave national security, second that security would have been seriously compromised had industrial action . . . taken place, third, that consultation with the appellants . . . would have served only further to reveal the vulnerability of the GCHQ, fourth, that it was in the interests of national security that that should not be allowed to take place and fifth, that . . . the respondent was justified [not to consult] . . . [T]he appeal should be dismissed.

Lord Scarman and Lord Brightman also made speeches in favour of dismissing the appeal. Like Lord Fraser, Lord Brightman reserved for a future occasion the question whether courts can review a direct exercise of prerogative power rather than a delegated exercise of power of the type that this case was concerned with.

ASSESSING THE HOUSE OF LORDS' DECISION

It is unlikely that the decision came as a great surprise to the CCSU, although no doubt it was something of a relief to the government. Did it, however, have any great significance beyond the particular facts? The main issues arising from the decision may be summarized as follows.

1. The majority decision established that the jurisdiction of courts to review prerogative powers extends beyond merely establishing the existence and scope of prerogative powers. Since the *GCHQ* decision the courts can review the *manner* in which such powers are exercised on the same grounds as they can review the manner in which statutory powers are exercised. Note on the scope and existence of prerogative powers that the majority in the House of Lords approached the case on the basis that the relevant prerogative powers were those which allowed the executive to regulate the civil service, rather than those which concern the defence of the realm. Sir William Wade has criticized the decision on the ground that such prerogative powers are not true prerogatives because they are not unique to the Crown: all large employers must regulate the terms and conditions of their employees.[20]

2. Whether the courts will be prepared to intervene, therefore, no longer depends on whether the powers are granted by statute or prerogative. What matters is not the source of the power, but the nature of the decision which has been taken.

3. The *GCHQ* case shows that the courts are extremely reluctant to intervene in decisions taken by the executive in the interests of national security. Such decisions are regarded as being non-justiciable because:

(a) government and not the courts is responsible for national security matters; and
(b) the courts lack the information and expertise to question executive discretion in this field.

Factor (a) is to do with the constitutional role of the courts and factor (b is to do with the competence of the courts.

4. Whether a decision has in fact been taken in the interests of natio security is a matter of evidence. The mere assertion by government th has acted in the interests of national security does not protect the gov ment from judicial review. Judges must be satisfied, usually on the ba the affidavit evidence, that national security was involved. The *GCH* shows that courts may be satisfied of this even where the affidavit ev does not explicitly refer to national security as the basis of the actio challenged.

[20] H. W. R. Wade, 'Procedure and Prerogative in Public Law' (1985) 101 LQR And see Chapter 12.

5. Had the government's decision not been based on national security, the judges would have intervened on the ground that the Minister for the Civil Service had acted unfairly in not consulting prior to imposing the ban. The decision, therefore, also illustrates that if a public body has in the past adopted procedures which have benefited individuals, those individuals may have a legitimate expectation that those procedures will benefit them in the future. Failure to follow these procedures may lead to a judicial review challenge on grounds of unfairness.

Criticisms of the decision

Several criticisms have been levelled at this decision: first, that the judges were too ready to accept the government's argument on the national security issue; secondly, that the reliance placed on Armstrong's affidavit revealed shortcomings in the judicial review procedure; and thirdly, that the judge's approach to the prerogative power issues was flawed. On the national security issue, the main criticism has been that the judges too readily allowed the national security claim to be used by government to prevent judicial review. In this context, it has been argued that there was no legal authority to support the view that national security arguments justify excluding review.[21]

It may be remembered the question was not whether the government was right to impose a ban on trade union membership. Rather, it was whether the government was justified in not consulting with individuals and the unions about the imposition of a ban, in circumstances in which the unions would ·robably have been prepared to accept an agreement not to strike at GCHQ. ·tics of the judgment emphasize that:

- Sir Robert Armstrong had not specifically referred to national security the reason for not consulting;
- ·onal security had not been specifically relied on at first instance; and
- was a view, considered by the Employment Select Committee, ·e decision not to consult had been taken as a negotiating device extra concessions from the unions.[22]

suggested that following the conviction of Geoffrey Prime, ·e (who, incidently, was not a union member), a year earl- behind the ban was 'not least to restore the NSA's [the ·gency] confidence' in the United Kingdom's security ·nt has never admitted the relevance of this factor.[23]

·view, the Royal Prerogative and National Security' (1985) 36 ·. Leigh, *In from the Cold: National Security and Parliamentary* ·See now *Chahal v UK, The Times*, 28 November 1996: the ·s indicated willingness, in limited circumstances, to review ·the interests of national security.

·tee's report).

·ative MP), *GCHQ: The Secret Wireless War 1900–1986* ·and I. Leigh, *In from the Cold: National Security and* ·n. 192).

J. A. G. Griffith has argued that the reliance placed on Sir Robert Armstrong's affidavit shows a weakness in the judicial review procedure which prevents the courts from getting to the real facts. He argues that the judges would have been better informed, and in a stronger position to decide what the public interest required, had the CCSU been able to cross-examine those who actually took the decision:

> . . . two people knew the real reason why the government did not consult with the trade unions: the Prime Minister and the Foreign Secretary. Neither could be required to give evidence.[24]

ECHR AND THE ILO

Failure in the House of Lords represented the end of the legal road for the employees and the unions, so far as the domestic courts were concerned. The political campaign was, however, continued, as was the complaint to the ILO and the European Commission of Human Rights.

European Convention on Human Rights

It was also decided to petition the European Commission of Human Rights on the grounds that the government's ban constituted a breach of Art 11 of the ECHR which provides:

> 1. Everyone has the right to freedom of peaceful assembly and to freedom of association with others, including the right to join trade unions for the protection of his interests.
> 2. No restrictions shall be placed on the exercise of these rights other than such as are prescribed by law and are necessary in a democratic society in the interests of national security or public safey, for the prevention of disorder or crime, for the protection of health or morals or for the protection of the rights and freedoms of others. This article shall not prevent the imposition of lawful restrictions on the exercise of these rights by members of the armed forces, of the police or of the administration of the state.

The unions, however, got little comfort from the Commission. In January 1987, three years after the ban on unions was imposed, it found that the unions' application was 'manifestly ill-founded' and rejected it as inadmissible. The case did not therefore proceed to be considered by the Human Rights Court. Here are extracts from its admissibility decision.[25]

> 1. The applicants complaint under Art 11 of the Convention that the respondent Government removed the right of individual employees at GCHQ to belong to a trade union. [The Commission considered several preliminary issues, including whether employees at GCHQ could be considered to be members of 'the

[24] J. A. G. Griffith, 'Judicial Decision-Making in Public Law' [1985] PL 564–95. See also Chapter 21.

[25] 10 EHHR 269.

administration of the state' within the meaning of Art 11. The Commission held that they were and continued.] It must therefore examine whether the further conditions of the second sentence of Art 11(2) have been met, in particular whether the restrictions at issue were lawful within the meaning of that provision. The applicants have pointed out that this must mean lawful under the Convention, having regard to the aim of the latter to prevent the interference with fundamental rights other than by means which are prescribed by law and which are necessary in a democratic society. They submit that the term prescribed by law in the first sentence of Art 11(2) is not met in that s 121(4) of the 1975 Act and s 138(4) of the 1978 Act[26] grant to the state discretionary powers without any indication how these powers should be exercised. Moreover, the powers conferred by Art 4 of the Order in Council of 1982 do not adequately indicate the conditions on which contractual terms and conditions may be regulated. Further no provisions are made for judicial control of the State assertion that national security is at stake . . . The Commission recalls that it has so far not expressed an opinion in its case law on the meaning of the term lawful in this particular context. In the Commission's view, however, lawful . . . means in the first place that the measures in issue must at least have been in accordance with national law . . . It is true that [the Order in Council] is rather broad in that it does not specifically refer to the regulation of trade union membership. However, these powers of the Minister must be seen in connection with the two Employment Protection Acts which restrict the exercise of the powers under the Civil Service Order in Council and on the basis of which provisions the Foreign Secretary . . . signed and issued certificates. In particular, s 138(4) of the 1978 Act and the corresponding s 121(4) of the 1975 Act expressly refer to the issuing of such certificates for the purpose of safeguarding national security. The Commission finds that the measure at issue met this condition in that the staff at GCHQ were concerned with vital functions of national security. Against this legislative background the Commission considers that the relevant legal provisions provided an adequate and sufficient indication to those employed at GCHQ as to the possibility of steps being taken to regulate trade union membership. In this respect the Commission notes, in addition, that the measures at issue were subject to judicial control by the domestic courts. In the Commission's opinion, the measures were, therefore, taken in accordance with national law . . . [T]he Comission finds that, even if the term lawful (*legitimate*) should require something more than basis in national law, in particular a prohibition of arbitrariness, there can be no doubt that this condition was in any event also observed in the present case. The Commission recalls its case law according to which States must be given a wide discretion when ensuring the protection of their national security. . . . [T]he Commission notes in particular the House of Lords, in its judgment of 2 November 1984, unanimously accepted that the basis of the Government's actions related to the interest of national security. The Commission considers that in this light and against the whole background of industrial action and the vital functions of GCHQ the action taken, although drastic, was in no way arbitrary. The measures would

[26] These are references to the Employment Protection Acts under which the Foreign Secretary was empowered to issue certificates barring employees from complaining to an industrial tribunal that they were being discriminated against because of their union membership: for an explanation, look back at the statement made by the Foreign Secretary to the House of commons set out at p. 16. The issuing of certificates happened after Mrs Thatcher had issued her oral instruction under prerogative power delegated to her by the Civil Service Order in Council.

therefore also be lawful within a wider meaning of that term in the second sentence of Art 11(2). The Commission is thus satisfied that the measures at issue, while interfering with the applicants' rights under Art 11(1), were justified under the second sentence of Art 11(2) . . . It follows that this part of the application is manifestly ill-founded within the meaning of Art 27(2) of the Convention.

[*The Commission then went on to consider another aspect of the application, namely the unions' argument that judicial review in the national courts had not provided them with an effective remedy.*]

2. The applicants complain that there was no effective remedy under domestic law for the alleged breach of Art 11(2), by which a municipal court can judge the validity of a particular administrative action. No remedy allowed an assessment of whether the Government acted in response, or proportionately, to a pressing social need, or whether the powers exercised were prescribed by English law and the English courts have no power to determine whether the Convention has been breached. Judicial review applied criteria much less onerous for the State to satisfy. The applicants rely on Art 13[27] . . . In the present case the Commission . . . observes that [the applicants] were able to bring a case before the High Court, the Court of Appeal and the House of Lords. In dealing with the case, these courts examined whether the measures at issue fell within the 1982 Civil Service Order in Council and the 1975 and 1978 Acts. The courts also examined the rights of trade union members as well as the manner in which the measures were taken, for instance, whether the Government should first have consulted the trade unions. Moreover, the court reviewed the justification of the measures, in particular on the grounds of national security. The Commission has also taken account of the fact that, since the Convention is not part of the domestic law of the United Kingdom, the High Court, the Court of Appeal and the House of Lords, as the national authorities referred to in Art 13 of the Convention, did not decide upon arguments which were made with express reference to the Convention. However, the Commission concludes that in the present case the relevant rights were substantially relied upon [by] the applicants in the domestic proceedings and that the national authorities were capable of affording the complainants an effective remedy within the meaning of Art 13. . . . In particular, the Commission considers that the Court of Appeal and the House of Lords were able to consider the essence of the applicants' present complaints under Art 11 of the Convention. The courts would have been able to quash the action taken by the Prime Minister under the 1982 Civil Service Order in Council had they found for the applicants in the proceedings in question. In fact, this course was followed by the High Court in its decision of 16 July 1984 which was subsequently set aside, on appeal by the Court of Appeal. The Commission concludes that effective remedies were in fact available to the applicants and that the proceedings concerned satisfied the requirements of Art 13 of the Convention. It follows that this part of the application is also manifestly ill-founded within the meaning or Art 27(2) of the Convention.

[27] This provides: 'Everyone whose rights and freedoms as set forth in this Convention shall have an effective remedy before national authority notwithstanding that the violation has been committed by persons acting in an official capacity.'

The International Labour Organization

As well as making an application to the European Commission of Human Rights, the unions also made a complaint to the ILO claiming that the government had infringed rights protected by the ILO Convention on Freedom of Association. This differed from the ECHR in two important respects. First, right to trade union membership is expressed differently. Art 9(1) of that treaty provides:

> The extent to which the guarantees provided for in the Convention shall apply to the armed forces and the police shall be determined by national law and regulations.

Unlike Art 11 of the ECHR, it makes no express reference to 'the administration of the state'. A second difference is that no mechanism exists to enforce the decision of the adjudicatory tribunal set up by the ILO Convention (the Freedom of Association Committee).

When giving evidence to the Employment Select Committee in February 1985, the Secretary of State for Employment (Tom King MP, one of the small group of ministers involved in deciding to impose the ban) was eager to tell the parliamentary committee that the government had carefully considered all its international treaty obligations and was confident that the union ban did not infringe them.[28] As we have seen, the ILO Convention was also mentioned, in passing, by the Court of Appeal and the House of Lords where several of their Lordships expressed the opinion that the government had not breached its obligation under this treaty. The ILO held otherwise. Almost every year since the union ban, the ILO has called upon the UK government to reverse its policy. In June 1995 the ILO's criticisms of the union ban were repeated at its annual conference in Geneva: a statement 'deeply regretting and deploring ministers' failure to solve the problem' was issued.[29] The government's response was to dismiss the statement as the product of 'a politically inspired campaign by the TUC to manipulate the ILO for partisan purposes'. This comment by Michael Portillo MP (Secretary of State for Employment) did little to hide what Labour MPs claimed was 'open warfare' between the Employment Department and the Foreign Office over whether the United Kingdom should quit the ILO in protest at its sustained and embarrassing criticisms: earlier that week Foreign Office ministers had made commitments in Parliament that the United Kingdom's membership of the organization was not under threat, yet Portillo now seemed to suggest that the United Kingdom would withdraw.[30] The Speaker, Mrs Betty Boothroyd MP, told the Commons that she hoped ministers would 'take an early opportunity of clearing up this matter so we can all understand what the position is'.[31]

[28] See Chapter 17.
[29] See *The Independent*, 15 June 1995.
[30] See *The Independent*, 9 June 1995, p. 10.
[31] *The Independent*, 9 June 1995, p. 10.

Questions

1. Do you agree with Griffith that the courts should have enabled the unions to cross-examine the Prime Minister and the Foreign Secretary? Would the court be any more likely to discover what went on and why than the Employment Select Committee? (See Chapter 17 above.)

2. According to Lord Diplock, 'National security . . . is *par excellence* a non-justiciable question. The judicial process is totally inept to deal with the sort of problems which it involves.' What is it that makes a decision 'non-justiciable'? If a decision is non-justiciable is it immune from legal accountability? If so, what forms of accountability can be imposed on those taking such decisions?

3. Which of the following statements most accurately summarizes the *ratio* of the *GCHQ* case on the national security point?

(a) The courts will not review any decision, even one impinging on the rights or important interests of citizens, that might have been taken in the interests of national security.
(b) The courts will not review any decision, even one impinging on the rights or important interests of citizens, when the government says that it took the decision in the interests of national security.
(c) The courts will not review any decision, even one impinging on the rights or important interests of citizens, where there is evidence that it was taken on the basis of national security.
(d) The courts will not review any decision, even one impinging on the rights or important interests of citizens, where there is reasonable evidence that it was taken on the basis of national security.
(e) The courts will review a decision impinging on the rights or important interests of citizens, unless the government can establish that the decision could reasonably have been taken in the interests of national security.
(f) The courts will review a decision impinging on the rights or important interests of citizens, unless the government can establish that the decision was justified on the grounds of national security.

4. Which of the above statements is closest to what you regard as being the desirable law? Why?

5. In what ways are select committees in a different position to the courts when it comes to investigating national security issues?

6. We have noted Lord Diplock's previous experience as Chairman of the Security Commission. Do you agree with the following statement of Lustgarten and Leigh?[32]

> . . . A judge publicly to have been a party to state secrets is one of the initiated. Overall there is a curious paradox between the self-denying judicial ordinance on substantive consideration of issues of national security in court and the preparedness to use the judiciary to serve as Security Commissioners [and in other similar roles] . . . the appearance of justice would be better served if they [judges who had served in such roles] declined to sit in all cases associated with official secrecy.

7. 'Judicial review is concerned, not with the decision, but with the decision-making process' (*per* Lord Brightman, *R v Chief Constable of the North Wales Police, ex p Evans*). In the light of the decisions in the *GCHQ* case, how true is this?

8. In what sense was judicial review an effective remedy under Art 13 of the ECHR?

[32] L. Lustgarten and I. Leigh, *In from the Cold: National Security and Parliamentary Democracy*, p. 491.

29

EURO-LITIGATION

... the Treaty is like an incoming tide. It flows into the estuaries and up the rivers. It cannot be held back.

Lord Denning MR, H. P. Bulmer Ltd v J. Bollinger SA [1974] Ch 401, 418

Ministers believe that the European Court of Justice has seized powers that must be sharply curbed. The Luxembourg-based court has heaped repeated humiliations on the British Government and cost taxpayers billions. Yet it has no democratic accountability—a situation Ministers plan to change.

David Hughes, political editor, Daily Mail, 3 February 1995

GENERAL INTRODUCTION

This chapter is about how membership of the European Community has affected public law litigation.

National courts and tribunals

Most 'euro-litigation', that is litigation which involves Community law issues, takes place not in the ECJ in Luxembourg, but in the courts and tribunals of the member states. In the United Kingdom, questions of Community law arise in many different types of proceedings in diverse courts and tribunals including prosecutions in magistrates' courts[1] and the Crown Court, in Order 53 applications for judicial review,[2] in industrial tribunals[3] and in civil actions for damages[4] and other remedies[5] against both public bodies and commercial organizations. Maher explains that:[6]

[1] For example, the prosecution of B&Q plc (a retailer of DIY goods) for Sunday trading brought by Torfaen Borough Council in Cwmbran Magistrates' Court: see p. 710.

[2] For example *R v Secretary of State for Transport, ex p Factortame (No 1)* [1990] 2 AC 85, *ex p Factortame (No 2)* (Case C-213/89) [1991] 1 AC 603 and *R v Secretary of State for Employment, ex p Equal Opportunities Commission* [1995] 1 AC 1.

[3] See e.g. *Marshall v Southampton and SW Hampshire Area Health Authority (Teaching)* (Case C-152/84) [1986] ECR 723.

[4] For example the claim made in *Bourgoin SA v Ministry of Agriculture, Fisheries and Food* [1986] QB 716. (The House of Lords has since doubted whether this judgment is correct: see *Kirklees Metropolitan Borough Council v Wickes Building Supplies Ltd* [1993] AC 227, 281.)

[5] For example, *Stoke-on-Trent City Council v B&Q plc* [1993] AC 900 (injunction sought in Chancery Division of the High Court).

[6] Imelda Maher, 'National Courts as European Community Courts' (1994) 14 Legal Studies 226, 242.

> As a new legal order which creates rights for individuals as well as states, the Community needed to make EC law, and the rights created thereunder, accessible to individuals. This could best be achieved through the national courts because they were already *in situ*; they were inexpensive because the member states bore the cost of running them; they enjoyed the respect of their citizens and if they enforced EC law it would help to ground EC and its legitimacy with the people of Europe.

In other words, just as the Community does not rely on a large staff of its own civil servants to implement Community law, but instead relies on the administrations in the member states, so too with adjudication: the work is largely carried out by national courts and tribunals. This chapter therefore looks at how courts in the United Kingdom have responded to membership of the EC, as well as examining the work of the ECJ.

The European Court of Justice

Even though national courts and tribunals are the workhorse of euro-litigation, the ECJ nevertheless plays a vitally important role. From the perspective of this book (looking at the impact of the EC on the constitutional and administrative law of the United Kingdom), three types of proceedings involving the ECJ need to be considered.

First, Art 177 references.[7] If in the course of hearing a case, a court or tribunal in the United Kingdom has to determine what rights or obligations flow from a piece of Community legislation, then it often decides to seek guidance on how to interpret it from the ECJ. This entails adjourning the proceedings, formulating a question for the ECJ, waiting 18 months or so for the ECJ to decide the issue, then resuming the proceedings in the national court or tribunal by applying the guidance given by the ECJ to the particular facts of the case. This Art 177 reference procedure is examined in more detail later in this chapter. It played a central role in the litigation tactics of those who campaigned for the legalization of Sunday trading.[8] Some commentators suggest that Art 177 is in need of radical reform.

Secondly, there are challenges (annulment proceedings) under Art 173 to the validity of Community regulations and directives.[9] The UK government, like those in the other member states, is entitled to challenge the legality of legislation made by the Council of Ministers and the Commission. Individuals and businesses can also, in theory, bring proceedings under Art 173—but in practice this can happen only in extremely limited circumstances. The United Kingdom's challenge to the validity of the Working Time Directive was made under Art 173.[10]

Thirdly, there are infraction proceedings under Art 169.[11] Where it is claimed that a member state is failing to comply with Community law, either

[7] See further p. 696 below.
[8] See Chapter 30.
[9] See further p. 698 below.
[10] See Chapter 14.
[11] See further p. 699 below.

the Commission or another member state may commence proceedings in the ECJ to ensure compliance. The United Kingdom has been subject to numerous such proceedings. Since the Maastricht Treaty, the ECJ has had power to impose financial penalties for some breaches.

Before looking at these three types of ECJ proceedings in more detail, we need to examine first the work of national courts and tribunals in handling Community law.

EURO-LITIGATION IN UK COURTS AND TRIBUNALS

Two legal principles of great importance underpin the way in which Community law issues are handled by the UK courts and tribunals:

(a) the principle of the supremacy (or primacy) of Community law; and
(b) the principle of 'direct effect' of some provisions in Community treaties and directives.

We begin by examining these concepts, though as will become apparent, other important principles also operate in this sphere.

Supremacy of Community law

As noted earlier,[12] the ECJ had asserted the principle of supremacy of Community law above that of the member states as long ago as the mid-1960s, long before the United Kingdom joined the EC:[13]

> By creating a Community of unlimited duration, having its own institutions, its own personality, its own legal capacity of representation on the international plane and, more particularly, real powers stemming from a limitation of sovereignty or transfer of powers from the States to the Community, the Member States have limited their sovereign rights, albeit within limited fields, and have thus created a body of law which binds both their nationals and themselves.
>
> The integration into the laws of each Member State of provisions which derive from the Community, and more generally the terms and spirit of the Treaty, make it impossible for the States, as a corollary, to accord precedence to a unilateral and subsequent measure over the legal system accepted by them on a basis of reciprocity. Such a measure cannot therefore be inconsistent with that legal system. The executive force of Community law cannot vary from one State to another in deference to subsequent domestic laws, without jeopardising the attainment of the objectives of the Treaty set out in Art 5(2) and giving rise to the discrimination prohibited by Art 7.

[12] See p. 116.

[13] *Costa v ENEL* (Case 6/64) [1964] ECR 585. Costa, an Italian lawyer, refused to pay a bill levied against him by the Italian electricity corporation on the ground that the Italian legislation nationalizing the electricity industry was contrary to provisions in the EC Treaty, and therefore invalid.

In a later case, the ECJ made it clear that Community law was supreme over national law, whether that national law was made before or after (as in *Costa*'s case) the Community law in question.[14]

The European Communities Act 1972, which incorporated Community law into the legal systems of the United Kingdom, alluded to the supremacy of Community law over UK law only in the obscure langauge used by s 2(4).[15] It came as a considerable surprise to many people outside the legal profession when in 1989 a UK court for the first time held that an Act of Parliament was incompatible with Community law and would therefore not be applied by the court.[16] British newspapers at the time spoke of a 'constitutional revolution'. The reality was rather more prosaic, though still of great constitutional significance.

The UK courts find themselves in a potentially sensitive position: on the one hand they are faced with the long-established principle of parliamentary supremacy under which a court cannot question the validity of an Act of Parliament;[17] on the other, UK courts—as part of the EC legal order—have an obligation to give effective protection to Community law rights and enforce obligations created by Community law. In large part this stems from Art 5 of the EC Treaty, which provides that member states (which includes their courts) are required to 'take all appropriate measures, whether general or particular, to ensure fulfilment of the obligations arising out of this Treaty or resulting from action taken by the institution of the Community'. How have the courts reconciled these two constitutional demands made of them? The result has been to stress that, in the United Kingdom, courts do not decide that an Act of Parliament inconsistent with Community law is 'invalid' or 'unconstitutional'. Rather, they either merely make a declaration stating that there is an inconsistency or they 'dis-apply' the offending sections of the Act. That is, they determine the outcome of the particular dispute before them on the basis of the Community law disregarding the statute.[18] The government, in due course, then introduces a bill into Parliament to amend the inconsistent statute. In this subtle way, two competing constitutional requirements can to some extent be reconciled.

The supremacy of Community law is very clearly accepted by the UK courts. This means, as Bradley puts it, that 'so long as the United Kingdom wishes to remain in the EC, the supremacy of the law made by Parliament must if necessary give way to the greater supremacy of Community law'.[19] For the judges, this has involved an enormous sea-change to the constitutional framework within which they work. Can you imagine what it must

14 *Simmenthal SA* (*No 2*) Case 106/77 [1978] ECR 629.

15 See p. 116.

16 *R v Secretary of State for Transport, ex p Factortame* (*No 2*) (Case C-213/89) [1991] 1 AC 603.

17 See Chapter 5.

18 See further J. Rinze, 'The Role of the ECJ as a Federal Constitutional Court' [1993] PL 426.

19 A. W. Bradley, 'Sovereignty of Parliament—in Perpetuity', in J. Jowell and D. Oliver (eds.), *The Changing Constitution* (3rd edn., 1994), p. 97. See also N. G. Gravells, 'Disapplying an Act of Parliament pending a Preliminary Ruling: Constitutional Enormity or Community Law Right?' [1989] PL 568.

have been like to be a judge in 1972 when, overnight, Community law suddenly became part of the UK legal systems?

The principle of direct effect

The UK courts have dis-applied Acts of Parliament on the ground of inconsistency with Community law in only a handful of cases. Much more important to the day-to-day work of the legal system is the other fundamental principle, that of the 'direct effect' of provisions in Community treaties and directives. As with supremacy, the doctrine of direct effect had begun to be developed in ECJ case law long before the United Kingdom joined the EC in 1973.

The starting point for much euro-litigation in national courts and tribunals is the rights and obligations created by Community legislation. The three main types of Community legislation (treaties, regulations and directives) each have a rather different status in the domestic legal system and so need to be considered separately. In short, it can be said that the principle of direct effect determines the situations in which a litigant appearing in a UK court or tribunal can claim that rights or obligations are created *directly* by Community legislation itself, without the need for any national legislation to have implemented it into the legal system of the member state.[20] A court needs 'to consider the spirit, the general scheme and the wording' of the Community legislation in order to determine whether a directly effective right or obligation has been created.[21]

Treaty provisions

For high-street solicitors in their daily legal practice, the provisions of treaties establishing the Community institutions, determining the legislative procedure for secondary legislation and so on, are of little day-to-day practical importance. Other articles in the treaties, however, confer rights and impose obligations on individuals, businesses and the governments of the member states. Such provisions are described as 'directly effective', meaning that they can be relied on by a person in a UK court or tribunal in the same way as if the rights were contained in an Act of Parliament:[22]

> . . . the Community constitutes a new legal order of international law for the benefit of which the states have limited their sovereign rights, albeit within limited fields, and the subjects comprise not only member states, but also their nationals. Independently of the legislation of member states, Community law therefore not only imposes obligations on individuals but is also intended to confer upon them rights which have become part of their legal heritage. These rights arise not only where they are expressly granted by the Treaty, but also by reason of obligations which the Treaty imposes in a clearly defined way upon individuals as well upon the member states and upon the institutions of the Community.

[20] See p. 314.
[21] *Van Gend en Loos v Nederlandse Belastingadministratie* (Case 26/62) [1963] ECR 1.
[22] *Van Gend en Loos*, above.

Not all the treaty provisions are directly effective, but in numerous cases the ECJ has held that those which establish clear, precise and complete obligations and rights are so effective. These include the following:

- Art 30 which prohibits quantitative restrictions on imports and measures having equivalent effect;[23]
- Art 48 covering freedom of movement;[24]
- Art 52 conferring the right of freedom of establishment;[25]
- Parts of Arts 85 and 86 which prohibit anti-competitive practices and abuses of dominant position;[26]
- Art 119 conferring the right of equal pay for equal work for men and women.[27]

These rights can all be relied on directly by a person in a British court 'vertically' against the government; some are also capable of applying 'horizontally' against another private citizen or business. And, of course, the rights and obligations under the treaties take precedence over any existing UK law which happens to be inconsistent with them.[28] By way of brief illustration, consider the *Factortame* litigation.[29] There, one of the arguments put forward by the Spanish trawler owners was that provisions in the Merchant Shipping Act 1988, which required UK-registered vessels to be substantially owned by British nationals, were inconsistent with Art 52 which created a right to freedom of establishment.

Regulations

As noted in a previous chapter, the legal status of Community regulations and directives are different.[30] Article 189 of the EC Treaty states: 'A regulation shall have general application. It shall be binding in its entirety, and *directly applicable* in all member states.' The concept of direct applicability is different to that of direct effect;[31] it means that, unlike directives, regulations are a source of law in the UK legal systems without any further steps needed to incorporate them into domestic law; in other words, regulations are 'self-executing' or 'automatically binding'. Although regulations are in this way 'directly applicable', they are not *necessarily* 'directly effective'. As with the treaty provisions, not all regulations create rights and obligations enforceable by litigants appearing in national courts. This is because, like the treaty articles just considered, a provision in a regulation must be clear and precise, unconditional and leave no room for the exercise of discretion in its implementation.

[23] See further Chapter 30.
[24] See *Van Duyn v Home Office* Case 41/74 [1975] CH 358.
[25] See e.g. *R v Secretary of State for Transport, ex p Factortame* (*No 2*) (Case C-213/89) [1991] 1 AC 603.
[26] See *Garden Cottage Foods Ltd v Milk Marketing Board* [1982] QB 1114.
[27] See *Defrenne v Sabena* (*No 2*) Case 149/77 [1978] ECR 1365.
[28] See p. 682 above.
[29] See p. 117.
[30] See p. 315.
[31] See Winter, 'Direct Applicability and Direct Effect—Two Distinct and Different Concepts in Community Law' (1972) 9 CMLRev 425.

Directives

The principle of direct effect is most complex when it is applied to directives. Article 189 of the EC Treaty provides that 'a directive shall be binding, as to the result to be achieved, upon each member state to which it is addressed, but shall leave to the national authorities the choice of form and methods'. Thus, directives apparently create rights and confer obligations enforceable in UK courts *only through the Act of Parliament or SI which specifically incorporates their provisions into domestic law*. On the face of it, this may suggest that litigants in national courts cannot readily rely *directly* on a directive to establish they enjoy a Community law right or are owed a duty under Community law. In fact, directives can be used in legal argument in several different ways:

(a) To a limited extent some provisions in some directives may be directly effective, that is they can be relied upon directly in a UK court or tribunal.
(b) The text of a directive may in some situations be used in argument to persuade a court or tribunal to interpret an Act of Parliament or subordinate legislation in a particular way.
(c) A person may sometimes be able to claim damages against the government if it has failed to incorporate a directive into UK law.

Here we examine (a), the principle of direct effect.[32]

The principle that a directive *may* be directly effective was established by the ECJ in *Van Duyn v Home Office*.[33] As with articles in the EC Treaty and regulations, the starting point is that a provision in a directive must be clear and precise, unconditional and leave no room for the exercise of discretion in its implementation before a litigant can rely upon it directly in court. Further, a directive can only have direct effect if the time for its implementation into national law has passed and the national government has failed to implement it, either adequately or at all. The UK government may, for example, have failed to incorporate the directive into domestic law by the set date.[34] Generally the United Kingdom has a very good record of managing to do this on time, unlike some other member states (such as Italy) where many directives remain to be incorporated several years after the due date. Another situation in which a lawyer may want to rely directly on the text of a directive itself is when an Act of Parliament or SI, although purporting to incorporate the provisions of a directive, fails to do so properly. This may be due to a mistake in drafting (where, for example, a right conferred by a directive is erroneously omitted from the domestic legislation) or because the UK

[32] On interpretation, see p. 688 below; on damages for failure to implement directives, see p. 691 below.
[33] Case 41/74 [1974] ECR 1377.
[34] One example is the Unfair Terms in Consumer Contracts Directive 93/13/EEC which ought to have been given effect to by 1 January 1995; the SI incorporating its provisions into English law, the Unfair Terms in Consumer Contracts Regulations 1994 (SI 1994 No 3159) did not come into force until 1 July 1995. The Working Time Directive was not incorporated into law by the UK on the set date.

government deliberately took an overly narrow or broad view of the policy contained in the directive when it was drafting the Act or SI designed to implement it. In summary, then, a directive may have direct effect when UK legislation fails to incorporate it into domestic law either properly or at all, after the date set for its implementation. This general position is, however, subject to an important caveat.

Unlike articles in the EC Treaty[35] or a Community regulation, a directive can never have 'horizontal effect'. In other words, individuals cannot directly rely on the provisions of a directive against other individuals or private businesses, only against a:[36]

> body, whatever its legal form, which is made responsible, pursuant to a measure adopted by the State, for providing a public service under the control of the State and has for that purpose special powers beyond those which result from the normal rules applicable in relations between individuals.

This is because of the wording used in Art 189 of the EC Treaty to define directives, which stresses that a directive is binding 'upon each member state to which it is addressed'. Vertical direct effect may be justified by the principle that if a member state fails in its obligations to give effect to a directive, it should be prevented from taking advantage of its own failure to comply with Community law.[37] But as Sir Patrick Neill points out, this type of estoppel-based explanation is really only convincing in relation to central government which can control legislative activity in a state.[38] The practical consequences of the distinction between vertical and horizontal direct can also be anomalous. For instance, an employee working for a private business cannot rely directly on a directive against their employer[39] (in the event of, say, a conflict between domestic legislation conferring certain rights on workers and those contained in a directive), whereas an employee working for a public body (as defined by *Foster v British Gas*) who has been treated in the same way, may do so.[40]

It is also arguable that the absence of a rule allowing horizontal direct effect of directives hinders uniformity of law throughout the Community. The Commission can, however, take proceedings in the ECJ to compel a member state to implement a directive correctly. Also, from the point of view

[35] See p. 684 above.

[36] See *Foster v British Gas* Case C-188/89 [1990] ECR I-3313, 3348–9. For an argument that directives ought to be directly effective horizontally, see J. Coppel, 'Rights, Duties and the End of *Marshall*' (1994) 57 MLR 859.

[37] See *Pubblico Ministero v Ratti* (Case 148/78) [1979] ECR 1629, 1642.

[38] Sir Patrick Neill QC, *The European Court of Justice: A Case Study in Judicial Activism* (1995); also published in Minutes of Evidence of the House of Lords European Communities Committee (Sub-committee on the 1996 Inter-governmental conference), 18th Report 1994–95; HL 88.

[39] See e.g. *Duke v GEC Reliance Ltd* [1988] AC 618.

[40] See e.g. *Marshall v Southampton and South-West-Hampshire Area Health Authority* (*Teaching*) (*No 2*) Case C-271/91 [1986] QB 401. Mrs Marshall, a physiotherapist, was required to retire at the age of 60 whereas her male colleagues could continue to work until 65. As she was an NHS employee, she was able to argue that the imposition of different retirement ages was contrary to directives on equal treatment of men and women.

of individuals and businesses, the absence of horizontal direct effect is mitigated by a range of other possible remedies in the UK courts:

(a) an individual or business can commence an application for judicial review in the High Court for an order declaring that national law is not in conformity with the directive;[41]
(b) there may be a right to claim damages against the government to compensate for loss suffered as a result of its failure to implement a directive; and also
(c) although national courts do not give horizontal direct effect to directives, they may be able to give effect to the 'spirit' of a directive by the way in which they interpret national legislation.[42]

Interpreting Community legislation

Having now considered the two fundamental principles of supremacy of Community law and direct effect, we can move on to examine how UK courts and tribunals set about interpreting Community legislation. Chapter 23 considered the techniques used by judges to interpret Acts of Parliament. Somewhat different approaches have been used to construe Community legislation. In particular, the courts have been far more willing to adopt purposive techniques.[43] One important reason for this is the different styles of drafting used in Community legislation in comparison to UK Acts of Parliament. British legislation tends to be drafted 'with utmost exactness', as if an attempt has been made to cover every eventuality, thereby reinforcing the impression that the courts' task is essentially limited to a literary exercise of applying the words of enactment to the facts which have arisen. Community legislation, like much continental legislation, is drafted much more broadly.[44] In attempting to understand the purpose of Community legislation, the courts may consider the preambles to the treaties and directives,[45] which set out reasons for the legislation having been made:[46]

> The [EC] Treaty is quite unlike any of the enactments to which we are accustomed. . . . It lays down general principle. It expresses its aim and purposes. All in sentences of moderate length and commendable style. But it lacks precision . . . All the way through the Treaty there are gaps and lacunae. These have to be filled by the judges, or by regulations or directives. It is the European way . . . of seeing

[41] See p. 690 below.
[42] See below.
[43] See further V. Sachs and C. Harlow, 'Interpretation European Style' (1977) 40 MLR 578; Lord Slynn, 'Looking at EC Texts' (1993) 14 *Statute Law Review* 12; and T. Rensen, 'British Statutory Interpretation in the Light of Community and Other International Obligations' (1993) 14 *Statute Law Review* 186. G. de Bùrca warns that 'what the UK courts mean by a purposive approach is not the same as the method of teleological or purposive interpretation of EC law which is used by the ECJ': see 'Giving Effect to EC Directives' (1992) 55 MLR 215, 222.
[44] See Chapter 8 and compare e.g. the Sunday Trading Act 1994 (Chapter 9, above) and the Directive on Working Time (Chapter 14, above).
[45] See e.g. the preamble ('Whereas . . .') to the Working Time Directive.
[46] *H. P. Bulmer v J. Bollinger SA* [1974] 1 Ch 401, 425.

> these differences, what are the English courts to do when they are faced with a problem of interpretation? They must follow the European pattern. No longer must they argue about the precise grammatical sense. They must look to the purpose and intent . . . They must divine the spirit of the Treaty . . . If they find a gap they must fill it as best they can.

Not all UK lawyers are enamoured of this sort of approach. For Sir Patrick Neill QC, 'the methods of interpretation adopted by the ECJ appear to have liberated the Court from the customarily accepted discipline of endeavouring by textual analysis to ascertain the meaning of the language of the relevant provision'.[47] National courts are obliged to follow the interpretations of the ECJ.

Membership of the Community has also involved the UK courts making changes to the ways in which they interpret *national* legislation in areas also regulated by Community law. Section 2(4) of the European Communities Act 1972 requires UK courts to interpret national law 'subject to' Community law.[48] In the early years of the United Kingdom's membership of the Community, UK courts took this principle to mean that where there was an ambiguity in national legislation, it should be interpreted to conform with any relevant Community treaty articles, regulations and directives. This is a similar rule of construction as that used by the court in relation to international treaties.[49] In the mid-1980s in the *Von Colson* case,[50] the ECJ held that national courts had a duty to interpret national legislation in accordance with the words and purpose of any directive covering the same subject matter. This decision, and later ones, left many unanswered questions and in a series of cases the UK courts adopted a variety of approaches.[51] De Bùrca argues that, overall, 'the UK courts have not been prepared to apply the presumption that Parliament intends to comply with EC law to domestic measures which are not specifically designed to implement EC law, and have limited the *Von Colson* principle accordingly'.[52]

The ECJ then laid down a new approach in *Marleasing*.[53] This was an Art 177 reference from a Spanish court in a case where there was a conflict between the Spanish civil code and a directive. The ECJ judgment made it clear that a national court had to interpret national legislation in accordance with directives whether the national legislation was made before or after the directive in question. The *Von Colson* approach does not, therefore, apply only to national legislation which is intended to implement a directive. Moreover, a passage in the *Marleasing* judgment (as de Bùrca expresses it) 'appears as a rule requiring domestic courts to give effect to the provisions of directives in actions between private parties, regardless of the terms of the

[47] *The European Court of Justice: A Case Study in Judicial Activism* (1995), p. 47.
[48] See p. 116.
[49] See Chapter 23.
[50] *Von Colson and Kamann v Land Nordrhein-Westfahlen* Case 14/83 [1984] ECR 1891.
[51] For a more detailed account, see G. de Bùrca (1992) 55 MLR 215, 217–18.
[52] (1992) 55 MLR 215, 221.
[53] *Marleasing SA v La Comercial Internacional de Alimentacion SA* Case C-106/89 [1990] ECR I-4135.

national legislation which is being interpreted'.[54] In the United Kingdom, the House of Lords has added a gloss to the approach laid down by the ECJ: courts must carry out their task of interpretation 'without distorting the meaning of the domestic legislation' and words of the Act or SI must actually be capable of supporting an interpretation consistent with the directive.[55] In other words, the UK courts apply the *Marleasing* principle to choose an interpretation of legislation consistent with a directive where this is one of several plausible interpretations. Nevertheless, *Marleasing* can be seen as a way in which directives and treaty provisions, even those which are not apt to create directly effective rights and obligations, can now form part of legal argument in UK courts.

Community law and judicial review in UK courts

Having looked so far at the general principles of supremacy, of the direct effect of provisions in the treaties and directives, and at the changing techniques of legislative interpretation, we can now move on to consider other impacts of Community law on judicial review litigation in the United Kingdom.

Judicial review to enforce compliance with Community law

Perhaps most obviously, an application for judicial review in the High Court can be used to challenge the failure of UK government ministers and other public bodies to comply with Community law. Well-known examples of this include the Spanish owners of trawlers who challenged the Secretary of State's refusal to register their vessels in the United Kingdom[56] and the challenge by the Equal Opportunities Commission to the Secretary of State for Employment's refusal to introduce a bill amending provisions of the Employment Protection (Consolidation) Act which, they rightly argued, were inconsistent with Community law prohibiting sex discrimination.[57]

New grounds of judicial review

Membership of the Community has also required UK courts to 'import' what some regard as novel grounds of judicial review. These include proportionality,[58] equality[59] and the principle of legal certainty.[60] Detailed consideration of the latter two grounds falls outside the scope of this book, but note

[54] (1992) 55 MLR 215, 223.

[55] *Webb v EMO Air Cargo (UK) Ltd* [1994] QB 718.

[56] See *R v Secretary of State for Transport, ex p Factortame (No 2)* [1991] 1 AC 603.

[57] See *R v Secretary of State for Employment, ex p Equal Opportunities Commission* [1995] 1 AC 1.

[58] The principle of proportionality is considered in Chapters 24 and 30 (proportionality applied to s 47 of the Shops Act 1950). See further Jürgen Schwarze, *European Administrative Law* (1992), Chapter 5 and N. Emiliou, *The Principles of Proportionality in European Law: A Comparative Study* (1996).

[59] Schwarze, Chapter 4.

[60] Schwarze, Chapter 6.

that some argue that these principles already exist in English common law.[61] The courts have, however, stressed recently that proportionality cannot be used as an independent ground of judicial review in cases which raise no Community law issues.[62]

In some circumstances, breach of the ECHR may also be a ground for review under Community law.[63] The ECHR and its enforcement mechanisms (the Human Rights Commission and Human Rights Court) are separate from the Community institutions. Nevertheless, the Community has attached importance to the ECHR, including the preamble to the Single European Act, where member states pledge themselves to 'work together to promote democracy on the basis of the fundamental rights recognised in the Convention', and Art F2 of the Maastricht Treaty.[64] In several cases, the ECJ has applied human rights principles in reviewing the actions of Community institutions[65] and public authorities in the United Kingdom are bound, as a matter of *Community* law, to comply with the ECHR in areas which are within the scope of Community law.[66]

Remedies for breaches of Community law

Community law does not, as a rule, specify remedies for breaches of Community law rights. Instead, it relies on national law. Generally speaking, the UK courts protect Community law rights and enforce obligations using the same sorts of remedies as are available to do similar tasks in cases which do not involve Community law issues. Some important innovations have nevertheless occurred.

First, the courts have awarded damages in a range of situations for breach of Community law. From the perspective of public law the most important of these is the right to claim damages against a member state, in some circumstances, for losses resulting from a failure to implement a directive properly by the specified date. This was established by the ECJ's decision in *Francovich v Republic of Italy*.[67] The Italian government should have set up a scheme as outlined in a directive to guarantee that employees received unpaid wages if their employer became insolvent. Italy failed to do this by the due date. Francovich's employer went into liquidation and he was not paid. The directive was not directly effective against the Italian government because the provisions lacked sufficient 'unconditionality'; the directive did not identify who precisely was to guarantee the unpaid wages, this being a

[61] See e.g. J. Jowell, 'Is Equality a Constitutional Principle?' (1994) 47 CLP Part II 1 and Jowell and A. Lester, 'Proportionality: Neither Novel nor Dangerous' in Jowell and Oliver (eds.), *New Directions in Judicial Review* (1988).

[62] See p. 573.

[63] On the Convention, see pp. 78 and 160.

[64] See p. 702 below.

[65] For a review, see T. Hartley, *The Foundations of European Community Law* (1994, 3rd edn.), pp. 139–49.

[66] For further discussion, see Nicholas Grief, 'The Domestic Impact of the European Convention on Human Rights as Mediated through Community Law' [1991] PL 555.

[67] Joined Cases C-6 & 9/90 [1995] ICR 722 or [1991] ECR I-5357.

matter for national governments to decide. But Francovich sued the Italian government for its failure to establish any scheme. The ECJ held that a person may in principle claim damages against a member state for its failure to comply with a directive if three conditions are satisfied in a case:

(a) the directive had to create individual rights;
(b) the content of those rights must be ascertainable from the directive itself; and
(c) there was a causal link between the government's failure to transpose the directive and the individual's loss.

The right to reparation laid down by the ECJ in *Francovich* was applied and extended in *R v Secretary of State for Transport, ex p Factortame Ltd* (*No 4*).[68] Here the Spanish fishermen claimed damages in the High Court for the financial losses resulting from the deregistration of their trawlers after the enactment of the Merchant Shipping Act 1988, Part II. One plaintiff company also claimed exemplary damages. An Art 177 reference was made to the ECJ (which considered the case at the same time as one brought against Germany). The situation in *Factortame* (*No 4*) differed from that in *Francovich*: here, the breach of Community law was of Art 52, a directly effective provision in the EC Treaty. The ECJ rejected an argument that member states were required to make good loss caused to people only where the provisions breached were not directly effective and that in *Francovich* (where the directive was not directly effective) the court had simply been concerned to 'fill a lacuna in the system for safeguarding the rights of individuals':[69]

> That argument cannot be accepted. The court has consistently held that the right of individuals to rely on the directly effective provisions of the Treaty before national courts is only a minimum guarantee and is not sufficient in itself to ensure the full and complete implementation of the Treaty. . . . The purpose of that right is to ensure that provisions in Community law prevail over national provisions. It cannot, in every case, secure for individuals the benefit of the rights conferred on them by Community law and, in particular, avoid their sustaining damage as the result of a breach of Community law attributable to a member state.

The ECJ also rejected the notion that there was no right to compensation when the breach of Community law was by the legislature of a member state (here, Parliament in enacting the offending provisions of the Merchant Shipping Act 1988):[70]

> . . . in international law a state whose liability for breach of an international commitment is in issue will be viewed as a single entity, irrespective of whether the breach which gave rise to the damage is attributable to the legislature, the judiciary or the executive. That must apply *a fortiori* in the Community legal order since all

[68] *Brasserie du Pêcheur SA v Federal Republic of Germany; R v Secretary of State for Transport, ex p Factortame Ltd* (*No 4*) Joined Cases C-46/93 & C-48/93 [1996] 2 WLR 506. Cf. *R v HM Treasury, ex p British Telecommunications plc* [1996] All ER (EC) All and *R v Secretary of State for the Home Department, ex p Gallagher*, [1996] 2 CMLR 951 where limitations were imposed.

[69] Paras 19–20.

[70] Para. 34.

> state authorities, including the legislature, are bound in performing their tasks to comply with the rules laid down by Community law directly governing the situation of individuals.

The court concluded that the existence of the following conditions were necessary and sufficient to give a person a right to compensation against a member state:

(a) the rule of Community law breached was intended to confer rights on individuals;
(b) the breach of Community law was sufficiently serious in that the legislature had 'manifestly and gravely disregarded the limits on its discretion';[71] and
(c) there was a direct causal link between the breach and the damage suffered.

If these conditions are satisfied, then the national court must award damages in accordance with its national law on liability; these rules of national law 'must not be less favourable than those relating to similar domestic claims or framed in such a way as in practice to make it impossible or excessively difficult to obtain reparation'.[72] Similar conditions and principles apply where a member state has breached Community law through some administrative action such as the refusal of an export licence.[73]

Apart from rights to damages, a second innovation in the United Kingdom was when the House of Lords held, following an Art 177 reference, that it had jurisdiction to grant an interim injunction against a minister.[74] Previously it had been thought that provisions in the Crown Proceedings Act 1947 prevented such relief being ordered against ministers on an application for judicial review. After the *Factortame* (*No 2*) decision, for a while it seemed as if in English law there were going to be two different approaches to granting interim remedies against ministers. Where litigation concerned rights under Community law, the court had power to grant interim relief. This was because member states, including their courts, are required to provide effective remedies to protect Community law rights. Where, however, litigation solely concerned national law, then the courts continued to believe they had no power to grant interim injunctions against ministers. In 1994, in the landmark case of *M v Home Office*,[75] the House of Lords put an end to the unsatisfactory distinction between injunctions in EC cases and purely domestic

71 The ECJ stressed that it was not its role, on an Art 177 reference, to find the facts in the main proceedings and decide how to characterize the breaches of Community law in question (para. 58). The ECJ did however indicate some of the factors the High Court would have to take into account, including that the provisions in the 1988 Act were 'prima facie incompatible with Art 52' and that the Commission had warned the UK government of its view that those provisions were unlawful.

72 Para. 74.

73 *R v Ministry of Agriculture, Fisheries and Food, ex p Hedley Lomas (Ireland) Ltd* (Case C-5/95) [1996] All ER (EC) 493.

74 *R v Secretary of State for Transport, ex p Factortame* (*No 2*) [1991] 1 AC 603. On the nature and purpose of interim remedies, see further Chapter 26.

75 [1994] 1 AC 377 (discussed at p. 619 above).

ones by revising earlier interpretations of the Crown Proceedings Act 1947; it held that the court did, indeed, have power to make interim injunctions against ministers in applications for Judicial review, even in cases governed solely by national law.[76]

THE EUROPEAN COURT OF JUSTICE

So far in this chapter, the focus has been on the ways in which Community law issues are handled by courts and tribunals within the United Kingdom. Even here, it should be apparent that ECJ case law plays a central role in establishing principles of law to be applied by national courts. Now we can move on to consider the more direct role of the ECJ.

The ECJ as an institution

There are now 15 judges nominated by the governments of the member states[77] and formally appointed by the Council of Ministers. On appointment, the judges swear the following oath: 'I swear that I will perform my duties impartially and conscientiously; I swear that I will preserve the secrecy of the deliberations of the court.' Almost everyone agrees that once appointed, the judges do indeed show remarkable independence from the member states which nominated them. One of the judges is elected President by the other judges for a term of three years.

The court is aided in its work by nine Advocates General;[78] these are distinguished lawyers nominated by member states and appointed by the Council of Ministers, who have the same status, and are subject to similar conditions, as the judges.[79] They represent the public interest and prepare advisory opinions on cases which are used by the court as its starting point for deliberations; the court is not, however, bound by the observations or arguments put forward by the Advocates General.[80] Nor do the parties to the case have any opportunity to comment on the Advocates General's submissions to the court. The Advocates General's opinions often contain much fuller legal analysis than the actual judgment handed down by the court and for this reason are regarded as persuasive authority; the opinions are published in the law reports together with the ECJ's judgment in a case.

[76] See further Chapter 26.

[77] UK nominees to the court have included Lord McKenzie-Stuart (a judge 1972–84 and president of the court 1984–88) and Sir Gordon Slynn (Advocate General at the ECJ 1981–88 then judge 1988–92). At the conclusion of his term of office at the ECJ, Lord Slynn became a member of the House of Lords.

[78] See Art 166.

[79] Francis Jacobs, formerly a British legal academic and barrister, has been one of the Advocates General since 1988.

[80] For instance, in 1963, in possibly the most significant decision handed down by the ECJ, *Van Gend en Loos* Case 26/62 [1963] ECR 1, Advocate General Roemer advised against the principle of direct effect of Art 12 of the EC Treaty (customs duties), arguing that it did not create rights enforceable by an individual appearing before a Dutch tax tribunal, but imposed obligations exclusively on member states.

Situated in a modern building in Luxembourg, the ECJ sits and deliberates sometimes in plenary session (at least nine judges present), sometimes in chambers of three, five or seven judges, depending on the nature of the case before it.

In 1989 a Court of First Instance, now staffed by 15 additional judges, was set up to help deal with a backlog of cases waiting to be heard. It does not determine Art 177 references.[81] So far as annulment actions[82] are concerned, it does hear proceedings brought by private parties, but not those brought by member states or other Community institutions. It almost always sits in chambers and there is a right of appeal to the ECJ on points of law.

Contrasts with domestic proceedings

The methods of working adopted by the ECJ differ in several important respects from that of UK courts. First, oral submissions to the court are a much less prominent part of ECJ procedure, where emphasis is given to written submissions. Secondly, the role played by the Advocates General in the ECJ have no real parallel in the United Kingdom.[83] Thirdly, the court is not formally bound by any system of precedent, though in practice it is normal for the court to decide cases consistently with its own past decisions.

Fourthly, and linked, the institutional style of judicial decision-making is quite distinct. The ECJ judges always decide cases collegially; a single judgment has to be handed down by the court and so there is no possibility for dissenting judgments or even for individual judges to indicate that they agree with the court's conclusion in a case, but arrive at that point for different reasons.

Fifthly, the ECJ is multilingual. The court may use any of the Community's official languages, though in practice French is regarded as the working language of the court. All judgments are first drafted in French, and when the judges meet in private to discuss a case no interpreters are present and French is again the normal language of choice. Multi-lingualism creates many problems, but these fall outside the scope of this chapter. Finally, unlike most UK courts, there is no appeal from decisions of the ECJ; its decisions are final.

Types of proceedings

As already noted, from the perspective of the UK constitution the ECJ can be seen as exercising its influence through three main types of proceedings:

[81] See p. 696 below.

[82] See p. 698 below.

[83] Cf. the suggestion by Lord Woolf for a Director of Civil Proceedings in domestic judicial review cases: Lord Woolf, *Protection of the Public—A New Challenge* (1992), pp. 109–13 and J. A. G. Griffith's proposal for a similar officer: 'Judicial Decision-making in Public Law' [1986] PL 564, 582.

(a) Art 177 references from national courts;
(b) proceedings for the annulment of directives or regulations; and
(c) infringement proceedings in which the Commission or another member state may seek to compel the United Kingdom to comply with Community law.

ART 177 REFERENCES FROM NATIONAL COURTS

Litigation involving Community law may arise entirely within the courts and tribunals of the United Kingdom; drawing on the case law of the ECJ where necessary, UK judges are able to interpret Community legislation and apply principles of Community administrative law to the dispute before them. Often, however, proceedings in a national court or tribunal have to be adjourned while the guidance of the ECJ is sought. This takes place under Art 177 of the EC Treaty. From the perspective of a national legal system, one of the most important functions of the ECJ is to give such 'preliminary rulings' on questions of Community law. Article 177 provides:

> The Court of Justice shall have jurisdiction to give preliminary rulings concerning:
> (a) the interpretation of this Treaty;
> (b) the validity and interpretation of acts of the institutions of the Community . . .;
> (c) the interpretation of the statutes of bodies established by an act of the Council, where those statutes so provide.
>
> Where such a question is raised before any court or tribunal of a Member State, that court or tribunal may, if it considers that a decision on that question is necessary to enable it to give judgment, request the Court of Justice to give a ruling thereon.
>
> Where any such question is raised in a case pending before a court or tribunal of a Member State, against whose decisions there is no judicial remedy under national law, that court or tribunal shall bring the matter before the Court of Justice.

In practice this enables any UK court or tribunal—from a bench of lay magistrates to the House of Lords—to request authoritative guidance from the ECJ on legal questions to do with the interpretation of Community law. One or other party to the litigation before the UK court may be particularly keen on the UK court making an Art 177 reference as this inevitably halts progress in the litigation for 18 months or more; thus, shops prosecuted for breaches of s 47 of the Shops Act 1950 for unlawful Sunday trading tried to persuade magistrates' courts to make references to the ECJ as this would halt the prosecution for a considerable time, during which they continued to trade.[84]

It is clear from the EC Treaty itself (see above) that the House of Lords, because it is the United Kingdom's final court of appeal, *must* make an Art

[84] See Chapter 30.

177 reference where the case it has to decide turns on the interpretation of the EC Treaty or secondary Community legislation or one of the parties questions the validity of Community legislation or administrative action.[85] In *R v International Stock Exchange of the United Kingdom and Republic of Ireland, ex p Else (1982) Ltd*, the Court of Appeal laid down new guidelines for other UK courts and tribunals as to how they should approach deciding whether to refer a preliminary question to the ECJ. Sir Thomas Bingham MR held:[86]

> . . . if the facts have been found and the Community law issue is critical to the court's final decision, the appropriate course is ordinarily to refer the issue to the Court of Justice unless the national court can with complete confidence resolve the issue itself. In considering whether it can with complete confidence resolve the issue itself the national court must be fully mindful of the differences between national and Community legislation, of the pitfalls which face a national court venturing into an unfamiliar field, of the need for uniform interpretation throughout the Community and of the great advantages enjoyed by the Court of Justice in construing Community instruments. If the national court is in any doubt, it should ordinarily refer.

In other words, there is a strong presumption in favour of a UK court or tribunal making an Art 177 reference. Only if the UK court or tribunal is satisfied that the matter is *acte clair* will it proceed directly to decide the Community issue itself without the benefit of a preliminary ruling from the ECJ. Thus, in *R v Secretary of State for Employment, ex p Equal Opportunities Commission*,[87] the House of Lords decided, without making an Art 177 reference to the ECJ, that provisions of the Employment Protection (Consolidation) Act were inconsistent with Community law.

Once a court or tribunal decides to make a reference, it formulates a question or questions. These do not deal in detail with the particular facts of the case before the court but are in general, abstract terms.[88] The parties to the litigation in the national court, and often the national government concerned, make written submissions to the ECJ and, several months later, they have an opportunity to make brief oral submissions. Some time later one of the Advocates General, having considered the parties' submissions to the ECJ, delivers a reasoned opinion advising the ECJ as to how questions posed by the national court or tribunal ought to be answered. The ECJ then deliberates and issues its judgment. The ECJ does not rule *directly* on the compatibility of national law with Community law, it merely 'interprets' the relevant treaty provisions or directive. Armed with this, the national court may resume hearing the case before it. Thus, in relation to Art 177 references, 'the events in the European Court are only an episode in the national proceedings'.[89]

[85] Even a lower court *must* make a reference where the issue concerns the validity of *Community* legislation.

[86] [1993] QB 534.

[87] [1995] 1 AC 1.

[88] For the questions referred to the ECJ by magistrates during the battles of Sunday trading, see Chapter 30.

[89] T. Hartley, *The Foundations of European Community Law*, p. 73.

By way of general assessment, it can be said that Art 177 references provide a useful mechanism to ensure a high degree of uniformity in the interpretation of Community law by courts and tribunals in member states. The down side is that referrals lead to considerable delays and increase the costs of litigation considerably.

For a more detailed study of Art 177 references in the particular context of the Sunday trading saga, turn to the case study in Chapter 30. For an examination of other types of proceedings in the ECJ, read on.

ART 173: ANNULMENT PROCEEDINGS

A second type of legal challenge determined by the ECJ which has constitutional significance are proceedings under Art 173 of the EC Treaty. This gives the ECJ power to determine whether Community regulations and directives are valid:

> The Court of Justice shall review the legality of acts adopted jointly by the European Parliament and the Council, of acts of the Council, of the Commission . . . and of acts of the European Parliament intended to produce legal effects vis-à-vis third parties.
>
> It shall for this purpose have jurisdiction in actions brought by a Member State, the Council or the Commission on the grounds of lack of competence, infringement of an essential procedural requirement, infringement of this Treaty or of any rule of law relating to its application, or misuse of powers.
>
> . . . Any natural or legal person may, under the same conditions, institute proceedings against a decision which, although in the form of a regulation or a decision addressed to another person, is of direct and individual concern to the former.
>
> The proceedings provided for in this Article shall be instituted within two months of the publication of the measure, or of its notification to the plaintiff, or, in the absence thereof, of the day on which it came to the knowledge of the latter, as the case may be.

If the court determines such Community secondary legislation is not in conformity with the EC Treaty, it may declare the legislation void. There has been considerable dispute in the past over which Community institutions may use the procedure, but detailed consideration of this falls outside the scope of this chapter. Our focus instead is on

(a) the ability of member states to use the procedure; and
(b) the limited extent to which individuals, groups and businesses in the United Kingdom have rights to challenge Community legislation in this way.

Art 173 proceedings by the United Kingdom

The UK government is able to use Art 173 to challenge the validity of Community secondary legislation. A recent example is its challenge to the validity of the Working Time Directive; the arguments put forward, the procedures used, and the ECJ's judgment are considered in more detail in Chapter 14.

Art 173 proceedings by individuals, groups and businesses

Individuals, groups and businesses cannot easily use the Art 173 procedure to challenge legislation in the form of directives and regulations (though there is no problem with applying for review of decisions addressed to them). As neither of these types of Community legislation is addressed to any particular person personally, extremely strict rules for standing require the applicants to demonstrate 'direct and individual concern'. It must be shown that the act in question will affect the individual or business organization differently to anyone else. This is impossible in relation to a directive. In respect of regulations, it has been possible in some cases for an individual or business applicant to demonstrate to the ECJ that, although the legislative act is in the form of a regulation, in substance it is a 'decision' (another type of act) addressed to them individually.

Mancini, a judge of the ECJ, writing extra-judicially, has criticized the consequences of the court's approach to *locus standi* as 'bizarre and paradoxical, if not downright perverse'.[90] But he points out that it may well be open to the individual or business affected by the allegedly unlawful Community legislation to refuse to comply with it, and then if and when proceedings are brought against them in a national court (such as prosecution in a magistrates' court) it is open to the citizen or business to argue that the Community legislation is void. The national court then makes an Art 177 reference to the ECJ for guidance and so, in the end, the ECJ may still intervene even given the restrictive standing rules under Art 173.

ART 169: ENFORCEMENT ACTIONS AGAINST MEMBER STATES

One of the functions of the Commission is to ensure that member states comply with Community law, as set out in the treaties, secondary legislation (regulations and directives) and the jurisprudence of the ECJ. In practice this is often done relatively informally, through administrative negotiation between officials at the Commission and civil servants in the member state.[91] If this fails, then Art 169 provides:

> If the Commission considers that a Member State has failed to fulfil an obligation under this treaty, it shall deliver a reasoned opinion on the matter after giving the State concerned the opportunity to submit its observations.

[90] G. F. Mancini and D. T. Keeling, 'Democracy and the ECJ' (1994) 57 MLR 175, 188. See also H. Rasmussen, 'Why is Article 173 Interpreted Against Private Plaintiffs?' (1980) 5 ELRev 112.

[91] See further F. Snyder, 'The Effectiveness of EC Law: Institutions, Processes, Tools and Techniques' (1993) 56 MLR 19, 27.

> If the State concerned does not comply with the opinion within the period laid down by the Commission, the latter may bring the matter before the Court of Justice.

Like most member states, the United Kingdom has been subject to numerous Art 169 actions brought by the Commission: after applications for judicial review brought by Spanish-owned trawler operators against the Secretary of State for Transport, in which the House of Lords held parts of the Merchant Shipping Act 1988 to be incompatible with Community law, the Commission commenced Art 169 proceedings against the United Kingdom. The Commission has also brought infraction proceedings in relation to the United Kingdom's alleged non-compliance with the Environmental Assessment Directive in respect of the government's plans for a new bridge across the Thames in East London;[92] for an oil installation near Falkirk in Scotland;[93] in respect of breaches of the Bathing Water Directive resulting from polluted sea at Blackpool;[94] and for the failure to designate adequate special protection areas under the Birds Directive.[95]

Under Art 170, one member state may also bring similar proceedings before the ECJ alleging that another state has failed to fulfil an obligation under the EC Treaty; there have hardly been any such proceedings such as this. Since the Maastricht Treaty, the ECJ has had power under Arts 171 and 172 to impose fines on member states.

The use in Art 169 of the phrase 'member state has failed to fulfil an obligation under this treaty' refers not only to central government, but also to a national Parliament,[96] national courts[97] and any other public authority. Thus, in theory, either the Commission or another member state could commence Art 169 proceedings against the United Kingdom if Parliament refused to pass an Act implementing a directive into UK law or if a court refused to give effect to the supremacy of Community law, for example by not dis-applying an Act of Parliament which was contrary to Community law. Courts and tribunals in the United Kingdom, like other organs of the state, are obliged to comply with Community law.[98]

EVALUATING THE ROLE OF THE ECJ

Many critics, including government ministers in several member states, have questioned the legitimacy of the ECJ—both as an institution and the ways in

92 See [1993] JPL 823.
93 *EC Commission v UK* [1992] 6 LMELR 192.
94 See *EC Commission v UK* [1993] Env L Rep 472.
95 *EC Commission v UK* [1992] 6 LMELR 192.
96 See *Commission v Belgium* Case 77/69 [1970] ECR 237 where the Belgian Parliament had delayed passing national legislation needed to comply with Community law. The ECJ held that this provided no defence for the Belgian state.
97 See Maher (1994) 14 Legal Studies 226, 230.
98 See Chapter 5.

which it has developed its case law.[99] Commentators have, however, suggested that national governments ought to be cautious about criticizing the court or calling for radical reforms; they need to 'be aware of the delicacy of the system' and 'the trust generated by the on-going fruitful co-operation between the ECJ and national courts'.[100] New powers conferred on the court by the Maastricht Treaty might suggest that national governments do, in fact, have considerable confidence in the ECJ as an institution. The treaty endorses the court's case law on fundamental rights.[101] It confirms the court's ruling that the European Parliament has the right to bring annulment proceedings to challenge the validity of Community legislation.[102] Also the new co-decision legislative procedure[103] 'will inevitably produce a further growth in litigation between the institutions over the correct legal basis of legislation'.[104] Moreover, the ECJ was given new powers to impose financial penalties on member states which fail to comply with Community law.[105] Also of great potential importance is the new concept of subsidiarity: arguably, this seems to demonstrate a willingness on the part of the member states to allow the courts to deal with the matter as a legal issue rather than leaving it to be a purely political one.[106]

As well as political criticism from member states and others, the ECJ also faces the severe practical problem of a rapidly growing caseload which has led to unacceptable delays in determining cases. Indeed, Arnull suggests that 'perhaps the greatest threat to the Court's place in the institutional structure of the community . . . comes not from the politicians, but from the sheer number of cases it is called upon to resolve'.[107] A number of proposals have been made as to how this might be contained; the Court of First Instance has done a little to relieve pressure. Thought has also been given to ways of limiting the number of Art 177 references. Ideas include restricting the power to make a reference to national courts from which there is no further appeal (in the United Kingdom, most often the House of Lords) or introducing some sort of 'filter' procedure to ensure that only important questions are

[99] For strong criticism of the ECJ see Trevor C. Hartley, 'The European Court, Judicial Objectivity and the Constitution of the European Union' (1996) 112 LQR 95; Sir Patrick Neill QC, *The European Court of Justice: a Case Study in Judicial Activism* (1995); and J. Coppel and A. O'Neill, 'The European Court of Justice: taking rights seriously?' (1992) 12 Legal Studies 227—a slightly different version of this article appears in (1992) 29 CMLRev 669. For rebuttals of some of these arguments, see Anthony Arnull, 'The European Court and Judicial Objectivity: a Reply to Professor Hartley' (1996) 112 LQR 411 and J. Weiler and N. Lockhart, '"Taking Rights Seriously" Seriously: the ECJ and its Fundamental Rights Jurisprudence' (1995) 32 CMLRev 51.

[100] See Editorial comment, '*Quis Custodiet* the ECJ?' (1993) 30 CMLRev 899.

[101] Art F2: 'The Union shall respect fundamental rights, as guaranteed by the European Convention for the Protection of Human Rights and Fundamental Freedoms . . . and as they may result from the constitutional traditions common to the Member States, as general principles of Community law.'

[102] Art 173, as amended.

[103] See Chapter 13.

[104] A. Arnull, 'Judging the New Europe' (1994) 19 ELRev 3, 14.

[105] Art 171, as amended.

[106] See Arnull (1994) 19 ELRev 3, 14.

[107] Arnull (1994) 19 ELRev 3, 15.

referred to the ECJ. (While reading the Sunday trading case study in the next chapter, consider whether it was really appropriate for the ECJ to determine the several Art 177 references made in that context.)

Undemocratic and unaccountable?

It is claimed by some that the ECJ is a 'political' institution which is undemocratic and unaccountable. Critics argue that it is a *political* institution which has done more to threaten the sovereignty of the United Kingdom than the Commission or the European Parliament, through the development of the principle of supremacy of Community law over national law (nowhere expressly stated in the EC Treaty) and the principle of direct effect of treaty provisions and directives (again, not expressly provided for in the EC Treaty). The critics say that little is known about the judges, who are all appointees of the governments of the member states, acting collectively through the Council of Ministers. For instance, the European Parliament has no power to hold hearings before the appointment of the judges. O'Neill makes the case against the court:

> Once they have been appointed, we learn nothing of the judges as individuals, because the European Court decides as a collegiate body. The court's judgments are drafted by committee and read as such—terse, not always coherent and concealing more than they say . . . In addition to swearing to keep their deliberations secret, the judges undertake to sign any judgment in a case which is supported by a majority of their brethren (no matter what their own particular opinions or reservations) and they pledge themselves not to dissent publicly from the decision of the majority. Dissent is concealed so that the illusion of monolithic unanimity might be maintained.[108]

Against this view, it can be argued that criticisms of the ECJ as 'undemocratic' are misplaced. The Community was not, in its foundation, a directly 'democratic' organization; rather it was based on cooperation between independent sovereign states. Despite this, however, *the judgments* of the ECJ reveal a real commitment to democratic principles.[109] Thus, the ECJ has upheld the role of the European Parliament in the Community legislative process and declared invalid directives and regulations made by the Council without proper consultation with the European Parliament.

A guardian of fundamental rights?

A connected, but distinct, further criticism levelled at the ECJ is that it has paid insufficient attention to individuals and their fundamental legal rights.

[108] A. O'Neill, 'The European Court of Justice: on justice not being seen to be done' (1992), *Journal of the Law Society of Scotland* 169, 170.

[109] The account which follows draws heavily on the arguments advanced by G. Frederico Mancini (a judge of the ECJ) and David T. Keeling, 'Democracy and the European Court of Justice' (1994) 57 MLR 175.

As we have seen, the court has chosen to develop extremely stringent rules of *locus standi* which may prevent individuals, pressure groups and businesses getting access to the court. In a provocative article, Coppel and O'Neill are extremely scathing in their criticisms of how the ECJ views fundamental rights.[110] They argue that 'references to fundamental rights are now being made by the [ECJ] in order to extend its jurisdiction into areas previously reserved to Member States' courts and to expand the influence of the Community over the activities of the Member States'. Their hypothesis is that the ECJ 'has employed fundamental rights instrumentally, so as to accelerate the process of legal integration in the Community. It has not protected fundamental rights for their own sake. It has not taken those rights seriously.' The authors are critical of the way the ECJ has applied fundamental rights principles to the domestic legislation of member states. For instance, in 1991 the ECJ held on an Art 177 reference from courts in the Republic of Ireland that the prohibition of abortion contained in the Irish constitution might be a restriction on Community law rights to freedom to provide and receive services.[111] 'In so doing the court effectively ignored the clear wording of the Irish constitution which explicitly extends human rights protection to the unborn,' Coppel and O'Neill argue. The ECJ, they claim, 'now sees itself as being able to review national legislation wherever this operates in an area touched by Community law'.[112] Set against this, however, is the trend for the court to 'clearly subordinate human rights to the end of closer economic integration in the Community'.[113] They conclude saying:

> By using the term 'fundamental rights' in such an instrumental way the court refuses to take the discourse of fundamental rights seriously. It thereby both devalues the notion of fundamental rights and brings its own standing into disrepute.

Other commentators have strongly criticized Coppel and O'Neill, both for their methodology and their conclusions.[114] It can be argued that ECJ case law has, indeed, helped to protect the rights of individuals. This it has done through the doctrine of direct effect which, to take one example, enabled Mrs Marshall to vindicate her rights not to be discriminated against on the grounds that she was a woman.[115] In the United Kingdom, injunctions may now be obtained against a minister of the Crown as the result of a ruling by the ECJ;[116] and following the *Francovich* ruling, UK citizens now have rights to claim compensation against the UK government if they suffer loss as a result of the government's failure to give effect to a directive.[117]

[110] J. Coppel and A. O'Neill, 'The European Court of Justice: taking rights seriously?' (1992) 12 Legal Studies 227; a slightly different version of this article appears in (1992) 29 CMLRev 669.

[111] *Society for the Protection of Unborn Children (Ireland) Ltd v Grogan* (Case C-159/90) [1991] 3 CMLR 689.

[112] p. 244.

[113] p. 245.

[114] See J. Weiler and N. Lockhart, '"Taking Rights Seriously" Seriously: the ECJ and its Fundamental Rights Jurisprudence' (1995) 32 CMLRev 51.

[115] See n. 3 above.

[116] See n. 53 above.

[117] See n. 67 above.

Overly powerful?

It is sometimes suggested that the ECJ has too much power *vis-à-vis* the other Community institutions and national governments. During 1995, the UK government was reported to be discussing proposals for curbing the powers of the ECJ, for discussion at the 1996 intergovernmental conference. The court's judgment in 1996 upholding the validity of the Working Time Directive added impetus to these demands. The proposals included redrafting the EC Treaty to give the Council of Ministers power, by majority vote, to overturn decisions of the ECJ. The tensions are captured by Seurin who writes that the 'ECJ has made great efforts not to trespass upon the prerogatives of the member states and it considers itself to be a guardian of the interest of the states'[118] yet 'where the question of Euro-pean union is concerned, the court has not hesitated to push in the direction of "the idea of Europe" . . .'.

Too creative?

Everyone accepts that the ECJ has, on many occasions, adopted a 'creative' approach to its role of developing the law. As Hartley puts it, the ECJ 'has not hesitated to remodel the law even when this has entailed adopting a solution different from that envisaged in the treaties'.[119] Criticisms have been made of this judicial activism and greater restraint has been urged by some. The court has not, it is said, stuck to its appropriate task of interpreting the treaties, but has meddled in politics. Little support is found in the language of the treaties for many principles developed by the ECJ, such as supremacy of Community law over national law and of direct effect. Sir Patrick Neill QC is particularly trenchant in his criticism of the court:[120]

> A court with a mission is not an orthodox court. It is a potentially dangerous court —the danger being that inherent in uncontrollable judicial power. Some instances of judicial legislation may produce welcome results; others may prove controversial and be the source of further strife. However, the essential point is that it is the Court which forms its own view as to the desirable scope of its own jurisdiction, as to the new remedies which should be created to benefit individuals, and as to the general principles which should be imported into Community law and use as a standard against which to assess the validity of national laws. There is no appeal and no challenge available in the national courts against excess of jurisdiction.

Others view things quite differently. The development by the ECJ of the principles of the supremacy of Community law and of direct effect can be seen as both courageous and inspired:

> Courageous, because no-one could have foreseen how the Member States and the national courts would react; inspired, because they enabled the Community to

[118] Jean Louis Seurin, 'Towards a European Constitution? Problems of Political Integration' [1994] PL 625, 634.

[119] T. Hartley, 'Federalism, Courts and Legal Systems: The Emerging Constitution of the European Community' (1986) 34 American Journal of Comparative Law 229, 247.

[120] *The European Court of Justice: A Case Study in Judicial Activism*, p. 48. See also Hartley (1996) 112 LQR 95.

leave behind the traditional model of the intergovernmental organisation for the uncharted waters of a 'new legal order', with all its potential rewards and associated risks.[121]

Questions

1. What impact has membership of the European Community had on courts in the United Kingdom?

2. What is the constitutional role of the ECJ?

WHERE TO GO FROM HERE

The next chapter examines 'euro-litigation' in the context of the campaigns to reform the restrictions on Sunday trading which used to be imposed by s 47 of the Shops Act 1950 before its repeal in 1994.

[121] A. Arnull (1994) 19 ELRev 3, 4.

30

CASE STUDY: SUNDAY TRADING LITIGATION

INTRODUCTION

The previous chapter examines in general terms how membership of the European Community has affected adjudication in the United Kingdom. This chapter turns to look in more detail at 'euro-litigation' in the specific context of the cat-and-mouse court-room battles between local authorities and retailers over Sunday trading.[1]

SUNDAY TRADING AND THE ENFORCEMENT OF REGULATION

As with the other case studies in this book, the aim is not primarily to consider the substantive law; indeed, the statutory provisions at the heart of the saga, ss 47 and 71 of the Shops Act 1950, have now been repealed. The focus is on understanding what the events reveal about aspects of the modern public law process, in particular the following:

(1) the principle of supremacy of Community law over national law, even statute law;[2]
(2) the principle of direct effect of provisions in the EC Treaty;[3]
(3) the operation of the Art 177 reference procedure and the relationship between national courts and the ECJ;[4] and
(4) proportionality as a ground of judicial review in cases involving Community law issues.[5]

This case study also highlights some of the problems surrounding the *enforcement* of law. Ministers may initiate legislation, and Parliament may pass a bill, to give legal effect to a policy choice (here, that Sunday trading should be regulated or deregulated). But the practical impact of law, especially

[1] See further R. Rawlings, 'The Eurolaw Game: Some Deductions from a Saga' (1993) Journal of Law and Society 309; P. Diamond, 'Dishonourable Defences: The Use of Injunctions and the EEC Treaty—Case Study of the Shops Act 1950' (1991) 54 MLR 72; A. Arnull, 'What Shall We Do on Sunday?' (1991) 16 ELRev 112.

[2] See pp. 116 and 682.

[3] See p. 684.

[4] See p. 696.

[5] See p. 572.

where it is contentious, depends largely on how the institution responsible for its implementation carries out its task.[6]

THE PROTAGONISTS

The main court-room battles over Sunday trading during the 1980s and 1990s were fought between local authorities (which were responsible for enforcing the restrictions) and a handful of large retailers, mainly from the DIY stores sector. We need to consider what motivated these players to act as they did, especially their use of the law.

Local authorities

For most of the 20th century, it was illegal for shops to open on Sundays in England and Wales, except for the sale of a very limited range of goods.[7] This policy was decided by central government, but responsibility for enforcing the law was placed on local authorities. Under s 71(1) of the Shops Act 1950:

> It shall be the duty of every local authority to enforce within their district the provisions of this Act . . . and for that purpose to institute and carry on such proceedings in respect of contraventions of the said provisions . . . as may be necessary to secure observance thereof.

In practice, different local authorities around the country adopted different policies on enforcement. Some were very strict; others only initiated prosecutions if several members of the public complained about unlawful Sunday trading by a particular shop. Section 71 of the 1950 Act made it a criminal offence for a shop to sell goods contrary to s 47, so in many cases where enforcement was attempted by local authorities, instituting a prosecution in the magistrates' court was the obvious method. The maximum fine which magistrates could impose was however only £1,000—for larger retailers, a relatively small sum to pay for a very profitable day's trading.[8]

Prosecutions, then, were of only quite limited effectiveness in curbing unlawful opening. This led some local authorities to try an alternative enforcement strategy: applying to the High Court for an injunction (a civil law remedy) to restrain a shop owner from trading illegally on Sundays. Power to do this stemmed from s 222(1) of the LGA 1972:[9]

[6] On implementation, see Chapter 4.

[7] See Chapter 9.

[8] The fine was increased to £2,500 by the Criminal Justice Act 1991.

[9] Before the enactment of this section, a local authority could not bring civil proceedings in its own name. It had to apply to the Attorney-General who had a discretion to permit a relator action to be brought (i.e. legal proceedings formally brought in the name of the Attorney-General, one of whose constitutional functions is to protect the public interest).

> Where a local authority consider it expedient for the promotion or protection of the interests of the inhabitants of their area—
>
> (a) they may prosecute or defend in any legal proceedings and, in the case of civil proceedings, may institute them in their own name . . .

The advantage of this approach was that if the shop breached the injunction, this would amount to contempt of court. The High Court would then have power to impose an unlimited fine and, at least in theory, to imprison the shop owner (or a director of a company that owned a shop). There were, however, numerous legal problems associated with obtaining injunctions for this purpose.[10]

Questions

1. Why do you think central government has chosen local authorities as the agency responsible for enforcing Sunday trading laws? (The Sunday Trading Act 1994 continues to make them responsible for this.) What other bodies might have been given the task?

2. Can you speculate on the reasons why some local authorities were zealous in enforcing the ban on Sunday trading whereas others were not? Do you think it would be wrong for a local authority to give more weight to:

(a) the fact that public opinion generally favoured Sunday opening and
(b) the fact that bringing a prosecution or seeking an injunction was costly and probably ineffective at preventing trading, than to
(c) their statutory obligation to enforce the law?

What does your answer tell you about public 'law'?

3. Did local authorities have any 'discretion' under s 71 of the Shops Act 1950? If so, what kind of discretion is it?[11]

4. Suppose you were a member of a pressure group opposed to Sunday trading, yet the local authority in whose area you lived did little or nothing to enforce s 47 of the Shops Act. What, if anything, could you do to force the authority to act?

The DIY retailers

During the 1980s, one of the most successful sectors in the retail trade were large shops selling home improvement goods and garden products. For millions of people, a visit to a local DIY store became part of weekend life. Many such stores deliberately flouted the apparently clear prohibitions under s 47 of the Shops Act. Sunday was often their busiest and most profitable day. The stores pressed government to change the legislation, which they saw as

[10] Detailed consideration of these falls outside the scope of this chapter. Briefly, one problem was that local authorities were required, when applying for an interim injunction to prevent Sunday trading, to give a cross-undertaking in damages to the retailer; in other words, if several months later at the full trial to decide whether a permanent injunction should be granted, the court decides that no injunction should be issued and so the local authority loses its case, the local authority has to pay damages to the retailer for any loss he incurred as a result of the *interim* injunction.

[11] You may find it helpful to refer back to Chapter 24.

outdated. Retailers such as B&Q were leading members of the Shop Hours Reform Council which was active in lobbying first for the abortive 1986 Shops Bill and, later, for the successful Sunday Trading Act 1994.[12] After the defeat of the 1986 bill, litigation became the focus of the campaign to change the law.[13]

Question

Given that the United Kingdom is a parliamentary democracy, do you think it was proper for retailers on the one hand to campaign for legislative reform of Sunday trading, while at the same time deliberately choosing to break the existing law?[14]

The legal advisors

In his analysis of the litigation over the Shops Act, Rawlings draws attention to the parties' legal advisors:[15]

> Sunday trading . . . provides us with the ideal type of 'repeat player', in Galanter's celebrated phrase.[16] B&Q not only has the resources to become experienced and proficient in eurolitigation, it has the economic incentive to litigate repeatedly, provided as a minimum that this helps postpone the evil day. The clue lies in the stability and quality of its legal team. Amongst the small segment of the English Bar which may be considered expert in Community law, counsel David Vaughan QC, Gerald Barling QC and David Anderson are leading lights, appearing together on behalf of the Spanish fishermen in the celebrated *Factortame* cases. Depending on the significance of the case, one or more of them has always appeared for B&Q. The instructing solicitor, Tony Askham, has even published a book on EC Sunday trading rules; co-author David Ramsden is B&Q's controller of retail services.

Rawlings goes on to show that *at first sight* local authorities may appear to be 'one-shooters', because they have power to enforce the law through litigation only in their areas, and therefore their use of law in this context may be sporadic compared to a regular litigant such as B&Q. The reality, however, Rawlings argues was that the identity of the lawyers representing the various local authorities in the different cases remained the same: Stuart Isaacs QC and Neil Calver. This leads Rawlings to conclude that:[17]

> In consequence, we could typify the eurolitigation on Sunday trading as involving a private battle of wits between two expert legal teams taking place . . . across the

[12] See Chapter 9.

[13] The most important cases on Sunday trading include *Rochdale Borough Council v Anders* [1988] 3 All ER 490; *Torfaen Borough Council v B&Q plc* (Case C-145/88) [1990] 2 QB 19; *WH Smith Do-It-All Ltd v Peterborough City Council* [1991] 1 QB 304; *Stoke-on-Trent City Council v B&Q plc* [1991] Ch 48; *Kirklees Metropolitan Borough Council v Wickes Building Supplies Ltd* [1993] AC 227.

[14] See p. 127.

[15] R. Rawlings, 'The Eurolaw Game: Some Deductions from a Saga' (1993) Journal of Law and Society 309.

[16] This is a reference to M. Galanter, 'Why the "Haves" Come Out Ahead: Speculations on the Limits of Legal Change' (1974) 9 Law and Society Review 95.

[17] Rawlings (1993) Journal of Law and Society 309, 315.

length and breadth of the country. Needless to say, this is of profound significance for the character of legal argument and in turn of the judgments.

Courts and judges

A final set of players in the court-room contests was, of course, the courts themselves. The events of the case study should demonstrate clearly that public law litigation is not synonymous with applications for judicial review in the High Court. Instead we see how the criminal law in the magistrates' courts is used by government to regulate activity and that local authorities resorted to civil proceedings (injunctions obtained in the Chancery Division) in their attempts to stop unlawful Sunday trading. There was also frequent resort to the ECJ in Luxembourg through the Art 177 reference procedure.

THE USE (AND ABUSE?) OF COMMUNITY LAW

When a local authority sought to prosecute or obtain an injunction to prevent Sunday trading, retailers such as B&Q and others raised a series of ingenious legal arguments in their defence. One of these became known as the 'European defence'. In short, the retailers argued that s 47 of the Shops Act 1950 was incompatible with provisions in the EC Treaty, in particular Arts 30 and 36:

> Art 30: Quantitative restrictions on imports and all measures having equivalent effect shall, without prejudice to the following provisions, be prohibited between Member States.
>
> Art 36: The provisions of Articles 30 to 34 shall not preclude prohibitions or restrictions on imports, exports or goods in transit justified on grounds of public morality, public policy or public security . . . Such prohibitions or restrictions shall not, however, constitute a means of arbitrary discrimination or a disguised restriction on trade between Member States.

The Torfaen prosecution and Art 177 reference

In 1988 Torfaen Borough Council in Wales laid an information before Cwmbran Magistrates' Court alleging that a B&Q store in its area had contravened s 47. B&Q's defence was based on the basic propositions that Art 30 of the EC Treaty had direct effect in English law and that in criminal proceedings a person could not be convicted on the basis of a national law which was incompatible with Community law. Approximately 10 per cent of all the goods sold by B&Q were manufactured in other member states of the Community. B&Q claimed that if their shops were unable to open on Sundays, some would sell up to 25 per cent fewer goods in a week. The company argued that s 47 was a 'measure having an effect equivalent to a quantitative restriction on imports' within the meaning of Art 30 because prohibition on

Sunday trading was capable of hindering, directly or indirectly, actually or potentially, intra-Community trade. B&Q also contended that the infringement of Art 30 could not be justified under Art 36. Article 36 was also subject to the principle of proportionality[18] in so far as the measure in question (here, s 47 of the Act) must be no more restrictive of trade than is necessary in order to attain the protection of the principle in Art 36; the prohibition of Sunday trading could not be regarded as reasonable in view of the extraordinary anomalies in its application and effect.

Faced with such complex and important questions of Community law, in April 1988 the magistrates' court decided to adjourn hearing the prosecution and make a reference to the ECJ under Art 177 of the EC Treaty.[19] The magistrates' court formulated three questions on which it sought preliminary rulings.

> 1. Where a Member State prohibits retail premises from being open on Sunday for the sale of goods to customers, save in respect of certain specified items, sales of which are permitted, and where the effect of the prohibition is to reduce in absolute terms the sales of goods in those premises, including goods manufactured in other Member States, and correspondingly to reduce the volume of imports of goods from other Member States, is such a prohibition a measure having equivalent effect to a quantitative restriction on imports within the meaning of Art 30 of the Treaty?
> 2. If the answer to Question 1 is in the affirmative, does such a measure benefit from any of the exceptions to Art 30 contained in Art 36, or from any other exception recognised by Community law?
> 3. Is the answer to Question 1 or Question 2 above affected by any factor so as to render the measure in question a means of arbitrary discrimination or a disguised restriction on trade between Member States or a measure lacking in proportionality or otherwise justified?

Notice how the questions are framed in abstract terms; the magistrates' court was not asking the ECJ to rule *directly* on whether s 47 was contrary to Community law. In the months which followed, written observations were submitted by the local authority, B&Q, the UK government and the EC Commission.

In May 1989, over a year after the magistrates had made the Art 177 reference, the Judge Rapporteur presented the facts to the ECJ.[20] A month later Advocate General Van Gerven delivered his opinion (which was closely reasoned and several times longer than the court's judgment that followed). His conclusions were as follows:

> *Proposed reply to the preliminary questions*
> In conclusion, I propose that the court should reply to the preliminary questions asked by Cwmbran Magistrates' Court as follows:
>
> > 'A national rule which prohibits retail premises from being open on Sunday for the sale of goods to customers, save in respect of certain specified items, is not

[18] Considered in more detail below.

[19] For the text of Art 177, see p. 696.

[20] *Torfaen Borough Council v B&Q plc* [1990] 1 All ER 129, 131–9.

covered by the prohibition laid down in Art 30 if the rule does not cause imported goods to be discriminated against or placed at an actual disadvantage compared with domestic goods and if it does not screen off the domestic market of the member state in question or make access to that market substantially more difficult or unattractive for imported goods to which the rule applies.'

In the event that the court should nevertheless decide that such a rule is in principle a measure caught by Art 30, I propose in the alternative that the court should answer the preliminary question as follows:

'Arts 30 and 36 of the Treaty do not preclude a national rule which prohibits retail premises from being open on Sunday for the sale of goods to customers, save in respect of certain specified articles, if the rule does not cause imported goods to be discriminated against or placed at an actual disadvantage compared with domestic goods and if any obstacles to intra-Community trade which may be caused by the application of that prohibition are not greater than is necessary for encouraging non-working activities and social contact on a specified day which is already devoted to those purposes by a large part of the population.'

In November 1989, over 18 months after the Cwmbran Magistrates' Court had made the Art 177 reference, the ECJ delivered its terse judgment. Commentators were unimpressed. Rawlings' comment is that 'the judgment was brief even by the standards of the Court, was in places delphic, and failed to address the considered view of the Advocate General'.[21] For Diamond, the ECJ 'did not answer the reference . . . as clearly and concisely as could have been hoped for' and 'it is as if the judgment asks more questions than it answers'.[22] Here are some extracts:

The first question

10. By its first question the national court seeks to establish whether the concept of measures having an effect equivalent to quantitative restrictions within the meaning of Art 30 of the Treaty also covers provisions prohibiting retailers from opening their premises on Sunday if the effect of the prohibition is to reduce in absolute terms the sales of goods in those premises, including goods imported from other member states.

11. The first point which must be made is that national rules prohibiting retailers from opening their premises on Sunday apply to imported and domestic products alike. In principle, the marketing of products imported from other member states is not therefore made more difficult than the marketing of domestic products.

12. Next, it must be recalled that in *Cinéthèque SA v Fédération Nationale des Cinémas Français*[23] the court held, with regard to a prohibition on the hiring of video-cassettes applicable to domestic and imported products alike, that such a prohibition was not compatible with the principle of the free movement of goods provided for in the Treaty unless any obstacle to Community trade thereby created did not exceed what was necessary in order to ensure the attainment of the objective in view and unless that objective was justified with regard to Community law.

[21] Rawlings (1993) Journal of Law and Society 309.

[22] Diamond (1991) 54 MLR 72, 80 and 82.

[23] Joined Cases 60 and 61/84 [1985] ECR 2065. The case concerned French legislation which banned the sale of video cassettes of any film for a year after it received its performance certificate for screening in cinemas; the aim was to protect the cinema industry.

13. In those circumstances it is therefore necessary in a case such as this to consider first of all whether rules such as those at issue pursue an aim which is justified with regard to Community law. As far as that question is concerned, the court has already stated in *Re Oebel*[24] that national rules governing the hours of work, delivery and sale in the bread and confectionery industry constitute a legitimate part of economic and social policy, consistent with the objectives of public interest pursued by the Treaty.

14. The same consideration must apply as regards national rules governing the opening hours of retail premises. Such rules reflect certain political and economic choices in so far as their purpose is to ensure that working and non-working hours are so arranged as to accord with national or regional socio-cultural characteristics, and that, in the present state of Community law, is a matter for the member states. Furthermore, such rules are not designed to govern the patterns of trade between member states.

15. Second, it is necessary to ascertain whether the effects of such national rules exceed what is necessary to achieve the aim in view. As is indicated in Art 3 of Commission Directive (EEC) 709/50 of 22 December 1969, the prohibition laid down in Art 30 covers national measures governing the marketing of products where the restrictive effect of such measures on the free movement of goods exceeds the effects intrinsic to trade rules.

16. The question whether the effects of specific national rules do in fact remain within that limit is a question of fact to be determined by the national court.

17. The reply to the first question must therefore be that Art 30 of the Treaty must be interpreted as meaning that the prohibition which it lays down does not apply to national rules prohibiting retailers from opening their premises on Sunday where the restrictive effects on Community trade which may result therefrom do not exceed the effects intrinsic to rules of that kind.

The second and third questions

18. In the light of the reply given to the first question, it is unnecessary to answer the second and third questions. . . .

Questions

1. Did the magistrates' court have any choice but to adjourn hearing the prosecution and make an Art 177 reference to the ECJ?

2. What are the respective roles of the ECJ and the national court on an Art 177 reference?

3. What was the Advocate General's opinion? Did the ECJ follow it?

4. Does the ECJ give adequate guidance to the UK courts on how the test of proportionality should be applied? Imagine you were sitting as a magistrate in Cwmbran Magistrates' Court: explain carefully how you would set about applying the ECJ's preliminary ruling to the facts of the adjourned prosecution of B&Q.

5. Should a magistrates' court, quite probably lay magistrates advised by a legally qualified clerk, really be left to decide whether an Act of Parliament is consistent with Community law and, if not, to dis-apply it? How does this fit with the policy of the so-called 'exclusivity principle' that issues of public law normally have to be decided in

[24] Case 155/80 [1981] ECR 1993.

applications for judicial review under RSC, Order 53 by one of the specialist nominated High Court judges?[25]

6. A spokesman for B&Q was reported as saying that the judgment represented a partial victory for the company. Was he correct? Do you think B&Q wanted the ECJ ruling to clarify the law, or was it beneficial for it to be confused and uncertain? Consider the following comment.[26]

> The whole purpose of the 'European Defence' was to delay the administration of justice and allow some traders to continue to trade in breach of the criminal law. After the first referral to Luxembourg, magistrates' courts throughout the country began adjourning *sine die* in anticipation of a judgment from [the ECJ]. Local authorities were hesitant to prosecute in a situation where complex points of law were being raised and justices were not convicting. Lay magistrates were clearly having difficulties with complex legal argument . . .

The aftermath of the Art 177 ruling: *Stoke City Council v B&Q*

The ECJ decision in the *Torfaen* case did very little to promote certainty in the domestic courts. The retailers continued to raise the 'European defence' when they were prosecuted. Hearings often became very lengthy because factual and expert evidence was adduced on the proportionality question (that is, whether s 47 of the Shops Act had a disproportionately severe impact on imports having regard to the gravity of the problem against which it was directed); the ECJ had held that this was a 'question of fact to be determined by the national courts'. In other words, courts in England and Wales attempted to carry out a kind of cost-benefit analysis of s 47. Perhaps not surprisingly, they often came to different conclusions.

In July 1990, Stoke City Council, perhaps the local authority with the toughest enforcement policy, applied to the Chancery Division of the High Court for an injunction; their case was joined with those of two other local authorities seeking to take similar action in their own areas. The case came before Hoffmann J.[27] In his judgment, in which the local authorities were successful, Hoffmann J attempted to clarify the law. Here are extracts.

> *(1) The issue*
> Who is to decide whether shops should be allowed to open on Sundays? Is it to be Parliament or this court? That is an incomplete, somewhat tendentious but not entirely inaccurate way of stating the question before me. The plaintiffs in these two actions are local authorities which seek injunctions to restrain B&Q plc from contravening s 47 of the Shops Act 1950 by opening do-it-yourself shops in Hanley and Norwich on Sundays. Section 47 makes Sunday trading a summary criminal offence punishable by fine. But the local authorities take the view that fines would be ineffective to stop B&Q from breaking the law and that nothing short of an injunction will do. They have therefore brought these civil proceedings under the

[25] On the exclusivity principle, see p. 514.
[26] P. Diamond, 'Dishonourable Defences: The Use of Injunctions and the EEC Treaty—Case Study of the Shops Act 1950' (1991) 54 MLR 72, 82.
[27] *Stoke-on-Trent City Council v B&Q plc; Norwich City Council v B&Q plc* [1991] *Ch 48*.

powers conferred by s 222 of the Local Government Act 1972. B&Q say that s 47 is unenforceable because it infringes Art 30 of the EEC Treaty. It also says this is not a case in which a court can or should exercise the civil jurisdiction to grant an injunction. But I shall first deal with the substantive point on the Treaty.

(2) The EEC Treaty

The EEC Treaty is the supreme law of this country, taking precedence over Acts of Parliament. Our entry into the Community meant that (subject to our undoubted but probably theoretical right to withdraw from the Community altogether) Parliament surrendered its sovereign right to legislate contrary to the provisions of the Treaty on the matters of social and economic policy which it regulated. The entry into the Community was in itself a high act of social and economic policy, by which the partial surrender of sovereignty was seen as more than compensated by the advantages of membership.

The member states of the Community differ widely in their histories, customs and social and cultural values. It was certainly not the object of the Community to introduce uniformity in all these matters. The purpose of the Treaty was to bring about a European common market but not to interfere with national law and customs which did not constitute obstacles to the establishment of such a market. But there are many provisions in the Treaty expressed in language capable of being given a wider or narrower interpretation. According to the way they are interpreted, they may have more or less of an impact on questions of social policy which in member states are strongly felt to be matters for national decision. It is the function of the Court of Justice of the European Communities in Luxembourg to interpret the Treaty and for the national court to apply it. In its interpretation of the Treaty the European Court has tried to tread a careful line which permits both boldness in advancing the objects of the Community and sensitivity to the domestic interest of member states. In applying the Treaty as interpreted by the court, the national court has to be aware of another division of powers: not between European and national jurisdiction, but between legislature and judiciary. The fact that the European court has said that a particular question is one for decision by the national court does not endow that court with quasi-legislative powers. It must confine itself within the area of judicial intervention required by the Treaty and not trespass on questions which are for democratic decision in Parliament.

. . .

(6) Interpretation of the Torfaen ruling

The judgment of the European Court was intended to be an authoritative interpretation of the Treaty sufficient to enable the domestic court to decide the case. But 'every decoding is another encoding' and there have been arguments over what the judgment means. It was even suggested that in the last resort I might have to make another reference to find out. In my judgment however its effect, in the light of the developing jurisprudence to which I have referred, is tolerably plain.

The court has decided that the validity of the English Sunday trading law depends on the answers to two questions. (1) Does the law pursue an aim which is justified with regard to Community law? (2) Does the effect of the law exceed what is necessary to achieve the end in view? In my judgment the court has itself answered the first question. It is true that in para 14 it said that rules governing the opening hours of retail premises were a matter for the member states '*in so far* as their purpose is to ensure that working and non-working hours are so arranged as to accord with national or regional socio-cultural characteristics . . .' (see [1990]

2 QB 19 at 53 (my emphasis)). If one reads 'in so far' as meaning 'if it is the case that', it could be said that the national court was being left to decide whether this condition was met. In my judgment, however, 'in so far' was intended to mean 'because' and the court was deciding that the purpose of s 47 of the Shops Act 1950 satisfied the description. This was the view of Mustill LJ and Schiemann J in a recent decision of the Divisional Court, *WH Smith Do-It-All Ltd v Peterborough City Council* [1991] 1 QB 304, and I respectfully agree. Both judgments also contain illuminating obiter dicta on the questions addressed in this case. In any case, it seems to me plain and obvious that the purpose of s 47 was to arrange working and non-working hours in shops in England and Wales so as to accord with the 'regional socio-cultural characteristic' by which people generally do not work on Sundays. . . .

(7) The question of fact

In *R v Goldstein* [1983] 1 WLR 151 at 155 Lord Diplock said that to satisfy the requirement of proportionality in a prosecution brought under a measure falling with an art 36 exception, it was necessary for the Crown—

> to adduce factual evidence (1) to identify the various mischiefs which the challenged restrictive measures were intended to prevent, (2) to show that these mischiefs could not have equally effectively been cured by other measures less restrictive of trade and (3) to show that the measures were not disproportionately severe having regard to the gravity of the mischiefs against which they were directed.

This accords with the European Court's view that proportionality was a question of fact. But I do not think, when Lord Diplock spoke of factual evidence, that he intended to require the prosecution to prove matters of which the court could properly take judicial notice. It follows that if the court is satisfied on the basis of judicial notice that the requirements of proportionality have been met, there is no need for the prosecution to adduce oral or documentary evidence. Judicial notice is not confined to questions which everyone would be able to answer of his own knowledge. It includes matters of a public nature such as history, social customs and public opinion, which may have to be culled from works of reference. As the late Professor Sir Rupert Cross said, judicial notice is important for two reasons:

> In the first place, it expedites the hearing of many cases. Much time would be wasted if every fact which was not admitted had to be the subject of evidence which would, in many instances, be costly and difficult to obtain. Secondly, the doctrine tends to produce uniformity of decision on matters of fact where a diversity of findings might sometimes be distinctly embarrassing.

(See *Cross on Evidence* (5th edn., 1979) p. 160. This was the last edition prepared by Sir Rupert. It appears in the sixth edition (1985) at p. 70.)

The second point is particularly important here. Since *Torfaen* there have been numerous prosecutions for Sunday trading in magistrates' courts and the Crown Court. In many of these, evidence has been led on the question of proportionality. A troupe of experts has toured the country giving their views over periods of several days and as a result some courts have convicted and others have acquitted. . . .

(8) The objectives of the Shops Act

In order to decide whether the effects of s 47 exceed what is necessary to achieve the aim in view, I must first decide what the aim was. There was a good deal of argument about it but the dispute seemed to me largely semantic. The aim is in my view clear enough from the terms of the 1950 Act itself, namely to ensure that, so far as possible, shopkeepers and shop assistants did not have to work on Sunday. The fact that the promoters of the 1950 Act embraced this aim suggests that they must have thought in general terms that it was undesirable to have to work on Sunday—there could be no rational basis for confining this view to shop workers. In that sense they were seeking to maintain what they regarded as the traditional English Sunday. But the immediate aim of the legislature was not universal. They may have thought that other trades were not subject to the same pressures or that they had sufficient protection from trade unions or other legislation or simply that other trades were not their concern. No doubt some would have supported the measure for other or wider reasons or because they hoped to gain from its incidental effects. Sabbatarians, for example, may have approved on the general ground that work on Sunday profaned the Lord's Day and bus drivers who disliked working on Sundays might have liked the idea that fewer buses would be needed if people could not go shopping. People who lived in shopping districts might like the quiet Sunday atmosphere. But these wider or incidental effects were not the aims of the legislation.

This view is supported by the parliamentary history and subsequent judicial comment. The Shops Act 1950 was a consolidation Act. Section 47 was derived from the Shops (Sunday Trading Restrictions) Act 1936, which originated in a private member's Bill. B&Q invited me to read the speech in *Hansard* of the sponsor, Mr Loftus, when introducing the second reading debate (see 308 *HC Official Report* (5th series) cols 2158–2170). The debate is summarised by Frankfurter J in his opinion upholding the constitutionality of American Sunday trading laws in *McGowan v Maryland* (1961) 366 US 420 at 480–482. The learned justice says in particular (at 481): 'Speakers asserted the necessity for maintaining "the traditional quality of the Sunday in this country".' To which he then added in a footnote 'Throughout the debates it is emphasized that the bill was "a Sunday Trading Restriction Bill" and not . . . a Bill to have one day's rest in seven.' I had some doubt about whether this was permissible but Mr Vaughan QC for B&Q said that in the exceptional case in which the court is concerned with the purpose of the legislation rather than its construction, consultation of *Hansard* is permitted: see *Pickstone v Freemans plc* [1989] AC 66 and *Conerney v Jacklin* (1985) 129 SJ 285. . . .

As for judicial comment, I need cite only Donovan J in *Waterman v Wallasey Corpn* [1954] 1 WLR 771 at 773 where he said: 'The purpose of the Act is to protect shop assistants . . .' If I might be allowed to enlarge this remark in a brief unreserved judgment to include shopkeepers, it is entirely consistent with what I have said so far. . . .

B&Q argue that these exceptions, some of which have turned out to give rise to very arbitrary distinctions, show that the object of the legislation was not to relieve shop workers from having to work on Sunday but to produce a situation in which some worked and some did not. This submission is used to support the argument that various alternative systems, such as exempting DIY shops and garden centres, would produce a situation which did not give shop workers materially less protection than the present law but would be much less restrictive of Community trade. I think that it is fallacious. So far as the Shops Act 1950 allows goods to be sold on Sundays, this is not in furtherance of its objectives but by way of recognition that its objectives could not be fully achieved.

(10) The division of powers

By far the most important question in this case concerns the function of the court in applying the proportionality tests. This is a case of a sovereign legislature acting to further what the European Court has held to be legitimate objectives. It is subject only to a requirement that the measure should not be disproportionate to the importance of its objective. The question is one on which strong and differing views may be held and which has been the subject of frequent parliamentary debate. Is the court to apply its own opinion of the importance of ensuring that shop workers do not have to work on Sundays and weigh that against its opinion of the importance of selling more Dutch bulbs or Italian furniture? If the legislature has declined to adopt any modification of the existing exceptions, is the court to say that modifications should nevertheless be introduced because in its opinion they would not detract from the legislative object and would mean that the 1950 Act was less of a hindrance to Community trade?

In my judgment it is not my function to carry out the balancing exercise or to form my own view on whether the legislative objective could be achieved by other means. These questions involve compromises between competing interests, which in a democratic society must be resolved by the legislature. The duty of the court is only to inquire whether the compromise adopted by the United Kingdom Parliament, so far as it affects Community trade, is one which a reasonable legislature could have reached. The function of the court is to review the acts of the legislature but not to substitute its own policies or values.

This is not an abdication of judicial responsibility. The primacy of the democratic process is far more important than the question of whether our Sunday trading laws could or could not be improved. I cannot imagine that in *Cinéthèque SA v Fédération Nationale des Cinémas Français* joined Cases 60 and 61/84 [1985] ECR 2065 the French court in applying the ruling of the European Court considered that it was under a duty to form an independent view of the importance of the cinema industry to France or whether that industry could be better protected by other means. These are also essentially legislative questions involving a balancing of interests and the judiciary cannot do more than decide whether the view of the legislature is one which could reasonably be held. It seems to me that unless both the European Court and the national courts exercise this kind of restraint, it will be impossible to avoid the concerns expressed by Mr Advocate General Van Gerven in *Torfaen* [1990] 2 QB 19 about the justiciability of some of the questions raised by the wide construction given to Art 30. . . .

These extracts, in which I have emphasised the significant passages, confirm my opinion that in this case the court's duty goes no further than to decide whether it is a reasonably tenable view that preventing shop workers from having to work on Sundays is a sufficiently important objective to justify the consequent reduction in Community trade and that no means other than requiring shops to shut would achieve the same objective with less hindrance to trade.

(11) Applying the proportionality tests

In passing the Shops (Sunday Trading Restrictions) Act 1936 and in refusing to accept any modifications since that date, Parliament must be taken to have decided that the objective of preventing shop workers from being or feeling under any economic pressure to work on Sunday was sufficient to outweigh the inconvenience which would thereby be caused to people who wanted to shop or work or any loss of trade for the economy as a whole. This view continues to be strongly held by a large number of people. Whether I personally agree with it or not, it would be presumptuous of me to characterise it as untenable. On the contrary, I accept that it is capable of forming a rational basis for legislation. And if Parliament was willing to accept the detriments I have mentioned, it must I think follow that (if the question had arisen) it would have been equally willing to accept the reduction in Community trade as a part of the wider effect on trade as a whole.

These considerations are sufficient to resolve the balancing test in favour of the validity of the 1950 Act. A similar approach produces the same result when the necessity test is applied. B&Q submitted that in considering alternative measures which might have a lesser effect on Community trade, it was wrong to compare the effect they would have with an Arcadian idyll in which no one worked on Sundays. The comparison must be with the current reality in which anyone can work in any shop as long as it is not open for the serving of customers, in which shops (including DIY shops and garden centres) can open lawfully for the sale of Sch 5 goods and in which the law is in any case widely disobeyed.

This argument is in my judgment mistaken. The object of the legislation was to secure that as few shop workers as possible worked on Sundays. The need for exceptions was recognised but the exceptions were not part of the legislative purpose; they were considered to be unavoidable concessions. Any enlargement of the exceptions must result in more shop workers falling outside the protection of the 1950 Act. It cannot therefore be argued that because exceptions already exist, a few more would do no harm. The irrelevance of the exceptions is confirmed by the opinion of Mr Advocate General Van Gerven in the *Torfaen* case [1990] 2 QB 19 at 49 (para. 32):

> B&Q's line of argument, however, concerns primarily the effectiveness and consistency of the rule. Community law lays down a different type of requirement: the obstacle which in practice results from the rule must be proportionate to the aim pursued, that is to say no more restrictive for intra-Community trade than is necessary for the intended purpose; whether the rule *achieves* its purpose in this respect is irrelevant. (The Advocate General's emphasis.)

It seems to me that the history of the Sunday trading law shows that the existing exceptions are regarded by Parliament as the limits of what is necessary to achieve the legislative object. Of course there are illogicalities in Sch 5 and opinions may differ about whether it draws the line in the right place. On the other hand, illogical compromise tends to be a British 'socio-cultural characteristic', to adopt the language of the European Court. That may also explain why Sunday trading is permitted in Scotland but not in England and Wales. In my judgment Parliament was entitled to decide that the present restrictions were necessary to attain the objects of the 1950 Act and that different restrictions would be inadequate, even though they might have less effect on Community trade.

I should mention that some reliance was placed on a decision by a stipendiary magistrate at Pendle that the object of s 47 was intended to protect Sunday leisure activities and that since many people regarded Sunday shopping in DIY and garden centre shopping as a leisure activity, a ban on such shopping was disproportionate. That seems to me based on a misconception. It was never the purpose of s 47 to protect shoppers from the pain of having to buy things on Sunday and the fact that certain kinds of shopping may be a pleasure is irrelevant. The 1950 Act was to protect shop workers and there is no evidence that anyone regards Sunday work, even in a DIY shop, as a leisure activity.

The result is that although I accept that the burden is upon the prosecution to justify the proportionality of the measure, that burden is in my judgment fully discharged on the basis of facts of which the court is entitled to take judicial notice. The factual and expert evidence adduced by B&Q does not disturb that conclusion.

No order. Undertaking given by B&Q not in future to trade on Sundays in Norwich or Stoke-on-Trent. The court certified under s 12 of the Administration of Justice Act 1969 that a question of general public importance relating to the construction of an enactment was involved in the decision and that a sufficient case for an appeal direct to the House of Lords had been made out.

Questions

1. Bearing in mind the confusion which followed the *Torfaen* case, would it have been better if the ECJ had had power to rule *directly* on whether s 47 of the Shops Act was consistent with the EC Treaty, rather than leaving it to the national courts?

2. Summarize Hoffmann J's approach to applying the proportionality principle to s 47. Does it help clarify the law?

3. Hoffmann J said: 'In my judgement it is not my function to carry out the balancing exercise or to form my own view on whether the legislative objective could be achieved by other means.' Is the perception of the role of the judge in accord with what the ECJ expected of the national courts in *Torfaen*?

4. Hoffmann J seems very clear that it is 'plain and obvious' that the object of the legislation was 'to secure that as few shop workers as possible worked on Sundays' and that s 47 was a proportionate method of achieving this aim. Is this really so? Look back at the 1984 report of the Auld Committee of Inquiry into Proposals to Amend the Shops Act.[28] Does not the enactment of the Sunday Trading Act 1994 show that it was possible to attain this end in a less drastic way?

5. One reason for the UK courts rejecting the principle of proportionality as a ground of judicial review in cases which do not raise Community law issues is that it 'must ultimately result in the question—is the particular decision acceptable?—and this must involve a review of the merits of the decision'.[29] What exactly is objectionable about this? Does Hoffmann J avoid the 'merits' in the *Stoke-on-Trent City Council* case? Was he, in reality, judicially reviewing Parliament?

6. How would you answer, in general terms, Hoffmann J's opening questions: 'Who is to decide whether shops should be allowed to open on Sundays? Is it to be Parliament or this court?' What does he mean when he says (at p. 714 above) that Community law does not endow a UK court with 'quasi-legislative powers'?

To the House of Lords and (again) the ECJ

Hoffmann J's attempt to give certainty to the law was only a very partial success; the lower courts did not always adopt his approach to proportionality and some doubted whether it was compatible with Community law! At the close of the hearing in the *Stoke-on-Trent City Council* case, Hoffmann J had certified under s 12 of the Administration of Justice Act 1969 that a question of general public importance relating to the construction of an enactment was involved in the decision and that a sufficient case for an appeal direct to the House of Lords had been made out. In May 1991, the Appeal Committee of the House of Lords decided that it was necessary to

[28] See p. 201.

[29] Per Lord Ackner in *R v Secretary of State for the Home Department, ex p Brind* [1991] 1 AC 696.

make *another* Art 177 reference to the ECJ and adjourned further consideration of the appeals until the ECJ gave its preliminary ruling. The ECJ gave its judgment on 16 December 1992, holding that Art 30 of the EC Treaty did not apply to national rules on Sunday trading as these did not have restrictive effects on trade which exceeded the effects intrinsic to such rules in relation to their socio-cultural aims.[30] The ECJ sent out a clear signal that it would not, in future, hear Art 177 references concerning the Shops Act. This helped bring an end to the 'European defence' tactics of the retailers and their legal advisors.

Question

Consider the following comment by Diamond:[31]

> In a democratic society, it is legitimate to use pressure to obtain legislative change. What cannot be acceptable is a deliberate and determined strategy to flout an Act of Parliament and bring the law into disrepute. Many local authorities have in effect been intimidated into not enforcing the 1950 Act. . . . What is alarming to any society that purports to be guided by the principles of the rule of law is that, if you are rich and determined enough, you can apparently disregard those public laws which are not perceived to be in your interest. . . . The tactics of these retailers have sunk to unacceptable levels of moral and public behaviour.

THE ISSUE RETURNS TO PARLIAMENT

Whatever the rights and wrongs of the tactics used by the retailers, euro-litigation had enabled them to carry on trading. It was now clear to them, however, that new legislation was the way forward. The campaign to persuade government and MPs to support a repeal of s 47 of the Shops Act 1950 therefore resumed with vigour. Look back at p. 215 to follow what happened next.

[30] *Stoke-on-Trent v B&Q plc* Case C-169/91 [1993] 1 All ER 481.
[31] P. Diamond (1991) 54 MLR 72, 86–7.

INDEX